European Americana

Volume I: 1493–1600

*Preparation of the present volume
has been made possible by
funds provided by the
Division of Research Grants for
Research Materials of the
National Endowment for the Humanities
with the further assistance of
The Readex Microprint Corporation
and
Brown University*

The John Carter Brown Library

EUROPEAN AMERICANA:

*A Chronological Guide to Works Printed in
Europe Relating to the Americas,
1493–1776*

Volume I: 1493–1600

Edited by

John Alden

with the assistance of

Dennis C. Landis

*New York:
Readex Books
A Division of the Readex Microprint Corporation*
1980

Copyright © 1980 by the
Readex Microprint Corporation
ISBN 0-918414-03-2
Library of Congress Card No. 80-51141

Printed in the United States of America

For

ALBERT BONI

whose wide-ranging imagination and enterprise
have placed American letters and scholarship
profoundly in his debt

Table of Contents

Foreword

The earliest known list of books relating to America appeared at the same time that the Old World became fully conscious of the presence of a New World. In 1548 the 'father of bibliography', Konrad Gesner, included in his *Pandectarum . . . libri xxi* a list of seven items under the heading 'De novo orbe, & insulis nostro saeculo repertis'. By that date the outline of all but the northwest part of the Americas had been laid down on maps, coasts had been probed from the Saint Lawrence to La Plata, while, in the Caribbean, Mexico and Peru, Spain's overseas empire had taken form. With the five hundredth anniversary of Columbus's discovery approaching we can look back and see the term 'America' growing from a purely geographical concept to the powerful and complex meaning it has today. As succeeding generations of Europeans brought two continents under their domination, the literature describing that experience expanded to touch every facet of human experience. In 1566 Jean Bodin gave recognition to the writings of Columbus and Vespucci in his *Methodus ad facilem historiarum cognitionem* and the centenary of the announcement of the discovery of the New World saw the publication of Antonio Possevino's *Bibliotheca selecta* (Rome: 1593) with its section on the 'Ratio agendi cum reliquis gentibus, praecipue Indis novi terrarum orbis, & Japoniis'.

It was not, however, till 1629 that a genuinely substantial record of publications treating the Americas appeared at Madrid in Antonio Rodríguez de León Pinelo's *Epitome de la Biblioteca Oriental i Occidental,* drawn from a larger list he had compiled in order to write a history of the Council of the Indies. Not surprisingly the contents of the 'Occidental' section deal almost exclusively with Spanish America.

But the first work devoted exclusively to the Americas was the *Bibliothecae Americanae Primordia* (London: 1713). Compiled by White Kennett, Bishop of Peterborough, it was based principally upon the library he had accumulated for the purpose of writing a history of the Society for the Propagation of the Gospel in Foreign Parts, founded in 1701 to support Anglican missionary activities in British North America. Though the collection consisted chiefly of writings about English America, others relating to Spanish or French America are also present. But of primary importance was the catalogue's strict chronological arrangement.

Though the 18th century also saw the appearance of bibliographies derived from the historical studies of Catholic clergy, it was not until 1832 that Obadiah Rich, erstwhile American consul at

Foreword

Valencia turned antiquarian bookseller in London, began to issue his series of catalogues offering Americana for sale, expansively including Continental as well as British publications. Arranged chronologically, the descriptions reveal a warm appreciation of the content of the works in question.

Such a chronological approach was to receive an even finer treatment in Henry Harrisse's *Bibliotheca Americana Vetustissima, A Description of Works Relating to America Published between the Years 1492 and 1551* (New York: 1866), known affectionately as the 'B.A.V.'. Brief though the span of years covered may be, the intense drama reflected in the works described can scarcely be exaggerated. They fully merit the treatment they are accorded, including typographic facsimiles of the title pages, detailed collations, and scholarly commentary. Of especial value is Harrisse's lucid introductory essay on the place of bibliography in the study of history, which also contains a survey of earlier bibliographies that, with minor revisions, can still serve, as far as it goes, as the basic work on the subject.

In the subsequent section Harrisse deals with a question that had not been fully confronted before. 'What books should enter into this bibliography?' Dismissing as inadequate the inclusion solely of 'works relating exclusively to America' alone, he acknowledges that 'to admit every book which contains a passage or chapter concerning the subject . . . especially among those published within the last three centuries, would compel the bibliographer to insert the titles of more than fifty thousand volumes.' But he then goes on to say, 'the wants and duties of the historian are such that he cannot neglect to consult every source of information, however apparently insignificant.' Choosing the more exhaustive approach Harrisse confined himself to a period when a limited number of works were printed; avoiding the impossible, he established firmly the intellectual framework for future bibliographers of Americana.

Undaunted and, by his own confession, unaware of the magnitude of his undertaking, yet another individual plunged into the morass Harrisse had avoided. The prospectus for Joseph Sabin's *Bibliotheca Americana: A Dictionary of Books Relating to America from its Discovery to the Present Time* (New York: 1868–1936) appeared in the same year as Harrisse's B.A.V., that of 1866. The arrangement was that of a dictionary, alphabetically by author (or appropriate equivalent). It provides a work for reference that answers specific questions already framed. It is not a guide to the literature of the subject by means of which one can gain insight into the sense and flow of history. The shortcomings of the work, both in concept and execution, are too well known to require elaboration here, but in Sabin's day an alphabetical arrangement was probably the only practical way of attacking the problem. The work's primary function was to accumulate, not to organize, data. As such it has been an extraordinarily useful tool. However, for those interested in the first three centuries of American history, its use is particularly frustrating. Of the 140,000 entries only a quarter treat works printed before 1801, and they are squirreled away among a mass of 19th century material, much of which is of negligible importance.

Toward the close of the 19th century the writing of American history began to be more nationally oriented, as Americans came to view their history in terms of their own countries, rather than as part of a larger unit or earlier empire. The phenomenon found its counterpart in the emergence of bibliographies of works printed in individual areas of the Americas. Of their compilers the two most notable were José Toribio Medina and Charles Evans. The former's eighteen imprint bibliographies record the output of thirty-four Spanish-American cities or towns. The latter's *American Bibliography*, ultimately completed through the year 1800, is an essential companion for anyone seriously studying the history of the United States prior to that date. Both men, it must be noted, made use of a chronological arrangement.

Amongst those not fully conversant with bibliographies of Americana there is a disturbing tendency to link Sabin and Evans together, as if somehow they dealt with the same kind of material. Were one to exclude government documents and newspapers, a remarkably small proportion of the books listed by Evans treat America in their subject matter. Many of them, such as the swarm of theological works, are American by implication, but they do not discuss America explicitly. Harrisse and Sabin, on the other hand, concern themselves with America as such, although Sabin is not altogether consistent, and apologizes for the inclusion of 'various works by early New England Divines' to which, he notes, some will take 'serious and proper objection'. This statement, indeed, is the closest he comes to providing anything specific about his standards of inclusion or exclusion.

The present work represents an attempt to impose and enlarge upon material accumulated by Sabin, and those who have followed him, the framework set forth by Henry Harrisse. (The latter's full descriptions have not been attempted for reasons set forth by Mr Alden in his Preface.)

The need for a bibliographical tool more satisfactory than 'Sabin' was recognized two years after the late R.W.G. Vail produced the final volume. In November of 1938 representatives of fifteen American libraries possessing major collections of Americana met, with assistance from the Carnegie Foundation, in New York to explore the possibility of creating a union catalogue of their holdings in the field. World War II and changing American cataloguing practices made the undertaking impractical, although the concept was again explored in the early phases of the present project.

In 1967 Mr Albert Boni of the Readex Microprint Corporation approached the John Carter Brown Library. In collaboration with the American Antiquarian Society he was about to complete the successful publication in microprint form of the works listed by

Foreword

Evans, complemented by an index to them, incorporating revisions, prepared by Clifford K. Shipton and published as the *National Index of American Imprints through 1800, the Short-Title Evans* (Worcester: 1969). Mr Boni hoped that it would be possible to produce something similar based upon 'Sabin'.

From the outset it was clear that a revision and updating of 'Sabin' itself would serve little purpose. The whole bibliographical concept needed to be recast. Hence the decision, in addition to returning to a chronological arrangement, to confine the work to European texts about the Americas, a body of material over which bibliographical control had become increasingly confused.

It is Albert Boni who had the imagination to recognize and appreciate the need for a large scale undertaking in further service to scholarship, and to commit himself to its support. To him this and the volumes to follow owe their inception. In 1968 he began by making possible, by computerization, a chronological index to 'Sabin' by entry number. This was followed by creation of files comprising copies of Sabin's entries supplemented by information growing out of this Library's collecting experience and other sources.

When Mr William F. Boni succeeded his father as President of the Readex Microprint Corporation, he urged us to move forward with the project. At the same time the retirement of Mr John Alden, Keeper of Rare Books for the Boston Public Library, made his services available. Mr Alden has long been acknowledged as one of this country's most perceptive and versatile bibliographers. With a scholarly career extending over forty years his writings on diverse aspects of the world of books are regarded as authoritative. And his experience has permitted a reappraisal of the essential needs for a work of this kind. If, as we believe it does, the present volume establishes some new patterns for handling certain bibliographical situations, the achievement is entirely his.

With Mr Alden in place as editor, funds were obtained from the Division of Research Grants for Research Materials of the National Endowment for the Humanities. These were supplemented by a further substantial contribution from the Readex Microprint Corporation, and work began in earnest in the autumn of 1977. The preparation of subsequent volumes is well in hand, and we foresee their publication in the near future.

Thomas R. Adams, Librarian
The John Carter Brown Library

Preface

The present volume, the first of a projected series designed ultimately to cover the period from the year 1493 through 1776, represents an effort to record in chronological form those works printed in Europe which depict the Americas in verbal terms. It constitutes, we venture to believe, a response to a need by historians for a more comprehensive statement of the varied ways in which the continents were perceived, in a sequence which reveals the development of those images.

To be sure, Joseph Sabin's *Bibliotheca Americana* has rewarded generations of scholars who have seen fit to consult its twenty-nine volumes, but its usefulness has been limited by its dictionary arrangement. Not uncharitably, the late Lawrence C. Wroth in his discussion of early Americana in *Standards of Bibliographical Description* (Philadelphia: 1949), while acknowledging Sabin's merits, could also say, 'Sabin's decision to make a dictionary rather than a chronological catalogue was a step backward in the progress of American bibliography.' But even as it stands, it has served its users well, while the lasting contributions to it by Wilberforce Eames alone ensure that it will never be fully superseded.

The fact remains that a chronological bibliography serves an invaluable purpose, providing a unique form of social history. Superficial it may be, yet no other means has yet been devised to bring together, within an assimilable compass, the diverse strands of the experience of the past as embodied in the printed word. One senses, furthermore, an increasing recognition that while the historian may himself be preoccupied with particular ideas or events, these cannot be fully comprehended outside the broadest possible context — material or physical, as well as abstractly intellectual — of their times.

Admittedly, there are other approaches to the same concept. One such is the brilliantly conceived and splendidly executed symposium organized by Fredi Chiappelli at the University of California at Los Angeles in 1975. Made possible by a grant from the National Endowment for the Humanities, the congress brought together as speakers over fifty specialists in a wide spectrum of disciplines. The papers presented, published in two volumes as *First Images of America: The Impact of the New World on the Old* (Berkeley: 1976), represent a milestone in American historiography. Yet the circumscribed focus of the individual scholars within their discrete fields does not always permit fusion or synthesis of the varied topics within an organic whole. Nor do the approaches employed always allow a quantitative evaluation of the impact involved. One ventures to believe that a chronological guide can help meet the latter goals.

That our scope has been confined to European publications, it will be readily recognized, reflects the availability of other works which already perform in their way a comparable service. The existence of Charles Evans's *American Bibliography,* Marie Tremaine's *Bibliography of Canadian Imprints, 1751-1800,* and of José Toribio Medina's numerous works for South and Central America fulfill their purposes well in recording chronologically works of all types published within the geographic areas concerned, and in doing so provide access to indigenous Americana by the scholar. But apart from those segments covered by Henry Harrisse's *Bibliotheca Americana Vetustissima* — even with its supplements less than exhaustive — and Medina's *Biblioteca Hispano-Americana (1493-1810),* how Europeans of a particular period envisaged the New World, and how their perceptions developed with the passage of time, has hitherto been less than clear.

Drawing from the resources of the John Carter Brown Library — both its splendid collections in themselves and records long garnered there — and from a wide range of bibliographic sources, including a computerized chronological listing by entry number of Sabin's descriptions, in January, 1976, work was begun on preparation of copy for the present volume.

In establishing the methodology and formulas to be employed, numerous factors were considered. Not the least of these were the economic exigencies of our day which none of us is spared. One recalls, in addition, an observation by the distinguished historian Carl Bridenbaugh that too few historians make appropriate use of Evans's *American Bibliography.* Insofar as this is perhaps true, one surmises that this may in part be the fault of the bibliographer who, to meet his own objectives, howsoever valid within themselves, places obstacles in the path of others whom he purports also to serve. In the light of both economics and utility, decisions were made to attempt to achieve a practical and pragmatic presentation of the materials in question, consciously departing from time to time from conventional practice.

Basic to the undertaking has been, needless to say, a definition of what constitutes the Americas as such. Sabin and his successors appear to have taken a somewhat ambiguous attitude towards their extent, though one can readily understand their inclusion of attractive works relating to islands — the Canaries amongst them — off the African coast and to the East as contrasted to the West Indies. While recognising the relationship of these works to the discovery and exploration of the New World, we have restricted ourselves on the other hand to a more rigid geographic scope, that of the area from Greenland to the Straits of Magellan, comprising the two Americas, Central America, and geologically related islands in the Caribbean and elsewhere. And while we are aware that an individual may consider as Americana those works which led or guided the explorer to the western world without mentioning it, we have ourselves resisted their appeal. At the same time we have considered indispensable the inclusion of works describing American topics, even though their authors were not aware of the fact or did not designate them as such.

A parallel problem is the extent to which one should include works in which the Americas appear at best tangentially or in the most tenuous of terms. Here it was decided that for this period to attempt to include any such reference was valid, to record in what ways and in what terms an awareness of the New World was developed or, one might even say 'insinuated', in the European consciousness in its early stages. To maintain this practice for succeeding centuries would be, we would agree, more difficult to justify, and a burden not necessarily to be assumed.

That the norms we have adopted for describing the individual items here included frequently represent a departure from custom will be apparent. Conditioned as a bibliographer is to deference to the past, and to its bibliographic practices as well, it is extremely difficult to liberate oneself from the latter, representing as they do — but chiefly to those alone familiar with the particular idiom invoked — the fruits of past experience. We have, however, sought independent means for providing a terse and unencumbered presentation of salient American content which at the same time permits identification of the work itself. If anything, we may have erred in offering more than a necessary minimum in this regard.

In such terms indeed the volume does not purport to be a 'bibliography' but to the contrary a 'guide' for those seeking what a contemporary reader may have encountered at a given period of time. Though one has the greatest of admiration for those who within this century, working in the sphere of analytical bibliography, have provided us with more authoritative texts and a highly sophisticated technical vocabulary, such concerns seem inappropriate here. An awareness of printing house practices will be found reflected, however, where they are pertinent to the historian's purposes. Thus, to describe a work as 'another issue' of a text can spare him unprofitable pursuit of copies lacking appreciable differences, at the same time saying something about the distribution of the text.

Departures from standard American practice notwithstanding, these are, we trust, not incompatible with American usage, and, in the selection of the form of an author's name, it has been followed, though where more recent or more authoritative information has become available we have utilized it.

In the transcriptions of titles, modifications have been rather more amply employed. Type abbreviations or printing house practices have been silently expanded and spellings modified, partly to spare present-day compositors typographic hurdles, partly in the belief that such refinements often obscure more than they reveal to

Preface

the eyes of the historian, howsoever knowledgeable in such matters he may himself be. And in the extent of transcription, the aim has been less that of revealing the full nature of the work than what is American about it.

In the recording of imprints—of place, printer or bookseller, and date—emboldened by the example of the Wellcome Historical Medical Library we have given these in a highly simplified form, normally, regardless of the original, in English, incorporating information which may be found not on the title page alone but also elsewhere in the work. Only when it is derived from an external source is this indicated by the use of brackets.

Similarly—rather than ignoring the matter altogether—collations, when available, have been provided only to the extent of indicating the last page number of the body of the text, errors being reported only when there is a substantial departure from reality. In the hope that they may serve as a point of departure for further study, the presence of illustrations, portraits and maps has been indicated in general terms. And, treacherous though reliance on past cataloguing practice here may be, the format is also shown. That we have not always been able to meet these modest norms will, however, be self-evident, but in such cases to try to do so would have been disproportionate to potential utility.

As will be apparent, not always do the titles of the works described reveal their American content. When necessary, such content is indicated by an annotation of the earliest edition recorded. To repeat it for subsequent editions would at best be impractical. The fact is that of an extraordinarily high proportion of works published in the 16th century there were multiple editions or issues. To such an extent indeed that one might infer that almost any work of any substance was seized upon—when not protected by regional privilege—and republished or translated, so greedy were printers and booksellers for copy. In any event, for subsequent editions or translations of a given work reference is made to the earliest edition, where such explanatory notes will be found. Where in our opinion additional annotations will benefit the user, we have provided them, and, with the fine precedent of Miss Katharine F. Pantzer's puckish wit, even allowed ourselves an occasional unacademic aside.

Deprived though bibliographers or cataloguers may feel themselves to be by the simplified descriptions produced, they will perhaps find solace in bibliographical references to selected works where one may find fuller information. Bearing in mind, however, the comment of the great Benedictine scholar, the Abbé Mabillon, that the zealous collecting of bibliographical references in itself does not constitute scholarship, restraint has been exercised: where available these have been given to those works which are likely to be the most helpful in providing detailed descriptions and collations and, not infrequently for the knowledgeable, further recognition of the nature of a work. At the same time we have viewed as supererogatory references to those catalogues with which the reader may be assumed to be familiar, such as that of the National Library of Medicine for its 16th-century holdings, to say nothing of those of various national libraries.

Supplementing the above, locations of copies are indicated. It cannot be too strongly emphasized that a census of copies has not been undertaken but simply, as far as the United States are concerned, their presence in those libraries with an enduring commitment to Americana, supplemented, when lacking there, by copies found in geographically related institutions. (Here propinquity has been judged by local standards: what in the West may be considered close at hand will not be in Boston!) Insofar as dependence has of necessity been placed upon the National Union Catalog we cannot claim to be authoritative in such locations.

For libraries outside of the United States, we have sought modest ends. Where known, locations in the British Library, or when not, elsewhere in the British Isles, and in the Bibliothèque Nationale, or, again when not, elsewhere on the Continent are added. One hopes one's colleagues on both sides of the Atlantic will not be too annoyed at not finding credited to their institutions copies which these possess. Needless to say, for some items known to have once existed, no copy can be today traced, while at the same time we have sought to avoid raising bibliographic ghosts by describing works which never were, and have silently laid to rest others found elsewhere.

That of the works thus described, some 4300 in number, only a fourth appear already in 'Sabin' may come as a surprise. This is not a matter for self-congratulation but reflects a wider recognition, with the passage of time, of the multiple aspects of the Americas' impact on Europe, and one need not condemn Sabin or his successors for overlooking or being unaware of topics which today one must perforce confront.

Not the least of these is that of literature, which, while not unrepresented in 'Sabin', appears there sparsely. Any attempt at explaining this weakness must remain conjecture, yet it may stem from a variety of causes. The simplest is that of lack of knowledge. Yet another is a possible preoccupation with first-hand descriptions or with history *per se*. From experience one can also add that attempting to record works of literature, in the vast number of editions published, is to open up a Pandora's box of immense dimensions. If anything, this very fact suggests that a European's image of the Americas may have been shaped by the literary imagination of a Montaigne, a Du Bartas or even a Simon Goulart rather than directly by an Oviedo or a López de Gomara. While the difficulties inherent to identifying and recording literary references to the New World will be apparent, so far as has been feasible these have been sought out, yet much may indeed still remain lost to view.

Equally sparse was Sabin's inclusion of American materials in the natural sciences, but let us acknowledge that an interest in them is relatively recent, and that historians had previously failed fully to appreciate the rôle of material circumstance and natural phenomena in the unfolding of civilisation. The impact of American foodstuffs upon Europe may in fact have been as important as the ideas the Americas generated, for, as pointed out a century and a half ago by Augustin de Candolle, Central America and its adjoining areas are one of the three most significant sources in the world in terms of botany and agriculture.

As with literature, to try to do justice to the Americas' botanical contributions to Europe is extremely complicated, the more so, unfortunately, because of Linnaeus's 18th-century taxonomy, the compulsion of 16th-century botanists (classically oriented as they were) to try to fit newly introduced plants into Dioscorides's classifications, and obscurity surrounding the arrival in Europe of American plants. Is the reason that maize (corn) was initially designated 'fruticum turcicum' (Turkish wheat) due simply to ignorance, or could it somehow have reached Europe by way of the Near East, where Leonhard Rauwolf found both it and other American plants flourishing by 1582? Whatever the means of their transmission or their nomenclature, the importance of American introductions has been emphasized as a major factor in Europe's population growth — and its attendant consequences — by Alfred W. Crosby, Jr, in his stimulating *The Columbian Exchange* (Westport, Conn.: 1972).

Closely related to botany is another aspect of 16th-century science: that of medicine (to which botany was viewed contemporaneously as an adjunct). The vigorous efforts of the medical men of the period to find in new plants of the New World therapeutic uses, exemplified with such distinction by Nicolás Monardes, are a striking facet of the age.

But when one turns to disease itself, one wishes that a convincing rebuttal were available to Francisco Guerra's statement in *First Images of America*, that 'Venereal syphilis and yaws were brought back to Spain and Portugal by the discoverers [of America]'! Long a matter of controversy, whatever or wherever its ultimate origins in the prehistoric past, the appearance in Europe of syphilis at the end of the 15th century seems, all too inexorably, due to its transmission from Hispaniola, beginning with Columbus and his men: modern diagnostic techniques and paleobiologic investigations lend little support to the contention that syphilis was known in Europe prior to the year 1493.

The consequences for the bibliographer will be readily evident, for as the armies of European powers traipsed across the Continent they spread this new scourge, reflected in the writings of the period. Not without reason did the personal physician to Charles V, Luís Lobera de Avila, in his *Libro delas quatro enfermedades cortesanos* (Toledo: 1544), describe syphilis as one of the principal diseases which the courtier was likely to experience.

As a result it is a relatively rare medical work of the 16th century, other than classical texts, that does not include reference to the disease. And even if it were at best dubiously American, treatment for it usually employed medicines derived from American sources, chiefly Guaiacum (*lignum vitae, palo de India*, the holy wood, logwood, or other variants), introduced from the Caribbean. Not in fact without valid therapeutic uses, its popularity as a specific remedy owes far more to the press-agentry of Ulrich von Hutten and Lorenz Fries than to its actual merits, and offers a curious footnote to history. To compensate the great Augsburg family of international merchant bankers, the Fuggers, who had provided funds to help purchase his election as Holy Roman Emperor, Charles V granted them a monopoly for the importation of Guaiacum from the Spanish Indies. In turn the family set up 'hospitals' utilizing it to treat syphilis, at the same time commissioning Hutten (better known as a poet and theologian) to write his *De Guaiaci medicina* (Mainz: 1519) advocating its use, a work widely reprinted and translated.

Suffice it to say that so copious is the literature of syphilis as to reveal its extraordinary impact on Europe. We do not, it should be said, propose to carry the recording of references to syphilis as such beyond the year 1600—by which time Europe can be described as having made the disease its own—save where the Americas are specifically cited, as later, for instance, in Voltaire's *Candide*. (To do otherwise would perhaps unnecessarily recapitulate the work of Johann Proksch on the literature of syphilis in general.) We confess to not having pursued, even within the 16th century, every possible presence in Catholic Missals of a special Mass, that of Blessed Job, 'contra morbum gallicum', to be offered on behalf of sufferers of the disease. First found in a Missal for the diocese of Passau printed at Augsburg in 1505, it appears elsewhere as well.

In such terms then it may be recognized how much more broadly by far, and in how many dimensions, it has been necessary to explore the horizons of the New World to produce something more than a perfunctory scissors-and-paste accumulation of what has previously if disparately been identified as Americana, though, insofar as this is the case, we have sought to evaluate the accuracy of ascriptions and descriptions, amending and omitting as need be. Actually one cannot purport to have succeeded in devising more than a fresh and more comprehensive statement of how the Americas were reflected and displayed to a European audience. The eventual completion of the *Index Aureliensis* will unquestionably reveal omissions; one regrets that Oxford has not found an equally hardy, indefatigable and practiced bibliographer to perform for it what H.M. Adams has achieved for Cambridge.

* * *

The appendices also offered, we venture to hope, may lend an additional dimension to our undertaking. The geographic index, by country, place and printer or bookseller, in unabashed imitation of similar indices in the British Museum's various short-title catalogues, should, we believe, contribute to an awareness and further understanding of the means by which knowledge of the Americas was disseminated throughout Europe. To enhance its utility, this has been supplemented by an alphabetic index to the individuals concerned and their locale, conceived as well as a step towards a tool which would be of service to many a bibliographer: an index of printers and booksellers, peripatetic as they often were, extending beyond a single country alone.

The provision of these appendices is a response to a confidence that we shall increasingly witness an intensified investigation of the entrepreneurial role of both printers and booksellers in the instigation as well as the production and distribution of an author's work. Studies of the practices of compositors in the printing room itself have profitably carried further the researches of the philologist in establishing more authentic texts—in terms such as that of Fredson Bowers carrying on where his early mentor George Lyman Kittredge left off. Now, one suspects, we are likely to see—as aleady adumbrated by David Foxon's rewarding enquiries into Alexander Pope's relations with his publishers—more concentrated exploration of author/printer relationships, acknowledging anew that ideas and their expression should be considered in terms of concrete circumstance and not in a purely intellectual context alone.

* * *

Insofar as the present volume may prove to be a more comprehensive and authoritative statement of the Americas' impact upon Europe, it is the product of many hands. These range from those whose works figure in the list of references which follows on to one's immediate colleagues and staff. Of the latter we are above all indebted to Mr Samuel J. Hough, Assistant Librarian of the John Carter Brown Library. His preliminary spadework for the period at hand has proven invaluable, not merely because of his professional competence but also in the panoramic scope of his erudition. Credit should also be given to Mr Donald L. Farren, now Curator of Rare Books at the University of New Mexico, who as a member of the John Carter Brown Library staff supervised the preparation of the computerized chronological index by entry number to 'Sabin', providing a skeleton upon which this work is structured.

For such restraint upon inconsistency and upon error as may be found here the reader is beholden to Dr Dennis C. Landis, the Assistant Bibliographer for this segment. To him furthermore much of the work with German, Dutch and Polish materials has fallen. The patience of Miss Lynne A. Southwick as typist and in entering the computerized index likewise merits commendation.

Further afield we are also grateful to those colleagues who have replied to burdensome queries. To all of them we can scarcely do justice, but special appreciation is due to Dr Dennis E. Rhodes of the British Library and to Mr Francis O. Mattson of the New York Public Library. In the unending demands made upon them the staff of the Reading Room of the Houghton Library at Harvard University have in turn displayed unflinching courtesy. A more hidden debt is owed one Priscilla Cabot, whose well-being provided motivation when any other was lacking.

Without, however, the dynamism and imagination of Mr Thomas R. Adams, the Librarian of the John Carter Brown Library, this work would never have been undertaken. His recognition of the need, his marshalling of resources and his unflagging courage have made possible its inception and sustained its development at all stages.

John Alden

References

Adams (Cambr.)   Adams, Herbert Mayow. *Catalogue of books printed on the continent of Europe, 1501-1600, in Cambridge libraries.* London: Cambridge University Press, 1967. 2v.

Adams (Laudonnière)   Laudonnière, René Goulaine de. *A notable history containing four voyages made by certain French captains unto Florida by . . . René Laudonnière with a survey of the sixteenth-century printed French accounts of the attempt to establish a French colony in Florida, by Thomas R. Adams.* Farnham, Surrey: H.Stevens, 1964.

Alcocer (Valladolid)   Alcocer y Martínez, Mariano. *Catálogo razonado de obras impresas in Valladolid, 1481-1800.* Valladolid: Casa Social Católica, 1926.

Allison & Rogers   Allison, Antony Francis, & David Morrison Rogers. *A catalogue of Catholic books in English . . . 1558-1640.* London: Dawson, 1964.

Anselmo   Anselmo, António Joaquim. *Bibliografia das obras impressas em Portugal no século XVI.* Lisbon: Biblioteca Nacional, 1926.

Arents   Arents, George. *Tobacco, its history.* New York: Rosenbach Co., 1937-52. 5v.

Arents (Add.)   New York. Public Library. Arents Tobacco Collection. *Tobacco; a catalogue.* New York: New York Public Library, 1958-69. 10 pts.

Armstrong   Armstrong, Charles E. 'Copies of Ptolemy's geography in American libraries'. *Bulletin of the New York Public Library,* LXVI (1962) 104-114.

Atkinson (Fr.Ren.)   Atkinson, Geoffroy. *La littérature géographique française de la Renaissance; répertoire bibliographique.* Paris: A.Picard, 1927. (Repr., Geneva: Slatkine Reprints, 1972).

References

BMC — British Museum. Dept of Printed Books. *Catalogue of books printed in the XVth century now in the British Museum.* London: 1908-71. 10v.

BN (Hist. de France) — Paris. Bibliothèque Nationale. Département des imprimés. *Catalogue de l'histoire de France.* Paris: Firmin Didot frères, 1855-79. 11v.

Backer — Backer, Augustin de. *Bibliothèque de la Compagnie de Jésus.* Bruxelles: O.Schepens; Paris: A.Picard, 1890-1932. 11v.

Baginsky (German Americana) — Baginsky, Paul. 'German works relating to America, 1493-1800; a list compiled from the collections of the New York Public Library'. *Bulletin of the New York Public Library*, XLII-XLIV (1938-40), *passim.*

Balsamo (Scinzenzeler) — Balsamo, Luigi. *Giovanni Angelo Scinzenzeler, tipografo in Milano (1500-1526).* Florence: Sansoni, 1959.

Baudrier (Lyons) — Baudrier, Henri Louis. *Bibliographie Lyonnaise; recherches sur les imprimeurs, libraires, relieurs et fondeurs de lettres de Lyon au XVI siècle.* Lyons: A.Brun, 1895-1921. 13v. (Repr., Paris: F.De Nobele, 1964-65).

Baudrier (Lyons) Suppl. — *Supplément provisoire à la 'Bibliographie Lyonnaise' du president Baudrier.* Paris: Bibliothèque Nationale, 1967-.

Baumgartner (Fracastoro) — Baumgartner, Leona, & Fulton, John F. *A bibliography of the poem* Syphilis, sive Morbus gallicus *by Girolamo Fracastoro, of Verona.* New Haven: Yale University Press, 1935.

Becker — Becker, Carl. *Jobst Amman, Zeichner und Formschneider, Kupferätzer und Stecher.* Leipzig: R.Weigel, 1854. (Repr., Nieuwkoop: B.de Graaf, 1961).

Belg.typ. — Cockx-Indestege, Elly & Glorieux, Geneviève. *Belgica typographica 1541-1600;* v.1. Nieuwkoop: B.de Graaf, 1968.

Benzing — Benzing, Joseph. *Die Buchdrucker des 16. und 17. Jahrhunderts im deutschen Sprachgebiet.* Wiesbaden: O.Harrassowitz, 1963. (Beiträge zum Buch- und Bibliothekswesen, XII).

Benzing (Fries) — ——. 'Bibliographie der Schriften des Colmarer Arztes Lorenz Fries'. *Philobiblon*, VI (1962) 121-140.

Benzing (Hutten)   ———. *Ulrich von Hutten und seine Drucker; eine Bibliographie der Schriften Huttens im 16. Jahrhundert*. Wiesbaden: O.Harrassowitz, 1956. (Beiträge zum Buch- und Bibliothekswesen, VI).

Benzing (Ryff)   ———. *Walter H.Ryff und sein literarisches Werk, eine Bibliographie*. Hamburg: 1959.

Bibl.belg.   *Bibliotheca Belgica; bibliographie générale des Pays-Bas*. Ghent: Vanderpoorten (1.sér.. C.Vyt); The Hague: M.Nijhoff, 1880-1967. 240 pts.

Bibl. mar. esp.   Instituto nacional del libro español. *Ensayo de bibliografía marítima española*. Barcelona: Casa Provincial de Caridad, 1943.

Bolaño e Isla (Veracruz)   Bolaño e Isla, Anáncio. *Contribución al estudio biobibliografico de fray Alonso de la Vera Cruz*. Mexico, D.F.: Libr. Robredo, 1947.

Bongi (Giolito)   Bongi, Salvatore. *Annali di Gabriel Giolito de' Ferrari da Trino di Monferrato, stampatore in Venezia*. Rome: 1890-97. 7 pts.

Borba de Moraes   Moraes, Rubens Borba de. *Bibliographie Brasiliana; a bibliographical essay*. Amsterdam: Colibris Editora, 1958. 2v.

Borsa   Borsa, Gedeon. 'Die Ausgaben der "Cosmographia" von Johannes Honter'. *Essays in honour of Victor Scholderer*, Mainz: K.Pressler, 1970, p.90-105.

Brunet   Brunet, Jacques-Charles. *Manuel du libraire et de l'amateur de livres*. Paris: Firmin Didot frères, 1860-80. 9v. (Repr., Copenhagen: Rosenkilde & Bagger, 1966-67).

Burmeister (Gasser)   Burmeister, Karl Heinz. *Achilles Pirmin Gasser*. Wiesbaden: G.Pressler, 1970-75. 3v. 'Bibliographie': v.2

Burmeister (Münster)   ———. *Sebastian Münster; eine Bibliographie*. Wiesbaden: G.Pressler, 1964.

Canto (Azores)   Canto, Ernesto do. *Bibliotheca açoriana*. Ponta Delgada: Archivo dos Açores, 1890.

Cartier (de Tournes)   Cartier, Alfred. *Bibliographie des éditions des de Tournes, imprimeurs lyonnais*. Paris: Bibliothèques Nationales de France, 1937-38. 2v. (Repr., Geneva: Slatkine Reprints, 1970).

Choptrayanovitch   Šoptrajanov, Gorgi. *Etienne Tabourot des Accords [par] Georges Choptrayanovitch*. Dijon: J.Belvet, 1935. (Repr., Geneva: Slatkine Reprints, 1970).

References

Church   Church, Elihu Dwight. *A catalogue of books relating to the discovery and early history of North and South America, forming a part of the Library of E.D.Church* [1482-1884]. New York: Dodd, Mead & Co., 1907. 5v. (Repr., Gloucester, Mass.: P.Smith, 1951).

Church (Eng.lit.)   ——. A catalogue of books, consisting of English literature and miscellanea. New York: Dodd, Mead & Co., 1902. 2v.

Cioranescu (XVI)   Cioranescu, Alexandre. *Bibliographie de la littérature française du seizième siècle.* Paris: C.Klincksieck, 1959.

Cioranescu (XVII)   ——. *Bibliographie de la littérature française du dix-septième siècle.* Paris: Centre National de la Recherche Scientifique, 1965-66. 3v.

Coccia   Coccia, Edmondo Maria. *Le edizioni delle opere del Mantovano.* Rome: Institutum Carmelitanum, 1960. (Collectanea bibliographica carmelitana, II).

Collijn (Sver.bibl.)   Collijn, Isak G.A. *Sveriges bibliografi intil år 1600.* Uppsala: Svenska Litteratursällskapet, 1927-38. 3v.

Coote (Schöner)   Schöner, Johann. *Johann Schöner, professor of Mathematics at Nuremburg . . . with an introduction and bibliography by C.H. Coote.* London: H.Stevens & Son, 1888.

Darlow & Moule   British and Foreign Bible Society. Library. *Historical catalogue of the printed editions of Holy Scripture in the library of the British and Foreign Bible Society;* comp. by T.H.Darlow and H.F.Moule. London: The Bible House, 1903-11. 2v. in 4. (Repr., Nendeln, Liechtenstein: Kraus, 1963).

De Ricci (Ronsard)   Maggs Bros., London. *Catalogue d'une collection unique des éditions originales de Ronsard,* par Seymour de Ricci. Paris, London: Maggs Bros., 1925.

Desgraves (Les Haultin)   Desgraves, Louis. *Les Haultin,* 1571-1623. Geneva: E.Droz, 1960. (L'imprimerie à La Rochelle, II).

Droz (Vve Berton)   Droz, Eugénie. *La veuve Berton et Jean Portau, 1573-1589.* Geneva: E.Droz, 1960. (L'imprimerie à La Rochelle, III).

Eames (Columbus)   New York. Public Library. *Two important gifts to the New York Public Library by Mr.George F.Baker, Jr.: Columbus' letter on the discovery of America (1493-1497)* [by

Wilberforce Eames], *& Daniel Denton's description of New York in 1670.* New York: New York Public Library, 1924.

Escudero (Seville) — Escudero y Perosso, Francisco. *Tipografía Hispalense; anales bibliográficos de la ciudad de Sevilla desde el establecimiento de la imprenta hasta fines del siglo XVIII.* Madrid: Sucesores de Rivadeneyra, 1894.

Fairfax Murray (France) — Murray, Charles Fairfax. *Catalogue of a collection of early French books in the library of C.Fairfax Murray;* comp. by Hugh W.Davies. London: Priv. print., 1910. 2v.

Fairfax Murray (Germany) — Murray, Charles Fairfax. *Catalogue of a collection of early German books in the library of C.Fairfax Murray;* comp. by Hugh W.Davies. London: Priv. print., 1913. 2v. (Repr., London: Holland Press, 1962).

Ferguson (Bibl. chem.) — Glasgow. Royal Technical College. Library. Young Collection. *Bibliotheca chemica: a catalogue of the alchemical, chemical and pharmaceutical books in the collection of the late James Young of Kelly and Durris* . . . by John Ferguson. Glasgow: J.Maclehose and Sons, 1906. 2v.

Ferguson (Reisch) — Ferguson, John. 'The Margarita philosophica of Gregorius Reisch; a bibliography'. *The Library*, 4th ser., X (1929) 194-216.

GW — *Gesamtkatalog der Wiegendrucke*; hrsg. von der Kommission für den Gesamtkatalog der Wiegendrucke. Leipzig: K.W.Hiersemann, 1925-. 8v. (Vols. 1-7 repr., Stuttgart: A.Hiersemann; New York: H.P.Kraus, 1968).

GW (Einbl.) — Prussia. Kommission für den Gesamtkatalog der Wiegendrucke. *Einblattdrucke des XV. Jahrhunderts; ein bibliographisches Verzeichnis.* Halle: S.Karras, 1914. (Sammlung bibliothekswissenschaftlicher Arbeiten, Hefte 35-36).

Garcia (Alcalá de Henares) — García López, Juan Catalina. *Ensayo de una tipografía Complutense.* Madrid: M.Tello, 1889.

Gibson (More) — Gibson, Reginald Walter. *St. Thomas More: a preliminary bibliography of his works . . . With a bibliography of Utopiana*; compiled by R.W.Gibson and J.Max Patrick. New Haven: Yale University Press, 1961.

References

Goff   Goff, Frederick Richmond. *Incunabula in American libraries; a third census of fifteenth century books recorded in North American collections.* New York: Bibliographical Society of America, 1964. (Repr., with emendations, Millwood, N.J.: Kraus Reprint Co., 1973).

Goldschmidt   Goldschmidt, Ernest Philip. 'Not in Harrisse'. *Essays honoring Lawrence C. Wroth,* Portland, Me.: 1951, p.129-141.

Graesse   Grässe, Johann Georg Theodor. *Trésor de livres rares et précieux.* Dresden: R.Kuntze, 1859-69. 7v. in 4. (Repr., Milan: G.Görlich, 1951).

Greg   Greg, Sir Walter Wilson. *A bibliography of the English printed drama to the Restoration.* London: The Bibliographical Society, 1939-59. 4v.

Grolier Club (Langland to Wither)   Grolier Club, New York. *Catalogue of original and early editions of some of the poetical and prose works of English writers from Langland to Wither.* New York: Grolier Club, 1893.

Guerra (Monardes)   Guerra, Francisco. *Nicolás Bautista Monardes: su vida y su obra.* Mexico, D.F.: Comp. fundidora de Fierro y Acero de Monterrey, 1961. (Yale University. Dept. of the History of Medicine. Publication no. 41).

Haebler (Bibl.Iber.)   Haebler, Konrad. *Bibliografía Ibérica del siglo XV.* The Hague: M.Nijhoff; Leipzig: K.Hiersemann, 1903-17. 2v. (Repr., New York: B.Franklin, 1963).

Hain   Hain, Ludwig Friedrich Theodor. *Repertorium bibliographicum . . . ad annum MD.* Stuttgart: J.G.Cotta, 1826-38. 2v. in 4. (Repr., Berlin: J.Altmann, 1925).

Hain/Copinger   Copinger, Walter Arthur. *Supplement to Hain's Repertorium bibliographicum.* London: H.Sotheran, 1895-1902. 2v. in 3. (Repr., Berlin: J.Altmann, 1926; Milan: G.Görlich, 1950).

Hanke/Giménez   Hanke, Lewis, & Giménez Fernández, Manuel. *Bartolomé de las Casas, 1474-1566; bibliografía crítica y cuerpo de materiales.* Santiago de Chile: Fondo José Toribio Medina, 1954.

Harrisse (BAV)	Harrisse, Henry. *Bibliotheca Americana vetustissima; a description of works relating to America published between the years 1492 and 1551.* New York: G.P.Philes, 1866. (Repr., with the *Additions*, Paris: Maisonneuve & Cie., 1922; Madrid: V.Suárez, 1958).
Harrisse (BAV) Add.	——. *Bibliotheca Americana vetustissima . . . Additions.* Paris: Libr. Tross. 1872. (Repr. with preceding, q.v.)
Harrisse (NF)	——. *Notes pour servir à l'histoire, à la bibliographie et à la cartographie de la Nouvelle-France et des pays adjacents, 1545-1700.* Paris: Libr. Tross, 1872. (Repr., Dubuque, Ia.: Brown, 1964).
Henning (Wagner)	Henning, Hans. 'Bibliographie der Wagner-Bücher des 16. Jahrhunderts'. In his *Beiträge zur Druckgeschichte der Faust- und Wagner-Bücher des 16. und 18. Jahrhunderts.* Weimar: Arion Verlag, 1963, p.69-73. (Beiträge zur deutschen Klassik, XVI).
Henrey (Brit.bot.)	Henrey, Blanche. *British botanical and horticultural literature before 1800.* London: Oxford University Press, 1975. 3v.
Holmes (Du Bartas)	Du Bartas, Guillaume de Salluste, seigneur. *The works . . . a critical edition . . .* by Urban Tigner Holmes, Jr., John Coriden Lyons, Robert White Linker. Chapel Hill: University of North Carolina Press, 1935-40. 3v. 'Bibliography': III:565-576.
Hoskins (Polonica)	Hoskins, Janina W. *Early and rare Polonica of the 15th-17th centuries in American libraries; a bibliographical survey.* Boston: G.K.Hall, 1973.
Hunt (Bot.)	Hunt, Rachel McM.M. *Catalogue of botanical books.* Pittsburgh: Hunt Botanical Library, 1958-61. 2v. in 3.
Ind.aur.	*Index Aureliensis; catalogus librorum sedecimo saeculo impressorum*, I-VI (A-Carr). Geneva: Fondation Index Aureliensis, 1962-. In progress.
Isaac	Proctor, Robert. *An index to the early printed books in the British Museum.* Pt II, 1501-1520. Sections II, Italy; III, Switzerland & Eastern Europe; by Frank Isaac. London: Quaritch, 1938. Continues Proctor's Section I below.

References

JCB AR	Brown University. John Carter Brown Library. *Annual report.* Providence: The Library, 1901-75. (Years 1901-1966, repr., with index, The Library, 1972).
JCB (101 Bks.)	———. *Rare Americana: a selection of one hundred & one books, maps & prints* not in *the John Carter Brown Library.* Providence: Associates of the John Carter Brown Library, 1974.
JCB (3)	———. *Bibliotheca Americana; catalogue of the John Carter Brown Library.* 3rd ed. Providence: The Library, 1919-31. 3 pts in 5v.
JCB (STL)	———. *Bibliotheca Americana: catalogue of the John Carter Brown Library . . . Short-title list of additions, books printed 1471-1700.* Providence: Brown University Press, 1973.
Jones (Goulart)	Jones, Leonard Chester. *Simon Goulart, 1543-1628; étude biographique et bibliographique.* Geneva: Georg & cie, 1917.
Kebabian	Kebabian, John S. *The Henry C. Taylor Collection.* New Haven: Yale University Library, 1971.
King Manuel	Manuel II, King of Portugal. *Livros antigos portuguezes, 1489-1600, da bibliotheca de Sua Majestade Fidelissima,* descriptos por S.M. el-rei D.Manuel. London: Maggs Bros., 1929-35. 3v.
Klebs	Klebs, Arnold Carl. *Incunabula scientifica et medica; short title list.* Bruges: Saint Catherine press, 1938. (Osiris, IV, pt 1).
Knuttel	The Hague. Koninklijke Bibliotheek. *Catalogus van de pamfletten-verzameling berustende in de Koninklijke Bibliotheek,* bewerkt . . . door Dr. W.P.C.Knuttel. The Hague: Algemeene Landsdrukkerij, 1889-1920. 9v.
Koeman (Braun & Hogenberg)	'Braun & Hogenberg'. In Koeman, Cornelis. *Atlantes Neerlandici; bibliography of terrestrial, maritime, and celestial atlases and pilot books, published in the Netherlands up to 1880,* Amsterdam: Theatrum Orbis Terrarum, 1967-71, II:15-25.
Koeman (Jod)	'Gerard and Cornelis de Jode'. As in the above, II:205-212.
Koeman (Lan)	'Langenes, Barent'. As in the above, II:252-261.

Koeman (Me)	'Mercator-Hondius-Janssonius'. As in the above, II:281-549.
Koeman (Ort)	'Ortelius, Abraham'. As in the above, III:25-83.
Koeman (Wyt)	'Wytfliet, Cornelis van'. As in the above, III:219-220.
Koeman (Z.Hey)	'Heyns, Zacharias'. As in the above, II:132-134.
Kraus (Drake)	Kraus, Hans Peter. *Sir Francis Drake, a pictorial biography . . . with . . . a detailed catalogue of the author's collection.* Amsterdam: N.Israel, 1970.
Kress	Harvard University. Kress Library of Business and Economics. *Catalogue.* Boston: Baker Library, Harvard Graduate School of Business Administration, 1940-67. 5v.
Langer	Langer, Edward, ed. *Bibliographie der österreichischen Drucke des XV. und XVI. Jahrhunderts.* I.Bd, 1.Heft. Vienna: Gilhofer & Rauschburg, 1913.
Leclerc (1867)	Leclerc, Charles. *Bibliotheca Americana: Catalogue raisonné d'une très-précieuse collection de livres.* Paris: Maisonneuve & Cie., 1867.
Leclerc (1878)	——. *Bibliotheca Americana: Histoire, géographie, voyages . . . des deux Amériques.* Paris: Maisonneuve & Cie., 1878.
Le Moine	Le Moine, Roger. *L'Amérique et les poètes français de la Renaissance.* Ottawa: Université d'Ottawa, 1972.
Madan (Oxford)	Madan, Falconer. *Oxford books; a bibliography of printed works relating to the university and city of Oxford or printed or published there.* Oxford: Clarendon Press, 1895-1931. 3v.
Maggs	Maggs Bros., London. Bibliotheca Americana et Philippina. London: 1922-1930. 9v. in 8.
Medina (Arau.)	Ercilla y Zúñiga, Alonso de. *La Araucana . . . Edición del centenario, ilustrada con grabados . . . y bibliográficas y una biografía del autor.* La publica José Toribio Medina. Santiago de Chile: Impr. Elzeviriana, 1910-18. 5v. 'Bibliografía de la Araucana': IV:1-60.

References

Medina (BHA)	Medina, José Toribio. *Biblioteca Hispano-Americana (1493-1810)*. Santiago de Chile: The Author, 1898-1907. 7v. (Repr.: Amsterdam: N.Israel, 1958-62).
Medina (BHA) (Ampl.)	'Ampliaciones'. In the preceding, VI:507-30.
Medina (Chile)	——. *Biblioteca Hispano-Chilena (1523-1817)*. Santiago de Chile: The Author, 1897-99. 3v.
Moranti (Urbino)	Moranti, Luigi. *Le cinquecentine della Biblioteca universitaria di Urbino*. Florence: L.S.Olschki, 1977. 3v. (Biblioteca di bibliografia italiana, LXXX).
Mortimer (France)	Harvard University. Library. Dept. of Graphic Arts. *Catalogue of books and manuscripts. Part I. French 16th century books*. Compiled by Ruth Mortimer. Cambridge, Mass.: Belknap Press of Harvard University Press, 1964. 2v.
Mortimer (Italy)	——. *Catalogue of books and manuscripts. Part II. Italian 16th century books*. Compiled by Ruth Mortimer. Cambridge, Mass.: Belknap Press of Harvard University Press, 1974. 2v.
Muller (1872)	Muller, Frederick. *Catalogue of books, maps, plates on America*. Amsterdam: F.Muller, 1872-75. 3 pts. (Repr., Amsterdam: N.Israel, 1966).
Nijhoff/Kronenberg	Nijhoff, Wouter, & Kronenberg, M.E. *Nederlandsche bibliographie van 1500 tot 1540*. The Hague: M.Nijhoff, 1923-61. 3v. in 7.
Nissen (Birds)	Nissen, Claus. *Die illustrierten Vogelbücher, ihre Geschichte und Bibliographie*. Stuttgart: Hiersemann Verlag, 1953.
Nissen (Bot.)	——. *Die botanische Buchillustration, ihre Geschichte und Bibliographie*. Stuttgart: Hiersemann Verlags-Gesellschaft, 1951. 2v.
Nissen (Zool.)	——. *Die zoologische Buchillustration, ihre Bibliographie und Geschichte*. Stuttgart: A.Hiersemann, 1966-69.
Ortroy (Apian)	Ortroy, Fernand Gratien van. *Bibliographie de l'oeuvre de Pierre Apian*. Besançon: P.Jacquin, 1902. (Repr., Amsterdam: Meridian, 1963).
Palau	Palau y Dulcet, Antonio. *Manual del librero Hispano-Americano*. 2da ed. Barcelona: A.Palau, 1948-77. 28v.

Palmer — Palmer, Philip Motley. *German works on America, 1492-1800.* Berkeley: University of California Press, 1952. (University of California Publications in modern philology, XXXVI (10):271-412).

Pardo de Tavera — U.S. Library of Congress. *Bibliography of the Philippine Islands.* Washington, D.C.: Govt. Print. Off., 1903. Pt 2: *Bibliotheca Filipina,* by T.H.Pardo de Tavera.

Peeters-Fontainas (Impr.esp.) — Peeters-Fontainas, Jean. *Bibliographie des impressions Espagnoles des Pays-Bas méridionaux.* Nieuwkoop: B.de Graaf, 1965. 2v.

Pellechet — Pellechet, Marie Léontine Cathérine. *Catalogue générale des incunables des bibliothèques publiques de France.* Paris: A.Picard et fils, 1897-1909. 3v. (A-Gr only).

——. ——. Nendeln, Liechtenstein: Kraus-Thomson, 1970. 26v. Includes a photoreproduction of the unpublished manuscript by Louis Polain continuing the work from Gregorius to Z.

Pérez Pastor (Madrid) — Pérez Pastor, Cristóbal. *Bibliografía Madrileña; descripción de las obras impresas en Madrid.* Madrid: Tip. de los Huérfanos, 1891-1907. 3v.

Pérez Pastor (Medina del Campo) — ——. *La imprenta en Medina del Campo.* Madrid: Sucesores de Rivadeneyra, 1895.

Pérez Pastor (Toledo) — ——. *La imprenta en Toledo; descripción bibliográfica de las obras impresas en la imperial ciudad desde 1483 hasta nuestros días.* Madrid: M.Tello, 1887.

Pforzheimer — Pforzheimer, Carl Howard. *The Carl H.Pforzheimer Library: English literature, 1475-1700.* New York: Priv.print., 1940. 3v.

Phillips (Atlases) — U.S. Library of Congress. Map Division. *A list of geographical atlases in the Library of Congress* . . . compiled under the direction of Philip Lee Phillips. Washington: Govt. Print. Off., 1909-20. 4v.

Plan (Rabelais) — Plan, Pierre Paul. *Bibliographie Rabelaisienne: Les éditions de Rabelais de 1532 à 1711.* Paris: Imprimerie Nationale, 1904. (Repr., Nieuwkoop: B.de Graaf, 1965).

Pogo (Conquista) — Pogo, Alexander, ed. 'The anonymous La conquista del Peru (Seville, April 1534) and the Libro ultimo del summaria dell Indie Occidental (Venice, October 1534)'. *Proceedings of the American Academy of Arts and Sciences,* LXIV (1930) 177-286.

References

Polain   Polain, Louis. *Catalogue des livres imprimés au quinzième siècle des bibliothèques de Belgique.* Brussels: Soc. de Bibliophiles, 1932. 4v.

Pritzel   Pritzel, Georg August. *Thesaurus literaturae botanicae.* Leipzig: F.A.Brockhaus, 1872-77. (Repr., Milan: G.Görlich, 1950).

Proctor   Proctor, Robert. *An index to the early printed books in the British Museum.* Pt II, 1501-1520. Section I. Germany. London: K.Paul 1898-1899. (Repr., London: Holland Press, 1960).

Proctor (Doesborgh)   ———. *Jan van Doesborgh, printer at Antwerp; an essay in bibliography.* London: The Bibliographical Society, 1894.

Proksch   Proksch, Johann Karl. *Die Litteratur über die venerischen Krankheiten von den ersten Schriften über Syphilis aus dem Ende des fünfzehnten Jahrhunderts bis zum Jahre 1889.* Bonn: P.Hanstein, 1889-91. 5 pts. (Repr., Nieuwkoop: B.de Graaf, 1966).

Racc.Tassiana   Bergamo. Biblioteca civica A.Mai. *La raccolta Tassiana della Biblioteca civica "A.Mai" di Bergamo.* Bergamo: Banca Piccolo Credito Bergamasco, 1960.

Reichling   Reichling, Dietrich. *Appendices ad Hainii-Copingeri Repertorium bibliographicum; additiones et emendationes.* Munich: J.Rosenthal, 1905-11. 7v. (Repr., Milan: G.Görlich, 1953).

Renouard (Aldus)   Renouard, Antoine Augustin. *Annales de l'imprimerie des Alde.* 2me éd. Paris: A.A.Renouard, 1825. 3v.

Renouard (Badius Ascensius)   Renouard, Philippe. *Bibliographie des impressions et des oeuvres de Josse Badius Ascensius, imprimeur et humaniste, 1462-1535.* Paris: E.Paul et fils et Guillemin, 1908. 3v. (Repr., New York: B.Franklin, 1967).

Renouard (de Colines)   ———. *Bibliographie des éditions de Simon de Colines, 1520-1546.* Paris: E.Paul, L.Huard et Guillemin, 1894. (Repr., Nieuwkoop: B.de Graaf, 1962).

Renouard (Estienne)   Renouard, Antoine Augustin. *Annales de l'imprimerie des Estienne.* 2me éd. Paris: J.Renouard & Cie., 1843. (Repr., New York: B.Franklin, 1960; Geneva: Slatkine Reprints, 1971).

Rép. bibl.   *Répertoire bibliographique des libres imprimés en France au seizième siècle.* Baden-Baden: Libr. Heitz; V.Koerner, 1968-77. 22v.

Retana (Filipinas)   Retana y Gamboa, Wenceslao Emilio. *Aparato bibliográfico de la historia general de Filipinas.* Madrid: Minuesa de los Ríos, 1906. 3v.

Riccardi   Riccardi, Pietro. *Bibliotheca matematica italiana, dalla origine della stampa ai primi anni del secolo XIX.* Modena: Tip. Soliana, 1870-80. 2v. (Repr., Milan: M.Görlich, 1952).

Ritter (Strasbourg)   Ritter, François. *Répertoire bibliographique des livres du XVIe siècle qui se trouvent à la Bibliothèque Nationale et Universitaire de Strasbourg.* Strasbourg: P.H.Heitz, 1932-57. 4v.

Ríus (Cervantes)   Ríus y de Llosellas, Leopoldo. *Bibliografía crítica de las obras de Miguel de Cervantes Saavedra.* Madrid: M.Murillo, 1895-1905. 3v. (Repr., New York: B.Franklin, 1970).

Rothschild   Rothschild, Nathan James Edouard, baron de. *Catalogue des livres composant la bibliothèque de feu M.le baron James de Rothschild.* Paris: D.Morgand, 1884-1920. 5v. (Repr., New York: B.Franklin, 1967).

STC   Pollard, A.W. & Redgrave, G.R., comps. *A short-title catalogue of books printed in England, Scotland, & Ireland and of English books printed abroad, 1475-1640.* London: The Bibliographical Society, 1926. (Repr., Oxford: Oxford University Press, 1946). Refs for entries 14045.5 ff. are to the following edn.

———. ———. 2nd edn, rev. & enl., begun by W.A.Jackson & F.S.Ferguson, completed by Katharine F.Pantzer; v.2, I-Z. London: The Bibliographical Society, 1976.

Sabin   Sabin, Joseph. *Bibliotheca Americana; a dictionary of books relating to America . . .* Begun by Joseph Sabin, continued by Wilberforce Eames and completed by R.W.G. Vail, for the Bibliographical Society of America. New York: Sabin, 1868-92; Bibliographical Society of America, 1928-36. 29v. (Repr., Amsterdam: N.Israel; New York: Barnes & Noble, 1961-62).

References

Salvá   Salvá y Pérez, Vicente. *Cátalogo de la biblioteca de Salvá,* escrito por D.Pedro Salvá y Mallen. Valencia: Ferrer de Orga, 1872. 2v. (Repr., Barcelona: Porter-Libros, 1963).

Sánchez (Aragon)   Sánchez, Juan Manuel. *Bibliografía Aragonesa del siglo* XVI. Madrid: Impr. Clásica Española, 1913-14. 2v.

Sánchez (Saragossa)   ———. *Bibliografía Zaragozana del siglo XV.* Madrid: Impr. Alemana, 1908.

Sander   Sander, Max. *Le Livre à figures italien depuis 1467 jusqu'à 1530.* Milan: U.Hoepli, 1942-43. 6v. in 5. (Also issued, New York: G.E.Stechert, 1941, i.e., 1942-43. Repr., Nendeln, Liechtenstein: Kraus, 1969).

Sanz (Ult.ad)   Sanz, Carlos. *Bibliotheca Americana vetustissima; últimas adiciones.* Madrid: V.Suárez, 1960. 2v.

Schorbach (Lucidarius)   Schorbach, Karl. *Studien über das deutsche Volksbuch Lucidarius und seine Bearbeitungen in fremden Sprachen.* Strassburg: K.J.Trübner, 1894.

Shaaber   Shaaber, Matthias Adam. *Sixteenth-century imprints in the libraries of the University of Pennsylvania.* Philadelphia: University of Pennsylvania Press, 1976.

Serra — Zanetti   Serra-Zanetti, Alberto. *L'arte della stampa in Bologna.* Bologna: 1959.

Sherrington (Fernel)   Sherrington, Sir Charles Scott. *The endeavour of Jean Fernel, with a list of the editions of his writings.* Cambridge: Cambridge University Press, 1946.

Silva (Camões)   Silva, Innocencio Francisco da. *Diccionario bibliographico portuguez,* XIV. Lisbon: Imprensa Nacional, 1886.

Stevens (Ptolemy)   Stevens, Henry Newton. *Ptolemy's Geography; a brief account of all the printed editions down to 1730.* 2nd edn. London: H.Stevens, Sons & Stiles, 1908. (Repr., Amsterdam: Theatrum Orbis Terrarum, 1972).

Stillwell (Science)   Stillwell, Margaret Bingham. *The awakening interest in science during the first century of printing, 1450-1550; an annotated checklist of first editions.* New York: Bibliographical Society of America, 1970.

Streit	Streit, Robert. *Bibliotheca Missionum.* Münster i.W., Aachen: 1916-74. 30v. (Veröffentlichungen des Internationalen Instituts für missionswissenschaftliche Forschung).
Sudhoff (Paracelsus)	Sudhoff, Karl. *Bibliographia Paracelsica; Besprechung der unter Hohenheims Namen 1527-1893 erschienenen Druckschriften.* Graz: Akademische Druck- und Verlagsanstalt, 1958.
Szabo	Szabó Károly. *Régi Magyar Könyvtár.* Budapest: A Magyar Tudományos Akadémia Könyvkiadó Hivatala, 1879-98. 3v.
Taylor (Regiment)	Bourne, William. *A regiment for the sea;* ed. by E.G.R. Taylor. Cambridge: Hakluyt Society, 1963. (Hakluyt Society Publications, 2nd ser., CXXI).
Tazbir	Tazbir, Janusz. 'La conquête de l'Amérique à la lumière de l'opinion polonaise'. *Acta Poloniae historica,* XVII (1968) 5-22.
Tchémerzine	Tchémerzine, Avenir. *Bibliographie d'éditions originales et rares d'auteurs français des XVᵉ, XVIᵉ, XVIIᵉ, et XVIIIᵉ siècles.* Paris: M.Plee, 1927-34. 10v.
Thickett (Pasquier)	Thickett, Dorothy. *Bibliographie des oeuvres d'Estienne Pasquier.* Geneva: E.Droz, 1956. (Travaux d'humanisme et renaissance, XXI).
Thiébaud (La chasse)	Thiébaud, Jules. *Bibliographie des ouvrages français sur la chasse.* Paris: E.Nourry, 1934.
Tiele	Tiele, Pieter Anton. *Nederlandsche bibliographie van land- en volkenkunde.* Amsterdam: F.Muller, 1884. (Repr., Amsterdam: Theatrum Orbis Terrarum, 1966).
Tiele-Muller	Muller, Frederik. *Mémoire bibliographique sur les journaux des navigateurs néerlandais . . . en la possession de Frederik Muller . . .* Rédigé par P.A.Tiele. Amsterdam: F.Muller, 1867. (Repr., Amsterdam: Theatrum Orbis Terrarum, 1969).
Vail (Frontier)	Vail, Robert W.G. *The voice of the old frontier.* Philadelphia: University of Pennsylvania Press, 1949.
Vindel	Vindel, Francisco. *Manual gráfico-descriptivo del bibliófilo Hispano-Americano (1475-1850).* Madrid: Impr. Gógora, 1930-34. 12v.

References

Wagner (Grijalva)   Wagner, Henry Raup. *The discovery of New Spain in 1518 by Juan de Grijalva, a translation of the original texts with an introduction and notes.* Berkeley, Calif.: The Cortes Society, 1942.

Wagner (NW)   ———. *The cartography of the northwest coast of America to the year 1800.* Berkeley, Calif.: University of California Press, 1937. 2v. (Repr., Amsterdam: B.M. Israel, 1968).

Wagner (SW)   ———. The Spanish Southwest, 1542-1794. Albuquerque: The Quivira Society, 1937. 2v.

Waller   Sallander, Hans. *Bibliotheca Walleriana; the books illustrating the history of medicine and science collected by Dr. Erik Waller and bequeathed to the Library of the Royal University of Uppsala. A catalogue.* Stockholm: Almquist & Wiksell, 1955. 2v. (Repr., New York: Arno Press, 1967).

Weale/Bohatta   Weale, William Henry James. *Bibliographia liturgica: catalogus missalium ritus latini ab anno MCCCCLXXV impressorum; iterum edidit Hanns Bohatta.* London: B.Quaritch, 1928.

Weber (Jobin)   Weber, Bruno. "'Die Welt begeret allezeit Wunder"; Versuch einer Bibliographie der Einblattdrucke von Bernhard Jobin in Strassburg'. *Gutenberg Jahrbuch*, 1976, p.270-290.

Weller (Ersten d. Zeitungen)   Weller, Emil Ottokar. *Die ersten deutschen Zeitungen.* Tübingen: H.Läupp, 1872. (Bibliothek des litterarischen Vereins in Stuttgart, CXI).

Weller (Falsch. & fing. Druckorte)   ———. *Die falschen und fingierten Druckorte.* 2te verm. und verb. Aufl. Leipzig: W.Engelmann, 1864. 2v. (Repr. Hildesheim: G.Olms, 1960).

Wierzbowski   Wierzbowski, Teodor. *Bibliographia Polonica XV ac XVI ss.* Warsaw: C.Kowalewski, 1889-94. 3v. (Repr., Nieuwkoop: B.de Graaf, 1961).

Winship (Cabot)   Winship, George Parker. *Cabot bibliography; with an introductory essay.* London: H.Stevens, Son & Stiles; New York: Dodd, Mead & Co., 1900. (Repr., New York: B.Franklin, 1967).

Wolfenbüttel   Wolfenbüttel. Herzog-August Bibliothek. *Die Neue Welt in den Schätzen einer alten europäischen Bibliothek.* Wolfenbüttel: 1976.

Wroth (Frampton)   Wroth, Lawrence Counselman. 'An Elizabethan merchant and man of letters'. *Huntington Library Quarterly,* XVII (1954) 299-314.

Wroth & Annan   Wroth, Lawrence C., & Annan, Gertrude L. *Acts of the French royal administration concerning Canada, Guiana, the West Indies and Louisiana, prior to 1791.* New York: New York Public Library, 1930.

Yarmolinsky (Early Polish Americana)   Yarmolinsky, Avrahm. *Early Polish Americana; a bibliographical study.* New York: New York Public Library, 1937.

Woodfield   Woodfield, Denis B. *Surreptitious printing in England, 1550-1640.* New York: Bibliographical Society of America, 1973.

Locations

North America

California

C	California State Library, Sacramento
CCamarSJ	St. John's Seminary, Camarillo
CLCo	Los Angeles County Public Library, Los Angeles
CLSU	University of Southern California, Los Angeles
CLU	University of California at Los Angeles
CLU-C	—William Andrews Clark Memorial Library
CLU-M	—Biomedical Library
CSdS	San Diego State College, San Diego
CSmH	Henry E. Huntington Library, San Marino
CSt	Stanford University Libraries, Stanford
CSt-L	—Lane Medical Library
CU	University of California, Berkeley
CU-A	—University of California, Davis
CU-B	—Bancroft Library, Berkeley
CU-L	—Law Library, Berkeley
CU-M	—University of California Medical Center, San Francisco
CU-S	—University of California, San Diego, La Jolla

Colorado

CoU	University of Colorado, Boulder

Connecticut

CtHT	Trinity College, Hartford
CtHT-W	—Watkinson Library
CtU	University of Connecticut, Storrs
CtY	Yale University, New Haven
CtY-D	—Divinity School
CtY-L	—Law School
CtY-M	—Medical School

District of Columbia

DAS	Atmosphere Sciences Library, U.S.Dept. of Environmental Science, Silver Springs, Md.

Locations

DCU	Catholic University of America Library, Washington
DDO	Dumbarton Oaks Research Library of Harvard University
DFo	Folger Shakespeare Library
DGU	Georgetown University
DHN	Holy Name College
DLC	U.S. Library of Congress
DNAL	U.S. National Agricultural Library
DNLM	U.S. National Library of Medicine
Delaware	
DeU	University of Delaware, Newark
Florida	
FU	University of Florida, Gainesville
Illinois	
ICJ	John Crerar Library, Chicago
ICN	Newberry Library
ICU	University of Chicago
IEG	Garret Theological Seminary, Evanston
IEN	Northwestern University
IEN-M	—Medical School Library, Chicago
IMunS	Saint Mary of the Lake Seminary, Mundelein
IU	University of Illinois, Urbana
Iowa	
IaAS	Iowa State University of Science and Technology, Ames
IaU	University of Iowa, Iowa City
Indiana	
InRenS	St. Joseph's College, Rensselaer
InU-L	Indiana University: Lilly Library, Bloomington
Kansas	
KMK	Kansas State University, Manhattan
KStMC	Saint Mary's College, Saint Marys
KU	University of Kansas, Lawrence
KU-M	—Medical Center Library, Kansas City
Massachusetts	
MB	Boston Public Library
MBAt	Boston Athenaeum, Boston
MBCo	Countway Library of Medicine (Harvard Boston Medical Libraries)
MBH	Massachusetts Horticultural Society, Boston
MBMu	Museum of Fine Arts

MH	Harvard University, Cambridge
MH-A	—Arnold Arboretum. Note: Early materials are largely on deposit in the Houghton Library.
MH-AH	—Andover-Harvard Theological School
MH-BA	—Graduate School of Business Administration
MH-Ed	—Graduate School of Education
MH-G	—Gray Herbarium
MH-L	—Law School
MH-Z	—Museum of Comparative Zoology
MHi	Massachusetts Historical Society, Boston
MShM	Mount Holyoke College, South Hadley
MWA	American Antiquarian Society, Worcester
MWelC	Wellesley College, Wellesley
MWiW-C	Chapin Library, Williams College, Williamstown

Maryland

MdBJ	Johns Hopkins University, Baltimore
MdBJ-G	—John Work Garret Library
MdBP	Peabody Institute. Now incorporated in Enoch Pratt Free Library
MdBWA	Walters Art Gallery

Michigan

MiD	Detroit Public Library
MiD-B	—Burton Historical Collection
MiDSH	Sacred Heart Seminary, Detroit
MiDW	Wayne State University
MiEM	Michigan State University, East Lansing
MiU	University of Michigan, Ann Arbor
MiU-C	—William L.Clements Library
MiU-L	—Law Library

Minnesota

MnCS	St. John's University, Collegeville
MnHi	Minnesota Historical Society, St. Paul
MnS	St. Paul Public Library
MnU	University of Minnesota, Minneapolis
MnU-B	—James Ford Bell Collection

Missouri

MoSB	Missouri Botanical Garden, St. Louis
MoSW	Washington University
MoU	University of Missouri, Columbia

Locations

New York

N	New York State Library, Albany
NBB	Brooklyn Museum Libraries, Brooklyn
NBC	Brooklyn College
NBuG	Buffalo and Erie County Public Library: Grosvenor Reference Division, Buffalo
NCH	Hamilton College, Clinton
NHi	New-York Historical Society, New York
NIC	Cornell University, Ithaca
NN-A	New York Public Library: Arents Collection
NN-RB	—Rare Book Division
NN-S	—Spencer Collection
NNBG	New York Botanical Garden, Bronx Park, New York
NNC	Columbia University, New York
NNC-M	—Medical Library
NNE	Engineering Societies Library
NNG	General Theological Seminary of the Protestant Episcopal Church
NNH	Hispanic Society of America
NNNAM	New York Academy of Medicine
NNPM	Pierpont Morgan Library
NNU	New York University Libraries
NNU-W	—Washington Square Library
NNUT	Union Theological Seminary
NPV	Vassar College, Poughkeepsie
NSyU	Syracuse University, Syracuse

North Carolina

NcD	Duke University, Durham
NcD-M	—Medical Center Library
NcU	University of North Carolina, Chapel Hill

New Hampshire

NhD	Dartmouth College, Hanover

New Jersey

NjN	Newark Public Library
NjP	Princeton University, Princeton
NjPT	Princeton Theological Seminary

Ohio

OCH	Hebrew Union College, Cincinnati
OCU	University of Cincinnati

OCl	Cleveland Public Library
OU	Ohio State University, Columbus
Oklahoma	
OkU	University of Oklahoma, Norman
Oregon	
OrU	University of Oregon, Eugene
Pennsylvania	
PBL	Lehigh University, Bethlehem
PBa	Academy of the New Church, Bryn Athyn
PBm	Bryn Mawr College, Bryn Mawr
PCarlD	Dickinson College, Carlisle
PHC	Haverford College, Haverford
PHi	Historical Society of Pennsylvania, Philadelphia
PLatS	Saint Vincent College and Archabbey, Latrobe
PP	Free Library of Philadelphia
PPAN	Academy of Natural Sciences
PPAmP	American Philosophical Society
PPC	College of Physicians of Philadelphia
PPD	Drexel Institute of Technology
PPDrop	Dropsie College for Hebrew and Cognate Learning
PPF	Franklin Institute
PPFr	Friends' Free Library of Germantown, Philadelphia
PPG	German Society of Pennsylvania
PPHa	Hahnemann Medical College and Hospital
PPJ	Jefferson Medical College
PPL	Library Company of Philadelphia
PPLT	Lutheran Theological Seminary
PPPD	Divinity School of the Protestant Episcopal Church in Philadelphia
PPPH	Pennsylvania Hospital Medical Library
PPRF	Rosenbach Foundation
PPT	Temple University
PPiHB	Rachel McMasters Miller Hunt Botanical Library, Carnegie-Mellon University, Pittsburgh
PSC	Swarthmore College, Swarthmore
PSC-Hi	—Friends Historical Library
PSt	Pennsylvania State University, University Park
PU	University of Pennsylvania, Philadelphia
PU-D	—Evans Dental Library

Locations

PU-F	—H.H.Furness Memorial Library
PU-L	—Biddle Law Library
PV	Villanova College, Villanova

Rhode Island

RP	Providence Public Library
RPB	Brown University, Providence
RPJCB	John Carter Brown Library, Providence

Tennessee

TU	University of Tennessee, Knoxville

Texas

TxU	University of Texas, Austin

Virginia

ViHarEM	Eastern Mennonite College, Harrisonburg
ViU	University of Virginia, Charlottesville

Vermont

VtU	University of Vermont, Burlington

Wisconsin

WU	University of Wisconsin, Madison

Washington

WaU	University of Washington, Seattle

Canada

CaBVaU	University of British Columbia, Vancouver

Other Locations

Amsterdam: NHSM	Nederlandsch Historisch Scheepvaart Museum, Amsterdam
Amsterdam: KAW	Koninklijke Nederlandse Akademie van Wetenschappen
Amsterdam: UB	Universiteitsbibliotheek
Antwerp: B.Communale	Bibliothèque Communale (Stadsbibliothek), Antwerp
Antwerp: Plantin Mus.	Musée Plantin-Moretus
Augsburg: StB	Staats- und Stadtbibliothek, Augsburg
Avignon: Mus.Calvet	Muséum Calvet, Avignon
Barcelona: BU	Biblioteca Universitaria, Barcelona, Spain

BL	British Library, London
BM (NH)	British Museum (Natural History)
BN	Bibliothèque Nationale, Paris
Basel: UB	Öffentliche Bibliothek der Universität, Basel, Switzerland
Bergamo: BC	Biblioteca Civica "A.Mai", Bergamo, Italy
Berlin: Kupf.Kab	Kupferstichkabinett. Now distributed between the Kupferstichkabinett Staatliche Museen Preussischer Kulturbesitz, West Berlin, and the Kupferstichkabinett und Sammlung der Zeichnungen, Staatliche Museen zu Berlin, East Berlin.
Berlin: StB	Staatsbibliothek. Now distributed between the Preussischer Kulturbesitz, West Berlin, and the Deutsche Staatsbibliothek, East Berlin.
Berwick y Alba, Duquesa de	Private collection, Madrid
Besançon: BM	Bibliothèque Municipale, Besançon, France.
Bibl.Cataluña	Biblioteca Central de la Diputación, Barcelona
Bonn: UB	Universitätsbibliothek, Bonn, Germany (West)
Bordeaux: BU	Bibliothèque Universitaire, Bordeaux
Bremen: StB	Staatsbibliothek, Bremen, Germany (West)
Breslau: BU	Staats- und Universitätsbibliothek, Breslau, Lower Silesia (1937); now replaced by Biblioteka Uniwersytecka, Wroclaw, Poland.
Breslau: StB	Stadtbibliothek, Breslau, Lower Silesia (1937), now Wroclaw
Brunswick: StB	Stadtarchiv und Stadtbibliothek, Braunschweig, Germany (West)
Brussels: BR	Bibliothèque Royale Albert 1er, Brussels
Budapest: OSK	Országos Széchényi Könyvtar (National Széchényi Library), Budapest, Hungary
Cambridge: Christ's	Christ's College, Cambridge
Cambridge: Clare	Clare College
Cambridge: Corp.Chr.	Corpus Christi College
Cambridge: Emmanuel	Emmanuel College
Cambridge: Fitzwilliam Mus.	Fitzwilliam Museum

Locations

Cambridge: Gonville & Caius	Gonville and Caius College
Cambridge: Jesus	Jesus College
Cambridge: King's	King's College
Cambridge: Magdalene	Magdalene College
Cambridge: Pembroke	Pembroke College
Cambridge: Pepys	Pepys Library, Magdalene College
Cambridge: Peterhouse	Peterhouse College
Cambridge: Queen's	Queen's College
Cambridge: St.John's	St.John's College
Cambridge: Sidney Sussex	Sidney Sussex College
Cambridge: Trinity	Trinity College
Cambridge: Trinity Hall	Trinity Hall
Cambridge: UL	Cambridge University Library
Cambridge: Westminster	Westminster College
Cambridge: Whipple Mus.	Whipple Science Museum
Chantilly: Mus. Condé	Bibliothèque du Musée Condé au Chateau de Chantilly, Oise, France
Coimbra: BU	Biblioteca Geral da Universidade, Coimbra, Portugal
Cologne: StB Cologne: UB	Universitäts- und Stadtbibliothek, Cologne, Germany (West)
Copenhagen: KB	Kongelige Bibliothek (The Royal Library), Copenhagen
Cracow: AkB Cracow: Akademie	Bibliotheka PAN w Krakowie (Polish Academy of Sciences), Cracow, Poland
Cracow: BCzart	Czartoryski Library & Archives
Cracow: BJ Cracow: Jagellon Univ.	Biblioteka Jagiellónska (Jagellonian Library), Jagellon University
Dresden: LB	Sächsische Landesbibliothek, Dresden, Germany (East)
Dublin: Trinity	Trinity College, Dublin
Edinburgh: NL	National Library of Scotland, Edinburgh
Edinburgh: PL	Edinburgh Public Library
Escorial	Biblioteca del Monasterio de San Lorenzo el Real del Escorial, Madrid
Florence: BN	Biblioteca Nazionale Centrale, Florence

•Frankfurt a.M.: StUB	Stadt- und Universitätsbibliothek, Frankfurt a.M., Germany (West)
Freiburg i.Br.: UB	Universitätsbibliothek, Freiburg im Breisgau, Germany (West)
Fulda: LB	Landesbibliothek, Fulda, Germany (West)
Fulda: Sem.	Bischöfliches Priesterseminar
Geneva: BP Geneva: UB	Bibliothèque Publique et Universitaire, Geneva
Ghent: BU	Bibliotheek van de Rijksuniversiteit, Ghent, Belgium
Göttingen: UB	Niedersächsische Staats- und Universitäts-bibliothek, Göttingen, Germany (West)
Granada: BU	Biblioteca de la Universidad, Granada, Spain
Grenoble: BM	Bibliothèque Municipale, Grenoble, France
Groningen: UB	Rijksuniversiteit, Groningen, The Netherlands
The Hague: KB	Koninklijke Bibliotheek, The Hague
The Hague: Mus. Meerm.West.	Rijksmuseum Meermanno-Westreen-ianum/Museum van het Boek
Halle: UB	Universitäts- und Landesbibliothek Sachsen-Anhalt, Halle, Germany (East)
Hatfield, Eng.: Hatfield House	Private Collection of the Marquess of Salis-bury, Hatfield House, Hatfield, England
Heidelberg: UB	Universitätsbibliothek, Heidelberg
Helsinki: UL	Helsingin Yliopiston Kirjasto (Helsinki University Library), Helsinki, Finland
Horblit	Private collection of Harrison D.Horblit
Innsbruck: UB	Universitätsbibliothek, Innsbruck, Austria
Kraus, H.P.	Private collection, New York
Landévennec: Abbaye	Abbaye, Landévennec, France
Lausanne: B.Cantonale	Bibliothèque Cantonale et Universitaire, Lausanne, Switzerland
LeMans: BM	Bibliothèque Municipale, LeMans, France
Leipzig: UB	Universitätsbibliothek der Karl-Marx-Universität, Leipzig, Germany (East)
Leyden: UB	Bibliotheek der Rijksuniversiteit, Leyden, The Netherlands
Lima: BN	Biblioteca Nacional, Lima, Peru
Lincoln: Cathedral	Lincoln Cathedral, Lincoln, England

Locations

Lisbon: Acad. das Ciencias	Biblioteca da Academia das Ciências de Lisboa, Lisbon
Lisbon: Ajuda	Biblioteca da Ajuda
Lisbon: Arquivo Nacional	Biblioteca e Arquivo da Assembleia Nacional
Lisbon: BN	Biblioteca Nacional
London: College of Surgeons	Royal College of Surgeons Library, London
London: Dr.Williams's Library	Dr. Williams's Library
London: Lambeth	Lambeth Palace Library
London: Soc. of Antiquaries	Society of Antiquaries Library
London: UL	University of London Library
London: V.& A.	Victoria and Albert Museum
London: Wellcome	Wellcome Historical Medical Library
London: Westminster School	Westminster School
Louvain: BU	Bibliothèque Centrale de l'Université Catholique, Louvain, Belgium. Now distributed between French and Dutch units
Lyons: BM	Bibliothèque Municipale, Lyons, France
Lwow: Baworowski Libr.	Biblioteka Fundacji Wiktora hr.Bawarowskiego, Lwow, Poland
Madrid: Acad. de la Hist.	Biblioteca de la Real Academia de la Historia, Madrid
Madrid: BN	Biblioteca Nacional
Madrid: BU	Biblioteca de la Universidad
Madrid: BU (San Isidro)	—San Isidro Collection
Madrid: Bibl.Palacio	Biblioteca del Palacio de Oriente
Madrid: Centro del Ejército y la Armada	Biblioteca del Centro del Ejército y la Armada
Madrid: Facultad de Medecina	Biblioteca de la Facultad de Medecina de la Universidad
Madrid: Ministerio del Ultramar	Museo Biblioteca de Ultramar, Ministerio del Ultramar, Madrid (Collections now distributed among the Museo Arqueológico Nacional, the Museo Naval, the Museo de Ciencias Naturales, the Biblioteca Nacional, etc.)
Madrid: Museo Naval	Biblioteca del Museo Naval

1

Manchester: Rylands Manchester: UL	John Rylands University Library, Manchester, Eng. (Combined in 1972)
Milan: Bibl. Ambrosiana	Biblioteca Ambrosiana, Milan
Milan: Bibl. Trivulziana	Biblioteca dell'Archivo Storico Civico e Biblioteca Trivulziana
Montpelier: BM	Bibliothèque de la Ville et du Musée Fabre, Montpelier, France
Munich: StB	Bayerische Staatsbibliothek, Munich
Munich: UB	Universitätsbibliothek
Münster: UL	Westfälische Universitätsbibliothek, Münster, Germany (West)
Nancy: BM	Bibliothèque Municipale, Nancy, France
Naples: BN	Biblioteca Nazionale Vittorio Emanuele III, Naples
Newcastle-upon-Tyne	Newcastle University, Newcastle-upon-Tyne
Nuremberg: StB	Stadtbibliothek, Nuremberg
Oslo: UB	Universitetsbiblioteket (Royal University Library) Oslo, Norway
Oviedo: BU	Biblioteca de la Universidad, Oviedo, Spain
Oxford: Bodl.	Bodleian Library, Oxford University
Oxford: Corpus	Corpus Christi College
Oxford: Oriel	Oriel College
Oxford: Queen's	Queen's College
Oxford: Worcester	Worcester College
Paris: Arsenal	Bibliothèque de l'Arsenal, Paris
Paris: BU	Bibliothèque de l'Université de Paris
Paris: Bibl. du Protestantisme Français	Bibliothèque de la Société de l'Histoire du Protestantisme Français
Paris: Faculté de Médicine	Université de Paris. Bibliothèque de la Section médecine
Paris: Inst. de France	Bibliothèque de l'Institut de France
Paris: Jesuites	Bibliothèque des Pères Jesuites
Paris: Mazarine	Bibliothèque Mazarine
Paris: Ste Geneviève	Bibliothèque Sainte-Geneviève
Paris: Sorbonne	Bibliothèque de la Sorbonne
Poznan: TPNB	Poznańskie Towarzystwo Przyjaciól Nauk (Poznan Learned Society), Poznan, Poland

Locations

Prague: Strahov Monastery	Strahovska Knihovna (Strahov Library), Prague
Rennes: BM	Bibliothèque Municipale, Rennes, France
Rome: BN	Biblioteca Nazionale Centrale Vittorio Emanuele II, Rome
Rome: B. Alessandrina	Biblioteca Universitaria Alessandrina
Rome: Bibl. Casanatense	Biblioteca Casanatense
Rome: Vatican	Biblioteca Apostolica Vaticana, Vatican City
Rostock: UB	Universitätsbibliothek, Rostock, Germany (East)
Rothenburg: Lateinschule	Lateinschule, Rothenburg ob der Tauber, Germany (West)
Rouen: BM	Bibliothèque Municipale, Rouen, France
Salamanca: BU	Biblioteca Universitaria, Salamanca, Spain
Santander: BM.yP.	Biblioteca Menéndey y Pelayo, Santander, Spain
Santiago: BU	Biblioteca Provincial y Universitaria, Santiago de Compostela, Spain
Santiago de Chile: BN	Biblioteca Nacional, Santiago, Chile
Saragossa: BU	Biblioteca Provincial y Universitaria, Saragossa, Spain
Seville: Archivo de Indias	Archivo General de las Indias, Seville, Spain
Seville: BM	Biblioteca Municipal
Seville: BU	Biblioteca de la Universidad
Seville: Bibl. Colombina	Biblioteca Colombina
Seville: Seminario	Biblioteca del Seminario
Sherrington	Sir Charles Scott Sherrington, Private Collection, Cambridge, Eng. (1945)
Soria: Bibl. Prov.	Biblioteca Provincial, Soria, Spain
Strasbourg: BM	Bibliothèque Municipale, Strasbourg, France
Strasbourg: BN	Bibliothèque Nationale et Universitaire
Torun: BU	Uniwersytet im Mikołaja Kopernika (Copernicus University), Torun, Poland
Toulouse: BM	Bibliothèque Municipale, Toulouse, France
Tours: BM	Bibliothèque Municipale, Tours, France
Uppsala: UB	Uppsala Universitetsbiblioteket, Uppsala, Sweden

Urbino: BU	Biblioteca Universitaria, Urbino, Italy
Utrecht: UB	Bibliotheek der Rijksuniversiteit, Utrecht, The Netherlands
Valencia: BM	Biblioteca Municipal, Valencia, Spain (now incorporated in the Universidad de Valencia library)
Valencia: BU	Biblioteca de la Universidad
Venice: Bibl. Marciana	Biblioteca Nazionale Marciana, Venice
Vicenza: Bibl. Bertoliana	Biblioteca Civica Bertoliana, Vicenza, Italy
Vienna: NB	Österreichische Nationalbibliothek, Vienna
Vienna: UB	Universitätsbibliothek
Warsaw: UB (UL)	Biblioteka Uniwersytecka w Warszawie (Warsaw University Library)
Weimar: Zentralbibliothek der deutschen Klassik	Zentralbibliothek der Deutschen Klassik, Weimar, Germany (East)
Wolfenbüttel: HB	Herzog August Bibliothek, Wolfenbüttel, Germany (West)
Würzburg: UB	Universitätsbibliothek, Würzburg, Germany (West)
Zerbst: Oberschule	Oberschule, Zerbst, Germany (East)
Zurich: StB	Stadtbibliothek, Zurich (now incorporated in the Zentralbibliothek Zürich)
Zurich: ZB	Zentralbibliothek Zürich, Kantons-, Stadt-und Universitätsbibliothek

European Americana

1493

Almeida, Ferdinando, Bp of Ceuta. Ad Alexandrum vi. Pont. Max. . . . Oratio. [*Rome:*] *J.Besicken & S.Mayr* [1493?]. [8]p.;4to. Suggests that the kings of Spain & Portugal reward the Pope for his arbitration of their claims by gift of possessions in the New World. Harrisse (BAV) 12; GW 1553; Goff A-523. NNH, RPJCB; Oxford: Bodl., BN. 493/1

Carvajal, Bernardino López de, Cardinal. Oratio super praestanda solemni obedientia . . . Alexandro Papae. [*Rome: S.Plannck,* 1493?]. 8 lvs;4to. Includes ref. to New World. Sabin 11175; Harrisse (BAV) 11; Medina (BHA) 11; GW 6145; Goff C-221; Church 3; JCB (3) I:16. CSmH, DLC, InU-L, NN-RB, RPJCB; BL, BN 493/2

Colombo, Cristoforo. Senor por que se que aureis plazer de la grand vitoria. [*Barcelona: P.Posa,* 1493]. [4]p.;fol. Letter to Santangel. Medina (BHA) 1; Eames (Columbus) 1; GW 7171; Goff C-756; JCB (101 Bks) 1. NN-RB. 493/3

————. Epistola . . . de insulis Indie supra Gangem nuper inventis. [*Rome: S. Plannck,* 1493]. 4 lvs;4to. Transl. by Leandro di Cosco from preceding. Has 34 lines to page. Sabin 14628; Harrisse (BAV) 1; Medina (BHA) 4; Eames (Columbus) 3; GW 7173; Church 3A; JCB (3) I:17. CSmH, ICN, InU-L, MB, MnU-B, NN-RB, RPJCB; BL. 493/4

——[Anr edn]. [*Rome: S.Plannck,* 1493]. 4 lvs;4to. Printed 33 lines to page. Sabin 14630; Harrisse (BAV) 4; Medina (BHA) 17; Eames (Columbus) 4; GW 7177; Goff C-758; Church 5; JCB (3) I:18-19. CSmH, DLC, ICN, InU-L, MiU-C, NN-RB, RPJCB; BL. 493/5

——[Anr edn]. *Rome: E.Silber,* 1493. 3 lvs;4to. Sabin 14631; Harrisse (BAV) 3; Medina (BHA) 6; Eames (Columbus) 5; GW 7178; Goff C-759; Church 4; JCB (3) I:19. CSmH, NN-RB, RPJCB; BL, BN. 493/6

——[Anr edn]. Epistola . . . de insulis Indie. [*Antwerp: T.Martens,* 1493]. 4 lvs;4to. Printed 38 lines to page. Medina (BHA) 11; Eames (Columbus) 6; GW 7176; Church 3A (8); cf. JCB (3) I:20. Brussels: BR. 493/7

——[Anr edn]. De insulis inventis Epistola. [*Basel: J.Wolff,* 1493]. [18]p.;illus.;4to. Sabin 14629; Harrisse (BAV) 2; Medina (BHA) 5; Eames (Columbus) 7; GW 7174; Goff C-760; Church 3A (7), JCB (3) I:18. NN-RB, RPJCB; BL. 493/8

——[Anr edn]. Epistola de insulis repertis de novo. *Paris: G.Marchant* [1493]. 8p.;4to. Cf. Sabin 14633; Medina (BHA) 8; Eames (Columbus) 9; GW 7175a; Church 3A (5). Göttingen: UB, Turin: BN. 493/9

——[Anr issue]. Epistola de insulis de novo repertis. *Paris: G.Marchant* [1493]. 8p.;1 illus.;4to. Sabin 14632; Harrisse (BAV) 5; Medina (BHA) 9; Eames (Columbus) 10; GW 7175b; Goff C-761; Church 3A (6); JCB (3) I:19. NN-RB, RPJCB; BN. 493/10

——[Anr issue]. Epistola de insulis noviter repertis. *Paris: G.Marchant* [1493]. 8p.;2 illus.;4to. Sabin 14633; Harrisse (BAV) 6; Medina (BHA) 10; Eames (Columbus) 11; GW 7175; Church 3A (7). Oxford: Bodl. 493/11

————. [Letra enviada al escrivano de Racio. *Barcelona?* 1493?]. In Catalan. Harrisse (BAV) Add. p.xii; Medina (BHA) 3. No copy known; described by Ferdinand Columbus as in his personal library. 493/12

Dati, Giuliano, Bp of S.Leone. Omnipotente idio ch'l tutto regie [Storia della inventione delle nuove insule di Channaria indiane]. *Rome: E.Silber,* 1493]. 4 lvs;illus.;4to. Verse paraphrase of the Columbus letter. Cf.Sabin 18656; Eames (Columbus) 13; GW 7999; Church 3A (10). BL. 493/13

——[Anr edn]. Questa e la hystoria della inventione delle diese isole di Cannaria Indiane. [*Rome: S.Plannck,* 1493]. 4 lvs;4to. Eames (Columbus) 14: GW 8002; Church 3A (11). BL(imp.). 493/14

——[Anr edn]. La lettera dell isole che ha trovate nuovamente il Re di Spagna. *Florence:* [*L.de'*

Morgiani & J. Petri] 1493. 4 lvs;4to. Sabin 18656; Harrisse (BAV) 9; Eames (Columbus) 15; GW 8000; Church 3A (12). BL.   493/15

Maino, Giasone del. Oratio habita apud . . . Alexandrinum . . . Pont. maximum. *Rome: S.Plannck* [1493?]. 10 lvs;4to. On recto of lf b1 a passage may refer to America—if not to Africa. Hain 10975; Goff M-407. CSmH, DLC, InU-L, NN-RB, PU, RPJCB; BL, BN.
493/16

—[Anr edn]. [*Rome: A.Freitag*, 1493]. 8 lvs;4to. Hain/Copinger 10976; Goff M-408. InU-L, MdBWA; BL, BN.   493/17

—[Anr edn]. *Leipzig:* [*G.Böttiger*, 1493?]. 10 lvs;4to. Hain 10977; Goff M-409. CSmH; BL.   493/18

—[Anr edn]. [*Pavia: A.de Carcano*, 1493]. 10 lvs;4to. Hain 10978; Goff M-410. InU-L, MnU-B.   493/19

Ortiz, Alonso. Los tratados. *Seville: J.Pegnitzer,M.Herbst,T.Glockner,* 1493. c lvs;fol. A ref. to discovery of New World appears on verso of lf xliii. Sabin 57714; Harrisse (BAV) 10; Medina (BHA) 12; Hain 12109; Goff 0-106; Escudero (Seville) 37; Church 6; JCB (3) I:21-22. CSmH, InU-L, MB, MiU-C, MnU-B, NN-RB, RPJCB; BL, BN.   493/20

Schedel, Hartmann. Liber chronicarum. *Nuremberg: A.Koberger,* 1493. ccxcix lvs;illus., maps;fol. Mentions African voyage of Cam & Behaim, a passage (not present in German text of this year) mistakenly interpreted as evidence the pair reached the New World. Sabin 77523; Harrisse (BAV) 13; Hain/Copinger 14508; Goff S-307; Church 7; Fairfax Murray (Germany) 394; JCB (3) I:22. CSmH, CtY, DLC, ICN, InU-L, MH, MiU-C, MnU-B, NN-RB, RPJCB; BL, BN.   493/21

1494

Brant, Sebastian. Das Narren Schyff. *Basel: J.Bergmann,* 1494. 158 lvs;illus.; 4to. In the 66th section, 'Von erfarung aller land', is a passage beginning 'Des lands so man erkundet hat' referring to the New World. Harrisse (BAV) Add. 2; GW 5041; Goff B-1080. DLC, NNPM.   494/1

—[Anr edn]. *Nuremberg: P.Wagner*, 1494. 180 lvs;illus.;8vo. GW 5042. BL.   494/2

—[Anr edn]. *Reutlingen:* [*M.Greyff*]1494. 158 lvs;illus.;4to. GW 5043. Berlin: Kupf.Kab.
494/3

—[Anr edn]. Cf. preceding. *Reutlingen:* [*M.Greyff*] 1494. 158 lvs;illus.;4to. GW 5044. Berlin: StB.   494/4

—[Anr edn]. *Augsburg: J.Schönsperger,* 1494. 180 lvs;illus.;8vo. GW 5045. Augsburg: StB.
494/5

—[Anr edn]. *Das nüu schiff von Narragonia. Strassburg: J.Grüninger,* 1494. 110 lvs;illus.; 4to. Includes unauthorized interpolations in text. GW 5048; Goff B-1081. NNPM; Brussels: BR.   494/6

Dati, Giuliano, Bp of S.Leone. El secondo cantare dell India. *Rome:* [*J.Besicken & S.Mayr*, 1494 or '95]. 4 lvs;illus.;4to. Continues the author's *Lettera delle isole nuovamente trovate* of 1493. Harrisse (BAV) p.43n; GW 7994. InU-L; Rome: Bibl. Casanatense.   494/7

Scillacio, Niccolò. De insulis meridiani atque Indici maris . . . nuper inventis. [*Pavia: F. Girardengus*, 1494?]. 10 lvs;4to. Describes Columbus's 2nd voyage. Sabin 94095; Harrisse (BAV) 16; Medina (BHA) 16; Sanz (Ult. ad.) 175-208; Reichling 320; Goff S-351; Church 9. CSmH, NN-RB.   494/8

Verardi, Carlo. In laudem . . . Ferdinandi Hispaniarum regis . . . et de insulis in Mari Indico nuper inventis. *Basel: J.Bergmann,* 1494. 36 lvs;illus.;4to. Includes the Columbus letter. Sabin 98923; Harrisse (BAV) 15; Medina (BHA) 15; Eames (Columbus) 8; Hain/Copinger 15942; Goff V-125; Church 8; Fairfax Murray (Germany) 424; JCB (3) I:25. CSmH, CtY, DLC, ICN, InU-L, MnU-B, NN-RB, RPJCB; BL. BN.   494/9

1495

Brant, Sebastian. Das Narrenschiff. *Basel:* [*J.Bergmann*] 1495. 164 lvs;illus.; 4to. 1st publ., Basel, 1494. GW 5046; Goff B-1082. NNPM.   495/1

—[Anr edn]. Das neü narrenschiff von Narragonia. *Augsburg: J.Schönsperger*, 1495. 102 lvs;illus.;4to. 1st publ. under above title, incl. unauthorized interpolations, Strassburg, 1494. GW 5049. CtY, NN-S; Berlin: StB.
495/2

Dati, Giuliano, Bp of S.Leone. Isole trovate novamente per el re di Spagna. *Florence:* 1495. 4 lvs;illus.;4to. 1st publ., Rome, 1493, under title *La lettera dell isole . . . trovate nuovamente.* Harrisse (BAV) 17 bis (p.461) &

Add. 3; Eames (Columbus) 16; GW 8003; Church 3A(13). Milan: Bibl. Trivulziana. 495/3

—[Anr edn]. La lettera dellisole che ha trovato nuovamente el Re di Spagna. *Florence: [L.de' Morgiani & J.Petri]* 1495. 4 lvs;illus.;4to. Eames (Columbus) 17; GW 8002; Goff D-46; Church 10. CSmH, ViU. 495/4

Schellig, Conrad. In pustulas malas morbum quem malum de Francia vulgus appelat consilium. *[Heidelberg: F.Misch, 1495/96?].* [20] p.;4to. Reichling 727; BMC III:668; Goff S-313; Klebs 891.1; Stillwell (Science) 518. CtY-M, DNLM, ICJ, MBCo, PPC; BL. 495/5

1496

Brant, Sebastian. Eulogium de scorra pestilentiali sive mala de Franczos. *Basel: J.Bergmann,* 1496. bds. In verse. GW 5038; Klebs 214.1; Stillwell (Science) 316. Augsburg: StB. 496/1

——. Das nüu schiff von Narragonia. *Strassburg: [J.Grüninger]* 1494 [i.e., ca.1496?]. 98 lvs;illus.;4to. 1st publ. in this version with unauthorized additions, Strassburg, 1494. GW 5050; Goff B-1084. DLC; The Hague: Mus. Meerm. West. 496/2

Corvinus, Laurentius. Cosmographia dans manuductionem in tabulas Ptholomei. *[Basel: N. Kesler,* not bef. 1496]. [110]p.;4to. A phrase referring to an unknown land, possibly designating America, appears on verso of lf 53. Goldschmidt (Not in Harrisse) 130-131; GW 7799; Goff C-941. CtY, DLC, InU-L, MB, NN-RB, RPJCB; BL. 496/3

Grünpeck, Joseph. Ein hübscher Tractat von dem ursprung des Bösen Franzos. *Augsburg: J.Schaur,* 1496. [42]p.;4to. Transl. from following title. Hain 8095; BMC II:393; Klebs 477.1. BL,Uppsala: UB. 496/4

—[Anr edn]. *[Nuremberg: C.Hochfeder,* 1496?-97?]. 12 lvs;4to. Hain 8094; Klebs 477.2; Goff G-518. MBCo. 496/5

——. Tractatus de pestilentiali scorra, sive Mala de Franzos. *[Augsburg: J.Schaur,* 1496]. [35]p.;illus.;4to. Comprises commentary on Sebastian Brant's *Eulogium* of this year, the text of which is also included. Hain 8090; BMC III:393; Klebs 476.1; Stillwell (Science) 395. BL, Uppsala: UB. 496/6

—[Anr edn]. *[Nuremberg: C.Hochfeder,*

1496-97] 4to. Hain 8091; Goff G-516; Klebs 476.2. MBCo, NNNAM, PPC. 496/7

—[Anr edn]. *[Leipzig: G.Böttiger,* 1496?]. 4to. Hain 8093; BMC III:648; Goff G-515; Klebs 476.2. CSmH; BL, BN. 496/8

Leonardi, Camillus. Expositio canonum equatorii celestium absque calculo. *Venice: G.Arrivabene,* 1496. 42 lvs;4to. On lf e2 a recently discovered region is mentioned, perhaps referring to Columbus's voyages. Goldschmidt (Not in Harrisse) 132-133; Reichling 4283; Goff L-139. MBCo. 496/9

Lilio, Zaccaria, Bp. De origine & laudibus scientiarium . . . Contra antipodes. *Florence: F.Bonaccorsi,for P.Pacini,* 1496. 72 lvs; 4to. On verso of lf 40 a ref. to recent Spanish discoveries in New World appears. Sabin 41067; Harrisse (BAV) 17; Hain/Copinger 10103; Goff L-221; Church 11; JCB (3) I:25. CSmH, CtY, DLC, ICN, InU-L, MB, MiU-C, NN-RB, RPJCB; BL, BN. 496/10

Scillacio, Niccolò. De foelici philosophorum paupertate appetenda. *[Pavia:J.A.de Boscho]* 1496. [92]p.;8vo. Includes ref. to syphilis at Barcelona and at Naples. Hain/Copinger 14572; BMC VII:1017; Stillwell (Science) 520.BL. 496/11

Sommariva, Giorgio. Del mal franzoso. *Venice: C.de Bottis,* 1496. 4to. In verse. Reichling 1632; Klebs 923.1; Stillwell (Science) 525. Vicenza: Bibl. Bertoliana. 496/12

Ulsenius, Theodorus. Vaticinium in epidemicam scabiem. *Nuremberg:* 1496. bds.;illus.; fol. In verse. Hain 16089; Proksch I:79. 496/13

1497

Baptista Mantuanus. De patientia aurei libri tres. *Brescia: B.Misintis,* 1497. 116 lvs;4to. On recto of lf m3 is a ref. to Spanish discoveries in New World. GW 3304; Goff B-76. CSmH, CtY, DLC, InU-L, MnU-B, NN-RB, RPJCB; Oxford: Bodl. 497/1

Brant, Sebastian. Dat narren schyp. *Lübeck: [The Poppy printer]* 1497. 238 lvs;illus.;4to. Transl. by Herman Barkhusen from Basel High German text of 1494. GW 5053. BL. 497/2

——. Das nuw schiff von Narragonia. *Strassburg: J.Grüninger,* 1497. 92 lvs;illus.; 4to. 1st publ. in this unauthorized version,

Strassburg, 1494. GW 5051. Berlin: StB.
497/3

____. La nef des folz du monde. *Paris:*
[*F.Baligault? for*] *G.de Marnef & J.Philippe,*
1497. cxix lvs;illus.;fol. Transl. by Pierre
Rivière from *Der Narrenschiff,* 1st publ.
Basel, 1494. Harrisse (BAV) Add. 6; GW
5058; Goff B-1094; Fairfax Murray (France)
66. DLC, MnU-B, NN-RB; BL, BN.   497/4

____. Stultifera navis. *Basel: J.Bergmann,* 1497.
cxlv lvs;illus.;4to. Transl. by Jakob Locher
from *Der Narrenschiff,* 1st publ., Basel, 1494.
Harrisse (BAV) Add. 5; GW 5054; Goff
B-1086. CSmH, CtY, DLC, ICN, InU-L, MB,
MiU, NN-RB; BL, BN.   497/5

__[Anr edn, counterfeiting preceding]. *Basel:*
J.Bergmann [i.e., *Nuremberg: G.Stuchs?*]
1497. cxlv lvs;illus.;8vo. GW 5055; Goff
B-1087. DLC, MnU-B, NN-RB, RPJCB; BL.
497/6

__[Anr edn]. *Augsburg: J.Schönsperger,* 1497.
cxiv lvs;illus.;8vo. GW 5056; Goff B-1088;
JCB (3) I:27. DLC, NN-RB, RPJCB; BL.
497/7

__[Anr edn]. *Strassburg: J.Grüninger,* 1497. 112
lvs; illus.;4to. GW 5057; Goff B-1089; JCB (3)
I:28. CSmH, DLC, MiU-C, NN-RB, RPJCB;
BL   497/8

__[Anr edn]. *Basel: J.Bergmann,* 1497. clix
lvs;illus.;4to. Notes by Thomas Beccadelli.
GW 5061; Goff B-1090; JCB (3) I:28. CSmH,
DLC, MH, RPJCB; Paris: Ste Geneviève.
497/9

Colombo, Cristoforo. Eyn schön hübsch lesen
von etlichen insslen. *Strassburg: B.Kistler,*
1497. 7 lvs;illus.;4to. Transl. from Spanish
text 1st publ., Barcelona, 1493. Sabin 14638;
Harrisse (BAV) 19; Medina (BHA) 11n (I:26);
Eames (Columbus) 12; GW 7179; Goff C-762;
Church 14; JCB (3) I:29. CSmH, InU-L, NN-
RB, PP, RPJCB; BL.   497/10

____. Señor por que se que aureis plazer de la
grand victoria. [*Valladolid: P.Giraldi & M.de*
Planes, ca.1497]. [8]p.;4to. 1st publ.,
Barcelona, 1493. Harrisse (BAV) 7; Medina
(BHA) 2; Eames (Columbus) 2; GW 7172;
Alcocer (Valladolid) 8. Milan: Bibl. Ambro-
siana.   497/11

Gilino, Corradino. De morbo quem gallicum
noncupant. [*Ferrara: L.de Rubeis,* 1497?]. 4
lvs;4to. Klebs 463.1; Stillwell (Science) 390;
Goff G-306. PPC; London: Wellcome. 497/12

Leoniceno, Niccolò. Libellus de epidemia

quam vulgo morbum gallicum vocant.
Venice: A.Manuzio, 1497. [57]p.;4to.
Hain/Copinger 10019; Goff L-165; Klebs
599.1; JCB (3) I:30. CSmH,CtY,DNLM,MH,
NNNAM, PPC, RPJCB; BL, BN.   497/13

__[Anr edn]. De morbo gallico. *Milan:*
G.LeSignerre,for J.Legnano, 1497. 32 lvs;4to.
Reichling 10020; Goff L-166. CU, CtY,
DNLM, MB, NNNAM, MnU-B, PPC; BN.
497/14

Montesauro, Natale. De dispositionibus quas
vulgares mal franzoso appellant. [*Bologna:*
G.da Ruberia, 1497?]. [31]p.;4to. Reichling
1284; BMC VI:850; Klebs 691.1; Stillwell
(Science) 457. DNLM; BL.   497/15

Schedel, Hartmann. Liber cronicarum, cum
figuris. *Augsburg: J. Schönsperger,* 1497.
338 numb.lvs;illus.,maps;fol. 1st publ.,
Nuremberg, 1493. The refs to Cam & Behaim
here appear on verso of lf 326. Sabin 77524;
Goff S-308. CSmH, CtY, DLC, ICN, MiU,
MWiW-C, NN-RB, PBL; BL.   497/16

Spain. Sovereigns, etc., 1479-1504 (Ferdinand
V and Isabella I). Este es traslado bien y
fielmente sacado de una carta de privilegio.
[*Burgos:* 1497?]. [5]p.;fol. Confirms Columbus's privileges in lands discovered. Duquesa
de Berwick y Alba (1920).   497/17

Torrella, Gaspar. Tractatus cum consiliis
contra pudendagram, seu morbum gallicum.
Rome: P.de Turre, 1497. [46]p.;4to.
Hain/Copinger 15558; Polain 3789; Klebs
979.1; Stillwell (Science) 537. BN.   497/18

Widman, Johann, called Mechinger. Trac-
tatus . . . de pustulis et morbo qui vulgato
nomine mal de franzos appellatur.
[*Strassburg: J. Grüninger,* 1497]. 10 lvs;4to.
Hain/Copinger 16160; BMC I:111; Goff
W-17; Klebs 1048.1; Stillwell (Science) 551.
DLC, MBCo, PP; BL.   497/19

__[Anr edn]. *Rome:* [*S.Plannck,* 1497].
[15]p.;4to. Klebs 1048.2; Pellechet 11808.
Paris: Mazarine.   497/20

1498

Baptista Mantuanus. De patientia aurei.
Lyons: F.Fradin & J.Pivard] 1498.
[127]p.;4to. 1st publ., Brescia, 1497. GW
3305; Goff B-77. CSmH, MH, NN-RB;
BL,BN.   498/1

__[Anr edn]. *Deventer: R.Pafraet,* 1498. GW
3306; Goff B-78. CtY, DFo, NN-RB.   498/2

Brant, Sebastian. La nef des folz du monde. *Lyons: G.Balsarin*, 1498. 84 lvs;illus.;fol. Transl. by J.Drouyn from *Der Narrenschiff*, 1st publ., Basel, 1494. GW 5059; Goff B-1095; Baudrier (Lyons) XII:54-55. NNPM; Oxford: Bodl., BN.   498/3

____. Das neü narren schiff. *Augsburg: J.Schönsperger*, 1498. 102 lvs;illus.;4to. 1st publ. in this unauthorized version, Augsburg, 1494. GW 5052; Goff B-1085. DLC, NNPM; BL.   498/4

____. Stultifera navis. *Basel: J.Bergmann*, 1498. 159 numb.lvs;illus.;4to. 1st publ. in this translation, Basel, 1497. GW 5062; Goff B-1091. DLC, IU, MH, NN-RB, RPJCB; BN.   498/5

—[Anr edn]. Salutifera [!] navis. *Lyons: J.Saccon*, 1488 [i.e., 1498]. 152 numb. lvs;illus.;4to. GW 5063; Goff B-1093; Baudrier (Lyons) XII:313-314. CSmH, DLC, ICN, MH, NN-RB; BL, BN.   498/6

—[Anr edn]. *Paris: [G.Wolff,for] G.de Marnef*, 1498/99. 156 lvs; illus.;4to. GW 5064; Goff B-1092. MH, RPJCB: BL. BN.   498/7

____. Varia . . . carmina. *Basel: J.Bergmann*, 1498. 140 lvs;illus.;4to. Includes 'Ad ornatissimum . . . Johannem Reuchlin . . . de pestilentiali scorra . . . elogium', 1st publ., Basel, 1496. For variant issues see GW 5068. GW 5068; Goff B-1099; Proksch I:79. CtY, DLC, MH, NN-RB; BL, BN.   498/8

—[Anr edn]. *Strassburg: J.Grüninger*, 1498. 128 lvs;illus.;4to. GW 5069; Goff B-1100. MH, PP; BL, Munich: StB.   498/9

Grünpeck, Joseph. Tractatus de pestilentiali scorra. *Magdeburg: M.Brandis*, 1498. 4to. 1st publ., Augsburg, [1496?]. Hain/Copinger 2801; BMC II:600; Klebs 476.4. BL.   498/10

Inghirami, Tomasso Fedra. De obitu illustrissimi Joannis Hispaniae principis, ad Senatum Apostolicum Oratio. [*Rome: E.Silber*, 1498]. 12 lvs;4to. On verso of lf 11 is a ref. to the Antipodes. Sabin 34757; Harrisse (BAV) Add. 4; Reichling 568; Goff I-79; JCB (3) I:29. NNH, RPJCB; BL.   498/11

Lebrija, Elio Antonio de. In cosmographiae libros introductorium Pomponii Melae. [*Salamanca: Printer of Lebrija's Gramatica*, ca. 1498]. 14 lvs;4to. At end of chapt.1 is a ref. to new lands. Sabin 52205; Harrisse (BAV) Add. 7; Medina (BHA) 17; GW 2236; Goff A-908. DLC, NN-RB; BL.   498/12

López de Villalobos, Francisco. Sumario de la medecina en romance trovado, con un tratado sobre las pestiferas bubas. *Salamanca: [Printer of Lebrija's Gramatica] for A.de Barreda*, 1498. 28 lvs;fol. In verse. On syphilis. Medina (BHA) 19; Hain/Copinger 10208; Goff L-286; Proksch I:79. NNH; BL, BN.   498/13

Mela, Pomponius. Cosmographia. *Salamanca: [Printer of Lebrija's Gramatica]* 1498. 70 lvs; map;4to. Ed. by Francisco Núñez de la Yerba. Ref. to New World on 1st page of preface. Sabin 63955; Harrisse (BAV) Add. 8; Medina (BHA) 18; Sanz (Ult.ad.) 241-247; Reichling 11021; Goff M-455; JCB AR51: 3-5. CSmH, InU-L, NN-RB, RPJCB; BL.   498/14

Pistoris, Simon. Positio de malo franco. *Leipzig: M.Brandis*, 1498. Hain 13020; cf.Klebs 781.1.   498/15

Sacro Bosco, Joannes de. Uberrimum sphere mundi, comentum intersetis etiam questionibus . . . Petri de Aliaco [i.e., P.Ciruelo]. *Paris: G.Marchand,for J.Petit*, 1498. 100 lvs;illus.;fol. On recto of lf h2 despatch of expedition reporting new lands in west is mentioned. Goldschmidt (Not in Harrisse) 139-141; Reichling 14120; Goff J-418; Fairfax Murray (France) 66. CtY, ICN, InU-L, MH, MnU-B, NN-RB, RPJCB; BL, BN.   498/16

Scanaroli, Antonio. Disputatio utilis de morbo gallico. *Bologna: [B.Hectoris]* 1498. [32]p.;4to. Hain 14505; BMC VI:844; Klebs 887.1; Goff S-304; Stillwell (Science) 517. DNLM, MBCo, PPC; BL, BN.   498/17

Steber, Bartholomaeus. A mala franczos morbo Gallorum praeservatio ac cura. [*Vienna: J.Winterburg*, 1498?]. [15]p.;illus.;4to. Hain/Copinger 15053; Klebs 931.1; Goff S-762; Stillwell (Science) 529; Langer (Winterburg) 147. DNLM; BL, BN.   498/18

1499

Baptista Mantuanus. De patientia. *Basel: J.Bergmann*, 1499. 118 lvs;4to. 1st publ., Brescia, 1497. GW 3307; Goff B-79. CtY, DLC, ICN, InU-L, MH, NN-RB, RPJCB; BL,BN.   499/1

—[Anr edn]. *Venice: J.Pencio*, 1499. [271]p.;4to. GW 3308; Goff B-80. CSmH, DLC, ICN, InU-L, MBCo, MiU-C, NN-RB; BL, BN.   499/2

Brant, Sebastian. La grant nef des folz. *Lyons: G.Balsarin*, 1499. 84 lvs;illus.;fol. 1st publ. in this translation by J.Drouyn, Lyons, 1498. GW 5060; Baudrier (Lyons) XII:55-56. BL, BN.   499/3

____. Das Narrenschiff. *Basel:J.Bergmann*, 1499. 164 lvs;illus.;4to. 1st publ., Basel, 1494. GW 5047. BL.   499/4

Leoniceno, Niccolò. Libellus de epidemia quam vulgo morbum gallicum vocant. [*Leipzig: W.Stoeckel*, ca.1499]. 4to. 1st publ., Venice, 1497. Hain 10018; Goff L-167. NNNAM.   499/5

Pollich, Martin. Defensio Leoniceniana nuper edita. *Magdeburg:* 1499. 16 lvs;4to. Proksch I:8.   499/6

Vagad, Gauberte Fabricio de. Corónica de Aragón. *Saragossa: P.Hurus*, 1499. clxxx lvs;fol. On recto of lf B4 is a ref. to the New World. Sabin 98286; Harrisse (BAV) Add. 9; Sanz (Ult.ad.) 1398-1401; Medina (BHA) 20; Reichling 15758; Goff V-1; Sánchez (Saragossa) 66. NN-RB; BL, Paris: Mazarine.   499/7

1500

Brant, Sebastian. Der narren scip. *Paris: G.Marchant*, 1500. [238]p.;illus.;4to. Transl. from *Der Narrenschiff*, 1st publ., Basel, 1494. GW 5066. BN.   500/1

Dati, Giuliano, Bp of S.Leone. La hystoria della inventione delle diese isole di Cannaria. [*Brescia:*1500?]. 4 lvs;4to. 1st publ. Rome, 1493, under title *La lettera dell isole . . . trovate nuovamente.* Sabin 18656; Harrisse (BAV) 8; Eames (Columbus) 14; GW 8001. BL(imp.).   500/2

Grünpeck, Joseph. Tractatus de pestiential scorra sive mala de Franczos. [*Cologne: C.de Zierikzee*, ca.1500]. 4to. 1st publ., Augsburg, 1496. Hain 8092; BMC I:306; Goff G-517; Klebs 476.5. DNLM, PPC; BL, Uppsala: UB.   500/3

Maino, Giasone del. Oratio habita apud . . . Alexandrinum . . . Pont. maximum. [*Rome?* ca. 1500?]. 10 lvs;4to. 1st publ., Rome, [1493?]. Goff M-411. DLC, NN-RB.   500/4

Manardo, Giovanni. De erroribus Symonis Pistoris . . . circa morbum gallicum. [*Leipzig?*] 1500. 8 lvs;4to. Proksch I:9.   500/5

Marineo,. Lucio, Siculo. De Hispaniae laudibus. *Burgos: F.Biel* [ca.1500]. lxxv lvs;fol. Refs to the New World are found on lvs xxxvii-xxxix. Haebler (Bibl. Iber.) 399; Goff M-273; Sanz (Ult.ad.) 1393-1397. ICN; BL.   500/6

Pintor, Petrus. De morbo foedo et occulto his temporibus affligente. *Rome: E.Silber*, 1500. 4to. On syphilis. Hain/Copinger 13010; Goff P-649. PPC.   500/7

Pistoris, Simon. Declaratio defensiva cujusdam positionis de malo franco. *Leipzig:*

[*C.Kachelofen*] 1500. 9 lvs;4to. Hain/Copinger (Add.) 13021; Klebs 781.8; Goff P-653. DNLM; BL.   500/8

Pollich, Martin. Castigationes in alabandicas declarationes d. S. Pistoris nuper editae. [*Leipzig?*] 1500. 31 lvs;4to. Proksch I:9; Hain 11053; Klebs 796.1. Berlin: StB. 500/9

Torrella, Gaspar. Dialogus de dolore cum tractatu de ulceribus in pudendagra evenire solitis. *Rome: J.Besicken & Martin of Amsterdam*, 1500. 4to. Hain/Copinger 155559; BMC IV:142; Klebs 980.1; Goff T-391; Stillwell (Science) 536. MBCo; BL, BN.   500/10

1501

Alpharabius, Jacobus. Panaegyricus in divi Ludovici Regis. [*Rome? J.Besicken?* 1501?]. 10 lvs;4to. Includes letter dated 31 Aug. 1501 to Ferdinand & Isabella referring to discovery of New World. Isaac 12048;Ind.aur. 103.847. MiU-C, NN-RB; BL, BN.   501/1

Baptista Mantuanus. De patientia aurei libri tres. *Deventer: R.Pafraet*, 1501. [140]p.;4to. 1st publ., Brescia, 1497. Nijhoff/Kronenberg 210; Ind.aur.112.337. DNLM; BL, BN.501/2

Pasqualigo, Pietro. Ad Hemanuelem Lusitaniae Regem Oratio. *Venice: B.dei Vitali*, 1501. [8]p.;4to. Points out superior merits of combatting Turks over mere discoveries of new lands. Isaac 12723. RPJCB; BL, BN.   501/3

Pistoris, Simon. Confutatio conflatorum circa positionem . . . Martini Mellerstadt [i.e. Pollich] de male franco. [*Leipzig?*] 1501. 10 lvs; 4to. Proksch I:9.   501/4

Pollich, Martin. Responsio . . . in superaddits errores Simoni Pistoris. [*Leipzig:*] 1501.

[79]p.;4to. Includes also text of Pistoris's *Confutatio conflatorum . . . de male franco* above. Klebs 797.1; Proksch I:9. DNLM,PPC.
501/5

Regimen sanitatis salernitanum. Regimen sanitatis en françois. *Lyons:* 1501. [227]p.;fol. The earliest edn with American implications. 'Remede tresutile pour ceulx qui ont la maladie appelle en hebreu malfranzos, & en latin variola croniqua, & en françois la grosse verolle': lvs p3v-p4r. DNLM.   501/6

Schellig, Conrad. Ein kurtz Regiment wie man sich vor der Pestilenz enthalten sol. *Heidelberg:* [*J.Stadelberger*] 1501. 4to. Transl. from author's *In pustulas malas,* 1st publ. [Heidelberg: 1495/96?]. Klebs 892.1; Stillwell (Science) 518n. DNLM; BL.   501/7

1502

Almenar, Juan. Libellus ad evitandum et expellendum morbum gallicum. *Venice: B.dei Vitali,* 1502. [42]p.;4to. Ind.aur. 103.787. DNLM; BL.   502/1

Sacro Bosco, Joannes de. Sphaera mundi. [*Leipzig: M. Landsberg or C. Kachelofen,* ca.1502?]. 42 lvs;map;4to. Contains an apparently early state of the Johann Ruysch world map. Goff J-424. MB.   502/2

Schellig, Conrad. Eyn kurtz Regiment . . . wie man sich vor der Pestilenz enthalten . . . sol. [*Speyer? C.Hist?* 1502]. [48]p.; illus.;4to. 1st publ., Heidelberg, 1501. Stillwell (Science) 518. DNLM.   502/3

—[Anr edn?]. *Speyer: H.Biber,* 1502. BL. 502/4

1503

Baptista Mantuanus. De patientia aurei libri tres. *Deventer: R.Pafraet,* 1503. [139]p.;4to. 1st publ., Brescia, 1497. Nijhoff/Kronenberg 211; Ind. aur.112.364. CtY; BL, BN.   503/1

Foresti, Jacopo Filippo, da Bergamo. Novissime hystoriarum omnium repercussiones, noviter . . . editae. *Venice: A.Vercellensis,* 1503. 452 lvs;illus.;fol. Refs to Columbus appear on lvs 441-442. Sabin 25083; Harrisse (BAV) 22 bis (p.461-462) & Add. 11; Sanz (Ult.ad.) 1402; Mortimer (Italy) 195; Isaac 12387; JCB (3) I:36. MH, RPJCB; BL.
503/2

Grünpeck, Joseph. Libellus . . . de mentulagra alias morbo gallico. [*Reutlingen? M.Greyff?* 1503?]. [27]p.;4to. Attrib. also to press of A.Kunne at Memmingen. Hain 8089; Proctor 11256; Stillwell (Science) 394; Goff G-513. CtY, DNLM; BL, BN.   503/3

Orden de Santiago. Compilación de los establecimientos de la Orden de la Caballeria de Santiago del Spada. *Seville: J.Pegnitzer,* 1503. 2pts;port.;fol. In the dedication by the compiler, Juan Fernández de la Gama, the Indies are mentioned. Sanz (Ult.ad.) 1403-1407; Escudero (Seville) 132. MH; BL.   503/4

Polo, Marco. Cosmographia, breve introductoria enel libro d' Marco paulo; el libro del famoso Marco paulo . . . d'las cosas maravillosas que vido enlas partes orientales. *Seville: L.Polono & J. Cromberger,* 1503. xxxiiii lvs;fol. Transl. by R.Fernández de Santa Ella. In prologue Santa Ella protests against use of term 'Indies' for newly found lands. Sanz (Ult.ad.) 296-298; Escudero (Seville) 128; Palau 151203. NNH; BL.   503/5

Reisch, Gregor. Margarita philosophica. *Freiburg i.Br.: J.Schott,* 1503. [604]p.;illus., map;4to. Map contains inscription interpreted as designating America. Sabin 69122; Sanz (Ult.ad.) 283-284; Ferguson (Reisch) 197-201; Proctor 11717; Shaaber R68. CSmH, CtY-M, DLC, InU-L, MH, MnU-B, NN-RB, PU; BL.   503/6

Spain. Laws, statutes, etc., 1479-1504 (Ferdinand V and Isabella I). Libro en que esta copiladas algunas bullas. *Alcalá de Henares: L.Polono,for J.Ramírez,* 1503. ccclxxv lvs;fol. Includes edict of 22 June 1493, decreeing that certain convicts be transported to West Indies as settlers. Sabin 40958; cf.Harrisse (BAV) Add. 10; García (Alcalá de Henares) 3. InU-L, MnU-B, NNH; BL.   503/7

—[Anr edn]. [*Salamanca? J.de Porras?* 1503?]. 257 numb.lvs;illus.;fol. Cf.Sabin 40959; cf. Harrisse (BAV) Add. 10; Sanz (Ult.ad.) 293-295; cf. Medina (BHA) 36; JCB (3) I:37. CtY, InU-L, MnU-B, NN-RB, RPJCB; BL.
503/8

Vespucci, Amerigo. Petri Francisci de Medicis Salutem plurimam. *Paris: F.Baligaut & J.Lambert,* 1503. [11]p.;4to. On Vespucci's 3rd voyage. Sabin 99327; Harrisse (BAV) 26 & Add., p.19; JCB (3) I:40. CSmH, InU-L, NN-RB, RPJCB; BL, BN.   503/9

1504

Anghiera, Pietro Martire d'. Libretto de tutta la navigatione de re de Spagna de le isole et terreni nuovamente trovati. *Venice: A.Vercellensis*, 1504. [31]p.;4to. Comprises the author's 1st Decade, an unauthorized piracy, in Italian translation by Angelo Trivigiano. Sabin 1547 (& 40955); Harrisse (BAV) 32 & Add. 16; Sanz (Ult.ad.) 301-336. InU-L, RPJCB; Venice: Bibl. Marciana.   504/1

Reisch, Gregor. Aepitoma omnis phylosophiae, alias Margarita phylosophica. *Strassburg: J.Grüninger*, 1504. 287 lvs;illus.,map; 4to. 1st publ., Freiburg, 1503. Sabin 69123; Ferguson (Reisch) 201-202; Proctor 9891. MH, NN-RB; BL, The Hague: KB.   504/2

___[Anr edn]. Margarita philosophica. [*Freiburg i.Br.:*] *J.Schott*, 1504. 330 lvs;illus.,map;4to. Sabin 69124; Ferguson (Reisch) 202-205; Proctor 11718; Adams (Cambr.) R333. CtY, DLC, InU-L, NN-RB, RPJCB; BL, BN.504/3

Sabellico, Marco Antonio Coccio, called. Secunda pars Enneadum. *Venice: B.Vercellensis*, 1504. cxci lvs;fol. The 1st part, without American refs, had appeared in 1498. On recto & verso of lf clxxi are described voyages of Columbus & P.A.Nuño. Sabin 74659; Harrisse (BAV) 2ln. CSmH, CtY, DLC, MiU-C, MnU-B, NN-RB, RPJCB; BN.   504/4

Vespucci, Amerigo. Mundus novus. *Venice: G.B.Sessa*, 1504. [7]p.;4to. 1st publ.,Paris, 1503. For variant states see Sabin 99328 under this title. Sabin 99328; Harrisse (BAV) Add. 14; Medina (BHA) 33; Church 19; JCB (3) I:39-40. CSmH, ICN, NN-RB, RPJCB; BL, BN.   504/5

___[Anr edn]. [*Augsburg: J.Otmar*, 1504]. [8]p.;4to. Sabin 99329; Harrisse (BAV) 22; Medina (BHA) 21; Church 16. CSmH, NN-RB.   504/6

___[Anr issue, with imprint]. *Augsburg: J.Otmar*, 1504. [8]p.;4to. Sabin 99330; Harrisse (BAV) 31; Medina (BHA) 30; Proctor 10662; Church 20; JCB (3) I:39. CSmH, InU-L, NN-RB, RPJCB; BL. [For other variant Augsburg issues or states see Sabin as here cited].   504/7

___[Anr edn]. [*Rome: E.Silber*, 1504]. [8]p.;4to. Sabin 99331; Harrisse (BAV) 23; Medina (BHA) 22; Isaac 12016; Church 17; JCB (3) I:40. CSmH, ICN, InU-L, NN-RB; BL. 504/8

1505

Baptista Mantuanus. De patientia libri tres. *Paris: J.Badius,for J.Petit* [1505]. lxvii lvs;4to. 1st publ., Brescia, 1497. MH, NN-RB; BL, BN.   505/1

Catholic Church. Liturgy and ritual. Missal. Missale pro Patavensis. *Augsburg: E.Ratdolt,* 1505. ccxii lvs;fol. Contains a 'Missa de beato Job, contra morbum gallicum', for the use of the diocese of Passau. PLatS.   505/2

Colombo, Cristoforo. Copia de la lettera . . . mandata ali . . . Re & Regina di Spagna: de le insule et luoghi per lui trovate. *Venice: S.de Luere,for C.Bayuera*, 1505. [11]p.;4to. Sabin 14642; Harrisse (BAV) 36 & Add. 17; Sanz (Ult.ad.) 339-377; Medina (BHA) 34n (I:49). Venice: Bibl. Marciana.   505/3

Manuel I, King of Portugal. Copia di una lettera del Re di Portugallo . . . del viaggio & successo de India. *Rome: J.Besicken*, 1505. [16]p.;4to. Cabral's discovery of Brazil is mentioned. Sabin 22407; Harrisse (BAV) Add. 18; Sanz (Ult.ad.) 381-400; Borba de Moraes II:16-18; Isaac 12041. MnU-B, NN-RB; BL.   505/4

___[Anr edn]. *Milan: P.M. de Mantegatiis & Bros, for J.J.Legnano & Bros*, 1505. [16]p.;4to. Sabin 22408; Harrisse (BAV) Add. 19; Sanz (Ult.ad.) 401-418; Borba de Moraes II:16-18. MnU-B.   505/5

Pacheco, Diogo. Obedientia potentissimi Emanuelis Lusitaniae Regis . . . ad Julium. II. Ponti. Max. . . . M.D.V. [*Rome: J.Besicken*, 1505?]. [8]p.;4to. Contains refs to the Indies. Cf. Sabin 56407; Isaac 12057; cf. Streit XV:683. RPJCB; BL, BN.   505/6

___[Anr edn]. [*Rome: E.Silber*, 1505?]. [8]p.;4to. Cf. Sabin 56407; Isaac 12022; cf. Streit XV:683. BL.   505/7

Sacro Bosco, Joannes de. Opus sphaericum. *Cologne: Sons of H.Quentel*, 1505. [74]p.;illus.;4to. The earliest edn to refer to America, on verso of lf 33. Ed. by Wencelaus Fabri. Proctor 10386; JCB (3) I:40-41. CU, DLC, NN-RB, RPJCB; BL.   505/8

Torrella, Gaspar. Consilium de egritudine pestifera & contagiosa ovina cognominata nuper cognita quam Hispani modorillam vocant. *Rome: J.Besicken*, 1505. [18]p.;4to. 1st publ., Rome, 1497. Palau 335985. DNLM; BL.   505/9

___[Anr edn]. *Salamanca:* [*H.Gysser*] 1505.
[19]p.;4to. Palau 335986; Adams (Cambr.)
T813. DNLM; Cambridge: UL, Madrid: BN.
505/10

Vespucci, Amerigo. Das sind die new gefunden menschen oder volcker. [*Nuremberg: G.
Stuchs, 1505-06*]. bds.;illus.;fol. Extracted
from the Basel, 1505, *Von der neu gefunden
Region* below. Sabin 99360; Sanz (Ult.ad.)
430-431. Wolfenbüttel: HB.   505/11

___. Be [i.e., De] ora antarctica per regem Por-
tugallie pridem inventa. *Strassburg: M.Hup-
fuff,* 1505. [11]p.;illus.;4to. 1st publ., Paris,
1503; other edns have title *Mundus Novus.* Sabin 99333; Harrisse (BAV) 39; Medina (BHA)
37; Proctor 10011; Church 21; Ritter
(Strasbourg) 2406; JCB (3) I:41. CSmH, DLC,
InU-L, MB, NN-RB, RPJCB; BL,
Strasbourg: BN.   505/12

___. Dise figur anzaight uns das volck und in-
sel. [*Augsburg: H.Froschauer, 1505-06*]. bds.;
illus.; obl.fol. Presumably extracted from the
Basel *Von der neu gefunden Region* of this
year, described below. In the title the reading
'cristenlichen' appears. Sabin 99361 (&
20257); cf. Borba de Moraes II:354-355.
Munich: StB.   505/13

___[Anr edn]. [*Augsburg: J.Froschauer,
1505-06*]. bds.; illus.; obl.fol. In this edn the
reading in the title is 'christenlichen'. Sabin
99362; Harrisse (BAV) 20; Borba de Moraes
II:354-355. NN-S.   505/14

___. Epistola Albericij. De novo mundo.
[*Rostock: H.Barkhusen,* 1505]. [8]p.;
illus.;fol. 1st publ., Paris, 1503. Sabin 99334;
Harrisse (BAV) Add. 13; Medina (BHA) 32;
Borba de Moraes II:352. BL.   505/15

___. Lettera . . . delle isole nuovamente
trovate. [*Florence: A.Tubini & A.Ghirlandi,
1505?*]. [32]p.;illus.;4to. Sabin 99353 (as
printed by P.Pacini); Harrisse (BAV) 87 &
Add.,p.xxiii-xxvi; Sanz (Ult.ad.) 419-429;
Medina (BHA) 46n (I:65); Borba de Moraes
II:353; Isaac 13324. NjP; BL, BN.   505/16

___. Mundus novus. [*Cologne: J.Landen,*
1505]. [8]p.;illus.;4to. Sabin 99335; Harrisse
(BAV) Add. 12; Medina (BHA) 31. CSmH;
Cologne: StB.   505/17

___[Anr edn]. [*Antwerp: W.Vorsterman, 1505?*].
[8]p.;4to. 1st publ., Paris, 1503; here
reprinted from Cologne edn above. Sabin
99336; Harrisse (BAV) 29; Medina (BHA) 28;
Nijhoff/Kronenberg 4055; JCB AR22:4-5.

CSmH, InU-L, MH, NN-RB, RPJCB;
Brussels: BR.   505/17a

___[Anr edn]. [*Nuremberg:* 1505]. [8]p.;illus.;
4to. Here reprinted from Rome, 1504, edn.
Sabin 99332; Harrisse (BAV) 24; Medina
(BHA) 23. NN-RB; Würzburg: UB.   505/18

___. Spis o nowych zemiech a o novem swiertie.
[*Pilsen: M.Bakalar, 1505-06*]. [16]p.;8vo.
Czech abridgment of the *Mundus Novus,* 1st
publ., Paris, 1503. Sabin 99367. Prague: Stra-
hov Monastery.   505/19

___. Von den nüwen Insulen und landen.
Strassburg: M. Hupfuff, 1505. [15]p.;illus.;
4to. Transl. from *Mundus Novus,* Paris, 1503.
Sabin 99345; Church 22. CSmH; Berlin: StB.
505/20

___[Anr edn]. Von den nawen Insulen unnd
Landen. *Leipzig: W.Müller* (i.e., *Stöckel*),
1505. [15]p.;illus.;4to. Reprinted from Strassburg edn above. Sabin 99346; Harrisse (BAV)
Add. 20. Leipzig: UB.   505/21

___. Von der neü gefunden Region. [*Basel:
M.Furter,* 1505]. [16]p.;4to. Transl. from au-
thor's *Mundus novus* 1st publ., Paris, 1503.
Sabin 99340; Harrisse (BAV) 37; Isaac 14133;
JCB (3) I:41. RPJCB; BL.   505/22

___[Anr edn]. Von der neuw gefunden Region.
[*Augsburg: J.Schönsperger,* ca. 1505].
[14]p.;illus.;4to. Sabin 99341; Harrisse (BAV)
34; Proctor 10613. BL.   505/23

___[Anr edn]. Von der neüwen gefunden Region.
[*Munich: J. Schobser,* 1505]. [20]p.;4to. Sabin
99342; Harrisse (BAV) Add. 21. Munich: StB.
505/24

1506

Bolognini, Angelo. Libellus de cura ulcerum
exteriorum. *Venice: J.Tacuinus,* 1506. [56]p.;
4to. On syphilis. Ind. aur. 121.499; Waller
1260. DNLM, NNNAM, PPC; Uppsala: UB,
Vienna: NB.   506/1

Brant, Sebastian. Narrenschiff. [*Basel: N.
Lamparter*] 1506. clxiiii lvs; illus.;8vo. 1st
publ., Basel, 1494. Wolfenbüttel 2; Ind.
aur.123.668. The Hague: KB, Wolfenbüttel:
HB.   506/2

Foresti, Jacopo Filippo, da Bergamo. Noviter
historiarum omnium repercussiones . . . noviter . . . edite. *Venice: G.dei Rusconi,* 1506.
499 numb.lvs;fol. 1st publ. with refs to New
World, Venice, 1503. American refs: lvs 440v-
441r. Sabin 25084; Harrisse (BAV) 42; Isaac

13042; JCB (3) I:42. NN-RB, RPJCB; BL, BN.   506/3

Maffei, Raffaele. Commentariorum urbanorum liber i[-xxxviii]. *Rome: J.Besicken*, 1506. dxlvii lvs;fol. Bk xii includes ref. to Columbus. Sabin 43763; Harrisse (BAV) 43 & Add. 22; Sanz (Ult. ad.) 440; Isaac 12043. DLC, MnU-B, RPJCB; BL.   506/4

Pico della Mirandola, Giovanni Francesco. De rerum praenotione libri novem. *Strassburg: J.Knobloch*, 1506-07. 294 lvs;fol. Refs to the New World appear on lvs T2v, s6v & p3v. Proctor 10052; Moranti (Urbino) 2596. NN-RB, RPJCB; BL, BN.   506/5

Sacro Bosco, Joannes de. Introductorium compendiosum in tractatum spere . . . per . . . Joannem Glogoviensem. *Cracow: J.Haller*, 1506. [143]p.;illus.;12mo. On lf g3 is a ref. to the 'Mundus novus', identified as America. Cf. Sabin 74800; Yarmolinsky (Early Polish Americana) 10. CSmH, DLC, InU-L, MB, MnU-B, NN-RB, RPJCB. 506/6

Torrella, Gaspar. De morbo gallico. *Rome: [J.Besicken, 1506?]*. [44]p.;4to. 1st publ., Rome, 1497, under title *Tractatus cum consiliis contra pudendagram seu morbum gallicum.* Isaac 12058. DNLM; BL.   506/7

Vespucci, Amerigo. Mundus novus. *[Paris: G.de Gourmont, 1506]*. [16]p.; 8vo. 1st publ., Paris, 1503. Sabin 99337; Harrisse (BAV) 28; Medina (BHA) 27. NN-RB; BN.   506/8

___[Anr edn]. *[Paris: D.Roce, 1506]*. [16]p.;8vo. Sabin 99338; Harrisse (BAV) 27; Medina (BHA) 28. NN-RB; BL.   506/9

___[Anr edn]. *[Paris: U.Gering & P.Rembolt, 1506]*. [16]p.;8vo. Sabin 99339; Harrisse (BAV) 25; Medina (BHA) 24; Church 18. CSmH, NN-RB, RPJCB; BL, BN.   506/10

____. Van den nygen Insulen und landen. *Magdeburg: J.Winter*, 1506. [15]p.; illus.;4to. 1st publ. in this Strassburg version, 1505. Sabin 99350. Brunswick: StB.   506/11

____. Van der nieuwer werelt oft landtscap. *Antwerp: J.van Doesborch, [1506-07]*. [16]p.; illus.;4to. Transl. prob. from Vorsterman's Antwerp, 1505, *Mundus novus.* Sabin 99352; Harrisse (BAV) Add. 15; Nijhoff/Kronenberg 2154; Proctor (Doesborgh) 3; JCB (3) I:48. RPJCB.   506/12

____. Von den newen Insulen und landen. *Leipzig: M.Landsberg*, 1506. [12]p.; illus.;4to. 1st publ. in this Strassburg version, 1505. Sabin 99348; Harrisse (BAV) 41; Proctor 11278. CSmH; BL.   506/13

___[Anr edn]. *Leipzig: M.Landsberg*, 1506. [12]p.;illus.;4to. In the title 'Insulen' reads 'Iusulen', etc. Sabin 99349. Bremen: StB.   506/14

___[Anr edn]. Von den nüwen Insulen und landen. *Strassburg: [M.Hupfuff]* 1506. [16]p.; illus.;4to. Sabin 99347; Harrisse (BAV) 40. NN-RB; Berlin: StB.   506/15

____. Von der neu gefunden Region. *[Nuremberg: W.Huber, 1506]*. [14]p.; illus.;4to. 1st publ. in this Basel version, 1505. Sabin 99343; Harrisse (BAV) 38; Medina (BHA) 46n (I:61); Proctor 10982; JCB (3) I:41-42. NN-RB, RPJCB; BL.   506/16

___[Anr edn]. Von der new gefunnden Region. *Nuremberg: W.Huber [1506]*. [11]p.;illus.; 4to. Sabin 99344; Harrisse (BAV) 33; Medina (BHA) 46n (I:60); JCB AR20:1505. RPJCB; Munich: StB.   506/17

1507

Baptista Mantuanus. Quae in hoc volumine infrascripti libri continentur. Vita Dionysii Areopagitae . . . Objurgatio cum exhortatione pro expeditione contra infideles. *Milan: P.M.de Mantegatiis*, 1507. 104 lvs;4to. The 'Objurgatio' contains a ref. to the New World. Ind. aur.112.454; Coccia 114. NN-RB; The Hague: KB.   507/1

Benivieni, Antonio. De abditis non nullis ac mirandis morborum et sanationum causis. *Florence: F.Giunta*, 1507. [107]p.;4to. On treatment of syphilis. Ind. aur. 116.785; Isaac 13341. DNLM, MiU, NNNAM; BL, BN.
                                             507/2

Dandolo, Marco. Apud Serenissimum Ferdinandum Hispaniae . . . Oratio. *[Naples? 1507?]*. 8 lvs;4to. On verso of 6th lf is a ref. to newly found lands. Harrisse (BAV) Add. 28; Palau 68243; JCB (3) I:43. NN-RB, RPJCB; BN.   507/3

Fracanzano da Montalboddo. Paesi novamenti retrovati. Et Novo Mondo da Alberico Vesputio. *Vicenza: H.& G.M.de Sancto Ursio*, 1507. 126 lvs;illus.;4to. Collection of voyages, incl. accounts of Columbus & Vespucci. Sabin 50050; Harrisse (BAV) 48 & Add. 26; Medina (BHA) 46n (I:64); Isaac 13917; Church 25; JCB (3) I:43. CSmH, CtY, DLC, InU-L, MB, NN-RB, RPJCB; BL, BN.   507/4

Lud, Gualtherus. Erclarnis und usslegung der Figur und Spiegels der Welt. *Strassburg:*

J.Grüninger, 1507. 8 lvs;4to. Transl. from following item. Breslau: UB.   507/5

____. Speculi orbis . . . declaratio. *Strassburg: J.Grüninger*, 1507. iv lvs;illus.;fol. On verso of lf iii are 'Versiculi de incognita terra' with ref. to America. Sabin 42638; Harrisse (BAV) 49; Proctor 9904. BL.   507/6

Petrarca, Francesco. Spurious and doubtful works. Chronica delle vite de pontefici et imperatori romani. *Venice: J.Pencio*, 1507. xc lvs;4to. On lf lxxxviii is a ref. to Columbus. Sabin 61290; Harrisse (BAV) Add. 27; Sanz (Ult.ad.) 653-654; Isaac 12915; Adams (Cambr.) P847. CSmH, CtY, DLC, ICN, MH, MiU-C, MnU-B, NN-RB, RPJCB; BL, BN.   507/7

Pico della Mirandola, Giovanni Francesco. Hymni heroici tres ad sanctissimam trinitatem. [*Milan: A.Minutianus*, 1507]. [176]p.; fol. American refs appear on lvs d2v & m2. Sanz (Ult.ad.) 651-652; Isaac 13583. MH, MnU-B, NN-RB; BL.   507/8

Vespucci, Amerigo. Quatuor navigationes. Issued as an integral part of the Martin Waldseemüller *Cosmographiae introductio*, which see below.

Vochs, Johann. De pestilentia anni presentis et eius cura. *Magdeburg: J.Winter*, 1507. 4to. Includes discussion of syphilis. Sherrington (Fernel) p.124. BL.   507/9

Waldseemüller, Martin. Cosmographiae introductio . . . Insuper quatuor Americi Vespucij navigationes. Universales cosmographiae descriptio . . . eis etiam insertis quae Ptholomaeo ignota a nuperis reperta sunt. *St.Dié: G.Lud*, 25 Apr.1507. [167]p.; diagr.;4to. Designed to accompany globe & map showing world, the New World being designated America. Sabin 101017 (& 99354); Harrisse (BAV) Add. 24; Sanz (Ult.ad.) 443-450; Medina (BHA) 42; Stillwell (Science) 250. NN-RB; BN.   507/10

__[Anr edn]. *St.Dié: G.Lud*, 25 Apr.1507. [104]p.;diagr.;4to. The preceding with 1st 6 lvs reset, 'cosmographiae' in the title reading 'cbosmographiae'. Sabin 101018; Harrisse (BAV) 45; Sanz (Ult.ad.) 453-456 & 469-573; Medina (BHA) 39; Arents 1; Church 23; JCB (3) I:45. CSmH, DLC, NN-A, RPJCB; BL, BN.   507/11

__[Anr edn]. *St.Dié:G.Lud*, 29 Aug. 1507. [167]p.;diagr.;4to. 1st line of title reads 'Cosmographiae.' Sabin 101019 (& 99355); Harrisse (BAV) 46; Sanz (Ult. ad.) 456-461;

Medina (BHA) 40; Church 24; JCB (3) I:45. CSmH, CtY, ICN, InU-L, MH, MiU-C, NN-RB, RPJCB; BL, BN.   507/12

__[Anr edn]. *St. Dié: G. Lud*, 29 Aug.1507. [167]p.;diagr.;4to. 1st line of title reads 'Cosmographiae Intro-'. Sabin 101020; Harrisse (BAV) 47; Medina (BHA) 41. NN-RB; Munich: StB.   507/13

__[Anr issue]. *St. Dié: G. Lud*, 29 Aug.1507. Possibly adventitious copy with 1st gathering of 6 lvs from 25 Apr.edn with 1st line of title 'Cosmographiae Introductio,' the remaining text being from 29 Aug.edn. Sabin 101021. Innsbruck: UB.   507/14

Wellendarfer, Virgilius, Bp of Salzburg. Decalogium . . . de metheorologicis impressionibus. *Leipzig: W. Stöckel*, 1507. cxvii lvs;illus.; 4to. On verso of lf lxvi is a ref. to Vespucci's 1501 New World voyage. Sabin 102560; Proctor 11447. CSmH, NN-RB; BL (Virgil, Saint).   507/15.

1508

Baptista Mantuanus. Ad potentas christianos exhortatio. *Paris: M. de Porta*, 1508. 17 lvs; 8vo. 1st publ., Milan, 1507, as 'Objurgatio cum exhortatio' with the author's *Vita Dionysii Areopagitae*. Coccia 125. The Hague: KB, Munich: UB.   508/1

Dionysius Periegetes. Situs orbis . . . Ruffo Avieno interprete. *Vienna: J. Winterburg, for J. Cuspian*, 1508. 26 lvs; illus.;4to. Includes allusions to New World on verso of t.p. Sabin 20209; Harrisse (BAV) 93 (misdated 1518); Isaac 14405. RPJCB; BL.   508/2

Foresti, Jacopo Filippo, da Bergamo. Supplemento supplementi de le Chroniche . . . infino al anno . . . MCCCCCIII. diligentemente vulgarizato per . . . Francesco C. [i.e., Francesco Sansovino]. *Venice: G. dei Rusconi*, 1508. cccl lvs;fol. Transl. from author's *Novissime hystoriarum omnium*, 1st publ., Venice, 1503. Sabin 25085 (& 24395); Harrisse (BAV) 53. DLC, NNH.   508/3

Fracanzano da Montalboddo. Itinerarium Portugallensium e Lusitania in Indiam & inde in occidentem & demum ad aquilonem. [*Milan: J.A. Scinzenzeler*, 1508?]. lxxviii lvs;illus., map;fol. Transl. by A.Madrignano from author's *Paesi novamente ritrovati*, 1st publ., Vicenza, 1507. Sabin 50058; Harrisse (BAV) 58; Streit XV:713; Church 27; JCB (3) I:46.

CSmH, CtY, DLC, ICN, InU-L, MH, MiU-C, MnU-B, NN-RB, RPJCB; BL, BN. 508/4

____. Newe unbekanthe landte und ein newe weldte in kurtz verganger Zeythe erfunden. *Nuremberg: G. Stuchs*, 1508. 68 lvs;illus.;fol. Transl. by J. Ruchamer from author's *Paesi novamente ritrovati*, 1st publ., Vicenza, 1507. Sabin 50056; Harrisse (BAV) 57; Church 28; JCB (3) I:46. CSmH, CtY, DLC, InU-L, MH, MiU-C, MnU-B, NN-RB, RPJCB; BL. 508/5

____. Nye unbekande Lande unde ein nye Werldt in korter vergangener tyd gefunden. *Nuremberg: G.Stuchs*, 1508. 68 lvs;fol. Transl. into Low Saxon by H.Ghetel from the author's *Paesi novamente trovati*, 1st publ., Vicenza, 1507. Sabin 50057; Harrisse (BAV) Add. 29; Church 29; JCB (3) I:46. CSmH, RPJCB. 508/6

____. Paesi nuovamente retrovati. & Novo Mondo da Alberico Vesputio. *Milan: J.A.Scinzenzeler, for J.J.Legnano & Bros*, 1508. 83 lvs;4to. 1st publ., Vicenza, 1507. Sabin 50051 (& 41055); Harrisse (BAV) 55; Isaac 13533; Balsamo (Scinzenzeler) 72; Church 30; JCB (3) I:46. CSmH, ICN, MH, NN-RB, RPJCB; BL, BN. 508/7

Fur die platern Malafrantsosa. [*Vienna: J.Winterburg*, ca.1508?]. bds.;fol. 'Diss gepet ist guet und bewert fur die platern Malafrantsosa.' Langer (Winterburg) 148. Munich: StB. 508/8

Montesino, Ambrosio, Bp. Cancionero de diversas obras de nuevo trobadas. *Toledo:* [*Successor of P.Hagembach*]1508. lxxiii lvs;illus.; 4to. In the poem 'Coplas de sant Juan Evangelista' is a passage (lf lvii r) beginning 'Los hombres que navegando/hallan yslas muy remotas', viewed as the earliest ref. to the New World in Spanish literature. Pérez Pastor (Toledo) 38; Palau 178942. NNH; Madrid: BN. 508/9

Ptolemaeus, Claudius. Geographiae . . . a plurimis viris . . . emendata . . . Nova & universalior orbis cogniti tabula Joan. Ruysch germano elaborata. *Rome: B.dei Vitali*, 1508. 209 lvs;maps;fol. A reissue of a 1507 edn with cancel t.p., added text 'Nova orbis descriptio' and new Ruysch map depicting New World. Sabin 66476; Harrisse (BAV) 56; Sanz (Ult.ad.) 660-669; Stevens (Ptolemy) 43; Armstrong 10; Phillips 357; Isaac 12097; JCB (3) I:47. CtY, DLC, InU-L, NN-RB, RPJCB; BL, BN. 508/10

Reisch, Gregor. Margarita philosophica cum additionibus novis. *Basel: M.Furter & J.Schott*, 1508. [632]p.;illus.,map;4to. 1st publ., Freiburg, 1503. Sabin 69125; Ferguson (Reisch) 205-206; Isaac 4119. DNLM, MH, NN-RB; BL, BN. 508/11

_[Anr edn]. *Strassburg: J.Grüninger*, 1508. [639]p.;illus.,map;4to. Sabin 69126; Ferguson (Reisch) 206-208; Proctor 9907; Adams (Cambr.) R334. CLU-C, CtY, DLC, IU, MH, NN-RB, PP; BL, The Hague:KB. 508/12

Reitter, Conrad. Mortilogus . . . epigrammata ad eruditissimos vaticolas. *Augsburg: E.Oeglin & G.Nadler*, 1508. [67]p.;illus.;4to. Included is an ode to the Virgin Mary seeking preservation from syphilis. Proctor 10703; Adams (Cambr.) R341; Proksch I:79. DNLM, MBCo; BL, BN. 508/13

Sacro Bosco, Joannes de. Opus sphericum. *Paris: R.de Gourmont*, 1508. 91 lvs;illus.;4to. 1st publ. as here ed. by Wencelaus Fabri, Cologne, 1505. TU. 508/14

_[Anr edn]. *Cologne: Heirs of H.Quentel*, 1508. [74]p.;illus.;4to. Proctor 10415. NN-RB; BL. 508/15

____. Uberrimum sphere mundi commentum, insertis etiam questionibus . . . Petri de Aliaco. *Paris:* [*J.Petit*] 1508. 80 lvs;illus.;fol. 1st publ. in this version referring to New World, Paris, 1498. Goldschmidt (Not in Harrisse) 140; Adams (Cambr.) H716. DLC, NN-RB; Cambridge: UL, BN. 508/16

Springer, Balthasar. Die reyse van Lissebone om te varen na den eylandt Naguaria. *Antwerp: J.van Doesborch*, 1508. [24]p.;illus.; 4to. A plagiary of Springer's Latin narrative of a voyage to India, substituting a Dutch translation of Vespucci's introductory words in his *Mundus Novus* and adding at end Vespucci's chapter on cosmography. Sabin 99364; JCB (3) I:48. RPJCB. 508/17

_[Anr issue]. *Antwerp: J.van Doesborch*, 1508. [24]p.;illus.;4to. On the t.p. 3 lines beginning 'Welcke reyse gheschiede' have been added, &c. Sabin 99364; Proctor (Doesborgh) 4; Nijhoff/Kronenberg 1800. BL. 508/18

Stamler, Joannes. Dyalogus . . . de diversarum gencium sectis et mundi religionibus. *Augsburg: E.Oeglin & J.Nadler*, 1508. xxxii lvs;illus;fol. On verso of lf aiii is a brief ref. to Columbus & Vespucci. Sabin 90127; Harrisse (BAV) 51; Proctor 10704; Church 26; Shaaber S552; JCB (3) I:47-48. CSmH, DLC, ICN,

InU-L, MH, NN-RB, PPL, RPJCB; BL, BN.
509/19

Téllez, Fernando. Razonamiento de los embaradores de España en la obediencia que dieron al Papa. *Rome*: 1508. [7]p.;4to. Includes ref. to exploration of New World. Sabin 94623; Harrisse (BAV) Add. 30; Medina (BHA) 44; Palau 329470. InU-L, MB.
508/20

Vespucci, Amerigo, alleged author. Die reyse van Lissebone. *Antwerp*: 1508. See Springer, Balthasar.

1509

Baptista Mantuanus. Opera nova. *Paris: J.Badius, for self & de Marnef Bros*, 1509. cxv lvs; 8vo. (The author's *Opera*, pt 5, 1507-10). On verso of lf lxxxv, in the 'Exhortatio regum christianorum ut ducant in barbaros', is a ref. to Columbus. Sabin 44403; Harrisse (BAV) Add. 35; Ind. aur.112.460; Renouard (Badius Ascensius) II:136. MH, MiU, NN-RB; BN.
509/1

Brant, Sebastian. Narrenschiff. *Basel: N.Lamparter*, 1509. clxiii lvs;illus.;4to. 1st publ., Basel, 1494. Ind.aur.123.675; Isaac 14254. BL.
509/2

_____. The shyp of folys of the worlde. *London: R.Pynson*, 1509. cclxxiiii lvs;illus.;fol. Comprises Locher's 1497 Latin translation of the 1494, Basel, *Narrenschiff* and Alexander Barclay's English translation. The refs to the New World appear on lvs cxxxix-cxl. Ind.aur. 123.676; STC 3545. CSmH, CtY, DFo, ICN, NN-RB; BL.
509/3

_____. The shyppe of fooles. *London: W.de Worde*, 1509. [338]p.;illus.;4to. Transl. by Henry Watson from the 1499 French paraphrase by Jehan Drouyn. The ref. to the New World—the earliest in English— appears in ch.lxiiii (p. [190]). Harrisse (BAV) Add. 33; Ind.aur. 123.677; STC 3547. BN.
509/4

Catholic Church. Liturgy and ritual. Missal. Missale Pataviense. *Vienna: J.Winterburg*, 1509. 272 numb.lvs; illus.;4to. 1st publ. with special Mass of Blessed Job, Augsburg, 1505. Langer (Winterburg) 61; Proksch I:79. NjN; BL (destroyed), Munich: StB.
509/5

Fregoso, Battista. De dictis factisque memorabilibus collectanea . . . a Camillo Gilino latina facta. *Milan: J. J.*

Ferrariis, 1509. 335 lvs;fol. Transl. from unpublished Italian text. On verso of lf 112 is a ref. to Columbus. Sabin 26140; Harrisse (BAV) Add. 34; Isaac 13634; JCB (3) I:49. NN-RB, RPJCB; BL, BN.
509/6

Gatinaria, Marco. De curis egritudinum particularium noni Almansoris practica uberrima . . . Sebastiani Aquilani Tractatus de morbo gallico celeberrimus. *Pavia: J.de Burgofranco*, 1509. 214 numb.lvs;illus.;8vo. CtY-M, DNLM, NNNAM.
509/7

Sabellico, Marco Antonio Coccio, called. Rapsodie historiarum Enneadum . . . ab orbe conditio ad annum . . . 1504. *Paris: J.Badius, for self & J.Petit*, 1509. 3v.;fol. 1st publ., Venice, 1504, with refs to Columbus in pt 2, these now appearing in pt 3 on verso of lf cxcvi. Sabin 74660; Harrisse (BAV) 59; Adams (Cambr.) S21; Renouard (Badius Ascensius) III:222-224. ICN, NN-RB, RPJCB (v.3 only); Cambridge: Gonville & Caius.
509/8

Seitz, Alexander. Ein nutzlich regiment vuider die bosen frantzosen. *Pforzheim: T.Anshelm*, 1509. 8 lvs;4to. BL.
509/9

Simonetta, Bonifacio. De christiane fidei et Romanorum Pontificium persecutionibus. *Basel: N.Kesler*, 1509. 156 lvs;fol. On verso of lf 101 are refs to West Indies. Adams (Cambr.) S1184; Proctor 14078. NN-RB, NNH, WU; BL.
509/10

Vespucci, Amerigo. Diss büchlin saget wie die zwen durchlüchtigsten herren her Fernandus K. zü Castilien und herr Emanuel. K. zü Portugal haben das weyte mör ersüchet unnd funden vil Insulen unnd ein Nüwe welt . . . vormals unbekant. *Strassburg: J.Grüninger*, 1509. [63]p.;illus.;4to. Translated from the 1507, St.Dié, Latin *Quattuor . . . navigationes.* Prob. prepared for issue with Waldseemüller's *Welt kugel* below. In this state the colophon has phrase 'uff mitfast'. Sabin 99356; Harrisse (BAV) Add. 31; Medina (BHA) 46n (I:62); Borba de Moraes II:354-355; Proctor 9914; Church 33. CSmH, ICN, NN-RB; BL.
509/11

—[Anr state]. As above, having reading 'uff Letare' in colophon. Sabin 99357; Harrisse (BAV) 62; Ritter (Strasbourg) 2407. NN-RB; Munich: StB.
509/12

Waldseemüller, Martin. Cosmographie introductio . . . Insuper quattuor Americi Vespucij navigationes. *Strassburg: J.Grüninger*, 1506. 32 lvs;illus.;4to. 1st publ., St.Dié,

1507. Sabin 101022; Harrisse (BAV) 60; Sanz (Ult.ad.) 461; Proctor 9915; Arents 1-a; Church 32; Fairfax Murray (Germany) 438; JCB (3) I:50. CSmH, ICN, InU-L, MH, MiU-C, RPJCB; BL, BN.   509/13

————. Globus mundi. Declaratio sive descriptio mundi et totius orbis terrarum . . . permultis de quarta orbis terrarum parte nuper ab Americo reperta. *Strassburg: J.Grüninger,* 1509. 14 lvs;illus.;4to. Prob. issued with the author's *Cosmographie introductio* of this year. Sabin 27583; Harrisse (BAV) 61; Proctor 9917; JCB (3) I:49. MH, RPJCB; BL, The Hague: KB.   509/14

————. Der welt kugel, Beschrybung der welt und dess gantzen Ertreichs. *Strassburg: J.Grüninger,* 1509. [31]p.;illus.;4to. Transl. from the author's Latin *Globus mundi* above. Prob. prepared for issue with Vespucci's *Diss büchlin* above. Sabin 102623; Harrisse (BAV) Add. 32. CSmH, InU-L; BL.   509/15

Wollich, Nicholas. Enchiridion musices. *Paris: J.Petit* [1509?]. On t.p. is punning distich citing 'americos . . . tractus'. See Charles Singer, 'An early use of the word "America" ', *TLS,* 14 July 1945, p. 336. Wm Dawson & Sons, London (1945).   509/16

1510

Albertini, Francesco degli. Opusculum de mirabilibus novae & veteris urbis Romae. *Rome: J.Mazochius,* 1510. [206]p.;4to. On p.[201], in section 'De laudibus civitatum Florentiae & Saonensis', is a brief ref. to Vespucci. Sabin 663; Harrisse (BAV) 64; Ind. aur.102.416; Isaac 12101; Adams (Cambr.) A502; JCB (3) I:50. CSmH, CtY, DLC, ICN, MH, MnU-B, RPJCB; BL, BN.   510/1

————. Septem mirabilia orbis et urbis Romae et Florentiae civitatis. *Rome: J.Mazochius,* 1510. [16]p.;4to. The dedication contains a ref. to Vespucci's voyages. Ind.aur. 102.417; Sander 165. CSmH, CtY, MH.   510/2

Baptista Mantuanus. De patientia. *Strassburg: M.Schürer,* 1510. cxxxvi lvs;4to. 1st publ., Brescia, 1497. Ind.aur. 112.492; Ritter (Strasbourg) 135. DCU, ICU, InU-L, NN-RB; BL, BN.   510/3

Foresti, Jacopo Filippo, da Bergamo. Suma de todas las cronicas del mundo. *Valencia: G.Costilla,* 1510. ccccxlvi lvs;illus.;fol. Transl.

by Narcis Viñoles from Latin & Italian texts of 1508. Palau 325000. MB; BL, BN.   510/4

Geiler, Johannes, von Kaisersberg. Navicula, sive Speculum fatuorum prestantissimi sacrarum literarium. *Strassburg: M.Schürer* [1510]. 248 lvs;4to. Ref. to America on lf Z2r, lines 9-10. Proctor 10177; Adams (Cambr.) G315; Ritter (Strasbourg) 955. NN-RB; BL, Strasbourg:BN.   510/5

Vespucci, Amerigo. De novo mondo. *Antwerp: J.van Doesborch* [ca.1510?]. [2]p.;illus.; fol. Extracted & transl. in part from the [1505-06] Nuremberg *Das sind die new gefunden menschen.* Sabin 99365. Rostock: UB.   510/6

1511

Anghiera, Pietro Martire d'. Opera: Legatio babylonica, Oceani decas, poemata epigrammatica. *Seville: J.Cromberger,* 1511. 74 lvs;map;fol. The 'Oceani decas' 1st publ., Venice, 1504. Sabin 1548; Harrisse (BAV) 66; Medina (BHA) 47; Escudero (Seville) 159; JCB (3) I:52. InU-L, RPJCB.   511/1

——[Anr edn]. *Seville: J.Cromberger,* 1511. In the title the reading 'Occeana' appears. Sabin 1549; Harrisse (BAV) Add. 41; Medina (BHA) 48; Church 35. CSmH, DLC, ICN, MiU-C; BL.   511/2

Catholic Church. Pope, 1492-1503 (Alexander VI). Copia dela bula dela concession que hizo el papa Alexandre sexto al Rey & ala Reyna nuestros señores: delas Indias. [*Logroño: A.G.de Brocar,* ca.1511]. bds.;fol. On division of newly found lands between Spain & Portugal. Harrisse (BAV) Add. 1; GW (Einbl.) 107m; Goff A-370; JCB (3) I:51. CSmH, DLC, RPJCB.   511/3

——[Anr edn]. Copia de la bula del decreto y concession que hizo el papa Alexandro sexto . . . [*Logroño? A.G.de Brocar?* ca.1511?]. bds.;fol. CCamarSJ.   511/4

Geiler, Johannes, von Kaisersberg. Navicula, sive Speculum fatuorum. *Strassburg: J.Prüss,* 1511. [560]p.;illus.; 4to. 1st publ., Strassburg, 1510; American ref. here appears on lf e2v. Proctor 9995; Adams (Cambr.) G316; Ritter (Strasbourg) 959; JCB (3) I:51-52. CSmH, CtY, DLC, MB, NN-RB, RPJCB; BL, BN.   511/5

Maffei, Raffaele. Commentariorum Urbanorum . . . octo et triginta libri. *Paris:*

J.Badius, for self & J.Petit, 1511. ccccxiiii lvs;fol. 1st publ., Rome 1506; the ref. to Columbus here appears on verso of lf cxxv. Sabin 43765; Harrisse (BAV) 67 & Add. 40; Renouard (Badius Ascensius) III: 384-385; Adams (Cambr.) M99. NN-RB, RPJCB; BL, BN.   511/6

Pico della Mirandola, Giovanni Francesco. Hymni heroici tres. *Strassburg: M.Schürer,* 1511. xcvi lvs;fol. 1st publ., Milan, 1507. Proctor 10190; Adams (Cambr.) P1157. CSt, MH, NN-RB; BL.   511/7

Ptolemaeus, Claudius. Liber geographiae. *Venice: J.Pencio,* 1511. 92 lvs; maps;fol. Contains world map depicting America, here designated 'regalis domus'. Sabin 66477; Sanz (Ult. ad.) 687-693; Isaac 12924; Adams (Cambr.) P2218; JCB (3) I:52-53. CSmH, CtY, DLC, InU-L, MH, MiU-C, MnU-B, NN-RB, RPJCB; BL.   511/8

Sobrarius, Joannes. Panegyricum carmen de gestis heroicis divi Ferdinandi catholici. *Saragossa: J.Coci,* 1511. xxv lvs;4to. 'Invento novarum insularum': verso of lf viii. Sabin 85670; Harrisse (BAV) Add. 39; Medina (BHA) 49; Sánchez (Aragon) 40. CSmH, NNH; Madrid: BN.   511/9

Waldseemüller, Martin. Instructio manuductionem prestans in cartam itinerariam Martini Hilacomili. *Strassburg: J.Grüninger,* 1511. xxi lvs;4to. Dedication dated at end. Sabin 101025; Proctor 9922. RPJCB; BL, BN.
                                    511/10

—[Anr state]. *Strassburg: J.Grüninger,* 1511. Dedication undated at end. Sabin 101026. BN.   511/11

1512

Aristoteles. Meteorologia. *Nuremberg: F.Peypus,* 1512. xciiii lvs; illus.,map;4to. Includes description of newly discovered lands. Goldschmidt (Not in Harrisse) 135-136; Sanz (Ult.ad.) 694-697; Ind.aur.107.806. MH, MnU-B; BN.   512/1

Baptista Mantuanus. Joannis Corrunni . . . Enarrationes . . . in Fra. Baptistae Mant. . . . . Exhortatio ad potentatus christianos. *Paris: J.Marchand,for F.Regnault & E.Gourmont* [1512?]. xxviii lvs;8vo. 1st publ., Milan, 1507, as *Objurgatio cum exhortatio* with the author's *Vita Dionysii Areopagitae.* Coccia 211 (& 276?). BL.   512/2

Brant, Sebastian. Das Narrenschiff. *Strassburg: M.Hupfuff,* 1512. clxiiii lvs; illus.;4to. 1st publ., Basel, 1494. Proctor 10032. BL.
                                    512/3

Catholic Church. Liturgy and ritual. Missal. Missale Pataviensis. *Vienna: J.Winterburg,* 1512. fol. 1st publ., Augsburg, 1505. Cf. Proksch I:79. BL.   512/4

Eusebius Pamphili, Bp of Caesarea. Chronicon . . . complura quae ad haec usque tempora subsecuta sunt adjecere. *Paris: H. Estienne, for J.Badius,* 1512. 175 numb.lvs; illus.;4to. On lf 172v is a passage prob. referring to Indians brought from Canada to Rouen in 1509. Sabin 23114; Harrisse (BAV) 71 & Add. 43; Sanz (Ult. ad.) 698-702; cf. Mortimer (France) 217; Renouard (Badius Ascensius) II:429-430; JCB (3) I:53-54. MH, MiU-C, MnU-B, RPJCB; BL, BN.   512/5

Fracanzano da Montalboddo. Paesi novamente retrovati. *Milan: J.A.Scinzenzeler,for J.J.Legnano & Bros,* 1512. 75 lvs;illus.;4to. 1st publ., Vicenza, 1507. Sabin 50052; Harrisse (BAV) 70; Isaac 13538; Balsamo (Scinzenzeler) 103. ICN, InU-L, NN-RB, RPJCB; BL.
                                    512/6

Jan ze Stobnicy. Introductio in Ptholomei Cosmographiam. *Cracow: F.Unglerius,* 1512. xl lvs;illus., map;4to. In text are refs to Vespucci's discoveries; map of western hemisphere depicts America. Sabin 91866; Harrisse (BAV) 69 & Add. 42; Sanz (Ult. ad.) 703-704; Yarmolinsky (Early Polish Americana) 15-30; JCB AR29: 28-31. CtY, DLC, MiU-C, NN-RB, RPJCB; Vienna: NB.   512/7

Pico della Mirandola, Giovanni Francesco. Staurostichon, hoc est Carmen de mysteriis dominicae crucis. *Tübingen: T.Anshelm,* 1512. lxxx lvs;4to. Earlier incl. in the author's *Hymni heroici tres.* Refs to New World are on lvs lxxvii(v)-lxxviii(r). Proctor 11728; Adams (Cambr.) P1159. CSt, CtY, DFo, ICN, MH, NN-RB, RPJCB; BL.   512/8

Prudentius Clemens, Aurelius. Opera. *Logroño: A.G.de Brocar,* 1512. 196 lvs; illus.;4to. The dedicatory epistle (not present in all copies) contains ref. to New World. Sabin 66411; Harrisse (BAV) Add. 44; Palau 239820; JCB (3) I:55. NN-RB, RPJCB; BL.
                                    512/9

Reisch, Gregor. Margarita philosophica nova. *Strassburg: J.Grüninger,* 1512. [747]p.;illus., map;4to. 1st publ., Strassburg, 1504. Sabin

69127; Ferguson (Reisch) 207-212; Proctor 9924; Adams (Cambr.) R335; JCB AR20: 1512. DLC, MnU-B, NN-RB, PPPH, RPJCB; BL, BN. 512/10

1513

Baptista Mantuanus. De patientia aurei libri tres. *Paris: J.Badius*, 1513. xlix lvs;4to. 1st publ., Brescia, 1497. Ind.aur.112.580. BN. 513/1

____. Opera. *Paris: J.Badius*, 1513. 3v.;fol. In v.1 is the 'Exhortationis in Turcas lib.I', 1st publ., Milan, 1507, as *Objurgatio cum exhortatio*, and *De patientia*, 1st publ., Brescia 1497. Printed by Badius, other issues were prepared for the Paris booksellers Denis Roce, Jean Petit, and the brothers de Marnef. Ind. aur.112.579; Coccia 232. MH (Roce); BL (de Marnef & Roce), BN (de Marnef & Petit). 513/2

Foresti, Jacopo Filippo, da Bergamo. Supplementum supplementi chronicarum . . . usque . . . .M.ccccc.X. editum. *Venice: G.dei Rusconi*, 1513. cccxxxv lvs;fol. 1st publ. in this version, Venice, 1503. 'De quattuor permaximis insulis in India extra orbem nuper inventis': verso of lf 329 ff. Sabin 25086; Harrisse (BAV) 73; Isaac 13042; Shaaber F357. InU-L, MBAt, MiU-C, NN-RB, PU; BL, BN. 513/3

Geiler, Johannes, von Kaisersberg. Navicula, sive speculum fatuorum. *Strassburg: J.Knobloch*, 1513. [482] p.;4to. 1st publ., Strassburg, 1510. Proctor 10080; Adams (Cambr.) G317; Ritter (Strasbourg) 964. CtY, ICU, MH; BL, Strasbourg: BN. 513/4

Paulus Middelburgensis. De recta Paschae celebratione. *Fossombrone: O.Petruccio*, 1513. 2pts;port.;fol. Refs to Columbus & Vespucci appear on lf FFiiiir. Sabin 59232; Sanz (Ult.ad.) 705-707; Isaac 14040; Adams (Cambr.) P504. CSmH, DLC, ICN, InU-L, MH, MnU-B, RPJCB; BL, BN. 513/5

Ptolemaeus, Claudius. Geographiae opus novissima. *Strassburg: J.Schott*, 1513. 2pts; maps;fol. Incorporates new material deriving from M. Waldseemüller & M.Ringmann relating to, the New World. Sabin 66478; Sanz (Ult.ad.) 708-731; Proctor 10271; Fairfax Murray (Germany) 348 & 348A; JCB (3) I:57-58. DLC, InU-L, MiU-C, MnU-B, NN-RB, RPJCB; BL, BN. 513/6

Sabellico, Marco Antonio Coccio, called. Rapsodie historiarum Enneadum. *Paris: J.Badius,for self & J.Petit*, 1513. 2v.;fol. 1st publ. with American refs, Venice, 1504. Sabin 74661; Harrisse (BAV) 72; Renouard (Badius Ascensius) III:224-225; Adams (Cambr.) R22-R23. Cambridge: Jesus, BN. 513/7

Sacro Bosco, Joannes de. Introductorium compendiosum in tractatum sphere· . . . per Joannem Glogoviensem recollectum. *Cracow: F.Ungler, for J.Haller*, 1513. 79 lvs;illus.;4to. 1st publ. in this version, Cracow, 1506. Wierzbowski 22. DLC. 513/8

Spain. Laws, statutes, etc., 1504-1516 (Ferdinand V). [Declaracion y moderacion de las ordenanzas hechas para el buen gobierno de las Indias, promulgadas en Valladolid. *Valladolid?* 1513?]. Medina (BHA) 51; António Muro Obrejón, 'Ordenanzas reales sobre los Indios (las leyes de 1512-13); estudio y edición', *Anuario de Estudios americanos*, XIII (1956) 417-471. 513/9

Widman, Johann, called Mechinger. Ain nützlichs Büchlin von dem Wildpad. [*Tübingen: T.Anshelm*, 1513]. [13]p.;4to. Transl. from 1497, Strassburg, *Tractatus de pustulis*. DNLM; BL. 513/10

1514

Albertus Magnus, Saint, Bp of Ratisbon. De natura locorum. *Vienna: H.Vietor & J.Singriener, for L. & L.Alantse*, 1514. [104]p.; illus.;4to. Ed. by G.Tannstetter. On final page Vespucci is mentioned by editor in confirmation of author's theories. Sabin 671; Harrisse (BAV) 76; Isaac 14440; JCB (3) I:58. CU, DNLM, ICN, MH, MiU-C, MnU-B, RPJCB; BL, BN. 514/1

Bolognini, Angelo. Libellus de cura ulcerum exteriorum. *Bologna: B.Hectoris*, 1514. [50]p.;4to. Contains section on unguents for treating syphilis. Ind.aur. 121.500; Waller 1261. BL, Uppsala: UB. 514/2

Cataneo, Giovanni Maria. Genua. *Rome: J.Mazochius*, 1514. [22]p.;4to. Poem praising Genoa, containing, on lf C2, verses on Columbus & his voyages. Sabin 11494; Harrisse (BAV) 75; Isaac 12119. CtY, DLC, MH, RPJCB; BL, BN. 514/3

Catholic Church. Liturgy and ritual. Missal. Missale Pataviense. *Nuremberg: J.Heller, for J.Gutknecht*, 1514. 356 numb.

lvs;illus.;fol. 1st (?) publ., Augsburg, 1505, the 'Missa de beato Job' here appearing on lvs 336v-337r. DLC. 514/4

Copia der Newen Zeytung auss Presillg Landt. [Woodcut: seaport with ships]. [*Nuremberg: H.Höltzel*, 1514?]. [6]p.;illus.;4to. Extract from letter of Fugger agent in Madeira Islands, describing return there of Portuguese vessel on 12 Oct. 1514 from exploration of Brazil. Sabin 7559; Harrisse (BAV) 99; Weller (Ersten d. Zeitungen) 1n; Borba de Moraes II:98-99; Baginsky (German Americana) 38; JCB (3) I:63-64. NN-RB, RPJCB; BL. 514/5

—[Anr edn]. [Woodcut: arms of Portugal]. *Augsburg: E.Oeglin* [1514?]. [4] p.;illus.;4to. Sabin 7560; Harrisse (BAV) 100; Sanz (Ult.ad.) 734-736; Weller (Ersten d. Zeitungen) 1; Borba de Moraes II:98-99; cf.Baginsky (German Americana) 36; cf.JCB (3) I:63. MnU-B; BL. 514/6

—[Anr edn, counterfeiting preceding, with erroneous reading 'eytung' for 'Zeytung' in title, & other faults in text]. '*Augsburg: E.Oeglin*' [1514?]. 4 lvs;4to. Weller (Ersten d. Zeitungen) 1; Borba de Moraes II:99, cf. Baginsky (German Americana) 36. InU-L; BL. 514/7

Gaguin, Robert. Les grandes chroniques . . . translatées . . . de latin [par Pierre Desrey] . . . ensemble aussi plusieurs additions. *Paris: P.LePreux & G.DuPré*, 1514. ccliii lvs;illus.; fol. Contains ref. in bk 11 to American savages brought to Rouen in 1509. Adams (Cambr.) G21. Cambridge: FitzWilliam Mus., BN. 514/8

Hock von Brackenau, Wendelin. Mentagra, sive Tractatus de causis preservativis regímine & cura morbi gallici. [*Strassburg: J.Schott*] 1514. 52 numb. lvs.;4to. Stillwell (Science) 423; Proctor 10275; Ritter (Strasbourg) 1176. DNLM, MiU; BL, BN. 514/9

Jan ze Stobnicy. Introductio in Ptholomei Cosmographiam. *Cracow: F.Unglerius* [ca.1514]. xxxiiiiiii lvs;illus.;4to. 1st publ., Cracow, 1512; save for 4 final lvs, printed from same setting of type as 1512 edn. Sabin 91866n; cf. Harrisse (BAV) 69 & Add. 42. NN-RB. 514/10

Ptolemaeus, Claudius. Opere . . . Nova translatio . . . Joanne Vernero . . . interprete. *Nuremberg: H.Stuchs*, 1514. [135]p.;illus.; fol. Contains J.Werner's 'De quattuor aliis planis terrarum orbis descriptionibus', lvs 43-48. Sabin 66479; Sanz (Ult.ad.) 732-733;

Proctor 11095; JCB (3) I:60-61. DLC, NN-RB, MiU-C, RPJCB; BL. 514/11

Stiborius, Andreas. Super requisitione Leonis Papae X . . . de romani calendarii correctione consilium. *Vienna: J.Singriener* [1514]. 10 lvs;illus.;4to. Jointly written with Georg Tannstetter; ref. is made to 'novas terras et insulas inventas'. Goldschmidt (Not in Harrisse) 138; Isaac 14460; Adams (Cambr.) S1864. NN-RB; BL. 514/12

Vigo, Giovanni da. Practica in chirurgica. *Rome: S.Guileretus & E.Nani*, 1514. ccxx lvs;fol. Includes, as bk 5, 'De morbo gallico'. BN. 514/13

—[Anr edn]. *Rome: S.Guileretus & E.Nani*, 1514. 162 numb. lvs;fol. DNLM; BN. 514/14

1515

Agricola, Rudolf. Ad Joachimum Vadianum epistola. *Vienna: J.Singriener*, 1515. [31]p.; 4to. Incorporates letter of Vadianus in which the New World is designated America. Sabin 98283; Harrisse (BAV) p.147n; Proctor 14455; Church 38; JCB AR20:1515. CSmH, CtY, ICU, MH, NN-RB, RPJCB; BL. 515/1

Albertini, Francesco. Opusculum de mirabilibus novae & veteris urbis Romae. *Rome: J.Mazochius*, 1515. [206]p.;4to. 1st publ., Rome, 1510. Ref. to Vespucci on p.[205]. Sabin 665; Harrisse (BAV) 79; Ind. aur.102.418; Isaac 12124; Adams (Cambr.) A503. DLC, ICN, MB, NN-RB, MiU-C, PU; BL, BN. 515/2

Albertus Magnus, Saint, Bp of Ratisbon. De natura locorum. *Strassburg: M.Schürer, for L. & L.Alantse*, 1515. xlviii lvs;4to. 1st publ., as ed. by G.Tannstetter, Vienna, 1514. Sabin 673; Harrisse (BAV) 78; Proctor 10224. DLC, NN-RB; BL, BN. 515/3

Baptista Mantuanus. De patientia aurei. *Deventer: A.Pafraet*, 1515. 90 lvs;4to. 1st publ., Brescia, 1497. Nijhoff/Kronenberg 212; Ind. aur.112.623. Brussels:BR. 515/4

Campani, Niccolò, called Lo Strascino. Lamento . . . sopra il mal francioso. [*Siena? ca.1515*]. [64]p.;8vo. In verse. Ind. aur.130.747; Sander 1570. Florence: BN. 515/5

Catholic Church. Liturgy and ritual. Missal. Missale Saltzeburgensis. *Venice: P.Liechenstein*, 1515. 324 numb.lvs;illus.,music;fol. Included (lvs 319v-320r) is the 'Missa de beato Job, contra morbum gallicum', 1st (?) publ., Augsburg, 1505. Weale/Bohatta 1385. MH, NNC; BL (destroyed), Paris: Jesuites. 515/6

Fracanzano da Montalboddo. Sensuyt de Nouveau monde & navigations: faictes par Emeric de Vespuce . . . des pays & isles nouvellement trouvez . . . translate de italien en langue françoise par Mathurin du Redouer. *Paris:* [*Widow of J.Trepperel*, 1515?]. 'lxxxx' (i.e., lxxxviii) lvs;4to. Transl.from the author's *Paesi novamente trovati*, 1st publ., Vicenza, 1507. Sabin 50059; Harrisse (BAV) 83; Atkinson (Fr.Ren.) 10. NN-RB; BN. 515/7

___[Anr edn]. *Paris:* [*Widow of J.Trepperel*, 1515?]. xc lvs;illus.;4to. Sabin 50060; Harrisse (BAV) Add.46;Atkinson (Fr.Ren.) 12. BL, BN. 515/8

___[Anr edn.]. *Paris: J.Janot* [1515?]. lxxxviii lvs;illus.;4to. Sabin 50061; Harrisse (BAV) 84; Atkinson (Fr.Ren.) 11. BL. 515/8a

___[Anr edn]. *Paris:* [*Widow of J.Trepperel*, 1515?]. lxxxix lvs;illus.;4to. Atkinson (Fr.Ren.) 13. BN. 515/9

Gaguin, Robert. Les croniques de France . . . translatées de latin [par Pierre Desrey]. *Paris: G.DuPré*, 1515. ccxliiii lvs;illus.;fol. 1st publ., Paris, 1514, under title *Les grandes croniques*, in this version with (here on recto of lf ccxxxiii) ref. to American savages brought to Rouen in 1509. BN. 515/10

___[Anr issue]. *Paris: P.LePreux*, 1515. CSmH. 515/11

Macrobius, Ambrosius Aurelius Theodosius. Macrobius intiger . . . a Joanne Rivio restitutus. *Paris: J.Badius,for self & J.Petit*, 1515. cxvii lvs;illus.,map;fol. Includes a world map with rendering of New World. Sabin 43657; Renouard (Badius Ascensius) III:53-55. CtY, DLC, MnU-B, NNC; BL, BN. 515/12

Maffei, Rafaele. Comentarium Urbanorum . . . octo et triginta libri. *Paris: J.Badius,for self & J. Petit*, 1515. ccccxxii lvs;fol. 1st publ., Rome, 1506. Renouard (Badius Ascensius) III:385-386; Adams (Cambr.) M99. CSt, ICN, MB, NN-RB, PPL; BL, BN. 515/13

Reisch, Gregor. Margarita philosophica nova. *Strassburg: J.Grüninger* [1515]. 348 lvs;illus.,maps;4to. 1st publ., Freiburg, 1503. Sabin 69128; Harrisse (BAV) 82 & Add. 45; Sanz (Ult.ad.) 737; Proctor 9935; Ferguson (Reisch) 211-213; JCB (3) I:62-63. DLC, MnU-B, NN-RB, RPJCB; BL, BN. 515/14

Sacro Bosco, Joannes de. Sphere textum . . . una cum additionibus . . . Petri Cirueli. *Paris: J.Petit*, 1515. lxxxi lvs;illus.;4to. 1st publ. in this version, Paris, 1498. Goldschmidt (Not in Harrisse) 140. NN-RB. 515/15

Schöner, Johann. Luculentissima quaedam terrae totius descriptio. *Nuremberg: H.Stuchs*, 1515. 65 numb.lvs;illus.;4to. Designed to accompany Schöner's terrestrial globe. 'De America': lvs 60-61. Sabin 77804; Harrisse (BAV) 80 (&81,an imperfect copy); Sanz (Ult.ad.) 738-740; Proctor 11096; Adams (Cambr.) S682; JCB (3) I:63. CSmH, CtY, DLC, ICN, InU-L, MH, MnU-B, NN-RB, RPJCB; BL. 515/16

Téllez, Fernando. Razonamiento de las embaxadores de España en la obediencia que dieron al Papa. *Barcelona:* [*J.Amoros?*] 1515. 4to. 1st publ., Rome, 1508. Palau 329470n. Seville:Bibl.Colombina. 515/17

Trithemius, Johannes. Liber octo questionum ad Maximilianum Caesarem. *Oppenheim: J.Kobel,for H.Haselberg, at Reichenau*, 1515. 39 lvs;illus.;4to. On verso of 9th lf is a ref. to New World. Sabin 97005; Adams (Cambr.) T977; Shaaber T356. MH, NN-RB, PU; Cambridge: UL. 515/18

Vella, Giorgio. Consilium medicum pro egregio . . . Aloysio Mantuano, qui morbo gallico laborant. *Mantua:* 1515. 4to. Proksch I:10. 515/19

1516

Anghiera, Pietro Martire d'. De orbe novo . . . decades. *Alcalá de Henares: A.G.de Brocar,for A.de Nebrija*, 1516. 64 lvs;fol. Contains all three Decades; cf. Seville, 1511, edn. Sabin 1550; Harrisse (BAV) 88; Sanz (Ult.ad.) 742-743; Medina (BHA) 53; García (Alcalá de Henares) 25; Arents 2; JCB (3) I:66. CSmH, DLC, InU-L, MH, NN-A, RPJCB; BL, BN. 516/1

Aureum opus et sublime ad medellam non parum utile Plinii philosophi et medici intigerrimi. *Pavia: B.de Garaldis*, 1516. 87 lvs;illus.;fol. Includes also J.Almenar's *Libellus ad evitandum . . . morbum gallicum*, 1st publ., Venice, 1502; N.Leoniceno's *Libellus de epidemia*, 1st publ., Venice, 1497; and A.Bolognini's *De cura ulcerum exteriorum*, 1st publ., Venice, 1506. DNLM, MiU; BL. 516/2

Baptista Mantuanus. Fastorum libri duodecim [& opera alia]. *Lyons: E.de Basignana,for B.Lescuyer*, 1516. 8vo. In bk vi, for June, the section 'De Pentecoste' refers to Spain's opening up new lands to christianize. Also publ., 1540, under title *De sacris diebus*. Baudrier (Lyons) II: 6,9,& 153; Ind. aur.112.640; Coccia 286. CU, DFo, ICN, MiU, NNC; BL, BN. 516/3

Bible. O.T. Psalms. Polyglot. 1516. Psalterium hebreum, grecum, arabicum, & chaldeum, cum tribus latinis interpretationibis & glossis. *Genoa: P.P.Porrus, for N. J.Paulus*, 1516. [399]p.;fol. Ed. by Augustino Giustiniani. A marginal note at verse 4 of Psalm xix gives a biography of Columbus (lvs C8v-D1r). Issued both printed on paper (2000 copies) & on vellum (50 copies). Sabin 66468; Harrisse (BAV) 88 (p.154-158); Isaac 13835; Darlow & Moule 1411; JCB (3) I:64. DLC, MH, MiU-C, NN-RB, RPJCB (both issues); BL. 516/4

Catholic Church. Pope, 1513-1521 (Leo X). Breve . . . Leonis . . . Pape decimi ad principes super correctione calendarii pro recta Pasche celebratione. *Rome*: 1516. 4to. Includes 'Compendium correctionis calendarii pro recta Pasche celebratione', by Paulus Middelburgensis, 1st publ., Fossombrone, 1513, as *De recta Paschae celebratione*. BN. 516/5

Corsali, Andrea. Lettera . . . allo illustrissimo signore Duca Juliano de Medici venuta dell' Indie del mese di octobre nel M.D.XVI. *Florence: G.S.di Carlo*, 1516. 6 lvs;4to. Included are refs to Brazil & Spanish West Indies. Isaac 13435. NjP; BL. 516/6

Ferdinand V, King of Spain. Epistola . . . ad Carolum Regem Castilie &c. . . . per Riccardum Bartholinum . . . translata. [*Rome? E. Silber?* 1516?]. 4 lvs;4to. Purported translation, in verse, of letter written to grandson, including a ref. to New World. Title in gothic type. Palau 89992. NN-RB; Seville: Bibl. Colombina. 516/7

—[Anr edn]. [*Augsburg: S.Otmar*, 1516?]. 4 lvs;4to. Title in roman type. Palau 89992. MH, RPJCB; BN. 516/8

Fracanzano da Montalboddo. Le nouveau monde et navigacions faites per Emeric de Vespuce . . . translaté de italien en langue francoyse par Mathurin Du Redouer. *Paris: G.DuPré* [1516]. cxxxii lvs;8vo. 1st publ. in this version, Paris, 1515. Sabin 50062; Har-

risse (BAV) 86; Church 40; JCB (3) I:64. CSmH, ICN, InU-L, MH, NN-RB, RPJCB; BN. 516/9

Gaguin, Robert. Les croniques de France . . . translatées de latin [par Pierre Desrey]. *Paris: M.LeNoir*, 1516. ccxliiii lvs;illus.;fol. 1st publ., Paris, 1514, under title *Les grandes croniques*, in this version with (here on recto of lf ccxxxiii) ref. to American savages brought to Rouen in 1509. CSmH, RPJCB. 516/10

Gatinaria, Marco. Contenta in hoc volumine . . . Sebastiani Aquilani De morbo gallico . . . Nicolai Leoniceni De morbo gallico . . . Joannis Almenar . . . De morbo gallico. *Venice: B.Locatellus, for Heirs of O.Scoto*, 1516. 79 numb. lvs;illus.; fol. 1st publ., Pavia, 1509, Aquilano's work being there included, under title *De curis egritudinum . . . practica*. Here also included are Leoniceno's *De morbo gallico*, 1st publ., Venice, 1497, as *Libellus . . . de morbum gallicum*; and Almenar's work, 1st publ., Venice, 1502, as *Libellus ad evitandum . . . morbum gallicum*. DNLM, PPC; BL. 516/11

—[Anr edn]. De curis egritudinum particulari noni Almansoris practica uberrima. *Lyons: S.Bevilacqua,for V.de Portonariis*, 1506 [i.e.,1516]. xci lvs;4to. Includes S.Aquilano's *Tractatus de morbo gallico*, 1st publ., Pavia, 1509, in M. Gatinaria's *De curis*. On erroneous imprint date, see Baudrier. Baudrier (Lyons) V:403; Waller 3429. DNLM; BL, Uppsala: UB. 516/12

Isolani, Isidoro. De imperio militantis ecclesiae. *Milan: G.da Ponte*, 1516. 126 lvs;illus.;fol. Includes chapt. on New World. Cf. Sabin 35264; cf. Harrisse (BAV) Add. 49; Streit I:9. BN. 516/13

Magno, Marco Antonio. Oratio in funere Regis Catholici [Ferdinandi] Hispaniarum. *Naples: S.Mayr*, 1516. 12 lvs;4to. On recto of lf 7 is a ref. to Columbus. Harrisse (BAV) Add. 47; Isaac 13809; JCB (3) I:65-66. NN-RB, RPJCB; BL. 516/14

More, Sir Thomas, Saint. Libellus . . . de optimo reip. statu, deque nova insula Utopia. [*Louvain:*] *T.Martens*, 1516. [108]p.;map; 4to. Set in New World, with ref. on recto of 3rd lf to Vespucci's voyages. Sabin 50542; Harrisse (BAV) Add. p.62-63n; Gibson (More) 1. CtY, MH, NNPM; BL, BN. 516/15

Orationes Viennae Austriae ad divum Maximilianum Caes. Aug. aliosque illustrissimos principes habitae. *Vienna: H.Vietor for L. & L. Atlantse*, 1516. [176]p.;4to. On verso of lf 5 is the phrase 'novae insulae, nova loca, novae terrae'. Sabin 57447. MH. 516/16

Portugal. Laws, statutes, etc. Regimentos e ordenações de fazenda. *Lisbon: H.de Campos*, 1516. cxvii lvs;fol. Sabin 68809n; Anselmo 441. ICN; Lisbon: BN. 516/17

Sabellico, Marco Antonio Coccio, called. Rapsodie historiarum Enneadum. *Paris: J.Badius,for self & J.Petit*, 1516-17. 2v.;fol. 1st publ. with American refs (here found in v.2 on lf cccxxxiii) Venice, 1504. Sabin 74662; Harrisse (BAV) 89 & Add. 51; Renouard (Badius Ascensius) III: 225-226. MH, MiU-C, NN-RB: The Hague: KB, BN. 516/18

Vigo, Giovanni de. Practica in arte chirurgica copiosa. *Lyons: J.Myt, for V.de Portonariis*, 1516. cxciii lvs;4to. 1st publ., Rome, 1514. Baudrier (Lyons) V:413-414. DNLM; London: Wellcome, BN. 516/19

1517

Breydenbach, Bernhard von. Le grant voyage de Jherusalem. *Paris: N.Hygman, for F. Regnault*, 1517. cxcvii lvs;illus.;fol. Adapted & transl. by Nicole LeHuen from the author's *Peregrinatio in terram sanctam*. Includes (recto of lf clxxxvii) letter of Pietro Pasqualigo describing G. Cortereal's discovery of Labrador. Harrisse (BAV) Add. 48; Atkinson (Fr. Ren.) 19. MH, NN-RB; BN. 517/1

Fracanzano da Montalboddo. Paesi nuovamente ritrovati per la navigazione di Spagna . . . Et da Albertutio Vesputio . . . intitulato Mondo Novo. Nuovamente impressa. *Venice: G.dei Rusconi*, 1517. [247]p.;8vo. 1st publ., Venice, 1507. Sabin 50053; Harrisse (BAV) 90 & Add. 52; Isaac 13065; Church 41; JCB (3) I:68. CSmH, DLC, NN-RB, RPJCB; BL. 517/2

Gatinaria, Marco. De curis egritudinum particularium noni Almansoris practica uberrima . . . Sebastiani Aquilani Tractatus de morbo gallico celeberrimus. *Bologna: B.Hectoris*, 1517. 3pts;8vo. 1st publ., Pavia, 1509. DNLM; London: Wellcome, BN. 517/3

Herrera, Fernando Alonso de. Disputatio adversus Aristotelem Aristotelisque sequaces.

Salamanca: [*J.de Porras*] 1517. 55 lvs;4to. Text in Latin & Castilian. On recto of lf d4 is an account of Pietro Martire d'Anghiera. Sabin 31564; Harrisse (BAV) Add. 50; Medina (BHA) 55; Palau 114070. Santander: BM.y P. 517/4

Isolani, Isidoro. De imperio militantis ecclesiae. *Milan: G.da Ponte*, 1517. 129 lvs;illus.;fol. 1st publ., Milan, 1516. On recto of lf B3 is section on New World. Sabin 35264; Harrisse (BAV) Add. 49; Streit I:13; Isaac 13595. DLC, ICN, InU-L, NN-RB, RPJCB; BL. 517/5

More, Sir Thomas, Saint. De optimo reipublicae statu, deque nova insula Utopia. [*Paris:*] *G.de Gourmont* [1517]. cx lvs;8vo. 1st publ., Louvain, 1516. Adams (Cambr.) M1755; Gibson (More) 2. CtY, MH, RPJCB; BL, BN. 517/6

Reisch, Gregor. Margarita philosophica cum additionibus novis: ab auctore suo . . . revisione quarto superadditis . . . m.d.xvii. *Basel: M.Furter*, 1517. 292 lvs;illus.,map;4to. 1st publ., Freiburg, 1503. Sabin 69129; Ferguson (Reisch) 213-214; Isaac 14132; Adams (Cambr.) B336; Fairfax Murray (Germany) 354. DLC, ICN, NN-RB, PP, RPB; BL, Strasbourg: BN. 517/7

Waldseemüller, Martin. Cosmographiae introductio . . . insuper Americi Vespucci navigationes. [*Lyons:*] *J.de La Place* [1517-18?]. 33 lvs;diagr.;4to. 1st publ., St Dié, 1507. Sabin 101023; Harrisse (BAV) 63; Sanz (Ult.ad.) 461-463; JCB (3) I:69. InU-L, NN-RB, RPJCB; BL. 517/8

1518

Baptista Mantuanus. Fastorum libri duodecim. *Strassburg: M.Shürer*, 1518. 163 lvs;ports;4to. 1st publ., 1516, in the Lyons edn of the author's works. Sanz (Ult.ad.) 779; Ind.aur.112.663; Coccia 308. DLC, MH, NN-RB; BL. 518/1

Eyn bewert Recept wie man das holtz Gnagacam [i.e., Guayacum] fur die Frantzosen brauchen sol. [*Nuremberg? J.Gutknecht?* 1518?]. 4 lvs;4to. On use of Guaiacum for treatment of syphilis. NN-RB. 518/2

Eusebius Pamphili, Bp of Caesarea. Chronicon. [*Paris:*] *H.Estienne* [1518?]. 175 numb.lvs;4to. 1st publ., Paris, 1512, with ref.

(verso of lf 172) to American savages brought to Rouen in 1509. Cf. Sabin 23114; Harrisse (BAV) Add. 54; Renouard (Estienne) I:20-21; JCB (3) I:69. MH, MiU-C, NN-RB, RPJCB; BL, BN.   518/3

Fregoso, Battista. De dictis factisque memorabilibus collectanea. latina facta. [*Paris:*] *P.Vidoue,for G.DuPré*, 1518. cccxxxii lvs;illus.;4to. 1st publ., Milan, 1509. The American ref. here appears on verso of lf cclx. Sabin 26140; Harrisse (BAV) Add. 53; JCB (3) I:70. RPJCB; BL.   518/4

Gaguin, Robert. La mer des croniques et mirouer historial de France . . . Nouvellement translatée de latin [par Pierre Desrey]. *Paris: N.de LaBarre*, 1518. ccxlvi lvs;illus.;fol. 1st publ., Paris, 1514, under title *Les grandes croniques* in this version with ref. to American savages brought to Rouen in 1509. Fairfax Murray (France) 184. ICN, NNC; BN.   518/5

Mela, Pomponius. Libri de situ orbis tres; adjectis Joachimi Vadiani . . . in eosdem scholiis. *Vienna: J.Singriener,for L.Alantse*, 1518. 132 numb.lvs;fol. Vadianus's notes contain refs to Vespucci and to Spanish & Portuguese discoveries; includes also editor's correspondence with Agricola of 1515. Sabin 63956; Harrisse (BAV) 92; Isaac 14461; JCB (3) I:71. DLC, MH, NN-RB, RPJCB; BL.   518/6

More, Sir Thomas, Saint. De optimo repu. statu, deque nova insula Utopia. *Basel: J.Froben*, March, 1518. 355p.;illus.;4to. 1st publ., Louvain, 1516. Gibson (More) 3; Isaac 14177; Adams (Cambr.) M1756. CtY, DLC, InU-L, MH; BL.   518/7

—[Anr issue]. *Basel: J.Froben*, December, 1518. Sabin 50543; Isaac 14196; Adams (Cambr.) M1757; Fairfax Murray (Germany) 304. CSmH, CtY, DLC, MH, MiU, MnU-B, NN-RB, RPJCB; BL.   518/8

Polo, Marco. Cosmographia, breve introductoria. *Seville: J.Varela*, 1518. xxxi lvs;illus.;fol. 1st publ. in this translation by R.Fernández de Santa Ella, with ref. to Indies, Seville, 1503. Medina (BHA) 55; Sanz (Ult.ad.) 768-778; Escudero (Seville) 201. InU-L, NNH; Madrid: BN.   518/9

Ain recept von ainem holtz zu brauchen für die kranckhait der frantzosen . . . aus hispanischer sprach zu teütsch gemacht. [*Augsburg: S.Grimm & M.Wirsung*, 1518]. 4 lvs;4to. On use of Guaiacum wood for

treating syphilis. Cf.Sabin 68347; Stillwell (Science) 492. NN-RB.   518/10

Sacro Bosco, Joannes de. Introductorium compendiosum in tractatum sphere . . . per . . . Joannem Glogoviensem recollectum. *Strassburg: H.Gran,for J. Knoblauch*, 1518. 56 lvs;illus.;4to. 1st publ. in this version, Cracow, 1506. Yarmolinsky (Early Polish Americana) 14; Proctor 11675. NN-RB; BL.
518/11

Schmaus, Leonardus. Lucubratiuncula de morbo gallico et cura eius noviter reperta cum ligno indico. *Augsburg: S.Grimm & M.Wirsung*, 1518. 6 lvs;4to. Refers specifically to West Indies. Sabin 77661; Harrisse (BAV) Add. 55; Stillwell (Science) 519; JCB (3) I:72. DNLM, NN-RB, RPJCB; BN.   518/12

Schöner, Johann. Appendices . . . in opusculum Globi astriferi nuper ab eodem editum. *Nuremburg: H.Stuchs*, 1518. .6 lvs;illus.;4to. Includes woodcut of terrestrial globe showing America; issued as supplement to author's *Solidi ac sphaerici corpus* from same publisher, 1517. Sabin 77799; Proctor 11103; Coote (Schöner) 4. DFo, MH, NN-RB, WU; BL.   518/13

1519

Albertini, Francesco. Opusculum de mirabilibus novae & veteris urbis Romae. *Basel: T.Wolff*, 1519. 99 numb.lvs;illus.;4to. 1st publ., Rome, 1510. Sabin 666; Harrisse (BAV) 96 & Add. 56; Ind.aur. 102. 419; Fairfax Murray (Germany) 23; Isaac 14354; Adams (Cambr.) A504. ICN, NN-RB; BL, BN.   519/1

Baptista Mantuannus. Selectiora. *Ghent:* 1519. See the year 1520.

Brant, Sebastian. Dat nye schip van narragonien. *Rostock: L.Dietz*, 1519. clxxv lvs;illus.;4to. 1st publ. in Low German, Lübeck, 1497. Ind.aur.123.696; Fairfax Murray (Germany) 90. DLC; Berlin: StB.
519/2

Brassicanus, Johannes Alexander. π α̃ ν. Omnis. *Haguenau: T.Anshelm,for J.Knobloch at Strassburg*, 1519. [24]p.;4to. Latin elegiacs, including refs to susceptibility of poets to syphilis. Ind.aur.123.888. CtY, MH; BL, Vienna: NB.   519/3

Enciso, Martín Fernández de. Suma de geographia que trata de todas las partidas &

provincias del mundo: en especial de las Indias. *Seville: J.Cromberger*, 1519. 76 lvs;illus.;fol. Sabin 22551; Harrisse (BAV) 97; Sanz (Ult. ad.) 780-804; Medina (BHA) 56; Escudero (Seville) 203; Church 42; JCB (3) I:73. CSmH, CtY, DLC, MH, NN-RB, RP-JCB; BL, BN.   519/4

Fracanzano da Montalboddo. Paesi nuovamente retrovati, & Novo Mondo da Alberico Vesputio. *Milan: G.A.Scinzenzeler, for J.J.Legnano & Bros*, 1519. 84 lvs;port.;4to. 1st publ., Vicenza, 1507. Sabin 50050; Harrisse (BAV) 94; Isaac 13547; Balsamo (Scinzenzeler) 157; Church 43; JCB (3) I:74. CSmH, DLC, ICN, InU-L, NN-RB, RPJCB; BL, BN.   519/5

Hutten, Ulrich von. De Guaiaci medicina et morbo gallico, liber unus. *Mainz: J.Schoeffer*, 1519. [88]p.;illus.,port.;4to. Sabin 34095; Proctor 9865; Stillwell (Science) 540; Fairfax Murray (Germany) 213; Benzing (Hutten) 103. CtY-M, DNLM, MiU, NN-RB; BL.   519/6

—[Anr edn]. *[Paris] P.Vidoue, for C.Resch*, 1519. 40 lvs;4to. Benzing (Hutten) 104. BN.   519/7

———. Von der wunderbarlichen Artzney des Holtz Guaiacum . . . Durch . . . Thomam Murner . . . geteutschet und verdolmetschet. *Strassburg: J.Grüninger*, 1519. [83]p.;4to. Transl. from preceding item. Benzing (Hutten) 111; Ritter (Strasbourg) 1226. DNLM, MnU-B, NN-RB; Munich: StB, Strasbourg: BN.   519/8

Jan ze Stobnicy. Introductio in Ptolomei Cosmographiam. *Cracow: H.Vietor*, 1519. 44 numb.lvs;illus.;4to. 1st publ., Cracow, 1512. Sabin 91867; Harrisse (BAV) 95; Yarmolinsky (Early Polish Americana) 22-24; Fairfax Murray (Germany) 349; Isaac 14398; JCB AR20:1519. MH, RPJCB; BL, BN.   519/9

Lucianus Samosatensis. Opuscula, Erasmo Roterodamo interprete . . . Thomae Mori: De optimo reip. statu deque nova insula Utopia. *Florence: Heirs of F.Giunta*, 1519. 279 numb.lvs;8vo. More's *Utopia* 1st publ., Louvain, 1516. Gibson (More) 82. CSt, DFo; Oxford: Bodl., BN.   519/10

Macrobius, Ambrosius Aurelius Theodosius. Macrobius Aurelius intiger . . . a Joanne Rivio . . . restitutus. *Paris: J.Badius*, 1519. c lvs;illus.,map;fol. 1st publ. in this version, Paris, 1515, the world map here appearing on

verso of lf Dvii. Sabin 43657n; Renouard (Badius Ascensius) III:53-55; Adams (Cambr.) M74. CSmH, DFo, MH, MnU-B, NN-RB; BL, BN.   519/11

Oviedo y Valdés, Gonzalo Fernández de. Libro del muy esforçado y invencible cavallero . . . don Claribalte. *Valencia: J.Viñao*, 1519. lxxiiii lvs;illus.;fol. A romance of chivalry; the dedication includes a ref. to author's West Indies experiences. Sabin 57995; Harrisse (BAV) Add. 57; Medina (BHA) 57. BL, BN.   519/12

Ain Recept von ainem holtz zu brauchen für die kranckhait der Frantzosen. *Augsburg: Hans, von Erfurt*, 1519. 6 lvs;4to. 1st publ., Augsburg, 1518. Cf. Sabin 68347. NN-RB.   519/13

Sensuyent lordonnance des royaumes . . . appertenans a la Ma. Imperiale Charles . . . roycatholique Despaigne. *[Geneva: W.Köln, 1519?]*. 12 lvs; port.;4to. Includes (lvs aii-aiii) a description of Spanish possessions in America. Rothschild 2714. BN.   519/14

Vigo, Giovanni de. Practica in arte chirurgica copiosa. *Lyons: J.Myt, & J.Moylin de Cambray, for V.de Portonariis*, 1519. cxciii lvs;4to. 1st publ., Rome, 1514. Baudrier (Lyons) V:418; Adams (Cambr.) V760. DNLM; BL.   519/15

1520

Albertini, Francesco. Mirabilia Rome, opusculum de mirabilibus nove et veteris Rome. *[Lyons:] J.Marion, for R.Morin*, 1520. 56 numb. lvs;illus.;4to. 1st publ., Rome, 1510. Sabin 667; Harrisse (BAV) 103; Baudrier (Lyons) V:366; Fairfax Murray (France) 6; Adams (Cambr.) A505; JCB (3) I:75. CSmH, ICN, MH, NN-RB, RPJCB; BL, BN.   520/1

—[Anr edn]. Opusculum de mirabilibus novae et veteris urbis Romae. *Bologna: [H.de Benedictis]*, 1520. 4to. Sabin 668; Harrisse (BAV) 106; Serra-Zanetti (Bologna) 20. 520/2

Angliara, Juan de. Die schiffung mitt dem Lanndt der Gulden Insel. *[Augsburg: J.Nadler, 1520?]*. [6]p.;4to. Transl. from following item. Sabin 1560; Harrisse (BAV) 102; Medina (BHA) 100n (I:154); Proctor 10858; Church 44; JCB (3) I:75. CSmH, InU-L, NN-RB, RPJCB; BL.   520/3

———. El viaggio: col paese de lisola del oro tro-

vato. [*Venice: A.Bindoni*, 1520?]. [4]p.;illus.;
4to. The 'Golden Island' designates Peru. Sabin 36789; Harrisse (BAV) 102 & Add. 65;
Isaac 13218. BL.   520/4

Ein auszug ettlicher sendbrieff dem . . . Fürsten und Herren Herren Carl Römischen und
Hyspanischen König. *Nuremberg: F.Peypus*,
1520. 7 lvs;illus.;4to. Includes account of expedition of Francisco Hernández de Córdova,
Grijalva & Cortés to Yucatan, seemingly
drawn from P.M. d'Anghiera's Decades, 1st
publ., Alcalá de Henares, 1516. Sabin 2442&
22086; Harrisse (BAV) 105; Proctor 11135;
JCB (3) I:76. CtY, InU-L, NN-RB, RPJCB;
BL.   520/5

Baptista Mantuanus. Fastorum libri duodecim. *Strassburg: M.Hupfuff*, 1520. 157
lvs;4to. 1st publ., Lyons, 1516, in author's
Opera. Ritter (Strasbourg) 150. Strasbourg:
BN.   520/6

——. Selectiora quaedam opuscula. *Ghent:
P.de Keyser*, 1519 [i.e., 1520]. 70 lvs;8vo. Included is the 'Exhortatio ad potentatus christianos', 1st publ., Milan, 1507, as 'Objurgatio
cum exhortatione'. Nijhoff/Kronenberg 2352;
Ind.aur.112.680; Coccia 330. BN.   520/7

Capitulo over Recetta delo arbore over legno
detto Guiana [i.e., Guaiaco]: remedio contra
el male gallico. [*Venice:*] *A.Bindoni*, 1520. 7
lvs;8vo. On use of Guaiacum for treating syphilis. RPJCB.   520/8

Catholic Church. Liturgy and ritual. Missal.
Missale Romanum. *Venice: L.Giunta*, 1520.
4to. Includes a 'Missa de beato Job, contra
morbum gallicum', found also in the 1505 and
later Passau missals. In view of their vast range
the possible presence of this special mass in the
numerous missals of the period has not been
fully explored. Cf. Proksch I:79-80. BL. 520/9

Díaz, Juan. Littera mandata della insula de
Cuba de India in laquale se cotiene de le insule, citta, gente et animali novamente trovate
de lanno .M.d.xix. per li Spagnoli. [*Venice?*
1520?]. 8 lvs;illus.;4to. Describes Grijalva's
Yucatan expedition. Harrisse (BAV) Add. 60;
Wagner (Grijalva) 5-7. Venice: Bibl. Marciana.   520/10

——. Provinciae sive regiones in India Occiden-
tali noviter repertae in ultima navigatione.
[*Rome? 1520?*]. 14 lvs;4to. Transl. by Ferdi-
nand Flores from preceding item. Harrisse
(BAV) 101; Medina (BHA) 58; JCB (3) I:76.
NN-RB, RPJCB.   520/11

Foresti, Jacopo Filipo, da Bergamo. Supplementum. Supplementi de le Chroniche . . .
per Francesco C., fiorentino, vulgarizato.
Venice: G.dei Rusconi, 1520. 356
numb.lvs;illus.;fol. 1st publ. in Italian,
Venice, 1508. Cf. Sabin 25087. ICN, MH,
MnU-B; BL.   520/12

Gaguin, Robert. La mer des croniques et
miroir historial de France . . . translaté de
latin [par Pierre Desrey]. *Paris: R.
Chaudière* [1520]. ccxxxv lvs;illus.;fol. 1st
publ., Paris, 1514, under title *Les grandes
croniques*, with ref. to American savages
brought to Rouen in 1509. BN.   520/13

Geiler, Johannes, von Kaisersberg.
Narrenschiff. *Strassburg: J.Grüninger*, 1520.
cxxiiii lvs;illus.;fol. Transl. by I. Pauli from
the author's *Navicula sive speculum
fatuorum*, 1st publ., Strassburg, 1510. Proctor 9955. BL, BN.   520/14

Hutten, Ulrich von. Guaiacum. L'experience
et approbation . . . touchant la medicine du
boys dict Guaiacum. Pour circonvenir . . . la
maladie indeuement appellee françoyse . . .
traduicte & interpretee par Jehan Cheradame.
Lyons: E.Gueynard, for C.Nourry [ca. 1520].
40 lvs;4to. Transl. from author's 1519, Mainz,
Latin *De Guaiaci medicina*. Baudrier (Lyons)
XI:186 etc.; Benzing (Hutten) 112. CtY-M,
NN-RB; BL, Paris: Mazarine.   520/15

Karl V, Emperor of Germany. Caroli. Ro.
regis, recessuri adlocutio in. conventu.
Hispaniarum. [*Rome: J.Mazochius*, 1520?].
[6]p.;4to. Address, perhaps that delivered 31
March 1520 on his behalf by Pedro Rúiz de
Mota, on leaving Spain for Germany on election as Holy Roman Emperor, mentioning
'alio poene aurifero', a possible American
allusion. MH.   520/16

——[Anr edn]. [*Augsburg? 1520?*]. 2 lvs;4to.
Palau 44419;Rothschild 3137. NN-RB; BN.
                                         520/17

Margallo, Pedro. Phisices compendium.
Salamanca: [J.de Porras?] 1520. xxxvi lvs;fol.
On recto of lf iiii is a ref.to America. Sabin
44525; Harrisse (BAV) Add. 61; Medina
(BHA) 59. Madrid: BN.   520/18

Montesino, Ambrosio, Bp. Cancionero de
diversas obras. *Toledo: J.de Villaquirán, for Alonso de Esquivias*, 1520. 184
lvs;4to. 1st publ., Toledo, 1508. Pérez Pastor
(Toledo) 85; Palau 178942n. NNH.   520/19

Nature of the four elements. A new iuterlude [i.e., interlude] and a mery of the nature of the .iiij. elements. [*London: J.Rastell*, 1520?] [64]p.;8vo. In verse, in part referring to America. Sabin 53023; Harrisse (BAV) Add. 50; Winship (Cabot) 5; STC 20722. BL (imp).
520/20

Pico della Mirandola, Giovanni Francesco. Examen vanitatis doctrinae gentium, et veritatis christinae doctrinae. *Mirandola: J.Mazochius*, 1520. ccviii lvs;fol. Includes 4 refs to America — A.Schill, *Pico della Mirandola und die Entdeckung Amerikas* (Berlin, 1929). Isaac 14050; Adams (Cambr.) P1156; Shaaber P312. MH, MiU, NN-RB, PU, RP-JCB; BL.
520/21

Pighius, Albertus. De aequinoctiorum solsticiorumque inventione. *Paris:* [*C.Resch*, 1520]. 2pts;fol. The 2nd pt, the 'De ratione paschalis celebrationis', contains, p.xxviii, a ref. to Vespucci. Sabin 62809-10; Harrisse (BAV) 107. CtY, DLC; BL, BN.
520/22

Ptolemaeus, Claudius. Ptolemaeus auctus restitutus . . . Cum tabulis veteribus ac novis. *Strassburg: H.Schott*, 1520. 151 numb.lvs; maps;fol. 1st publ. in this version, Strassburg, 1513. Sabin 66480; Harrisse (BAV) 104 & Add. 58; Proctor 10289; Phillips (Atlases) 360; Stevens (Ptolemy) 46; JCB (3) I:76. DLC, ICN, MBMu, MiU-C, MnU-B, NN-RB, RP-JCB; BL.
520/23

Seyssel, Claude de, Abp. De divina providentia tractatus. *Paris: R.Chaudière*, 1520. 152 lvs;4to. On the problem of converting the heathen, created by discovery of the New World. Streit I:23; Adams (Cambr.) S1031. Cambridge: UL, BN.
520/24

Solinus, Caius Julius. Joannis Camertis . . . in C. Julii Solini πολνιστωρα enarrationes. *Vienna: J.Singriener,for L. Alantse*, 1520. [336]p.;map;fol. Includes Petrus Apianus's world map. Sabin 86390; Harrisse (BAV) 108; Isaac 14471; Church 45; JCB (3) I:77. CSmH, CtY, DLC, InU-L, MH, MiU-C, MnU-B, NN-RB, RPJCB; BL, BN.
520/25

Spain. Laws, statutes, etc. Las pragmaticas del reyno. Recopilacion de algunas bulas de nuestro sancto padre. *Seville: J.Varela*, 1520. cxcii lvs;fol. 1st publ., Alcalá de Henares, 1503. Sabin 64914; Harrisse (BAV) Add. 63; Medina (BHA) 61; Escudero (Seville) 217. MH, NN-RB; BL, Madrid: BN.
520/26

Varthema, Lodovico di. Itinerario . . . Buelto de latin en romance por Christoval de Arcos . . . nunca hasta aqui impresso en lengua castellana. *Seville: J.Cromberger*, 1520. lv lvs;fol. Cf. following Italian version, of which this is a translation. Escudero (Seville) 204; JCB AR20: 1520. CSmH, CtY, InU-L, MnU-B, NN-RB, RPJCB; BL.
520/27

———. Itinerario . . . ne lo Egypto ne la Suria . . . Et al presente agiontovi alcune isole nuovamente ritrovate. *Venice: G.dei Rusconi*, 1520. 103 lvs;8vo. Includes Juan Díaz's account of Grijalva's 1518 expedition (lvs M1v-N4v) publ. separately earlier this year. Sabin 98643; Harrisse (BAV) Add. 59; Isaac 13079; JCB (3) I:77. MiU-C, NN-RB, RPJCB; BL.
520/28

Vigo, Giovanni de. Practi[ca] . . . copiosa in arte chirugica. *Venice: Heirs of O.Scoto*, 1520. 2pts;fol. 1st publ., Rome, 1514. DFo, DNLM; BN.
520/29

1521

Anghiera, Pietro Martire d'. De nuper sub D. Carolo repertis insulis . . . enchiridion. *Basel: A. Petri*, 1521. 43p.;illus.;4to. Continues author's 1516 Decades through the year 1520. Sabin 1553; Harrisse (BAV) 110; Sanz (Ult. ad.) 829-830; Medina (BHA) 62; JCB (3) I:79. DLC, InU-L, MH, MiU-C, MnU-B, NN-RB, RPJCB; BL.
521/1

Apianus, Petrus. Isagoge in typum cosmographicum seu Mappam mundi. *Landshut: J. Weissenburger* [1521?]. 4 lvs;map;4to. Ortroy (Apian) 10; Ind.aur.106.403; JCB AR24:4-5. CtY, ICN, MH, MiU-C, MnU-B, NN-RB, RPJCB; BN.
521/2

Baviera, Baverio. Consilia Baverii. *Pavia: B.de Garaldis*, 1521. 104 numb. lvs;fol. Includes 'Consilium Gasparis Torelle . . . de peste ovina', 1st publ., Rome, 1505. DNLM; BL.
521/3

Campani, Niccolò, called Lo Strascino. Lamento . . . sopre el male incognito: el quale tratta de la patientia et impatientia. *Venice: N.&V.Zoppino*, 1521. [56]p.;illus.;8vo. 1st publ., [Siena? ca. 1515]. In verse. Ind. aur. 130.749; Sander 1565. Florence: BN.
521/4

Fracanzano da Montalboddo. Paesi novamente ritrovati per la navigatione di Spagna . . . et da Albertutio Vesputio . . . intitolato Mondo Novo, nuovamente impressa. *Venice:*

G.dei Rusconi, 1521. [247]p.;illus.;4to. 1st publ., Vicenza, 1507. Sabin 50055; Harrisse (BAV) 109 & Add. 26; Church 46; JCB (3) I:78. CSmH, DLC, InU-L, MiU-C, MnU-B, NN-RB, RPJCB; BL. 521/5

____. Sensuyt le Nouveau monde et navigations . . . translate . . . par Mathurin du Redouer. *Paris: P.LeNoir* [1521]. 88 lvs;4to. 1st publ. in this translation, Paris, [1515?]. Sabin 50063; Atkinson (Fr. Ren.) 21. MH; BN. 521/6

Gatinaria, Marco. De curis egritudinum particularium noni Almasoris practica uberrima . . . Sebastiani Aquilani Tractatus de morbo gallico celeberrimus. *Venice: A.& B.Bindoni*, 1521. 3pts;8vo. 1st publ., Pavia, 1509. DNLM; BL. 521/7

Hutten, Ulrich von. De Guaiaci medicina et morbo gallico liber unus. *Bologna: H.de Benedictis*, 1521. xxxix lvs;4to. 1st publ., Mainz, 1519. Benzing (Hutten) 105. DNLM, NN-RB; BN. 521/8

Manardo, Giovanni. Epistolae medicinales. *Ferrara: B.de Odonino*, 1521. 72 numb.lvs; 4to. Includes two letters on syphilis & also two on Guaiacum. CtY-M, DNLM, NNNAM; BL, BN. 521/9

Padilla, Juan de. Los doce triumfos de los doce apostoles. *Seville: J.Varela*, 1521. 62 numb.lvs;illus.;fol. In verse. The 9th 'Triumfo' contains in cap.2 a ref. to Columbus's voyages. Harrisse (BAV) Add. 67; Medina (BHA) 63; Escudero (Seville) 221. NN-RB; BL, BN. 521/10

Vigo, Giovanni de. Opera . . . in chyrurgia. *Lyons: J.Myt,for J.Giunta*, 1521. 2pts;4to. Includes 'De morbo gallico', 1st publ., Rome, 1514, in the author's *Practica*. Baudrier (Lyons) VI:109-110. BN. 521/11

1522

Apianus, Petrus. Declaratio: et usus typi cosmographici Mappa mundi. [*Regensburg: P.Kohl*, 1522]. [16]p.;illus.;4to. The author's foreword begins 'Petrus Apianus Leysnicus mathematicus lectori'. 'America': lvs 4v-5r. Harrisse (BAV) 69; Ortroy (Apian) 11; Ind. aur.106.397. Munich: UB. 522/1

__[Anr edn]. *Regensburg: P.Kohl* [1522]. [16]p.;illus.;4to. The author's foreword begins 'Petrus Apianus Leysnicus liberalium artium baccalaureus'. Harrisse (BAV) 68; Ortroy

(Apian) 12; Ind.aur. 106.398; JCB (3) I:80. DLC, NN-RB, RPJCB. 522/2

Berengario, Jacopo. Isagoge brevis . . . in anatomiam humani corporis. *Bologna: B.Hectoris*, 1522. 72 lvs;illus.;4to. Includes discussion of syphilis as treated with mercury. Ind.aur.117.160. DNLM, PPC; London: Wellcome, Vienna: NB. 522/3

Breydenbach, Bernhard von. Le grant voyage de Hierusalem. *Paris: F.Regnault*, 1522. ccix lvs;illus.;4to. 1st publ. with Pasquaglio's account of Cortereal's discovery of Labrador, Paris, 1517. Harrisse (BAV) Add. 71; Atkinson (Fr.Ren.) 26; Ind.aur.124.182; Fairfax Murray (France) 625. CtY, ICN, MB, NN-RB, ViU; BN. 522/4

Cortés, Hernando. Carta de relacion embiada a su .S. Majestad . . . Enla qual haze relacion d'las tierras y provincias sin cuento que han descubierto nuevamente enel Yucatan del año de .xix. *Seville: J.Cromberger*, 1522. [56]p.;illus.,port.;fol. Comprises Cortés's second letter. Sabin 16933; Harrisse (BAV) 118; Sanz (Ult.ad.) 851-908; Medina (BHA) 64; Escudero (Seville) 224; Church 47; JCB (3) I:81. CSmH, NN-RB, RPJCB; BL. 522/5

____. [Des marches, ysles et pays trouvees et conquise par les capitaines du tres illustre . . . Charle. V]. [*Antwerp: M.Hillen*, 1522?]. 15 lvs; 4to. Transl. from preceding. Neither extant copy bears a printed title, that found in each being in manuscript. Sabin 16952; Harrisse (BAV) Add. 73; Sanz (Ult.ad.) 847-850; Nijhoff/Kronenberg 620; Church 48. CSmH, InU-L. 522/6

____. Nove de le isole & terra ferma novamente trovate in India. *Milan: A.Calvo*, 1522. 6 lvs;4to. Extracted & transl. from the *Carta de relacion* above. Sabin 16950 & 56052; Harrisse (BAV) 119. BL. 522/7

Lannoy, Charles de. Translation uss hispanischer sprach zü Frantzösisch gemacht, so durch den Vice Rey in Neapols, Fraw Margareten Hertzoginn inn Burgundi zü geschriben. [*Basel: P.Gengenbach*, 1522?]. 4 lvs;illus.,port.;4to. Includes ref to Cortés's conquest of Yucatan. Sabin 16954; Harrisse (BAV) 113. NN-RB. 522/8

Mela, Pomponius. De orbis situ libri tres . . . cum commentariis Joachimi Vadiani . . . castigatioribus . . . Epistola Vadiani . . . ad Rudolphum Agricolam. *Basel: A.Cratander*, 1522. 220p.;map;fol. 1st publ., Vienna, 1518;

here revised. Sabin 63957; Harrisse (BAV) 112; JCB (3) I:82. DLC, InU-L, MH, MiU-C, MnU-B, RPJCB; BL, BN.   522/9

Newe zeitung. von dem lande. das die Sponier funden haben ym 1521. iare genant Yucatan. Newe zeittung von Prussla. [*Augsburg?* 1522?]. 6 lvs; illus.;4to. Sabin 54946 (& 106221n); Harrisse (BAV) Add. 70; Weller (Ersten d. Zeitungen) 14; JCB AR29:6-9. RPJCB; Berlin: StB.   522/10

___[Anr edn]. [*Augsburg?* 1522?]. [8]p.;illus.; 4to. CU-B.   522/11

Ptolemaeus, Claudius. Opus Geographiae noviter castigatum & emaculatum. *Strassburg: J.Grüninger*, 1522. 194 lvs;maps; fol. Comprises Lorenz Fries's revision of the J.Angelus Latin text; cf.1513, Strassburg, edn. Sabin 66481; Harrisse (BAV) 117; Sanz (Ult.ad.) 913-918; Stevens (Ptolemy) 47; Phillips (Atlases) 361; Benzing (Fries) 51; JCB (3) I:83. DLC, MH, NN-RB, RPJCB; BL, BN.   522/12

Sacro Bosco, Joannes de. Sphaericum opusculum, cum . . . expsitione [sic] per Matthaeum Shamotulienn. *Cracow: J.Haller*, 1522. 70 numb.lvs;illus.;4to. Lf 54 contains substantial passage on America. Sabin 74800; Wierzbowski 59; Yarmolinsky (Early Polish Americana) 32; Church 49. CSmH, NN-RB; BL.   522/13

Ein schöne newe zeytung so Kayserlich Mayestet auss Indiat yetz newlich zükommen seind. [*Augsburg: M.Ramminger*, 1522]. 8 lvs;4to. Abridged account of Columbus, and of Cortés's conquest of Mexico, with ref. to the Magellan circumnavigation. Sabin 16956; Harrisse (BAV) 115; Sanz (Ult.ad.) 909-912; Weller (Ersten d. Zeitungen) 15; JCB (3) I:81. CSmH, CtY, InU-L, MnU-B, NN-RB, RPJCB; BL.   522/14

Springer, Balthasar. Of the newe landes and of ye people founde by the messengers of the kynge of Portygale named Emanuel. [*Antwerp:*] *J.van Doesborch* [1522?]. 24 lvs;illus.;4to. Transl. from p.[4-17] & [47] of Springer's 1508, *Die reyse van Lissebone*, from the same printer. On p.[3] is a ref. to 'Armenica' and its savages. Sabin 99366; Harrisse (BAV) 116; Nijhoff/Kronenberg 1311; Proctor (Doesborgh) 22; STC 7677. CSmH; BL.   522/15

Varthema, Lodovico di. Itinerario . . . Et al presente agiontovi alchune isole novamente ritrovatte. *Venice: Heirs of G. dei Rusconi*, 1522. 103 lvs;8vo. 1st publ., Venice, 1520. Includes, as earlier, Juan Díaz's account of Grijalva's Yucatan expedition. Sabin 98644; Harrisse (BAV) 114. MiU-C, NN-RB.   522/16

1523

Berengario, Jacopo. Isagoge brevis . . . in anatomiam humani corporis. *Bologna: B.Hectoris*, 1523. 80 lvs;illus.;4to. 1st publ., Bologna, 1522. Ind.aur. 117.160. DNLM, MiU; BL, BN.   523/1

Campani, Niccolò, called Lo Strascino. Lamento . . . sopra el male incognito el quale tratta de la patientia et impatientia. *Venice: N.&V.di P.Zoppino*, 1523. [56]p.;illus.;8vo. 1st publ., [Siena? ca. 1515]. In verse. Ind. aur.130.750; Sander 1566; Adams (Cambr.) C469. Cambridge: Trinity, Florence: BN.   523/2

Cortés, Hernando. Carta de relacion embiada a su S. Magestad del Emperador. *Saragossa: J.Coci* [1523]. [56]p.;fol. 1st publ., Seville, 1522. Sabin 16934; Harrisse (BAV) 120; Medina (BHA) 65; Sánchez (Aragon) 115; JCB (3) I:86. RPJCB; BL.   523/3

____. Carta tercera de relacion: embiado . . . del Yucatan llamado la Nueva España. *Seville: J. Cromberger* [1523]. 30 lvs;port.;fol. Sabin 16935; Harrisse (BAV) 121; Sanz (Ult.ad.) 919; Medina (BHA) 66; Escudero (Seville) 230; Church 50; JCB (3) I:86. CSmH, ICN, InU-L, NN-RB, RPJCB; BL, BN. 523/4

____. De contreyen vanden eylanden ende lantdouwen. *Antwerp: M.Hillen*, 1523. 30 lvs;illus.;4to. Transl. from printer's [1522] French version, *Des marches, ysles et pays*. Harrisse (BAV) 86; Nijhoff/Kronenberg 2713. BN.   523/5

De Roma prisca et nova, varii auctores. *Rome: J.Mazochius*, 1523. 2pts;4to. Includes F.Albertini's *Mirabilia Romae*, 1st publ., Rome, 1510, with mention of Vespucci. Sabin 72884; Harrisse (BAV) Add. 74. ICN, MH, NN-RB, RPJCB.   523/6

Maximilianus, Transylvanus. De Moluccis insulis, itemque aliis pluribus mirandis, quae novissima Castellanorum navigatio suscepta, nuper invenit. *Cologne: E.Cervicornus*, 1523. [31]p.;8vo. An account of the Magellan circumnavigation. Sabin 47038; Harrisse (BAV)

122; Medina (BHA) 68; Church 51; JCB (3) I:88. CSmH, CtY, DLC, ICN, InU-L, MH, MnU-B, NN-RB, RPJCB; BL, BN. 523/7

—[Anr edn]. *Paris: P.Viart*, 1523. 16 lvs;8vo. Church 52. CSmH. 523/8

—[Anr.edn]. Epistola, de admirabili & novissima Hispanorum in Orientem navigatione. *Rome: F.M.Calvo*, 1523. 19 lvs;4to. Sabin 47039; Harrisse (BAV) 123; Medina (BHA) 67; JCB (3) I:88. CU, CtY, DLC, InU-L, MnU-B, RPJCB; BL, BN. 523/9

Maynardus, Petrus. De preservatione hominum a pestiphero morbo. [*Venice? 1523?*]. [14]p.;4to. On syphilis. Cf. Proksch I:12. CtY-M, DNLM; London: Wellcome, BN. 523/10

Pico della Mirandola, Giovanni Francesco. Strix, sive de Ludificatione daemonum. *Bologna: H.de Benedictis*, 1523. 48 lvs;4to. 'De navigatione hispana': lvs F2v-F3r. Adams (Cambr.) P1155. NN-RB, RPJCB; BL, BN. 523/11

Schöner, Johann. De nuper sub Castiliae ac Portugalliae regibus . . . repertis insulis ac regionibus . . . epistola & globus geographicus, seriem navigationum annotantibus. *Timiripae* [*i.e., Cologne? E.Cervicornus?*] 1523. 4 lvs;8vo. To accompany author's terrestrial globe. Sabin 77800; Sanz (Ult.ad.) 920; Coote (Schöner) 7. MiU-C, NN-RB; BL. 523/12

Spain. Cortes. Quaderno de las cortes que en Valladolid tuvo su Magestad, este presente año de MDXXIII. *Burgos: A.de Melgar*, 1523. 13 lvs;fol. Petition xvi comprises banning of sale of Indians and of trade by foreigners in Indies. Palau 242573 (&63139). BL. 523/13

1524

Anghiera, Pietro Martire d'. De rebus, et insulis noviter repertis. *Nuremberg: F.Peypus*, 1524. xii lvs;fol. Extracted from the author's 4th Decade, 1st publ., Basel, 1521. Usually bound with, as issued, H.Cortés's *De nova maris Oceani Hyspania narratio*. Sabin 16947n; JCB (3) I:90. DLC, NN-RB, RPJCB; BL. 524/1

Apianus, Petrus. Cosmographicus liber. *Landshut: J.Weissenburger,for P.Apianus,*

1524. 104p.;illus.;4to. Chapt.4 relates to America. Sabin 1738; Harrisse (BAV) 127 & Add. p. 87; Sanz (Ult.ad.) 921-931; Ortroy (Apian) 22; JCB (3) I:89. CtY, DLC, MB, MiU-C, MnU-B, NN-RB, RPJCB; BL, BN. 524/2

———. Ein kunstlich Instrument. *Landshut: J. Weissenburger*, 1524. [38]p.;illus.,map;4to. Volvelle on p. [4] comprises map incl. America. Ortroy (Apian) 21. CtY, MH; Munich: StB. 524/3

Ein bewert Recept wie man das holtz Gnagacam [i.e., Guayacum] für die Krannckheit der Frantzosen brauchen sol. [*Bamberg: G.Erlinger*] 1524. 4 lvs;4to. 1st publ., Nuremberg?, 1518. Sabin 29155; JCB (3) I:92. NN-RB, RPJCB. 524/4

Cortés, Hernando. Praeclara . . . de nova maris Oceani. Hyspania narratio. *Nuremberg: F.Peypus*, 1524. xlix lvs;illus.,port.,map;fol. Transl. by P. Savorgnanus from Cortés's Seville, 1522, *Carta de relacion*. With this is usually bound, as issued, the printer's P.M. d'Anghiera's *De rebus, et insulis noviter repertis* above. Sabin 16947; Harrisse (BAV) 125; Sanz (Ult.ad.) 933-934; Medina (BHA) 70; Church 53; JCB (3) I:90. CSmH, CtY, DLC, InU-L, MH, MiU-C, NN-RB, RPJCB; BL. 524/5

———. La preclara narratione . . . della Nuova Hispagna. *Venice: B.Vercellensis,for G.B.Pederzano*, 1524. [145]p.;map;4to. Transl. by N. Liburnio from P. Savorgnanus's Latin version of this year of the Seville, 1522, *Carta de relacion.* Sabin 16951; Harrisse (BAV) 129; Sanz (Ult.ad.) 935-936; Medina (BHA) 86n (I:129); Church 55; JCB (3) I:91. CSmH, DLC, InU-L, MiU-C, NN-RB, RPJCB; BL. 524/6

—[Anr issue, with cancel t.p.]. *G.A.Nicolini da Sabbio,for G.B.Pederzano*, 1500 [i.e., 1524?]: [145]p.;map;4to. Sabin 16951n; Harrisse (BAV) 130; Medina (BHA) 86n (I:130). BL. 524/7

———. Tertia . . . in nova maris Oceani Hyspania generalis praefecti preclara narratio. *Nuremberg: F.Peypus*, 1524. li lvs;illus.;fol. Transl. by P. Savorgnanus from the Seville, 1523, *Carta tercera.* Sabin 16948; Harrisse (BAV) 126; Sanz (Ult.ad.) 937-938; Medina (BHA) 71; Church 54; JCB (3) I:90. CSmH, CtY, ICN, InU-L, MiU-C, MnU-B, NN-RB, RPJCB; BL, BN. 524/8

Foresti, Jacopo Filippo, da Bergamo. Supplementum supplementi de le Chroniche . . . per Francesco C., fiorentino, vulgarizato. *Venice: G.F. & G.A.dei Rusconi*, 1524. ccclx-vi lvs;illus.;fol. 1st publ. in Italian with American material, Venice, 1508; additions here bring the chronicles up to October, 1524. Included is a chapt. on America. Cf. Sabin 25087; JCB (3) I:93. RPJCB; BL.   524/9

—[Anr issue, with variant title omitting translator's name]. *Venice: G.F. & G.A.dei Rusconi*, 1524. Sabin 25087; Harrisse (BAV) 128. NN-RB; BL.   524/10

Giovio, Paolo, Bp of Nocera. De romanis piscibus libellus. *Rome: F.M.Calvo*, 1524. 53 lvs;fol. Chapter on sturgeon contains ref. to Portuguese & Spanish voyages on verso of 15th lf. Adams (Cambr.) G634; Moranti (Urbino) 1659. DFo, NN-RB; BL, BN.   524/11

Hutten, Ulrich von. De Guaiaci medicina et morbo gallico liber unus. *Mainz: J.Schoeffer*, 1524. [87]p.;4to. 1st publ., Mainz, 1519. Adams (Cambr.) H1222; Benzing (Hutten) 106; Waller 5031. DNLM, MiU, MnU-B; BL, Uppsala: UB.   524/12

Maximilianus, Transylvanus. Epistola, de admirabili & novissima Hispanorum in Orientem navigatione. *Rome: F.M.Calvo*, 1524. 18 lvs;4to. 1st publ., Cologne, 1523. Sabin 47040; Harrisse (BAV) 124; Medina (BHA) 69; Church 56. CSmH, DLC, ICN, InU-L, NN-RB; BL, BN.   524/13

More, Sir Thomas, Saint. Von der wunderbarlichen Innsel Utopia genant. *Basel: J.Bebel*, 1524. [128]p.;illus.,map;4to. Transl. by C.Cantiuncula from Louvain, 1516, *Utopia*. Gibson (More) 34. MH, NNUT; BL.   524/14

Pico della Mirandola, Giovanni Francesco. Libro detto Strega, o Delle illusioni del demonio. *Bologna: H.de Benedictis*, 1524. 55 lvs;4to. Transl. by L.Alberti from the Bologna, 1523, Latin *Strix*. The American ref. is on lvs 35v-36r. Adams (Cambr.) P1160. CtY, DFo, NN-RB; BL.   524/15

Ponti, Antonino. Rhomitypion . . . ubi dum omnia, quae notata sunt digna urbis Romae & nova, & vetera breviter . . . scribuntur. *Rome: A.Blado*, 1524. 62 lvs;illus.;4to. A ref. to America appears on lf L1. Sabin 64020; Adams (Cambr.) P1894; JCB (3) I:94. ICN, MB, MnU-B, NN-RB, RPJCB; Cambridge: UL, BN.   524/16

Ayn recept von ainem holtz zü brauchen für die kranckheit der frantzosen und ander flüssig offen Schäden auss Hispanischer Sprach zü teutsch gemacht. *Augsburg:* 1524. 4 lvs;4to. 1st publ., Augsburg, 1518. On use of Guaiacum for treating syphilis. CU-B, RP-JCB; London: Wellcome.   524/17

1525

Avila, Pedro Arias d'. Lettere . . . della conquista del paese del mar Oceano scripte . . . dalla cipta di Panama delle cose ultimamente scoperte nel mar meridiano decto el Mar Sur, 1525. [*Florence? 1525?*]. 4 lvs;8vo. In verse; describes Pizarro & discovery of Peru. Sabin 1974; Harrisse (BAV) 132 & Add. 76; Medina (BHA) 95n (I:145); Ind.aur. 107.282. BL.   525/1

Bolognini, Angelo. Libellus de cura ulcerum exteriorum, et de unguentis . . . de quorum numero nonnulla in morbum gallicum inserta sunt. *Bologna: Heirs of B.Hectoris*, 1525. [51]p.;4to. 1st publ. with section on treatment for syphilis, Bologna, 1514. Ind.aur.121.501. DNLM.   525/2

Ciminelli, Serafino dei, Aquilano. Traictez singuliers . . . les trois comptes intitulez de Cupido et de Atropos . . . le premier . . . par Serafin, le second & tiers de Jean LeMaire. *Paris: A.Cousteau, for G.DuPré*, 1525. 107 lvs;8vo. LeMaire's contributions contain refs to syphilis. The presumptive Italian text of the 1st work, transl. by LeMaire from Ciminelli, is unknown. Brunet III:966 (13338); Proksch I:80; Fairfax Murray (France) 547; Rothschild 487. BL, BN.   525/3

Cortés, Hernando. La quarta relacion que Fernando Cortes . . . embio al . . . don Carlos emperador . . . enla qual estan otras cartas o relaciones que los capitanes Pedro de Alvarado & Diego Godoy embiaron al . . . capitan Fernando. *Toledo: G.de Avila* [1525]. 21 lvs;illus.;fol. Sabin 16936; Harrisse (BAV) 135; Sanz (Ult.ad.) 939-978; Medina (BHA) 73; Streit II:194; Pérez Pastor (Toledo) 104; Church 57; JCB (3) I:94. CSmH, InU-L, NN-RB, RPJCB; BL.   525/4

Fossetier, Julien. De la glorieuse victoire divinement obtenue devant Pavie par lempereur Charles Quint. [*Antwerp? S.Cock? 1525?*]. 24p.;4to. Includes refs to Columbus,

Yucatan, etc. Sabin 25190; Harrisse (BAV) Add. 77; Nijhoff/Kronenberg 0522. 525/5

Fries, Lorenz. Ein clarer bericht wie man alte scheden, löcher und bülen heylen soll mit dem holtz Guaiaco. *Strassburg: J.Grüninger,* 1525. [11]p.;4to. Benzing (Fries) 18. Frankfurt a.M.: StUB. 525/6

____. Uslegung der Mer carthen. *Strassburg: J.Grüninger,* 1525. 32 lvs;illus.,maps;fol. Text designed to accompany the author's version of the Waldseemüller marine chart of this year. In chapt.I is an account of Vespucci's 1st voyage. Sabin 25964; Harrisse (BAV) 133; Borba de Moraes I:282; Benzing (Fries) 55; JCB AR37:4-8. DLC, NN-RB, RPJCB; Munich: StB. 525/7

Gaguin, Robert. La mer des croniques et miroir historial de France . . . nouvellement additionne [par Pierre Desrey]. *Paris: P.Gaudoul* [1525]. ccxxxv lvs;illus.;fol. 1st publ., Paris, 1514, under title *Les grandes croniques,* with ref. to American savages brought to Rouen in 1509. BN. 525/8

___[Anr issue]. *Paris: [A.Girault,* 1525]. CSt. 525/9

Gatinaria, Marcos. De curis egritudinum particularium noni Almansoris practica uberrima . . . Sebastiani Aquilani Tractatus de morbo gallico celeberrimus. *Lyons: J.Moylin, of Cambray,* 1525. c lvs;illus.;8vo. 1st publ., Pavia, 1509. DNLM; London: Wellcome, BN. 525/10

Mocenigo, Andrea. Bellum camaracense. *Venice: B.dei Vitali,* 1525. [375]p.;8vo. On lf q8v is a ref. to Spanish in Hispaniola & New World. Adams (Cambr.) M1518. CtY, DLC, IU, InU-L, NN-RB, RPJCB; BL, BN. 525/11

Pigafetta, Antonio. Le voyage et navigation faict par les Espaignolz es isles de Mollucques. *Paris: S.de Colines* [ca.1525]. 76 numb. lvs;8vo. Transl. by J.A.Fabre from an Italian ms. Sabin 62803; Harrisse (BAV) 134 & Add. p.xxviii-xxxiv; Medina (BHA) 69n (I:98-99); Borba de Moraes II:144-145; Renouard (de Colines) 421-422; JCB (3) I:95. CtY, MiU-C, NN-RB, RPJCB; BL, BN. 525/12

Poliziano, Angelo Ambrogini, known as. Oratio pro oratoribus Senesium ad Alexandrinum Sextum. *Rome: [F.M.Calvo?* 1525?]. [26]p.;4to. Includes also G.del Maino's *Oratio . . . apud . . . Alexandrinum,* 1st publ., Rome, 1493. Adams (Cambr.) P1775. CtY, ICN, NN-RB; BL. 525/13

Ptolemaeus, Claudius. Geographicae enarrationis libri octo, Bilibaldo Pirckeymo interprete. *Strassburg: J.Grüninger, for J.Koberger, at Nuremberg,* 1525. 82 lvs;illus.,maps;fol. Sabin 66482; Harrisse (BAV) 136 & Add. 78; Sanz (Ult.ad.) 979-987; Stevens (Ptolemy) 47; Phillips (Atlases) 362; JCB (3) I:95. CSmH, CtY, DLC, ICJ, InU-L, MH, MiU-C, MnU-B, RPJCB; BL, BN. 525/14

Salignac, Barthélemy de. Itinerarii Terrae sanctae . . . descriptio. *Lyons: G.de Villiers,* 1525. 70 numb.lvs;illus.;8vo. On verso of lf 56 is a passage on 'Noviter terre invente'. Rothschild 3090; Fairfax Murray (France) 499; JCB AR21:7. MH, NN-RB, RPJCB; BL, BN. 525/15

Spain. Laws, statutes, etc., 1516-1556 (Charles I). Las Cortes de Toledo. deste presente año: de mil y quinientos y .xxv. años. Quaderno. *Burgos: A.de Melgar,* 1525. 18 lvs;fol. 'Peticion' xxii' relates to need for coastal protection for ships carrying provisions and gold from the Indies. Palau 63123. BL. 525/16

Vigo, Giovanni de. Opera . . . in chirurgia. *Lyons: A.DuRy, for J.& F.Giunta & Co.,* 1525. 3pts;illus.;8vo. 1st publ., Rome, 1514. Baudrier (Lyons) VI:118. DNLM. 525/17

____. Sensuit la practique & cirurgie . . . nouvellement translatee de latin [par Nicolas Godin]. *Lyons: B.Bonyn,for self & J.Planfoys,* 1525. 2pts;4to. Transl. from author's *Practica,* 1st publ., Rome, 1514. Baudrier (Lyons) I:344. DNLM; BN. 525/18

1526

Baptista Mantuanus. Opus absolutissimum de sacris diebus, mendis . . . emaculatum, ope . . . Nicolai Parvo. *Poitiers: J.Bouchet,* 1526. 80 lvs;4to. 1st publ., Lyons, 1516, in S.de Basignana's edn of the author's *Opera.* Ind. aur.112.719; Coccia 360. BN. 526/1

Cortés, Hernando. La quarta relacion que Fernando Cortes governador . . . en la Nueva España del mar oceano . . . embio. *Valencia: G.Costilla,* 1526. 26 lvs;illus.;fol. 1st publ., Toledo, 1525. Sabin 16937; Harrisse (BAV) 138; Sanz (Ult.ad.) 988-989; Medina (BHA) 74; Church 58; JCB (3) I:95. CSmH, ICN, NN-RB, RPJCB. 526/2

Fernel, Jean. Monalosphaerium, partibus constans quatuor. *Paris: S.de Colines,* 1526. 36 numb.lvs;fol. Address in verse to reader by Jean LeLieur refers to America. Harrisse (BAV) Add. 84; Renouard (de Colines) 85-86. CtY, MH, NN-RB; BL, BN.   526/3

Maffei, Raffaele. Commentarii Urbanorum . . . octo & triginta libri. *Paris: J.Badius, for self J.Petit, C.Chevallon & C.Resch,* 1526. ccccxxii lvs;fol. 1st publ., Rome, 1506, the passage on Columbus here appearing on verso of lf cxxv. Sabin 43766; Harrisse (BAV) Add. 82; Renouard (Badius Ascensius) III:386; Adams (Cambr.) M101; JCB (3) I:96. NN-RB, RPJCB; BL.   526/4

Oviedo y Valdés, Gonzalo Fernández de. De la natural hystoria de las Indias. *Toledo: R.de Petras,* 1526. lii lvs;fol. Sabin 57987; Harrisse (BAV) 139; Sanz (Ult.ad.) 990-991; Medina (BHA) 75; Pérez Pastor (Toledo) 124; Pogo (Conquista) A; Nissen (Zool.) 3031; Church 59; JCB (3) I:96. CSmH, CtY, DLC, MH, RPJCB; BL, BN.   526/5

Petrarca, Francesco. Spurious and doubtful works. Chronica delle vite de pontefici et imperatori romani. *Venice: G.de Gregoriis [for N.Garanta?]* 1526. 120 numb.lvs;4to. 1st publ. in this version, Venice, 1507, with ref. to Columbus, here found on recto of lf 116. Sabin 61291; Harrisse (BAV) Add. 79; Adams (Cambr.) P849. CtY, ICN, MH, NN-RB, RPJCB; Cambridge: UL, BN.   526/6

Sacro Bosco, Joannes de. Opusculum de sphera mundi . . . cum additionibus: y . . . commentario Petri Ciruelli. *Alcalá de Henares: M.deEguia,* 1526. lxxiii lvs;illus.;fol. 1st publ., as ed. by Ciruelo, with American ref., Venice, 1498. Ref.to Columbus's 1st voyage on verso of lf xlii. Medina (BHA) 76; García (Alcalá de Henares) 87. CtY, DLC, MB, MiU, MnU-B, NN-RB, RPJCB.   526/7

Spain. Laws, statutes, etc., 1516-1556 (Charles I). Las leys & prematicas hechas en las Cortes de Toledo [1525]. *Burgos: A.de Melgar,* 1526. 22 lvs;fol. 1st publ., Burgos, 1525. In the title the reading 'hizierō' appears. Palau 63124. BL.   526/8

__[Anr edn]. *Burgos: A.de Melgar,* 1526. 22 lvs;fol. In the title the reading 'hizieron' appears. BL.   526/9

Varthema, Lodovico di. Itinerario . . . Et al presente agiontovi alcune isole novamente ritrovate. *Venice:* 1526. 103 lvs;8vo. 1st publ.,

Venice, 1520, with account by Juan Díaz of Grijalva expedition to Yucatan. Sabin 98645; Harrisse (BAV) 137; JCB (3) I:96. MiU-C, NN-RB, RPJCB; BL.   526/10

1527

Béthencourt, Jacques de. Nova penitentialis quadragesima, necnon purgatorium in morbum gallicum. *Paris: N.Savetier,* 1527. [115]p.;4to. Proksch I:12; Ind.aur. 118.212. DNLM; BL, BN.   527/1

Dialogo aquae argenti ac ligni guaiaci colluctantium super dicti morbi curationis praelatura. *Paris:* 1527. 8vo. Proksch I:12.   527/2

Fernel, Jean. Cosmo-theorica. *Paris:* 1527. See the year 1528.

Fries, Lorenz. Uslegung der Mercarthen. *Strassburg: J.Grüninger,* 1527. xxvi lvs;map;fol. 1st publ., Strassburg, 1525, with account of Vespucci's 1st voyage. Sabin 98184; Harrisse (BAV) 141 & Add. 83; Borba de Moraes I:283; Benzing (Fries) 57; JCB (3) I:97. CtY, NN-RB, RPJCB; BL.   527/3

Gaguin, Robert. La mer des croniques et miroir historial de France . . . nouvellement additionné jusques en l'an mil cinq. cens et xxvii [par Pierre Desrey]. *Paris: N.de La Barre [for J.Petit]a la rue sainct Jacques a la seigne de la fleur de lys dor,* 1527. ccxxxv lvs;illus.;fol. 1st publ., Paris, 1514, under title *Les grandes croniques* in this version with ref. (here on recto of lf ccxix) to American savages brought to Rouen in 1509. Fairfax Murray (France) 182; JCB (3) I:97-98. RPJCB.   527/4

__[Anr issue]. *Paris: N.de La Barre, a la rue neuve Nostre Dame a lenseigne Saint Nicolas pour Jehan de Sainct Denys,* 1527. CtY.   527/5

Giovio, Paolo, Bp of Nocera. De piscibus marinis . . . liber. *Rome: F.M.Calvo,* 1527. [85]p.;4to. 1st publ., Rome, 1524. In chapt. 4, 'De sturione', is a ref. (here on verso of lf Di) to Spanish & Portuguese voyages 'dum novas incogniti orbis terras inusitata, ac admirabili navigatione per immensam oceanum'. Adams (Cambr.) G636. DFo, MH, NN-RB, RPJCB; BL, The Hague: KB.   527/6

Glareanus, Henricus. De geographia liber unus. *Basel: J.Faber,* 1527. 35 numb.lvs;illus.;4to. A ref. to America appears on recto of lf 35. Sabin 27536; Harrisse (BAV) 142; Sanz (Ult.ad.) 997-998; Adams (Cambr.)

G758; JCB (3) I:98. CSmH, CtY, IU, MH, MnU-B, NN-RB, RPJCB; BL. 527/7

Maynardus, Petrus. De quiditate morbi gallici causis et accidentibus et curationibus libellus. [*Venice?*] 1527. 11 lvs;4to. 1st publ. [Venice? 1523?]. Proksch I:12. 527/8

Montesino, Ambrosio, Bp. Cancionero de diversas obras. *Toledo: M.de Eguía,* 1527. 86 lvs;port.;4to. 1st publ., Toledo, 1508. Pérez Pastor (Toledo) 142; Palau 178943. NNH. 527/9

Sabellico, Marco Antonio Coccio, called. Rapsodiae historiarum Enneadum. *Paris: J.Badius, for self & J.Petit,* 1527-28. 2v.;fol. 1st publ. with American refs, Venice, 1504. Renouard (Badius Ascensius) III:226; Adams (Cambr.) S24-S25. CtY; Cambridge: UL, Paris: Arsenal. 527/10

Schöner, Johann. Appendices . . . in opusculum Globi astriferi nuper . . . aeditum. *Antwerp: M.de Keyser,for R.Bollaert,* 1527. 32 lvs;8vo. 1st publ., Nuremberg, 1518. Sabin 77799; Nijhoff/Kronenberg 3859; Coote (Schöner) 10; Adams (Cambr.) S680. BL. 527/11

1528

Almenar, Juan. Libelli duo di morbo gallico. *Lyons: A.Blanchard,for B.Trot,* 1528. xl lvs;8vo. 1st publ., Venice, 1502. Includes also Nicolai Leoniceni's *De curatione morbi quam Itali gallicum vocant,* 1st publ., Venice, 1497. Adams (Cambr.) A775; Ind.aur.103.788; Baudrier (Lyons) V:103 (&VIII:438). Cambridge: UL, BN. 528/1

Bordone, Benedetto. Libro . . . nel qual si ragiona de tutte l'isole del mondo. *Venice: N.Zoppino,* 1528. 73 lvs;illus.,maps;fol. On Mexico, Cuba & Spanish America; subsequent edns bear title *Isolario.* Sabin 6417; Harrisse (BAV) 145; Sanz (Ult.ad.) 1003; Borba de Moraes I:98-99; Phillips (Atlases) 162; Ind. aur.122.344; JCB (3) I:98-99. CtY, DLC, ICN, MH, MiU-C, NN-RB, RPJCB; BL, BN. 528/2

Coppo, Pietro. Portolano. *Venice: A.Bindoni,* 1528. 47 lvs;maps;16mo. In addition to map showing New World, a passage on Columbus appears on verso of lf F3. Sabin 16715; Harrisse (BAV) 144. NN-RB; BL. 528/3

Delicado, Francisco. Retrato de la Loçana: andaluza. [*Venice?* 1528?]. 54 lvs;illus.;4to.

Includes passage on Guaiacum, 'el legno de las Indias'. Palau 70179. Vienna: NB. 528/4

Fernel, Jean. Cosmotheorica, libros duos complexa. *Paris: S.de Colines,* 1527 [i.e., 1528]. 46 numb.lvs;illus.;fol. Dedicatory letter, dated 4 Feb. 1528 & addressed to King John of Portugal, praises country's navigators & exploits in New World. On recto of 3d lf is a specific ref. to America. Harrisse (BAV) Add. 85; Sanz (Ult.ad.) 1004-1006; Renouard (de Colines) 97-98. DLC; BL. 528/5

—[Anr issue]. *Paris: S.de Colines,* 1528. Renouard (de Colines) 116-117. MH, MnU-B, NN-RB, RPJCB; BN. 528/6

Giovio, Paolo, Bp of Nocera. De romanis piscibus libellus. *Antwerp: J.Grapheus,* 1528. [126]p.;8vo. 1st publ., Rome, 1524. Nijhoff/Kronenberg 1238. MH, NN-RB; BL, BN. 528/7

Glareanus, Henricus. De geographia liber unus. *Basel: J.Faber,* 1528. 35 numb.lvs;illus.;4to. 1st publ., Basel, 1527. The American ref. is on recto of lf 35. Sabin 27537; Harrisse (BAV) 143. ICN, NN-RB, RPJCB. 528/8

Manardo, Giovanni. Epistolae medicinales. *Paris: S.DuBois, for C.Wechel,* 1528. [224]p.;8vo. Includes Manardo's *De erroribus Symonis Pistoris . . . circa morbum gallicum,* 1st publ., [Leipzig?], 1500. CtY-M, DNLM, NNNAM. 528/9

Mura, Petrus de. Catecismo de la doctrina cristiana en lengua mexicana. *Antwerp:* 1528. Sabin 59518; Harrisse (BAV) Add. p.95n; Peeters-Fontainas (Impr. esp.) 820; Nijhoff/Kronenberg 0976. Cf. 1553 edn, Medina (Mexico) 20. 528/10

Spain. Laws, statutes, etc. Las pramaticas del reyno. *Alcalá de Henares: M.de Eguía,* 1528. ccxxviii lvs;fol. 1st publ., Alcalá de Henares, 1503. Passage on convicts to be sent to America is on verso of lf xciii. Sabin 64915; Harrisse (BAV) Add. 86; Medina (BHA) 77; García (Alcalá de Henares) 105. InU-L, NN-RB, NNH. 528/11

1529

Almenar, Juan. Libelli duo di morbo gallico. *Lyons: A.Blanchard,* 1529. xl lvs;8vo. 1st publ., Venice, 1502, the present edn being a reissue with altered imprint date of Lyons, 1528, edn. Includes also Nicolai Leoniceni's

De curatione morbi quam Itali gallicum vocant, 1st publ., Venice, 1497. Baudrier (Lyons) V:105-107. NN-RB, PPC; London: Wellcome.   529/1

—[Anr issue]. *Lyons: A.Blanchard, for B.Trot*, 1529. Baudrier (Lyons) V:105-107; Waller 366. Uppsala: UB.   529/1a

Apianus, Petrus. Cosmographicus liber . . . studiose correctus . . . per Gemmam Phrysiam. *Antwerp: J.Grapheus,for R.Bollaert*, 1529. lv lvs;illus.,maps;4to. 1st publ., Landshut, 1524. 'De America': lf xxxiiii. Sabin 5260; Harrisse (BAV) 148 & Add. 88; Sanz (Ult.ad.) 1007-1014; Nijhoff/Kronenberg 121; Ortroy (Apian) 25; JCB (3) I:99. DLC, ICN, MnU-B, NN-RB, RP-JCB; BL, Paris: BU.   529/2

Brant, Sebastian. La grand nef des folz. *Lyons: F.Juste*, 1529. civ lvs;illus.;4to. 1st publ., Lyons, 1499, in this translation from Locher's 1497 Latin version of the Basel, 1494, German original. Ind.aur. 123.706. BL, BN.   529/3

Campani, Niccolò, called Lo Strascino. Lamento . . . sopra il male incognito, il quale tratta della patientia & impatientia. *Venice: N.Zoppino*, 1529. [56]p.;illus.;8vo. 1st publ., [Siena? ca.1525]. In verse. Sander 1567; Ind. aur. 130.752; Waller 1715. DNLM; BL, Uppsala: UB.   529/4

Delicado, Francisco. Il modo de adoperare el legno de India occidentale, salutifero remedio a ogni piaga e mal incurabile. [*Venice: The author*] 1529. [17]p.;4to. Palau 70184. 529/5

Franciscus, o.f.m. De orbis situ ac descriptione. *Antwerp: M.de Keyser,for R. Bollaert* [1529?]. 15 lvs;maps;4to. Sabin 25465; Harrisse (BAV) 131; Sanz (Ult.ad.) 992-996; Nijhoff/Kronenberg 3040; JCB (3) I:93. RPJCB; BL, BN.   529/6

Fries, Lorenz. Eyn clarer bericht yetzt nüw von dem holtz Guaiaco. *Strassburg: J.Grüninger*, 1529. 8 lvs;illus.;4to. 1st publ., Strassburg, 1525. Ritter (Strasbourg) 1234. Strasbourg: BN (Hutten, Ulrich). 529/7

—[Anr edn]. Ein clarer bericht. *Strassburg: J.Grüninger*, 1529. 8 lvs;illus.;4to. Ritter (Strasbourg) 1767. BL (Bericht), Strasbourg: BN (Paracelsus).   529/7a

Grimaldi, Giovanni Battista. Copey eynes brieffes . . . Ansaldo de Grimaldo und andern Edlen von Genua auss Hispanien zugeschrieben. [*Speyer: J.Schmidt*, 15]29. 4

lvs;4to. Mentions arrival of two ships at Seville from Indies with pearls worth 50,000 ducats. Stuttgarter Antiquariat, Cat.94 (1977) no.4. BL.   529/8

Hock von Brackenau, Wendelin. Mentagra, sive tractatus excellens de causis, preservativis, regimine & cura morbi gallici. *Lyons: A.Blanchard, for B.Trot*, 1529. lxv lvs;8vo. 1st publ., Strassburg, 1514. Baudrier (Lyons) VIII:440. DNLM; BL, BN.   529/8a

Karl V, Emperor of Germany. Ain ernstliche red Keyselicher Maiestet, Caroli des fünften, die er zu den Hispanien gethon hat, von seinem Abschid auss Hispania . . . yetz new inn Teutsche zung vertolmetschet. [*Augsburg? ca. 1529*]. 4 lvs;4to. Shaaber H178. PU. 529/9

Manardo, Giovanni. Medicinales epistolae. *Strassburg: J.Schott*, 1529. 129 numb.lvs;8vo. Includes Manardo's *De erroribus Symonis Pistoris . . . circa morbum gallicum*, 1st publ., [Leipzig?], 1500. Bibl. belg., 2nd ser., XVII,M233; Ritter (Strasbourg) 1468. CtY-M, DNLM; London: Wellcome, BN.
                                        529/10

Padilla, Juan de. Los doce triumfos de los doce apostoles. *Seville: J.Varela*, 1529. fol. 1st publ., Seville, 1521. Escudero (Seville) 284.
                                        529/11

Paracelsus. Vom Holtz Guaiaco gründlicher heylung. *Nuremberg: F.Peypus*, 1529. 7 lvs;illus.;4to. Stillwell (Science) 468; Sudhoff (Paracelsus) 1. BL.   529/12

——. Von der französischen krankheit. *Nuremberg: J.Gutknecht*, 1529. 4to Proksch I:12.   529/13

Polo, Marco. Libro . . . delas cosas maravillosas que vido enlas partes orientales . . . con otro tratado de micer Pogio florentino. *Logroño: M.de Eguïa*, 1529. xxxii lvs;fol. 1st publ. as transl. by R.Fernández de Santa Ella, Seville, 1503. Harrisse (BAV) Add. 89; Medina (BHA) 79. CSmH, InU-L, NN-RB; BL.   529/14

Sichardus, Joannes. En damus Chronicon divinum . . . ab ipso mundi initio, ad annum . . . M.D.XII. *Basel: H.Petri*, 1529. 207 numb.lvs;fol. On verso of lf 153 is an account of the American savages brought to Rouen in 1509. JCB (3) I:100. CSmH, CtY, DFo, ICJ, MH, MiU-C, MnU-B, NN-RB, PPAmP, RP-JCB; BL.   529/15

Spain. Cortes. Quaderno de las cortes: que en Valladolid tuvo su magestad del Emperador

. . . el año de M.D.xxiii. *Burgos: J.de Junta,* 1529. 18 lvs;fol. 1st publ., Burgos, 1523. Cf.Palau 242574 (& 63141). BL.   529/16

Vives, Juan Luis. De concordia & discordia in humano genere. *Antwerp: M.Hillen,* 1529. 275 lvs;8vo. In bk iii is a passage, citing navigators in the [West?] Indies, on the harmony of Indians in their natural state amongst themselves. Nijhoff/Kronenberg 2163; Adams (Cambr.) V945; Palau 371643. BL, Paris: Arsenal.   529/17

1530

Anghiera, Pietro Martire d'. De orbe novo . . . decades. *Alcalá de Henares: M.de Eguía,* 1530. cxvii lvs;fol. Contains all 8 Decades of complete work. In some copies a map produced at Antwerp, 1530, appears. Sabin 1551 & 45010; Harrisse (BAV) 154; Sanz (Ult.ad.) 1053-1058; Medina (BHA) 84; García (Alcalá de Henares) 134; Church 62; JCB (3) I:101. CSmH, ICN, InU-L, MH, MiU-C, NN-RB,RPJCB; BL, BN.   530/1

_____. Opus epistolarum. *Alcalá de Henares: M.de Eguía,* 1530. 199 numb.lvs;fol. Included are letters referring to Columbus & the New World. Sabin 1555; Harrisse (BAV) 160; Sanz (Ult.ad.) 1059-1084; Medina (BHA) 85; García (Alcalá de Henares) 135; JCB (3) I:101. DLC, ICN, MH, NN-RB, RPJCB; BL, BN.   530/2

Berengario, Jacopo. Isagogae breves . . . in anatomiam humani corporis. *Strassburg: H.Sybold,* 1530. [271]p.;illus.;8vo. 1st publ., Bologna, 1522. Ind.aur.117.161. DNLM, MiU, MnU, NNNAM; BL, BN.   530/3

Beroaldo, Filippo. Carminum . . . libri iii. *Rome:A.Blado,* 1530. 66 lvs;4to. Includes ode 'In laudem Ferdinandi et Emanuelis Hispaniae regum', commenting on overseas discoveries and praising simplicity of savages there. Ind.aur.117.899. MH, RPJCB; The Hague: KB.   530/4

Brant, Sebastian. La grand nef des folz du monde. *Paris: D.Janot,for* [*P.LeNoir*] *a l'enseigne de la Rose blanche couronnée* [ca. 1530]. 124 lvs;illus.;4to. 1st publ., Lyons, 1498, in this French translation of Locher's 1497 Latin version of the 1494 German original. That other issues were produced for other booksellers seems likely. BN.   530/5

Brunfels, Otto. Herbarum vivae eiconeb [sic]

ad nature imitationum. *Strassburg: J.Schott,* 1530. 266p.;illus.;fol. On p. 15 are refs to Guaiacum & U.von Hutten. Ind.aur. 125.632; Pritzel 1283; Nissen (Bot.) 257,Ia; Fairfax Murray (Germany) 462; Ritter (Strasbourg) 287. DNLM, MH, MnU-B, RPB; BL, BN.   530/6

Catholic Church. Pope, 1492-1503 (Alexander VI). Alfonsus de Fonseca, miseratione divina archiepiscopus. [*Toledo:* 1530?]. 3 numb.lvs;4to. Transmits, as of 9 May 1530, text of bull 'Dudum siquidem' of Pope Alexander issued 26 Sept. 1493 in respect to Spanish lands newly discovered, revoking early grants to Portugal of lands not yet actually possessed. Palau 6640 (dated 'ca. 1600'). NNPM.   530/7

Enciso, Martín Fernández de. Suma de geographia que trata de todas las partidas y provincias del mondo: en especial de las Indias . . . nuevamente emendada. *Seville: J.Cromberger,* 1530. lviii lvs;illus.;fol. 1st publ., Seville, 1519. In this edn the colophon reads 'mil y quinientos. y .xxx.'. Sabin 22552; Harrisse (BAV) 153; Sanz (Ult.ad.) 26-27; Medina (BHA) 81; Church 61; JCB AR57: 5-14. CSmH, NN-RB, RPJCB; BL.   530/8

—[Anr edn]. The colophon has reading 'mill & quiniẽtos y .xxx.'. Escudero (Seville) 290; Church 61n. NN-RB; Madrid: BN.   530/9

Erasmus, Desiderius. Utilissima consultatio de bello Turcis inferendo. *Cologne* [*i.e. Antwerp: M.Keyser?*]1530. 8vo. Opening passage includes description of horrors of syphilis. BL.   530/10

—[Anr edn]. *Antwerp: M.Hillen* [1530?]. 28 lvs;8vo. Nijhoff/Kronenberg 803. BL. 530/11

—[Anr edn]. *Basel: Froben Office,* 1530. 118p.;8vo. MH, MnU-B; BL.   530/12

—[Anr edn]. *Paris: C.Wechel,* 1530. [64]p.;4to. Adams (Cambr.) E413. DFo, ICN, MH; Cambridge: UL.   530/13

Fracastoro, Girolamo. Syphilis, sive Morbus gallicus. *Verona:* [*S.dei Nicolini da Sabbio & Bros*] 1530. 36 lvs;4to. In verse. In bk 3 is an allegorical description of the discovery of the West Indies by the Spanish & their encounter with both the disease syphilis & Guaiacum ('Hyacum'). Harrisse (BAV) Add. 91; Baumgartner (Fracastoro) 1; Waller 3173; JCB (3) I;100. CtY-M, DNLM, ICJ, InU-L, MBCo, MiU, NN-RB, RPJCB; BL, BN.   530/14

Fries, Lorenz. Ein clarer Bericht wie man alte Schaden, Löcher und Bülen heylen soll mit dem Holtz Guaicaco. [*Strassburg: J.Prüss*, 1530]. [11]p.;4to. 1st publ., Strassburg, 1525. Benzing (Fries) 19; Waller 3261. DNLM; Uppsala: UB.   530/15

____. Hydrographiae; hoc est, Charta marinae totiusque orbis . . . descriptio. *Strassburg: J.Grüninger*, 1530. [32]p.;4to. Transl. by Nicolas Prugner from the author's *Underweisung und usslegunge der Cartha marina*, the following item. Borba de Moraes I:283-284; Benzing (Fries) 59. NN-RB. 530/16

____. Underweisung und usslegunge der Cartha marina. *Strassburg: J.Grüninger*, 1530. 22 lvs;illus.;fol. 1st publ., Strassburg, 1525, under title *Uslegung der Mercarthen.* 'Von den nuen land auch America genant': verso of 6th lf. Sabin 25965; Harrisse (BAV) 151,158 & Add. 90; Borba de Moraes I:283; Benzing (Fries) 58. InU-L, NN-RB; BL.   530/17

Fuchs, Leonhart. Errata recentiorum medicorum ix numero, adjectis eorundem confutationibus. *Haguenau: J.Secerius*, 1530. lxxix lvs;4to. In bk 2, Error 45 reports 'Morbus gallicus non estis, quem Graeci Lichenen nominant', i.e., denying that syphilis & impetigo are the same disease. DNLM, MBCo, NNNAM, PPC; BL, BN.   530/18

Gaguin, Robert. La mer des cronicques et mirouer hystorial de France . . . nouvellement traduict de latin . . . et augmenté de nouveau [par Pierre Desrey]. *Paris: J.Nyverd* [1530]. ccxxviii lvs;illus.;fol. 1st publ., Paris, 1514, under title *Les grandes croniques*, with ref. to American savages brought to Rouen in 1509. Shaaber G2. MH, PU; BN.   530/19

Gemma, Reinerus, Frisius. De principiis astronomiae . . . Item de orbis divisione, & insulis, rebusque nuper inventis. *Antwerp: J.Grapheus, for S.Zassenus,at Louvain & G. de Bonte,at Antwerp*, 1530. [84]p.;4to. Sabin 26853; Harrisse (BAV) 156 & Add. 92; Nijhoff/Kronenberg 971; Adams (Cambr.) G387; JCB (3) I:100-101. CtY-M, ICN, NN-RB, RPJCB; BL, BN.   530/20

Glareanus, Henricus. De geographia liber unus, ab ipso autore recognitus. *Freiburg i.Br.: J.Faber*, 1530. 35 numb. lvs; illus.;4to. 1st publ., Basel, 1527. Sabin 27538; Harrisse (BAV) 147; JCB (3) I:101. MH, NN-RB, RP-JCB; BN.   530/21

Holy Roman Empire. Sovereigns, etc., 1519-1556 (Charles V). Carolus Quintus divina favente clementia Romanorum imperator . . . Bononiae . . . millesimo quingentesimo trigesimo die vero mensis Martii. [*Bologna*: 1530]. bds., on vellum;fol. Form for ecclesiastical appointment, citing Pope Clement VII's bulls of 8 May 1529 & letter of 20 Feb. 1530 as authority for such appointments in the New World. Sabin 10984 & 13624; Harrisse (BAV) 152; Medina (BHA) 80. NN-RB.   530/22

Honter, Johannes. Rudimentorum cosmographiae libri duo. *Cracow: M.Scharffenberg*, 1530. 16 lvs;maps;8vo. In verse. Includes mention of America. Cf.Sabin 32792; Sanz (Ult.ad.) 1027-1029; Haskins (Polonica) 408; Wierzbowski 2140. NN-RB.   530/23

Hutten, Ulrich von. L'experience et approbation . . . touchant la medicine du boys dict Guaiacum . . . traduicte & interpretee par Jean Cheradame. *Paris: P.LeNoir* [ca.1530?]. [84]p.;illus.;4to. 1st publ., in French, Lyons, [ca. 1520?]. Benzing (Hutten) 113. DNLM; BL.   530/24

____[Anr issue]. *Paris: J.Trepperel* [ca.1530?] Benzing (Hutten) 114. NN-RB; BN.   530/25

____[Anr issue]. *Paris: M.de LaPorte* [ca.1530?]. Fairfax Murray (France) 284; Benzing (Hutten) 115. Uppsala: UB.   530/26

Maffei, Raffaele. Commentariorum . . . octo & triginta libri. *Basel: Froben Office*, 1530. 468 numb.lvs;illus.;fol. 1st publ., Rome, 1506, the ref. to Columbus here appearing on verso of lf 139. Sabin 43767; Harrisse (BAV) 161 & Add. 93; Adams (Cambr.) M102. DLC, MnU-B, NN-RB; Cambridge: St John's, BN.
                                              530/27

Marineo, Lucio, Siculo. Obra . . . de las cosas memorables de España. *Alcalá de Henares: M.de Eguía*, 1530. 253 numb.lvs;fol. Cf. Latin edn of this year. Includes biographies of notable Spaniards, for which it was subsequently censured. Sabin 44583; Harrisse (BAV) 159; Sanz (Ult.ad.) 1034-1052; Medina (BHA) 82; García (Alcalá de Henares) 126. Madrid: BN (t.p. wanting; title from colophon).   530/28

____. Opus de rebus Hispaniae memorabilibus. *Alcalá de Henares: M.de Eguía*, 1530. 175 numb.lvs;fol. 1st publ., 1497; here revised with additional biographies, e.g., of Cortés,& with account of early Spanish exploration. In 1553 lvs 128-175 were ordered suppressed. Cf.Sabin 44583; Medina (BHA) 83; Palau 152133.   530/29

Mela, Pomponius. De orbis situ libri tres . . . emendati, unà cum commentariis Joachimi Vadiani. *Paris:* [*C.Wechel*] 1530. 196p.; map;fol. 1st publ. in this version, Vienna, 1518; here reprinted from 2nd, 1522, edn. Sabin 63958; Harrisse (BAV) 157; Moranti (Urbino) 2165; JCB (3) I:102. CSmH, CtY, DLC, MH, NN-RB, RPJCB; BL, BN. 530/30

Paracelsus. Von der Frantzösischen kranckheit, drey Bücher. *Nuremberg: F. Peypus,* 1530. [146]p.;4to. Sudhoff (Paracelsus) 7. IaU, NcD-M; BL. 530/31

Pirckheimer, Wilibald. Germaniae ex variis scriptoribus perbrevis explicatio. *Nuremberg: J.Petrejus,* 1530. 36 lvs;8vo. On lvs [34-35] appear an account of Hispaniola & Central America. Sabin 63016; Shaaber P360. CU, CtY, ICN, MH, NN-RB, PU; BL. 530/32

—[Anr edn]. *Strassburg: H.Steiner,* 1530. 36 lvs;8vo. Sabin 63017; JCB (3) I:102. CtY-M, MnU-B, NN-RB, RPJCB. 530/33

Vigo, Giovanni de. Opera . . . in chirurgia. *Lyons: A.Blanchard* (v.1) *& J.Crespin* (v.2) *for J.& F.Giunta & Co.,* 1530. 2v.;8vo. Includes Vigo's *De morbo gallico,* 1st publ., Rome, 1514. Baudrier (Lyons) VI:135-136. DNLM; BL. 530/34

———. Sensuit la practique & cirurgie . . . nouvellement translatee de latin [par Nicolas Godin]. *Paris: D.Janot,for P.LeNoir,* 1530. 224 lvs;fol. 1st publ. in French, Lyons, 1525. BN. 530/35

1531

Fracastoro, Girolamo. Syphilis, sive Morbus gallicus. *Rome: A.Blado,* 1531. [61]p.;4to. 1st publ., Verona, 1530. In verse. Harrisse (BAV) 95; Baumgartner (Fracastoro) 2. CU, DNLM, NN-RB, MiU; BL. 531/1

—[Anr edn]. *Paris: L.Cynaeus,* 1531. 25 numb.lvs;8vo. Harrisse (BAV) 94; Baumgartner (Fracastoro) 3; Waller 3174. CtY-M, PPC; BL, BN. 531/2

Giovio, Paolo, Bp of Nocera. De romanis piscibus libellus. *Basel: H.Froben & N.Episcopius,* 1531. 144p.;8vo. 1st publ., Rome, 1524. The ref. to newly discovered lands here appears on p.44. Adams (Cambr.) G635. MH, NN-RB, PPAN; BL, BN. 531/3

Hutten, Ulrich von. De guaici medicina et morbo gallico liber unus. *Mainz: J.Schoeffer,* 1531. 123p.;8vo. 1st publ., Mainz, 1519. Benzing (Hutten) 107. DFo, DNLM; BN. 531/4

Jan ze Stobnicy. Introductio in Ptolomei Cosmographiam. [*Cracow?* 1531?] 32 numb.lvs; 4to. 1st publ., Cracow, 1512. Sabin 91868. Cracow: Jagellon Univ. 531/5

Parmentier, Jean. Description nouvelle des merveilles de ce monde . . . en rithme francoyse . . . faisant sa derniere navigation . . . en lisle Taprobanc, autrement dicte Samatra. *Paris:* 1531. 48 lvs;4to. In the prologue is a ref. to America, which the author was the earliest Frenchman to visit. Sabin 58825; Harrisse (BAV) Add. 96. BN. 531/6

Spain. Laws, statutes, etc., 1516-1556 (Charles I). Las leys & prematicas reales hechas . . . en las Cortes de Toledo [1525]. *Burgos: J.de Junta,* 1531. 8 lvs;fol. 1st publ., Burgos, 1525. Palau 63125. 531/7

Vigo, Giovanni de. Opera . . . in chirurgia. *Lyons: J.Moylin,of Cambray,* 1531. 3pts;illus.;8vo. 1st publ., Rome, 1514. DNLM. 531/8

Vives, Juan Luis. De disciplinis. *Antwerp: M.Hillen,* 1531. 2pts;fol. In pt 2, bk v, chapt.2, is a ref. to Pietro Martire d'Anghiera's writings on the New World. Nijhoff/ Kronenberg 4063; Adams (Cambr.) V946; Palau 371654. BL, BN. 531/9

1532

Anghiera, Pietro Martire d'. Extraict ou recueil des isles nouvellement trouvées en la grand mer Oceane . . . Item trois Narrations. *Paris: S.de Colines,* 1532. 207 numb.lvs;8vo. Transl. & abridged from the 1st three Decades of the author's *De orbe novo,* 1st publ., Alcalá de Henares, 1516. The 'Narrations' comprise similar versions of Cortés's 2nd & 3rd letters publ., 1524, at Nuremberg. Sabin 1554 & 16952n (& 23542?); Harrisse (BAV) 167; Medina (BHA) 86n (I:131-132); Renouard (de Colines) p.196-198; Church 64; JCB (3) I:105. CSmH, CtY, ICN, InU-L, MH, MnU-B, NN-RB, RPJCB; BL, BN. 532/1

Antonio de Olave, o.f.m. Hystoire et lettres du glorieux & bienheure frere Andre de Spolete . . . Est contenu aussi . . . lettres de la . . . conversion & augmentation de la foy catholicque au pays de Huketan aultrement dict terre neufve, ou bien Neufve Hespaigne. *Toulouse: J.Colomiès,for J.Barril,* 1532. [12]p;illus.;4to. Transl. from the following item. The letters are those of Martín de Valencia and of Juan de Zumárraga relating to

Franciscan missions in Yucatan and Mexico. Cf. Sabin 44932; cf. Harrisse (BAV) Add. 98; Atkinson (Fr. Ren.) 44; Streit II:280; Rép. bibl., XX:70. BN.   532/2

———. Passio gloriosi martyris beati patris fratris Andree de Spoleto. *Toulouse: J. Colomiès, for J. Barril*, 1532. [8]p.;4to. Based on letters written by Fernando de Meneses to the King of Portugal; also included are letters by Martín de Valencia & Juan de Zumárraga relating to Franciscan missions in Yucatan & Mexico. Sabin 44931; Harrisse (BAV) Add. 97; Medina (BHA) 87; Atkinson (Fr. Ren.) 50; Streit II:279; Rép.bibl.XX:70; Pérez Pastor (Medina del Campo) 34n. NN-RB; BN. 532/3

——[Anr edn]. *Bologna: G. da Ruberio*, 1532. [8]p.;4to. RPJCB.   532/4

Apianus, Petrus. Cosmographiae intróductio. *Ingolstadt: [P. & G. Apianus]* 1529 [i.e.,1532]. 32 lvs;illus.,maps;8vo. The presumptive copy of a 1531 edn is in fact from the present printing. An abridgment of the author's Ingolstadt, 1524, *Cosmographicus liber*. Sabin 1740; Harrisse (BAV) 149; Ortroy (Apian) 82; Ind. aur.106.408; JCB (3) I:99-100. MH, RPJCB; BL.   532/5

Bartolomeo da li Sonetti. [Isolario]. Al divo cinquecento e diece tre cinque. [*Venice:*] 1532. 28 numb.lvs;maps;fol. In verse. Includes a world map by F. Rosello, incorporating recent discoveries. G.F.Nunn, *World Map of Francesco Roselli* (Philadelphia, 1924); JCB AR57:20-22. RPJCB.   532/6

Brunfels, Otto. Contrafayt Kreüterbüch. *Strassburg: J. Schott*, 1532. cccxxxii p.;illus.; fol. Abridged & transl. from the 1530, Strassburg, *Herbarum vivae eicones*. Ind. aur.125.641; Nissen (Bot.) 258 v.l; Ritter (Strasbourg) 289. MnU-B; BL, Strasbourg: BN.   532/7

———. Herbarium vivae eicones [Vol.I]. *Strassburg: J. Schott*, 1532. 266p.;illus.;fol. 1st publ., Strassburg, 1530. Ind.aur.125.642; Nissen (Bot.) 257 Ib; Hunt (Bot.) 30; Ritter (Strasbourg) 289. CU, CtY-M, DNLM, ICJ, MH, PU; BL, BN.   532/8

Cortés, Hernando. De insulis nuper inventis . . . cum alio quodam Petri Martyris. *Cologne: Melchior von Neuss, for A. Birckmann*, 1532. 82 lvs;fol. Comprises the 2nd & 3rd letters as translated into Latin by Savorgnanus, 1st publ. thus, Nuremberg, 1524; d'Anghiera's *De rebus et insulis* of the same

year; and the letters of Martín de Valencia and of Juan de Zumárraga as published at Toulouse in António de Olave's *Passio* . . . *Andree de Spoleto* of the present year. Sabin 16949; Harrisse (BAV) 168; Medina (BHA) 86; Streit I:27; Church 63; JCB (3) I:103. CtY, DLC, ICN, InU-L, MiU-C, MnU-B, NN-RB, RPJCB; BL, BN.   532/9

Díaz de Lugo, Juan Bernardo, Bp. Lettres envoyees au chapitre general des freres mineures . . . en la cite de Tholose . . . lan mil.D.xxxii. [*Toulouse: J. Barril*, 1532]. [20]p.;illus.;4to. Preface exhorts readers to undertake missions to New World. Sabin 44932; Harrisse (BAV) Add. 98; Medina (BHA) 87n (I:134); Atkinson (Fr.Ren.) 43; Streit II:281; Rép. bibl. XX:105; JCB AR46:51-52. RPJCB; BN.   532/10

Fries, Lorenz. Epitome opusculi de curandi pusculis, ulceribus, & doloribus morbi gallici. *Basel: H. Petri*, 1532. 63p.;4to. Transl. from Fries's 1529, Strassburg, *Ein clarer Bericht*. Benzing (Fries) 22; Proksch I:15. CtY, DNLM, MHi, MiU, NN-RB, PPC; BL, BN.   532/11

Gasser, Achilles Pirminius. Historiarum et chronicorum mundi epitome. *Basel: H. Petri*, 1532. 122p.;8vo. On p.119 is a ref. to America. Burmeister (Gasser) 27. NN-RB.   532/12

Gatinaria, Marco. De curis egritudinum particularium noni Almansoris practica uberrima . . . Sebastiani Aquilani Tractatus de morbo gallico celeberrimus. *Lyons: B. Bonyn, for V. de Portonariis*, 1532. xcv lvs;8vo. 1st publ., Pavia, 1509. CtY, DNLM, ICJ.   532/13

Leoniceno, Niccolò. Opuscula . . . Per d. Andream Leenium . . . repurgata, atque annotationibus illustrata. *Basel: A. Cratander & J. Bebel*, 1532. 157 numb.lvs;fol. Includes the author's *De morbo gallico*, 1st publ., Venice, 1497. Adams (Cambr.) L497. DNLM, ICN, MH-A, MiU, NNNAM; BL.   532/14

Manardo, Giovanni. Epistolarum medicinalium tomus secundus. *Lyons: S. Gryphius*, 1532. 589p.;8vo. 1st publ., Paris, 1528; here ed. by François Rabelais. Cioranescu (XVI) 18015. DNLM; Paris: Mazarine.   532/15

Massa, Niccolò. Contenta. Nicolai Massae . . . Liber de morbo gallico . . . Joannis Almenar . . . Liber perutilis, de morbo gallico . . . Nicolai Leoniceni . . . Compendiosa eiusdem morbi cura. Angeli Bolognini . . . Libellus de cura ulcerum . . . et de unguentis.

[*Venice?* 1532]. [415]p.;8vo. Almenar's work had been 1st publ., Venice, 1502; Leoniceno's, Venice, 1497; Bolognini's in this text, Bologna, 1514. DNLM; BN.   532/16

Novus Orbis regionum. Novus Orbis regionum ac insularum veteribus incognitarum. *Basel: J.Herwagen,* 1532. 584p.;illus.,map; fol. A collection of voyages, including those initiated by Spain, ed. by Simon Grynaeus from materials compiled by Johann Huttich. On the various states of the map, see Sabin. Sabin 34100; Harrisse (BAV) 171; Medina (BHA) 46n (I:68-69); Streit I:28; JCB (3) I:104. DLC, InU-L, MH, NN-RB, RPJCB; BL, BN.   532/17

___[Anr edn]. *Paris: A.Augereau,for G.DuPré,* 1532. 507p.;map;fol. Sabin 34101; Harrisse (BAV) 172; Burmeister (Münster) 61; Streit I:29. DLC, InU-L, MH, MiU-C; BL, BN.   532/18

___[Anr issue of preceding]. *Paris: A.Augereau,for J.Petit,* 1532. Sabin 34102; Harrisse (BAV) 173; Streit I:30; JCB (3) I:104. CSmH, DLC, ICN, InU-L, MH, NN-RB, RPJCB; BL, BN.   532/19

Pirckheimer, Wilibald. Germaniae ex variis scriptoribus perbrevis explicatio . . . postremum ab ipso [authore] recognita. *Nuremberg: J.Petrejus,* 1532. 36 lvs;8vo. 1st publ., Nuremberg, 1530, with account of Hispaniola & Central America at end. Sabin 63018; JCB (3) I:105. ICN, MiU-C, NN-RB, RPJCB.   532/20

___[Anr edn]. *Frankfurt a.M.: C.Egenolff,* 1532. 40 lvs;8vo. A reprinting of the preceding with two additional treatises relating to America. Sabin 63019. MiU-C, NN-RB; BL, BN.   532/21

Tollat von Vochenberg, Johann. Artzney Buchlein der kreuter. *Leipzig: M.Blum,* 1532. [91]p.;4to. The earliest edn with American material. Includes chapt. (p.[85-91]) on Guaiacum, identified as growing in the Antilles. Pritzel 9388n. DNLM, NN-RB; London: Wellcome.   532/22

___[Anr edn]. Artzney Biechleinn der Kreutter. *Augsburg: H.Steiner,* 1532. 2pts;4to. DNLM; London: Wellcome.   532/23

Vives, Juan Luis. De concordia & discordia in humano genere. *Lyons: M. & G.Trechsel,* 1532. [536]p.;8vo. 1st publ., Antwerp, 1529. Passage on Indies here appears on recto of lf O7. Palau 371644. MH; Madrid: BN.   532/24

___. De disciplinis libri xx. *Cologne: J.Gymnich,* 1532. 622p.;12mo. 1st publ., Antwerp, 1532. Palau 371655. Madrid: BN.   532/25

Ziegler, Jacob. Quae intus continentur. Syria . . . Schondia, tradita ab auctoribus, qui in eius operis prologo memorantur. *Strassburg: P.Schoeffer,the Younger,* 1532. 108 numb. lvs;maps;fol. By 'Schondia' is designated Greenland and other northern regions. Sabin 106330 (&106294); Harrisse (BAV) 170; Adams (Cambr.) Z153; Ritter (Strasbourg) 2527; JCB (3) I:105. DLC, NN-RB, RPJCB; BL, Strasbourg: BN.   532/26

1533

Anghiera, Pietro Martire d'. De rebus oceanicis & orbe novo; decades tres . . . Praeterea Legationis Babylonicae libri tres. *Basel: J.Bebel,* 1533. 93 numb.lvs;fol. 1st publ., Basel, 1516; here supplemented by abridgment of 4th Decade. Sabin 1557; Harrisse (BAV) 176; Medina (BHA) 92; Borba de Moraes II:31; Church 65; JCB (3) I:108. CSmH, CtY, DLC, InU-L, MH, MiU-C, MnU-B, NN-RB, RPJCB; BL, BN.   533/1

Apianus, Petrus. Cosmographiae introductio. *Ingolstadt: [G.&P.Apianus]* 1529 [i.e., 1533]. 32 lvs;illus.,maps;8vo. 1st publ., Antwerp, 1532. Dated at end, the title page notwithstanding, 1533. Sabin 1741; Harrisse (BAV) 150; Ind.aur.106.409; Ortroy (Apian) 83; Church 60; JCB (3) I:100. CSmH, DLC, ICN, MH, MiU-C, MnU-B, NN-RB, RPJCB; Munich: StB.   533/2

___[Anr edn]. *Venice: G.A.Nicolini da Sabbio & Bros,for M.Sessa,* 1533. [63]p.;illus.,maps; 8vo. Refs to America appear on lvs 22r-23v & 28v. Harrisse (BAV) Add. 100; Ind.aur. 106.420; Ortroy (Apian) 84; JCB (3) I:107. CtY, DLC, ICN, MHi, MiU-C, NN-RB, RPJCB.   533/3

___. Cosmographicus liber . . . restitutus per Gemmam Phrysiam. *Antwerp: J.Grapheus,for G. de Bonte,* 1533. lxvi lvs;illus.,maps;4to. 1st publ., Antwerp, 1524; in this version, Antwerp, 1529. Sabin 1742; Harrisse (BAV) 179; Sanz (Ult.ad.) 1139; Ind.aur.106.414; Nijhoff/Kronenberg 122; Ortroy (Apian) 26. MH; BL.   533/4

___[Anr issue]. *Antwerp: J.Grapheus,for A.Birckmann,* 1533. Harrisse (BAV) 179n; Ind.

aur. 106.415; Nijhoff/Kronenberg 123; Ortroy (Apian) 27; JCB (3) I:106. DLC, MnU-B, NN-RB, RPJCB; Brussels: BR.   533/5

Bellum Christianorum principum, praecipue Gallorum, contra Saracenos, anno salutis M.LXXXVIII. *Basel: H.Petri,* 1533. 152p.; fol. 'Christopheri Colom de insulis nuper inventis': p.116-121. Sabin 72023; Harrisse (BAV) 175; Sanz (Ult.ad.) 1157; Medina (BHA) 89; Streit XV:951; Church 66; JCB (3) I:108. CSmH, MH, NN-RB, RPJCB; BL, BN.   533/6

Capella, Galeazzo Flavio. L'anthropologia. *Venice: Heirs of A.Manuzio & of A.Torresano,* 1533. 74 numb.lvs;8vo. Mentions Portuguese voyages to New World. Adams (Cambr.) C578. BL.   533/7

Gasser, Achilles Pirminius. Een cronijcke waer in als in een tafel seer cortelic begrepen wort alle tgene dat bescreven een gheschiet is. *Antwerp: A.van Berghen,for W.van Lin* 1533. 78 lvs;8vo. Transl. from the author's *Historiarum . . . epitome,* 1st publ., Basel, 1532. Nijhoff/Kronenberg 956; Burmeister (Gasser) 38. Ghent: BU.   533/8

____. Historiarum et chronicorum mundi epitome. *Antwerp: J.Grapheus,for M.Hillen,* 1533. 56 numb.lvs;8vo. 1st publ., Basel, 1532. Nijhoff/Kronenberg 952; Adams (Cambr.) G268; Burmeister (Gasser) 28. Cambridge: King's,Paris: Ste Geneviève.   533/9

__[Anr issue]. *Antwerp: J.Grapheus,for J.Steels,* 1533. Nijhoff/Kronenberg 953; Burmeister (Gasser) 29. BN.   533/10

__[Anr edn]. *Antwerp: M.Hillen,* 1533. 60 lvs;8vo. Nijhoff/Kronenberg 954; Burmeister (Gasser) 30. Utrecht: BU.   533/11

__[Anr edn]. *[Antwerp? 1533?].* 111p.;8vo. Adams (Cambr.) G269; Burmeister (Gasser) 31. Cambridge: St John's, BN.   533/12

__[Anr edn]. Historiarum et chronicarum mundi epitomes libellus. *Venice: G.A.Nicolini da Sabbio & Bros,for M.Sessa,* 1533. 60 numb. lvs;8vo. Burmeister (Gasser) 32; JCB AR20: 1533. CtY, IU, InU-L, NN-RB, RPJCB; BL.   533/13

Glareanus, Henricus. De geographia liber unus . . . ab ipso authore iam tertio recognitus. *Freiburg i.Br.: J.Faber,* 1533. 36 lvs;illus.;4to. 1st publ., Basel, 1527. Sabin 63179; Harrisse (BAV) 183. CSmH, DLC, MiU-C, MnU-B, NN-RB; BL.   533/14

González de Mercado, Luis. Copia di una let-

tera . . . sopra la presa del'India del Peru. *Florence: A.de Mazochius* [1533?]. [6]p.;4to. Prob. transl. from a now lost Spanish text. Sabin 63179; Palau 105536. NN-RB.   533/15

Haselberg, Johann. Von den welschen Purppeln. *[Mainz: I.Schoeffer]* 1533. [15]p.;4to. Includes refs to syphilis. Proksch I:81. DNLM; BL.   533/16

Honter, Johannes. Rudimentorum cosmographiae libri duo. *Basel: H.Petri,* 1533. 1st publ., Cracow, 1530. Munich: StB.   533/17

Hortus sanitatis [Minor]. Den groten herbarius . . . Item noch eenen . . . tractaet van die spaensche pocken [ghescreven door Wendelin Höck von Brackenau]. *Antwerp: C.de Grave,* 1533. clxviii lvs;illus.;fol. The earliest edn to include Hock von Brackenau's 1514, Strassburg, *Mentagra* in Dutch. Nijhoff/Kronenberg 1053; Nissen (Bot.) 2291. DNLM.   533/18

Hutten, Ulrich von. De morbo gallico. *London: T.Berthelet,* 1533. 79 numb.lvs;8vo. Transl. into English by T.Paynell from author's *De Guaiaci medicina,* 1st publ., Mainz, 1519. Cf. Sabin 34096; Benzing (Hutten) 116; STC 14024. CSmH; BL.   533/18a

Marineo, Lucio, Siculo. Obra . . . de las cosas memorables de España. *Alcalá de Henares: M.de Eguía,* 1533. cxc lvs;fol. 1st publ., Alcalá de Henares, 1530; here reissued with lf cxc a cancel & lvs cxci-cclii deleted. Sabin 44584; Harrisse (BAV) 182; Sanz (Ult.ad.) 1144-48; Medina (BHA) 91; García (Alcalá de Henares) 144; Adams (Cambr.) M594. CtY, NNH, RPB; Cambridge: UL, The Hague: KB.   533/19

____. Opus de rebus Hispaniae memorabilibus. *Alcalá de Henares: M.de Eguía,* 1533. cxxviii numb.lvs;fol. 1st publ. with a ref. to Columbus's discoveries (here on verso of lf cvi), Alcalá de Henares, 1530. Sabin 44585; Harrisse (BAV) Add. 101; Medina (BHA) 90; García (Alcalá de Henares) 143; Shaaber M147. MB, PU, RPJCB; BL, BN.   533/20

Mattioli, Pietro Andrea. Morbi gallici novum ac utilissima opusculum. *Bologna: Heirs of H.de Benedictis,* 1533. [103]p.;4to. DNLM, NN-RB, MnU-B; London: Wellcome. 533/21

Petrarca, Francesco. Spurious and doubtful works. Chronica delle vite de pontifici et imperadori romani . . . alla quale sono state aggiunte quelle . . . insido alla eta nostra. *Venice: M.Sessa,* 1533. 120 numb.lvs;8vo. 1st publ., Venice, 1507, with ref. to Columbus. CtY.   533/22

Schöner, Johannes. Opusculum geographicum. [*Nuremberg: J.Petrejus*] 1533. [40]p.;illus.,maps;4to. Produced to accompany terrestrial globe; includes references to Brazil & Vespucci (pt 2, chapt.i) and to 'regionibus extra Ptolemaeum' (pt 2, chapts xx-xxi) with mention of Columbus and of newly discovered lands. Sabin 77802; Harrisse (BAV) 178; Borba de Moraes II:243; Church 68; JCB (3) I:110. CSmH, InU-L, MiU-C, NN-RB, RPJCB; BL, BN.   533/23

Zumárraga, Juan de, Bp of Mexico. Universis et singulis R.P. ac fratribus in Christo . . . Salute. [*Rome?* 1533?] [8]p.;4to. An account of the author's missionary labors in Mexico. That the text is set in italic suggests Italian printing. Sabin 106401; Harrisse (BAV) Add. 102; Medina (BHA) 88; Streit I:31. Seville: Bibl. Colombina.   533/24

1534

Amandus von Kirikzee. Chronica compendiossima. *Antwerp: S.Cock*, 1534. 128 numb. lvs;8vo. 'In Nova Hispania' (lvs 122v- 127r) comprises letters of Martín de Valencia & Juan de Zumárraga, 1st publ., 1532, in António de Olave's *Passio gloriosi martyris . . . Andree de Spoleto*, supplemented by a letter dated 29 June 1529 of Pedro de Gante (or, de Mura), otherwise unlocated. Sabin 994; Harrisse (BAV) 186 & Add., p.95n; Medina (BHA) 93; Streit I:32. DLC, NN-RB, RPJCB; BL, BN.   534/1

Bordone, Benedetto. Isolario . . . nel quale si ragiona di tutte l'isole del mondo. *Venice: N. Zoppino*, 1534. lxxiiii lvs;maps;fol. 1st publ., Venice, 1528, under title *Libro di Benedetto Bordone*. Sabin 6419; Harrisse (BAV) 187; Borba de Moraes I:98; JCB (3) I:112. CSmH, DLC, ICN, MB, MiU-C, RPJCB; BL, BN.   534/2

Brunfels, Otto. Kreuterbuch contrafayt. *Strassburg: J.Schott*, 1534. ccxiii p.;illus.;4to. 1st publ. in German, Strassburg, 1532. Ind. aur.125.654; Nissen (Bot.) 259; Ritter (Strasbourg) 295. NNNAM; Munich: StB.   534/3

La conquista del Peru, llamada la nueva Castilla. *Seville: B.Pérez*, 1534. [14]p.;illus.;

fol. Sabin 61097; Harrisse (BAV) 199; Medina (BHA) 94; Pogo (Conquista) B; Escudero (Seville) 350. MH, NN-RB; BL.   534/4

Copia delle lettere del prefetto della India la nuova Spagna. [*Venice?*] 1534. [4]p.;4to. Dated 'M D XXXIIII' at end. On Pizarro's conquest of Peru. Sabin 63177. NN-RB.534/5

——[Anr state]. [*Venice? 1534?*]. [4]p.;4to. Without date or privilege statement at end. Sabin 16669. NN-RB.   534/6

Dionysius, Periegetes. De totius orbis situ, Antonio Becharia interprete . . . Joannis praeterea Honteri . . . de cosmographiae rudimentis libri duo. *Basel: H.Petri*, 1534. 99p.;4to. In Honter's work, on p.91 ff. is a section on 'Nomina insularum oceani et maris', referring in part to America. Sabin 20210; Harrisse (BAV) 194; Yarmolinsky (Early Polish Americana) 34. MnU-B, RPJCB; BL.
534/7

Francesco da Bologna, o.f.m. La letera mandata dal rev. padre frate Francesco da Bologna, da Lindia, over nova Spagna: & dalla città di Mexico. *Venice: P.Danza* [1534]. 7 lvs.;8vo. Transl. from a presumptive Latin text. Sabin 25435; Harrisse (BAV) 185; Medina (BHA) 87n (I:135); Streit II:330. NN-RB.   534/8

Franck, Sebastian. Weltbüch: spiegel und bildtniss des gantzen erdtbodens. *Tübingen: U.Morhart*, 1534. ccxxxvii lvs;fol. American material appears on lvs ccx-ccxxxvii. Sabin 25468; Harrisse (BAV) 197; JCB (3) I:112. CU, DLC, ICN, NN-RB, RPJCB; BL, Strasbourg: BN.   534/9

Gasser, Achilles Pirminius. Brief recueil de toutes chroniques & hystoires. *Antwerp: M.de Keyser*, 1534. [175]p.;8vo. Transl. from Basel, 1532, Latin text. Nijhoff/Kronenberg 960; Burmeister (Gasser) 42. ICN; BN.534/10

——. Een chronijcke waer in als in een tafel seer cortelic begrepen wort alle tghene dat bescreven en geschiet is. *Antwerp: A.van Berghen*, 1534. 84 lvs;8vo. 1st publ. in Dutch, Antwerp, 1533. Nijhoff/Kronenberg 957; Burmeister (Gasser) 39. Brussels: BR. 534/11

——[Anr issue]. *Antwerp: A.van Berghen,for W.van Lin*, 1534. 84 lvs;8vo. Nijhoff/Kronenberg 958; Burmeister (Gasser) 40. Brussels: BR.   534/12

——[Anr edn]. *Leyden: J.Severszoon* [1534?]. 84 lvs;8vo. Nijhoff/Kronenberg 959; Burmeister (Gasser) 41. The Hague: KB.   534/13

Glareanus, Henricus. De geographia liber unus ab ipso authore iam tertio recognitus. *Venice: G.A.Nicolini da Sabbio, for M.Sessa,* 1534. 45 numb.lvs;illus.;8vo. 1st publ. in this revision, Freiburg, 1533. The section 'De regionibus extra Ptolemaeum' occupies lvs 44-45. Sabin 27450; Harrisse (BAV) 184 & Add. 103; JCB (3) I:113. DLC, InU-L, MiU-C, NN-RB, PSt, RPJCB; BL.   534/14

Honter, Johannes. Rudimentorum cosmographiae libri duo. *Cracow: M.Scharffenberg,* 1534. 16 lvs;8vo. 1st publ., Cracow, 1530. Sabin 32792; Haskins (Polonica) 409. MiU-C, NN-RB.   534/15

León, Juan de. Relacion de lo que se truxo del Perú con dos menores de coplas. *Medina del Campo:* 1534. 4to. Medina (BHA) 96; Pérez Pastor (Medina del Campo) 9; Palau 135187. No copy known, that once in the Bibliotheca Colombina having disappeared.   534/16

Massa, Niccolò. Liber de morbo neapolitano, noviter editus. [*Lyons: B.Trot*] 1534. 86 numb.lvs;4to. 1st publ., Venice?, 1532. DNLM.   534/17

Newe Zeytung aus Hispanien und Italien, mense Februario, 1534. [*Nuremberg?* 1534]. 4 lvs;4to. Describes conquest of Peru. Sabin 54945; Harrisse (BAV) 195; Medina (BHA) 95n (I:145); Weller (Ersten d. Zeitungen) 73. MH, NN-RB; BL.   534/18

Nouvelles certaines des isles du Peru. *Lyons: F.Juste,* 1534. [16]p.;illus.;8vo. Presumably transl. from an unidentified Spanish text. Sabin 63178; Harrisse (BAV) 196; Medina (BHA) 95n (I:145-146); Atkinson (Fr.Ren.) 46; Baudrier (Lyons) Suppl. I,p.97. BL.

534/19

Novus Orbis regionum. Die new welt, der landschaften unnd Insulen, so bis hie her allen Altweltbeschrybern unbekant. *Strassburg: G.Ulricher,* 1534. 242 numb.lvs;fol. Transl. by Michael Herr from 1532, Basel, Latin text, slightly modified. Sabin 34106; Harrisse (BAV) 188; Medina (BHA) 46n (I:70); Streit I:33; Arents (Add.) 2; Richter (Strasbourg) 1048; JCB (3) I:113. InU-L, MH, NN-A, RP-JCB; BL, Strasbourg: BN.   534/20

Oppianus. Alieuticon, sive De piscibus libri quinque. *Strassburg: J.Cammerlander,* 1534. 152 lvs;4to. Includes Paolo Giovio's *De piscibus liber,* 1st publ., Rome, 1524. Adams (Cambr.) O202. CU, CtY, DNLM, ICU, InU-L, MH, PPAmP; BL, BN.   534/21

Paschalis, Joannes. Liber de morbo composito, vulgo gallico appelato. *Naples: J.A.de Caneto,* 1534. 31 numb.lvs;4to. Cf.Medina (BHA) 72. CtY-M, DNLM; BL.   534/22

Petrarca, Francesco. Spurious and doubtful works. Chronica delle vite de pontefici et imperatori romani . . . alla quale sono state aggiunte quelle che da tempi del Petrarca infino alla eta nostra mancavano. *Venice: F. Bindoni & M.Pasini,* 1534. 120 numb.lvs; 8vo. 1st publ. in this version, Venice, 1507, the ref. to Columbus here appearing on recto of lf 116. Sabin 61292; Harrisse (BAV) Add. 105; JCB (3) I:115. RPJCB; BL.   534/23

—[Anr edn]. *Venice: M.Sessa,* 1534. 120 numb.lvs;8vo. Adams (Cambr.) P849. CtY, DLC, ICN, MiU, NN-RB; BL, BN.   534/24

Pius II, Pope. Asiae Europaeque elegantissima descriptio . . . Accessit H. Glareani Compendiaria Asiae, Africae, Europaeque descriptio. *Paris: C.Chevallon,* 1534. 522p.;12mo. The earliest edn to include Glareanus's work, 1st publ., Basel, 1527, the ref. to America here appearing on p.521. Sabin 63164. RPJCB, ViU; BL, BN.   534/25

—[Anr issue]. *Paris: G.DuPré,* 1534. CtY, ICN, MH, NN-RB; BL.   534/26

Río, Baldassare del, Bp. Copia de una lettera . . . alla S. di N.S. delle richezze & thesoro ritrovato in India. [*Rome: A.Blado,* 1534?]. 4 lvs;4to. On Pizarro's conquest of Peru and transmittal of treasure to Spain. Sabin 63176n; Harrisse (BAV) Add. 109 (as 'Lettere di Pizarro'); Medina (BHA) 94 (I:146). InU-L; BL.   534/27

Summario de la generale historia de l'Indie Occidentali cavato da libri scritti dal signor Don Pietro Martyre . . . et da molte altre particulari relationi. *Venice:* [*A.Pincio?*] 1534. 3pts in l v.;illus.,maps;4to. General title from verso of 1st lf. Pt 1, transl. from P.M.d'Anghiera's *De orbe novo Decades* of 1530, has title 'Libro primo della historia de l'Indie Occidentali'; pt 2, transl. by A. Navigero from G.F.Oviedo y Valdés's *Dela natural hystoria delas Indias,* 1st publ., 1530, has title 'Libro secondo delle Indie Occidentali' with at end a privilege lf with statement 'Stampato in Vinegia, nel mese di Decembre, del .1534.'.Pt 3, transl. with modifications, from the anon. *La conquista del Peru,* 1st publ.this year at Seville, has title 'Libro ultimo del Summario delle Indie Occidentali', and, at end, colophon 'In Vinegia, del mese d'Ottobre .M D XXXIIII.' Sabin 1565; Harrisse (BAV) 190: Sanz (Ult.ad.) 1162-1166; Borba de Moraes II:32; Church 69; Arents 3; Pogo (Conquista) D-F; JCB (3)I:114. CSmH, DLC, IU, MH, MiU-C, MnU-B, NN-RB, RPJCB; BL, BN.   534/28

Tomic, Pere. Historias e conquestas dels excellentissims e catholics reys de Arago. *Barcelona: C.Amoros*, 1534. 74 numb.lvs;fol. Contains an appendix not found in earlier edns that mentions discovery and exploration of the New World. Palau 334030. NNH; BL, BN.   534/29

Trithemius, Johannes. Liber octo questionum quas illi dissolvendas proposuit Maximilianus. *Cologne: Melchior von Neuss*, 1534. 64 lvs; 8vo. 1st publ., Oppenheim, 1515. Sabin 97005n; Adams (Cambr.) T978. BL.   534/30

Vadianus, Joachim von Watt, called. Epitome trium terrae partium, Asiae, Africae, et Europae. *Zurich: C.Froschauer*, 1534. 273p.; map;fol. On p.267 (misnumbered 567) is a ref. to America. Sabin 98279; Harrisse (BAV) 189; Adams (Cambr.) V10; JCB (3) I:115. CtY, DLC, MH, NN-RB, RPJCB; BL, BN.   534/31

__[Anr edn]. *Zurich: C.Froschauer*, 1534. 564p.;map;8vo. Sabin 98280; Harrisse (BAV) 189bis (p.464) & Add. 104; Adams (Cambr.) V9; JCB AR41:53-55. NN-RB, RPJCB; BL, BN.   534/32

Vigo, Giovanni de. Opera . . . in chyrurgia. *Lyons: J.Moylin,for J.Giunta*, 1534. 2pts;8vo. Includes 'De morbo gallico', 1st publ., Rome, 1514, in the author's *Practica*. Baudrier (Lyons) VI:158-159. BL.   534/33

Vives, Juan Luis. Wannenher Ordnungen menschlicher Beywoning. [*Strassburg?* 1534]. 59 lvs;4to. Transl. from Vives's *De concordia*, 1st publ., Antwerp, 1529. Palau 371649. BL.   534/34

Xérez, Francisco de. Verdadera relacion de la conquista del Peru y . . . la nueva Castilla: conquistada por . . . Francisco Piçarro. *Seville: B.Pérez*, 1534. [38]p.;illus.;fol. Exists in 2 issues, the latter of which, (B), contains numerous typographic errors in sheet B, ostensibly created by careless composition following an accident at press. Sabin 105720; Harrisse (BAV) 198; Medina (BHA) 95; Escudero (Seville) 350; Church 70; Pogo (Con-

quista) C; JCB (3) I:116. CSmH (B), NN-RB (A), RPJCB (B); BL (B).   534/35

1535

Apianus, Petrus. Cosmographiae introductio cum quibusdam geographiae ac astronomiae principiis. *Venice: G.A. Nicolini da Sabbio, for M.Sessa*, 1535. 31 numb.lvs;illus.,maps; 8vo. 1st publ., Ingolstadt, 1532. Sabin 1743; Harrisse (BAV) 202; Ind.aur.106.424; Ortroy (Apian) 85; JCB (3) I:117. DLC, MH, MiU-C, NN-RB, RPJCB; London: Wellcome   535/1

Berengario, Jacopo. Anatomia Carpi. Isagoge brevis . . . in anatomiam humani corporis. *Venice: B.dei Vitali*, 1535. 61 numb. lvs;illus.;4to. 1st publ., Bologna, 1522. Ind. aur.117.163. CtY, DLC, MBCo, NNNAM; BL, BN.   535/2

Copey etlicher brieff, so auss Hispania kummen seindt. [*Augsburg?* 1535]. [7]p.;4to. Translation from an untraced Spanish original, describing the conquest of Peru. Though referred to at the end of the present work, similar French & Dutch versions are unlocated. Sabin 16663 & 63176; Harrisse (BAV) Add. 108; Medina (BHA) 95n (I:146); JCB (3) I:117. MH, NN-RB, RPJCB.   535/3

Egenolff, Christian, comp. Chronica, Beschreibung, und gemeyne anzeyge vonn aller Welt herkommen. *Frankfurt a.M.: C.Egenolff*, 1535. cxxxvii lvs;illus.;fol. Includes refs to America, e.g., on verso of lf ciii, 'Von America dem vierdten Theyl der Welt'. Sabin 12957; Harrisse (BAV) 211; Fairfax Murray (Germany) 117. DLC, ICN, NN-RB; BL.   535/4

Foresti, Jacopo Filippo, da Bergamo. Supplementum supplementi delle chroniche. *Venice: B.Bindoni*, 1535. cccxcii lvs;illus.;fol. The earliest edn with continuation by Marco Guazzo to 1535; cf.1524, Venice, edn. ICN, MiU-C, NN-RB; BL, BN.   535/5

Fracanzano da Montalboddo. Sensuyt le nouveau monde & navigations faictes par Emeric de Vespuce . . . Translate . . . par Mathurin du Redouer. *Paris: D.Janot* [ca. 1535?]. lxxxviii lvs;4to. 1st publ., Paris, [1515?]. The printer Denis Janot was active at the address given from 1532 till 1545. Sabin 50064; Harrisse (BAV) 146 & Add. 87.   535/6

Gasser, Achilles Pirminius. Historiarum et chronicarum totius mundi epitome. *Basel:*

H.Petri, 1535. 169p.;8vo. 1st publ., Basel, 1532. Burmeister (Gasser) 33. CtY, DLC, ICN, InU-L, NN-RB.   535/7

Letera de la nobil cipta: nuovamente ritrovata alle Indie con li costumi & modi del suo re & soi populi. [*Rome: A.Blado*, 1535?]. [8] p.;4to. Signed at end: El .V.S.V. al suo .D.L.S. Data in Peru adi .xxv. de Novembre. de .MDXXXIIII. Describes an unidentified city named Zhaval; quite possibly a work of fiction. Reprinted, 1536 & 1539, under title *Lettera de la nobil citta* . . . Sabin 40244; Harrisse (BAV) 191. NN-RB; BL.   535/8

Liber de morbo gallico. *Venice: G.Padovano & V.Ruffinello*, 1535. [384]p.;8vo. Contains N.Leoniceno, *De epidemia quam Itali morbum gallicum* . . . *vocant* (1st publ., Venice, 1497); U. von Hutten, *De admiranda guaiaci medicina* (1st publ., Mainz, 1519); P.A. Mattioli, *Morbi gallici novum* . . . *opusculum* (1st publ., Bologna, 1533); L.Fries, *Epitome opusculi de curandis pustulis* (1st publ., Basel, 1532); Scribonius Largus: excerpts from Basel, 1529, *De compositione medicamentorum liber*; J.Almenar, *Libellus de morbo gallico* (1st publ., Venice, 1502); A.Bolognini, *Liber de cura ulcerum exteriorum* (1st publ., Bologna, 1514). Normally bound with this is Nicolaus Pol's *De cura morbi gallici* of this year; bibliographically distinct, it is described separately below. Benzing (Hutten) 108; JCB AR20:1535. CLU-C, CtY-M, DNLM, MiU, RPJCB;BL, BN.   535/9

Lucidarius. Eyn newer M.Lucidarius von allerhandt geschöpffen Gottes . . . und wie alle creaturen geschaffen seind auff erden. Auch wie die Erd in drei teyl geteilt. *Strassburg: J.Cammerlander* [ca.1535]. [80]p.;illus.;4to. A reworking of the mediaeval text which here contains a mention of America in ch.8, citing Apianus. Schorbach (Lucidarius) 30; Ritter (Strasbourg) 1404. OCl; Munich: StB, Strasbourg: BN.   535/10

Manardo, Giovanni. Epistolarum medicinalium libri duoviginti. *Basel: J.Bebel*, 1535. 467p.;fol. Includes Manardo's *De erroribus Symonis Pistoris* . . . *circa morbum gallicum*, 1st publ., [Leipzig?], 1500. Adams (Cambr.) M315. CtY-M, DNLM, NN-RB; BL.   535/11

Oviedo y Valdés, Gonzalo Fernández de. La historia general de las Indias. *Seville: J.Cromberger*, 1535. cxciii lvs;fol. A distinct

work from the author's 1526 *De la natural hystoria de las Indias*. Sabin 57988; Harrisse (BAV) 207; Sanz (Ult.ad.) 1187-1194; Medina (BHA) 97; Escudero (Seville) 361; Streit II:342; Pogo (Conquista) J; Nissen (Zool.) 3032; Arents 4; Church 71; JCB (3) I:118. CSmH, CtY, InU-L, MH, NN-A, RPJCB; BL, BN.   535/12

Pol, Nicolaus. De cura morbi gallici per lignum guaycanum. [*Venice: G.Padovano & V.Ruffinelli*] 1535. [15]p.;8vo. Normally bound with the publishers' *Liber de morbo gallico* of this year. Stillwell (Science) 488. CLU-C, CtY-M, DNLM, MiU, RPJCB; BL, BN.   535/13

Ptolemaeus, Claudius. Geographicae enarrationes libri octo. Ex Bilibaldi Pirckeymheri translatione, sed ad Graeca & prisca exemplaria à Michaele Villanovano [i.e., Servetus] iam primum recogniti. *Lyons: G.& M. Trechsel*, 1535. 149p.;maps;fol. Of the maps, four, with textual commentary, relate to America. Sabin 66483; Harrisse (BAV) 210; Sanz (Ult.ad.) 1174; Stevens (Ptolemy) 48; Phillips (Atlases) 364; Benzing (Fries) 53; JCB (3) I:119. CtY, DLC, ICN, InU-L, MH, MiU-C, MnU-B, NN-RB, RPJCB; BL, BN.   535/14

Reisch, Gregor. Margarita philosphica . . . nuper aut ab Orontio Fineo . . . castigata & aucta. *Basel: H.Petri,for C.Resch*, 1535. 1498p.;illus.,maps;4to. The earliest edn with supplementary text; originally publ., Freiburg, 1503. In the appendices are sections and map relating to America. Included also, p.1440-1463, is J.Honter's *Rudimentorum cosmographiae libri duo*, 1st publ., 1530. Sabin 69130; Harrisse (BAV) 208; Ferguson (Reisch) 214-215; Adams (Cambr.) R337. DLC, MiU-C, MnU-B, NN-RB; BL, BN.   535/15

Sabellico, Marco Antonio Coccio, called. Rapsodiae historiarum Enneadum. *Lyons: N. Petit & H.Penet,for V.de Portonariis*, 1535. 506(i.e.,606)p.;fol. 1st publ. with American refs, Venice, 1504. In this edn the account of Columbus, etc., appears in v.2, p.526-527. Sabin 74663; cf.Harrisse (BAV) 203; Baudrier (Lyons) VI:166-167; Renouard (Badius Ascensius) III: 226-227. CtY, DFo, ICU, MiU-C, NN-RB; Paris: Mazarine.   535/16

—[Anr issue]. *Lyons: N.Petit & H.Penet,for J.Giunta*, 1535. Baudrier (Lyons) V:455-456;

Renouard (Badius Ascensius) III:226-227.
BL. Above locations may apply to this issue.
535/17

Spain. Cortes.   Quaderno de las cortes: que en
Valladolid tuvo su magestad del Emperador
. . . el año de .M.d.xxiii. *Burgos: J. de Junta*,
1535. [35]p.;fol. 1st publ., Burgos, 1523. The
1525 edn cited by Palau as a note to his
no.242574 may be an error for the present
edn. Palau 63142. DLC, NNH, RPJCB; BL.
535/18

Vadianus, Joachim von Watt, called.   Epitome
topographica totius orbis. *Antwerp:
J. Grapheus*, 1535. 220 numb.lvs;8vo. 1st
publ., Antwerp, 1534, under title *Epitome
trium terrae partium*. 'Insulae Oceani
praecipue', relating to America: lvs 205-213.
Sabin 98278; Harrisse (BAV) 209; Nij-
hoff/Kronenberg 2093; Church 72; JCB
AR20:1535. CSmH, DLC, NN-RB, RPJCB;
BL, BN.   535/19

Varthema, Lodovico di.   Itinerario . . . Et al
presente agiontovi alcune isole novamente
ritrovate. *Venice: F. Bindoni & M. Pasini*,
1535. 100 numb.lvs;8vo. 1st publ. with
American material, Seville, 1520, Juan Díaz's
account of Grijalva's Yucatan expedition of
1518 here occupying lvs 89-100. Sabin 98646;
Harrisse (BAV) 205. MiU-C, NN-RB, RPJCB;
BL.   535/20

Xérez, Francisco del.   Libro primo de la con-
quista del Peru & provincia del Cuzco de le In-
die occidentali. *Venice: S. dei Nicolini da Sab-
bio*, 1535. 62 lvs;illus.;4to. Transl. by D. de
Gaztelu from the Seville 2nd issue of 1534.
Sabin 105721; Harrisse (BAV) 200; Sanz
(Ult.ad.) 1185-1186; Medina (BHA) 95n
(I:144); Pogo (Conquista) G; Church 73; JCB
(3) I:119. CSmH, DLC, ICN, InU-L, MH,
MiU-C, MnU-B, NN-RB, RPJCB; BL. 535/21

—[Anr edn]. *Milan: G. da Ponte, for J. A. da Borsano*, 1535. 40 lvs;illus.;4to. Reprinted from
preceding. Sabin 105722; Harrisse (BAV) 201;
Medina (BHA) 95n (I:144-145); Pogo (Conquista) H. InU-L, NN-RB; BL.   535/22

1536

Brant, Sebastian.   Le grand nauffrage des folz
qui sont en la nef d'insipience. *Paris: D. Janot*
[ca.1536?]. 52 lvs;illus.;4to. Abridged from
P. Rivière's 1497 translation of the Basel,
1494, *Narrenschiff*. BL, BN.   536/1

Brasavola, Antonio Musa.   Examen omnium
simplicium medicamentorum quorum in officinis usus est. *Rome: A. Blado*, 1536. 120
lvs;fol. Includes discussion of Guaiacum,
referring to Hispaniola as the source of
syphilis. Stillwell (Science) 317; Ind.aur.
123.773. CtY-M, ICJ, NNNAM; London:
Wellcome, BN.   536/2

Burchardus, de Monte Sion.   Descriptio terrae
sancta exactissima . . . De Novis insulis nuper
repertis . . . per Petrum Martyr. *Antwerp: J.
Grapheus, for J. Steels*, 1536. [96]p.;8vo. Includes Anghiera's *De nuper . . . repertis
insulis*, 1st publ., Basel, 1521. Sabin 8150;
Harrisse (BAV) 218; Medina (BHA) 100; Nij-
hoff/Kronenberg 500; Ind.aur.127.836; JCB
(3) I:119. DLC, ICN, NN-RB, RPJCB; BL,
Cologne: UB.   536/3

Flaminio, Giovanni Antonio.   Epistola ad
Paulum III. Pont. Max. *Bologna: V. Bonardo
& M. A. da Carpo*, 1536. [40]p.;4to. Includes
(lvs D2 ff.) letter describing Santa Cruz &
Nicaragua. Sabin 24663; Harrisse (BAV) 216
& Add. 110. InU-L, NN-RB, RPJCB; BL.
536/4

Fracastoro, Girolamo.   Syphilis, sive Morbus
gallicus. *Basel: J. Bebel*, 1536. [55]p.;8vo. 1st
publ., Verona, 1530. Harrisse (BAV) Add.
111; Baumgartner (Fracastoro) 4; Waller
3175. CtY-M, DNLM, NN-RB; BL, BN.
536/5

Gaguin, Robert.   La mer des cronicques et
mirouer hystorial de France . . . nouvellement
traduict . . . du latin . . . augmenté de
nouveau [par Pierre Desrey]. *Paris:
[J. Kerver?] a l'enseigne des deux cochetz rue
Sainct-Jacques*, 1536. cclvi lvs;fol. 1st publ.,
Paris, 1514, under title *Les grandes croniques*,
with ref. to American savages brought to
Rouen in 1509. BN.   536/6

—[Anr issue]. *Paris: [P. Sergent?] en la rue
neufve Nostre-Dame, à l'enseigne sainct
Nicolas*, 1536. BN.   536/7

—[Anr issue]. *Paris: [A. Girault] a la rue Sainct
Jacques au Pellican*, 1536. CSmH.   536/8

Gasser, Achilles Pirminius.   Historiarum et
chronicarum totius mundi epitome. *Antwerp:
J. Grapheus, for J. Steels*, 1536. 120p.;8vo. 1st
publ., Basel, 1532. Nijhoff/Kronenberg 955;
Burmeister (Gasser) 34. BL, BN.   536/9

Glareanus, Henricus.   De geographia liber
unus . . . tertio recognitus. *Freiburg i. Br.:
J. Faber*, 1536. 35p.;illus.;4to. 1st publ. in this

revision, Freiburg, 1533. Sabin 27451; Harrisse (BAV) 212; Sanz (Ult.ad.) 1195-1196. CtY, MnU-B, NN-RB. 536/10

Hutten, Ulrich von. Of the wood called Guaiacum, that healeth the French pockes. *London: T.Berthelet*, 1536. 82 numb.lvs;8vo. 1st publ., as translated by T. Paynell, under title *De morbo gallico*, London, 1533. Sabin 34096; STC 14025; Benzing (Hutten) 117. CSmH, NN-RB; BL. 536/11

Lettera de la nobil citta nuovamente ritrovata alle Indie con li suoi costumi & modi del suo re & soi popolo . . . Data in Zhaval. adi .xxv. di Settembre .M.D.XXXV. [*Florence?* 1536?]. 4 lvs;4to. 1st publ., [Rome, 1535?], with title *Letera de la nobil cipta* and dated 'Peru adi .xxv. de Novembre de .M.D.XXXIIII.' The city called 'Zhaval' has not been identified, and the work may well be fictitious. Sabin 40558; Harrisse (BAV) 206. BL. 536/12

Massa, Niccolò. Liber de morbo neapolitano. *Venice: F.Bindoni & M.Pasini*, 1536. 50 numb.lvs;4to. 1st publ., 1532. Stillwell (Science) 449. DNLM, ICU, InU-L, MBCo, MnU-B, NN-RB. 536/13

Maximilianus, Transylvanus. Il viaggio fatto da gli Spagniuoli a torno del mondo. [*Venice: L.Giunta*] 1536. [103]p.;4to. Transl. from author's *De Moluccis insulis*, Cologne, 1523, and, in an abridged version, Pigafetta's *Voyage et navigation*, Paris, ca. 1525. Sabin 47041 & 47042; Harrisse (BAV) 192 & 215; Borba de Moraes II:46-47; Church 74; JCB (3) I:120. CSmH, CtY, ICN, InU-L, MnU, NN-RB, RPJCB; BL, BN. 536/14

Monardes, Nicolás. Dialogo llamado Pharmacodilosis o declaracion medicinal. *Seville: J.Cromberger*, 1536. 8 lvs;fol. Comments unfavorably on medicinal herbs imported from New World, etc. Escudero (Seville) 379; Palau 17548; Guerra (Monardes) 1. Madrid: Facultad de Medecina. 536/15

Morbi gallici curandi ratio exquisitissima a variis . . . medicis conscripta: nempe Petro Andrea Matthaeolo . . . Joanne Almenar . . . Nicolo Massa . . . Nicolao Poll . . . Benedicto de Victoriis . . . His accessit Angeli Bolognini De ulcerum exteriorum medela opusculum . . . Eiusdem De unguentis ad cuiusvis generis maligna ulcera conficiendis lucubratio. *Basel: J.Bebel*, 1536. 299p.;4to. Ed.by Josephus Tectander, bringing together works earlier published separately. Adams (Cambr.) M913.

CtY-M, DNLM, NNNAM; BL. 536/16

—[Anr edn]. *Lyons: S.de Gabiano & Bro.*, 1536. 299p.;8vo. Baudrier (Lyons) VII:183-184. CtY-M, DNLM, InU-L, NN-RB, PPC; BL. 536/17

Prudentius Clemens, Aurelius. Opera . . . Aelii Antonii Nebrissensis commentariis . . . illustrata. *Antwerp: M.de Keyser*, 1536. 563p.;8vo. 1st publ., Logroño, 1512. Nijhoff/Kronenberg 1768; Adams (Cambr.) P2181. CSt, OrU; BL. 536/18

Ruel, Jean. De natura stirpium libri tres. *Paris: S.de Colines*, 1536. 884p.;fol. In bk 1, ch.45 discusses 'Hebenus' (Ebony), 'Guaiacum' & 'Bersilicum' (Brazil wood), describing syphilis as derived from islands where Guaiacum is found, i.e., the West Indies; in bk 2, ch.27 describes corn (maize). Renouard (de Colines) 267-268. DFo, MH, NNPM; BL, BN. 536/19

Trithemius, Johannes. Epistolarium familiarium libri duo. *Hagenau: P.Braubach*, 1536. 344p.;4to. In letter of 12 Aug. 1507, Trithemius mentions (p.296) purchase of global sphere and map, produced at Strassburg and ostensibly Waldseemüller's, depicting islands & regions newly discovered by Vespucci. Sabin 97006; Harrisse (BAV) 213; Sanz (Ult.ad.) 1197-1200; Adams (Cambr.) T976; Ritter (Strasbourg) 2361; Shaaber T354. CtY, ICN, MH, MiU, NN-RB, PU, RPJCB; BL, BN. 536/20

Vives, Juan Luis. De disciplinis libri xx. *Cologne: J.Gymnich*, 1536. 654p.;8vo. 1st publ., Antwerp, 1531. Adams (Cambr.) V947. NN-RB; Cambridge: UL, BN. 536/21

Ziegler, Jacob. Terrae sanctae . . . Syriae, Arabiae, AEgypti & Schondiae doctissima descriptio. *Strassburg: W.Rihel*, 1536. cxlii lvs;maps;fol. 1st publ., Strassburg, 1532. By 'Schondia' is meant Greenland & other northern regions. Sabin 106331; Harrisse (BAV) 217; Adams (Cambr.) Z154; Ritter (Strasbourg) 2526; JCB (3) I:121. MH, NN-RB, RPJCB; BL, Strasbourg: BN. 536/22

1537

Apianus, Petrus. Cosmographiae introductio. *Venice: F.Bindoni & M.Pasini*, 1537. 31 numb.lvs;illus.;8vo. 1st publ., Ingolstadt, 1532. Harrisse (BAV) Add. 133; Medina

(BHA) 102; Ortroy (Apian) 86; JCB AR34:25. CtY, DLC, ICN, MH, NN-RB, RPJCB. 537/1

____. De cosmographie . . . Enn hoemen de carten der lantscapen maect van Gemma Phrysio bescreven. *Antwerp: G.de Bonte,* 1537. lvi lvs;illus.,maps;4to. Transl. from author's *Cosmographiae introductio,* 1st publ., Ingolstadt, 1532. Nijhoff/Kronenberg 127; Ind.aur.106.425; Ortroy (Apian) 29; JCB (3) I:121. NN-RB,RPJCB. 537/2

Brasavola, Antonio Musa. Examen omnium simplicium medicamentorum quorum in officinis usus est. *Lyons: J.Barbou for J. & F.Frellon,* 1537. 542p.;8vo. 1st publ., Rome, 1536. Ind.aur.123.774; Baudrier (Lyons) V:9; Stillwell (Science) 317n. CSt-L, CtY, DNLM, MH-A, NNNAM; BL, BN. 537/3

Campani, Niccolò, called Lo Strascino. Lamento . . . sopra il male incognito . . . corretto et nuovamente ristampato. *Venice: F.Bindoni & M.Pasini,* 1537. [56]p.;8vo. 1st (?) publ., Venice, 1523. In verse. Ind. aur.130.753. DNLM; London: Wellcome. 537/4

Carion, Johann. Chronica . . . conversa ex germanico . . . à . . . Hermanno Bono. *Hall (Swabia): P.Brubach,* 1537. 308 numb.lvs; 8vo. The mutations of this chronology 1st publ. in German, Wittenberg, 1532, and later expanded by Melanchthon & Peucer as a medium for a Lutheran reinterpretation of history, and as widely translated, offer wide scope for the historiographer. Its American relevance is however confined to a brief ref. to Columbus & Vespucci under the year 1492, not found in all editions; we have confined ourselves to including those editions we have examined or those we may infer to contain this ref. Ind. aur.132.263; Adams (Cambr.) C705. NN-RB; BL, Berlin: StB. 537/5

__[Anr edn]. *Antwerp: J.Grapheus,for J.Steels,* 1537. 166 numb.lvs;8vo. Ind.aur.132.262; Nijhoff/Kronenberg 4205. Amsterdam:UB. 537/6

Catholic Church. Pope, 1534-1549 (Paul III). Bull, 1 June 1537. De baptizandis incolis Occidentalis et Meridionalis Indiae. *Rome:* 1537. bds.;fol. Medina (BHA) 101n; Streit I:39. BL. 537/7

Ferri, Alfonso. De ligni sancti multiplici medicina et vini exhibitione. *Rome: A.Blado,* 1537. [115]p.;4to. On medicinal use of Guaiacum. Harrisse (BAV) Add. 116; JCB

AR23:5-6. DNLM, MH, NN-RB, RPJCB; BL, BN. 537/8

Garcés, Julien, Bp of Tlaxcala. De habilitate et capacitate gentium, sive Indorum Novi mundi nuncupati ad fidem Christi capessendam, & quam libenter suscipiat. *Rome:* 1537. 8 lvs;4to. Harrisse (BAV) Add. 112; Medina (BHA) 101. RPJCB. 537/9

Gatinaria, Marco. Summi medici omnes, quos scripsit, libri [i.e., De curis aegritudinum totius corporis] . . . Sebastianum Aquilam De morbo gallico. *Basel: H.Petri* [1537]. 291p.;fol. 1st publ., Pavia, 1509. Adams (Cambr.) G283. CtY-M, DNLM, NNNAM; Cambridge: Gonville & Caius. 537/10

Giustiniani, Agostino, Bp of Nebbio. Castigatissimi annali . . . della eccelsa & illustrissima republi. di Genoa [ed. L. L. Sorba]. *Genoa: A.Bellone,* 1537. cclxii lvs;fol. On lf ccxlix is a ref. to Columbus. Sabin 27518; Harrisse (BAV) 220; Adams (Cambr.) G751; JCB (3) I:122. GtY, DLC, InU-L, MH, MiU-C, MnU-B, NN-RB, RPJCB; BL, BN. 537/11

Montesino, Ambrosio, Bp. Cancionéro de diversas obras. *Toledo: J.de Ayalá,* 1537. lxxxvii lvs;port.;4to. 1st publ., Toledo, 1508. Pérez Pastor (Toledo) 172; Palau 178945. NNH; Madrid: Bibl.Palacio. 537/12

__[Anr edn]. *Seville: D.de Robertis,* 1537. 4to. Escudero (Seville) 388; Palau 178944. BL. 537/13

Novus Orbis regionum. Novus Orbis regionum ac insularum veteribus incognitarum. *Basel: J.Herwagen,* 1537. 559p.;illus.,map;fol. 1st publ., Basel, 1532. Sabin 34103; Harrisse (BAV) 223; Burmeister (Münster) 62; Streit I:38; Adams (Cambr.) G1337; JCB (3) I:123. CtY, DLC, InU-L, MH, MiU-C, NN-RB, RPJCB; BL, BN. 537/14

Nunes, Pedro. Tratado da sphera com a theorica do sol e da lua, e ho primeiro livro da Geographia de Claudio Ptolomeu . . . Tirados novamente de latim . . . e acrecentados de muitas annotações e figuras . . .Item dous tratados . . . sobre a carta de marear. *Lisbon: G.Galharde,* 1537. 90 lvs;fol. Comprises new translations of Sacro Bosco's *Tractatus de sphera mundi* & other works, with refs to navigational problems respecting Brazil (lvs Blr & B7r). Sabin 56320; Harrisse (BAV) Add. 177; Borba de Moraes II:109; Anselmo 614; King Manuel 36; Church 76; JCB

AR37:9-12. CSmH, CtY, DLC, MH, RPJCB; Lisbon: BN.   537/15

Rangoni, Tommaso. Mali galeci. *Venice:* 1537. See the year 1538.

Ruel, Jean. De natura stirpium libri tres. *Basel: Froben Office,* 1537. 666p.;fol. 1st publ., Paris, 1536. Pritzel 7885n; Adams (Cambr.) R873; Moranti (Urbino) 2976. CtY-M, DNLM, ICJ, MH-A, NN-RB, PPC; BL, BN.   537/16

Sacro Bosco, Joannes de. Sphera volgare novamente tradotta, con molte notande additioni . . . auctore M. Mauro. *Venice: B.Zanetti,for J.Ortega de Carrion,at Florence,* 1537. [112]p.;illus.,maps;4to. Contains (twice) a woodcut globe on which America appears. Sabin 32677; Harrisse (BAV) 219; Mortimer (Italy) 452; Church 75; JCB (3) I:123-124. CSmH, CtY-M, IU, MH, MiU, MnU-B, NN-RB, RPJCB; BL.   537/17

—[Anr issue]. *Venice: B.Zanetti,for S.dei Nicolini da Sabbio,* 1537. Mortimer (Italy) 452n. Above locations may include this issue.
537/18

Vigo, Giovanni de. Libro, o Pratica en cirurgia . . . Traduzido de lengua latina en castellana por el doctor Miguel Juan Pascual. *Valencia:* 1537. 3pts;fol. Transl. from Vigo's *Practica in chirurgia,* 1st publ., Rome, 1514. Palau 364933. London: Wellcome, Madrid: BN.   537/19

Vives, Juan Luis. Ein gar schon . . . Büchlin in Latin ussgangen . . . wohar Eintrechechtikeit [!] und ouch Zwitracht, des die Welt voll ist komme unnd erwachse, vertütscht durch Leo Jud. *Basel: W.Friess,* 1537. 181 lvs;4to. Transl. from author's Antwerp, 1529, *De concordia & discordia.* Palau 371650. BN.   537/20

Vochs, Johann. Opusculum praeclara de omni pestilentia . . . & de diuturna peste morbi gallici . . . per Dryandrum novissime repurgatum. [*Cologne: E.Cervicornus?*] 1537. 125p.;8vo. 1st publ., Magdeburg, 1507, under title *De pestilentia anni presentis.* DNLM; BL.   537/21

1538

Berni, Francesco. Tutte le opere . . . in terza rima. *Venice: C.Navò & Bros,* 1538. 59 numb.lvs;8vo. Includes Berni's 'Capitolo

secondo de la peste' referring to syphilis. With this was issued, though bibliographically distinct, Giovanni dalla Casa's *Terze rime,* described below. Ind.aur.117.692. MH, RPB; BL, Vienna: BN.   538/1

Casa, Giovanni dalla, Abp. Le terze rime de messer Giovanni dalla Casa, di messer Bino et d'altri. *Venice: C.Navò & Bros,* 1538. 80 numb.lvs;8vo. Includes Giovanni Francesco Bini's 'Capitolo del mal francese'. Though issued with Francesco Berni's *Tutte le opere . . . in terza rima,* described above, bibliographically a distinct work. Ind. aur.117.692; cf.Proksch I:82. MH, RPB; BL, Vienna: NB.
538/2

Copia di una lettera di Sybilia [i.e., Sevilla] venuto al signor don Lope, imbasciatore cesareo in Venetia. [*Florence?* 1538]. 2 lvs;illus.;8vo. Dated at end, Seville, 8 Feb. 1538, & describing discoveries of gold in Peru by Diego de Almagro. Sabin 41966 & 63180; Harrisse (BAV) Add. 118; Sotheby cat.: 6/7 Dec. 1976, lot 270.   538/3

Estienne, Charles. Sylva. frutetum. collis. *Paris: F.Estienne,* 1538. 56 numb.lvs;8vo. In the 'Sylva', in section on Anarcardum (recto of lf 29), are refs to Brasil wood & Guaiacum. MBCo, MH, NNBG; BL.   538/4

Ferri, Alfonso. De ligni sancti multiplici medicina et vini exhibitione. *Basel: J.Bebel,* 1538. 201p.;8vo. 1st publ., Rome, 1537. DNLM, NN-RB; BL, BN.   538/5

Gasser, Achilles Pirminius. Historiarum et chronicarum totius mundi epitome. [*Strassburg: K.Müller (Mylius)*] 1538. 277p.; 8vo. 1st publ., Basel, 1532. Adams (Cambr.) G271; Burmeister (Gasser) 35. IU, InU-L, NN-RB; BL, Paris: Arsenal.   538/6

Glareanus, Henricus. De geographia liber unus ab . . . authore iam tertio recognitus. *Venice: G.A.dei Nicolini da Sabbio,for M.Sessa,* 1538. 39 numb.lvs;illus.;8vo. 1st publ. in this revision, 1533. Sabin 27542; Harrisse (BAV) 225 & Add. 120; JCB AR19:10-11. DLC, ICN, InU-L, MiU-C, NN-RB, RPJCB; BN.   538/7

Rangoni, Tommaso. Mali galeci [i.e., gallici] sanandi, vini ligni, & aquae. *Venice: G.A.dei Nicolini da Sabbio,* 1537 [i.e., 1538]. [67]p.;4to. DNLM.   538/8

—[Anr issue]. *Venice: G.A.dei Nicolini da Sabbio,* 1538. CtY-M, DNLM, NN-RB; BL.
538/9

Rithaymer, Georg. De orbis terrarum situ compendium. *Nuremberg: J.Petrejus*, 1538. 111p.;illus.;4to. 'De terris et insulis nuper repertis': p.111. Sabin 71582; Harrisse (BAV) Add. 119; JCB (3) I:124. CtY, DLC, NN-RB, RPJCB; BL, Strasbourg: BN.   538/10

Ruel, Jean. De natura stirpium libri tres. *Venice: G.A.dei Nicolini da Sabbio,for B.Bindoni,on behalf of G.B.Pederzano*, 1538. 3pts;8vo. 1st publ., Paris, 1536. Pritzel 7885n. DNLM; BL, BN.   538/11

Sabellico, Marco Antonio Coccio, called. Opera Rapsodiae historicae Enneadum xi . . . cum D.C. Hedionis historica synopsi. *Basel: J.Herwagen & J.E.Froben*, 1538. 2v.;fol. Brings the *Enneades* up to date; cf.earlier edns of 1504, etc. Sabin 74665; Harrisse (BAV) 224. DFo, MiU; BL, BN.   538/12

Vigo, Giovanni de. Opere. . .in chirurgia. *Lyons: J.Giunta*, 1538. 3pts;illus.;8vo. 1st publ., Rome, 1514. Baudrier (Lyons) VI:181-182. DNLM.   538/13

1539

Apianus, Petrus. Cosmographia, per Gemmam Phrysiam . . . restituta. *Antwerp: A. Coppens,for A.Birckmann*, 1539. lxi lvs;illus.;4to. 1st publ. in this version, Antwerp, 1529. On lf xxix is a diagr. with western hemisphere designated America; on lf xxxi, a passage of text relating to America. Sabin 1744; Harrisse (BAV) 229; Sanz (Ult. ad.) 1204-1207; Nijhoff/Kronenberg 125; Ind. aur.106.429; Ortroy (Apian) 30; Church 77; JCB (3) I:125. CSmH, MiU-C, MnU-B, RP-JCB; BL, BN.   539/1

Bock, Hieronymus. New Kreütter Buch von underscheydt, würckung und namen der kreütter so in teutschen landen wachsen. *Strassburg: W.Rihel*, 1539. 2pts; fol. Includes numerous refs to American plants. Pritzel 864; Nissen (Bot.) 182; Ind.aur.120.584; Stillwell (Science) 604; Ritter (Strasbourg) 211. DNLM, MH-A, NN-RB; Berlin: StB.   539/2

Brasavola, Antonio Musa. Examen omnium simplicium medicamentorum quorum in officinis usus est. *Venice: Comin da Trino,for A.Arrivabene*, 1539. 542p.;8vo. 1st publ., Rome, 1536. Ind.aur.123.779. CtY, DNLM, PPC; BL.   539/3

—[Anr issue]. *Venice: Off.Erasmiana* [i.e.,*V.Valgrisi*], 1539. MH-A.   539/4

Brunfels, Otto. Herbarium [Tomus I]. *Strassburg: J.Schott*, 1539. 266p.;illus.;fol. 1st publ., Strassburg, 1530. Ind. aur.125. 670;Nissen (Bot.) 257, Ic; Adams (Cambr.) B2926; Ritter (Strasbourg) 304. Cambridge: UL, Strasbourg: BN.   539/5

____. Kreüterbuch contrafeyt. *Strassburg: J. Schott*, 1539-40. 2v.;illus.;4to. 1st publ., Strassburg, 1532. Ind.aur.125.671; Nissen (Bot.) 260. MWelC; BL.   539/6

Carion, Johann. Chronicorum libellus . . . per Hermannum Bonum in latinum conversus. *Hall (Swabia): P.Brubach*, 1539. 259 numb.lvs;8vo. 1st publ., Hall, 1537. Ind. aur.132.270. BN.   539/7

Díaz de Isla, Ruy. Tractado contra el mal serpentino: que vulgarmente en España es llamado bubas. *Seville: D.de Robertis*, 1539. liii lvs;fol. Specifies Hispaniola as the source of syphilis. Harrisse (BAV) Add. 122; Medina (BHA) 104: Escudero (Seville) 401. CSmH, ICN, NNH; Madrid: BN.   539/8

Ferri, Alfonso. De ligni sancti multiplici medicina. *Paris: J.Foucher*, 1539. 201p.;16mo. 1st publ., Rome 1537. Baumgartner (Fracastoro) 5. DNLM.   539/9

Fries, Lorenz. Ein gruntlich und bestendig heilung Alter schäden . . . mit dem tranck des holtzes Guaiaco. *Strassburg: J.Prüss*, 1539. [16]p.;4to. 1st publ., Strassburg, 1525. Benzing (Fries) 20. Strasbourg: UB.   539/10

Gatinaria, Marco. De curis egritudinum particularium noni Almansoris practica uberrima . . . Sebastiani Aquilani Tractatus de morbo gallico celeberrimus. *Lyons: J.Flajollet,for J. Giunta*, 1539, xcv lvs;illus.;8vo.1st publ., Pavia, 1509. Baudrier (Lyons) VI:184 & XII:433. CtY, DNLM, ICU; London: Wellcome, BN.   539/11

Giambullari, Pietro Francesco. Apparato et feste nelle noze dello illustrissimo signor Duca di Firenze. *Florence: B.Giunta*, 1539. 171p.; 8vo. On p.13-14 are refs to Vespucci & his discoveries. Adams (Cambr.) G584; Shaaber G163. DFo, MH, NIC, PU, WU; BL, BN.   539/12

Glareanus, Henricus. De geographia liber unus . . . novissime recognitus. *Freiburg i.Br.: J.Faber*, 1539. 35 numb.lvs;illus.;4to. 1st publ. in this revision, Freiburg, 1533. Sabin 27548; Harrisse (BAV) 228. DLC, ICN, NN-RB, RPJCB; BL, BN.   539/13

__[Anr edn]. *Venice: G.A.dei Nicolini da Sabbio*, 1539. 35 lvs;illus.,map;4to. Cf. printer's 1538 edn. BN.   539/14

Goes, Damião de. Avisi de le case fatte da Portuguesi ne l'India di quà del Gange. *Venice:* 1539. 24 lvs;8vo. Transl. by G. Palus from the following *Commentarii.* BL,BN.   539/15

____. Commentarii rerum gestarum in India citra Gagem a Lusitanis. *Louvain: R.Rescius*, 1539. [43]p.;4to. On lf E3r is a ref. to Portuguese colonization of Brazil. Borba de Moraes I:302; Nijhoff/Kronenberg 678; Adams (Cambr.) G819. ICN, MH, MnU-B, NN-RB; BL.   539/16

Hutten, Ulrich von. Of the wood called Guaiacum, that healeth the French pockes. *London: T.Berthelet*, 1539. 82 numb.lvs;8vo. 1st publ., under title *De morbo gallico*, London, 1533, as transl. by T.Paynell. Cf.Sabin 34096; STC 14026; Benzing (Hutten) 118. DNLM, NN-RB; BL.   539/17

Lettera dela nobil citta nuovamente ritrovata alle Indie con li suoi costumi & modi del suo re & soi popoli. [*Florence?* 1539?]. 2 lvs;4to. 1st publ., [1535?] under title *Letera de la nobil cipta.* Dated at end 'xxx di Settembre M.D.XXXIX', the text is otherwise identical with that of an edn dated '.xxv. de Novembre. de .MDXXXIIII' & another of '.xxv. di Settembre .M.D.XXXV', described above under the years 1535 & 1536. Purporting to describe a city named Zhaval, otherwise unidentified, this is probably a work of fiction. Sabin 40559; Harrisse (BAV) 227. NN-RB.   539/18

Lucidarius. Eyn newer M.Lucidarius, von allerhandt geschöpffen Gottes . . . und wie alle Creaturen geschaffen seint auff erden. *Strassburg: J.Cammerlander* [ca.1539]. [80]p.;illus.;4to. 1st publ., Strassburg, [ca.1535]. Schorbach (Lucidarius) 31. MB; Bamberg: StB.   539/19

Marineo, Lucio, Siculo. Obra . . . de las cosas memorables de España. *Alcalá de Henares: J.de Brocar*, 1539. 192 numb.lvs;fol. 1st publ., Alcalá de Henares, 1530. Sabin 44586; Harrisse (BAV) 226; Sanz (Ult.ad.) 1208-1212; Medina (BHA) 103; García (Alcalá de Henares) 167. DLC, ICU, InU-L, MH, MiU-C, NNH, RPJCB; BL, BN. 539/20

Le triumphe de tres haulte et puissante dame Verolle, royne du puy d'amours. *Lyons: F.*

Juste, 1539. 40 lvs;8vo. In verse. LeMoine 111; Baudrier (Lyons) Suppl. 108. BN.   539/21

1540

Albergati, Vianesio. La pazzia. [*Bologna?*] 1540. [42]p.;8vo. Includes comparison of New World natives with citizens of Plato's Republic. Ind.aur.102.237. Berlin: StB.   540/1

Apianus, Petrus. Cosmographia, per Gemmam Phrysium . . . denuo restituta. *Antwerp: A.Coppens,for A.Birckmann*, 1540. lxi lvs; map;4to. 1st publ. in this version, Antwerp, 1529. Sabin 1745; Harrisse (BAV) 230; Sanz (Ult. ad.) 1213-1214; Nijhoff/Kronenberg 126; Ind.aur.106.430; Ortroy (Apian) 31 (cf.32); Fairfax Murray (Germany) 40; Church 78; JCB (3) I:125. CSmH, ICN, MH, NN-RB, RPJCB; BL, BN.   540/2

Baptista Mantuanus. De sacris diebus. *Milan: F.M.Calvo*, 1540. 238p.;8vo. 1st publ., Lyons, 1516, under title *Fastorum libri.* Ind. aur.112.748; Coccia 392. IU, MH, MiU; BL.
540/3

Berni, Francesco. Tutte le opere . . . in terza rima. [*Venice?*], 1540. 2v.;8vo. 1st publ., Venice, 1538. Includes both Berni's 'Capitolo secondo de la peste' & also G.F.Bini's 'Capitolo del mal francese'. Cf.Proksch I:82; Ind. aur.117.693; Adams (Cambr.) B753; Shaaber B260. PU; BL, Vienna: NB.   540/4

Bordone, Benedetto. Isolario . . . nel qual si ragiona di tutte le isole del mondo . . . Ricorretto et di nuova ristampata con la gionta del Monte del Oro nuovamente ritrovato. *Venice: F.de Leno* [ca.1540?]. lxxiiii lvs;illus.,maps; fol. 1st publ., Venice, 1528. Sabin 6420; Harrisse (BAV) 221; Ind.aur.122.346; Adams (Cambr.) B2483; JCB (3) I:122. DLC, ICN, MnU, NN-RB, RPJCB; BL, BN.   540/5

Carion, Johann. Chronica . . . ex lingua germanica . . . ab Hermanno Bono . . . transfusa. *Antwerp: J.Grapheus,for J.Steels*, 1540. 168 numb.lvs;8vo. 1st publ., Hall (Swabia), 1537. Ind.aur.132.271. Brussels:BR.   540/6

Erasmus, Desiderius. Omnia opera. *Basel: Froben Office*, 1540[-42]. 9v.;fol. Included in v.5 is the author's *De bello Turcis inferendo*, 1st publ., Antwerp, 1530. Adams (Cambr.) E309. CU, CtY, DFo, MH, MiU, MnU, NNUT; BL.   540/7

Ferri, Alfonso. De l'administration du sainct-boys . . . trad. . . . par . . . Nicoles Michel. *Poitiers: J.& E.de Marnef*, 1540. 219p.;8vo. Transl. from author's Rome, 1537, *De ligni sancti*. Harrisse (BAV) Add. 129; Church 79. CSmH; BN. 540/8

Foresti, Jacopo Filippo, da Bergamo. Supplemento delle chroniche . . . novamente revisto, vulgarizato, corretto, & emendata . . . insino a tutto l'anno MDXXXIX. *Venice: B.Bindoni [for M.Sessa]*, 7 May 1540. ccclxxxix lvs;fol. Includes supplementary material to year 1540. Chapter on America: lvs cccxxxii-cccxxxiii. Shaaber F356. DFo, ICN, InU-L, NN-RB, PU; BL. 540/9

__[Anr issue]. *Venice: B.Bindoni [for M.Sessa]*, 29 May 1540. From same setting of type as 7 May issue save for final 2 lvs. NN-RB; BL. 540/10

Gallo, Antonio. De ligno sancto non permiscendo. *Paris: S.de Colines*, 1540. 116 numb. lvs;8vo. Renouard (de Colines) 330. DNLM, ICN, NN-RB; BL, BN. 540/11

Gasser, Achilles Pirminius. Historiarum et chronicarum totius mundi epitome. *Venice: G.A.dei Nicolini da Sabbio,for M.Sessa*, 1540. 60 numb.lvs;8vo. 1st publ.,Basel, 1532. Burmeister (Gasser) 36. CtY, InU-L, NN-RB; BL. 540/12

Goes, Damião de. Fides, religio, moresque Aethiopum. *Louvain: R.Rescius*, 1540. [103]p.;4to. On verso of lf A4 is a ref. to Columbus & his voyages. Sabin 27690n; Nijhoff/Kronenberg 679; Adams (Cambr.) G819[A]. ICN, MH, NN-RB; BL. 540/13

Guazzo, Marco. Historie di tutte le cose degne di memoria quai del anno .M.D.XXIIII. sino questo presente sono occorse. *Venice: N.Zoppino*, 1540. 215 numb.lvs;port.;4to. Continues J.F. Foresti's *Supplementum supplementi de le Croniche*, & its anonymous continuation of 1524. On lvs 103v-104r is an account of Pizarro's 1533 conquest of Peru. Harrisse (BAV) Add. 124; Mortimer (Italy) 227; Adams (Cambr.) G1452. InU-L, MH, MiU-C, NN-RB, RPJCB; BL. 540/14

Hutten, Ulrich von. Of the wood called Guaiacum, that healeth the French pockes. *London: T.Berthelet*, 1540. 58 numb.lvs;4to. 1st publ., London, 1533, as transl. by Paynell, under title *De morbo gallico*. Sabin 34097; STC 14027; Benzing (Hutten) 119. CSmH, CtY-M, InU-L, NNNAM; BL. 540/15

Lucidarius. M.Elucidarius von allerhandt geschöpffen Gottes, den Engeln den Himeln, Gestirns, Planeten, unnd wie alle Creaturen geschaffend sein auff erden. *Augsburg: H. Steiner*, 1540. [79]p.;illus.;4to. 1st publ., Strassburg, [ca.1535]. Schorbach (Lucidarius) 49. BL, Munich: UB. 540/16

__[Anr edn]. *Augsburg: H.Steiner*, 1540. [79]p.;illus.;4to. In the title the reading 'geschaffen seint' appears. Schorbach (Lucidarius) 50. Heidelberg: UB. 540/17

Malo de Briones, Juan. De los hombres monstruosos de las Indias. *Valencia*: 1540. fol. Medina (BHA) 109. 540/18

Manardo, Giovanni. Epistolarum medicinalium libros xx. *Basel: M.Isengrin*, 1540. 603p.;fol. Includes Manardo's *De erroribus Symonis Pistoris . . . circa morbum gallicum*, 1st publ., [Leipzig?] 1500. Adams (Cambr.) M316. DNLM, NN-RB; BL, BN. 540/19

Mela, Pomponius. De orbis situ libri tres, accuratissimi emendati, una cum commentariis Joachimi Vadiani . . . castagatioribus, & multis in locis auctioribus factis. *Paris: C.Wechel*, 1540. 196p.;map;fol. 1st publ. in this version, Basel, 1522. At end are 36 unnumbered lvs., with part title 'Loca aliquot', which include Vadianus's letter to R. Agricola (1st publ., 1518, in the latter's *Ad Joachimum Vadianum epistola*), with, on verso of 25th lf, a mention of America. The world map, based on that prepared by Oronce Finé for the 1532, Paris, edn of the *Novus orbis regionum*, here appears with caption 'Christianus Wechelus lectori' and dated 'sub scuto Basiliensi, M.D.XL' (in some copies 'M.D. XLI'). Sabin's implication that the map was intended for this issue alone is not supported by evidence of copies seen. Sabin 63960; Harrisse (BAV) Add. 127. CtY, ICN, MH, MnU-B, NN-RB; BL, BN. 540/20

__[Anr. issue, with altered printer's device & imprint]. *Paris: J.Roigny*, 1540. 196p.;map;fol. Sabin 63959; Harrisse (BAV) Add. 126; JCB (3) I:126. ICN, MH, MiU-C, MnU-B, NN-RB, RPJCB; BN. 540/21

Ptolemaeus, Claudius. Geographia universalis, vetus et nova complectens . . . libros viii. Quorum primus nova translatione Pirckheimeri . . . redditus est . . . Succedunt Tabulae Ptolemaece, opera Sebastiani Munsteri novo paratae modo. *Basel: H.Petri*, 1540. 195p.; maps;fol. Contains Münster's significant revisions & new maps, of which 3 relate to America. Sabin 66484; Harrisse (BAV) 231; Sanz (Ult.ad.) 1215-1220; Stevens (Ptolemy) 48; Phillips (Atlases) 365; Burmeister (Münster) 166; JCB (3) I;127. CtY, DLC, NN-RB, RP-JCB; BL, BN. 540/22

Ryd, Valerius Anshelmus. Catalogus annorum et principum . . . in praesentem annum continuatus. *Berne: M.Apiarius,* 1540. lxviii lvs;illus.;fol. Ref. to America on lf lx. Adams (Cambr.) R984; Shaaber R388. CLU, DLC, ICN, MnU-B, PU; BL. 540/23

Spain. Laws, statutes, etc. Las pragmaticas del reyno. *Valladolid: J.de Villaquirán,* 1540. ccxxvi lvs;fol. 1st publ., Alcalá de Henares, 1503. On verso of lf cxiii is edict of Ferdinand & Isabella of 22 June 1497 commuting sentences of convicts willing to work in Hispaniola mines. Sabin 64915n; Harrisse (BAV) Add. 131; Medina (BHA) 108 & VII:313; Alcocer (Valladolid) 98; JCB (3) I:128. RPJCB; Madrid: BN. 540/24

Stamler, Joannes. Dialogo . . . de le sette diverse genti, e de le religioni del mondo. *Venice: [Comin da Trino] for G.Padovano* [1540?]. 151p.;16mo. Transl. from author's *Dyalogus,* 1st publ., Augsburg, 1508. Ref. to America is on p.3. Sabin 90128; Harrisse (BAV) 52. NN-RB; BL, BN. 540/25

Sylvius, Petrus. Tfundament der medicinen ende chyrurgien. *Antwerp: W.Vorsterman,* 1540. clxii lvs;illus.;fol. Includes, lvs lxxxv-xciii, in Dutch translation, Giovanni de Vigo's *De morbo gallico tractatus,* 1st publ., Rome, 1514, in his *Practica in chirurgia.* Nijhoff/Kronenberg 1952. DNLM; Louvain: UB. 540/26

Venegas de Busto, Alejo. Primera parte de las diferencias de libros que ay en el universo. *Toledo: J.de Ayalá,* 1540. ccxl lvs;illus.;4to. Refs to America, Columbus, etc., appear on lvs lxi (r-v), lxv(v)-lxvi(v), lxxii(r) & lxxix(v). Sabin 98501; Harrisse (BAV) Add. 130; Medina (BHA) 107; Pérez Pastor (Toledo) 187. NN-RB, RPJCB; BN. 540/27

1541

Albergati, Vianesio. La pazzia. *[Bologna?]* 1541. [48]p.;8vo. 1st publ. in dated edn, [Bologna?] 1540, the West Indian refs here appearing on lf C3v. Ind.aur.102.238. RPJCB; Berlin: StB. 541/1

—[Anr edn]. *Venice: G.A.& F.Valvassori,* 1541. [48]p.;8vo. Ind. aur.102.239. Munich: StB. 541/2

Alfonso X, el Sabio, King of Castile and Leon. Las quatro partes enteras dela Cronica de España . . . vista y emendada . . . por . . . Florian Docampo. *Zamora: A.de Paz & J.Picardo,for J.de Spinosa of Medina,* 1541. ccccxxvii lvs;fol. The earliest edn as ed. by Ocampo. Chapt.xix contains ref. to Spanish exploration of New World. Sabin 56618; Medina (BHA) 113; JCB AR20:1541. DLC, ICN, MH, MiU, NNH, RPJCB; BL, BN. 541/3

Ferri, Alfonso. New erfundene heylsame, und bewärte Artzney, gewisse Hilff unnd Radt, nit allein die frantzosen oder bösen Blatern, sunder auch andere sorgliche schwere Kranckheyt . . . Gebrauch und Würckung des indianischen Holtz Guaiacum . . . Durch m. Gualtherum H. Ryff . . . verfasst. *[Strassburg: B.Beck]* 1541. [227]p.;illus.;8vo. Transl. from Ferri's *De ligni sancti,* 1st publ., Rome, 1537. Benzing (Ryff) 109. DNLM, NN-RB. 541/4

Fregoso, Battista. De dictis & factis memorabilibus. *Basel: B.Westheimer,* 1541. 8vo. 1st publ., Milan, 1509. ICN, NNC; BL. 541/5

Fusch, Remaclus. Morbi hispanici quem alii gallicum, alii neapolitanum appellant, curandi per ligni indici, quod guayacum vulgo dicitur, decoctum. *Paris: C.Wechel,* 1541. 80p.;4to. DNLM; BL. 541/6

Goes, Damião de. Fides, religio, moresque Aethiopum. *Paris: C.Wechel,* 1541. 95p.;8vo. 1st publ., Louvain, 1540. Adams (Cambr.) G820. CU-S, ICN, MH, NN-RB; BL, BN. 541/7

Honter, Johannes. Rudimenta cosmographica. *Kronstadt* [now Stalin, Rumania]: *J. Honter,* 1541. 46 lvs;maps;8vo. 1st publ., Cracow, 1530. In verse. Vienna: NB. 541/8

Ptolemaeus, Claudius. Geographicae enarrationis, libri octo. Ex Bilibaldi Pirckeymheri tralatione sed . . . à Michaële Villanovano [i.e., Serveto] . . . castigati. *Vienne (France): G.Trechsel, for H.de LaPorte,at Lyons,* 1541. 149p.;50maps;fol. 1st publ. in this version, Lyons, 1535. Maps 28, 34, 49 & 50 relate to America, with text on Columbus on verso of no.28. Sabin 66485; Harrisse (BAV) 233; Sanz (Ult.ad.) 1249-51; Benzing (Fries) 54; Stevens (Ptolemy) 49; Phillips (Atlases) 366; JCB (3) I:129. CtY, DLC, ICN, InU-L, MH, MiU-C, MnU-B, NN-RB, RPJCB; BL, BN. 541/9

Ribaldus, Petrus, Peruanus, pseud. Satyrarum liber prior, et Reinoldi Guisco de Goa Americani elegiarum et epigrammatum cum miscellaneis liber posterior, Indiarum Occident. poetarum cum Rubeo Ense. *Utopia*: *R.Arabalida*, MM.DD.XL.IoI. 4to. Actual place of printing unknown. Sabin 70787; Weller (Falsch.& fing.Druckorte) I:244. 541/10

1542

Berni, Francesco. Tutte le opere . . . in terza rima. [*Venice: B.Zanetti*, 1542]. 3pts;8vo. 1st publ., Venice, 1538. Includes both Berni's 'Capitolo secondo de la peste' & G.F.Bini's 'Capitolo del mal francese'. Cf.Proksch I:82; Ind.aur.117.698 (& 117.699). DLC; BL, BN. 542/1

Biondo, Michelangelo. De partibus ictu sectis citissime sanandis . . . Idem . . . De origine morbi gallici deque ligni Indici ancipiti proprietate. *Venice: G.A.& P.dei Nicolini da Sabbio*, 1542. [95]p.;8vo. Ind.aur.119.486. DNLM; BL, Oslo: UB. 542/2

Boemus, Johann. Omnium gentium mores, leges & ritus . . . Praeterea, Epistola Maximiliani Transylvani . . . de Moluccis insulis. *Antwerp: J.Steels*, 1542. 123 numb.lvs;8vo. The earliest edn to contain American material. In addition to Maximilianus Transylvanus's *De Moluccis insulis*, 1st publ., Cologne, 1523, includes also Jacob Ziegler's 'De regionibus septentrionalibus', 1st publ. Strassburg, 1532. Sabin 106330n; Harrisse (BAV) Add. 136; Ind.aur.120.941; Palau 31246; JCB (3) I:130. MH, MnU-B, NN-RB, RPJCB; Brussels: BR. 542/3

__[Anr edn]. *Venice: G.A.& P.dei Nicolini da Sabbio*, 1542. 294p.;12mo. Ind.aur.120.943; Adams (Cambr.) B2267; Moranti (Urbano) 615. RPJCB; Cambridge: UL, Nuremberg: StB. 542/4

Bolognini, Angelo. Livre . . . de la curation des ulceres exterieures, traduit de latin. *Paris: O.Mallard*, 1542. 32 lvs;8vo. Transl. from author's *Libellus de cura ulcerum*, 1st publ., Venice, 1506, but here from Bologna, 1514, text. Ind.aur.121.502. DNLM; BN. 542/5

Díaz de´Isla, Ruy. Tractado llamado fructo de todos los sanctos contra el mal serpentino. *Seville: A.de Burgos*, 1542. lxxxii lvs;fol. 1st publ., Seville, 1539. Sabin 106219; Harrisse

(BAV) Add. 137; Medina (BHA) 115; Escudero (Seville) 431; Waller 2432. NNH; Madrid: BN, Uppsala: UB. 542/6

Ferri, Alfonso. De ligni sancti multiplici medicina . . . Nunc primum additus est Hieronymi Fracastori Syphilis. *Paris: J. Foucher*, 1542. 2 pts;16mo. 1st publ., Rome, 1537; Fracastoro's *Syphilis* 1st publ., Verona, 1530. NN-RB. 542/7

__[Anr issue]. *Paris: V.Gaultherot*, 1542. Adams (Cambr.) F309; Baumgartner (Fracastoro) 8. CtY-M, NcD-M; Cambridge: UL, BN. 542/8

Franck, Sebastian. Weltbüch, Spiegel und bildtnis des gantzen Erdtbodens . . . nämlich in Asiam, Aphricam, Europam und Americam. [*Tübingen: U.Morhart*] 1542. ccxxxvii lvs;fol. 1st publ., Tübingen, 1534. Sabin 25469; Harrisse (BAV) 238; Adams (Cambr.) F946; JCB (3) I:181. MiU-C, NN-RB, RPJCB; BL, Strasbourg: BN. 542/9

Fuchs, Leonhard. De historia stirpium commentarii insignes. *Basel: M.Isengrin*, 1542. 896p.;illus.,ports;fol. Includes accounts of American plants: Tagetes (marigold), Siliquastrum (pimento) & Turcico frumento (maize). Pritzel 3138; Nissen (Bot.) 658; Fairfax Murray (Germany) 175; Hunt (Bot.) 48. CSt, CtY-M, DLC, ICN, MH, MnU-B, NN-RB, PPL, RPB; BL, BN. 542/10

Gatinaria, Marco. De curis aegritudinum particularium noni Almansoris practica uberrima . . . Sebastiani Aquilani Tractatus de morbo gallico celeberrimus. *Lyons: G.& J. Huguetan*, 1542. 132 numb.lvs;8vo. 1st publ., Pavia, 1509. Baudrier (Lyons) XI:326. DNLM. 542/11

Glareanus, Henricus. Brevissima totius habitabilis terrae descriptio. *Paris: C. Wechel*, 1542. [40]p.;4to. 1st publ. in this version, Freiburg i.Br., 1533, under title *De geographia*. The final chapt. describes America & its discoverers. DLC, MnU-B. 542/12

____. De geographia liber unus, ab ipso authore iam novissime recognitus. *Paris: J.Loys*, 1542. 35 numb.lvs;map;4to. 1st publ. in this version, Freiburg, 1533. Adams (Cambr.) G760. NN-RB; Cambridge: Corpus Christi. 542/13

__[Anr issue]. *Paris: J.Loys,for G.Richard*, 1542. Adams (Cambr.) G759. Cambridge: Peterhouse, BN. 542/14

Goes, Damião de. Hispania. *Louvain: R. Rescius*, 1542. [59]p.;4to. Refs to Cortés &

Pizarro appear on lf E3v, to Brazil on G5r-
G6r. Sabin 27689; Harrisse (BAV) Add. 141;
Borba de Moraes I:302. DLC, MH, MnU-B,
NNH; BL, BN.   542/15

Honter, Johannes. Rudimenta cosmographica. *Kronstadt* [now Stalin, Rumania]: *J.
Honter*, 1542. 46 lvs;maps;8vo. 1st publ., Cracow, 1530, under title *Rudimentorum cosmographiae libri duo.* In verse. JCB AR25:10.
RPJCB.   542/16

_[Anr edn]. *Breslau:* 1542. Reprinted from
Kronstadt, 1541, edn. Borsa 94-95; Szabo
III:338. Budapest:OSK.   542/17

Manardo, Giovanni. Epistolarum medicinalium lib. xx. *Venice: P.Schoeffer*, 1542.
469p.;fol. Includes Manardo's *De erroribus
Symonis Pistoris . . . circa morbum gallicum*,
1st publ., [Leipzig?], 1500. Adams (Cambr.)
M317. CtY-M, DNLM, MiU, NN-RB, PPC;
BL.   542/18

Muñon, Sancho de. Tragicomedia de Lysandro y Rosellia. *Salamanca: J.de Junta*, 1542.
106 lvs;4to. Includes ref. to American parrot
'rasura del ara'. Palau 14442.   542/19

_[Anr edn]. [*Madrid:*] 1542. 281 lvs;4to. Palau
14443.   542/20

Núñez Cabeza de Vaca, Alvar. La relacion
que dio Alvar Nuñez Cabeça de Vaca de lo
acaesido enlas Indias enla armada donde y va
por governador Pamphilo de Narbaez, desde
el año de veynte y siete hasta el año d'treynta y seys. *Zamora: A.de Paz & J.Picardo,for J.
P.Musetti,at Medina del Campo*, 1542. 68
lvs;4to. Sabin 9767; Harrisse (BAV) 239; Medina (BHA) 114; Wagner (SW) 1; Vail (Frontier) 1; Streit II:465; JCB AR30:19-23. NN-
RB, RPJCB; BL.   542/21

Ptolemaeus, Claudius. Geographia universalis, vetus & nova . . . Succedunt tabulae ptolemaicae, opera Sebastiani Munster novo
paratae modo. *Basel: H.Petri*, 1542.
195p.;maps;fol. 1st publ. in this version,
Basel, 1540. Sabin 66486; Harrisse (BAV)
233; Sanz (Ult.ad.) 1252-1254; Stevens
(Ptolemy) 49; Phillips (Atlases) 367; Burmeister (Münster) 167; JCB (3) I:132. CSmH,
DLC, InU-L, MnU-B, NN-RB, RPJCB; BL,
BN.   542/22

Rodríguez, Juan. Relacion cierta y verdadera, sacada y traslada de una carta que a esta
cibdad de Sevilla fue embiada sobre la terrible
y tempestuosa tormenta que sucedio en la cibdad de Guatimala . . . a diez dias del mes de

setiembre del año passado de mil y quinientos y quaranta y uno. [*Seville?* 1542].
[7]p.;4to. Medina (BHA) 117; Palau 257157.
Madrid: Private collection (1898).   542/23

_[Anr edn]. Relacion del espantable terremoto
que agora nuevamente ha acontescido en las
Yndias en la ciudad llamada Guatimala.
[*Medina del Campo: P.de Castro*, 1542?].
[8]p.;4to. Imprint deduced from printer's device. Medina (BHA) 112; Pérez Pastor (Medina del Campo) 24; Palau 257158. The Escorial.   542/24

_[Anr edn of preceding]. [*Valladolid? J.de Vil-
laquirán?* 1542?]. [7]p.;4to. Type & initial on
p.[2] permit tentative attribution to printer.
Harrisse (BAV) Add. 134; Medina (BHA)
111; Palau 257159. MH.   542/25

Vigo, Giovanni de. La practique et cirurgie.
Paris: O.Petit, 1542. 505 numb.lvs;8vo. 1st
publ. in this translation by N. Godin, Lyons,
1525. DNLM.   542/26

_[Anr issue]. *Paris: M.de La Porte*, 1542.
DNLM.   542/27

1543

Albergati, Vianesio. La pazzia. *Venice: G.A.
& Florio Valvassori*, 1543. [47]p.;8vo. 1st dated
edn, Bologna, 1540. Ind.aur.102.239. DFo,
NN-RB, RPJCB.   543/1

**Alfonso X, el Sabio, King of Castile and
Leon.** Los quatro libros primeros de la
Cronica general de España. *Zamora: J.Picar-
do,for J.P.Musetti,at Medina del Campo*,
1543. ccxxxv lvs;fol. 1st publ., Zamora, 1541.
Authorship frequently ascribed to its editor,
Florián de Ocampo. Sabin 56620; Harrisse
(BAV) 242; Medina (BHA) 118. CtY, DCU,
ICU, MH, NN-RB, RPJCB; BL.   543/2

Copernicus, Nicolaus. De revolutionibus orbium coelestium, libri vi. *Nuremberg: J.Petre-
jus*, 1543. 196 numb.lvs;illus.;fol. In bk I,
chapt.iii, ref. is made to the newly found islands of the New World. Sabin 16662; Harrisse (BAV) 241; Stillwell (Science) 47. CtY,
DLC, InU-L, MH, MiU, RPB; BL, BN. 543/3

Dionysius, Periegetes. De situ habitabilis orbis, a Simone Lemnio . . . nuper latinus. *Venice: B.& F.Imperadore*, 1543. 40 lvs;illus.;
4to. Cf.1508 & 1534 versions. Title illustration
contains figure of globes, one labelled America. Sabin 20211; Harrisse (BAV) 245; Adams

(Cambr.) D650. CtY, DLC, MB, MnU-B, NN-RB, RPJCB; BL, BN.   543/4

Dioscorides, Pedanius. De medicinali materia libri sex, Joanne Ruellio . . . interprete . . . Additis etiam annotationibus . . . per Gualtherum H. Ryff. *Marburg: C.Egenolff,for C.Egenolff,at Frankfurt a.M.*, 1543. 2pts;illus.;fol. Includes discussion of Guaiacum. Pritzel 2307; Nissen (Bot.) 496. CtY-M, DNLM, MH, MiU, MnU-B, PPC; BL.   543/5

Ferri, Alfonso. De ligni sancti multiplici medicina . . . Nunc primum additus est Hieronymi Fracastori Syphilis. *Paris: J. Foucher*, 1543. 2pts;16mo. 1st publ., Rome, 1537; Fracastoro's *Syphilis*, 1st publ., 1530. A reissue of printer's 1542 edn with altered imprint date. NN-RB.   543/6

—[Anr issue]. *Paris: V.Gaultherot*, 1543. Baumgartner (Fracastoro) 8a. As with preceding, a reissue of 1542 edn. DNLM, NN-RB.   543/7

Fuchs, Leonhart. De historia stirpium commentarii insignes. *Paris: J.Bogard*, 1543. 368 numb.lvs;8vo. 1st publ., Basel, 1542. Cf. Pritzel 3138n. BN.   543/8

—[Anr issue]. *Paris: J.Gazeau*, 1543. CtY, DNLM, MH-A, MiU, PPJ, RPB; BN. 543/9

____. New kreüterbuch. *Basel: M.Isengrin*, 1543. 680p.;illus.,ports.;fol. Transl. from printer's 1542 Latin edn of Fuchs's *De Historia stirpium*. Pritzel 3139; Nissen (Bot.) 659; Adams (Cambr.) F1107. CLU-M, DLC, NNBG; BL.   543/10

Glareanus, Henricus. De geographia liber unus, ab ipso authore iam novissime recognitus. *Freiburg i.Br.: S.M.Graf*, 1543. 36 lvs;illus.;4to. 1st publ. in this revision, Freiburg, 1533. Sabin 27544. CtY-M, ICN, RPJCB.   543/11

Isla, Alonso de la. Libro llamado Thesoro de virtu. *Medina del Campo: P.de Castro*, 1543. cxxxv lvs;4to. Includes 1st Spanish translation of António de Olave's *Passio . . . Andree de Spoleto* of 1532, incorporating letters of Martin de Valencia & Juan de Zumárraga regarding Franciscan missions in Yucatan & Mexico. Sabin 40960; Harrisse (BAV) 243; Medina (BHA) 119; Streit II:474; Pérez Pastor (Medina del Campo) 34; JCB (3) I:133. ICN, MH, NNH, RPJCB.   543/12

Lucidarius. M. Elucidarius, von allerhandt geschöpffen Gottes . . . und wie alle Creaturen geschaffen seind auff erden. *Augsburg: H.Steiner*, 1543. [79]p.;illus.;4to. 1st publ.,

Strassburg, [ca.1535]. Baginsky (German Americana) 64; Schorbach (Lucidarius) 51. NN-RB; BL, Munich: StB.   543/13

Maurolico, Francesco. Cosmographia . . . in tres dialogos distincta. *Venice: Heirs of L.Giunta*, 1543. 103 numb.lvs;illus.;4to. Refs to Vespucci, Columbus & the New World appear on lvs 18v, 34v & 63v. Sabin 46957; Harrisse (BAV) Add. 142; Stillwell (Science) 79; JCB (3) I:133. CSmH, DLC, ICN, InU-L, MH, MiU-C, NN-RB, RPJCB; BL, BN.   543/14

Postel, Guillaume. Quatuor librorum de orbis terrae concordia. [*Paris:*] *P.Gromors* [1543?]. 143 numb.lvs;8vo. Adams (Cambr.) P2031. ICU, InU-L, MH; Cambridge: UL, BN.   543/15

Ruel, Jean. De natura stirpium libri tres. *Basel: Froben Office*, 1543. 666p.;fol. 1st publ., Paris, 1536. Pritzel 7885n; Adams (Cambr.) R874. DLC, ICJ, MH-A, MnU-B; Cambridge: UL, BN.   543/16

Sacro Bosco, Joannes de. Trattato della sfera . . . raccolto da Giovanni di Sacrobusto e altri astronomi . . . & tradotto . . . per Antonio Brucioli. *Venice: F.Brucioli & Bros*, 1543. 24 numb.lvs;illus.;4to. On lf 24r a woodcut globe depicts America. Sabin 32678 & 74810; Harrisse (BAV) p.390n; Sanz (Ult.ad.) 1257-1260; JCB (3) I:135. CtY, DLC, ICN, MnU-B, NN-RB, RPJCB; BL.   543/17

Spain. Laws, statutes, etc., 1516-1556 (Charles I). Leyes y ordenanças nuevamente hechas por su Magestad por la governacion de las Indias y buen tratamiento y conservacion delos Indios. *Alcalá de Henares: J.de Brocar*, 1543. xiii lvs;fol. On distribution of lands among Conquistadors. Sabin 40902; Harrisse (BAV) 247; Sanz (Ult.ad.) 1255-1256; Medina (BHA) 120; Streit I:46; Church 8; JCB (3) I:135. CSmH, DLC, InU-L, NN-RB, RPJCB; BL.   543/18

Tagault, Jean. De chirurgica institutione libri quinque. *Paris: C.Wechel*, 1543. 421p.;fol. In bk 1, ch.2, is a ref. to syphilis (morbus neapolitanus) and its 1st appearance at Naples in 1493. DNLM; BL, BN.   543/19

Vigo, Giovanni de. The most excellent workes of chirurgerye. [*London:*] *E.Whytchurch*, 1543. cclxx lvs;fol. Transl. by B.Traheron; based in part on author's *Practica . . . copiosa*, 1st publ., Rome, 1514. STC 24720. DNLM, MH; BL.   543/20

1544

Apianus, Petrus. La cosmographie . . . nouvellement traduict de latin en françois. Et par Gemmam Frison . . . corrigé. *Antwerp: G.Coppens v.Diest,for G.de Bonte & Gemma Frisius*, 1544. lxv lvs;illus.,maps;4to. Transl. from author's *Cosmographiae introductio*, 1st publ., Ingolstadt, [1532]. Includes (lvs xxx-xxxii), refs to America. In this state in title reading 'nouvellemēt' appears. Sabin 1752; Harrisse (BAV) 253; Sanz (Ult.ad.) 1262-1265; Atkinson (Fr.Ren.) 70; Ortroy (Apian) 33; JCB (3) I:136-137. MBAt, MiU-C, NN-RB, RPJCB; BN.   544/1

__[Anr state]. *Antwerp: G.Coppens v.Diest,for G.de Bonte & Gemma Frisius*, 1544. Minor typographic variants, e.g., reading 'nouvellement' in title. Ortroy (Apian) 34. RPJCB.
544/2

Brasavola, Antonio Musa. Examen omnium simplicium medicamentorum. *Lyons: J.Pullon*, 1544. 520p.;8vo. 1st publ., Rome, 1536. Baudrier (Lyons) V:193; Ind.aur.123.788. NN-RB; BL.   544/3

__[Anr issue]. *Lyons: J.Pullon,for G.de Millis,at Medina del Campo*, 1544. Baudrier (Lyons) IV:195; Ind.aur.123.789. BN.   544/4

Cabot, Sebastian. Declaratio chartae novae navigatoriae Domini Almirantis. [*Antwerp?* ca.1544?]. [47]p.;4to. Text, in Latin & Spanish, found also in margins of Cabot map of 1544; perhaps written by one Dr Grajales from information supplied by Cabot. Includes both sailing directions & accounts of lands depicted. Winship (Cabot) 55; Church 81. CSmH.   544/5

Dioscorides, Pedanius. Libri cinque della historia, & materia medicinale tradotti . . . da m. Pietro Andrea Matthiolo . . . con amplissimi discorsi, et comenti. *Venice: N.de Bascarini*, 1544. 442p.;fol. In commenting on Dioscorides' description of ebony, Mattioli discusses Guaiacum. Pritzel 2316 & 5986; Adams (Cambr.) D677. CtY, DNLM, MH-A, PSC-Hi, RPB; Cambridge: UL, BN.   544/6

Gemma, Reinerus, Frisius. De principiis astronomiae & cosmographie . . . Item de orbis divisione, & insulis, rebusque nuper inventis. *Antwerp: J.Grapheus,for J.Richard*, 1544. 92 lvs;illus.;8vo. 1st publ., Antwerp, 1530. Sabin 26855; Harrisse (BAV) 252; Belg.typ. (1541-1600) I:1255. ICN, MWiW-C, NN-RB; Brussels: BR.   544/7

Giambullari, Pietro Francesco. De'l sito, forma, & misura, dello Inferno di Dante. *Florence: N.Dortelata*, 1544. 153p.; illus.,map; 8vo. On p.18 is a map with area 'Terra incognita', interpreted as America. Sabin 27265; Harrisse (BAV) 260; Adams (Cambr.) G589; Shaaber G164. CSt, DLC, InU-L, MH, MiU, NN-RB, PU, RPB; BL, BN.   544/8

Goes, Damião de. Aliquot opuscula. *Louvain: R.Rescius*, 1544. [306]p.;illus.;4to. Includes author's *Fides . . . Aethiopum*, 1st publ., Louvain, 1540. Sabin 27690; Harrisse (BAV) Add. 144; Adams (Cambr.) G817; Belg.typ. (1541-1600) I:1287. DFo, InU-L, MH, MnU-B, NN-RB; BL, BN.   544/9

Guazzo, Marco. Historia di tutte le cose degne di memoria quai del anno .M.D.XXIIII. sino questo presente anno sono occorse. *Venice: Comin da Trino*, 1544. 408 numb.lvs;8vo. 1st publ, Venice, 1540. Adams (Cambr.) G1453. InU-L; BL, BN.   544/10

Lobera de Avila, Luis. Libro delas quatro enfermedades cortesanos que son catarro, gota arthetico, mal de piedra y de risiones e hijada, e mal de bubas. *Toledo: J.de Ayalá*, 1544. 2pts;fol. The 2nd pt has title *Libro de experiencias de medecina*. In addition to the section on syphilis in pt 1, pt 2 contains descriptions of various unguents for treating syphilis, including (recto of lf xxii) a 'Recepta de curar morbo gallico conel palo delas Indias'. Medina (BHA) 121; Pérez Pastor (Toledo) 202; Palau 139424. DNLM, MBCo, NNH; London: Wellcome, BN.   544/11

Lucidarius. M.Elucidarius von allerhand geschöpffen Gottes . . . und wie alle Creaturen geschaffen seind auff erden. *Augsburg: H.Steiner*, 1544. [79]p.;illus.;4to. 1st publ., Strassburg, [ca.1535]. Schorbach (Lucidarius) 52. Frankfurt a.M.: StB.   544/12

Maffei, Raffaele. Commentariorum . . . octo & triginta libri, accuratius quam antehac excusi. *Basel: H.Froben & N.Episcopius*, 1544. 468 numb.lvs;fol. 1st publ., Rome, 1506, the ref. to Columbus here appearing on lf 139v. Sabin 43768; Harrisse (BAV) 257 & Add. 146; Adams (Cambr.) M103; Moranti (Urbino) 2043. CSmH, ICN, NN-RB; Cambridge: Trinity, BN.   544/13

Mocenigo, Andrea. La guerra di Cambrai . . . Tradotta di latino [per Andrea Arrivabene]. *Venice: G.Padovano*, 1544. 140 numb.lvs;8vo. 1st publ. in Latin, Venice, 1525. The ref. to the New World here appears

on lf L8v. Adams (Cambr.) M1519. RPJCB;
BL.   544/14

___[Anr edn]. Le guerre fatte a nostri tempi in
Italia. *Venice: G.Padovano*, 1544. 140
numb.lvs;8vo. Adams (Cambr.) M1520. CtY,
DLC, InU-L, NN-RB; Cambridge: Trinity.
                                          544/15

Münster, Sebastian. Cosmographia. Beschreibung aller Lender. *Basel: H.Petri*, 1544. dclix
lvs;illus.,maps;fol. 'Von den neüwen inseln':
lvs dcxxxvi-dcxlii. Sabin 51385; Harrisse
(BAV) 258; Sanz (Ult.ad.) 1271-1275; Borba
de Moraes II:90; Burmeister (Münster) 66.
InU-L, MnU-B, NN-RB; BL, BN.   544/16

Postel, Guillaume. De orbis terrae concordia
libri quatuor. [*Basel: J.Oporinus*, 1544].
427p.;fol. On p.350-353 are refs to need to
christianize American natives. Sabin 64525;
Harrisse (BAV) Add. 145; Adams (Cambr.)
P2020. CU, CtY, ICN, MH, MiU-C, RPJCB;
BL, BN.   544/17

Tagault, Jean. De chirurgica institutione libri
quinque, iam denuò accuratius recogniti.
Venice: V.Valgrisi, 1544. 417 numb.lvs; illus.;
8vo. 1st publ., Paris, 1543. DNLM, WU;
BL.   544/18

1545

Albergati, Vianesio. La pazzia. *Venice:*
[ca.1545?]. 24 lvs;8vo. 1st dated edn, Bologna, 1540. Florence:BN.   545/1

___[Anr edn]. '*India Pastinaca*' [ca. 1545?].
Shaaber A120. PU; Rome: BN.   545/2

Apianus, Petrus. Cosmographia . . . per
Gemmam Frisium . . . iam demum ab omni-
bus vindicata mendis. *Antwerp: G.Coppens
v.Diest,for G.de Bonte*, 1545. 66 numb.lvs;
illus.,maps;4to. 1st publ. in this version, Ant-
werp, 1529. Sabin 1748; Harrisse (BAV) 262;
Sanz (Ult.ad.) 1284-1285; Ind.aur.106.441;
Ortroy (Apian) 36; Church 84; JCB (3) I:140.
CSmH, CtY, DLC, MiU-C, MnU-B, NNE,
RPJCB; BL.   545/3

____. Cosmographie, oft Beschryvinghe der ge-
helder werelt . . . Anderwerf gecorrigeert van
Gemma Phrysio. *Antwerp:G. Coppens v.Diest
for G.de Bonte*, 1545. lxviii lvs;illus.,map;4to.
1st publ. in Dutch, Antwerp, 1537. Ind.
aur.106.442; Ortroy (Apian) 35. DLC; Louvain: BU.   545/4

Berni, Francesco. Tutte le opere . . . in terza
rima. [*Venice?*], 1545. 3pts;8vo. 1st publ.,
Venice, 1538. Includes both Berni's 'Capitolo
secondo de la peste' & also G.F. Bini's 'Capito-

lo del mal francese'. Cf.Proksch I:82; Ind.
aur.117.701. NNH; BL.   545/5

Brant, Sebastian. Der Narren Spiegel; Das
gross Narrenschiff. *Strassburg: J.Cammer-
lander*, 1545. 140 numb.lvs;illus.;4to. 1st
publ., Basel, 1494. Ind.aur.123.722. BL.
                                          545/6

Brasavola, Antonio Musa. Examen simpl[icium]. medicament[orum]. *Venice: V.
Valgrisi*, 1545. 629p.;8vo. 1st publ., Rome,
1536. Ind.aur.123.793. CLU-M, DNLM,
MH-A, MnU, PPC; London: Wellcome.545/7

Cartier, Jacques. Brief recit, & succincte nar-
ration, de la navigation faicte es ysles de Cana-
da, Hochelage & Saguenay & autres, avec par-
ticulieres meurs, langaige, & ceremonies des
habitans d'icelles. *Paris: P.Roffet & A.
LeClerc*, 1545. 48 numb.lvs;8vo. More prob-
ably written by Jehan Poullet than Cartier—
C.A. Julien, *Les Français en Amérique*
(Paris, 1946), p.20-21. Sabin 11138; Harrisse
(BAV) 267; Harrisse (NF) 1; Atkinson
(Fr.Ren.) 74; Arents 4-a; JCB (101 Bks) 11.
NN-A; BL, Paris: Mazarine.   545/8

Ferrer, Jaume, de Blanes. Sentencias catholicas del divi poeta Dant florenti. *Barcelona:
C.Amoros*, 1545. 64 lvs;8vo. Includes discussion of cosmography with refs to papal demarcation line of 1495 and world map depicting
it. Sabin 24174; Harrisse (BAV) 261 & Add.
154; Medina (BHA) 122. BN.   545/9

Ferri, Alfonso. Methode curative de plusieurs
et diverses maladies par nouvelle industrie et
administration de la potion du boys de guiac
. . . traduict en françoys, corrigé et amendé
. . . par . . . Nicoles Michel. *Rouen: J.
Petit,for N.LeBourgeois* [ca.1545]. 321p.;
16mo. 1st publ. in this French version,
Poitiers, 1540. NN-RB; London: Wellcome.
                                          545/10

Fuchs, Leonhart. Läbliche abbildung und
contrafaytung aller kreüter. *Basel: M.Isen-
grin*, 1545. 516 lvs;illus.;8vo. A German version of the author's *Primi de stirpium historia*
of this year. Pritzel 3140; Nissen (Bot.) 660.
                                          545/11

____. Den nieuwen Herbarius. *Basel: M.Isen-
grin* [ca.1545]. 556p.;illus.,port.;fol. Transl.
from author's Basel, 1542, *De historia stirpium*. Pritzel 3139n; Nissen (Bot.) 662. DFo,
MH-A, MnU, NN-RB.   545/12

____. Primi de stirpium historia commentario-
rum tomi vivae imagines. *Basel: M.Isengrin*,
1545. 516p.;illus.;8vo. Includes illus. of

American plants: marigold, tomato & corn (maize). Pritzel 3140n; Nissen (Bot.) 661; cf. Hunt (Bot.) 63. CtY-M, DNLM, MH-A, NN-RB; BL, BN. 545/13

Gasser, Achilles Pirminius. Epitome historiarum & chronicorum mundi. *Lyons: S. Sabon, for A. Constantin* [ca. 1545?]. 241p; 8vo. 1st publ., Basel, 1532, ref. to Vespucci & Columbus here appearing on ɒ.236. Sabin 76906; Harrisse (BAV) 155; Baudrier (Lyons) II:30-31; Burmeister (Gasser) 37. CtY, IU, InU-L, MH, RPB; BN. 545/14

Gesner, Konrad. Bibliotheca universalis, sive Catalogus omnium scriptorum locupletissimus. *Zurich: C. Froschauer*, 1545. 631 numb. lvs;fol. Includes entries for Columbus, Ulrich von Hutten, P.M. d'Anghiera & Vespucci. Adams (Cambr.) G516; Shaaber G139. CU, DLC, ICU, InU-L, MH, MiU, MnU-B, NN- RB, PU; BL, BN. 545/15

Guazzo, Marco. Historie di tutte le cose degne di memoria. *Venice: Comin da Trino*, 1545. 408 numb.lvs;illus.;12mo. 1st publ., Venice, 1540, the ref. to Pizarro's conquest of Peru here appearing on lf 167. Sabin 44401; Harrisse (BAV) Add. 153. NN-RB, WU; BL. 545/16

L'Histoire de la terre neuve du Perù en l'Inde Occidentale . . . Traduitte de l'italien [par J. Gohory]. *Paris: P. Gaultier, for J. Barbé & V. Sertenas*, 1545. 56 lvs;map;4to. A translation based on the anonymous *Libro ultimo del Summario delle Indie Occidentali* found in the 1534 *Summario de la generale historia de l'Indie Occidentali*, itself a translation from *La conquista del Peru* of that year. It is not, though so stated by the French translator, and by both Sabin & Medina, a translation from Oviedo y Valdés. Cf.W.H. Bowen, 'L'Histoire de la terre neuve du Peru,' *Isis*, XXVIII (1938) 330-340. Sabin 57994 (& 32018); Harrisse (BAV) 264; Medina (BHA) 75n (I:111-112); Pogo (Conquista) K; JCB (3) I:142. NN-RB, PPL, RPJCB; BL, BN. 545/17

Marineo, Lucio, Siculo. Sumario dela serenissima vida, y heroycos hechos de . . . don Fernando y doña Ysabel. *Seville: D. de Robertis*, 1545. lxxix lvs; 4to. Extracted from author's *De las cosas memorables de España*, Alcalá de Henares, 1530. Includes chapt. 'De otras yslas apartadas del hemispherio llamadas Indias'. Sanz (Ult.ad.) 1286-1289; Shaaber M148. PU. 545/18

Medina, Pedro de. Arte de navegar. *Valladolid: F. Fernández de Córdova*, 1545. c lvs;illus.,map;fol. Instructional manual for those voyaging to the Americas, with map of New World. Sabin 47344; Harrisse (BAV) 266; Sanz (Ult.ad.) 1290-1299; Medina (BHA) 123; Alcocer (Valladolid) 122; Borba de Moraes II:47-48; JCB (3) I:142. CtY, DLC, InU-L, MnU-B, NN-RB, RPJCB; BL, BN. 545/19

Mexía, Pedro. Historia ymperial y cesarea. *Seville: J. de León*, 1545. ccccxxiii lvs;fol. Includes American ref. on lf ccccxiii. Escudero (Seville) 452. CSmH, NNH; Madrid: BN. 545/20

Münster, Sebastian. Cosmographia. Beschreibung aller Lender . . . Weiter . . . fast seer gemeret und gebessert. *Basel: H. Petri*, 1545. dcccxviii p.;illus.,maps;fol. 1st publ., Basel, 1544. Sabin 51386; Harrisse (BAV) Add. 152; Burmeister (Münster) 67. DCU; BL. 545/21

Ptolemaeus, Claudius. Geographia universalis, vetus et nova . . . libros viii. quorum primus nova translatione Pirckheimheri . . . redditus est . . . Succedunt tabulae ptolemaicae opera Sebastiani Munsteri novo paratae modo. *Basel: H. Petri*, 1545. 195p.;maps;fol. 1st publ. in this version, Basel, 1540, with new maps here added. Sabin 66487; Harrisse (BAV) Add. 155; Sanz (Ult.ad.) 1300-1302. Stevens (Ptolemy) 49; Phillips (Atlases) 368; Burmeister (Münster) 168; JCB (3) I:143. DLC, InU-L, MH, MiU-C, NN-RB, RPJCB; BL, BN. 545/22

Rangoni, Tommaso. Mali galeci [i.e., gallici] sanandi, vini, ligni et aquae. *Venice: G. Padovano, for M. Pagan*, 1545. 40 lvs;8vo. 1st publ., Venice, 1538. London: Wellcome, BN. 545/23

Resende, Garcia de. Lyvro . . . que trata da vida e grandissima virtudes . . . do . . . principe el Rey don Joao o segundo deste nome. [*Lisbon:*] *L. Rodrigues*, 1545. cliii lvs;fol. Includes account of encounter between King John II of Portugal and Columbus. Sabin 70061; Harrisse (BAV) 265; Borba de Moraes II:199-200; Anselmo 1047; King Manuel 59. BL, Lisbon: Arquivo Nacional. 545/24

Sacro Bosco, Joannes de. Tractado de la sphera . . . con muchas addiciones. Agora nuevamente traduzido . . . por . . . Hieronymo de Chaves. *Seville: J. de León*, 1545. 109 numb.lvs; illus.,map;4to. On lf 25 are refs to

Peru & Magellan's Straits; on lf 27, a map showing America. Sabin 74808 (&32684); Harrisse (BAV) Add. 149; Sanz (Ult.ad.) 1303-1312; Medina (BHA) 124; Escudero (Seville) 453. MnU-B; BL, Madrid: BN.

545/25

1546

Albergati, Vianesio. La pazzia. [*Venice?*] 1546. 23 lvs;8vo. 1st dated edn, Bologna, 1540. Ind.aur.102.240; Adams (Cambr.) A436. Cambridge: Clare, Florence: BN. 546/1

Beuter, Pedro Antonio. Primera parte de la Coronica general de toda España. *Valencia: J.Mey,* 1546. cxviii lvs;fol. Records, in chapt. 28, theory that, following Moorish invasion in early 8th cent., some Spaniards took refuge in the islands & lands of Yucatan, now recently discovered & called New Spain. Ind. aur.118.415; Palau 28824. DLC, MnU-B; BL, Vienna: NB. 546/2

Biondo, Michelangelo. De ventis et navigatione . . . Cum accuratissima descriptione distantiae locorum interni maris, & oceani, a Gadibus ad novum orbem. *Venice: Comin da Trino,* 1546. 18 numb.lvs;illus.;4to. The earliest edn, a purported 1544 edn being a ghost. Sabin 5518; Harrisse (BAV) 274; Ind. aur.119.498; JCB (3) I:144. CtY, MH, MiU-C, MnU-B, NN-RB, RPJCB; BL, BN. 546/3

Bock, Hieronymus. Kreüter Buch. *Strassburg: W.Rihel,* 1546. cccliii lvs;illus.;fol. Cf.Strassburg, 1539, edn with title *New Kreütter Buch.* Here depicted (verso of lf cccxlvii) is a marigold ('Indianisch Negelin'); a ref. to pepper from Spanish Indies appears on verso of lf cccl. Pritzel 865; Nissen (Bot.) 182n; Ind.aur.120.587; Ritter (Strasbourg) 213. DNLM, MH-A, MiU; BL, Strassbourg: BN. 546/4

Brasavola, Antonio Musa. Examen omnium simplicium medicamentorum . . . Ab ipso authore recognitum & auctum. *Lyons: J.& F. Frellon,* 1546. 862p.;16mo. 1st publ., Rome, 1536. Ind.aur.123.797; Baudrier (Lyons) V:202. CtY-M, DNLM, MH; BL. 546/5

__[Anr issue]. *Lyons: A.Vincent,* 1546. Baudrier (Lyons) V:202. 546/6

Catholic Church. Liturgy and ritual. Missal. Missale Romanum. *Venice: Heirs of L.Giunta,* 1546. 309 numb.lvs;illus., music; fol. Cf.1505 edn for usage of Passau, publ. at

Augsburg. Includes (lvs 299v-300v) 'Missa de beato Job contra morbum gallicum'. Weale/ Bohatta 1102. MH. 546/7

Cervantes de Salazar, Francisco. Obras que Francisco Cervantes de Salazar ha hecho, glosado, y traduzido. *Alcalá de Henares: J.de Brocar,* 1546. 3pts in 1 v.;4to. Author's dedication to Hernando Cortés includes refs to latter's exploits in New World. Sabin 75567; Harrisse (BAV) 158; Medina (BHA) 129; García (Alcalá de Henares) 209. IU, InU-L, MB, NN-RB, RPJCB; BL. 546/8

Enciso, Martín Fernández de. Suma de geographia que trata de todos las partidas & provincias del mundo: en especial de las Indias . . . agora nuevamente emendada de algunos defectos. *Seville: A.de Burgos,* 1546. lviii lvs; illus.;fol. 1st publ., Seville, 1519. Sabin 22553; Harrisse (BAV) 272; Medina (BHA) 127; Escudero (Seville) 473; JCB (3) I:146. NN-RB, RPJCB, ViU; BL. 546/9

Ferri, Alfonso. De l'administration du sainct boys . . . trad. . . . par . . . Nicoles Michel. *Poitiers: J.& E.de Marnef,* 1546. 495p.; 16mo. 1st publ. in French, Poitiers, 1540. Harrisse (BAV) Add. 160. CtY, MHi, NN-RB; BL, BN. 546/10

Focard, Jacques. Paraphrase de l'astrolabe . . . Le miroir du monde. *Lyons: J.de Tournes,* 1546. 187p.;illus.,map;8vo. Text on p.155 discusses America, figured also in world map. Sabin 24933; Harrisse (BAV) 272; Fairfax Murray (France) 167; Mortimer (France) 234; Cartier (de Tournes) 54. CtY, MH, NN-RB; BL, BN. 546/11

Fracastoro, Girolamo. De sympathia et antipathia rerum liber unus. De contagione et contagiosis morbis et curatione libri iii. *Venice: Heirs of L.Giunta,* 1546. 76 numb. lvs;4to. In bk ii of the 'De contagione' chapts xi-xii discuss syphilis, citing its American origin. Elsewhere, in discussing its cure by Guaiacum, the wood is described as coming 'ad nos . . . ex hispana vocata insula novi orbis, & adjacentibus'. CtY, DNLM, ICJ, NNNAM; BL. 546/12

Fuchs, Leonhart. De historia stirpium commentarii insignes. [*Lyons:*] *B.Arnoullet,for M.DuPuys at Paris,* 1546. 851p.;illus.;8vo. 1st publ., Basel, 1542. Pritzel 3138n; Baudrier (Lyons) X:116. CU, MoSB. 546/13

__[Anr edn]. *Paris: O.Petit,* 1546. 304 numb. lvs;8vo. DNLM. 546/14

—[Anr issue of preceding?] *Paris: J.Bogard,* 1546. BL. 546/15

Gómez de Ciudad Real, Alvár. El vellocino dorado: y la historia dela orden del Tuson . . . Assi mismo el summario d'los catholicos reyes don Fernando y doña Ysabel . . . sacado dela obra grande Delas cosas memorables d'España, q. escrivio Lucio Marineo. *Toledo: J.de Ayalá,* 1546. 2pts;illus.;4to. Marineo's *Summario,* 1st publ., Seville, 1545, includes chapt. 'De otras islas apartadas del hemisferio llamadas Indias'. Sabin 44587; Harrisse (BAV) 268; Sanz (Ult.ad.) 1315-1319; Medina (BHA) 126; Pérez Pastor (Toledo) 214. CU, ICN, NN-RB; BN. 546/16

Guazzo, Marco. Historie . . . di tutti i fatti degni di memoria. *Venice: G.Giolito de' Ferrari,* 1546. 375 lvs;12mo. 1st publ. with ref. to Pizarro's conquest of Peru, Venice, 1540. Sabin 44402; Harrisse (BAV) 157; Adams (Cambr.) G1454; Shaaber G374. DFo, ICN, InU-L, NN-RB, PU; Cambridge: UL, BN. 546/17

Honter, Johannes. Rudimenta cosmographica. *Zurich: C.Froschauer,* 1546. [88]p.; maps;8vo. 1st publ. in this version, Kronstadt, 1542. Sabin 32794; Harrisse (BAV) 271; Sanz (Ult.ad.) 1313-1314; Adams (Cambr.) H831; JCB (3) I:147. CtY, IU, MiU-C, NN-RB, RPJCB; BL. 546/18

Mexía, Pedro. Historia imperial y cesarea. *Basel: J.Oporinus,* 1546. 717p.;fol. 1st publ., Seville, 1545. Moranti (Urbino) 2204. Urbino: BU. 546/19

Münster, Sebastian. Cosmographia; Beschreibung aller Lender. *Basel: H.Petri,* 1546. 818p.;maps;fol. 1st publ., Basel, 1544. Sabin 51386n; Harrisse (BAV) Add. 152; Burmeister (Münster) 68. MnU-B; Basel: UB. 546/20

Sacro Bosco, Joannes de. La sphere . . . traduicte [par M. de Perer] de latin . . . augmentee de nouvelles figures. *Paris: J.Loys,* 1546. 48 lvs.illus.;8vo. NN-RB. 546/21

Venegas de Busto, Alejo. Primera parte de las diferencias de libros que ay enel universo . . . Ahora nuevamente emendada y corregida por el mismo autor. *Toledo: J.de Ayalá,* 1546. ccxxiiii lvs;4to. 1st publ., Toledo, 1540. Sabin 98502; Harrisse (BAV) Add. 156; Medina (BHA) 128; Pérez Pastor (Toledo) 219; JCB (3) I:148. MH, MiU-C, NN-RB, RPJCB; BL. 546/22

1547

Albergati, Vianesio. La pazzia. *Venice: G.A. Valvassori,* 1547. [47]p.;8vo. 1st dated edn, Bologna, 1540. CtY, ICN, NNC. 547/1

Bordone, Benedetto. Isolario . . . nel quale si ragiona di tutte l'isole del mondo . . . Ricoreto, & di nuovo ristampato. *Venice: P.Manuzio,for F.Torresano,* 1547. lxxiiii lvs;illus., maps;fol. 1st publ., Venice, 1528. Includes for 1st time 'Copia delle lettere del prefetto della India la nuova Spagna detta', describing Pizarro's conquest of Peru. Sabin 6421; Harrisse (BAV) 275; Sanz (Ult.ad.) 1327-1329; Phillips (Atlases) 164; Mortimer (Italy) 82; Church 86; JCB (3) I:149. CSmH, CtY, ICU, MH, MnU-B, NN-RB, RPJCB; BL, BN. 547/2

Ferri, Alfonso. De ligni sancti multiplici . . . Hieronymi Fracastori Syphilis. *Lyons: J.& F. Frellon,* 1547. 168p.;8vo. 1st publ., Rome, 1537; Fracastoro's *Syphilis* 1st publ., Verona, 1530. Baumgartner (Fracastoro) 9; Baudrier (Lyons) V:208; Waller 3008. CtY-M, DNLM, MiU, NN-RB, PPC; BL, BN. 547/3

Fuchs, Leonhart. De historia stirpium commentarii insignes. *Paris: C.Guillard,* 1547. 492 lvs;12mo. 1st publ., Basel, 1542. NNBG; BN. 547/4

—[Anr edn]. *Paris: V.Gaultherot,* 1547. 16mo. BL. 547/5

—[Anr edn]. *Paris: J.Foucher,* 1547. 484 lvs; 16mo. Adams (Cambr.) F1101. Cambridge: UL. 547/6

—[Anr edn]. *Lyons: B.Arnoullet, for G.Gazeau,* 1547. Baudrier (Lyons) X:117–118, Adams (Cambr.) F1100. CtY, DNLM, IU, MH-A; Cambridge: St John's, BN. 547/7

—[Anr issue of preceding]. *Lyons: B.Arnoullet,* 1547. Pritzel 3138n. BN. 547/8

Fuentes, Alonso de. Summa de philosophia natural. *Seville: J.de León,* 1547. cxxviii lvs; illus.,map;4to. The global map includes America. Escudero (Seville) 480; Palau 95383. NN-RB; BL, Madrid: BN. 547/9

Gemma, Reinerus, Frisius. De principiis astronomiae. *Paris:* 1547. See the year 1548.

Mexía, Pedro. Colóquios o dialogos nuevamente compuesta. *Seville: D.de Robertis,* 1547. clxxiii lvs;12mo. The 1st colloquy, concerning physicians, includes a ref. to 'el mal de las bubas' (syphilis) & its cure by 'palo . . . sancto' (Guaiacum); the 3rd colloquy, on the sun, contains a ref. to Magellan's circumnavigation. Sabin 48235; Harrisse (BAV) Add. 161; Medina (BHA) 132; Escudero (Seville) 487. MB, NNH; BL, Madrid: BN.   547/10

—[Anr edn]. *Antwerp: M.Nuyts,* 1547. ciii lvs; 8vo. Peeters-Fontainas (Impr.esp.)781. InU-L; BL, Madrid: BN.   547/11

—[Anr edn]. *Saragossa: B.de Nagera,* 1547. xc lvs;8vo. Sánchez (Aragon) 265; Palau 167365. CtY-M, NN-RB.   547/12

——. Historia ymperial y cesarea . . . enmendada y corregida por el mismo autor. *Seville: D.de Robertis,* 1547. ccccxxiii lvs;fol. 1st publ., Seville, 1545, the American ref. here appearing on lf ccccxiii. Sabin 48249n; Medina (BHA) 106n; Escudero (Seville) 485. BL, BN.   547/13

—[Anr edn]. *Basel: J.Oporinus,* 1547. 719p.; fol. Palau 167342. CU-S, IU, InU-L; BL, Madrid: BN.   547/14

Oviedo y Valdés, Gonzalo Fernández de. Coronica de las Indias. La hystoria general de las Indias agora nuevamente impressa, corregida y emendada. 1547. y con la Conquista del Peru [por F. de Xérez]. *Salamanca: J.de Junta,* 1547. cxcii & xxii lvs;illus.;fol. 1st publ., Seville, 1535, under title *La historia general de las Indias.* In some copies the phrase 'y con la Conquista del Peru' does not appear on t.p. Xérez's *Conquista del Peru,* 1st publ., Seville, 1534; included also is M.Estete's 'La relacion del viaje que hizo . . . Hernando Piçarro', here first printed. Sabin 57989 (& 105724); Harrisse (BAV) 277 & Add. 162; Medina (BHA) 131; Streit II:569; Pogo (Conquista) M-N; Arents 4-a; JCB (3) I:150–152. CSmH, DLC, InU-L, MH, MiU-C, NN-RB, PPL, RPJCB; BL, BN.   547/15

Tagault, Jean. De chirurgica institutione libri quinque. *Lyons: E.Rufin & J. Ausoult, for G. Rouillé,* 1547. 446p.;illus.;8vo. 1st publ., Paris, 1543. Baudrier (Lyons) IX:135. DNLM; BN.   547/16

Xérez, Francisco de. Conquista del Peru. Verdadera relacion de la conquista del Peru y provincia del Cuzco. [*Salamanca? J.de Junta?* 1547?]. 37 lvs;illus.;4to. 1st publ., Seville, 1534; see also G.F. de Oviedo y Valdés's *Coronica de las Indias* of this year, described above. Sabin 105723; Harrisse (BAV) Add. 162; Medina (BHA) 130; Pogo (Conquista) L. MiU-C.   547/17

1548

Apianus, Petrus. Libro de la cosmographia . . . el qual trata la descripcion del mundo . . . augmentado por Gemma Frisio . . . con otros dos libros del dicho Gemma. Agora nuevamente traduzidos en romance castellano. *Antwerp: G.de Bonte,* 1548. 68 numb.lvs; illus.,map;4to. Transl. from Antwerp, 1545, Latin text. Sabin 1753; Harrisse (BAV) 283; Sanz (Ult.ad.) 1330-1338; Medina (BHA) 133; Ind.aur.106.443; Ortroy (Apian) 37; Peeters-Fontainas (Impr.esp.) 61; JCB (3) I:152. CtY, DLC, ICJ, NN-RB, RPJCB; BL.   548/1

Augustus, Hieronymus Oliverius. De imperio romano . . . liber unicus . . . De partitione orbis: libri quattuor. *Augsburg: P.Ulhart,* 1548. [123]p.;port.;4to. In verse. The 'De partitione orbis liber quartus' contains refs to Labrador & New World. Sabin 2383; Harrisse (BAV) 284 & Add. 166. NN-RB, RPJCB; BL, BN.   548/2

Brant, Sebastian. Der sottenschip oft Dat narrenschip. [*Antwerp: M.Ancxt,for P.Lens,* 1548]. [239]p.;illus.;4to. Transl. from *Das Narren Schyff,* 1st publ., Basel, 1494. Ind. aur.123.728; Belg.typ. (1541-1600) I:389. DLC; Brussels: BR.   548/3

Cabrera, Cristóbal. Meditatiunculae, ad serenissimum Hispaniarum Principem Philippum. *Valladolid: F.Fernández de Córdova,* 1548. lxxx lvs;4to. In verse. On versos of lvs lxxiii & lxxv are refs to Indies & Mexico. Harrisse (BAV) Add. 169; Medina (BHA) 135; Alcocer (Valladolid) 140. Madrid: BN.   548/4

Cardano, Girolamo. Contradicentium medicorum liber primer [-secundus]. *Lyons: S.Gryphius,* 1548. 2v.;4to. The earliest edn to include, in v.2, Cardano's 'De sarza parilia' & his 'De cina radice'. Ind.aur.132.055; Baudrier (Lyons) VIII:223; Adams (Cambr.) C655. DNLM, ICJ; London: Wellcome, BN.   548/5

Carion, Johann. Chronicorum libri tres, in latinum sermonem conversi, Hermanno Bonno interprete. *Paris: J.Bogard,* 1548. 16mo. 1st publ., Hall (Swabia), 1537. Ind. aur.132.303. Vienna: NB.   548/6

Chaves, Jerónimo de. Chronographia o Repertorio de los tiempos. *Seville: J.de León,* 1548. ccxv lvs;maps;4to. On lf lix is a map representing America. Sanz (Ult.ad.) 1344-1346; Palau 67450.   548/7

Dioscorides, Pedanius. Il Dioscoride, dell' eccellente dottor medico m. Andrea Matthioli . . . con li suoi discorsi . . . la seconda volta illustrati. *Venice: V.Valgrisi*, 1548. 2pts;4to. 1st publ.in this version, Venice, 1544. Pritzel 2318 & 5986n. CtY-M, DNLM, MH-A; BL, BN.   548/8

Dodoens, Rembert. Cosmographica in astronomiam et geographiam isagoge. *Antwerp: J. van der Loe*, 1548. [112]p.;illus.;8vo. In bk ii, chapt. xii, is a ref. to America as being on the Equator; in bk iii, chapt. xii, a ref. to Peru appears. Bibl.belg.,1st ser.,IX:D98. ICN, MB, NN-RB; BL.   548/9

Emili, Paolo. De rebus gestis Francorum libri x . . . Arnoldi Ferroni . . . De rebus gestis Gallorum libri quatuor. *Paris: O.Petit*, 1548-49. 3pts;8vo. The earliest edn to contain Le Ferron's appendix of 1549. See also that work as separately issued in that year. BN.   548/10

Fernel, Jean. De abditis rerum causis libri duo. *Paris: C.Wechel*, 1548. 255p.;fol. Chapt.xiiii of bk ii comprises 'De lue venerea dialogus'; in addition the preface to bk i discusses the effect of the New World upon classical knowledge. For variant title pages, see Sherrington. Sherrington (Fernel) 17.Fl. BN.   548/11

—[Anr issue]. *Paris: C.Wechel & C.Perier*, 1548. Adams (Cambr.) F243. Cambridge: Corpus Christi.   548/12

Gasca, Pedro de la. Este es un traslado de una carta que fue embiada de la ciudad del Cuzco, provincia del Peru a esta . . . ciudad de Seville, en que cuenta . . . la victoria que vico . . . el señor de la Gasca . . . contra Gonçalo Piçarro. [*Seville*: 1548]. 7p.;illus.; 4to. Maggs, Cat.429, no.56.   548/13

Gemma, Reinerus, Frisius. De principiis astronomiae et cosmographiae . . . De orbis divisione & insulis, rebusque nuper inventis. Eiusdem De annuli astronomica usu. Joannis Schoneri De usu globi astriferi opusculum. *Antwerp: J.Grapheus,for J.Steels*, 1548. 119 numb.lvs;illus.;8vo. 1st publ., Antwerp, 1530. Sabin 26856 (& 77801); Harrisse (BAV) 279; Belg.typ. (1541-1600) I:1256. DLC, InU-L, NN-RB; BL, Brussels: BR.   548/14

—[Anr edn]. *Paris: T.Richard*, 1547 [colophon: 1548]. 179p.;illus.;8vo. 'De America': p.137-140; 'De insulis apud Americam': p.140-142. Sabin 62588; Harrisse (BAV) Add.

168; JCB (3) I:150. MH, NN-RB, RPJCB.   548/15

Gesner, Konrad. Pandectarum, sive Partitionum universalium . . . libri xxi. *Zurich: C. Froschauer*, 1548. 374 numb.lvs;fol. The section 'De geographia' includes 'Titulus viii. De novo orbe, & insulis nostro saeculo repertis' comprising 7 titles, constituting the earliest known bibliographic listing of Americana. Adams (Cambr.) G553; Moranti (Urbino) 1625. DLC, MH, MnU-B, NN-RB; BL, BN.   548/16

Giovio, Paolo, Bp of Nocera. Descriptio Britanniae, Scotiae, Hyberniae, et Orchadum. *Venice: M.Tramezzino*, 1548. 125 numb.lvs; illus.;4to. Refs to New World appear on verso of 2nd lf & to Columbus on recto of lf 42. Adams (Cambr.) G638; Shaaber G190. DLC, ICU, NN-RB, MiU, MnU-B, PU, RPJCB; BL, BN.   548/17

Guazzo, Marco. Historie . . . di tutte le cose degne di memoria. *Venice: Comin da Trino*, 1548. 104 numb.lvs;8vo. 1st publ. with ref. to Peru, Venice, 1540. Adams (Cambr.) G1455. DLC, NN-RB, RPB; BL.   548/18

Honter, Johannes. Rudimenta cosmographica. *Zurich: C.Froschauer*, 1548. [96]p.;illus.,maps;8vo. 1st publ. in this version, Kronstadt, 1542. In verse. Borsa 95. NN-RB, RPB.   548/19

—[Anr issue]. Rudimentorum cosmographicorum . . . libri iii. *Zurich: C.Froschauer*, 1548. Sabin 32795; Harrisse (BAV) 287; Adams (Cambr.) H832; Borsa 95. CSmH, DLC, MiU-C, MnU-B, NN-RB, RPJCB; BL. 548/20

Lucidarius. M.Lucidarius, von allerhand geschöpffen Gottes . . . und wie alle Creaturn schaffen seind auff erden. *Augsburg: V.Otmar*, 1548. [79]p.;illus.;4to. 1st publ., Strassburg, [ca.1535]. Schorbach (Lucidarius) 53. Munich: StB.   548/21

Medina, Pedro de. Libro de grandezas y cosas memorables de España. *Seville: D.de Robertis*, 1548. clxxxvi lvs;illus.,maps;fol. Includes refs to New World discoveries & conquests & to Magellan's circumnavigation. Cf.Sabin 47348; cf.Harrisse (BAV) 281; Sanz (Ult.ad.) 1348-1363. CSmH, ICN, InU-L, NN-RB; BL.   548/22

—[Anr edn]. [*n.p., no pr.*] 1548. clxxxii lvs; map;fol. Lacking an imprint & possibly a piracy produced at a later date. Sabin 47348; Harrisse (BAV) Add. 165. BN.   548/23

Mexía, Pedro. Los dialogos o Colóquios . . . nuevamente corregidas . . . añedido un excelente tratado de Isocrates, llamado Paranesis. *Seville: D.de Robertis*, 1548. xc lvs;8vo. 1st publ., Seville, 1547, under title *Colóquios o dialogos*. Sabin 48236; Harrisse (BAV) Add. 164; Medina (BHA) 134; Escudero (Seville) 503. MB; BN, Madrid: BN. 548/24

More, Sir Thomas, Saint. De optimo reipu. statu, deque nova insula Utopia. *Louvain: S. Zassenus,for Widow of A. Birckmann*, 1548. 182p.;12mo. 1st publ., Louvain, 1516. Sabin 50543n; Belg.typ. (1541-1600) I:4526; Adams (Cambr.) M1758; Gibson (More) 5. CSmH, CtY, DFo, ICN, RPJCB; BL, BN. 548/25

———. La republica nuovamente ritrovata, del governo dell' isola Eutopia. *Venice: [A.F.Doni]*, 1548. 60 numb.lvs;8vo. Gibson (More) 37; JCB (3) I:153. CSmH, CtY, DFo, ICN, MH, RPJCB; BL. 548/26

Münster, Sebastian. Cosmographia: Beschreibung aller Lender. *Basel: H.Petri*, 1548. 818p.;maps;fol. 1st publ., Basel, 1544. Burmeister (Münster) 69. Munich: StB, Vienna: NB. 548/27

Opere burlesche . . . ricorrette. *Florence: B. Giunta*, 1548. 293p.;8vo. Included are F. Berni's 'Capitolo secondo de la peste' & G.F. Bini's 'Capitolo del mal francese', both 1st publ., Venice, 1538. Cf. Proksch I:82; Ind. aur.117.702. NjP; Vienna: NB. 548/28

Paradin, Guillaume. Memoriae nostrae libri quatuor. *Lyons: J.de Tournes*, 1548. 182p.; fol. In bk 3 (p.97) Pizarro's discovery of Peru is mentioned. Cartier (de Tournes) 123; Adams (Cambr.) P307. CtY, DLC, MH, NN-RB; BL, BN. 548/29

Portugal. Laws, statutes, etc. Regimento & ordenacões da fazenda. *Lisbon: G.Galharde*, 1548. cxvi lvs;fol. 1st publ., Lisbon, 1516. Sabin 68809; Harrisse (BAV) 286; King Manuel 283. CtY, MH, NN-RB. 548/30

Ptolemaeus, Claudius. La geografia . . . con alcuni comenti & aggiunti fattevi da Sebastiano Munstero . . . con le tavole non solamente antiche & moderne . . . ma altre nuove aggiuntevi di . . . Jacopo Gastaldo . . . ridotta in volgare italiano da m. Pietro Andrea Mattiolo. *Venice: N.de Bascarini,for G.B.Pederzano*, 1548. 214 numb.lvs;maps;fol. Maps 54-58, with descriptive text, relate to America. Sabin 66502; Harrisse (BAV) 285; Sanz (Ult.ad.) 1368-1373; Stevens (Ptolemy) 50;

Phillips (Atlases) 369; Burmeister (Münster) 170; JCB(3) I:153. CSmH, CtY, DLC, InU-L, MiU-C, MnU-B, NN-RB, RPJCB; BL, BN. 548/31

Vadianus, Joachim von Watt, called. Epitome trium terrae partium, Asiae, Africae et Europae. *Zurich: C.Froschauer*, 1548. 524p.; illus.,maps;8vo. 1st publ., Zurich, 1534. Sabin 98281; Harrisse (BAV) Add. 170; JCB (3) I:154. CSmH, DLC, NN-RB, RPJCB; BL, BN. 548/32

Venero, Alonso. Enchiridion de los tiempos . . . Agora nuevamente por el mismo auctor añadido, corregido y emendado. Mas lleva aora de nuevo añadido el descubrimiento de las Indias y quien fue primero que las hallo y en que se año se començaron a ganar. *Saragossa: D.Hernández*, 1548. 180 numb.lvs;8vo. The earliest edn to contain American refs; 1st publ., Burgos, 1526. Sabin 98863; Palau 358451. Private collection (cf.Palau). 548/33

Vigo, Giovanni de. Libro, o Pratica en cirugía . . . Traduzido . . . por el doctor Miguel Juan Pascual. *Toledo: F.de Sancta Catalina,for J.de Spinosa*, 1548. cclxiii numb.lvs; fol. 1st publ. in Spanish [Valencia], 1537. Pérez Pastor (Toledo) 232; Palau 364934. NNH; London: Wellcome, Madrid: BN. 548/34

1549

Albenino, Nicolao de. Verdadera relacion: de lo sussedido en los reynos e provincias del Peru desde la yda a ellos del virey Blasco Nuñez Vela hasta el desbarato y muerte de Gonçalo Piçarro. *Seville: J.de León*, 1549. 80 lvs;8vo. Sabin 647; Harrisse (BAV) 290 & Add. 173; Medina (BHA) 137; Ind.aur.102.141; JCB AR39:2-8. NN-RB, RPJCB; BN. 549/1

Brant, Sebastian. Der Narren Spiegel. *Strassburg: W.Rihel*, 1549. [332]p.;illus.;4to. 1st publ., Basel, 1494. Ind.aur.123.730; Ritter (Strasbourg) 249. N; BL, Strasbourg: BN. 549/2

Dioscorides, Pedanius. De medicinali materia libri sex, Joanne Ruellio . . . interprete . . . Additis etiam annotationibus . . . per Gualtherum Rivium. *Frankfurt a.M.: C. Egenolff*, 1549. 554p.;illus.;fol. 1st publ. as here ed., Frankfurt, a.M., 1543. Pritzel 2308; Nissen (Bot.) 496n. CtU, DNLM, MH-A, NNBG; BL, BN. 549/3

____. Il Dioscoride, dell'eccellente dottor medi-
co m. P. Andrea Matthioli . . . con li šuoi discorsi. *Mantua: G.Ruffinelli*, 1549. 2pts;illus.;
4to. 1st publ., Venice, 1544. Pritzel 2319 &
5986n. BL.　　　　　　　　　　　　　549/4

Firenzuola, Agnolo. Rime. *Florence: B.Giun-
ta*, 1549. 135 numb.lvs;8vo. Includes (lvs
118v-120v) ode 'In lode del legno santo', on
treatment of syphilis by use of Guaiacum.
Adams (Cambr.) F503. CU, DLC, IU, MH,
MnU-B, NjP, RPJCB; BL, BN.　　　　549/5

Fontanon, Denys. De morborum internorum
curatione, libri tres. *Lyons: J.Frellon*, 1549.
438p.;8vo. Included is mention of syphilis of
the brain. Baudrier (Lyons) V:214. CtY-M,
DNLM, NNNAM; London: Wellcome. 549/6

Fornari, Simone. La spositione sopra . . .
l'Orlando furioso di m. Ludovico Ariosto. *Florence: L.Torrentino*, 1549[-50]. 2v.;8vo. In
v.1, p.313-320, a section discusses Portuguese
navigators, the voyages of Columbus & Vespucci, and the discovery of America. Shaaber
F363. DLC, InU-L, PU, RPJCB; BL, BN.
　　　　　　　　　　　　　　　　　　549/7

Fuchs, Leonhart. Commentaires tres excellens de l'hystoire des plantes, composez premierement en latin . . . et depuis, nouvellement traduictz . . . par [Eloy de Maignan].
Paris: J.Gazeau, 1549. 278 lvs;illus.;fol. Pritzel 3139n; Nissen (Bot.) 663; Hunt (Bot.) 60.
MH-A, NNNAM; BM(NH).　　　　　549/8

____. De historia stirpium commentarii insignes.
Lyons: B.Arnoullet, 1549. 852p.;illus.,port.;
8vo. 1st publ., Basel, 1542. Pritzel 3138n; Nissen (Bot.) 667; Baudrier (Lyons) X:120; Fairfax Murray (France) 181. CtY, DNLM, IU,
MH-A, NN-RB, PPC, RPB; BL, BN.　549/9

____. Histoire des plantes . . . Nouvellement
traduict en françoys. *Paris: Widow of A.
Birckmann*, 1549. 519p.;illus.;8vo. Transl.
from the author's *De historia stirpium commentarii*, 1st publ., Basel, 1543. Nissen (Bot.)
665. DLC, MH-A; BN.　　　　　　　549/10

____. Plantarum effigies . . . ac quinque diversis
linguis redditae. *Lyons: B.Arnoullet*, 1549.
516p.;illus.;port.;16mo. Anr edn of the Basel
work 1st publ., 1545, under title *Primi de stirpium historia*. Included are illus. & descriptions of the marigold, tomato & corn (maize).
Cf.Pritzel 4140n; Nissen (Bot.) 670n; Baudrier (Lyons) X:122. MoSB,
PPiH; BL, BN.　　　　　　　　　　549/11

__[Anr edn]. Stirpium imagines. *Lyons: B.Ar-*

noullet, 1549. 516p.; illus.;port.;16mo. Nissen (Bot.) 669; Baudrier (Lyons) X:122. DLC;
BL.　　　　　　　　　　　　　　　549/12

____. Primi de stirpium historia commentar-
iorum tomi vivae imagines. *Basel: M.Isengrin*,
1549. 516p.;illus.;8vo. 1st publ., Basel, 1545.
Pritzel 3140n; Nissen (Bot.) 661n; Hunt (Bot.)
63; Shaaber F513a. MH-A, PU; BL, BN.
　　　　　　　　　　　　　　　　　549/13

Garimberto, Girolamo, Bp of Gallese.
Problemi naturali, e morali. *Venice: V.Val-
grisi*, 1549. 230p.;8vo. On p.113-116 the lost
Atlantis is discussed, with mention of Columbus. Sabin 26668n; Harrisse (BAV) 292 & Add.
174. CU, CtY, DLC, ICN, InU-L, NN-RB,
RPJCB; BL, BN.　　　　　　　　　　549/14

Glareanus, Henricus. De geographia liber
unus ab ipso authore iam tertio recognitus.
*Venice: P.G.M. & C.dei Nicolini da Sabbio,
for M.Sessa*, 1549. 39 numb.lvs;illus.;8vo. 1st
publ. in this version, Freiburg, 1533. Sabin
27545 (misdated 1544); JCB (3) I:156. CSt,
DFo, ICN, InU-L, MH, MiU-C, NN-RB,
RPJCB; BL.　　　　　　　　　　　　549/15

Honter, Johannes. Rudimentorum cosmographicorum . . . libri iii. cum tabellis geographicis. *Zurich: C.Froschauer*, 1549. [58]p.;
maps;8vo. 1st publ. in this version, Kronstadt,
1542. In verse. Sabin 32796; Harrisse (BAV)
Add. 175; JCB (3) I:156. DLC, InU-L,
RPJCB; BN.　　　　　　　　　　　　549/16

Le Ferron, Arnoul. De rebus gestis Gallorum
libri quatuor. *Paris: M.de Vascovan*, 1549. 70
numb.lvs;8vo. Issued also as pt 3 of Paolo
Emili's *De rebus gestis Francorum*, Paris,
1548. In bk 2 is an account of appearance of
syphilis at Naples & elsewhere, with subsequent discussion of Columbus's role in this &
its treatment with Guaiacum; in bk 8 capture
of a Spanish ship returning from the Indies by
a Dieppe force is mentioned. BN.　　549/17

__[Anr issue]. *Paris: O.Petit*, 1549. Adams
(Cambr.) F318. ICN; Cambridge: UL, BN.
　　　　　　　　　　　　　　　　　549/18

Lucidarius. M.Elucidarius, von allerhand
geschöpffen Gottes . . . unnd wie alle Creaturen geschaffen sein auff erden. *Frankfurt
a.M.: H.Gülfferich*, 1549. [88]p.;4to. 1st
publ., Strassburg, [ca.1535]. Schorbach (Lucidarius) 54. NIC; Munich: StB.　　549/19

Manardo, Giovanni. Epistolarium medicinalium libri viginti. *Basel: M.Isengrin*, 1549.
603p.;fol. Includes Manardo's *De erroribus*

Symonis Pistoris . . . circa morbum gallicum, 1st publ., [Leipzig?], 1500. Adams (Cambr.) M319. DNLM; BL. 549/20

__[Anr edn]. *Lyons: G.. & M.Beringen,* 1549. 653p.;8vo. Adams (Cambr.) M318; Baudrier (Lyons) III:49. DNLM; BL, BN. 549/21

Medina, Pedro de. Libro de grandezas y cosas memorables de España. *Seville: D.de Robertis,* 1549. clxxxvi lvs;illus.,maps;fol. 1st publ., Alcalá de Henares, 1548. Medina (BHA) 138; Escudero (Seville) 511; JCB (3) I:157. ICN, NNH, RPJCB; BL. 549/22

Spain. Laws, statutes, etc. Pragmaticas y leyes . . . compuesto y añadido por . . . Diego Perez. *Medina del Campo: P.de Castro,* 1549. 180 numb.lvs;fol. 1st publ., with edict concerning convict labor for Hispaniola, Alcalá de Henares, 1503. Sabin 64915n; Harrisse (BAV) Add. 171; Medina (BHA) 139; Pérez Pastor (Medina del Campo) 68. InU-L; BL. 549/23

Spain. Laws, statutes, etc., 1516-1556 (Charles I). Las pregmaticas y capitulos que su Magestad . . . hizo en las Cortes . . . en Valladolid . . . M. D. XL Viii. *Valladolid: F.Fernández de Córdova,* 3 Feb. 1549. lxii lvs;fol. The 'Peticion ccxiiii' considers inflation & other effects of trade with New World. Alcocer (Valladolid) 150; Palau 63146. MH; BL. 549/24

__[Anr edn]. *Valladolid: F.Fernández de Córdova,* Dec., 1549. lv lvs;fol. Alcocer (Valladolid) 143; Palau 63147; JCB (3) I:155-156. ICN, RPJCB; BL. 549/25

Tagault, Jean. De chirurgica institutione libri quinque . . . Secunda editio. *Lyons: G. Rouillé,* 1549. 572p.;illus.;8vo. 1st publ., Paris, 1543. Baudrier (Lyons) IX:160. DNLM; London: Wellcome. 549/26

__[Anr edn]. *Venice: V.Valgrisi,* 1549. 660p.; illus.;8vo. DNLM, MiU; London: Wellcome. 549/27

____. Les institutions chirurgiques . . . Nouvellement traduictes de latin. *Lyons: [P.Rollet for] G.Rouillé,* 1549. 732p.;illus.;8vo. Transl. from Tagault's *De chirurgica institutione,* 1st publ., Paris, 1543. Baudrier (Lyons) IX:166-167. DNLM; BL. 549/28

Venero, Alonso de. Enchiridion de los tiempos . . . Agora nuevamente por el mismo auctor añadido, corregido y emendado. Mas lleva aora de nuevo añadido el descubrimiento de las Indias. *Saragossa: J.Milian (widow of D.Hernández),* 1549. 195 numb.lvs;8vo. 1st publ. with American material, Saragossa, 1548. Sabin 98864; Harrisse (BAV) Add. 172; Medina (BHA) 140; Sánchez (Aragon) 292. 549/29

Vigo, Giovanni de. Pratica universale in cirugia . . . Novamente tradotte per m. Lorenzo Chrisaorio. *Venice: F. Torresano,* 1549. 258 numb. lvs; illus.;4to. Transl. from author's *Practica in arte chirurgica copiosa,* 1st publ., Rome, 1514. DNLM. 549/30

1550

Albergati, Vianesio. La pazzia. [*Italy?* ca.1550?]. [46]p.;8vo. 1st dated edn., Bologna, 1540. Ind.aur.102.241; Adams (Cambr.) A437. BL, Munich: StB. 550/1

Alberti, Leandro. Descrittione di tutta Italia. *Bologna: A.Giaccarelli,* 1550. 469 numb.lvs; illus.,port.;fol. On lf 43 r/v is a passage on Vespucci. Sabin 659; Harrisse (BAV) 302; Ind.aur.102.338. DLC, IU, MH, MiU, PPL, RPJCB; BL, BN. 550/2

Apianus, Petrus. Cosmographia . . . per Gemmam Frisium . . . iam demum ab omnibus vindicata mendis. *Antwerp: G.Coppens v.Diest,for G.de Bonte,* 1550. 65 numb.lvs; illus.,maps;4to. 1st publ. in this version, Antwerp, 1529. Ortroy (Apian) 38. CtY; BL. 550/3

__[Anr edn]. *Antwerp: G.Coppens v. Diest,for G.de Bonte,* 1550. 64 numb. lvs; illus.,maps; 4to. Sabin 1749; Harrisse (BAV) 298; Sanz (Ult.ad.) 1383; Ortroy (Apian) 39; Ind. aur.106.444; JCB (3) I:158. DLC, ICN, MiU-C, NN-RB, RPJCB; Cambridge: UL, BN. 550/4

____. Cosmographiae introductio. *Paris: G.Cavellat,* 1550. 46 numb.lvs;illus.;8vo. 1st publ., Ingolstadt, 1532. Harrisse (BAV) Add. 180; Ind.aur.106.445; Ortroy (Apian) 89. ICN, MH, MiU, NN-RB. 550/5

Cabrera, Cristóbal de. Flores de consolacion. *Valladolid: F.Fernández de Córdova,* 1550. 97 numb.lvs;illus.;8vo. The anonymous translator (from the Latin), in covering epistle from Cuernavaca, refers to barbarous language of Indians of New Spain. Harrisse (BAV) Add. 181; Medina (BHA) 143; Alcocer (Valladolid) 156. 550/6

Cardano, Girolamo. De subtilitate libri xxi. *Nuremberg: J.Petrejus,* 1550. 371p.;illus., port.;fol. The 8th bk, on plants, includes refs to the West Indies. Pritzel 1528; Ind. aur.132.058. DLC, ICJ, InU-L, MB, NN-RB, PPAmP; BL, BN.	550/7

—[Anr edn]. *Lyons: P.Rollet,for G.Rouillé*, 1550. 621p.;8vo. Baudrier (Lyons) IX:173; Ind.aur.132.056; Shaaber C130. PU; Berlin: StB.	550/8

—[Anr edn]. *Paris: M.Fezandot & R.Granjon*, 1550. 312 numb.lvs;illus.;8vo. Ind. aur.132.057; Shaaber C129. NN-RB, PU; BL, Munich: StB.	550/9

Chaves, Jerónimo de. Chronographia, o Repertorio de los tiempos. *Seville: C.Alvárez*, 1550. ccvi lvs;4to. 1st publ., Seville, 1548. Palau 67450n; Shaaber 368. PU.	550/10

Cortés, Hernando. Von dem Newen Hispanien, so im Meer gegen Nidergang . . . Erstlich in hispanischer Sprach . . . nachmals von Doctor Peter Savorgnan . . . in lateinische sprach transferiert, entlich aber in hochteütsche sprach . . . von Xysto Betuleio und Andrea Diethero. *Augsburg: P.Ulhart*, 1550. 2pts.;fol. The 1st pt, transl. by Sixt Birck (xxxix lvs) comprises Cortés's 2nd narration. The 2nd, with title 'Ander histori' (lx lvs), transl. by Andreas Diether, contains 12 chapts (lvs i-xi) taken from P.M. d'Anghiera's 4th Decade, followed by Cortés's 3rd narration. In turn this is followed by letters describing events in Venezuela dated 20 Oct. 1538 & 16 Jan. 1540 from Coro, the writer of which, though not here identified, was Philipp von Hutten. Lvs lvii ff. contain letter dated 20 Jan. 1543 from Santo Domingo of G.F. d'Oviedo y Valdës, also found (lvs 345r-346r) in Ramusio's *Terzo volume delle Navigationi*, Venice, 1556. Sabin 16957; Harrisse (BAV) 197; Medina (BHA) 86; JCB (3) I:158. CU, DLC, InU-L, MH, MiU, MnU-B, NN-RB, RPJCB; BL, BN.	550/11

Dioscorides, Pedanius. Il Dioscoride, dell'eccellente dottor medico m. P. Andrea Matthioli . . . con li suoi discorsi. *Venice: V. Valgrisi*, 1550. 2pts;4to. 1st publ., Venice, 1544. Pritzel 2318 & 5906. DNLM, NNBG; BL, BN.	550/12

Emili, Paolo. De rebus gestis Francorum . . . libri decem . . . Arnoldi Ferroni . . . De rebus gestis Gallorum libri ix. *Paris: M.de Vascovan*, 1550. 3pts;fol. 1st publ. with Le Ferron's appendix, Paris, 1548. Adams (Cambr.) A238; Ind.aur.100.830. ICU, RPB; Cambridge: UL, BN.	550/13

Fernel, Jean. De abditis rerum causis libri duo. *Venice: P. & G.M.dei Nicolini da Sabbio,for A.Arrivabene*, 1550. 310p.;8vo. 1st publ., Paris, 1548. Sherrington (Fernel) 18.F2. CtY, DNLM, ICN, MH, NNNAM; BN.	550/14

Fontanon, Denys. De morborum internorum curatione libri quatuor. *Lyons: J.Frellon*, 1550. 381p.;8vo. 1st publ. (in 3 bks), Lyons, 1549. Baudrier (Lyons) V:218. DNLM, PPC; London: Wellcome.	550/15

Fracastoro, Girolamo. Liber I, De sympathia & antipathia rerum. De contagione, & contagiosis morbis & eorum curatione, libri tres. *Lyons: N.Bacquenois,for G.Gazeau*, 1550. 558p.;16mo. 1st publ., Venice, 1546. Waller 3164. CSmH, CtY, DNLM, IU, MnU, NNNAM, PPC; London: Wellcome, BN.	550/16

Franck, Sebastian. Wereltboeck. Spiegel ende beeltenisse des gheheelen aertbodems. [*Antwerp? 1550?*]. fol. Transl. from author's *Weltbüch*, 1st publ., Tübingen, 1542. BL.	550/17

Fuchs, Leonhart. L'histoire des plantes . . . nouvellement traduict de latin . . . [par Guillaume Guéroult?]. *Lyons: B.Arnoullet*, 1550. 607p.;illus.;4to. Transl. from author's *De historia stirpium commentarii*, 1st publ., Basel, 1542. Cf.Pritzel 3139n; Nissen (Bot.) 668; Baudrier (Lyons) X:125-126. DNLM, MH, OkU, RPB; BN.	550/18

Garimberto, Girólamo, Bp of Gallese. Problemi naturali, e morali. *Venice: V. Valgrisi*, 1550. 239p.;8vo. 1st publ., Venice, 1549. Sabin 26668; Harrisse (BAV) 293; Adams (Cambr.) G251. ICN, NN-RB, PU, RPB; BL.	550/19

Giovio, Paolo, Bp of Nocera. Historiarum sui temporis, tomus primus[-secundus]. *Florence: L.Torrentino*, 1550-52. 2v.;fol. Refs to American discovery, exploration & conquest appear in v.2 on p.251-254. Adams (Cambr.) G649. CtY, ICN,MH, NN-RB, RPB; BL, BN.	550/20

Glareanus, Henricus. De geographia liber unus. *Paris: G.Cavellat*, 1550. 40 lvs;illus.; 4to. 1st publ. in this version, Freiburg, 1533. Fairfax Murray (France) 197. NN-RB. 550/21

Le Ferron, Arnoul. De rebus gestis Gallorum libri ix. *Paris: M.de Vascovan*, 1550. 151 numb.lvs;fol. 1st publ. Paris, 1548, as supplement to Paolo Emili's *De rebus gestis Francorum*. Adams (Cambr.) F319. CSt, DLC,

ICN, RPB; Cambridge: UL, BN.   550/22
___[Anr edn]. *Paris: M.de Vascovan*, 1550. 190 numb.lvs;8vo. Adams (Cambr.) F320. BL, BN.   550/23

Lucidarius. M.Elucidarius, von allerhand geschöpffen Gottes . . . unnd wie alle Creaturen geschaffen sein auff erden. *Frankfurt a.M.: H.Gülfferich*, 1550. [88]p.;4to. 1st publ., Strassburg, [ca.1535]. Schorbach (Lucidarius) 55. Wolfenbüttel:HB.   550/24

More, Sir Thomas, Saint. La description de l'isle de l'Utopie. *Paris: C.L'Angelier*, 1550. 105 numb.lvs;illus.,port,;8vo. Transl. by Jehan Le Blond from Latin text, 1st publ., Louvain, 1516. Gibson (More) 19; Adams (Cambr.) M1759; Fairfax Murray (France) 391. CtY, DLC, ICN, MH, NNPM; BL, BN.   550/25

Münster, Sebastian. Cosmographei, oder beschreibung aller länder. *Basel: H. Petri*, 1550. mccxxxiii p.;illus.,ports.,maps;fol. 1st publ. in German, Basel, 1544; the 1st edn to contain views of towns. Sabin 51387; Harrisse (BAV) 294 & Add. 179; Burmeister (Münster) 70. CSmH, ICU, PPG; Basel: UB.   550/26

___. Cosmographiae universalis lib. vi. *Basel: H.Petri*, 1550. mclxii p.; illus.,port.,maps;fol. Transl. from author's German *Cosmographia*, 1st publ., Basel, 1544. Sabin 51379; Harrisse (BAV) 300; Burmeister (Münster) 87. CtY, DLC, ICN, InU-L, MH, NN-RB, RPJCB; BL, Paris: Ste Geneviève.   550/27

Pantaleon, Heinrich. Chronographia ecclesiae christianae. *Basel: N.Brylinger*, 1550. 129p.;4to. Includes ref. to Columbus & Vespucci. BL, BN.   550/28

Paradin, Guillaume. Histoire de nostre temps. *Lyons: J.de Tournes & G.Gazeau*, 1550. 183p.;fol. Transl. from author's *Memoriae nostrae libri quatuor*, 1st publ., Lyons, 1548. Cartier (de Tournes) 176. ICN; BL, BN.   550/29

Peucer, Kaspar. De dimensione terrae, et fontibus doctrinae longitudinis et latitudinis locorum. *Wittenberg: Heirs of P.Seitz*, 1550. 61 lvs;8vo. Includes chapt. on America. Sabin 61311; Harrisse (BAV) Add. 184. NN-RB; BN.   550/30

Ramusio, Giovanni Battista, comp. Primo volume delle Navigationi et viaggi nel qual si contiene la descrittione dell'Africa, et del paese del Prete Ianni, con varii viaggi, dal mar Rosso à Calicut, & infin all'isole Molucche . . . et la navigatione attorno il mondo.

Venice: Heirs of L.Giunta, 1550. 405 numb. lvs;maps,plans;fol. The 2nd vol., published in 1559, is itself without American content, but cf.3rd vol. of 1556. Of the contents, the following relate to the Americas: 'Di Amerigo Vespucci . . . lettera prima . . . di due viaggi' (lvs 139v-140v), 'Di Amerigo Vespucci lettera II' (lf 141r-v), 'Sommario di Amerigo Vespucci' (lvs 141v-144v), 'Discorso sopra il viaggio fatto da gli spagnuoli intorno al mondo' (lvs 382v-383r), 'Epistola di Massimiliano Transilvano' (lvs 383v-389v), 'Viaggio atorno il mondo fatto et descritto per m. Antonio Pigafetta' (lvs 389v-408v), 'Narratione di un portoghese . . . qual fu sopra la nave Vittoria del anno MDXIX' (lvs 408v-409r). See also G.B.Parks, 'The contents and sources of Ramusio's *Navigationi*', New York Public Library *Bulletin*, L(1955) 279-313. Sabin 67730; Harrisse (BAV) 304; Sanz (Ult.ad.) 1386-1390; Streit I:55; JCB AR20:1550. CSmH, DLC; MB, MnU-B, NN-RB, RPJCB; BL, BN.   550/31

Ryd, Valerius Anselmus. Catalogus annorum et principum, sive Monarcharum mundi geminus plerisque in locis obscurioribus illustratus. *Berne: M.Apiarius*, 1550. xcix lvs;fol. 1st publ., Berne, 1550, the American ref. here appearing on lf xciiii. Adams (Cambr.) R985. MH, NN-RB, RPJCB; Cambridge: UL, BN.   550/32

Sabellico, Marco Antonio Coccio, called. Coronica geral . . . des ho começo do mundo ate nosso tempo. Treslado de latim em lingoagem portugues por Dona Lianor, filha do marques de Vila Real. *Coimbra: J.de Bareira e J.Alvárez*, 1550-53. 2v.;fol. Transl. from author's *Enneades*, 1st publ. with ref. to Columbus, Venice, 1504. Sabin 74667; Harrisse (BAV) 296; Anselmo 271 & 294. MH; BL, Lisbon: BN.   550/33

Sacro Bosco, Joannes de. Annotationi sopra la lettione della Sfera . . . authore M. Mauro. *Florence: L.Torrentino*, 1550. 219p.;4to. 1st publ. in this translation, with Mauro's annotations, Venice, 1537. Sabin 74810n (&32683); Harrisse (BAV) Add. 182; JCB (3) I:135. NN-RB, RPJCB; BL.   550/34

Sepúlveda, Juan Gines de. Apologia . . . pro libro de justis belli causis. *Rome: V. & L.Dorici*, 1550. [48]p.;8vo. Pages [39-48] contain a 'Decretum et indultum Alexandri Sexti super expeditione in barbaros novi orbis quos Indos vocant'. Presumably the work elsewhere described by its author as his 'Democrates secundus'. Justifies waging war on Indians. Sabin 79125 (cf.79126); Harrisse (BAV) 303; Medina (BHA) 142; Streit I:56. InU-L; Rome: Bibl. Casanatense.   550/35

Spain. Laws, statutes, etc. Recopolacion de algunas bullas del summo pontife, concedidas, en favor dela jurisdicíon real, con todas las pragmaticas, y algunas leyes del reyno. *Toledo: J.Ferrer,for M. Rodríguez*, 1550. ccxxiv lvs;fol. Includes, as 'Ley .cii.', edict 1st publ., 1503, on transport of convicts to Indies in Columbus's service. Sabin 64915n; Harrisse (BAV) Add. 178; Medina (BHA) 141; Pérez Pastor (Toledo) 246; JCB AR20:1550. NN-RB, RPJCB.   550/36

Spain. Laws, statutes, etc., 1516-1556 (Charles I). Las leyes y prematicas reales hechas . . . en las cortes . . . de Toledo [1525]. *Salamanca: J.de Junta*, 1550. [43]p.;fol. 1st publ., Burgos, 1525. Palau 63129; JCB (3) I:160. CtY-L, InU-L, NNH, RPJCB.   550/37

Tagault, Jean. La chirurgia . . . tradotta in buona lingua volgare. *Venice: M.Tramezzino*, 1550. 421 numb. lvs;illus.;8vo. Transl. from Tagault's *De chirurgica institutione*, 1st publ., Paris, 1543. Moranti (Urbino) 3221. DNLM, MiU; Urbino: BU.   550/38

Vadianus, Joachim von Watt, called. Epitome trium terrae partium, Asiae, Africae et Europae. *Zurich: C. Froschauer* [ca.1550?]. 524p.;illus.,maps;8vo. 1st publ., Zurich, 1534. Sabin 98282; Adams (Cambr.) V11. DLC (lacks maps), NN-RB (lacks maps), NNH; Cambridge: UL, BN.   550/39

Varthema, Lodovico di. Itinerario. *Venice: M.Pagan* [1550?]. 100 numb. lvs;8vo. 1st publ., with Juan Díaz's account of Grijalva's 1518 expedition, Venice, 1520. Sabin 98647; Medina (BHA) 98; JCB (3) I:120. NN-RB, RPJCB; BL.   550/40

Vigo, Giovanni de. The most excellent workes of chirurgerie. [*London:*] *E.Whytchurch*, 1550. cclxx lvs;fol. 1st publ. in this translation by B.Traheron, London, 1543. STC 24721. CSmH, DFo, MH, NNPM; BL.   550/41

1551

Alberti, Leandro. Descrittione di tutta Italia. *Venice: P. & G.M.dei Nicolini da Sabbio*, 1551. 424 numb.lvs;4to. 1st publ., Bologna, 1550. Ind.aur.102.339; Adams (Cambr.)

A472. CU, IU, MH, NN-RB; Cambridge: UL, BN.   551/1

Amatus Lusitanus. Curationum medicinalium centuria prima. *Florence: L. Torrentino*, 1551. 391p.;8vo. The 45th, 49th, 50th & 54th 'Curationes' deal with syphilis and the use of Guaiacum. Ind.aur.104.552. DNLM, MBCo, NNNAM, PPC; BN.   551/2

Apianus, Petrus. Cosmographia . . . per Gemmam Frisium . . . iam demum ab omnibus vindicata mendis. *Paris: V. Gaultherot*, 1551. 74 numb.lvs;illus.,maps;8vo. 1st publ,. in this version, Antwerp, 1529. Sabin 1749n; Ind.aur.106.446; Ortroy (Apian) 41. CtY, DLC, ICN, MH, NN-RB, RPJCB; BL, BN.   551/3

——. Cosmographiae introductio. *Paris: G. Cavellat*, 1551. 38 numb. lvs;illus.,maps;8vo. 1st publ., Ingolstadt, 1532. 'De America et circumiacentibus insulis': lvs 36v-37v. Also issued as pt 2 of M.Borrhaus's *Elementale cosmographicum* of this year, q.v. Sabin 1749n; Ortroy (Apian) 91; Ind.aur.106.448. CtY, NN-RB; BL.   551/4

——[Anr edn]. *Venice: P.Nicolini da Sabbio & Bros,for M.Sessa*, 1551. 24 numb.lvs;illus., maps;8vo. 1st publ. in this version, Venice, 1533. Ind.aur.106.449; Ortroy (Apian) 92. DLC, ICN.   551/5

——. La cosmographie . . . nouvellement traduicte de latin . . . par Gemma Frisius. *Paris: V.Gaultherot*, 1551. 70 numb.lvs;illus.,map; 4to. 1st publ. in this French edn, Antwerp, 1544. Sabin 1752n; Ind.aur.106.447; Ortroy (Apian) 40. DLC, MiU-C, RPJCB; Paris: Ste Geneviève.   551/6

Bembo, Pietro, Cardinal. Historiae Venetae libri xii. *Venice: Sons of A.Manuzio*, 1551. 203 numb.lvs;fol. Bk vi (lvs 82-99) includes an account of Portuguese & Spanish explorations, cited as a cause of the economic decline of Venice. In this issue, an Aldine anchor device appears on the t.p., the verso being blank. For reasons for assigning priority to this issue, see C.H.Clough, 'Pietro Bembo's L'Histoire du Nouveau Monde,' *British Library journal*, IV (1978) 8-21. Sabin 4619; Renouard (Aldus) I:364-365 (no.17); Ind. aur.116.419; JCB (3) I:162. CLU, MH, NNC, RPJCB; BN.   551/7

——[Anr issue]. *Venice: Sons of A.Manuzio* [*for C.Gualteruzzi?*] 1551. The license on verso of the t.p. is to Gualteruzzi; on the t.p. is the

Hermes & Athena device found elsewhere in works published by Gualtiero Scoto (cf.Mortimer, Italy, 449n). Cf.Sabin 4619; Renouard (Aldus) I:364-365 (no.17n); Adams (Cambr.) B597. CLU, CtY, DLC, ICN, MH, MiU, MnU-B, NN-RB, RPJCB; BL, BN. 551/8

___[Anr edn]. Rerum Venetarum historiae libri xii. *Paris: M.de Vascovan*, 1551. 311 numb. lvs;4to. Sabin 4619n; Ind.aur.116.417; Adams (Cambr.) B598. DLC, ICN, InU-L, MnU-B, PPL; Cambridge: UL, BN. 551/9

Bielski, Marcin. Kronika wszystkiego swiata. *Cracow*: 1551. 327 numb. lvs;map;fol. On verso of lf 20 is passage referring to Vespucci & New World, on lf 110 one to Columbus. Yarmolinsky (Early Polish Americana) 37-42; cf. Hoskins (Early Polonica) 68. Lwow: Baworowski Libr. 551/10

Bock, Hieronymus. Kreüter Buch. *Strassburg: W.Rihel*, 1551. ccccxxiiii lvs; illus.;fol. 1st publ. with illus., Strassburg, 1546. Pritzel 866; Nissen (Bot.) 182n; Ind. aur.120.590; Ritter (Strasbourg) 215. MnU, PPAN; BL, Strasbourg: BN. 551/11

Borrhaus, Martin. Elementale cosmographicum . . . Adjunximus . . . Cosmographiae introductio [Petri Apiani]. *Paris: G.Cavellat*, 1551. 2pts;illus.,map;8vo. Apianus's work was 1st publ. in this form, Ingolstadt, 1532. Though, as indicated by the above title, an integral part of the larger work, the *Introductio* is believed to have also been issued separately. Ortroy (Apian) 90; Burmeister (Gasser) 23; JCB (3) I:162. DLC, MH, MiU, MnU-B, NN-RB, RPJCB; BL, BN. 551/12

Cardano, Girolamo. De subtilitate libri xxi. *Lyons: P.Rollet,for G.Rouillé*, 1551. 621p.; illus.;8vo. 1st publ., Nuremberg(?), 1550. Here a reissue of the bookseller's 1550 edn with altered imprint date. Baudrier (Lyons) IX:190; Ind.aur.132.059. Paris: Arsenal. 551/13

___[Anr edn]. *Paris: M.Fezandat & R.Granjon*, 1551. 312 numb.lvs;illus.;8vo. A reissue of the printers' 1550 edn with altered imprint date. Ind.aur.132.061. CtY, MiU, MnU-B, NNBG; BN. 551/14

___[Anr issue of preceding?]. *Paris: J.DuPuys*, 1551. Ind.aur.132.060; Adams (Cambr.) C669; Arents (Add.) 9. NN-A; BL. 551/15

Cortés, Martín. Breve compendio de la sphera y de la arte de navegar, con nuevos instrumentos y reglas. *Seville: A.Alvárez*, 1551.

xcv lvs;illus.,maps;fol. On lf xxi(r) appear refs to Brazil, Magellan Straits, etc.; on lf lxvii(r) is a world map including New World. Sabin 16966; Medina (BHA) 145; Borba de Moraes I:185-186; Escudero (Seville) 532; JCB (3) I:163. CtY, DLC, InU-L, MH, MiU-C, NN-RB, RPJCB; BL, Madrid: BN. 551/16

Dioscorides, Pedanius. Il Dioscoride, dell'eccellente dottor medico m. P. Andrea Matthioli . . . con li suoi discorsi . . . la terza volta illustrati. *Venice: V.Valgrisi*, 1551. 2pts;4to. 1st publ. in this version, Venice, 1544. Cf. Pritzel 2320. NcD; BL. 551/17

Fernel, Jean. De abditis rerum causis libri duo . . . Aeditio secunda. *Paris: C.Wechel*, 1551. 181p.;fol. 1st publ., Paris, 1548. Sherrington (Fernel) 19.F3; Adams (Cambr.) F244. Oxford: Bodl., Paris: Faculté de Médecine. 551/17a

___[Anr issue]. *Paris: C.Wechel,for J. Dupuys*, 1551. Sherrington (Fernel) 19.F3n. Sherrington. 551/18

Fuchs, Leonhart. De historia stirpium commentarii insignes. *Lyons: B.Arnoullet*, 1551. 851p.;illus.,port.;8vo. 1st publ., Basel, 1542. Pritzel 3138n; Baudrier (Lyons) X:128. DNLM, MH-A, NNNAM; BL, BN. 551/19

_____. L'histoire des plantes . . . nouvellement traduict de latin. *Lyons: B.Arnoullet*, 1551. 607p.;illus.;4to. 1st publ. in French, Paris, 1549; here a reissue with altered imprint date of Arnoullet's 1550 edn. Nissen (Bot.) 670; Baudrier (Lyons) X:128. 551/20

_____. Plantarum eefigies [i.e., effigies] . . . ac quinque diversis linguis redditae. *Lyons: B. Arnoullet*, 1551. 516p.; illus.,port.;16mo. 1st publ., Lyons, 1549. Cf.Pritzel 3140n; Nissen (Bot.) 670; Baudrier (Lyons) X:129-130. DNLM, MH-A, NNC, PPAN; BL, Paris: Ste Geneviève. 551/21

Gesner, Konrad. Elenchus scriptorum omnium, veterum scilicet ac recentiorum . . . redactus . . . per Conradum Lycosthenem [i.e., C. Wolffhart]. *Basel: J.Oporinus*, 1551. 1096cols;4to. Includes entries for P.M. d'Anghiera, Columbus, U.von Hutten, Vespucci, etc. Adams (Cambr.) W248; Shaaber G143. CtY, ICN, MH, PU; BL, BN. 551/22

Giovio, Paolo, Bp of Nocera. Elogia virorum bellica virtute illustrium veris imaginibus supposita, quae apud Musaeum spectantur. *Florence: L.Torrentino*, 1551. 340p.;fol. Includes accounts of Columbus & Hernando

Cortés. For variant states, see Mortimer. Adams (Cambr.) G639; Mortimer (Italy) 213; Shaaber G193. CLSU, CtY, DLC, InU-L, MH, MiU-C, NN-RB, PU, RPJCB; BL.
　　　　　　　　　　　　　　　　551/23
____. La prima[-seconda] parte dell'Istorie del suo tempo . . . Tradotta per m. Lodovico Domenichi. *Venice: B. & F.Imperadore* (v.2, *B. Cesano*), 1551-54. 4to. Transl. from author's *Historiarum sui temporis*, Venice, 1550-52. CtY.　　　　　　　　　　　　551/24

Glareanus, Henricus. De geographia liber . . . novissime recognitus. *Freiburg i.Br.: S. M.Graf*, 1551. 33 numb.lvs;4to. 1st publ. in this version, Freiburg, 1533. Sabin 27546; JCB (3) I:164. DLC, NNH, RPJCB.　551/25

Interiano, Paolo. Inventione del corso della longitudine . . . col Ristretto della sphera. *Lucca: V.Busdrago*, 1551. 2pts(16 lvs);4to. In dedication Columbus is mentioned. Riccardi I:649. MH, NN-RB; BL, BN.　　551/26
____. Ristretto delle historie genovese. *Lucca: V.Busdrago*, 1551. 233 numb. lvs;4to. On lf 227 is a brief note on Columbus. Sabin 34905; Adams (Cambr.) I146; JCB (3) I:164. CU, CtY, DLC, ICU, MH, MiU, MnU-B, NN-RB, RPJCB; BL, BN.　　　　　551/27

Lonitzer, Adam. Naturalis historiae opus novum. *Frankfurt a.M.: C.Egenolff*, 1551. 352 numb.lvs;illus.;fol. Included are descriptions of American plants, e.g. Guaiacum, 'Indicum frumentum' (corn), 'Siliquastrum' (pepper), etc. Pritzel 5598; Nissen (Bot.) 1229. DNLM, MH, MnU-B, RPB; BL.　　551/28

Lopes de Castanheda, Fernão. Historia do descobrimento e conquista de India pelos Portuguezes [Livro primeiro]. *Coimbra: J.da Barreira & J.Alvares*, 1551. 267p.;8vo. Refs to Brazil appear on p.91-93. For continuation, see year 1552. Sabin 11381-82; Borba de Moraes I:140; King Manuel 72. ICN, RPJCB; BL.　　　　　　　　　　　　551/29

Mexía, Pedro. Dialogos o coloquios. *Seville: C.Alvárez*, 1551. clviii numb.lvs;8vo. 1st publ., Seville, 1547, under title *Colóquios o dialogos*. Escudero (Seville) 531. MH; BL, Madrid: BN.　　　　　　　　551/30

More, Sir Thomas, Saint. A fruteful and pleasant worke . . . called Utopia . . . translated . . . by R. Robinson. *London: S.Mierdman,for A.Veale*, 1551. 144 numb.lvs;12mo. 1st publ., in Latin, Louvain, 1516. Sabin 50544; STC 18094; Gibson (More) 25; JCB (3)

I:165. CSmH, CtY, DFo, ICN, NN-RB, RPJCB; BL.　　　　　　　　551/31

Pantaleon, Heinrich. Chronographia ecclesiae christianae. *Basel: N.Brylinger*, 1551. 157p.;fol. 1st publ., Basel, 1550. Adams (Cambr.) P173. CtY, IU; BL.　　551/32

Rouen. Cest la deduction du somptueux ordre, plaisantz spectacles et magnifiques theatres, et exhibes par les citoiens de Rouen . . . a la sacree Maiesté du . . . Roy de France, Henry second . . . lors de leur triumphant, joyeulx & nouvel advenement en icelle ville. *Rouen: J.LePrest,for R.LeHoy & R. & J. DuGort*, 1551. [137]p.;illus.,music;4to. Included in the spectacles was a Brazilian village with Tupinamba Indians. The title given by Sabin at entry 57538 is derived from the colophon of this work. Sabin 73458; Borba de Moraes I:151-154; Mortimer (France) 203. DLC, MH; BL.　　　　　　　551/33

Sacro Bosco, Joannes de. Sphaera . . . auctior quam antehac . . . castigatior, cum annotationibus et scholiis Eliae Vineti. *Paris: G.Cavellat*, 1551. 104 numb.lvs;illus.;8vo. Includes Vinet's *Scholia* with ref. to Portuguese & Spanish discoveries in East & West Indies. Cf. Sabin 32681. NN-RB; London: Wellcome.
　　　　　　　　　　　　　　　　551/34

Schöner, Johann. Opera mathematica. *Nuremberg: J.vom Berg & U.Neuber*, 1551. 3pts;illus.,port.,maps;fol. Includes the author's *Opusculum geographicum* describing a terrestrial globe, 1st publ., Nuremberg, 1533. Sabin 77805; Adams (Cambr.) S678; Coote (Schöner) 41. CtY, DLC, ICN, MH, MiU, NN-RB; BL, BN.　　　　　　551/35

Spain. Cortes. Quaderno de las cortes: que en Valladolid tuvo su magestad del Emperador . . . el año de .1523. *Salamanca: J.de Junta*, 1551. [36]p.;fol. 1st publ., Burgos, 1523. Palau 63148; JCB (3) I:163-164. InU-L, MH-L, RPJCB.　　　　　551/36

Venero, Alonso. Enchiridion de los tiempos. *Burgos: J.de Junta*, 1551. 199 numb. lvs;8vo. 1st publ. with American refs, Saragossa, 1549. Sabin 98865n; Medina (BHA) 140n; Palau 358453.　　　　　　551/37
____[Anr edn]. *Medina del Campo: J.de Espinosa*, 1551. 151 numb.lvs;8vo. Perhaps printed for Espinosa at Valladolid by F.Fernández de Córdova. Palau 358454.　　　551/38
____[Anr edn]. *Antwerp: M.Nuyts*, 1551. 212 numb.lvs;8vo. Peeters-Fontainas (Impr. esp.)

1357; Palau 358452. Antwerp: Plantin Mus., Madrid: BN.   551/39

Vittori, Benedetto, alleged author. De morbo gallico liber . . . De curatione pleuritidis. *Florence: L.Torrentino*, 1551. 316p.;8vo. 1st publ., Basel, 1536, in *Morbi gallici curandi ratio*. Authorship here denied (see p.133) by Vittori. DNLM.   551/40

1552

Amatus Lusitanus. Curationum medicinalium centuria prima. *Paris: P.Gaulthier*, 1552. 432p.;16mo. 1st publ., Florence, 1551. OCH.   552/1

—[Anr issue?]. *Paris: [P.Gaulthier for?] G. Cavellat*, 1552. 432p.;16mo. DNLM.   552/2

————. Curationum medicinalium centuria secunda. *Venice: G.Griffio, for V.Valgrisi*, 1552. 232p.;8vo. Continues 1st *Centuria* of 1551. In discussing syphilis, ref. appears in Curatio 95 to Guaiacum 'ex insulis noviter repertis'. Ind. aur.104.553. DNLM; BL, BN.   552/3

Barros, João de. Asia . . . dos fectos que os Portugueses fizeram no descobrimento & conquista dos mares & terras do Oriente. *Lisbon: G.Galharde*, 1552. 128 numb.lvs;fol. In bk 1, chapt.xi describes Columbus's 1st voyage; in bk 2, chapt.ii describes discovery of Brazil. Continued by 2nd Decade of following year. Sabin 3646; Borba de Moraes I:71-72; Streit IV:667; Ind.aur.113.423; King Manuel 74. MH, MnU-B, NN-RB; BL, BN.   552/4

Bembo, Pietro, Cardinal. Della istoria vinitiana . . . volgarmenta scritta. Libri xii. *Venice: G.Scoto*, 1552. 179 numb.lvs;4to. Transl. from Venice, 1551, Latin text. Sabin 4620; Ind. aur.116.428; Adams (Cambr.) 599; Shaaber B188. DLC, ICN, MH, MnU-B, NN-RB; BL, BN.   552/5

Bock, Hieronymus. De stirpium, maxime earum, quae in Germania nostra nascuntur. *Strassburg: W.Rihel*, 1552. 1200p;illus.;4to. Transl. by David Kyber from author's *Kreuter Buch*, 1st publ., Strassburg, 1539. For American plants here described see Enrique Álvarez López, 'Las plantas de América en la botánica europea del siglo XVI', *Revista de Indias*, VI (1945) 231-233. Pritzel 867; Nissen (Bot.) 183; Adams (Cambr.) T895 (Tragus); Ritter (Strasbourg) 216. CtY, DNLM, InU-L, MH-A, NNNAM; London: Wellcome, BN.   552/6

Brasavola, Antonio Musa. De medicamentis tam simplicibus, quam compositis catharticis. *Venice: Heirs of L.Giunta*, 1552. 220 numb. lvs;8vo. 1st publ., Rome, 1536, under title *Examen omnium simplicium*. Ind.aur. 123.806; Adams (Cambr.) B2680. DNLM, IJC, NNNAM; BL.   552/7

Casas, Bartolomé de las, Bp of Chiapa. Brevissima relacion de la destruycion de las Indias. *Seville: S.Trugillo*, 1552. [108] p.;4to. The final 4 lvs comprise an appendix of unknown authorship with title 'Lo que se signe es un pedaço de una carta y relacion'. Usually given separate recognition, it is bibliographically an intrinsic part of the *Brevissima relacion*, which is here given priority amongst the group of Las Casas's writings on the cruelties inflicted on the Indians, since by it are they collectively known. The sequence in which they were individually printed is obscure, for though some bear month and date in their colophon, others do not; nor does the order in which the items are found bound up together in whole or in part offer a basis for judgment. Though inconsistent with the colophon dates, the sequence adopted by Sabin, derived from inferred periods of original composition, has been followed. Sabin 11227 & 11228; Medina (BHA) 151; Escudero (Seville) 542 (5); Streit I:59; Church 87 & 88; JCB (3) I:167-168. CSmH, CtY, DLC, InU-L, MH, MiU-C, NN-RB, PU, RPJCB; BL, BN.   552/8

————. Entre los remedios que don fray Bartolome delas Casas . . . refirio . . . para reformacion delas Indias. *Seville: J.Cromberger*, 1552. [106]p.;4to. Though printed by Cromberger, the title page is set within the same woodcut border used by Trugillo for preceding item, implying collaboration. Sabin 11229; Medina (BHA) 146; Streit I:62; Church 89; JCB (3) I:169-170. CSmH, CtY, DLC, InU-L, MH, MiU-C, NN-RB, PU, RPJCB; BL, BN. 552/9

————. Este es un tratado . . . sobre la materia de los Yndios que se han hecho . . . en los esclavos. *Seville: S.Trugillo*, 1552. [71]p.;4to. Sabin 11230; Medina (BHA) 149; Escudero (Seville) 542 (3); Streit I:61; Church 93; JCB (3) I:169. CSmH, CtY, DLC, InU-L, MH, MiU-C, NN-RB, PU, RPJCB; BL, BN.552/10

————. Tratado comprobatorio. *Seville*: 1552 [i.e., 1553]. Though 4th in sequence of composition, not printed till the year 1553, which see.

____. Aqui se contienen unos avisos y reglas para los confessores. *Seville: S.Trugillo,* 1552. [31]p.;4to. Sabin 11232; Medina (BHA) 148; Escudero (Seville) 542 (4); Streit I;62; Church 90; JCB (3) I:170. CSmH, CtY, DLC, InU-L, MH, MiU-C, NN-RB, PU, RPJCB; BL, BN.
552/11

____. Aqui se contienen treynta proposiciones muy juridicas. *Seville: S.Trugillo,* 1552. [20]p.;4to. Sabin 11233; Medina (BHA) 150; Escudero (Seville) 542 (6); Streit I:63; Church 94; JCB(3) I:169. CSmH, CtY, DLC, InU-L, MH, MiU-C, NN-RB, PU, RPJCB; BL, BN.
552/12

____. Aqui se contiene una disputa . . . entre el obispo . . . Bartholome de las Casas . . . y el doctor Gines de Sepulveda. *Seville: S.Trugillo,* 1552. [122]p.;4to. The last line of the t.p. reads 'Año 1552'. Sabin 11234; Medina (BHA) 147; Escudero (Seville) 542 (2); Streit I:60: Church 91; JCB (3) I:168. CSmH, CtY, DLC, InU-L, MH, MiU-C, MnU-B, NN-RB, RPJCB; BL, BN.
552/13

__[Anr edn]. *Seville: S.Trugillo,* 1552. [122]p.;4to. The last line of the t.p. reads solely '1552'. Sabin 39115; Church 92. CSmH, CtY, DLC, MB, MiU-C, PU.
552/14

____. Principia quedam ex quibus procedendum est in disputatione ad manifestandam et defendendam justiciam Yndorum. *Seville: S. Trugillo* [1552?]. [20]p.;4to. Sabin 11235; Medina (BHA) 152; Escudero (Seville) 542 (7); Streit I:58; Church 95; JCB (3) I:170. CSmH, CtY, DLC, InU-L, MiU-C, NN-RB, PU, RPJCB; BL, BN.
552/15

Dioscorides, Pedanius. Il Dioscoride, dell'eccellente dottor medico m. P. Andrea Matthiolo . . . con li suoi discorsi de esso la terza volta illustrati. *Venice: V.Valgrisi,* 1552, 2pts;4to. 1st publ., Venice, 1544. Pritzel 2320. DNLM, NNBG; London: Wellcome.
552/16

Fuchs, Leonhart. Plantarum effigies. *Paris: B.Arnoullet,* 1552. 516p.;illus.,port.;16mo. 1st publ., Lyons, 1549; here a reissue of 1551 edn with altered imprint date. Pritzel 3140n; Nissen (Bot.) 670n; Baudrier (Lyons) X:130-131; Adams (Cambr.) F1126. MH-A; Cambridge: UL, Paris: Arsenal.
552/17

Gambara, Lorenzo. Chorineus. *Rome: V.& L.Dorici,* 1552. 7 lvs; 4to. In verse, describing newly found islands, principally Cuba & its inhabitants. Leclerc (1878) 230. ICN, InU-L; BL.
552/18

Gesner, Konrad. Thesaurus Euonymi Philiatri [pseud.]. De remediis secretis liber physicus, medicus et partim etiam chymicus et oeconomicus . . . Nunc primum in lucem editus. *Zurich: A.Gessner & R.Wyssenbach,* 1552. 580p.;illus.;8vo. Included are refs to Guaiacum & syphilis, citing Monardes. DNLM, WU; BN.
552/19

Giovio, Paolo, Bp of Nocera. Histoires . . . sur les choses faictes et avenues de son temps en toutes les parties du monde. Traduictes de latin . . . par le seigneur du Parq Champenois [Denis Sauvage]. *Lyons: G.Rouillé,* 1552. 2 pts (604p.);fol. Transl. from author's Florence, 1550-52, *Historiarum sui temporis tomus primus-secundus.* Atkinson (Fr.Ren.) 87; Baudrier (Lyons) IX:197 & 224. BL, BN.
552/20

____. Historiarum sui temporis. Tomus primus[-secundus]. *Venice: G.Griffio,for P.Bosello* (v.1);*Comin da Trino* (v.2), 1552-53. 2v. 1st publ., Venice, 1550-52. Moranti (Urbino) 1660. Urbino: BU.
552/21

Gómara, Francisco López de. La istoria de las Indias, y la conquista de Mexico. *Saragossa: A.Millán,* 1552. 2pts;maps;fol. Pt 2 has special t.p. with title *La conquista de Mexico.* Reissued, 1553, under title *Primera y segunda parte dela Historia general de las Indias.* Sánchez (Aragon) 331; Wagner (SW) 2; JCB AR40:11-15. InU-L, RPJCB; BL, Madrid: BN.
552/22

Guazzo, Marco. Historie . . . de le cose degne di memoria . . . successe del mdxxiiii sino a l'anno mdlii. nuovamente reviste. *Venice: G. Giolito de' Ferrari & Bros,* 1552. 734p.;8vo. 1st publ. with refs to Pizarro & Peru (here found on p.250-251), Venice, 1540. CSt, ICN, InU-L, MH, MiU, MnU-B, NN-RB, PU, RPJCB; BL, BN.
552/23

Héry, Thierry de. La methode curatoire de la maladie venerienne. *Paris: M.David & A. L'Angelier,* 1552. 272p.;8vo. CtY, DNLM, NNNAM, PPC; London: Wellcome, BN.
552/24

Honter, Johannes. Rudimentorum cosmographicorum . . . libri iii, cum tabellis geographicis elegantissimis. *Zurich: C.Froschauer,* 1552. [58]p;illus.,maps;8vo. 1st publ. in this version, Kronstadt, 1542. In verse. Sabin 32796n; Adams (Cambr.) H833; JCB (3) I:171. MnU-B, NN-RB, RPJCB; Cambridge: UL, BN.
552/25

__[Anr edn]. *Antwerp: A.Coppens v.Diest, for J.Richard* [1552]. 2pts;maps; 8vo. Belg.typ. (1541-1600) I:1483. Brussels: BR.   552/26

Jesuits. Letters from missions (Brazil). Copia de unas cartas embiadas del Brasil, por el padre Nobrega . . . y otros padres . . . Tresladada de portugues en castellano. Recebidas el año de M.D.LI. [*Coimbra?* 1552?]. 27p.;4to. Cf. Italian edn publ. this year at Rome, the following item. Addressed to the Jesuit prefect in Portugal and members of the Society in Coimbra. For reasons similar to those given in King Manuel's Catalogue (entry 71) for attributing the 'Copia de una carta . . . de la India' written by the Jesuit Gaspar Barzeo, and similarly translated from Portuguese into Castilian, it seems plausible to ascribe this as well to J.da Barreira and J.Alvares. Sabin 55393 (&16672); Medina (BHA) 420; Borba de Moraes I:175-176; Streit II:1209. Lisbon: BN.   552/27

Jesuits. Letters from missions (The East). Avisi particolari delle Indie di Portugallo ricevuti in questi doi anni del 1551 et 1552. *Rome: V.& L.Dorico,for B.di Rossi,* 1552. 317p.;8vo. Cf. preceding item. Includes 7 letters from Brazil, also publ. separately in Spanish (the preceding item). Sabin 7523; Medina (BHA) 170n; Borba de Moraes I:49-50; Streit II:1221 (& IV:669); JCB (3) I:166. DLC, InU-L, MH, NN-RB, RPJCB; BL.   552/28

Lopes de Castanheda, Fernão. Historia do livro segundo do descobrimento & conquista da India pelos Portugeses. *Coimbra: J.da Barreira & J.Alvares,* 1552. 239p.;illus.;fol. For v.1 see the year 1551. The subsequent v.3 of this year contains no American refs. Refs to Brazil appear on p.62 & 144. Sabin 11384; Borba de Moraes I:141. CSmH, MH, MnU-B, NN-RB, RPJCB; BL, BN.   552/29

Maffei, Raffaele. Commentariorum . . . octo et triginta libri. *Lyons: S.Gryphius,* 1552. 1218 numb.cols;illus.;fol. 1st publ., Rome, 1506, the refs to Columbus & New World here appearing in col.368. Cf.Sabin 43765; cf.Harrisse (BAV) 67; Baudrier (Lyons) VIII:259; Shaaber M25. CtY, NN-RB, PU, RPJCB; BN.   552/30

Medina, Pedro de. Regimiento de navegacion, en que se contienen las reglas, declarationes y avisos del libro del arte de navegar. *Seville: J.Canalla,* 1552. 43 lvs;illus.,map;

4to. 1st publ., Valladolid, 1545, under title *Arte de navegar.* Medina (BHA) 154; Borba de Moraes II:48; Escudero (Seville) 546. CtY, NN-RB; Madrid: Centro del Ejército y la Armada.   552/31

Mexía, Pedro. Historia imperial y cesarea . . . agora nuevamente impressa. *Antwerp: M.Nuyts,* 1552. 400 numb.lvs;4to. 1st publ., Seville, 1545. Peeters-Fontainas (Impr.esp.) 783; Palau 167343. NNH; Brussels: BR, Madrid: BN.   552/32

Mizauld, Antoine. De mundi sphaera, seu Cosmographia libri tres. *Paris: G.Cavellat,* 1552. 96p.;illus.,maps;8vo. In verse. Ref.to America on p.7. Sabin 49773; Cioranescu (XVI) 15131. DLC, InU-L, MH, MiU, NN-RB; BL, BN.   552/33

Münster, Sebastian. Cosmographiae universalis lib. vi. *Basel: H.Petri,* 1552. 1162p.; maps; fol. 1st publ. in Latin, Basel, 1550. Sabin 51380; Burmeister (Münster) 88. CSmH, ICN, MH, NN-RB; Oxford: Bodl., BN.   552/34

____. La cosmographie universelle. *Basel: H. Petri,* 1552. 1429p.;maps,port.;fol. Transl. from German text, 1st publ., Basel, 1544. Sabin 51397; Atkinson (Fr.Ren.) 88; Burmeister (Münster) 92. CSmH, MiU-C; BL, Paris: Ste Geneviève.   552/35

Opere burlesche . . . Ammendato, e ricorretto, e . . . ristampato. *Florence: Heirs of B. Giunta,* 1552-55. 2v.;8vo. 1st publ. as here collected, Florence, 1548. Included are F.Berni's 'Capitolo secondo de la peste' & G.F.Bini's 'Capitolo del mal francese', both 1st publ., Venice, 1538. Proksch I:82; Ind.aur.117.704 & 117.706. OU; BL, Vienna: NB.   552/36

Paracelsus. Von der Frantzösischen kranckheit drey Bücher. *Nuremberg: H.Andreae,* 1552. [198]p.;8vo. 1st publ., Nuremberg, 1530. Sudhoff (Paracelsus) 28. Munich: StB.   552/37

Paradin, Guillaume. Histoire de nostre temps . . . revue & augmentee. *Lyons: J.de Tournes & G.Gazeau,* 1552. 757p.;16mo. 1st publ. in French, Lyons, 1550. Cartier (de Tournes) 227. ICN; BL, BN.   552/38

Postel, Guillaume. De universitate liber. *Paris: J.Gueullart,* 1552. 56 numb. lvs;illus.;4to. In the section 'Divisio terrae' ref. is made to the New World; also included is section 'De regionibus extra Priscorum cognitionem' with American refs. Cf.Sabin 64531;

Adams (Cambr.) P2024. MH, NN-RB; Cambridge: UL, BN.　　　　　　552/39

Ptolemaeus, Claudius. Geographiae . . . libri viii . . . Conradi Lycosthenis . . . opera adjecti. Quibus praefixa est epistola in qua de utilitate tabularum geographicarum ac duplici indicis usu latè disseritur. Tabulae novae . . . per Sebastianum Munster. *Basel: H. Petri*, 1552. 195p.;illus.,maps;fol. 1st publ. in this version ed. by Münster, Basel, 1540. Sabin 66488; Burmeister (Münster) 169; JCB (3) I:172. CSmH, DLC, ICN, InU-L, MH, MiU-C, NN-RB, PP, RPJCB; BL, BN. 552/40

Rabelais, François. Le quart livre des faicts et dicts heroiques du bon Pantagruel. *Paris: M. Fezandat*, 1552. 144 numb.lvs;8vo. Describes a voyage perhaps inspired by that of Jacques Cartier, & interpreted as a search for a Northwest Passage—cf.Gilbert Chinard, *L'exotisme américain dans la littérature française au XVIe siècle* (Paris, 1911). Plan (Rabelais) 78; Rothschild 1514. BL, BN.
　　　　　　　　　　　　　　552/41

—[Anr edn]. Reveu & corrigé pour la seconde edition. [*Lyons?*], 1552. 375p.;16mo. Plan (Rabelais) 79. BL, Chantilly: Mus. Condé.
　　　　　　　　　　　　　　552/42

—[Anr edn]. *Lyons: B.Aleman*, 1552. 166 numb. lvs;8vo. Plan (Rabelais) 81. CtY, MH, NN-RB; BL, Paris: Arsenal.　　552/43

—[Anr edn]. *Rouen: R.Valentin*, 1552. 144 lvs; 16mo. Plan (Rabelais) 80. BN.　　552/44

—[Anr edn]. *Paris* [i.e., *Lyons?*]: *M.Fezandat*, 1552. 182 numb.lvs;16mo. Piracy of 1st edn above. Plan (Rabelais) 82. BN.　　552/45

1553

Alberti, Leandro. Descrittione di tutta l'Italia. *Venice: G.M.Bonelli*, 1553. 464 numb. lvs;4to. 1st publ., Bologna, 1550, with ref. to Vespucci. Sabin 660; Ind.aur.102.340. ICN; BL.　　　　　　　　　　553/1

Alfonso X, el Sabio, King of Castile and Leon. Hispania vincit. Los cinco libros primeros de la Cronica general de España. *Medina del Campo: G.de Millis*, 1553. cccxxxvi lvs;fol. The earliest edn to contain 5 bks; cf. Zamora, 1543, edn containing 4. Chapt.xix relates to the Americas. Authorship frequently attributed to Florián d'Ocampo, editor & con-

tinuator of the work. Sabin 56621; Medina (BHA) 118n; Pérez Pastor (Medina del Campo) 101; Shaaber O1. InU-L, MnU-B, NN-RB, PU; BL, BN.　　　　　553/2

Amatus Lusitanus. In Dioscoridis . . . De medica materia libros quinque . . . enarrationes eruditissimae. *Venice: G.Scoto*, 1553. 514p.; 8vo. 'Enarratio xviii', on balsam, describes 'opobalsam . . . è Peru noviter inventa regione'; 'Enarratio cxix' treats 'Secunda species Ebeni. Lignum Guaiacum . . . Holtz auss Indien', citing sources in newly found lands, e.g., San Juan (i.e., Puerto Rico). Pritzel 124; Ind. aur.104.554. DNLM; London: Wellcome, Munich: StB.　　　　　　　553/3

Apianus, Petrus. Cosmographia . . . per Gemmam Phrysiam . . . ab omnibus vindicata mendis. *Antwerp: G.Coppens v. Diest,for G.de Bonte*, 1553. 64 numb.lvs;illus.,map; 4to. 1st publ., as ed. by Gemma, Antwerp, 1529. Ortroy (Apian) 42; Ind. aur.106.450; JCB (3) I:173. NN-RB, RPJCB; Brussels: BR.
　　　　　　　　　　　　　　553/4

—[Anr edn]. *Paris: V.Gaultherot*, 1553. 74 numb. lvs;illus.,map;8vo. A reissue, with cancel t.p., of the printer's 1551 edn. Sabin 1749n; Ind. aur.106.452; Ortroy (Apian) 44; Fairfax Murray (France) 15; JCB (3) I:172-173. DLC, MH, NN-RB, RPJCB; BL, BN.　　　　　　　　　　　　　553/5

——. La cosmographie . . . nouvellement traduicte de latin en françois par Gemma Frisius . . . de nouveau augmentee. *Paris: V. Gaultherot*, 1553. 70 numb. lvs;illus.,map; 4to. 1st publ. in this translation, Antwerp, 1544. Sheets of the printer's 1551 edn reissued with cancel t.p. Cf.Sabin 1752; Ind.aur. 104.542; Ortroy (Apian) 45. DLC, MH, NN-RB; BN.　　　　　　　　　　553/6

——. Cosmographie, oft Beschrijvinghe der gheheelder werelt . . . ghecorrigeert van Gemma Frisio. *Antwerp: G.de Bonte*, 1553. lxxv lvs;illus.,map;4to. 1st publ. in Dutch, Antwerp, 1545. Cf.Sabin 1754; Ind.aur.106.451; Ortroy (Apian) 43; JCB (3) I:173. RPJCB; Brussels: BR.　　　　　　　　　　553/7

Barot, Jean de, baron de Taye Peilhot. Devis poictevin dicte a Tholose aux jeux floraux . . . L'affutiman de Pelhot . . . et Le blason de la verole. *Toulouse: G.Boudeville* [1553]. 8vo. Proksch I:81; Rép. bibl.,XX: 137.　　553/8

Barros, João de. Segunda decada da Asia. *Lisbon: G.Galharde*, 1553. 143 numb.lvs;fol.

Continues 1st Decade of previous year. In bk 7, chapt.2 contains a passing mention of Brasil. The author's subsequent 3rd Decade was publ. in 1563. Sabin 3646; Borba de Moraes I:71-72; Streit IV:667; Ind.aur.113.424; King Manuel 74. MH, MnU-B, NN-RB; BL, BN.

553/9

Beausard, Pierre. Annuli astronomici instrumenti cum certissimi tum commodissimi usus. *Antwerp: J.Steels*, 1553. 96p.;maps;8vo. The maps are probably from blocks, or based on them, which had been used for Zurich, 1546, edn of Honter's *Rudimenta cosmographica*, with world map showing America. Ind. aur.115.171. MiU-C, NN-RB; BL, BN.

553/10

Belon, Pierre. Les observations de plusieurs singularitez et chose memorables, trouvées en Grece, Asie . . . & autres pays estranges. *Paris: B.Prevost, for G.Corrozet*, 1553. 210 numb.lvs;illus.;4to. In bk 1 chapt.51 is captioned 'Autre discours de l'or de Peru et des Indes'. Atkinson (Fr.Ren.) 90; Cioranescu (XVI) 3483; Ind.aur.116.316. DLC, InU-L, NN-RB, PPAN; BL, BN.

553/11

—[Anr issue]. *Paris: B.Prevost, for G.Cavellat*, 1553. Atkinson (Fr.Ren.) 90n. Paris: Arsenal.

553/12

Bock, Hieronymus. Verae atque ad vivum expressae imagines omnium herbarum. *Strassburg: W.Rihel*, 1553. cccxxxiii p.;illus.;4to. Pritzel 868; Nissen (Bot.) 184; Ind. aur.120.592; Adams (Cambr.) T896 (Tragus). NNNAM; BL.

553/13

Bon, Baltasar Manuel de. De sphaera mundi libri tres. *Valencia: J.Mey*, 1553. 8vo. Medina (BHA) 155; Palau 32338; Bibl.mar.esp. 1521.

553/14

Bonacossa, Ercole. De humorum exuperantium signis ac serapiis . . . liber . . . De modo praeparandi aquam ligni sancti. *Bologna: A. Giaccarelli*, 1553. [136]p.;4to. Ind. aur.121.601. DNLM.

553/15

Brant, Sebastian. Das Narrenschiff. *Frankfurt a.M.: H.Gülfferich*, 1553. 158 numb.lvs; illus.;8vo. 1st publ., Basel, 1494. Ind.aur. 123.733. Zurich: StB.

553/16

Brasavola, Antonio Musa. Examen omnium loch . . . ubi de morbo gallico . . . tractatur. *Venice: The Giuntas*, 1553. 292 numb.lvs; 8vo. Ind.aur.123.808; Adams (Cambr.) B2687; Moranti (Urbino) 679. DNLM, WU; BL, BN.

553/17

Cardano, Girolamo. De subtilitate libri xxi. *Basel: S.Henricpetri*, 1553. 626p.;4to. 1st publ., Nuremberg, 1550. Ind.aur.132.062. NjP, PPL; Berlin: StB.

553/18

Casas, Bartolomé de las, Bp of Chiapa. Tratado comprobatorio del imperio soberano . . . que los reyes de Castilla y Leon tienen sobre las Indias. *Seville: S.Trugillo*, 1553. [160]p.;4to. For earlier tracts of the series of which this forms part, see the year 1552. Sabin 11231; Medina (BHA) 156; Escudero (Seville) 542 (8); Streit I:67; Church 67; JCB (3) 174-175. CSmH, CtY, DLC, InU-L, MH, MiU-C, NN-RB, RPJCB; BL, BN.

553/19

Cieza de León, Pedro de. Parte primera dela Chronica del Peru. *Seville: M.de Montesdoca*, 1553. cxxxiii lvs;illus.;fol. No more published. Sabin 13044; Medina (BHA) 157; Escudero (Seville) 555; Streit II:644; JCB (3) I:175. DLC, ICN, InU-L, NN-RB, RPJCB; BL, BN.

553/20

Dodoens, Rembert. Trium priorum stirpium historia. *Antwerp: J.van der Loe*, 1553-54. 2v.;illus.,port.;8vo. On recto of lf Ee2 in v.1 is the earliest picture of the tobacco plant, designated 'Hyoscyamus luteus', mistakenly identified as a henbane described by Dioscorides. Pritzel 2650; Nissen (Bot.) 507; Bibl. belg.,1st ser.,IX, D105; Adams (Cambr.) D723; Arents (Add.) 10; Hunt (Bot.) 68. CtY-M, DNAL, NN-A; BL, BN.

553/21

Ferrier, Auger. De pudendagra, lue hispanica, libri duo. *Toulouse: J.Colomiès*, 1553. [120]p.;8vo. Cioranescu (XVI) 9952; Rép. bibl.XX:82; Proksch I:16.

553/22

Fontanon, Denys. De morborum internorum curatione libri quatuor. *Lyons: J.Frellon*, 1553. 381p.;8vo. 1st publ., Lyons, 1549. Baudrier (Lyons) V:226-227. London: Wellcome.

553/23

—[Anr issue]. *Lyons: J.Frellon, for A.Vincent*, 1553. Adams (Cambr.) F716. CLU-M, DNLM; BL.

553/24

—[Anr edn]. *Venice: G.Griffio, for B.Costantino*, 1553. 207 numb.lvs;8vo. CLU-M, CtY-M, DNLM, MnU; London: Wellcome.

553/25

Foresti, Jacobo Filippo da Bergamo. Supplementum supplementi delle croniche. *Venice: B. & F.Imperadore*, 1553. 419p.;illus.;fol. 1st publ. in Italian with ref. to America, Venice, 1508. Cf.Sabin 25086. CtY, ICN, MH, MiU; BL, BN.

553/26

García Matamoros, Alonso. De asserenda Hispanorum eruditione, sive De viris Hispaniae doctis narratio apologetica. *Alcalá de Henares: J.Brocar,* 1553. 62 numb.lvs;8vo. Lvs 56 ff. discuss Columbus & son Fernando. Medina (BHA) 158 (citing author's copy not found in 1942); García (Alcalá de Henares) 261; Palau 99339. Madrid: BN.   553/27

Gemma, Reinerus, Frisius. De principiis astronomiae & cosmographiae . . . De orbis divisione, & insulis, rebusque inventis . . . Opus . . . ab ipso auctore multis in locis auctum, ac sublatis omnibus erratis . . . restitutum. *Antwerp: J.Graphaeus,for J.Steels,* 1553. 185p.; illus.;8vo. 1st publ., Antwerp, 1530. Cf.Sabin 26856; Adams (Cambr.) G388; Moranti (Urbino) 1613; JCB(3) I:175. CtY, DLC, InU-L, MiU, MnU-B, NN-RB, RPJCB; BL, BN.
                                                      553/28

Giovio, Paolo, Bp of Nocera. Historiarum sui temporis tomus primus[-secundus]. *Paris: M.de Vascovan,* 1553-54. 2v.;fol. 1st publ., Florence, 1550-52. Adams (Cambr.) G650 (v.1). MH, NN-RB, ViU; BL, BN   553/29

Gómara, Francisco López de. Primera y segunda parte dela Historia general de las Indias . . . ata el año de 1551. Con la conquista de Mexico y de la Nueva España. *Saragossa: A.Millán,for M.Capila,* 1553. 2pts;maps;fol. 1st publ., Saragossa, 1552. A reissue of the printer's prior edn, with the title and following leaf cancelled by a newly set sheet. Sabin 27724; Harrisse (BAV) p.193n; Medina (BHA) 153; Wagner (SW) 2a; Streit II:632; Sánchez (Aragon) 348; Church 97; JCB (3) I:175-176. CSmH, DLC, ICN, InU-L, RPJCB.   553/30

—[Anr edn]. Hispania victrix. Primera y segunda parte de la Historia general de las Indias . . . Con la conquista de Mexico, y de la Nueva España. *Medina del Campo: H.de Millis,* 1553. 2pts;fol. Sabin 27725; Medina (BHA) 159; Wagner (SW) 2b; Streit II:645; Pérez Pastor (Medina del Campo) 100;JCB (3) I:176. DLC, ICN, InU-L, MB, MnU-B, NN-RB, RPJCB; BL, BN.   553/31

Guazzo, Marco. Cronica . . . ne la quale ordinatamente contiensi l'essere de gli huomini illustri antiqui, & moderni, le cose & i fatti di eterna memoria. Prima editione. *Venice: F.Bindoni,* 1553. 435 numb.lvs;fol. Cf. author's *Historie di tutte le cose degne di memoria,* 1st publ., Venice, 1540. On verso of

If 396 is ref. to Pizarro. Adams (Cambr.) G1451; Shaaber G372. CSt, DFo, ICN, InU-L, MH, MiU, NN-RB, PU, RPJCB; BL, BN.   553/32

Jesuits. Letters from missions. Novi avisi di piu lochi de l'India et massime de Brazil, ricevuti quest'anno del .M.D.LIII. *Rome: A.Blado,for B.di Rossi,* 1553. 22 lvs;8vo. Sabin 56200; Leclerc (1878) 1625; cf.Borba de Moraes I:50; cf.Streit II:1229; JCB (3) I:174. MnU-B, NN-RB, RPJCB.   553/33

Lopes de Castanheda, Fernão. Os livros quarto & quinto da Historia do descobrimento & conquista da India pelos Portugueses. *Coimbra: J.da Barreira & J.Alvares,* 1553. ccx p.;fol. Continues 3rd vol. of 1552. In bk 4 a ref. to Brazil appears on p.xxxv, in bk 5 on p.xcvii–ciiii. Sabin 11385; Borba de Moraes I:141; Anselmo 297; King Manuel 72. DLC, RPJCB; BL, BN.   553/34

——. Le premier livre de l'Histoire de l'Inde . . . traduict de portugues . . . par Nicolas de Grouchy. [*Paris:*] *M.de Vascovan,* 1553. 346p.; 4to. Transl. from 1552, Coimbra, text. Sabin 11387; Atkinson (Fr.Ren.) 91; Borba de Moraes I:142. InU-L, MnU-B, NN-RB; BL, BN.   553/35

Medina, Pedro de. L'art de naviguer . . . contenant toutes les reigles, secrets, & enseignemens necessaires a la bonne navigation. Traduit . . . par Nicolas de Nicolai. *Lyons: G. Rouillé,* 1553. 115 numb.lvs;illus.,map;4to. Transl. from Valladolid, 1545, Spanish text. Sabin 47345n; Mortimer (France) 369. MH.
                                                      553/36

Mizauld, Antoine. De mundi sphaera, seu Cosmographia, libri tres. *Paris: G.Cavellat,* 1553. 95p.;illus.,maps;8vo. 1st publ., Paris, 1552. In verse. Cf.Sabin 49773; Cioranescu (XVI) 15131; JCB (3) I:176. RPJCB; BN.
                                                      553/37

Münster, Sebastian. Cosmographei oder beschreibung aller länder. *Basel: H.Petri,* 1553. 1233p.;maps;fol. 1st publ.,Basel, 1544. Sabin 51388; Burmeister (Münster) 71. Munich: StB.   553/38

——. A treatise of the newe India, with other new founde lands and islands, as well eastwarde as westwarde . . . Translated . . . by Rycharde Eden. *London: S.Mierdman,for E. Sutton,* 1553. 102 lvs;8vo. Extracted and transl. from Paris, 1550, edn, in turn a translation from the Basel, 1544, German text.

Sabin 51404 (& 21826); STC 18244; Burmeister (Münster) 107; JCB (3) I:177. MiU-C, NN-RB, PHi, RPJCB; BL.   553/39

Natta, Marco Antonio. De pulchro libri sex. *Pavia: F.Moscheni*, 1553. 148 numb.lvs;fol. Includes mentions in bk 5 of Spanish explorations of New World & of Pacific. NjP, RPJCB.
553/39a

Ovidius Naso, Publius. Metamorphoses. Italian. Le trasformationi di m. Lodovico Dolce. *Venice: G.Giolito de' Ferrari*, 1553. 311p.;illus.,map;4to. On verso of lf *6 is a world map showing New World as 'Nueva Hispania'. For variant issues and states, see Mortimer. Mortimer (Italy) 342; Shaaber O133. CSmH, MH, MnU, NN-RB, PU; BL, BN.
553/40

—[Anr edn]. . . . Di novo ristampate, e da lui [Dolce] ricorrette, e in diversi luoghi ampliate. *Venice: G.Giolito de' Ferrari*, 1553. 312p.;illus.,map;4to. Adams (Cambr.) O508; Mortimer (Italy) 342n. CU, ICU, MH; Cambridge: Trinity, BN.   553/41

Paracelsus. Von der Frantzösischen kranckheit drey Bücher. *Frankfurt a.M.: H.Gülfferich*, 1553. [146]p.;4to. 1st publ., Nuremberg, 1530. Sudhoff (Paracelsus) 29. Berlin:StB.   553/42

Postel, Guillaume. Des merveilles du monde, et principalement des admirables choses des Indes et du Nouveau monde. *[Paris? 1553?]*. 96 lvs;12mo. Sabin 64525; Atkinson (Fr.Ren.) 93; Cioranescu (XVI) 17841. BN(t.p. mutilated, removing imprint).   553/43

Rabelais, François. Les oeuvres. *[Paris?]* 1553. 932p.;16mo. Includes 'Le quart livre', 1st publ., Paris, 1552. Plan (Rabelais) 92. MH, NjP; BL, BN.   553/44

———. Le quart livre des faicts & dictz heroiques du bon Pantagruel . . . Nouvellement reveu & corrigé, par ledict autheur, pour la deuxiesme edition. *[Lyons?]* 1553. 294p.;8vo. 1st publ., Paris, 1552. Plan (Rabelais) 83. BN.   553/45

Soto, Domingo de. De justitia & jure libri decem. *Salamanca: A.à Portonariis*, 1553 [colophon: 1554]. 904p.;fol. In bk 4, 'De dominio', quaest.4, art.2 mentions 'Antipodas & Insulares à nobis repertos'; in bk 5; quaest.3, art.5 mentions newly found western world. Palau 320138. BL, Madrid: BN.   553/46

Spain. Casa de Contratación de las Indias. Ordenanzas reales para la casa de contractacion de Sevilla y para otras cosas de las Indias: y de la navegacion y contractacion dellas. *Seville: M.de Montesdoca,for A.de Carvajal*, 1553. L lvs;fol. Medina (BHA) 160; Escudero (Seville) 556; Palau 203197. InU-L, NN-RB; Madrid: BN.   553/47

Tarafa, Francisco. De origine, ac rebus gestis regum Hispaniae liber. *Antwerp: H.de Laet, for J.Steels*, 1553. 201p.; port.;8vo. Refs to America appear on p. 183 & 196. Sabin 94398; Palau 327552; Adams (Cambr.) T131; Shaaber T28; JCB (3) I:177. DLC, NN-RB, PU, RPJCB; Cambridge: UL, BN.   553/48

Treslado de una carta embiado, de la ciudad de los Reyes a esta ciudad de Sevilla contando de como se ha alcado en el Cuzco Francisco Hernandez contra la S.C.C.M. de Emperador . . . y assi mismo de como entonelaron a Ventura Beltran porque mato su muger. *[Seville: 1553?]*. 8p.;illus.;4to. Sabin 96789; Medina (BHA) 419; Escudero (Seville) 855. CSmH.
553/49

1554

Amatus Lusitanus. Curationum medicinalium centuriae duae, prima & secunda . . . Omnia nunc . . . cujusdam doctissimi medici Galli infinitis mendis . . . expurgata. *Paris: B.Prévost,for S.Nivelle*, 1554. 2v.;16mo. 1st Century 1st publ., Florence, 1551; 2nd Century, Venice, 1552. CtY, DNLM, MBCo.
554/1

—[Anr issue]. *Paris: B.Prévost,for G.Gourbin*, 1554. WaU.   554/2

—[Anr issue]. *Paris: B.Prévost,for F.Barthélemy*, 1554. Ind.aur.104.555. MBCo; Munich: StB.   554/3

———. In Dioscoridis . . . De medica materia libros quinque . . . enarrationes eruditissimae. *Strassburg: W.Rihel*, 1554. 536p.;4to. 1st publ., Venice, 1553. Pritzel 124n; Ind.aur. 104.556; Ritter (Strasbourg) 1415. DNLM, NN-RB; BL, BN.   554/4

Apianus, Petrus. Cosmographiae introductio. *Venice: F.Bindoni*, 1554. [63]p.;illus.,maps; 8vo. 1st publ., Ingolstadt, 1532, the present edn reproducing the printer's 1537 edn. Ind. aur.106.454; Ortroy (Apian) 94. ICN, MH, NN-RB; London: Wellcome, Vienna: NB.
554/5

Belon, Pierre. Les observations de plusieurs singularitez & choses memorables, trouvées en Grece, Asie . . . & autres pays estranges . . .

Reveuz de nouveau & augmentez de figures. *Paris: B.Prévost,for G.Cavellat*, 1554. 211 numb. lvs;illus.;4to. 1st publ., Paris, 1553. Atkinson (Fr.Ren.) 96; Ind.aur.116.325; Adams (Cambr.) B564. NcD-M; BL, BN.

554/6

___[Anr issue]. *Paris: B.Prévost,for G.Corrozet*, 1554. Atkinson (Fr.Ren.) 96n; Adams (Cambr.) B562. MH-A, NjP; Cambridge: Trinity, Paris: Arsenal.   554/7

Bielski, Marcin. Kronika wssythyego swyata . . . y swyata nowego wypisanye. *Cracow: H. Scharffenberg*, 1554. 333 numb.lvs;illus., map;fol. 1st publ., Cracow, 1551; here expanded with added matter on New World, lvs 305 ff. Yarmolinsky (Early Polish Americana) 39-40; Ind.aur.119.176. Cracow: AkB. 554/8

Brasavola, Antonio Musa. Examen omnium loch . . . ubi de morbo gallico . . . tractatur. *Lyons: J.Faure,for S.Honorat*, 1554. 750p.; 8vo. 1st publ., Venice, 1553. Ind.aur. 123.809; Baudrier (Lyons) IV:164. BL, Oslo: UB.   554/9

Cardano, Girolamo. De subtilitate libri xxi. *Basel: L.Lucius*, 1554. 561p.;illus.,port.;fol. 1st publ., Nuremberg(?), 1550. Ind.aur. 132.064; Adams (Cambr.) C670; Moranti (Urbino) 814. CU-S, DLC, MH, NNE; BL, BN.

554/10

___[Anr edn]. *Lyons: G.Rouillé*, 1554. 813p.; illus.;8vo. Ind.aur.132.065; Adams (Cambr.) C671; Shaaber C131. DNLM, PU; Cambridge: UL, BN.   554/11

Carion, Johann. Chronicorum libri tres. Appendix eorum quae à fine Carionis ad haec usque tempora contigere. *Lyons: M.Dubois, for J.Frellon*, 1554. 560p.;16mo. 1st publ. in this version, Hall (Swabia), 1537. Ind.aur. 132.317; Baudrier (Lyons) V:228-229. IU.

554/12

___[Anr issue]. *Lyons: M.Dubois,for A.Vincent*, 1554. RPJCB; Berlin StB.   554/13

Chaves, Jerónimo de. Chronographia o Repertorio de los tiempos. *Seville: M.de Montesdoca*, 1554. cciv lvs;maps;4to. 1st publ., Seville, 1548. The Seville edn of this year purportedly printed by A.Bexarano is probably a ghost — cf. Escudero (Seville) 561. Palau 67451.   554/14

Cieza de León, Pedro de. La chronica del Peru, nuevamente escrita. *Antwerp: M. Nuyts* 1554. 204 numb.lvs;illus.;8vo. 1st publ., Seville, 1553. Sabin 13045; Medina (BHA) 161;

Streit II:651; Peeters-Fontainas (Impr.esp.) 256; JCB (3) I:179. CSmH, MH, MnU-B, NN-RB, RPJCB; BL, BN.   554/15

___[Anr edn]. Parte primera de la Chronica del Peru. *Antwerp: H.de Laet, for J. Steels*, 1554. 285 numb.lvs;illus.;8vo. Sabin 13046n; Medina (BHA) 163; Streit II:653; Bibl.belg.,1st ser., IV:C16; Peeters-Fontainas (Impr.esp.) 254. DLC, MH, NN-RB, RPJCB; BL, BN.   554/16

___[Anr issue]. *H.de Laet,for J.Bellère*, 1554. 285 numb.lvs;illus.,map;8vo. The map (showing New World) appears in this issue only. Sabin 13046; Medina (BHA) 162; Streit II;652; Peeters-Fontainas (Impr.esp.) 255; JCB (3) I:179. NN-RB, RPJCB; BL.   554/17

Dioscorides, Pedanius. De materia medica libri sex, innumeris locis ab Andrea Matthiolo emendati ac restituti. *Lyons: B.Arnoullet*, 1554. 564p.;8vo. Transl. by Jean Ruel from Italian text, 1st publ., Venice, 1544. For subsequent edns of this text with commentaries so expanded and enlarged as to constitute an independent work, see entries under Mattioli, Pietro Andrea. Baudrier (Lyons) X: 145. BL.

554/18

___[Anr issue]. *Lyons: B.Arnoullet,for J. Frellon*, 1554. Pritzel 2310; Baudrier (Lyons) V:229.   554/19

___[Anr issue]. *Lyons: B.Arnoullet,for A.Vincent*, 1554. DNLM; BN.   554/20

___[Anr issue]. *Lyons: B.Arnoullet,for G. Rouillé*, 1554. DNLM.   554/21

Dodoens, Rembert. Cruijde boeck. *Antwerp: J.van der Loe*, 1554. cccccccxviii p.;illus., port.;fol. Includes numerous refs to American plants. Pritzel 2344; Nissen (Bot.) 509; Bibl. belg.,1st ser.,IX:D108; Arents 5-A. MH-A, MiU, NN-A; BL, Brussels: BR.   554/22

Fontaine, Charles. Les nouvelles, & antiques merveilles. *Paris: G.LeNoir*, 1554. [192]p.; 16mo. The 'nouvelles merveilles' comprise 'isles, & terres neuves'. Atkinson (Fr.Ren.) 98; Cioranescu (XVI) 10098. RPJCB; BL, BN.

554/23

Fracastoro, Girolamo. Liber unus, De sympathia & antipathia rerum. Item, De contagione, & contagiosis morbus, & eorum curatione, lib.iii. *Lyons: J.de Tournes & J. Gazeau*, 1554. 351p.;16mo. 1st publ., Venice, 1546. Cartier (de Tournes) 276. CtY-M, DNLM, ICJ, MBCo, NNNAM, PPC; BL, BN.   554/24

Gesner, Konrad. Thesaurus Euonymi Philiatri [pseud.], de remediis secretis. *Zurich: A.Gessner*, 1554. 580p.; illus.;8vo. 1st publ., Zurich, 1552. Adams (Cambr.) G527. DNLM, MBCo; BL, BN. . 554/25

___[Anr edn]. *Lyons: B.Arnoullet*, 1554. 498p.; illus.;16mo. Baudrier (Lyons) X:147. MBCo; Toulouse: BM. 554/26

Giovio, Paolo, Bp of Nocera. Gli elogi vite brevemente scritti d'huomini illustri di guerra, antichi et moderni . . . tradotte per m. Lodovico Domenichi. *Florence: L.Torrentino*, 1554. 439p.;4to. Transl. from printer's 1551 edn of *Elogia virorum bellica*, with accounts of Columbus (p.218-223) & Cortés (p.392-397). Sabin 27478. CtY, DLC, ICN, MH, MiU, RPJCB; BL, BN. 554/27

Gómara, Francisco López de. La historia general delas Indias y nuevo mundo, con mas la conquista del Peru y de Mexico: agora nuevamente añadida y emendada por el mismo autor. *Saragossa: P.Bernuz & A.Millán, for M.de Zapila*, 1554. 2v.;illus.;fol. 1st publ., Saragossa, 1552. Vol.2 (pr. by Millán) has special t.p.: *Cronica de la nueva españa con la conquista de Mexico*. Sabin 27727 & 27728; Wagner (SW) 2c; Streit II:654 & 656; JCB (3) I:180. CU-S, NNH; BL, Madrid: BN. 554/28

___[Anr issue, with variant t.p. for v.2] La segunda parte dela historia general delas Indias. *Saragossa: A.Millán*, 1554. cxiij lvs;fol. Cf. Medina (BHA) 164; Wagner (SW) 2d; cf.Streit II:655. NN-RB. 554/29

___[Anr edn]. *Antwerp: M.Nuyts*, 1554. 2v.;8vo. 1st publ., Saragossa, 1552. Sabin 27729 & 27732; Medina (BHA) 165; Wagner (SW) 2j-2k; Streit II:658; Peeters-Fontainas (Impr. esp.) 714; JCB (3) I:180. DLC (v.2), ICN (v.1), MH, NN-RB, RPJCB; BL, BN. 554/30

___[Anr edn]. *Antwerp: H.de Laet, for J.Bellère*, 1554. 2v.;map;8vo. Vol.2 has title *Historia de Mexico*. The map is that found also in Bellère's issue of Cieza de León of this year. Sabin 27730(2) & 27731(1); Medina (BHA) 167; Wagner (SW) 2f-2g; Streit II:659; Peeters-Fontainas (Impr.esp.) 715; JCB (3) I:180. DLC, NN-RB, RPJCB; BL, BN. 554/31

___[Anr issue]. *Antwerp: H.de Laet, for J.Steels*, 1554. 2v.;8vo. As with Steels's Cieza de León of this year, does not contain the map found in Bellère's issue. Sabin 27730(1)& 27731(2); Medina (BHA) 168; Wagner (SW)

2h-2i; Streit II:657 (v.2) & 659n; Peeters-Fontainas (Impr.esp.) 716; JCB (3) I:180. CSmH, CtY, DLC, MiU-C, MnU-B, NN-RB, PPL, RPJCB; BL, BN. 554/32

Haschaert, Pierre. Morbi gallici compendiosa curatio. *Louvain: R.Velpius, for J. Waen*, 1554. 24 lvs;8vo. Includes also directions for use of Guaiacum. Bibl. belg.,1st ser.,X-II,H44; Proksch I:16. London: Wellcome. 554/33

Honter, Johannes. Rudimentorum cosmographicorum . . . libri iii. *Antwerp: J.Richard*, 1554. 2pts;maps;8vo. 1st publ. in this version, Kronstadt, 1542. In verse. Cf.Sabin 32793; Belg.typ. (1541-1600) I:1484. CSmH, DLC, NN-RB; Brussels: BR. 554/34

___[Anr edn]. *Antwerp: J.Richard* [ca. 1554?] Belg.typ. (1541-1600) I:1482; Borsa 97. BL, Brussels: BR. 554/35

Laguna, Andrés de. Annotationes in Dioscoridem Anazarbeum. *Lyons: G.Rouillé*, 1554. 340p.;16mo. Includes numerous references to American plants. Pritzel 4992; Baudrier (Lyons) IX:212. DNLM, MiU; BL, BN. 554/36

Le Ferron, Arnoul. De rebus gestis Gallorum libri ix . . . Tertia editio. *Paris: M.de Vascovan*, 1554. 183 numb.lvs;fol. 1st publ., Paris, 1549. Adams (Cambr.) F321. DLC, ICU, MH; Cambridge: Corp. Chr., BN. 554/37

Lopes de Castanheda, Fernão. L'histoire des Indes de Portugal . . . traduict . . . par Nicolas de Grouchy. *Antwerp: J. Steels*, 1554. 211 numb.lvs; 8vo. 1st publ. in this translation, Paris, 1553. Sabin 11388; Borba de Moraes I:142; Atkinson (Fr.Ren.) 97. NN-RB; BL, BN. 554/38

___. Historia del descubrimiento y conquista de la India por los Portugueses. *Antwerp: M. Nuyts*, 1554. 220 numb.lvs;8vo. Transl. from Coimbra, 1551, Portuguese text. Contains bk 1 only. Borba de Moraes I:142; Peeters-Fontainas (Impr.esp.) 712; Adams (Cambr.) L1467; Palau 140958. CtY, InU-L, MnU-B, NN-RB, RPJCB; BL, BN. 554/39

___. Ho livro primeiro dos dez da historia do descobrimento & conquista da India pelos Portugueses. *Coimbra: J.da Barreira*, 1554. ccii p.;fol. 1st publ., Coimbra, 1551, the ref. to Brazil here appearing on p.lxiiii. Sabin 11383; Borba de Moraes I:140-141; Anselmo 130. CSmH, MH, MnU-B, NN-RB, RPJCB. 554/40

____. Ho sexto livro da Historia do descobrimento & conquista da India, pelos Portugueses. *Coimbra: J.da Barreira*, 1554. cxcviii p.;fol. Continues earlier vols publ., Coimbra, 1551-53. Chapts vi-x & xli (p.v-xv & lviii-lix) describe Magellan's circumnavigation. The subsequent vols seven (1554) & eight (1561) lack refs to America. Sabin 11385n; Borba de Moraes I:141; Anselmo 131; King Manuel 72. CSmH, ICN, MH, MnU-B, NN-RB, RPJCB; BL, BN.   554/41

Lucidarius. M.Elucidarius, von allerhandt geschöpffen Gottes . . . und wie alle Creaturn geschaffen sein auff erden. *Frankfurt a.M.: H.Gülfferich*, 1554. [88]p.;4to. 1st publ., Strassburg, [ca.1535]. Schorbach (Lucidarius) 56. Wolfenbüttel: HB.   554/42

Mattioli, Pietro Andrea. Commentarii in libros sex Pedacii Dioscoridis de medica materia. *Venice: V.Valgrisi*, 1554. 707p.;illus.;fol. A revision of Mattioli's earlier edns of Dioscorides' work, so extended & expanded as to constitute an independent work in its own right, whilst retaining Dioscorides' text (cf.Lyons edn of Dioscorides of this year described above). In bk 1, chapt.18, on Balsam, refers to a West Indian source; bk 1, chapt.111, on Ebony, discusses Guaiacum & its American origins, with mention of sarsaparilla. In bk 3, chapt.22 describes & illustrates an Opuntia (Prickly pear cactus). Pritzel 2309 & 5985; Nissen (Bot.) 1305; Adams (Cambr.) D665; Moranti (Urbino) 2136. CSmH, DNLM, MH, MnU-B, NNBG; BL, BN.   554/43

Medina, Pedro de. L'art de naviguer . . . contenant toutes les reigles secrets, & enseignements necessaires à la bonne navigation. Trad. . . . par Nicolas de Nicolai. *Lyons: G. Rouillé*, 1554. 115 numb.lvs;illus.,map;fol. 1st publ. in French, Lyons, 1553. Sabin 47345; cf. Mortimer (France) 369; Cioranescu (XVI) 16568; Baudrier (Lyons) IX:216; JCB (3) I:182. CtY, DLC, MH, RPJCB; BL.
                                                                    554/44

____. L'arte del navegar, in laqual si contengono le regole, dechiarationi, secreti, & avisi, alla bona navegation necessarii. *Venice: A. Pincio,for G.B.Pederzano*, 1554. cxxxvii lvs; illus.,maps;4to. Transl. from Valladolid, 1545, Spanish text by Vicenzo Paletino. Cf. Sabin 47346; Mortimer (Italy) 300; Adams (Cambr.) M1025; Church 98; JCB (3) I:182. CSmH, CtY, DLC, ICN, InU-L, MnU-B, NN-

RB, RPJCB; Cambridge: UL, Strasbourg: BN.   554/45

Miranda, Luis de. Comedia prodiga. *Seville: M.de Montesdoca*, 1554. [48]p.;4to. Verse drama, with mention of the Indies. Said to have been 1st publ. in 1532, the present edn alone survives. Escudero (Seville) 560; Palau 172127. Madrid: BN.   554/46

Münster, Sebastian. Cosmographiae universalis lib. vi. *Basel: H.Petri*, 1554. 1162p.; illus.,maps;fol. 1st publ. in Latin, Basel, 1550. Sabin 51381; Borba de Moraes II:90; Burmeister (Münster) 89; JCB (3) I:183. CSmH, DLC, MH, NNC, RPJCB; BL, BN.
                                                                    554/47

____. Kozmograffia cżeska. *Prague: J. Kosorsky ze Skosoře*, 1554. 883 numb.lvs;illus.,map; fol. Transl. into Bohemian by Jan & Zikmund ze Púchova. Sabin 51401; Burmeister (Münster) 98. InU-L, MH, RPJCB; Vienna: NB.   554/48

Peucer, Kaspar. De dimensione terrae et geometrice numerandis. *Wittenberg: J.Krafft*, 1554. 287p.;illus.;8vo. 1st publ., Wittenberg, 1550, the discussion of America here appearing on p.63 & 65-66. Sabin 61312; JCB (STL) 9. CtY, DLC, MH, MiU, MnU-B, NN-RB, RPJCB; BN.   554/49

—[Anr edn]. *Frankfurt a.M.*: 1554. 8vo. Sabin 61312n.   544/50

Ramusio, Giovanni Battista. Primo volume, & seconda edizione delle Navigationi et viaggi in molti luoghi corretta, et ampliata. *Venice: Heirs of L.Giunta*, 1554. 436 numb.lvs;illus., maps;fol. 1st publ., Venice, 1550. Here 1st appears the 'Navigation d'un Portoghese compagno d'Odoardo Barbosa che fu sopra la nave Vittoria attorno al mondo'. Sabin 67331; Streit I:69; Adams (Cambr.) R135; Church 99a; JCB (3) I:183. CSmH, CtY, DLC, ICN, MH, NN-RB, RPJCB; BL.   554/51

Renner, Frantz. Ein köstlich und bewärtes Artzney-Büchlein aller inner-unnd eusserlicher Artzney, wider die abschewliche kranckheit der Frantzosen und Lähmung: auch vor alle andre Seuchten. *Nuremberg: G.Hain*, 1554. 4to. Proksch I:17.   554/52

Resende, Garcia de. Livro . . . que tracta da vida . . . do . . . principe el Rey don Joam ho segundo. *Evora: A.de Burgos*, 1554. 2pts;fol. 1st publ., Lisbon, 1545, with mention of Columbus's encounter with the King. Sabin 70062; Borba de Moraes II: 200; Anselmo

383; King Manuel 80. DCU, MH, MnU-B; BL, Paris: Ste Geneviève.   555/53

Rondelet, Guillaume. Libri de piscibus marinis. *Lyons: M.Bonhomme*, 1554-55. 2v.;illus., port.;fol. In v.l, bk 16, ch.18 describes the manatee; in v.2, discussion of crocodile mentions alligator. Baudrier (Lyons) X:239-241; Adams (Cambr.) R746 & R757; Moranti (Urbino) 2954 (v.l). CU, CtY, DLC, ICJ, InU-L, MH, MiU, MnU-B, NNC, PPL, RPB; BL, BN.   555/54

Valleriola, François. Enarrationum medicinalium libri sex. *Lyons: S.Gryphius*, 1554. 466p.;fol. In bk 4, 'Enarratio 8' contains a ref. to 'ebeni Indicae, quam lignum sanctum nostri vocant', i.e., Guaiacum. Baudrier (Lyons) VIII: 268; Adams (Cambr.) V209. DNLM, MBCo; BL, Paris: Arsenal.   555/55

Villegas, Alonso de. Comedia llamado Selvagia. *Toledo: J.Ferrer*, 1554. lxxvi lvs;4to. Among the characters is an Indian chief, Flerinardo, a native of Mexico. Pérez Pastor (Toledo) 275; Palau. 369103. BL, Madrid: BN.   555/56

1555

Belon, Pierre. Les observations de plusieurs singularitez & choses memorables, trouvées en Grece, Asie . . . & autres pays estranges. *Antwerp: C.Plantin*, 1555. 375 numb.lvs;8vo. 1st publ., Paris, 1553. Atkinson (Fr.Ren.) 100; Ind.aur.116.326. DNAL, MH, NN-RB; BL, BN.   555/1

—[Anr issue]. *Antwerp: C.Plantin, for J.Steels*, 1555. 375 numb.lvs;8vo. Atkinson (Fr.Ren.) 100n; Ind.aur.116.327. BL, Antwerp: Plantin Mus.   555/2

—[Anr edn]. *Paris: B.Prévost,for G. Cavellat*, 1555. 224 numb.lvs;4to. Printed, like edns of 1553 & 1554, for both Cavellat & Corrozet; no copy with Corrozet's t.p. has been located. Atkinson (Fr.Ren.) 101; Ind.aur.116.317; Shaaber B174. PU; BL, BN.   555/3

Boileau de Bouillon, Gilles. La sphere des deux mondes, composée . . . par Darinel pasteur des Amadis. *Antwerp: J.Richard*, 1555. 58 numb.lvs;illus., maps;4to. In verse. Refs to Peru appear on verso of lvs 55-56; contains also the Bellère map of New World found in edns of Cieza de León & Gómara of

1554. Sabin 18576; Cioranescu (XVI) 4251; Ind.aur.121.307; Church 101; JCB (3) I:185. CSmH, DLC, MiU-C, NN-RB, RPJCB; BL, BN.   555/4

Brant, Sebastian. Das Narrenschiff. *Frankfurt a.M.: H.Gülfferich*, 1555. 158 numb.lvs; illus.;8vo. 1st publ., Basel, 1494. Ind.aur.123.736. Wolfenbüttel: HB, Uppsala: UB.   555/5

Brasavola, Antonio Musa. Examen omnium loch . . . ubi de morbo gallico . . . tractatur. *Lyons: J.Fauré,for S.Honorat*, 1555. 750p.; 8vo. 1st publ., Venice, 1553; here a reissue of Lyons, 1554, edn with altered imprint date. Ind. aur.123.813; Adams (Cambr.) B2689; Baudrier (Lyons) IV:165. Cambridge: UL, Oslo: UB.   555/6

—[Anr issue]. *Lyons: J.Fauré,for J. Temporal*, 1555. Ind.aur.123.814; Baudrier (Lyons) IV:383. MH; BL, BN.   555/7

Castile, Laws, statutes, etc., 1252-1284 (Alfonso X). Las siete partidas . . . nuevamente glosadas por . . . Gregório Lopez. *Salamanca: A.de Portonariis*, 1555. 7v.;fol. The earliest edn to contain López's annotations, which contain refs to New World. Palau 7091. DLC, MH-L.   555/8

Cieza de León, Pedro de. La prima parte de la Cronica del . . . Peru . . . tradotta per Augustino da Cravaliz. *Rome: V.& L.Dorici*, 1555. 32 & 541p.;8vo. Transl. from 1553, Seville, Spanish text. Sabin 13047; Medina (BHA) 157n; Streit II:674; JCB (3) I:184. KU, NN-RB, RPJCB.   555/9

Dioscorides, Pedanius. Acerca de la materia medicinal . . . Traduzido de lengua griega . . . & illustrado con . . . substantiales annotationes, y con las figuras de innumeras plantas . . . por el doctor Andres de Laguna. *Antwerp: J.de Laet*, 1555. 616p.;illus.;fol. The earliest edn in this form, with both Dioscorides' text and Laguna's annotations, the latter having been publ. separately at Lyons in 1554. Pritzel 2313; Nissen (Bot.) 500; Peeters-Fontainas (Impr.esp.) 349. MiU; Brussels: BR, Madrid: BN.   555/10

Duval, Pierre, Bp of Seez. De la grandeur de Dieu. *Paris: M.de Vascovan*, 1555. 8vo. In verse. Included is a ref. to the Americas as evidence of God's handiwork. BL.   555/11

—[Anr edn]. *Antwerp: C.Plantin*, 1555. 15 lvs;8vo. Cioranescu (XVI) 9388. Brussels: BR.   555/12

Eden, Richard, ed. & tr. The decades of the new world or West India. *London: W.Powell*, 1555. 361 numb.lvs;4to. Contains 1st three Decades of P. Martyr d'Anghiera, his 'De nuper . . . repertis insulis', Pope Alexander VI's Demarcation Bull of 1493, Oviedo's *Hystorie of the West Indies*, Pigafetta's circumnavigation account, 'The stryfe betwene the Spanyardes and Portugales' from Gómara, etc. In some copies a map appears, enlarged from that which appears in the Antwerp editions publ. by Bellère of Cieza de León, Gómara & Darinel of 1554 & 1555. Four different colophons are found, with names & addresses of differing printers: R. Jug (Jugge), W.Seres, E.Sutton & R.Toye. Borba de Moraes II:32-33; STC 645-648; Church 102; JCB (3) I:186. CSmH (Seres, Sutton & Toye), CtY (Seres & Sutton), DLC (Jug), ICN, MH, MiU-C (Jug), MnU-B (Toye), NN-RB (Jug), RPJCB (Sutton & Toye); BL (Jug & Toye).
555/13

Emili, Paolo. De rebus gestis Francorum libri x. Arnoldi Ferroni . . . De rebus gestis Gallorum libri ix. *Paris: M.de Vascovan*, 1555. 2pts;8vo. 1st publ. with Le Ferron's appendix, Paris, 1548. Adams (Cambr.) A239; Ind. aur.100.831. ICN, PPL; Cambridge: King's, BN.
555/14

Focard, Jacques. Paraphrase de l'astrolabe . . . Le miroir du monde . . . Revue et corrigé par Jaques Bassentin. *Lyons: J.de Tournes*, 1555. 192p.;illus.,map;4to. 1st publ., Lyons, 1546. Sabin 58546; Cartier (de Tournes) 296; cf.Mortimer (France) 234. MH, NN-RB, PPF; BL, BN.
555/15

Fracastoro, Girolamo. Opera omnia. *Venice: Heirs of L.Giunta*, 1555. 285 numb.lvs; ports;4to. Includes author's *De contagione* (1st publ., Venice, 1546) and his *Syphilidis* (1st publ., Verona, 1530). Baumgartner (Fracastoro) 32; Shaaber F375; Waller 3168. CU-S, DLC, ICJ, MH, MiU, NNC, PU, RPB: BL, BN.
555/16

Fuchs, Leonhard. De historia stirpium commentarii insignes. *Lyons: J.de Tournes & G.Gazeau*, 1555. 991p.;12mo. 1st publ., Basel, 1542. Cartier (de Tournes) 297; Hunt (Bot.) 74. CtY, DLC, MH-A, NNNAM; BL.
555/17

――――. De usitata huius temporis componendorum miscendorumque medicamentorum ratione libri quatuor. *Basel: J.Oporinus*

[1555]. 398p.;fol. Expanded from earlier, 1541, edn. Included are refs to Brazil wood & Guaiacum. DNLM; BN.
555/18

Gesner, Konrad. Appendix Bibliothecae. *Zurich: C.Froschauer*, 1555. 105 numb.lvs;fol Supplements author's *Bibliotheca*, Zurich, 1545. Includes entries for Albericus [*sic*] Vespucius & Gonzalus Fernandus Oviedus. CU, CtY-M, DLC, ICU, InU-L, MH, NNNAM; BL, BN.
555/19

――――. Chirurgia. De chirurgia scriptores optimi quique veteres et recentiores, plerique in Germania antehac non editi. *Zurich: A.& J.Gessner*, 1555. 408 numb.lvs;illus.;fol. Included are J.Tagault's *De chirurgica institutione libri quinque* (1st publ., Paris, 1543) and M.Biondo's 'De origine morbi gallici, deque Ligni indici ancipiti proprietate' (1st publ., Venice, 1542, in his *De partibus ictu sectis citissime sanandis*). Adams (Cambr.) G520; Shaaber G141. CtY-M, DNLM, ICJ, MBCo, MnU-B, NNNAM, PU, RPB; BL, BN.
555/20

――――. Historiae animalium liber iii., qui est de avium natura. *Zurich: C.Froschauer*, 1555. 779p.;illus.,port.;fol. Includes description of turkey. Nissen (Birds) 349. CtY, DLC, ICJ, MH; BN.
555/21

――――. Icones avium omnium quae in Historia avium Conradi Gesneri describuntur. *Zurich: C.Froschauer*, 1555. 125p.;illus.;fol. Included is illus. of turkey. Nissen (Birds) 352; Adams (Cambr.) G545. DLC, MH, NcD; BL. 555/22

――――. Schatz. Ein kostlicher theürer Schatz Euonymi Philiatri [pseud.] . . . neüwlich verteütscht durch Joannem Rüdolphum Landenberger . . . vormals in teütscher Spraach nie gesähen. *Zurich: A.& J.Gessner*, 1555. 390p.;illus.;4to. Transl. from Gesner's *Thesaurus*, 1st publ., Zurich, 1552. DNLM, MBCo, MiU, NNNAM; BL.
555/23

――――. Thesaurus Euonymi Philiatri [pseud.], de remediis secretis. *Lyons: B.Arnoullet*, 1555. 498p.;illus.;16mo. 1st publ., Zurich, 1552, here a reissue of the Lyons, 1554, edn with altered imprint date. Baudrier (Lyons) X:149n Shaaber G149. CU, CtY-M, MnU, NNC, PU.
555/24

―[Anr issue]. *Lyons: B.Arnoullet,for A.Vincent*, 1555. Baudrier (Lyons) X:149; Adams (Cambr.) G528. MH-A; Cambridge: UL, BN.
555/25

Giovio, Paolo, Bp of Nocera. Histoire . . . sur les choses . . . de son temps. Traduictes de latin . . . & revueues pour la seconde edition, par Denis Sauvages, seigneur du Parc-Champenois. *Lyons: G.Rouillé*, 1558,'55. 2v.; fol. 1st publ. in French, Lyons, 1552-53, the American refs here appearing in v.2. Atkinson (Fr.Ren.) 119; Baudrier IX:224; cf. Adams (Cambr.) G662. BL (v.2), BN (v.1).   555/26

——. Historiarum sui temporis tomus primus [-secundus]. [*n.p.*] 1555. 2v.;8vo. 1st publ., Venice, 1550-52. BN.   555/27

——. La prima parte delle Historie del suo tempo . . . Tradotte per m. Lodovico Domenichi. *Venice: D.Farri [for P.Pietrasanta]* 1555. 557p.;8vo. Transl. from Giovio's *Historiarum sui temporis, tomus primus*, 1st publ., Venice, 1550. For 2nd pt, see year 1557. Moranti (Urbino) 1661. IU, NcD; BL, Urbino: BU.555/28

Gómara, Francisco López de. La historia general de las Indias y Nuevo Mundo . . . agora añadida y emendada por el mismo autor. *Saragossa: P.Bernuz & A.Milán,for M.de Zapila*, 1555. 2v.;illus.;fol. A reissue of the 1554 edn, with altered imprint date on t.p., the 1554 date appearing in colophon of both parts. Pt 2 has been special t.p. dated 1554 with title *Cronica de la Nueva España con la conquista de Mexico*. Cf.Sabin 27727 & 27728; Medina (BHA) 171; Wagner (SW) 2e; Streit II:675; Sánchez (Aragon) 374; JCB (3) I:181 (as 1554 issue). CU-B, ICN, InU-L, MB, NN-RB, PPL, RPJCB; Madrid: BN.   555/29

Honter, Johannes. Rudimentorum cosmographicorum . . . libri iii . . . cum tabellis geographicis. *Antwerp: J.Richard*, 1555. 2pts; maps;8vo. 1st publ. in this version, Kronstadt, 1542. In verse. Cf.Sabin 32793. NN-RB; BL.
555/30

Jesuits. Letters from missions. Copia de unas cartas de algunos padres y hermanos de la Compañia de Jesus que escrivieron de la India, Japon, y Brasil . . . trasladados de portugues en castellano. Fueron recibidas el año de mil y quinientos y cincuenta y cinco. [*Coimbra?*] *J.Alvárez*, 1555. 32 lvs;4to. Translated perhaps from manuscript sources, no printed Portuguese text being known. King Manuel plausibly preferred Coimbra to Lisbon as probable place of printing. Medina (BHA) 170; Streit II:1241; Borba de Moraes I:175; Anselmo 66; King Manuel 87. NN-RB; Lisbon: BN.   555/31

Le Ferron, Arnoul. De rebus gestis Gallorum libri ix . . . Tertia editio. *Paris: M.de*

Vascovan, 1555. 309 numb.lvs;8vo. 1st publ., Paris, 1549. Adams (Cambr.) F321. CtY, DLC, ICN, MHi; BL, BN.   555/32

Lucidarius. M.Elucidarius, von allerhandt geschöpffen Gottes . . . und wie alle Creaturn geschaffen sein auff erden. *Frankfurt a.M.: H.Gülfferich*, 1555. [88]p.;4to. 1st publ., Strassburg, [ca.1535]. Schorbach (Lucidarius) 57.   555/33

Macchelli, Niccolò. Tractatus de morbo gallico. *Venice: A.Arrivabene*, 1555. 55 lvs;8vo. DNLM, MBCo, MnU, PPC; BL.
555/34

Macer, Joannes. Indicarum historiarum ex oculatis et fidelissimis testibus perceptarum libri tres. *Paris: G.Guillard*, 1555. 87p.;12mo. Cf.French version, the following item. Sabin 43229n; Atkinson (Fr.Ren.) 103n; Cioranescu (XVI) 13885. DFo; BL, BN.   555/35

——. Les trois livres de l'Histoire des Indes. *Paris: G.Guillard,,* 1555. 96 numb.lvs;16mo. Cf.Latin version, the preceding item, of which this is a translation. Sabin 43229; Atkinson (Fr.Ren.) 103; Cioranescu (XVI) 138851. CSmH, ICN, MnU-B, RPJCB; Paris: Arsenal.
555/36

Magnus, Olaus, Abp of Upsala. Historia de gentibus septentrionalibus. *Rome: G.M.de Viottis*, 1555. 815p.;illus.,map;fol. Includes description of Greenland, geologically at least related to North America. Sabin 43830; Collijn (Sver.bibl.) II:221-227; Adams (Cambr.) M140. CU, CtY, DFo, ICN, InU-L, MH, MiD, MnU-B, NN-RB, PPAmP, RPJCB; BL, BN.   555/37

Mattioli, Pietro Andrea. I discorsi . . . ne i sei libri della materia medicinale di Pedacio Dioscoride. *Venice: V.Valgrisi*, 1555. 741p.; illus.;fol. Transl. from Venice, 1554, Latin edn. Pritzel 5987; Nissen (Bot.) 1304. DNLM, MH-A; London: Wellcome.   555/38

Medina, Pedro de. L'arte del navegar . . . tradotta de lingua spagnola [da Vicenzo Paletino]. *Venice: A.Pincio,for G.B.Pederzano*, 1555 [colophon: 1554]. cxxxvii lvs;illus., maps;4to. 1st publ. in Italian, Venice, 1554; here reissued with altered imprint date on t.p. Sabin 47346; Palau 159679; JCB (3) I:187. DLC, InU-L, MH, MiU-C, NN-RB, RPJCB; BL, BN.   555/39

Meneses, Felipe de. Luz de alma christiana. *Seville: M.de Montesdoca*, 1555. cxxix lvs;4to. Compares ignorance found in Spain to that of the Indies. Palau 16443. Madrid: BN. 555/40

Münster, Sebastian. La cosmographie universelle. *Basel: H.Petri*, 1555. 1402p.;maps;fol. 1st publ. in French, Basel, 1552. InU-L.
555/41

Natto, Marco Antonio. De pulchro et obiter de universa mundi fabrica. *Venice: F.Portonari*, 1555. 148 numb.lvs;fol. 1st publ., Pavia, 1553. Adams (Cambr.) N70. CLSU, ICN, InU-L, NNC; BL. 555/41a

Novus orbis regionum. Novus orbis regionum ac insularum veteribus incognitarum una cum tabula cosmographica, & aliquot aliis consimilis argumenti libellis. *Basel: J.Herwagen*, 1555. 677p.;illus.,map;fol. Contains, in addition to text 1st publ., Basel, 1532, as comp. by Simon Grynaeus, Cortés's 2nd & 3rd narratives and letters of Juan Zumárraga, Martín de Valencia, etc.; prob. reprinted from the Cologne, 1532, edn of Cortés's *De insulis noviter inventis*, itself derived in part from António de Olave's *Passio . . . Andree de Spoleto*, publ. that year at Toulouse. Sabin 34104; Streit I:73; Burmeister (Münster) 63; Adams (Cambr.) G1338; JCB (3) I:185-186. DLC, ICJ, InU-L, MB, MiU-C, MnU-B, NN-RB, PPL, RPJCB; BL, BN. 555/42

Núñez Cabeza de Vaca, Alvaro. La relacion y comentarios del governador Alvar Nuñez Cabeça de Vaca, de lo acaescido en las dos jornadas que hizo a las Indias. *Valladolid: F.Fernández de Córdova*, 1555. clxiiii lvs;4to. Lvs i-lvi 1st publ., Zamora, 1542. Sabin 9768; Medina (BHA) 172; Vail (Frontier) 2; Wagner (SW) la; Streit II:677; Alcocer (Valladolid) 202; JCB (3) I:188. CSmH, CtY, DLC, ICN, InU-L, MH, MiU-C, NN-RB, RPJCB; BL, BN. 555/43

Ovidius Naso, Publius. Metamorphoses. Italian. Le trasformationi di m. Lodovico Dolce. *Venice: G.Giolito de' Ferrari & Bros*, 1555. 4to. 1st publ. in this version with world map, Venice, 1553. Mortimer (Italy) 342n. MH;BL. 555/44

Oviedo y Valdés, Gonzalo Fernández de. L'histoire naturelle et generalle des Indes, isles, et terre ferme de la grand mer Oceane. *Paris: M.de Vascovan*, 1555. 134 numb.lvs;illus.;fol. Transl. by Jean Poleur from Seville, 1535, *Historia general de las Indias*. Sabin 57992; Medina (BHA) 97n; Atkinson (Fr.Ren.) 104. ICN, MH, NN-RB, RPJCB; BL. 555/45

Pico della Mirandola, Giovanni Francesco. Dialogo intitolato La strega, overo De gli inganni de demoni. *Pescia: L.Torrentino*, 1555. 126p.;4to. Transl. by Turino Turini from author's Latin *Strix*, 1st publ., Bologna, 1523. DLC, NN-RB. 555/46

Ronsard, Pierre de. Les hymnes. *Paris: A.Wechel*, 1555. 195p.;4to. Includes poem 'L'hymne de l'or', referring to 'ce gayac estranger', i.e., Guaiacum. Le Moine 92; Adams (Cambr.) R764; Rothschild 672. BL, BN. 555/47

Trithemius, Johannes. Antwort . . . auff acht fragstuck. *Ingolstadt: A.& S.Weissenhorn*, 1555. 4to. Transl. from author's *Liber octo questionum ad Maximilianum Cesarem*, 1st publ., Oppenheim, 1515. Sabin 97005; Shaaber T357. PU; BL. 555/48

Valleriola, François. Enarrationum medicinalium libri sex. *Venice: G.Griffio,for B.Costantini*, 1555. 511 numb.lvs;8vo. 1st publ., Lyons, 1554. DNLM. 555/49

Zárate, Augustín de. Historia del descubrimiento y conquista del Peru. *Antwerp: M.Nuyts*, 1555. 273 numb. lvs;illus.;8vo. Sabin 106268; Medina (BHA) 173 & Ampl., V,p.109; Peeters-Fontainas (Impr.esp.) 1343; Church 103; JCB (3) I:189. CSmH, DLC, MH, MWA, NN-RB, RPJCB; BL. 555/50

1556

Amatus Lusitanus. Curationum medicinalium centuriae duae, tertia & quarta . . . enchiridii forma nunc primum editae. *Lyons: P.Fradin,for J.F.de Gabiano*, 1556. 318 numb.lvs;16mo. Cf.1st Century, 1st publ., Florence, 1551, & 2nd Century, 1st publ., Venice, 1552. In the 4th 'Centuria' the 'Curatio 69' discusses syphilis & its treatment with Guaiacum. Ind.aur.104.558; Baudrier (Lyons) VII:196-197. KU-M; BN. 556/1

―――. Curationum medicinalium centuriae quatuor, quarum duae priores, ab auctore sunt recognitae, duae posteriores nunc primum editae. *Basel: Froben Office*, 1556. 406p.;fol. 1st Century 1st publ., Florence, 1551; 2nd Century 1st publ., Venice, 1552; 3rd & 4th Centuries 1st publ. at Lyons, the preceding item. Ind.aur.104.557. DNLM, MnU, NNNAM, PPC; BL, Munich: StB. 556/2

Bembo, Pietro, Cardinal. L'histoire du nouveau monde descouvert par les Portugaloys . . . Premiere impression. *Lyons: J.d'Ogerolles*, 1556. 24p.;8vo. Transl. from Bk 6 of the author's Venice, 1551, *Historiae Venetae*; no more publ. Borba de Moraes I:84; Atkinson (Fr.Ren.) 107; Ind. aur.116.444. BL, Grenoble: BM. 556/3

__[Anr edn]. *Paris: O.de Harsy,for E.Denise*, 1556. 32p.;8vo. Borba de Moraes I:84; Ind. aur.116.445; Church 104. CSmH, NN-RB. 556/4

____. Quaecumque usquam prodierunt opera. *Basel: M.Isengrin*, 1556. 3v.;8vo. Includes author's *Historiae Venetae*, 1st publ., Venice, 1551. Sabin 4619n; Ind.aur.116.443; Adams (Cambr.) B569. ICU, IU; Cambridge: UL (v.1 & 3), Trinity (v.2), BN. 556/5

Beuter, Pedro Antonio. Cronica generale d'Hispagna . . . nuovamente tradotta . . . dal s. Alfonso d'Ulloa. *Venice: G.Giolito de' Ferrari & Bros*, 1556. 533p.;map;8vo. Transl. from Beuter's *Primera parte de la Coronica general de toda España*, Valencia, 1546. Ind.aur.118.413; Palau 28828; Shaaber B295. CU, DLC, ICU, MH, NN-RB, PU, RPB; BL, BN. 556/6

Bock, Hieronymus. Kreüter Buch. *Strassburg: J.Rihel*, 1556. ccccxxiiii lvs;illus.;fol. 1st publ. with illus., Strassburg, 1546. Pritzel 866n; Nissen (Bot.) 182n; Ind.aur.120.594. MiU, NNBG; London: Wellcome. 556/7

Brasavola, Antonio Musa. Examen omnium simplicium medicamentorum. *Lyons:M.Dubois,for J.Frellon*, 1556. 862p.;16mo. 1st publ., Rome, 1536. Ind.aur.123.818; Baudrier (Lyons) V:235. MH; BL. 556/8

__[Anr issue]. *Lyons: M.Dubois,for A.Vincent*, 1556. MH-A. 556/9

Cardano, Girolamo. Les livres . . . intitulés De la subtilité & subtiles inventions . . . traduis de latin . . . par Richard Le Blanc. *Paris: G.LeNoir*, 1556. 391 numb.lvs;illus.; 4to. Transl. from Cardano's *De subtilitate rerum*, 1st publ., Nuremberg (?), 1550. The privilege to print was assigned to LeNoir. Ind.aur.132.069. InU-L; BN. 556/10

__[Anr issue]. *Paris: [G.LeNoir,for] C.L'Angelier*, 1556. Ind.aur.132.069. DLC, MH, PPF; BL, BN. 556/11

__[Anr issue]. *Paris: [G.LeNoir,for] J.Foucher*, 1556. Ind.aur.132.069. DLC, MH, NN-RB. 556/12

Cieza de León, Pedro de. La prima parte dell'Istorie del Peru. *Venice: D.Farri,for A.Arrivabene*, 1556. 215 numb.lvs;8vo. 1st publ. in this translation by A.de Cravaliz, Rome, 1555. Sabin 13048; Medina (BHA) 157n (I:256-257); Streit II:687; JCB (3) I:190. DLC, MnU-B, NN-RB, PPL, RPJCB; BL. 556/13

Cortés, Martín. Breve compendio de la sphera y de la arte de navegar. *Seville: A.Alvárez*, 1556. xcv lvs;illus.;8vo. 1st publ., Seville, 1551. Cf.Sabin 16966; cf.Medina (BHA) 145; Bibl.mar.esp. 208; Palau 63379n. NN-RB; BL (imp.), Madrid: BN. 556/14

Fuchs, Leonhart. De componendorum miscendorumque medicamentorum ratione libri quatuor. *Lyons: [S.Barbier,for?] J.Frellon*, 1556. 910p.;16mo. 1st publ., Basel, 1555, under title *De usitata huius temporis componendorum . . . medicamentorum ratione*. Baudrier (Lyons) V:237. MH-A; London: Wellcome. 556/15

__[Anr issue]. *Lyons: [S.Barbier,for?] A.Vincent*, 1556. Baudrier (Lyons) V:237. DNLM, ICJ; BN. 556/16

Gemma, Reinerus, Frisius. De principiis astronomiae et cosmographiae . . . Item de orbis divisione et insulis rebusque nuper inventis. *Paris: B.Prévost,for G.Cavellat*, 1556. 171 numb.lvs;illus.;8vo. 1st publ., Antwerp, 1530. Sabin 62588n. NhD; BN. 556/17

____. Les principes d'astronomie & cosmographie . . . mis en langage françois par m. Claude de Boissier. *Paris: G.Cavellat*, 1556. 128 numb.lvs;illus.;8vo. Transl. from preceding item. Cioranescu (XVI) 4286. CtY, DLC, InU-L, MH, MiU-C, NN-RB. 556/18

Gesner, Konrad. Tesauro di Euonomo Filatro [pseud.] de rimedii secreti . . . Tradotto di latino . . . per m. Pietro Lauro. *Venice: G.B. & M.Sessa*, 1556. 152 numb.lvs;illus.;8vo. Transl. from Gesner's *Thesaurus*, 1st publ., Zurich, 1552. CtY, DNLM, ICU, NNC; London: Wellcome. 556/19

Giovio, Paolo, Bp of Nocera. Historiarum sui temporis. Tomus primus[-secundus]. *Strassburg: A.Fries*, 1556. 2v.;8vo. 1st publ., Florence, 1550-52. Ritter (Strasbourg) 1285. Strasbourg: BN. 556/20

Girava, Gerónimo. Dos libros de cosmographia. *Milan: G.A.da Castiglione & C.Caron*, 1556. 271p.;illus.,map;4to. 'India ó Nuevo mundo': p.186-242. Cf.Sabin 27504; Medina

(BHA) 176; Borba de Moraes I:299; Wagner (NW) II:279. CU, CtY, DLC, InU-L, MH, MnU-B, NN-RB, RPJCB; BL.   556/21

Gómara, Francisco López de. La historia generale delle Indie Occidentali . . . Tradotta . . . per Augustino de Cravaliz. *Rome: V.& L.Dorici*, 1556. 2v.;4to. Transl. from Saragossa, 1552, Spanish text. Vol.2 has title *Historia del illustriss. et valoriss. capitano Ferdinando Cortes.* Copies of v.2 with title *Historia di Mexico* and imprint dated 1555 are imperfect, lacking the 1st 8 lvs — Wagner. Sabin 27736 & 27735 (cf.27734); Medina (BHA) 159n (I:270-271); Wagner (SW) 2n-o; Streit II:689-690 (cf.676); JCB (3) I:192 (cf.p.186). DLC, ICN, InU-L, MH (v.2), MiU-C, MnU-B, NN-RB, RPJCB; BL. 556/22

Jesuits. Letters from missions. Copia de diversas cartas de algunas padres y hermanos de la Compañia de Jesus. Recibidas el año de mil y quinientos cincuenta y cinco. De las grandes maravillas, que Dios . . . obra . . . en las Indias del Rey de Portugal, y en . . . Japon, y en . . . Brasil. *Barcelona: C.Bornat*, 1556. 32 lvs;4to. 1st publ., [Coimbra?], 1555. Medina (BHA) 174; Borba de Moraes I:174; Streit II:1248. BL, Lisbon: BN.   556/23

———. L'institution des loix, coutumes et autres choses merveilleuses & memorables tant en royaume de la Chine que des Indes. *Paris: S.Nivelle*, 1556. 116 numb.lvs;16mo. Transl. from [Coimbra?], 1555, *Copia de unas cartas.* Borba de Moraes I:354; Atkinson (Fr.Ren.) 106; Streit IV:808. DCU, NNH; BL.   556/24

Leo Africanus, Joannes. Historiale description de l'Afrique . . . Escrite de nostre temps par Jean Leon . . . premierement en langue arabesque, puis en toscane, et à present mise en françois [par Jean Temporal]. *Lyons: J.Temporal*, 1556. 2v.;fol. Extracted & transl. from Ramusio's Venice, 1550, *Primo volume delle navigationi*, and including also Vespucci's narratives. The latter are not found in the Antwerp edns of Leo Africanus of this year. Sabin 40044; Borba de Moraes I:398; Atkinson (Fr.Ren.) 108; Streit I:77; Baudrier (Lyons) IV: 386-387;JCB (3) I:191-192. DLC, MH, NN-RB, RPJCB; BL, BN.   556/25

Macchelli, Niccolò. Tractatus de morbo gallico. *Venice: A.Arrivabene*, 1556. 55 lvs;8vo. 1st publ., Venice, 1555, this being a reissue of that edn. DNLM; London: Wellcome. 556/26

Meneses, Felipe de. Luz de alma christiana. *Medina del Campo: G.de Millis*, 1555

[colophon:1556]. cxlvii lvs;4to. 1st publ., Seville, 1555. Pérez Pastor (Medina del Campo) 128; Palau 164444. BL.   556/27

Merula, Gaudenzio. Memorabilium . . . cum emendatione et scholiis P. Castali. *Lyons: M. Bonhomme*, 1556. 432p.;illus.;8vo. On p.417-418 is a brief notice of 'insulae Americae'. Sabin 48033; Adams (Cambr.) M1356. CU, DNLM, InU-L, MiU, NN-RB; BL, BN.   556/28

Mexía, Pedro. Les diverses leçons . . . mis en françois par Claude Gruget . . . de nouveau revues, corrigées et augmentées de trois dialogues, touchant la nature du soleil, de la terre et des météores. *Paris: M.Prévost*, 1556. 634 numb.lvs;12mo. Contains supplementary dialogues referring to Magellan, etc., 1st publ. in Spanish, Seville, 1547, with title *Colóquios o dialogos.* Palau 167310. BN.   556/29

More, Sir Thomas, Saint. A frutefull, pleasaunt, & wittie worke . . . called Utopia . . . translated into Englishe by Ralph Robinson . . . nowe by him at this seconde edition newlie perused and corrected, and also with divers notes . . . augmented. *London: [R.Tottell,for] A.Veale* [1556]. 131 numb.lvs;8vo. 1st publ. in English, London, 1551. Without colophon. Sabin 50545; STC 18095; Gibson (More) 26a; JCB (3) I:165. CSmH, CtY, RPJCB; BL.   556/30

—[Anr state]. *London: [R.Tottell,for] A.Veale*, 1556. With colophon, dated 1556. STC 18095.5; Gibson (More) 26b. CSmH, DFo, IU, MH; BL.   556/31

Münster, Sebastian. Cosmographei, oder Beschreibung aller länder. *Basel: H.Petri*, 1556. 1233p.;illus.,maps;fol. 1st publ., Basel, 1544. Sabin 51389; Burmeister (Münster) 72. BL, Munich: StB.   556/32

———. La cosmographie universelle. *[Basel:] H.Petri*, 1556. 1429p.;illus.,port.,maps;fol. 1st publ. in French, Basel, 1552. Sabin 51398; Atkinson (Fr.Ren.) 110; Adams (Cambr.) M1913; Burmeister (Münster) 93. NN-RB; Cambridge: Trinity, BN.   556/33

Oviedo y Valdés, Gonzalo Fernández de. L'histoire naturelle et generalle des Indes, isles, et terre ferme de la grande mer Oceane. *Paris: M.de Vascovan*, 1556. 134 numb.lvs; illus.;fol. 1st publ., Paris, 1555, as transl. by J.Poleur, here differing only in altered imprint date on t.p. Sabin 57993; Atkinson (Fr.Ren.) 104n; Streit II:688; Arents 7; JCB (3)

I:190-191. CSmH, CtY, InU-L, MiU-C, MnU-B, NN-RB, RPJCB; BL, BN.   556/34

Pico della Mirandola, Giovanni Francesco. Libro detto Strega, overo De le illusioni del demonio. *Venice: Al segno de la Speranza*, 1556. 68 numb.lvs;8vo. 1st publ., Bologna, 1524, as here transl. by Leandro Alberti, the passage referring to the Indies appearing on lvs 43v-44r. OU, RPJCB; BN.   556/35

Rabelais, François. Les oeuvres. *Troyes: L. Vivant*, 1556. 2pts;16mo. Includes 'Le quart livre', 1st publ., Paris, 1552. Plan (Rabelais) 93. BL, Chantilly: Mus. Condé.   556/36

__[Anr edn]. [*Lyons?*] 1556. 740p.;16mo. Plan (Rabelais) 94; Rothschild 1515. MWiW-C; BN.   556/37

Ramusio, Giovanni Battista, comp. Terzo volume delle Navigatione et viaggi nel quale si contengono le navigationi al Mondo Novo, alli antichi incogniti. *Venice: Heirs of L. Giunta*, 1556. 456 numb.lvs;illus.,maps;fol. Includes narratives relating to America by P.M. d'Anghiera, Oviedo, Cortés, Vázquez de Coronado, Xérez, Verrazano, Cartier, etc. For detailed contents, see Sabin, and also G. B. Parks, 'The contents and sources of Ramusio's *Navigationi*', New York Public Library *Bulletin*, L (1955) 279-313. Sabin 67740; Borba de Moraes II:172-173; Wagner (SW) 3-6; Streit I:75; Church 99; Shaaber R20; JCB (3) I:194. CSmH, CtY, DLC, ICN, NN-RB, PU, RPJCB; BL, BN.   556/38

Rostinio, Pietro. Trattato di mal franceso. *Venice: A. de Carnaccioli, for L. Avanzi*, 1556. 182p.;8vo. Based on A.M. Brasavola's *Examen omnium decoctionum*, itself 1st publ. as part of his *Examen omnium loch*, Venice, 1553. CtY-M, DFo; BL.   556/39

Sacro Bosco, Joannes de. Sphaera . . . emendata Eliae Vineti . . . Scholia. *Paris: G. Cavellat*, 1556. 102 numb.lvs;illus.;8vo. 1st publ. with Vinet's *Scholia*, Paris, 1551. Cf.Sabin 32681. CU; BL, BN.   556/40

Scaliger, Julius Caesar. In libros duos, qui inscribuntur De plantis, Aristotele autore, libri duo. *Paris: M. de Vascovan*, 1556. 266 numb. lvs;4to. Included is mention of the Spanish Indies, of Guaiacum as cure of syphilis, and of cacao. Pritzel 8088; Adams (Cambr.) S587. CtY-M, DNLM, MH-A, NNNAM, PPL; BL.   556/41

Scandianese, Tito Giovanni. I quattro libri della caccia. *Venice: G. Giolito de' Ferrari*, 1556. 2pts;illus.,map;4to. The earliest edn to contain (on p.23) the world map, including the Americas, 1st used in the Venice, 1553, *Trasformationi* of Ovid. Mortimer (Italy) 211. CtY, DLC, ICN, MH, MiU, NN-RB, RPJCB; BL.   556/42

Soto, Domingo de. De justitia & jure libri decem. Nunc primum ab ipso authore innumeris in locis emendati atque multo auctiores redditi. *Salamanca: A. de Portonariis, for J. Moreno*, 1556. 916p.;fol. 1st publ., Salamanca, 1553. Adams (Cambr.) S1482; Palau 320139. DCU; Cambridge: UL, Madrid: BN.   556/43

Spain. Laws, statutes, etc., 1556-1598 (Philip II). La ultima nueva orden y ordenanças: que la.S.C.C. Magestad del Emperador . . . dio: para la buena orden de justicia y governacion . . . de Sevilla . . . en diez de Enero deste año de .1556. [*Seville? M. de Montesdoca?* 1556?]. 4 lvs;fol. Though stated by Vindel, followed by Palau, to have been printed at Valladolid, the t.p. bears a coat-of-arms and borders with monogram AB, also employed at Seville by Andrés de Burgos & then by Antón Alvárez, 1544-1551. Text contains prohibition of shipping fictional histories, etc., to Indies. Vindel 3.031; Palau 203198. NNH (t.p. wanting).   556/44

Tamara, Francisco. El libro de las costumbras de todas las gentes del mundo, y de las Indias. Traduzido y copilado por . . . Francisco Thamara. *Antwerp: M. Nuyts*, 1556. 349 numb.lvs;8vo. A reworking of Johann Boemus's *Mores, leges, et ritus omnium gentium*, with the addition, lvs 249-328, of materials relating to the Americas. Sabin 94273 (&6117); Medina (BHA) 177; Ind. aur.120.951; Peeters-Fontainas (Impr.esp.) 134; JCB (3) I:194. MH, NN-RB, RPJCB; BL.   556/45

Vigo, Giovanni de. Prattica universale in cirugia . . . novamente tradotte per m. Lorenzo Chrisaorio. *Venice: D. Farri, for F. Torresano*, 1556. 758 (i.e., 258) numb.lvs;illus.;4to. 1st publ. in this translation, Venice, 1549. London: Wellcome.   556/46

1557

Alberti, Leandro. Descrittione di tutta l'Italia. *Venice: D. Farri*, 1557. 464 numb.lvs; 4to. 1st publ., Bologna, 1550. Ind.aur. 102.341. IU; BL.   557/1

Alvares, Francisco. Historia de las cosas de Etiopia . . . Agora nuevamente traduzido de portuges en castellano, por . . . Thomas de Padilla. *Antwerp: H.de Laet,for J.Steels*, 1557. 207 numb.lvs;8vo. The earliest edn to contain American refs, here found in translator's dedicatory epistle, the Portuguese original (Lisbon, 1540) being without them. Sabin 974n; Borba de Moraes I:25; Streit XV:1572; Peeters-Fontainas (Impr.esp.) 43; Ind.aur. 104.034. CU, RPJCB; BN, Madrid: BN.557/2

Amatus Lusitanus. Curationum medicinalium . . . centuriae quatuor . . . omnia nunc accuratius rec. *Venice: G.Costantini*, 1557. 645p.;8vo. 1st publ., Basel, 1556, in edn containing 4 centuries. Ind.aur.104.559. DNLM; BL, BN.   557/3

_____. In Dioscoridis . . . De medica materia libros quinque . . . Enarrationes eruditissime. *Venice: G.Scoto,for G.Ziletti*, 1557. 514p.;4to. 1st publ., Venice, 1553. A reissue of the 1553 edn, with cancel t.p. Ind.aur. 104.560. BL   557/4

Barré, Nicolas. Copie de quelques letres sur la navigation du Chevalier de Villegaignon es terres de l'Amerique . . . avec les moeurs & façons de vivre des sauvages du pais. *Paris: M.LeJeune*, 1557. 38p.;8vo. Sabin 99728n; Borba de Moraes I:67-68; Atkinson (Fr.Ren.) 114; Ind.aur.113.370; Arents (Add.) 12; JCB (3) I:195. NN-A, RPJCB; BL.   557/5

Cardano, Girolamo. De rerum varietate libri xvii. *Basel: H.Petri*, 1557. 707p.;illus.,port.; 8vo. Includes numerous scattered refs to American persons, places, plants, etc., deriving at least in part from F.L.Gómara's *Istoria de las Indias*. Ind.aur.132.070; Adams (Cambr.) C662 (misdated 1577); Arents (Add.) 14. CU, DLC, ICJ, MH, MnU-B, NN-RB, PU; BL, BN.   557/6

—[Anr edn]. *Basel: H.Petri*, 1557. 1194p.; illus.,port.;8vo. Ind.aur.132.071. CLSU, DLC, MH-A, MiU, RPB; BL, BN.   557/7

Carvajal, Miguel de. Cortes d' casto amor: y Cortes d' la muerte. *Toledo: J.Ferrer*, 1557. 2pts;illus.;4to. Drama. In the *Cortes de la muerte*, by Carvajal & Luis Hurtado de Toledo, American Indians appear. Pérez Pastor (Toledo) 282; Palau 117311. Paris: Mazarine, Madrid: BN.   557/8

Couillard, Antoine, seigneur du Pavillon. Les antiquitez et singularitez du monde. *Paris: J.Dallier*, 1557. 136 numb.lvs;8vo. 'De l'isle Americ, ou la nouvelle Castille': lf 89r/v.

Cioranescu (XVI) 7009; JCB (3) I:196; JCB AR16:8. NN-RB, RPJCB; BN.   557/9

—[Anr issue]. *Paris: A.LeClerc*, 1557. BN.
557/10

Dodoens, Rembert. Histoire des plantes . . . Nouvellement traduite de bas aleman . . . par Charles de l'Escluse. *Antwerp: J.van der Loe*, 1557. 584p.;illus.;fol. Transl. with emendations & additions supplied by Dodoens, from his 1554 *Cruijde boeck*. Pritzel 2345n; Nissen (Bot.) 510; Bibl.belg.,1st ser.,IX:D109; Adams (Cambr.) D718; Arents (Add.) 15. CtY, DNLM, MH, NN-A; BL, BN.   557/11

Duval, Pierre, Bp of Seez. De la grandeur de Dieu. *Paris: F.Morel*, 1557. 8vo. 1st publ., Paris, 1555. In verse. BL.   557/12

Federman, Nicholas. Indianische historia. Ein schön kurtzweilige Historia . . . erster Raise . . . von Hispania und Andolosia auss in Indias des Occeanischen Mors. *Hagenau: S. Bund*, 1557. 63 numb.lvs;4to. Narrates experiences as Welser agent in Venezuela, 1529-32. Sabin 23997; Baginsky (German Americana) 68; Palau 23997; JCB (3) I:197. InU-L, MH, NN-RB, RPJCB; BL.   557/13

Francisco de Vitoria. Relectiones theologicae xii. *Lyons: J.Boyer*, 1557. 2v.;8vo. 'De Indis insulanis relectio prior': v.l,p.282-374; 'De Indis, sive De jure belli Hispanorum in barbaros, relectio posterior': v.l,p.375-485. Sabin 100618; Medina (BHA) 180 (& Ampl., VI, p.509-510); Streit I:79; Palau 371064; JCB (3) I:197. DGU, ICN, MH-L, MiU-L, NNH, RPJCB; Madrid: BN.   557/14

Fuchs, Leonhart. Historia de yervas, y plantas . . . Traduzidos nuevamente en español. *Antwerp: H.de Laet,for Heirs of A.Birckmann*, 1557. 520p.;illus.;8vo. 1st publ. in Latin, Basel, 1542. Cf.Nissen (Bot.) 666; Peeters-Fontainas (Impr.esp.) 350; Fairfax Murray (Germany) 473. DLC; Antwerp: Plantin Mus.   557/15

—[Anr issue]. Historia de las yervas, y plantas . . . Traduzida nuevamente . . . por Juan Jarava. *Antwerp: H.de Laet,for Heirs of A. Birckmann*, 1557. Nissen (Bot.) 666; Peeters-Fontainas (Impr.esp.) 351. MH-A, NNH.
557/16

Gemma, Reinerus, Frisius. Les principes d'astronomie & cosmographie . . . mis en langage françois par m. Claude de Boissier. *Paris: G.Cavellat*, 1557. 128 numb.lvs;illus.; 8vo. 1st publ. in French, Paris, 1556; here reissued with altered imprint date. Adams

(Cambr.) G389; Moranti (Urbino) 1611. ICN, MH, NN-RB; Cambridge: Trinity, Urbino: BU. 557/17

Gesner, Konrad. Tresor de Euonime Philiatre des remedes secretz, par Euonyme Philiatre [pseud.]. *Lyons: Widow of B.Arnoullet*, 1557. 440p.;8vo. Transl. by Barthélemy Aneau from Gesner's *Thesaurus*, 1st publ., Zurich, 1552. Baudrier (Lyons) X:151. 557/18

—[Anr issue]. *Lyons: Widow of B.Arnoullet,for A.Vincent*, 1557. Baudrier (Lyons) X: 151; Adams (Cambr.) G531. CtY-M, MH; BL. 557/19

——. Vogelbüch . . . neüwlich aber durch Rudolff Heüsslin in das teutsch gebracht. *Zurich: C.Froschauer*, 1557. cclxxii lvs;illus.;fol. Transl. from Gesner's *Historiae animalium liber iii. qui est de avium natura*, 1st publ., Zurich, 1555. Here the turkey is designated as 'Indianische Hün'. Nissen (Birds) 350. MH; BL. 557/20

Giovio, Paolo, Bp of Nocera. La seconda parte dell' Historie del suo tempo . . . Tradotte per m. Lodovico Domenichi. *Venice: Comin da Trino*, 1557. 398 numb.lvs;8vo. 1st publ. as here transl., Venice, 1553. Moranti (Urbino) 1663. Urbino: BU. 557/21

Gómara, Francisco López de. La seconda parte delle Historie dell' India . . . nuovamente tradotte di spagnuolo. Venice: [*D.Farri,for*] *A.Arrivabene*, 1557. 324 numb.lvs;8vo. This translation differs from that by A. de Cravaliz, 1st publ., Rome, 1556. Continues the same publisher's 1556 edn of P. de Cieza de León's *La prima parte dell' Istorie del Peru*. A preface by Arrivabene identifies him as instigator of this version. Sabin 27737 (cf. 13049n); Medina (BHA) 159n (I:270); Wagner (SW) 2p; Streit II:702; JCB (3) I:196. MnU-B, NN-RB, PHi, RPJCB. 557/22

—[Anr issue]. *Venice:* [*D.Farri,for*] *G.Ziletti*, 1557. Differs only in imprint and device from preceding. Sabin 13049n; cf.Medina (BHA) 159n; Wagner (SW) 2q; cf.Streit II:702; JCB (3) I:196. CtY, NN-RB, RPJCB. 557/23

Jesuits. Letters from missions. Avisi particulari dell' Indie di Portugallo nuovamente hauti [i.e., havuti] quest' anno del 1557. *Rome: Society of Jesus*, 1557. 48 lvs;8vo. Includes 4 letters from Brazil. Borba de Moraes I:50; Streit II:1253. BL. 557/24

Lonitzer, Adam. Kreuterbuch, neu zugericht. *Frankfurt a.M.: C.Egenolff*, 1557. 342 numb.lvs;illus.;fol. Transl. from author's *Na-*

turalis historiae opus novum, Frankfurt a.M., 1551. Pritzel 5599; Nissen (Bot.) 1227. NNBG; London: Wellcome. 557/25

Manardo, Giovanni. Epistolarum medicinalium libri xx. *Venice: G.F.Camocio*, 1557. 900p.;8vo. Includes Manardo's *De erroribus Symonis Pistoris . . . circa morbum gallicum*, 1st publ., [Leipzig?], 1500. DNLM, NNNAM. 557/26

Manuzio, Paolo. De gli elementi, e di molto loro notabili effetti. *Venice: P.Manuzio*, 1557. xxxiiii lvs;4to. Includes ref. to Columbus. Sabin 44434; Renouard (Aldus) I:410; Adams (Cambr.) M470; JCB (3) I:198. CtY, DFo, MH, NN-RB, RPJCB; BL, BN. 557/27

Mattioli, Pietro Andrea. I discorsi . . . ne i sei libri della materia medicinale di Pedacio Dioscoride. *Venice: V.Valgrisi & B.Costantini*, 1557. 741p.;illus.;fol. 1st publ., Venice, 1555. Cf.Pritzel 5987; cf.Nissen (Bot.) 1304; Mortimer (Italy) 294. CtY-M, DFo, MH. 557/28

Mexía, Pedro. Dialoghi . . . tradotti nuovamente . . . da Alfonso d'Ulloa. *Venice: P. Pietrasanta*, 1557. 125p.;4to. 1st publ. in Spanish, Seville, 1547. Palau 167380; Shaaber M324. CtY, DFo, ICN, NN-RB, PU; BL, BN. 557/29

Ovidius Naso, Publius. Metamorphoses. Italian. Le trasformationi di m. Lodovico Dolce . . . Quarta impressione. *Venice: G. Giolito de' Ferrari*, 1557. 312p.;illus., map;4to. 1st publ. in this version with world map, Venice, 1553. Mortimer (Italy) 342n. ICN, MH; BL, BN. 557/30

Oviedo y Valdés, Gonzalo Fernández de. Libro xx. de la segunda parte de la General historia de las Indias . . . que trata del estrecho de Magallans. *Valladolid: F.Fernández de Córdova*, 1557. lxiiii lvs; illus.;fol. Continues the author's *Historia general de las Indias*, 1st publ., Seville, 1535. Further text publ. from mss only in 1851-55. Sabin 57991; Harrisse (BAV) 207n; Medina (BHA) 179; Alcocer (Valladolid) 209; Streit II:701; Nissen (Zool.) 4111; Church 106; JCB (3) I:197. CSmH, CtY, DLC, MiU-C, MnU-B, NN-RB, RPJCB; BL, BN. 557/31

Paracelsus. Een excellent tracktaet leerende hoemen alle ghebreken der pocken sal moghen ghenesen. *Antwerp: J.Roelants*, 1557. 32 lvs;illus.4to. The earliest extant edn, though privilege dated 1553 implies an earlier edn of this Dutch translation, by Philipp Hermann, from the *Von der französischen Krankheit*, 1st publ., Nuremberg, 1530. Sudhoff (Paracelsus) 38. Cologne: StB. 557/32

Relaçam verdadeira dos trabalhos que ho governador don Fernando de Souto e certos fidalgos portugueses passarom no descobrimento da provincia da Frolida [i.e., Florida]. Agora novamente feita per hum fidalgo Delvas. *Evora: A.de Burgos*, 1557. clxxx lvs;8vo. Sabin 24895; Vail. (Frontier) 3; Anselmo 388; Palau 256843; JCB AR50:5-12. NN-RB, RPJCB; BL, Lisbon: Ajuda. 557/33

Renner, Franz. Ein new wolgegründet nützlichs unnd haylsams Handtbüchlein, gemeiner Practick, aller innerlicher und eusserlicher Ertzney, so wider die erschröckliche, abscheuliche, Kranckheit der Frantzosen unnd Lemung, auch für all ander Seuchten. *Nuremberg: G.Hain*, 1557. 157 numb.lvs;4to. 1st publ., Nuremberg, 1554. Proksch I:17. KU-M; London: Wellcome. 557/34

Rouen. Les pourtres et figures du sumptueux ordre, plaisantz spectacles et magnifiques theatres dresses et exhibes par les citoiens de Rouen . . . a l'entree de . . . Henry second. *Rouen: J.DuGort*, 1557. 24 lvs;illus.;4to. Versified rendering of 1551 account, reusing illus. from the earlier prose text. Brunet II:1001. 557/35

Soto, Domingo de. Commentarium . . . in quartum Sententiarum [Petri Lombardi] tomus primus[-secundus]. *Salamanca: J.à Canova*(v.1) & *A.de Portonariis*(v.2), 1557-60. 2v.;fol. In v.1, dist.5, Art.10 adverts to Pope Alexander's concession of West Indies to Ferdinand & Isabella to be christianized; in v.2, dist.39, Art.3 refers to conversion of their natives. Palau 320167. 557/36

Staden, Hans. Warhaftige Historia und beschreibung eyner Landtschafft der Wilden, Nacketen, Grimmigen Menschfresser, Leuthen in der Newenwelt America gelegen. *Marburg: A.Kolbe*, 1557. [178]p.;illus.,map;4to. Deals chiefly with author's voyages in Brazil & captivity by Tupi Indians there. Sabin 90036; Vail (Frontier) 4; Borba de Moraes II:280-282; Baginsky (German Americana) 70; JCB (3) I:199. CSmH, InU-L, MB, NN-RB, RPJCB; BL. 557/37

—[Anr edn]. Varhaftige beschreibung eyner Landschafft. *Marburg: A.Kolbe*, 1557. [178]p.;illus.;4to. Sabin 90039; Borba de Moraes II:281-282; Baginsky (German Americana) 69. NN-RB. 557/38

—[Anr edn]. Warhafftig Historia unnd beschreibung einer Landtschafft. *Frankfurt a.M.: W.Han* [1557?]. [168]p.;illus.;4to. Sabin 90037; Borba de Moraes II:283; Arents (Add.) 20; JCB (3) I:198. DLC, MnU-B, NN-A, RPJCB; BL. 557/39

—[Anr issue of preceding]. Warhafftige Historia. *Frankfurt a.M.: W.Han* [1557]. Sabin 90038; Borba de Moraes II:282; Baginsky (German Americana) 71; Church 105. CSmH, NN-RB; BL. 557/40

Thevet, André. Les singularitez de la France Antarctique, autrement nommée Amerique: et de plusieurs terres & isles decouverts de nostre temps. *Paris: Heirs of M.de LaPorte*, 1557. 166 numb. lvs;illus.;4to. Sabin 95339; Borba de Moraes II:303-304; Atkinson (Fr.Ren.) 116n; Arents (Add.) 21; Church 107. CSmH, DLC, NN-A; Edinburg: NL. 557/41

1558

Alfonce, Jean, i.e., Jean Fonteneau, known as. Les voyages avantureux du Capitaine Ian Alfonce, sainctongeois. *Poitiers: J.de Marnef* [ca.1558?]. 68 numb.lvs;4to. In part derived from 1544-45 Roberval expedition; describes coasts of the Americas from Labrador to Magellan's Straits. In this issue the final paragraph on verso of lf 68 ends 'marchāt d'Honfleur Fin.' Sabin 100828; Church 111. CSmH. 558/1

—[Anr issue]. *Poitiers: J.de Marnef* [ca.1558?]. In this issue the final paragraph ends 'marchant d'Honfleur. Fin.' Sabin 100828n; Ind. aur. 103.629; Rothschild 1957. InU-L; BN. 558/1a

Alvares, Francisco. Historiale description de l'Ethiopie. *Antwerp: C.Plantin*, 1558. 341 numb.lvs;illus.;8vo. Includes also commentary by G.B.Ramusio mentioning Columbus (lf 39v) and letters of Andrea Corsali adverting to Brazil & Spanish West Indies (lf 16r), the whole translated by Jean Bellère from v.1 of Ramusio's *Navigationi et viaggi*, 1st publ., Venice, 1551. Atkinson (Fr.Ren.) 117; Streit XV:1589; Ind.aur.104.036. ICN, NN-RB, RPJCB; BL, BN. 558/2

—[Anr issue]. *Antwerp: [C.Plantin,for] J. Bellère*, 1558. Atkinson (Fr.Ren.) 117n; Ind. aur. 103.035; Adams (Cambr.) A847. MH, MnU-B, NN-RB; BL, BN. 558/3

Amatus Lusitanus. In Dioscoridis . . . De medica materia libros quinque . . . enarrationes eruditissimae. *Lyons: Widow of B.Arnoullet,* 1558. 807p.;illus.;8vo. 1st publ.; Venice, 1553. Pritzel 124n; Ind.aur.104.561; Shaaber C230a. MBCo, PU; London: Wellcome.558/4

___[Anr issue]. *Lyons: Widow of B.Arnoullet,for M.Bonhomme,* 1558. Cf.Ind.aur.104.561; Baudrier (Lyons) X:258. Avignon: Musée Calvet. 558/5

___[Anr issue]. *Lyons: Widow of B.Arnoullet,for T.Payen,* 1558. Cf.Ind.aur.104.561. MH-A. 558/6

___[Anr issue]. *Lyons: Widow of B.Arnoullet,for G.Rouillé,* 1588. Cf.Ind.aur.104.561; Baudrier (Lyons) IX:248. London: Wellcome. 558/7

Amerbach, Georg. Threnodia de morte Caroli .V. Rom. Imperatoris. *Dillingen: S.Mayer,* 1558. [19]p.;4to. Includes, p.[10], refs to Charles's role in exploration of Indies. Ind. aur.104.718. RPJCB; Munich: StB. 558/8

Barré, Nicolas. Copie de quelques letres sur la navigation du Chevalier de Villegaignon es terres de l'Amerique outre l'aequinoctial. *Paris: M.LeJeune,* 1558. 38p.;4to. 1st publ., Paris, 1557. Sabin 99728n; Cf.Atkinson (Fr.Ren.) 114. MH. 558/9

Boemus, Johann. Gli costumi, le leggi, et l'usanze di tutte le genti . . . tradotti per Lucio Fauno . . . Aggiuntovi di nuovo gli costumi, & l'usanze dell'Indie occidentali, overo Mundo Nuovo, da p. Gironimo Giglio. *Venice: G.Giglio & Co.,* 1558. 236 numb.lvs;8vo. Contain Giglio's description of the New World, lvs 189-236; condensed from the Rome, 1556, Italian translation of F.L.de Gómara's *Historia general de las Indias.* Sabin 6119n; Borba de Moraes I:95; Ind. aur. 120.955; Arents (Add.) 22. DLC, MiU, NN-A, RPJCB; BL. 558/10

Cardano, Girolamo. De rerum varietate libri xvii. A prima editione ab ipso denuo recogniti. *Avignon: M.Vincent,* 1558. 883p.;illus., port.;8vo. 1st publ., Basel, 1557. Ind. aur.132.074; Adams (Cambr.) C663. DNLM, ICU, InU-L, MnU-B, NNC; BL, BN. 558/11

___. De subtilitate libri xxi. *Lyons: G.Rouillé,* 1558. 718p.;illus.;8vo. 1st publ., Nuremberg, 1550. Ind.aur.132.075. Venice: BN. 558/12

Franck, Sebastian. Chronica, tytboeck ende gheschiet bibel van aenbegin der werelt tot den Jare M.D.XXXVI. [*Antwerp?* 1558].

2pts;fol. 1st publ. in Dutch, [Antwerp? 1550?], under title *Wereltboeck.* Brussels: BR. 558/13

Fuchs, Leonhart. L'histoire des plantes. *Lyons: Widow of B.Arnoullet,for G.Rouillé,* 1558. 607p.;illus.;4to. 1st publ. in French, as transl. by Guillaume Guéroult (?), Lyons, 1550. Pritzel 3139n; Nissen (Bot.) 671; Baudrier (Lyons) IX:250. MH-A, RPB; BN. 558/14

Gesner, Konrad. Thesaurus Euonymi Philiatri [pseud.], de remediis secretis. *Lyons: B.Arnoullet,for A.Vincent,* 1558. 498p.;illus.;8vo. 1st publ., Zurich, 1552; here a paginary reprint of Lyons, 1555, edn. CU, CtY, MnU, NNC. 558/15

___. Tresor des remedes secretz, par Euonyme Philiatre [pseud.]. *Lyons: Widow of B.Arnoullet,* 1558. 440p.; illus.;8vo. 1st publ., Lyons, 1557, here reissued with altered imprint date. Baudrier (Lyons) X:151. MnU-B. 558/16

___[Anr issue]. *Lyons: Widow of B.Arnoullet,for A.Vincent,* 1558. MH. 558/17

Giovio, Paolo, Bp of Nocera. Historiarum sui temporis tomus primus-secundus. *Paris: M.de Vascovan,* 1558-60. 2v.;8vo. 1st publ., Florence, 1550-52. Adams (Cambr.) G654. CtY, ICN, MiU, NN-RB, PPL; BL, BN. 558/18

___. La prima parte delle Historie del suo tempo . . . Tradotte per m. Lodovico Domenichi. *Venice: Comin da Trino,* 1558. 1st publ. in Italian, Venice, 1555. Adams (Cambr.) G659; Moranti (Urbino) 1662. Cambridge: Trinity, Urbino: UL. 558/19

Hiel, Laurentius. Dissertatio inauguralis de morbo gallico. *Jena:* 1558. Proksch I:83. 558/20

Honter, Johannes. Rudimentorum cosmographicorum . . . libri iii. *Zurich: C.Froschauer,* 1558. [96]p.; illus.,maps;8vo. 1st publ. in this version, Kronstadt, 1542. In verse, NN-RB; BL. 558/21

Interiano, Paolo. Ristretto delle historie genovesi. *Lucca: V.Busdrago,* 1558. 233 numb. lvs;4to. 1st publ., Lucca, 1551. A reissue of sheets of 1551 edn, with lvs [1-4] reset. DFo, NN-RB, RPJCB. 558/22

Lobera de Avila, Luis. Libro delle quatro infermita cortegiane . . . catarro, gotta, artetica, sciatics, mal di pietre, et di reni, dolori di fianchi e mal francese . . . Tradotto . . . per Pietro Lauro. *Venice: G.B.& M.Sessa,* 1558.

272 numb.lvs;fol. Transl. from author's Toledo, 1544, *Libro de las quatro enfermedades cortesanos* and his *Libro de experiencias de medicina.* Palau 139424. CLU-M, CtY-M, DNLM, MBCo, NNNAM; BL, BN.   558/23

Magnus, Olaus, Abp of Upsala. Historia de gentibus septentrionalibus . . . a C.Scribonio Graphaeo in epitomen redacta. *Antwerp: C. Plantin,* 1558. 192 numb.lvs;illus.;8vo. Condensed from Magnus's *Historia,* with section on Greenland, 1st publ., Rome, 1555. Sabin 43833; Collijn (Sver.bib.) II:250-252; Adams (Cambr.) M143; Belg.typ. (1541-1600) I:2022. CLU, CtY, IEN, InU-L, MH, MiU, MnU-B, RPJCB; BL, BN.   558/24

Manuzio, Paolo. De elementis et variis eorum effectis . . . latinus factus per Jac. Carpentarium. *Paris: M.David,* 1558. 38p.;4to. Transl. from Venice, 1557, Italian text. BL, BN.
558/25

Marguérite d'Angoulême, Queen of Navarre. Histoires des amans fortunez [éd. par Pierre Boaistuau]. *Paris: G.Gilles,* 1558. 184 numb. lvs;4to. Subsequent edns have title *L'Heptaméron.* The 67th tale, naming Canada, recounts an episode from Cartier's voyage there in 1542-44. Issued also with imprints of J.Caveiller, G.Robinot & V.Sertenas. Tchémerzine VII:390. MH;BN.   558/26

Mattioli, Pietro Andrea. Commentarii secundo aucti, in libros sex Pedacii Dioscoridis . . . De medica materia. *Venice: V.Valgrisi,* 1558. 2pts;illus.;fol. 1st publ., Venice, 1554. Pritzel 2309n; Nissen (Bot.) 1305n; Adams (Cambr.) D667. CtHT, DNLM, MH, MoSB, RPB; BL, BN.   558/27

Maurolico, Francesco. Cosmographia. *Paris: G.Cavellat,* 1558. 168 numb.lvs;12mo. 1st publ., Venice, 1543. Sabin 46958; Adams (Cambr.) M918; JCB (3) I:201. InU-L, NNH, RPJCB; BL, BN.   558/28

Mexía, Pedro. Le vite di tutti gl'imperadori . . . tratte del libro spagnuolo par Lodovici Dolce. *Venice: G.Giolito de' Ferrari,* 1558. 1054p.;4to. Transl. from Mexía's *Historia imperial y cesarea,* 1st publ., Toledo, 1545. Palau 167348. ICN, NNC; BL.   558/29

Monteux, Jérôme de. Halosis febrium, quae omnium morborum gravissimae sunt, libri ix . . . Morbi item venerei, ac eorum, qui huic vicini sunt, curationes. *Lyons: J.de Tournes & G.Gazeau,* 1558. 3pts;4to. Proksch I:18; Cartier (de Tournes) 410; Mortimer (France) 382.

CtY-M, DNLM, ICJ, MH, NNNAM; BL, BN.
558/30

Münster, Sebastian. Cosmographei, oder beschreibung aller länder. *Basel: H.Petri,* 1558. 1233p.;illus.,maps;fol. 1st publ., Basel, 1544. Burmeister (Münster) 73. DLC, IU; Munich: StB.   558/31

____. Sei libri della Cosmografia universale. *Basel: H.Petri,* 1558. 1237p.;illus.,maps;fol. 1st publ., Basel, 1544, in German. On printing variants, see H.J.W.Horch, 'Bibliographische Notizien zu den Ausgaben der "Kosmographie" Sebastian Münsters in italienischer Sprache', *Gutenberg Jahrbuch,* 1976, p.237-247. Sabin 51402; Burmeister (Münster) 99. NN-RB; BL, BN.   558/32

Ovidius Naso, Publius. Metamorphoses. Italian. Le trasformationi di m. Lodovico Dolce . . . Quinta impressione. *Venice: G.Giolito de' Ferrari,* 1558. 312p.;illus.,map;4to. 1st publ. in this version with world map, Venice, 1553. Cf.Mortimer (Italy) 342n. CtY, DFo; BN.   558/33

Paradin, Guillaume. Histoire de notre tems. *Lyons: J.de Tournes & G.Gazeau,* 1558. 909p.;16mo. 1st publ. in French, Lyons, 1550. Cartier (de Tournes) 413; Adams (Cambr.) P305. BL.   558/34

__[Anr edn]. *Lyons: P.Michel,* 1558. 835p.; 16mo. Shaaber P63. PU.   558/35

Piccolomini, Alessandro. Della grandezza della terra et dell'acqua . . . Nuovamente mandato in luce. *Venice: G.Ziletti,* 1558. 43 numb.lvs;4to. On lf 9 is a discussion of western discoveries and, on verso of lf 28, of New Spain, Yucatan & Peru. JCB AR20:1558; JCB (STL):10. CtY, DLC, MiU, MnU-B, NN-RB, RPJCB; BL.   558/36

Rondelet, Guillaume. L'histoire entiere des poissons, composé . . . en latin . . . Maintenant traduite [par Laurent Joubert] en françois. *Lyons: M.Bonhomme,* 1558. 2v.; illus.,port.;4to. Transl. from author's *Libri de piscibus marinis,* 1st publ., Lyons, 1554-55. Baudrier (Lyons) X:259. CU, CtY, DLC, ICU, MH-Z, PPAN; BL, BN.   558/37

Sacro Bosco, Joannes de. Sphaera . . . emendata. Eliae Vineti . . . scholia . . . ab ipso authore restituta. *Paris: G.Cavellat,* 1558. 102 numb.lvs;illus.;8vo. 1st publ. with Vinet's *Scholia,* Paris, 1551. NSyU, IU, MiU.   558/38

Staden, Hans. Warachtige historie ende beschrivinge eens lants in America ghelegen.

Antwerp: C.Plantin, 1558. 104 lvs;illus.;8vo. Transl. from German text, 1st publ., Marburg, 1557. Sabin 90040; Borba de Moraes II:283; JCB (3) I:202. RPJCB; BL.   558/39

Thevet, André. Les singularitez de la France Antarctique. *Paris: Heirs of M.de LaPorte*, 1558. 166 numb.lvs;illus.;4to. 1st publ., Paris, 1557; here reissued with altered imprint date. Sabin 95339; Borba de Moraes II:303-304; Atkinson (Fr.Ren.) 116; Arents (Add.) 21; Church 109; Shaaber T187; JCB (3) I:202. CSmH, ICN, MiU-C, NN-RB, PU, RPJCB; BL, BN.   558/40

___[Anr end]. *Antwerp: C.Plantin*, 1558. 163 numb.lvs;illus.;8vo. Sabin 95440; Borba de Moraes II:304; Atkinson (Fr.Ren.) 121; Arents 8; Church 108; Fairfax Murray (France) 537; Shaaber T188; JCB (3) I:202. CSmH, CtY, DLC, MH, NN-RB, PU, RPJCB, BL, BN.   558/41

Valtanas Mexía, Domingo de. Compendio de algunas cosas notables de Espana. *Seville: M. de Montesdoca*, 1558. Includes chapter 'Cuando se descubrieron las Indias'. Cf. Medina (BHA) 144; Escudero (Seville) 594; Palau 349178.   558/42

Vigo, Giovanni de. Prattica utilissima et necessaria di cirugia . . . Tradotta nuovamente . . . per . . . Pietro Rostinio. *Venice: V.Valgrisi & B.Costantini*, 1558. 391p.;illus.; 4to. Transl. from author's *Practica in arte chirurgica copiosa*, 1st publ., Rome, 1514. DNLM.   558/43

Zeno, Niccolò. De i commentarii del viaggio in Persia . . . Et dello scoprimento dell'isole Frislanda, Eslanda, Engrovelanda, Estotilanda & Icaria fatto sotto il polo artica, da due fratelli Zeni, m. Nicolò il K. e m. Antonio. *Venice: F.Marcolini*, 1558. 58 numb.lvs; map;8vo. The designations Estotilanda & Droga have been tentatively identified as referring to Labrador & Newfoundland. Sabin 106317; Church 110; JCB (3) I:202-203. CSmH, InU-L, MH, NN-RB, MiU-C, RPJCB; BL.   558/44

1559

Alfonce, Jean, i.e., Jean Fonteneau, known as. Les voyages avantureux du Capitaine Ian Alfonce, sainctongeois. *Poitiers: J.de Marnef* [1559]. 68 numb.lvs;4to. 1st publ., Poitiers, [ca. 1558]. Printed, except for 1st sheet

(signed ā), from same setting of type as earlier edn, with date of printing here appearing on verso of t.p. Sabin 100829; Harrisse (NF) 2. MH, NN-RB; BL, BN.   559/1

___[Anr edn]. *Poitiers: J.de Marnef*, 1559. 68 numb.lvs;4to. Sabin 100830; Harrisse (NF) 3; Borba de Moraes I:17;Ind. aur.103.630. BL, BN.   559/2

___[Anr issue?] *Poitiers: J.de Marnef & Bouchetz frères*, 1559. 68 numb.lvs;4to. Sabin 100831; Ind.aur.103.631. BL   559/3

Amatus Lusitanus. Curationum medicinalium centuriae II. priores. *Lyons: G.Rouillé*, 1559. 693p.;16mo. 1st Century 1st publ., Florence, 1551; 2nd Century, Venice, 1552. Baudrier (Lyons) IX:252.   559/4

Cardano, Girolamo. De subtilitate libri xxi. *Lyons: G.Rouillé*, 1559. 718p.;illus.;8vo. 1st publ., Nuremberg(?), 1550. Ind.aur.132.079; Baudrier (Lyons) IX:258; Adams (Cambr.) C672. DNLM, PPAN, RPB; London: Wellcome, BN.   559/5

____. Offenbarung der Natur unnd natürlicher dingen auch mancherley subtiler würckungen . . . durch Heinrich Pantaleon . . . verteütscht. *Basel: H. Petri*, 1559. dccccxxxiiii p.;fol. Transl. from Cardano's *De rerum varietate libri xvii*, 1st publ., Basel, 1557. Ind. aur.132.078. ICU, IU; BL, Munich: StB.   559/6

Cuningham, William. The cosmographical glasse, conteinyng the pleasant principles of cosmographie, geographie, hydrographie, or navigation. *London: J.Day*, 1559. 202p.;illus.,port.,maps;fol. 'A particular description of such partes of America, as are by travaile found out': p.200-202. Sabin 17971; STC 6119; JCB (3) I:204. CSmH, CtY, DLC, ICN, NN-RB, MB, PU, RPJCB; BL.   559/7

Dodoens, Rembert. De stirpium historia commentariorum, imagines . . . supra priorem aeditionem . . . recognitae. *Antwerp: J.van der Loe*, 1559. 2v.;illus.;8vo. 1st publ., Antwerp, 1553-4; here reissued, in part reset, with supplementary material. Pritzel 2343n; Nissen (Bot.) 511; Bibl.belg., 1st ser.,IX:D106. DNAL, MH-A; BL, Brussels: BR.   559/8

Ferri, Alfonso. New erfundene heylsame, und bewärte Artzney . . . nit allein die frantzosen oder bösen Blatern, sonder auch andere . . . Kranckheyt . . . gründtlichen . . . zü vertreiben . . . mit . . . Gebrauch unnd Würckung des indianischen Holtz, Guaiacum oder frantzosen Holtz genennet . . . Durch m. Gualtherum H. Ryff in teutsche Sprach verfasst. *Strassburg: S.Emmel*, 1559. [236]p.;illus.; 8vo. 1st publ. in German, Strassburg, 1541. Benzing (Ryff) 110. DNLM, NN-RB.   559/9

Fontaine, Charles. La description des terres trovees de nostre temps. *Lyons: J.Pullon,for B.Rigaud*, 1559. [80]p.;8vo. 1st publ., Paris, 1554, under title *Les nouvelles, & antiques merveilles.* Atkinson (Fr.Ren.) 124; Baudrier (Lyons) III:208; Cioranescu (XVI) 10108. BL. 559/10

Garimberto, Girolamo. Les problèmes . . . traduitz . . . par Jean Louveau. *Lyons: G. Rouillé*, 1559. 296p.;8vo. Transl. from Venice, 1549, Italian text. FU;BL,BN.   559/11

Gesner, Konrad. Thesauri Euonymi Philiatri [pseud.], de remediis secretis. *Lyons: Widow of B.Arnoullet,for A.Vincent*, 1559. 498p.; illus.;8vo. 1st publ., Zurich, 1552. Baudrier (Lyons) X:152.   559/12

____. The treasure of Euonymus, conteyninge the wonderfull hid secretes of nature . . . Translated . . . out of Latin, by Peter Morwyng. *London: J.Day* [1559]. 408p.;illus.;4to. Transl. from Gesner's *Thesaurus*, 1st publ., Zurich, 1552. STC 11800. CtY, DFo, MH, MiU, MnU, PPC; BL.   559/13

____. Tresor des remedes secretz; par Euonyme Philiatre [pseud.]. *Lyons: Widow of B.Arnoullet,for A.Vincent*, 1559. 440p.;illus.;8vo. 1st publ. in French, Lyons, 1557. Baudrier (Lyons) X:152. DNLM, MH.   559/14

Giovio, Paolo, Bp of Nocera. Gli elogi, vite brevemente scritte d'huomini illustri. *Venice: F.Lorenzini*, 1559. 192 numb.lvs;8vo. 1st publ. in Italian, Florence, 1554. Sabin 27478n; Adams (Cambr.) G642. CU, InU-L, MnU-B, NN-RB; Cambridge: Trinity. 559/15

__[Anr edn].*Venice: F.Bindoni*, 1559. 574p.; 8vo. CtY,IU.   559/16

Jesuits. Letters from missions. Diversi avisi particolari dall' Indie di Portogallo ricevuti, dall anno 1551. fino al 1558. *Venice: M.Tramezzino*, 1559. 286 numb.lvs;8vo. The earliest edn to contain letter from Brazil of Diego Jacobo & account of death of Pietro Correa; otherwise reprinted from the 1553 *Nuovi avisi* & the 1557 *Avisi particolari.* Cf.Sabin 20333; Borba de Moraes I:50-51; Streit II:1263 (& IV:850); Arents (Add.) 25; JCB (3) I:203. CtY, ICN, InU-L, MH, NN-A, RPJCB; BL.   559/17

Lucidarius. M.Elucidarius, von allerhandt geschöpffen Gottes . . . unnd wie alle Creaturen geschaffen sein auff Erden. *Frankfurt a.M.: W.Han*, 1559. [87]p.;4to. 1st publ., Strassburg, [ca.1535]. Schorbach (Lucidarius) 58. DAS; Munich: StB.   559/18

Marguérite d'Angoulême, Queen of Navarre. L'heptameron des nouvelles . . . Remis en son ordre . . . par Claude Gruget. *Paris: B.Prévost,for J.Caveiller*, 1559. 212 numb. lvs;4to. 1st publ., Paris, 1558, under title *Histoire des amans fortunez* in a less authoritative text. Sabin 44535; Harrisse (NF) 382; Tchémerzine VII:391. CtY, MWiW-C; BL, BN.   559/19

__[Anr issue]. *Paris: B.Prévost,for G. Robinot*, 1559. Tchémerzine VII:391. BL. 559/20

__[Anr issue]. *Paris: B.Prévost,for V.Sertenas*, 1559.   559/21

__[Anr issue]. *Paris: B.Prévost, & E.Gibier,at Orleans*, 1572. Adams (Cambr.) M563. Cambridge:St John's.   559/22

__[Anr issue]. [*Paris?* 1559?]. 12mo. Tchémerzine VII:392.   559/23

Martínez, Andrés. Relacion verdadera de los trabajos y fortunas que an passado los que fueron el viaje del Rio de La Plata. *Seville: A. de Coca* [1559?]. 2 lvs;fol. At end: Fecha en Sancto Domingo, à quince dias de Agosto de m.d.l.jx. Medina (BHA) 182; Escudero (Seville) 598; Palau 154202. CtY.   559/24

Massa, Niccolò. De morbo gallico liber. *Venice: G.Ziletti*, 1559. 50 numb.lvs;4to. 1st publ., Venice, 1532. The present edn is a reissue of that of 1536, with the 1st 4 lvs reset and the final lf cancelled. DNLM.   559/25

Mattioli, Pietro Andrea. Commentarii secundo aucti, in libros sex Pedacii Dioscoridis . . . De materia medica. *Venice: V.Valgrisi*, 1559. 2pts;illus.;fol. 1st publ., Venice, 1554; here reissued with altered imprint date from Valgrisi's 1558 edn. Cf.Pritzel 2309; Nissen (Bot.) 1305n; Adams (Cambr.) D668. DNLM, MH, NN-RB, RPB; BL.   559/26

____. I discorsi . . . ne i sei libri di Pedacio Dioscoride . . . della materia medicinale. *Venice: V.Valgrisi*, 1559. 802p.;illus.;fol. 1st publ., Venice, 1555. Cf.Pritzel 5987; Nissen (Bot.) 1304n. DNLM, ICJ, MH-A, NNBG; London: Wellcome, BN.   559/27

Mexía, Pedro. Della selva. di varia lettione, parti cinque . . . di nuovo ristampate et corrette. *Venice: F.Sansovino & Co.*, 1559-60.

438 numb.lvs;8vo. Contains a 5th pt on the Indies by F. Sansovino, 'Della grandezza dell Indie, & chi le trovò, & perche furono chiamate Indie'. Cf.Sabin 48239. Strasbourg: BN. 559/28

More, Sir Thomas, Saint. La republique d'Utopie. *Lyons: J.Saugrain*, 1559. 352p.; 8vo. 1st publ. in French, as transl. by J. LeBlond, Paris, 1550. Gibson (More) 20. CtY, MH; BL, BN. 559/29

Münster, Sebastian. Cosmographiae universalis lib. vi . . . in hunc usque annum 1559. *Basel: H.Petri*, 1559. 1162p.;illus.,maps;fol. Contains newly revised text (p.1099-1113) relating to the Americas. Sabin 51382; Burmeister (Münster) 90; Adams (Cambr.) M1911. DLC, ICN, WU; Cambridge: Emmanuel, Paris: Arsenal. 559/30

Rabelais, François. Les oeuvres. [*Paris?*] 1559. 2v.;16mo. Includes 'Le quart livre', 1st publ., Paris, 1552. Plan (Rabelais) 97. NNPM. 559/31

Renner, Franz. Ein new wolgegründet nützlichs unnd haylsams Handtbüchlein, gemeiner Practick, aller innerlicher und eusserlicher Ertzney, so wider die erschröckliche, abscheuliche Kranckheit der Frantzosen und Lemung, auch für all ander Seuchten . . . von newen ubersehen. *Nuremberg: G.Hain*, 1559. clvii lvs;4to. 1st publ., Nuremberg, 1554. DNLM. 559/32

Robortello, Francesco. Oratio in funere Imperatoris Caroli V. Augusti in . . . Hispanorum Collegio Bonon. habita. *Bologna: A.Benacci*, 1559. 82p.;4to. Pages 28-29 include description of New World. Adams (Cambr.) R624. BL. 559/33

Rostinio, Pietro. Trattato del mal francese . . . aggiuntovi di nuovo molte cose, & con diligenze ristampato. *Venice: L.Avanzi*, 1559. 87 numb.lvs;8vo. 1st publ., Venice, 1559. Moranti (Urbino) 2961. DNLM, MnU-B; BN. 559/34

Soto, Domingo de. Libri decem De justitia & jure. *Lyons: N.Edoard,for G.Rouillé*, 1559 [colophon: 1558]. 738p.;fol. 1st publ., Salamanca, 1553. Palau 320140. 559/35

—[Anr issue]. *Lyons: N.Edoard,for Heirs of J. Giunta*, 1559. Palau 320141. BN. 559/36

—[Anr edn]. De justitia & jure libri decem. *Salamanca: J.M.à Terranova,for J. Moreno*, 1559. 942p.;fol. Palau 320142. Madrid: BN. 559/37

Székely, István. Krónika ez világnak yełes dolgairól. *Cracow*: 1559. 4to. Includes refs to Columbus & Vespucci. E.Igloi, 'Die ersten polnischen, ungarischen und russischen Berichte über die Entdeckung Amerikas', *Slavica*, IV (1964), 128-130. BL. 559/38

Terraube, Galard de. Brief discours des choses plus necessaires & dignes d'estre entendues en la cosmographie. *Paris: F.Morel*, 1559. 38 numb.lvs;8vo. Includes section relating to the Americas. Atkinson (Fr.Ren.) 125; Cioranescu (XVI) 21051; Adams (Cambr.) T402. BL, BN. 559/39

1560

Albergati, Vianesio, supposed author. La pazzia. [*Bologna?*] 1560. [46]p.;8vo. 1st dated edn, [Bologna?], 1540. Florence: BN. 560/1

Amatus Lusitanus. Curationum medicinalium . . . centuriae duae, quinta videlicet ac sexta. *Venice: V.Valgrisi*, 1560. 380p.;8vo. The present Centuries continue those earlier printed variously, 1551-1557. In the 5th Century, Curationes xxii, xxv, xlix, lvi & lxviii discuss syphilis and its treatment, as also in the 6th, Curationes xliiii, xlviii & lxxxv. The subsequent 7th Century, Venice, 1566, contains no related material. Ind.aur.104.563; Adams (Cambr.) A917. DNLM, MH-A; Cambridge; UL, BN. 560/2

——. Curationum medicinalium centuriae II. priores. *Lyons: G.Rouillé*, 1560. 693p.;12mo. 1st Century 1st publ., Florence, 1551; 2nd Century, Venice, 1552. A reissue of Rouillé's 1559 edn. Ind.aur.104.562. DNLM; BL, Paris: Ste Geneviève. 560/3

Bock, Hieronymus. Kreüter Büch. *Strassburg: J.Rihel*, 1560. ccccxiii lvs;illus.;fol. 1st publ. with illus., Strassburg, 1546. Pritzel 866n; Nissen (Bot.) 182n; Ind.aur.120.595; Ritter (Strasbourg) 218. CU, CtY-M, ICU, MH-A, MiU, NNNAM, PPC; BL, Strasbourg: BN. 560/4

Boemus, Johann. Gli costumi, le leggi, et l'usanze di tutti le genti . . . tradotti per Lucio Fauno. Aggiontovi di nuovo gli costumi e l'usanze dell'Indie Occidentali, overo Mondo Nuovo, da p. Gieronimo Giglio. *Venice: F.Lorenzini*, 1560. 236 numb.lvs;12mo. 1st publ. with Giglio's section on New World, Venice, 1558. Sabin 6119; Ind.aur.120.956; Palau

31252; JCB (3) I:208. DLC, ICN, MH, MnU-B, NN-RB, RPJCB; BL.   560/5

Brant, Sebastian. Das Narrenschiff. *Frankfurt a.M.: W.Han*, 1560. 158 numb.lvs;illus.;8vo. 1st publ., Basel, 1494. Ind.aur.123.739. BL, Berlin: StB.   560/6

Cardano, Girolamo. De subtilitate libri xxi. *Basel: H.Petri*, 1560. 1426p.;illus.;8vo. 1st publ., Nuremberg(?), 1550. Ind.aur.132.081; Adams (Cambr.) C674. MH-A, NN-RB; BL, BN.   560/7

__[Anr edn]. *Basel: H.Petri*, 1560. 603p.;illus.; fol. Ind.aur.132.080; Adams (Cambr.) C673. DNLM, MH; BL, Berlin: StB.   560/8

Chaumette, Antoine. Enchiridion chirurgicum . . . Quibus, Morbi venerei curandi methodus probatissima accessit. *Paris: A.Wechel*, 1560. 584 (i.e., 184) numb.lvs;8vo. DNLM;BL.   560/9

Cieza de León, Pedro de. Cronica del gran regno del Peru . . . Parte prima . . . Tradotta . . . per Agostino di Cravaliz. *Venice: F.Lorenzini*, 1560. 219 numb.lvs;8vo. 1st publ. in this translation, Rome, 1555. Sabin 13050; Streit II:725. CSmH, DLC, MH, MiU-C, NN-RB, PPL; BL.   560/10

__[Anr issue]. *Venice: P.Bosello*, 1560. BN.   560/11

____. La prima parte dell'Historie del Peru [trad. per L.Mauro]. *Venice: G.Ziletti*, 1560. 215 numb.lvs;8vo. 1st publ. in Mauro's translation, Venice, 1556. Continued by F.López de Gómara's *Seconda parte delle Historie dell'India*, issued, 1565, by Ziletti. Sabin 13052 (& in error 13051); Medina (BHA) 157n (I:257); Streit II:724; JCB (3) I:208. CtY, DLC, NN-RB, MH, RPJCB; BL.   560/12

Domingo de Santo Tomás. Grammatica, ò Arte de la lengua general de los Indios . . . del Peru. *Valladolid: F.Fernández de Córdova*, 1560. 96 numb.lvs;8vo. The earliest grammar of the Kechua language. Sabin 20564; Medina (BHA) 183; Alcocer (Valladolid) 226; JCB (3) I:209-210. DLC, InU-L, RPJCB; BL, BN.   560/13

____. Lexicon, ò Vocabulario de la lengua general de Peru. *Valladolid: F.Fernández de Córdova*, 1560. 179 numb.lvs;8vo. Cf. preceding item. Sabin 20565; Medina (BHA) 184; Alcocer (Valladolid) 227; JCB (3) I:210. DLC, InU-L, NNH, RPJCB; BL, BN.   560/14

Fernel, Jean. De abditis rerum causis libri duo. *Paris: A.Wechel*, 1560. 426p.;8vo. 1st

publ., Paris, 1548. Sherrington (Fernel) 20.F4. DNLM, KU-M; London: Wellcome, BN.   560/15

Fontanon, Denys. De morborum internorum curatione libri iiii. *Lyons: S.Barbier,for A.Vincent*, 1560. 381p.;8vo. 1st publ., Lyons, 1549. Adams (Cambr.) F717. CtY-M, DNLM.   560/16

__[Anr issue]. *Lyons: S.Barbier,for J.Frellon*, 1560. Baudrier (Lyons) V:249.   560/17

Fries, Lorenz. Pocken boecxken, inholdende een grontliche end heylsame gheneesinghe der grusamigher pocken . . . allen mit dem dranck del hilligen holts gwayci. *Kampen: P.Warnerus* [ca.1560?]. [24]p.;4to. Transl. from author's *Ein clarer bericht*, 1st publ., Strassburg, 1525. Date of printing inferred from Warnerus's known period of activity. Benzing (Fries) 21. BN.   560/18

Gesner, Konrad. Icones avium. *Zurich: C.Froschauer*, 1560. 237 (i.e., 137)p.;illus., port.; fol. 1st publ., Zurich, 1555. Nissen (Birds) 352n; Adams (Cambr.) G546. CtY, RPB; BL.   560/19

____. Nomenclator aquatilium animantiam. Icones animalium aquatilium. *Zurich: C.Froschauer*, 1560. 374p.;illus.;fol. Described as American are the 'Ostracion Americae' (p.318), a 'Hyperus homicida' (p.365) and the 'Crocodilus terrestris' (p.356-357), found in Brazil. Adams (Cambr.) G551; Nissen (Zool.) 1554; Moranti (Urbino) 1622. CU, CtY, DLC, MH, PPC, NN-RB, RPB; BL, BN.   560/20

____. Tesauro di Euonomo Filiatro [pseud.] de rimedii secreti . . . Tradotto di latino . . . per m. Pietro Lauro. *Venice: G.B. & M.Sessa*, 1560. 152 numb.lvs;illus.;8vo. 1st publ. in Italian, Venice, 1556. CtY, MH, MnU-B, NNNAM; BL.   560/21

Giovio, Paolo, Bp of Nocera. Gli elogi vite brevemente scritti d'huomini illustri di guerra . . . tradotte per m. Lodovico Domenichi. *Venice: F.Bindoni*, 1560. 574p.;8vo. 1st publ. in Italian, Venice, 1554. Shaaber G194. PU.   560/22

____. Historiarum sui temporis tomus primus [-secundus]. *Basel: H.Petri & P.Perna*, 1560. 3v.;8vo. 1st publ., Florence, 1550-52. Adams (Cambr.) G655. Cambridge: St John's. 560/23

____. Libro de' pesci romani. *Venice: The Gualtieri*, 1560. 197p.;4to. Transl. by C.Zancaruolo from Giovio's *De romanis piscibus*, 1st publ., Rome, 1524. Adams (Cambr.) G637;

Shaaber G199. DFo, NN-RB, PU; BL, BN.
560/24

____. Ein warhafftige beschrybung aller namm-
hafftigen geschichten . . . verteütscher und in
truck geferriger durch Heinrych Pantaleon.
Basel: 1560. 409p.;fol. Transl. from Giovio's
Historiarum sui temporis, 1st publ., Florence,
1550-52. CtY, NCH.   560/25

Gómara, Francisco López de. Historia delle
nuove Indie Occidentali . . . Parte seconda
. . . Tradotta . . . da Agostino de Cravaliz.
Venice: F.Lorenzini, 1560. 306 numb.lvs;8vo.
1st publ. in this version, Rome, 1556. The 1st
pt, to which the 'seconda' pt in the above title
refers, is Cieza de León's *Cronica del gran
regno del Peru* of this year. Continued in turn
by the *Historia di Don Ferdinando Cortes*, the
following item. Sabin 27738; Medina (BHA)
159n (I:270): Wagner (SW) 2r; Streit II:727;
JCB (3) I:209. CSmH, InU-L, MH, MiU-C,
NN-RB, PPL, RPJCB; BL.   560/26

—[Anr issue]. *Venice: P.Bosello*, 1560. Wagner
(SW) 2s. DLC, ICN.   560/27

____. Historia di Don Ferdinando Cortes . . .
Tradotta . . . da Agostino di Cravaliz. *Ven-
ice: F.Lorenzini*, 1560. 348 numb.lvs;8vo. 1st
publ. in this version, Rome, 1556, as pt 2 of
La historia generale delle Indie Occidentali. A
continuation of the author's *Historie delle
nuove Indie Occidentali*, the preceding item.
Sabin 27739; Medina (BHA) 159n (I:271);
Wagner (SW) 2t; Streit II:726, JCB (3) I:209.
DLC, ICN, InU-L, MiU-C, NNH, RPJCB;
BL.   560/28

Honter, Johannes. Rudimentorum cosmogra-
phicorum . . . libri iii. *Antwerp: J.Richard*,
1560. 2pts;maps;8vo. 1st publ. in this version,
Kronstadt, 1542. In verse. Cf.Sabin 32793;
Belg.typ. (1541-1600) I:1485. BN, Brussels:
BR.   560/29

—[Anr edn]. *Antwerp: J.Richard* [1560?]. 74p.;
maps;12mo. InU-L, MH.   560/30

Le Court, Benoit. Hortorum libri triginta.
Lyons: J.de Tournes, 1560. 683p.;fol. In bk
xx, chapts xiv-xv deal with Brazil wood &
Guaiacum respectively. Pritzel 5132; Cartier
(de Tournes) 454. CU, DFo, MH-A, MnU,
NN-RB; BL, BN.   560/31

Marguérite d'Angouleme, Queen of Navarre.
L'heptameron des nouvelles. *Paris: B.Prévost*,
1560. 212 numb.lvs;4to. 1st publ. in this version, Paris, 1559; here a new impression with
altered imprint date? Tchémerzine VII:

392-393; Adams (Cambr.) M564; Rothschild
1697. CtY, ICN, MH; Cambridge: Emmanuel.   560/32

—[Anr issue]. *Paris: B.Prévost, for J.Caveiller*,
1560. Shaaber M140. PU; BL.   560/33

—[Anr issue].*Paris: B.Prévost, for G.Robinot*,
1560. Tchémerzine VII:392-393; Fairfax
Murray (France) 353.   560/34

—[Anr issue]. *Paris: B.Prévost, for V.Sertenas*,
1560. Tchémerzine VII:392-393.   560/35

—[Anr edn] [*Paris?*] 1560. 726p.;8vo. Tchémerzine VII:392-393.   560/36

Mattioli, Pietro Andrea. I discorsi . . . ne i sei
libri di Pedacio Dioscoride . . . della materia
medicinale. *Venice: V.Valgrisi*, 1560.
802p.;illus.;fol. 1st publ., Venice, 1555; here
a reissue of the 1559 edn with altered imprint
date. Cf. Pritzel 5987; cf.Nissen (Bot.) 1304.
DNLM, MH-A.   560/37

Mexía, Pedro. Le vite di tutti gl'imperadori
. . . da m. Lodovico Dolce tradotte e ampliate. *Venice: G.Giolito de' Ferrari*, 1560.
1054p.;4to. 1st publ. as here translated, Venice, 1558. Palau 167349.   560/38

Mocenigo, Andrea. La guerra di Cambrai.
[Tradotta di latino per Andrea Arrivabene].
Venice: [Heirs of G.Padovano?] 1560. 140
numb.lvs;8vo. 1st publ. in Italian, Venice,
1544; here a reissue with cancel t.p.? Adams
(Cambr.) M1521. DFo; Cambridge: UL, BN.
560/39

Münster, Sebastian. La cosmographie universelle. *Basel: H.Petri*, 1560. 1337p.;illus.,
maps;fol. 1st publ. in French, Basel, 1552.
Burmeister (Münster) 94. NN-RB; Paris: Ste
Geneviève.   560/40

**Ovidius Naso, Publius. Metamorphoses.
Italian.** Le trasformazioni . . . di m.
Lodovico Dolce. *Venice: G.Giolito de' Ferrari*,
1560. 320p.;illus.,map;4to. 1st publ. with
world map depicting America, Venice, 1553.
Cf. Mortimer (Italy) 342n; Bongi (Giolito)
II:123. BL.   560/41

Peucer, Kaspar. Commentarius de praecipuis
generibus divinationum. *Wittenberg: J.Crato*,
1560. 456 numb.lvs;8vo. On basis of collation,
this appears to be an enl. edn which includes
a passage in section on Astrology mentioning
Columbus & contrasting time required for east
& west voyages between Spain & West Indies.
It is not found in the printer's 1553 edn.
Adams (Cambr.) P930. ICU, MnU-B, NNC;
Cambridge: UL, BN.   560/41a

Sabellico, Marco Antonio Coccio, called. Opera omnia . . . cum supplemento Rapsodiae historiarum . . . per C.S. Cerionem . . . confecta. *Basel: J.Herwagen,* 1560. 4v.;fol. The *Rapsodiae*, with their mention of Columbus & discovery of New World, 1st publ., Venice, 1504, as *Seconda pars Enneadum.* Sabin 74666; Adams (Cambr.) S12. MdBJ, NN-RB; BL, BN.   560/42

Tagault, Jean. Der chirurgijen instructie oft onderrechtinghe . . . Nu eerst uuten Latijne . . . overgheset door Lambrecht van Tuylt. *Antwerp:* [Heirs of A.Birckmann, ca.1560?]. ccccxxiii p.;illus.;fol. Transl. from Tagault's *De chirurgica institutione,* 1st publ., Paris, 1543. DNLM.   560/43

———. De chirurgica institutione libri cinque. *Lyons: G.Rouillé,* 1560. 487p.;illus.;8vo. 1st publ., Paris, 1543. DNLM; London: Wellcome.   560/44

Ulloa, Alfonso de. La vita dell'invitissimo imperator Carlo Quinto . . . nuovamente mandata in luce . . . Nelle quale vengono comprese le cose piu notabili . . . dall'anno MD. infino al M D LX. *Venice: V.Valgrisi,* 1560. 752p.;4to. Includes numerous scattered refs to the Americas. Sabin 97679; Palau 343390; Adams (Cambr.) U41. NcD, RPB; BL.560/45

Valtanas Mexía, Domingo de. Compendio de algunas cosas notables de España. *Seville: S.Trugillo* [ca.1560?]. [56]p.;4to. 1st publ., Seville, 1558. Though the present edn has been assigned to the year 1550 by Medina & others, Trugillo's address given here as 'junto a la casa de Pedro de Pineda' is not found prior to 1558, whilst the author's works in his lifetime were uniformly printed by M. de Montesdoca, responsible for the 1558 edn. Sabin 98396; Harrisse (BAV) Add. 183; Medina (BHA) 144; Palau 349177.   560/46

Vigo, Giovanni de. La pratica universale in cirugia. *Venice: F.Sansovino & Co.,* 1560. 3v.;illus.;8vo. Includes in Italian translation the author's *Practica in arte chirurgica copiosa,* 1st publ., Rome, 1514. DNLM.   560/47

———. Prattica universale in cirugia . . . Tradotte per m. Lorenzo Chrisaorio. Di nuovo ristampate, et . . . recorette per m. Borgaruccio de' Borgarucci. *Venice: D.& C.dei Nicolini da Sabbio,* 1560. 258p.;illus.;4to. 1st publ. in this translation, Venice, 1549. DNLM.   560/48

Villegagnon, Nicolas Durand de. Ad articulos Calvinianae, de sacramento eucharistiae . . . ab eius ministris, ab eius ministris in Francia Antarctica evulgatae, Responsiones. *Paris: A.Wechel,* 1560. 422p.;4to. Includes (prel.lvs 10-11) Pierre Richer's 'Articuli . . . in Francia Antarctica scripto traditi'. A defence of the author's views on the Eucharist, the basis for an extended controversy with Calvin deriving from the former's conduct in Brazil. From the ensuing exchanges of accusations only those items relating to Brazil itself will be cited. Sabin 99724n; Cioranescu (XVI) 21821. NN-RB.   560/49

1561

Alberti, Leandro. Descrittione di tutta l'Italia. *Venice: L.degli Avanzi,* 1561. 503 numb.lvs;4to. 1st publ., Bologna, 1550. Ind. aur.102.342; Moranti (Urbino) 45; Shaaber A125. ICU, PU; BL, Urbino: BU.   561/1

—[Anr edn]. *Venice: P.& G.M.dei Nicolini da Sabbio,* 1561. 424 numb.lvs;4to. A reissue of printers' 1551 edn. CtY, ICN, MiU.   561/2

Alvares, Francisco. Historia de las cosas de Etiopia. *Saragossa: A.Millán,for M.de Zapilla,* 1561. lxxx lvs;fol. 1st publ. as here transl. by Thomas de Padilla, Antwerp, 1557, but here containing (lvs lxvi-lxxx) material relating to Brazil drawn from the Jesuit *Copia de diversas cartas,* Barcelona, 1556. Medina (BHA) 185; Borba de Moraes I:25; Streit II:1274; Ind.aur.104.037; Palau 9250. MH, NN-RB; BL.   561/3

Apianus, Petrus. Cosmographie, oft Beschrijvinghe der gheheelder Werelt. *Antwerp: J.Verwithagen,* 1561. lxxvi lvs;illus.,map;4to. 1st publ. in Dutch, Antwerp, 1545. Sabin 1754; Ind.aur.106.455; Ortroy (Apian) 46; JCB (3) I:210-211. RPJCB; BL, Brussels: BR.   561/4

Barreiros, Gaspar. Chorographia de alguns lugares que stam em hum caminho que fez Gaspar Barreiros. *Coimbra: J.Alvarez,* 1561. 247 lvs;4to. Includes, with special t.p., the author's 'Commentarius de Ophyra regione' which denies the then current theory that King Solomon's Ophir designated America. Sabin 3596 (&3595); Anselmo 82-83; Ind. aur.113.371 & 113.373; King Manuel 310. DLC, MH, NN-RB; BL, BN.   561/5

Barros, João de. Asia . . . nuovamente . . . tradotta . . . dal s. Alfonso Ulloa. *Venice: V.Valgrisi*, 1561. 2v.;4to. Transl. from 1st & 2nd Decades, 1st publ., Lisbon, 1552-53, with refs to Columbus, discovery of America & of Brazil in 1st Decade. Cf.Sabin 3647; cf.Borba de Moraes I:71-72; Adams (Cambr.) B254; King Manuel 74n (II:295). CU, DLC, NN-RB, PPDrop, RPJCB; Cambridge: UL. 561/6

Brasavola, Antonio Musa. Examen omnium loch . . . ubi de morbo gallico . . . tractatur. *Lyons: P.Michel,for S.Honorat*, 1561. 716p.;8vo. 1st publ., Venice, 1553. Ind. aur.123.824. DNLM; London: Wellcome, Oslo: UB. 561/7

Cortés, Martín. The arte of navigation . . . Translated out of Spanish . . . by Richard Eden. *London: R.Jug*, 1561. lxxxiiii lvs;illus.,map;4to. Transl. from the author's *Breve compendio de la sphera*, Seville, 1551. Sabin 16967; Medina (BHA) 145n; STC 5798; JCB (3) I:211. CtY, MB, NN-RB, RPJCB; BL. 561/8

Dolce, Lodovico. Vita dell' invittiss. e gloriossis. imperador Carlo Quinto. *Venice: G.Giolito de' Ferrari*, 1561. 168p.;4to. Includes (p.166-167) passage on Columbus & Spanish exploits in the New World. Adams (Cambr.) D755. CtY, DLC, MH, MiU, PU, RPJCB; BL, BN. 561/9

__[Anr edn]. *Venice: G.Giolito de' Ferrari*, 1561. 96p.;4to. DLC, InU-L; BL. 561/10

DuBellay, Joachim. L'olive et autres oeuvres poetiques. *Paris: F.Morel*, 1561. Includes poem 'A André Thevet' with ref. to French voyages to America. LeMoine 37. 561/11

Du Pinet, Antoine, sieur de Norey. Historia plantarum. *Lyons: G.Cotier*, 1561. 2pts;illus.;12mo. Based upon P.A.Mattioli's *Commentarii in libros sex Pedacii Dioscoridis de medica materia*, 1st publ. in this version, Venice, 1554. Pritzel 2539; Nissen (Bot.) 565 & 1307; Baudrier (Lyons) IV:72. DNLM, MH-A, MnU, NN-RB; BL, BN. 561/12

Fioravanti, Leonardo. Capricci medicinali. *Venice: L.degli Avanzi*, 1561. 183 numb.lvs; illus.;8vo. In bk 1, ch.26, 'Come gli antichi non hebbero cognitione del mal francese', are refs to the Spanish Indies & to sarsaparilla. Syphilis is attributed to cannibalism, found in the Indies. Also included are recipes for treatment of syphilis. Adams (Cambr.) F483. DNLM; London: Wellcome. 561/13

Fuchs, Leonhart. De componendorum miscendorumque medicamentorum ratione libri quatuor. *Lyons: S.Barbier,for A.Vincent*, 1561. 910p.;16mo. 1st publ., Basel, 1555, under title *De usitata huius temporis componendorum . . . medicamentorum ratione.* DNLM, MH-A. 561/14

__[Anr issue]. *Lyons: S.Barbier,for J.Frellon*, 1561. Baudrier (Lyons) V:254. Rouen: BM. 561/15

Giovio, Paolo, Bp of Nocera. Descriptiones quotquot extant, regionum atque locorum. *Basel: H.Petri & P.Perna*, 1561. 2v.;8vo. Includes Giovio's *Descriptio Britanniae*, 1st publ., Venice, 1548, and his *De romanis piscibus*, 1st publ., Rome, 1524. CSt, DLC, ICN, MiU, NCH; BL, BN. 561/16

____. Elogia virorum bellica virtute illustrium. *Basel: [P.Perna?]*, 1561. 82, [592]p.;8vo. 1st publ., Florence, 1551. Sabin 36773; Adams (Cambr.) G640. MH; Cambridge: Trinity. 561/17

____. Historiarum temporis sui tomus primus & tertius. *Lyons: Heirs of S.Gryphius*, 1561. 3v.;16mo. 1st publ., Florence, 1550-52. Baudrier (Lyons) VIII:302; Adams (Cambr.) G656. ICU; Cambridge: UL, BN. 561/18

____. Le second tome des histoires . . . sur les choses faictes et avenues de son temps. *Lyons: G.Rouillé*, 1561. 910p.;fol. 1st publ. in French, Lyons, 1552-53. Atkinson (Fr.Ren.) 134. Paris: Mazarine. 561/19

Guicciardini, Francesco. La historia di Italia. *Florence: L.Torrentino*, 1561. 665p.;port.; fol. In bk 6, chapt.9 comprises a discussion of Portuguese & Spanish explorations, citing Columbus & Vespucci. Adams (Cambr.) G1508. CSmH, CtY, DLC, IU, NN-RB; BL, BN. 561/20

__[Anr edn].Dell' historia de'Italia. *Florence: L.Torrentino*, 1561. 1295p.;port.;8vo. Adams (Cambr.) G1507. NIC, NNC; BL, BN. 561/21

Histoire des choses memorables advenues en la terre du Bresil, partie de l'Amerique australe, sous le gouvernement de N. de Villeg[agnon]. depuis l'an 1555. jusque à l'an 1558. *[Geneva?]* 1561. 48 numb.lvs;12mo. On possible authorship see Borba de Moraes. Sabin 99728n; Atkinson (Fr.Ren.) 131; Borba de Moraes I:342-343; JCB (3) I:212. NN-RB, RPJCB; BL, Paris: Arsenal. 561/22

Lucidarius. M.Elucidarius, von allerhandt geschöpffen Gottes . . . unnd wie alle Creaturen geschaffen seyn auff Erden. *Frankfurt a.M.: W.Han & G.Rab* [ca.1561]. 44 lvs;4to. 1st publ., Strassburg, [ca.1535]. Schorbach (Lucidarius) 32. Wolfenbüttel: HB.   561/23

Magnus, Olaus, Abp of Upsala. Histoire des pays septentrionaux . . . traduite du latin. *Antwerp: C.Plantin*, 1561. 264 numb.lvs; illus.;8vo. Transl. from Magnus's *Historia de gentibus septentrionalibus*, as condensed by C.Scribonius, 1st publ., Antwerp, 1558. Sabin 43834; Collijn (Sver.bibl.) II:271-272. CtY, MH, MnU-B; BL.   561/24

__[Anr issue]. *Antwerp: C.Plantin,for M.Le-Jeune,at Paris*, 1561. Sabin 43834n; Collijn (Sver.bibl.) II:272-273; Belg.typ. (1541-1600) I:2026. CSt, CtY, DFo, ICN, MH, MnU-B, NN-RB, PPAmP; Brussels: BR.   561/25

____. Storia . . . de'costumi de' popoli setten-trionali. Tradotta per m. Remigio [Nannini]. *Venice: F.Bindoni*, 1561. 511p.;8vo. Transl. from C.Scribonius's Antwerp, 1558, abridge-ment of Magnus's *Historia de gentibus septen-trionalibus*, 1st publ., Rome, 1555. Collijn (Sver.bibl.) II:290-292; JCB AR20:1561. CtY, MnU-B, NIC, RPJCB; BL.   561/26

Marguérite d'Angoulême, Queen of Navarre. L'heptameron. *Lyons: G.Rouillé*, 1561. 12mo. 1st publ. in this version, Paris, 1559. Tchémerzine VII:394. BL.   561/27

__[Anr edn]. *Paris: G.Gilles*, 1561. 733p.;16mo. Tchémerzine VII:394.   561/28

Mattioli, Pietro Andrea. Les commentaires . . . sur les six livres des simples de Pedacius Dioscoride . . . Nouvellement traduits de latin [par Antoine Du Pinet]. *Lyons: J.d'Ogerol-les,for G.Cotier*, 1561. 538p.;illus.;fol. Transl. from Ruel's version of the author's *Commentarii*, 1st publ., Venice, 1554. Pierre Haultin is named in colophon as sharing in this edn with Cotier. Pritzel 5991; Nissen (Bot.) 1312; Baudrier (Lyons) IV:72-73; Adams (Cambr.) D676. CU, DNLM, KU, MH-A; Cambridge: Trinity.   561/29

Medina, Pedro de. L'art de naviguer . . . con-tenant toutes les reigles & annotations, par Nicolas de Nicolai. *Lyons: G.Rouillé*, 1561. 225p.;illus.;4to. 1st publ. in French, Lyons, 1553. Baudrier (Lyons) IX:280; Adams (Cam-br.) M1028. Cambridge: Emmanuel, BN.   561/30

Mexía, Pedro. Colóquios o Dialogos. *Ant-werp: Widow of M.Nuyts*, 1561. 165 numb. lvs;12mo. 1st publ., Seville, 1547. Sabin

48249; Peeters-Fontainas (Impr.esp.) 782; Palau 167370. DNLM; BN.   561/31

____. Historia imperial y cesarea. *Antwerp: Widow of M.Nuyts*, 1561. 366 numb.lvs;fol. 1st publ., Seville, 1545. Sabin 48249n; Peeters-Fontainas (Impr.esp.) 784. DFo, MoSW, MH; BL, BN.   561/32

____. Le vite di tutti gl'imperadori romani. *Ve-nice: G.Giolito de' Ferrari*, 1561. 2v.;4to. In-cludes also another issue of Lodovico Dolce's *Vita dell' invitissimo Carlo Quinto* also publ. separately this year as described above. BL.
561/33

____. Vite di tutti gli imperadori . . . nuova-mente . . . tradotte dal signor Alfonso Ulloa. *Venice: V.Valgrisi*, 1561. 1119p.;4to. Transl. from Mexía's *Historia ymperial y cesarea*, 1st publ., Seville, 1545. Palau 167359. DCU, IU, RPB.   561/34

Moleti, Giuseppe. Discurso universale . . . nel quale son raccolti, & dichiarati tutti i termini, & tutte le regole appartenenti alla geographia. *Venice: V.Valgrisi*, 1561. 47p.;4to. *In* C.Pto-lemaeus, *La geografia*, Venice, 1561, q.v. In-cluded in the tables are calculations for the 'terra nuovamente trovata.'   561/34a

Münster, Sebastian. Cosmographei oder be-schreibung aller länder . . . biss auff das M.D.LXI. jar . . . gemehret. *Basel: H.Petri*, 1561. 1475p.;illus.,maps;fol. 1st publ., Basel, 1544. Burmeister (Münster) 74. Munich: StB.
561/35

Ovidius Naso, Publius. Metamorphoses. Ital-ian. Le trasformationi di m. Lodovico Dolce . . . Sesta impressione. *Venice: G.Giolito de' Ferrari*, 1561. 320p.;illus.,map; 4to. 1st publ. in this version with world map, Venice, 1553. Cf.Mortimer (Italy) 342n. CtY, DLC. 561/36

Pantaleon, Heinrich. Chronographia chris-tianae ecclesiae. *Basel: N.Brylinger*, 1561. 157p.;fol. 1st publ., Basel, 1550. Adams (Cambr.) P174. MH; BL.   561/37

Paradin, Guillaume. Histoire de nostre temps. *Paris: L.Breyer*, 1561. 16mo. 1st publ. in French, Lyons, 1560. BL.   561/38

__[Anr issue]. *Paris: J.Longis & R.LeMangnier*, 1561. Cartier (de Tournes) 413n.   561/39

Postel, Guillaume. Cosmographicae discipli-nae compendium. *Basel: J.Oporinus*, 1561. 79p.;illus.;4to. Contains scattered refs to New World. Sabin 64522; Cioranescu (XVI) 17855. DLC, InU-L, MH, MnU-B, NN-RB, RPJCB; BL, BN.   561/40

Proclus Diadochus. De sphaera. *Basel: H.Petri* [1561]. 985p.;illus.,maps;8vo. The earliest edn of this compendium of astronomic works, ed. by Marcus Hopper, to contain also Johannes Honter's *De cosmographiae rudimentis*, 1st publ. in this version, Kronstadt, 1541. Sabin 65940; Yarmolinsky (Early Polish Americana) 34. DLC, MiU-C, MnU-B, NN-RB, RPJCB; BL, BN. 561/41

Ptolemaeus, Claudius. La geografia . . . Nuovamente tradotta di greco . . . de Jeronimo Ruscelli. *Venice: V.Valgrisi,* 1561. 3pts;illus.,maps;4to. The earliest edn of this translation with freshly executed maps. Includes, with text & maps relating to New World, Ruscelli's *Espositioni et introduttioni universali . . . sopra tutta la geografia*; and also G.Moleto's *Discorso universale*. Sabin 66503; Stevens (Ptolemy) 50; Phillips (Atlases) 371; Adams (Cambr.) P2235; JCB (3) I:214. CSmH, CtY, DLC, ICN, InU-L, MH, MiU-C, NN-RB, PPF, RPJCB; BL, BN. 561/42

La response aux lettres de Nicolas Durant, dict le chevalier de Villegaignon, addressés à la Reyne mere du Roy. [*Geneva?* 1561?]. 46 lvs; 8vo. Includes, lvs 2-11, an 'Ode contenant une briefve description du voyage de Villegaignon au Bresil, & des cruautes qu'il y a exercee'. Borba de Moraes II:200-201; Rothschild 1988. MH, NN-RB; BL, BN. 561/43

___[Anr edn]. *Paris: A.Wechel*, 1561. 4to. BL. 561/44

Richer, Pierre. Libri duo apologetici ad refutandas naenias, & coarguendos blasphemos errores, detegendáque mendacia Nicolai Durandi qui se Villagagnonem cognominat. '*Hierapoli, per Thrasybulum phoenicum*' [i.e., *Geneva: J. Crespin*] 1561. 235p.;illus.; 4to. An attack on Villegagnon's theology, describing him as 'King of America', including also author's recollections of Brazil. Borba de Moraes II:207-208; Adams (Cambr.) R513. Cambridge: UL, BN. 561/45

___. La refutation des folles resveries, execrables blasphemes, erreurs & mensonges de Nicolas Durand, qui se nomme Villaigagnon. [*Geneva?*] 1561. 176 numb.lvs;illus.;8vo. Transl. from preceding item. Borba de Moraes II:207-208. CtY; BN. 561/46

Ruscelli, Girolamo. Espositioni et introduttioni universali . . . sopra tutta la Geografia di Tolomeo. *Venice: V.Valgrisi,* 1561. [54]p.; maps;4to. *In* C.Ptolemaeus, *La geografia,*

Venice, 1561, q.v. Included are a ref. to America & maps relating to it. 561/46a

Sacro Bosco, Joannes de. Sphaera . . . emendata Eliae Vineti . . . Scholia. *Paris: G. Cavellat,* 1561. 102 numb.lvs;illus.;8vo. 1st publ. with Vinet's *Scholia,* Paris, 1551. Cf.Sabin 32681; Adams (Cambr.) H729. NN-RB; Cambridge: UL. 561/47

Schitler, Joannes. Tractatus methodicus de morbo gallico seu scabie hispanica. *Breslau: C.Scharffenberg,* 1561. 8vo. Proksch I:18. 561/48

Schöner, Johann. Opera mathematica. *Nuremberg: J.vom Berg & U.Neuber,* 1561. 3pts; illus.,port.,maps;fol. 1st publ. in this collective edn, Nuremberg, 1551. Includes the author's *Opusculum geographicum,* 1st publ., Nuremberg, 1533. Sabin 77806; Adams (Cambr.) S679; Coote (Schöner) 44; JCB (3) I:214-215. CSmH, DLC, InU-L, NN-RB, RPJCB; BL. 561/49

Soto, Domingo de. Commentariorum . . . in quartum Sententiarum tomus primus [-secundus]. *Salamanca: J.M.à Terranova,for J.Moreno,* 1561-62. 2v.;fol. 1st publ., Salamanca, 1557-60. Palau 320168. BL(v.l). 561/50

Spain. Cortes. Quaderno de las cortes: que en Valladolid tuvo su magestad del Emperador . . . el año .1523. *Salamanca: J.à Cánova,* 1561. 14 lvs;fol. 1st publ., Burgos, 1523. Palau 63150. Madrid: BN. 561/51

Thevet, André. Historia dell'India America, detta altramente Francia Antartica . . . tradotta . . . da m. Giuseppe Horologgi. *Venice: G.Giolito de' Ferrari,* 1561. 363p.;8vo. Transl. from Thevet's *Les singularitez de la France Antarctique,* 1st publ., Paris, 1557. Sabin 95336; Borba de Moraes II:304-305; Church 112; Arents 9; Shaaber T190; JCB (3) I:215. CSmH, CtY, DLC, ICN, MH, MiU-C, NN-A, PU, RPJCB; BL, BN. 561/52

Villegagnon, Nicolas Durand de. Responce par le Chevalier de Villegaignon aux remonstrances faictes à la Royne mere du Roy. *Paris: A.Wechel,* 1561. 221p.;4to. A reply to the anonymous *Remonstrance à la Reyne Mère* of this year described above, here citing Pierre Richer, 'nostre ministre au Bresil'. Sabin 99726; JCB (3) I:212. RPJCB; BN. 561/53

___. Response aux libelles d'injures publiez contre le chevalier de Villegaignon. *Paris: A. Wechel,* 1561. [11]p.;4to. Refers to author's execution in Brazil of 3 abjuring priests and asserting own orthodox religious conduct there. Sabin 99727; Borba de Moraes II:360; Cioranescu (XVI) 21851; JCB (3) I:212. NN-RB, RPJCB; BL, BN.   561/54

____[Anr edn]. *Lyons: B.Rigaud*, 1561. 8p.;8vo. Sabin 99728; Borba de Moraes II:360; Baudrier (Lyons) III:212. NN-RB.   561/55

Wecker, Johann Jakob. Antidotarium speciale . . . ex optimorum authorum . . . scriptis fideliter congestum. *Basel: [N.Episcopius the Younger?]*, 1561. Included are recipes for treatment of syphilis. Ferguson (Bibl.chem.) II:534, citing Johann Werner Herzog, *Athenae Rauricae*, Basel, 1778-80.   561/56

1562

Alonso de la Veracruz, Father. Physica speculatio. *Salamanca: J.M.à Terranova*, 1562. 344p.;illus.;fol. 1st publ., Mexico City, 1557. With other of the author's works, the earliest such reprintings of writings originally publ. in the Americas; cf.following items. In the section 'De coelo' is a geographic description of the New World. Sabin 98915; Medina (BHA) 190; Bolaño e Isla (Veracruz) 56-57 no.2; Palau 359155. Seville: BU.   562/1

____. Recognitío sumularum, cum textu Petri Hispani, et Aristotelis . . . Nunc secondò . . . revisa ab autore. *Salamanca: J.M.à Terranova*, 1562. 170p.;fol. 1st publ., Mexico City, 1554. Cf.other works by author reprinted in this year. Sabin 98918n; Medina (BHA) 188; Bolaño e Isla (Veracruz) 48-49 (no.2); Palau 359141. Seville: BU.   562/2

____. Speculum conjugiorum . . . Nunc secondò opus elaboratum, & ab authore . . . limatum. *Salamanca: A.de Portonariis*, 1562. 573p.;fol. 1st publ., Mexico City, 1556; cf.other works likewise reprinted in this year. On the moral theology of marriage, with particular reference to application to Indian converts. Sabin 98919n; Medina (BHA) 191; Streit I:88; Bolaño e Isla (Veracruz) 60 (no.2); Palau 359150. Seville: Seminario.   562/3

Aristoteles. Organum. Latin (Selections). Resolutiò dialectica cum textu Aristotelis, admodum . . . fratris Alphonsi à Vera Cruce . . . Nunc secondò . . . revisa ab autore. *Salamanca: J.M.à Terranova*, 1562. 161p.;fol. 1st publ., Mexico City, 1554, under title *Dialectica resolutio*; cf.other works by Alonso de la

Veracruz likewise reprinted in this year. Medina (BHA) 189; Bolaño e Isla (Veracruz) 53 (no.2); Palau 359146. Seville: BU.   562/4

Ayalá, Gabriel. Carmen pro vera medicina . . . Ad eundum: De lue pestilenti elegiarum liber unus. *Antwerp: C.Plantin, for W.Silvius*, 1562. 28 lvs;4to. In verse. The *De lue pestilenti* is on syphilis. Ind.aur.110.969. NNNAM; BL, BN.   562/5

Barros, João de. L'Asia . . . Nuovamente . . . tradotta . . . dal s. Alfonso Ulloa. *Venice: V.Valgrisi*, 1562. 2v.;4to. 1st publ. in this translation, 1561, and here reprinted from same setting of type, the imprint date alone being altered. Cf.Sabin 3647; Borba de Moraes I:71-72; Ind.aur.113.426; Adams (Cambr.) B255. DLC, ICN, MH, NN-RB, RPJCB; BL, BN.   562/6

Díez, Diego. Relacion muy verdedera trayda por Diego Diez y Juan Rodriguez y Pedro Morzillo, maestre y piloto y escrivano del navio numbrado Nuestra Señora de la Luz, viniendo de Sancto Domingo. *Seville: A.de Coca* [1562?]. bds.;fol. Describes volcanic eruption, Sept. 1562, on island of Pico in the Azores. Medina (BHA) 187; Escudero (Seville) 606; Palau 257180.   562/7

____. Een warachtighe ende seer verschickelijcke geschiedenisse, te weten, vanden grooten viere ofte brant, gheschiet in een eylandt, ghenoemt del Pico, den xx. dach Septembris inden jare. .M.D.LXII. *Antwerp: J.Mollyns* [1562?] [8]p.;8vo. Transl. from preceding item. Sabin 101271; cf.Medina (BHA) 187; JCB (STC) 11. RPJCB.   562/8

Eisenmenger, Samuel, called Siderocrates. Libellus geographicus, locorum numerandi intervalla rationem in lineis rectis & sphaericis complectens. *Tübingen: Widow of U.Morhart*, 1562. 74 numb.lvs; illus.;4to. Refs to America appear on lvs 20-22, etc. JCB (3) I:217. MH, MiU, NN-RB, RPJCB; BL. 562/9

Franck, Sebastian. Dat Wereltboeck, spiegel ende beeltnisse des gheheelen Aertbodems. *[Amsterdam?]* 1562. cxcviii lvs;fol. 1st publ. in Dutch [Antwerp? 1550?]. Sabin 25470n. MB, MnU-B, NN-RB.   562/10

Gastaldo, Jacopo. La universale descrittione del mondo. *Venice: M.Pagan*, 1562. [23]p.; illus.;12mo. Cf.following item. Descriptive text to accompany author's world map, with refs to America on p.[5] & [19]. JCB AR47: 16,25-29,31-33. MH, MnU-B, RPJCB. 562/11

____. Universalis mundi descriptio . . . descripta. *Venice: M.Pagan*, 1562. 10 lvs;illus.;8vo. Transl. from preceding item. Descriptive text to accompany author's world map. MnU-B, RPJCB; BN. 562/12

Giovio, Paolo, Bp of Nocera. Historia general de todas las cosas succedidas en el mundo en estos cincuenta años de nuestro tiempo. Traducido por Gaspar Baeça. *Salamanca: A.de Portonariis*, 1562-63. 2v.;fol. Transl. from Giovio's *Historiarum sui temporis tomus primus-secundus*, 1st publ., Florence, 1550-52. Sabin 36775; Palau 125417. 562/13

____. Libro de las historias, y cosas acontescidas en Alemaña, España . . . India, y mundo nuevo . . . traduzido en romance castellano por Antonio Joan Villafranca. *Valencia: J.Mey,for H.Ulzina*, 1562. cclx lvs;illus.;fol. Transl. from Giovio's *Historiarum sui temporis tomus primus-secundus*, 1st publ., Florence, 1550-52. Salva 3251; Palau 125419. NNH; BL. 562/14

Guicciardini, Francesco. La historia d'Italia. *Venice: G.M.Bonelli*, 1562. 470 numb.lvs; 4to. 1st publ., Florence, 1561. ICN, NN-RB, PPL. 562/15

Jesuits. Letters from missions. Nuovi avisi dell'Indie di Portogallo . . . tradotti dalla lingua spagnuola . . . Terza parte. *Venice: M. Tramezzino*, 1562. 316 lvs;8vo. Continues the publisher's *Diversi avisi* of 1559. Included are 10 reports from Brazil. Sabin 5640; Borba de Moraes I:51; Streit II:1280; Arents (Add.) 25; JCB (3) I:216. NN-A, RPJCB; BL. 562/16

Magnus, Olaus, Abp of Upsala. Historia de gentibus septentrionalibus . . . a C.Scribonio Graphaeo in epitomen redacta. *Antwerp: [C.Plantin,for] J.Bellère*, 1562. 192 numb. lvs;illus.;8vo. 1st (?) publ. in this condensed form, Antwerp, 1558. Sabin 43833n; Collijn (Sver.bibl.) I:306-308; Adams (Cambr.) M144; Belg.typ. (1541-1600) I:2024. CtY, IU, MH, MnU-B, NN-RB; BL, Brussels: BR. 562/17

____. De wonderlijcke historie van de noordersche landen . . . Nu eerst overghestelt uuten latijn in ons nederlantsche duytsche sprake. *Antwerp: W.Silvius*, 1562. cclxxxv lvs;illus., maps;8vo. Transl. from Magnus's *Historia de gentibus septentrionalibus* as condensed by C.Scribonius, 1st publ., Antwerp, 1558. Sabin 43835; Collijn (Sver.bibl.) II:308-309. BL. 562/18

Mattioli, Pietro Andrea. Commentarii denuo aucti, in libros sex Pedacii Dioscoridis . . . De materia medica. *Lyons: J.d'Ogerolles,for G. Cotier*, 1562. 2pts;illus.;fol. 1st publ., Venice, 1554. Copies exist with colophon dated 1563, made up apparently of mixed sheets of this & the 1563 issue. Baudrier (Lyons) IV:73-74; cf.Adams (Cambr.) D670. CtY-M, DNLM, MBH. 562/19

____. Herbárz . . . na czeskau rzec, od Doktora Thadeásse Hágka. *Prague: J.Melantrich*, 1562. cccxcii lvs;illus.,ports;fol. Transl. from the author's *Commentarii in sex libros . . . Dioscoridis*, 1st publ., Venice, 1554. Pritzel 5992; Nissen (Bot.) 1314. DNLM, MBH, NNBG; London: Wellcome. 562/20

Mexía, Pedro. Colóquios o Dialogos. *Seville: S.Trugillo*, 1562. clxvii lvs;8vo. 1st publ., Seville, 1547. Escudero (Seville) 608; Palau 167370. 562/21

__[Anr edn]. *Saragossa: Widow of B.de Nagera*, 1562. lxxxviii lvs;8vo. Palau 167371. 562/22

Paracelsus. Der dritte Theil der grossen Wundtartzney. *[Frankfurt a.M.: W.Han & G.Rab*, 1562?]. [146]p.;4to. 1st publ., Nuremberg, 1530. A reissue of sheets of the 1553 edn with title *Von der frantzösischen Kranckheit*, printed by H.Gülfferich. Sudhoff (Paracelsus) 51. DNLM; BL. 562/23

____. Spittal Büch. *Mülhausen: P.Schmid*, 1562. [83]p.;4to. Includes discussion of syphilis. Sudhoff (Paracelsus) 44. DNLM; BL. 562/24

Ptolemaeus, Claudius. Geographia . . . olim a Bilibaldo Pirckheimherio traslata, at nunc multis codicibus graecis collatis collata, pluribusque in locis ad pristinam veritatem redacta a Josepho Moletio. *Venice: V.Valgrisi*, 1562. 286p.;maps;4to. Of the maps 10, with descriptive text, relate to America. Sabin 66489; Stevens (Ptolemy) 51; Phillips (Atlases) 372; Armstrong 31; JCB (3) I:217. CSmH, CtY, DLC, ICN, MH, MWA, MiU-C, NN-RB, PP, RPJCB; BL, BN. 562/25

Recueil de la diversité des habits qui sont a present en usaige tant es pays d'Europe, Asie, Affrique et Illes sauvages. *Paris: R.Breton*, 1562. [127]p.;illus.;8vo. Comprises woodcut illustrations of costumes, each accompanied by verses in French; included is a representation of Brazilian Indian couple. The dedication is signed by 'François deserpz', almost certainly the Paris bookseller François Desprez (cf.1567 issue sold by him). Sabin 19689 & 68432; Atkinson (Fr.Ren.) 136; Borba de Moraes I:220-222. NN-RB; Paris: Mazarine.   562/26

Ronsard, Pierre de.   Continuation du Discours des miseres de ce temps. *Paris: G.Buon,* 1562. [20]p.4to. Supplements the author's *Discours* of this year. Includes ref. to 'Perou, Canada, Callicuth, Canibales' where Christianity is unknown. Tchémerzine IX,440; Adams (Cambr.) R763. BL, BN.   562/27

__[Anr edn]. *Toulouse: J.Colomiès,* 1562. 12 lvs;4to. DeRicci (Ronsard) 472.   562/28

Ruscelli, Girolamo, comp.   Lettere di principi. *Venice: G.Ziletti,* 1562. 230 numb.lvs; 4to. Includes letter to Cardinal Bembo from G.F. de Oviedo y Valdés from Santo Domingo, 20 Jan. 1543, describing Pizarro, El Dorado, etc., 1st publ. (lvs 345r-346r) in Ramusio's *Terzo volume delle Navigationi,* Venice, 1556; cf. German version found in H.Cortés, *Von dem Newen Hispanien,* Augsburg, 1550. Cf.Sabin 40563. CtY, DFo, ICN, MH, PU, RPB; BL, BN.   562/29

Sacro Bosco, Joannes de.   Sphaera . . . emendata. Eliae Vineti . . . Scholia. *Paris: G.Cavellat,* 1562. 102 numb.lvs.;illus.;8vo. 1st publ. with Vinet's *Scholia,* Paris, 1561. Cf. Sabin 32681. DLC, ICJ, NN-RB.   562/30

Soto, Domingo de.   De justitia & jure. Libri decem. *Salamanca: J.M.à Terranova,for J. Moreno,* 1562. 942p.;fol. 1st publ., Salamanca, 1553. Palau 320143.   562/31

Tarcagnota, Giovanni.   Delle historie del mondo. *Venice: M.Tramezzino,* 1562. 3pts; 4to. In the 2nd pt, bk xxi contains an extended account of Columbus & the New World; in pt 3, bk i gives a further account of Columbus. Cf.Adams (Cambr.) T139. ICN; BL.   562/32

Ulloa, Alfonso de.   Vita dell'invitissimo Emperador Carlo Quinto. *Venice: V.Valgrisi,* 1562. 336 numb.lvs;8vo. 1st publ., Venice, 1560. Sabin 97680; Palau 343391. CSmH, DLC, NNH, RPJCB;BL.   562/33

Valleriola, François.   Loci medicinae communes, tribus libris digesti. *Lyons: Heirs of S. Gryphius,* 1562. 3pts;port.;fol. In bk 3 a new venereal disease, i.e., syphilis, is cited. Baudrier (Lyons) VIII:305-306; Adams (Cambr.) V210. DNLM, MBCo; BL, BN.   562/34

Villegagnon, Nicolas Durand de.   Ad articulos Calvinianae, de sacramento eucharistae . . . ab eius ministris in Francia Antarctica

evulgatae, Responsiones.   *Paris: A.Wechel,* 1562. 438p.;4to. 1st publ., Paris, 1560. Sabin 99724; Borba de Moraes II:360-361; JCB (3) I:216. RPJCB; BL, BN.   562/35

__[Anr edn]. *Venice: G.Bindoni,* 1562. 2v.;8vo. Sabin 99724n. InU-L.   562/36

1563

Barros, João de.   Terceira decada da Asia. *Lisbon: J.de Barreira,* 1563. 266 numb.lvs;fol. Continues 1st & 2nd Decades earlier publ., Lisbon, 1552-53. In bk 5, chapts 8-10 describe Magellan and his circumnavigation. The subsequent 4th Decade did not appear till 1615. Cf.Sabin 3646; Borba de Moraes I:71; Streit IV:667; Ind.aur.113.428; King Manuel 101. MH, MnU-B, NN-RB; BL, BN.   563/1

Botallo, Leonardo.   Luis venereae curandae ratio. *Paris: J.Foucher,* 1563. 109 numb.lvs; 8vo. Proksch I:18; Adams (Cambr.) B2544; Ind.aur.122.671. NNNAM; Cambridge: UL, BN.   563/2

Dioscorides, Pedanius.   Acerca de la material medicinal . . . traduzido de lengua griega . . . & illustrado con . . . substantiales annotationes y con las figuras de innumeras plantas . . . por el doctor Andres de Laguna. *Salamanca: M.Gast,* 1563. 616p.;illus.,port.; fol. Laguna's annotations, with numerous refs to American plants, 1st publ. separately, Lyons, 1554, & in the present form, Antwerp, 1555. Pritzel 2313n; Palau 74022n. BN, Madrid: BN.   563/3

Dodoens, Rembert.   Cruijde boeck. *Antwerp: J.van der Loe,* 1563. vcclxxxii (i.e., dclxxxii) p.;illus.,port.;fol. 1st publ., Antwerp, 1554. Pritzel 2345; Nissen (Bot.) 512; Bibl.belg.,1st ser., IX: D108; Arents (Add.) 16. CU, DNLM, NN-A; BL, BN.   563/4

Falloppius, Gabriel.   Secreti diversi, et miracolosi. *Venice: M.di Maria,* 1563. 215 numb. lvs;8vo. Included are recipes for ointments, etc., for treatment of syphilis. DNLM.   563/5

Fuchs, Leonhart.   De componendum miscendorumque medicamentorum ratione libri quatuor. *Lyons: A.Vincent,* 1563. 910p.; 16mo. 1st publ. under this title, Lyons, 1556. CtY-M, DNLM, MnU.   563/6

Galvão, António.   Tratado . . . dos diversos & desvayrados caminhos. *[Lisbon:] J.de Barreira,* 1563. 80 numb.lvs;8vo. 'Descobrimiento das Antilhas & Indias pollos Espanhões feytas': lvs 23-80. Sabin 26467; Borba de Moraes I:288-289; Anselmo 177; JCB (3) I:218. CtY, InU-L, RPJCB; BL, Lisbon: BN. 563/7

Guicciardini, Francesco. La historia d'Italia. *Venice: N.Bevilacqua*, 1563. 470 numb.lvs; 4to. 1st publ., Florence, 1561. Adams (Cambr.) G1509. CtY, DLC, ICN, ICU; BL, BN. 563/8

Lucidarius. M. Elucidarius, von allerhand Geschöpffen Gottes . . . und wie alle Creaturen geschaffen seyn auff Erden. *Frankfurt a.M.: Heirs of W.Han* [ca.1563?]. [87]p.;4to. 1st publ., Strassburg, [ca.1535]. Schorbach (Lucidarius) 33. CtY, NIC; Munich: UB, Strasbourg: UB. 563/9

Massa, Niccolò. Liber de morbo gallico . . . Cui . . . multa addita sunt ab autore de vi ac potestate ligni indici. *Venice: G.Ziletti*, 1562. 73 numb.lvs;4to. 1st publ., Venice, 1532. DNLM, MBCo, NNNAM; London: Wellcome. 563/10

Mattioli, Pietro Andrea. Commentarii denuo aucti, in libros sex Pedacii Dioscoridis . . . De medica materia. *Lyons: J.d'Ogerolles,for G. Cotier*, 1563. 2pts;illus.;fol. 1st publ., Venice, 1554; here a reissue of the 1562 edn with altered imprint date. Nissen (Bot.) 1305n; Baudrier (Lyons) IV:74; Adams (Cambr.) D671. DNLM, NNBG; BL. 563/11

——. I discorsi . . . ne i sei libri di Pedacio Dioscoride . . . della materia medicinale. *Venice: V.Valgrisi*, 1563. 802p.;illus.;fol. 1st publ., Venice, 1555. Pritzel 5987n; Nissen (Bot.) 1304n. NNBG. 563/12

——. New Kräuterbuch . . . durch Georgium Handsch verdeutscht. *Prague: G.Melantrich, & for V.Valgrisi at Venice*, 1563. 1149p.; illus.,port.;fol. Transl. from author's *Historia plantarum*, 1st publ., Lyons, 1561. Includes account and cut of tobacco ('Hyoscyamus'). Pritzel 5989; Nissen (Bot.) 1310; Arents 9-A. CtY-M, DNAL, ICJ, NN-A; BL. 563/13

Medina, Pedro de. Regimiento de navegacion. *Seville: S.Carpintero*, 1563. lxxviii lvs; illus.,map;8vo. 1st publ., Valladolid, 1545, under title *Arte de navegar*. Medina (BHA) 192; Borba de Moraes II:48; Escudero (Seville) 614; Bibl.mar.esp.210. CtY, InU-L, NN-RB, TxU, ViU; BL, BN. 563/14

Mexía, Pedro. Della selva di varia lettione, parti cinque . . . Di nuovo ristampate, et cor-

rette. *Venice: D.Nicolini*, 1563. 438 numb. lvs;8vo. 1st publ., Venice, 1559-60, with Sansovino's pt 5, on West Indies. Cf.Sabin 48239. DFo, RPJCB, WU. 563/15

——. Les diverses leçons . . . mises en françois par Claude Gruget . . . augmentées de trois dialogues. *Lyons: G.Cotier*, 1563. 1272p.;8vo. 1st publ. in this version with supplementary dialogues, Paris, 1556. Baudrier (Lyons) IV:74. BL. 563/16

More, Sir Thomas, Saint. Lucubrationes. *Basel: N. & E.Episcopius*, 1563. 530p.;8vo. Includes the author's *Utopia*, 1st publ., Louvain, 1516. Gibson (More) 74; Adams (Cambr.) M1752; Fairfax Murray (Germany) 305; JCB (3) I:220. CSmH, CtY, DLC, ICU, MH, MiU, NNC, RPJCB; BL. 563/17

Navagero, Andrea. Il viaggio fatto in Spagna, et in Francia. *Venice: D.Farri*, 1563. 68 numb.lvs;8vo. Description of Seville (lvs 15v-16r) contains refs to West Indian trade, natives, etc. Palau 187929; Moranti (Urbino) 2289; Shaaber N78. CSt, CtY, MH, MiU, MnU-B, NN-RB, PU, RPJCB; BL, BN. 563/18

Novus Orbis regionum. Die nieuwe weerelt der landtschappen ende eylanden. *Antwerp: J.van der Loe*, 1563. dcccxiii p.;illus.;fol. Transl. by Corneille Ablyen, with additional material, from German text, 1st publ., Basel, 1532. Sabin 34107 (&16961); Streit I:92; Adams (Cambr.) N268; Belg.typ. (1541-1600) I:2218; JCB (3) I:219. DLC, InU-L, MnU-B, NN-RB, RPJCB; BL, Brussels: BR. 563/19

Orta, Garcia da. Coloquios dos simples, e drogas he cousas mediçinais da India. *Goa: J.de Endem*, 1563. 217 numb.lvs;4to. Included are scattered refs to New World plants, to Magellan, Brazilian rubber, and relative merits of Guaiacum & ginseng ('raiz de China') in treatment of syphilis. Though printed in Portuguese India, ostensibly distributed in Europe. Sabin 57662; Pritzel 4316; Anselmo 535; Adams (Cambr.) O323. InU-L; BL, BN. 563/20

Postel, Guillaume. De universitate liber . . . Secunda aeditio. *Paris: M.LeJeune*, 1563. 77p.;4to. 1st publ., Paris, 1552. Adams (Cambr.) P2025. ICN, MH, NN-RB; BL, BN. 563/21

Ramusio, Giovanni Battista. Primo volume, & terza editione delle Navigationi et viaggi. *Venice: Heirs of L.Giunta*, 1563. 394 lvs;

illus.,maps;fol. 1st publ., Venice, 1554. Apart from new pref. with account of compiler, an unchanged text. Sabin 67732; Borba de Moraes II:271-272; Streit I:91; Adams (Cambr.) R136; Shaaber R16; JCB (STC) 11. InU-L, MB, NN-RB, PU, RPJCB; BL, BN.
563/22

Ribaut, Jean. The whole and truè discoverye of Terra Florida . . . written in Frenche . . . and nowe newly set forthe in Englishe. *London: R.Hall, for T.Hacket* [1563]. 23 lvs;8vo. The original French text is unknown. Sabin 70792; Adams (Laudonnière) 1; JCB (101 Bks) 12; STC 20970. MH; BL.   563/23

Rondelet, Guillaume. Methodus curandorum omnium morborum corporis humani . . . Ejusdem . . . De morbo gallico. *Paris: J.Macé* [1563?]. 7pts;8vo. Adams (Cambr.) R751. DNLM, NNNAM; Cambridge: UL.   563/24

Ronsard, Pierre de. Continuation du Discours de ce temps. *Paris: G.Buon*, 1563. 10 lvs;4to. 1st publ., Paris, 1562. There appear to be varying edns or issues of this title in this year, not feasibly differentiated. Tchémerzine IX: 440. MH; BN.   563/25

____. Remonstrance au peuple de la France. *Paris: G.Buon*, 1563. 17 numb.lvs;4to. In verse. Includes ref. to Villegagnon's Brazilian venture. LeMoine 99; Cioranescu (XVI) 19429; Rothschild 676. BN.   563/26

Seall, Robert. A commendation of the adventurous viage of the wurthy captain of the land called Terra Florida. *London: J.Allde* [1563?]. bds.,fol. Ballad. Sabin 78597; STC 22139. CSmH.   563/27

Staden Hans. Warachtighe historie ende beschrivinghe eens lants in America gelegen. *Antwerp: J.Roelants*, 1563. 108 lvs;illus.;8vo. 1st publ. in Dutch, Antwerp, 1550. Sabin 90041; Borba de Moraes II:283; Palau 321856. MH.   563/28

Valleriola, François. Loci medicinae communes. *Venice: V.Valgrisi*, 1563. 2pts;8vo. 1st publ., Lyons, 1562. DNLM; London: Wellcome.   563/29

Voerthusius, Joannes. Academiae . . . gratulantionis. *Frankfurt a.M.:* 1563. See the year 1573.

Zárate, Agustín de. Le historie . . . Dello scoprimento et conquista del Peru . . . Nuovamente . . . tradotte dal s. Alfonso Ulloa. *Venice: G.Giolito de' Ferrari*, 1563. 294p.;8vo. Transl. from Zárate's *Historia*, 1st

publ. in Spanish, Antwerp, 1555. Sabin 106270 (&106271); Medina (BHA) 249n (I:412-413); Adams (Cambr.) 73; JCB (3) I:233. DLC, MH, MiU-C, NN-RB, RPJCB; BL, BN.   563/30

____. De wonderlijcke ende warachtighe historie van coninckrijck van Peru. *Antwerp: W.Silvius,for J.Verwithagen*, 1563. 206 numb. lvs;illus.,map;8vo. Transl. by Rumoldus de Baquerre from the *Historia del descubrimiento . . . del Peru*, Antwerp, 1555. Sabin 106273; cf.Medina (BHA) 249n (I:414); JCB (3) I:222. DLC, NN-RB, RPJCB.   563/31

1564

Amatus Lusitanus. Curationum medicinalium centuriae duae, quinta videlicet ac sexta. *Lyons: G.Rouillé*, 1564. 648p.;16mo. 1st publ., Venice, 1560. Ind.aur.104.563; Baudrier (Lyons) IX:293; Moranti (Urbino) 124. ICJ; BL, Urbino: BU.   564/1

Antwerp. Ordinancie inhoudende die oude en nieuwe poincten, van onser vrowen ommegande, der stadt van Antwerpen, gheschiet inden Jare. 1564. *Antwerp: H.de Laet* [1564]. 4to. Describes tableau depicting 'Theatre du monde' which includes allegorical figure of America. Belg.typ. (1541-1600) I:2261. BL, Brussels: BR.   564/2

Apianus, Petrus. Cosmographia . . . per Gemmam Frisium . . . iam demum ab omnibus vindicata mendis. *Antwerp: A.Coppens v.Diest,for Heirs of A.Birckmann*, 1564. 64p.;illus.,map;4to. 1st publ. in this version, Antwerp, 1529. Sabin 1749n; Ortroy (Apian) 47; Belg.typ. (1541-1600) I:130; Ind.aur. 106.456; Adams (Cambr.) A1282; JCB (3) I:223. CtY, DLC, ICN, MH, MiU-C, NN-RB, PPL, RPJCB; BL, Munich: StB.   564/3

__[Anr issue]. *Antwerp: A.Coppens v.Diest,for J.Verwithagen*, 1564. Ortroy (Apian) 48; Ind.aur.106.457; JCB (3) I:223-224. PPL, RPJCB; Paris: Mazarine, Strasbourg: BN.
   564/4

Bielski, Marcin. Kronika, tho iesth, Historia Swiátá. *Cracow: M.Siebeneycherá*, 1564. 467 numb.lvs;illus.,map.;fol. 1st publ., Cracow, 1551. Ind.aur.119.178; Wierzbowski 246. Cracow: Akademie.   564/5

Boemus, Johann. I costumi, le leggi, et l'usanze di tutte le genti . . . tradotti per Lucio Fauno . . . Et aggiuntovi di nuovo il quarto libro nel qual si narra i costumi, et l'usanze dell'Indie Occidentali, overo Mondo Nuovo, da . . . Gieronimo Giglio. *Venice: G. Bonadio*, 1564. 240 numb.lvs;8vo. 1st publ. in this version, Venice, 1560. Sabin 6119n; Ind. aur.120.960; Adams (Cambr.) B2274; JCB (3) I:224. DLC, MiU, RPJCB; Cambridge: UL. 564/6

Brant, Sebastian. Das gross Narren Schiff. *Strassburg: J.Rihel*, 1564. 164 numb.lvs;4to. 1st publ., Basel, 1494. Ind.aur.123.742. Wolfenbüttel: HB. 564/7

Camilla, Giovanni. Enthosiasmo . . . de' misterii, e maravigliose cause della compositione del mondo. *Venice: G.Giolito de' Ferrari*, 1564. 110p.;illus.;8vo. In ch.xix, 'Della cosmographia', is a ref. to Peru. Ind. aur.130.621. CtY, ICN, InU-L, MH; Manchester: UL, Florence: BN. 564/8

Cardano, Girolamo. Ars curandi parva. *Basel: S.Henricpetri*, 1564. 2v.;8vo. Included are Cardano's 'Ventriculi dolore cum aliis dispositionibus ob morbum gallicum . . . consilium' & his 'De cyna radice', i.e., American ginseng, 1st publ., Lyons, 1548, in his *Contradicentium medicorum*. Ind.aur.132.094. Berlin: StB, Rome: BN. 564/9

_____. Contradicentium medicorum libri duo. *Paris: J.Macé*, 1564-65. 2v.;8vo. 1st publ. with American refs, Lyons, 1548. Ind.aur.132.096; Adams (Cambr.) C656. DLC, MH, NNNAM; London: Wellcome, BN. 564/10

Carion, Johann. Chronicorum ab orbe condito ad hanc usque nostram aetatem libri iii. *Basel*: 1564. 688p.;8vo. 1st publ. in this version, Hall (Swabia) 1537. MH. 564/11

Chaumette, Antoine. Enchiridion chirurgicum . . . quibus Morbi venerei curandi methodus probatissima accessit. *Paris: J.Kerver*, 1564. 191 numb.lvs;8vo. 1st publ., Paris, 1560. CtY; BL, BN. 564/12

Cieza de León, Pedro de. Historia, over Cronica del gran regno del Peru . . . Tradotta per Agostino di Cravaliz. *Venice: G.Bonadio*, 1564. 216 numb.lvs;8vo. 1st publ. in this version, Rome, 1555. With this were published uniformly in this year, as pts 2 & 3, F.L. de Gómara's *Historia, delle nuove Indie Occidentali*, & his *Historia, di Don Ferdinando Cortes*. Sabin 13053; Medina (BHA) 157n (I:257); Streit II:774; JCB (3) I:224. DLC, MnU-B, NN-RB, RPJCB; Göttingen: UB. 564/13

Crespin, Jean. Actes des martyrs deduits en

sept livres, depuis le temps de Wiclef & de Hus. [*Geneva:*] *J.Crespin*, 1564. 1084p.;fol. Includes text of anonymous *Histoire des choses memorables advenues en . . . Bresil*, on Villegagnon's attempted settlement, 1st publ., [Geneva?], 1561. Borba de Moraes I:199n. NNC; BL. 564/14

Du Pinet, Antoine, sieur de Norey. Plantz, pourtraitz, et descriptions de plusieurs villes et forteresses, tant de l'Europe, Asie & Afrique, que des Indes & terres-neuves. *Lyons: J.d'Ogerolles*, 1564. xxxvi, 308p.;illus.,ports,maps; fol. Descriptive text & views of Cusco, Peru, & Mexico City (Temistitan): p.292-305. Sabin 62940; Atkinson (Fr.Ren.) 141; Baudrier (Lyons) X:140; Mortimer (France) 191; JCB (STC) 11. DLC, MH, NN-RB, RPJCB; BL, BN. 564/15

Estienne, Charles. L'agriculture et maison rustique. *Paris: J.DuPuys*, 1564. 155 numb. lvs;4to. Edited by Jean Liébault. Included are refs to American plants. Thiébaud (La chasse) 337-338; cf.Arents 12. CtY; BN. 564/16

Fallopius, Gabriel. De morbo gallico liber . . . a Petro Angelo Agatho [i.e., Giovanni Bonacci] . . . scriptus . . . Additum etiam est . . . De morbo gallico tractatus, Antonii Fracanciani. *Padua: L.Bertellio & Co., & C. Griffio*, 1564. 2pts;illus.;4to. The 1st chapt., 'Praefatio de origine eius [i.e., of syphilis]', discusses American source & Columbus's interpretation of wind currents (later adopted by Guicciardini) as basis for voyages. Pt 2 has t.p. dated 1563 but 1564 colophon. Adams (Cambr.) F140. CtY-M, DFo, NNAM; BL, BN. 564/17

Ferrier, Auger. De lue hispanica sive morbo gallico lib. 2. *Paris: G.Gilles*, 1564. 121p.;8vo. 1st publ., Toulouse, 1553. DNLM, MnU-B, NNNAM; BL, BN. 564/18

___[Anr edn]. De pudendagra, lue hispanica, libri duo. Adjecimis De radice cina & sarza parilla Hieronymi Cardani judicimus. *Antwerp: Widow of M.Nuyts*, 1564. 53 numb. lvs;8vo. Adams (Cambr.) F310; Waller 3010. DNLM; BL, BN. 564/19

Fioravanti, Leonardo. De capricci medicinali . . . Di nuovo corretti, et in molti luoghi ampliati, & ristampati. *Venice: L.degli Avanzi*, 1564. 271 numb.lvs;illus.;8vo. 1st publ., Venice, 1561. DNLM. 564/20

_____. Del compendio de i secreti rationali . . . libri cinque. *Venice: V.Valgrisi*, 1564. 183

numb.lvs;8vo. In bk 1, ch.46 describes syphilis & its treatment, utilizing Guaiacum & sarsaparilla. Adams (Cambr.) F488. DNLM, MiU; BL.   564/21

Fracanzano, Antonio.   De morbo gallico fragmenta quaedam elegantissima ex lictionibus anni 1563 Bononiae. *Padua: C.Griffio*, 1563 [colophon: 1564]. 16 numb.lvs;4to. Issued as pt 2 of Gabriel Falloppius's *De morbo gallico* of this year. Includes chapts on use of sarsaparilla & Guaiacum. CtY-M, DNLM, NNNAM; BL.   564/22

—[Anr edn]. . . . Nunc recens a mendis, quibus in prima editione circunfluebat vindicatus . . . a Camillo Cochio. *Bologna: P.Bonardo*, 1564. 26 numb.lvs;4to. DNLM.   564/23

Gómara, Francisco López de.   Historia delle nuove Indie Occidentali . . . tradotta . . . per Agostino di Cravaliz. *Venice: G.Bonadio*, 1564. 312 numb.lvs;8vo. 1st publ. in this version, Rome, 1556. Published uniformly, as pt 2, in this year with P.Cieza de León's *Historia, over Cronica del . . . Peru*. Sabin 27740; Medina (BHA) 159n (I:270); Wagner (SW) 2u; Streit II:775; JCB (3) I:224-225. DLC, MnU, NN-RB; Göttingen: UB.   564/24

——. Historia, di Don Fernando Cortes . . . con le sue maravigliose prodezze . . . che discoprî, & acquistò la Nuova Spagna. *Venice: G.Bonadio*, 1564. 355 numb.lvs;8vo. 1st publ. in this version as pt 2 of the author's *Historia generale delle Indie Occidentali*, Rome, 1555. Published uniformly, as pt 3, in this year with P. Cieza de León's *Historia, over Cronica del . . . Peru*. Sabin 27741; Medina (BHA) 159n (I:271); Wagner (SW) 2v; Streit II:776. DLC, ICN, MiU-C, NNH (imp.); Göttingen: UB.
                                        564/25

Guicciardini, Francesco.   Dell' historia d'Italia. *Venice: G.Giolito de' Ferrari*, 1564. 477p.;4to. 1st publ., Florence, 1561. CtY, ICN, InU-L, MH; BN.   564/26

Honter, Johannes.   Rudimentorum cosmographicorum . . . libri iii. *Zurich: C.Froschauer*, 1564. [60]p.;illus.,maps;8vo. 1st publ. in this version, Kronstadt, 1542. In verse. DLC, InU-L.   564/27

Lonitzer, Adam.   Kreuterbuch, neu zugericht. *Frankfurt a.M.: C.Egenolff*, 1564. 343 numb.lvs;illus.;fol. 1st publ. in German, Frankfurt a.M., 1557. Pritzel 5599n; Nissen (Bot.) 1227n. MnU-B.   564/28

Maggi, Girolamo.   Variarum lectionum, seu Miscellaneorum libri iiii. *Venice: G.Ziletti*, 1564. 220 numb.lvs;8vo. On recto of lf 20 is ref. to discovery by Vespucci of an island of giants. Adams (Cambr.) M127. CU, DLC, MiU, NN-RB, RPJCB; BL, BN.   564/29

Meneses, Felipe de.   Luz de alma christiana. *Seville: S.Trugillo*, 1564. 148 numb.lvs;4to. 1st publ., Seville, 1555. Palau 164444n. BN.
                                        564/30

Mexía, Pedro.   Della selva di varia lettione. *Venice: G.de' Cavalli*, 1564. 4to. 1st publ. with section on New World by F.Sansovino, Venice, 1559-60. Cf.Sabin 48239; Palau 167291. BL.   564/31

——. Historia ymperial y cesarea . . . nuevamente emendada y corregida. *Seville: S.Trugillo*, 1564. 334 numb.lvs;fol. 1st publ., Seville, 1545. Escudero (Seville) 615; Adams (Cambr.) M1383. CU, IU; Cambridge: Corp. Christ., Madrid: BN.   564/32

——. Vilvaltige Beschreibung christenlicher unnd heidnischer Keyseren Künigen . . . verteutscht [von Luc. Zoleckhofer]. *Basel: H.Petri & P.Perna*, 1564. ccclix p.;fol. 1st publ. in Spanish, Seville, 1545. Palau 167360. MnU-B, NNG.   564/33

Moleti, Giuseppe.   Discorso universale . . . nelquale son raccolti, & dichiarati tutti i termini, & tutte le regole appartenenti alla geografia. *Venice: G.Ziletti*, 1564. 47p.;4to. *In* C.Ptolemaeus, *La geografia*, Venice, 1564, q.v.   564/34

Münster, Sebastian.   Cosmographey oder beschreibung aller länder. *Basel: H.Petri*, 1564. 1475p.;illus.,maps;fol. 1st publ. in German, Basel, 1544. Sabin 51390; Burmeister (Münster) 75; JCB (3) I:225. DLC, MH, PPAmP, RPJCB; BL, Munich: StB.   564/35

Nauclerus, Johannes.   Chronicon . . . Cum appendice usque ad 1564 per L. Surium congesta. *Cologne: Heirs of J. Quentel & G.Calenius*, 1564. 2v.;fol. The earliest edn to include, under years 1500 & 1558, refs to Columbus, Vespucci & New World. Adams (Cambr.) N73-74. MdBP; Cambridge: UL.   564/36

Opere burlesche . . . *Venice: D.Giglio*, 1564-66. 2v.;8vo. 1st publ. as here collected, Florence, 1548. Included are F.Berni's 'Capitolo secondo de la peste', & G.F.Bini's 'Capitolo del mal francese', both 1st publ., Venice, 1538. Cf.Proksch I:82; Ind.aur.117.707 & 117.709; Shaaber B259(v.1). CSt, ICN, MH, PU(v.1); BL.   564/37

Paracelsus. Holtzbüchlein . . . darinnen gründtlich der recht nutz und gebrauch des Frantzosen holtzes . . . reichlich würt angezaight. *Strassburg: C.Müller*, 1564. [45]p.; 8vo. Sudhoff (Paracelsus) 61. BL.　　564/38

Polo, Gaspar Gil. Primera parte de Diana enamorada. *Valencia: J.Mey*, 1564. 150 numb.lvs;8vo. In verse. Includes refs to New World & its riches. Palau 102074. NNH; BL.　　564/39

Ptolemaeus, Claudius. La geografia . . . Nuovamente tradotta di greco . . . de Jeronimo Ruscelli. *Venice: G.Ziletti*, 1564. 3pts; illus.,maps;4to. 1st publ., Venice, 1561. Includes also Ruscelli's *Espositioni et introduttioni universali . . . sopra tutta la geografia* & G.Moleto's *Discorso universale*. A reissue of the 1561 edn, with altered title pages. Sabin 66504; Stevens (Ptolemy) 51; Phillips (Atlases) 373; Shaaber P603; JCB (3) I:225. DLC, ICN, MH, NN-RB, PU, RPJCB; BL, BN.　　564/40

Rabelais, François. Les oeuvres. *Lyons:* 1564. 2pts;16mo. Includes 'Le quart livre,' 1st publ., Paris, 1552. Plan (Rabelais) 98. CtY, MH; BL.　　564/41

Recueil de la diversité des habits qui sont de present en usaige tout és pays d'Europe, Asie, Affrique et Illes sauvages. *Paris: R.Breton*, 1564. 64 lvs;illus.;8vo. 1st publ., Paris, 1562. Sabin 68432n; Mortimer (France) 453. MH, NNC.　　564/42

Ronsard, Pierre de. Continuation du Discours des miseres de ce temps. *Paris: G.Buon*, 1564. 10 lvs;4to. 1st publ., Paris, 1562. Tchémerzine IX:440.　　564/43

__[Anr edn]. *Lyons:* 1564. 8 lvs;8vo. A piracy. Tchémerzine IX:440. Paris: Arsenal.　　564/44

Ruscelli, Girolamo. Espositioni et introduttioni universali . . . sopra tutta la Geografia di Tolomeo. *Venice: G.Ziletti*, 1564. [54]p.; maps;4to. *In* C.Ptolemaeus, *La geografia*, Venice, 1564, q.v. 1st publ., Venice, 1561.　　564/45

____, comp. Lettere di principi . . . Libro primo . . . Seconda edizione. *Venice: G.Ziletti*, 1564. 230 numb.lvs;4to. 1st publ., Venice, 1562, the letter of Oviedo y Valdés to Cardinal Bembo here appearing on lvs 149-152. Sabin 40563. DFo, MB, NN-RB, RPJCB; BL, BN.　　564/46

Sacro Bosco, Joannes de. Sphaera . . . emendata. Eliae Vineti . . . Scholia. *Paris: G.Cavellat*, 1564. 102 numb.lvs;illus;8vo. 1st publ.

with Vinet's *Scholia*, Paris, 1551. Cf. Sabin 32681; Adams (Cambr.) H732. NN-RB; BL.　　564/47

__[Anr edn]. *Lyons: S.Barbier, for Heirs of J. Giunta*, 1564. 107p.;illus.;8vo. Baudrier (Lyons) VI:312. CU, NN-RB, WU; Avignon: Mus. Calvet.　　564/48

Zárate, Augustín de. De wonderlijcke ende warachtighe historie vant coninckrijck van Peru. *Antwerp: W.Silvius*, 1564. 206 numb. lvs;illus.,map;8vo. 1st publ. in Dutch, Antwerp, 1563, here a reissue with altered imprint date. Sabin 106273n. MB; Strasbourg: BN.　　564/49

1565

Amatus Lusitanus. Curationum medicinalium centuriae duae, tertia et quarta. *Lyons: G.Rouillé*, 1565. 647p.;16mo. 1st publ., Lyons (?), 1556. Ind.aur.104.565; Baudrier (Lyons) IX:300; Adams (Cambr.) A914. DNLM, PPC; Cambridge: UL, Munich: StB.　　565/1

Benzoni, Girolamo. La historia del Mondo Nuovo . . . la qual tratta dell' isole, & mari nuovamente ritrovati, et delle nuove città da lui proprio vedute . . . in quattordeci anni. *Venice: F.Rampazetto*, 1565. 175 numb.lvs; illus.,port.;8vo. Sabin 4790; Medina (BHA) 250n (I:418); Streit II:789; Ind.aur.116.985; Arents 10. CtY, DLC, MH, MiU-C, MnU, NN-A, RPJCB; BL, BN.　　565/2

__[Anr issue]. *Venice: F.Rampazetto, for Gabriel Benzoni*, 1565. Ind.aur.116.985n. BL.　　565/3

Bock, Hieronymus. Kreutterbuch. *Strassburg: J.Rihel*, 1565. ccccxiii lvs;illus.;fol. 1st publ. with illus., Strassburg, 1546. Pritzel 866n; Nissen (Bot.) 182n; Ind.aur.120.596. NcD; Berlin: StB.　　565/4

Botallo, Leonardo. Commentarii duo, alter de medici, alter de aegroti munere. *Lyons: S. Gryphius*, 1565. 627p.;illus.;8vo. Includes Botallo's *Luis venereae curandae ratio*, 1st publ. separately, Paris, 1563. Adams (Cambr.) B2541; Ind.aur.122.674. DNLM, PPC; BL, BN.　　565/5

Bref recueil de l'affliction et dispersion de l'eglise des fideles au pays du Bresil . . . ou est contenu . . . le voyage & navigation, faicte par Nicolas de Vill'gaignon. [*Orléans:*] 1565. [72]p.;8vo. Abridged from the [Geneva?] 1561

Histoire des choses memorables advenues en la terre du Bresil. Sabin 99728n; Borba de Moraes I:109; Atkinson (Fr.Ren.) 151; Cioranescu (XVI) 21853. BL.   565/6

Castile. Laws, statutes, etc., 1252-1284. Las siete partidas . . . nuevamente glosadas, por . . . Gregório López. *Salamanca: A. de Portonariis*, 1565. 7v.;fol. 1st publ. with López's notes with American refs, Salamanca, 1555. Palau 7092. C, DLC, IU, MH.   565/7

Coppie d'une lettre venant de la Floride envoyée a Rouen, et depuis au seigneur d'Everon: ensemble le plan et portraict du fort que les François y ont faict. *Paris: V. Normant & J.Bruneau*, 1565. [16]p.;12mo. Sabin 24854 & 99605n; Atkinson (Fr.Ren.) 143A; Adams (Laudonnière) 3; JCB (3) I:227. RPJCB.   565/8

Cooper, Thomas, Bp of Winchester. Thesaurus linguae romanae & britannicae. *London: H.Wykes*, 1565. [1086]p.;fol. Includes definition & discussion of Guaiacum, & in 'Dictionarium historicum' describes America as discovered by Vespucci. STC 5686; Shaaber C667. CSmH, CtY, DFo, ICU, MWA, NNRB, PU, RP; BL.   565/9

Crespin, Jean. Actes des martyrs deduits en sept livres, depuis le temps de Wiclef & de Hus. *[Geneva:] J.Crespin*, 1565. 1084p.;fol. 1st publ., [Geneva], 1564; here a reissue with altered imprint date. BN.   565/10

Du Bois, Jean. De morbi articularii curatione tractatus quatuor . . . De morbo gallico declamatio. *Antwerp: C.Plantin*, 1565. 102p.; 8vo. DNLM, NNNAM; BL.   565/11

Emili, Paolo. De rebus gestis Francorum libri x. Arnoldi Ferroni . . . De rebus item gestis Gallorum libri novem. *Paris: M.de Vascovan*, 1565. 2pts;fol. 1st publ. with LeFerron's appendix, Paris, 1548. Ind.aur. 100.833. BN.
565/12

Estienne, Charles. L'agriculture et maison rustique. *Antwerp: C.Plantin*, 1565. 155 numb.lvs;4to. 1st publ., Paris, 1564; here a reissue with cancel t.p. Cf.Bibl.belg.,1st ser.,X:38; Thiébaud (La chasse) 338-339; Adams (Cambr.) S1720; cf.Arents (Add.) 28. Cambridge: Sidney Sussex.   565/13

—[Anr issue]. *Paris: J.DuPuys*, 1565. Thiébaud (La chasse) 339; Arents (Add.) 28n.   565/14

—[Anr edn]. *Lyons: J.Martin*, 1565. 565p.;8vo. Thiébaud (La chasse) 339.   565/15

Falloppius, Gabriel. De morbo gallico liber

absolotissimus . . . Additum etiam est . . . De morbo gallico tractatus, Antonii Fracanciani . . . 2da ed. *Venice: F.Lorenzini*, 1565. 2pts; 8vo. 1st publ., Padua, 1564; Fracanzano's work 1st publ. separately, Bologna, 1564. Moranti (Urbino) 1427. DNLM, WU; BL, Urbino: BU.   565/16

____. Secreti diversi et miracolosi, nuovamente ristampati. *Venice: M.di Maria*, 1565. 366p.;8vo. 1st publ., Venice, 1563. BL.
565/17

Fernel, Jean. Opera medicinalia. *Venice: R. Borgominieri*, 1565. 659p.;4to. Includes also Fernel's De abditis rerum causis, 1st publ., Paris, 1548. Sherrington (Fernel) 55.H1. CtY, DNLM, MB, PPC.   565/18

Fioravanti, Leonardo. De capricci medicinali . . . Di nuovo corretti, et in molti luoghi ampliati, & ristampati. *Venice: L.degli Avanzi*, 1565. 271 numb.lvs;8vo. 1st publ., Venice, 1561; here a reissue of printer's 1564 edn? BL.
565/19

Fracanzano, Antonio. De morbo gallico fragmenta. *Venice: F.Lorenzini*, 1565. 14 [i.e., 24] numb.lvs;8vo. 1st publ., Padua, 1564. Issued as pt 2 of Gabriel Falloppius's De morbo gallico of this year, q.v.   565/20

Francisco de Vitoria. Relectiones undecim. Per . . . Alfonsum Muñoz . . . a . . . vitiis . . . repurgatae. *Salamanca: J.à Cánova*, 1565. 423 numb.lvs;8vo. 1st publ., Lyons, 1557. Sabin 100619; Palau 371066. DCU, MH, MiU-L; BL, Madrid: BN.   565/21

Fregoso, Battista. Factorum, dictorumque memorabilium libri ix. *Antwerp: J.Bellère*, 1565. 798p.;8vo. 1st publ., Milan, 1509. Sabin 26140n; Belg.typ. (1541-1600) I:1197. BL, BN.   565/22

Gesner, Konrad. Euonymus [pseud.] . . . de remediis secretis. *[Zurich: C.Froschauer*, ca. 1565]. 202 numb.lvs;illus.:8vo. 1st publ., Zurich, 1552. Adams (Cambr.) G529. Cambridge: UL.   565/23

____. A new booke of destillatyon of waters, called the Treasure of Euonymus . . . Translated . . . out of Latin, by Peter Morwyng. *London: J.Day*, 1565. 408p.;illus.;4to. 1st publ. in English, London, 1559, under title *The treasure of Euonymus.* STC 11801. CtY-M, DFo, NNNAM; BL.   565/24

Giglio, Girolamo. Nuova seconda selva di varia lettione. *Venice: C. & F.Franceschini*, 1565. 207 numb.lvs;4to. Supplements Pedro

Mexía's *Selva di varia lettione*. Provides account of discovery of New World; discusses introduction of syphilis to Europe by Columbus's crew & use of Guaiacum in its treatment. Palau 167292; Adams (Cambr.) G606. ICU, InU-L; BL. 565/25

Gómara, Francisco López de. La seconda parte delle Historia dell' India. *Venice: G.Ziletti*, 1565. 324 numb.lvs;8vo. 1st publ. as here transl. by Lucio Mauro, Venice, 1557. Continues the same printer's edn of Pedro Cieza de León's *La prima parte dell'Historie del Peru* of 1560. The 3d pt, also by Gómara, appeared in 1566. Sabin 27739 & 13052; Wagner (SW) 2x; Streit II:790; JCB (3) I:227. CU-B, DFo, ICN, NN-RB, RPJCB; BL. 565/26

Guicciardini, Francesco. La historia d'Italia. *Venice: N.Bevilacqua*, 1565. 470 lvs;4to. 1st publ., Florence, 1561. DFo, ICN; BN. 565/27

Hese, Joannes de. Peregrinatio . . . ab urbe Hierusalem instituta, et per Indiam, Aethiopiam, aliasque . . . nationes ducta. *Antwerp: J.Verwithagen*, 1565. [79]p.;8vo. Includes (lvs F1-H3), with special t.p., the 'De orbis situ, ac descriptione' of Franciscus, o.f.m., 1st publ., Antwerp [1529?]. Sabin 25465n & 57642; Harrisse (BAV) 131n; Belg.typ. (1541-1600) I:1425. CtY, DLC, MH, NN-RB (Franciscus only), RPJCB (Franciscus only); BL. 565/28

Honter, Johannes. Rudimentorum cosmographicorum . . . libri iii. *Zurich: C.Froschauer*, 1565. [60]p.;illus.,maps;8vo. 1st publ. in this version, Kronstadt, 1542. In verse. Sabin 32797; JCB (3) I:228. MnU-B, NN-RB, RPJCB. 565/29

Jesuits. Letters from missions. Diversi avisi particolari dall' Indie di Portogallo, ricevuti dall'anno 1551. sino al 1558. *Venice: M.Tramezzino*, 1565. 294 numb.lvs;8vo. Includes 19 letters written from Brazil. Cf.Sabin 56340; Borba de Moraes I:53; Streit II:1284. CSmH, DLC, MH, MiU, MnU-B, NN-RB. 565/30

————. Nuovi avisi delle Indie di Portogallo . . . Quarta parte. *Venice: M.Tramezzino*, 1565. 189 numb.lvs;8vo. Continues the Jesuit *Nuovi avisi* of 1562. Included are 3 letters written from Brazil. Sabin 56340n; Borba de Moraes I:51; Streit II:1285 (& IV:913); Arents (Add.) 25. CU, ICN, MH, MdBP, NN-RB; Munich: StB. 565/31

La Place, Pierre de. Commentaires de l'estat de la religion et republique soubs les rois Henry & François seconds, & Charles neufieme. [*Rouen? A. Clémence*] 1565. 287 lvs;8vo. Includes an account of Villegagnon's attempted Brazilian colony. On reasons for assigning priority to this edition, and its printing to Clémence, see George Clutton, ' "Abel Clemence" of "Rouen": a sixteenth-century secret press', *The Library*, 4th ser., XX (1939) 136-153. The numerous editions of this account of France's religious wars, all without place of printing or printer's name, await the attention of a zealous bibliographer, with a view to identifying both. It is probable that they were, at least in part, produced by Huguenot presses at Geneva. BL. 565/32

——[Anr edn]. [*Geneva?*] 1565. 312 numb.lvs;8vo. BN. 565/33

——[Anr edn]. [*France?*] 1565. 309 numb.lvs;8vo. MiEM, NcD. 565/34

——[Anr edn]. [*Geneva?*] 1565. 304 numb.lvs;8vo. Adams (Cambr.) L183. Cambridge: UL, BN. 565/35

——[Anr edn] [*Geneva?*] 1565. 282 numb. lvs;8vo. Adams (Cambr.) L184. ICN, MH, NjP; Cambridge: King's. 565/36

——[Anr edn]. [*France?*] 1565. 262 numb.lvs;8vo. IU; BN. 565/37

——[Anr edn]. [*France?*] 1565. 130 numb.lvs;8vo. Adams (Cambr.) L182. Cambridge: Christ Church. 565/38

Lopes de Castanheda, Fernão. Warhafftige und volkomene Historia, von erfindung Calecut und andere Königreich Landen und Inseln in Indien . . . Auss frantzösischer Sprach . . . gebracht. [*Augsburg?*] 1565. 765p.;8vo. Transl. from French edn, 1st publ., Paris, 1553; orig. publ. in Portuguese, Coimbra, 1551. Includes 1st book only, with passing refs to Brazil. Sabin 11390; Borba de Moraes I:142; JCB (3) I:229. InU-L, NNH, RPJCB. 565/39

Magnus, Olaus, Abp of Upsala. Historia delle genti e della natura delle cose settentrionali . . . nuovamente tradotta. *Venice: D. Nicolini,for the Heirs of L.A.Giunta*, 1565. 286 numb.lvs;illus.,map;fol. Transl. from Magnus's *Historia de gentibus septentrionalibus*, 1st publ., Rome, 1555. Sabin 43831n; Collijn (Sver.bibl.) II:330-332; JCB (3) I:229. CLU, DLC, InU-L, MH-Z, MnU-B, NN-RB, RPJCB; BL, BN. 565/40

Massa, Niccolò. Il libro del mal francese . . . Nuovamente tradotto . . . di latino. *Venice:*

G.*Ziletti*, 1565. 320p.;8vo. Transl. from Massa's *Liber de morbo gallico*, 1st publ., [Venice?], 1532. NcD-M; London: Wellcome.
565/41

Mattioli, Pietro Andrea. Commentarii in sex libros . . . Dioscoridis Anazarbei De medica materia. *Venice: V.Valgrisi*, 1565. 1459p.; illus.,port.;fol. 1st publ., Venice, 1554. Cf.Pritzel 2309; Nissen (Bot.) 1305n; Adams (Cambr.) D672. CtY-M, DNLM, MH, NN-RB, RPB; BL, BN.
565/42

Mexía, Pedro. Della selva di varia lettione. *Venice: N.Bevilacqua*, 1565. 438 numb.lvs; 8vo. 1st publ. with section on New World by F.Sansovino, Venice, 1559-60. Cf.Sabin 48239; Adams (Cambr.) M1386. InU-L; Cambridge: UL.
565/43

____. Ragionamenti . . . nei quali . . . trattandosi di diverse materie, si ha cognitione di molte, & varie cose . . . Tradotti dal sig. Alfonso Ulloa. *Venice: A.Ravenoldo*, 1565. 111 numb.lvs;8vo. 1st publ. in Italian, Venice, 1557, under title *Dialoghi*. Palau 167381. CtY, ICN, InU-L; BN.
565/44

Monardes, Nicolás. Dos libros. El uno trata de todos las cosas que traen de nostras Indias Occidentales, que sirven al uso de medicina . . . El otro libro, trata de dos medicinas maravillosas. *Seville: S.Trugillo*, 1565. [263]p.;8vo. Medina (BHA) 194; Guerra (Monardes) 7; Escudero (Seville) 618; JCB AR30:16-18. DNLM, NN-RB, PPC, RPJCB; London: Wellcome, BN.
565/45

More, Sir Thomas, Saint. Omnia . . . latina opera. *Louvain: P.Zangrius*, 1565. 136 numb.lvs;fol. Includes the *Utopia*, 1st publ., Louvain, 1516. Belg.typ. (1541-1600) I:4524; Gibson (More) 75b. CtY, RPJCB; BL, BN.
565/46

—[Anr issue] *Louvain: J.Bogardus*, 1565. Belg.-typ. (1541-1600) I:4523; Adams (Cambr.) M1749; Gibson (More) 75a. ICN; BL, Brussels: BR.
565/47

Münster, Sebastian. La cosmographie universelle. *Basel: H.Petri*, 1565. 1337p.;illus., maps,ports;fol. 1st publ. in French, Basel, 1552. Atkinson (Fr.Ren.) 158; Burmeister (Münster) 95. MH, MiU-C; BN.
565/48

Nel Bresil di san Vicenzo nella citta di Santes . . . è apparso questo mostro su la riva del mare. *Venice*: 1565. bds.;illus.;fol. Cf. German edns of this year with title *Newe Zeytung*

von einem seltzamen Meerwunder. Borba de Moraes II:98. Zurich: StB.
565/49

Newe Zeytung von einem seltzamen Meerwunder so sich diss nechst verschienen lxiiii Jar in Land Bresilia bei der State Santes. *Augsburg: M.Franck* [1565]. bds.;illus.;fol. Borba de Moraes II:97-98; Weller (Ersten d. Zeitungen) 287. Zurich: StB.
565/50

__[Anr edn]. [*Frankfurt*: 1565?]. bds.;illus.;fol. Borba de Moraes II:97-98. Zurich: StB.
565/51

Opere burlesche, Il primo libro delle. *Venice: D.Giglio*, 1565. 8vo. A reissue (?) of the printer's 1564 edn of this vol. Ind.aur. 117.708. Milan: Bibl. Trivulziana.
565/52

Paracelsus. Drey Bücher . . . Wider getruckt, und gemehrt. *Strassburg: C.Müller*, 1565. [87]p.;8vo. Includes the author's *Höltzbüchlin*, 1st publ., Strassburg, 1564. Sudhoff (Paracelsus) 68. CLSU, DNLM, NNNAM, PPHa; BL.
565/53

____. Drey nützlicher Bücher . . . von der Frantzösischen kranckheyt. *Nuremberg: C. Heussler*, 1565. [198]p.;8vo. 1st publ., Nuremberg, 1530; here reprinted from 1552 edn. Sudhoff (Paracelsus) 72. Rothenburg: Lateinschule.
565/54

____. Opus chirurgicum . . . Wund und Artzney Buch. Darinnen begriffen welchermassen allerhandt Kränck . . . als offne Wunden . . . Frantzosen . . . und dergleichen gefährliche kranckheiten. *Frankfurt a.M.: M.Lechler,for S.Feyerabend & S.Hüter*, 1565. cccccccvi p.; illus.;fol. Sudhoff (Paracelsus) 69. DNLM; London: Wellcome.
565/55

Pysière, Giles de. Discours de l'entreprinse et saccagement que les forsaires de l'isle Floride avoient conclud de faire à leurs capitaines & gouverneurs, estans mis en liberté. Avec la descriptions des bestes sauvages tant marines que terrestres . . . dans le circuit de la Floride. *Paris: P.de Langres*, 1565. [14]p.;illus.;4to. Atkinson (Fr.Ren.) 160. Paris: Mazarine.
565/56

Rabelais, François. Les oeuvres. *Lyons*: 1565. 3pts;16mo. Includes 'Le quart livre,' 1st publ., Paris, 1552. Plan (Rabelais) 99. NjP.
565/57

Ramusio, Giovanni Battista. Terzo volume delle Navigationi et viaggi. *Venice: Heirs of L.Giunta*, 1565. 453 numb.lvs;illus.,maps;fol. 1st publ., Venice, 1556, but with illus. & maps here re-engraved. Sabin 67741; Streit I:96;

Adams (Cambr.) R140; Church 99; Shaaber R21; JCB (STL) 11. CSmH, InU-L, MH, PU, RPJCB; Cambridge: UL, BN. 565/58

Ronsard, Pierre de. Bergerie dediée à la Majesté de la Royne d'Escosse. [*Paris*: 1565]. In verse. Mentions enrichment of France through American commerce. Reprinted in v.1 of Ronsard's *Oeuvres*, Paris, 1567, etc. Le Moine 100. 565/59

Rostinio, Pietro. Trattato del mal francese. *Venice: G.de' Cavalli*, 1565. 87 numb.lvs;8vo. 1st publ., Venice, 1556. DNLM, MnU, PPC; BL. 565/60

1566

Alberti, Leandro. Descriptio totius Italiae . . . ex italica lingua nunc primum . . . conversa, interprete Guilelmo Kyriando Hoenigeno. *Cologne: N.Schreiber*, 1556. 826p.;fol. Transl. from author's *Descrittione di tutta Italia*, 1st publ., Bologna, 1550. Ind. aur.102 344; Adams (Cambr.) A470. Cambridge: Trinity, BN. 566/1

Amatus Lusitanus. Curationum medicinalium . . . tomus primus-secundus. *Venice: V. Valgrisi*, 1556. 3v.;8vo. Contains all 7 Centuries; cf.years 1551, 1552, & 1556 for earlier separate printings. Ind.aur.104.566. DNLM, NNNAM, PPC; Munich: StB. 566/2

Antwerp. Ordonantie inhoudende de niew poincten vanden ommeganck halff ooght .1566. ghenaempt den tijt present. *Antwerp: H.de Laet*, 1566. Describes ceremonial tableau representing the world, incl. America. Belg.typ. (1541-1600) I:2262. Brussels: BR. 566/3

Apollonius, Levinus. De Peruviae regionis . . . libri v. *Antwerp: A.Tavernier,for J.Bellère*, 1566. 236 numb.lvs;map;8vo. Plagiarized from Augustín de Zárate's *De wonderlijcke ende warachtige historie vant coninckrijck van Peru*, Antwerp, 1563. Sabin 1761; Medina (BHA) 197; Ind.aur.106.493; Belg.typ. (1541-1600) I:145. DLC, MH, MnU-B, NN-RB, PPL; BL, BN. 566/4

Bodin, Jean. Methodus ad facilem historiarum cognitionem. *Paris: M.LeJeune*, 1566. 463p.;4to. In chapt.6 is a favorable ref. to Spanish undertakings in Africa & America; in chapt. 10 historians of the Americas are named: Columbus & Vespucci. Ind.aur. 120.802; Adams (Cambr.) B2241. DLC, ICN,

InU-L, MH, MiU, NN-RB; BL, BN. 566/5

Boemus, Johann. I costumi, le leggi et l'usanze di tutte le genti. *Venice: D. & A.Giglio*, 1566. 240 numb.lvs;8vo. 1st publ. in this version with G.Giglio's 4th book on the New World, Venice, 1558. Sabin 6119n; Ind. aur.120.961; Palau 31252n; JCB (3) I:230. DLC, ICN, MH-L, RPJCB; BL. 566/6

Brant, Sebastian. Das Narrenschiff. *Frankfurt a.M.: G.Rab & Heirs of W.Han*, 1566. 158 numb.lvs;illus.;8vo. 1st publ., Basel, 1494. Ind.aur.123.743. BL, Berlin: StB. 566/7

Cardano, Girolamo. Ars curandi parva. *Basel: S.Henricpetri*, 1566. 2v.;8vo. 1st publ. as here collected, Basel, 1564. Ind.aur.132.094; Adams (Cambr.) C650. CtY, DNLM, MH; BL, BN. 566/8

———. Les livres . . . intitulés De la subtilité, & subtiles inventions . . . traduis de latin . . . par Richard LeBlanc. *Paris: S.Calvarin*, 1566. 478 numb.lvs;illus.;8vo. 1st publ. in French, Paris, 1556; 1st published, Nuremberg, 1550, as *De subtilitate rerum*. Ind. aur.132.101. BL. 566/9

—[Anr issue]. *Paris: C.Micard*, 1566. Ind. aur.132.101. DLC, MH. 566/10

Chaves, Jerónimo de. Chronographia, ó Repertorio de los tiempos. *Seville: J.Gutiérrez*, 1566. 243 numb.lvs;illus.,maps,port.;4to. 1st publ., Seville, 1548. Medina (BHA) 196 (misn. 156); Escudero (Seville) 1566; Palau 67453. BL, Valencia: BM. 566/11

Copernicus, Nicolaus. De revolutionibus orbium coelestium libri vi. *Basel: H.Petri*, 1566. 213 numb.lvs;illus.;fol. 1st publ., Nuremberg, 1543. Adams (Cambr.) C2603. CU, CtY, DLC, InU-L, MH, MiU-C, NNNAM, RPB; BL, BN. 566/12

Copia de una carta venida de Sevilla a Miguel Salvador de Valencia. La qual narra el venturoso descubrimiento que los Mexicanos han hecho, navegando con la armada que su Magestad mando hazer en Mexico. *Barcelona: P.Cortey*, 1566. 2 lvs;4to. On expedition of M.López de Legazpi from Mexico to Philippines. Medina (BHA) 195; Retana (Filipinas) 7; JCB (101 Bks) 13. 566/13

Dioscorides, Pedanius. Acerca de la material medicinal . . . traduzido de lengua griega . . . & illustrado con . . . substantiales annotationes, y con las figuras de innumeras plantas . . . por el doctor Andres de Laguna. *Salamanca: M.Gast*, 1566. 616p.;illus.,port.;fol.

Laguna's annotations, with numerous refs to American plants, 1st publ. separately, Lyons, 1554, & in the present form, Antwerp, 1555. Cf.Pritzel 2313n; Palau 74023. DNLM, MH-A; BL, BN.   566/14

Discours des choses plus necessaires & dignes d'estre entendues en la cosmographie. *Paris: F.Morel*, 1566. 8vo. *See below*, Terraube, Galard de.   566/15

Dodoens, Rembert. Frumentorum, leguminum, palustrium et aquatilium herbarum ac eorum, quae eo pertinent historia. *Antwerp: C.Plantin*, 1566. 271p.;illus.;8vo. Includes (p.73-75) discussion of 'Frumentum turcicum', i.e., corn (maize). Pritzel 2346; Nissen (Bot.) 513n; Bibl.belg.,1st ser.,IX:D111; Adams (Cambr.) D716; Fairfax Murray (Germany) 136. DLC, ICJ, MH-A, MnU, NNNAM, PPL; BL, BN.   566/16

Emili, Paolo. De rebus gestis Francorum libri x. Arnoldi Ferroni . . . De rebus item gestis Gallorum libri novem. *Paris: M.de Vascovan*, 1566. 2pts;fol. 1st publ., Paris, 1548-49. Ind. aur.100.834; Adams (Cambr.) A240. DLC, ICN; Cambridge: King's.   566/17

Estienne, Charles. De landtwinninge ende hoeve . . . Uut de fransoysche sprake . . . overgheset. *Antwerp: C.Plantin*, 1566. 415p.;8vo. Transl. by Martin Everaert from the Plantin issue of previous year. Bibl. belg.,1st ser.,X:E38; Thiébaud (La chasse) 359. NNBG; Brussels: BR.   566/18

Falloppius, Gabriel. Opuscula . . . Accedit Gulielmi Rondeletii tractatus De fucis . . . Omnia haec Petri Angeli Agathi [i.e., Giovanni Bonacci] opera . . . edita. *Padua: L.Bertellio*, 1566. 2pts;4to. Includes the author's *De morbo gallico*, 1st publ., Padua, 1564, as well as Rondelet's work on the same subject, 1st publ., Paris, [1563?]. CtY-M, DNLM, NNNAM, PPC; BL, BN.   566/19

Fernel, Jean. Opera medicinalia. *Venice: F. Portonariis*, 1566. 659p.;4to. A reissue, with cancel t.p., of 1565 edn. Includes also Fernel's *De abditis rerum causis*, 1st publ., Paris, 1548. DNLM, ICU.   566/20

Fioravanti, Leonardo. Del compendio dei secreti rationali . . . libri cinque. *Venice: A.Ravenoldo*, 1566. 184 numb.lvs.;8vo. 1st publ., Venice, 1564. Adams (Cambr.) F489. London: Wellcome.   566/21

Goes, Damião de. Chronica do felicissimo rei Dom Emanuel. *Lisbon: F.Correa*, 1566-67.

4pts;fol. Includes account of Cabral's discovery of Brazil. For variant issue consult King Manuel's catalog. Sabin 27686; Borba de Moraes I:302-303; Adams (Cambr.) G818; Streit XV:1805; Anselmo 491; Arents (Add.) 26; King Manuel 115. DCU, InU-L, MH, MnU-B, NN-A, RPJCB; BL, BN.   566/22

Gómara, Francisco López de. La terza parte delle Historie dell' Indie. *Venice: G.Ziletti*, 1566. 402 numb.lvs;4to. Transl. by L.Mauro. Continues uniformly the author's *Seconda parte* of 1565, itself a continuation of P.de Cieza de León's *Prima parte* of 1560. Sabin 13052 (misdated 1556); Wagner (SW) 2y; JCB (3) I:233. ICN, NN-RB, RPJCB.   566/23

Guicciardini, Francesco. Historiarum sui temporis libri viginti . . . ex italico . . . conversi et editi, Caelio Secundo Curione interprete. *Basel: H.Petri & P.Perna*, 1566. 2v.; fol. Transl. from author's *La historia d'Italia*, 1st publ., Florence, 1561. Adams (Cambr.) G1522. ICN, MnU-B, PPL; BL, BN.   566/24

Le Challeux, Nicolas. Discours de l'histoire de la Floride, contenant la trahison des Espagnols. *Dieppe: J.LeSellier*, 1566. 54p.;12mo. An account of Jean Ribaut's final voyage. Sabin 39631; Atkinson (Fr.Ren.) 169A; Adams (Laudonnière) 4; JCB (101 Bks) 15. MH, NN-RB.   566/25

—[Anr edn]. Discours de l'histoire de la Floride, contenant la cruauté des Espagnols. [*Paris?*] 1566. 62p.;8vo. Sabin 39633; Atkinson (Fr.Ren.) 169; Adams (Laudonnière) 5; JCB (3) I:231-232. RPJCB; BN.   566/26

—[Anr edn]. Discours et histoire de ce qui est advenu en la Floride. [*Paris?*] 1566. 56p.;8vo. Cf.Sabin 39633; Atkinson (Fr.Ren.) 170; Adams (Laudonnière) 6. BL, Paris: Arsenal.   566/27

—[Anr edn]. Histoire memorable du dernier voyages aux Indes, lieu appelé la Floride. *Lyons: J.Saugrain*, 1566. 71p.;8vo. Sabin 39634; Atkinson (Fr.Ren.) 168A; Adams (Laudonnière) 7; JCB (3) I:232. RPJCB.   566/28

———. A true and perfect description, of the last voyage . . . attempted by . . . French men into Terra Florida. *London: H.Denham,for T.Hacket* [1566]. [56]p.;8vo. Transl. from preceding work. Sabin 39635; STC 15347; Adams (Laudonnière) 8. BL.   566/29

Lucidarius. M. Elucidarius von allerhand Geschöpffen Gottes . . . und wie alle

Creaturen geschaffen seind auff erden. *Frankfurt a.M.: Heirs of C.Egenolff*, 1566. [102]p.; illus.;4to. 1st publ., Strassburg, [ca.1535]. Schorbach (Lucidarius) 59. Munich: StB.
566/30

Luisini, Luigi, comp. De morbo gallico omnia quae extant apud omnes medicos. *Venice: G.Ziletti*, 1566-67. 3v.;fol. Includes, *infra alia*, G.F.de Oviedo y Valdés's 'De guaicano ligno', 1st publ., in Spanish, Toledo, 1526, in his *De la natural historia de las Indias*; U.von Hutten's *De Guaiaci medicina*, 1st publ., Mainz, 1519; and G.Torrella's work of same title, 1st publ:, Rome, 1497. Contains references to use of 'ligno indico' (Guaiacum) & sarsaparilla. Palau 335981; Adams (Cambr.) L1693; Sherrington (Fernel) 22.F6; Benzing (Hutten) 109. CtY, DNLM, ICJ, MH, NNNAM, PPL; BL, BN.
566/31

Massa, Niccolò. Il libro del mal francese . . . Nuovamente tradotto . . . di latino. *Venice: G.Ziletti*, 1566. 320p.;8vo. 1st publ. in Italian, Venice, 1565. Moranti (Urbino) 2133. CtY-M, DFo, DNLM; Urbino: BU.
566/32

Mattioli, Pietro Andrea. Les commentaires . . . sur les six livres des simples de Pedacius Dioscoride . . . Traduit du latin [par Antoine Du Pinet] . . . Seconde impression, revue et augmentee. *Lyons: J.d'Ogerolles, for the Widow of G.Cotier*, 1566. 538p.;illus.;fol. 1st publ. in French, Lyons, 1561. Cf.Pritzel 5991; Nissen (Bot.) 1312n; Baudrier (Lyons) IV:77-78. DNLM, MH-Ed.
566/33

Medina, Pedro de. Libro de grandezas y cosas memorables de España. *Alcalá de Henares: P. de 'Robles & J. de Villanueva, for L.Gutiérrez*, 1566. clxxxvii lvs;illus.,map;fol. 1st publ., Alcalá de Henares, 1548. Medina (BHA) 198; García (Alcalá de Henares) 395. DLC, InU-L, MnU-B, NN-RB; Madrid: BN.
566/34

Mellini, Domenico. Descrizione dell' entrata della sereniss. Reina Giovanna d'Austria et dell' apparato, fatto in Firenze. *Florence: Heirs of B.Giunta*, 1566. 119p.;8vo. Includes mention of Vespucci & accounts of maritime discoveries, incl. Peru. Sabin 47453; Adams (Cambr.) M1224; Shaaber M283. DLC, MH, NHi, PU; BL.
566/35

—[Anr edn]. . . . Ristampata & riveduta dal proprio autore. *Florence: Heirs of B.Giunta*, 1566. 128p.;8vo. Adams (Cambr.) M1225. CtY, DLC, InU-L, RPJCB; BL.
566/36

—[Anr edn] . . . Rivedutta, & corretta & . . . stampata la terza volta. *Florence: Heirs of B. Giunta*, 1566. 128p.;8vo. NN-RB.
566/37

Mexía, Pedro. Trois dialogues . . . touchant la nature du soleil, de la terre et de toutes les choses qui se font et apparoissent en l'air. *Paris: F.Morel*, 1566. 32 lvs;8vo. Transl. by Marie de Coste-Blanche from the author's *Colóquios o Dialogos*, 1st publ., Seville, 1547. Palau 167383.
566/38

Mizauld, Antoine. Cosmographie seu Mundo sphaerae, libri tres. *Paris: F.Morel*, 1566. 72p.;8vo. 1st publ., Paris, 1552, under title *De mundi sphaera*. NN-RB; BN.
566/39

More, Sir Thomas, Saint. Omnia . . . latina opera. *Louvain: P.Zangrius*, 1566. 136 numb.lvs;fol. Includes the *Utopia*, 1st publ., Louvain, 1516; here a reissue of the bookseller's 1565 edn. Belg.typ. (1541-1600) I:4525; Adams (Cambr.) M1750; Gibson (More) 76b. CSmH, CtY, DLC, NNUT, MH; BL, BN.
566/40

—[Anr issue]. *Louvain: J.Bogardus*, 1566. Like the above, a reissue of the bookseller's 1565 edn. Adams (Cambr.) M1751; Gibson (More) 76a. CLSU, CtY, MH, NNU-W; BL.
566/41

Requeste au Roy, faite en forme de complainctes par les femmes vefves, & enfans orphelins, parens & amis de ses subiects, qui ont esté cruellement massacrez par les Espagnols, en la France antartique, nommee la Floride. [*Paris?*] 1566. [12]p.;8vo. On the Ribaut massacre. Atkinson (Fr.Ren.) 169B; Adams (Laudonnière) 13. Aix-en-Provence: Bibl. Méjanes.
566/41a

Ruscelli, Girolamo, comp. Le imprese illustri, con espositioni et discorsi. *Venice: F. Rampazetto, for D.Zenaro*, 1566. 567p.; illus.;4to. The section on Charles V contains refs to Columbus & Sebastian Cabot. Mortimer (Italy) 449. ICN, InU-L, MH, NN-RB; BL, BN.
566/42

Sacro Bosco, Joannes de. Sphaera . . . emendata . . . Intersecta etiam sunt Eliae Vineti . . . Scholia. *Antwerp: Heirs of A.Birckmann*, 1566. 2 pts;illus.;8vo. 1st publ. with Vinet's *Scholia*, Paris, 1551. Cf.Sabin 32681. DLC, DFo, ICJ; London: Wellcome.
566/43

—[Anr edn]. *Antwerp: J.Richard*, 1566. 144p.;illus.;8vo. NN-RB.
566/44

—[Anr edn]. *Cologne: M.Cholinus*, 1566. 101 numb.lvs;illus.;8vo. Sabin 32680. MiU.
566/45

Scaliger, Julius Caesar. In libros de plantis Aristoteli inscriptos, commentarii. [*Geneva*:] *J.Crespin*, 1566. 143p.;fol. 1st publ., Paris, 1556. Adams (Cambr.) S584; Shaaber S235. DNLM, MH, PU; Cambridge: Emmanuel, BN.   566/46

——[Anr issue]. *Geneva: J.Crespin*, 1566. Pritzel 8088n; Adams (Cambr.) S585. Cambridge: UL, BN.   566/47

——[Anr issue]. [*Geneva: J.Crespin,for*] *G.Rouillé,at Lyons*, 1566. Adams (Cambr.) S586. ICU, InU, MBH, MiU, MnU, RPB; Cambridge: Trinity.   566/48

Soto, Domingo de. Commentariorum . . . in quartum librum Sententiarum. Tomus primus[-secundus]. *Salamanca: J.M.à Terranova*, 1566. 2v.;fol. 1st publ., Salamanca, 1557-60. Adams (Cambr.) S1473 (v.2); Palau 320169. Cambridge: UL(v.2).   566/49

————. De justitia & jure libri decem. *Salamanca: J.M.à Terranova,for B.Boyer*, 1566. 895p.; fol. 1st publ., Salamanca, 1553. Palau 320144. MH-L.   566/50

Surius, Laurentius. Commentarius brevis rerum in orbe gestarum ab anno . . . millesimo quingentesimo, usque ad annum LXVI. *Cologne: Heirs of J.Quentel & G.Calenius*, 1566. 641p.;8vo. 1st publ., Cologne, 1564, as supplement to Nauclerus's *Chronicon*. Under year 1500 (p.79) refs to Columbus & Vespucci appear; under 1550 (i.e., 1558;p.578-587), extended discussion of New World. Cf.Sabin 93887. ICN, NN-RB, RPJCB.   566/51

Teluccini, Mario. Artemidoro . . . Dove si contengono le grandezze de gli antipodi. *Venice: D.& G.B.Guerra*, 1566. 467p.;4to. Chivalric poem, the hero being the son of an American emperor. DFo, MWelC, NN-RB, RPJCB; BL.   566/52

Terraube, Galard de. Discours des choses plus necessaires et dignes d'estre entendues en la cosmographie. *Paris: F.Morel*, 1566. 39 numb.lvs;8vo. 1st publ., Paris 1559. Cf.Sabin 94865; cf. Atkinson (Fr.Ren.) 125. BN.   566/53

Ulloa, Alfonso de. Vita dell'invitissima, e sacratissimo imperator Carlo V. *Venice: V.Valgrisi*, 1566. 344 numb.lvs;8vo. 1st publ., Venice, 1560. Sabin 97681; Adams (Cambr.) U42; Shaaber U21. ICN, InU-L, NNH, PU; Cambridge: Trinity.   566/54

Warhafftige Contrafey einer wilden Frawen gefunde in der Landtschafft Nova terra. *Nur-*emberg: H.W.Glaser [1566?]. bds.;port.;fol. Describes & depicts Eskimo woman & child captured in Newfoundland 20 Aug. 1566. Sabin 101422. BL.   566/55

——[Anr edn]. *Augsburg: M.Franck* [1566?]. bds.;port.;fol. Weber (Jobin) p.274. Zurich: StB.   566/56

Zapata, Luis de. Carlo famoso. *Valencia: J. Mey*, 1566. 289 numb.lvs;4to. A metrical romance relating in part to Mexico. Sabin 106252; Palau 379348; Shaaber Z15. MH, NNH, PU; BL.   566/57

1567

Alberti, Leandro. Descriptio totius Italiae. . . interprete Guilelmo Kyriandro Hoeningeno. *Cologne: T.Baum*, 1567. 815p.;fol. 1st publ. in Latin, Cologne, 1566. Ind.aur.102.345; Adams (Cambr.) A471. DFo;BL, Munich: StB.   567/1

Amatus Lusitanus. Curationum medicinalium, centuriae II priores. *Lyons: G.Rouillé*,1567. 686p.;8vo. 1st Century 1st publ., Florence, 1561; 2nd Century, Venice, 1562. Ind.aur.104.567; Baudrier (Lyons) IX:310. PPC.   567/2

Apollonius, Levinus. De Peruviae regionis. . . libri v. *Antwerp: A.Tavernier,for J.Bellère*, 1567. 236 numb.lvs;map;8vo. 1st publ., Antwerp, 1566; here a reissue with altered imprint date. Sabin 1761n; Medina (BHA) 200; Ind.aur.106.492; Adams (Cambr.) A1318; JCB (3) I:233. CU-S, CtY, DLC, ICN, MH, NN-RB, PPL, RPJCB; BL, BN.   567/3

Arias de Benavides, Pedro. Secretos de chirurgia, especial de las enfermedades de morbo galico y lamparones y mirrarchia, y assi mismo la manera como se curan los Indios de llagas y heridas . . . en las Indias. *Valladolid:F. Fernández*, 1567. clxv lvs;8vo. Sabin 4639;Medina (BHA) 199; Alcocer (Valladolid) 254;Ind.aur.107.283; JCB (3) I:233. DNLM, NNH, RPJCB; BL, BN.   567/4

Bembo, Pietro, Cardinal. Opera . . . ab C. Augustino Curione . . . collata. *Basel: T. Guarin*, 1567. 3v.;8vo. Includes the author's *Historiae Venetae*, 1st publ., Venice, 1551. Sabin 4619n; Ind.aur.116.482. CtY, DFo, InU-L, MH, NNU-W; BL, BN.   567/5

Caracciolo, Virgilio. Compendio della descrittione di tutto il mondo. *Naples:*

M.Cancer,1567. 76p.;4to. Ind.aur.131.899. NN-RB, NNH; Rome: Vatican. 567/6

Catholic Church. Pope, 1566-1572 (Pius V). Bulla confirmationis et novae concessionis privilegiorum omnium ordinum mendicatium. *Rome: Heirs of A.Blado*, 1567. 12 lvs;4to. Grants special privileges to mendicant orders to facilitate missionary efforts in New World. DHN. 567/7

—[Anr edn]. *Barcelona: F.Cantarelli*, 1567. 12 lvs;4to. Palau 37007. 567/8

—[Anr edn]. Bulla . . . extensionis omnium privilegiorum ordinibus mendicantium concessorum cum eorum concessione. *Rome:Heirs of A.Blado*, 1567. 14 lvs;illus.;4to. NcU. 567/9

Chaumette, Antoine. Enchiridion chirurgicum . . . quibus, Morbi venerei curandi methodus probatissima accessit. *Paris: A.Wechel*, 1567. 343p.;8vo. 1st publ., Paris, 1560. DNLM, PPC. 567/10

Cruz, Juan de la, fray. Coronica dela Orden de Predicadores. *Lisbon: M.João*, 1567. cclvii lvs;4to. Lvs cxxvi-cxxx describe Dominicans in Santo Domingo. Streit I:99; Anselmo 718; Palau 65209. Göttingen: BU. 567/11

Dolce, Lodovico. Immortalita dell' invitissimo et glorioss. imperator Carlo Quinto . . . .*Venice: G.Giolito de' Ferrari*, 1567. 315p.;4to. 1st publ.,Venice, 1567. Adams (Cambr.) D756. NN-RB, RPB; BL, BN. 567/12

Du Pinet, Antoine, sieur de Norey. Historia plantarum. *Lyons: Widow of G.Cotier*, 1567. 2pts;illus.;12mo. 1st publ., Lyons, 1561. Pritzel 2539n; Nissen (Bot.) 565n & 1307n; Baudrier (Lyons) IV:78-79; Adams (Cambr.) D1146; Hunt (Bot.) 100. CU, DLC, NNBG, RPB; BL, BN. 567/13

Estienne, Charles. L'agriculture et la maison rustique. *Paris: J.DuPuys*, 1567. 264 numb. lvs;illus.;4to. 1st publ., Paris, 1564, but here further rev. & enl. by Liébault, with accounts of turkey & tobacco added. Thiébaud (La chasse) 340-341; Adams (Cambr.) S1721.CtY, MH; Cambridge: UL. 567/14

Fernel, Jean. Universa medicina . . . diligentia Guil. Plantii . . . eliminata. *Paris: A.Wechel*, 1567. 2pts;port.;fol. Includes Fernel's *De abditis rerum causis*, 1st publ., Paris,1548. Sherrington (Fernel) 57.J1; Adams (Cambr.) F256. DNLM; London: Wellcome,Paris: Faculté de Médicine. 567/15

Franck, Sebastian. Warhafftige Beschrei-bunge aller theil der welt. *Frankfurt a.M.:M. Lechler,for S.Feyerabend & S.Hüter*, 1567. 2v.;fol. 1st publ., Tübingen, 1534, under title *Weltbüch*. Sabin 25472 (&25471) & 77677; JCB (3) I:234. CtY, DLC, MH, MnU-B, NN-RB, RPJCB; BL. 567/16

Fregoso, Battista. Exemplorum, hoc est, Dictorum factorumque memorabilium ex historiarum probatis autoribus, lib. ix. *Basel: H. Petri*, 1567. 1365p.;8vo. 1st publ., Milan,1509, under title *De dictis factisque memorabilibus*. Sabin 26140n; Adams (Cambr.)F1149. Cambridge: Trinity. 567/17

Genebrard, Gilbert, Abp of Aix. Chronographia in duos libros distincta. *Paris: M.LeJeune*, 1567. 2v.;fol. The 2nd vol.,comp. by A.de. Pontac, contains refs to Columbus, Vespucci, Magellan, etc. Adams (Cambr.) G395. ICN, NIC; BL. 567/18

Giovio, Paolo, Bp of Nocera. Historiarum sui temporis tomus primus[-secundus]. *Basel: [H.Petri & P.Perna?]* 1567. 3v.;8vo. 1st publ., Florence, 1550-52. Adams (Cambr.) G657. IU, NNG; Cambridge: Trinity, BN. 567/19

Gonsalvius, Reginaldus, Montanus. Sanctae Inquisitionis Hispanicae artes aliquot detectae. *Heidelberg: M.Schirat*, 1567. 297p.;8vo. Includes account of Juan de León, formerly a missionary priest in Mexico. Palau 105548; Adams (Cambr.) G854; Shaaber G270. DLC, MH, NN-RB, PU; Cambridge: UL, BN. 567/20

Guicciardini, Francesco. La historia d'Italia. *Venice: G.Giolito de' Ferrari*, 1567. 2v.; port.;4to. 1st publ., Florence, 1561. DLC, IU; BL. 567/21

———. Historiarum sui temporis libri viginti . . . ex italico . . . conversi et editi, Caelio Secundo Curione interprete. *Basel: H.Petri & P.Perna*, 1567. 2v.;8vo. 1st publ. in this translation, Basel, 1566. Adams (Cambr.) G1523. BL. 567/22

LeRoy, Louis. Consideration sur l'histoire françoise, et l'universelle de ce temps. *Paris: F.Morel*, 1567. 27 numb.lvs;8vo. Contains ref. to Florida. Atkinson (Fr.Ren.) 177. BN. 567/23

Lumnius, Joannes Fredericus. De extremo Dei judicio et Indorum vocatione ii. *Antwerp: A.Thielens*, 1567. 269p.;8vo. The author's refs to the Spanish Indies, Vespucci & Magellan confirm that he has the New World in view in advocating missionary activity, and in identifying American Indians as the lost tribes of Israel. Sabin 42675; Streit I:100: Adams (Cambr.) L1713. MH; BL.   567/24

Magnus, Olaus, Abp of Upsala. Beschreibüng [sic] allerley Gelegenheyte, Sitten, Gebräuchen und Gewonheyten, der Mitnächtigen Völcker in Sueden, Ost unnd Westgothen unnd andern . . . Erstlich in latinischer Sprache beschriben . . . Jetz erst . . . ins Teutsch bracht, durch Israelem Achatium. *Strassburg: T.Rihel* [1567]. cccxxxvii lvs;illus.;8vo. Transl. from Magnus's *Historia de gentibus septentrionalibus*, as condensed by C.Scribonius, 1st publ., Antwerp, 1558. Cf.Sabin 43833; Collijn (Sver.bibl.) II:366-367. MnU-B, NN-RB.   567/25

——. Historia . . . de gentium septentrionalium. *Basel: H.Petri*, 1567. 854p.;illus.,map; fol. 1st publ., Rome, 1555. Sabin 43831; Collijn (Sver.bibl.) II:363-366; Adams (Cambr.) M141; Shaaber M43; JCB (3) I:235-236. CSt, CtY, DFo, MH, MnU-B, NN-RB, PU, RPJCB; BL, BN.   567/26

——. Historien der mittnächtigen Länder . . . ins Hochteüsch gebracht . . . durch Johann Baptisten Ficklern. *Basel: H.Petri* [1567]. dcxxiii p.;map;fol. Transl. from Magnus's *Historia de gentibus septentrionalibus*, as condensed by C.Scribonius, Antwerp 1558. Collijn (Sver.bibl.) II:358-363. CtY, DLC, MiU, MnU-B, NIC.   567/27

Marguérite d'Angoulême, Queen of Navarre. L'heptameron. *Paris: V.Normant & J.Bruneau*, 1567. 16mo. 1st publ. in this version, Paris, 1559. Tchémerzine VII:394. BL.
567/28

—[Anr issue]. *Paris: G.Gilles*, 1567. Tchémerzine VII:394. BL.   567/29

Meneses, Felipe .de. Luz de alma christiana. *Alcalá de Henares: J.de Villanueva,for L.Gutiérrez*, 1567. 151 numb.lvs;4to. 1st publ., Seville, 1555. García (Alcalá de Henares) 411. Madrid: BN.   567/30

—[Anr edn]. *Medina del Campo: F.del Canto*, 1567. clii lvs;fol. Pérez Pastor (Medina del Campo) 146.   567/31

Mexía, Pedro. Les diverses leçons . . . mises en françois par Claude Gruget . . . augmentées de trois dialogues. *Paris: C.Micard*, 1567. 634 numb.lvs;16mo. 1st publ. in this version with supplementary dialogues, Paris, 1556. Cf.Sabin 48244; Palau 167313n. MH, NN-RB.   567/32

——. Trois dialogues . . . touchant la nature du soleil, de la terre et de toutes les choses qui se font et apparoissent en l'air. *Paris: F.Morel*, 1567. 32 lvs;8vo. 1st publ. as here transl. by Marie de Coste-Blanche, Paris, 1566. Palau 167383n. MH; BL.   567/33

Mizauld, Antoine. Cosmographie, seu Mundi sphaerae, libri tres. *Paris: F.Morel*, 1567. 71p.;8vo. 1st publ., Paris, 1552, under title *De mundi sphaera*. In verse. Cf.Sabin 49773; JCB AR20:1567. CtY, MH, RPJCB, WU.
567/34

Münster, Sebastian. Cosmographey oder beschreibung aller Länder. *Basel: H.Petri*, 1567. 1467p.;illus.,maps;fol. 1st publ. in German, Basel, 1544. Borba de Moraes II:91; Burmeister (Münster) 76; JCB (3) I:236. NN-RB, RPJCB; BN.   567/35

Orta, Garcia da. Aromatum, et simplicium aliquot medicamentorum apud Indos nascentium Historia: ante biennium quidem lusitanica lingua per dialogos conscripta . . . nunc verò primùm latina facta, & in epitomen contracta à Carolo Clusio. *Antwerp: C.Plantin*, 1567. 250p.;illus.;8vo. Transl. from Orta's *Coloquios dos simples*, Goa, 1563, but substantially modified, with added material relating to the New World, derived from Oviedo & Thevet & a ref. to introduction of 'lues venerea' (syphilis) by the Spanish in 1493. Sabin 57663; Pritzel 4613n; Nissen (Bot.) 949; Bibl. belg.1st ser.,XX:05; Adams (Cambr.) 0319; Moranti (Urbino) 2365; JCB (3) I:236. CtY, DNLM, MH, NN-RB, PU, RPJCB; BL, BN.
567/36

Paracelsus. Medici libelli. *Cologne: A. Birckmann*, 1567. 261p.;4to. Includes (p.218-235) *De ligno Guaiaco*, 1st publ., 1529. Sudhoff (Paracelsus) 87. DNLM, PPHa; Munich: StB.
567/37

——. Tgasthuys boec. *Antwerp: H.de Laet*, 1567. 36 lvs;8vo. Transl. from the author's *Spittal Büch*, 1st publ., Mülhausen, 1562. Normally bound with the author's 1568, *De cleyne chirurgie*. Belg.typ. (1541-1600) I:3930; Sudhoff (Paracelsus) 93. BL, Brussels: BR.   567/38

Polo, Gaspar Gil. Primera parte de Diana enamorada. *Antwerp: Widow & Heirs of J. Steels*, 1567. 120 lvs;12mo. 1st publ., Valencia, 1564. In verse. Peeters-Fontainas (Impr. esp.) 501; Palau 102075. NIC, CaBVaU; Louvain: BU.   567/39

Pulgar, Hernando del. Chronica de los muy altos, y esclarecidos reyes católicos Don Hernando y Doña Ysabel. *Saragossa: J.Millán, for M.de Suelves*, 1567. ccxlix lvs; illus.;fol. Contains supplement (lvs ccxiiii ff.) by [Pedro?] Valles, with brief account of discovery of the Indies. Sabin 66621; Sánchez (Aragon) 471; Adams (Cambr.) P2257. CtY, MiU-C, NN-RB; BL, BN. 567/40

Rabelais, François. Les oeuvres. *Lyons: J. Martin*, 1567. 3pts;16mo. Includes 'Le quart livre', 1st publ., Paris, 1552. Plan (Rabelais) 100. 567/41

Recueil de la diversité des habits. *Paris: R. Breton*, 1567. [127]p.;illus.;8vo. 1st publ., Paris, 1562. In this edn, on verso of lf A2, reading 'Cancer' appears. Sabin 68432; Atkinson (Fr.Ren.) 174; Borba de Moraes I:222; cf.Mortimer (France) 453. BN. 567/42

___[Anr edn]. *Paris: R.Breton*, 1567. [127]p.;illus.;8vo. In this edn, on verso of lf A2, reading 'Cācer' appears. Atkinson (Fr.Ren.) 175; Borba de Moraes I:222. Grenoble: BM. 567/43

___[Anr issue]. *Paris: F.DesPrez*, 1567. Fairfax Murray (France) 478. DLC. 567/44

Rondelet, Guillaume. Methodus curandorum omnium morborum corporis humani . . . Ejusdem . . . De morbo gallico. *Paris: J.Macé* [1567?]. 7pts;8vo. 1st (?) publ., Paris [1563?]. DNLM, NNNAM. 567/45

Ronsard, Pierre de. Oeuvres. *Paris: G.Buon*, 1567. 6v.;port.;4to. Includes, in v.6, the *Continuation du Discours des misères de ce temps*, 1st publ., Paris, 1562. Tchémerzine IX:472; Rothschild 667. MH; BL, BN. 567/46

Rueda, Lope de. Compendio llamado el deleytoso. *Valencia: J.Mey, for J.Timoneda*, 1567. 32 lvs;8vo. Comedy. Includes mention of land of Xauxa (i.e., Jauja, Peru) as one of plenty & prosperity. Palau 281019. 567/47

Sacro Bosco, Joannes de. Sphaera . . . emendata . . . Interserta etiam sunt Eliae Vineti . . . Scholia. *Lyons: Heirs of J.Giunta*, 1567. 207p.;8vo. 1st publ. with Vinet's *Scholia*, Paris, 1551. Baudrier (Lyons) VI:322-323. CU-M, CtY, MiU, MnU-B, NN-RB, RPJCB; Rennes: BM. 567/48

___. La sphera . . . nueva y fielmente traduzido de latin en romance, por Rodrigo Saenz de Santayana y Spinosa. *Valladolid: A.Ghemart, for P.de Corcuera*, 1567. 78 numb.lvs; illus.;8vo. The earliest Spanish edn. Medina (BHA) 201; Alcocer (Valladolid) 255. Madrid: BN. 567/49

Schmidel, Ulrich. Neuwe Welt, das ist, Warhafftige Beschreibunge aller schönen Historien von erfindung viler unbekanten Königreichen. *Frankfurt a.M.: M.Lechler, for S.Feyerabend & S.Hüter*, 1567. 2pts;fol. A reissue, with cancel t.p., of v.2 of Sebastian Franck's *Warhafftige Beschreibunge aller theil der welt* of this year. Sabin 77678; Palau 304834; JCB (3) I:237. RPJCB; BL. 567/50

Soto, Domingo de. Libri decem De justicia & jure. *Antwerp: P.Nuyts*, 1567. 344p.;fol. 1st publ., Salamanca, 1553. Palau 320145. BN. 567/51

Surius Laurentius. Commentarius brevis rerum in orbe gestarum. *Cologne: G.Calenius & Heirs of J.Quentel*, 1567. 936p.;8vo. 1st publ. separately, Cologne, 1566; here expanded to include year 1567. Sabin 93881; Adams (Cambr.) S2097; Shaaber S686. PU; Cambridge: UL. 567/52

___[Anr edn]. *Louvain: J.Bogardus*, 1567. 641p.;8vo. BN. 567/53

Tagault, Jean. De chirurgica institutione libri quinque. *Lyons: G.Rouillé*, 1567. 487p.; illus.;8vo. 1st publ., Paris, 1543. Baudrier (Lyons) IV:314. DNLM; BL. 567/54

Terraube, Galard de. Vray discours des choses plus necessaires & digne d'estre entendues en la cosmographie. *Lyons: B.Rigaud*, 1567. 69p.;8vo. 1st publ., Paris, 1559. Sabin 94866; cf.Atkinson (Fr.Ren.) 125; cf.Cioranescu (XVI) 21051-52. NNH. 567/55

1568

Alberti, Leandro. Descrittione di tutta Italia. *Venice: L.degli Avanzi*, 1568. 504 numb.lvs; 4to. 1st publ., Bologna, 1550. Ind.aur. 102.347; Adams (Cambr.) A474. NNU; BL, BN. 568/1

Bizzarri, Pietro. Historia . . . della guerra fatta in Ungheria . . . Con la narratione di tutte quelle cose che sono avvenute in Europa, dall' anno 1564, insino all'anno 1568. *Lyons: G.Rouillé*, 1568. 213p.;8vo. On p.190-194 is an account of the Indians of Florida & French attempts to settle there. Ind.aur.119.704; Adams (Cambr.) B2086; Baudrier (Lyons) IX:318; JCB (3) I:238. CSmH, RPJCB; Cambridge: St John's, BN. 568/2

Catholic Church. Pope, 1566-1572 (Pius V). Bulla . . . extensionis omnium privilegiorum ordinibus mendicantium. *Rome: Heirs of A. Blado*, 1568. 10 lvs;illus.;4to. 1st publ., Rome, 1567. NN-RB; BL. 568/3

___[Anr edn]. Confirmatio et nova concessio privilegiorum omnium mendicantium. *Seville: J.Gutiérrez*, 1568. 11 lvs;4to. Palau 359160.
568/4

Centorio degli Hortensii, Ascanio. La seconda parte de' Commentarii delle guerre & de' successi più notabili avvenuti cosi in Europa come in tutte le parti del mondo dall'anno 1553. fino à tutto il 1560. *Venice: G.Giolito de' Ferrari*, 1568. 298p.;4to. The 1st pt, without American refs, has title *Commentarii della guerra di Transilvania*. BN. 568/5

Dodoens, Rembert. Florum, et coronarium odoratarumque nonnularum herbarum historia. *Antwerp: C.Plantin*, 1568. 308p.; illus.;8vo. Includes refs to American plants, e.g., marigolds, sunflowers, etc. Pritzel 2347; Nissen (Bot.) 514; Bibl.belg.,1st ser., IX: D113; Adams (Cambr.) D714; Hunt (Bot.) 101. DLC, MH-A, NN-RB, PPAN, RPB; BL, BN. 568/6

Dordoni, Giorgio. De morbi gallici curatione tractatus quatuor. *Pavia: G.Bartoli*, 1568. 115 numb.lvs;8vo. In 'Tractatus 3, cap. 1. De inventione ligni indici, & eius ortu, & natura', i.e., Guaiacum, Columbus is mentioned. DNLM, MH; London: Wellcome. 568/7

Fioravanti, Leonardo. De capricci medicinali . . . libri quattro . . . Con molta diligenza revisti, corretti, & ristampati. *Venice: L.degli Avanzi*, 1568. 283 numb.lvs;8vo. 1st publ., Venice, 1561. Adams (Cambr.) F484. NNC-M; BL. 568/8

Giovio, Paolo, Bp of Nocera. Elogios o vidas breves, de los cavalleros antiguos y modernos . . . que estan al bivo pintados en el Museo de Paulo Jovio . . . Traduxolo de latin . . . Gaspar de Baeça. *Granada: H.de Mena*, 1568. 222 numb.lvs;fol. Transl. from Giovio's *Elogia*, 1st publ., Florence, 1551. Medina (BHA) 203; Palau 125422. DLC, MH, NN-RB. 568/9

Gómara, Francisco López de. Histoire generalle des Indes Occidentales & terres neuves . . . Traduite . . . par m. Fumée, sieur de Marly le Chastel. *Paris: M.Sonnius*, 1568. 252 numb.lvs;8vo. 1st publ. in Spanish, Saragossa, 1554. Sabin 27746n; Wagner (SW)

2dd; Atkinson (Fr.Ren.) 180; Streit II:824. MH, NN-RB; BL, Brussels: BR. 568/10

Gonsalvius, Reginaldus, Montanus. A discovery and playne declaration of sundry subtill practises of the Holy Inquisition of Spagne. *London: J.Day*, 1568. 99 numb.lvs; 4to. Transl. by Vincent Skinner from author's *Sanctae Inquisitiones Hispanicae artes*, 1st publ., Heidelberg, 1567. STC 11996; Shaaber G271. CSmH, CtY, DLC, ICN, NN-RB, PU; BL, BN. 568/11

___. Histoire de l'Inquisition d'Espagne. [*Geneva?*] 1568. 255p.;8vo. Transl. from author's Heidelberg, 1567, *Sanctae Inquisitiones Hispanicae artes*, the account of Jean de León, 'premierement . . . cousturier a Mexique, ville de la nouvelle Espagne', here appearing on p.215-220. Adams (Cambr.) G855. NNH, RPJCB; Cambridge: Sidney Sussex, BN. 568/12

Guicciardini, Francesco. L'histoire d'Italie . . . translatée d'italien . . . par Hiérosme Chomedey. *Paris: B.Turrisan*, 1568. ccccxv lvs;fol. Transl. from author's *L'historia d'Italia*, 1st publ., Florence, 1561. Tchémerzine IX:458; Shaaber G409. PU; BL, BN. 568/13

___. La historia d'Italia. *Venice: N.Bevilacqua*, 1568. 470 numb.lvs;4to. 1st publ., Florence, 1561. Adams (Cambr.) G1510. CU, CtY, MH, IU, PPD; Cambridge: UL. 568/14

___[Anr edn]. *Venice: G.Giolito de' Ferrari*, 1568, '67. 2v.;port.;4to. A reissue of the publisher's 1567 edn. Adams (Cambr.) G1511. NhD; Cambridge: UL, BN. 568/15

Héry, Thierry de. La methode curatoire de la maladie venerienne. *Lyons: T.Payan*, 1568. 298p.;8vo. 1st publ., Paris, 1552. London: Wellcome. 568/16

Histoire memorable de la reprinse de l'isle de la Floride, faicte par les François, sous la conduite du Capitaine Gorgues . . . le 24. & 27. d'avril de ceste annee, 1568. [*Paris?*] *Imprimé nouvellement*, 1568. [24]p.;4to. Atkinson (Fr.Ren.) 179; Adams (Laudonnière) 14. Paris: Mazarine. 568/17

Jesuits. Letters from missions. Nuovi avisi dell'Indie di Portogallo . . . tradotti dalla lingua spagnuola. *Venice: M.Tramezzino*, 1568. 59 numb.lvs;8vo. 1st publ., Venice, 1559, as pt 2 of publisher's *Diversi avisi*. Borba de Moraes I:51; Streit II:1288; Shaaber J32;

JCB AR20:1568. CSmH, ICN, MH, MiU, NN-RB, PU, RPJCB; BL. 568/18

LeRoy, Louis. Consideration sur l'histoire françoise, et l'universelle de ce temps. *Paris: F.Morel,* 1568. 15 numb.lvs;8vo. 1st publ., Paris, 1567. Atkinson (Fr.Ren.) 181. BN. 568/19

___[Anr edn]. *Lyons: B.Rigaud,* 1568. 46p.;8vo. Atkinson (Fr.Ren.) 182; Baudrier (Lyons) III:253. CtY, ICN; BN. 568/20

Lucidarius. M.Elucidarius. Von allerhand Geschöpffen Gottes . . . und wie alle Creaturen geschaffen seynd auf Erden: auch wie die Erd in vier Theil getheilet. *[Basel: J.Oporinus,* ca.1568]. [76]p.;illus.;4to. 1st publ., Strassburg, [ca.1535], but here with added matter, including a chapt.14, 'Von der neuen Welt, America genant'. Schorbach (Lucidarius) 34. 568/21

Malestroict, Jehan Cherruyt de. Les paradoxes . . . sur le faict des monnoyes, présentez a Sa Majesté au mois de mars M.D.LXVI. avec la response de m. Jean Bodin ausdicts paradoxes. *Paris: M.LeJeune,* 1568. 2pts;4to. Bodin's *Response* attributes current price inflation chiefly to the abundance of gold & silver, due in part to Spanish conquests in the New World. BN. 568/22

Mattioli, Pietro Andrea. I discorsi . . . nelli sei libri di Pedacio Dioscoride . . . della materia medicinale. Hora di nuovo dal suo istesso autore ricorretti, & . . . aumentati. *Venice: V.Valgrisi,* 1568. 1527p.;illus.,port.; fol. 1st publ., Venice, 1555. Pritzel 5987n; Nissen (Bot.) 1304n; Adams (Cambr.) D678; Arents (Add.) 27; Shaaber M199. CU, CtY-M, DNLM, MH-A, NN-A, PU; BL, BN. 568/23

Münster, Sebastian. La cosmographie universelle. *[Basel:] H.Petri,* 1568. 1402p.;illus., maps;fol. 1st publ. in French, Basel, 1552. Sabin 51399; Atkinson (Fr.Ren.) 183; Borba de Moraes II:91; Burmeister (Münster) 96. InU-L, MnU-B, RPJCB; Oxford: Worcester. 568/24

Pantaleon, Heinrich. Chronographia ecclesiae Christi . . . ad praesentem hunc 1568 annum usque. *Basel: Heirs of N.Brylinger,* 1568. 157p.;fol. 1st publ., Basel, 1550. Adams (Cambr.) P175. BL. 568/25

Ronsard, Pierre de. Discours des miseres de ce temps. *Antwerp: P.Strout* [i.e., *Lyons: B.Rigaud*], 1568. 32 lvs;8vo. Includes the *Continuation du Discours,* 1st publ., Paris, 1562.

On fictitious imprint, see L. Scheler, 'Une supercherie de Benoît Rigaud, l'impression anversoise du "Discours des misères de ce temps" ', *Bibliothèque d'humanisme et renaissance,* XVI (1954), 331-335. Tchémerzine IX:439-440. BN. 568/26

Sacro Bosco, Joannes de. La sphera . . . nueva . . . traduzida de latin . . . por Rodrigo Sáenz de Santayana y Spinosa. *Valladolid: A.Ghemart,for P.de Corcuera,* 1568. 78 numb.lvs;4to. 1st publ. in this version, Valladolid, 1567. Sabin 74809; Medina (BHA) 201; Alcocer (Valladolid) 260. DLC, MB, NN-RB. 568/27

Soto, Domingo de. Libri decem De justitia & jure. *Venice: G.Perchacino,* 1568. 280 numb. lvs;fol. 1st publ., Salamanca, 1553. Palau 320146. DLC; Rome: BN. 568/28

Surius, Laurentius. Commentarius brevis rerum in orbe gestarum. *Cologne: G.Calenius & Heirs of J.Quentel,* 1568. 548p.;fol. 1st publ. separately, Cologne, 1566; here expanded to cover year 1568. Cf.Sabin 93882; Adams (Cambr.) S2098. NjP; Cambridge: UL, BN. 568/29

___[Anr edn]. *Cologne: G.Calenius & Heirs of J. Quentel,* 1568. 938p.;8vo. Adams (Cambr.) S2099. CSt, DLC, ICN; BL. 568/30

_____. Kurtze Chronick . . . der vornembsten händeln . . . so sich . . . in der Welt zugetragen. *Cologne: G.Calenius & Heirs of J.Quentel,* 1568. 377p.;fol. Transl., by H.Fabricius, from the publishers' Latin edn of this year. Sabin 93888; Shaaber S688. CtY, PU; BL. 568/31

Thevet, André. The new found worlde, or Antarctiche, wherein is contained wonderful and strange things, as well of humaine creatures, as beastes, fishes, foules, and serpents, trees, plants, mines of golde and silver . . . now newly translated [by T.Hacket]. *London: H.Bynneman,for T.Hacket,* 1568. 138 numb.lvs;4to. Transl. from Thevet's *Singularitez de la France Antarctique,* Paris, 1557. For printing variants see Church as cited. Sabin 95338; Borba de Moraes II:305; STC 23950; Arents 11-A; Church I:113; Shaaber T189; JCB (3) I:238. CSmH, CtY, DLC, ICN, MH, NN-RB, PU, RPJCB; BL. 568/32

Turner, William. The first and seconde partes of the Herbal . . . lately oversene, corrected and enlarged with the thirde parte.

Cologne: [*Heirs of*] *A.Birckmann*, 1568. 4pts;illus.;fol. Includes new 3d pt with its account (p.34) of Guaiacum and of sarsaparilla (p.65). Pritzel 9570n; Nissen (Bot.) 2013n; STC 24367; Henrey (Brit.bot.) 368. CSmH, DFo, IEN-M, MH-A, NNNAM, WU; BL.

568/33

1569

Alonso de la Veracruz, Father. Physica speculatio . . . Nunc tertiò ab eodem auctore edita. *Salamanca: J.B.à Terranova,for S.de Portonariis*, 1569. 444p.;fol. 1st publ., Mexico City, 1557; cf.1562, Salamanca, edn. Sabin 98916; Medina (BHA) 211; Bolaño e Isla (Veracruz) 57-58 (no.3); JCB AR25: 16-17. RPJCB; Seville: BU.   569/1

———. Recognitio summularum . . . Nunc tertiò . . . revisa ab authore. *Salamanca: D.de Portonariis,for S.de Portonariis*, 1569. 157p.;fol. 1st publ., Mexico City, 1554; cf.Salamanca, 1562, reprinting. Sabin 98918n; Medina (BHA) 209; Bolaño e Isla (Veracruz) 49-50 (no.3); Palau 359142. Seville: BU.   569/2

Arias Montanus, Benedictus. Rhetoricorum libri iiii . . . Cum annotationibus Antonii Moralii. *Antwerp: C.Plantin*, 1569. 158p.;8vo. The annotator has been identified by Medina & others, perhaps mistakenly, as Antonio Rúiz de Morales y Molina, successively Bishop of Michoacán and of Puebla de los Angeles in Mexico. Cf.Medina (BHA) 225; Belg.typ. (1541-1600) I:164; Ind.aur.107.285; Palau 16465. NjP; BL, Brussels: BR.   569/3

Aristoteles. Organum. Latin (Selections). Resolutio dialectica cum textu Aristotelis, admodum . . . fratris Alphosi à Vera Cruce . . . Nunc tertio . . . revisa ab autore. *Salamanca: J.B.à Terranova,for S.de Portonariis*, 1569. 259p.;illus.;fol. 1st publ., Mexico City, 1554; cf.Salamanca, 1562, edn. Medina (BHA) 210; Bolaño e Isla (Veracruz) 53-54 (no.3); Palau 359147. MiU.   569/4

Baten, Carel. Propositiones de morbo gallico. *Rostock: J.Lucius*, 1569. 8vo. Ind.aur. 114.739; Proksch I:83. BL.   569/5

Bizzarri, Pietro. Historia della guerra fatta in Ungheria. *Lyons: G.Rouillé*, 1569. 213p.;8vo. 1st publ., Lyons, 1568. Ind.aur.119.704; Baudrier (Lyons) IX:325. ICN; BL, Paris: Arsenal.   569/6

Catholic Church. Pope, 1566-1572 (Pius V). Bullas . . . confirmationis et novae concessionis privillegiorum omnium ordinum mendicantium motu proprio. *Alcalá de Henares: A.de Angulo*,1569. [32]p.;4to. 1st publ., Rome, 1567. Includes here additional text relating privileges to Franciscan Order. JCB (3) I:240. RPJCB.   569/7

Centorio degli Hortensii, Ascanio. La seconda parte de' Commentarii delle guerre & de' successi più notabili avvenuti cosi in Europa come in tutte le parti del mondo dall'anno 1553 fino à tutto il 1560. *Venice: G.Giolito de' Ferrari*, 1569. 298p.;4to. 1st publ., Venice, 1568; here reissued with altered imprint date. BL.   569/8

Colón, Fernando. Historie . . . nelle quali s'hà particolare . . . della vita . . . dell'ammiraglio D. Christoforo. Colombo . . . E dello scoprimento, ch'egli fece dell'Indie Occidentali, detto Mondo Nuovo . . . Esattamente di lingua spagnuola tradotta . . . dal sign. Alfonso Ulloa. *Venice: Il Prodocino*, 1569. 494p.;8vo. For discussion, see the 1571 edn with its refs. DLC, NjP.   569/8a

Córdoba, Antonio de. Opera. *Venice*, 1569. See the year 1570.

Dodoens, Rembert. Florum, et coronarium odoratumque nonnularum herbarum historia . . . Altera editio. *Antwerp: C.Plantin*, 1569. 309p.;illus.;8vo. 1st publ., Antwerp, 1509. Pritzel 2347n; Nissen (Bot.) 514n; Bibl. belg.,1st ser.,IX:D114; Adams (Cambr.) D715; Hunt (Bot.) 104. CU, DFo, ICU, MH-A, MiU, NNNAM, PPC; BL, BN. 569/9

———. Historia frumentorum, leguminum, palustrium et aquatilium herbarum. *Antwerp: C.Plantin*, 1569. 293p.;illus.;8vo. 1st publ., Antwerp, 1566, under title *Frumentorum . . . historia*; here included is new section 'De panico indico' (Penicillaria spicata) & 'Trifolium ex America' (Psoloralea americana). Pritzel 2346n; Nissen (Bot.) 513; Bibl.belg.,1st ser., IX:D112; Adams (Cambr.) D717; Hunt (Bot.) 105. CU, DNLM, MH-A, MiU, MnU, NN-RB, PPAN; BL, Brussels: BR.   569/10

Donati, Marcello. De variolis et morbillis tractatus . . . De radice purgante quam Mechioacan vocant. *Mantua: P.& C.Philoponi*, 1569. 2pts;4to. CLU-M, CtY-M, DNLM; BL, BN.   569/11

Emili, Paolo. Historiae jam denuo emendatae

. . . de rebus gestis Francorum . . . Arnoldi Ferroni . . . De rebus gestis Gallorum libri ix. *Basel: S.Henricpetri,* 1569. 2v.;fol. 1st publ. with Le Ferron's appendix, Paris, 1548, under title *De rebus gestis Francorum.* Adams (Cambr.) A241; Ind.aur.100.835; Shaaber E63. CU, CtY, ICN, MH, PU; BL, BN.
569/12

Ercilla y Zúñiga, Alonso de. La Araucana [Primera parte]. *Madrid: P.Cosin,* 1569. 205p.;port.;8vo. Narrative poem on Chilean efforts to subdue Araucanian Indians. Sabin 22718; Medina (BHA) 205; Pérez Pastor (Madrid) 26; Medina (Arau.) 1; JCB (101 Bks) 16. CSmH, MiU-C, NNH; BL, BN.   569/13

Gabrielli, Giulio, of Gubbio. Orationum et epistolarum . . . libri duo . . . Epistola de rebus Indicis à quodam Societatis Jesu italicè scripta, & nunc primum in latinum conversa. *Venice: F.Ziletti,* 1569. 52 numb.lvs;4to. Relates in part to Jesuits in Brazil. Sabin 26283. DLC, NIC; BL, BN.   569/14

Gesner, Konrad. Euonymus, sive de Remediis secretis, pars secunda: nunc primum opera & studio Caspari·Wolphii . . . in lucem editus. *Zurich: C.Froschauer,* 1569. 427 (i.e.,247) numb.lvs;illus.;8vo. Continues Gesner's *Euonymus,* 1st publ., Zurich, 1552. In addition to mention of syphilis ('Gallicus morbus'), the chapter 'De oleis e lignis extrahendis', citing Monardes, discusses Guaiacum. MBCo, NIC; BL, BN.   569/15

Gómara, Francisco López de. Histoire generalle des Indes Occidentales & terres neuves . . . Traduite . . . par m. Fumee, sieur de Marly le Chastel. *Paris: M.Sonnius,* 1569. 252 numb.lvs;8vo. 1st publ. in this version, Paris, 1568; here reissued with altered imprint date. Sabin 27746; Medina (BHA) 159n (I:272); Wagner (SW) 2ee; Atkinson (Fr.Ren.) 180n; Streit II:836; Arents (Add.) 24; JCB (3) I:239. DLC, NN-RB, RPJCB; BL, BN.
569/16

—[Anr issue]. *Paris: B.Turrisan,* 1569. As above, a reissue of 1568 edn. Sabin 27746n; Medina (BHA) 159n (I:272); Wagner (SW) 2ff; Atkinson (Fr.Ren.) 180n. ICN, NN-RB, RPJCB; BL.   569/17

Gómez de Castro, Alvar. De rebus gestis a Francisco Ximeno Cisnerio, Archiepiscopo Toletano, libri octo. *Alcalá de Henares: A.de Angulo,* 1569. 240 numb.lvs;port.;fol. In-cludes refs to Ximénez de Cisneros's voyages to

America. Streit II:385; García (Alcalá de Henares) 439; Palau 103905; Adams (Cambr.) G851; Shaaber G264. ICN, MH, NN-RB, PU; BL, BN.   569/18

Gonsalvius, Reginaldus, Montanus. A discovery and playne declaration of sundry subtil practices of the Holy Inquisition of Spayne. *London: J.Day,* 1569. 99 numb. lvs;illus.;fol. 1st publ. in English, London, 1568. STC 11997; Palau 105552n. CSmH, DFo, RPJCB; BL.   569/19

——. Der heiligen hispanischen Inquisition, etliche entdeckte, und offentliche an tag gebracte ränck und Practiken. *Heidelberg: J.Mayer,* 1569. 228p.;4to. Transl. from author's *Sanctae Inquisitionis Hispanicae artes,* Heidelberg, 1567. Palau 105559.   569/20

——. Der heyliger Hispanischer Inquisitie, etliche listighe consten int licht ghebract. [*Norwich, Eng.? A.Solemne?*] 1569. 143 numb. lvs;8vo. Cf.other translations of this year. Palau 105557; STC 12001. Cambridge: UL.   569/21

——. De heylighe Spaensche inquisitie. *London: J.Day,* 1569. 175 numb.lvs;8vo. Cf.other translations of this year. Palau 105556; STC 12000. BL.   569/22

——. Historie van de Spaensche Inquisitie. [*Antwerp?*] 1569. 301p.;8vo. Transl. from [Geneva?], 1568, French translation of author's *Sanctae Inquisitionis Hispanicae,* 1st publ., Heidelberg, 1567. Palau 105555; Belg. typ. (1541-1600) I:1307. NNH; Brussels: BR.
569/23

——. Inquisitio hispanica . . . aus dem Letein verdeutscht durch Wolffgangum Kauffman. *Eisleben: A.Petri,* 1569. 159 numb.lvs;8vo. Cf.other translations of this year. Palau 105561. NNH.   569/24

Guicciardini, Francesco. La historia d'Italia. *Venice: G.Giolito de' Ferrari,* 1569. 2v.; port.;4to. 1st publ., Florence, 1561; here a reissue of the publisher's 1567 edn. Adams (Cambr.) G1512. MH; BL.   569/25

Hawkins, Sir John. A true declaration of the troublesome voyage of m. John Hawkins to the partes of Guynea and the West Indies, in . . . 1567. and 1568. *London: T.Purfoot,for L. Harrison,* 1569. 16 lvs;8vo. Sabin 30954; STC 12961; Church 113A; JCB (101 Bks) 17. CSmH, MiU-C; BL.   569/26

Héry, Thierry de. La methode curatoire de la maladie venerienne. *Paris: G.Gourbin,* 1569.

272p.;8vo. 1st publ., Paris, 1552. DNLM, MnU; London: Wellcome. 569/27

Jesuits. Letters from missions (The East). Epistolae Japonicae, de multorum gentilium in variis insulis ad Christi fidem . . . conversione. *Louvain: R.Velpius,* 1569. 2pts;8vo. Included is 1549 letter of Manuel de Nobrega from Brazil, 1st publ., Venice, 1559, in Italian, in the *Diversi avisi.* Sabin 35780; Borba de Moraes I:246; Streit II:1290; Shaaber J30; JCB AR20:1569. DLC, MnU-B, NN-RB, PU, RPJCB; BL. 569/28

Lonitzer, Adam. Kreuterbuch, neu zugericht. *Frankfurt a.M.: C.Egenolff,* 1569. ccclxxxiv lvs;illus.;fol. 1st publ., Frankfurt a.M., 1557. Pritzel 5599n; Nissen (Bot.) 1228. NcU.

569/29

Lucidarius. M.Elucidarius von allerhand Geschöpffen Gottes . . . und wie alle Creaturen geschaffen seynd auff Erden. [*Basel: J.Oporinus,* ca.1569]. [75]p.;illus.; 4to. 1st publ. in this enl. version, [Basel, ca.1568]. In this edition the title contains reading 'GOTTes'. Schorbach (Lucidarius) 35. Zurich: StB. 569/30

Lumnius, Joannes Fredericus. De extremo Dei judicio et Indorum vocatione libri ii. *Venice: D.Farri,* 1569. 80 numb.lvs;8vo. 1st publ., Antwerp, 1567. Cf.Sabin 42675; Streit I:104; Adams (Cambr.) L1714; JCB (STL) 12. DLC, InU-L, MH, NN-RB, RPJCB; Cambridge: UL, BN. 569/31

Medina, Pedro de. L'art de naviguer . . . Traduict . . . par Nicolas de Nicolai. *Lyons: G.Rouillé,* 1569. 225p.;illus.,map;4to. 1st publ. in French, Lyons, 1554. Sabin 47345n; Baudrier (Lyons) IX:326; JCB (3) I:240. DLC, MiU-C, RPJCB; BL, BN. 569/32

Mercado, Thomas de. Tratos y contratos de mercaderes. *Salamanca: M.Gast,* 1569. 249 numb.lvs;4to. Includes chapts 'De los tratos de Indias, y tratantes en ellas', 'De la navegacion a las Indias, ansi Orientales, como Occidentales', 'De los cambios que se usan de aqui a Indias', etc. Medina (BHA) 206; Streit I:105. CLCo, CtY, DLC, ICU, InU-L, MnU-B, NN-RB, RPJCB; BL, BN. 569/33

Mexía, Pedro. Les diverses leçons . . . mises en françois par Claude Gruget . . . augmentées de trois dialogues. *Paris: C.Micard,* 1569. 634 numb.lvs;16mo. 1st publ. in this version with supplementary dialogues, Paris,

1556. Palau 167314; Cioranescu (XVI) 11190. NIC, RPJCB; BL, BN. 569/34

——. Le vite di tutti gl'imperadori. *Venice: G.Sansovino,* 1569. 531 numb.lvs:4to. 1st publ. as transl. by Lodovico Dolce with addition of life of Charles V, Venice, 1561. Palau 167352; Adams (Cambr.) M1387. NcU; Cambridge: Trinity. 569/35

Monardes, Nicolás. Dos libros, el uno que trata de todas que traen de nuestras Indias Occidentales, que sirven de uso de la medicina, y el otro que trata de la pedra bezaar, y de la yerva escuerçonera. *Seville: F.Díaz,* 1569. [280]p.;port.;8vo. 1st publ., Seville, 1565. Sabin 49936; Medina (BHA) 207; Guerra (Monardes) 8; Escudero (Seville) 630; JCB (3) I:240. DLC, ICN, InU-L, MH, RPJCB; BL. 569/36

Münster, Sebastian. Cosmographey, oder Beschreibung aller Länder. *Basel: H.Petri,* 1569. mcccclxvii p.;illus.,ports.,maps;fol. 1st publ., Basel, 1544. Burmeister (Münster) 77. CSt, TxU, WU; Munich: StB. 569/37

Rabelais, François. Les oeuvres. *Lyons: J. Martin,* 1569. 3pts;port.;16mo. Includes 'Le quart livre', 1st publ., Paris, 1552. Plan (Rabelais) 101. Besançon: BM. 569/38

Román y Zamora, Jerónimo. Chronica de la Orden de los Ermitanos del glorioso padre Sancto Agustin. *Salamanca: J.B.de Terranova,* 1569. 157 numb.lvs;port.;fol. Includes refs to activities of Augustinian friars in New World. Medina (BHA) 208; Streit I:106; Palau 276579. InU-L, NNH, TxU; Strasbourg: BU. 569/39

Sacro Bosco, Joannes de. Sphaera . . . emendata. Eliae Vineti . . . Scholia. *Paris: J.de Marnef & G.Cavellat,* 1569. 94 numb.lvs; illus.;8vo. 1st publ. with Vinet's *Scholia,* Paris, 1551. Cf.Sabin 32681. CtY, NN-RB; BN. 569/40

——[Anr edn]. *Venice: G.Scoto,* 1569. 168p.; illus.;8vo. Cf.Sabin 32681. MoU, NN-RB.

569/41

Soto, Domingo de. Commentariorum . . . in quartum Sententiarum. Tomus primus[-secundus]. *Salamanca: J.M.à Terranova,for B.Boyer,* 1569. 2v.;fol. 1st publ., Salamanca, 1557-60. Adams (Cambr.) S1474; Palau 320170. DCU, IMunS, MH; Cambridge: Pembroke. 569/42

——. De justitia & jure libri decem. *Salamanca: J.B.à Terranova,for B.Boyer,* 1569 [colophon:

1568]. 895p.;fol. 1st publ., Salamanca, 1553. Adams (Cambr.) S1483; Palau 320147. OU, WU; Cambridge: UL. 569/43

—[Anr edn]. Libri decem De justitia et jure. *Lyons: G.Rouillé*, 1569. 2v.;fol. Moranti (Urbino) 3155; Palau 320149. BN. 569/44·

—[Anr issue of preceding]. *Lyons: Heirs of J.Giunta*, 1569. 344 numb.lvs;fol. Adams (Cambr.) S1484; Palau 320148. MH-BA, NjP; BL. 569/45

—[Anr edn]. *Antwerp: P.Nuyts*, 1569. 344 numb.lvs;fol. Adams (Cambr.) S1485. Cambridge: Corpus Christi. 569/46

Terraube, Galard de. Brief discours des choses plus necessaires & dignes d'estre entendues en la cosmographie. *Paris: F.Morel*, 1569. 20 lvs;8vo. 1st publ., Paris, 1559. Sabin 94865; cf.Atkinson (Fr.Ren.) 125. BL. 569/47

Venegas de Busto, Alejo. Primera parte de las differencias de libros que ay en el universo. *Madrid: A.Gómez*, 1569. 242 numb.lvs; illus.;4to. 1st publ., Toledo, 1540. Sabin 98502; cf.Harrisse (BAV) Add. 156; cf.Medina (BHA) 128; Pérez Pastor (Madrid) 40. BL. 569/48

Venero, Alonso de. Enchiridion de los tiempos. *Toledo: F.de Guzmán, for M.Rodríguez*, 1569. 213 numb.lvs;8vo. 1st publ. with American contents, Saragossa, 1548. Pérez Pastor (Toledo) 320; Palau 358456. 569/49

1570

Alderhande habijt ende cleedinge . . . by onsen tijde . . . in den landen van Europa, Asia, Africa, ende in den wilden eylanden . . . Eerst gedruct de Parijs, ende nu overghesedt in onse brabantsche tale. *Antwerp: G.van Parijs*, 1570. 64 lvs;illus.;8vo. 1st publ., Paris, 1562, under title *Recueil de la diversité des habits*. Authorship attributed to François Desprez. Belg.typ. (1541-1600) II:5610. Antwerp: Plantin Mus. 570/1

Ambasciata del gran re de Chicorani. *Padua: L.Pasquato*, 1570. 24p.;4to. In verse; purports to relate to area today comprising the Carolinas, mentioning Columbus. CSmH; BL. 570/2

Belleforest, François de. L'histoire universelle du monde. *Paris: G.Mallot*, 1570. 317 numb.lvs;4to. In part transl. from J.Boemus's

Omnium gentium mores, the 4th bk (lvs 245-317) describes recent discoveries in both Indies. Sabin 4506; Borba de Moraes I:82; Atkinson (Fr.Ren.) 196; Ind.aur.110.096. DLC, MH, MiU-C, MnU-B, NN-RB; BL, Paris: Arsenal. 570/3

Bembo, Pietro, Cardinal. Della historia vinitiana. Aggiuntovi di nuovo la tavola delle cose piu notabili . . . per m. Alemanio Fino. *Venice: G.Ziletti*, 1570. 179 numb.lvs;4to. A reissue, with additional prelim.matter, of sheets of the printer's 1552 edn. Sabin 4620; Ind.aur.116.486. CSt, CtY, ICN, MH, MnU-B; BN. 570/4

Brant, Sebastian. Stultifera navis . . . The ship of fooles . . . Transl. out of Latin . . . by Alexander Barclay. *London: J.Cawood*, 1570. 259 numb.lvs;fol. 1st publ. in this version, London, 1509. STC 3546; Ind.aur.123.748; Pforzheimer 41; JCB (3) I:241. CSmH, CtY, DLC, ICN, MH, NN-RB, RPJCB; BL. 570/5

Bugati, Gasparo. Historia universale: nella quale . . . si racconta . . . tutto quel ch'é successo dal principio del mondo fino all'anno MDLXIX. *Venice: G.Gioliti de' Ferrari*, 1570. 1090p.;illus.,map;4to. Includes accounts of Columbus, Vespucci, Magellan, etc. Ind. aur.126.801. IU; BL, Munich: StB.

570/6

Centorio degli Hortensii, Ascanio. La seconda parte de' Commentarii delle guerre & de' successi più notabili avvenuti cosi in Europa come in tutto le parti del mondo dall'anno 1553 fino à tutto il 1560. *Venice: G.Giolito de' Ferrari*, 1570. 298p.;4to. 1st publ., 1568; here reissued with altered imprint date. Adams (Cambr.) C1269. MiU-C, NN-RB; Cambridge: UL. 570/7

Chaumette, Antoine. Enchiridion chirurgicum . . . Quibus morbi Venerei curandi methodus probatissima accessit. *Lyons: G.Rouillé*, 1570. 450p.;illus.;8vo. 1st publ., Paris, 1560. Baudrier (Lyons) IX:330-331. DNLM, NNC; BL, BN. 570/8

Clavius, Christoph. In Sphaeram Joannis de Sacro Bosco commentarius. *Rome: V.Eliano*, 1570. 499p.;illus.;4to. Included are scattered refs to New World. Backer II:1212. CtY, ICJ, NN-RB. 570/9

Córdoba, Antonio de. Opera. *Venice: G.Ziletti (Toledo: J.de Ayala Cano)* 1569 [i.e., 1570]. 2v.;fol. Colophon, v.2, states that p.289ff. were printed at Toledo. 'Quaestio 57. De bello infidelium et insularum': v.l,p.491-508. Streit I:107; Ind.aur.106.075; Palau 61829. DCU; BL, BN.   570/10

Crespin, Jean. Histoire des martyrs persecutez et mis a mort. [*Geneva: J.Crespin*] 1570. fol. 1st publ. in this version, [Geneva], 1564. Brunet II:420.   570/11

__[Anr edn]. Histoire des vrays temoins de la verité de l'Evangile. [*Geneva: `P.Aubert*, 1570*]. 709p.;fol. Brunet II:420. IEG. 570/12

Dioscorides, Pedanius. Acerca de la material medicinal . . . traduzido de lengua griega . . . & illustrado con . . . substantiales annotationes, y con las figuras de innumeras plantas . . . por el doctor Andres de Laguna. *Salamanca: M.Gast*, 1570. 616p.;illus.,port.; fol. Laguna's annotations, with numerous refs to American plants, 1st publ. separately, Lyons, 1554, & in the present form, Antwerp, 1555. Pritzel 2313n; Palau 74023n. DLC, MH-A, NNH, PPAmP; BN.   570/13

Estienne, Charles. L'agriculture et maison rustique . . . augmentée par m. Jean Liebaut. *Paris: J.DuPuys*, 1570. 252 numb.lvs;4to. 1st publ., Paris, 1567. Thiébaud (La chasse) 343; cf.Arents 12 & Add. 28. CtY-M, MH, NN-RB.   570/14

__[Anr edn]. *Paris: J.DuPuys* [i.e., *Geneva: F. Estienne*], 1570. 255 numb.lvs;illus.;4to. A piracy of 1567, Paris, edn. Thiébaud (La chasse) 343-344; Arents 12 & Add. 28. NN-A; BL.   570/15

Fioravanti, Leonardo. La cirurgia . . . Di nuovo posta in luce. *Venice: Heirs of M.Sessa*, 1570. 200 numb.lvs;8vo. In bk 1, chapts 24 & 90 discuss syphilis. CtY, DNLM, NNNAM, PPC; London: Wellcome.   570/16

____. Il tesoro della vita humana . . . Di nuovo posto in luce. *Venice: Heirs of M.Sessa*, 1570. 327 numb.lvs;8vo. Included are numerous chapts on nature & cures of syphilis. CtY-M, DNLM, NNC, PPC; BL.   570/17

Gesner, Konrad. Euonymus, sive de Remediis secretis, pars secunda: nunc . . . studio Caspari Wolphii . . . editus. [*Zurich: C.Froschauer*, 1570?]. 237 numb.lvs;illus.;8vo. 1st publ., Zurich, 1569. Adams (Cambr.) G530. CtY, DNLM, NNNAM, WU; BL.   570/18

Genebrard,` Gilbert, Abp of Aix. Chronographia. *Louvain: J.Fowler*, 1570. 290 numb. lvs;12mo. 1st publ., Paris, 1567. CtY; BN.
570/19

Giovio, Paolo, Bp of Nocera. Histoires . . .

sur les choses faictes et avenues de son temps . . . Traduictes de latin . . . & reveües pour la seconde edition, par Denis Sauvage. *Paris: O.de Harsy*, 1570. 2v.;fol. 1st publ. in French, Lyons, 1552-53. Atkinson (Fr.Ren.) 197. BN.
570/20

__[Anr issue]. *Paris:* [*O.de Harsy,for*] *J.DuPuys*, 1570. Atkinson (Fr.Ren.) 197n. IU; BN.
570/21

____. Warhafftige Beschreibunge aller Chronickwirdiger Historien. *Frankfurt a.M.: G.Rab* [*for*] *P.Perna,at Basel*, 1570. 2pts;8vo. 1st publ. in German, Basel, 1560. Sabin 36776. RPJCB; BL.   570/22

Girava, Gerónimo. La cosmographia, y geographia . . . en la qual se contiene la descripcion de todo el mundo, y de sus partes, y particularmente de las Indias, y tierra nueva. *Venice: G.Ziletti*, 1570. 271p.;illus.,map;4to. 1st publ., Milan, 1556, under title *Dos libros de cosmographia*. Sabin 27504; Medina (BHA) 212; Borba de Moraes I:299; cf.Wagner (NW) II:279n; JCB (3) I:242. CtY, DLC, InU-L, MH, MiU-C, NN-RB, RPJCB; BN.   570/23

Honter, Johannes. Rudimentorum cosmographicorum . . . libri iii. [*Zurich: C.Froschauer*] 1570. 44 lvs;maps;8vo. 1st publ. in this version, Kronstadt, 1542. In verse. Borsa 96; Szabo III:605; Adams (Cambr.) H835. Cambridge: Trinity.   570/24

Jesuits. Letters from missions (The East). Epistolae Japanicae, de multorum in variis insulis gentilium ad Christi fidem conversione. *Louvain: R.Velpius*, 1570. 401p.;8vo. 1st publ., Louvain, 1569. Sabin 36082n; Streit II:1294; Borba de Moraes I:246-247; Adams (Cambr.) J97. MH, MnU-B; Cambridge: St. John's.   570/25

____. Nuovi avisi dell'India . . . recevuti quest'anno MDLXX. *Rome: Heirs of A.Blado* [1570]. 45 numb.lvs;8vo. Includes Pietro Díaz's account of massacre of missionaries en route to Brazil. Borba de Moraes I:52; Streit II:1295. BL.   570/26

LeRoy, Louis. Consideration sur l'histoire françoise, et l'universelle de ce temps. *Paris: F.Morel*, 1570. 15 numb.lvs;8vo. 1st publ., Paris, 1567. Atkinson (Fr.Ren.) 198; Shaaber L153. ICN, PU; BN.   570/27

Lucidarius. M. Elucidarius von allerhand Geschöpffen Gottes . . . und wie alle Creaturen geschaffen seynd auff Erden. [*Basel:*

J.Oporinus, ca.1570]. [75]p.;illus.; 4to. 1st publ. in this enl. edn, [Basel, ca.1568]. In this edn the title contains reading 'Gottes'; cf. that of 1569. Schorbach (Lucidarius) 36.   570/28

Magnus, Olaus, Abp of Upsala. Historiae de gentibus septentrionalibus, a C.Scribonio Graphaeo in epitome redacta. *Antwerp: [C.Plantin,for] J.Bellère* [ca.1570?]. 512p.; illus.;8vo. 1st publ. in this condensed version, Antwerp, 1558. Collijn (Sver.bibl.) III:215-217; Belg.typ. (1541-1600) I:2023; Adams (Cambr.) M142. CtY, MH, OCl; Cambridge: UL, Brussels: BR.   570/29

Marcos da Lisboa, Bp, o.f.m. Tercera parte de las Chronicas de la Orden de los frayles menores del . . . padre sant Francisco. *Salamanca: A.de Cánova*, 1570. 280 numb. lvs;fol. The earlier parts had appeared in Portuguese at Lisbon in 1556 & 1562. In bk ix, chapts viii & x-xi describe Franciscans in Mexico. Medina (BHA) 213; Streit I:108. BL (Silva, M.da).   570/30

Mattioli, Pietro Andrea. Commentarii in sex libros . . . Dioscoridis Anazarbei De medica materia . . . Adjectis plantarum & animalium iconibus. *Venice: V.Valgrisi*, 1570. 956p.; illus.;fol. 1st publ., Venice, 1554; here newly illustrated. Pritzel 2309n; Nissen (Bot.) 1305n; Adams (Cambr.) D673. DNLM, MH, MoSB; Cambridge: UL, BN.   570/31

——. I discorsi . . . nelli sei libri di Pedacio Dioscoride . . . della materia medicinale. *Venice: V.Valgrisi*, 1570. 956p.;illus.;fol. 1st publ., Venice, 1555. Pritzel 5988; Nissen (Bot.) 1304n.   570/32

Meneses, Felipe de. Luz de alma christiana. *Medina del Campo: F.del Canto*, 1570. 4to. 1st publ., Seville, 1555. Palau 164444n. Saragossa: BU.   570/33

—[Anr edn]. *Seville: M.Montesdoca*, 1570. 4to. Escudero (Seville) 642; Palau 164444n. 570/34

Mexía, Pedro. Dialogos . . . nuevamente enmendados. *Seville: F.Díaz*, 1570. 269p.;8vo. 1st publ., Seville, 1547. Escudero (Seville) 639; Palau 167372. MH, NNH; BL, Valencia: BM.   570/35

——. Les diverses lecons . . . mise en françois par Claude Gruget . . . De nouveau reveuës, corrigees, & augmentees de trois Dialogues, touchant la nature du soleil, de la terre & des metheores. *Lyons: J.Marcorelle,for the Widow of G.Cotier*, 1570. 1272p.;8vo. 1st publ. in this version with supplementary dialogues,

Paris, 1556. Palau 167314; Baudrier (Lyons) IV:80. Lyons: BM.   570/36

——. Trois dialogues . . . touchant la nature du soleil, de la terre et de toutes les choses qui se font et apparoissent en l'air. *Paris: F.Morel*, 1570. 32 lvs;4to. 1st publ. as here transl. by Marie de Coste-Blanche, Paris, 1566. MH.   570/37

Monardes, Nicolás. Modo et ordine come si ha de usare la radice Mechoacane . . . cavato da un trattato de alcuni simplici che vengono dalle Indie Occidentali. *Milan*: 1570. 7 lvs;4to. 1st publ., in Spanish, Seville, 1565, in author's *Dos libros*. Guerra (Monardes) 9. DNLM(missing).   570/38

Ortelius, Abraham. Theatrum orbis terrarum. *Antwerp: G.Coppens v.Diest*, 1570. 38 lvs;53maps;fol. Includes list of errata (corrected in later edns) at end of 'Index tabularum'; in 'Catalogus auctorum' 87 names appear. For this & all subsequent edns Koeman's descriptions, though susceptible of variants, have been followed. Sabin 57693; Koeman (Ort.) 1A; Phillips (Atlases) 3389; Adams (Cambr.) 0331; JCB (3) I:243. 570/39

—[Anr edn, with imprint & collation as above]. In the 'Catalogus auctorum' 91 names appear. Koeman (Ort.) 1B.   570/40

—[Anr edn with imprint, &c., as above]. The 'Catalogus auctorum' has 92 names. Koeman (Ort.) 1C.   570/41

—[Anr edn, as above]. The 'Catalogus auctorum' has 94 names. Koeman (Ort.) 1D. Without distinction of edn: CSmH, DLC, ICN, InU-L, MH, MiU-C, MnU-B, NN-RB, RPJCB; BL.   570/42

Peña, Pierre. Stirpium adversaria nova. *London*: 1570. See the year 1571.

Portugal. Laws, statutes, etc. Leys, e provisoes. *Lisbon: F.Correa*, 1570. 223p.;8vo. Included is a 'Ley sobre a liberdade dos gentios do Brasil: & em que casos se poden ou nam poden captivar'. Borba de Moraes I:114; Anselmo 498; King Manuel 127. MH; Lisbon: BN.   570/43

Ruscelli, Girolamo, comp. Lettere di principi. *Venice: G.Ziletti*, 1570. 247 numb.lvs; 4to. 1st publ., Venice, 1562. Moranti (Urbino) 2986. NNC; BN.   570/44

Serres, Jean de. Rerum in Gallia ob religionem gestarum, libri tres. [*Geneva: E.Vignon*] 1570. 117 (i.e., 177) numb.lvs;8vo. Bks 1-2 derive from Pierre de La Place's *Commen-*

taires de l'estat de la religion, 1st publ., [Rouen?] 1565. On textual history and printing, see B.A.Vermaseren, 'La première edition des *Commentaires* de Jean de Serres', *Bibliothèque d'humanisme et renaissance*, XXIII (1961), 117-120. Contains abbreviated account of Villegagnon's attempted Brazil settlement. 570/45

—[Anr edn]. Commentariorum de statu religionis et reipublicae in regno Galliae . . . Prima partis, libri iii. [*Geneva: E.Vignon*] 1570. Brunet II:187-188; see also Vermaseren as cited above. Paris:Bibl. du Protestantisme français,Geneva: BP. 570/46

Soto, Domingo de. Commentariorum . . . in quartum Sententiarum, tomus primus[-secundus]. *Venice: D.Nicolini*, 1570. 2v.;4to. 1st publ., Salamanca, 1557-60. Adams (Cambr.) S1476; Palau 320171. CU-L(v.1.), DCU; Cambridge: UL, Rome: BN. 570/47

—[Anr edn]. *Salamanca: J.M.à Terranova*, 1570-72. 2v.;fol. Palau 320172. MH-L, NcU(v.2); Madrid: BN. 570/48

Tagault, Jean. Institutione di cirurgia. *Venice: G.Angelieri*, 1570. 421 numb.lvs;illus.; 8vo. 1st publ. in Italian, Venice, 1550. DNLM. 570/49

Torquemada, Antonio de. Jardin de flores curiosas. *Salamanca: J.B.de Terranova*, 1570. 286 numb.lvs;8vo. In verse. Included are numerous refs to various aspects of America, e.g., Columbus, Magellan, Hispaniola, etc. Palau 334907; Shaaber T274. MB, NNH, PU; BL, Madrid: BN. 570/50

Ulloa, Alfonso de. Die historie ende het leven vanden . . . keyser Kaerle de Vijfde . . . Eerstmael in italiaensche sprake beschreven . . . nieuwelijk in nederlatsche sprake overgheset [door Peeter Bellaert]. *Antwerp: Widow & Heirs of J.Steels*, 1570. 229 numb.lvs;port.;fol. Transl. from Ulloa's *Vita dell' . . . imperator Carlo Quinto*, 1st publ., Venice, 1560. Sabin 97678; Belg.typ. (1541-1600) I:4567. BL, BN. 570/51

1571

Alonso de la Veracruz, Father. Appendix ad Speculum conjugorum. *Madrid: P.Cosin*, 1571. 143p.;4to. Relates decisions of Council of Trent to author's *Speculum conjugiorum* (cf.Salamanca, 1562, edn). Included also are papal bulls of Leo X, Hadrian VI & Pius V granting privileges to missionary orders in America. Sabin 98919; Medina (BHA) 221; Pérez Pastor (Madrid) 55; Bolaño e Isla (Veracruz) 60; JCB AR67:7-9. RPJCB; BL, Madrid: BU. 571/1

Boaistuau, Pierre. Histoires prodigeuses, extraictes de plusieurs fameux autheurs grecs & latins . . . divisees en trois tomes. Le premier mis en lumiere par P.Boaistuau, le second par Claude de Tesserant: & le troisieme par François de Belle-Forest. *Paris: J.de Bordeaux*, 1571. 2v.;illus.;16mo. The earliest edn to contain Belleforest's contribution in 'Illusion faite aux Indies Occidentaux', v.2, p.231-232. Ind.aur.120.062. PU-F; BL. 571/2

—[Anr issue]. *Paris: G.Buon*, 1571. Ind.aur. 120.063. DFo, OU; Vienna: UB. 571/3

Bugati, Gasparo. Historia universale. *Venice: G.Giolito de' Ferrari*, 1571. 1092p.;illus., map;4to. 1st publ., Venice, 1570. Ind. aur.126.802; Adams (Cambr.) B3157. ICN; BL, BN. 571/4

Burgos. Relación verdadera del recebimiento, que . . . Burgos hizo a la Magestad Real de la Reyna nuestra Señora, doña Anna de Austria. *Burgos: P.de Junta*, 1571. liv lvs;4to. On lf xxxviii is a description of a float containing an Indian cacique & natives. Palau 257198. NNH. 571/5

Casas, Bartolomé de las, Bp of Chiapa. Erudita & elegans explicatio quaestionis Utrùm reges vel principes jure aliquo . . . cives . . . à regio corona alienare . . . possint . . . Edita cura . . . Wolffgangi Griestetteri. *Frankfurt a.M.: G.Corvinus,for H.Feyerabend*, 1571. 67p.;4to. Americana only as inferential of Las Casas's basic views. Sabin 39118 (& 11237); Hanke/Giménez 471; Streit I:111. DFo, MH, MiU-C, NN-RB; BL. 571/6

Chaumette, Antoine. Enchiridion, ou Livret portatif des chirurgiens . . . Ausquels est adjousté de nouveau une methode . . . pour guerir la verole . . . de nouveau . . . traduit de latin. *Lyons: L.Cloquemin*, 1571. 384p.;8vo. Transl. from Chaumette's *Enchiridion chirurgicum*, 1st publ., Paris, 1560. Baudrier (Lyons) IV:45. BN. 571/7

Colón, Fernando. Historie . . . nelle quali s'ha particolari, & vera relatione della vita, & de' fatti dell' ammiraglio D.Christoforo Colombo, suo padre: et dello scoprimento, ch'egli fece dell'Indie Occidentali, detto Mon-

do Nuovo . . . Nuovamente di lingua spagnuolo tradotte . . . dal s.Alfonso Ulloa. *Venice: F.de' Franceschi*, 1571. 247 lvs;8vo. Whether or not this is, as represented, from Columbus's son's pen has, in the absence of the Spanish original, long been a matter of dispute (cf.Palau 57209 & 221828n). Sabin 14674; Streit II:874; Church 114; Arents 14; Shaaber C608; JCB (3) I:244. CSmH, CtY, DLC, MH, MiU-C, MnU-B, PU, RPJCB; BL.
571/8

Falloppius, Gabriel. Künstbuch . . . in teutsche Sprach verferttiget durch Hieremiam Martium. *Augsburg: M.Manger,for G. Willers*, 1571. 665p.;8vo. Transl. from author's *Secreti diversi*, 1st publ., Venice, 1563. CtY-M, DNLM; London: Wellcome. 571/9

Fernández, Diego. Primera, y segunda parte, de la Historia del Peru. *Seville: F.Díaz*, 1571. 2pts;fol. Distribution forbidden shortly after publication by Council of the Indies, but permitted in 1729—Medina. Sabin 24133; Medina (BHA) 214; Escudero (Seville) 649-650; Palau 89549; JCB (3) I:244. CtY, DLC, ICN, MH, MiU-C, NNH, RPJCB; BL, BN. 571/10

Fioravanti, Leonardo. Del compendio de i secreti rationali . . . libri cinque. *Venice: Heirs of M.Sessa*, 1571. 187 numb.lvs;port.; 8vo. 1st publ., Venice, 1564. DNLM, NNNAM. 571/11

Flores, Bartholomé de. Obra nuevamente compuesta, en la qual se cuenta, la felice victoria que Dios . . . fue servido de dar al . . . señor Pedro Melendez . . . contra Juan Ribao [i.e., Ribaut] de la nanaccion [sic] frances . . . con otras curiosidades . . . de las viviendas de los Indios dela Florida. *Seville: F.Díaz*, 1571. [8]p.;4to. In verse. Colonization tract favoring settlement of Florida. Medina (BHA) 215; Vail (Frontier) 5; Palau 92459; JCB AR40:29-33. RPJCB. 571/12

Garibáy y Zamálloa, Esteban de. Los xl. libros d'el compendio historial de las chronicas y universal historia de todos los reynos de España. *Antwerp: J.Verwithagen & T.Lyndanus,for C.Plantin*, 1571. 4v.;port.;fol. In bks 19-20 substantial accounts of Columbus & the New World appear. Sabin 26666; Peeters-Fontainas (Impr.esp.) 499; Adams (Cambr.) G244; Palau 100101. DLC, MH, MiU, NNH; BL, BN. 571/13

Giovio, Paolo, Bp of Nocera. Descriptiones, quotquot extant, regionum atque locorum,

quibus . . . De piscibus romanis libellus . . . adiunximus. *Basel: [H.Petri & P.Perna?]*, 1571. 520p.;8vo. Includes Giovio's *Descriptio Britanniae*, 1st publ., Venice, 1548, and his *De romanis piscibus*, 1st publ., Rome, 1524. CU-A, MnU; BL. 571/14

——. Elogia virorum bellica virtute illustrium. *Basel: [P.Perna?]* 1571. 592p.;8vo. 1st publ., Florence, 1551. Cf.Sabin 36773. CU-A, NcD, RPJCB; BL. 571/15

Jesuits. Letters from missions. Sendtschreiben und warhaffte zeytungen . . . inn teutsche spraach transsferiert . . . durch d. Philipp Dobereiner. *Munich: A.Berg*, 1571. 111 lvs;8vo. Transl. from the *Nuovi avisi*, Rome, 1570. Sabin 79097; Streit IV:950; JCB (3) I:247. MH, NN-RB, RPJCB; Munich: UB. 571/16

Jesuits. Letters from missions (The East). Nuovi avisi dell'India. *Brescia: G.P.Bozzola*, 1571. 46 numb.lvs;8vo. 1st publ., Rome, 1570. Borba de Moraes I:52; Streit II:1298. BL. 571/17

——. Recueil des plus fraisches lettres, escrites des Indes Orientales. *Paris: M.Sonnius*, 1571. 131p.;8vo. Transl. by P.M.Coyssard from the Rome, 1570, *Nuovi avisi*, with Pietro Díaz's account of massacre of missionaries to Brazil. Borba de Moraes II:175; Streit II:1299. BN. 571/18

La Boétie, Estienne de. La mesnagerie de Xenophon . . . ensemble quelques vers latins et françois de son invention. *Paris: F.Morel*, 1571. 131 numb.lvs;8vo. In the Latin poems, the 1st, addressed 'Ad Belotium & Montanum', contains refs to New World as 'solemque alium terrasque recentes' & to 'novum orbem'; the 20th, addressed to Montaigne alone, refers to syphilis, 'Nota lues, Italis si credis, Gallica'. MWiW-C; BN. 571/19

LeRoy, Louis. Consideration sur l'histoire françoise, et l'universelle de ce temps. *Paris: F.Morel*, 1571. 15 numb.lvs;8vo. 1st publ., Paris, 1567. Atkinson (Fr.Ren.) 215. ICN; BN. 571/20

Marguérite d'Angoulême, Queen of Navarre. L'heptaméron. *Paris: M.de Roigny*, 1571. 726p.;16mo. 1st publ. in this version, Paris, 1559. Adams (Cambr.) M565. Cambridge: Trinity. 571/21

Mattioli, Pietro Andrea. Compendium de plantis omnibus. *Venice: V.Valgrisi*, 1571. 921p.;illus.;4to. Included are descriptions of

American plants. Pritzel 6661; Nissen (Bot.) 1306; Adams (Cambr.) M908; Arents (Add.) 45. CU, DNLM, MH-A, MiU, NN-A; BL, BN.   571/22

Mercado, Thomas de. Summa de tratos, y contratos. *Seville: F.Díaz*, 1571. 2pts;4to. 1st publ., Salamanca, 1569, under title *Tratos y contratos de mercaderes.* Medina (BHA) 216; Streit I:112; Escudero (Seville) 652; Kress 105; JCB (3) I:245. DLC, InU-L, MH, MnU-B, NN-RB, RPJCB; Madrid: BN.   571/23

Mexía, Pedro. Della selva di varia lettione. *Venice: F.Rampazetto*, 1571. 8vo. 1st publ. with section on New World by F.Sansovino, Venice, 1559-60. Sabin 48239; Palau 167294.   571/24

Monardes, Nicolás. Segunda parte del libro de las cosas que se traen de nuestras Indias Occidentales, que sirven al uso de medicina. *Seville: A.Escrivano*, 1571. 2pts;illus.;8vo. 1st publ., Seville, 1565, as bk 2 of the author's *Dos libros*, here supplemented by his 'Libro que trata de la nieve'. Sabin 49937; Medina (BHA) 219; Guerra (Monardes) 10-11; Escudero (Seville) 647 & 655; Arents 15; JCB (3) I:246. DLC, ICN, MH, NN-RB, RPJCB; BL, BN.   571/25

Nores, Giasone de. Breve trattado del mondo, et delle sue parti. *Venice: A.Muschio*, 1571. 74 numb.lvs;8vo. Chapt.17 contains description of America. Sabin 55465 (& 19603); Adams (Cambr.) N334; JCB (3) I:247. DLC, ICN, InU-L, MH, MiU, NN-RB, RPJCB; BL, BN.   571/26

Ortelius, Abraham. Theatre, ofte Toonnel des aerdt-bodems waer inne te seine sijn de landt-tafelen van de geheele weerelt. *Antwerp: G.Coppens v.Diest*, 1571. 8 lvs; 53maps;fol. Transl. by Pieter Heyns from Latin text, 1st publ., Antwerp, 1570. Sabin 57705; Koeman (Ort.) 3. CSmH, DLC; BL.   571/27

———. Theatrum orbis terrarum. *Antwerp: G.Coppens v.Diest*, 1571. 39 lvs;53maps;fol. 1st publ., Antwerp, 1570. Sabin 57694; Koeman(Ort.) 2. CU, PBL; BL.   571/28

Osorio, Jerónimo, Bp of Silves. De rebus, Emmanuelis Regis Lusitaniae invictissimi virtute et auspicio gestis libri duodecim. *Lisbon: J.Gonçalves*, 1571. 480p.;fol. Includes discussion of Brazil & of tobacco. Sabin 57804; Borba de Moraes II:120; Streit IV:941; Anselmo 694; King Manuel 133; Arents (Add.) 47;

JCB AR20:1571. CtY, DLC, InU-L, MB, MiU, MnU-B, NN-A, RPJCB; BL, Paris: Arsenal.   571/29

Peña, Pierre. Stirpium adversaria nova, perfacilis vestigatio . . . Authoribus Petro Pena & Mathia de Lobel. *London: T.Purfoot*, 1570 [i.e., 1571]. 455p.;illus.;fol. Colophon dated 1571. Describes not only tobacco but also other American plants, e.g. Prickly pear cactus (Opuntia) citing its American source. Pritzel 7029; Nissen 1502; Henrey (Brit.bot.) 289; STC 19595; Arents 13; Shaaber P150; JCB AR51:53-54. CSt, CtY-M, DLC, MH, MiU, NN-A, PU, RPJCB; BL, BN.   571/30

Portugal. Laws, statutes, etc. Ley de como ham de hir armados os navios que destes reynos navegarem. *Lisbon: J.de Barreira*, 1571. 24 numb.lvs;8vo. In addition to regulations for voyages to Brazil, contains also laws against sodomy and against traffic in heretical works, the latter punishable by banishment or exile to Brazil. Anselmo 211; King Manuel 128. Coimbra: BU.   571/31

Rabelais, François. Oeuvres. *Lyons: P.Estiard*, 1571. 3pts;port.;16mo. Includes 'Le quart livre', 1st publ., Paris, 1552. Plan (Rabelais) 102. DeU; BL.   571/32

Renner, Franz. Ein sehr nützlichs und heilsams, wolgegründets Handtbüchlein, gemeiner Practick, aller innerlicher unnd eusserliche Ertzney, so wider die abscheuliche Kranckheyt der Frantzosen und Lemung, auch für all ander Seuchten . . . von newen ubersehen, augirt und gebessert. *Nuremberg: C.Heussler*, 1571. 217 numb.lvs;illus.;4to. 1st publ., Nuremberg, 1554. Proksch I:17. DNLM; BL.   571/33

Ronsard, Pierre de. Oeuvres. *Paris: G.Buon*, 1571. 6v.;8vo. Includes, v.6, the *Continuation du Discours des misères de ce temps*, 1st publ., Paris, 1562. Tchémerzine IX:473. MH; BN.   571/34

Sarrasin, Jean Antoine. De peste commentarius. *Geneva: J.Grégoire*, 1571. 345p.;8vo. Among plants recommended for treatment of plague sores is tobacco. Arents (Add.) 49. NN-A.   571/35

Serres, Jean de. Commentariorum de statu religionis & reipublicae in regno Galliae . . . Ia partis, libri iii. *[Geneva: E.Vignon]* 1571. 356p.;8vo. 1st publ., [Geneva], 1570. Adams (Cambr.) L185. CLSU, MH, WU; Cambridge: UL.   571/36

Soto, Domingo de. De justitia & jure libri decem. *Salamanca: J.B.à Terranova,for B. Boyer,* 1571. fol. 1st publ., Salamanca, 1553. Palau 320150.   571/37

Spain. Consejo de las Indias. Ordenanças reales del Consejo de las Indias. [*Madrid:* 1571?]. xxii lvs;fol. Dated 24 Sept. 1571. Comprises code for civil administration of the Council, including designation of official chronicler & cosmographer for the Indies. Medina (BHA) 220; Pérez Pastor (Madrid) I:50& 50 bis (p.402); JCB AR45:17-26. RPJCB.
                                    571/38

Surius, Laurentius. Histoire, ou Commentaires de toutes choses memorables avenues depuys lxx ans . . . par toutes les parties du monde . . . nouvellement mis en françois par Jacq. Estourneau. *Paris: G.Chaudière,* 1571. 444 numb.lvs;4to. Transl. from the author's *Commentarius brevis rerum in orbe gestarum,* 1st publ. separately, Paris, 1566. Cf.Sabin 93887; Cioranescu (XVI)9735.1; Atkinson (Fr.Ren.) 218. RPJCB; BN.   571/39

Teluccini, Mario. Artemidoro. *Venice: D.& G.B.Guerra,* 1571. 467p.;4to. Chivalric poem. 1st publ., Venice, 1566.   571/40

Torquemada, Antonio de. Jardín de flores curiosas. *Saragossa: Widow of B.de Nágera,* 1571. 276 numb.lvs;8vo. 1st publ., Salamanca, 1570. In verse. Sánchez (Aragon) 501; Palau 334908.   571/41

Vigo, Giovanni de. The most excellent workes of chirurgerie. *London: T.East & H.Middelton,* 1571. cclxx lvs;fol. 1st publ. in this translation by B.Traheron, London, 1543. STC 24722. CLU, CtY, DNLM, NNNAM; BL.
                                    571/42

1572

Alonso de la Veracruz, Father. Speculum conjugiorum. *Alcalá de Henares: J.Gracián* 1572. 658p.;4to. 1st publ., Mexico City, 1557; cf.Salamanca, 1562, reprinting. Sabin 29332 (& 98919n); Medina (BHA) 226; Bolaño e Isla (Veracruz) 61 (no.3); Streit I:113; García (Alcalá de Henares) 481. Madrid: BN. 572/1

Arfe y Villafañe, Juan de. Quilatador de la plata, oro, y piedras. *Valladolid: A. & D. Fernández de Córdoba,* 1572. 71 numb. lvs; illus.;4to. Includes refs to precious metals & jewels received from New World. Alcocer

(Valladolid) 271; Ind.aur.107.216; Adams (Cambr.) A2004; Kress S.204; Palau 16053. CtY-M, MH, NN-RB; BL, BN.   572/2

Arias Montanus, Benedictus. In Benedicti Ariae Montani adnotationes, a D. Antonio Ruiz Morales y Molina. *Antwerp:* 1572. 8vo. 1st publ., Antwerp, 1569. The annotator has been identified, perhaps mistakenly, by Medina & others, as António Rúiz de Morales y Molina, successively Bishop of Michoacán and of Puebla de los Angeles. Not recorded in the *Index aureliensis,* this edition may be a ghost. Medina (BHA) 225; Palau 282127 & 16465n.
                                    572/3

Aristoteles. Organum. Latin (Selections). Resolutio dialectica cum textu Aristotelis admodum . . . fratris Alphonsi à Vera Cruce . . . Nunc quarto . . . revisa ab autore. *Salamanca: J.B.à Terranova,* 1572. 255p.;fol. 1st publ., Mexico City, 1554; cf.Salamanca, 1562, edn. Palau 359148.   572/4

Belleforest, François de. L'histoire universelle du monde . . . nouvellement augmentee. *Paris: G.Mallot;* 1572. 325 numb.lvs;port.; 4to. 1st publ., Paris, 1570. Atkinson (Fr.Ren.) 227; cf.Borba de Moraes I:82; Ind.aur. 116.108. MBAt, NNH; Munich: StB.   572/5

—[Anr issue]. *Paris: J.Hulpeau,* 1572. Atkinson (Fr.Ren.) 227n. MnU-B.   572/6

Benzoni, Girolamo. La historia del Mondo Nuovo . . . Nuovamente ristampata et illustrata con la giunta d'alcune cose notabile dell'isole di Canaria. *Venice: Heirs of G.M. Bonelli,for P.& F.Tini,* 1572. 179 numb. lvs;illus.,port.;8vo. 1st publ., Venice, 1565. Sabin 4791; Streit II:887; Ind.aur.116.986; Adams (Cambr.) B688; Arents (Add.) 51; JCB (3) I:248. CSmH, MH, NN-A, RPJCB; BL, BN.   572/7

Bock, Hieronymus. Kreutterbuch. *Strassburg: J.Rihel,* 1572. fol. 1st publ. with illus., Strassburg, 1546. Pritzel 866n; Nissen (Bot.) 182n; Ind.aur.120.597. IU, PPL; BL.   572/8

Bodin, Jean. Methodus ad facilem historiarum cognitionem, ab ipso recognita et multo . . . locupletior. *Paris: M.LeJeune,* 1572. 614p.;8vo. 1st publ., Paris, 1566. Ind.aur. 120.803; Adams (Cambr.) B2242. CtY, ICN, MH, PPL, RPJCB; Cambridge: UL, BN.
                                    572/9

Bolognini, Angelo. De la curation des ulcères exterieurs du corps humain. *Lyons: B. Rigaud,* 1572. 16mo. 1st publ. in French,

Paris, 1542. Ind.aur.121.503; Baudrier (Lyons) III:277.   572/10

Brant, Sebastian. Stultifera navis mortalium . . . per Jacobum Locher . . . latinitati donatus: nunc vero revisus, & elegantissimis figuris recens illustratus. *Basel: H.Petri*, 1572. 284p.;illus.;8vo. 1st publ., Basel, 1497. Ind. aur.123.749; Adams (Cambr.) B2673. RPJCB; BL, BN.   572/11

Braun, Georg. Civitates orbis terrarum [Liber primus]. *Cologne: T.Graminaeus,for the authors & P.Galle,at Antwerp*, 1572. 59 double pls;fol. Views of cities engraved by Frans Hogenberg, with descriptions by Braun. Included are Mexico City & Cusco, Peru. The subsequent 5 vols. are without American interest. Sabin 7448; Koeman (Braun & Hogenberg) 1; Ind.aur.123.943. DLC, NNC; BL, BN.   572/12

Caro, Annibale. De le lettere familiari . . . volume primo. *Venice: A.Manuzio*, 1572. 296p.;4to. A letter of 10 May 1539 refers to 'legno d'India,' i.e., Guaiacum. Ind.aur. 132.470; Adams (Cambr.) C740. DLC; Cambridge: UL, Berlin: StB.   572/13

Chaumette, Antoine. Enchiridion, ou Livret portatif des chirurgiens . . . Ausquels est adjouste de nouveau une methode . . . pour guerir la verole. *Lyons: L.Cloquemin*, 1572. 569p.;8vo. 1st publ. in French, Lyons, 1571. Baudrier (Lyons) IV:46. CtY-M; Bordeaux: BM.   572/14

Chaves, Jerónimo de. Chronographia; ó, Reportorio de los tiempos. *Seville: A.Escrivano*, 1572. 272 numb.lvs;illus.,port.,map;4to. 1st publ., Seville, 1548. Sabin 12351; Medina (BHA) 222; Palau 67454; Adams (Cambr.) C1422. DLC, MB, NN-RB; Cambridge: Sidney Sussex.   572/15

Cortés, Martín. The arte of navigation . . . Written in the Spanish tongue . . . Translated . . . by Richarde Eden, and now newly corrected and amended in dyvers places. [*London:*] *R.Jug*, 1572. lxxxiii lvs;illus.,map;4to. 1st publ. in English, London, 1561. STC 5799. NN-RB; BL.   572/16

Costa, Manuel da. Historia rerum a Societate Jesu in Oriente gestarum. *Paris: M.Sonnius*, 1572. 246 numb.lvs;8vo. 1st publ., Dillingen, 1571, but with here added a letter of Pietro Díaz, 1st publ., Rome, 1570, describing martyrdom of Inácio de Azevedo & other Jesuits en route to Brazil. Subsequent edns with addi-

tional text will be found under heading: Jesuits. Letters from Missions (The East). Streit IV:956; Ind.aur.100.471. CtY, MH; BL, BN.   572/17

Donati, Marcello. Traité de l'admirable vertue . . . de la racine nouvelle de l'Inde de Mechiaacan . . . écrit en latin . . . traduit par Pierre Tolet. *Lyons: M.Jouve*, 1572. 8vo. Transl. from author's *De Mechoacanna*, 1st publ., Mantua, 1569. Baudrier (Lyons) II:130.   572/18

Emili, Paolo. Französischer und anderer Nationen . . . Historien . . . durch Johann Thomas Frey biss auff . . . 1572 . . . verlengert. *Basel: S.Henricpetri*, 1572. 2pts;illus.; fol. Transl. by Christian Wurstisen from author's *De rebus gestis Francorum*, 1st publ., Paris, 1548-49. The present edn is prob. translated from the Basel, 1569, edn of the larger work with title *Historiae . . . de rebus gestis Francorum*. Ind.aur.100.836. ICN, NNC; Munich: StB.   572/19

Estienne, Charles. L'agriculture et maison rustique, . . . augmentée par m. Jean Liebault. *Paris: J.DuPuys*, 1572. 252 numb. lvs;illus.;4to. 1st publ. in this version, Paris, 1567. Thiébaud (La chasse) 344. DNLM, MH.   572/20

Falloppius, Gabriel. Secreti diversi et miracolosi, nuovamente ristampati. *Venice: G.F. Camozio*, 1572. 366p.;8vo. 1st publ., Venice, 1563. DFo, DNLM.   572/21

Foglietta, Uberto. Clarorum Ligurum elogia. *Rome: Heirs of A.Blado*, 1572. 84p.;4to. Included among the Ligurians here praised is Columbus, for his discoveries. Adams (Cambr.) F664. BL.   572/22

Fragoso, Juan. Discursos de la cosas aromaticas y de medicinas simples de la India Oriental. *Madrid: F.Sánchez,for S.Ibáñez*, 1572. 211 numb.lvs;8vo. Though ostensibly discussing Eastern herbs, etc., includes numerous references to those of the New World, based on Monardes. Sabin 25418a; Medina (BHA) 223; Pérez Pastor (Madrid) 58; Pritzel 3000; Arents 16. CU, CtY, DNLM, MH-A, NN-A; BL, BN.   572/23

Genebrard, Gilbert, Abp of Aix. Chronographia. *Louvain: J.Fowler*, 1572. 390 (i.e.,293) numb.lvs;12mo. 1st publ., Paris, 1567. Adams (Cambr.) G396. BL, BN.572/24

Gesner, Konrad. Euonymus . . . De remediis secretis, pars secunda. *Lyons: J.Marcorelle,for*

B.Vincent, 1572. 531p.;illus.;12mo. 1st publ., Zurich, 1569. MnU-B, NNC; BN. 572/25

Gohory, Jacques. Instruction sur l'herbe Petum ditte en France de la Royne ou Medicée: et sur la racine Mechiocan. *Paris: G.duPré*, 1572. 2pts;illus.;8vo. The 2nd pt, the 'Brief traitté de la racine Mechoacan', is a translation from Nicolás Monardes. Atkinson (Fr.Ren.) 228; Guerra (Monardes) 12; Arents 17. CU, CtY, ICN, MH, NN-A; BL, BN. 572/26

Guilandini, Melchior. Papyrus, hoc est, Commentarius in tria C.Plinii majoris de papyro capita. *Venice: M.Olmo*, 1572. 280p.;4to. Included are refs to plants introduced from New World, e.g. cocoa, marigolds & Guaiacum. Pritzel 3639; Adams (Cambr.) G1562. ICN, MH, MiU, MnU, NN-RB; BL. 572/27

Honter, Johannes. Rudimentorum cosmographicorum . . . libri iiii. *Rostock: J.Stöckelmann & A.Gutterwitz*, 1572. [60]p. 1st publ. in this version, Kronstadt, 1542. In verse. Borsa 97; Szabo III:739. Copenhagen: KB. 572/28

Jesuits. Portugal. Epistola patrum lusitanorum Societatis Jesu . . . de duodecim eiusdam Societatis . . . interfectis, mense septembri 1571. *Naples: G.Cacchi*, 1572. 22p.;8vo. Signed at end by Franciscus Henricus, 'v. id. decembris MDLXXI', includes 'Exitum Ignatii Azebedii et sociorum novem et triginta', i.e., the Jesuit group murdered en route to Brazil by French Calvinists. Sabin 31382; Borba de Moraes I:246; Streit II:1302. Munich: StB. 572/29

La Popelinière, Lancelot Voisin, sieur de. La vraye et entiere histoire des troubles . . . avenues tant en France qu'en Flandres . . . depuis l'an 1562. Comprinse en quatorze livres: les trois premiers, & dernier desquels sont nouveau. *Basel: P.Davantes*, 1572. 2v.(481 numb.lvs);8vo. The earliest edn to contain, in bk 3, an account of the seizure of a Portuguese ship en route to Brazil, 1570, by French Calvinists, and subsequent murder of Inácio Azevedo & his fellow Jesuits. DFo, MnU-B, NN-RB; BL, BN. 572/30

Lucidarius. M. Elucidarius von allerhand Geschöpffen Gottes . . . und wie alle Creaturen geschaffen seind auff Erden. *Frankfurt a.M.: M.Lechler,for Heirs of C.Egenolff*, 1572. [102]p.;illus.;4to. 1st publ., Strassburg, [ca.1535]. Schorbach (Lucidarius) 60. Bonn: UB. 572/31

Marguérite d'Angouleme, Queen of Navarre. L'heptameron ou Histoires des amans fortunez. *Lyons: L.Cloquemin*, 1572. 812p.; 16mo. 1st publ. in this version, Paris, 1559. Adams (Cambr.) M566; Tchémerzine VII:394; Baudrier (Lyons) IV:46-47. Cambridge: Trinity. 572/32

Mattioli, Pietro Andrea. Commentaires . . . sur les six livres de Ped. Dioscoride . . . De la matiere medicinale . . . mis en françois sur la derniere edition latine de l'autheur, par m. Jean des Moulin. *Lyons: [P.Roussin,for] G. Rouillé*, 1572. 819p.;illus.;fol. Transl. from author's *Commentarii*, 1st publ., Venice, 1554. Pritzel 5991n; Nissen (Bot.) 1313; Baudrier (Lyons) IX:339-40. DLC, MiU, NNBG; BL, BN. 572/33

——. Commentaires . . . sur les six livres de Pedacius Dioscoride . . . de la matiere medicinale: traduits de latin . . . par m. Antoine du Pinet. *Lyons: Widow of G.Cotier*, 1572. 599p.;illus.;fol. Cf.the preceding item, representing a different translation. Baudrier (Lyons) IV:81-82. BN. 572/34

Meerman, Arnould. Theatrum conversionum gentium totius orbis. *Antwerp: C.Plantin*, 1572. 192p.;8vo. On p.141 is a ref. to New World. Streit I:114; Belg.typ. (1541-1600) I:2098. DHN; BL, Brussels: BR. 572/35

Mexía, Pedro. Les diverses leçons . . . mises en françois par Claude Gruget . . . augmentées de trois dialogues. *Paris: C.Micard*, 1572. 472 numb.lvs;16mo. 1st publ. in this version with supplementary dialogues, Paris, 1556. Adams (Cambr.) M1382; Palau 167315. Cambridge: UL, BN. 572/36

Münster, Sebastian. A briefe collection and compendious extract of straunge and memorable thinges, gathered oute of the Cosmo-. graphye of Sebastian Munster. *London: T.Marsh*, 1572. 100 numb.lvs;8vo. Transl. by Richard Eden from the author's *Cosmographei*, 1st publ., Basel, 1544. Sabin 51405; Burmeister (Münster) 111; STC 18242. BL(imp.). 572/37

——. Cosmographey, oder Beschreibung aller Länder. *Basel: H.Petri*, 1572. 1467p.;illus., maps;fol. 1st publ., Basel, 1544. Burmeister (Münster) 78. Freiburg i. Br.: UB, Groningen: UB. 572/38

_____. Cosmographiae universalis lib. vi. *Basel: H.Petri*, 1572. 1333p.;illus.,maps;fol. 1st publ. in Latin, Basel, 1550. Sabin 51383; Burmeister (Münster) 91; JCB (3) I:249. CSmH, DLC, InU-L, MH, NHi, RPJCB; BL, Munich: StB.   572/39

Ortelius, Abraham. Theatrum oder Schawplatz des erdbodens. *Antwerp: G.Coppens v.Diest*, 1572. 193 lvs,incl.maps;fol. The earliest authorized German edn; transl. from the author's Antwerp, 1570, Latin edn. Cf.Sabin 57706; Koeman (Ort.) 5; Phillips (Atlases) 376. DLC, InU-L, MiU-C.   572/40

_____. Théatre de l'univers. *Antwerp: G.Coppens v.Diest*, 1572. 10 lvs;53maps;fol. Transl. from the author's Antwerp, 1570, Latin edn. Atkinson (Fr.Ren.) 231; Koeman(Ort.) 4; Phillips (Atlases) 3391; JCB (3) I:249. DLC, InU-L, RPJCB.   572/41

Pantaleon, Heinrich. Diarium historicum. *Basel: H.P[etri].*, 1572. 394p.;port.;fol. 1st publ., Basel, 1550, under title *Chronographia ecclesiae christianae*. Adams (Cambr.) P176. BL, BN.   572/42

Paracelsus. De medicamentorum simplicium gradibus et compositionibus. *Zurich: C.Froschauer*, 1572. 26 numb.lvs;8vo. Ed. by B. Aretus. Includes chapter on Guaiacum. Sudhoff (Paracelsus) 139. DNLM, IaU; BL.   572/43

Peucer, Kaspar. Commentarius de praecipuis generibus divinationum. *Wittenberg: J.Lufft*, 1572. 440 numb.lvs;8vo. 1st (?) publ. in enl. edn, Wittenberg, 1560. Adams (Cambr.) P931; Shaaber P249. DFo, NNG, PU; Cambridge: UL, BN.   572/43a

Porcacchi, Tommaso. L'isole piu famose del mondo . . . intagliate da Girolamo Porro. *Venice: S.Galignani & G.Porro*, 1572. 117p.; maps;fol. Includes text describing maps showing Temistitan (Mexico), Spagnuola, Cuba, etc. Sabin 64148; Palau 23891; JCB (3) I:250. MH, NNH, RPJCB; BL, BN.   572/44

Recueil de la diversite des habits. Omnium fere gentium nostraeque aetatis nationum, habitus & effigies. In eosdem Joannis Sluperius . . . epigrammata. *Antwerp: G.van den Rade,for J.Bellère*, 1572. 135 lvs;illus.; 8vo. Contains Sluperius's Latin translation, accompanying original French text, 1st publ., Paris, 1562. Borba de Moraes II:265; Belg.typ. (1541-1600) I:4361; Fairfax Murray

(France) 479. DLC, NN-RB; BL, Brussels: BR.   572/45

Renner, Franz. Ein sehr nützlichs und heilsams, wolgegrundets Handtbüchlein, gemeiner Practick, aller innerlicher unnd eusserliche Ertzney, so wider die abscheuliche Kranckheyt der Frantzosen und Lemung, auch für all ander Seuchten . . . von newen ubersehen, augirt und gebessert. *Nuremberg: C.Heussler*, 1572. 217 numb.lvs;illus.;4to. Anr issue, with altered imprint date, of the publisher's 1571 edn; 1st publ., Nuremberg, 1554. Proksch I:17. DNLM.   572/46

Rivadeneira, Pedro de. Vita Ignatii Loiolae, Societatis Jesu fundatoris, libris quinque comprehensa. *Naples: G.Cacchi*, 1572. 217 numb. lvs;8vo. In bk 3, chapt. xix describes Jesuit mission to Brazil. Sabin 70782; Streit I:115; Palau 266202. MH, NIC; BL, BN.   572/47

Román y Zamora, Jerónimo. Primera parte de la Historia de la Orden de los frayles hermitaños de sant Augustin. *Alcalá de Henares: A.de Angulo*, 1572. 365 numb.lvs; fol. 1st publ., Salamanca, 1569. Medina (BHA) 224; cf.Streit I:106; García (Alcalá de Henares) 479; Palau 276580. NNH, RPJCB; BL.   572/48

Ronsard, Pierre de. Oeuvres. *Paris: G.Buon*, 1572-73. 6v.;ports;8vo. Includes, v.6, the *Continuation du Discours des misères de ce temps*, 1st publ., Paris, 1562. Tchémerzine IX:474. DFo, MH; BN.   572/49

Rúiz de Morales y Molina, Antonio, Bp of Michoacan. In Benedicti Ariae Montani Rhetoricam annotationes. *Antwerp*: 1572. 8vo. Cf. entry under year 1569 above for Arias Montanus. Medina (BHA) 225; Palau 282127.   572/50

Ruscelli, Girolamo, comp. Epistres des princes . . . Recueillies d'italien par Hieronyme Ruscelli, & mises en françois par François de Belle Forest. *Paris: J.Ruelle*, 1572. 209 numb.lvs;4to. Transl. from compiler's *Lettere di principi*, 1st publ., Venice, 1562. Cioranescu (XVI) 3419. ICU, NN-RB; BL, BN.   572/51

_____. Le imprese illustri con espositioni, et dicorsi . . . Con la giunta di altre impresse tutto riordinato et corretto da Fran[ces].co Patritio. *Venice: Comin da Trino*, 1572. 288 numb.lvs;illus.,port.;4to. 1st publ., Venice, 1566. Adams (Cambr.) R953; Moranti (Urbino) 2984; cf.Mortimer (Italy) 449. CSmH,

CtY, DFo, ICN, MH, MiU, NN-RB; BL, BN.
572/52

____. Lettere di principi. *Venice: G.Ziletti*, 1572. 246 numb.lvs;4to. 1st publ., Venice, 1562. BN. 572/53

Sacro Bosco, Joannes de. La sfera . . . tradotta, emendata in capitoli da Piervincentio Dante de Rinaldo con molte . . . annotazioni . . . Rivista da frate Egnatio Danti. *Florence: The Giuntas*, 1571 [colophon: 1572]. 68p.; illus.;port.,4to. Danti's annotations include refs to Columbus & the New World in those for bk 1, ch.8, bk 2, ch.7 & bk 3, ch.12. In the last, Seneca's *Medea* prediction of new worlds is cited. Sabin 32683; Adams (Cambr.) H740; JCB (3) I:297. CtY, DLC, MiU, NN-RB, PPC, RPJCB; BL. 572/54

____. Sphaera . . . emendata. Eliae Vineti . . . Scholia. *Paris: J.de Marnef & G.Cavellat*, 1572. 94 numb.lvs;illus.;8vo. 1st publ. with Vinet's *Scholia*, Paris, 1551. Sabin 32681. BL, BN. 572/55

Sarrasin, Jean Antoine. De peste commentarius. [*Geneva*:] *G.Grégoire*, 1572, 345p.; 8vo. 1st publ., Geneva, 1571; here reissued with altered imprint date. Arents (Add.) 50. CtY-M, DLC, NN-A; BL, BN. 572/56

__[Anr issue]. [*Geneva: G.Grégoire, for*] *L.Cloquemin, at Lyons*, 1572. Baudrier (Lyons) IV:46. Paris: Ste Geneviève. 572/57

Serres, Jean de. Commentariorum de statu religionis et reipublicae in regno Galliae . . . I. partis, libri iii. [*Geneva: E.Vignon*] 1572. 184 numb.lvs;8vo. 1st publ., [Geneva], 1570. Adams (Cambr.) L186. CtY, MH-AH, PCarlD; Cambridge: UL. 572/58

Surius, Laurentius. Histoire, ou Commentaire de toutes choses memorables avenue . . . par toutes les parties du monde. *Paris: G.Chaudière*, 1572. 446 numb.lvs;8vo. 1st publ. as here transl. by Jacques Lestourneau, Paris, 1571. Cf.Sabin 93887; Atkinson (Fr.Ren.) 232. ICN; BN. 572/59

1573

Albornoz, Bartolomé de. Arte de los contractos. *Valencia: P.de Huete*, 1573. 176 numb. lvs;4to. Includes discussion of slave trade. Medina (BHA) 227; Streit I:117; Ind.aur. 102.802; Palau 5357. MH-L; Berlin: StB.
573/1

Alonso de la Veracruz, Father. Physica speculatio . . . Quarta editio. *Salamanca: J.B.à Terranova*, 1573. 430p.;fol. 1st publ., Mexico City, 1557; cf.1562, Salamanca, edn. Sabin 98917; Medina (BHA) 232; Bolaño e Isla (Veracruz) 58 (no.4). Seville: BU. 573/2

____. Recognitio summularum, cum textu Petri Hispani, & Aristotelis . . . Nunc quartò . . . revisa ab authore. *Salamanca: J.B.à Terranova, for V.& S.de Portonariis*, 1573. 159p.; illus.;fol. 1st publ., Mexico City, 1554; cf.Salamanca, 1562, reprinting. Sabin 98918n; Medina (BHA) 230; Bolaño e Isla (Veracruz) 50-51 (no.4); Palau 159143. N; Salamanca: BU. 573/3

Anania, Giovanni Lorenzo d'. L'universale fabbrica del mondo . . . in quattro trattati. *Naples: G.Cacchi*, 1573. 8vo. The 4th treatise describes the New World. Cf.Sabin 1364; Ind.aur.105.085. Berlin: StB. 573/4

Apianus, Petrus. Cosmographie, oft Beschrijvinghe der gheheelder werelt . . . ghecorrigeert van Gemma Frisio. *Antwerp: J.Verwithagen*, 1573. lxxv lvs;illus.,maps;4to. 1st publ. in this Dutch version, Antwerp, 1561. Cf.Sabin 1754; Ortroy (Apian) 49; Ind.aur. 106.459. MnU-B; Ghent: BU. 573/5

Aristoteles. Organum. Latin (Selections). Resolutio dialectica cum textu Aristotelis admodum . . . fratris Alphonsi à Vera Cruce . . . Nunc quarto . . . revisa ab autore. *Salamanca: J.B.à Terranova, for V.& S.Portonariis*, 1573. 231p.;fol. 1st publ., Mexico City, 1554; cf.Salamanca, 1562, edn. Medina (BHA) 231; Bolaño e Isla (Veracruz) 54-55 (no.4); cf.Palau 359148. Seville: BU. 573/6

Baptista Mantuanus. Opera. *Frankfurt a.M.: Lucienberg*, 1573. 4v.;8vo. Vol.1 contains 'Fastorum libri 12', 1st publ., Lyons, 1516; v.2, 'Exhortationes ad reges et principes christianos', 1st publ., Milan, 1507; and, v.4, 'De patientia', 1st publ., Brescia, 1497. Ind.aur. 112.775; Coccia 430. Munich: UB. 573/7

Bellinato, Francesco, supposed author. Discorso di cosmografia in dialogo. *Venice: A.Manuzio*, 1573. 58p.;8vo. On p.48-49 is a brief description of the New World. Ind. aur.116.208; Renouard (Aldus) 245-246n; Adams (Cambr.) B526. CtY, NNH, NN-RB; Cambridge: Trinity. 573/8

Bizzarri, Pietro. Pannonicum belli . . . Una cum epitome illarum rerum, quae in Europa insigniores gestae sunt . . . ab anno LXIIII usque ad LXXIII. *Basel: S.Henricpetri*, 1573. 322p.;8vo. Transl. & expanded from author's *Historia . . . della guerra fatta in Ungaria*, 1st publ., Lyons, 1568. Includes, p.238-278, account of French in Florida & Canada. Ind. aur.119.707; Adams (Cambr.) B2087; JCB AR55:16-20. CtY, ICN, MH, MiU, MnU-B, RPJCB; BL, Munich: StB.   573/9

Boemus, Johann. I costumi, le leggi, et l'usanze di tutte le genti . . . Aggiuntovi di nuovo il quarto libro, nelquale si narra i costumi & l'usanze dell'Indie Occidentali, overo Mondo Novo, da . . . Gieronimo Giglio. *Venice: D.Farri*, 1573. 8vo. 1st publ. with Giglio's 4th bk on New World, Venice, 1558. Ind.aur.120.964. ICN, NN-RB; Vienna: NB.
573/10

Bordini, Francesco. Quaesitorum et responsorum mathematicae disciplinae chilias. *Bologna: A.Benacci*, 1573. [390]p.;4to. Includes passages relating to Brazil, Florida, Newfoundland & Peru. Ind. aur.122.341; Adams (Cambr.) B2481. CtY, ICN, MiU, NN-RB; BL, BN.   573/11

Caro, Annibale. De le lettere familiari . . . volume primo. *Venice: A.Manuzio*, 1573. 296p.;4to. 1st publ., Venice, 1572. Ind.aur. 132.474. BL.   573/12

Castillejo, Cristóbal de. Obras. *Madrid: P. Cosin*, 1573. 912p.;8vo. Includes in bk 2 the author's 'Alabanza del palo de las Indias' (i.e., Guaiacum), as a cure for syphilis. Pérez Pastor (Madrid) 68; Palau 48017. NNH; BL, Madrid: BN.   573/13

Cooper, Thomas, Bp of Winchester. Thesaurus linguae romanae & britannicae. *London: [J.Charlewood?]*, 1573. [1716]p.;fol. 1st publ., London, 1565. STC 5687; Shaaber C668. CSmH, CtY, DFo, ICU, MB, MiDSH, NN-RB, PU-F; BL.   573/14

Danti, Antonio, da Santa Maria in Bagno. Osservationi di diverse historie et d'altri particolari degni di memoria. *Venice: G.Angelieri,for M.Boselli*, 1573. 168 numb. lvs;4to. Includes chapters on syphilis & how it reached Italy from the New World, on Portuguese & Spanish navigations, & on the Indians of the New World. Sabin 18508. CtY, DLC, IU, MBAt; BL.   573/15

Dictionaire françois-latin . . . Recuelli des observations de plusieurs hommes doctes: entre autres de m. [Jean] Nicot. *Paris: J.DuPuys*, 1573. 781p.;fol. Included is the

word 'Nicotiane' designating tobacco. Arents (Add.) 55. DLC, NN-A, WaU.   573/16

Estienne, Charles. L'agriculture et maison rustique. *Paris: J.DuPuys*, 1573. 255 numb. lvs;4to. 1st publ. in this edn enlarged by Jean Liébault, Paris, 1565. Thiébaud (La chasse) 344n; Arents (Add.) 29. NN-A.   573/17

Falloppius, Gabriel. Kunstbuch. *Augsburg: M.Manger,for G.Willers*, 1573. 366(i.e., 466) p.;8vo. 1st publ. in German, Augsburg, 1571. DNLM.   573/18

Fioravanti, Leonardo. De capricci medicinali . . . Di nuovo, dall'istesso autore . . . ampliati . . . revisti, corretti, & ristampati. *Venice: L.degli Avanzi*, 1573. 283 numb.lvs;illus.;8vo. 1st publ., Venice, 1561. Shaaber F93. DNLM, MiU, PU.   573/19

Foglietta, Uberto. Clarorum Ligurum elogia. *Rome: Heirs of A.Blado*, 1573. 265p.;4to. 1st publ., Rome, 1572. Sabin 24942; Adams (Cambr.) F665; Shaaber F335. JCB (3) I:250. CtY, ICN, MnU-B, PU, RPJCB; BL, BN.
573/20

Fontanon, Denys. De morborum internorum curatione libri iiii. *Lyons: A.de Harsy*, 1573. 635p.;8vo. 1st publ., Lyons, 1549. CtY-M.
573/21

Gesner, Konrad. Quatre livres des secrets de medecine . . . Faicts françois par m. Jean Liébault. *Paris: J.Sevestre,for J.DuPuys*, 1573. 297 numb.lvs;illus.;8vo. Paraphrased and enlarged by Liébault from Gesner's *Euonymus. De remediis secretis, pars secunda*, 1st publ., Zurich, 1569. CtY, DNLM, MH; London: Wellcome.   573/22

Geuffroy, Antoine. Aulae Turcicae Othomannicicae imperii, descriptio . . . Item, Bellum Pannonicum . . . Una, cum Epitome insigniorum . . . historiam, hinc inde gestarum, ab anno M.D.LXIIII. usque LXXIII. deducta. Authore, Petro Bizaro. *Basel: S.Henricpetri*, 1573. 3v.;8vo. Transl. from author's 1542 *Estat de la cour*. The American refs are found, however, in v.l, in Baptista Mantuanus's 'Objurgatio', 1st publ., Milan, 1507, &, in v.3 (with its distinct t.p.) in Bizzarri's *Pannonicum belli*. The latter comprises the 1st Latin edn (transl. & expanded from Bizzarri's *Historia . . . della guerra fatta in Ungaria*, Lyons, 1568), with, in the 'Epitome' an extended account of French activity in Florida & Canada. Ind.aur.119.707; Adams (Cambr.) B2087 & G559; Shaaber G156. JCB

AR55:16-20. CtY, ICJ(v.3 only) MH, MnU-B, NN-RB, PU, RPJCB(v.3 only); BL, BN.

573/23

Giglio, Girolamo. Nuova seconda selva de varia lettione che segue Pietro Messia. *Venice: C.Zanetti*, 1573. 207 numb.lvs;8vo. 1st publ., Venice, 1565. Sabin 48240; JCB (3) I:250. NcD, RPJCB; BL.

573/24

Gómara, Francisco López de. Historia di Messico, con il discoprimento della nuova Spagna. *Venice: [G.Ziletti?]* 1573. 402 numb. lvs;8vo. 1st publ. in this Italian version transl. by L.Mauro, Venice, 1566, under title *La terza parte delle Historie dell'Indie.* Cf.Sabin 27742; Wagner (SW) 2z. NN-RB(imp.).

573/25

Honter, Johannes. Rudimentorum cosmographicorum . . . libri iii. *Zurich: C. Froschauer*, 1573. 44 lvs;maps,illus.;8vo. 1st publ. in this version, Kronstadt, 1542. In verse. CtY, IU; BL.

573/26

Jesuits. Letters from missions (The East). Rerum a Societate Jesu in Oriente volumen. *Naples: H.Salviani*, 1573. 236 numb.lvs;4to. 1st publ., Dillingen, 1571, with here 1st added letters on the martyrdom of Inácio de Azevedo & other Jesuits en route to Brazil, that of Pietro Diaz, 1st publ., Rome, 1570, in the *Nuovi avisi*, and that of Francisco Henriques, 1st publ., Naples, 1572, in the *Epistola patrum Lusitanorum.* Streit IV:958; Ind. aur.100.472. MnU-B, NN-RB; BL. 573/27

La Popelinière, Lancelot Voisin, sieur de. La vraye et entière histoire des troubles . . . avenues depuis l'an 1562. *La Rochelle: P. Davantes* [i.e., *Geneva? J.Stoer?*] 1573. 426 numb.lvs;8vo. 1st publ., Basel, 1572. On probable false imprint, see E.Droz, 'Fausses adresses typographiques', *Bibliothèque d'humanisme et renaissance*, XXIII (1961) 144-146. Rép.bibl.,XVI:33. ICN; BL, BN.

573/28

Lonitzer, Adam. Kräuterbuch . . . zum fünften Mal durchsehen, gebessert und gemahret. *Frankfurt a.M.: M.Lechler,for Heirs of C.Egenolff*, 1573. fol. 1st publ., Frankfurt, 1557. Pritzel 5599n; Nissen (Bot.) 1228n. BL.

573/29

Mainoldus, Jacobus. De titulis Philippi Austrii Regis . . . liber. *Bologna: P.Bonardo*, 1573. 120 numb.lvs;illus.;4to. Includes section (lvs 26-37) 'De regnis insularum, terrae firmae & maris oceani', covering events there

from Columbus's discoveries through the year 1541. CtY, DLC, ICU, InU-L, NN-RB, RPJCB; BL, BN.

573/30

Mattioli, Pietro Andrea. Commentaires . . . sur les six livres de Pedacius Dioscoride De la matiere medicinale . . . Traduits de latin . . . par Antoine DuPinet. *Lyons: Widow of G. Cotier*, 1573. 2pts;illus.,port.;fol. 1st publ. in this version, Lyons, 1561; here a reissue of the Widow Cotier's 1572 edn? MH-A.

573/31

————. I discorsi . . . nelli sei libri di Pedacio Dioscoride . . . della materia medicinale. *Venice: Heirs of V.Valgrisi*, 1573. 971p.; illus.;fol. 1st publ., Venice, 1555. Cf.Pritzel 5988; Nissen (Bot.) 1304n. DNLM; BL, BN.

573/32

Medina, Pedro de. L'art de naviguer. *Rouen: J.Crevel,B.Belis,G.Pavie & R.Mallard*, 1573. 274p.;illus.,map;4to. 1st publ. in French, Lyons, 1554. Sabin 47345n; Palau 159672. NN-RB.

573/33

Meerman, Arnould. Theatrum conversionum gentium totius orbis. *Antwerp: C.Plantin*, 1573. 192p.;8vo. 1st publ., Antwerp, 1572. Cf.Streit I:114; Belg.typ (1541-1600) I:2099. NN-RB; Brussels: BR.

573/34

Moleti, Giuseppe. Discorso . . . nel quale con via facile . . . si dichiarano & insegnano tutti i termini . . . appartenenti alla geografia. Di nuovo dal proprio autore ricorretto. *Venice: G.Ziletti*, 1573. 65p.;4to. *In* C.Ptolemaeus, *La geografia*, Venice, 1573, q.v.

Ortelius, Abraham. Theatre, oft Toonneel des aertbodens. *Antwerp: G.Coppens v.Diest*, 1573. 9 lvs;69maps;fol. 1st publ. in Dutch, Antwerp, 1571. Cf.Sabin 57705; Koeman (Ort.) 10. NN-RB; BL.

573/35

————. Theatrum oder Schawplatz des erdbodens. *Antwerp: G.Coppens v.Diest*, 1573. 143 lvs, incl. maps;fol. 1st publ. in German, Antwerp, 1572. Sabin 57706; Koeman (Ort.11); Phillips (Atlases) 377. CtY, DLC, ICN, InU-L, NN-RB; BL.

573/36

————. Theatrum orbis terrarum . . . & quamplurimis novis tabulis atquè commentarius auctum. *Antwerp: A.Coppens v.Diest*, 1573. 10 lvs;70maps;fol. 1st publ., Antwerp, 1570. Sabin 57694; Koeman (Ort.) 9; Phillips (Atlases) 378; Adams (Cambr.) 0333; JCB (3) I:251. CtY, DLC, ICN, InU-L, MnU-B, RPJCB; BL, BN.

573/37

Paracelsus. Chirurgia magna . . . nunc recens à Joaquino Dalhemio . . . latinitate donata.

Strassburg [i.e., *Basel: P.Perna*], 1573. 2v.; fol. Includes, v.2, p.166-250, author's *De causis et origine luis gallicae.* Sudhoff (Paracelsus) 146-147. DNLM, MBCo, MnU, PPL; BL, BN.   573/38

Pérez de Moya, Juan. Tratado de cosas astronomia, y cosmographia, y philosophia natural. *Alcalá de Henares: J.Gracián*, 1573. 248p.;illus.;fol. (*In his* Tratado`de matematicas. Alcalá de Henares, 1573). Includes refs to Spanish America. García (Alcalá de Henares) 486; Palau 221732. CU, DLC, InU-L, MB, MiU, NN-RB; BL, BN.   573/39

Rabelais, François. Les oeuvres. *Lyons: P. Estiard*, 1573. 3pts;16mo. Includes 'Le quart livre', 1st publ., Paris, 1552. The t.p. is without border. Plan(Rabelais) 103. Paris: Arsenal.   573/40

—[Anr edn]. *Lyons: P.Estiard*, 1573. 3pts; 16mo. The t.p. has wood-engraved border. Plan(Rabelais) 104. Paris: Inst.de France.
                                                    573/41

—[Anr edn]. *Antwerp: F.Niergue* [i.e., *Montluel: C.Pesnot*], 1573. 3pts;16mo. Plan (Rabelais) 105; Belg.typ. (1541-1600) I:4085. NjPT; Brussels: BR.   573/42

Rondelet, Guillaume. Methodus curandorum omnium morborum corporis humani . . . Ejusdem . . . De morbo italico. *Paris: C. Macé*, 1573. 2v.;8vo. 1st (?) publ., Paris [1563?]. Adams (Cambr.) R752. DNLM; Cambridge: Trinity, BN.   573/43

Ruscelli, Girolamo. Espositioni et introduttioni universali . . . sopra tutta la Geografia di Tolomeo. *Venice: G.Ziletti*, 1573. [53]p.; maps;4to. *In* C.Ptolemaeus, *La geografia*, Venice, 1573, q.v.

——,**comp.** Lettere di principi, libro primo. *Venice: F.Toldi*, 1573. 247 numb.lvs;4to. 1st publ., Venice, 1562. Adams (Cambr.) L563; Shaaber R376. ICN, MiU-C, PU; BL. 573/44

Sacro Bosco, Joannes de. Sphaera . . . emendata. In eandem Francisci Junctini . . . et Eliae Vineti . . . Scholia. *Antwerp: G.van den Rade,for J.Bellère*, 1573. 294p.;illus.;8vo. 1st publ. with Vinet's *Scholia*, Paris, 1551. Cf. Sabin 32681; Adams (Cambr.) H733; Belg. typ. (1541-1600) I:1640. MiU; Cambridge: Emmanuel, BN.   573/45

Serres, Jean de. The fyrst parte of the Commentaries, concerning the state of religion, and the common wealth of Fraunce. *London: H.Bynneman,for F.Coldocke*, 1573. 4to.

Transl. by T.Tymme from author's *Commentariorum de statu religionis et reipublicae in regno Galliae . . . I.partis, libri iii*, 1st publ., [Geneva], 1570. Includes account of Villegagnon's attempted Brazilian settlement. STC 22241. CSmH; Oxford: Bodl.   573/46

Soto, Domingo de. In quartum Sententiarum commentarii. *Louvain: J.Maes,for J.Bogardus*, 1573. 1054p.;fol. 1st publ., Salamanca, 1557-60. Palau 320173. BN.   573/47

—[Anr issue]. *Louvain: J.Maes,for H.Welle*, 1573. Adams (Cambr.) S1477. Cambridge: King's.   573/48

——. Libri decem De justitia & jure. *Venice: G. Perchacino,for B.Rubini*, 1573. 279 numb. lvs;fol. 1st publ., Salamanca, 1553. Palau 320151. MH-L; Rome: BN.   573/49

—[Anr edn]. De justitia & jure libri decem. *Salamanca: J.B.à Terranova,for B.Boyer*, 1573. 896p.;fol. Palau 320152.   573/50

Spain. Sovereigns, etc., 1556-1598 (Philip II). Instruccion y orden para la publicacion, predicacion, administracion y cobrança de la Bula de la Santa Cruzada en las Indias, islas y tierra firme del mar Oceano . . . 23 agosto 1573. [*Madrid?* 1573]. 8 lvs;fol. Pérez Pastor (Madrid) 69; Palau 120112. BN.   573/51

Surius, Laurentius. Histoire, ou Commentaires de toutes choses memorables . . . par toutes les parties du monde. *Paris: G. Chaudière*, 1573. 447 numb.lvs;8vo. 1st publ. as here transl. by Jacques Lestourneau, Paris, 1571. Sabin 93887; Atkinson (Fr.Ren.) 242. MnU-B; BN.   573/52

Tarcagnota, Giovanni. Delle historie del mondo. *Venice: M.Tramezzino*, 1573. 3pts.; 4to. 1st publ., Venice, 1562. ICN, MiU-C; BL(pts 1 & 3).   573/53

Valleriola, François. Observationum medicinalium libri sex, nunc primum editi. *Lyons: A.Gryphius*, 1573. 264p.;fol. In bk 5 the 7th Observation discusses syphilis. Baudrier (Lyons) VIII:360; Adams (Cambr.) V211. DNLM; London: Wellcome, BN.   573/54

Voerthusius, Joannes. Academiae veteris et novae ad Maximilianum Austrium II, in coronatione Francofurtensi gratulationis ergo legatio. *Frankfurt a.M.: L.Lucius*, 1563 [i.e., 1573]. 99p.;4to. Colophon dated '1573'. On p.81-82 are refs to Columbus & New World. Adams (Cambr.) V995. MH; BL, BN. 573/55

Zárate, Agustín de. De wonderlijcke ende warachtige historie vant coninckrijck van Peru geleghen in Indien. *Antwerp: W.Silvius, for J. Verwithagen*, 1573. 206 numb.lvs;illus.,map; 4to. 1st publ. in Dutch, 1563; here a reissue with cancel t.p. Sabin 106274; Belg.typ. (1541-1600) I:4911. MH; BL(Peru), Brussels: BR.   573/56

1574

Anghiera, Pietro Martire d'. De rebus oceanicis et novo orbe, decades tres . . . Item . . . de Babylonica legatione, libri iii, et item de rebus aethiopicis, indicis, lusitanicis & hispanici . . . Damiani a Goes. *Cologne: G. Calenius & Heirs of J. Quentel*, 1574. 655p.; 8vo. Anghiera's work 1st publ., Basel, 1521; that of Goes, here amended & enlarged, Louvain, 1544, as *Aliquot opuscula.* Sabin 1558 (& 27689a); Medina (BHA) 235; Streit XV:1888; Arents (Add.) 3; JCB (3) I:253. CU, CtY, DLC, MH, MiU-C, MnU-B, NN-RB, RPJCB; BL, BN.   574/1

Apianus, Petrus. Cosmographia . . . per Gemmam Frisium . . . ab omnibus vindicata mendis. *Antwerp: J.Verwithagen*, 1574. 64 numb.lvs;illus., map;4to. 1st publ. in this version, Antwerp, 1540. Cf.Sabin 1749n; Ortroy (Apian) 52; JCB (3) I:251-252. MiU-C, RPJCB.   574/2

—[Anr issue]. *Antwerp: J.Verwithagen, for J. Bellère*, 1574. Ortroy (Apian) 50; Bibl.belg., 1st ser.,I:A38; Ind.aur.106.460. BL, BN.
                                                574/3

—[Anr issue]. *Antwerp: J.Verwithagen, for C. Plantin*, 1574. Ortroy (Apian) 51; Bibl. belg.,1st ser.,I:A38; Ind.aur.106.461; JCB (3) I:251-252. CtY, ICN, MH,MiU-C, NN-RB, RPJCB; BL, BN.   574/4

—[Anr edn]. *Cologne: Heirs of A.Birckmann*, 1574. 64 numb.lvs;illus.,map;4to. See Ortroy 54 for variant imprint date. Sabin 1750; Ortroy (Apian) 53; Bibl.belg.,1st ser.,I:A39; Ind.aur.106.462; Shaaber A315. CtY, DLC, ICN, MH, MiU-C, NN-RB, PU, RPJCB; BL, BN.   574/5

Bessard, Toussainct de. Dialogue de la longitude est-ouest . . . contenant tous les moyens que l'on pourrait avoir tenus en la navigation jusqu'à maintenant. *Rouen: M.Le Mégissier, the Younger*, 1574. 104p.;illus., port.; 4to. Includes, p.8-9, refs to Magellan's cir-

cumnavigation, Peru, etc. Ind.aur.118.154. BL, BN.   574/6

Boaistuau, Pierre. Histoires prodigeuses. *Paris: J.de Bordeaux*, 1574. 396 numb.lvs;illus.; 16mo. 1st publ. with American ref. in section by François de Belleforest, Paris, 1571. Ind. aur.120.071; Shaaber B424. PU-F; BL. 574/7

Bock, Hieronymus. Kreutterbuch. *Strassburg: J.Rihel*, 1574. 1st publ. with illus., Strassburg, 1546. Nissen (Bot.) 182n.   574/8

Boissard, Jean Jacques. Poemata. *Basel: T. Guarin*, 1574. 127 numb.lvs;16mo. The various works by Boissard with this title vary in contents. In the elegies here published, no.xv, 'De discessu Caroli V.Imperatoris in Hispaniam', refers to Indies. Ind.aur.121.321; Cioranescu (XVI) 4260. ICN, MH, MiU, RPB; BL, BN.   574/9

Brant, Sebastian. Welt Spiegel oder Narren Schiff. *Basel: S.Henricpetri*, 1574. 400 numb. lvs;illus.;8vo. 1st publ., Basel, 1494. Ind. aur.123.750. DLC, ICN, NN-RB; BL, Munich: StB.   574/10

Braun, Georg. Beschreibuug [!] und Contrafactur der vornembster Stätt der Welt. Liber primus. *Cologne: H.von Ach*, 1574. 59 double pls;fol. Transl. from 1572, Cologne, Latin edn. Koeman (Braun & Hogenberg) 7; Ind.aur.123.944. CSmH, RPB; BL, Munich: StB.   574/11

—[Anr edn]. [*Cologne:*] 1574. fol. BL. 574/12

——. Théatre des cités du monde. [*Cologne?*] 1574. 59 double lvs;fol. Transl. from 1572, Cologne, Latin text. Ind.aur.123.945. NNH; Vienna: NB.   574/13

Capilupi, Ippolito, Bp of Fano. Carmina. *Antwerp: C.Plantin*, 1574. 130p.;4to. Includes (p.114-115) three epitaphs on Columbus. Ind.aur.131.589; Belg.typ. (1541-1600) I:564. ICU; BL, Brussels: BR.   574/14

Caro, Annibale. De le lettere familiari . . . volume primo. *Venice: A. Manuzio*, 1574. 296p.;4to. 1st publ., Venice, 1572. Ind.aur. 132.475; Adams (Cambr.) C741. CtY, MH; Cambridge: Trinity, BN.   574/15

Dodoens, Rembert. Purgantium aliarumque eo facientium, tum et radicum, convolvulorum ac deleterarium herbarum historiae. *Antwerp: C.Plantin*, 1574. 505p.;illus.;8vo. Included (in bk 3) are chapts on 'Hyoscyamus Peruvianus' (tobacco) & 'Zarsae Parillae' (sarsaparilla) also designated as Peruvian. Pritzel 2348; Nissen (Bot.) 515; Bibl.belg.,1st ser.,

IX:D115; Adams (Cambr.) D721; Hunt (Bot.) 116. CLU-M, CtY, DNLM, MH-A, MiU, PPC, RPB; BL, BN. 574/16

Ercilla y Zúñiga, Alonso de. La Araucana [Primera parte]. *Salamanca: D.de Portonariis, for V.& S.de Portonariis*, 1574. 392p.; port.;8vo. 1st publ., Madrid, 1569. Sabin 22719; Medina (BHA) 233; Medina (Arau.) 2. NNH, RPJCB. 574/17

Emili, Paolo. Französischer und anderer Nationen . . . Historien . . . durch Johann Thomas Frey . . . biss in das 1574 jar verlengert. *Basel: S.Henricpetri*, 1574. 2pts; illus.;fol. 1st publ. in this translation by Christian Wurstisen, Basel, 1572. Ind.aur.100.837. Berlin: StB. 574/18

Estienne, Charles. L'agriculture et maison rustique de . . . Charles Estienne et Jean Liebault. *Paris: J.DuPuys*, 1574. 291 numb. lvs;illus.;4to. 1st publ. in this version, Paris, 1567. Thiébaud (La chasse) 344; Arents (Add.) 30. CSmH, DNLM, NN-A; BN. 574/19

Falloppius, Gabriel. De morbo gallico liber absolutissimus, a Petro Angelo Agatho Materate . . . editus . . . Additum etiam est . . . De morbo gallico tractatus, Antonii Fracanciani. *Venice: E.Regazzola*, 1574. 239p.; 8vo. 1st published, Padua, 1564; Fracanzano's work 1st publ. separately, Bologna, 1564. DNLM, MBCo. 574/20

Fernel, Jean. De abditis rerum causis. *Frankfurt a.M.: A.Wechel*, 1574. 272p.;port.;8vo. 1st publ., Paris, 1548. CtY, MnU. 574/21

——. Universa medicina. *Frankfurt a.M.: A. Wechel*, 1574. 2v.;ports;8vo. Includes Fernel's *De abditis rerum causis*, 1st publ., Paris, 1548. Sherrington (Fernel) 59.J3; Adams (Cambr.) F257. Cambridge: Whipple Mus., BN. 574/22

Foglietta, Uberto. Clarorum Ligurum elogia. *Rome: V.Accolto & V.Panizza*, 1574. 223p.; 4to. 1st publ., Rome, 1572. Adams (Cambr.) F666. CtY, DFo, IU, MiU, RPJCB; BL, BN. 574/23

Fontanon, Denys. De morborum internorum curatione, libri iiii. *Lyons: A.de Harsy*, 1574. 635p.;8vo. 1st publ., Lyons, 1549; here a reissue of 1573 edn with altered imprint date. DNLM; BN. 574/24

Foucher, Jean. Itinerarium catholicum proficiscentium, ad infides convertandos . . . Nuper summa cura . . . auctum, expurgatum

. . . per fratrem Didacum Valadesium . . . provinciae Sancti Evangelii in nova Hyspania. *Seville: A.Escrivano*, 1574. 99 numb.lvs; illus.;8vo. Sabin 24934; Medina (BHA) 234; Streit I:119; Escudero (Seville) 670; JCB (3) I:252. CSmH, CtY, ICN, InU-L, NN-RB, RPJCB; Madrid: BN. 574/25

Fracastoro, Girolamo. Opera omnia . . . 2da ed. *Venice: Heirs of L.Giunta*, 1574. 213 numb.lvs;illus.;4to. 1st publ. in coll. edn, Venice, 1555; includes the author's 'De contagione' (1st publ., Venice, 1546) and his 'Syphilidis' (1st publ., Verona, 1530). Baumgartner (Fracastoro) 33; Moranti (Urbino) 1525. CSmH, CtY, DNLM, ICJ, MBCo, MnU, NN-RB; BL, BN. 574/26

Gesner, Konrad. Bibliotheca . . . in epitomen redacta & novorum librorum accessione locupletata . . . per Josiam Simlerum. *Zurich: C. Froschauer*, 1574. 691p.;fol. 1st publ., Zurich, 1545. Adams (Cambr.) G514. CU-S, CtY, DLC, ICJ, MH, MnU, PBL; BL, BN. 574/27

Girard, Bernard de, sieur du Haillan. Discours sur l'extreme cherté qui est aujourd'hui en France. *Paris: P.L'Huillier*, 1574. 80p.;8vo. Reiterates Bodin's thesis regarding influx of gold & silver as cause of inflated prices, citing Peru and America. BL, BN. 574/28

Guicciardini, Francesco. Gründtliche unnd warhafftige beschreibüng aller fürnemen historienn die in viertzig jaren, nemlich von dem 1493 biss auff das 1533 . . . geschehen sind . . . in . . . Teutsch gebracht, durch Magistrum Georgium Forberger. *Berne: S. Apiarius,for H.Petri & P.Perna at Basel*, 1574. cccclxv lvs;fol. Transl. from author's *La historia d'Italia*, 1st publ., Florence, 1561. MH, NcU. 574/29

——. La historia d'Italia. *Venice: G.Angelieri*, 1574. 488 numb.lvs;4to. 1st publ., Florence, 1561. CSt, CtY, IU, MB, PPL; BL, BN. 574/30

Jesuits. Letters from missions (The East). Rerum a Societate Jesu in oriente gestarum volumen. *Cologne: G.Calenius, & Heirs of J. Quentel*, 1574. 472p.;8vo. 1st publ. in this version containing letters of both Pietro Díaz & Franciscus Henriques on martyrdom of Inácio de Azevedo & other Jesuits, Naples, 1573. Sabin 31382n; Streit IV:959 (& II:1300n); Ind.aur.100.473. CtY-D, DLC,

MH, MnU-B, NN-RB; BL, Munich: StB.
574/31

Jodelle, Etienne. Oeuvres & meslanges poetiques. *Paris: N.Chesneau & M.Patisson,* 1574. 309 numb.lvs;4to. 'Ode sur les singularitez de la France Antarctique, d'André Thevet': lvs 130r-131r. Rothschild 696. CtU, DFo, MH, NjP; BL, BN.   574/32

Léry, Jean de. Histoire memorable de la ville de Sancerre. [*Geneva:*] 1574. 253p.;8vo. In describing the siege and surrender of Calvinist Sancerre, Léry draws upon his earlier experiences in Brazil, subsequently recounted at fuller length. In the prelim. matter variant readings occur. DFo, InU-L, MH, MiU, NN-RB(2 variants), RPJCB; BL, BN.   574/33

Marguérite d'Angoulême, Queen of Navarre. L'heptameron ou Histoires des amans fortunez. *Paris: M.de Roigny,* 1574. 812p.; 16mo. 1st publ. in this version, Paris, 1559. Tchémerzine VII:394. DLC.   574/34

Meneses, Felipe de. Luz de alma christiana. *Alcalá de Henares: J.Gracián,* 1574. 8vo. 1st publ., Seville, 1555. Palau 164444n. Soria: Bibl. Prov.   574/35

Mercado, Luis. Libri duo. De communi et peculiari praesidiorum artis medicae indicatione. *Valladolid: D.Fernández de Córdova,* 1574. 654p.;fol. Describes medicinal use of tobacco. Arents (Add.) 57-A; Palau 164997. CtY-M, NN-A; London: Wellcome, Madrid: BU.   574/36

Monardes, Nicolás. De simplicibus medicamentis ex Occidentali India delatis, quorum in medicina usus est . . . interprete Carolo Clusio. *Antwerp: C.Plantin,* 1574. 88p.; illus.;8vo. Transl. from pts 1-2 of the author's Spanish texts (cf.following item), rearranged, condensed, & otherwise adapted. Sabin 49941; Medina (BHA) 237; Guerra (Monardes) 14; Pritzel 6366n; Nissen (Bot.) Suppl. 1397na; Arents 18; JCB (3) I:254. CU, CtY-M, DNLM,ICN, InU-L, MH-A, MnU-B, NN-RB, RPJCB; BL, BN.   574/37

――――. Primera y secunda y tercera partes de la Historia medicinal de las cosas que se traen de nuestras Indias Occidentales. *Seville: A.Escrivano,* 1574. 206 numb.lvs;illus.;4to. The earliest edn to contain 3 pts. Sabin 49938; Medina (BHA) 263; Pritzel 6366n; Nissen (Bot.) Suppl. 1397n(n); Guerra (Monardes) 13; Arents 19; JCB (3) I:254. CU-B, CtY,

DLC, InU-L, MH-A, NN-RB, RPJCB; BL, BN.   574/38

Münster, Sebastian. A briefe collection and compendious extract of straunge and memorable thinges, gathered out of the Cosmographeye. *London: T.Marsh,* 1574. 102 numb. lvs;8vo. 1st publ., London, 1572. Sabin 51406; Burmeister (Münster) 112; STC 18243. DFo, MB; BL.   574/39

――――. Cosmographey oder beschreibung aller Länder. *Basel: H.Petri,* 1574. 1414p.;illus., maps;fol. 1st publ., Basel, 1544. Sabin 51391; Burmeister (Münster) 79. DLC, NjP; Munich: StB.   574/40

Orta, García da. Aromatum, et simplicium aliquot medicamentorum apud Indos nascentium Historia . . . nunc vero latino sermone in epitomen contracta . . . locupletiorisque annotatiunculis illustrata a Carolo Clusio. *Antwerp: C.Plantin,* 1574. 227p.;illus.;8vo. 1st publ. as ed., transl. & annotated by L'Ecluse, Antwerp, 1567. Sabin 57664; Pritzel 4316n; Nissen (Bot.) 949n; Bibl.belg.,1st ser.,XX:06; Hunt (Bot.) 120; Adams (Cambr.) 320; JCB (3) I:254. CtY, DLC, InU-L, MB, NNNAM, PPC, RPJCB; BL, BN. 574/41

Ortelius, Abraham. Theatrum orbis terrarum. *Antwerp: G.Coppens v.Diest,* 1574. 10 lvs;70maps;fol. 1st publ., Antwerp, 1570. Sabin 57695; Koeman (Ort.) 12; Phillips (Atlases) 379; Adams (Cambr.) 0334; JCB (3) I:255. CtY, DLC, ICN, InU-L, MH, MiU-C, RPJCB; BL, BN.   574/42

Osorio, Jerónimo, Bp of Silves. De rebus Emmanuelis Regis . . . Lusitaniae . . . gestis; libri duodecim. *Cologne: Heirs of A.Birckmann,* 1574. 412p.;8vo. The earliest edn to contain dedicatory epistle by Joannes Metellus describing Portuguese and Spanish explorations in both East & West Indies; 1st publ., Lisbon, 1571. Sabin 57804; Borba de Moraes II:120; Adams (Cambr.) 0380; Shaaber O93. CSmH, DLC, InU-L, MnU-B, PU, RPJCB; BL, BN.   574/43

Polo, Gaspar Gil. Primera parte de Diana enamorada. *Antwerp: G.van den Rade,for G.Steels,* 1574. 120 lvs;12mo. 1st publ., Valencia, 1564. In verse. Peeters-Fontainas (Impr. esp.) 502; Palau 102075n. CU, KMK, NNH; BN.   574/44

Portugal. Laws, statutes, etc. Ley de como ham de hir armados os navios que destes reynos navegarem. *Lisbon: J.de Barreira,* 1574.

12mo. 1st publ., Lisbon, 1571. Cf. Anselmo 211. Maggs Cat.508, no.21.   574/45

Ptolemaeus, Claudius. La geographia . . . già tradotta di greco . . . da m. Giero. Ruscelli . . . Con l'espositioni del Ruscelli . . . sopra tutto il libro . . . Et con un discorso di m. Gioseppe Moleto. *Venice: G.Ziletti*, 1574. 350p.;maps;4to. 1st publ. in this translation— here rev. & corr. by Giovanni Malombra— Venice, 1561. Sabin 66505; Stevens (Ptolemy) 52; Phillips (Atlases) 380; JCB (3) I:255. CU, DLC, MH, NNH, PPL, RPJCB; BL, BN.

574/46

Rabelais, François. Les oeuvres. *Lyons: P. Estiard*, 1574. 3pts;16mo. 1st publ., Paris, 1552. Plan (Rabelais) 106. BN.   574/47

Riquel, Hernando. Relacion muy cierta . . . de lo que agora nuevamente se ha sabido de las nuevas yslas del poniente y descubrimiento . . . de la China. *Seville: A.de la Barrera*, 1574. [4]p.;fol. Report addressed to Mexico on Spanish discoveries in Far East. Medina (BHA) 238; Pardo de Tavera 2397; Palau 269326. BL.   574/48

Rondelet, Guillaume. Methodus curandorum omnium morborum corporis humani . . . Ejusdem . . . De morbo italico. *Paris: C.Macé*, 1574. 2v.;8vo. 1st (?) publ., Paris [1563?]; here a reissue with altered imprint date of 1573 edn. Adams (Cambr.) R753. DNLM, NNNAM; Cambridge: Trinity, BN.

574/49

—[Anr edn]. *Paris: J.Macé*, 1574. 350p.;fol. CU.   574/50

Ruscelli, Girolamo, comp. Epistres des princes . . . mises en françois par François de Belle-Forest. *Paris: J.Ruelle*, 1574. 447 numb.lvs;8vo. 1st publ. in French, Paris, 1572. ICN, NjP; BL, BN.   574/51

———. Lettere di principi. *Venice: F.Toldi*, 1574. 247 numb.lvs;4to. 1st publ., Venice, 1562. A reissue of printer's 1573 edn? DLC.   574/52

Sacro Bosco, Joannes de. La sfera . . . tradotta da Pier-Vincentio Dante de Rinaldi . . . con l'aggiunta . . . d'altre annotazioni [da Ignazio Dante]. *Perugia: G.B.Rastelli*, 1574. 60p.;illus.,port.;4to. 1st publ., Florence, 1572. Cf.Sabin 32683. ICJ, MB, MiU-C, NN-RB.   574/53

———. Sphaera . . . emendata. Eliae Vineti . . . Scholia. *Venice: G.Scoto*, 1574. 168p.; illus.;8vo. 1st publ. with Vinet's *Scholia*, Paris, 1551. Cf.Sabin 32681. ICJ, MiU, NN-RB.   574/54

Saint-Gelais, Mellin de. Oeuvres poëtiques. *Lyons: A.de Harsy*, 1574. 25p.;8vo. Includes sonnet 'Pour mettre au devant de l'Histoire des Indes' (*i.e.*, of Jean Alfonce's *Voyages avantureux*, Poitiers [ca. 1558?]), with reference to Columbus. Rothschild 630. CtY, MH; BL, BN.   574/55

Serres, Jean de. The three partes of Commentaries, containing the whole and perfect discourse of the civill warres of Fraunce. *London: H.Bynneman* (pt 1) & [*H.Middelton*] (pts 2-3) *for F.Coldocke*, 1574. 3pts;4to. Transl. by T.Tymme. A reissue of pt 1, 1st publ., London, 1573, with the addition here of pts 2-3. STC 22241. 5. CU, DFo, ICN, NN-RB; BL.   574/56

—[Anr issue]. *London*: [*H.Middelton*] 1574. A reissue of pts 2-3 above, with pt 1 newly reset, the 1st line of text on lf A1r ending 'commenta-'. STC 22242. CSmH, DFo, MH; BL.   574/57

Surius, Laurentius. Commentarius brevis rerum in orbe gestarum. *Cologne: G.Calenius & Heirs of J.Quentel*, 1574. 622p.;fol. 1st publ. separately; Cologne, 1566; here expanded to include the year 1574. Cf.Sabin 93883; Adams (Cambr.) S2100. RPJCB; BL.

574/58

—[Anr edn]. *Cologne: G.Calenius & Heirs of J. Quentel*, 1574. 838p.;8vo. Sabin 93883; Adams (Cambr.) S2101. DLC, MnCS, NN-RB; Cambridge: UL, BN.   574/59

Tagault, Jean. Gründtliche und rechte Underweisung der Chirurgie oder Wundartzney. *Frankfurt a.M.: G.Rab & S.Feyerabend*, 1574. ccxliiii numb. lvs;fol. Transl. by G. Zechendorffer from Tagault's *De chirurgica institutione*, 1st publ., Paris, 1543. BL.

574/60

Torquemada, Antonio de. Jardin de flores curiosas. *Lérida: P.de Robles & J.de Villanueva*, 1573 [colophon: 1574]. 256 numb.lvs; 8vo. 1st publ., Salamanca, 1570. In verse. Palau 334909. NNH.   574/61

Ulloa, Alfonso de. Vita dell'invittissimo . . . Imperator Carlo V. di nuovo ristampata, e . . . ricoretta. *Venice: Heirs of V.Valgrisi*, 1574. 341 numb.lvs;4to. 1st publ., Venice, 1560. BN.   574/62

Wecker, Johann Jakob. Antidotarium speciale . . . ex optimorum authorum . . .

scriptis fideliter congestum. *Basel: E. Episcopius & Heirs of N.Episcopius,* 1574. 799p.;4to. 1st publ., Basel, 1561. London: Wellcome. 574/63

1575

Albergati, Vianesio. Les louanges de la folie . . . traduict . . . par . . . Jean du Thier. *Paris: N.Bonfons,* 1575. [96]p.;16mo. Transl. from author's *La pazzia,* 1st publ. in dated edn, [Bologna?], 1540. Ind.aur.102.242; Rothschild 1827. BN. 575/1

Apianus, Petrus. La cosmographia . . . corregida y añadida por Gemma Frisio. *Antwerp: J.Verwithagen,* 1575. 68 numb.lvs; illus.,map;4to. 1st publ. in Spanish, Antwerp, 1548, with minor additions derived from F.L.de Gómara & J.Girava. Sabin 1756; Ortroy (Apian) 56; Peeters-Fontainas (Impr. esp.) 62; Bibl.belg.1st ser.,I:A40n. CU, DLC, MH, NN-RB; BL, Brussels: BR. 575/2

___[Anr issue]. *Antwerp: J.Verwithagen,for J.Bellère,* 1575. Cf. Sabin 1756; Medina (BHA) 239; Ortroy (Apian) 55; Peeters-Fontainas (Impr.esp.) 63; Bibl.belg.,1st ser.,I:A40; Ind.aur.106.463. CU-B, MnU-B, NNH, RPJCB; Paris: Mazarine. 575/3

Banister, John. A needefull, new, and necessarie treatise of chyrurgerie . . . drawen foorth of sundrie worthy wryters, but especially of Antonius Calmetus . . . and Joannes Tagaltius. *London: T.Marsh,* 1575. 138 numb.lvs;8vo. Included are refs to Guaiacum & syphilis ('morbus gallicus'). STC 1360; Ind. aur.112.271. CSmH, CtY-M, DNLM; BL. 575/4

Boaistuau, Pierre. Histoires prodigeuses. *Paris: C.Macé,* 1575. 175 numb.lvs;8vo. 1st publ. with American ref. in section by François de Belleforest, Paris, 1571. Ind. aur.120.071. MH, NN-RB; BN. 575/5

Braun, Georg. Civitates orbis terrarum, liber primus. *Antwerp: G.van den Rade,for the authors at Cologne & P.Galle at Antwerp,* 1575. 1st publ., Cologne, 1572. Cf.Koeman (Braun & Hogenberg) 1; Ind.aur.123.946; Belg.typ. (1541-1600) I:392. RPJCB; Brussels: BR. 575/6

___. Theatre des principales villes de tout l'univers. Premier volume. [*Cologne?* ca.1575]. 59 double pls;fol. 1st publ. in French, [Co-

logne?], 1574. Ind.aur.123.948. BL. 575/7

Clavius, Christoph. In sphaeram Joannis de Sacro Bosco commentarius. *Rome: V.Eliano,* 1575. 499p.;illus.;4to. 1st publ., Rome, 1570. Backer II:1212. 575/8

Ercilla y Zúñiga, Alonso. La Araucana [Primera parte]. *Antwerp: T.Lyndanus,for P.Bellère,* 1575. 333p.;12mo. 1st publ., Madrid, 1569. Medina (BHA) 240; Peeters-Fontainas (Impr.esp.) 389; Medina (Arau.) 3. NNH; BL, Madrid: BN. 575/9

Fernel, Jean. Universa medicina. *Frankfurt a.M.: A.Wechel,* 1575. 2v;ports;8vo. A reissue of Wechel's 1574 edn. Includes Fernel's *De abditis causis rerum,* 1st publ., Paris, 1548. Sherrington (Fernel) 60.J4. NIC; BN. 575/10

Foresti, Jacopo Filippo, da Bergamo. Sopplimento delle croniche universali del mondo . . . tradotto nuovamente da m. Francesco Sansovino. *Venice:* 1575. 2v.;4to. 1st publ. in this translation, Venice, 1508. MH; BN. 575/11

Fuchs, Leonhart. L'histoire des plantes. *Lyons: C.Pesnot,* 1575. [580]p.;illus.;fol. 1st publ. in French, Paris, 1549. Pritzel 3139n; Nissen (Bot.) 673; Baudrier (Lyons) III:140; Adams (Cambr.) F1106. KU; Cambridge: UL, BN. 575/12

Giglio, Geronimo. Nuova seconda selva di varia lettione, che segue Pietro Messia . . . Nuovamente posta in luce, & . . . corretta. *Venice: C.Zanetti,* 1575. 207 numb.lvs;8vo. 1st publ., Venice, 1565. Adams (Cambr.) G607; Palau 167296. RPJCB; Cambridge: UL. 575/13

Giovio, Paolo, Bp of Nocera. Elogia virorum bellica virtute illustrium . . . et nunc eiusdem Musaeo ad vivum expressis imaginibus exornata. *Basel: P.Perna & H.Petri,* 1575. 391p.; ports;fol. 1st publ., Florence, 1551, but here 1st illustrated with portraits, by Tobias Stimmer, for sections on Columbus & Cortés. Sabin 36773; Adams (Cambr.) G644. CtY, DLC, ICN, MH, MiU-C, PPT, RPJCB; Cambridge: UL, BN. 575/14

Honter, Johannes. Rudimentorum cosmographicorum . . . libri iii. [*Zurich: C. Froschauer*] 1575. 1st publ. in this version, Kronstadt, 1542. In verse. Borsa 96; Szabo III:633. 575/15

LeRoy, Louis. De la vicissitude ou variete des choses en l'univers. *Paris: P.L'Huillier,* 1575. 118 numb.lvs;fol. Includes refs to Americas.

Atkinson (Fr.Ren.) 246; Cioranescu (XVI) 13472. CU, ICN; BN. 575/16

Monardes, Nicolás. Delle cose che vengono portate dall'Indie Occidentali pertinenti all'uso della medicina . . . Nuovamente recata dalla spagnola [da Annibale Briganti]. *Venice: G.Ziletti*, 1575. 2pts;illus.;8vo. Transl. from author's *Dos libros*, 1st publ. Seville, 1565. Sabin 49939; Medina (BHA) 237; cf.Pritzel 6366n; Nissen (Bot.) 1397nb; Guerra (Monardes) 16; Arents 20; JCB (3) I:258. DLC, MH, MnU-B, NN-RB, RPJCB; London: Wellcome. 575/17

Münster, Sebastian. Cosmographia universale . . . corretta & repurgata. per gli censori ecclesiastici, & quei del Re cattolico nelli Paesi basi, & per l'Inquisitore di Venetia. *Cologne: Heirs of A.Birckmann*, 1575. 1237p.;illus., maps;fol. 1st publ. in Italian, Basel, 1558. Sabin 51403; Borba de Moraes II:91; Burmeister (Münster) 101; JCB (3) I:260. DLC, ICN, NN-RB, PPL, RPJCB; BL, Munich: StB. 575/18

—[Anr edn]. *Venice: G.F.Thomasini* [1575]. 1237p.;illus.,maps;fol. Burmeister (Münster) 100. DLC; BN. 575/19

——. La cosmographie universelle, augmentée, ornée & enrichie, par François de Belle-Forest. *Paris: M.Sonnius*, 1575. 2v.;illus., maps;fol. The earliest edn as ed. by Belle-Forest. Sabin 51400; Burmeister (Münster) 97n; Atkinson (Fr.Ren.) 247; Adams (Cambr.) M1914. BL, BN. 575/20

—[Anr issue]. *Paris: M.Chesneau*, 1575. Sabin 51400n; Burmeister (Münster) 97; Borba de Moraes I:82-83; Atkinson (Fr.Ren.) 247n. RPJCB. Issues not differentiated:DLC, ICN, MH. 575/21

Ortelius, Abraham. Theatrum orbis terrarum. *Antwerp: G.van den Rade*, 1575. 58 lvs;70maps;fol. 1st publ., Antwerp, 1570, but here containing for 1st time the author's *Synonomia locorum*. Koeman (Ort.) 13; Phillips (Atlases) 382; Adams (Cambr.) 0335. DLC, ICN, InU-L, MH; BL, BN. 575/22

Osorio, Jerónimo, Bp of Silves. De rebus Emmanuelis Regis Lusitaniae . . . gestis, libri duodecem. *Cologne: Heirs of A. Birckmann*, 1575. 374 numb.lvs;8vo. 1st publ. with Metellus's dedication, as here, Cologne, 1574. Cf. Sabin 57804. KU, MH, NN-RB. 575/23

Porcacchi, Tommaso. L'isole piu famoso del mondo. *Venice: G.Angelieri,for S.Galignani*, 1575. 201p.;maps;fol. 1st publ., Venice, 1572. Adams (Cambr.) P1905; Moranti (Urbino) 2804. Cambridge: UL, Urbino: BU. 575/24

Rangoni, Tommaso. Malum gallecum [!] depilativam . . . usque ad contortos sanans, ligni Indi, aquae . . . spartae parillae . . . mechoacan . . . praecipitati seminis Indi, ac additorum Mundi novi, et reliquorum . . . Tertia impressio. *Venice: P.dei Franceschi*, 1575. 66 lvs;8vo. 1st publ., Venice, 1538. DNLM; BL. 575/25

Román y Zamora, Jerónimo. Republicas del mundo. *Medina del Campo: F.del Canto*, 1575. 2v.;fol. 'De la republica de las Indias Occidentales': v.2,lvs 353-423. Sabin 72894; Medina (BHA) 241; Streit I:122; Pérez Pastor (Medina del Campo) 174; Adams (Cambr.) R687. DLC, InU-L; Cambridge: Pembroke (v.2 only), BN. 575/26

Rondelet, Guillaume. Methodus curandorum omnium morborum corporis humani . . . Ejusdem . . . De morbo italico. *Paris: C.Macé*, 1575. 2v.;8vo. 1st (?) publ., Paris [1563?]; here a reissue, with altered imprint date, of 1573 edn. Adams (Cambr.) R754. DNLM; Cambridge: Gonville & Caius, BN. 575/27

—[Anr edn]. *Lyons: G.Rouillé*, 1575. 1277p.; 8vo. Moranti (Urbino) 2956. DNLM, MnU-B; London: Wellcome, Urbino: BU. 575/28

Serres, Jean de. Commentariorum de statu religionis et reipublicae in regno Galliae . . . I. partis, libri iii . . . 4. editio emendatior, & longé locupletior. *Leyden: J.Jucundus* [i.e., *Geneva: E.Vignon*], 1575. 8vo. 1st publ., [Geneva], 1570. CU-S, ICU, NNG. 575/29

Soto, Domingo de. In quartum (quem vocant) Sententiarum. Tomus primus[-secundus]. *Venice: G.M.Leni*, 1575. 2v.;4to. 1st publ., Salamanca, 1557-60. Moranti (Urbino) 3153; Palau 320174. BN. 575/30

Terraube, Galard de. Bref discours des choses plus necessaires et dignes d'estres entendues en la cosmographie. *Paris: F.Morel*, 1575. 20 lvs;8vo. 1st publ., Paris, 1559. Sabin 94865; cf.Atkinson (Fr.Ren.) 125; Cioranescu (XVI) 21052. BL, BN. 575/31

Thevet, André. La cosmographie universelle. *Paris: P.L'Huillier*, 1575. 2v.;illus.,ports, maps; fol. The 4th section (v.2, lvs 903-1025) deals with the Americas. Sabin 95335; Atkinson (Fr.Ren.) 249n; Borba de Moraes

II:305-306; Adams (Cambr.) T623; Mortimer (France) 517; JCB (3) I:261. DLC, MH, RPJCB; Cambridge: UL, BN. 575/32

___[Anr issue]. *Paris: G.Chaudière,* 1575. Sabin 95335n; Atkinson (Fr.Ren.) 249; Arents 21. NN-A; BL, BN. 575/33

Torquemada, Antonio de. Jardin de flores curiosas. *Antwerp: G.Smits,for J.Cordier,* 1575. 538p.;12mo. 1st publ., Salamanca, 1570. In verse. Exists in both thick & thin paper issues. Peeters-Fontainas (Impr.esp.) 1309; Palau 334910; Adams (Cambr.) T812. DLC, MH, NNH; BL, BN. 575/34

Ulloa, Alfonso de. Vita dell'invitissimo . . . Imperator Carlo V. . . . Di nuovo ristampato, & . . . ricorretta. *Venice: Aldine Press,* 1575. 344 numb.lvs;8vo. 1st publ., Venice, 1560. Sabin 97682; Adams (Cambr.) U43; Shaaber U22. DLC, MBAt, NIC, PU; BL, BN. 575/35

1576

Anania, Giovanni Lorenzo d'. L'universale fabrica del mondo, overo Cosmografia . . . Di nuovo posta in luce. *Venice: G.Vidali,for A. San Vito,at Naples,* 1576. 336p.;4to. 1st publ., Naples, 1573. Sabin 1364; Ind.aur. 105.086; Adams (Cambr.) A1006; Moranti (Urbino) 1145. DFo, ICN, InU-L, NN-RB, RPJCB; BL, Munich: StB. 576/1

Baptista Mantuanus. Opera omnia. *Antwerp: J.Bellère,* 1576. 4v.;8vo. Collected edn containing, v.1, 'Exhortatio ad reges', 1st publ., Milan, 1507, with title 'Objurgatio cum exhoratione'; in v.2, 'Fastorum libri', 1st publ., Lyons, 1516; & in v.4, 'De patientia', 1st publ., Brescia, 1497. Ind.aur.112.777; Adams (Cambr.) M390; Coccia 432. DFo, ICN, MiU; BL, BN. 576/2

Boaistuau, Pierre. Histoires prodigeuses. *Paris: C.Macé,* 1576. 175 numb.lvs;8vo. 1st publ. with American ref. in section by François de Belleforest, Paris, 1571. Ind. aur.120.075. DFo; BL, Copenhagen: KB. 576/3

Bodin, Jean. Methodus historica. *Basel: P. Perna,* 1576. 1140p.;8vo. 1st publ., Paris, 1566, under title *Methodus ad facilem historiarum cognitionem.* Ind.aur.120.804; Adams (Cambr.) B2243. ICN, MH; Cambridge: Trinity, BN. 576/4

_____. Les six livres de la Republique. *Paris: J.DuPuys,* 1576. 759p.;fol. Included in bk 1,

chapt.5, are refs to West Indian slavery, drawn from Gómara's *Histoire générale;* & in bk 5, chapt. 1, to the New World as a whole. Ind.aur.120.805. CtY, MH-L, NNC; BN. 576/5

Capelloni, Lorenzo. Ragionamenti varii. *Genoa: M.A.Bellone,* 1576. 192p.;4to. Pages 191-192 describe harmful social effects of introduction from New World of gold & silver. Ind.aur.131.534. DFo, ICN, MH, MiU, RPJCB; BL, BN. 576/6

Castile. Laws, statutes, etc., 1252-1284 (Alfonso X). Las siete partidas . . . glosadas por . . . Gregorio López. *Salamanca: D.de Portonariis,* 1576. 7v.;fol. 1st publ. in this version with American refs, Salamanca, 1555. Palau 7093. CtY, MH, NN-RB. 576/7

Chaves, Jerónimo de. Chronographia, o Repertorio de los tiempos. *Lisbon: A.Ribeiro,for J.de Hespanha,* 1576. 188 numb. lvs;illus.;4to. 1st publ., Seville, 1548. According to Palau copies occur misdated (in colophon) 1566. Anselmo 930; Palau 67455. CU, MH; BL, BN. 576/8

___[Anr edn]. *Seville: A.Escrivano,* 1576. 272 numb.lvs;illus.,port.,map;4to. Medina (BHA) 242; Escudero (Seville) 684; Palau 67454n. 576/9

Cheyne, James. De geographia libri duo; accessit Gemmae Phrysii De orbis divisione & insulis. *Douai: L.de Winde,* 1576. 2pts;illus.; 8vo. Incorporates Gemma's 'De orbis divisione', 1st publ., Antwerp, 1530, in his *De principiis astronomiae.* Adams (Cambr.) C1452. CSmH, ICN; BL, BN. 576/10

Cieza de León, Pedro de. Cronica del gran regno del Peru con la descrittione di tutte le provincie, costumi, e riti . . . Tradotta . . . por Agostino di Cravaliz. *Venice: C.Franceschini,* 1576. 219 numb.lvs;8vo. 1st publ. in this translation, Venice, 1560. Uniformly publ. with this edn in this year were the two works of Gómara described below. Sabin 13054; Medina (BHA) 157n (I:257); Streit II:930; JCB (3) I:261. DFo, NN-RB, RPJCB; BL, BN. 576/11

Duchesne, Joseph. Sclopetarius, sive, De curandis vulneribus . . . liber. *Lyons* [i.e., *Geneva:*] *J.Lertout,* 1576. 209p.;8vo. Included are directions for medicinal use of tobacco. CtY, DNLM, MiU; BL. 576/12

_____. Traitté de la cure generale et particuliere des arcbusades. *Lyons* [i.e., *Geneva:*] *J.Ler-*

tout, 1576. 248p.;8vo. Transl. from preceding Latin text. Arents (Add.) 58. CtY, DNLM, MiU, NN-A; BL, BN.   576/13

Emili, Paolo. De rebus gestis Francorum libri x. Arnoldi Ferroni . . . De rebus item gestis Gallorum libri ix. *Paris: M.de Vascovan,* 1576. 2pts;fol. 1st publ. with A. LeFerron's appendix, Paris, 1549. Pt.2, LeFerron's *De rebus . . . Gallorum* is a reissue of the Paris, 1554, edn above. Ind.aur.100.838. MH.
                                              576/14

Estienne, Charles. L'agriculture, et maison rustique de mm. Charles Estienne et Jean Liebault. [*Lyons: Printed for*] *J.DuPuys,at Paris,* 1576. 312 lvs;illus.;4to. 1st publ., Paris, 1567. Thiébaud (La chasse) 344; Baudrier (Lyons) I:365; Arents (Add.) 31. NN-A.
                                              576/15

General chronicen, das ist: Warhaffte eigentliche und kurtze beschreibung, vieler namhaffter, und zum theil biss daher unbekannter landtschafften. *Frankfurt a.M.: J.Schmidt & P.Reffeler,for S.Feyerabend,* 1576. 3pts;illus.;fol. Comprises three works, also issued separately, here brought together with collective t.p. Part 2, with title *Cosmographia . . .* is a German version of Ortelius's *Theatrum orbis terrarum* described below. Sabin 26870. DLC, MB, MnU-B, NN-RB.   576/16

Gesner, Konrad. The newe jewell of health . . . Faithfully corrected, and published in Englishe, by George Baker. *London: H.Denham,* 1576. 258 numb.lvs;illus.;4to. Transl. from author's *Euonymus, sive de Remediis secretis, pars secunda,* 1st publ., Zurich, 1569; subsequently reprinted under title *The practice of . . . phisicke.* STC 11798. CSmH, CtY, DFo, ICN, MH, MiU, MnU-B, NNNAM, PPC; BL.   576/17

Gilbert, Sir Humphrey. A discourse of a discoverie for a new passage to Cataia [i.e., Cathay]. *London: H.Middelton,for R.Jones,* 1576. [88]p.;map;4to. Advocates search for northwest passage to Asia; prelim.sonnet by George Gascoigne refers to Columbus, Vespucci & Magellan. Sabin 27351; STC 11881; Church 117; JCB (3) I:261. CSmH, CtY, DLC, MnU-B, NN-RB, PPL, RPJCB; BL.   576/18

Gómara, Francisco López de. Historia delle nuove Indie Occidentali . . . Parte seconda . . . Tradotta . . . per Agostino di Cravaliz.

Venice: C. Franceschini, 1576. 306 numb.lvs; 8vo. 1st publ. in this translation, Rome, 1556. Continues, as pt 2, Cieza de León's *Cronica* of this year; see also the following entry. Sabin 13054 & 27743 (& in error 27741); Medina (BHA) 159n (I:270-271); Wagner (SW) 2aa; Streit II:931; JCB (3) I:262. NN-RB, RPJCB; BL, Urbino: BU.   576/19

_____. Historia di Don Ferdinando Cortes . . . Tradotta . . . per Agostino di Cravaliz. *Venice: C.Franceschini,* 1576. 1st publ. in this translation, Rome, 1556; continues preceding entry. Sabin 13054 (& 27744); Medina (BHA) 159n (I:271); Wagner (SW) 2bb; Streit II:932; JCB (3) I:262. ICU, NN-RB, RPJCB; BL.
                                              576/20

Guilandini, Melchior. In C. Plinii majoris capita aliquot . . . commentarius. *Lausanne: F.LePreux,* 1576. 151p.;4to. 1st publ., Venice, 1572, under title *Papyrus.* Pritzel 3639n. DNLM, ICN; BN.   576/21

L'Ecluse, Charles de. Rariorum aliquot stirpium per Hispanias observatarum historia. *Antwerp: C.Plantin,* 1576. 529p.;illus.;8vo. Includes refs to American origin of certain species, notably the 'Aloe americana', p.442-446. Sabin 13802; Pritzel 1756; Nissen (Bot.) 370; Adams (Cambr.) C2242; Hunt (Bot.) 125; JCB (3) I:262. CSt, CtY-M, DLC, ICJ, MH-A, NN-RB, PPL, RPJCB; BL, BN.
                                              576/22

LeRoy, Louis. De la vicissitude ou variete des choses en l'univers. *Paris: P.L'Huillier,* 1576. 118 numb.lvs;8vo. 1st publ., Paris, 1575; here reissued with altered imprint date. Atkinson (Fr.Ren.) 246n; Adams (Cambr.) L533. NN-RB; Cambridge: Trinity, BN.   576/23

L'Obel, Matthias de. Plantarum seu Stirpium historia . . . Cui annexum est Adversariorum volumen. *Antwerp: C.Plantin,* 1576. 2v.; illus.;fol. The earliest edn of v.1, v.2, with title *Nova stirpium adversaria . . . auctoribus Petro Pena et Matthia de Lobel,* being an enlarged reissue with cancel t.p. of Pena's *Stirpium adversaria nova,* London, 1571. Pritzel 5548; Nissen (Bot.) 1218; STC 19595.3; Bibl. belg. 1st ser.,XVIII:L118; Adams (Cambr.) L1382; Arents (Add.) 60. CSmH, CtY-M, DLC, MH-A, MnU, NN-RB, PPL, RPB; BL, BN.   576/24

Lopes de Castanheda, Fernão. L'histoire des Indes de Portugal . . . traduict . . . par Nicolas de Grouchy. [*Antwerp: J.Steels,for*] *J.*

Parant,Paris, 1576. 211 numb.lvs;8vo. 1st publ. in this translation, Paris, 1553. A reissue of Steels's 1554, Antwerp, edn with cancel t.p. Atkinson (Fr.Ren.) 97n. BN. 576/25

Magalhães de Gandavo, Pedro de. Historia da provincia sancta Cruz a que vulgarmente chamamos Brasil. *Lisbon: A.Gonsalvez,for J. Lopes*, 1576. 48 numb.lvs;illus.;4to. Sabin 43794; Borba de Moraes I:293; Streit II:1305; Anselmo 709; Church 118; JCB (3) I:262. CSmH, MH, NN-RB, RPJCB; BL, Lisbon: BN. 576/26

Medina, Pedro de. L'art de naviguer . . . traduict . . . avec augmentation & illustration . . . par Nicolas de Nicolai. *Lyons: G.Rouillé*, 1576. 222p.;illus.,map;4to. 1st publ. in French, Lyons, 1553. Sabin 47345n; Baudrier (Lyons) IX:357-358, Palau 159673. CU, CtY, InU-L; BL. 576/27

Mexía, Pedro. Della selva di varia lettione, parti cinque . . . Ampliata, et di nuovo riveduta, per Francesco Sansovino. *Venice: G.Griffio*, 1576. 444 numb.lvs;8vo. 1st publ. in this version with American material, Venice, 1559-60. Palau 167297. CU. 576/28

____. Les diverses leçons . . . mises en françois par Claude Gruget . . . augmentées . . . de trois dialogues. *Paris: N.Bonfons*, 1576. 591 numb.lvs;8vo. 1st publ. in this version with supplementary dialogues referring to Magellan, etc., Paris, 1556. Palau 167316. MoU. 576/29

Münster, Sebastian. A briefe collection and compendious extract of straunge and memorable thinges. *London: T.Marsh*, 1576. 4to. 1st publ., London, 1572, in this version comp. by Richard Eden. Cf.Sabin 51406; cf.Burmeister (Münster) 112; STC 19595.3. VtU. 576/30

Orta, Garcia da. Due libri dell'historia de i semplici, aromati, et altre cose, che vengono portate dall'Indie Orientali, perti alla medicina . . . con alcuni brevi annotationi di Carlo Clusio. Et due altri libri parimente di quelle che si portano dall'Indie Occidentali di Nicolo Monardes . . . Hora tutti tradotti . . . da m. Annibale Briganti. *Venice: [G.&A. Zenari?]* 1576. 2pts;illus.;4to. Orta's work 1st publ. in L'Ecluse's Latin version, Antwerp, 1567; that of Monardes is an incomplete translation of his *Dos libros*, 1st publ., Seville, 1565. Sabin 57667; Guerra (Monardes) 17; Palau 99518; JCB (3) I:263. CtY-M, DNLM,

ICN, NNNAM, RPJCB; BL, BN. 576/31

Ortelius, Abraham. Cosmographia; das ist, Warhaffte . . . beschreibung dess gantzen erdbodens . . . und die . . . neuw erfundenen inseln Americe und Magellane. *Frankfurt a.M.: P.Reffeler,for S.Feyerabend*, 1576. 71 numb.lvs;fol. 1st publ., Antwerp, 1572, as text of Ortelius's *Theatrum oder Schawplatz des erdbodens*. This version also issued as pt 2 of the publisher's *General chronicen* of this year, described above under title. Cf.Sabin 26870; Koeman (Ort.) p.29. DLC, NNH. 576/32

Osório, Jerónimo, Bp of Silves. De rebus Emmanuelis Regis Lusitaniae . . . gestis, libri duodecim . . . Adcessit huic . . . editioni Jo. Metelli . . . epistola. *Cologne: Heirs of A. Birckmann*, 1576. 374p.;8vo. 1st publ. with Matal's preface, Cologne, 1574. Sabin 57804n; Borba de Moraes II:121n; Adams (Cambr.) 0381. InU-L; Cambridge: UL, BN. 576/33

Peña, Pierre. Nova stirpium adversaria. *Antwerp: C.Plantin*, 1576. 471p.;illus.;fol. 1st publ., London, 1571; here largely a reissue of that edn. Pritzel 7029; Nissen (Bot.) 1502; Adams (Cambr.) P616; Arents (Add.) 59. CU, DNLM, MH-A, NN-A, PU, RPB, WU; BL, BN. 576/34

Peucer, Kaspar. Commentarius de praecipuis generibus divinitiarum. *Wittenberg: J. Schwertel*, 1576. 452 numb.lvs;8vo. 1st (?) publ. in this enl. edn, Wittenberg, 1560. Adams (Cambr.) P931; Shaaber P250. ICN, NIC, PU; BL, BN. 576/34a

Porcacchi, Tommaso. L'isole piu famose del mondo . . . con l'aggiunta di molte isole. *Venice: G.Angelieri,for S.Galignani & G. Porro*, 1576. 201p.;illus.,maps;fol. 1st publ., Venice, 1572. Sabin 64149; Phillips (Atlases) 167; Adams (Cambr.) P1905; JCB (3) I:263-264. DLC, RPJCB; Cambridge: UL, Strasbourg: BN. 576/35

Rondelet, Guillaume. Methodus curandorum omnium morborum corporis humani . . . Ejusdem . . . De morbo gallico. *Lyons: G. Rouillé*, 1576. 1277p.;8vo. 1st (?) publ., Paris [1563?]; here a reissue with altered imprint date of Rouillé's 1575 edn. DNLM, PPL. 576/36

____. Traité de vérole . . . Traduit . . . et remis au net, par Estienne Maniald. *Bordeaux: S. Millanges*, 1576. 94p.;8vo. Transl. from the

author's *Methodus curandorum omnium morborum*, 1st (?) publ., Paris [1563?]. BN.
576/37

Surius, Laurentius. Kurtze Chronick . . . der
vornembsten händeln so sich . . . in der . . .
Welt zugetragen. *Cologne: H.von Ach*, 1576.
2pts;8vo. 1st publ. in German, Cologne, 1568,
as transl. by H.Fabricius; text here extended
to year 1575. Sabin 93888n. BL. 576/38

Vigo, Giovanni de. La pratica universale in
cirugia . . . di nuova ristampata, & corretta.
Venice: G.M.Bonelli, 1576. 307 numb.lvs;
illus.;4to. Includes in Italian translation the
author's *Practica in arte chirurgica copiosa*,
1st publ., Rome, 1514. DNLM; London:
Wellcome. 576/39

1577

Alberti, Leandro. Descrittione di tutta
l'Italia. *Venice: G.M.Leni*, 1577. 501 lvs;4to.
1st publ., Bologna, 1550. Ind.aur.102.349;
Adams (Cambr.) A475. DFo, ICN, MH,
MnU-B; Cambridge: Fitzwilliam Mus., BN.
577/1

Anghiera, Pietro Martire d'. The history of
travayle in the West and East Indies . . . With
a discourse of the Northwest passage.
Gathered in parte, and done into English by
Richard Eden. Newly set in order, aug-
mented, and finished by Richard Wiles. *Lon-
don: R.Jug*, 1577. 466 numb.lvs;4to. Includes
Anghiera's Decades 1-4 & abridgements of
5-8; & also Oviedo's *History of the West
Indies*. Sabin 102837 (&1562); Borba de
Moraes II:33; Streit I:123; Burmeister
(Münster) 113; STC 649; Arents 23; Church
119; JCB (3) I:266. CSmH, CtY, ICN, MH,
NN-RB, PPL, RPJCB; BL. 577/2

Bock, Hieronymus. Kreütterbuch. *Strassburg: J.Rihel*, 1577. 470 numb.lvs;illus.;fol.
1st publ. with illus., Strassburg, 1546; here
ed. for 1st time by Melchior Sebitzius. Pritzel
866n; Nissen (Bot.) 182n; Ind.aur.120.598.
BL, Munich: StB. 577/3

Bodin, Jean. Les six livres de la Republique.*Paris: J.DuPuys*, 1577. 797p.;fol. 1st
publ., Paris, 1576. Ind.aur.120.807n; Adams
(Cambr.) B2235. CtY, DFo, MH, NN-RB;
Cambridge: Trinity. 577/4

—[Anr edn]. *Paris: J.DuPuys*, 1577. 759p.;fol.

Ind.aur.120.807n; Adams (Cambr.) B2234.
ICN; Cambridge: Pepys, BN. 577/5

—[Anr edn]. [*Geneva: C.de Juge*] 1577. 547 lvs;
8vo. On variant settings of 1st 112 pages, see
M. Reulos, 'L'édition de 1577 de la République', *Bibliothèque d'humanisme et renaissance*, XIII (1951) 343. Ind.aur.120.806;
Adams (Cambr.) B2233. MiU, NN-RB; Cambridge: King's, Vienna: NB. 577/6

Braun, Georg. Civitates orbis terrarum, liber
primus. *Cologne: G.von Kempen*, 1577. 58
double pls;fol. 1st publ., Cologne, 1572. Cf.
Koeman (Braun & Hogenberg) 1; Ind.aur.
123.951; Adams (Cambr.) B2709. Cambridge: UL, BN. 577/7

Castillejo, Cristóbal de. Obras. *Madrid: F.
Sánchez*, 1577. 404 numb.lvs;12mo. 1st publ.,
Madrid, 1573. Pérez Pastor (Madrid) 112;
Palau 48017n. InU-L; BN. 577/8

Dee, John. General and rare memorials per-
tayning to the perfect arte of navigation. *London: J.Day*, 1577. 80p.;illus.;fol. Includes ref.
to Francis Drake's forthcoming voyage, & ad-
vances argument for English claims to North
America. The 1st vol. of a larger work never
completed. STC 6459. CSmH, CtY, DLC,
MiU, NN-RB; BL. 577/9

Du Verdier, Antoine. Les diverses leçons
. . . suivans celles de Pierre Messie. *Lyons:
B.Honorat*, 1577. 422p.;port.;8vo. Issued as
pt 2 of Pedro Mexía's *Diverses leçons* described below. In bk 4 are chapters on beliefs
of New World natives & origin of syphilis.
Sabin 48245n; Cioranescu (XVI) 9400;
Baudrier (Lyons) IV:134. DFo, WU; BN.
577/10

Emili, Paolo. De rebus gestis Francorum libri
x. Arnoldi Ferroni . . . De rebus item gestis
Gallorum libri novem. *Paris: M.de Vascovan*,
1577. 244 numb.lvs;fol. 1st publ. with Le Ferron's appendix, Paris, 1548. Ind.aur.100.839.
MBAt, MiU; BL, BN. 577/11

Ercilla y Zúñiga, Alonso de. La Araucana
[Primera parte]. *Saragossa: J.Soler*, 1577.
328p.;8vo. 1st publ., Madrid, 1569. Medina
(BHA) 244; Medina (Arau.) 4; Sánchez (Aragon) 537. NN-RB; Madrid: BN. 577/12

Fernel, Jean. De abditis rerum causis. *Frankfurt a.M.: A.Wechel*, 1577. 101p.;port.;fol.
1st publ., Paris, 1548. DNLM, ICU,
NNNAM, PPL. 577/13

——. Universa medicina. *Frankfurt a.M.: A.
Wechel*, 1577. 2v.;port.;fol. Includes Fernel's

De abditis causis rerum, 1st publ., Paris, 1548. Sherrington (Fernel) 61.J5; Adams (Cambr.) F258. DNLM, NNNAM, PPL; Cambridge: Emmanuel. 577/14

___[Anr edn]. [*Geneva:*] *J.Stoer*, 1577. 657p.;fol. CaBVaU. 577/15

Fischart, Johann. Das glückhafft Schiff von Zürich. *Strassburg: B.Jobin*, 1577. 14 lvs;8vo. Fictional narrative which includes ref. to discovery of America. Ritter (Strasbourg) 847. Berlin: StB. 577/16

Foglietta, Uberto. Clarorum Ligurum elogia. *Rome: G.degli Angeli*, 1577. 264p.;8vo. 1st publ., Rome, 1572. BN. 577/17

Gesner, Konrad. Epistolarum medicinalium . . . libri iii . . . Omnia nunc primum per Casparum Wolphium . . . in lucem data. *Zurich: C.Froschauer*, 1577. 140 numb.lvs; 4to. Included are refs to Guaiacum, tobacco, & the New World. Adams (Cambr.) G526; Arents 22. CtY, DNLM, ICJ, MH-A, MiU, MnU, NN-A; BL, BN. 577/18

Giovio, Paolo, Bp of Nocera. Eigentliche und gedenckwurdige Contrafacturen oder Anbildungen, wolverdienter unnd weitberumpter Kriegshelden auss des hochwirdigen Bischoffs Pauli Jovii Elogiis . . . gezogen . . . Durch Theobaldum Muller. *Basel: P.Perna*, 1577. [144]p.;ports;4to. Transl. from Giovio's *Musaei Joviani imagines*, the following item. Fairfax Murray (Germany) 184. CtY, MiU-C, MnU-B, PP; BL (Mueller, Theobald). 577/19

____. Musaei Joviani imagines. *Basel: P.Perna & H.Petri*, 1577. 133ports;4to. Reprints portraits, with verse captions, 1st publ. in Perna's 1575 edn of Giovio's *Elogia virorum bellica virtute illustrium*. They were the work of Tobias Stimmer. DLC, NN-RB. 577/20

Gómara, Francisco López de. Histoire generalle des Indes Occidentalles et terres neuves . . . Traduite . . . par m. Fumée sieur de Marley le Chastel. *Paris: M.Sonnius*, 1577. 355 numb.lvs;8vo. 1st publ. in this translation, Paris, 1568. Sabin 27747; Medina (BHA) 159n (I:272) Wagner (SW) 2gg; Streit II:938; Atkinson (Fr.Ren.) 252; JCB (3) I:265. DLC, ICN, NN-RB, RPJCB; BL. 577/21

Guicciardini, Francesco. L'histoire des guerres d'Italie . . . translatée . . . par Hiérosme Chomedey. *Paris: J.Kerver*, 1577. 479 numb.lvs;fol. 1st publ. in this version, Paris, 1568. Adams (Cambr.) G1524. BL. 577/22

___[Anr issue]. *Paris: J.Kerver,for M.Sonnius*, 1577. Adams (Cambr.) G1525. DLC, PPL; Cambridge: St John's, BN. 577/23

___[Anr edn]. *Lyons: P.de Saint-André*, 1577. 2v.;8vo. CtY; BN. 577/24

Heyns, Peeter. Spieghel der werelt, ghestelt in ryme. *Antwerp: C.Plantin,for P.Galle*, 1577. 70 numb.lvs;illus.,maps;obl.4to. A 'reduction and generalization' by Philip Galle of the maps in Ortelius's *Theatrum orbis terrarum* in pocket atlas form, with versified text by Heyns. Koeman (Ort) 47; Bibl.belg.,1st ser., XII:H53. NN-RB, RPJCB; BL, Brussels: BR. 577/25

LeRoy, Louis. De la vicissitude ou variete des choses en l'univers. *Paris: P.L'Huillier*, 1577. 119 numb.lvs;fol. 1st publ., Paris, 1575. MH, NjP; Chantilly: Mus. Condé. 577/26

Liébault, Jean. Thesaurus sanitatis paratu facilis. *Paris: J.DuPuys*, 1577. 422 numb.lvs; 16mo. Includes Auger Ferrier's *De morbo gallico libri duo*, 1st publ., Toulouse, 1553. Adams (Cambr.) L664; Proksch I:16. CtY-M, DNLM, NNNAM; BL, BN. 577/27

Lonitzer, Adam. Kreuterbuch . . . zum sechsten Mal von neuwem ersehen . . . durch Adamum Lonicerum. *Frankfurt a.M.: M. Lechler,for Heirs of C.Egenolff*, 1577. ccclviii lvs;illus.,port.;fol. 1st publ. in German, Frankfurt a.M., 1557. Pritzel 5599n; Nissen (Bot.) 1228n. DNLM, NNBG. 577/28

Lopes de Castanheda, Fernão. Historia dell' Indie Orientali, scoperte, & conquistate da' Portoghesi . . . Nuovamente di lingua portoghese . . . tradotti dal signor' Alfonso Ulloa. *Venice: G.Ziletti*, 1577. 2v.;4to. Transl. from the author's *Historia do descobrimento e conquista da India pelos Portuguezes*, Coimbra, 1551-61. Sabin 11387; Borba de Moraes I:142-143; Streit IV:972; JCB (3) I:265. ICN, NN-RB, RPJCB; BL(v.1), BN. 577/29

Mexía, Pedro. Les diverses leçons . . . mises en françois par Claude Gruget . . . augmentées de trois dialogues. *Paris: N.Bonfons*, 1577. 592 numb.lvs;16mo. 1st publ. in this version with supplementary dialogues, Paris, 1556. Palau 167317. ICN; BN. 577/30

___[Anr edn]. Les diverses leçons . . . avec trois dialogues, mises en français par Claude Gruget . . . augmentees . . . de la suite d'icelles, faite par Antoine Verdier. *Lyons: B. Honorat*, 1577. 2pts;port.;8vo. The earliest edn with DuVerdier's continuation. Baudrier

(Lyons) IV:134-135; Palau 167319. DFo, WU;
BN.   577/31

Monardes, Nicolás. The three books written
in the Spanish tongue . . . translated . . . by
Jhon Frampton. *London: W.Norton,* 1577.
109 numb.lvs;illus.;4to. Transl. from the author's *Primera y segunda y tercera partes,* Seville, 1574, with additional text on tobacco derived from Estienne's *Agriculture,* Paris, 1567.
Guerra (Monardes) 18; STC 18005; Palau
175497. DFo, NN-RB; BL.   `   577/32

___[Anr issue]. *London: W.Norton,* 1577. Sheets
of above reissued with cancel t.p. Sabin
49944; Medina (BHA) 237n (I:392); Guerra
(Monardes) 19; STC 18005a; Palau 175509;
Arents 24; JCB (3) I:266. CSmH, CtY, DLC,
ICN, MB, NN-A, RPJCB; BL, BN.   577/33

**Newe Zeyttung auss den new erfundenen In-
seln,** wie daselbst grosser Schaden durch Erd-
bidem geschehen. [*Augsburg?* 1577?]. 4 lvs;
4to. On Chilean earthquake of 1576. NN-RB.
                                             577/34

Ortelius, Abraham.   Spieghel der werelt. *Antwerp:* 1577. See entry under Heyns, Peeter,
above.

Paracelsus.   Schreiben von der Frantzosen in ix
Bücher verfasset. *Basel: P.Perna,* 1577. 234p.;
8vo. 1st publ., 1564. Sudhoff (Paracelsus)
178. BL.   577/35

Polo, Gaspar Gil.   Primera parte de Diana
enamorada. *Saragossa: J.Millán,* 1577. 147
numb.lvs;8vo. 1st publ., Valencia, 1564. In
verse. Sánchez (Aragon) 538; Palau 102076.
BL, Madrid: BN.   577/36

___[Anr issue]. *Lérida: J.Millán,* 1577. Palau
102076n.   577/37

Sacro Bosco, Joannes de.   Sphaera . . . emen-
data. Eliae Vineti . . . Scholia. *Paris: J.de
Marnef & Widow of G.Cavellat,* 1577. 94
numb.lvs;illus.;8vo. 1st publ. with Vinet's
Scholia, Paris, 1551. Cf.Sabin 32681; Adams
(Cambr.) H734. ICJ, NN-RB; BL.   577/38

Salazar, Esteban de.   Veynte discursos sobre el
Credo. *Granada: H.de Mena,* 1577-78. 240
numb.lvs;4to. Describes at length missionary
efforts among Indians in Mexico & Peru, as
cited & quoted by Medina. Medina (BHA)
248; Streit II:939; Palau 286516. RPJCB.
                                             577/39

Schylander, Cornelius.   Medicina astrologica
. . . unà cum practica chirurgiae brevi & fa-
cili. *Antwerp: A.Thylens,for J.Verwithagen,*

1577. 2pts;illus.;8vo. Pt 2 has special t.p.:
*Practica chirurgiae . . . & . . . modum ex-
trahendi olea ex floribus, herbis vulnariis, ligno guiaco, & cera continens.* Belg.typ. (1541-
1600) I:4309. DNLM, PPC; BL, Brussels: BR.
                                             577/40

Serres, Jean de.   Commentariorum de statu religionis et reipublicae in regno Galliae. [*Geneva: E.Vignon*] 1577. 122 numb.lvs; 8vo. 1st
publ., [Geneva], 1570. Adams (Cambr.)
L187. Cambridge: UL.   577/41

Settle, Dionyse.   A true reporte of the last voyage into the West and Northwest regions, &c.
1577 worthily atchieved by Capteine Frobisher. *London: H.Middelton,* 1577. 24 lvs;
8vo. Collates A⁴, B-C⁸, D⁴. Sabin 79341;
Church 119A; STC 22265; JCB (3) I:315.
CSmH, PPL, RPJCB; BL.   577/42

___[Anr edn]. *London: H.Middelton,* 1577. Col-
lates A-C⁸. Sabin 79341n; STC 22266. NN-
RB.   577/43

**Spain. Sovereigns, etc., 1556-1598 (Philip
II).**   Instruccion para la observacion del
eclypse de luna, y cantidad de las sombras que
su Magestad mandó hazer . . . en las ciudades
y pueblos de Españoles de las Indias.
[*Madrid?* 1577]. Supposedly drawn up by
Juan López de Velasco; cf.following item. Medina (BHA) 246; Pérez Pastor (Madrid) 115.
                                             577/44

_____. Instruction, y memoria, de las relaciones
que se han de hazer, para la descripcion de las
Indias. [*Madrid?* 1577?]. [3]p.;fol. A ques-
tionnaire seeking information, drawn up by
Juan López de Velasco, 'Chronista cosmogra-
pho mayor' of the Council of the Indies.
Medina (BHA) 245; Pérez Pastor (Madrid)
113; JCB AR45:17-26. RPJCB; Madrid: BN.
                                             577/45

Torquemada, Antonio de.   Jardin de flores curiosas. *Salamanca: J.B.de Terranova,for A.de
Terranova y Neyla,* 1577. 286 numb.lvs;8vo.
1st publ., Salamanca, 1570. In verse. Palau
334912. BL.   577/46

Weigel, Hans.   Habitus praecipuorum populorum, tam virorum quam foeminarum singu-
lari arte depicti. *Nuremberg: H.Weigel,* 1577.
ccxix pl.;illus.;fol. Of the plates, the work of
Jost Amman, 2 depict Brazilian natives;
cf.Paris, 1562, *Recueil de la diversité des
habits.* The text (in German verse) describing
the plates is attributed to the publisher. Borba

de Moraes II:373; Fairfax Murray (Germany) 32; Becker (Amman) 140. NN-S; BL. 577/47

Zárate, Agustín de. Historia del descubrimiento y conquista de las provincias del Peru. *Seville: A.Escrivano,* 1577. 117 numb.lvs;fol. 1st publ., Antwerp, 1555. Sabin 106269; Medina (BHA) 249; Escudero (Seville) 692; Church 120; JCB (3) I:267. CSmH, CtY, DLC, MH, NN-RB, RPJCB; BL. 577/48

1578

Alfonce, Jean, i.e., Jean Fonteneau, known as. Les voyages avantureux du Capitaine Jean Alfonce. *Rouen: T.Mallard,* 1578. 64 numb.lvs;4to. 1st publ., Poitiers, 1559; here reissued with additional text. Sabin 100832; Harrisse (NF) 4; Atkinson (Fr.Ren.) 257; Shaaber A179. PU; BN. 578/1

Alfonso X, el Sabio, King of Castile and Leon. Los cinco libros primeros dela Coronica general de España. *Alcalá de Henares: J.Iñiguez de Lequérica, for D.Martínez,* 1578. 222 numb.lvs;fol. 1st publ. in 5 bks, Medina del Campo, 1553. Authorship frequently ascribed to Florián d'Ocampo, editor of the work. Sabin 56621; Medina (BHA) 118n; García (Alcalá de Henares) 534. CU, DLC, MH, MiU, NjP; BL, BN. 578/2

Benzoni, Girolamo. Novae Novi Orbis historiae, id est, Rerum ab Hispanis in India Occidentali hactenus gestarum . . . libri tres, Urbani Calvetonis opera . . . ex italicis . . . latini facti . . . His ab eodem adjuncta est, De Gallorum in Floridam expeditione, & insigni Hispanorum in eos saevitiae exemplo, Brevis historiae. [*Geneva:*] *E.Vignon,* 1578. 480p.;8vo. Transl. from Benzoni's *Historia del Mondo Nuovo,* 1st publ., Venice, 1565, with addition here of Nicolas Le Chailleux's *Discours de l'histoire de la Floride,* 1st publ., Dieppe, 1565, here transl. by L.Apollonius. Sabin 4792; Medina (BHA) 250; Adams (Laudonnière) 9; Streit II:946; Ind. aur.116.987; Adams (Cambr.) B685; Arents 25; JCB (3) I:268. CU-B, CtY, DLC, MH, MiU-C, MnU-B, NN-A, RPJCB; BL, BN. 578/3

Best, George. A true discourse of the late voyages of discoverie, for the finding of a passage to Cathaya by the Northwest under the conduct of Martin Frobisher. *London: H.Byn-*

neman, 1578. 3pts;illus.,maps;4to. For variant states see Church cat. Sabin 5051; STC 1972-1973; Ind.aur. 118.201; Church 122; JCB (3) I:268. CSmH (3 states), CtY, ICN, MH, MnU-B, NN-RB, RPJCB; BL(2 states). 578/4

Boaistuau, Pierre. Histoires prodigeuses. *Paris: J.de Bordeaux,* 1578. 3v.;illus.;8vo. 1st publ. with American ref. in section by François de Belleforest, Paris, 1571. MH, RPB. 578/5

Bodin, Jean. Discours . . . sur le rehaussement et dimunition des monnoyes . . . & reponce aux Paradoxes de monsieur de Malestroict. *Paris: J.DuPuys,* 1578. [247]p.;8vo. 1st publ., Paris, 1568, in de Malestroict's *Paradoxes;* here expanded to include fuller ref. to gold derived from Peru. Ind.aur.120.809. ICU, MH-BA, NN-RB; BL, BN. 578/6

_____. Les six livres de la Republique . . . Revue, corrigee et augmentee de nouveau. Troisieme edition. *Paris: J.DuPuys,* 1578. 773p.;fol. 1st publ., Paris, 1576. Ind.aur.120.208; Adams (Cambr.) B2236. MH-L, NN-RB, PPL, RPB; Cambridge: King's, BN. 578/7

Cardano, Girolamo. Les livres . . . intitulez De la subtilite . . . Traduits . . . par Richard le Blanc. Nouvellement reveuz, corrigez, & augmentez. *Paris: G.Beys,* 1578. 478 numb. lvs;illus.;8vo. 1st publ. in French, Paris, 1556. Ind.aur.132.113. BN. 578/8

__[Anr issue]. *Paris: S.Calvarin,* 1578. Ind. aur.132.113. DNLM, MH; BN. 578/9

__[Anr issue]. *Paris: G.Chaudière,* 1578. London: Wellcome. 578/10

__[Anr issue]. *Paris: G.Julian,* 1578. Ind. aur.132.113; Adams (Cambr.) C677. Cambridge: Trinity. 578/11

__[Anr issue]. *Paris: G.LaNouë,* 1578. Ind. aur.132.113. BN. 578/12

Casas, Bartolomé de las, Bp of Chiapa. Seer cort verhael vande destructie van d'Indien . . . uyte spaensche overgeset. [*Antwerp?*] 1578. [139]p.;4to. Transl. from the author's *Brevissima relacion de la destruycion de las Indias* and his *Treynta proposiciones muy juridicas,* Seville, 1552. Sabin 11249; Medina (BHA) 1085n (II:475); Streit I:126; JCB (3) I:270. DLC, NN-RB, RPJCB; BL. 578/13

Centellas, Joachin de. Les voyages et conquestes des roys de Portugal. *Paris: J.d'Ongois,* 1578. 60 numb.lvs;8vo. Included are refs to Brazil. Atkinson (Fr.Ren.) 258. MnU-B; BL, BN.   578/14

Chaumette, Antoine. Enchiridion ou Livret portatif des chirurgiens . . . Auquel est adjouste . . . une methode . . . pour guérir la verole. *Lyons: L.Cloquemin,* 1578. 8vo. 1st publ. in French, Lyons, 1571. Baudrier (Lyons) IV:51-52. London: Wellcome. 578/15

Churchyard, Thomas. A discourse of the Queenes Majesties entertainment in Suffolk and Norffolk . . . Whereunto is adjoyned a commendation of Sir Humfrey Gilberts ventrous journey. *London: H.Bynneman* [1578]. 44 lvs;4to. For description of variant issue, see Church catalog. Sabin 13032; STC 5226; Church 120B. CSmH; BL.   578/16

————. A prayse, and reporte of maister Martyne Forboishers voyage to Meta Incognita. *London: A.Maunsell,* 1578. 24 lvs;8vo. Sabin 13034; STC 5251; Church 120A. CSmH; BL.
                                              578/17

Cooper, Thomas, Bp of Winchester. Thesaurus linguae romanae & britannicae. *London:* 1578. [1716]p.;fol. 1st publ., London, 1565. STC 5688; Shaaber C669. CSmH, CtY, DLC, ICN, MH, MnU, NN-RB, PU; BL.
                                              578/18

Costa, Christovam da. Tractado delas drogas, y medicinas de las Indias Orientales, con sus plantas debuxadas al bivo . . . En el qual se verifica mucho de lo que escrivio el Doctor Garcia de Orta. *Burgos: M.de Victoria,* 1578. 448p.;illus.,port.;4to. In ch.16, 'Del lacre', is a ref. to Brazilian rubber; ch.58, 'Del ananas', describes pineapple, introduced to East Indies from West Indies. Sabin 113; Pritzel 13; Nissen (Bot.) 3n; Hunt (Bot.) 130. CU, CtY, DLC, ICN, InU-L, MH, MnU-B, NN-RB, RPJCB; BL, BN.   578/19

Costeo, Giovanni. De universali stirpium natura libri duo. *Turin: Heirs of N.Bevilacqua,* 1578. 496p.;4to. In bk 1, chapt.4, the cactus Opuntia, 'ficus Indiae', is discussed; in chapt.24, 'Agnacat' (tobacco), found near the 'Istmum Dariem'. Pritzel 1921; Hunt (Bot.) 131. DFo, MH-A, NNNAM, PPC; BL. 578/20

Couilliard, Antoine, seigneur du Pavillon. Les antiquitez et singularitez du monde. *Lyons: B.Rigaud,* 1578. 337 numb. lvs;8vo. 1st publ., Paris, 1557. Cioranescu (XVI) 7010; Baudrier (Lyons) III:344-345. BL.   578/21

Dodoens, Rembert. A niewe herball, or Historie of plantes . . . translated out of French

. . . by Henry Lyte. *London: H.van der Loe,Antwerp,for G.D'Ewes,* 1578. 779p.; illus.;fol. Transl. from Charles de L'Ecluse's 1557 French translation of the 1554 Dutch *Cruijde boeck.* Cf.Pritzel 2345n; Nissen (Bot.) 516; Bibl.belg.,1st ser.,IX:D110; STC 6984; Henrey (Brit.bot.) 110; Arents (Add.) 17; Hunt (Bot.) 132. CLSU, CtY, DFo, ICN, MH, MiU, MnU, NN-A, PPC, RPB; BL, BN.
                                              578/22

Du Bartas, Guillaume de Salluste, seigneur. La sepmaine, ou Creation du monde. *Paris: J.Février,* 1578. 224p.;4to. In verse. Includes numerous scattered refs to New World, e.g. to corn, Columbus & Vespucci, derived from Benzoni, Gómara, Oviedo, &c. Holmes (DuBartas) I:70 no.1n. BL, BN.   578/23

—[Anr issue]. *Paris: M.Gadoulleau,* 1578. Holmes (DuBartas) I:70, no.1; Adams (Cambr.) D960. Cambridge: Trinity, BN.
                                              578/24

—[Anr edn]. Troisiéme edition. *Turin: J.Farine* [i.e., *Lyons: A.de Harsy*] 1578. 8vo. On false imprint, see E.Droz, 'Fausses adresses typographiques', *Bibliothèque d'humanisme et renaissance,* XXIII (1961) 148-150. Holmes (DuBartas) I:70 no.2. Montpelier: BM.578/25

Ellis, Thomas. A true report of the third and last voyage into Meta incognita, atchieved by the worthie Capteine, M. Martin Frobisher. *London: T.Dawson,* 1578. 20 lvs;8vo. Sabin 22330; STC 7607; Church 120C. CSmH.
                                              578/26

Enciso, Martín Fernández de. A briefe description of the portes, creekes, bayes, and havens, of the Weast India: translated out of the Castlin tongue by J.F[rampton]. *London: H.Bynneman,* 1578. 27p.;4to. Extracted & transl. from Enciso's *Suma de geographia,* 1st publ., Seville, 1519. Wroth (Frampton) 309-311; STC 10823; Palau 88437. CSmH, NN-RB, RPJCB.   578/27

Ercilla y Zúñiga, Alonso de. Primera parte de la Araucana. *Saragossa: J.Soler,* 1578. 328p.;8vo. 1st publ., Madrid, 1569. With colophon dated 1577, presumably a reissue with cancel t.p. of Soler's 1577 edn, so prepared to accompany the *Segunda parte* of this year. Medina (Arau.) 7; Sánchez (Aragon) 551. BN.
                                              578/28

————. Primera y segunda parte dela Araucana. *Madrid: P.Cosin,* 1578. 729p.;8vo. The earliest edn to contain the 2nd pt, the 1st having

been 1st publ., 1569, at Madrid. With license dated 10 June 1578, ostensibly publ. prior to Saragossa edn of this year. Sabin 22720; Medina (BHA) 252; Pérez Pastor (Madrid) 124; Medina (Arau.) 5. NNH; BL, Madrid: BN.
578/29

__[Anr edn]. *Madrid: P.Cosin*, 1578. 2pts;4to. Medina (BHA) 253; Pérez Pastor (Madrid) 125; Medina (Arau.) 6. MH, NN-RB, RPJCB; Madrid: BN. 578/30

____. Segunda parte de la Araucana. *Saragossa: J.Soler*, 1578. 335p.;8vo. With privilege dated 22 Aug., postdates 1st Madrid edn of this pt described above. Medina (BHA) 251; Sánchez (Aragon) 552; Medina (Arau.) 7. MiU-C, NNH, RPJCB; Madrid: BN. 578/31

Estienne, Charles. L'agriculture, et maison rustique de mm. Charles Estienne et Jean Liebault. [*Lyons: Printed for*] *J.DuPuys,at Paris*, 1578. 347 numb.lvs;illus.;4to. 1st publ. in this version, Paris, 1574. Thiébaud (La chasse) 347; Baudrier (Lyons) I:366. DNAL, MH.
578/32

Falloppius, Gabriel. Secreti diversi et miracolosi, nuovamente ristampata. *Venice: A. Gardano*, 1578. 366p.;8vo. 1st publ., Venice, 1563. Moranti (Urbino) 1428. DFo, DNLM; Urbino: BU. 578/33

Fernel, Jean. Universa medicina. *Frankfurt a.M.: A.Wechel*, 1578. 2v.;port.;fol. A reissue with altered imprint date of Wechel's 1577 edn. Includes Fernel's *De abditis rerum causis*, 1st publ., Paris, 1548. Sherrington (Fernel) 62.J6. Sherrington. 578/34

__[Anr edn]. [*Geneva:*] *J.Stoer*, 1578. 2v.;port.; fol. Sherrington (Fernel) 65.J9. DNLM, ICU, NNC; BN. 578/35

__[Anr issue of preceding]. [*Geneva: J.Stoer*] *for A.Marsilius,at Lyons*, 1578. Sherrington (Fernel) 63.J7. DNLM. 578/36

Fregoso, Battista. Factorum dictorumque memorabilium libri ix. *Paris: P.Cavellat*, 1578. 380 numb.lvs;8vo. 1st publ., Milan, 1509. Adams (Cambr.) F1150. ICN, InU-L, MH, NNC; Cambridge: UL, BN. 578/37

Giovio, Paolo, Bp of Nocera. Opera quotquot extant omnia. *Basel: H.Petri & P.Perna*, 1578. 3v.;port.;fol. The earliest collected edn of Giovio's works, including his *Historiarum sui temporis*, 1st publ., Florence, 1550-52, etc. Adams (Cambr.) G632; Shaaber G185. CU, CtY, DLC, ICU, MH, MiU, NN-RB, PU, RPB; BL, BN. 578/38

____. Regionum et insularum atque locorum: descriptiones. *Basel: P.Perna*, 1578. 156p.; fol. Includes Giovio's *Descriptio Britanniae*, 1st publ., Venice, 1548, and his *De romanis piscibus*, 1st publ., Rome, 1524. Adams (Cambr.) G676. CtY, DFo, ICU, MH, NN-RB, PU; Cambr.: Gonville & Caius, BN.
578/39

Gómara, Francisco López de. Histoire generalle des Indes Occidentalles et terres neuves . . . Traduite par m. Fumée sieur de Marley le Chastel. *Paris: M.Sonnius*, 1578. 355 numb.lvs;8vo. 1st publ. in this translation, Paris, 1568; here anr issue of the bookseller's 1577 edn with altered imprint date. Cf.Sabin 27747; Medina (BHA) 159n (I:272); Wagner (SW) 2hh; Streit II:947; Atkinson (Fr.Ren.) 252n; JCB (3) I:271. DLC, MH, RPJCB; Nancy: BM. 578/40

____. The pleasant historie of the conquest of the Weast India, now called New Spayne, atchieved by . . . Hernando Cortes . . . translated by . . . T.N[icholas]. *London: H.Bynneman*, 1578. 405p.;4to. Transl. from 2nd pt of Gómara's *Historia general de las Indias*, 1st publ., Saragossa, 1552. Sabin 27751; Wagner (SW) 2pp; Streit II:948; STC 16807; Church 123; JCB (3) I:271. CSmH, CtY, DLC, ICN, MH, MiU-C, MnU-B, NNH, RPJCB; BL.
578/41

Honter, Johannes. Rudimentorum cosmographicorum . . . libri iii. [*Zurich? C.Froschauer?*] 1578. 46 lvs;illus.,maps;8vo. 1st publ. in this version, Kronstadt, 1542. In verse. Borsa 96; Szabo III:676. DFo, IU.
578/42

Informacion de derecho en favor de las provincias de la Nueva España, y nuevo reyno de Galizia, sobre la perpetuydad de los repartimientos de Indios, fechos a los conquistadores, y pobladores dellas. *Madrid: G.Drouy*, 1578. 36 numb.lvs;fol. Signed by Ascensio López & 4 other lawyers; issued with the petition of Juan Velásquez de Salazar described below. Medina (BHA) 255; LeClerc (1867) 2985n.
578/43

Jesuits. Letters from missions. Lettres du Jappon, Peru, et Brasil. *Paris: T.Brumen*, 1578. 110p.;8vo. Borba de Moraes I:408-409; Atkinson (Fr.Ren.) 260; Streit II:949. DLC, NNH, RPJCB; BL, Paris: Mazarine. 578/44

Jode, Gérard de. Speculum orbis terrarum. *Antwerp: G.Smits,for G.de Jode*, 1578. 2v.;

maps;fol. The descriptive text is by Daniel Cellarius. Cf.Sabin 36826; Koeman (Jod) 1; Phillips (Atlases) 383; Adams (Cambr.) C1238. CtY, DLC, MiU-C, NNH, RPJCB; BL, Munich: StB.   578/45

Le Paulmier de Grentemesnil, Julien. De morbis contagiosis libri septem. *Paris: D. Duval*, 1578. 443p.;4to. Includes discussion of syphilis. CtY-M, DNLM, PPC; BL.   578/46

Léry, Jean de. Histoire d'un voyage fait en la terre du Bresil, autrement dite Amerique. *La Rochelle: A.Chuppin*, 1578. 424p.;illus.;8vo. An account of Villegagnon's Brazilian colony. On verso of lf a3 variant readings, described by Borba de Moraes, occur. Sabin 40148; Borba de Moraes I:400-402; Atkinson (Fr.Ren.) 261; Arents 26; Church 124. CSmH, NN-A; BL, BN.   578/47

—[Anr issue]. [*La Rochelle:*] *A.Chuppin*, 1578. Perhaps designed for sale by Chuppin at Geneva. Borba de Moraes I:400-402; Atkinson (Fr.Ren.) 261n; Arents 26n; Church 124n; Rothschild 1989; JCB (3) I:271. CSt, DLC, InU-L, MH, MiU-C, MnU-B, RPJCB; BN.
                                             578/48

Lopes de Castanheda, Fernão. Historia dell'Indie Orientali, scoperte, & conquistate da' Portoghesi . . . Nuovamente di lingua portoghese . . . tradotti dal signor' Alfonso Ulloa. *Venice: F.Ziletti*, 1578. 2v.;4to. 1st publ., 1577; here reissued with imprints altered. Cf. Sabin 11389. DLC, ICN, InU-L, MH, MnU-B; BL(v.2).   578/49

Lucidarius. M. Elucidarius, von allerhand Geschöpffen Gottes . . . unnd wie alle Creaturen geschaffen seind auff Erden. *Frankfurt a.M.: Heirs of C.Egenolff,for A.Lonicer,J.Cnipius & P.Steinmeyer*, 1578. [102]p.; illus.;4to. 1st publ., Strassburg, [ca.1535]. Schorbach (Lucidarius) 61. Freiburg i.Br.: UB.   578/50

Malestroict, Jehan Cherruyt de. Les paradoxes . . . sur le faict des monnoyes, presentez à Sa Majesté au mois de mars 1566, avec la response de m. Jean Bodin. *Paris: M. LeJeune*, 1578. 128p.;8vo. 1st publ. with Bodin's *Response*, Paris, 1568. MH-BA; BL, BN.   578/51

—[Anr edn]. *Paris: J.DuPuys*, 1578. 2pts;8vo. BN.   578/52

Marguérite d'Angoulême, Queen of Navarre. L'heptaméron. *Lyons: L.Cloquemin*, 1578. 812p.;16mo. 1st publ., Paris, 1558, under title *Histoire des amans fortunez*. Tchémerzine VII:395; Baudrier (Lyons) IV:52; Adams (Cambr.) M567. ICN, MH; Cambridge: UL, BN.   578/53

Meneses, Felipe de. Luz de alma christiana. *Salamanca: P.Lasso*, 1578. 294p.;4to. 1st publ., Seville, 1555. Palau 164444n. Santiago: BU.   578/54

Merckliche Beschreibung sampt eygenlicher Abbildung eyes frembden unbekanten Volcks eyner neu-erfundenen Landschafft oder Insul neulicher zeit vom Herren Martin Frobiser . . . erkündigt. *Strassburg: [B.Jobin]* 1578. bds.;ports;fol. Apparently based on an unidentified English news sheet with text & commentary by John Fischart, the woodcut also being based on an English original. Weber (Jobin) 59. Zurich: StB.   578/55

Mexía, Pedro. Historia imperial y cesarea . . . nuevamente impressa. *Antwerp: P.Bellère*, 1578. 615p.;fol. 1st publ., Seville, 1545. Palau 167346; Peeters-Fontainas (Impr.esp.) 785. CU, DFo, ICN, NN-RB; BL, BN.   578/56

——. Trois dialogues . . . touchant la nature du soleil, de la terre et de toutes les choses qui se font et apparoissent en l'air. *Paris: F.Morel*, 1578. 32 lvs;8vo. 1st publ. as here transl. by Marie de Coste-Blanche, Paris, 1566. Palau 167383n.   578/57

——. Le vite di tutti gl'imperatori . . . da m. Lodovico Dolce nuovamente tradotte e ampliate. *Venice: A.Griffio*, 1578. 546 numb.lvs; 4to. 1st publ. in enlarged form, Venice, 1561. Palau 167353. InU-L.   578/58

Monardes, Nicolás. Herba tabaco, d'Indie trattato . . . che serve per uso di medicina . . . tradutto di spagnolo. *Genoa: M.A.Bellone*, 1578. 15 lvs;8vo. Extracted & transl. from author's Seville, 1574, *Historia medicinal*. Guerra (Monardes) 20; Palau 175509. Leyden: UB.
                                             578/59

Münster, Sebastian. Cosmographey, oder beschreibung aller Länder . . . biss in das M.D. LXXVIII. jar gemehret. *Basel: H.Petri*, 1578. 1414p.;illus.,maps;fol. 1st publ., Basel, 1544. Sabin 51392; Burmeister (Münster) 80. NjP; BL.   578/60

Ortelius, Abraham. Synonomia geographica, sive Populorum, regionum, insularum, urbium . . . appellationes & nomina. Opus non tantùm geographis, sed etiam historiae . . . utile ac necessarium. *Antwerp: C.Plantin*, 1578. 417p.;4to. Includes refs to America, e.g., in entries for 'Atlantis insula', 'India', 'Oceanus' & 'Ophir'. Sabin 57692; Adams (Cambr.) 0330. CtY, DLC, MH, NNH, PPL, RPJCB; BL, BN.   578/61

Paracelsus. De morbe gallico. Warhaffte Cur der Frantzosen . . . Durch D. Toxiten corrigirt. *Strassburg: C.Müller,* 1578. 348p.;8vo. Includes also author's *Von dem Holtz Guaiaco,* 1st publ., Nuremberg, 1529. Sudhoff (Paracelsus) 180. DNLM, PPH.   578/62

Polo, Gaspar Gil. Primera parte de Diana enamorada. *Pamplona: T.Porralis,* 1578. 2pts;12mo. 1st printed, Valencia, 1564. In verse. Palau 102076n.   578/63

Renner, Franz. Wundartzneybuch. Ein sehr nützliches unnd heilsames, wolgegründetes Handtbüchlein gemeiner Practick, aller innerlicher und eusserlicher ärtzney, so wider die abscheuliche Kranckheit der Frantzosen und Lemung, auch für alle ander seuchten . . . wieder umb von neuwem mit sonderm fleiss, ersehen, augirt und gebessert. *Frankfurt a.M.: C.Heussler,* 1578. 217 numb.lvs;4to. 1st publ., Nuremberg, 1554, under title *Ein köstlich . . . Artzney-Buchlein.* Proksch I:17. MiU.   578/64

Ronsard, Pierre de. Les oeuvres. *Paris: G. Buon,* 1578. 7v.;ports;8vo. Appearing for the 1st time in v.1, as dedication to 'Les amours diverses', is an ode addressed 'A tres-respectueux N. de Neufville, seigneur de Villeroy', containing ref. to Spanish discovery of America. Included in v.6 is the *Continuation du Discours des miseres de ce temps,* 1st publ., Paris, 1562. Cioranescu (XVI) 19310; Tchémerzine IX:475. BN.   578/65

Sacro Bosco, Joannes de. Sphaera . . . emendata a Fr. Junctino . . . In calci libri habes Scholia Eliae Vineti. *Lyons: P.Tinghi,* 1578. 107p.;illus.;8vo. 1st publ. with Vinet's *Scholia,* Paris, 1551. Cf.Sabin 32681. ICJ, NN-RB; BN.   578/66

Settle, Dionyse. La navigation du Capitaine Martin Forbisher anglois, és regions de west & nordwest, en l'annee M.D.LXXVII. [*Geneva?*] *A.Chuppin,* 1578. 40 lvs;illus.;8vo. Transl. by Nicolas Pitou from author's *A true reporte of the laste voyage,* London, 1577. Sabin 79343 (also 5052 & 52120); Atkinson (Fr. Ren.) 259; Church 121. CSmH, CtY, InU-L, MH, NN-RB, RPJCB; BL.   578/67

Surius, Laurentius. Histoire de toutes choses memorables advenues depuis soixante dix-

huict ans. Traduite . . . & continuee jusques aujourd'hui, par I.Estourneau. Edition derniere. *Paris: G.Chaudière,* 1578. 468 numb. lvs;8vo. Transl. from author's *Commentarius brevis,* 1st publ., Cologne, 1566. Cf.Sabin 93887; Adams (Cambr.) S2106. Cambridge: Trinity Hall, BN.   578/68

Thurneisser, Leonard. Historia, sive Descriptio plantarum omnium. *Berlin:M.Hentzke,* 1578. clvi p.;illus.;fol. Transl. from author's *Historia unnd Beschreibung* below. On p.123, in section 'De sironibus atun' is a ref. to islands of America, where animalcules are generated from human perspiration. Pritzel 9338; Nissen (Bot.) 1964; Adams (Cambr.) T690. DNLM, MH-A; BL, BN.   578/69

——. Historia unnd Beschreibung influentischer, elementischer und natürlicher Wirckungen, aller fremden unnd heimischen Erdgewechssen. *Berlin: M.Hentzke,* 1578. 156p.; illus.,port.;fol. Cf.preceding item. Pritzel 9339; Nissen (Bot.) 1964. DNLM; BL. 578/70

Toscana, Giovanni Matteo. Peplus Italiae . . . in quo illustres viri . . . (quotquot trecentis ab hinc annis tota Italia floruerunt) . . . recensentur. *Paris: F.Morel,* 1578. 128p.;8vo. Comprises verses, with prose notes. 'Americus Vespucius': p.28-29. RPJCB; BL, BN. 578/71

Velázquez de Salazar, Juan. Peticion que Juan Velazquez de Salazar, procurador general de la Nueva España y Nuevo reyno de Galizia dio, en nombre de las dichas provincias, a . . . Phelippe segundo . . . sobre la perpetuacion de las encommiendas de Indios, fechas a los conquistadores y pobladores de las dichas provincias. [*Madrid: G.Drouy,* 1578]. 9 lvs;fol. With this was issued the *Informacion* signed by A.López & others described above. Sabin 98817; Medina (BHA) 257; LeClerc (1867) 2985; Palau 357630-II.   578/72

1579

Beale, Robert. Rerum Hispanicarum scriptores aliquot . . . ex bibliotheca . . . Roberti Beli angli, nunc accuratius emendatiusque recusi. *Frankfurt a.M.: A.Wechel,* 1579. 3v.; fol. Included, with their American refs, are Lucio Marineo's *De rebus Hispaniae memorabilibus,* 1st publ., Alcalá de Henares, 1531, & Damião de Goes's *Hispania,* 1st publ., Antwerp, 1542. Sabin 4477 (& 32004);

Shaaber B127. CU-B, CtY, DLC, InU-L, MH, NN-RB, PU; BL, BN.   579/1

Benzoni, Girolamo. Histoire nouvelle du Nouveau Monde, contenant en somme ce que les Hespagnols ont fait . . . aux Indes Occidentalles, & le rude traitement qu'ils font à ces povres peuples-la. Extraite de l'italien . . . & enrichie de plusieurs discours & choses dignes de memoire, par m. Urbain Chauveton. Ensemble, Une petite histoire d'un massacre commis par les Hespagnols sur quelques François en la Floride. [*Geneva:*] *E.Vignon,* 1579. 2pts;8vo. Transl. from Benzoni's *Historia del Mondo Novo,* 1st publ., Venice, 1565; supplemented by Nicolas Le Challeux's *Discours . . . de la Floride,* 1st publ., Dieppe, 1566. Sabin 4795 (& 39630); Medina (BHA) 250n (I:418); Streit II:964; Adams (Cambr.) B689; Adams (Laudonnière) 10; Arents (Add.) 52; JCB (3) I:273. CtY, DLC, MH, MiU-C, MnU-B, NN-A, RPJCB; BL, BN.
                                                    579/2

____. Der Newen Weldt und Indianischen Königreichs . . . History . . . Auss dem Latein . . . durch Nicolaum Höniger . . . gebracht. *Basel: S.Henricpetri,* 1579. ccxix p.;fol. Transl. from publisher's 1578 *Novae Novi Mundi,* 1st publ., in Italian, Venice, 1565. Sabin 4797; Baginsky (German Americana) 79; Ind.aur.116.988; JCB (3) I:273. DLC, InU-L, MnU-B, NN-RB, RPJCB; BL, Berlin: StB.   579/3

Bizzarri, Pietro. Senatus populique Genuensis rerum domi foresque gestarum historiae atque annales. *Antwerp: C.Plantin,* 1579. 802p.; fol. On p.371-376 is a substantial account of Columbus & Spanish exploration; p.383 contains ref. to possible New World source of syphilis. Sabin 5663; Ind.aur. 119.710; Adams (Cambr.) B2089. DLC, ICN, MH, NN-RB, RPJCB; BL, BN.   579/4

__[Anr issue]. *Antwerp: C.Plantin,for M.Sonnius,at Paris,* 1579. Belg.typ. (1541-1600) I:321. Brussels: BR.   579/5

Bodin, Jean. Les six livres de la Republique. *Lyons: J.de Tournes,for J.DuPuys,at Paris,* 1579. 739p.;fol. 1st publ., Paris, 1576. Ind. aur.120.811; Baudrier (Lyons) I:366. DLC, MH-L, MnU, NN-RB; BL, BN.   579/6

__[Anr edn]. Quatrieme edition, revue et augmentee. *Paris: J.DuPuys,* 1579. 1058p.;8vo. Ind.aur.120.812. NN-RB; BN.   579/6a

Brant, Sebastian. La grand nef des fols du

monde . . . Reveuë nouvellement & corrigee. *Lyons: J.d'Ogerolles,* 1579. 259p.;illus.;4to. 1st publ. as here transl. by J.Drouyn, Lyons, 1498. NjP; BL.   579/7

Braun, Georg. Théâtre des cités du monde, premier volume. *Cologne: G.van Kempen,* 1579. 59 double pls;fol. 1st publ. in French, [Cologne?], 1574. Cf.Koeman (Braun & Hogenberg) 13; Ind.aur.123.952. BN.   579/8

Carion, Johann. Chronique et histoire universelle . . . Dressée premierement par Jean Carion, puis augmentee . . . & enrichie . . . par Ph. Melanchton & Caspar Peucer . . . Plus deux livres adjoustez de nouveau aux cinq autres. [*Geneva:*] *J.Bérion,* 1579[-80]. 2v.; port.;8vo. Transl. by Simon Goulart with additional text, containing, in bk 6, chapter on 'Conqueste du Nouveau Monde'. Cf. Cioranescu (XVI) 10886; Jones (Goulart) 15; Ind.aur.132.367; Adams (Cambr.) C721. MH; BL, BN.   579/9

Casas, Bartolomé de las, Bp of Chiapa. Spieghel der spaenscher tiranije. [*Antwerp?*] 1579. [139]p.;4to. 1st publ., [Antwerp?], 1578; here a reissue with altered imprint date. Sabin 11250; Streit I:130; Palau 46972. DLC.
                                                    579/10

____. Tyrannies et cruautez des Espagnols, perpetrees és Indes Occidentales . . . fidelement traduites par Jaques de Miggrode. *Antwerp: F.Raphelengius,* 1579. 184p.;8vo. Transl. from the author's *Brevíssima relación,* with portions of other tracts, 1st publ., Seville, 1552. Sabin 11267; Medina (BHA) 1085n (II:471); Streit I:129; Palau 46961; Adams (Cambr.) C1420; JCB (3) I:274. CU, CtY, DLC, MB, MiU-C, NN-RB, PU, RPJCB; BL, BN.   579/11

Clowes, William. A short and profitable treatise touching the cure of the morbus gallicus by unctions. *London: J.Day,* 1579. 58p.; 8vo. STC 5447. PPC; BL.   579/12

Cortés, Martín. The arte of navigation . . . Englished . . . by Richard Eden, and now newly corrected and amended. *London: Widow of R.Jug,* 1579. 72 numb.lvs;illus., map;4to. 1st publ. in English, London, 1561. STC 5800. NN-RB; Oxford: Bodl.   579/13

Daneau, Lambert, comp. Geographiae poeticae, id est, Universae terrae descriptionis . . . libri quatuor: quorum, primus Europeam: secundus, Africam: tertius, Asiam, quartus, mare universum, & maris insulas continet.

[*Geneva:*] *J.Stoer*, 1579. 322p.;8vo. Adams (Cambr.) D44. Cambridge: Emmanuel. 579/14

Du Bartas, Guillaume de Salluste, seigneur. Joannis Edoardi Du Monin . . . Beresithias, sive Mundi creatio ex gallico . . . Heptamero expressa. *Paris: J.Parant*, 1579. 2pts;8vo. Transl. from Paris, 1578, *La sepmaine.* In verse. Holmes (DuBartas) I:106-107 no.1. ICN, MH; BL, BN. 579-14a

__[Anr issue]. *Paris: H.LeBouc*, 1579. Holmes (DuBartas) I:107 no.1n. MH; BN. 579/15

____. La sepmaine, ou Creation du monde. *Paris: J.Février*, 1579. 108 numb.lvs;8vo. 1st publ., Paris, 1578. In verse. Holmes (DuBartas) I:70 no.4n. CtY, MH, NNC; Paris: Mazarine. 579/16

__[Anr issue]. *Paris: M.Gadoulleau*, 1579. Holmes (DuBartas) I:70 no.4. Paris: Mazarine. 579/17

__[Anr edn]. *Villefranche: C.DuMont* [i.e., *Blois? B.Gomet?*] 1579. On probable false imprint, see E.Droz, 'Fausses adresses typographiques', *Bibliothèque d'humanisme et renaissance*, XXIII (1961) 139. Holmes (DuBartas) I:70-71,no.6. Paris: Ste Geneviève. 579/18

__[Anr edn]. *Antwerp: P.:LaMotte* [i.e., *Lyons? L.Cloquemin?*] 1579. 576p.;8vo. On probable false imprint, see E.Droz as cited for preceding item. Holmes (DuBartas) I:71, no.7. Antwerp: Plantin Mus. 579/19

Estienne, Charles. L'agriculture et maison rustique. *Luneville* [i.e., *Geneva?*] *C.de LaFontaine*, 1579. 459p.;illus.;4to. 1st publ. in this version, Paris, 1570. Both place & printer in imprint are undoubtedly fictitious. Arents (Add.) 32; Thiébaud (La chasse) 347. NN-A. 579/20

____. Siben Bücher von dem Feldbau, und vollkommener bestellung eynes ordenlichen Mayerhofs oder Landguts . . . Nun . . . von Melchiore Sebizio . . . inn Teutsch gebracht. *Strassburg: B. Jobin*, 1579. 643p.;illus.;fol. Transl. from expanded version of Jean Liébault, 1st publ., Paris, 1574, but here based prob. on 1578 edn. Thiébaud (La chasse) 358; Ritter (Strasbourg) 1355; Arents 28. NN-A; Strasbourg: BN. 579/21

Fernel, Jean. De luis venereae curatione . . . liber. *Antwerp: C.Plantin*, 1579. 126p.;8vo. Published posthumously. Proksch I:19. DNLM, MnU-B, NNNAM, PPC; London: Wellcome. 579/22

Foglietta, Uberto. Gli elogi . . . degli huomini chiari della Liguria, tradotti da Lorenzo Conti. *Genoa: [C.Bellone]*, 1579. 133 numb.lvs; 8vo. Transl. from Latin text, 1st publ., Rome, 1572. Cf.Sabin 24942. ICN, NN-RB, RPJCB; BL, BN. 579/23

____. Opera subsciciva. *Rome: F.Zanetti*, 1579. 351p.;4to. Included is the author's *Clarorum Ligurum elogia*, 1st publ., Rome, 1573. Sabin 24942n; Adams (Cambr.) F663. ICU, MH, NNC, PPRF; BL, BN. 579/24

Gesner, Konrad. Quatre livres des secrets de medecine . . . Faicts francois par m. Jean Liebault. *Paris: J.Sevestre,for J.DuPuys*, 1579. 297 numb.lvs.;illus.;8vo. 1st publ. in French, Paris, 1573. A reissue of the 1573 edn? DNLM, MH, MnU-B; London: Wellcome, BN. 579/25

Guicciardini, Francesco. The historie of Guicciardin . . . Reduced into English by Geffray Fenton. *London: T.Vautrollier*, 1579. 1184p.;fol. 1st publ. in Italian, Florence, 1561, with ref. to Columbus in bk 6. STC 12458a. CSmH, DFo, IU, MH, MnU-B; BL. 579/26

__[Anr issue]. *London: T.Vautrollier,for W. Norton*, 1579. STC 12458; Shaaber G407. CtY, DFo, ICN, InU-L, MH, MnU-B, NjP, PU-F; BL. 579/27

Heyns, Peeter. Le miroir du monde, reduict premierement en rithme brabaçonne . . . et maintenant tourne en prose françoise. *Antwerp: C.Plantin,for P.Galle*, 1579. 23 numb. lvs;maps;obl.4to. Transl. from author's *Spieghel der werelt*, 1st publ., Antwerp, 1577. Atkinson (Fr.Ren.) 270; Koeman (Ort.) 48; Bibl.belg.,1st ser.,XII:H55; Phillips (Atlases) 385; JCB (3) I:276. DLC, MiU-C, RPJCB; Brussels: BR. 579/28

Hoyarsabal, Martin de. Les voyages avantureux du Capitaine Martin Hoyarsabal. *Bordeaux: J.Chouin*, 1579. 115p.;4to. 'Les routtes, lieuës, sondes, entrées, cognoissances des pors de terre neufve': p.98-114. Atkinson (Fr.Ren.) 271. BN. 579/29

La Popelinière, Lancelot Voisin, sieur de. La vraye et entiere histoire des troubles . . . avenues . . . depuis l'an mil. cinq cents soixante & deux. *Basel: B.Germain*, 1579. 2v.;8vo. 1st publ., Basel, 1572. Adams (Cambr.) L204. MiU; Cambridge: UL.579/30

Le Pois, Antoine. Discours sur les medalles [!] et graveurs antiques. *Paris: M.Patisson,at*

lodging of R.Estienne, 1579. 147 numb.lvs; illus.,port.;4to. Included in ch.1 are refs to Columbus, Vespucci & New World, esp. Brazil. Adams (Cambr.) L522; Fairfax Murray (France) 667. CU-S, CtY, DLC, MH, NN-RB, PBL; BL, BN.   579/31

LeRoy, Louis. Consideration sur l'histoire françoise, et l'universelle de ce temps. *Paris: F.Morel*, 1579. 46p.;8vo. 1st publ., Paris, 1567. Atkinson (Fr.Ren.) 272. BL.   579/32

_____. De la vicissitude ou variete des choses en l'univers . . . Troisiesme edition reveüe & corrigee. *Paris: P.L'Huillier*, 1579. 116 numb. lvs;fol. 1st publ., Paris, 1575. Atkinson (Fr. Ren.) 273. BL, BN.   579/33

Mattioli, Pietro Andrea. Commentaires . . . sur les six livres de Ped. Dioscor. de la Matiere medecinale . . . Mis en françois sur la derniere edition latine de l'autheur, par m. Jean des Moulins . . . et de nouveau reveuz par iceluy & augmentes. *Lyons: [P.Roussin,for] G. Rouillé*, 1579. 852p.;illus.,port.;fol. 1st publ. in this French version, Lyons, 1572. Cf.Pritzel 5991; cf.Nissen (Bot.) 1313; Baudrier (Lyons) IX:369. DNLM, MH, NN-RB, RPB; London: Wellcome, BN.   579/34

Mexía, Pedro. Historia imperial y cesarea . . . Agora nuevamente impressa. *Antwerp: P. Nuyts*, 1579. 615p.;fol. 1st publ., Seville, 1545. Peeters-Fontainas (Impr.esp.) 786. BL.
                                          579/35

_____. Le vite di tutti gl'imperatori. *Venice: Brigonci*, 1579. 980p.;4to. 1st publ. as here transl. by Lodovico Dolce, Venice, 1558. BN.
                                          579/37

Monardes, Nicolás. Simplicium medicamentorum ex Novo Orbe delatorum, quorum in medicina usus est, Historia. *Antwerp: C.Plantin*, 1579. 84p.;illus.;8vo. 1st publ., Antwerp, 1574, as here ed. & transl. by Charles L'Ecluse. Sabin 49942; Medina (BHA) 258; Guerra (Monardes) 21; Pritzel 6366; Nissen (Bot.) 1397na(n); Adams (Cambr.) M1593; Arents 27. DLC, MH-A, NN-RB; BL.   579/38

Orta, Garcia da. Aromatum, et simplicium aliquot medicamentorum apud Indos nascentium historia . . . latino sermone in epitomen contracta . . . locupletiorisque annotatiunculis illustrata a Carolo Clusio . . . Tertia editio. *Antwerp: C.Plantin*, 1579. 217p.; illus.;8vo. 1st publ. as ed., transl. & annotated by L'Ecluse, Antwerp, 1567. Sabin 57665; Pritzel 4316n; Nissen (Bot.) 949n; Adams

(Cambr.) O321; Bibl.belg.1st ser., XX:O7. DNLM, InU-L, MH-A, MnU-B, NN-RB; BL, Brussels: BR.   579/39

Ortelius, Abraham. Additamentum Theatri orbis terrarum. *Antwerp: [C.Plantin]*, 1579. 23maps;fol. Includes 2 new maps of Spanish America. Koeman (Ort.) 14A. Antwerp: Plantin Mus.   579/40

_____. Le miroir du monde. *Antwerp:* 1579. See entry under Heyns, Peeter, above.

_____. Theatrum orbis terrarum. *Antwerp: C. Plantin*, 1579. 79p.;maps;fol. 1st publ., Antwerp, 1572. Sabin 57696n; Koeman (Ort.) 15B; Phillips (Atlases) 3393; JCB (3) I:276. DLC, ICN, NN-RB, RPJCB; BL.   579/41

Paracelsus. Kleine Wundartzney . . . drei Bücher begreiffendt. *Basel: P.Perna*, 1579. 285p.;8vo. Includes *De morbo gallico*, 1st publ., Nuremberg, 1530. Sudhoff (Paracelsus) 182. DNLM; Berlin: StB.   579/42

Rabelais, François. Les oeuvres. *Antwerp: F.Niergue [i.e., Montluel: C.Pesnot]*, 1579. 1150p.;16mo. Includes 'Le quart livre', 1st publ., Paris, 1552. Plan (Rabelais) 107; Belg. typ. (1541-1600) I:4086. BN.   579/43

Sacro Bosco, Joannes de. La sfera . . . tradotta, emendata, & distinta in capitoli da Piervincenzio Dante de' Rinaldi con molte . . . annotazioni [da Egnazio Danti]. *Florence: The Giuntas*, 1579. 70p.;illus.,port.;4to. 1st publ., Florence, 1571. Cf.Sabin 32683; JCB AR22:5. DLC, MiU-C, NN-RB, RPJCB; BL, BN.   579/44

Skarga, Piotr. Zywoty świętych. *Vilna: Radziwil*, 1579. fol. Said to contain a ref. to Brazil. Backer VII:1266.   579/45

Sleidanus, Johannes. Der erste[-ander] Theyl Ordenlicher Beschreibunge unnd Verzeychnisse, allerley fürnemer Händel. *Strassburg: T.Rihel*, 1579. 909p.;fol. 1st publ. in German, Strassburg, 1574. Ritter (Strasbourg) 2149. Strasbourg: BN.   579/46

Soto, Domingo de. Commentariorum . . . in quartum Sententiarum. Tomus primus[-secundus]. *Medina del Campo: F.à Canto,for B.Boyer*, 1579. 2v.;fol. 1st publ., Salamanca, 1557-60. Pérez Pastor (Medina del Campo) 189; Adams (Cambr.) S1478. BL(v.2), Cambridge: UL(v.1)   579/47

Taisnier, Joannes. A very necessarie and profitable booke concerning navigation, compiled in Latin . . . Translated . . . by Richard Eden. *London: R.Jug* [1579]. [176]p.;illus.;

4to. In his dedicatory epistle Eden mentions Sebastian Cabot, if not the Americas, hence its relevance. Sabin 94220; STC 23659; JCB (3) I:277. DFo, MiU, RPJCB; BL.   579/48

Torquemada, Antonio de. Hexameron, ou Six journees contenans plusieurs doctes discours . . . Fait en hespagnol . . . et mis en françois par Gabriel Chappuys. *Lyons: J. Béraud*, 1579. 16mo. Transl. from author's *Jardin de flores curiosas*, 1st publ., Salamanca, 1570. Baudrier (Lyons) V:37; Palau 334917.   579/49

Valadés, Diego. Rhetorica christiana ad concionandi, et orandi usum accommodata. *Perugia: P.G.Petrucci*, 1579. 378p.;illus.;4to. Manual for instruction of missionaries to Mexico, describing indigenous religious rites & customs, etc. Sabin 98300 (& 25934n); Medina (BHA) 259; Streit I:131; Adams (Cambr.) V18; Mortimer (Italy) 510; JCB (3) I:277-278. DLC, MH, NN-RB, RPJCB; BL, BN.   579/50

158–?

Apuntamiento del hecho, sobre el pleyto de Veragua, por doña Francisca Colon de Toledo. [*Madrid*? 158-?]. 5 numb.lvs;fol. On succession to honors bestowed on Columbus by Spanish Crown. Medina (BHA) 433; cf. Palau 57253. Santiago, Chile: BN.   58-/1

Aunque parece a la marquesa de Guadaleste, y sus letrados, que bestantemente deffendida la razon y justicia con que se le ha de dar la executoria que tiene pedida. [*Madrid*? 158-?]. 15 numb.lvs;fol. On claims to succession to Columbus's honors; cf.*Apuntamiento* above. Medina (BHA) 434. Santiago, Chile: BN.
          58-/2

Catholic Church. Pope, 1492-1503 (Alexander VI). [Sanè pro parte (16 Dec. 1501)]. Bula de la concession de los diezmos. [*Madrid*? 158-?]. [2]p.;fol. Dated at Rome, 16 Dec. 1501. Medina (BHA) 427.   58-/3

__[Anr edn]. Copia de la bula de la concession que hizo el Papa Alexandro sexto al Rey y a la Reyna nuestros señores de las Indias. [*Madrid*? 158-?]. 6p.;fol. Medina (BHA) 428. Seville: Archivo de Indias.   58-/4

Por don Alonso Fernandez de Cordova, escrivano mayor de la governacion del Piru, contra Alvaro Ruiz de Navamuel. [*Madrid*? 158-?].

31 numb.lvs;fol. Medina (BHA) 425. Santiago, Chile: BN.   58-/5

1580

Alfonce, Jean, i.e., Jean Fonteneau, known as. Les voyages avantureux du Capitaine Jean Alfonce . . . Reveue & de nouveau augmenté outre les precedentes impressions. *La Rochelle: J.Portau* [ca.1580?]. 62 numb.lvs; 4to. 1st publ., Poitiers, [ca.1558?]. Atkinson (Fr.Ren.) 352; Droz (Vve Berton) 74-75. BL, Paris: Arsenal.   580/1

__[Anr issue]. *La Rochelle: [J.Portau, for] M. Villepoux* [ca.1580?]. Sabin 100832n; Atkinson (Fr.Ren.) 352n; Droz (Vve Berton) 75; Ind.aur.103.634. BL.   580/2

Amatus Lusitanus. Curationum medicinalium centuriae II. priores. *Lyons: G.Rouillé*, 1580. 685p.;16mo. 1st Century 1st publ., Florence, 1551; 2nd Century 1st publ., Venice, 1552. Baudrier (Lyons) IX:373-374. BN.
          580/3

____. Curationum medicinalium centuriae duae, tertia et quarta. *Lyons: G.Rouillé*, 1580. 647p.;16mo. 1st publ., Lyons (?) 1556. Baudrier (Lyons) IX:373-374. DLC, MBCo; BN.   580/4

____. Curationum medicinalium centuriae, quinta et sexta. *Lyons: G.Rouillé*, 1580. 639p.;16mo. Baudrier (Lyons) IX:374. DLC, MBCo; London: Wellcome.   580/5

Boaistuau, Pierre. Histoires prodigeuses. *Paris: J.de Marnef & Widow of G.Cavellat*, 1580-82. 5v.;illus.;16mo. 1st publ. with American ref. in section by François de Belleforest, Paris, 1571. DFo.   580/6

Bock, Hieronymus. Kreutterbuch. *Strassburg: J.Rihel*, 1580. 450 lvs;illus.;fol. 1st publ. with illus., Strassburg, 1546; here ed. by Melchior Sebitzius. Pritzel 866n; Nissen (Bot.) 182n; Ind.aur.120.599. ICJ; Berlin: StB.
          580/7

Bodin, Jean. Les six livres de la Republique. *Lyons: J.de Tournes, for J.DuPuys, at Paris*, 1580. 739p.;8vo. 1st publ., Paris, 1576. Ind. aur.120.814; Baudrier (Lyons) I:366. MH-L, NN-RB; BL, Besançon: BM.   580/8

__[Anr edn]. *Paris: J.DuPuys*, 1580. 1060p.;8vo. Ind.aur.120.815; Adams (Cambr.) B2237. DLC, MH-BA; BL, BN.   580/9

Calvo, Jean. Primera y segunda parte de la cirugia universal y particolar. *Seville*: 1580. 4to.

Includes section on syphilis, stating that it had been imported from the New World. Medina (BHA) 260; Escudero (Seville) 707; Palau 40551. No copy known; cf.Barcelona, 1592, edn. 580/10

Cardano, Girolamo. De rerum varietate libri xvii. *Lyons: B.Honorat*, 1580. 883p.;illus.; 8vo. 1st publ., Basel, 1557. Baudrier (Lyons) IV:137; Ind.aur.132.116; Adams (Cambr.) C664. DNLM, IaU, NjP; Cambridge: Trinity, BN. 580/11

__[Anr issue]. *Lyons: E.Michel*, 1580. Ind. aur.132.116; Adams (Cambr.) C665. DNLM; London: Wellcome. 580/12

____. De subtilitate libri xxi. *Lyons: B.Honorat*, 1580. 718p.;illus.;8vo. 1st publ., Nuremberg (?), 1550. Baudrier (Lyons) IV:137; Ind. aur.132.115; Adams (Cambr.) C675. MH-A; Cambridge: Trinity Hall. 580/13

__[Anr issue]. *Lyons: E.Michel*, 1580. Ind. aur.132.115. DLC, MH, NNNAM, RPJCB; BL, BN. 580/14

Carion, Johann. Chronique et histoire universelle . . . Dressee premierement par Jean Carion, puis augmentee . . . & enrichie . . . par Ph. Melanchton & Caspar Peucer . . . Plus deux livres adjoustez de nouveau aux cinq autres. [*Geneva*:] *J.Berion*, 1580. 2v.;port.; 8vo. 1st publ. as transl. here by Simon Goulart, with added text on New World, Geneva, 1579. Cioranescu (XVI) 100886; cf. Jones (Goulart) 15; Ind.aur.132.368. BL, Geneva: BP. 580/15

Cartier, Jacques. A shorte and briefe narration of the two navigations and discoveries to the northweast partes called Newe France: first translated out of French into Italian, by . . . Gio: Bapt: Ramutius, and now turned into English by John Florio. *London: H.Bynneman*, 1580. 80p.;4to. 1st publ., Venice, 1556, in the 3rd vol. of Ramusio's *Navigationi et viaggi*. Sabin 11144 & 80706; Harrisse (NF) 5; STC 4699; Church 125; JCB (3) I:278. CSmH, DFo, MiU-C, NN-RB, RPJCB; BL. 580/16

Chassanion, Jean. De gigantibus eorumque reliquiis. *Basel*: 1580. 75p.;8vo. In ch.6 is a statement that in the New World no one has, in a century, reported actual giants. Cioranescu (XVI) 6485; Adams (Cambr.) C1407. ICN, MH, NN-RB; BL, BN. 580/17

Chaves, Jerónimo de. Chronographia o Repertorio de los tiempos. *Seville: F.Díaz, for J.F.*

de Cisneros, 1580. 284 numb.lvs;illus.;4to. 1st publ., Seville, 1548. Escudero (Seville) 705. ICN, MB; BL, Madrid: BN. 580/18

Coignet, Michel. Nieuwe onderwijsinghe, op de principaelste puncten der zee-vaert. 1580. *See below* Medina, Pedro de, *De zeevaert*, 1580.

Daneau, Lambert, comp. Geographiae poeticae, id est Universae terrae descriptionis . . . libri quatuor. [*Geneva*:] *J.Stoer*, 1580. 322p.; 8vo. 1st publ., Geneva, 1579; here a reissue with altered imprint date. Adams (Cambr.) D45. Cambridge: Emmanuel. 580/19

__[Anr issue]. *Lyons: L.Cloquemin*, 1580. Cioranescu (XVI) 7318; Baudrier (Lyons) IV:56-57. CtY, DLC, MH, NjP; BN. 580/20

Du Bartas, Guillaume de Salluste, seigneur. La sepmaine, ou Creation du monde. *Paris: J.Février*, 1580. 104 numb.lvs; 4to. 1st publ., Paris, 1578. In verse. Holmes (DuBartas) I:70 no.5. BN. 580/21

__[Anr issue]. *Paris: M.Gadoulleau*, 1580. Holmes (DuBartas) I:70 no.5n. ICN; Tours: BM. 580/22

Du Verdier, Antoine. Les diverses leçons . . . suivans celles de Pierre Messie . . . Seconde edition. *Lyons: B.Honorat*, 1580. 422p.;port;8vo. 1st publ., Lyons, 1580. Cf. Sabin 48245; Baudrier (Lyons) IV:139. CtY, ICN, NN-RB. 580/23

Estienne, Charles. Siben Bücher von dem Feldbau . . . Nun . . . von Melchiore Sebizio . . . in Teutsch gebracht. *Strassburg: B.Jobin*, 1580. 321 numb.lvs;illus.,port.;fol. 1st publ. in German, Strassburg, 1579. Thiébaud (La chasse) 358; Ritter (Strassbourg) 1356. ICJ; Strasbourg: BN. 580/24

Falloppius, Gabriele. Secreti diversi et miracolosi, nuovamente ristampata. *Turin*: [*G.Varrone & M.Morello?*] 1580. 331p.;8vo. 1st publ., Venice, 1563. DNLM. 580/25

Fernel, Jean. De luis venereae, sive morbi gallici curatione liber. *Padua: P.Meietti*, 1580. 111p.;8vo. 1st publ., Antwerp, 1579. Sherrington (Fernel) 99.N2. CtY-M, DNLM; London: Wellcome. 580/26

____. Universa medicina . . . His accessit . . . febrium ac luis venereae curatio methodica libris duobus comprehensa. *Geneva: J.Stoer*, 1580. 2pts;port.;fol. In addition to Fernel's *De abditis rerum causis* found earlier edns of this work, includes also his *De luis venereae curatione*, 1st publ., Antwerp, 1579. Sherrington

(Fernel) 67.J11; Adams (Cambr.) F259. DNLM, PPL; Cambridge: St John's, BN.
580/27

Fioravanti, Leonardo. A short discours of . . . Leonardo Phioravanti . . . upon chirurgerie . . . Translated out of Italyan . . . by John Hester. *London: T.East*, 1580. 64 numb.lvs;4to. Transl. from the author's *Tesoro della vita humana*, 1st publ., Venice, 1570. STC 10881. CSmH, CtY-M, DFo, NNNAM; BL. 580/28

Francisco de Vitoria. Relectiones tredecim. *Ingolstadt: W.Eder*, 1580. 648p.;8vo. 1st publ., Lyons, 1557. Sabin 100619; Streit I:132; Palau 371068; Adams (Cambr.) F935. Cambridge: Gonville & Caius, Madrid: BN.
580/29

Freigius, Johann Thomas. Historiae synopsis, seu Praelectionum historicarum in Altofiano Noribergensium gymnasio delineatio. *Basel: S.Henricpetri*, 1580. 102p.;8vo. Includes passage on New World discoveries, citing Columbus, Cortés, Pizarro & Magellan. Adams (Cambr.) F1010. BL, BN. 580/30

Genebrard, Gilbert, Abp of Aix. Chronographiae libri quatuor. *Paris: M.LeJeune*, 1580. 568p.;fol. 1st publ., Paris, 1567. Adams (Cambr.) G397. ICN, PLatS; Cambridge: UL, BN. 580/31

__[Anr issue]. *Paris*: [*M.LeJeune for*] *G.Gourbin*, 1580. NNC. 580/32

__[Anr issue]. *Paris*: [*M.LeJeune,for*] *M.Sonnius*, 1580. CLU. 580/33

Giovio, Paolo, Bp of Nocera. Histoires . . . sur les choses faictes et avenues de son temps . . . traduictes de latin . . . par Denis Sauvage. *Paris*: [*O.de Harsy,for*] *J.DuPuys*, 1580. 2v.;fol. A reissue, with altered imprint date, of the bookseller's 1570 edn. Atkinson (Fr. Ren.) 197n. BN. 580/34

_____. Icones sive Imagines virorum bellica ex Museo Joviano. [*Basel: P.Perna*, ca. 1580]. [144]p.;4to. 1st publ., Basel, 1577, under title *Musaei Joviani imagines*; comprises ports, with verse captions, 1st publ. in Perna's 1575 edn of Giovio's *Elogia virorum bellica virtute illustrium*. They were the work of Tobias Stimmer. DLC, NNH(Stimmer, Tobias); BL(Mueller, Theobald). 580/35

Gohory, Jacques. Instruction de la congnoisce . . . de lherbe Petum . . . et sur la racine Mechiocan [par N.Monardes]. *Paris: J.Parant*, 1580. 2pts;illus.;8vo. 1st publ.,

Paris, 1572; here a reissue with cancel t.p. of that edn. Cf.Atkinson (Fr.Ren.) 228; cf. Guerra (Monardes) 12. MH(2nd pt, by Monardes, wanting). 580/36

Gómara, Francisco López de. Histoire generalle des Indes Occidentales et terres neuves . . . Traduite . . . par M.Fumee. *Paris: M.Sonnius*, 1580. 355 numb.lvs;8vo. 1st publ. in French, Paris, 1568. Sabin 27748; Wagner (SW) 2ii; Streit II:973; Rothschild 1958; JCB (3) I:280. MB, RPJCB, ViU; BL, BN. 580/37

Guicciardini, Francesco. Della historia d'Italia. *Venice: G.A.Bertano*, 1580. 596 numb.lvs;4to. 1st publ., Florence, 1561. Adams (Cambr.) G1315. CSt, CtY, ICN, MH; Cambridge: Sidney Sussex, BN. 580/38

Jesuits. Compendium privilegiorum. Compendium Indicum. In quo continentur facultates, & aliae gratiae a Sede Apostolica Societati Jesu in partibus Indiarum concessae. *Rome: Jesuit College*, 1580. 33p.;12mo. Refers to both West & East Indies. Streit I:133; Backer V:92. Florence: BN. 580/39

Jesuits. Letters from missions. Lettres du Jappon, Peru et Brasil. *Lyons: B.Rigaud*, 1580. 109p.;8vo. 1st publ., Paris, 1578. Cf.Borba de Moraes I:408-409; Streit II:974. ICN; Toulouse: BM. 580/40

Léry, Jean de. Histoire d'un voyage faict en la terre du Bresil, autrement dite Amerique . . . Reveue, corrigee, et bien augmentee en ceste seconde edition. *Geneva: A.Chuppin*, 1580. 382p.;illus.;8vo. 1st publ., La Rochelle, 1578. Sabin 40149; Borba de Moraes I:402-403; JCB (3) I:279. DLC, ICN, NN-RB, RPJCB; BN.
580/41

__[Anr issue]. [*Geneva:*] *A.Chuppin*, 1580. Sabin 40149n; Atkinson (Fr.Ren.) 280; Borba de Moraes I:402-403. BL, BN. 580/42

Lucidarius. M. Elucidarius von allerhandt Geschöpffen Gottes . . . unnd wie alle Creaturen geschaffen seind auff Erden. *Frankfurt a.M.: Heirs of C.Egenolff,for A.Lonicer,J. Cnipius & P. Steinmeyer*, 1580. [102]p.; illus.;map;4to. 1st publ., Strassburg, [ca. 1535]. Schorbach (Lucidarius) 62. Breslau: StB. 580/43

Matienzo, Juan de. Commentaira [i.e., Commentaria] . . . in librum quintum recollectionis legum Hispaniae. *Madrid: F.Sánchez*, 1580. 485 numb.lvs;fol. Included are numerous glosses referring to New World, esp. status of Indians. The author was a senator in the

Argentine Chancery for the kingdom of Peru. Medina (BHA) 262; Pérez Pastor (Madrid) 157; Palau 158226; JCB (3) I:282. CtY, DLC, NN-RB, RPJCB; BL. 580/44

Medina, Pedro de. De zeevaert, oft Conste van ter zee te varen . . . Met noch een ander nieuwe onderwijsinghe, op de principaelste puncten der navigatien, van Michiel Coignet. *Antwerp: H.Hendricksen*, 1580. 2pts;illus., maps;4to. Transl. with introduction mentioning Peru, by Martin Everaert, purportedly from Spanish text of Medina's *Arte de navegar* (1st publ., Valladolid, 1545) but more probably from the Rouen, 1573, French version by Nicolas de Nicolai, whence the illus. are derived. Coignet's supplement, with special t.p. & separate paging, includes a ref. to West Indian voyages. Bibl.belg.,1st ser.,XX:M187; Palau 159682. NN-RB, RPJCB; Brussels: BR. 580/45

Mexía, Pedro. Dialogos . . . Agora nuevamente emendados. *Seville: F.Díaz*, 1580. 164 numb.lvs;port.;8vo. 1st publ., Seville, 1547. Escudero (Seville) 704; Palau 167373. DNLM, NNH; BL, Madrid: BN. 580/46

____. Les diverses leçons . . . avec trois dialogues, mises en françois par Claude Gruget . . . augmentees . . . de la suite d'icelles, faite par Antoine du Verdier. *Lyons: E.Michel*, 1580. 2pts;port.;8vo. 1st publ. in this enlarged version, Lyons, 1577. Baudrier (Lyons) IV:139; Palau 167321n. CU. 580/47

—[Anr issue]. *Lyons: [E.Michel,for] B.Honorat*, 1580. Baudrier (Lyons) IV:138-139; Palau 167321; Shaaber M326. PU; BL. 580/48

—[Anr edn]. *Rouen: G.Loyselet,for C. Micard,at Paris*, 1580. 620 numb.lvs;12mo. Sabin 48244; JCB (3) I:280-281. RPJCB. 580/49

____. A pleasaunt dialogue between two Spanish gentlemen, concerning phisicke and phisitions . . . translated out of the Castlin tongue by T[homas]. N[ewton]. *London: J. Charlewood*, 1580. [79]p.;8vo. Transl. from the 1st of the author's *Colóquios*, 1st publ., Seville, 1547, with mention of syphilis. Palau 167386; STC 17848. BL. 580/50

Monardes, Nicolás. Joyfull newes out of the newfound world . . . Englished by John Frampton, merchant. Newly corrected. *London: W.Norton*, 1580. 181 numb.lvs;illus.; 4to. The earliest complete English edn, enlarged from Seville, 1574, text. Sabin 49945;

Medina (BHA) 236n (I:393); Guerra (Monardes) 19; STC 18006 & 18006.5; Pritzel 6366; Nissen (Bot.) 1397nc(n); Hunt (Bot.) 137; Arents (Add.) 63; JCB (3) I:281 & AR56: 42-49. CSmH, CtY, DLC, ICN, MH, NN-RB, RPJCB; BL. 580/51

____. Primera y segunda y tercera partes de la Historia medicinal: de las cosas que se traen de nuestras Indias Occidentales que sirven en medicina . . . Van en esta impression la tercera parte y el dialogo del hierro nuevamente hechos, que no han sido impressos hasta agora. *Seville: F.Díaz*, 1580. 162 numb.lvs; illus.,port.;4to. 1st publ. in this enlarged version, Seville, 1574. Sabin 49938; Medina (BHA) 263; Guerra (Monardes) 22; Pritzel 6366n; Nissen (Bot.) 1397n(n); Arents 19a; JCB (3) I:281. CtY-M, ICJ, MH-A, NN-RB, PU, RPJCB; BL. 580/52

Montaigne, Michel Eyquem de. Les essais . . . Livres I et II. *Bordeaux: S.Millanges*, 1580. 2v.;8vo. In addition to scattered refs to the New World, includes in bk 1, chapt.31, 'Des cannibales', discussing those of Brazil. Tchémerzine VIII:402; Rép.bibl.I:37; Rothschild 138. CSmH, CtY, ICN, InU-L, MH, NjP; BL, BN. 580/53

Ortelius, Abraham. Additamentum Theatri orbis terrarum. *Antwerp: [C.Plantin]* 1580. 23maps;fol. 1st publ., Antwerp, 1579. Koeman (Ort.) 14B. Brussels: Plantin Mus.580/54

____. Theatrum oder Schawbüch des Erdtkreÿs; opus nunc denuò ab ipso auctore recognitum. *Antwerp: C.Plantin,for A.Ortelius*, 1580. 8 lvs;93maps;obl.fol. 1st publ. in German, Antwerp, 1572; here rev. & enl. Koeman records the existence of variants. Sabin 57707; Koeman (Ort.) 16A; Phillips (Atlases) 3394. CtY, DLC, InU-L, NjP; Antwerp: Plantin Mus. 580/55

Osório, Jerónimo, Bp of Silves. Historiae . . . de rebus Emmanuelis Lusitaniae Regis . . . gestis, libri duodecim . . . Item Jo. Matalii Metelli . . . praefatio et commentarius; de reperta ab Hispanis et Lusitanis in Occidentis et Orientis Indiam navigatione deque populorum eius vita, moribus ac ritibus. *Cologne: Heirs of A.Birckmann*, 1580. 368 numb.lvs; 8vo. 1st publ. with Matal's preface, Cologne, 1574. Sabin 57804n; cf.Borba de Moraes II:120; Streit IV:991. ICN, MB. 580/56

Palissy, Bernard. Discours admirables de la nature des eaux et fonteines. *Paris: M.Le-*

Jeune, 1580. 361p.;8vo. In chapt. 'Des pierres' the need to go to Newfoundland for cod is mentioned. Cioranescu (XVI) 16849. CtY, DFo, InU-L, MH, NNNAM; BL, BN. 580/57

Peucer, Kaspar. Commentarius de praecipuis generibus divinitianum. *Wittenberg: J.Lufft*, 1580. 448 numb.lvs;illus.;8vo. 1st (?) publ., Wittenberg, 1560. DNLM, IU, MH, NjP. 580/57a

Rabelais, François. Les oeuvres. *Lyons: P. Estiard*, 1580. 16mo. Includes 'Le quart livre', 1st publ., Paris, 1552. Plan (Rabelais) 108. NN-RB; BN. 580/58

Ruscelli, Girolamo. Le imprese illustri . . . tutto riordinato et corretto. *Venice: F.dei Franceschi*, 1580. 496p.;illus.,ports;4to. 1st publ., Venice, 1566. Adams (Cambr.) R954. CtY, ICN, MH, MnU-B; BL, BN. 580/59

Serres, Jean de. Commentariorum de statu religionis et reipublicae in regno Galliae libri. [*Geneva: E.Vignon*] *for J. Jucundus* [pseud.] *at Leyden*, 1580. 8vo. 1st publ., [Geneva], 1570. BL. 580/60

Settle, Dionyse. Beschreibung der Schiffart des Haubtmans Martini Forbissher . . . in die Lender gegen West und Nordtwest im Jar 1577 . . . Auss dem Frantzösischen . . . gebracht. *Nuremberg: K.Gerlach & Heirs of J.vom Berg*, 1580. 13 lvs;illus.;4to. Transl. from [Geneva?], 1578, *Navigation du Capitaine Martin Forbisher*, itself transl., by Nicolas Pitou, from the *True reporte of the laste voyage*, &c., 1st publ., London, 1577. Sabin 79344 (& 25996); Baginsky (German Americana) 80; JCB (3) I:279. DLC, InU-L, NN-RB, RPJCB; BL. 580/61

———. De Martini Forbisseri angli navigatione in regiones occidentis et septentrionis narratio historica, ex gallico sermone . . . translata per d. Joan. Tho. Freigium. *Nuremberg: K.Gerlach & Heirs of J.vom Berg*, 1580. [88]p.; illus.;8vo. Transl. from [Geneva?], 1578, *Navigation du Capitaine Martin Forbisher*, itself transl., by Nicolas Pitou, from the *True reporte of the laste voyage*, &c., 1st publ., London, 1577. Sabin 79345 (&25994); JCB (3) I:279. CSmH, CtY, DLC, ICN, InU-L, MH, MiU-C, MnU-B, NN-RB, RPJCB; BL. 580/62

Soto, Domingo de. De justitia & jure libri decem. *Medina del Campo: F.à Canto*, 1580. 896p.;fol. 1st publ., Salamanca, 1553. Pérez Pastor (Medina del Campo) 192; Palau 320156 (&320153). NNC. 580/63

Suárez de Peralta, Juan. Tractado de la cavalleria . . . Compuesto por don Juan Suarez de Peralta, vezino y natural de Mexico, en las Indias. *Seville: F.Díaz*, 1580. 101 numb.lvs; 4to. Sabin 93325; Medina (BHA) 264; Escudero (Seville) 702. MH, NNH; Madrid: BN. 580/64

Tagault, Jean. La chirurgie . . . Traduicte de latin. *Lyons: B.Honorat*, 1580. 738p.;illus.; 8vo. 1st publ. in French, Lyons, 1549, under title *Les institutions chirurgiques*. Baudrier (Lyons) IV:137. DNLM. 580/65

Tarcagnota, Giovanni. Delle historie del mondo . . . Supplemento, overo quinto volume. *Venice: Heirs of F.& M.Tramezzini*, 1580. 3pts in 5v.;4to. Contains, in the supplement, bk ix, an account of French & Spanish conflict in Florida, in addition to refs to Columbus & New World found in 1562 & subsequent edns. BN. 580/66

1581

Alberti, Leandro. Descrittione di tutta l'Italia. *Venice: G.B.Porta*, 1581. 501 numb. lvs;4to. 1st publ., Bologna, 1550. Sabin 660n; Ind.aur.102.351; Adams (Cambr.) A476; Moranti (Urbino) 46. ICU, MnU-B; BL, BN. 581/1

Apianus, Petrus. Cosmographie ou description des quatre parties du monde . . . Corrigée et augmentée par Gemma Frison . . . avec plusieurs autres traitez concernans la mesme matiere, composez par . . . Gemma Frison, & autres autheurs, nouvellement traduits en langue françoise. *Antwerp: J.Bellère*, 1581. 333p.;illus.,maps;4to. 1st publ. in French, Antwerp, 1544, but here substantially enlarged, including American material derived from Antwerp, 1575, Spanish edn. Sabin 1751n; Atkinson (Fr.Ren.) 283; Ortroy (Apian) 57; Ind.aur.106.465; JCB (3) I:283. DLC, ICN, MiU-C, NIC, RPJCB; BL,BN. 581/2

—[Anr issue]. *Antwerp: J.Verwithagen*, 1581. Atkinson (Fr.Ren.) 283n; Ortroy (Apian) 58; JCB (3) I:282-283. RPJCB. 581/3

Benzoni, Girolamo. Novae Novi Orbis historiae; id est, Rerum ab Hispanis in India Occidentali hactenus gestarum . . . libri tres, Urbani Calvetonis opera . . . ex italicis . . . latini facti . . . His ab eodem adjuncta est, De Gallorum in Floridam expeditione, & insigni Hispanorum in eos saevitiae exemplo, Brevis historiae. *Geneva: E.Vignon*, 1581. 480p.;8vo. 1st publ. in Latin, Geneva, 1578; here newly reset in type. The 'De Gallorum . . . Brevis historia' is by Nicolas LeChailleux. Sabin 4792n; Medina (BHA) 265; Streit II:991; Adams (Cambr.) B686; Ind.aur.116.990; Arents 25-a; JCB (3) I:283. DLC, IU, InU-L, MBAt, MnU-B, NN-RB, PPRF, RPJCB; BL, BN.   581/4

Bialobrzeski, Marcin. Postilla orthodoxa: to iest: Wyklad swientych ewánieliy niedzielnych. *Cracow: L.Andrysowicz*, 1581. 514p.;fol. On p.247 is a ref. to the New World. Wierzbowski 392a; Ind.aur.118.922. Copenhagen: KB.
581/5

Borough, William. A discours of the variation of the cumpas. *London: J.Kingston, for R.Ballard*, 1581. 4to. Issued with R.Norman's *The new attractive*. In ch.11 is a ref. to marine plats for voyages to Newfoundland. Ind.aur.122.490; STC 3389. DFo; BL.   581/6

Breton, Nicholas. A discourse in commendation of the valiant . . . Frauncis Drake, with a rejoysing of his happy adventures. *London: J. Charlewood*, 1581. 8 lvs;8vo. Kraus (Drake) 17 (p.197); STC 3646.5. H.P. Kraus.   581/7

Bruyn, Abraham de. Omnium pene Europae, Asiae, Aphricae et Americae habitus, elegantissime aeri incisi. *Antwerp: A.de Bruyn*, 1581. 58pl.;obl.fol. The earliest edn to incorporate plates illustrative of American dress. Sabin 8739; Ind.aur.126.149. ICN, NNH; BL.   581/8

Cardano, Girolamo. De rerum varietate libri xvii. *Basel: S.Henricpetri*, 1581. 1171p.; illus.,port.;8vo. 1st publ., Basel, 1557. Ind. aur.132.119; Adams (Cambr.) C666. CtY-M, MH, NNNAM, PBa; BL, BN.   581/9

Caro, Annibale. De le lettere familiari . . . volume primo. *Venice: B.Giunta & Bros*, 1581. 176p.;4to. 1st publ., Venice, 1572. Ind.aur.132.477; Adams (Cambr.) C742. CtY, DLC, MH, RPJCB; BL, BN.   581/10

Casas, Gonzalo de las. Libro intitulado Arte para criar seda . . . Hecho por Gonçalo de las Casas, señor dela provincia y pueblos de Yāguitan [i.e., Yucatan], que es en la mixteca de la nueva España, vezino de la ciudad de Mexico. *Granada: R.Rabat*, 1581. 96 lvs; 8vo. Sabin 11290; Medina (BHA) 266; Palau 47016; JCB (3) I:284. MH, NN-RB, RPJCB; BN.   581/11

Chaves, Jerónimo de. Chronographia o Repertorio de los tiempos. *Seville: F.Díaz, for J.de Cisneros*, 1581. 163 (i.e., 263) numb.lvs; illus.,maps;4to. 1st publ., Seville, 1548. Escudero (Seville) 714. MB; Seville: BM.
581/12

Clavius, Christoph. In Sphaeram Joannis de Sacro Bosco Commentarius . . . iterum ab ipso auctore recognitus. *Rome: D.Basa, for F. Zanetti*, 1581. 467p.;illus.;4to. 1st publ., Rome, 1570. Backer II:1212. DFo, ICJ, InU-L, MH, NN-RB; BL.   581/13

Coignet, Michel. Instruction nouvelle des poincts . . . necessaires, touchant l'art de naviguer. *Antwerp: H.Hendricksen*, 1581. 98p.;illus.,map;4to. Transl. from the author's *Nieuwe onderwijsinghe, op de principaelste puncten der zee-vaert*, 1st (?) publ. in Pedro de Medina, *De zeevaert*, Antwerp, 1580. Sabin 14234; Belg.typ. (1541-1600) I:669. CtY; BL, BN.   581/14

A compendious or briefe examination of certayne ordinary complaints . . . By [i.e., edited by?] William Stafford. *London: T.Marshe*, 1581. 55 numb.lvs;4to. Includes in 2nd dialogue a query on reasons for which people go to Peru & elsewhere in search of gold and silver. Authorship has been attributed to Sir Thomas Smith (1513-1577). STC 23133. DFo; Newcastle-upon-Tyne.   581/15

—[Anr issue, with altered t.p.]. By W.S., gentleman. *London: T.Marshe*, 1581. STC 23133.5. DFo, MB; London: UL.   581/16

—[Anr edn]. *London: T.Marshe*, 1581. Heading of lf A1r has reading 'Englande'. STC 23133a. CSmH, CtY, DFo, MH, NNC; BL.
581/17

—[Anr edn]. *London: T.Marshe*, 1581. Heading of lf A1r has reading 'England'. STC 23134. CSmH, DFo, ICU, MH; BL.   581/18

Conti, Natale. Universae historiae sui temporis libri triginta. *Venice: D.Zenaro*, 1581. 683p.;fol. Included is an account of Vespucci. Adams (Cambr.) C2438. IU, MB, NjP; BL, BN.   581/19

Du Bartas, Guillaume de Salluste, seigneur. La sepmaine, ou Creation du monde . . . Revue, augmentee, & embellie en divers par l'auteur mesme. En ceste quinzieme [sic] edition ont esté adjoustez l'argument general . . . annotations en marge, & indices propres pour l'intelligence des mot & matieres de tout l'oeuvre, par S[imon]. G[oulart]. [*Geneva:*] *J.Chouët*, 1581. 2pts;8vo. The

earliest edn with Goulart's notes & commentary. In verse. Holmes (DuBartas) I:71,no.8; Jones (Goulart) 20a. MiU; Paris: Arsenal.
581/20

__[Anr issue]. [*Geneva:*]*J.Durant*, 1581. MH.
581/21

__[Anr edn, without Goulart's notes]. *Paris: M. Gadoulleau*, 1581. 2pts; 12mo. Reprinted from Paris, 1580, edn. Holmes (DuBartas) I:71,no.9. BN.
581/22

Emili, Paolo. L'histoire des faicts, gestes et conquestes de roys, princes, seigneur et peuple de France . . . mise en françois par Jean Regnart . . . avec la suite . . . tirée du latin de . . . Arnold Le Ferron. *Paris: F.Morel*, 1581. 687p.;fol. Transl. from author's *De rebus gestis Francorum*, 1st publ. with Le Ferron's appendix containing American refs, Paris, 1548-49. Adams (Cambr.) A243. MnU-B; BL, BN.
581/23

Estienne, Charles. L'agricoltura et casa di villa . . . Nuovamente tradotta dal cavaliere Hercole Cato. *Venice:* [*A.Manuzio,the Younger*] 1581. 511p.;4to. Transl. from Estienne's *L'agriculture* as publ., Paris, 1574. Thiébaud (La chasse) 357-358; Adams (Cambr.) S1722; Arents (Add.) 38. CLSU, CtY, DNLM, MH, NN-A; BL.
581/24

Fernel, Jean. De abditis rerum causis. *Frankfurt a.M.: A.Wechel*, 1581. 272p.;8vo. 1st publ., Paris, 1548. DNLM, PBa.
581/25

____. Universa medicina. *Frankfurt a.M.: A. Wechel*, 1581. 3v.;ports;8vo. Includes both Fernel's *De abditis rerum causis*, 1st publ., Paris, 1548, and his *De luis venereae curatione*, 1st publ., Antwerp, 1579. CtY-M, DNLM, MHi; BL.
581/26

__[Anr issue]. [*Frankfurt a.M.: A.Wechel,for*] *A.Marsilius,at Lyons*, 1581. DNLM.
581/27

Fioravanti, Leonardo. Del compendio de i secreti rationali . . . libri cinque. *Venice: Heirs of M.Sessa*, 1581. 187 numb.lvs;port.;8vo. 1st publ., Venice, 1564. DNLM, PPC.
581/28

Gambara, Lorenzo. De navigatione Christophori Columbi libri quattuor. *Rome: F.Zanetti*, 1581. 112p.;8vo. In verse. Sabin 26500; Adams (Cambr.) G181; Palau 97340; JCB (3) I:286. CSmH, DLC, ICN, InU-L, MH, MiU-C, NN-RB, RPJCB; BL, BN.
581/29

Genebrard, Gilbert, Abp of Aix. Chronographiae libri quatuor. *Cologne: J.Gymnich*, 1581. 1191p.;8vo. 1st publ., Paris, 1567. Adams (Cambr.) G398. DLC, MiU-C; Cambridge: Gonville & Caius.
581/30

Gesner, Konrad. Vogelbuch . . . neüwlich aber durch Rudolff Heüsslin . . . in das teütsch gebracht. *Zurich: C.Froschauer*, 1581. cxlxi lvs;illus.;fol. 1st publ. in German, Zurich, 1557. Cf.Nissen (Birds) 350. DLC. 581/31

Giglio, Girolamo. Nuova seconda selva di varia lettione, che segue Pietro Messia. *Venice: F.& A.Zoppino*, 1581. 198 numb.lvs;8vo. 1st publ., Venice, 1565. ICU.
581/32

Giovio, Paolo, Bp of Nocera. Delle istorie del suo tempo. *Venice:* [*P.Pietrasanta*] 1581. 3pts;4to. 1st publ. in Italian, Venice, 1551-53. Adams (Cambr.) G661. Cambridge: Clare.
581/33

Gómez de Castro, Alvaro. De rebus gestis a Francisco Ximenio Cisnerio . . . libri octo. *Frankfurt a.M.: A.Wechel*, 1581. 271p.;fol. 1st publ., Alcalá de Henares, 1569. Streit II:992. MdBP, MnU-B, NN-RB; BN. 581/34

Guerreiro, Afonso. Das festas que se fizeram na cidade de Lisboa, na entrada del Rey D. Philippe primeiro de Portugal. *Lisbon: F.Correa*, 1581. 59 lvs;4to. A statue representing Brazil, with verse inscription, is described. Borba de Moraes I:319-320; Anselmo 514. MH; BL, Lisbon: BN.
581/35

Guicciardini, Francesco. La historia . . . traduzido por Antonio Florez de Benavides. *Baeza: J.B.de Montoya*, 1581. 184 numb.lvs; fol. Transl. from author's *Historia di Italia*, 1st publ., Florence, 1561; includes 1st 7 bks only. Palau 110715. CU, NNH; BN. 581/36

Honter, Johannes. Rudimentorum cosmographicorum . . . libri iii. [*Zurich: C.Froschauer*] 1581. [60]p.;illus.,maps;8vo. 1st publ. in this version, Kronstadt, 1542. In verse. Cf.Sabin 32799. DLC, MH, NN-RB.
581/37

La Popelinière, Lancelot Voisin, sieur de. L'histoire de France . . . Depuis lan 1550 jusques a ce temps. [*La Rochelle:*] *Abraham H.* [i.e., *P.Haultin*], 1581. 2v.;fol. In bk 5 is an account of Villegagnon's undertaking, with a substantial description of the New World; bk 10 describes Ribaut in Florida; bk 34 contains copious American references. Desgraves (Les Haultin) 45. CtY, MH, NjP, PBL; BL, BN.
581/38

L'Obel, Matthias de. Kruydtboeck oft Beschryvinghe van allerleye ghewassen, kruyderen, hesteren ende gheboomten. *Antwerp: C. Plantin*, 1581. 2v.;illus.;fol. The earliest Dutch edn; constitutes an expanded & re-arranged edn of the work 1st publ. in Latin, Antwerp, 1576. Pritzel 5548n; Nissen (Bot.)

1219; Bibl.belg.,1st ser.,XVIII:L119; Arents (Add.) 61; Shaaber L309a. DLC, MiU, MnU, NN-A, PU; BL. 581/39

____. Plantarum seu Stirpium icones. *Antwerp: C.Plantin*, 1581. 2v.;illus.;obl. 4to. Pritzel 5549; Nissen (Bot.) 1220; Bibl.belg.,1st ser.,XVIII:L120; Adams (Cambr.) L1383. CU-A, DLC, MH-A, PPL; BL. 581/40

Marguérite d'Angoulême, Queen of Navarre. L'heptameron ou Histoires des amans fortunez. *Lyons: L.Cloquemin*, 1581. 812p.;16mo. 1st publ. in this version, Paris, 1559. Tchémerzine VII:395; Baudrier (Lyons) IV:60. CSt, MH; BN. 581/41

__[Anr edn]. *Paris: G.Buon*, 1581. 801p.;16mo. Tchémerzine VII:395. MH. 581/42

__[Anr issue]. *Paris: A.L'Angelier*, 1581. Tchémerzine VII:395. 581/43

Mattioli, Pietro Andrea. I discorsi . . . nelli sei libri di Pedacio Dioscoride . . . della materia medica. *Venice: Heirs of V.Valgrisi*, 1581. 971p.;illus.;fol. 1st publ., Venice, 1555. Pritzel 5988n; Nissen (Bot.) 1304n. DNLM, ICJ, MH-A; BN. 581/44

Medina, Pedro de. The arte of navigation . . . translated out of Spanish . . . by John Frampton. *London: T.Dawson*, 1581. 83p.;fol. Transl. from Medina's *Arte de navegar*, 1st publ., Valladolid, 1545. Sabin 47347; STC 17771; Palau 159681. CtY, DFo; BL. 581/45

Norman, Robert. The new attractive, containing a short discourse of the magnes or lodestone. *London: J.Kingston,for R.Ballard*, 1581. 2pts;illus.;4to. Pt 2 comprises W.Borough's *A discourse of the variation of the cumpas*, described separately above. In ch.9 is a discussion of the effect of the arctic pole on compass variation in voyages to Newfoundland, West Indies, etc. Cf.Sabin 55496; STC 18647. BL. 581/46

Oczko, Wojeich. Przymiot. *Cracow: L.Andrysowicz*, 1581. 664p.;4to. On syphilis, referring to its American origin. Proksch I:20; Wierzbowski 1565. 581/47

Ortelius, Abraham. Theatre de l'univers. *Antwerp: C.Plantin*, 1581. 93maps;fol. 1st publ. in French, Antwerp, 1572. Atkinson (Fr.Ren.) 284; Koeman (Ort.) 17; Phillips (Atlases) 3395; Adams (Cambr.) 0341. DLC, MH; Cambridge: Trinity. 581/48

Osório, Jerónimo, Bp of Silves. De rebus; Emmanuelis Regis Lusitaniae . . . gestis. *Cologne: Heirs of A.Birckmann*, 1581. 368 numb.lvs;8vo. 1st publ. with commentary by

Metellus relating to New World, Cologne, 1574. Cf.Sabin 57804. CoU, InU-L; Strasbourg: BN. 581/49

____. Histoire de Portugal, contenant les entreprises, navigations, & gestes mémorables de Portugallois, tant en la conqueste des Indes Orientales par eux descouvertes, qu'ès guerres d'Afrique & autres exploits . . . Comprinse en vingt livres, dont les douze premiers sont traduits du latin de Jerosme Osorius . . . les huit suivants prins de Lopes Castagneda & d'autres historiens. Nouvellement mise en françois par S[imon]. G[oulart]. [*Geneva:*] *F.Estienne,for A.Chuppin*, 1581. 764p.;fol. Osorio's work transl. from his *De rebus Emmanuelis . . . gestis*, 1st publ., Lisbon, 1571; that of Lopes de Castanheda from his *Historia do descobrimento*, 1st publ., Lisbon, 1551. Cf. Sabin 57805; Borba de Moraes II:121; Atkinson (Fr.Ren.) 285; Jones (Goulart) 18a; Streit IV:1004; Adams (Cambr.) 0384; Arents (Add.) 48. DLC, NN-A; BL, BN. 581/50

__[Anr edn]. *Paris: P.Chevillot*, 1581. 680 numb.lvs;fol. Sabin 57805; Atkinson (Fr. Ren.) 286; JCB (3) I:287. RPJCB; Paris: Mazarine. 581/51

__[Anr edn]. *Paris: G.de La Noue*, 1581. 1360p.;8vo. Streit IV:1003. 581/52

____. Historiae . . . de rebus Emmanuelis, Lusitaniae Regis . . . gestis, libri duodecim . . . Item Jo. Matalii Metelli . . . praefatio et commentarius; de reperta ab Hispanis et Lusitanis in Occidentis et Orientis Indiam navigatione deque populorum eius vita, moribus ac ritibus. *Cologne: Heirs of A.Birckmann*, 1581. 368 numb.lvs;8vo. 1st publ. with Metellus's preface, Cologne, 1574. Sabin 57804n; Borba de Moraes II:120-121; Streit IV:991n; Adams (Cambr.) 0382; Palau 206492. RPJCB; BL, BN. 581/53

Pamphilus, Josephus, Bp of Segni. Chronica ordinis Fratrum Eremitarum S.Augustini. *Rome: G.Ferrario,for V.Accolti*, 1581. 144 numb.lvs;4to. Lvs 113-117 relate to Augustinians in America. Streit I:135; Adams (Cambr.) P134. PV; BL, BN. 581/54

Paracelsus. Opus chirigicum . . . darinn begriffen wie die Wunden, offnen Schäden . . . Frantzosen, Blatern . . . curiert werden sollend. *Basel: P.Perna*, 1581. 444p.;fol. Sudhoff (Paracelsus) 187. BL. 581/55

Peurbach, Georg von. Theoricae novae planetarum . . . Henrici Glareani, De geographia . . . liber unus. Omnia recognita, ac novis figuris illustrata. *Cologne: G.von Kempen,for the Heirs of A.Birckmann*, 1581. 256p.;illus.;8vo. Glareanus's *De geographia*, 1st publ. separately, Basel, 1527. Sabin 66670; Adams (Cambr.) P2280. CtY, NN-RB, PPL; Cambridge: Clare, BN.   581/56

Ruscelli, Girolamo, comp. Delle lettere di principi . . . Libro primo. *Venice: F.Ziletti*, 1581. 236 numb.lvs;4to. 1st publ., Venice, 1562. Sabin 40564; Adams (Cambr.) L564; Shaaber R371. CSt, ICN, MH, MiU, NNC, PU, RPB; BL.   581/57

Sánchez, Francisco. Quod nihil scitur. *Lyons: A.Gryphius*, 1581. 100p.;4to. Includes ref. to the ignorance found in the Indies. Baudrier (Lyons) VIII:380; Palau 294101. ICU; BL, Paris: Arsenal.   581/58

Soto, Domingo de. In quartum Sententiarum commentarii. Tomus primus[-secundus]. *Medina del Campo: F.à Canto,for B.Boyer*, 1581. 2v.;fol. 1st publ., Salamanca, 1557-60. Pérez Pastor (Medina del Campo) 194. BL, Madrid: BN.   581/59

Tasso, Torquato. Gerusalemme liberata . . . ultimamente emendata di mano dell'istesso auttore. *Parma: E.Viotti*, 1581. 496p.;4to. The earliest edn to include canto 15 with, stanzas 30-32, discussion of Columbus. In verse. Racc.Tassiana 152. Bergamo: BC.   581/60

—[Anr edn]. *Casalmaggiore: A.Canacci & E.Viotti*, 1581. 254p.;4to. Racc.Tassiana 153; Adams (Cambr.) T235; Shaaber T77. PU; BL, Bergamo: BC.   581/61

—[Anr edn]. *Lyons: P.Roussin,for A.Marsilius*, 1581. 336 numb.lvs;8vo. Racc.Tassiana 154; Baudrier (Lyons) II:168; Shaaber T78. MH, PU; BL, Bergamo: BC.   581/62

—[Anr edn]. *Ferrara: V.Baldini*, 1581. 208p.; 4to. Racc.Tassiana 155; Shaaber T79. PU; BL, Bergamo: BC.   581/63

—[Anr edn]. Il Goffredo . . . Novamente corretto. *Venice: G.Perchacino*, 1581. 112 numb. lvs;4to. Racc.Tassiana 156; Shaaber T80. PU; BL, BN.   581/64

—[Anr edn] Gierusalemme liberata. *Ferrara: Heirs of F.Rossi*, 1581. 266p.;4to. Racc.Tassiana 157; Adams (Cambr.) T236. Cambridge: Trinity, BN.   581/65

—[Anr edn]. *Parma: E.Viotti*, 1581. 242p.;4to. Racc.Tassiana 158; Shaaber T81. PU; BL.   581/66

Ulloa, Alfonso de. Vita dell'invittissimo e sacratissimo Imperator Carlo V. *Venice: Heirs*

of *F.Rampazetto*, 1581. 4to. 1st publ., Venice, 1560. DFo.   581/67

Vigo, Giovanni de. Libro, o Pratica en cirurgia . . . Traduzido . . . por el doctor Miguel Juan Pascual. *Saragossa: J.Soler*, 1581. fol. 1st publ. in this translation, Valencia, 1537. Palau 364935. Lisbon: BN.   581/68

——. La pratica universale in cirurgia . . . di nuovo ristampata et ricorreta. *Venice: F.& A.Zoppini*, 1581. 558p.;4to. Includes in Italian translation the author's *Practica in arte chirurgica copiosa*, 1st publ., Rome, 1514. BL, BN.   581/69

Zamorano, Rodrigo. Compendio. *Seville*: 1581. See the year 1582.

Zárate, Agustín de. The strange and delectable history of the discoverie and conquest of the provinces of Peru . . . Translated out of the Spanish tongue, by T.Nicholas. *London: [J.Charlewood,W.How, & J.Kingston,for] R.Jones*, 1581. 88 numb.lvs;illus.;4to. Transl. from Zárate's *Historia . . . del Peru*, 1st publ., Antwerp, 1555. Sabin 106272; STC 26123; Church 126; JCB (3) I:287. CSmH, CtY, DLC, ICN, MH, MiU-C, NN-RB, RPJCB; BL.   581/70

1582

Anania, Giovanni Lorenzo d', comp. & tr. Lo scoprimento dello stretto artico e di meta incognita ritrovato nel'anno 1577 e 1578 dal capitano Martino Forbisero . . . posto nuovamente in luce . . . dal sig. Gio Lorenzo Anania. *Naples: G.B.Capello*, 1582. 40 lvs; illus.;8vo. An account of Frobisher's 2nd voyage based on that of Dionyse Settle, and of the 3rd, from an unknown source. Sabin 78166. MnU-B, NN-RB, PBL; BN.   582/1

——. L'universale fabrica del mondo. *Venice: A.Muschio,for A.San Vito,at Naples*, 1582. 402p.;maps;4to. 1st publ., Naples, 1573. Sabin 1364; Ind.aur.105.088. DLC, MiU, MnU, NNH, RPJCB; BL, Vienna: NB. 582/2

Antist, Vicente Justiniano. Verdadera relación de la vida y muerte del padre fray Luis Bertran. *Valencia: Widow of P.Huete*, 1582. 268p.;8vo. Chapts vii-x describe Bertrán's missionary activities in New Granada, i.e., Colombia. Medina (BHA) 270; Streit II:1001; Palau 13079.   582/3

Argote de Molina, Gonzalo. Libro de la monteria . . . Acrecentado por Gonçalo

Argote de Molina. *Seville: A.Pescioni*, 1582. 2pts;illus.;fol. Authorship of the 1st pt has been attributed to King Alfonso el Sabio. In the 2nd pt, chapts 35-37 describe hunting in the New World. Ind.aur.107.260; Escudero (Seville) 726; Palau 16167; JCB (3) I:288. DLC, MH, NN-RB, RPJCB; BL, BN.   582/4

Bazán, Alvaro de, marqués de Santa Cruz. A discourse of that which happened in the battell fought between the two navies of Spaine and Portugall at the islands of Azores . . . 1582. *London: T.Purfoote* [1582?]. 24 lvs;8vo. Presumably transl. from *Lo succedido a la armada* described below, or from another of the translations here recorded. Sabin 76755; Canto (Azores) 524; STC 1103; Ind.aur.111.328; Palau 297849. BL.   582/5

——. Historia successus classis regiae, cui praefuit Marchio S.Crucis, et navalis praelii, quod commissium est cum D.Antonio in insulis, quas Hispani Açores vocant. Antea quidem ab ipso Marchione . . . per nepotem suum Petrum Ponce, ad Regem Hispanicè missa: postea verò ex hispano idiomate, in lat. diligenter conversa. *Cologne: G.von Kempen*, 1582. 22p.;8vo. Cf.Bazán's *Lo succedido a la armada* below. Ind.aur.111.325. Münster: UB.   582/6

——. Königliche Spanische Meerschlacht und Victoria. Warhaffte Beschreibung, welcher gestalt Don Antonii Armada, der sich dess Königreichs Portugal anmast, von dess Königs in Hispanien und Portugal Armada, den 23. 24. 25 Julii, diss 82 Jars, bey den Inseln Acores . . . angegriffen . . . Auch unterschiedliche vermeldung, was reichen Schatz die Flotta, diss Jars, auss Nova Hispania, von Berlein, Gold, Silber, etc., mitgebracht. *Nuremberg: L.Heussler* [1582?]. 12 lvs;4to. Cf.entry for Bazán's *Lo succedido a la armada* below, and also his *Warhaftige unn gründliche Beschreibung*. Sabin 76756; Palau 295850. BL.   582/7

——. Relacion verdadera del felice sucesso y vitoria, que tuvo la armada de su magestad contra la armada de don Antonio, en la batalla naval, que hubo en las islas de la Tercera, en 27 de Julio de 1582, las cuales recibieron los . . . señores Justicia y Regimiento de la ciudad de Burgos. [*Burgos:*] *P.de Giunta*, 1582. 4 lvs;fol. Cf.entry for Bazán's *Lo succedido a la armada* below. Palau 257217.   582/8

——. Lo subcedido a la armada de su Magestad.

[*Toledo?* 1582]. 4 lvs;fol. Cf.entry for Bazán's *Lo succedido a la armada* below. Sabin 76761; Palau 297852. BL.   582/9

——. Lo succedido a la armada de Su Magestad, de que es capitan general el marques de Sancta Cruz, en la batalla que dio a la armada que traya Don Antonio, en las islas de los Açores. *Saragossa: L.& D.de Robles*, 1582. [11]p.;fol. 'Este relacion embio el marques de sancta Cruz a S.M.'—p.[11]. So complex are the relationships of the various editions and translations of this news sheet, & so scarce are extant copies, that we are reduced to undertaking little more than recording their existence. This account of the naval engagement between Spanish forces under Bazán and Portuguese forces, with French allies, in an effort to withstand Philip II's assumption of the Portuguese crown manifestly caught the attention of all Europe, in part because of the brutality with which Bazán treated and executed prisoners captured. The strategic importance of the Azores for ships returning from both East and West Indies lend these works American relevance, though specific refs to the latter are not always present. For a final battle at Tercera, giving Spain total control of the Azores, see the year 1583. Sánchez (Aragon) 593; Palau 257215-II.   582/10

——[Anr edn]. *Valladolid:* 1582. 4to. Palau 257215.   582/10a

——[Anr edn]. Relacion: Copia de una carta que don Antonio escribio . . . Lo sucedido a la armada de S.M. . . . en las islas de los Açores. [*Spain:* 1582]. 6 lvs;fol. Palau 257216.   582/11

——. Successo dell'armata di Sua Maestà Catholica, della quale fu capitano, il marchese di Santa Croce nella giornata contra Don Antonio di Portugalo . . . tradotto nella italiana lingua da una copia spagnuola stampata in Milano. *Bologna: A.Benacci*, 1582. 8 numb. lvs;4to. Cf.entry for Bazán's *Lo succedido a la armada* above. Sabin 76763; Ind.aur. 111.323; Palau 297853. BL.   582/12

——[Anr edn]. Il successo de l'armata del Re Filippo. *Florence: At the Badian Steps* [1582?]. [11]p.;4to. RPJCB.   582/13

——. Warhaftige und gründliche Beschreibung, welcher massen des Don Antonio Armada in den Insulen las Açores genant, von des Königs Philippen in Hispanien unnd Portugal Armada, deren Obrister der Marggrave de S.

Cruz, Don Alvaro de Baciano gewesen, auff den 26. Julii diss 82. Jars geschlagen und vertrent worden. Sambt der verzeichnuss des Reichthumbs, so die Flotta diss 82. Jars auss den Newen Hispanien . . . Alles . . . treulich verdeutscht. *Munich: A.Berg* [1582]. 14 lvs; 4to. Cf.entry for Bazán's *Lo succedido a la armada* and also his *Königliche Spanische Meerschlacht* above. Sabin 76764; Palau 297851. NN-RB.   582/14

Benzoni, Girolamo. Erste[-ander] Theil der Newen Weldt und Indianischer Nidergängischen Königreichs newe und wahrhaffte History . . . Durch Hieronymum Bentzon . . . in lateinischer Sprach erstlich beschrieben . . . Ander Theil der Newen Welt und Indianischen Nidergängischen Königreichs . . . Erstlich durch Petrum Martyrem in lateinischen Sprach . . . verzeichnet. Jetz aber Alles . . . in das Teutsch gebracht durch Nicolaum Höniger. *Basel: S.Henricpetri*, 1582. dcii p.;fol. 1st pt, by Benzoni, 1st publ. in German, Basel, 1579; 2d pt here 1st publ. in German, transl. from Anghiera's *De orbe novo*, in text 1st publ., Alcalá de Henares, 1530. For a 3rd pt, see the year 1583, under Apollonius, Levinus. Sabin 4798; Medina (BHA) 100n (I:156-157); Baginsky (German Americana) 82-83; Ind.aur.116.991; Arents (Add.) 53; JCB (3) I:289-291. DLC, NN-RB, RPJCB; BL, Berlin: StB.   582/15

Beuther, Michael. Bildnisse viler zum theyle von uralten, zum theyle von newlichern zeiten her . . . in massen dieselbige Paulus Jovius . . . in seiner bibliotheca zusammen gebracht . . . abgemalt hinderlassen. *Basel: P.Perna*, 1582. 391p.;ports.;fol. Derived from Paolo Giovio's *Elogia . . . virorum bellica virtute illustrium* as publ., Basel, 1575. Includes ports, etc., of Columbus & Cortés. Ind.aur.118.439. MH; BL, Strasbourg: BM.   582/16

Boemus, Johann. Mores, leges, et ritus omnium gentium. *Lyons: J.de Tournes*, 1582. 2pts;16mo. Also included, as pt 2 (with continuing signatures), is Damião a Goes's *Fides, religio, moresque Aethiopum*, 1st publ., Louvain, 1540. Sabin 6117n; Ind.aur.120.966; Cartier (de Tournes) 625. IU, MH, RPJCB; Munich: StB, Tours: BM.   582/17

Braun, Georg. Beschreibung und Contrafactur der vornembster Stät der Welt, liber primus. *Cologne: G.von Kempen*, 1582. 59 double pls;fol. 1st publ. in German, Cologne,

1574. Cf.Koeman (Braun & Hogenberg) 7; Ind.aur.123.956. BN.   582/18

_____. Civitates orbis terrarum, liber primus. *Cologne: G.von Kempen*, 1582. 58 double pls; fol. 1st publ., Cologne, 1572. Cf.Koeman (Braun & Hogenberg) 1; Ind.aur.123.954; Adams (Cambr.) B2710. BL, Vienna: NB.
582/19

Cardano, Girolamo. De subtilitate rerum. *Basel: S.Henricpetri*, 1582. 1148p.;illus., port.;8vo. 1st publ., Nuremberg (?), 1550. Ind.aur.132.122; Adams (Cambr.) C676. ICN, NNC, PPC; BL.   582/20

_[Anr edn]. *Basel: S.Henricpetri*, 1582. 626p.; illus.,port.;fol. MH.   582/21

Caro, Annibale. De le lettere familiari. *Venice: G.Giunti*, 1582. 2v.;8vo. 1st publ., Venice, 1572. Ind.aur.132.478. Naples: BN.
582/22

Casas, Bartolomé de las, Bp of Chiapa. Histoire admirable des horribles insolences, cruautez, & tyrannies exercees par les Espagnols es Indes Occidentales . . . fidelement traduite par Jaques de Miggrode. [*Geneva:*] *G.Cartier*, 1582. 222p.;8vo. 1st publ. in French, Antwerp, 1579, under title *Tyrannies et cruautez des Espagnols*. Copies occur without printer's name on t.p. Sabin 11269; Medina (BHA) 1085n (II:471); Streit I:138; Atkinson (Fr.Ren.) 289; Palau 46961n; JCB (3) I:291. CtY, DLC, NN-RB, PU, RPJCB; BN.
582/23

_____. Tyrannies et cruautez des Espagnols, perpetrees es Indes Occidentales . . . fidelement traduites par Jaques de Miggrode. *Paris: G. Julien*, 1582. 184p.;8vo. 1st publ. in French, Antwerp, 1579. Sabin 11268; Medina (BHA) 1085n (II:471); Streit I:137; Palau 46961n; JCB (3) I:291. CtY, ICN, InU-L, MH, NN-RB, PU, RPJCB; BL, BN.   582/24

Costa, Christovam da. Aromatum & medicamentorum in Orientali India nascentium liber: plurimum lucis adferens iis quae à Doctore Garcia de Orta in hoc genere scripta sunt. Caroli Clusii . . . opera ex hispanico sermone latinus factus, in epitomem contractus, & quibusdam notis illustratus. *Antwerp: C. Plantin*, 1582. 88p.;illus.;8vo. An abridged translation of Costa's *Tractado delas drogas*, 1st publ., Burgos, 1578, with mention of Brazilian rubber & of pineapples. Sabin 57665n; Pritzel 13n; Nissen (Bot.) 3na; Hunt (Bot.) 139; JCB (3) I:288. CtY, DNLM, MH, MiU,

MnU-B, NNNAM, RPJCB; BL, BN. 582/25

Crespin, Jean. Histoire des martyrs persecutez et mis a mort . . . depuis le temps des Apotres jusques l'an 1574. Revue et augmentee d'un tiers. [*Geneva: J.Crespin*, 1582]. 732 numb. lvs;fol. 1st publ. in this version, [Geneva], 1564. Borba de Moraes I:199n; Adams (Cambr.) C2939. CtY, PPPD, ViHarEM; BL. 582/26

Du Bartas, Guillaume de Salluste, seigneur. Commentaires et annotations sur La sepmaine de la creation du monde [par Simon Goulart]. *Paris: A.L'Angelier*, 1582. 354 numb.lvs; 12mo. 1st publ. with Simon Goulart's commentary, Geneva, 1581, as *La sepmaine*; here an ostensibly illicit reprinting employing altered title, with Goulart's notes distributed throughout the text, which, notwithstanding the title, is also included. In verse. Holmes (DuBartas) I:72 no.13; Jones (Goulart) 20b. Paris: Arsenal. 582/27

—[Anr issue]. *Paris: T.Jouän*, 1582. Holmes (DuBartas) I:72 no.13n; Jones (Goulart) 20b(n). Paris: Arsenal. 582/28

____. La sepmaine, ou Creation du monde . . . Revue, corrigee et augmentee par l'autheur mesme, & embellie en divers passages. *Paris: J.Février*, 1582. 114 numb.lvs;12mo. 1st publ., Paris, 1578. In verse. Holmes (DuBartas) I:71 no.10n. BN. 582/29

—[Anr issue]. *Paris: M.Gadouleau*, 1582. Holmes (DuBartas) I:71 no.10. BL. 582/30

—[Anr edn]. [*Geneva:*] *J.Chouet*, 1582. 225p.; 8vo. Contains Goulart's notes, 1st publ., Geneva, 1581. NIC. 582/31

—[Anr issue]. [*Geneva:*] *J.Durant*, 1582. Jones (Goulart) 20c. Geneva: BP. 582/32

Ercilla y Zúñiga, Alonso de. Primera parte dela Araucana. *Lisbon: A.Ribeiro*, 1582. 149 numb.lvs;12mo. 1st publ., Madrid, 1569. Ribeiro's edn of pt 2 appeared in 1588. Medina (BHA) 273; Medina (Arau.) 8; Anselmo 953; Palau 80415; JCB (3) I:292. RPJCB. 582/33

Estienne, Charles. L'agricoltura e casa di villa . . . tradotta dal cavaliere Hercole Cato. *Turin: Heirs of N.Bevilacqua*, 1582. 4to. 1st publ. in Italian, Venice, 1581. Thiébaud (La chasse) 358. 582/34

____. De landtwinnighe ende hoeuve . . . Uut de fransoische spraecke . . . overgheset. Den laetsten druck, oversien ende vermeerdert. *Antwerp: C.Plantin*, 1582. 707p.;illus.;4to.

1st publ. in Dutch, Antwerp, 1566; transl. by Martin Everaert from *L'agriculture et maison rustique* as ed. by Jean Liébault. Bibl.Belg.1st ser.,X:E39; Arents (Add.) 40. DNAL, NN-A; Antwerp: Plantin Mus. 582/35

Falloppius, Gabriel. Secreti diversi, et miracolosi. *Venice: C.Franceschini*, 1582. 360p.; 8vo. 1st publ., Venice, 1563. NNNAM; London: Wellcome. 582/36

Fioravanti, Leonardo. La cirurgia . . . Con una gionta de secreti nuovi, dell'istesso autore. *Venice: Heirs of M.Sessa*, 1582. 182 numb. lvs;port.;8vo. 1st publ., Venice, 1570. CtY-M, DNLM, NNC, PPC; BL. 582/37

____. A compendium of the rationall secretes, of . . . Leonardo Phiorovante . . . *London: J.Kingston,for G.Pen & J.H[ester].*, 1582. 2pts;8vo. Transl. by J.Hester from author's *Del compendio dei secreti rationali*, 1st publ., Venice, 1564. Ferguson (Bibl.chem.) I:277-278; STC 10879. CSmH, DFo; BL. 582/38

____. De' cappricc [!] medicinali . . . Di nuovo, dall'istesso autore . . . ampliati . . . revisti, corretti, & ristampati. *Venice: Heirs of M. Sessa*, 1582. 267 numb.lvs;illus.;8vo. 1st publ., Venice, 1561. Adams (Cambr.) F486. DNLM; BL. 582/39

____. Della fisica . . . Di nuovo posta in luce. *Venice: Heirs of M.Sessa*, 1582 [colophon:1581]. 391p.;port.;8vo. A medical treatise, including much material on therapeutic uses of tobacco, Mexican balsam (*taccamacca*), Guaiacum, & sarsaparilla, etc., as well as on the treatment of syphilis, based in part upon Monardes. Adams (Cambr.) F490; Arents (Add.) 70; Ferguson (Bibl.chem.) I:278. DFo, MH, NN-A; BL, BN. 582/40

____. Il tesoro della vita humana . . . Diviso in libri quattro . . . Di nuovo posto in luce. *Venice: Heirs of M.Sessa*, 1582. 327 numb.lvs;8vo. 1st publ., Venice, 1570. Adams (Cambr.) F494. NNNAM, WU; BL. 582/41

Gesner, Konrad. Quatre livres des secrets de medecine . . . Faicts françois par m. Jean Liebault. *Paris: J.Sevestre,for J.DuPuys*, 1582. 297 numb.lvs;illus.;8vo. 1st publ. in this version, Paris, 1573. London: Wellcome. 582/42

Gumiel, Pablo de. La victoria que tuvo don Alvaro Baçan marques de Sancta Cruz contra Felipe Stroço en la ysla de S.Miguel a 26. de Julio 1582. [*Lisbon: A.Ribeiro*, 1582]. Anselmo 955. 582/43

Hakluyt, Richard. Divers voyages, touching the discoverie of America, and the ilands adjacent unto the same, made first of all by our Englishmen, and afterwards by the Frenchmen and Britons. *London: T.Dawson,for T. Woodcocke*, 1582. 60 lvs;2maps;4to. Sabin 29592; STC 12624; Church 128; JCB (3) I:292. CSmH, DLC, ICN, MH, MiU-C, MnU-B, NN-RB, RPJCB; BL.   582/44

Herrera, Fernando de. Algunas obras. *Seville: A.Pescioni*, 1582. 56 numb.lvs;4to. In verse. Refs to America appear in Elegias 7 & 11 and in Canción 5. Escudero (Seville) 719. CtY, NNH; Madrid: BN.   582/45

La Boétie, Estienne de. La mesnagerie de Xenophon . . . Ensemble quelques vers latins & françois, de son invention. *Paris: F.Morel*, 1582. 2pts;8vo. 1st publ., Paris, 1571. MH.
582/47

La Popelinière, Lancelot Voisin, sieur de. L'histoire de France . . . depuis l'an 1550 jusques à ces temps. [*Geneva?*] 1582. 3v. in4;8vo. 1st publ., [La Rochelle], 1581. ICN, NN-RB; BL, BN.   582/48

____. Les trois mondes. *Paris: P.L'Huillier*, 1582. 3pts;map;8vo. Pt 2 describes voyages of Columbus, Pizarro, Ribaut, etc.; pt 3 describes voyages of Villegagnon, Vespucci & Magellan. Cf.Sabin 39008; Borba de Moraes II:160-161; Adams (Laudonnière) 16; Atkinson (Fr.Ren.) 292; Adams (Cambr.) L202; Church 129; JCB (3) I:293. CSmH, DLC, MiU-C, MnU-B, NNH, PPL, RPJCB; BL, BN.   582/49

__[Anr issue]. 'La seconde édition'. *Paris: P. L'Huillier*, 1582. Sabin 39008n; Borba de Moraes II:161; Adams (Laudonnière) 17; Atkinson (Fr.Ren.) 292; Church 129n; Rothschild 1959. DLC, MiU-C, NN-RB; BN.
582/50

__[Anr edn]. *Paris: P.L'Huillier*, 1582. 3pts; map;4to. Cf.Sabin 39008; Borba de Moraes II:160-161; Atkinson (Fr.Ren.) 291; Adams (Laudonnière) 14; Adams (Cambr.) L203; Arents (Add.) 71; Church 129n. MiU-C, NN-A, RPJCB; BL, BN.   582/51

L'Ecluse, Charles de. Aliquot notae in Garciae Aromatum historiam. Ejusdem descriptiones nonnullarum stirpium, & aliarum exoticarum rerum, quae à . . . Francesco Drake . . . & his observatae sunt, qui eum in longa illa navigatione, qua proximis annis universum

orbem circumivit, comitati sunt. *Antwerp: C. Plantin*, 1582. 44p.;illus.;8vo. Described are various American plants, e.g., cocoa & Mexican jasmine (Gelsemium). Sabin 13800; Pritzel 1757; Nissen (Bot.) 373; Adams (Cambr.) C2240; Arents (Add.) 69; JCB (3) I:294. CSmH, CtY, DLC, ICN, MH-A, MiU, MnU-B, NN-RB, RPJCB; BL,BN.   582/52

Lonitzer, Adam. Kreuterbuch. *Frankfurt a.M.: Heirs of C.Egenolff*, 1582. ccclviii lvs; illus.,port.;fol. 1st publ. in German, Frankfurt a.M., 1557. Cf.Pritzel 5599; Nissen (Bot.) 1228n. CSmH, DNLM, NNBG.   582/53

Lopes de Castanheda, Fernão. The first booke of the Historie of the discoverie and conquest of the East Indies . . . Set foorth in the Portingale language . . . and now translated . . . N[icholas]. L[ichefield]. *London: T.East*, 1582. 164 numb.lvs;4to. 1st publ., Coimbra, 1551, under title *Historia do descobrimento e conquista de India*. Sabin 11391; Borba de Moraes I:143; STC 16806; JCB AR65:21. CSmH, CtY, DLC, ICN, InU-L, MH, NN-RB, RPJCB; BL, BN.   582/54

Meneses, Felipe de. Luz de alma christiana. *Medina del Campo: F.del Campo,for P.Landry*, 1582. 294 numb.lvs;8vo. 1st publ., Seville, 1555. Pérez Pastor (Medina del Campo) 197; Palau 164444n.   582/55

__[Anr issue?] *Medina del Campo: F.del Campo,for B.Boyer*, 1582. BL.   582/56

Monardes, Nicolás. Delle cose, che vengono portate dall'Indie Occidentali pertinenti all'uso della medicina . . . Nuovamente recata dalla spagnola [da Annibale Briganti]. *Venice: G.Ziletti*, 1582. 249p.;illus.;8vo. 1st publ. in Italian, Venice, 1575. Sabin 49940; Medina (BHA) 237n (I:392); Guerra (Monardes) 26; Pritzel 6366n; Nissen (Bot.) 1397nb(n) Arents 20a. DLC, InU-L, MH, MnU-B, NN-A, PPC, RPJCB; BL, BN.   582/57

____. Simplicium medicamentorum ex Novo Orbe delatorum, quorum in medicina usus est, Historiae liber tertius . . . nunc verò primum latio donatus, & notis illustratus à Carolo Clusio. *Antwerp: C.Plantin*, 1582. 47p.;illus.;8vo. Transl. from 3d pt of Monardes's *Historia medicinal*, publ. at Seville, 1580. Continues L'Ecluse's translation of pts 1-2, publ. at Antwerp, 1579. Sabin 49943; Medina (BHA) 274; Guerra (Monardes) 24; Pritzel 6366n; Arents (Add.) 64. CU, CtY-M, DNLM, ICJ, MH, NN-RB; BL, BN.   582/57a

Montaigne, Michel Eyquem de. Les essais . . . édition seconde, reveue et augmentée. *Bordeaux: S.Millanges*, 1582. 807p.;8vo. 1st publ., Bordeaux, 1580. Rép.bibl. I:40; Tchémerzine VIII:403. ICU, MH, NN-RB; BL, BN.   582/58

Neander, Michael. Chronicon, sive Epitome historiarum. *Eisleben: U.Gubisius*, 1582. 95 numb.lvs;8vo. Includes (lvs 89r-92r) discussion of West & East Indies. BL, BN.   582/59

Nores, Giason de. Tavole . . . del mondo et della sphaera. *Padua: P.Meietto*, 1582. 24 numb.lvs;4to. On verso of lf 3 are refs to America. Shaaber N158. MB, MiU, NN-RB, PU; BN.   582/60

Orta, Garcia da. Due libri dell'historia de i semplici, aromati, et altre cose, che vengono portate dall'Indie Orientali, pertinenti alla medicina . . . con alcune brevi annotationi di Carlo Clusio. Et due altri libri parimente di quelle che si portano dall'Indie Occidentali, di Nicolo Monardes . . . Hora tutti tradotti . . . da Annibale Briganti. *Venice: F.Ziletti*, 1582. 347p.;illus.;8vo. 1st publ. in Italian, Venice, 1576. Sabin 57668; Medina (BHA) 237n (I:392); Guerra (Monardes) 25. CtY-M, DLC, MH-A, MiU-C, MnU-B, NN-A, PPC; BL, BN.   582/61

—[Anr issue]. [Printer's device of fountain on t.p.]. *Venice: [F.Ziletti]* 1582. Guerra (Monardes) 25n. DNLM.   582/62

Parmenius, Stephanus, Budeus. De navigatione illustris et magnanimi . . . Humfredi Gilberto, ad deducendam in novum orbem coloniam suscepta, carmen. *London: T.Purfoot*, 1582. [15]p.;4to. In verse. Sabin 8960; STC 19308 (formerly 4015); Church 127. CSmH; BL.   582/63

Rauwolf, Leonhard. Beschreibung der Reyss . . . in die Morgenländer. *Frankfurt a.M.: C. Rab*, 1582. 3pts;4to. Included are refs to plants of American origin—kidney beans, French beans, maize—found growing in the Near East. Pritzel 7430n; Adams (Cambr.) R188. ICU, NNBG; Cambridge: Trinity.
582/64

—[Anr edn]. Aigentliche Beschreibung der Raiss . . . inn die Morgenländer. *Lauingen: L.Reinmichel,for G.Willer,at Augsburg*, 1582. 487p.;4to. Pritzel 7430n. CtY, ICU, MBCo, NN-RB, PPAN; BL.   582/65

Relaçam de la infanteria y gente de guerra que se ha embarcado para la empresa y con-

quista de la ysla Tercera, en la . . . armada . . . de que va por Capitan General . . . el marques de Sancta Cruz. *Burgos: Santillana* [1582]. 4to. For reasons given for those items entered above under Alvaro de Bazán here also included. The present edn in its imprint is stated to have been first printed at Lisbon, but of the latter no copy is known. Cf.,however, item entered under Pablo de Gumiel above. Palau 257215.   582/66

Reusner, Jeremias. Decisiones. *Basel: Heirs of N.Brylinger*, 1582. 13 lvs;4to. Discusses medicinal use of tobacco. Arents (Add.) 72. NN-A.   582/67

Sacro Bosco, Joannes de. Sphaera . . . emendata. In eandem Francisci Junctini . . . Eliae Vineti . . . et Alberti Heronis Scholia. *Antwerp:J.Bellère*, 1582. 327p.;illus.;8vo. 1st publ. with Vinet's *Scholia*, Paris, 1551. Cf.Sabin 32681. NN-RB; BN.   582/68

Saint Gelais, Mellin de. Oeuvres poétiques. *Lyons: B.Rigaud*, 1582. 295p.;16mo. 1st publ., Lyons, 1574. Baudrier (Lyons) III:372; Rothschild 631. BL, BN.   582/69

Salazar, Estéban de. Veynte discursos sobre el Credo. *Granada: H.de Mena,for J.Díaz*, 1582. 240 numb.lvs;4to. 1st publ., Granada, 1577-78. Medina (BHA) 275; Streit II:1004; Palau 286517. CtY; BL.   582/70

Soto, Domingo de. Libri decem De justitia et jure. *Lyons: S.Béraud (at shop of P.Tinghi)*, 1582. 344 numb.lvs;fol. 1st publ., Salamanca, 1553. Baudrier (Lyons) V:62-63; Adams (Cambr.) S1492; Palau 320154. Cambridge: Magdalene.   582/71

—[Anr issue]. *Lyons: Jeanne Giunta*, 1582. Baudrier (Lyons) VI:380; Adams (Cambr.) S1488; Palau 320155. NNC; Cambridge: Jesus, BN.   582/72

—[Anr issue]. *Lyons: A.de Harsy*, 1582. Baudrier (Lyons) Suppl.34; Adams (Cambr.) S1486. Cambridge: UL, Toulouse: BM.
582/73

—[Anr issue]. *Lyons: B.Honorat*, 1582. Adams (Cambr.) S1487. Cambridge: Gonville & Caius.   582/74

—[Anr issue]. *Lyons: S.Marsilius*, 1582. Adams (Cambr.) S1489. Cambridge: UL.   582/75

—[Anr issue]. *Lyons: E.Michel*, 1582. Baudrier (Lyons) V:62-63n; Baudrier (Lyons) Suppl. 152. Paris: Mazarine.   582/76

—[Anr issue]. *Lyons: C.Pesnot*, 1582. Adams

(Cambr.) S1490; Palau 320158. Cambridge: Pembroke.   582/77

—[Anr issue]. *Lyons: G.Rouillé*, 1582. Adams (Cambr.) S1491; Palau 320157. Cambridge: UL.   582/78

—[Anr edn.]. De justitia et jure libri decem. *Salamanca: A.de Terranova*, 1582. 135 numb.lvs;fol. Palau 320159.   582/79

Spain. Sovereigns, etc., 1556-1598 (Philip II). Instruccion para la observacion del eclypse de la luna, y cantidad de las sombras, que su Magestad manda hazer el año de mil y quinientos y ochenta y dos. en las ciudades y pueblos de Españoles de las Indias. [*Madrid?* 1582?]. [2]p.;fol. Cf.similar instructions of 1577. Cf.Medina (BHA) 246; cf.Palau 120120; JCB (STL) 14. RPJCB.
                                                              582/80

Tasso, Torquato. Il Goffredo. *Venice: G.Perchacino*, 1582. 127 numb.lvs;4to. 1st publ., with American refs, Parma, 1581, under title *La Gerusalemme liberata*. In verse. Racc.Tassiana 159. BL, Bergamo: BC.   582/81

—[Anr edn]. Gierusalemme liberata. [*Venice?*] 1582. 221p.;4to. Racc.Tassiana 160. BN, Bergamo: BC.   582/82

—[Anr edn]. *Ferrara: D.Mammarelli & G.C. Cagnacini*, 1582. 576p.;12mo. Racc.Tassiana 161; Shaaber T82. PU; BN, Bergamo: BC.
                                                              582/83

—[Anr edn]. *Naples: G.B.Cappelli*, 1582. 333 numb.lvs;4to. Racc.Tassiana 162. Bergamo: BC.   582/84

—[Anr edn]. *Naples: G.B.Cappelli*, 1582. 208p.;4to. A reissue of the Ferrara, Baldini, 1581, edn, with cancel t.p., etc. Racc.Tassiana 163. Bergamo: BC.   582/85

—[Anr edn]. *Naples: H.Salviani,C.Cesare & Bros*, 1582. 196p. Racc.Tassiana 164. Bergamo: BC.   582/86

—[Anr edn]. *Naples: H.Salviani,C.Cesare & Bros*, 1582. 564p. Racc.Tassiana 165. Bergamo: BC.   582/87

Torquemada, Antonio de. Hexameron, ou Six journees contenans plusieurs doctes discours . . . Fait en hespagnol . . . et mis en françois par Gabriel Chappuys. *Lyons: A.de Harsy*, 1582. 490p.;8vo. 1st publ. in French, Lyons, 1579. Palau 334918. BL, BN. 582/88

Vigo, Giovanni de. Opera . . . in chirurgia. *Lyons: S.Béraud*, 1582. 930p.;8vo. 1st publ., Rome, 1514. DNLM.   582/89

Zamorano, Rodrigo. Compendio del arte de

navegar. *Seville: A.de la Barrera*, 1581 [colophon:1582]. 60 numb.lvs;illus.,port.;4to. The author, cosmographer to Philip II, dedicates the work to the president of the Casa de Contratacïon de las Indias. Sabin 106246; Medina (BHA) 269; Escudero (Seville) 713; Palau 379247; Adams (Cambr.) Z24. BL, Madrid: Museo Naval.   582/90

—[Anr edn]. *Seville: A. Pescioni*, 1582. 60 numb.lvs;illus.,port.;4to. Sabin 106246n; Medina (BHA) 276; Escudero (Seville) 725; Palau 379248. CtY; Madrid: BN.   582/91

1583

Alberti, Leandro. Descrittione di tutta Italia. *Venice: A.Salicato*, 1583. 2 pts;4to. 1st publ., Bologna, 1550. Moranti (Urbino) 47. Urbino: BU.   583/1

Antist, Vicente Justiniano. Vera relatione de la vita, et morte del p.f. Luigi Bertrando. *Genoa*: [*A.Roccatagliata,for*] *G.del Poggio*, 1583. 251p.;8vo. Transl. from Valencia, 1582, Spanish text. Medina (BHA) 277n (I:448); Streit II:1017; Ind.aur.106.037; Palau 13085n. BL, BN.   583/2

——. Verdadera relacion de la vida y muerte del padre fray Luys Bertran. *Pamplona: T.Porralis*, 1583. 365p.;4to. 1st publ., Valencia, 1582. Medina (BHA) 277; Streit II:1016; Ind. aur.106.038; Palau 13080. BL.   583/3

—[Anr edn]. *Valencia: Widow of P.de Huete*, 1583. 268p.;8vo. A reissue of 1st, Valencia, 1582, edn with altered imprint date on t.p. Ind.aur.106.039; Palau 13079n.   583/4

—[Anr edn]. *Saragossa: J.de Alterach*, 1583. 334p.;8vo. Ind.aur.106.040; Sánchez (Aragon) 596; Palau 13082.   583/5

Apollonius, Levinus. Dritte Theil der Newen Welt des Peruvischen Königreichs . . . Item, Von der frantzosen Schiffarth in der Landtschafft Floridam, und ihrer schröcklichen Niderlag die sie von den Spaniern im Jar M.D.LXV. . . . erlitten . . . verteutschet durch Nicolaum Höniger. *Basel: S.Henricpetri*, 1583. ccccvi p.;map;fol. Transl. from *De Peruviae regionis inventione*, 1st publ., Antwerp, 1566. Continues, as designated, G.Benzoni's *Erste & Ander Theil der Newen Weldt*, Basel 1582. Sabin 1762a (& 1762); Medina (BHA) 200n (I:318-319); Ind.aur.

106.494. DLC, NN-RB, RPJCB; BL, Berlin: StB.   583/6

Bazán, Alvaro de, marqués de Santa Cruz. Gründlicher Bericht, wellicher gestalt . . . durch . . . Don Alvaro de Baçan . . . die Insul Terzera . . . eingenommen. *Munich: A. Berg*, 1583. [24]p.;4to. Transl. from the *Relacion* below. Ind.aur.111.329.   583/7

_____. Narratio, sive quam vocant relatio trium nuntiorum, de capta Tercera . . .`. ex hispanico idiomate, ad verbum versa. [*Nuremberg?* 1583?]. 7 lvs;8vo. Transl. from following item. Includes, lvs 6v-7v, a 'Relatio Dominici de Campi' with ref. to 'exquirendum de navibus Indiae Occidentalis'. Sabin 76758. BL. 583/8

_____. Relacion de la jornada, expugnacion, y conquista de la isla Tercera . . . que hizo don Albaro de Baçan . . . a onze de Agosto, mil y quinientos y ochenta y tres. *Valencia: 1583.* [24]p.;illus.;4to. Describes final suppression of Portuguese resistance to Philip II's claims to Portuguese throne; cf.entries for Bazan under year 1582. Sabin 76759; Ind.aur.111.327; Palau 257221. InU-L; Oxford: Bodl.   583/9

—[Anr edn]. [*Milan? 1583?*]. 12 numb.lvs;fol. Typographically Italian in appearance, the possibility that this was printed at Milan, a center of Spanish influence, is strong. Sabin 76759; Palau 257221n. BL.   583/10

—[Anr edn]. Relacion de lo sucedido en la isla de Tercera. *Alcalá de Henares: S.Martínez*, 1583. 4 lvs;4to. Sabin 69203; Palau 257218.
583/11

—[Anr edn of preceding]. *Saragossa: J.Soler,for D.de Fuentes*, 1583. 2 lvs;fol. Sánchez (Aragon) 613; Palau 257218.   583/12

—[Anr edn]. Successo dela jornada, expugnacion, y conquista dela Tercera. [*Lisbon?* 1583?]. [24]p.;4to. Sabin 76762; Ind.aur. 111.330; Palau 257219. DLC; BL.   583/13

Bodin, Jean. Methodus ad facilem historiarum cognitionem: accurate denuo recusus. [*Lyons?*] *J.Mareschal*, 1583. 396p.;8vo. 1st publ., Paris, 1566. Baudrier (Lyons) XI:457; Ind.aur.120.823; Adams (Cambr.) B2244. CtY, DFo, ICN, InU-L, NNC; BL, BN.
583/14

_____. Les six livres de la Republique . . . Ensemble une apologie de René Herpin. *Paris: J.DuPuys*, 1583. 1060p.;8vo. 1st publ., Paris, 1576. Ind.aur.120.824; Adams (Cambr.) 2238; Shaaber B512. DLC, MiU, PU; BL, BN.
583/15

Bretonnayau, René. La génération de l'homme. *Paris: A.L'Angelier*, 1583. 186 numb.lvs;4to. Includes poem with ref. to 'peuple américain'. LeMoine 18; Ind.aur.124.923. BN, Vienna: BN.   583/16

Carleill, Christopher. A discourse upon the extended voyage to the hethermoste partes of America. [*London: 1583*]. [16]p.;4to. On advantages for the English & the Muscovy Company from northwest exploration & establishing a colony on North American coast. Sabin 10900; JCB (3) I:283. RPJCB.   583/17

Casas, Bartolomé de las, Bp of Chiapa. The Spanish colonie, or Briefe chronicle of the acts and gestes of the Spaniardes in the West Indies, called the newe World, for the space of xl yeeres . . . and now first translated into English, by M.M.S. *London: T.Dawson,for W.Brome*, 1583. 74 lvs;4to. Transl. from Antwerp, 1579, French translation, in turn transl. from the *Brevíssima relación*, 1st publ., Seville, 1552, with other material drawn from Las Casas' writings. Sabin 11287; Medina (BHA) 1085n (II:474-475); Streit I:141; STC 4739; Church 130; JCB (3) I:295. CSmH, CtY, DFo, ICN, MnU-B, NN-RB, PU, RPJCB; BL.
583/18

Cecchi, Giovanni Maria. Lezione o Vero cicalmente di Bartolino dal Canto de' Bischeri [pseud.] sopra'l sonetto Passere e beccafichi magri arrosto. *Florence: D.Manzani*, 1583. 59p.;8vo. Includes account of Columbus. CtY, DFo; BL.   583/19

Cesalpino, Andrea. De plantis libri xvi. *Florence: G.Marescotti*, 1583. 621p.;4to. In bk 5, chapt.22 describes 'Piper Indicum' (Siliquastrum), chapt.27 'Sarzaparilla'. In bk 8, chapt.43 discusses 'Tornabona' (tobacco). All are identified as American in origin. Pritzel 1640; Adams (Cambr.) C20; Arents (Add.) 73. DNAL, ICJ, MH-A, NN-A, PPC, RPB; BL, BN.   583/20

[**Copie d'une lettre missive** envoyée aux gouverneurs de la Rochelle, par les capitaines des galleres de France, sur la victoire qu'ils ont obtenue contre les Mores et sauvages faisant le voyage de l'isle de Floride, et du Bresil. Ensemble les manières de vivres . . . des sauvages. *La Rochelle: J.Portau*, 1583]. 1st publ., Paris, 1565, under title *Coppie d'une lettre venant de la Floride*. Description conjectured from undated edn with imprint 'suivant la coppie imprimée à la Rochelle par

Jean Porteau'. Cf.Sabin 24855; cf.Borba de Moraes I:176; Atkinson (Fr.Ren.) 294. 583/21

Crescenzi, Pietro de. New Feldt und Ackerbaw. *Frankfurt a.M.: P.Schmid,for S.Feyerabend*, 1583. 566p.;illus.;fol. Contains 2 chapts on tobacco, taken from M.Sebisch's translation of C.Estienne's *L'agriculture*, publ., Strassburg, 1579, as *Siben Bücher von dem Feldbau*. Arents (Add.) 41. MH, NN-A.
583/22

Dodoens, Rembert. Stirpium historiae pemptades sex. *Antwerp: C.Plantin*, 1583. 860p.; illus.;8vo. Definitive edn of Dodoens's writings, in part incorporating earlier works and refs to numerous American plants. Pritzel 2350; Nissen (Bot.) 517; Bibl.belg.,1st ser., IX,D117; Adams (Cambr.) D722; Arents (Add.) 74. CU, CtY-M, DNLM, ICJ, MH-A, MiU, NN-RB, PPAN, RPB; BL, BN. 583/23

Du Bartas, Guillaume de Salluste, seigneur. Les oeuvres . . . Reveuës & augmentées par l'autheur. En ceste derniere edition ont esté adjoustez commentaires sur la Sepmaine. *Paris: J.Février*, 1583. 415 numb. lvs; illus.;12mo. 1st publ. with Simon Goulart's commentaries, Geneva, 1581. Holmes (Du Bartas) I:70-71; Jones (Goulart) 20f. Paris: Ste Geneviève. 583/24

___[Anr issue]. *Paris: P.Huet*, 1583. Holmes (Du-Bartas) I:71; Jones (Goulart) 20d. MdBP; BN.
583/25

___. Commentaires et annotations sur la Sepmaine [par Simon Goulart]. *Paris: P.Chevillot,for A.L'Angelier*, 1583. 346 numb.lvs;4to. 1st publ. in this form, including text of *La Sepmaine* itself, Geneva, 1581. In verse. Holmes (DuBartas) I:72 no.14; Jones (Goulart) 20e; Adams (Cambr.) D967. BL, BN.
583/26

___[Anr issue]. [*Paris: P.Chevillot,for*] *T.Jouan*, 1583. Jones (Goulart) 20e(n). Zurich: StB.
583/27

___[Anr edn]. *Paris: P.L'Angelier*, 1583. 432 numb.lvs;12mo. Adams (Cambr.) D968. CSmH, ICN, MH, PPL; Cambridge: Magdalene. 583/28

___. Hebdomas . . . a Gabriele Lermeo . . . latinitate donatum. *Paris: M.Gadouleau*, 1573 [i.e.,1583]. Transl. from author's *La sepmaine*, 1st publ., Paris, 1578. Holmes (Du Bartas) I:107 no.2. MH; BL, BN. 583/29

___. La sepmaine, ou Creation du monde . . . Avec commentaires, argumens, & annota-

tions, par Simon Goulard. *Paris: M.Gadouleau*, 1583. 452p.;4to. 1st publ., Geneva, 1581, in this version. In verse. Holmes (Du Bartas) I:71 no.11; Rothschild 3269. DLC, MH; BN. 583/30

Du Verdier, Antoine. Les diverses leçons . . . suivans celles de Pierre Messie . . . Augmentée & revue par l'auteur en ceste troisieme edition. *Paris: N.Bonfons*, 1583. 365 numb. lvs;12mo. 1st publ., Lyons, 1577. Cf.Sabin 48245. DLC, NjP. 583/31

___[Anr edn]. *Paris: C.Micard*, 1583. 410 numb. lvs;8vo. MnU-B. 583/32

Estienne, Charles. L'agricoltura et casa di villa . . . nuovamente tradotta dal cavaliere Hercole Cato. *Turin: Heirs of N.Bevilacqua,for G.B.Ratteri*, 1583. 511p.;8vo. 1st publ. in Italian, Venice, 1581. Thiébaud (La chasse) 358. CU, ICU, MH. 583/33

___. L'agriculture et maison rustique . . . Edition derniere et augmentée de beaucoup. *Paris: J.DuPuys*, 1583. 294 (i.e., 394) numb. lvs;illus.;4to. 1st publ., Paris, 1567. Thiébaud (La chasse) 348. BN. 583/34

___[Anr edn]. *Lyons: [Printed for] J.DuPuys,at Paris*, 1583. 390 numb.lvs;illus.;4to. Thiébaud (La chasse) 348; Baudrier (Lyons) I:367; Arents (Add.) 33. DFo, NN-A. 583/35

Franck, Sebastian. Chronica, tytboeck en gheschiet bibel, van aenbegin der werelt tot . . . M.D.XXXVI. *Delft: A.Henricszoon*, 1583. 3 pts;fol. 1st publ. in Dutch, [Antwerp? 1550?], under title *Wereltboeck*. Belg.typ. (1541-1600) I:1180; JCB (3) I:296-298. RPJCB, ViHarEM; Brussels: BR. 583/36

Gambara, Lorenzo. De navigatione Christophori Columbi libri quattuor. *Rome: B.Bonfadini & T.Diani*, 1583. 64 numb.lvs;illus., map;4to. 1st publ., Rome, 1581. In verse. Sabin 26501; Adams (Cambr.) G182; JCB (3) I:298. ICN, InU-L, MH, NN-RB, RPJCB; BL, BN. 583/37

Gesner, Konrad. Bibliotheca . . . in epitome redacta . . . tertiò recognita . . . per Josiam Simlerum . . . amplificata, per Johannem Jacobum Frisium. *Zurich: C.Froschauer*, 1583. 835p.;fol. 1st publ., Zurich, 1545. Shaaber G140. DLC, IU, InU-L, MH, MiU, MnU, NN-RB, PPL; BL, BN. 583/38

___. Der erste[-ander] Theil dess köstlichen unnd theuren Schatzes Euonymi Philiatri. *St Gall: L.Straub,for J.Gessner at Zurich*, 1583. 2 pts;4to. Pt 1 1st publ. in German, Zurich,

1555; pt 2 here 1st publ., as transl. by J.J.Nüscheler from Gesner's *Euonymus . . . pars secunda*, Zurich, 1569. CtY; London: Wellcome. 583/39

Giglio, Girolamo. Nuova seconda selva di varia lettione. *Venice: F.& A.Zoppini*, 1583. 198 numb.lvs;8vo. 1st publ., Venice, 1565. Palau 167298. Madrid: BN. 583/40

Guicciardini, Francesco. La historia d'Italia. *Venice: G.Angelieri*, 1583. 488 numb.lvs;4to. 1st publ., Florence, 1561. Adams (Cambr.) G1514. InU-L, NSyU; Cambridge: Emmanuel, BN. 583/41

Heyns, Peeter. Le miroir du monde reduit premierement en rithme brabançonne . . . et maintenant tourné en prose françoise. *Antwerp: C.Plantin,for P.Galle*, 1583. 85 numb. lvs;illus.,maps;obl.4to. 1st publ., Antwerp, 1579. Cf.Sabin 31666; Koeman (Ort.) 50; Atkinson (Fr.Ren.) 50; Phillips (Atlases) 387. CSmH, DLC; BL, BN. 583/42

____. Spieghel der werelt ghestelt in ryme . . . Van nieuws oversien, ghebetert, ende vermeerdet met veel schoon caerten. *Antwerp: C.Plantin,for P. Galle*, 1583. 98 lvs;illus., maps;obl.4to. 1st publ., Antwerp, 1579. Sabin 31667; Koeman (Ort.) 49; Bibl.belg., 1st ser.,XII:H54. MiU-C; Ghent: BU. 583/43

Honter, Johannes. Rudimentorum cosmographicorum libri iii. *[Zurich: C.Froschauer]* 1583. 40 lvs;illus.,maps;8vo. 1st publ., in this version, Kronstadt, 1542. In verse. CU, DLC, NN-RB; BL, BN. 583/44

Jesuits. Letters from missions. Annuae litterae (1581) 1583. Annuae litterae . . . anni MDLXXXI. *Rome: Jesuit College*, 1583. 218p.;8vo. Includes sections on Brazilian & Mexican provinces. Sabin 1607 (& 41507); Medina (BHA) 278; Streit: I:144. MnU-B, NNH, RPJCB; BL. 583/45

Jodelle, Etienne. Oeuvres et meslanges poetiques . . . Reveuës & augmentees en ceste derniere edition. *Paris: N.Chesneau & M.Patisson*, 1583. 294 numb.lvs;12mo. 1st publ., Paris, 1574. Adams (Cambr.) J224; Shaaber J69. CLU-C, MH, NN-RB, PU-F; BL. 583/46

__[Anr issue]. *Paris: R.LeFizelier*, 1583. MH; BN. 583/47

LeRoy, Louis. De la vicissitude ou variete des choses en l'univers. *Paris: P.L'Huillier*, 1583. 255 numb.lvs;8vo. 1st publ., Paris, 1575. Atkinson (Fr.Ren.) 298. ICN, PBm; BN. 583/48

Marnix, Philippe de, seigneur de Sainte-Aldegonde. Ad potentissimos ac serenissimos reges, principes, reliquosque amplissimos christiani orbis ordines. *[Middelburg: R.Schilders]* 1583. [31]p.;4to. On p.[10] & [25] are refs to Spanish domination in the Indies & America. In addition to the translations described below, according to Hakluyt an Italian translation also appeared that today is untraced. Knuttel 626; Adams (Cambr.) A136. RPJCB; BL, Rome: BN. 583/49

____. Ernstighe vermaninghe vanden standt ende gheleghentheyt der christenheyt. *[Middelburg? R.Schilders?]* 1583. 28 lvs;4to. Transl. from author's *Ad potentissimos ac serenissimos reges* above. Knuttel 627. The Hague: KB. 583/50

____. A pithie and most earnest exhortation, concerning the estate of Christiandome. *Antwerp [i.e.,London: R.Waldegrave]*: 1583. Transl. from author's *Ad potentissimos ac serenissimos reges* above. STC 17450.7 (formerly 5147). CSmH, DFo; BL. 583/51

____. Remonstrance serieuse sur l'etat de la chrestienté . . . Par un gentil-homme allemand. *[Middelburg? R.Schilders?]* 1583. 30 lvs;4to. Transl. from author's *Ad potentissimos ac serenissimos reges* above. Knuttel 628. ICN; The Hague: KB. 583/52

Mattioli, Pietro Andrea. Commentarii in vi. libros Pedacii Dioscoridis . . . De medica materia. *Venice: Heirs of V.Valgrisi*, 1583. 2v.; illus.,port.;fol. 1st publ., Venice, 1554. Moranti (Urbino) 2137. DNAL, MH-A, MoSB; Urbino: BU. 583/53

Mexía, Pedro. Les diverses leçons . . . mises en françois par Claude Gruget . . . augmentées de trois dialogues. *Paris: N.Bonfons*, 1583. 616 numb.lvs;16mo. 1st publ. in this version with supplementary dialogues, Paris, 1556. Palau 167321n. DFo; BL, BN. 583/54

____. Vite di tutti gl'imperadori romani . . . da m. Lodovico Dolce nuovamente tradotte & ampliate , . . Sesta impressione. *Venice: [G. A.Rampazetto]* 1583. 547 numb.lvs;4to. 1st publ. with life of Charles V by Dolce & refs to Cortés & Spanish overseas ventures, Venice, 1561. Palau 167354; Moranti (Urbino) 2205. ICN, MH, WU; BL, Urbino: BU. 583/55

Neander, Michael. Chronicon. *[Eisleben? U. Gubisius?]* 1583. 184 numb.lvs;8vo. 1st publ.,

Eisleben, 1582. Adams (Cambr.) N107. Cambridge: UL. 583/56

____. Orbis terrae partium succincta explicatio. *Eisleben: U.Gubisius*, 1583. 212 lvs;8vo. In section 'Oceani insulae' is a description of the New World, with discussion of historical source material. Adams (Cambr.) N112. InU-L; BL. 583/57

Ortelius, Abraham. Le miroir du monde. *Antwerp:* 1583. See entry under Heyns, Peeter, above.

____. Spieghel der werelt. *Antwerp:* 1583. See entry under Heyns, Peeter, above.

Peckham, Sir George. A true reporte of the late discoveries, and possession, taken in the right of the Crowne of Englande, of the Newfound Landes: by . . . Sir Humfrey Gilbert. *London: J.C[harlewood]. for J.Hinde*, 1583. [55]p.;4to. For variant states see the STC. Sabin 97145 (& 59498); STC 19523. CSmH, CtY, DFo, ICN, MnU-B, NN-RB, PPRF; BL. 583/58

Ramusio, Giovanni Battista, comp. Secondo volume delle Navigationi et viaggi . . . hora in questa nuova editione accresciuto. *Venice: The Giuntas*, 1583. 256 numb.lvs;illus.,maps; fol. Contains American material not found in prior edns publ. earlier at Venice in 1558 & 1573. 'Navigatione di Sebastiano Cabota': lvs 211-219. See also G.B.Parks, 'The contents and sources of Ramusio's *Navigationi*', New York Public Library *Bulletin*, L (1955) 279-313. Sabin 67738; Streit I:143; Adams (Cambr.) R139; Shaaber R19. CtY, DLC, MH, NN-RB, PU, RPJCB; BL. 583/59

Rauwolf, Leonhard. Aigentliche Beschreibung der Raiss, so er . . . inn die Morgenländer . . . selbs vorbracht. *Lauingen: L. Reinmichel,for G.Willer [at Augsburg]* 1583. 4 pts;illus.;4to. A reissue of the publisher's 1582 edn with addition of a 'Vierte Thail etlicher aussländischer Kreüter', comprising illustrations of plants described in the text. This pt is also found bound with copies of both prior 1582 edns. Pritzel 7430; Nissen (Bot.) 1587; Hunt (Bot.) 146. CU, CtY, DNLM, MH-A, MnU-B, NN-RB, PPAmP; BL, BN. 583/60

Reisch, Gregor. Margarita filosofica . . . ab Orontio Finaeo locupletata. *Basel: S.Henricpetri*, 1583. 1403p.;map;4to. 1st publ., Strassburg, 1503. Sabin 69131; Ferguson (Reisch)

215-216; Adams (Cambr.) R338. BL, BN. 583/61

Rivadeneira, Pedro de. Vida del padre Ignacio de Loyola . . . aora nuevamente traduzida en romance, y añadida por el mismo autor. *Madrid: A.Gómez*, 1583. 304 numb. lvs;4to. 1st publ. in Latin, Naples, 1572. Backer VI:1726; Pérez Pastor (Madrid) 191; Palau 266222. CtY, MH. 583/62

San Román de Ribadeneyra, Antonio de. Consuelo de penitentes, o Mesa franca. *Salamanca: A.de Terranova y Neyla*, 1583. 2v.; 8vo. In v.2 is a description of the earliest missionaries in Mexico. Medina (BHA) 280; Streit II:1018; Palau 293608-609. Seville: BU. 583/63

Silva, Joanna de Saavedra de. Papel del pleyto entre Dona Joanna de Silva, viuda . . . vezina de Los Reyes en el Pyro, con Alvaro Ruyz de Navamuel, sobre los reditos de la Secretaria de governación del Peru. *Madrid:* 1583. 14p.;fol. On claims to right of appointment of chief notary for Peru, and revenues therefrom, as widow of Juan de Saavedra & sister of Alonso Fernández de Córdova— cf. Medina (BHA) 422, 424, 425 & 431. Maggs: Cat.496:259. 583/64

Tasso, Torquato. Il Goffredo. *Venice: F.dei Franceschi*, 1583. 2 pts;4to. 1st publ. with American refs, Parma, 1581. In verse. Racc. Tassiana 166; Adams (Cambr.) T239; Shaaber T83. CtY, MH, PU; BL, Bergamo: BC. 583/65

Torquemada, Antonio de. Hexameron, ou Six journees contenans plusieurs doctes discours . . . Fait en hespagnol . . . et mis en françois par Gabriel Chappuys. *Paris: P.Brachonier*, 1583. 319 numb.lvs;12mo. 1st publ. in French, Lyons, 1579. BL, BN. 583/66

Vairo, Leonardo. De fascino libri tres. *Paris: N.Chesneau*, 1583. 275p.;4to. In describing superstitions of West Indian natives, quotes Monardes on use of tobacco. Adams (Cambr.) V15. Cambridge: Emmanuel, BN. 583/67

____. Trois livres de charmes . . . faicts en latin . . . et mis en françois par Julian Baudon. *Paris: N.Chesneau*, 1583. 553p.;8vo. Transl. from preceding item. Adams (Cambr.) V17; Arents (Add.) 77; Shaaber V3. ICN, MH, NN-A, PU; BL, BN. 583/68

Venegas de Busto, Alejo. Primera parte de las diferencias de libros que hay en el universo.

Valladolid: D.Fernández de Córdova, for J. Boyer, 1583. 483p.;8vo. 1st publ., Toledo, 1540. Sabin 98502n; Alcocer (Valladolid) 306; Palau 351612. BL.   583/69

1584

Apianus, Petrus. Cosmographia, sive Descriptio universi orbis, Petri Apiani & Gemmae Frisii . . . iam demum integretati suae restituta. Adiecti´ sunt alii, tum Gemmae Frisii, tum aliorum auctorum eius argumenti tractatus ac libelli varii. *Antwerp: J.Verwithagen*, 1584. 478p.;illus.,map;4to. An enlarged Latin edn, with translations of American material found in 1575 Spanish edn, etc. Ortroy (Apian) 60; Bibl.belg.,1st ser.,I:A42; Ind.aur.106.466; Adams (Cambr.) A1285; JCB (3) I:299. MH, RPJCB; BL, BN.   584/1

___[Anr issue]. *Antwerp: J.Verwithagen, for J. Bellère*, 1584. Ortroy (Apian) 59; Bibl.belg., 1st ser.,I:A42n; Ind.aur.106.467; Adams (Cambr.) A1286; JCB (3) I:299. RPJCB; BL, Munich: StB.   584/2

___[Anr issue]. *Antwerp: J.Verwithagen, for A. Coninx*, 1584. Sabin 1751; Ortroy (Apian) 61; Ind.aur.106.468; Adams (Cambr.) A1287. Cambridge: UL, BN.   584/3

___. Cosmographie, ou Description du monde universel, par Pierre Apian et Gemma Frison . . . Traduite nouvellement de latin. *Antwerp: A.Coninx*, 1584. 333p.;illus.,map;4to. 1st publ. in this enlarged French version, Antwerp, 1581. Ortroy (Apian) 62; Ind.aur. 106.469; Adams (Cambr.) A1288. BL, BN.
                                    584/4

Bonardo, Giovanni Maria, conte. La grandezza, larghezza, e distanza di tutte le sfere . . . Con alcune chiare annotationi . . . di Luigi Grotto. *Venice: F.& A.Zoppini*, 1584. 134 numb.lvs;8vo. The earliest edn to contain Groto's annotations, mentioning America in ch.13 & in ch.19 citing 'corso del mare verso ponente' as aiding voyages to West Indies. Ind.aur.121.661. DLC, NN-RB, WU; London: Wellcome.   584/5

Brant, Sebastian. Navis stultorum: oft, Der sotten schip. *Antwerp: J.van Ghelen*, 1584. 234p.;illus.;4to. Transl. by Jan van Ghelen from Brant's *Narrenschiff*, 1st publ., Basel, 1494. Ind.aur.123.753; JCB (3) I:299. DLC, RPJCB; BL, Brussels: BR.   584/6

Bruno, Giordano. La cena de le Ceneri, des-

critta in cinque dialogi. [*London: J.Charlewood*] 1584. 128p.;8vo. An exposition of Copernican views, with ref. to Columbus in 1st dialog as fulfilling Seneca's prophecy in his *Medea* (cf.Dodoens's *De sphaera* of this year below). STC 3935; Ind.aur.125.906; Woodfield 7; Adams (Cambr.) B2942. CLSU, MH; BL, BN.   584/7

___. Spaccio de la bestia trionfante . . . Diviso in tre dialogi. *Parigi* [i.e.,*London: J.Charlewood*]: 1584. 261p.;8vo. In the 2d pt of the 3rd dialog is a ref. to the newly discovered New World, citing its ancient records as undermining Biblical accounts of the Flood. STC 3940; Adams (Cambr.) B2954; Ind. aur.125.903; Woodfield 11. CtY-M, MH; BL, BN.   584/8

Caradog, of Llancarvan. The historie of Cambria, now called Wales . . . written in the Brytish language above two hundred yeares past: translated . . . by H.Lhoyd . . . Corrected, augmented, and continued . . . by David Powel. *London: R.Newbery & H.Denham*, 1584. 401p.;4to. In life of David ap Owen is an account (p.228-229) of Madoc's voyage to Florida, antedating Spanish discoveries. Sabin 40914; Ind.aur.131.901; STC 4606; Shaaber C124. CSmH, CtY, DLC, ICN, InU-L, MH, MiU-C, MnU-B, PU, RPJCB; BL.   584/9

Cardano, Girolamo. Les livres . . . intitules De la subtilité . . . traduits . . . par Richard le Blanc. *Paris: P.Cavellat*, 1584. 478 numb. lvs.;8vo. 1st publ. in French, Paris, 1556. Ind.aur.132.124; Shaaber C132. MH, PU.
                                    584/10

___[Anr issue]. *Paris: R.LeFizelier*, 1584. IU, MH-A, NNE, PPC.   584/11

___[Anr issue]. *Paris: J.Houzé*, 1584. Ind.aur. 132.124. MH; BN.   584/12

___[Anr issue]. *Paris: A.L'Angelier*, 1584. Ind. aur.132.124.   584/13

Caro, Annibale. De le lettere familiari. *Mantua: F.Osanna*, 1584. 2v.;12mo. 1st publ., Venice, 1572. Ind.aur.132.480. BN.   584/14

Chaves, Jerónimo de. Chronographia o Repertorio de los tiempos. *Seville: F.Díaz, for F.de Magariño*, 1584. 262 numb.lvs;illus.,port.; 4to. 1st publ., Seville, 1548. Medina (BHA) 282; Escudero (Seville) 733; JCB AR20:1584. CtY, MH, PPC, RPJCB; BL.   584/15

Cooper, Thomas, Bp of Winchester. Thesaurus linguae romanae & britannicae. *Lon-*

don: H.Bynneman, 1584. [1784]p.;fol. 1st publ., London, 1565. STC 5689. CSmH, CtY, DFo, ICN, InU-L, MH, MiU, NNC, RPB; BL. 584/16

Cortés, Martĭn. The arte of navigation . . . Englyshed out of Spanishe by Richard Eden, and now newly corrected and amended in divers places. *London: Widow of R.Jug*, 1584. 82 numb.lvs;illus.,map;4to. 1st publ. in English, London, 1561. Sabin 16967n; STC 5801. CSmH, DFo, NN-RB. 584/17

Dictionaire françois-latin . . . recueilli des observations de plusieurs hommes doctes, entre autres de m. Nicot. *Paris: J.DuPuys*, 1584. 771p.;fol. 1st publ., Paris, 1573. BN. 584/18

Dioscorides, Pedanius. Acerca de la material medicinal . . . traduzido de lengua griega . . . & illustrado con . . . substantiales annotationes, y con las figuras de innumeras plantas . . . por el doctor Andres de Laguna. *Salamanca*: 1584. fol. 1st publ. with Laguna's annotations, Salamanca, 1563. Palau 74023n. 584/19

Discours au Roi Henri III, sur les moyens de diminuer l'Espagnol. [*Paris?*] 1584. Describes, *inter alia*, measures for attacking the Spanish silver fleet. Reprinted in Simon Goulart's *Premier Recueil*, [Geneva?], 1590. 584/19a

Dodoens, Rembert. De sphaera, sive De astronomiae et geographiae principiis cosmographica isagoge. *Antwerp: C.Plantin*, 1584. 109p.;illus.;8vo. 1st publ., Antwerp, 1548, under title *Cosmographica . . . isagoge;* here rev. & enl. by the author, with ref. to America on p.70. Appended is a new description of the habitable world (p.105-109) by Cornelius Valerius, with refs to America & Vespucci, whilst a final note by Dodoens quotes Seneca's *Medea* as referring to the New World, perhaps derived from Egnatio Danti's annotation to J. de Sacro Bosco's *La sfera*, Florence, 1572. Cf. also Ferdinand Columbus's annotated copy of Seneca's works in the Bibliotheca Colombina. Bibl.belg.,1st ser.,IX:D99. MH, MnU-B, NN-RB; BL, BN. 584/20

Du Bartas, Guillaume de Salluste, seigneur. Commentaires et annotations sur La sepmaine [par Simon Goulart]. *Paris: A. L'Angelier*, 1584. 434 numb.lvs;12mo. 1st publ. in this form, including text itself of *La sepmaine*, Geneva, 1581. In verse. Holmes (DuBartas) I:72 no.15; Jones (Goulart) 20(g), MH; Paris: Arsenal. 584/21

———. Hebdomas, opus gallicum a Gabriele Lermeo . . . latinitate donatum. *Paris: M.Gadoulleau*, 1584. 102 numb.lvs;12mo. 1st publ. in Latin, Paris, 1583. Holmes (DuBartas) I:107 no.2n. MH, NNC; BL, BN. 584/22

———. Premier[-septieme] jour de la Sepmaine . . . illustré de commentaires de Pantaleon Thévenin. *Paris: D.Cotinet*, 1584. 732p.; illus.;4to. The earliest edn to contain Thévenin's commentaries; 1st publ., Paris, 1578. BN (t.p. wanting). 584/23

———. La seconde sepmaine ou Enfance du monde. *Paris: P.L'Huillier*, 1584. 102 numb. lvs;4to. In verse. Includes numerous refs to New World, esp. in section 'Les colonies'. Holmes (DuBartas) I:84 no.1a; Adams (Cambr.) D962. MH, OU, RPJCB; BL, BN. 584/24

—[Anr edn]. *Douai: J.Bogard*, 1584. CtY. 584/25

—[Anr edn]. Reveüe par l'autheur. *Paris: P. L'Huillier*, 1584. 104 numb.lvs;4to. Holmes (DuBartas) I:84 no.1b. NcU; BL, BN. 584/26

—[Anr edn]. Troisième edition. *Antwerp: J. Henric* [i.e., *La Rochelle? P.Haultin?*] 1584. 194p.;8vo. On false imprint, see Anne Rouzet, *Dictionnaire des imprimeurs . . . de la Belgique* (Nieuwkoop, 1975) 92; cf.1588 Haultin edn. Holmes (DuBartas) I:84 no.3a. MH; Tours: BM. 584/27

———. La sepmaine ou Creation du monde . . . Avec commentaires, argumens, & annotations. *Paris: P.L'Huillier*, 1584. 1st publ. in this version, Paris, 1583. In verse. Holmes (DuBartas) I:72 no.17. 584/28

Du Pinet, Antoine, sieur de Norey. L'histoire des plantes, traduicte du latin . . . à laquelle sont adjoustees celles des simples aromatiques, animaux à quatre pieds, oiseaux, poissons, serpens, ensemble la distillation, par Geoffroy Linocier. *Paris: C.Macé*, 1584. 943p.;illus.; 16mo. The *Histoire des plantes* itself was transl. from Du Pinet's Lyons, 1561, *Historia plantarum;* of the further sections, that on aromatic herbs is drawn from L'Ecluse, Garcia d'Orta & N.Monardes, whilst the others derive from Gesner & P.A.Mattioli. Pritzel 2539n; Adams (Cambr.) L734. DNLM, MH; BL, BN. 584/29

Du Verdier, Antoine. Les diverses leçons . . . suivans celles de Pierre Messie. *Lyons: B. Honorat*, 1584. 478p.;port.;8vo. 1st publ., Lyons, 1577. Sabin 48245n. BN. 584/30

__[Anr edn]. *Paris: N.Bonfons,* 1584. 364 numb.lvs;12mo. Anr issue of bookseller's 1583 edn, with altered imprint date? BN. 584/31

__[Anr edn]. *Paris: C.Micard,* 1584. 410 numb. lvs;16mo. Anr issue of bookseller's 1583 edn with altered imprint date? Adams (Cambr.) D1216. Cambridge: Emmanuel. 584/32

Factor, Nicolás. Testimonios de la santidad,y bienaventuranza del Padre Fr. Luis Bertran. *Valencia: Heirs of J.Navarro,* 1584. 8vo. Bertrán's career included missionary activities in the New World, esp. Colombia. Medina (BHA) 283. 584/33

Falloppius, Gabriel. Opera . . . omnia. *Venice: F.Valgrisi,* 1584. 469 numb.lvs;illus.;fol. Includes the author's *De morbo gallico,* 1st publ., Padua, 1564. DNLM. 584/34

__[Anr edn]. *Frankfurt a.M.: Heirs of A.Wechel,* 1584. 848p.;illus.;fol. Shaaber F32. CtY, DNLM, ICJ, MnU, PU, RPB. 584/35

Ferri, Alfonso. Ein new Artzeneybuch: darinnen die newe erfundene heilsame, und bewerte Artzney . . . so nicht allein die frantzosen oder bösen Blatteren, sondern auch andere sorgliche schwere Krannckheit. *Dresden: [G.Bergen]* 1584. 132 numb.lvs;illus., port.;4to. 1st publ. in German, Strassburg, 1541. Includes section on 'Gebrauch und Wirckung des indianischen Holtzes, Guaiacum oder frantzosen Holtz genennet'. Benzing (Ryff) 111. DNLM; BL. 584/36

Fracastoro, Girolamo. Opera omnia . . . Ex tertia editione. *Venice: Heirs of L.Giunta,* 1584. 213 numb.lvs;port.;4to. 1st publ in coll.edn, Venice, 1555; includes the author's *De contagione* (1st publ., Venice, 1546) and his *Syphilidis* (1st publ., Verona, 1530). Baumgartner (Fracastoro) 34; Waller 3169. CtY, DNLM, ICU, MnS, NNNAM, PPPH; London: Wellcome, BN. 584/37

Gesner, Konrad. Epistolarum medicinalium . . . liber quartus. *Wittenberg: S.Gronenberg,*1584. 140 numb.lvs;4to. 1st publ., Zurich, 1577. DNLM; BL. 584/38

Gómara, Francisco López de. Histoire generalle des Indes Occidentales, et terres neuves . . . Augmentée en cette cinquiesme edition de la description de la nouvelle Espagne, et de la grande ville de Mexicque, autrement nommee, Tenuctilan. Composée en espagnol . . . et traduite . . . par . . . Mart. Fumee. *Paris: M.Sonnius,* 1584. 485 numb.lvs; 8vo. 1st publ. in French, Paris, 1568. Sabin 27748;

Medina (BHA) 159n (I:272); Wagner (SW) 2jj; Atkinson (Fr. Ren.) 304; Streit II:1030; Palau 141160; JCB(3) I:300. CU, NN-RB, RPJCB; Oxford: Bodl., BN. 584/39

Jesuits. Letters from missions. Annuae litterae (1582) 1584. Annuae litterae . . . anni .M.D.LXXXII. *Rome: Jesuit College,* 1584. 300p.;8vo. Includes sections on Mexican and Peruvian missions. Cf.Sabin 1607; Streit I:147. NNH; BL. 584/40

La Croix du Maine, François Grudé, sieur de. Premier volume de la Bibliotheque du Sieur de la Croix-du-Maine. Qui est un catalogue general de toutes sortes d'autheurs, qui ont escrit en françois depuis cinq cents& plus. *Paris: A.L'Angelier,* 1584. 558p.;fol. No more published. Included are works by or translated by French writers relating to the New World. Rothschild 2515; Shaaber G 351. CU, DLC, MH, MnU, NN-RB, PU; BL, BN. 584/41

La Popelinière, Lancelot Voisin, sieur de. L'amiral de France. Et par occasion, de celuy des autres nations. *Paris: T.Périer,* 1584. 92 numb.lvs;4to. Included are refs to Vespucci & Columbus. Adams (Cambr.) L200. ICN, MH, MnU-B, NN-RB; BL, BN. 584/42

LeRoy, Louis. De la vicissitude ou variete des choses en l'univers. *Paris: P.L'Huillier,* 1584. 255 numb.lvs;8vo. 1st publ., Paris, 1575; here a reissue of the 1583 edn with imprint date & t.p. slightly altered. Atkinson (Fr.Ren.) 298n. NNC, RPB; BL, BN. 584/43

Lucidarius. M.Elucidarius. Von allerhand Geschöpffen Gottes . . . und wie alle Creaturen geschaffen seind auff Erden. *Frankfurt a.M.: Heirs of C.Egenolff,for A.Lonicer, J.Cnipius & P.Steinmeyer,* 1584. [102]p.; illus.,map;4to. 1st publ., Strassburg, [ca. 1535]. Schorbach (Lucidarius) 63. Strasbourg: BU. 584/44

Marnix, Philippe de, seigneur de Sainte-Aldegonde. Ad potentissimos ac serenissimos reges, principes, reliquosque amplissimos christiani orbis ordines . . . Germani cuisdam nobilis et patriae amantis viri commonefactio. *[Middelburg? R.Schilders?]* 1584. [31]p.;4to. 1st publ., [Middelburg], 1583. *Primo Catalogo collettivo delle biblioteche italiane* (Rome, 1962) 1.7667. Rome: BN. 584/45

Martí, Luis. Primera parte de la historia del bienaventurado padre Luys Bertran . . . Compuesta en octava rima. *Valencia: V.de*

Miravet, in shop of Heirs of J. Navarro, for sale by M. de Esparza, 1584. 144 numb.lvs;8vo. Bertrán's career included missionary work in the New World, esp. Colombia. Medina (BHA) 284; Palau 153304 (cf. 153303, an apparent ghost). NNH. 584/46

Mexía, Pedro. Les diverses leçons . . . avec trois dialogues, mises en français par Claude Gruget . . . augmentees . . . de la suite d'icelles, faite par Antoine Verdier. *Lyons: B. Honorat*, 1584. 2 pts;8vo. 1st publ. in this version, Lyons, 1577. Palau 167321n. BN. 584/47

___[Anr edn]. *Paris: N. Bonfons*, 1584. 616 numb.lvs;8vo. A reissue of the printer's 1583 edn. Palau 167321n. BN. 584/48

Ortelius, Abraham. Additamentum III. Theatri orbis terrarum. *Antwerp: [C. Plantin?]* 1584. 24 maps;obl.fol. Includes map showing Peru, Florida, etc. Phillips (Atlases) 389; Koeman (Ort.) 18. CU-B, DLC, ICN, MiU-C; BN. 584/49

___. Der dritte Zusatz dess Theatri oder Schawbuchs dess Erdbodems. *Antwerp: [C. Plantin?]* 1584. 24 maps;obl.fol. Cf. preceding item. Phillips. (Atlases) 3396; Koeman (Ort.) 19. DLC, InU-L; BL, Antwerp: Plantin Mus. 584/50

___. Theatrum orbis terrarum; opus nunc tertio ab ipso auctorem recognitum. *Antwerp: C. Plantin*, 1584. 2 pts;maps;obl.fol. 1st publ., Antwerp, 1570. Phillips (Atlases) 388; Koeman (Ort.) 21; Adams (Cambr.) 0337. CtY, DLC, IU, MiU-C, NN-RB, RPB; BL, Madrid: BN. 584/51

Pedraza, Juan. Relacion cierta y verdadera que trata de la victoria y toma de la Parayva, que . . . Dieto Flores de Valdés tomó con la armada . . . Cuenta como corriendo la costa del Brasil halló un puerto que los franceses tenían gomado . . . y do como se lo ganó. *[Seville: F. Maldonado, 1584]*. In verse. Palau 257227. MnU-B. 584/52

Petrarca. Francesco. Spurious and doubtful works. Chronica delle vite de pontefici. *Venice: M. Sessa*, 1584. 120 numb.lvs;8vo. 1st publ., Venice, 1507. ICN. 584/53

Peucer, Kaspar. Les devins, ou Commentaires des principales sortes de devinations . . . Nouvellement tourné en françois par S[imon]. G[oulart]. *Antwerp: A. Coninx*, 1584. 653p.; 4to. Transl. from the author's *Commentarius de praecipuis generibus divinationum* as publ., Wittenberg, 1560, the refs to east &

west voyages between Spain & West Indies appearing in bk xiv, chapt. ii. Jones (Goulart) 24 (a); Shaaber P251. CU-M, DLC, NN-RB, PU; BL, BN. 584/54

___[Anr issue]. *Lyons: B. Honorat*, 1584. Jones (Goulart) 24 (a)n. MH; BN. 584/55

Rabelais, François. Les oeuvres. *Lyons: J. Martin*, 1584. 3 pts;16mo. Includes 'Le quart livre', 1st publ., Paris, 1552. Plan (Rabelais) 109. BL, BN. 584/56

___[Anr edn]. *Lyons: J. Martin*, 1584. 2 pts;16mo. Plan (Rabelais) 110. 584/57

Relacion del negocio entre los prelados y clero dela nueva España, y el Fiscal de su Magestad, coadjubando este derecho, por lo que toca a la conservacion del Patronazgo Real, de la una parte, y las tres ordenes mendicantes dela otra. Sobre la execucion de una cedula dada en Lisboa, en veynte y nueve de Enero passado, de .1583. años. Dirigida al Arçobispo de Mexico, y los demas prelados de la nueva España, cerca de la provision de los curatos y doctrinas delos Indios. *[Madrid?1584]*. [24]p.;fol. Palau 257226 (& 257225?). BL. 584/58

Rivadeneira, Pedro de. Vida del padre Ignacio de Loyola . . . Escripta primeramente en latin. *Madrid: Widow of A. Gómez*, 1854 [i.e.,1584]. 440 numb.lvs;8vo. 1st publ. in Spanish, Madrid, 1583. Backer VI:1726-1727; Pérez Pastor (Madrid) 211; Palau 266223. 584/59

Ronsard, Pierre de. Les oeuvres. *Paris: G. Buon*, 1584. 919p.;ports;fol. 1st publ. as here collected, Paris, 1578. Tchémerzine IX:476. CtY, ICN, MH, NjP; BL, BN. 584/60

Ruscelli, Girolamo. Le imprese illustri . . . Aggiuntovi nuovam[en].te il quarto libro da Vincenzo Ruscelli. *Venice: F. de'Franceschi*, 1584. 496p.;illus.;4to. 1st publ., Venice, 1566. Adams (Cambr.) R955. CU, CtY, DLC, NN-RB; BL, BN. 584/61

Sacro Bosco, Joannes de. Sphaera . . . emendata. Eliae Vineti . . . scholia . . . ab ipso auctore restituta. *Paris: J. de Marnef & Widow of G. Cavellat*, 1584. 187p.;illus.;8vo. 1st publ. with Vinet's *Scholia*, Paris, 1556. JCB (3) I:302. ICJ, MB, RPJCB. 584/62

San José, Gabriel de. Razones informativas de la necessidad que tienen las republicas christianas de Indias, que los religiosos no desistan del cargo spiritual que han tenido dellos. *[Seville? 1584?]*. 19 lvs;fol. Said to have been written jointly by San José & Andrés de Aguirre. Medina (BHA) 426; Streit II:1029; Palau 248833. Seville: Archivo de Indias.   584/63

Soto, Domingo de.   De justitia & jure libri decem. *Venice: F.Prati*, 1584. 1006p.;4to. 1st publ., Salamanca, 1553. Palau 320160. MH-L, NNUT.   584/64

——. In quartum Sententiarum, tomus primus[-secundus]. *Venice: G.Zenari & Bros*, 1584. 2v.;4to. 1st publ., Salamanca, 1557-60. Adams (Cambr.) S1479; Palau 320177. Oxford: Bodl.   584/65

Spain. Sovereigns, etc., 1556-1598 (Philip II). Instrucion para la observacion de los eclipses de la luna . . . que su magestad manda hazer este año de mil y quinientos y ochenta y quatro en las ciudades y puertos de Españoles de las Indias. [*Madrid?* 1584]. [3]p.;fol. Cf. similar instructions of 1577 & 1582. Medina (BHA) 279; Pérez Pastor (Madrid) 202; Palau 120120. Madrid: Acad. de la Hist.   584/66

Tasso, Torquato.   Gierusalemme liberata, poema heroico. *Mantua: F.Osanna*, 1584. 236p.;4to. 1st publ. with American refs, Parma, 1581. Racc.Tassiana 167; Shaaber T84. MH, PU; BL, Bergamo: BC.   584/67

—[Anr edn]. Il Goffredo, overo Gierusalemme liberata. *Venice: A.Salicato*, 1584. 2pts;12mo. Racc.Tassiana 168. CU-S, DFo, IU, MH, NNC; BL, Bergamo: BC.   584/68

Thevet, André.   Historia dell'India America detta altramente Francia Antarctica . . . tradotta di francese . . . da m. Giuseppe Horologgi. Di novo ristampata. *Venice: The Giuntas*, 1584. 363p.;8vo. 1st publ. in Italian, Venice, 1561. A reissue of sheets of the 1561 Giolito de' Ferrari edn (including colophon dated 1561), with prelim.lvs 1-8 here cancelled by newly set text. Sabin 95337; Borba de Moraes II:305; JCB (3) I:302. DLC, NN-RB, RPJCB.
584/69

—[Anr issue]. *Venice: The Giuntas*, 1584. As preceding but with final signature also cancelled, & with colophon reading 'In Venetia appresso i Giolitti'. Sabin 95337n; Shaaber T191. CSmH, NN-RB, PU.   584/70

——. Les vrais pourtraits et vies des hommes illustres. *Paris: Widow of J.Kerver & G.Chaudière*, 1584. 664 numb.lvs;ports;fol. Includes ports & biographical sketches of Columbus, Magellan, Vespucci, Cortés, etc. Sabin 95341; Borba de Moraes II:306; Adams (Cambr.)

T625; Mortimer (France) 518. DLC, MH, MiU-C, NN-RB; BL, BN.   584/71

Wujek, Jakub.   Postilla catholica; Kazánia ná Ewángelie niedzielne. *Cracow: Siebeneycher Press*, 1584. 448 numb.lvs;fol. On verso of lf 430 is a ref. to New World. Wierzbowski 470; Shaaber W 159. PU; Warsaw: BU.   584/72

1585

Alfonce, Jean, i.e., Jean Fonteneau, known as.   Les voyages avantureux du Capitaine Jean Alfonce . . . Reveu et corrige de nouveau selon la reformation faicte du calendrier, qui fut faict l'an mil cinq cens quatre vingtz-deux. *La Rochelle: J.Portau*[ca.1585?]. 62 numb. lvs;4to. 1st publ., Poitiers, [ca.1558?]. Sabin 100833.   585/1

—[Anr issue]. *La Rochelle: [J.Portau,for] M. Villepoux* [ca.1585?]. Sabin 100832n; Atkinson (Fr.Ren.) 353; Droz (Vve Berton) 75; Ind.aur.103.633. BL.   585/2

Antist, Vicente Justiano.   Verdadera relacion de la vida y muerte del padre fray Luys Bertran. *Seville: F.Díaz*, 1585. 180 numb.lvs;8vo. 1st publ., Valencia, 1582. Medina (BHA) 287; Streit II:1034; Palau 13083. RPJCB.   585/3

Avelar, André do.   Reportorio dos tempos. *Lisbon: M.de Lyra*, 1585. 137 numb.lvs; illus.;4to. Included is a brief chapt. on New World, esp.Brazil. Anselmo 743; Ind.aur. 109.699; King Manuel 182. MH; BL, Lisbon: Ajuda.   585/4

Beccadelli, Antonio.   De dictis & factis Alphonsi regis Aragonum et Neapolis libri quatuor . . . Editae studio Davidis Chytraei. *Wittenberg: Heirs of J.Krafft*, 1585. 298p.; 4to. The earliest edn to contain David Chytraeus's 'De Caroli V. Imperatore oratio' with refs to Spanish voyages & conquests & to the Magellan circumnavigation. Sabin 58428; Ind.aur.115.387. DLC, MH, MiU; BL, Munich: StB.   585/5

Blagrave, John.   The mathematical jewel. *London: T.Dawson,for W.Venge*, 1585. 124p.;illus.;fol. On p. 113 is a ref. to the Americas (cited for its store of Guaiacum). STC 3119. CSmH, CtY, DLC, MB, MiU, PBL, RPJCB, WU;BL.   585/6

Boemus, Johann.   I costumi, le leggi, et l'usanze di tutte le genti . . . Aggiuntovi di nuovo il quarto libro, nelquale si narra i costumi, & l'usanze dell'Indie Occidentali, overo Mondo Novo; da . . . Gieronimo Giglio. *Venice: G.Cornetti*, 1585. 240 numb.lvs;8vo. 1st publ. with Giglio's 4th bk on New World, Venice, 1558. Sabin 6119n; Arents 23. DFo, ICN, MShM, MiU, NN-RB. 585/7

Bonardo, Giovanni Maria. La minera del mondo . . . Mandate in luce . . . da Luigi Grotto. *Venice: F. & A.Zoppino*, 1585. 112 numb.lvs;8vo. Described are various New World medicinal plants. Ind.aur.121.663; Arents (Add.) 79; Shaaber B598. DFo, MH, MnU-B, NN-RB, PU; London: Wellcome. 585/8

Borough, William. A discourse of the variation of the cumpas. *London: T.East,for R. Ballard*, 1585. 4to. 1st publ., London, 1581. Ind.aur.122.491; STC 3390. CtHT-W, MH; BL. 585/9

Botero, Giovanni. Epistolarum . . . Caroli cardinalis Borromaei nomine scriptarum, libri ii. Eiusdem Epistolarum theologic. liber. *Paris: T.Périer*, 1585. 140 numb.lvs;12mo. The last of the 'epistolae theologicae' describes presumed vestiges and precursors of Christianity found by early travellers in Asia and America. Ind.aur.122.690. BN. 585/10

Catholic Church. Pope, 1572-1585 (Gregorius XIII). Actes exhibez publiquement au consistoire par nostre sainct pere Gregoire pape xiii, aus ambassadeurs des rois du Jappon à Rome, le xxiii mars 1585 . . . mis en françois par m. Georges Thourin. *Liège: G.Morberius*, 1585. 20 lvs;4to. Transl. from the *Acta consistorii . . . die xiii. Martii M.D.LXXXV*, 1st publ.,, Rome, 1585, without American refs, but here including a 'Petit recueil du nouveau monde, des Indes orientales, & principalement du Jappon, par M. George Thourin'. Atkinson (Fr.Ren.) 313; Streit IV:1624. BL, BN(Thourin). 585/11

Cervantes Saavedra, Miguel de. Primera parte dela Galatea. *Alcalá de Henares: J.Gracián,for B.de Robles*, 1585. 375 numb.lvs; 8vo. The 6th bk contains a 'Canto de Calíope' which contains refs to America & writers residing there. See J.T.Medina, *Escritores americanos celebrados por Cervantes en el Canto de Calíope* (Santiago, Chile, 1926). Ríus (Cervantes) 199; García (Alcalá de Henares) 600; Palau 51928. MH, NNH, NNPM; BL, Madrid: BN. 585/12

Chaves, Jerónimo de. Chronographia, o Rep-

ertorio de los tiempos. *Pamplona:* 1585. 4to. 1st publ., Seville, 1548. Palau 67456n. 585/13

Clavius, Christoph. In Sphaeram Joannis de Sacro Bosco commentarius . . . Nunc tertio ab ipso auctore recognitus. *Rome: D.Basa,for F.Zanetti*, 1585. 483p.;illus.;4to. 1st publ., Rome, 1570. Backer II:1212. MH, NN-RB, PPF. 585/14

Clowes, William. A briefe and necessarie treatise, touching the cure of the disease called Morbus gallicus, or Lues venerea . . . Newly corrected and augmented. *London: T.East, for T.Cadman*, 1585. 64 numb.lvs;illus.;4to. 1st publ., London, 1579. STC 5448. CSmH, CtY, MBCo; BL. 585/15

Conestaggio, Girolamo Franchi di. Dell'unione del regno di Portogallo alla corona di Castiglia. *Genoa: G.Bartoli*, 1585. 264 numb.lvs;4to. In bk 1 is a mention of Columbus's discoveries and of Portuguese settlement of Brazil. Adams (Cambr.) C2502; Shaaber C626. CtY, DLC, ICN, MH, NNH, PU; BL, BN. 585/16

Costa, Christovam da. Trattato . . . della historia, natura et virtù delle droghe medicinali et altri semplici rarissimi, che vengono portati dalle India Orientali . . . Nuovamente recato dalla spagnuola. *Venice: F.Ziletti*, 1585. 342p.;illus.;4to. Transl. from da Costa's *Tractado delas drogas*, 1st publ., Burgos, 1578. Sabin 114; Pritzel 13n; Palau 1964; Moranti (Urbino) 1093; Shaaber A28. CtY, DLC, ICN, MH-G, MnU-B, NN-RB, PU, RPJCB; BL, BN. 585/17

Du Bartas, Guillaume de Salluste, seigneur. Commentaires et annotations sur La sepmaine [par Simon Goulart]. *Paris: A. L'Angelier*, 1585. 416 numb.lvs;12mo. 1st publ. in this form, including text itself of *La Sepmaine*, Geneva, 1581. In verse. Holmes (DuBartas) I:72 no.16. ICU; Grenoble: BM. 585/18

———. Les oeuvres . . . Reveuës & augmentees par l'autheur. En ceste derniere edition ont esté adjoustez commentaires sur la Sepmaine [par Simon Goulart]. *Caen: P.LeChandelier*, 1585. 1st publ. in this version, Paris, 1583. In verse. Holmes (DuBartas) I:72 no. 18. Tours: BM. 585/19

———. La sepmaine, ou Creation du monde . . . illustree des Commentaires de Pantaleon Thevenin. *Paris: J.de Marnef & the Widow of G. Cavellat*, 1585. 731p.;4to. 1st publ. with Thévenin's commentaries, Paris, 1584. In verse.

Holmes (DuBartas) I:72-73 no.19. NcD; BN.
585/20

Du Fail, Noel, seigneur de La Herissaye. Les contes et discours d'Eutrapel. *Rennes: N. Glamet,* 1585. 224p.;8vo. In chapt.'Musique d'Eutrapel' appears description of discovery of Canada by Bretons, citing Jacques Cartier; that 'De la verole' discusses its origins, mentioning Guaiacum. Rép.bibl.,XIX,73. DLC, MH, PPL; BL, BN. 585/21

Durante, Castore. Herbario nuovo . . . con figure, che rappresentano le vive piante, che nascono in tutta Europa & nell'India Orientali & Occidentali. *Rome: B.Bonfadino & T. Diani,* 1585. 492p.;illus.,ports.;fol. Pritzel 2552; Arents (Add.) 82. DNAL, ICJ, MH, MiU, NN-A; BN. 585/22

—[Anr issue]. *Rome: B.Bonfadino & T. Diani,for J.Bericchia & J. Tornieri,* 1585. Nissen (Bot.) 569; Arents (Add.) 82n. DNLM, NN-A, PPiHB; BN, Rome: BN. 585/23

Du Verdier, Antoine. La bibliotheque . . . contenant le catalogue de tous ceux qui ont escrit, ou traduict en françois . . . ensemble leurs oeuvres imprimees & non imprimees. *Lyons: J.d'Ogerolles,for B.Honorat,* 1585. 1233p.;port.;fol. Discursive accounts of French authors and their writings, including those relating to America. Baudrier (Lyons) IV:148; Rothschild 2516; Shaaber D353. DLC, NNC, PU, RPB; BL, BN. 585/24

Ercilla y Zúñiga, Alonso de. La Araucana [Primera parte]. *Madrid: Widow of A. Gómez,* 1585. 197 numb.lvs;8vo. 1st publ., Madrid, 1569. In verse. Medina (BHA) 288; Medina (Arau.) 9; Palau 80415n. MiU-C, RPJCB.
585/25

Explanatio veri ac legitimi juris, quo Serenissimus Lusitaniae rex Antonius . . . ad bellum Philippo regi Castellae, pro regni recuperatione, inferendum: una cum historica quadam enarratione rerum eo nomine gestarum vaque ad annum MDLXXXIII. *Leyden: C.Plantin,* 1585. 79p.;4to. Included are brief mentions of the West Indies. Also published in this year in Dutch, French and English: see the following entry and those beginning 'Justificatie' & 'Justification'. BL, BN. 585/26

The explanation. of the true and lawfull right and tytle of . . . Prince Anthonie . . . King of Portugall, concerning his warres, against Phillip King of Castile . . . for the recoverie of his kingdome. Translated into English and conferred with the French and Latine copie. *Leyden: C.Plantin,* 1585. 54p.;4to. Cf.preceding entry. Cf.STC 689. RPJCB; BL. 585/27

—[Anr edn]. *Leyden: C.Plantin,* 1585. 55p.; 4to. Cf.STC 689. BL. 585/28

Falloppius, Gabriel. Secreti diversi et miracolosi . . . Nuovamenti ristampati. *Venice: V.de Salvador,* 1585. 355p.;8vo. 1st publ., Venice, 1563. KU-M. 585/29

Favolius, Hugo. Theatri orbis terrarium enchiridion, minoribus tabulis per Philippum Gallaeum exaratum: et carmine heroico, ex variis geographis & poëtis collecto. *Antwerp: C.Plantin,for P.Galle,* 1585. 170p.;maps;4to. Text in Latin verse, in a free rendering of Peeter Heyns's *Spieghel der Werelt,* Antwerp, 1583. Sabin 23935; Koeman (Ort.) 51; Adams (Cambr.) F189. DLC, MH, MiU-C, MnU-B, NNH, RPJCB; BL, Vienna: NB. 585/30

Foglietta, Uberto. Historiae Genuensium libri xii. *Genoa: G.Bartoli,* 1585. 314 numb.lvs; port.;fol. In bk xi, under year 1493, ref. is made to Columbus. Adams (Cambr.) F674; Moranti (Urbino) 1503; Shaaber F338. CtY, DLC, IU, InU-L, MnU-B, NN-RB, PU; BL, Urbino: BU. 585/31

Gambara, Lorenzo. De navigatione Christophori Colombi libri quatuor. Editio copiosor. *Rome: B.Bonfadini & T.Diani,* 1585. 117p.; 8vo. 1st publ., Rome, 1581. In verse. Sabin 26502; Palau 97340n; JCB (3) I:304. CtY, DLC, InU-L, MH, NN-RB, RPJCB; BL, BN.
585/32

Gesner, Konrad. Historiae animalium liber iii, qui est de avium natura. Nunc denuo recognita. *Frankfurt a.M.: J.Wechel,for R. Cambier,* 1585. 806p.;illus.;fol. 1st publ., Zurich, 1555. Nissen (Birds) 349n; Adams (Cambr.) G536. IU, NNNAM; BL. 585/33

—[Anr issue]. In imprint the reading 'Francofurdi' rather than 'Francofurti' appears. *Frankfurt a.M.: J.Wechel,* 1585. Adams (Cambr.) G537; Moranti (Urbino) 1623. IU, NNNAM; Cambridge: Magdalene. 585/34

Genebrard, Gilbert, Abp of Aix. Chronographiae libri quatuor. *Paris: G.Gourbin,* 1585. 2 pts;fol. 1st publ., Paris, 1567. Adams (Cambr.) G399. MiU-C; Cambridge: Peterhouse. 585/35

—[Anr issue]. *Paris: M.Sonnius,* 1585. RPB; BN. 585/36

González de Mendoza, Juan, Bp. Historia de las cosas mas notables, ritos y costumbres, del gran reyno dela China . . . Con un itinerario del nuevo Mundo [por Martín Ignacio de Loyola]. *Rome: V.Accolto,for B.Grassi*, 1585. 440p.;8vo. Sabin 47826 (& 27775); Medina (BHA) 289; Wagner (SW) 7; Streit IV:1972; Palau 105495; JCB (3) I:304. CtY, DLC, ICN, InU-L, MBAt, MiU-C, MnU-B, NN-RB, PPRF, RPJCB; BL, BN. 585/37

—[Anr edn]. *Valencia: Widow of P.de Huete*, 1585. 526p.;8vo. Medina (BHA) 290; Wagner (SW) 7a; Streit IV:1973. ICN, NN-RB; BL. 585/38

Heyns, Peeter. Theatri orbis terrarum enchiridion. *Antwerp:* 1585. See Favolius, Hugo, above.

Justificatie vanden doorluchtigen Don Antonio, Coninck van Portugael . . . nopende d'oorloghe die by ghenootdruct is teghens den Coninck van Spaignien te vueren, om in zijn conincrijck wederom ghestelt te werden. Met een corte ende summiere historie van alle t'ghene dat deshalven gheschiet is, totten jare 1583. incluys. *Dordrecht: P.Verhaghen*, 1585. 31 numb.lvs;4to. Cf.Latin text with title *Explanatio . . .* of this year described above. Knuttel 722. MnU-B; BL, The Hague: KB. 585/39

Justification de Sérénissime Don Antonio roi de Portugal . . . touchant la guerre qu'il faict à Philippe roi de Castille, ses subjetz & adhérens, pour estre remis en son roiaume. *Leyden: C.Plantin*, 1585. 98p.;4to. Cf.Latin text with title *Explanatio . . .* of this year described above. Knuttel 721. DFo, MnU-B; The Hague: KB. 585/40

La Popelinière, Lancelot Voisin, sieur de. L'amiral de France et par occasion, de celuy des autres nations. *Paris: T.Périer*, 1585. 92 numb.lvs;4to. 1st publ., Paris, 1584; here reissued with altered imprint date. Adams (Cambr.) L201. DLC; BL, BN. 585/41

Ledesma, Bartolomé de. Summarium . . . denuo ab authore recognitum. *Salamanca: Heirs of M.Gast*, 1585. 1622 cols;fol. 1st publ., Mexico, 1566. The Dominican author was a distinguished prelate in the New World. Medina (BHA) 292; Palau 134124n. Seville: BU. 585/42

LeRoy, Louis. La vicissitudine o mutabile varieta delle cose nell' universo, di Luigi Regio . . . tradotto dal sig. . . . Hercole Cato. *Venice: Aldine Press*, 1585. 327p.;4to. Transl. from author's *De la vicissitude ou variete des choses*, 1st publ., Paris, 1575. Adams (Cambr.) L534. CU, CtY-M, DFo, ICN, InU-L, MH, MiU, NN-RB, PBL; BL, BN. 585/43

Léry, Jean de. Histoire d'un voyage faict en la terre du Bresil, autrement dite Amerique . . . Avec les figures, reveue, corrigee & bien augmentee de discours notables en ceste troisiesme edition. *[Geneva:] A.Chuppin*, 1585. 427p.;illus.,map;8vo. 1st publ., [La Rochelle], 1578. Sabin 40150n; Borba de Moraes I:403; Atkinson (Fr.Ren.) 315; Rép.bibl.XVI:41-42; JCB (3) I:304. CSmH, DLC, RPJCB; BL, Paris: Arsenal. 585/43a

Mattioli, Pietro Andrea. Dei discorsi . . . nelli sei libri di Pedacio Dioscoride . . . della materia medicinale. *Venice: F.Valgrisi*, 1585 [colophon: 1584]. 1527p.;illus.,port.;fol. 1st publ., Venice, 1555. Cf.Pritzel 5988; Nissen (Bot.) 1304n; Adams (Cambr.) D679. DLC, MH-A, MiU; BL, BN. 585/44

Norman, Robert. The newe attractive, containing a short discourse of the magnes or lodestone . . . Newly corrected by m.W.B[orough]. *London: T.East,for R.Ballard*, 1585. 2 pts;illus.;4to. 1st publ., London, 1581. Sabin 55496; STC 18648(& 3390). CSmH, CtY, MH; BL. 585/45

Ortelius, Abraham. Theatri orbis terrarum enchiridion. *Antwerp:* 1585. See Favolius, Hugo, above.

Paracelsus. Cheirugia. Warhafftige Beschreibunge der Wundartzney . . . Der ander Theil. *Basel: C.Waldkirch*, 1585. 260p.;fol. Includes author's 'Der Frantzösischen kranckheiten'. Sudhoff (Paracelsus) 207. CtY, DNLM. 585/46

Pirckheimer, Wilibald. Descriptio Germaniae. *Antwerp: C.Plantin*, 1585. 144p.; 8vo. 1st publ., Nuremberg, 1530. Sabin 63019n. CtY, MiU, MnU; BL, BN. 585/47

Poza, Andrés de. Hydrographia la mas curiosa, que hasta aqui ha salido a luz. *Bilbao: M.Mares*, 1585. 2 pts;4to. Includes incidental refs to New World. Medina (BHA) 296; Bibl.mar.esp.215. InU-L; BL. 585/48

Proclus, Diadochus. De sphaera liber i . . . una cum Joan. Honteri . . . de cosmographiae rudimentis duplici editione, ligata scilicet & soluta. *Basel: S.Henricpetri*, 1585. 737p.; maps;8vo. 1st publ. with Honter's work, Basel, 1561. Sabin 65941; Adams (Cambr.) P2135. CtY, DLC, NN-RB, NcD; BL. 585/49

Río Riaño, Andrés del. Tratado de hidrografia, en que se enseña la navegación porla altura y derrota y la graduación de puertos. [*Madrid*?] 1585. Palau 268361; Bibl.mar. esp.216.   585/50

Roberts, Henry. A most friendly farewell, given by a welwiller, to . . . sir Frauncis Drake. *London*: [*T.East,for*] *W.Mantell & T.Lawe* [1585]. [17]p.;4to. Sabin 71893(& 51094); STC 21084. CSmH; Lincoln: Cathedral.   585/51

Rondelet, Guillaume. Methodus curandorum omnium morborum corporis humani . . . Ejusdem . . . De morbo italico. *Lyons: G. Rouillé,* 1585. 1152p.;8vo. 1st (?) publ., Paris, [1563?]. Adams (Cambr.) R755. Cambridge: UL.   585/52

San Román, Antonio de. Consuelo de penitentes, o Mesa franca de spirituales manjares . . . Aora nuevamente corregido y enmendado por el mismo autor. *Seville: A.Pescioni & J.de León,for A.Sagete,* 1585. 473 numb.lvs;8vo. 1st publ., Salamanca, 1583. Escudero (Seville) 745; Palau 293610.   585/53

Seville. Universidad de los mercaderes tratantes en las Indias. Ordenanzas para el Prior y consules de la universidad de los mercaderes de la ciudad de Sevilla. *Madrid: F.Sánchez,* 1585. xxiv lvs;fol. Medina (BHA) 7739; Palau 203048; JCB (3) I:306. MnU-B, RPJCB.   585/54

Skarga, Piotr. Zywoty swietych starego y nowego. *Cracow: A.Piotrkowczyk,* 1585. 1143p.; fol. 1st publ., Vilna, 1579. Backer VII:1267.
                                              585/55

Spain. Casa de Contratación de las Indias. Ordenanças reales, para la Casa de la contractacion de Sevilla, y para otras cosas de las Indias. Y de la navegacion y contractacion dellas. *Madrid: F.Sánchez,* 1585. liii lvs; fol. 1st publ., Seville, 1553. Medina (BHA) 295; Pérez Pastor (Madrid) 223n; Palau 203199; JCB(3) I:305. DLC, MH, MnU-B, RPJCB.
                                              585/56

———. Ordenanças reales para los juezes letrados de la Casa de la Contractacion de Sevilla. *Madrid: F.Sánchez,* 1585. 5 numb.lvs; fol. Medina (BHA) 7740; Palau 203200. RPJCB.   585/57

Spain. Cònsejo de las Indias. Ordenanzas reales del Consejo de las Indias. *Madrid: F.Sánchez,* 1585. xxii lvs;fol. 1st publ., [Madrid, 1571?]. Palau 202817; JCB (3) I:305. RPJCB; BL.   585/58

Spain. Laws, statutes, etc., 1516-1556 (Charles I). Leyes y ordenanzas nuevamente hechas por Su Magestad, para la governacion de las Indias. *Madrid: F.Sánchez,* 1585. xiv lvs;fol. 1st publ., Alcalá de Henares, 1543. Sabin 40903; Medina (BHA) 293; Streit I:150; Palau 137459;JCB (3) I:306. DLC, MH, RPJCB.
                                              585/59

Spain. Laws, statutes, etc., 1556-1598 (Philip II). Ordenanças de Su Magestad sobre el despacho de las flotas de Nueva España,y Tierra firme. *Madrid: F.Sánchez,* 1585. 4 numb.lvs;fol. Medina (BHA) 7741; Palau 202615; JCB (3) I:306. MH, RPJCB.   585/59a

Spain. Sovereigns, etc., 1556-1598 (Philip II). Instruction y memoria, de las relaciones que se han de hazer, para la descripcion de las Indias, que su Magestad manda hazer, para el buen gobierno y ennoblescimiento dellas. [*Madrid?* ca.1585]. [3]p.;fol. 1st publ., [Madrid, 1577]. Medina (BHA) 291; Pérez Pastor (Madrid) 222; Palau 120121. Madrid: BN.
                                              585/60

Stella, Giulio Cesare. Columbeidos, libri priores duo. *London: J. Wolfe,* 1585. 4to. In verse. Ed.by G.Castelvetri. Sabin 91216; STC 23246. CXmH; BL.   585/61

—[Anr issue]. *Lyons* [i.e.,*London: J.Wolfe*] 1585. 26 lvs;4to. Sabin 91216n; STC 23246.5. DFo; BL.   585/61a

Tabourot, Estienne. Les bigarrures . . . quatriesme livre. *Paris: J.Richer,* 1585. 118 numb.lvs;12mo. In verse & prose. In sonnet addressed to Jacques Gohory, ref. is made to Mechoacan & tobacco. Cioranescu (XVI) 20915; cf.Arents (Add.) 122. MH, NjP; BN.
                                              585/62

Tarcagnota, Giovanni. Delle istorie del mondo . . . Con l'aggiunta di m.Mambrino Roseo & . . . Bartolomeo Dionigi. *Venice: The Giuntas,* 1585. 3 pts in 5v. 1st publ. in this expanded edn, Venice, 1583. DLC, NIC; BL.
                                              585/63

Tasso, Torquato. Il Goffredo, overo Gerusalemme liberata, poema heroico. *Venice: A. Salicato,* 1585. 2 pts;4to. 1st publ. with American refs, Parma, 1581. Racc.Tassiana 169; Shaaber T85. MH, NNH, PU; BL, BN.
                                              585/64

—[Anr edn]. Gierusalemme liberata. *Ferrara:* [*G.C.Cagnacini & Bros*] 1585. 576p.;12mo. Racc.Tassiana 170; Adams (Cambr.) T240. Cambridge: Clare.   585/65

—[Anr issue]. *Ferrara: G.C.Cagnacini & Bros,*

1585. Adams (Cambr.) T241. Cambridge: UL.   585/66

Tornamira, Francisco Vicente de.· Chronographia, y repertorio de los tiempos. *Pamplona: T.Porràlis*, 1585. 560p.; illus.;4to. On p.40 is a ref. to the Magellan circumnavigation; on p.497, a list of midsummer's days of New World; on p.538-539, locations of New World cities. Medina (BHA) 297; Palau 334501; Adams (Cambr.) T803. DLC, NN-RB, RPJCB; BL.   585/67

Wecker, Johann Jacob. Practica medicinae generalis. *Basel: H.Froben, the Younger*, 1585. 337 (i.e.,437) p.;16mo. In bk 3, ch.74 discusses Mechoacan, 'radix Indica'. Adams (Cambr.) W36. DNLM, MBCo; BL, BN.
585/68

1586

Benzoni, Girolamo. Historia Indiae Occidentalis. *[Geneva:] E.Vignon*, 1586. 480p.;illus.; 8vo. 1st publ., Venice, 1565. With this is normally bound Vignon's edn of Jean de Léry's *Historia navigationis* of this year. Sabin 4793; Medina (BHA) 299; Borba de Moraes I:85; Streit II:1039; Ind.aur.116.992; Palau 27628; JCB (3) I:307. DLC, MH, MiU-C, NN-RB, PPL, RPJCB; BL, Geneva: BP.   586/1

Boaistuau, Pierre. Historias prodigiosas y maravillosas de diversos sucessos acaescidos en el mundo. Escriptas . . . por Pedro Bouistau, Claudio Tesserant, y Francisco Beleforest. Traduzidas . . . por Andrea Pescioni. *Medina del Campo: F.del Canto,for B.Boyer*, 1586. 390 numb.lvs;8vo. Transl. from author's *Histoires prodigeuses*, 1st publ., Paris, 1571. Pérez Pastor (Medina del Campo) 207; Ind. aur.120.090; Shaaber B425. NNH, PU; BL, Madrid: BN.   586/2

Bock, Hieronymus. Kreutterbuch. *Strassburg: J.Rihel*, 1586. 454 numb.lvs;illus.;fol. 1st publ. with illus., Strassburg, 1546; here ed. by Melchior Sebizius. Nissen (Bot.) 182n.
586/3

Bodin, Jean. De republica libri sex, latine ab autore redditi. *Lyons: For J.DuPuys at Paris*, 1586. 779p.;fol. Transl. from author's *Six livres de la Republique*, 1st publ., Paris, 1576. Ind.aur.120.826; Adams (Cambr.) B2228 (& B2229). CLSU, CtY, ICN, InU-L, MH, MnU, NNC; BL, BN.   586/4

Botero, Giovanni. Epistolarum . . . Caroli cardinalis Borromaei nomine scriptarum, libri

ii. Eiusdem Epistolarum theolog. liber. *Paris: T.Périer*, 1586. 140 numb.lvs;8vo. 1st publ., Paris, 1585; here a reissue with altered imprint date? Ind.aur.122.694; Adams (Cambr.) B2560. ICN; BL, BN.   586/5

Bruyn, Abraham de. Omnium pene Europae, Asiae, Aphricae atque Americae gentium habitus. *[Antwerp? A.de Bruyn? 1586?]*. 82 pls; fol. 1st publ., Antwerp, 1581. Cf.Sabin 8739. NBuG.   586/6

Costa, Manuel da. Kurtze Verzeichnuss und historische Beschreibung deren Dingen so von der Societät Jesu in Orient . . . gehandlet worden: erstlich durch Joannem Petrum Maffeium, auss portugalesischer sprach in Latein und jetzo neben etlichen japonischen Sendtschreiben vom Jar 1548 biss auff 1555 . . . ins Teutsch gebracht unnd zum ersten mal an Tag geben: durch Joannem Georgium Götzen. *Ingolstadt: D.Sartorius*, 1586. 2 pts;8vo. Transl. from the Latin compendium initially edited by Acosta, subsequently republished by Maffei, and here· enlarged to include letter of Manuel Nobrega from Salvador, Brazil, itself 1st publ., Rome, 1552, in the *Avisi particolari*. Sabin 43781; Streit IV:1041; Backer V:295; Ind.aur.100.474. ICN, NN-RB; BL, Munich: StB.   586/7

Cysat, Renwart. Warhafftiger Bericht von den new-erfundnen Japponischen Inseln . . . auch von andren zuvor unbekandten Indianischen Landen. *Freiburg i.Br.: A.Gemperlin*, 1586. 2 pts;illus.,map;8vo. Pt 2 comprises Jesuit letters from missions, including that of Pietro Díaz, 1st publ., Rome, 1570 in *Nuovi avisi*, that of Francisco Henriques, 1st publ., Brescia, 1579, in *Nuovi avisi*, and one from Brazil of Quiritius Caxa, apparently not previously published. Sabin 18220; Borba de Moraes I:203; Streit II:1314; Baginsky (German Americana) 86. MH, NN-RB; BL, BN.
586/8

—[Anr issue?] Title includes phrase 'von Brasilia und weytere beschreibung'. *Freiburg i.Br.: A.Gemperlin*, 1586: Streit II:1315. DLC.
586/9

De rebus Gallicis, Belgicis, Anglicis, Italicis, Hispanicis, Constantinopolitanis &c. recens allata. *[Cologne?]* 1586. [8]p.;4to. Newsletter, containing, p.[2-3], 'Mari verò classem habet piraticam: Francisco Draco'. JCB AR40:60. RPJCB.   586/10

Dioscorides, Pedanius. Acerca de la material medicinal . . . traduzido de lengua griega . . .

& illustrado con . . . substantiales annotationes, y con las figuras de innumeras plantas . . . por el doctor Andres de Laguna. *Salamanca: C.Bonardo*, 1586. 617p.;illus.,port.; fol. Laguna's annotations, with numerous refs to American plants, 1st publ. separately, Lyons, 1554, & in the present form, Antwerp, 1555. Cf.Pritzel 2313n; Palau 74023n. 586/11

Dodoens, Rembert. A new herball . . . translated out of the French, by Henrie Lyte. *London: N. Newton*, 1586. 916p.;4to. 1st publ. in English, London, 1578. STC 6985; Henrey (Brit.bot.) 111; Arents (Add.) 18. CSmH, CtY, DFo, MH, MiU, NN-A, PPC; BL.
586/12

Du Bartas, Guillaume de Salluste, seigneur. Commentaires et annotations sur la Sepmaine [par Simon Goulart]. *Paris: A. L'Angelier*, 1586. 416 numb.lvs;12mo. 1st publ. in this form, including text itself of *La sepmaine*, Geneva, 1581. In verse. Adams (Cambr.) D969. OrU; Cambridge: Trinity. 586/13

Du Fail, Noël, seigneur de La Hérissaye. Les contes et discours d'Eutrapel. *Rennes: N. Glamet*, 1586. 569p.;16mo. 1st publ., Rennes, 1585. Adams (Cambr.) D1059; Rép.bibl., XIX:73. ICN; Cambridge: Clare, BN. 586/14

—[Anr edn]. *Rennes: N.Glamet*, 1586. 540p.;16mo. Rép.bibl.,XIX:73. Landévennoc: Abbaye. 586/15

—[Anr edn]. *Rennes: N.Glamet*, 1586. 223 numb.lvs;8vo. Rép.bibl.,XIX:73. BN. 586/16

Du Hamel, Jacques. Acoubar, ou la Loyauté trahie. Tragédie tirée des amours de Pistion & de Fortunie en leur voyage de Canada. [*Rouen?*] 1586. 12mo. Probably a ghost; cf. year 1603. Sabin 29938; Harrisse (NF) 6; cf. Cioranescu (XVII) 26999. 586/17

Durante, Castor. Il tesoro della sanita. Nel quale si da il modo da conservar la sanità . . . & si tratta della natura de' cibi. *Rome: F.Zanetti,for J.Bericchia & G.Tornieri*, 1586. 296p.;port.;4to. Transl. from author's *De bonitate et vitio alimentorum centuria*, 1st publ., Pisauri, 1565. Includes discussion of the turkey; recommends diet of partridges for those with syphilis. CLU-M, DNLM, ICJ, MH-A; BL, Rome: BN. 586/18

—[Anr edn]. *Venice: A.Muschio*, 1586. 328p.; 8vo. CtY-M, DNLM; BL. 586/19

Ercilla y Zúñiga, Alonso de. Primera, y segunda parte de la Araucana. *Antwerp: A. Bacx,for P.Bellère*, 1586. 615p.;12mo. Pt 1 1st publ., Madrid, 1569; pt 2, Madrid, 1578.

In verse. Sabin 22721; Medina (BHA) 300; Medina (Arau.) 10; Peeters-Fontainas (Impr. esp.) 390; Palau 80416; Adams (Cambr.) E917. MnU-B, NN-RB; Cambridge: UL, Brussels: BR. 586/20

Espejo, Antonio de. Histoire des terres nouvellement descouvertes . . . lesquelles terres ont esté descouvertes par Antonio de Espejo & nommees le nouveau Mexico. Traduict de l'espagnol . . . par m.Basanier. *Paris: Widow of N.Roffet*, 1586. 46p.;4to. Transl. from Paris edn of this year in Spanish, described below. Sabin 69210n; Wagner (SW) 8a; Palau 82371. ICN, NN-RB. 586/21

——. El viaje que hizo Antonio de Espejo en el anno de ochenta y tres: el qual con sus companneros descubrieron una tierra . . . a quien pusieron por nombre nuevo Mexico. *Paris: R.Hakluyt*, 1586. 16 lvs;4to. Extracted from Q.Gerardo's edn of González de Mendoza's *Historia de las cosas mas notables . . . del China* of this year, where it 1st appeared. Sabin 69210n; Wagner (SW) 8; Palau 82370. BL. 586/22

Estève, José, Bp of Orihuela and of Vesti. Ad Sixtum Quint. Pont. Max. Philippi II nomine . . . Oratio habita. *Rome: A.Gardano & F. Coattino*, 1586. [12]p.;4to. Included are scattered refs to New World. Sabin 91231. CtY; BL, BN. 586/23

—[Anr edn]. Ad S.D.N. Sixtum Quintum . . . oratio habita. *Milan: M.Tini*, 1586. 4to. BL.
586/24

Estienne, Charles. L'agriculture et maison rustique, de mm. Charles Estienne et Jean Liebault. *Lyons: [Printed for] J.DuPuys,at Paris*, 1586. 394 numb.lvs;illus.;4to. 1st publ. in this version, Paris, 1567. Thiébaud (La chasse) 348-349; Baudrier (Lyons) I:367. MH-A.
586/25

Farissol, Abraham ben Mordecai. [Iggereth orhoth 'olam. *Venice: G.di Gara*, 1586]. [71]p.;illus.;8vo. Printed in Hebrew; title & imprint transliterated. Includes refs to New World derived from Vespucci. JCB AR50:45-49. NNH, RPJCB; BL. 586/26

Fernel, Jean. Universa medicina. *Lyons: Heirs of J.Giunta & P.Guissio*, 1586. 2 pts; ports;fol. Includes both Fernel's *De abditis rerum causis*, 1st publ., Paris, 1548, and his *De luis venereae curatione*, 1st publ., Antwerp, 1579. Sherrington (Fernel) 69.J13. DNLM; BL. 586/27

Francisco de Vitoria. Relectiones theologicae

tredecim . . . novissimè juxta Ingolstadiensem editionem castigatum. *Lyons: A.Duport,* 1586. 521p.;8vo. 1st publ., Lyons, 1557. Sabin 100620; Palau 321069. DLC. 586/28

____[Anr issue]. *Lyons: P.Landry,* 1586. Sabin 100620n; Baudrier (Lyons) V:318; Palau 371070. BN. 586/29

Girard, Bernard, sieur du Haillan. Discours sur l'extreme cherté qui est aujourd'hui en France. *Bordeaux:* 1586. 79p.;8vo. 1st publ., Paris, 1574. BN. 586/30

González de Mendoza, Juan, Bp. Dell'historia della China . . . tradotta . . . dal m. Francesco Avanzo. *Rome: B.Grassi,* 1586. 379p.;4to. Transl. from author's *Historia de las cosas mas notables . . . dela China,* 1st publ., Rome, 1585. Sabin 27778; Wagner (SW) 7g; cf.Streit IV:1985; Palau 105503n. DLC, InU-L, MH, MnU-B, NN-RB, RPJCB; BN. 586/31

____[Anr issue]. *Rome: G.A.Ruffinelli,* 1586. Wagner (SW) 7h. CU, NN-RB. 586/32

____[Anr issue]. *Rome: A.Calentano & C.Rasimo,* 1586. Wagner (SW) 7i. ICU. 586/33

____[Anr issue]. *Rome: G.Martinelli,* 1586. Wagner (SW) 7j. MnU-B, RPJCB; BN.586/34

____[Anr issue]. *Rome: G.Marsioni,* 1586. Wagner (SW) 7k. 586/35

____[Anr issue]. *Rome: V.Pelagallo,* 1586. Wagner (SW) 7k(n). CLSU, MnU-B. 586/36

____[Anr edn]. *Venice: A.Muschio,* 1586. 462p.; 8vo. Sabin 27779 (& 47828); Wagner (SW) 7l; Streit IV:1986; Woodfield B4; Palau 105504; JCB (3) I:307. CtY, DLC, InU-L, MiU-C, MnU-B, RPJCB; BL, BN. 586/37

____[Anr edn]. *Genoa: G.Bartoli,* 1586. 280p.; 4to. Sabin 27779n; Wagner (SW) 7m; Streit IV:1987; Palau 105505. DLC, ICN, InU-L, MnU-B, NN-RB; RPJCB: BN. 586/38

____. Historia de las cosas mas notables, ritos, y costumbres . . . de la China. *Barcelona: J. Cendrat,for J.P.Menescal,* 1586. 512p.;8vo. 1st publ., Rome, 1585. Cf.Sabin 27776; Medina (BHA) 302; Wagner (SW) 7b. Madrid: BN. 586/39

____[Anr issue]. *Barcelona: J.Cendrat,for F. Trincher,* 1586. CF.Sabin 27776; Wagner (SW) 7c. RPJCB. 586/40

____[Anr edn]. . . . Con un itinerario del Nuevo Mundo. *Madrid: Q.Gerardo,for B.de Robles,* 1586. 268 (i.e., 368) numb.lvs;8vo. The earliest edn to include also Antonio de Espejo's exploration of New Mexico. Sabin 27776; Medina (BHA) 301; Wagner (SW) 7y; Streit IV:1984; Pérez Pastor (Madrid) 236. CtY, InU-L, MH, MnU-B, NN-RB, RPJCB; BL, Madrid: BN. 586/41

____. Itinerario y compendio de las cosas notables que ay desde España, hasta el reyno de la China. *Lisbon: [A. Lobato?]* 1586. 136 numb.lvs;8vo. 1st publ., Madrid, 1586, under title *Historia de las cosas . . . de la China* in edn containing Espejo narrative. Wagner (SW) 8c; Anselmo 784; Palau 105498; JCB AR30:23-24. InU-L, RPJCB; Lisbon: BN. 586/42

Gracián, Jerónimo. Stimulo dela propagacion dela fee. Contiene el vinculo de hermandad entre los padres descalços, de nuestra Señora del Monte Carmelo, y del . . . Sant Francisco . . . Y una exortacion . . . hecho por fray Hieronymo Gracian. *Lisbon: A.Lobato,* 1586. 71 lvs;8vo. Includes refs to evangelization of Indians in Mexico. Streit I:155; Anselmo 785. CtY, InU-L; Lisbon: Acad.das Sciencias. 586/43

Jesuits. Compendiorum privilegiorum. Compendium facultatem et indulgentiarum . . . in Indiarum orientalium et occidentalium provinciis conceduntur. *Rome: Jesuit College,* 1586. 71p.;12mo. 1st publ., Rome, 1580. Streit I:161; Backer V:93. 586/44

Jesuits. Letters from missions. Annuae Litterae (1584) 1586. Annuae litterae . . . anni .M.D.LXXXIV. *Rome: Jesuit College,* 1586. 351p.;8vo. 'Provincia Brasilia': p.140-146; 'Provincia Peruana': p.286-295; 'Provincia Mexicana': p.295-336. Streit I:160; Backer V:1935. NNH, RPJCB; BL. 586/45

Laudonnière, René Goulaine de. L'histoire notable de la Floride . . . contenant les trois voyages faits . . . par certains capitaines & pilotes françois . . . à laquelle a esté adjousté un quatriesme voyage fait par le Capitaine Gourges. Mise en lumière par m. Basanier. *Paris: G.Auvray,* 1586. 123 numb.lvs;8vo. Sabin 39234; Atkinson (Fr.Ren.) 321; Adams (Laudonnière) 18; Church 131; JCB (3) I:308. CSmH, CtY, DLC, ICN, InU-L, MiU-C, MnU-B, NN-RB, PPRF, RPJCB; BL, BN. 586/46

Léry, Jean de. Historia navigationis in Brasiliam, quae et America dicitur. Qua describitur autoris navigatio . . . Villegagnonis in America gesta: Brasiliensium victus & mores. *[Geneva:]* E.Vignon, 1586. 341p.;illus.;8vo. Transl. from author's *Histoire d'un voyage* 1st publ., [La Rochelle], 1578, but containing material suppressed there. Imprint appears in 2 forms, one reading 'excud. Eustathius Vignon', the other 'apud. Eustathium Vignon'. Normally bound with Vignon's edn of G.Benzoni's *Historia Indiae Orientalis* of this year. Sabin 40153; Borba de Moraes I:405; Adams (Cambr.) L536 & L537; Arents 29; JCB (3) I:309. CU, CtY, DLC, ICN, MH, MnU-B, NN-RB, PPL, RPJCB; Cambridge: UL, BN. 586/47

Maisonfleur, Etienne de. Cantiques spirituels. *Paris: G.Auvray,* 1586. 2 pts;12mo. Includes, lvs 85-119, Pierre Duval's *La grandeur de Dieu,* 1st publ., Paris, 1555. Cioranescu (XVI) 13970. BN. 586/48
___[Anr issue]. *Paris: J.Houzé,* 1586. BL. 586/49

Mattioli, Pietro Andrea. De plantis epitome utilissima . . . novis iconibus et descriptionibus pluribus nunc primum diligenter aucta, à d. Joachimo Camerario. *Frankfurt a.M.: [S.Feyerabend]* 1586. 1003p.;illus.;4to. The earliest edn ed. by Camerarius, with his fresh description of tobacco. The title leaf exists in another state, with more fulsome wording, including reading 'novis plane, et ad vivum expressis inconibus' for 'novis iconibus'. Pritzel 5983; Nissen (Bot.) 1308; Adams (Cambr.) M909; Arents 30. CtY-M, DFo, MH, MiU, MnU, NN-A, PPT, RPB; BL, BN. 586/50
___. Kreuterbuch . . . gemehret und verfertiget durch . . . Joachimum Camerarium. *Frankfurt a.M.: S.Feyerabend,H.Tack & P.Fischer,* 1586. 460 numb.lvs;illus.;fol. Ed. by Camerarius from Georg Handsch's translation, 1st publ., Prague, 1563, as *New Kräuterbuch.* Cf.Pritzel 5990; Nissen (Bot.) 1311. DNLM, NNNAM, MoSB. 586/51

Neander, Michael. Chronicon sive Synopsis historiarum. *Leipzig: G.Deffner,* 1586. 3 pts;8vo. 1st publ., Eisleben, 1582. ICN, InU-L, NjP; BL. 586/52
___. Orbis terrae divisio compendiaria et plana in partes & regiones suas praecipuas . . . in usum studiosae juventutis, in scholia Ilfedensi. *Leipzig: [G.Deffner?]* 1586. 56 lvs;8vo. Sabin 52174. InU-L. 586/53
___. Orbis terrae partium succincta explicatio. *Leipzig: G.Deffner,* 1586. [648]p.;8vo. 1st publ., Eisleben, 1583. Adams N113. InU-L, MH; BL, BN. 586/54

Newe Zeittung auss Venedig . . . Daneben auch ein kurtze verzaichnuss der reichen Flot-

ta auss Terra Firme, und New Spanien. *Munich:* [1586]. [7]p.;4to. JCB AR21:8. NN-RB, RPJCB. 586/55

Osório, Jerónimo, Bp of Silves. De rebus Emmanuelis Lusitaniae Regis . . . gestis, libri duodecim . . . Item Jo. Matalii Metelli . . . praefatio et commentarius . . . Omnia iam recognita et emendata. *Cologne: House of Birckmann,for A.Mylius,* 1586. 368 numb.lvs;8vo. 1st publ. with Matal's preface, Cologne, 1574. Sabin 57804n. DLC, MB, MnU-B, NNC, RPJCB; BL, BN. 586/56

Paracelsus. Cheirugia. Warhafftige Beschreibunge der Wundartzney . . . Der ander Theil. *Basel: C.Waldkirch,* 1586. 260p.;fol. A reissue with altered imprint date of the publisher's 1585 edn. Sudhoff (Paracelsus) 211 586/57

Pasquier, Etienne. Les lettres. *Paris: A. L'Angelier,* 1586. 330 numb.lvs;ports.;4to. In bk 3, letter 3 contains a description of customs of Brazilian natives. Thickett (Pasquier) 19; Cioranescu (XVI) 17184. DLC, ICN, MH, NjP; BL, BN. 586/58

Rabelais, François. Les oeuvres. *Lyons: J.Martin,* 1586. 16mo. Includes 'Le quart livre', 1st publ., Paris, 1552. Plan (Rabelais) 111. BL. 586/59

Rivadeneira, Pedro de. Vita Ignatii Loiolae . . . nunc denuo recognita & locupletata. *Madrid: Widow of A.Gómez,* 1586. 347 numb.lvs;8vo. 1st publ., Naples, 1572. Cf.Sabin 70782; Backer VI:1726; Pérez Pastor (Madrid) 247; Palau 266203; Adams (Cambr.) R464. IU; Cambridge: UL. 586/60
___. Vida del padre Ignacio de Loyola . . . Descripta en latin y traducida en castellano, y aora mas acrecentada en esta tercera impression. *Madrid: Widow of A. Gómez,* 1586. 419 numb.lvs;8vo. 1st publ. in Spanish, Madrid, 1583. Backer VI:1727; Pérez Pastor (Madrid) 246; Palau 266224. MH, MnU-B. 586/61
___. Vita del .p. Ignatio Loiola . . . Descritta . . . prima in lingua latino, e dopo da lui ridutta nella castigliana, & ampliate in molte cose. E nuovamente traduatta dalla spagnuola . . . da Giovanni Giolito de' Ferrari. *Venice: The Gioliti,* 1586. 589p.;4to. 1st publ. in enl. Spanish text, Madrid, 1584. Backer VI:1730; Palau 266239. MH, NIC, RPJCB; BL. 586/62

Rondelet, Guillaume. Methodus curandorum omnium morborum corporis humani . . . Ejusdem . . . De morbo italico. *Lyons:*

G.Rouillé, 1586. 1152p.;8vo. 1st (?) publ., Paris [1563?]; here reissued with altered imprint date from Rouillé's 1585 edn? Baudrier (Lyons) IX:397. BL. 586/63

Salazar, Estéban de. Veinte discursos sobre el Credo. *Seville: A.Pescioni & J.de León*, 1586. 248 numb.lvs;4to. 1st publ., Granada, 1577-78. Medina (BHA) 303; Streit II:1040; Escudero (Seville) 747. InU-L; Madrid: BN. 586/64

Scherer, Georg. Rettung der Jesuiter Unschuld wider die Gifftspinnen Lucam Ostrander. *Ingolstadt: D.Sartorius*, 1586. 72p.; 4to. Includes refs to Jesuit missions in New World. Backer VII:751-752; Palmer 385; JCB (3) I:309. MH-AH, RPJCB; BL. 586/65

Surius, Laurentius. Commentarius brevis rerum in orbe gestarum. *Cologne: G.Calenius & Heirs of J.Quentel*, 1586. 1199p.;8vo. 1st publ. separately, Cologne, 1566; here expanded, by M.ab Isselt, to year 1586. Sabin 93884; Adams (Cambr.) S2102; Shaaber S687. DLC, MH, NN-RB, PU; BL, BN. 586/66

Tabourot, Estienne. Les bigarrures . . . Quatriesme livre. *Paris: J.Richer*, 1586. 154 numb.lvs;12mo. In verse & prose. 1st publ., Paris, 1585. Rothschild 1778. NjP;BN. 586/67

Vigo, Giovanni de. The whole work . . . newly corrected [by G.Baker & R.Norton]. *London: T.East*, 1586. 3v.;4to. 1st publ. in this translation by B.Traheron, London, 1543. STC 24723. CtY, DLC, MH; Cambridge: UL. 586/68

Whitney, Geffrey. A choice of emblemes. *Leyden: Plantin Press (F.Raphelengius)*, 1586. 2 pts;illus.;4to. In verse. Poem, with emblem, 'To Richard Drake esquier, in praise of Sir Francis Drake knight' describes latter's voyages. For variant states, see the STC. Grolier (Langland to Wither) 260; STC 25438. CSmH, DFo, ICN, MH, NN-RB; BL. 586/69

Zamorano, Rodrigo. Compendio del arte de navegar. *Seville: [A.Pescioni,for] J.de León*, 1586. 60 numb.lvs;illus.,port.;4to. 1st publ., Seville, 1582; here a reissue, with cancel t.p., of Pescioni's 1582 edn. Sabin 106246n; Medina (BHA) 305; Palau 379249. 586/70

Zurita, Fernando. Theologicarum de Indis quaestionum, enchiridion primum. *Madrid: Q.Gerardo*, 1586. 128 numb.lvs;8vo. Sabin 106406; Medina (BHA) 306; Streit I:159; Pérez Pastor (Madrid) 248. MH; BL. 586/71

1587

Anghiera, Pietro Martire d'. De orbe novo . . . decades octo . . . utilissimis annotationibus illustratae . . . labore & industria Richardi Hakluyti. *Paris: G.Auvray*, 1587. 605p.;map;8vo. 1st publ. with all 8 decades, Alcalá de Henares, 1530. Sabin 1552; Medina (BHA) 310; Borba de Moraes II:31; Adams (Cambr.) M753; Arents (Add.) 4; Church 133; JCB (3) I:311. CSmH, CtY, DLC, MH, MiU-C, MnU-B, NN-A, PU, RPJCB; BL, Strasbourg: BN. 587/1

Anguisola, Antonio. Compendium simplicium et compositorum medicamentorum. *Piacenza: G.Bazzachi*, 1587. 198p.;8vo. Included are sections on balsam & sarsaparilla, citing Monardes & New World sources. Ind. aur.105.866. CtY, DNLM, MH-A; BL, BN. 587/2

Beuther, Michael. Warhafftiger kurtzer Bericht von mannigerley Kriegs und anderen fürnemen Händeln . . . als deren eygentliche Bildnisse Paulus Jovius . . . abgemalt hinterlassen. *Basel: C.Waldkirch*, 1587. 2 pts;fol. 1st publ., Basel, 1582, under title *Bildnisse viler zum theyle von uralten*, etc. Ind.aur. 118.440. OrP; Göttingen: UB. 587/3

Bock, Hieronymus. Kreütterbuch. *Strassburg: J.Rihel*, 1587. 454 lvs;illus.;fol. 1st publ. with illus., Strassburg, 1546; here ed. by Melchior Sebitzius. Pritzel 866n; Nissen (Bot.) 182n; Ind.aur.120.600; Ritter (Strasbourg) 219. MH-A, NNBG; London: Wellcome, Strasbourg: BN. 587/4

Caro, Annibale. De le lettere familiari . . . volume primo. *Venice: B.Giunta*, 1587. 176p.;4to. 1st publ., Venice, 1572. Ind. aur.132.482; Adams (Cambr.) C743. Cambridge: Trinity, BN. 587/5

Castile. Laws, statutes, etc., 1252-1284 (Alfonso X). Las siete partidas . . . nuevamente glosadas por . . . Gregorio Lopez. *Valladolid: D.Fernández de Córdova*, 1587-88. 8pts;fol. 1st publ. with American refs, Salamanca, 1555. Alcocer (Valladolid) 318; Ind.aur. 103.658; Palau 7094; JCB (3) I:309-310. CU, DFo, MWelC, PHC, RPJCB; BN. 587/6

Chassanion, Jean. De gigantibus eorumque reliquiis. *Speyer: B.Albinus,* 1587. 80p.;8vo. 1st publ., Basel, 1580. Cf.Cioranescu (XVI) 6485; Adams (Cambr. C1408. CtY; BL, BN.
587/7

Cooper, Thomas, Bp of Winchester. Thesaurus linguae romanae & britannicae. [*London?*] 1587. [1710]p.;fol. 1st publ., London, 1565. STC 5690. IU; Oxford: Bodl. 587/8

Duchesne, Joseph. Le grand miroir du monde. *Lyons:* [*F.Forest,for*] *B.Honorat,* 1587. 206p.;4to. In verse. In bk 5 (p.182) tobacco ('petun visqueux') is mentioned. Baudrier (Lyons) IV:157; Cioranescu (XVI) 8600; Shaaber D313. MH, PU, WU; BN.
587/9

Du Fail, Noël, seigneur de La Hérissaye. Les contes et discours d'Eutrapel. *Rennes: N. Glamet,* 1587. 556p.;12mo. 1st publ., Rennes, 1585. Rép. bibl., XIX:73. BL. 587/10

Durante, Castore. Tractatus de usu radicis et foliorum Mechoacan. *Antwerp:* 1587. 8vo. Oxford: Bodl. 587/11

Espejo, Antonio de. New Mexico. Otherwise, The voiage of Anthony of Espejo . . . Translated out of the Spanish. *London: T.Cadman* [1587]. 16 lvs;8vo. Transl. from Espejo's *Viaje* as publ. at Paris, 1586. Sabin 53283; Wagner (SW) 8b; Palau 82372. CSmH. 587/12

Estienne, Charles. XV. Bücher von dem Feldbau . . . von Carolo Stephano und Johanne Liebhalto . . . von Melchiore Sebizio . . . ins Teutsch gebracht. *Strassburg: B.Jobin,* 1587. 773p.;illus.;fol. 1st publ. in German, Strassburg, 1579. DNAL. 587/13

Everard, Giles. De herba panacea quam alii tabacum, alii petum, aut nicotianum vocant, brevis commentarious. *Antwerp: G.van den Rade,for J. Bellère,* 1587. 2 pts;port.;8vo. In this edn pt 2 comprises 246p. Sabin 23218; Adams (Cambr.) E1149; JCB (101 Books) 21. Cambridge: Gonville & Caius. 587/14

—[Anr edn]. *Antwerp: G.van den Rade,for J.Bellère,* 1587. 2 pts;port.;8vo. In this edn pt 2 comprises 234p. Adams (Cambr.) E1150; Arents 32. DFo, MH, MnU-B, NN-A, RPJCB; BL, BN. 587/15

Francisco de Vitoria. Relectiones theologicae tredecim. *Lyons: P.Landry,* 1587. 521p.;8vo. 1st publ., Lyons, 1557; here a reissue with altered imprint date of edn of 1586. Sabin 100620n; Baudrier (Lyons V:321; Adams (Cambr.) F934. BL, BN. 587/16

Giglio, Girolamo. Nuova seconda selva di varia lettione. *Venice: G.Cornetti,* 1587. 198 numb.lvs;8vo. 1st publ., Venice, 1565. Palau 167299. DFo. 587/17

Girard, Bernard, sieur du Haillan. Discours sur l'extreme cherté qui est aujourd'hui en France. *Bordeaux:* 1587. 80p.;8vo. 1st publ., Paris, 1574. BN. 587/18

Gómara, Francisco López de. Histoire generalle des Indes Occidentales, et terres nueves . . . Augmentee en ceste cinquiesme edition. *Paris: M.Sonnius,* 1587. 485 numb. lvs;8vo. 1st publ. in this enlarged edn, Paris, 1584; transl. by Martin Fumée, sieur de Marly le Chastel. Sabin 27748; Medina (BHA) 159n (I:272); Wagner (SW) 2kk; Streit II:1046; JCB (3) I:310. DLC, ICN, InU-L, MnU-B, NN-RB, RPJCB; BL, BN. 587/19

Gonzaga, Francisco Bp. De origine seraphicae religionis franciscanae eiusque progressionibus. *Rome: D.Basa,* 1587. 1363p.; issus.;fol. Includes copious information on Franciscan missionary activities in New World. Sabin 27790; Borba de Moraes I:306-307; Streit I:163; Adams (Cambr.) G861; JCB (3) I:310. MB, NN-RB, RPJCB; BL, BN. 587/20

González de Mendoza, Juan, Bp. Historia de las cosas mas notables . . . dela China . . . Con un itinerario del nuevo Mundo. *Madrid: P.Madrigal,for B.de Robles,* 1586 [colophon: 1587]. 2 pts;8vo. 1st publ., Rome, 1585. Sabin 27776n; Medina (BHA) 308; Wagner (SW) 7z; Streit IV:1993; JCB (3) I:307-308. CtY, DLC, ICN, InU-L, MH, NN-RB, RPJCB: BN. 587/21

—[Anr edn]. *Saragossa: L. & D.de Robles,* 1587. 556p.;8vo. Sabin 27776n; Wagner (SW) 7d; Sánchez (Aragon) 656. ICN, MH; Avignon: BM. 587/22

——. L'historia del gran regno della China . . . fatto vulgare da Francesco Avanzi . . . Stampata la terza volta, & molto piu dell' altre emendata. *Venice: A.Muschio* [i.e.,*London: J. Wolfe*] 1587. 508p.;12mo. 1st publ. in Italian, Rome, 1586. Sabin 27779 (&47828n); Medina (BHA) 373n (I:544); Wagner (SW) 7n; Streit IV:1994; STC 12004; Woodfield 28; Adams (Cambr.) G869. CU-B, DLC, MWA, NN-RB, RPJCB; BL, Florence: BN. 587/23

Greepe, Thomas. The true and perfecte newes

of the woorthy and valiaunt exploytes, performed . . . by . . . Syr Frauncis Drake: not onely at Sancto Domingo, and Carthagena, but also nowe at Cales, and uppon the coast of Spayne. *London: J.Charlewood,for T.Hackett*, 1587. [23]p.;4to. In verse. Sabin 28701 (&20836); STC 12343. CSmH, CtY, DFo; BL. 587/24

Guicciardini, Francesco. La historia d'Italia. *Venice: D.Farri*, 1587. 488 numb.lvs;4to. 1st publ., Florence, 1561. Adams (Cambr.) G1515. DFo, KMK, NNC; Cambridge: Jesus, BN. 587/25

Haslop, Henry. Newes out of the coast of Spaine. The true report of the . . . service for England, perfourmed by Sir Frauncis Drake. *London: W.How,for H.Haslop*, 1587. 8 lvs; 4to. STC 12926; Palau 76141. DFo, MiU, NN-RB; BL. 587/26

Hercusanus, Joannes, Danus. Magnifico viro D.Francisco Draco. *London: J.Charlewood, for R. Wallie*, 1587. bds.;fol. STC 13193. BL. 587/27

Heurne, Johan van. Praxis medicinae nova ratio. *Leyden: Plantin Press (F.Raphelengius)*, 1587. 421p.;illus.;4to. Includes directions for medicinal use of tobacco. Arents (Add.) 85. DNLM, NN-A; London: Wellcome. 587/28

Jesuits. Letters from missions. Annuae litterae (1585) 1587. Annuae litterae . . . .M.D.LX-XXV. *Rome: Jesuit College*, 1587. 362p.;8vo. Included are reports from Brazil & Mexico. Cf.Streit I:175; Backer V:1935. DLC, NNH, RPJCB; BL. 587/29

La Noue, François de. Discours politiques et militaires. *Basel: F.Forest*, 1587. 848p.;8vo. In discourse 8 is a ref. to the mines of Peru, perhaps deriving from Jean Bodin. The British Museum suggests that the imprints for this & similar 'Forest' edns are fictitious, Forest being otherwise unknown. NN-RB; BN. 587/30

——[Anr edn]. *Basel: F.Forest*, 1587. 776p.;8vo. Adams (Cambr.) L156; Shaaber L47. DFo, PU-L; Cambridge: UL. 587/31

——[Anr edn]. *Basel: F.Forest*, 1587. 710p.;4to. MH; BN. 587/32

——[Anr edn]. *Geneva: F.Forest*, 1587. 710p.;4to. MH. 587/33

——. The politicke and militarie discourses . . . All faithfully translated out of the French tongue by E.A[ggas]. *London: T.Orwin for T.Cadman & E.Aggas*, 1587 [colophon:

1588]. 458p.;4to. Transl. from the preceding work. STC 15215. CSmH, CtY, DFo, ICN, MH, PPL; BL. 587/33a

Laudonnière, René Goulaine de. A notable historie containing foure voyages made by certayne French captaynes unto Florida . . . Newly translated out of French . . . by R[ichard]. H[akluyt]. *London: T.Dawson*, 1587. 64 numb.lvs;4to. Transl. from Paris, 1586, French text. Sabin 39236; Adams (Laudonnière) 19; STC 15316. CSmH, NN-RB; BL. 587/34

Lightfoot, William. The complaint of England. Wherein it is clearely prooved that the practises of Papists against . . . this realme . . . are . . . unlawfull. *London: J.Wolfe*, 1587. 34 lvs;4to. Included are accounts of Spanish cruelties practiced in the New World. Sabin 41050; STC 15595. CSmH, DLC, IU, MH, MiU, NN-RB; BL. 587/35

Lonitzer, Adam. Kräuterbuch. *Frankfurt a.M.: Heirs of C.Egenolff*, 1587. ccclxxxii lvs; illus.;fol. 1st publ. in German, Frankfurt a.M., 1557. Pritzel 5599n; Nissen (Bot.) 1228n. MH-A. 587/36

Mayerne, Louis Turquet de. Histoire genérale d'Espagne. *[Geneva:] J.de Tournes*, 1587. 1526p.;fol. Included are numerous refs to Spanish discoveries & conquests in the New World. Sabin 47117; Cartier (de Tournes) 673; Cioranescu (XVI) 21425. CSmH, CtHT, MiU, NjP; BN. 587/37

Mercado, Thomas de. Summa de tratos, y contratos. *Seville: F.Díaz,for D.Núñez*, 1587. 375 numb.lvs;4to. 1st publ., Salamanca, 1569. Medina (BHA) 311; Streit I:166; Escudero (Seville) 754. CtY, DLC, MH-L, NN-RB; BL, BN. 587/38

Montaigne, Michel Eyquem de. Les essais . . . reveus et augmentez. *Paris: J.Richer*, 1587. 1075p.;12mo. 1st publ., Bordeaux, 1580. Tchémerzine VIII:404; Rothschild 139. CLU-C, CtY, ICU, MH, NjP; BN. 587/39

Ortelius, Abraham. Theatre de l'univers, contenant les cartes de tout le monde . . . Le tout reveu, amendé & augmenté . . . par le mesme autheur. *Antwerp: C.Plantin,for A.Ortelius*, 1587. 112 maps;fol. 1st publ. in French, Antwerp, 1572. Sabin 57709n (& 57687); Koeman (Ort.) 22; Phillips (Atlases) 392. DLC, ICN, MiU-C; BL, BN. 587/40

——. Thesaurus geographicus. *Antwerp: C. Plantin*, 1587. 350 lvs;fol. 1st publ., Antwerp,

1578, under title *Synonymia geographica.* Sabin 57709n; Adams (Cambr.) 0347. CSt, CtY, DLC, ICN, MH, MiU, NN-RB; BL.

587/41

Osório, Jerónimo, Bp of Silves. Histoire de Portugal . . . Comprinse en vingt livres, dont les douze premiers sont . . . de Jerosme Osorius . . . les huits suivants prins de Lopez Castagneda & autres historiens. Nouvellement mise en françois par S[imon]. G[oulart]. *Paris: N.Bonnefons,* 1587. 680 (i.e.,580) numb.lvs;8vo. 1st publ. in French, [Geneva], 1581. Cf.Sabin 57805; Atkinson (Fr.Ren.) 328. BN.

587/42

—[Anr issue]. *Paris: G.Chaudière,* 1587. Borba de Moraes II:121.

587/43

—[Anr issue]. *Paris: J.Houzé,* 1587. Atkinson (Fr.Ren.) 328n; Borba de Moraes II:121. BN.

587/44

—[Anr issue]. *Paris: A.L'Angelier,* 1587. Atkinson (Fr.Ren.) 328n; Borba de Moraes II:121; Streit IV:104. BN.

587/45

—[Anr issue]. *Paris: G.LaNoue,* 1587. Atkinson (Fr.Ren.) II:328n; Jones (Goulart) 18b. BL.

587/46

—[Anr issue]. *Paris: F.LeMangnier,* 1587. Borba de Moraes II:121.

587/47

Padilla, Francisco de. Conciliorum omnium orthodoxorum, generalium, nationalium, et provincialium . . . index chronographia, seu epitome. *Madrid: F.Sánchez,* 1587. 2 pts;4to. An account of a 1585 Mexican ecclesiastical council occupies lvs 93r-94v. Pérez Pastor (Madrid) 263; Palau 208324. RPJCB. 587/48

Rivadeneira, Pedro de. Vita del p. Ignatio Loiola . . . Descritta . . . prima in lingua latina, e poi da lui trasportata nella castigliana, et ampliata in molte cose. E nuovamente volgarizata dalla spagnuola da Giovanni Giolitto de' Ferrari. *Venice: The Gioliti,* 1587. 684p.;8vo. 1st publ. in Italian, Venice, 1586. Backer VI:1730; Palau 266240. IEN.

587/49

——. Vita Ignatii Loiolae . . . nunc denuo recognita & locupletata. *Antwerp: C.Plantin,* 1587. 558p.;8vo. 1st publ., Naples, 1572. Sabin 70782n; Backer VI:1726; Palau 266204. DLC, ICU; BL, BN.

587/50

Ronsard, Pierre de. Oeuvres. *Paris: G.Buon,* 1587. 12v.;ports;12mo. 1st publ. as here collected, Paris, 1578. Tchémerzine IX:477. MH; BN.

587/51

Sleidanus, Johannes. Ordenliche besch-

reibung und verzeychniss allerlei fürnemer händel. *Strassburg: T.Rihel,* 1587. 400 numb.lvs;fol. MH, MdBP, MiU. 587/52

Tasso, Torquato. Jerusalem libertada, poema heroyco . . . Traduzido al sentido de lengua toscana . . . por Juan Sedeño. *Madrid: P.Madrigal,for E. & F.Bogia,* 1587. 341 numb.lvs;8vo. Transl. from Tasso's *Gerusalemme liberata.* 1st publ. with ref. to Columbus, Parma, 1581. Racc. Tassiana 952; Pérez Pastor (Madrid) 274. CU, InU, MH, NNH, PU; BL, Madrid: BN. 587/53

Thurneisser, Leonard. Historia, sive Descriptio plantarum omnium. *Cologne: J.Gymnich,* 1587. clvi p.;illus.;fol. 1st publ., Berlin, 1578; here reissued with altered imprint. Pritzel 9338n; Nissen (Bot.) 1963n; Adams (Cambr.) T691. BL. 587/54

Venero, Antonio do. Enchiridion de los tiempos . . . Va añadido en esta ultima impression todas las cosas notables succedidʹas hasta este año de mil y quinientos y ochenta y siete. *Toledo: J.Rodríguez,* 1587. 273 numb.lvs;8vo. 1st publ. with American refs, Saragossa, 1548. Sabin 98865; Pérez Pastor (Toledo) 381; Palau 358457. Madrid: BN. 587/55

Vera relatione di tutto quello che la flotta . . . del Rè Cattolico hà portato, tornando dalla terra ferma, Nova Spagna, & San Domenico, l'anno 1587. *Rome: Heirs of G.Gigliotti,* 1587. [8]p.;4to. Sabin 98907. NNH. 587/56

—[Anr edn]. . . . Con la relatione della regina d'Algiero. [*Ferrara? V.Baldini?* 1587]. 12mo. Sabin 98907n. BL. 587/57

Verheiden, Willem. Nootelijcke consideratien die alle goede liefhebbers des vaderlants behooren rijpelick te overwegen, opten voorgeslagen tractate van peys met den Spaengiarden. [*Amsterdam?*] 1587. [19]p.; 4to. In opposing treaty, Spanish cruelty to Indians is cited. Knuttel 816; Belg.typ (1541-1600) I:2224. NN-RB; BL, Brussels: BR, The Hague: KB. 587/58

—[Anr edn]. In title, readings 'vaderlandts', 'overweghen', & 'voorgheslaghen' occur. [*Amsterdam?*] 1587. [19]p.;4to. Knuttel 817; Belg.typ (1541-1600) I:2223. RPJCB; Brussels: BR, The Hague: KB. 587/59

—[Anr edn]. In title, readings 'vaderlandts', 'overwegen' & 'voorgheslagen' occur. [*Amsterdam?*] 1587. [24]p.;4to. Knuttel 818; Belg.typ. (1541-1600) I:2222. Brussels: BR, The Hague: KB. 587/60

Verstegen, Richard. Theatrum crudelitatem haereticorum nostri temporis. *Antwerp: A.Hubert,* 1587. 95p.;illus.;4to. Includes account of the martyrdom of Inácio de Azevedo & fellow Jesuits en route to Brazil. Belg.typ. (1541-1600) I:4728. MH, NN-RB; BL, BN.
587/61

1588

Acosta, José de. De natura Novi Orbis libri duo, et de promulgatione evangelii, apud barbaros, sive de procuranda Indorum salute libri sex. *Salamanca: G.Foquel,* 1588. 640p.;8vo. Cf.Sabin 118; Medina (BHA) VII:317 (319); Streit I:167; Palau 1978. CU-B, NN-RB; Santiago, Chile: BN.
588/1

Advertissement certain contenant les pertes advenues en l'armee d'Espagne . . . Avec deux lettres, l'une d'un Flamen . . . demeurant a Londres . . . et l'autre de monsieur Candiche [i.e., Thomas Cavendish], qui a passé par le Cap de Bonne-Esperance. [*Paris?*] 1588. 28p.;8vo. Sabin 11603; JCB (3) I:312. RPJCB; BL.
588/2

—[Anr edn]. [*Paris?*] 1588. 28p.;8vo. Kebabian 181. CtY.
588/3

Airebaudouze, Pierre de, seigneur du Cest. Orbis terrarum synoptica epitome, una cum geographia poetica: variis locorum, regionum, populorum, urbium, fluvium, insularum & montium synonymis . . . Quae . . . adjuncta est Geographia poetica, a viro doctissimo [Lamberto Danaeo]. [*Geneva:*] *J. Stoer,* 1588. 2 pts;8vo. Daneau's *Geographiae poeticae . . . libri* 1st publ., Geneva, 1579. Ind.aur.106.974; Adams (Cambr.) B381. NN-RB; Cambridge: UL, Munich: StB.
588/4

Alberti, Leandro. Descrittione di tutta Italia. *Venice: A.Salicato,* 1588. 495 numb.lvs; maps;4to. 1st publ., Bologna, 1550. Ind. aur.102.352; Adams (Cambr.) A477. DLC, NNUT, PSt; BL, Munich: StB.
588/5

Alvares, Francisco. Historia de las cosas notables de Ethiopia . . . traduzida por Miguel de Selves [i.e., Thomas de Padilla]. *Toledo: P.Rodríguez,for B.Pérez,* 1588. 362 numb.lvs;8vo. 1st publ. in Spanish, Antwerp, 1557. Cf.Sabin 974n; Pérez Pastor (Toledo) 382; Ind.aur.104.042. ICN, MH, MnU-B, NN-RB; BL, BN.
588/6

Banchieri, Adriano. La nobiltà dell'asino di Attabalippa dal Perù [pseud.]. [*Bologna?*] 1588. 4to. Americana only in choice of pseudonym. For the earliest recorded extant edn, see the year 1592. Brunet I:540; Graesse I:247.
588/6a

Belon, Pierre. Les observations de plusieurs singularitez et choses memorables, trouvées en Grece, Asie . . . & autres pays estranges. *Paris: L.Cavellat,for J.de Marnef & the Widow of G.Cavellat,* 1588. 468p.;illus., maps;4to. 1st publ., Paris, 1553. Atkinson (Fr. Ren.) 333; Ind.aur.116.333. DLC, MB, MnU-B, NBB; BL, BN.
588/7

Beuther, Michael. Warhafftiger kurtzer Bericht von mannigerley Kriegs und anderen fürnemen Händeln. *Basel: C.Waldkirch,* 1588. 2 pts; ports;fol. 1st publ., Basel, 1582, under title *Bildnisse viler zum theyle von uralten,* etc. Ind.aur.118.441. Halle: UB.
588/8

Bigges, Walter. Expeditio Francisci Draki equitis angli in Indias a. M.D.LXXXV. quâ urbes, Fanum D. Jacobi, D.Dominici, D.Augustini & Carthagena, captae fuere. *Leyden: Plantin Press (F.Raphelengius),* 1588. 21p.; maps,port.;4to. Transl. & condensed from ms. of English text printed only in 1589. On the t.p. either a group of type ornaments or a vignette of ship appears. Sabin 20828; Ind. aur.119.255; cf.STC 3171.6; Church 134A; Kraus (Drake) 20 (p.198); JCB (3) I:312; JCB AR37:12-13. CSmH, ICN, MiU-C, MnU-B, NN-RB, RPJCB; BL, Copenhagen: KB.588/9

———. Le voyage de messire François Drake chevalier, aux Indes Occidentales l'an M.D.LXXXV. auquel les villes de S.Iago, S.Domingo, S.Augustino, & Cartagena ont esté prisés. *Leyden: Plantin Press (F.Raphelengius),* 1588. 23p.;maps;4to. Cf.preceding entry. Sabin 20828n; Ind. aur.119.256. CSmH, NN-RB, NcU; BL.
588/10

Bodin, Jean. I sei libri della Republica . . . Tradotti . . . da Lorenzo Conti. *Genoa: G.Bartoli,* 1588. 691p.;illus.;fol. Transl. from Bodin's *Les six livres de la République,* 1st publ., Paris, 1576. Ind.aur.120.830. DLC, MiU; BL.
588/11

———. Les six livres de la Republique. *Lyons* [i.e.,*Geneva?*]: *G.Cartier,* 1588. [i.e., 1593?]. 1060p.;8vo. The imprint date as set in roman numerals may represent an error; cf.1593 entry. TxU.
588/12

Braun, Georg. Civitates orbis terrarum, liber primus. *Cologne: G.van Kempen*, 1588. 58 double pls;fol. 1st publ., Cologne, 1572. Cf.Koeman (Braun & Hogenberg) 1; Ind. aur.123.961; Adams (Cambr.) B2711. BL, Munich: StB.   588/13

Camerarius, Joachim, 1534-1598. Hortus medicus et philosophicus. *Frankfurt a.M.: J.Feyerabend,for S.Feyerabend,H.Tack & P.Fischer*, 1588. 2pts;illus.;4to. A dictionary of plants, including tobacco. Pritzel 1439/1440; Nissen (Bot.) 311; Ind. aur.130.576; Adams (Cambr.) C446; Arents (Add.) 88; Shaaber C69. CU, DNLM, MH-A, MnU-B, NN-A, PU; BL, BN.   588/14

Cavendish, Thomas. Copye, overgeset uut de Engelsche tael . . . ghescreven . . . van Mr. Thomas Candische . . . welcke in September verleden anno 1588. met zijne schepen . . . inghecomen is in Pleymuyt . . . ende in welcke manieren hy de werelt om is geseylt. *Amsterdam: C.Claeszoon* [1588?]. [4]p.;4to. Probably transl. from a ms. copy or unrecorded broadside; cf.English text found (p.808) in Hakluyt's *Principal navigations* of 1589 Sabin 11604; Knuttel 824. RPJCB; BL, The Hague: KB.   588/15

Chaumette, Antoine. Enchiridion chirurgicum . . . Ad haec accessit luis venereae cum . . . descriptione methodica curatio. *Lyons* [i.e., *Geneva*]: J.Lertout, 1588. 536p.;8vo. 1st publ., Paris, 1560. DNLM; BL, BN.   588/16

Chaves, Jerónimo de. Chronographia o Repertorio de los tiempos. Reduzido conforme al computo de Su Santitad por . . . Pedro de Luxan. *Seville: F.Díaz*, 1588. 271 numb. lvs;4to. 1st publ. Seville, 1548. Palau 67457.   588/17

Clowes, William. A prooved practise for all young chirurgians . . . Heereto is adjoyned a treatise of the French or Spanish pockes, written by John Almenar. *London: T.Orwyn,for T.Cadman*, 1588. 200p.;4to. Almenar's 'treatise' transl. from his *Libellus ad evitandum . . . morbum gallicum*, 1st publ., Venice, 1502. STC 5444. CSmH, CtY, DFo; London: Wellcome.   588/18

Discours politique, tres-excellent pour le temps present; composé par un gentilhomme françois, contreux ceulx de la Ligue, qui taschoyent de persuader au Roy, de rompre l'alliance qu'il a avec l'Angleterre, & la confirmer avec l'Espaigne. [*London: J.Wolfe*]

1588. 84p.;4to. Included are refs to cruelties of Spaniards towards both Indians & French in New World. STC 11267. RPJCB; BL.
                                         588/19

Du Bartas, Guillaume de Salluste, seigneur. La seconde semaine ou Enfance du monde. [*La Rochelle: J.Haultin*] 1588. 182p.;8vo. 1st publ., Paris, 1584. Desgraves (Les Haultin) 85. DFo; Edinburgh: NL.   588/20

——. La sepmaine, ou Creation du monde . . . Reveue, augmentee, & embellie . . . par l'auteur mesme. En cest derniere edition ont este . . . annotations . . . par S[imon]. G[oulart]. [*Geneva:*] J.Chouët, 1588. 623p.;12mo 1st publ. with Goulart's annotations, Geneva, 1581. In verse. Holmes (DuBartas) I:73 no. 20; Jones (Goulart) 20(h). CoU, MdBP; BL.   588/21

—[Anr issue]. [*Geneva:*] J.Chouët,for the Widow of J.Durant, 1588. Jones (Goulart) 20h(n); Adams (Cambr.) D961. Cambridge: Emmanuel, Heidelberg: UB.   588/22

Durante, Castore. Il tesoro della sanita. *Venice: A.Muschio*, 1588. 328p.;8vo. 1st publ., Rome (?), 1586. Hunt (Bot.) 157. DNLM, PPiHB; London: Wellcome, BN.
                                         588/23

—[Anr. issue]. *Venice: D.Farri*, 1588. CtY-M, DNLM, NNNAM; London: Wellcome.
                                         588/24

—[Anr edn]. *Bergamo: C.Ventura*, 1588. 175p.;4to. DNLM.   588/25

Ercilla y Zúñiga, Alonso de. Segunda parte de La Araucana. [*Lisbon*] A.Ribeiro, 1588. 130 numb.lvs;12mo. 1st publ., Saragossa, 1578. Medina (Arau.) 8n; Palau 80415; JCB (3) I:312-313. NNH, RPJCB; Valencia: BU.
                                         588/26

Estienne, Charles. XV. Bücher von dem Feldbaw . . . von Carolo Stephano und Joh. Libalto . . . vom . . . Melchiore Sebizio . . . inn Teutsch gebracht. *Strassburg: B.Jobin*, 1588. 773p.;illus.;fol. 1st publ. in German, Strassburg, 1579, under title *Siben Bücher von dem Feldbaw* here enl. to contain 15 pts. Thiébaud (La chasse) 358-359. NN-RB; BN.
                                         588/27

——. De veltbouw ofte lantwinninghe. *Amsterdam: C.Claeszoon*, 1588. 259p.;illus.;fol. 1st publ. in Dutch, Antwerp, 1566. Bibl.belg.1st ser.,X:E40. Amsterdam: UB.   588/28

Falloppius, Gabriel. Kunstbuch. *Augsburg: M.Manger*, 1588. 496 (i.e.,466) p.;8vo. 1st

publ. in German, Augsburg, 1571. DNLM.
588/29

____. Secreti diversi et miracolosi, nuovamente ristampata. *Venice: M.A.Zaltieri*, 1588. 366p.;8vo. 1st publ., Venice, 1563. DNLM, ICU, MH; BN. 588/30

Foglietta, Uberto. Clarorum Ligurum elogia. *Genoa: G.Bartoli*, 1588. 265p.;4to. 1st publ., Rome, 1572. Cf.Sabin 24942. NN-RB, RP-JCB. 588/31

Fricius, Valentinus. Indianischer Religionstandt der gantzen newen Welt, beider Indien gegen auff und nidergang der Sonnen . . . aussm Latein in hochteutsch verwendet: durch f. Valentinum Fricium. *Ingolstadt: W. Eder*, 1588. 199p.;8vo. In part transl. from Francisco Gonzaga's *De origine seraphicae religionis franciscanae* (Rome, 1587) & Diego Valades's *Rhetorica christiana* (Perugia, 1579). Sabin 25934; Baginsky (German Americana) 87; Borba de Moraes I:307; Streit I:169; JCB (3) I:313. CtY, ICN, NN-RB, RPJCB; BL. 588/32

Gallucci, Giovanni Paolo. Theatrum mundi, et temporis. *Venice: G.B.Somasco*, 1588. 488p.;illus.,maps;4to. Included is a map of the Western Hemisphere, showing America. Mortimer (Italy) 206; Adams (Cambr.) G168. CtY, DLC, ICJ, MH, MnU-B, NN-RB; BL. 588/33

Gesner, Konrad. Tesauro di Euonomo Filatro de rimedi secreti . . . Tradotto di latino . . . par m. Pietro Lauro. Di nuovo ristampato, & corretto. *Venice: G.B.Bonfadino*, 1588. 152 numb.lvs;illus.;8vo. 1st publ. in Italian, Venice, 1556. Moranti (Urbino) 1621; Shaaber G150. DFo, MH-A, MnU, PU; London: Wellcome, Urbino: BU. 588/34

Gómara, Francisco López de. Voyages et conquestes du Capitaine Ferdinand Courtois, es Indes Occidentales. Histoire traduite de langue espagnole, par Guillaume le Breton. *Paris: A.L'Angelier*, 1588. 416 numb.lvs;8vo. 1st publ., Saragossa, 1552, as v.2 of Gómara's *La istoria de las Indias*. Sabin 16955 (& 27750); Wagner (SW) 2ll; Atkinson (Fr.Ren.) 335; JCB (3) I:314. CtY, DLC, MH, NN-RB, RPJCB; BL, BN. 588/35

González de Mendoza, Juan, Bp. Dell'historia della China . . . tradotta . . . dal . . . m. Francesco Avanzo. *Venice: A.Muschio*, 1588. 462p.;8vo. 1st publ. in Italian, Rome, 1586. Sabin 27779n; Wagner (SW) 7o; Streit

IV:1998; Woodfield B5. CtY-D, DLC, ICN, InU-L, MnU-B, NN-RB; Barcelona: BC. 588/36

____. Histoire du grand royaume de la Chine . . . ensemble un itineraire du nouveau monde, & le descouvrement du nouveau Mexique en l'an 1583 . . . mise en françois avec des additions . . . par Luc de La Porte. *Paris: J.Périer*, 1588. 323 numb.lvs;8vo. Transl. from Madrid, 1586, edn, including Espejo relation. Sabin 27780; Wagner (SW) 7bb; Atkinson (Fr.Ren.) 339; Streit IV:1999. CU, CtY, DLC, ICN, InU-L, MB, MnU-B, RP-JCB; BL, BN. 588/37

____. Historia de las cosas mas notables . . . de la China . . . Con un itinerario del nuevo Mundo. *Saragossa: L.& D.de Robles*, 1588. 556p.;8vo. 1st publ., Rome 1585. Cf.Sabin 27776; Medina (BHA) 315; Wagner (SW) 7e; Streit IV:1997; Sánchez (Aragon) 681. 588/38

____. The historie of the great and mightie kingdome of China . . . Translated out of Spanish by R.Parke. *London: J.Wolfe,for E.White*, 1588. 410p.;4to. Transl. from Madrid, 1586, edn including Espejo relation. Sabin 27783; Wagner (SW) 7jj; Streit IV:2000; STC 12003; JCB (3) I:313. CSmH, CtY, DLC, ICN, MWiW-C, MiU-C, MnU-B, NN-RB, RPJCB; BL. 588/39

Hariot, Thomas. A briefe and true report of the new found land of Virginia . . . Discovered by the English colony there seated . . . in the yeare 1585. *London: [R.Robinson]* 1588. [48]p.;4to. Sabin 30377; STC 12785; Church 135. CSmH, MiU-C, NN-RB(imp.); BL, Leyden: UB. 588/40

Heyns, Peeter. Epitome du Theatre du monde. *Antwerp:* 1588. See Ortelius, Abraham, below.

Hurault, Michel, sieur de Bélesbat et du Fay. Discours sur l'estat de France. *[Paris?]* 1588. 104p.;8vo. Includes ref. to Spanish control of the riches of its own & of Portugal's Indies. Cioranescu (XVI) 11701. DFo; BN. 588/41

—[Anr edn]. Excellent et libre discours sur l'estat present de la France. *[Paris?]* 1588. 135p.;8vo. Cioranescu (XVI) 11702. BN. 588/42

—[Anr edn]. *[Paris?]* 1588. 93p.;8vo. BN. 588/43

—[Anr edn]. *[Paris?]* 1588. 91p.;8vo. ICN, RP-JCB. 588/44

___[Anr edn]. [*Paris?*] 1588. 89p.;8vo. BN.
588/45

___[Anr edn] [*Paris?*] 1588. 87p.;8vo. BN. 588/46

____. A discourse upon the present state of France. [*London: J.Wolfe*] 1588. 98p.;4to. Transl. from the *Discours sur l'estat de France*, the preceding item. STC 14003. CSmH, DFo, ICN, MH, NN-RB, RPJCB; BL.
588/47

___[Anr edn]. . . . Translated out of French . . . and now newly reprinted and corrected by E.Aggas. [*London: J.Wolfe*] 1588. 67p.;4to. In the title the 3rd line is set in roman. STC 14004. MH.   588/48

___[Anr edn]. [*London: J.Wolfe*] 1588. 67p.;4to. As preceding, the 3rd line in the title being set in black letter. STC 14004.2. MH.   588/49

La Noue, François de. Discours politiques et militaires. [*Paris?*] 1588. 1012p.;12mo. 1st publ., Basel, 1587. CtY; BN.   588/50

___[Anr edn]. [*Paris?*] 1588. 838p.;12mo. ICU; BN.   588/51

___[Anr edn]. [*Paris?*] 1588. 648p.;8vo. Adams (Cambr.) L157. ICN; Cambridge: Westminster.   588/52

___[Anr edn]. *La Rochelle: J.Haultin*, 1588. 648p.;8vo. Desgraves (Les Haultin) 109. MdBP.   588/53

LeRoy, Louis. Consideration sur l'histoire francoise, et l'universelle de ce temps. *Paris: F.Morel*, 1588. 46p.;8vo. 1st publ., Paris, 1567. Atkinson (Fr.Ren.) 336. BN.   588/54

Lobo Lasso de la Vega, Gabriel. Primera parte de Cortés valeroso, y Mexicana. *Madrid: P.Madrigal*, 1588. 193 numb.lvs;4to. In verse. Contains 1st 2 cantos only. Sabin 39139; Medina (BHA) 316; Pérez Pastor (Madrid) 283; JCB (3) I:313. DLC, ICN, MH, NN-RB, RPJCB; BL, Madrid: BN.   588/55

Macer Floridus. Les fleurs du livre des vertus des herbes . . . illustré des commentaires de m. Guillaume Guerolt . . . Le tout mis en françois par m. Lucas Tremblay. *Rouen: M.& H.Mallard*, 1588. 80 numb.lvs;illus., port.;8vo. The earliest edn with American reference, in 'Description de l'herbe nicotiane', lvs 76v-80r. Pritzel 5711n. DNLM, MH-A; BL.   588/56

Maffei, Giovanni Pietro. Historiarum Indicarum libri xvi. Selectarum item ex India epistolarum eodem interprete libri iv. *Florence: F.Giunta*, 1588. 570p.;fol. The

earliest edn as here ed. by Maffei, utilizing materials deriving from letters from Jesuit missions, and now including accounts of Inácio Azevedo and the Brazilian martyrs, etc. Sabin 43769; Borba de Moraes II:9; Backer V:298; Streit IV:1047; Adams (Cambr.) M90. CSt, DFo, ICN, InU-L, MnU-B, PBL, RPJCB; BL, BN.   588/57

____. Selectarum epistolarum ex India quatuor. *Venice: D.Zenaro*, 1588. 211 numb.lvs;4to. 1st publ. as part of the preceding; also issued as pt 2 of the Venice, 1589, edn of that work. Sabin 43776; Streit IV:1046; Backer V:298; JCB (3) I:314. RPJCB; BL.   588/58

Mercado, Luis. Libri ii de communi et peculiari praesidiorum artis medicae indicatione. *Cologne: J.B.Ciotti*, 1588. 952p.;8vo. 1st publ., Valladolid, 1574. Cf.Alcocer (Valladolid) 325; Palau 164998. DNLM, MBCo; BN.   588/59

Monardes, Nicolás. Brief traité de la racine Mechoacan, venue de l'Espagne nouvelle . . . Traduit d'espagnol . . . par J.G[ohory]. *Rouen: M.& H.Mallard*, 1588. 16 numb.lvs; 8vo. 1st publ., Seville, 1565, in the author's *Dos libros*. Guerra (Monardes) 28. DNLM, MH-A; BN.   588/60

Montaigne, Michel Eyquem de. Essais . . . cinquiesme [!] edition, augmentée d'un troisiesme livre: et de six cens additions aux deux premiers. *Paris: A.L'Angelier*, 1588. 496 numb.lvs;4to. The earliest edn to contain the 3rd bk; 1st publ., Bordeaux, 1580. Basis for designation as 5th edn today unknown. Tchémerzine VIII:405; Fairfax Murray (France) 677; Rothschild 140. CtY, MH, NN-RB, PPL; BN.   588/61

___[Anr issue]. *Paris: M.Sonnius*, 1588. Tchémerzine VIII:405.   588/62

Münster, Sebastian. Cosmographey, oder beschreibung aller Länder . . . Jetzt aber . . . bis in das M.D.LXXXVIII. Jar gemehret. *Basel: S.Henricpetri*, 1588. 1420p.;illus.,maps,port.; fol. 1st publ., Basel, 1544. Sabin 51393; Burmeister (Münster) 81. DLC, InU-L, NjP; BL, Munich: StB.   588/63

Ortelius, Abraham. Epitome du Theatre du monde . . . Reveu, corrigé & augmenté de plusieurs cartes, pour la troisiesme fois. *Antwerp: C.Plantin, for P.Galle*, 1588. 94 numb. lvs;maps;obl.4to. 1st publ. with French text, by Peeter Heyns, under title *Le miroir du*

monde, Antwerp, 1579. Sabin 57688; Atkinson (Fr.Ren.) 340; Koeman (Ort.) 52; Bibl. belg.,1st ser.,XII:H56; Phillips (Atlases) 3398. DLC, ICN, InU-L, NNH; BL, BN.
588/64

____. Theatro de la tierra universal. *Antwerp: C.Plantin*, 1588. 10 lvs;maps;fol. Transl. from Latin text, 1st publ., Antwerp, 1570. Koeman (Ort.) 23; Phillips (Atlases) 393; Peeters-Fontainas (Impr.esp.) 990; Palau 205363. DLC, ICN, RPJCB; BL, Madrid: BN.
588/65

Piccha, Gregorio. Oratio ad Sixtum V. Pont. Max. aliosque christianos principes et respublicas pro britannico bello indicendo. *Rome: V.Accolti*, 1588. 14 lvs; 4to. On the Spanish Armada, with refs to Sir Francis Drake. Sabin 62602. CSt, DFo, NN-RB; BL, BN.
588/66

Porta, Giovanni Battista della. Phytognomonica . . . octo libris contenta. *Naples: H.Salviani*, 1588. 320p.;illus.,port.;fol. Among plants described for medicinal use are Guaiacum & sarsaparilla. Pritzel 7273; Nissen (Bot.) 463; Adams (Cambr.) P1938. CtY-M, DNAL, IU, MH-A, MnU, NNBG; BL, BN.
588/67

Rabelais, François. Les oeuvres. *Lyons: J.Martin*, 1588. 3 pts;12mo. Includes 'Le quart livre', 1st publ., Paris, 1552. Plan (Rabelais) 112. ICN, OCl; BL, BN.   588/68

Ramusio, Giovanni Battista. Primo volume, & quarta editione. delle Navigationi et viaggi raccolto da m. Gio.Batt. Ramusio. *Venice: The Giuntas*, 1588 [colophon: 1587]. 394 numb.lvs;illus.,maps;fol. 1st publ., Venice, 1550. Sabin 67733; Streit I:171. CSt, DFo, ICU, MH, NN-RB; BL.   588/69

Rueda, Lope de. Compendio llamado El deleytoso . . . Recompilados por Juan Timoneda. *Logroño: M.Mares*, 1588. 38 numb.lvs;8vo. 1st publ., Valencia, 1567. Palau 281020. NNH.   588/70

Sanuto, Livio. Geografia . . . distinta in xii libri. *Venice: D.Zenaro*, 1588. 146 numb.lvs; maps;fol. Principally concerned with Africa, but with refs to Sebastian Cabot & New World. Sabin 76897; Adams (Cambr.) S378; Winship (Cabot) 209; JCB (3) I:314. DLC, MH, MnU-B, NN-RB, RPJCB; BL, BN.
588/71

Schwalenberg, Heinrich. Theses de morbo gallico et eius curatione. *Basel: Heirs of J.Oporinus*, 1588. 4to. Proksch I:83. BL.
588/72

Spain. Sovereigns, etc., 1556-1598 (Philip II). Instruccion y forma . . . en la publicacion, expendicion y cobranza de la Bula de Santa Cruzada . . . en los obispados de Guatemala, Onduras, etc. *Madrid*: 1588. 8 lvs;fol. Medina (BHA) 7742; Palau 120123.
588/73

Tabourot, Estienne. Les bigarrures . . . Quatriesme livre. *Paris: J.Richer*, 1588. 154 numb.lvs;12mo. In verse & prose. 1st publ., Paris, 1585. Choptrayanovitch (Tabourot) 212; Shaaber T1. MnU, PU.   588/74

Tasso, Torquato. Il Goffredo, overo Gierusalemme liberata, poema heroica. *Venice: A. Salicato*, 1588. 2 pts;12mo. 1st publ. with American refs, Parma, 1581. Racc.Tassiana 171; Adams (Cambr.) T242; Moranti (Urbino) 3250. CtY, MH, PU; Cambridge: Emmanuel, Bergamo: BC.   588/75

Theodorus, Jacobus, called Tabernaemontanus. Neuw Kreuterbuch mit schönen, künstlichen und leblichen Figuren und Konterfeyten aller Gewächss der Kreuter. *Frankfurt a.M.: N.Bassé*, 1588-91. 2v.;illus.; fol. Described are numerous American plants, e.g., beans & corn. Pritzel 9093; Nissen (Bot.) 1930; Arents (Add.) 89. CtY, MBH, NN-A; BL.
588/76

Valleriola, François. Observationum medicinalium lib. vi. [*Geneva?*] *A.Blanc*, 1588. 523p.;8vo. 1st publ., Lyons, 1573. Adams (Cambr.) V212. DNLM, MBCo; Cambridge: Clare.   588/77

Vera relatione di tutto quello che la flotta . . . del Rè Cattolico hà portato, tornando dalla terra ferma, Nova Spagna, & San Domenico, l'anno 1587. *Ferrara: V.Baldini*, 1588. [8]p.;4to. 1st publ., Rome, 1587. Sabin 98908. MiU-C.   588/78

Verheiden, Willem. Nootelijcke consideratien . . . opten . . . tractate van peys met den Spaengiarden. [*Amsterdam?*] 1588. [22]p.; 4to. 1st publ., [Amsterdam?], 1587. Knuttel 819. The Hague: KB.   588/79

Verstegen, Richard. Theatre des cruautez des hereticques de nostre temps. *Antwerp: A. Hubert*, 1588. 2 pts;illus.;4to. Transl. from author's *Theatrum crudelitatum haereticorum nostri temporis*, 1st publ. Antwerp, 1587.

Adams (Cambr.) T443. BL, BN.   588/80
____. Theatrum crudelitatum haereticorum
nostri temporis. *Antwerp: A.Hubert*, 1588.
95p.;illus.;4to. 1st publ., Antwerp, 1587. BL,
BN.   588/81
Zamorano, Rodrigo. Compendio del arte de
navegar. *Seville: J.de León*, 1588. 61
numb.lvs;illus.;4to. 1st publ., Seville, 1582.
Sabin 106246; Medina (BHA) 318; Palau
379250. CtY, RPJCB; BL, Madrid: BN.
                                          588/82

1589

Acosta, José de. De natura Novis Orbis libri
duo, et de promulgatione evangelii, apud barbaros, sive de precuranda Indorum salute libri
sex. *Salamanca: G.Foquel*, 1589. 640p.;8vo.
1st publ., Salamanca, 1588; here a reissue
with altered imprint date? Sabin 118; Medina
(BHA) 319; Streit I:176; Backer I:33; Ind.
aur.100.450; JCB (3) I:315. ICN, MH,
MnU-B, NN-RB, PBL, RPJCB; BL, BN.
                                           589/1
Airebaudouze, Pierre de, seigneur du Cest.
Orbis terrarum synoptica epitome . . . Quae
. . . adjuncta est Geographia poetica . . . a
viro doctissimo [Lamberto Danaeo]. [*Geneva:*] *J.Stoer*, 1589. 2 pts;8vo. 1st publ., Geneva, 1588. Ind.aur.106.975. BN.   589/2
Banister, John. An antidotarie chyrurgicall,
containing great varietie and choice of all sorts
of medicines. *London: T.Orwin,for T.Man*,
1589. 360p.;8vo. Includes directions for
medical use of tobacco. STC 1358; Ind.
aur.112.273; Arents (Add.) 91. CSmH,
DNLM, NN-A; London: Wellcome.   589/3
Beccadelli, Antonio. De dictis & factis
Alphonsi regis . . . libri quatuor . . . studio
Davidis Chytraei. *Rostock: S.Moelleman*,
1589. 188p.;4to. 1st publ. with American refs,
Wittenberg, 1585. Ind.aur.115.388. MBAt;
Munich: StB.   589/4
Belon, Pierre. Plurimarum singularium &
memorabilium rerum in Graecia, Asia . . .
aliisque exteris provinciis . . . Observationes
. . . Carolus Clusius . . . é gallicis latinas
faciebat. *Antwerp: C.Plantin*, 1589. 495p.;
illus.;8vo. 1st publ. in French, Paris, 1553;
here transl. from Plantin's 1555 edn. Bibl.
belg.,1st ser.,II:B123; Ind.aur.116.334.
MnU-B; BL, BN.   589/5

Beuther, Michael. Warhafftiger kurtzer
Bericht von mannigerley Kriegs und anderen
fürnemen Händeln. *Strassburg*: 1589. fol. 1st
publ., Basel, 1582, under title *Bildnisse viler
zum theyle von uralten*, etc. Ind.aur.118.442.
Göttingen: UB.   589/6
Bigges, Walter. Relation oder Beschreibung
der Rheiss und Schiffahrt auss Engellandt in
die . . . Indien gethan durch einen englischen
Ritter Franciscum Drack genant. [*Cologne:*]
1589. 23p.;maps;fol. Cf.Latin & French edns,
Leyden, 1588 & English edn of this year.
Sabin 20837; Baginsky (German Americana)
88; Ind.aur.119.259; Church 138; JCB (3)
I:315. CSmH, ICN, InU-L, MiU, NN-RB,
RPJCB; BL.   589/7
____. A summarie and true discourse of Sir
Frances Drakes West Indian voyage. Wherein
were taken, the townes of Saint Jago, Sancto
Domingo, Cartagena & Saint Augustine. *Lon-
don: R.Field*, 1589. 52p.;maps;4to. Con-
densed Latin & French translations from an
English ms had appeared in 1588. The maps,
engr. by Baptista Boazio, were probably
printed from plates used for the Latin version,
& are also found issued separately, with letter-
press descriptive text, and will be described at
entry 3171.6 in the (forthcoming) 2nd edn of
the STC. Sabin 93588 (&11505 & 20842);
Ind.aur.119.257; STC 3056; Church 136;
Kraus (Drake) 21 (p.199); JCB AR43:7-18.
CSmH, CtY, DFo, MHi, MiU-C, MnU-B,
NN-RB, RPJCB; BL.   589/8
—[Anr edn]. *London: R.Ward*, 1589. 37p.;4to.
Sabin 20841; Ind.aur.119.258; STC 3057;
Kraus (Drake) 22 (p.199). NN-RB; BL. 589/9
Blundeville, Thomas. A briefe description of
universal mappes and cardes, and of their use.
London: R.Ward,for T.Cadman, 1589. 4to.
Included are refs to American navigation.
Sabin 6022; Ind.aur.120.016; STC 3145;
Church 137. CSmH, DLC, ICN, MH, NN-
RB; BL.   589/10
Boazio, Baptista. The famous West Indian
voyadge made by the Englishe fleete.
[*London?* 1589?]. bds.;map;fol. Comprising
an engraved map with letterpress text, the
complex forms in which the two may be found
& their relation to Walter Bigges's *Summarie*
of this year (see above) will be described in the
(forthcoming) 2nd edn of the STC at entry
3171.6. The descriptive text has caption 'Sir

Francis Drake knight generall of the whole fleete'. JCB AR40:58-59 & AR48:17-20. NN-RB, RPJCB; BL. 589/11

Bonardo, Giovanni Maria, conte. La grandezza, larghezza, e distanza di tutte le sfere . . . Con alcune chiare annotazioni, per . . . Luigi Grotto. *Venice: F.& A.Zoppini,* 1589. 132 numb.lvs;8vo. 1st publ. with Groto's annotations mentioning New World, Venice, 1584. Ind.aur.121.669; Adams (Cambr.) B2379. DLC, NNC; Cambridge: Trinity, Vienna: NB. 589/12

____. La minera del mondo . . . Mandata in luce . . . da Luigi Grotto. *Venice: F. & A.Zoppini,* 1589. 112 numb.lvs;8vo. 1st publ., Venice, 1585. Ind.aur.121.668; Arents (Add.) 80. DNLM, ICU, NN-A; BL, BN. 589/13

Botero, Giovanni. Della ragion di stato. *Venice: The Gioliti,* 1589. 367p.;4to. In discussing statecraft mention is made of work of Jesuits in New World, and of Spanish colonization. Ind.aur.122.698; Adams (Cambr.) B2548; Moranti (Urbino) 667. CtY, ICN, MH, MnU-B, NNC, RPJCB; Bl, Copenhagen: KB. 589/14

__[Anr edn]. *Ferrara: V.Baldini,* 1589. See the year 1590.

Castellanos, Juan de. Primera parte de las Elegias de varones illustres de Indias. *Madrid: Widow of A. Gómez,* 1589. 382p.;port.;4to. In verse. No more published. Sabin 11402; Medina (BHA) 320; Pérez Pastor (Madrid) 303; JCB (3) I:315-316. DLC, MH, NN-RB, PBL, RPJCB; BL, BN. 589/15

Conestaggio, Girolamo Franchi di. Dell'unione del regno di Portogallo alla corona di Castiglia. *Genoa: G.Bartoli,* 1589. 412p.;4to. 1st publ., Genoa, 1585. IU, NNH, RPJCB; BL, BN. 589/16

____. Historien der Königreich, Hispanien, Portugal und Aphrica . . . Auss dem Italienischen, durch Albrecht Fürsten . . . gebracht. *Munich: A.Berg,* 1589. 126 numb.lvs;illus.;fol. Transl. from author's *Dell'unione del regno di Portugal a la corona di Castiglia,* 1st publ., Genoa, 1585. Sabin 32099; Shaaber C628. DLC, ICN, NNH, PU, RPJCB; BL. 589/17

Conti, Natale. Delle historie de' suoi tempi . . . Di latino . . . nuovamente tradotta da m.Giovan Carlo Saraceni. *Venice: D.Zenaro,* 1589. 491 numb.lvs;4to. Transl. from Conti's

Universae historiae sui temporis, 1st publ., Venice, 1581. Sabin 16161n. DLC, ICN, RPJCB; BL, BN. 589/18

Cortés, Martín. The arte of navigation . . . Translated out of Spanish . . . by Richard Eden. *London: R.Jug,* 1589. 83 numb.lvs; map;4to. 1st publ. in this translation, London, 1561. Sabin 16967; STC 5802; JCB (3) I:316. DLC, RPJCB; BL. 589/19

Du Bartas, Guillaume de Salluste, seigneur. Commentaires sur la Sepmaine de la creation du monde [par Simon Goulart]. *Rouen: T.Mallard,* 1589. 328 numb.lvs;12mo. 1st publ. in this form, including text itself of *La sepmaine,* Geneva, 1581. In verse. Holmes (DuBartas) I:73 no.21; Jones (Goulart) 20(j). BN. 589/20

____. La seconde sepmaine, ou Enfance du monde. *Geneva: J.Chouët,* 1589. 579p.;12mo. 1st publ., Paris, 1584. In verse. Holmes (DuBartas) I:84 no.5a; Jones (Goulart) 20(i); Adams (Cambr.) D963; Rothschild 3270. Cambridge: Sidney Sussex, BN. 589/21

Durante, Castore. Il tesoro della sanita. *Venice: A.Muschio,* 1589. 328p.;8vo. 1st publ., Rome (?), 1586; here a reissue of the publisher's 1588 edn? CtY-M. 589/22

Ercilla y Zúñiga, Alonso de. Tercera parte de la Araucana. *Madrid: P.Madrigal,* 1589. 365-434 numb.lvs;4to. The earliest edn of this pt, the foliation continuing the total number of leaves of the Madrid, 1578, edns of the 1st two pts. In verse. Medina (BHA) 321; Medina (Arau.) 11. MH; The Escorial, Santiago, Chile: BN. 589/23

Estienne, Charles. L'agriculture et maison rustique, de mm. Charles Estienne et Jean Liebault. [*Lyons: Printed for*] *J.DuPuys,at Paris,* 1589. 294 numb.lvs;illus.;4to. 1st publ. in this version, Paris, 1567. Thiébaud (La chasse) 349; Baudrier (Lyons) I:368. NjP. 589/24

Gabelkover, Oswald. Nützlich Artzneybuch für alle des menschlichen Leibes, Anligen und Gebrechen. *Tübingen:* 1589. 4to. Includes a recipe using tobacco as embrocation. Graesse III:1. 589/25

Gallucci, Giovanni Paolo. Theatrum mundi, et temporis. *Venice: G.B.Somasco,* 1589. 478p.;illus.,maps;4to. 1st publ., Venice, 1588; here a reissue with altered imprint date. Mortimer (Italy) 206n; Adams (Cambr.)

G169. InU-L, MiU; Cambridge: Whipple.
589/26

González de Mendoza, Juan, Bp. Histoire du grand royaume de la Chine . . . ensemble un Itineraire du nouveau monde, & le descouvrement du nouveau Mexique en 1583 . . . mise en françois . . . par Luc de la Porte. *Paris: J.Périer*, 1589. 2 pts;8vo. 1st publ. in French, Paris, 1588. Sabin 47829; Wagner (SW) 7cc; Atkinson (Fr.Ren.) 347; Streit IV:2005; JCB (3) I:316-317. ICN, NNH, RPJCB; BL, BN.
589/27

___[Anr issue]. *Paris: N.du Fossé*, 1589. Sabin 27780n; Wagner (SW) 7dd; Atkinson (Fr. Ren.) 347n; Streit IV:2005n. DLC, InU-L, MH, MnU-B, NN-RB; Paris: Mazarine.
589/28

____. Ein neuwe kurze doch warhafftige Beschreibung dess . . . bisshere unbekandten Konigreichs China. *Frankfurt a.M.: S.Feyerabend*, 1589. 181p.;4to. Transl. by Johann Kellner from author's *Historia de las cosas mas notables . . . de la China*, 1st publ., Valencia, 1585, but without 2nd pt describing New World; refs to America appear however in preface. Sabin 27781n; Wagner (SW) 7r; Streit IV:1985. DLC, InU-L, RPJCB; BL.
589/29

____. Nova et succincta, vera tamen historia de . . . regno China . . . Ex hispanica primum in italicum, inde in germanicam ex hac demùm in latinum . . . operâ Marci Henningi. *Frankfurt a.M.:* [*S.Feyerabend?* 1589]. 283p.;8vo. Transl. from preceding item, with its truncated text. Sabin 27781; Wagner (SW) 7s; Streit IV:2006. CtY, DLC, MH, MnU-B, NN-RB, RPJCB; BL.
589/30

Hakluyt, Richard, comp. The principall navigations, voiages and discoveries of the English nation, made by sea or over land. *London: G.Bishop & R.Newberie*, 1589. 825p.;map;fol. Two issues are known, in the earlier of which 'The ambassage of Sir Hierome Bowes', etc., comprises p. 491-505, the later being condensed to p.491-501. In addition, in some copies, 6 lvs, unpaged, with caption 'The famous voyage of Sir Francis Drake into the South Sea', is inserted between p.643 & 644. For the contents, sources, and detailed bibliographical analysis, etc., of this monumental work, see *The Hakluyt Handbook*, ed. by D.B.Quinn (London, 1974). Sabin 29594; Wagner (SW) 9; STC 12625;

Arents (Add.) 93; Church 139 & 139A; JCB (3) I:317-318. CSmH, CtY, DLC, ICN, InU-L, MH, MiU-C, MnU-B, NN-RB, PPL, RPJCB; BL, Helsinki: UL. 589/31

Heyns, Peeter. Epitome Theatri. *Antwerp:* 1589. See Ortelius, Abraham, below.

Hurault, Michel, sieur de Bélesbat et du Fay. Discours. Ein fürtreffliches frey rundes und ungescheuchtes Bedencken. *Kleine Rhuwart, H.Windstill* [i.e.,*Strassburg? B.Jobin?*] 1589. [70]p.;4to. Transl. from [*Paris?*], 1588, *Discours sur l'estat de France* IU. 589/32

____. Excellent et libre discours sur l'estat present de la France. [*Paris?*] 1589. 88 lvs;16mo. 1st publ., [*Paris?*], 1588. Adams (Cambr.) H1195. Cambridge: Clare. 589/33

Jesuits. Letters from missions. Annuae litterae (1586-7) 1589. Litterae . . . annorum M.D.LXXXVI et M.D.LXXXVII. *Rome: Jesuit College*, 1589. 592p.;8vo. Sabin 41509; Streit I:179; Backer I:1286; JCB (3) I:318. DLC, ICN, NNH, RPJCB; BL. 589/34

Lucidarius. M.Elucidarius. Von allerhand Geschöpffen Gottes . . . und wie alle Creaturen geschaffen sein auff Erden. *Frankfurt a.M.: Heirs of C.Egenolff*, 1589. 43 lvs;illus.,map;4to. 1st publ., Strassburg, [ca.1535]. Schorbach (Lucidarius) 64. Munich: StB, Wolfenbüttel: HB. 589/35

Lyly, John. Pappe with an hatchet. *London: J.Anoke & J.Astile,for* [*T.Orwin*, 1589]. 4to Includes ref. to tobacco used as snuff. In this issue, on lf B2v line 26 has reading 'abusde.'. STC 17463; Arents 33. CSmH, DFo, MH, NN-A; BL, BN. 589/36

___[Anr issue]. *London: J.Anoke & J.Astile,for* [*T.Orwin*, 1589]. In this issue lf B2v has reading 'abusde:'. STC 17463.3. CtY, InU-L; Oxford: Bodl. 589/37

___[Anr edn]. *London: J.Anoke & J.Astile,for* [*T.Orwin*, 1589]. In this edn lf B2v has reading 'abusde,'. STC 17463.7. CSmH, TxU; Oxford: Bodl. 589/38

Maffei, Giovanni Pietro. Historiarum Indicarum libri xvi. Selectarum, item, ex India, epistolarum . . . libri iv. Accesit Ignatii Loiolae vita. *Cologne: House of Birckmann,for A.Mylius*, 1589. 541p.;fol. 1st publ., Florence, 1588. Sabin 43770n; Streit IV:1053; Backer V:298; Adams (Cambr.) M92. CtY, DLC, ICN, InU-L, MH, MnU-B, NN-RB; BL, BN. 589/39

__[Anr edn]. *Lyons: The Giuntas*, 1589. 688p.;4to. Sabin 43770n; Streit IV:1054; Backer V:298; Baudrier (Lyons) VI:410; Adams (Cambr.) M93. MH, RPJCB; Cambridge: UL, BN. 589/40

__[Anr edn]. *Venice: D.Zenaro*, 1589,'88. 2 pts;4to. The 2nd pt comprises Maffei's *Selectarum epistolarum . . . libri quatuor*, 1st publ. separately, 1588. Sabin 43770n; Streit IV:1045; Backer V:298; Adams (Cambr.) M91. MnU-B, RPJCB; BL. 589/41

____. Le istorie delle Indie Orientali . . . Tradotte di latino . . . da m. Francesco Serdonati. *Florence: F.Giunta*, 1589. 930p.;4to. 1st publ. in Latin, Florence, 1588. Sabin 43777; Borba de Moraes II:10; Streit IV:1055; Backer V:299; JCB (3) I:318. CU, DLC, InU-L, MWelC, MiU, MnU-B, NN-RB, RPJCB; BL, BN. 589/42

__[Anr edn]. Le historie delle Indie Orientali. *Venice: D.Zenaro*, 1589. 416 numb.lvs;4to. Sabin 43778; Borba de Moraes II:10; Streit IV:1056; Backer V:299. CtY, ICU, InU-L, MnU-B, NN-RB. 589/43

Marquardus, Joannes. Practica theorica empirica morborum. *Spira: B.Albinus*, 1589. 464p.;8vo. Includes, p.422-464, Lucas Ghini's 'Morbi neapolitani curandi perbrevis'. DNLM; BL. 589/44

Martin, Anthony. A second sound, or warning of the trumpet unto judgement. *London: T.Orwin,for A.Maunsell*, 1589. 4to. On lf 17 is mentioned Spain's neglect in converting American natives. Sabin 44829; STC 17491. BL, Oxford: Bodl., Cambridge: UL. 589/45

Mexía, Pedro. Vite di tutti gl'imperadori romani . . . da m. Lodovico Dolce nuovamente tradotte & ampliate. *Venice: P.Ugolino*, 1589. 547 numb.lvs;4to. 1st publ. in enlarged form, Venice, 1561. Palau 167354n. 589/46

Neander, Michael. Orbis terrae partium succinta explicatio . . . Tertiae editioni addita sunt alia. *Leipzig: A.Lamberg*, 1589. 224 numb.lvs;8vo. 1st publ., Eisleben, 1583. Sabin 52175; Adams (Cambr.) N114. DLC, InU-L, MiU, MnU-B, RPJCB; Cambridge: St John's. 589/47

Nores, Giasone de. Discorso . . . intorno alla geographia. *Padua: P.Meietti*, 1589. 13 numb.lvs;4to. Included are refs to America. Sabin 55466. MB, RPJCB; BL. 589/48

Orta, Garcia da. Dell'historia de i semplici aromati. Et altre cose; che vengono portate dall'India. Orientali pertinenti all'uso della medicina . . . Et due altri libri parimente di quelle cose che si portano dall'Indie Occidentali; di Nicolò Monardes . . . tutti tradotti . . . da m. Annibale Briganti. *Venice: Heirs of F.Ziletti*, 1589. 2 pts;8vo. 1st publ. in Italian, Venice, 1576. Sabin 57669; Guerra (Monardes) 29; JCB (3) I:320. CtY-M, DNLM, MH-A, OCU, RPJCB; BL. 589/49

__[Anr issue]. *Venice: G.& A.Zenari*, 1589. Guerra (Monardes) 30. MiU-C. 589/50

Ortelius, Abraham. Epitome Theatri . . . praecipuarum regionum delineationes . . . continens. *Antwerp: C.Plantin,for P.Galle*, 1589. 103 lvs;maps;obl.16mo. 1st publ. with Latin version of text of Peeter Heyns, Antwerp, 1585. Sabin 57689; Koeman (Ort.) 53; Phillips (Atlases) 394; Adams (Cambr.) O344. DLC, ICN, PPL; BL, BN. 589/51

____. Theatrum oder Schawbuch des Erdtkreijs. *Antwerp: C.Plantin,for A.Ortelius*, 1580 [i.e., 1589?]. 101 lvs;maps;fol. 1st publ. in German, Antwerp, 1572. Though having colophon dated 1580, differs from that described above in containing renewed or altered maps dated as late as 1589, amongst them one of America of 1587. Koeman (Ort.) 16B (p.51-52); Phillips (Atlases) 3394. DLC; Brussels: BR. 589/52

Pasquier, Etienne. Remonstrance aux François sur leur sedition, rebellion et felonie, contre la majeste du Roy. [*Paris?*] 1589. 8vo. Contains passage contrasting dutiful obedience of barbarians in Indies & New World to their rulers with the recent disloyal conduct of the French. BN (Hist. de France) I:337 no.710. BN. 589/53

Peele, George. A farewell. Entituled to the famous and fortunate generalls of our English forces: Sir John Norris and Syr Frauncis Drake. *London: J.C[harlewood].*, 1589. 21p.;4to. In verse. Sabin 59526; STC 19537. CSmH; BL. 589/54

Poccianti, Michele. Catalogus scriptorum florentinorum. *Florence: F.Giunta*, 1589. 171p.;4to. Included are extracts of Vespucci's letters. Sabin 63505; Adams (Cambr.) P1677; Shaaber P479. CU-S, DLC, ICN, MH, MiU, NN-RB, PU; BL, BN. 589/55

Porta, Giovanni Battista della. Phytognomonics . . . octo libris contenta. *Naples: H.Salviani*, 1589 [colophon:1588]. 320p.;

illus.,port.;fol. 1st publ., Naples, 1588; here a reissue with altered imprint date. Cf.Pritzel 7273; cf.Nissen (Bot.) 463; cf.Adams (Cambr.) P1938. DNLM, PPC. 589/56

Response a un avis qui conseille aux François de se rendre sous la protection du Roi d'Espagne. [*Paris?*] 1589. Cites as an example of Spanish justice their treatment of Atabalipa (last Inca ruler of Peru) & of Temistitan (i.e., Mexico). Reprinted in Simon Goulart's *Quartriesme recueil,*[Geneva?], 1595. 589/56a

Sarrasin, Jean Antoine. De peste commentarius . . . Editio altera. *Geneva: J.de Tournes,* 1589. 369p.;8vo. 1st publ., Geneva, 1571. Cartier (de Tournes) 685. DNLM, MnU, NNNAM, PPC; BL, BN. 589/57

Soto, Domingo de. Commentarium in quartum Sententiarum tomus primus[-secundus]. *Venice: G.& A.Zenari,* 1589. 2v.;4to. 1st publ., Salamanca, 1557-60. Adams (Cambr.) S1480. Cambridge: St John's. 589/58

————. De justitia & jure, libri decem. *Medina del Campo: F.à Canto,for B.Boyer,* 1589. 896p.;fol. 1st publ., Salamanca, 1553. Pérez Pastor (Medina del Campo) 220; Palau 320162. MH-L. 589/59

——[Anr edn]. *Venice: F.Prato,* 1589. 1006p.;4to. Palau 320161. CtY-L, MH-L, MiU-L,. NN-RB. 580/60

Stella, Giulio Cesare. Columbeidos libri priores duo. *Rome: Santi & Co.,* 1589. 67p.;4to. 1st publ., London, 1585. In verse. Sabin 91217. DLC, NN-RB. 589/61

Tasso, Torquato. Il Goffredo, overo Gierusalemme liberata, poema heroico. *Venice: A. Salicato,* 1589. 2 pts;4to. 1st publ. with American refs, Parma, 1581. Racc.Tassiana 172; Shaaber T87. PU; Bergamo: BC. 589/62

Thilo, Valentin. Icones heroum bellica virtute illustrium. Joviani Musei heroes. *Basel: K.von Waldkirch,* 1589. 2 pts; ports;4to. Comprises ports deriving from Basel, 1575, edn of Paolo Giovio's *Elogia virorum bellica virtute illustrium,* here accompanied by verses by Thilo. Sabin 36774. BL. 589/63

Vairo, Leonardo. De fascino libri tres. *Venice: The Aldine Press,* 1589. 375p.;8vo. 1st publ., Paris, 1583. Adams (Cambr.) V16; Arents (Add.) 78; Shaaber V1. CtY, MH, NN-A, PU; BL, BN. 589/64

Valleriola, François. Enarrationum medicinalium libri sex. *Lyons: F.LeFèvre,* 1589. 984p.;8vo. 1st publ., Lyons, 1554. Baudrier

(Lyons) V:355. DNLM; BL, BN. 589/65

Wittich, Johann. Bericht von den wunderbaren bezoardischen Steinen . . . Welche alle mehrentheils den alten und newen Scribenten unbekandt, und erst innerhalb 30. Jahren aus India Orientali und Occidentali, durch Gartiam ab Horto, und Nicolaum Monardum kündig gemacht worden seind. *Leipzig: Heirs of H.Steinman,* 1589. 181p.;4to. Pages 141-181 have title 'Von dem ligno Guayaco . . . von der Sarsa parilla'. Sabin 104966. DNLM, MH; BL. 589/66

1590

Acosta, José de. Historia natural y moral de las Indias, en que se tratan las cosas notables del cielo, y elementos, metales, plantas, y animales dellas: y los ritos, y ceremonias, leyes, y govierno, y guerras de los Indios. *Seville: J.de León,* 1590. 535p.;4to. Sabin 121; Medina (BHA) 324; Streit II:1072; Backer I:34; Ind.aur.100.451; Escudero (Seville) 772; Pritzel 14; Arents 35; JCB (3) I:321. CU, DLC, MH, MiU-C, MnU-B, NN-RB, PPL, RPJCB; BL, BN. 590/1

Arnauld, Antoine. Anti-Espagnol, autrement Les Philippiques d'un Demostenes françois touchant les menees & ruses de Philippe roy d'Espagne. [*Paris?*] 1590. 32p.;12mo. In attacking dynastic designs of Philip II on French throne, ref. is made to Spanish expulsion of French from Florida. Palau 12985; Ind. aur.108.852. 590/2

——[Anr edn]. Copie de l'Anti-Espagnol, faict a Paris. [*Amsterdam?*] 1590. 56p.;12mo. RP-JCB. 590/3

——[Anr edn]. Coppie de l'Anti-Espagnol, faict a Paris. [*France?*] 1590. 81p.;8vo. Ind. aur.108.853; Cioranescu (XVI) 2635. NjP; BN. 590/3a

————. L'antiespagnol, odor Ausführliche Erklerunge . . . Trewlich auss frantzösischer Sprache, durch einen natürlichen Castilianern [Johann Fischart] verdeudscht. *Basilico, ausserhalb Madrill: G.Spinardus* [i.e., *Basel: S.Apiarius*] 1590. 20 lvs;4to. Transl. by Johann Fischart from preceding work. Ind. aur.108.854; Shaaber A787. PU; Munich: StB. 590/4

——[Anr edn]. [*Strassburg: B.Jobin*] 1590. 4to. Ind.aur.108.857. Halle: UB. 590/5

___[Anr edn]. Antihispanus. *Leyden* [i.e., *Strassburg: B.Jobin*] 1590. 20 lvs;4to. Ind. aur.108.856. NNH; Berlin: StB. 590/6

___. The coppie of the Anti-Spaniard, made at Paris, by a Frenchman. *London: J.Wolfe*, 1590. Transl. (by A.Munday?) from the author's *Anti-Espagnol* of this year (in edn with title *Coppie de l'Anti-Espagnol?*). STC 684; Palau 12987; Ind.aur.108.855. CSmH, CtY, MH, NNH; BL. 590/7

Avelar, André do. Reportorio dos tempos . . . segunda impressam reformado e acrescentado pelo mesmo autor. *Lisbon: M.de Lyra,for S.López*, 1590. 207 numb.lvs;illus.;4to. 1st publ., Lisbon, 1585; here enl. with additional American refs. Anselmo 753; Ind.aur. 109.700. MH; Lisbon: BN. 590/8

Banchieri, Adriano. La nobiltà dell'asino di Attabalippa dal Perù [pseud.]. *Venice:* 1590. Said to have been 1st publ., 1588, quite possibly at Bologna. *Dizionario biografico degli Italiani* (Rome, 1963) V:652. For the earliest extant recorded edn, see the year 1592. 590/8a

Bellinato, Francesco, supposed author. Discorso di cosmographia in dialogo. *Venice: A. Manuzio*, 1590. 48p.;8vo. 1st publ., Venice, 1573. Renouard (Aldus) 245.9; Ind.aur. 116.209. Berlin: StB. 590/9

Benzoni, Girolamo. Novae Novi Orbis historiae. Das ist, Aller Geschichten, so in der newen Welt, welche Occidentalis India . . . genent wird . . . Dessgleichen von der frantzosen Meerfahrten das Land Floridam . . . durch Abeln Scherdigern . . . auss dem Latein . . . gebracht. *Helmstadt: J.Lucius,for L.Brandes*, 1590. 517p.;4to. 1st publ. in Latin, [Geneva], 1578; as transl. from the Italian text, 1st publ., Venice, 1565. Sabin 4799; Medina (BHA) 250n (I:419); Streit II:1073; Ind.aur.116.993; Arents (Add.) 54; JCB (3) I:321. NN-RB, RPJCB; Berlin: StB. 590/10

Bigges, Walter. Narrationes due admodum memorabiles, quam prima continet diarium expeditionis Francisci Draki . . . in Indias Occidentales susceptae, anno MDLXXXV. Altera omnium rerum ab eodem Drake et Norreysio in Lusitanica irruptione gestarum fidelem continuationem subjicit. *Nuremberg: C.Lochner & H.Hofmann*, 1590. 36p.;maps; 4to. Bigges's *Narrationes* 1st publ., Leyden, 1588, with title *Expeditio* etc.; the 2nd pt 1st publ., London, 1589, with title *Ephemeris ex-*

peditio. . . . Sabin 20834; Church 247; JCB (3) I:322. CSmH, ICN, MB, NN-RB, RPJCB; BL. 590/11

Bodin, Jean. Los seis libros de la Republica . . . Traducidos . . . y emendados catholicamente por Gaspar de Añastro Ysunza. *Turin: Heirs of N.Bevilacqua*, 1590. 638p.;fol. 1st publ. in French, Paris, 1576. Ind.aur. 120.836; Palau 31205. MH; BL, BN. 590/12

Bonardo, Giovanni Maria. La minera del mondo . . . Mandato in luce . . . da Luigi Grotto. *Mantua: F.Osanna*, 1590. 8vo. 1st publ., Venice, 1585. Ind.aur.121.670; Arents (Add.) 81. NN-A; BN. 590/13

Botero, Giovanni. Della ragion di stato. *Ferrara: V.Baldini*, 1589 [colophon:1590]. 334p.; 8vo. 1st publ., Venice, 1589. Ind.aur.122. 697. ICN, MH; BL. 590/14

___[Anr issue]. *Ferrara: V.Baldini*, 1590. Ind. aur.122.699. CtY, ICN, MH, NN-RB; Milan: BT. 590/15

___[Anr edn]. . . . Revisti dall'autore. *Rome: V.Pelagallo*, 1590. 400p.;12mo. Ind. aur. 122.700; Moranti (Urbino) 668. BN. 590/16

Capilupi, Ippolito, Bp of Fano. Capiluporum carmina. *Rome: Heirs of G.O. Gigliotto*, 1590. 394p.;front.;4to. A collective edn of poems of Ippolito, Lelio, Alfonso & Giulio Capilupi, including 3 poems by Ippolito on Columbus, 1st publ., Rome, 1574. Shaaber C110. DFo, ICN, MH, NNC, PU; BL, BN. 590/17

Capivaccio, Girolamo. De lue venerea acroaseis. *Speyer: B.Albini*, 1590. 88p.;8vo. Proksch I:20; Ind.aur.131.668; Adams (Cambr.) C600. DNLM, NNNAM; BL, Berlin: StB. 590/18

Cervantes Saavedra, Miguel de. Primera parte de Galatea. *Lisbon:* 1590. 503 (i.e.,423) numb.lvs;8vo. 1st publ., Alcalá de Henares, 1585. Ríus (Cervantes) 200; Palau 51929. Barcelona: BC. 590/19

Daunce, Edward. A briefe discourse dialoguewise, shewing how false and dangerous their reports are, which affirm, the Spaniards' intended invasion to be, for the re-establishment of the Romish religion; for her Majestie's succours given to the Netherlanders, and for Sir Francis Drake's enterprise three yeares past into the West Indies. *London: R.Field*, 1590. 26p.;4to. Sabin 18668; STC 6290. DFo, NN-RB; BL. 590/20

Donati, Marcello. De variolis et morbillis tractatus . . . De radice purgante quam

Mechioacan vocant. *Mantua: F.Osanna,* 1590-91. 2 pts;8vo. 1st publ., Mantua, 1569. BN.   590/21

Duchesne, Joseph. The sclopotarie of Joseph Quercetanus, phisition, or his booke containing the cure of wounds received by shot of gunne . . . Published into English by John Hester. *London: R.Ward, for J.Sheldrake,* 1590. 95p.;4to. Transl. from ᐟ Duchesne's *Sclopetarius,* 1st publ., Lyons [i.e.,Geneva], 1576.STC 7277.DFo, NNNAM;BL.   590/22

Durante, Castore. Il tesoro della sanita. *Mantua: F.Osanna,* 1590. 334p.;8vo. 1st publ., Rome (?), 1586. DNLM.   590/23

Ercilla y Zúñiga, Alonso do. Primera, segunda, y tercera partes de la Araucana. *Madrid: P.Madrigal,* 1590.436 numb.lvs;8vo. The earliest edn as such to incorporate all 3 pts. In verse. Pt 1 1st publ., 1569; pt 2, 1578; pt 3, 1589, all at Madrid. Pts 2 & 3, though here foliated consecutively with pt 1, have special title pages dated 1589. Sabin 22722; Medina (BHA) 342; Medina (Arau.) 12; JCB (3) I:322-323. CtY, NHi, RPJCB; Madrid: BU(San Isidro).   590/24

_____. Tercera parte de la Araucana. *Saragossa: Widow of J.Escarilla,* 1590. 70 numb.lvs;8vo. 1st publ., Madrid, 1589. In verse. Medina (Arau.) 13. NNH; Barcelona: BU.   590/25

Estienne, Charles. L'agricoltura et casa di villa . . . tradotta dal cavaliere Hercole Cato. *Turin:* 1590. 8vo. 1st publ. in Italian, Venice, 1581. Thiébaud (La chasse) 358.   590/26

Gesner, Konrad. Quatre livres des secrets de medecine.*Rouen: T.Reinsart,* 1590.1st publ., Paris, 1573. NNNAM.   590/27

González de Mendoza, Juan, Bp. Dell'historia della China . . . tradotta nell'italiana dal magn. m. Francesco Avanzó . . . Dove . . . si tratta . . . d'altri luochi più conosciuti del mondo nuovo. *Venice: A.Muschio,* 1590. 462p.;8vo. 1st publ. in Italian, Rome, 1586. Sabin 27779n; Wagner (SW) 7p.;Streit IV:2013; Woodfield B6; JCB (3) I:323. DLC, ICN, InU-L, MnU-B, NNH, RPJCB; Florence: BN.   590/28

Goulart, Simon, comp. Le premier recueil, contenant les choses plus memorables advenuès sous la Ligue. [*Geneva?*] 1590. 805p.;8vo. Includes (p.771-805) Walter Bigges's 'Voyage de messiere Francois Drake', 1st publ. in French, Leyden, 1588; and also the *Discours au Roi Henri III,* 1st publ., [Paris?],

1584. Cf.Sabin 20929n; Jones (Goulart) 30(b); Adams (Cambr.) F868. MiU-C, NN-RB; BL, BN.   590/29a

___[Anr edn]. [*Geneva?*] 1590. 548p.;8vo. Jones (Goulart) 30(c). Paris: Ste Geneviève. 590/29b

___[Anr edn]. [*Geneva?*] 1590. 340 (i.e., 540) p.;8vo. Bigges's 'Voyage' occupies p.521-'340'. Cf.Jones (Goulart) 30(e). MH.   590/29c

_____. Le second recueil, contenant l'histoire des choses plus memorables advenues sous la Ligue. [*Geneva?*] 1590. 865p.;8vo. 'Du voyage & du retour notable du grand capitaine Drake des Indes, avec les riches dispouilles des Espagnols': p.295-299. Jones (Goulart) 30(b); Adams (Cambr.) F871. RPJCB; BL, BN.
                                             590/29d

___[Anr edn]. [*Geneva?*] 1590. 606p.;8vo. In the title 'plus' appears as 'pus'. The account of Drake's voyage here appears on p.206-208. Cf.Jones (Goulart) 30(e). MH.   590/29e

Guicciardini, Francesco. La historia d'Italia. *Venice: P.Ugolino,* 1590. 488 numb.lvs;4to. 1st publ., Florence, 1561. Adams (Cambr.) G1516. CU, NSyU; BL.   590/30

Hariot, Thomas. Admiranda narratio fida tamen, de commodis et incolarum ritibus Virginiae . . . Anglica scripta sermone . . . nunc autem primum latio donata à C.C[lusius]. *Frankfurt a.M.: J.Wechel, for T.de Bry, to be sold by S.Feyerabend,* 1590. 2pts;illus.,map;fol. (Theodor de Bry's *America.* Pt 1. Latin). 1st publ. in English, London, 1588. Cf.Sabin 8784; Church 140-141; Arents 37; JCB (3) I:383-384. CSmH, CtY, DLC, MH, NN-RB, PPL, RPJCB; BL, BN.
                                             590/31

_____. A briefe and true report of the new found land of Virginia. *Frankfurt a.M.: J.Wechel, for T.de Bry,to be sold by S.Feyerabend,* 1590. 2 pts;illus.,map;fol. (Theodor de Bry's *America.* Pt 1. English). 1st publ., London, 1588; here supplemented (as in the translations of this year) by plates derived from drawings by John White. Cf.Sabin 8784; STC 12786; cf.Church 203; cf.JCB (3) I:385. CSmH, DLC, ICN, InU-L, MH, MiU-C, MnU-B, NN-RB, RPJCB; BL, BN.   590/32

_____. Merveilleux et estrange rapport, toutefois fidele, des commoditez qui se trouvent en Virginia . . . Traduit nouvellement d'anglois. *Frankfurt a.M.: J.Wechel, for T.de Bry,* 1590. 2 pts;illus.,map;fol. (Theodor de Bry's *America.* Pt 1. French). 1st publ. in English,

London, 1588. Cf.Sabin 8784; Church 203; JCB (3) I:386. CSmH, DLC, ICN, MH, MiD-B, RPJCB; BL, BN. 590/33

____. Wunderbarliche, doch warhafftige Erklärung, von der Gelegenheit und Sitten der Wilden in Virginia, welche newlich von den Engelländern, so im Jar 1585 . . . ist erfunden worden. *Frankfurt a.M.: J.Wechel, for T.de Bry,& sold by S.Feyerabend*, 1590. 3 pts; illus.,map;fol. (Theodor de Bry's *America*. Pt 1. German). Transl. from English text, 1st publ., London, 1588. Cf.Sabin 8784; Arents (Add.) 96; cf.Church 178; cf.JCB (3) I:386-387. CSmH, DLC, IU, MH, MiU-C, NN-RB, RPJCB; BL. 590/34

Heurne, Johan van. Praxis medicinae nova ratio . . . Recognita et emendata ab auctore. *Leyden: Plantin Press (F.Raphelengius)*, 1590. 518p.;illus.;4to. 1st publ., Leyden, 1587. NNNAM; BL. 590/35

Heyns, Peeter. Epitome du Theatre du monde. *Antwerp:* 1590. See Ortelius, Abraham, below.

Honter, Johannes. Rudimentorum cosmographicorum libri iii. [*Zurich? House of Froschauer?* 1590?]. [60]p.;illus.,maps;8vo. 1st publ., in this version, Kronstadt, 1542. In verse. Sabin 32799. MH, NNH, OCl. 590/36

Jesuits. Letters from missions. Annuae litterae (1588) 1590. Annuae litterae . . . anni .M.D.LXXXVIII. *Rome: Jesuit College*, 1590. 336p.;8vo. Included are reports on Brazilian & Mexican provinces. Streit I:186; Backer I:1286 (Benci 10). MnU-B, NNH. 590/37

La Noue, François de. Discours politiques et militaires. *Basel:* 1590. 710p.;8vo. 1st publ., Basel, 1587. BN. 590/38

__[Anr edn]. *La Rochelle: J.Haultin*, 1590. 964 + p.;12mo. Desgraves (Les Haultin) 109. 590/39

Leo Hebraeus. La traduzion del Indio de los tres dialogos de amor . . . hecha de italiano . . . por Garcilasso Inga de la Vega, natural . . . del Cuzco. *Madrid: P.Madrigal*, 1590. 313 numb.lvs;4to. In his preface the translator refers to his projected work *La Florida del Ynca*, later publ. in 1605. Medina (BHA) 328; Adams (Cambr.) A64; Palau 417; JCB AR21:8. CtY, InU-L, NNC, RPJCB; Cambridge: Trinity, BN. 590/40

Lima (Ecclesiastical province). Council, 1583. Concilium provinciale Limense.

Celebratum in civitate regum, anno M.D.LXXII . . . Typis excusum, atq. ad Indos transmissum. *Madrid: P.Madrigal*, 1590. 88 numb.lvs;4to. Authorship attrib. to José de Acosta. Streit II:1074; Backer I:37; Ind. aur.100.454; Pérez Pastor (Madrid) 323; Palau 1997. Madrid: BU(San Isidro). 590/41

Maffei, Giovanni Pietro. Historiarum Indicarum libri xvi. Selectarum, item, ex Indiarum epistolarum libri iv. *Cologne: House of Birckmann, for A.Mylius*, 1590. 2 pts;8vo. 1st publ., Florence, 1588. Sabin 43771; Borba de Moraes II:9; Streit IV:1059; Backer V:298; JCB(3) I:323. MH, MnU-B, RPJCB; BL, BN. 590/42

__[Anr edn]. *Bergamo: C.Ventura*, 1590. 432p.;8vo. Borba de Moraes II:9; Streit IV:1060; cf.Backer V:298. DLC, MnU-B, RPJCB;BL. 590/43

Marlowe, Christopher. Tamburlaine the Great . . . Now first, and newlie published. *London: R.Jones*, 1590. 2 pts;8vo. In pt 1, Act 3, Scene 3 contains a ref. to Mexico; in pt 2, Act 1, Scene 2, 'gold of rich America' is mentioned. STC 17425; Greg 94. CSmH; Oxford: Bodl. 590/44

Mattioli, Pietro Andrea. Kreutterbuch . . . gemehret, und verfertigt durch Joachimum Camerarium. *Frankfurt a.M.: J.Feyerabend*, 1590. 460 numb.lvs;illus.;fol. 1st publ., Frankfurt, 1586. Pritzel 5990; Nissen (Bot.) 1311n. CtY, MH-A, PPL; London: Wellcome. 590/45

Mela, Pomponius. The rare and singuler worke of Pomponius Mela . . . Whereunto is added, that learned worke of Julius Solinus . . . Translated into Englishe, by Arthur Golding. *London: T.Hacket*, 1590. 124p.;4to. The earliest edn to contain (p. 122-124)'A perticular description of such parts of America, as are by travaile found out'. Sabin 63961; STC 17786. CSmH, DLC, MH, NNC; BL. 590/46

Montaigne, Michel Eyquem de. Essais . . . Cinquiesme [!] edition, augmentée d'un troisiesme livre. *Paris: P.L'Angelier* [ca.1590?]. 496p.;4to. 1st publ. in this edn, Paris, 1588; here a reissue with imprint date omitted? BN. 590/47

Myritius, Johannes. Opusculum geographicum rarum. *Ingolstadt: W.Eder*, 1590. 136p.;illus.,map;fol. Chapt.xx discusses 'De America, Spagnolia, Isabella, & aliis insulis'.

Sabin 51650; JCB (3) I:323. DLC, ICN, MiU-C, MnU-B, NN-RB, RPJCB; BL.   590/48

Neander, Michael. Chronicon sive Synopsis historiarum. *Leipzig:* 1590. 596p.;8vo. 1st publ., Eisleben, 1582. BN.   590/49

Ortelius, Abraham. Additamentum IV Theatri orbis terrarum. *Antwerp: Plantin Office,* 1590. 22 double maps;fol. Added is a map of the South Seas & adjacent lands. Koeman (Ort.) 25; Phillips (Atlases) 395; Adams (Cambr.) 0343. DLC, NN-RB; Cambridge: Trinity, Warsaw: BU.   590/50

_____. Epitome du Theatre du monde. Revue, corrigé, & augmenté de plusieurs cartes, pour la derniere fois. *Antwerp: C.Plantin,for P.Galle,* 1590. 94 numb.lvs;maps;obl.4to. 1st publ. with French text, by Peeter Heyns, under title *Le miroir du monde,* Antwerp, 1579. Atkinson (Fr.Ren.) 357; Koeman (Ort.) 54. BL, BN.   590/51

Paracelsus. An excellent treatise touching howe to cure the Frenchpockes . . . now put into English by John Hester. *London:* [J.Charlewood] 1590. 63p.;4to. 1st publ., Strassburg, 1530, as *De morbo gallico;* here transl. from Antwerp, 1557, Dutch version by P.Hermann. STC 13215 (Hermanni, Phillippus); Sudhoff (Paracelsus) 1590. DNLM; BL.   590/52

Pasquier, Etienne. Les lettres. *Avignon: J.Bramereau,* 1590. 438 numb.lvs;8vo. 1st publ., Paris, 1586. Thickett (Pasquier) 20; Adams (Cambr.) P380. MH, NjP; BL, Munich: StB.   590/53

Porcacchi, Tommaso. L'isole piu famose del mondo . . . e intagliate da Girolamo Porro . . . con l'aggiunta di molte isole. *Venice: G.Angelieri,for the Heirs of S.Galignani,* 1590. 201p.;maps;fol. 1st publ., Venice, 1572. Sabin 64150; Adams (Cambr.) P1906; JCB(3) I:324. CtY, DFo, ICN, InU-L, MH, MiU-C, MnU-B, NN-RB, RPJCB; BL, BN.   590/54

Rivadeneira, Pedro de. Historia von dem Leben und Wandel Ignatii Loiole . . . nachmals durch Johannem Jolitum inn die Welsche, und ferrner in unser hochteutsche Sprach versetzet [durch F.Alber?]. *Ingolstadt: D.Sartorius,* 1590. 563p.;port.;4to. Transl. from Venice, 1586, Italian edn, itself transl. from Spanish edn, 1st publ., Madrid, 1583. Though the dedication is signed by Ferdinand Alber, Sommervogel believed the translator to

be Theobald Stoz. Backer I:119; Palau 266258. NcD;BL.   590/55

_____. Vita Ignatii Loiolae. *Ingolstadt: D.Sartorius,* 1590. 514p.;8vo. 1st publ., Naples, 1572. Cf.Sabin 70782; Backer VI:1726; Palau 266205. PLatS;BL.   590/56

Sacro Bosco, Joannes de. Sphaera . . . emendata, aucta et illustrata. Eliae Vineti . . . scholia. *Cologne: P.Cholinus,* 1590. 262p.; illus.;8vo. 1st publ. with Vinet's *Scholia,* Paris, 1551. Cf.Sabin 32681. Strasbourg:BN.   590/57

Severt, Jacques. De orbis catoptrici seu Mapparum mundi principiis, descriptione, ac usu, libri tres. *Paris: B.Moreau,* 1590. 332(i.e., 232) p.;illus.;fol. Adams (Cambr.) S1020. NN-RB; Cambridge: Trinity.   590/58

Sfondrati, Pandolfo. Causa aestus maris. *Ferrara: B.Mammarello,* 1590. 44 numb.lvs;4to. Included are discussions of tides in American waters. Adams (Cambr.) S1038. ICN, InU-L, NN-RB, RPJCB; BL.   590/59

Skarga, Piotr. O rzadzie y iednosci Kosciola Bozego pod iednym pasterzem. *Cracow: A. Piotrkowczyk,* 1590. 363p.;8vo. On p. 19 is a ref. to missions in Brazil. Backer VII:1274.   590/60

Spenser, Edmund. The faerie queene. *London:* [J. Wolfe] for W.Ponsonbie, 1590. 600p.; 4to. In verse. On recto of 1f Gg5 are two stanzas describing tobacco. For variant states, see STC entries. STC 23080-23081a; Grolier Club (Langland to Wither) 231; Arents 38. CSmH, DFo; BL.   590/61

Stella, Giulio Cesare. Columbeidos libri priores duo. *Rome: Santi & Co.,* 1590. 67p.;4to. 1st publ., London, 1585; here a reissue of Rome, 1589, edn with altered imprint date. In verse. Sabin 91217; Adams (Cambr.) S1710; JCB (3) I:324. DLC, MH, RPJCB; Cambridge: Trinity, BN.   590/62

Szyszkowski, Marcin, Bp. Pro religiosissimis Societatis Jesu patribus . . . oratio. *Cracow: A.Piotrkowczyk,* 1590. 85p.;4to. On p.41 is a defense of Jesuits in the New World. Tazbir p.13. MH.   590/63

Tasso, Torquato. La Gierusalemme liberata. *Genoa: G.Bartoli,* 1590. 3 pts;illus.;4to. 1st publ. with American refs, Parma, 1581. In verse. Racc.Tassiana 173; Mortimer (Italy) 494; Adams (Cambr.) T243; Shaaber T89. CU, CtY, DLC, MH, NN-RB, PU; BL, BN.   590/64

__[Anr edn]. Il Goffredo, overo Gierusalemme liberata, poema heroico. *Venice: A.Salicato,* 1590. 2 pts;12mo. Racc.Tassiana 174; Shaaber T88. PU; Bergamo: BC.   590/65

Theodorus, Jacobus, called Tabernaemontanus. Eicones plantarum seu stirpium arborum, nempe fructicum, herbarum fructuum, lignorum, radicum omnis generis. *Frankfurt a.M.: N.Bassé,* 1590. 1128p.;illus.;obl. fol. 1st publ. in part in German, Frankfurt, 1588. Pritzel 9094; Nissen (Bot.) 1932; Arents (Add.) 90. MH-A, NN-A; BL.   590/66

Torquemada, Antonio de. Giardino di fiori curiosi . . . tradotto di spagnuolo . . . per Celio Malespina. *Venice: A.Salicato,* 1590. 262p.;4to. Transl. from author's *Jardin de flores curiosas,* 1st publ., Salamanca, 1570. Palau 334922; Shaaber T275. DFo, MiU, PU; BL.   590/67

Vique Manrique, Pedro. La vista que V[uestra]. S[eñoria]. vio en revista entre . . . Alonso Perez de Salazar . . . con don Pedro Vique Manrique, cabo y capitan que fue de las galeras de la costa de Cartagena, de las Indias. [*Madrid:* ca.1590]. 11 lvs;fol. Includes description of defense of Cartagena from attack by Sir Francis Drake. Kraus (Drake) 28 (p.202). H.P.Kraus.   590/68

1591

Acosta, José de. Historia natural y moral de las Indias. *Barcelona: J.Cendrat,* 1591. 345 numb.lvs;8vo. 1st publ., Seville, 1590. Sabin 122; Medina (BHA) 330; Streit II:1083; Backer I:34; Ind.aur.100.456; JCB (3) I:324. CU, CtY, ICN, MH, MiU-C, NN-RB, PPL, RPJCB; Vienna: NB.   591/1

__[Anr issue]. *Barcelona: J.Cendrat,for L.Marini,* 1591. Ind.aur.100.458; Adams (Cambr.) A126. BL.   591/2

__[Anr issue]. *Barcelona: J.Cendrat,for House of Garrich,at Gerona,* 1591. Ind.aur.100.457. BN.   591/3

Beccadelli, Antonio. De dictis & factis Alphonsi regis . . . libri quatuor . . . studio Davidis Chytraei. *Rostock: S.Moelleman,* 1591. 188p.;4to. 1st publ. with American refs, Wittenberg, 1585; here a reissue of printer's 1589 edn? NjP.   591/4

Bodin, Jean. De republica libri sex . . . Editio altera. *Frankfurt a.M.: J.Wechel & P.Fischer,*

1591. 1221p.;8vo. 1st publ., Paris, 1586. Ind. aur.120.839; Adams (Cambr.) B2231. ICN, MWelC, PPL; BL, Berlin: StB.   591/5

__[Anr edn]. [*n.p.*] *J. DuPuys* [i.e.,*Geneva: J.Stoer*] 1591. 1132p.;8vo. On false imprint, see E.Droz, 'Fausses adresses typographiques', *Bibliothèque d'humanisme et renaissance,* XXIII (1961) 146-148. Shaaber B513. CU, MH-L, MiU, PU.   591/6

____. Methodus ad facilem historiarum cognitionem, accurate denua recusa. [*Lyons?*] *Heirs of J.Mareschal,* 1591. 550p.;8vo. 1st publ., Paris, 1566. Baudrier (Lyons) XI:461; Ind. aur.120.841. MnU-B; Munich: StB.   591/7

Boemus, Johann. Mores, leges, et ritus omnium gentium . . . Fides, religio, et mores Aethiopum . . . Damiano à Goës auctore. [*Geneva:*] *J.de Tournes,* 1591. 495p.;16mo. Goes's work, with ref. to Columbus, 1st publ., Louvain, 1540. Sabin 6117n; Ind.aur. 120.968; Cartier (de Tournes) 689; Adams (Cambr.) B2271; JCB AR20:1591. DLC, RPJCB; Cambridge: UL, Munich: StB. 591/8

Boissard, Jean Jacques. Poemata. *Metz: A.Faber,* 1591. 406p.;8vo. 1st publ., Basel, 1574. Ind.aur.121.331. Rome: Vatican. 591/9

Botero, Giovanni. Delle relationi universale. *Rome: G.Faciotto,for G.Ferrari,* 1591-92. 2 pts;4to. In pt 1, bks 4-6 deal largely with the New World; in pt 2 are numerous scattered refs to it. Cf.Sabin 6803; Ind.aur.122.701 & 122.705; Adams (Cambr.) B2554. DLC, RPJCB; BL, Vienna: NB.   591/10

Bozio, Tommaso. De signis ecclesiae Dei libri xxiiii. *Rome: B.Bonfadini,for G.Tornieri* (v.1) *& A.& H.Donangeli* (v.2), 1591. 2v.;fol. In v.2, 'Signum lxxxiv' treats 'Insulae longinquae & novae', i.e., the New World, as evidence of superiority of Catholic faith. Streit I:187; Ind.aur.123.288. DCU, RPJCB; BL, Munich: StB.   591/11

Camoẽs, Luis de. Los Lusiadas . . . Tra duzidos de Portugues . . . por Henrique Garces. *Madrid: G.Drouy,* 1591. 851(i.e., 185) numb.lvs;4to. The earliest edn of this translation with sonnet addressed to Philip II adverting to Garcés's services on his behalf (i.e., in Peru). Medina (BHA) 334; Pérez Pastor (Madrid) 352; Ind.aur.130.698. DLC, IU, MH, NNH; BL, BN.   591/12

Cardano, Girolamo. Offenbarung der Natur und natürlicher Dingen. *Basel: S.Henricpetri,* 1591. 827p.;fol. 1st publ. in German, Basel,

1559. Ind.aur.132.127. CU, ICJ; London: Wellcome, Berlin: StB.   591/13

Chiabrera, Gabriello. Canzonette. *Genoa:* [*G.Bartoli*] 1591. 4to. Included is a poem on Columbus. CF.Sabin 12614. BL.   591/14

Clavius, Christoph. In Sphaeram Joannis de Sacro Bosco commentarius . . . Nunc tertio ab ipso auctore recognitus. *Venice: G.B. Ciotti*, 1591. 483p.;illus.;4to. 1st publ., Rome, 1570. Backer II:1212. CtY, DFo, NN-RB.   591/15

Clowes, William. A prooved practise for all young chirurgians . . . Hereunto is adjoyned a treatise of the French or Spanish pocks, written by John Almenar. [*London:*] *T.Orwyn,for Widow Broome*, 1591. 200p.;4to. A reissue, with cancel t.p., etc., of the 1588 edn. STC 5445. DFo; BL.   591/16

Cortusi, Giacomo Antonio. L'horto dei semplici di Padova. *Venice: G.Porro* 1591. 72 lvs;illus.,port.;8vo. Included in lists of plants grown are numerous ones of American origin. Pritzel 1896. DNAL, MH-A; BL.   591/17

Du Bartas, Guillaume de Salluste, seigneur. Commentaires sur la Sepmaine de la creation du monde [par Simon Goulart]. *La Rochelle: J.Haultin*, 1591. 2 pts;8vo. 1st publ. in this form, including text itself of *La Sepmaine*, Geneva, 1581. In verse. Tchémerzine X:189; Adams (Cambr.) D970; Desgraves (Les Haultin) 119; Holmes (DuBartas) I:73 no. 22. Cambridge: Clare, Paris: Arsenal.   591/18

___[Anr issue]. *Antwerp: T.Ruault* [i.e.,*La Rochelle: J.Haultin*], 1591. Desgraves (Les Haultin) 119 bis; Holmes (DuBartas) I:73 no.22n. Geneva: BP   591/19

___[Anr issue]. *Antwerp: H.Mersman* [i.e., *La Rochelle: J.Haultin*] 1591. Cf.'Mersman' edn of *La seconde sepmaine* below. Holmes (DuBartas) I:73 no.22n. CSt, NjP.   591/20

___. Hebdomas, a Gabriele Lermaeo latinitate donata. *London:* [*J.Windet? for*] *R.Dexter*, 1591. 112 numb.lvs;12mo. 1st publ. in this version, Paris, 1584; transl. from *La Sepmaine*, 1st publ., Paris, 1578. In verse. Holmes (DuBartas) I:107 no.3; STC 21656; Shaaber D300. CSmH, DFo, MH, PU; BL.
591/21

___. La seconde sepmaine . . . Revuë, augmentee et embellie en divers passages par l'autheur mesme. En ceste nouvelle edition ont esté adjoutez . . . annotations en marge, et ex-

plications continuelles . . . par S[imon]. G[oulart]. *La Rochelle: J.Haultin*, 1591. 576p.;8vo. 1st publ., Paris, 1588. In verse. Desgraves (Les Haultin) 122; Holmes (DuBartas) I:85 no.7; Jones (Goulart) 20 (k). BL.
591/22

___[Anr issue]. *Antwerp: H.Mersman* [i.e.,*La Rochelle: J.Haultin*] 1591. Borba de Moraes I:75-76; Desgraves (Les Haultin) 122; Holmes (DuBartas) I:85 no.7a(n); Jones (Goulart) 20k(n). CSt, MiU, NjP; Geneva: BP.   591/23

___. La seconde semaine . . . reveüe par l'autheur . . . avec les argumens, commentaires et annotations de C[laude]. D[uret]. *Nevers: P.Roussin*, 1591. 114 numb.lvs;4to. Includes 'Le premier jour: Eden' only; 1st publ., Paris, 1584. Duret's commentary discusses New World as Ophir, & includes extracts from Oviedo y Valdes on cochineal, Mexico, etc. Holmes (DuBartas) 84-85; Rép. bibl.III:82. BN.   591/24

Duchesne, Joseph. Opera medica. *Lyons* [i.e., *Geneva*]: *J.Lertout*, 1591. 2v.;8vo. Included is Duchesne's *Sclopetarius*, 1st publ., Lyons [i.e.,Geneva], 1576. Adams (Cambr.) D1012. CtY-M, DNLM; Cambridge: UL.   591/25

Espinel, Vicente. Diversas rimas. *Madris: L.Sánchez,for J.de Montoya*, 1591. 166 numb. lvs;8vo. Amongst the laudatory verses at front is a sonnet of Pedro de Montes de Oca, 'el Indiano', so designated for having seen military service in Peru. Pérez Pastor (Madrid) 353; Palau 82585. NNH; BL, Madrid: BN. 591/26

___[Anr edn]. *Madrid: L.Sánchez*, 1591. 166 numb.lvs;8vo. Pérez Pastor (Madrid) 354; Palau 82585n. BN.   591/27

Estienne, Charles. L'agricoltura nuova, et casa di villa . . . tradotta dal sr Hercole Cato. *Venice: A.Manuzio, the Younger*, 1591. 511p.;4to. 1st publ. in Italian, Venice, 1581. Thiébaud (La chasse) 358; Adams (Cambr.) S1723. Cambridge: UL, BN.   591/28

___. L'agriculture, et maison rustique de mm. Charles Estienne et Jean Liebault. *Lyons: J.Guichard*, 1591. 294 numb.lvs;illus.;4to. 1st publ. in this version, Paris, 1567. Thiébaud (La chasse) 349; Baudrier (Lyons) I:207.
591/29

Fracastoro, Girolamo. Operum pars prior posterior. *Lyons: F.LeFèvre*, 1591. 2v.;8vo. 1st publ. in coll.edn, 1555; includes the author's *De contagione* (1st publ., Venice,

1546) and his *Syphilidis* (1st publ., Verona, 1530). Baumgartner (Fracastoro) 35. CtY, DLC, MiU, MnU-B; BL, BN. 591/30

Herrera y Tordesillas, Antonio de. Cinco libros . . . de la Historia de Portugal, y conquista de . . . los Açores, en los años de. 1582. y 1583: *Madrid: P.Madrigal;sold by J.de Montoya,* 1591. 213 numb.lvs;4to. On recto of lvs 177 & 183 are refs to silver fleets from West Indies. Sabin 31538; Pérez Pastor (Madrid) 357; Palau 114283. ICN, MH, NN-RB, RPJCB; BL, BN. 591/31

Hortop, Job. The rare travailes of Job Hortop, an Englishman . . . Wherein is declared the dangers he escaped in his voiage to Gynnie, where after hee was set on shoare in a wilderness near to Panico, hee endured much slaverie and bondage in the Spanish galley. *London: [T.Scarlet] for W.Wright,* 1591. [23]p.;4to. Treats of Mexico & West Indies. STC 13828. DFo; BL. 591/32

Hurault, Michel, sieur de Bélesbat et du Fay. Discours sur l'estat de France. *[Paris?]* 1591. 152p.;8vo. A second discourse on theme of author's work of this title, 1st publ., [Paris?], 1588. Includes ref. to Spanish use of treasures of the Indies to support the Duke of Mayenne. BN. 591/33

—[Anr edn]. *Chartres: [C. Cottereau?]* 1591. 149p.;8vo. Cioranescu (XVI) 11705. ICN, RPB; BN. 591/34

____. Premier discours sur l'estat de la France . . . suivi d'un second, sur le mesme subject, de ceste annee 1591. *[Paris?]* 1591. 2 pts; 12mo. The 1st discourse had been 1st publ., [Paris?], 1588. Cioranescu (XVI) 11706. DLC; BN. 591/35

Jesuits. Letters from missions. Annuae litterae (1589) 1591. Annuae litterae . . . anni .M.D.LXXXIX. *Rome: Jesuit College,* 1591. 473p.;8vo. Included are reports on Brazil & Peru. Streit I:190; Backer I:1288. ICU, NNH. 591/36

La Noue, François de. Discours politiques et militaires. *Basel: F.LeFèvre,* 1591. 1019p.; 16mo. 1st publ. Basel, 1587. DFo, MH. 591/37

Laudonnière, René Goulaine de. Der ander Theil der newlich erfundenen Landtschafft Americae, von dreyen Schiffahrten, so die Frantzosen in Floridam . . . gethan . . . Auss dem Frantzösischen in Latein beschrieben, durch C.C[lusius].A. und jetzt auss dem Latein in Teutsch bracht, durch . . . Oseam Halen. *Frankfurt a.M.: J.Feyerabend,for T.de Bry,* 1591. xlii p.;illus.,map;fol. (Theodor de Bry's *America.* Pt 2. German). Transl. from following item. Cf.Sabin 8784; cf. Church 179a-179b; Arents 40; JCB (3) I:389. CSmH, DLC, MH, MiU-C, NN-RB, RPJCB; BL, BN. 591/38

____. Brevis narratio eorum quae in Florida Americae provincia Gallis acciderunt . . . Latio verò donata a C.C[lusius]. *Frankfurt a.M.: J. Wechel,for T.de Bry;for sale by S. Feyerabend,* 1591. 30p.;illus.,map;fol. (Theodor de Bry's *America.* Pt 1. Latin). 1st publ. in French, Paris, 1586. Cf.Sabin 8784; Church 145; Arents 39; Shaaber L132; JCB (3) I:387-388. CSmH, DLC, MH, MiU-C, NN-RB, PPL, RPJCB; BL, BN. 591/39

Lima (Ecclesiastical province). Council, 1583. Concilium provinciale Limense. Celebratum in civitate regum, anno M.D.LXXXII . . . Jussu . . . Philippi Secundi, editum. *Madrid: P.Madrigal,* 1591. 88 numb.lvs;4to. 1st publ., Madrid, 1590; here a reissue with new prelim. matter. Sabin 41086; Medina (BHA) 331; Streit II:1087; Ind. aur.100.455; Arents (Add.) 98; Palau 1997. NN-A; BL, Santiago, Chile: BN. 591/40

L'Obel, Matthias de. Icones stirpium seu Plantarum tam exoticarum quam indigenarum. *Antwerp: Widow of C.Plantin & J. Mourentorf,* 1591. 2v.;illus.;obl.4to. 1st publ., Antwerp, 1576, with title *Plantarum seu Stirpium historia;* here a re-impression with cancel t.p. of 1581 edn, & minor corrections in text. Pritzel 5549n; Nissen (Bot.) 1220n; Adams (Cambr.) L1384; Bibl.belg.,1st ser.,XVIII:L121; Arents (Add.) 62. DDO, ICJ, MH-A, NN-A, RPB; BL, The Hague: KB. 591/41

Lopes, Duarte. Relatione del reame di Congo . . . tratta dalli scritti . . . di Odoardo Lopez . . . per Filippo Pigafetta. *Rome: B.Grassi* [1591]. 82p.;illus.,maps;4to. Includes refs to Brazilian cannibals, and to explorers Drake & Cavendish. Tiele-Muller, p.318; Adams (Cambr.) L1468. DLC, ICN, InU-L, MH, MnU-B, NN-RB; BL. 591/42

Lorenzini, Niccolò. Il peccator contrito. *Florence: F.Giunta,the Younger,* 1591. 206p.; 4to. In verse. In stanza 125 is a ref. to Guaiacum ('di nobil merce il legno') & other treasures of the Indies. Shaaber L350. CtY, DFo, ICN, MH, NN-RB, PU; BL. 591/43

—[Anr edn]. *Venice: F.Giunta,the Younger,* 1591. 173 (i.e., 137) numb.lvs;8vo.RPJCB. 591/44

Marcos de Lisboa, o.f.m., Bp. Delle chroniche de Frati Minori del . . . p. S. Francesco; parte terza . . . hora tradotte di lingua spagnuola . . . dal sig. Horatio Diola. *Venice: E. Viotti,* 1591. 358 numb.lvs;4to. Transl. from Salamanca, 1570, Spanish text. Streit I:188 RPJCB. 591/45

Mercado, Thomas de. De'negotii, et contratti de mercati, et de negotianti . . . Trattato . . . tradotto dalla lingua spagnuola. *Brescia: P.M.Marchetti,* 1591. 763p.;8vo. Transl. from author's *Tratos y contratos de mercaderes,* 1st publ., Salamanca, 1569. Moranti (Urbino) 2188. ICN, MH-BA; BL, Urbino: BU. 591/46

Ortelius, Abraham. Der vierdte zusatzs dess Theatri oder Schawspiegels der gantzer Welt. *Antwerp: [Plantin Office]* 1591. 45 lvs;maps; fol. Based on Antwerp, 1590, Latin edn. Koeman (Ort.) 26; Phillips (Atlases) 3399. DLC, InU-L; Brussels: BR. 591/47

Pasini, Antonio. Annotationi & emendationi nella tradottione dell'eccell. P.Andrea Matthioli de' cinque libri Della materia medicinale di Dioscoride Anazerbeo. *Bergamo: C. Ventura,* 1591. 252p.;4to. Pritzel 6964. BN. 591/48

Patirzi, Francesco, Bp of Gaeta. De reyno, y de la institucion del que ha de reynar . . . Traduzido por Henrique Garces de latin. *Madrid: L.Sánchez,* 1591. 412 numb.lvs;4to. Garcés in his dedication refers to his experience in Peru in mining of mercury & silver. Medina (BHA) 332; Pérez Pastor (Madrid) 365; Adams (Cambr.) P460. WU; BL,BN. 591/49

Petrarca, Francesco. Los sonetos y canciones . . . que traduzia Henrique Garces de lengua thoscana. *Madrid: G.Drouy,* 1591. 178 numb. lvs;4to. Includes a *canción* by Garcés, addressed to Peru, recalling his experiences there. Medina (BHA) 333; Pérez Pastor (Madrid) 366; Adams (Cambr.) P841. NNH; BL, BN. 591/50

Petrycy, Sebastian. De natura, causis, symptomatibus morbi gallici eiusque curatione. *Cracow:* 1591. Proksch I:20. 591/51

Peucer, Kaspar. Commentarius de praecipuis generibus divinitiarum. *Zerbst: B.Schmidt,* 1591. 479 numb.lvs;4to. 1st (?) publ. in this enl. edn, Wittenberg, 1560. Adams (Cambr.) P933. NN-RB, MiU; Cambridge: Peterhouse. 591/52

Peurbach, Georg von. Theoricae novae planetarum . . . Henrici Glareani, De geographia . . . liber unus. *Cologne: G.von Kempen,for A.Mylius,* 1591. 256p.;8vo. 1st publ. with Glareanus's *De geographia,* Cologne, 1581. Adams (Cambr.) P2281. MH, NN-RB; Cambridge: Sidney Sussex, BN. 591/53

Porta, Giovanni Battista della. Phytognomonica . . . Nunc primum ab innumeris mendis . . . vindicata. *Frankfurt a.M.: J.Wechel & P.Fischer,* 1591. 552p.;illus., port.;8vo. 1st publ., Naples 1588. Pritzel 7273n; Nissen (Bot.) 463n; Adams (Cambr.) P1939. CU, DNLM, MH, NNNAM, PBL, WU; BL, BN. 591/54

Raleigh, Sir Walter. A report of the truth of the fight about the iles of Açores, this last sommer. Betwixt the Revenge . . . and an armada of the King of Spaine. *London: [J. Windet] for W.Ponsonbie,* 1591. 14 lvs; 4to. Included are refs to the West Indies & Sir Francis Drake. For variant settings of prelim. matter see the STC; for reprintings, see Sabin. Sabin 67585; STC 20651. CSmH, CtY, MH; BL. 591/55

Salazar, Estéban de. Veynte discursos sobre el Credo. *Alcalá de Henares: J.Gracián,* 1591. 248 numb.lvs;4to. 1st publ., Granada, 1577-78. Medina (BHA) 336; Streit II:1085; García (Alcalá de Henares) 671; JCB AR60:17-18. RPJCB; Madrid: BN. 591/56

—[Anr edn]. *Barcelona: J.Cendrat,* 1591. 351 numb.lvs;8vo. Medina (BHA) 337; Streit II:1086; Palau 286520. 591/57

Spain. Laws, statutes, etc., 1556-1598 (Philip II). Ordenanças para remedio de los daños e inconvenientes, que se siguen delos descaminos y arribadas maliciosas de los navios, que navegan a las Indias Ocidentales. *Madrid: P.Madrigal,* 1591. 26 numb.lvs;fol. Sabin 57482; Medina (BHA) 335 (VII:317). CU-B, DLC, ICN. 591/58

Suárez de Escobar, Pedro. Primera parte del libro intitulado Espejo de vida christiana . . . por el padre maestro Don Pedro Suarez de Excobar . . . Obispo de la nueva Viscaya, en el reyno de Mexico. *Madrid: Widow of A.Gó-*

mez, 1591. 528 numb. lvs;fol. No more published. Sabin 93310; Medina (BHA) 338; Pérez Pastor (Madrid) 373. Madrid: BU (San Isidro).   591/59

Tabourot, Estienne. Les bigarrures. *Rouen: J.Bauchu*, 1591. 2pts;8vo. In verse & prose. Includes *Le quatriesme livre*, 1st publ., Paris, 1585. NjP; BL.   591/60

Torquemada, Antonio de. Giardino di fiori curiosi . . . tradotto di spagnuolo . . . par Celio Malespina. *Venice: A.Salicato*, 1591. 262p.;4to. 1st publ. in Italian, Venice, 1590; here a reissue with altered imprint date. Palau 334922n. ICN; BL.   591/61

Zamorano, Rodrigo. Compendio del arte de navegar. *Seville: J.de León*, 1591. 63 numb. lvs;illus.;4to. 1st publ., Seville, 1582. Sabin 106246n; Medina (BHA) 340; Palau 379251.
591/62

1592

Airebaudouze, Pierre de, seigneur de Cest. Orbis terrarum synoptica epitome . . . Quae . . . adjuncta est Geographia poetica a viro doctissimo [Lamberto Danaeo]. [*Geneva*:] *J.Stoer*, 1592. 2 pts;8vo. 1st publ., Geneva, 1588. Ind.aur.106.977. Augsburg: StB. 592/1

Apianus, Petrus. Cosmographie, oft Beschrijvinge der geheelder Werelt . . . Gecorrigeert ende vermeerdert deur m.Gemma Frisius. *Antwerp: Widow of J.Verwithagen;for sale by C.Claeszoon,Amsterdam*, 1592. 121 numb. lvs;illus.,map;4to. 1st publ. in this Dutch edn, Antwerp, 1573, but here enlarged with material found in intervening Latin, French & Spanish edns. Sabin 1755n; Ortroy (Apian) 63; Bibl.belg.,1st ser.,I:A43. NN-RB; Brussels: BR.   592/2

Arnauld, Antoine. Anti-Espagnol, autrement Les philippiques d'un Demostenes françois. [*Paris?*] 1592. 39p.;8vo. 1st publ., [Paris?], 1590. Ind.aur.108.858; Cioranescu (XVI) 2636. BN.   592/3

Augenio, Orazio. Epistolarum et consultationum medicinalium . . . libri. Editio tertia. *Venice: D.Zenaro*, 1592. 2v.;fol. Vol.1 1st publ., Turin, 1579, but here suppl. by 2nd vol. containing refs to Guaiacum & to tobacco. Ind.aur.109.845; Adams(Cambr.) A2126; Moranti (Urbino) 320. CtY-M, DNLM, MBCo, NNNAM, PPC; Cambridge: Clare, Berlin: StB.   592/4

Banchieri, Adriano. La nobiltà dell'asino. Di Attabalippa dal Perù, provincia del Mondo novo [pseud.], tradotta in lingua italiana. *Venice: B.Barezzi*, 1592. 70p.;8vo. 1st (?) publ., [Bologna?], 1588. The present edn is the earliest of which extant copies are recorded. Brunet I:540; Ind.aur.112.131. MH, NN-RB; BL, Vienna: NB.   592/4a

Bassé, Nikolaus. Collectio in unum corpus, omnium librorum . . . qui in nundinis Francofurtensibus ab anno 1564 usque ad nundinas autumnales anni 1592 . . . venales extiterunt. *Frankfurt a.M.: N.Bassé*, 1592. 3v.;4to. Described are works relating to the New World. Sabin 14366; Ind.aur.114.650; Adams (Cambr.) B367. NN-RB, NNC; BL, BN.   592/5

Bodin, Jean. Methodus ad facilem historiarum cognitionem, accurate derecusa. [*Lyons?*] *Heirs of J.Mareschal*, 1592. 550p.;8vo. 1st publ., Paris, 1566; here a reissue of the printers' 1591 edn. Baudrier (Lyons) XI:461; Ind.aur.120.845; Adams (Cambr.) B2227. BL, BN.   592/6

———. Respublica . . . in . . . Teutsch . . . gebracht durch m.Johann Oswaldt. *Montbéliard: J.Foillet,for N.Bassé at Frankfurt a.M.*, 1592. 775p.;fol. 1st publ. in French, Paris, 1576. Ind.aur.120.844; Rép.bibl. III:52. ICN; Munich: StB.   592/7

Botero, Giovanni. Delle relationi universali . . . corrette, & ampliate in più luoghi. *Ferrara: B.Mammarelli*, 1592[-93]. 2 pts;4to. 1st publ., Rome, 1591-92. Ind.aur.122.702. DFo, DLC, RPJCB; BL, Vienna: NB.   592/8

Bozio, Tommaso. De signis ecclesiae Dei. *Cologne: J.Gymnich,the Younger*, 1592[-93]. 2v.; 8vo. 1st publ., Rome, 1591. Streit I:191; Ind. aur.123.290; Adams (Cambr.) B2641. InRenS, MH, MnCS; Cambridge: Trinity, BN.   592/9

Calvo, Juan. Libro de medicina y cirurgia . . . y . . . del morbo gallico, de la curacion de e, y de cada uno de sus accidentes. *Barcelona: J.Cendrat*, 1592. 216 numb.lvs;8vo. 1st publ., Seville, 1580, but the earliest extant edn. Ind.aur.130.302; Palau 40551n. BL.   592/10

Caro, Annibale. De le lettere familiari . . . volume primo. *Venice: B.Giunta & Bros*, 1592. 176p.;4to. 1st publ., Venice, 1572. Ind. aur.132.484; Adams (Cambr.) C744. IU, PV; BL, Venice: BN.   592/11

Conestaggio, Girolamo Franchi di. Dell'unione del regno di Portogallo alla corona di Castiglia. *Venice: P.Ugolino,* 1592. 295 numb. lvs;8vo. 1st publ., Genoa, 1585. Adams (Cambr.) C2503. DLC, NNH, PBL; BL.   592/12

Cysat, Renwart. Cosmographische und warhafftige Beschreibung der newerfundenen orientalischen, Japponischen . . . Inseln . . . somt ander bissher unbekante Indianische Länder. *Freiburg i.Br.: A.Gemperlin,* 1592. 2pts;8vo. 1st publ., Freiburg, 1586. Cf.Sabin 18220; Borba de Moraes I:203; Streit IV:1737. MH.   592/13

Du Bartas, Guillaume de Salluste, seigneur. Les oeuvres . . . Reveües & augmentees par l'autheur. *Rouen: P.Retif,* 1592. 4 pts;8vo. 1st publ. as here collected, Paris, 1583. OCU.
        592/14

____. La divina settimana [trad. da Ferrante Guisone]. *Tours: J.Mettayer,* 1592. 152 numb. lvs;12mo. Transl. from *La Sepmaine,* 1st publ., Paris, 1578. Holmes (DuBartas) I:109 no.18; Adams (Cambr.) D973. BL, Paris: Mazarine.   592/15

Du Verdier, Antoine. Les diverses leçons . . . suivans celles de Pierre Messie. *Lyons: E.Servain,for T.Soubron,* 1592. 602p.;port.; 8vo. 1st publ., Lyons, 1577. Adams (Cambr.) D1217. NNH; BL, BN.   592/16

Estienne, Charles. XV. Bücher von dem Feldbauw . . . von Carolo Stephano und Joh. Libalto . . . vom . . . Melchiore Sebizio . . . inn Teutsch gebracht. *Strassburg: B.Jobin,* 1592. 773p.;illus.;fol. 1st publ. in German, Strassburg, 1579, under title *Siben Bücher* . . . ; here a reissue of Jobin's expanded 1588 edn. Thiébaud (La chasse) 359; Ritter (Strasbourg) 1357. CU, DLC; Strasbourg: BN.
        592/17

Fernel, Jean. De abditis rerum causis. *Frankfurt a.M.: Heirs of A.Wechel,C.de Marne,& J.Aubry,* 1592. 142p.;port.;fol. 1st publ., Paris, 1548. CtY, ICJ, PPPH.   592/18

____. Universa medicina. *Frankfurt a.M.: Heirs of A.Wechel,& C.de Marne & J.Aubry,* 1592. 3v.;ports;fol. Includes both Fernel's *De abditis rerum causis,* 1st publ., Paris, 1548, and his *De luis venereae curatione,* 1st publ., Antwerp, 1579. Sherrington (Fernel) 70.J14; Adams (Cambr.) F260. DNLM, PPPH; Oxford: Bodl.   592/19

Fioravanti, Leonardo. Del compendio de i secreti rationali . . . libri cinque. *Turin:*

G.D.Tarino, 1592. 183 lvs;8vo. 1st publ., Venice, 1564. DNLM.   592/20

Girault, Simon. Globe du monde contenant un bref traité du ciel et de la terre. *Langres: J.DesPreyz,* 1592. 91 numb.lvs;illus.,maps; 4to. Included are numerous geographic refs to America. DLC, NN-RB, NNH; BL.   592/21

Guicciardini, Francesco. La Historia d'Italia. *Venice: P.Ugolino,* 1592. 488 numb.lvs;4to. 1st publ., Florence, 1561. CU, IU, InU-L.
        592/22

Hurault, Michel, sieur de Bélesbat et du Fay. Exactissimi discursus de rebus gallicis, anno 1588 editi, continuatio . . . gallice conscripta, nunc primum latine reddita. [*Strassburg:*] 1592. 8vo. Transl. from author's *Discours sur l'estat de France,* 1st publ., [Paris?], 1588, & its sequel with same title, 1st publ., [Paris?], 1591. BL.   592/23

____. An excellent discourse upon the now present estate of France. Faithfully translated out of French by E.A[ggas]. *London:* [*J.Wolfe*] 1592. 58 numb.lvs;4to. Transl. from Hurault's second *Discours,* [Paris?], 1591. STC 14005. CSmH, DLC, MH; BL.   592/24

Jesuits. Letters from missions. Ragguaglio d'alcune missioni dell'Indie Orientali, & Occidentali. Cavato da alcuni avvisi scritti gli anni 1590. & 1591. da i pp. Pietro Martinez provinciale dell'India Orientale, Giovanni d'Atienza provinciale del Perù, Pietro Diaz provinciale del Messico . . . raccolto dal padre Gasparo Spitilli. *Rome: A.Zanetti,* 1592. 63p.;8vo. Sabin 89536; Wagner (SW) 10; Streit IV:1066 (& II:1099); JCB (3) I:331-332. CSmH, DLC, NN-RB, RPJCB; BL, BN.
        592/25

LeRoy, Louis. Della vicissitudine o mutabile varieta delle cose nell'universo. *Venice: Aldine Press,* 1592. 327p.;4to. 1st publ. in Italian, Venice, 1585. Adams (Cambr.) L535; Moranti (Urbino) 1966; Shaaber L154. CSt, CtY, ICN, MH, NN-RB, PU; BL, BN.   592/26

Mariana, Juan de. Historiae de rebus Hispaniae libri xx. *Toledo: P.Rodríguez,* 1592. 959p.;fol. Included are chapts on the West Indies. Sabin 44543; Backer V:547; Pérez Pastor (Toledo) 402; Palau 151660; Adams (Cambr.) M580C. MWA, RPJCB, ViU; BL, BN.   592/27

__[Anr edn]. Historiae de rebus Hispaniae libri xxv. *Toledo: P.Rodríguez,* 1592. 1168p.;fol. The preceding work, with added text.

Cf.Sabin 44543; Backer V:547; Pérez Pastor (Toledo) 403; Palau 151661. CU, DLC, ICN, InU-L, MH, MiU, MnU-B, NN-RB, RPJCB; Madrid: BN.   592/28

Marquardus, Joannes. Practica theorica empirica morborum interiorum . . . Cui duo tractatus de lue venerea accesserunt, unus Lucae Ghini, alter Hieronymi Capivacci. *Spira: B.Albinus,* 1592. 460p.;8vo. Ghini's work 1st publ., in Spira, 1590, edn of Marquard; that of Capivaccio, Spira, 1590, under title *De leu venerea acroaseis.* DNLM, MnU.
592/29

Mercado, Luis. Libri ii de communi et peculiari praesidiorum artis medicae indicatione. *Cologne: J.B.Ciotti,* 1588. 952p.;8vo. 1st publ., Valladolid, 1574. Palau 16499. DNLM, MBCo.   592/30

Mexía, Pedro. Les diverses lecons . . . avec trois dialogues, mises en francais par Claude Gruget . . . augmentees . . . de la suite d'icelles, faite par Antoine Verdier. *Lyons: E.Servain,for T.Soubron,* 1592. 738p.;8vo. 1st publ. in this augmented version, Lyons, 1577. Sabin 48244n; Baudrier (Lyons) IV:348-349; Palau 167322. CSmH, CtY-M, NNH, WU; BL.   592/31

Moles, Juan Bautista. Memorial de la provincia de San Gabriel, de la orden de los frayles menores de observancia. *Madrid: P.Madrigal,* 1592. 307 numb.lvs;4to. Includes accounts of Franciscans in Mexico, etc. Medina (BHA) 345; Streit I:195; Pérez Pastor (Madrid) 388. BN.   592/32

Münster, Sebastian. Cosmographey, oder beschreibung aller Länder . . . Jetzt . . . biss in das M.D.XCII. jare gemehret. *Basel: S.Henricpetri,* 1592. 1421p.;illus.,maps,port.;fol. 1st publ., Basel, 1544. Sabin 51394; Burmeister (Münster) 82. IU, MBAt; BL, Munich: StB.   592/33

Nash, Thomas. Pierce Penilesse his supplication to the divell. *London: [J.Charlewood,for] R.Jones,* 1592. 46 lvs;4to. Includes ref. to tobacco. STC 18371; Arents (Add.) 100. DFo, MH, NN-A; BL.   592/34

__[Anr edn]. *London: A.Jeffes,for J.Busby,* 1592. 40 lvs;4to. STC 18372. DFo, ICN, MWiW-C; Oxford: Bodl.   592/35

__[Anr edn]. *London: A.Jeffes,for J.B[usby].,* 1592. 38 lvs;4to. STC 18373. CSmH; BL.
592/36

Norman, Robert. The newe attractive, con-

taining a short discourse of the magnes or lodestone. *London: E.Allde,for H.Astley,* 1592. 2 pts;illus.;4to. 1st publ., London, 1581. Cf.Sabin 55496; STC 18649. NN-RB, WU; London: Westminster School.   592/37

Ortelius, Abraham. Theatrum orbis terrarum. Opus nunc denuo ab ipso auctore recognitum. *Antwerp: Plantin Press,* 1592. 3 pts;maps,port.;fol. 1st publ., Antwerp, 1570. Sabin 57699; Koeman (Ort) 27B; Phillips (Atlases) 396; Adams (Cambr.) 0338; Fairfax Murray (Germany) 314; JCB (3) I:325. CtY, DLC, ICN, InU-L, MiU-C, NjP, RPJCB; BL.
592/38

Parsons, Robert. Elizabethae, Angliae reginae . . . edictum . . . Promulgatum Londini, 29 novembris. 1591. Cum responsione ad singula capita . . . Per D.Andream Philopatrum [pseud.]. *Lyons: [P.Roussin,for] J.Didier,* 1592. 278p.;8vo. Included are refs to Sir Francis Drake, Sir Richard Grenville & Sir Walter Raleigh. Cf.Sabin 58903; Backer VI:301; Baudrier (Lyons) IV:98-99. CLU-C, DLC, ICN; BL, Lyons: BM.   592/39

__[Anr edn]. *Augusta: J.Faber* [i.e.,*London, J.Smith?*] 1592. 268p.;8vo. Backer VI:301; Adams (Cambr.) E142. DFo, MH, NN-RB; Cambridge: UL.   592/40

Pasini, Antonio. Annotationi, & emendationi nella tradottione dell'eccell. P.Andrea Matthioli Della materia medicinale di Dioscoride Anazerbeo. *Bergamo: C.Ventura,* 1592. 252p.;4to. 1st publ., Bergamo, 1591; anr issue of earlier edn with altered imprint date? Cf.Pritzel 6964. BL.   592/41

Rivadeneira, Pedro de. Vida del padre Francisco de Borja . . . General de la Compañia de Jesus. *Madrid: P.Madrigal,* 1592. 237 numb.lvs;4to. In bk 3, chapt.6 describes Jesuits in Florida, chapt.7 their arrival in Peru & Mexico. Streit I:196; Backer VI:1733; Pérez Pastor (Madrid) 394; Palau 266307. CSmH, ICN, MH; BL.   592/42

Roberts, Henry. Our Ladys retorne to England, accompanied with saint Frances and the good Jesus of Viana in Portugall [captured ships], who comming from Brasell, arived at Clavelly in Devonshire. *London: A.J[effes]..for W.Barley,* 1592. 4 lvs;4to. In verse. Sabin 71894 (& 57926); STC 21087.3. CSmH.
592/43

Rondelet, Guillaume. Methodus curandorum omnium morborum corporis humani . . .

Ejusdem . . . De morbo italico. *Frankfurt a.M.: Heirs of A.Wechel,C.de Marne & J. Aubry*, 1592. 1277p.;8vo. 1st (?) publ., Paris [1563?]. Adams (Cambr.) R756. DNLM, NNNAM, PPL; BL.   592/44

Ronsard, Pierre de. Les oeuvres. *Lyons: T. Soubron*, 1592. 5v.;ports.;12mo. 1st publ. as here collected, Paris, 1578. Baudrier (Lyons) IV:351-353; Adams (Cambr.) R760. DFo, MH, RPB; Cambridge: UL, BN.   592/45

Rosaccio, Giuseppe. Teatro del cielo e della terra. *Brescia: V.Sabbio*, 1592. 65p.;illus., maps;8vo. Includes a description & map of America. Cf.Sabin 73198. NPV.   592/46

Schaller, Georg. Thierbuch, sehr künstliche und wolgerissene Figuren . . . in Reimen gestellt. *Frankfurt a.M.: J.Feyerabend,for Heirs of S.Feyerabend*, 1592. [215]p.;illus.; 4to. Includes, with descriptive verse, illus., by Jost Amman, of both cock & hen turkey. Nissen (Zool.) 431; Becker (Amman) 15c. MH(Amman,Jost), MWiW-C, NN-RB; BL.   492/47

Skarga, Piotr. Zywoty swiętych starego y nowego. [*Cracow?*] 1592-93. 2v. (1132p.);fol. 1st publ., Vilna, 1579. Backer VII:1267.   592/48

Staden, Hans. America tertia pars memorabilem provinciae Brasiliae historiam continens, germanico primùm sermone scriptam . . . nunc autem latinitate donatam à Teucrio, Annaeo Privato . . . Addita est Narratio profectionis Joannis Lerii in eamdem provinciam, quam ille initio gallicè conscripsit . . . His accessit Descriptio morum & ferocitatis incolarum illius regionis. *Frankfurt a.M.: J. Wechel,for T.de Bry*, 1592. 296p.;illus., map;fol. (Theodor de Bry's *America*. Pt 3. Latin). Staden's work 1st publ., Marburg, 1557; that of Léry, La Rochelle, 1578; and the 'Descriptio', by Nicolas Barré, Paris, 1558. Cf.Sabin 8784; Church 148; Arents 41 & (Add.) 13; JCB (3) I:390-391. CSmH, DLC, MH, MiU-C, NN-RB, RPJCB; BL, BN.   592/49

Tarcagnota, Giovanni. Delle istorie del mondo. *Venice: F.dei Franceschi*, 1592. 3 pts in 5v.;4to. 1st publ. in this expanded version, Venice, 1583. BL.   592/50

Tasso, Torquato. Goffredo, overo Gierusalemme liberata, poema heroico. *Venice: A.Salicato*, 1592. 2 pts;4to. 1st publ. with American refs, Parma, 1581. Racc.Tassiana 175. Bergamo: BC.   592/51

Verstegen, Richard. A declaration of the true causes of the great troubles . . . to be intended against the realme of England. [*Antwerp: J.Trognaesius*] 1592. 8vo. Authorship attributed to Robert Parsons & also to Richard Rowlands. Includes accounts of Sir Humphrey Gilbert, Sir Francis Drake, Cavendish & other early English explorers. Sabin 19182; STC 10005. CSmH, DFo; BL, Brussels: BR. 592/52

____. Theatrum crudelitatum haereticorum nostri temporis. *Antwerp: A.Hubert*, 1592. 95p.;4to. 1st publ., Antwerp, 1587. Adams (Cambr.) T445; Shaaber V136. PU; Cambridge: UL, BN.   592/53

Watson, Thomas. Amintae gaudia. *London: P.Short,for G.Ponsonby*, 1592. 4to. In verse. In 5th 'epistle' are refs to English explorers of the New World. STC 25117. CSmH, DFo, MH; BL.   592/54

Wittich, Johann. Bericht von den wunderbaren bezoardischen Steinen . . . Dessgleichen von den fürnembsten Edlen gesteinen, unbekandten hartzigen dingen, und des newen Armenischen Balsams, frembden wunder Kreutern, Holz und Wurtzeln . . . Welche alle mehrentheils den alten und newen Scribenten unbekandt, und erst innerhalb 30.Jahren aus India Orientali und Occidentali, durch Gartiam ab Horto, und Nicolaum Monardum kündig gemacht worden seind. *Leipzig: M.Lantzenberger*, 1592. 146p.;4to. 1st publ., Leipzig, 1589. Sabin 104966n. DNLM; BL.   592/55

1593

Arnauld, Antoine. La Fleur de lys, qui est un discours d'un François retenu dans Paris, sur les impietez et desguisemens contenus au manifeste d'Espagne. [*Paris?*] 1593. 32p.;8vo. Warns against Spanish dynastic ambitions regarding France, citing, in probable echo of Las Casas, Spain's 'cruautex, espouvantables qui ont depeuplé les Indes'. Ind.aur.108.860; Cioranescu (XVI) 2638. BL, BN.   593/1

Avelar, André do. Reportorio dos tempos . . . acrecentado & emendado de novo. *Coimbra: A.de Barreira*, 1593. 148p.;illus.;4to. Anselmo 113; Ind.aur.109.702; King Manuel 228. Lisbon: BN.   593/2

____. Spherae utriusque tabella, ad sphaerae huius mundi faciliorem enucleationem. *Coimbra: A.de Barreira*, 1593. 104 numb.lvs;illus., map;8vo. On the map America is depicted. Anselmo 116; Ind. aur.109.701; King Manuel 229. Lisbon: BN. 593/3

Bodin, Jean. Apologie de René Herpin [pseud.] pour la République de Jean Bodin . . . Discours . . . sur le rehaussement et diminution tant d'or que d'argent. *Lyons: B.Vincent,* 1593. 82p.;8vo. The *Discours* 1st publ., Paris, 1568, in J.C.de Malestroict's *Paradoxes.* MH; BN. 593/4

____. Les six livres de la République . . . Ensemble une apologie de René Herpin. *Lyons* [i.e.,*Geneva?*]: *G.Cartier,* 1593. 1060p.;8vo. 1st publ., Paris, 1576. Includes also Bodin's Paris, 1578, *Discours.* Ind.aur.120.849. Lausanne: B.Cantonalle. 593/5

__[Anr edn]. *Lyons: B.Vincent,* 1593. 1060p.; 8vo. Ind.aur.120.851. CtY, ICN, MH, MnU, PSC; BL. 593/6

Botero, Giovanni. Diez libros de la Razon de estado . . . Traduzido de italiano . . . por Antonio de Herrera. *Madrid: L.Sánchez,* 1593 [colophon: 1592]. 229 numb.lvs;8vo. Transl. from Venice, 1589, Italian text. Ind.aur. 122.706; Pérez Pastor (Madrid) 404. Madrid: BN. 593/7

Braun, Georg. Civitates orbis terrarum, liber primus. *Cologne: G.van Kempen,for authors & P.Galle at Antwerp,* 1593. 58 double pls;fol. 1st publ., Cologne, 1572. Cf.Koeman (Braun & Hogenberg) 1; Ind.aur.123.966; Belg.typ. (1541-1600) I:393. Brussels: BR, Munich: StB. 593/8

Chiocco, Andrea. Psoricon vel de scabie libri duo. *Verona: G.Discepolo,* 1593. 4to. Cf. Proksch I:82. BL. 593/9

Clavius, Christoph. In Sphaeram Joannis de Sacro Bosco commentarius. Nunc quarto ab ipso auctore recognitus. *Lyons: G.Julliéron, for the Gabiano Bros,* 1593. 551p.; illus.;4to. 1st publ., Rome, 1570. Backer II:1212-1213; Baudrier (Lyons) VII:228. BL, BN. 593/10

Du Bartas, Guillaume de Salluste, seigneur. Commentaires sur la Sepmaine [par Simon Goulart]. *Rouen: T.Mallard,* 1593. 1st publ. in this form, including text itself of *La sepmaine,* Geneva, 1581. In verse. Holmes (DuBartas) I:74 no.24. 593/11

__[Anr issue]. *Rouen:* [*T.Mallard,for*] *R.Du Petit Val,* 1593. Holmes (DuBartas) I:74 no.24n. Bordeaux: BU. 593/12

____. La divina settimana, cioè I sette giorni della creatione del mondo . . . tradotta di rima francese in verso sciolto italiano, dal sig.

Ferrante Guisone. *Venice: G.B.Ciotti,* 1593. 120 numb.lvs;12mo. 1st publ. in Italian, Tours, 1592. In verse. Holmes (DuBartas) I:109 no.19. MH; Edinburgh: UL, BN. 593/13

____. La seconde sepmaine, ou Enfance du monde. [*Geneva:*] *J.Chouët,* 1593. 577p.;12mo. 1st publ., Paris, 1584. In verse. Holmes (DuBartas) I:84 no.5an; Jones (Goulart) 201; Adams (Cambr.) D964. CU, MiU, MnU, NNC; Cambridge: Emmanuel, BN. 593/14

____. La sepmaine ou Creation du monde . . . Revue, augmentee, & embellie . . . par l'auteur mesme. En laquelle ont esté adjoustez . . . annotations en marge, & explications . . . par S[imon]. G[oulart]. [*Geneva:*] *J.Chouët,* 1593. 623p.;12mo. 1st publ. with Goulart's annotations, Geneva, 1581. In verse. Holmes (DuBartas) I:73-74 no.23; Jones (Goulart) 20(1). NNC, MiU, MnU; BN. 593/15

Duchesne, Joseph. Le grand miroir du monde . . . Deuxieme edition reveuë, corrigée et augmentée en divers endroits, & d'un livre entier, par l'auteur. A la fin de chasque livre sont de nouveau adjoustees amples annotations & observations sur le texte . . . par S[imon]. G[oulart]. *Lyons: For Heirs of E.Vignon,at Geneva,* 1593. 654p.;8vo. 1st publ., Lyons, 1587. Jones (Goulart)41; Cioranescu (XVI) 8601; Adams (Cambr.) D1014. DFo; BL, BN. 593/16

Durante, Castore. Il tesoro della sanita. *Venice: P.Ugolino,* 1593. 323p.;8vo. 1st publ., Rome (?), 1586. Adams (Cambr.) D1191. CtY-M, DNLM; Cambridge: Emmanuel. 593/17

Fernel, Jean. De abditis rerum causis. *Frankfurt a.M.: Heirs of A.Wechel,C.de Marne,& J.Aubry,* 1593. 272p.;port.;8vo. 1st publ., Paris, 1548. KU-M, NNNAM, NcD. 593/18

____. Universa medicina. *Frankfurt a.M.: Heirs of A.Wechel,& C.de Marne,& J.Aubry,* 1593. 3v.;ports;fol. Anr issue of the printers' 1592 edn, with altered imprint date. Includes both Fernel's *De abditis rerum causis,* 1st publ., Paris, 1548, and his *De luis venereae curatione,* Antwerp, 1579. Sherrington (Fernel) 71.J15. ICJ, NjP; London: College of Surgeons. 593/19

Flor de romances. Quarta, quinta, y sexta parte de Flor de romances nuevos, nunca hasta agora impresos, llamado, Ramillete de flores . . . Y demas desto, va alcabo la tercera parte de el Araucana. *Lisbon: A.Alvárez,for P.Flores*, 1593. 444 numb.lvs;12mo. 3rd pt of *El Araucana*, by Ercilla y Zúñiga, 1st publ., Madrid, 1589. Medina (BHA) 348; Anselmo 30; Palau 92884. NNH; Lisbon: BN.   593/20

Fuchs, Leonhart. Histoire générale des plantes. *Rouen: R.Mallard*, 1593. 373p.; illus.;16mo. 1st publ. in French, Paris, 1549. BN.   593/21

Gesner, Konrad. Quatre livres des secrets de medicine . . . Faicts françois par m.Jean Liebault. *Lyons: Heirs of P.Roussin,for B. Rigaud*, 1593. 293 numb.lvs;illus.;8vo. 1st publ., Paris, 1573. Baudrier (Lyons) III:430-431; Shaaber G151. DNLM, MnU, PU; London: Wellcome, BN.   593/22

Le grand dictionaire françois-latin, augmente outre les precedentes impressions . . . Recueilli des observations de plusieurs hommes doctes: entre autres de m.Nicod [i.e., Nicot]. [*Geneva:*] *J.Stoer*, 1593. 976p.;4to. 1st publ., Paris, 1573, under title *Dictionaire françois-latin.* DFo.   593/23

Guicciardini, Francesco. Histoire des guerres d'Italie . . . traduite . . . par Hiérosme Chomedey. [*Geneva:*] *Heirs of E.Vignon*, 1593. 2v.;8vo. 1st publ. in this version, Paris, 1568. Adams (Cambr.) G1526. DFo; BL, BN.   593/24

Harvey, Gabriel. Pierces supererogation, or A new prayse of the olde asse. *London: J.Wolfe*, 1593. 120 (i.e.,220) p.;4to. Included is a ref. to the smoking of tobacco. STC 12903; Arents 43. CSmH, CtY, DFo, MH, NN-A; BL.   593/25

Heyns, Peeter. Theatro . . . ridotta in forma piccola. *Antwerp:* 1593. See entry under Ortelius, Abraham, below.

Hurault, Michel, sieur de Bélesbat et du Fay. Quatre excellent discours sur l'estat present de la France. [*Paris?*] 1593. 2 pts;12mo. The earliest collective edn. Includes Hurault's *Discours sur l'estat de France*, 1st publ., [Paris?], 1588, and its sequel with same title 1st publ., [Paris?], 1591; followed by Antoine Arnauld's *La fleur de lys*, 1st publ., [Paris?], 1593, and his *Anti-Espagnol*, 1st publ., [Paris?], 1590. Cf.Cioranescu (XVI) 11707. BN.   593/26

Jesuits. Letters from missions. Bref discours d'aucunes missions, tant d'Orient que d'Occident, tiré d'aucunes lettres. *Douai: The*

Widow Boscard, 1593. [84]p.;12mo. Transl. from Antwerp, 1593, *Brevis et compendiosa narratio missionum quarundam*, itself transl. from Rome, 1592, *Ragguaglio d'alcuni missioni*. Sabin 44962; Streit II:1116n; Backer I:612; Palau 154579. DLC.   593/27

———. Brevis et compendiosa narratio missionum quarundam Orientis et Occidentis. *Antwerp: M.Nuyts, the Younger*, 1593. 52p.;8vo. Transl. from the *Ragguaglio d'alcune missioni*, 1st publ., Rome, 1592. Sabin 44963; Streit II:1108; Backer I:612; Belg.typ. (1541-1600) I:413. NNUT; BL, Brussels: BR.593/28

———. Fortsetzung der Zeytungen und historischen Berichts auss den fürtrefflichen unnd weitberühmbten Japonischen und Chinesischen Königreichen . . . wie auch beydes so wol auss den Orientalischen als Occidentalischen Indien. *Ingolstadt: D.Sartorius*, 1593. 477p.;8vo. Included are letters from Peru and Mexico, 1st publ. in Italian, Rome, 1592, in the *Ragguaglio d'alcune missioni*. Sabin 25178; Streit II:1109; JCB (3) I:328. ICN, NN-RB, RPJCB; BL, Munich: StB.   593/29

———. Lettres du Japon, et de la Chine, des annees 1589. & 1590. Et certains advis du Peru, des annees 1588. & 1589. *Lyons: J.Pillehotte*, 1593. 310p.;8vo. Includes letters of Giovanni d'Atienza, 1st publ., Rome, 1592, in the *Ragguaglio d'alcune missioni*. Atkinson (Fr.Ren.) 366; Streit II:1110; Backer II:1603. BL, Avignon: Mus.Calvet.   593/30

———. Ragguaglio d'alcune missioni dell'Indie Orientali y Occidentali. Cavato de alcuni avvisi scritti gli anni 1590. & 1591. *Bologna: V.Benacci*, 1593. 48p.;12mo. 1st publ., Rome, 1592. Sabin 89537 (& 18658); Wagner (SW) 10n; JCB (3) I:331-332. RPJCB. 593/31

—[Anr edn]. *Brescia: V.Sabbio*, 1593. 53p.;8vo. Sabin 89638; Wagner (SW) 10n; JCB (3) I:332. RPJCB.   593/32

—[Anr edn]. *Turin:* 1593. 54p.;8vo. Backer VIII:1703. MH.   593/33

Jode, Gérard de. Speculum orbis terrae. *Antwerp: A.Coninx,for the Widow & Heirs of G.de Jode*, 1593. 2v.;maps;fol. 1st publ., Antwerp, 1578; here a reissue with additional maps, in part American. Sabin 36826; Koeman (Jod) 2; Phillips (Atlases) 398-399; JCB (3) I:329. CtY, DLC, MiU-C, RPJCB; BL. BN.   593/34

La Charlonye, Gabriel de. De sphaera mundi, sive De cosmographia, libri ii. *Tours: J.*

Mettayer, 1593. 60 numb.lvs;8vo. Cioranescu (XVI) 12158. BN.   593/35

Lonitzer, Adam. Kreuterbuch . . . von neuwem ersehen . . . durch Adamum Lonicerum. *Frankfurt a.M.: Heirs of C.Egenolff*, 1593. ccclxxxii lvs;illus.,port.;fol. 1st publ. in German, Frankfurt a.M., 1557. Pritzel 5599n; Nissen (Bot.) 1228n. DNLM;BL.   593/36

Lucidarius. M.Elucidarius. Von allerhand Geschöpffen Gottes . . . und wie alle Creaturen geschaffen seind auff Erden. *Frankfurt a.M.: Heirs of C.Egenolff*, 1593. [87]p.;illus.; 4to. 1st publ., Strassburg, [ca.1535]. Schorbach (Lucidarius) 65. Munich: StB.   593/37

Maffei, Giovanni Pietro. Historiarum Indicarum libri xvi. *Cologne: House of Birckmann,for A.Mylius*, 1593. 541p.;fol. 1st publ., Florence, 1588. Sabin 43772; Borba de Moraes II:10; Streit IV:1070; Backer V:295; Palau 146981; JCB (3) I:329. CU, CtY, DLC, InU-L, MH, NN-RB, RPJCB; BL, BN.
593/38

Marlowe, Christopher. Tamburlaine the Great . . . Now newly published. *London: [R.Robinson,for] R.Jones*, 1593. 2 pts;8vo. 1st publ., London, 1590. STC 17426. NIC (t.p.wanting); BL.   593/39

Megiser, Hieronymus. Specimen quadraginta diversarum . . . linguarum & dialectorum; videlicet Oratio Dominica, totidem linguis expressa. *Frankfurt a.M.: J.Spiess*, 1593. 24 lvs;8vo. Amongst the languages for the text of the Lord's Prayer are those of North American Indians. Sabin 47384; Adams (Cambr.) M1038. NNC; Cambridge: UL.   593/40

Mexía, Pedro. Trois dialogues . . . touchant la nature du soleil, de la terre et de toutes les choses qui se font et apparoissent en l'air. *Lyons: J.Roussin,for B.Rigaud*, 1593. 32 lvs;8vo. 1st publ. as here transl. by Marie de Coste-Blanche, Paris, 1566. Palau 167383n. BL.   593/41

Minetti, Girolamo. Quaestio non minus pulchra, quam utilis de sarzaeparillae, et ligni sancti viribus. *Sienna: L.Bonetti*, 1593. 20p.; 4to. DNLM.   593/42

Molina, Luis de. De justitia tomus primus. *Cuenca: J.Masselini*, 1593. 1544 cols; fol. In tract.2, disp.33 discusses slavery, including that in Brazil. Palau 174615:I.   593/43

Montaigne, Michel Eyquem de. Livre des essais . . . dernière edition. *Lyons: For G.La-Grange,at Avignon*, 1593. 2 pts;8vo. 1st publ.

with 3 pts; Paris, 1588. Rép.bibl.,VI:52; Tchémerzine VIII:406; Baudrier (Lyons) I:227. BL, BN.   593/44

Morigia, Paolo. Historia de' personaggi illustri religiosi. *Bergamo: C.Ventura*, 1593. 344p.;4to. Bk 5 deals in part with native religious practices in New World. NIC, RPJCB; BN.   593/45

Nash, Thomas. Pierce Pennilesse his supplication to the divell. *London: A.Jeffes,for J. B[usby].*, 1593. 4to. 1st publ., London, 1592. STC 18734. BL, Oxford: Corpus.   593/46

Observations notables sur le titre & contenue de la Satyre Ménippée. *[Paris?]* 1593. Compares members of the League of French Catholics to the prickly-pear cactus ('figuier des Indes'; Opuntia), described by Mattioli & Fragoso. Reprinted in Simon Goulart's *Cinquiesme recueil* of 1598; cf.1594 edn of the *Satyre Ménippée*.   593/46a

Orta, Garcia da. Aromatum, et simplicium aliquot medicamentorum apud Indos nascentium historia. *Antwerp: Widow of C.Plantin & J.Mourentorff*, 1593. 456p.;illus.;8vo. 1st publ., as ed. & transl. by C.L'Ecluse, Antwerp, 1567. Also included, with special title pages, are Christovam da Costa's *Aromatum & medicamentorum in Orientali India nascentium* (p.[225]-312) 1st publ. in Latin, Antwerp, 1582, & Nicolas Monardes's *Simplicium medicamentorum ex Novo Orbe delatorum* (p.[313]-456), Antwerp, 1579. Sabin 49942 & 57666; Pritzel 4316n; Nissen (Bot.) 949n; Guerra (Monardes) 31; Adams (Cambr.) 0322; JCB (3) I:330-331. DLC, ICJ, InU-L, MH-A, MnU, NN-RB, PPC, RPJCB; BL, BN.   593/47

Ortelius, Abraham. Theatro . . . ridotta in forma piccola, augmentato di molte carte nuove . . . Tradotto . . . da Giovanni Paulet. *Antwerp: Plantin Press,for P.de Galle*, 1593. 106 numb.lvs;maps;obl.16mo. Text by Peeter Heyns 1st publ. as the *Spieghel der werelt*, Antwerp, 1577. Sabin 57701; Koeman (Ort.) 55; Bibl.belg.,1st ser.,XII:H58; Phillips (Atlases) 397. DLC, RPJCB; Brussels: BR, Madrid: BN.   593/48

Parsons, Robert. Elisabethen, der Königin inn Engellandt . . . Edict den neun und zweyntzigsten Novembris dess fünfftzehenhundert ein und neuntzigsten Jars . . . mit einer Erleutterung Andreae Philopatri. *Ingolstadt: D.Sartorius*, 1593. 271p.;4to. Transl. from

Lyons, 1592, Latin text. Backer VI:302. DFo, MH, NNUT; BN.   593/49

____. Elizabethae, Angliae reginae . . . edictum . . . Promulgatum Londini, 29 novembris, 1591. Cum responsione ad singula capita . . . Per Andream Philopatrum [pseud.]. *Lyons: [P.Roussin,for] J.Didier*, 1593. 278p.;8vo. 1st publ., Lyons, 1592; here a reissue with altered imprint date. Sabin 22188; Backer VI:301; Baudrier (Lyons) IV:99; Adams (Cambr.) E143. MH, NIC, WU; Cambridge: UL, BN.   593/50

—[Anr edn]. *Rome: A.Zanetti*, 1593. 485p.;4to. Sabin 58903; Backer VI:301; Adams (Cambr.) E144; Moranti (Urbino) 1385; Shaaber P75. CU-L, CtHT, IU, MH, PU; BL, Rome: BN.   593/51

—[Anr edn.]. [*Rome?*] 1593. 361p.;8vo. Backer VI:301; Adams (Cambr.) E145. CSmH, CtY, DFo, ICN, MH, MnU, NNUT; Cambridge: UL, BN.   593/52

—[Anr edn]. [*London?*] 1593. 341p.;8vo. CtY-L.   593/53

____. Responce à l'injuste et sanguinaire edict d'Elizabeth reyne d'Angleterre . . . Publié à Londres le 29 novembre 1591. En laquelle sont descouvertes et refutees les calomnies dont se servent les heretiques . . . Traduict du latin. *Lyons: J.Pillehotte*, 1593. 153 numb. lvs;8vo. Transl. from Latin text 1st publ., Lyons, 1592. Cf.Sabin 58903; Backer VI:301-302; Baudrier (Lyons) II:333. DFo, NNUT; BL, BN.   593/54

Peucer, Kaspar. Commentarius de praecipuis generibus divinitiarum. *Frankfurt a.M.: Heirs of A.Wechel,C.de Marne & J.Aubry*, 1593. 738p.;8vo. 1st (?) publ. in this enl. edn, Wittenberg, 1560. Adams (Cambr.) P934. CtY, DFo, MH, NNC, PPLT, WU; BL, BN.
                                    593/54a

Possevino, Antonio. Bibliotheca selecta. *Rome: D.Bassa,for Vatican Press*, 1593. 2 pts;fol. Bks x-xi comprise a 'Ratio agendi cum reliquis gentibus, praecipue Indis novi terrarum orbis, & Japoniis'. Streit I:198; Shaaber P556. PU.   593/55

Rabelais, François. Les oeuvres. *Lyons: J. Martin*, 1593. 3 pts;12mo. Includes 'Le quart livre', 1st publ., Paris, 1552. Plan (Rabelais) 113; Adams (Cambr.) R7-R8. DFo, NjP; Cambridge: UL, BN.   593/56

Rivadeneira, Pedro de. Vida del .p. Ignacio de Loyola. *Madrid: P.Madrigal*, 1593.

236p.;fol. 1st publ. in Spanish, Madrid, 1583. NcD.   593/57

____. Zywota Ignacego Lojoli. *Cracow: J.Siebencher*, 1593. 193 numb.lvs;4to. Transl. by Jacob Szafarzynski; 1st publ. in Latin, Naples, 1572. Backer VI:1731; Wierzbowski 1766; Palau 266246.   593/58

Rosaccio, Giuseppe. Le Sei età del mondo. *Brescia: V.Sabbio*, 1593. In chronology provided, under year 1492 Columbus is mentioned. Cf.Sabin 73197. NPV.   593/59

____. Teatro del cielo e della terra. *Brescia: V.Sabbio*, 1593. 65p.;illus.,maps;8vo. 1st publ., Brescia, 1592. Cf.Sabin 73198. N.
                                    593/60

Satyre Menippée. Satyre, Menippee. [*Paris?*] 1593. See the year 1594.

Schotus, Fridericus. Ander theil D. Johann Fausti Historien, darinn beschrieben ist, Christophori Wageners, Fausti gewesenen Discipels auffgerichter Pact mit dem Teuffel . . . Neben einer feinen Beschreibung der Newen Inseln, was für Leute darinn wohnen, was für Früchte darinn wachsen, was sie für Religion und Götzendienst haben, unnd wie sie von den Spaniern eingenommen werden. Alles aus seinen verlassenen schriften genommen . . . in druck verfertiget, durch Fridericum Schotum Tolet. *P[rague?].*: 1593. 160 lvs;8vo. Incorporates American material derived largely from Oviedo & Benzoni. Henning (Wagner) 1. Munich: StB.   593/61

Staden, Hans. Dritte Buch Americae, darinn Brasilia . . . auss eigener erfahrung in Teutsch beschrieben. Item Historia der Schiffart Ioannis Lerii in Brasilien welche er selbst publiciert hat jetzt von newem verteutscht durch Teuchrium Annaeum Privatum C. Vom Wilden unerhörten wesen der Innwoner von allerley frembden Gethieren und Gewächsen sampt einen Colloquio, in der wilden Sprach. *Frankfurt a.M.: T.de Bry*, 1593. 285p.;illus.,map;fol. (Theodor de Bry's *America*. Pt 3. German). The earliest German edns of Léry's work (1st publ. in French, La Rochelle, 1578) & of Barré's 'Colloquio' (1st publ. in French, Paris, 1558); Staden's text 1st publ., Marburg, 1557. Sabin 8784; Church 181; Arents 42; JCB (3) I:392-393. CSmH, CtY, DLC, ICN, MH, MiU-C, NN-RB, RPJCB; BL, BN.   593/62

Tasso, Torquato. Goffredo, overo Gierusalemme liberata, poema heroico. *Venice: A.*

Salicato, 1593. 2 pts;4to. 1st publ. with American refs, Parma, 1581. Racc.Tassiana 176; Shaaber T90. MH, PU; BL, Bergamo: BC.
593/63

1594

Arnauld, Antoine. The arrainment of the whole Society of Jesuits in France . . . Translated out of the French copie. *London: C.Yetsweirt*, 1594. 32 numb.lvs;4to. Transl. from Arnauld's *Plaidoyé* of this year. Ind. aur.108.863; STC 779. CSmH, CtY, DFo, MH, NN-RB; BL.
594/1

____. Coppie de l'Anti-Espagnol. *Lyons: P.Ferdelat*, 1594. 54p.;8vo. 1st publ., [Paris?], 1590. Ind.aur.108.865. BN.
594/2

____. La fleur de lys, qui est un discours d'un François retenu dans Paris. *Lyons: G.Julliéron & T.Ancelin*, 1594. 30p.;8vo. 1st publ., [Paris?], 1593. Ind.aur.108.867. BL, BN.
594/3

____. Oratio . . . pro Universitate Parisiensi actrice contrà Jesuitas . . . Nunc primum latine facta. *Leyden: J.J.Paets & L.Elzevir*, 1594. 84p.;4to. Transl. by François Junius from Arnauld's *Plaidoyé* of this year. Ind.aur. 108.862. Dublin: Trinity, Leyden: UB.
594/4

—[Anr edn]. Philippica . . . nomine Universitatis Parisiensis actricis, in Jesuitas reos. [*Frankfurt a.M.? J.Spiess?*] 1594. 108p.;8vo. Ind.aur.108.869; Adams (Cambr.) A1988; Shaaber A788. NNC, PU; BL, Munich: StB.
594/5

____. Plaidoyé . . . pour l'Université de Paris, demanderesse contre les Jésuites défendeurs. *Paris: M.Patisson*, 1594. 52p.;8vo. Included are refs to Jesuits in America. Ind.aur. 108.868; Adams (Cambr.) A1989. ICN, MH, NjP; BL, BN.
594/6

—[Anr edn]. *The Hague: A.Hendrickszoon*, 1594. [106]p.;8vo. Ind.aur.108.861. Brussels: BR, Göttingen: UB.
594/7

—[Anr edn]. *Lyons: T.Ancelin & G.Julliéron*, 1594. 52 numb.lvs;8vo. Ind.aur.108.864. BL, BN.
594/8

—[Anr edn]. La première Philippique, à la France. *Lyons: C.Morillon*, 1594. 64p.;8vo. Ind.aur.108.866. Munich: StB, Vienna: NB.
594/9

Avelar, André do. Chronographia ou Reportorio dos tempos . . . terceira impressaõ

reformado & acrecentado pello mesmo author. *Lisbon: S.Lopez*, 1594. 256 numb. lvs;illus.;4to. 1st publ., Lisbon, 1585. Anselmo 801; King Manuel 233. CtY, ICN, RPJCB; Lisbon: BN.
594/10

Benzoni, Girolamo. Americae pars quarta. Sive, Insignis & admiranda historia de reperta primùm Occidentali India à Christophoro Columbo anno M.CCCCXCII . . . Addita ad singula ferè capita, non contemnanda scholia. *Frankfurt a.M.: J.Feyerabend,for T.de Bry*, 1594. 145p.;illus.,map;fol. (Theodor de Bry's *America*. Pt 4. Latin). 1st publ., Geneva, 1578, as bk 1 (of 3) of Urbain Chauveton's translation, with annotations, of Benzoni's *Historia del Mondo Nuovo*, 1st publ., Venice, 1565. Cf.Sabin 8784; Church 153; Arents 44; JCB (3) I:393-394. CSmH, DLC, ICN, MH, MiU-C, NN-RB, PU, RPJCB; BL, BN.594/11

____. Das vierdte Buch von der neuwen Welt. oder Neuwe und gründtliche Historien von dem Nidergängischen Indien . . . Mit nützlichen Scholien und Ausslegungen fast auff jede Capitel. *Frankfurt a.M.: J.Feyerabend,for D.de Bry*, 1594. 141p.;illus.,map; fol. (Theodor de Bry's *America*. Pt 4. German). 1st publ. in this translation by Nicolaus Höniger as bk 1 of the Basel, 1579, *Der Newen Weldt . . . History* but here supplemented by annotations supplied by Urbain Chauveton in the Basel, 1578, Latin *Novae Novi Mundi historiae*, here 1st translated. Cf.Sabin 8784; Church 183; JCB (3) I:394. CSmH, DLC, IU, MH, MiU-C, NN-RB, RPJCB; BL, BN.
594/12

Blundeville, Thomas. M.Blundeville his exercises, containing six treatises . . . to have knowledge as well in cosmographie, astronomie, and geographie, as also in the arte of navigation. *London: J.Windet*, 1594. 350 numb.lvs;illus.;4to. Included are scattered refs to the New World, as well as John Blagrave's *Mathematical jewel*, 1st publ., London, 1585. Sabin 6023; STC 3146; Ind. aur.120.018. CSmH, CtY, DLC, MH, NN-RB; BL.
594/13

Boaistuau, Pierre. Histoires prodigeuses. *Antwerp: G.Janssens*, 1594. 720p.;illus.;12mo. 1st publ. with American ref. in section by François de Belleforest, Paris, 1571. Ind.aur. 120.103. ICN; BL, BN.
594/14

Bodin, Jean. De republica libri sex . . . Editio tertia. *Frankfurt a.M.: Widow of J.Wechel*,

for P.Fischer, 1594. 1221p.;8vo. Ind.aur. 120.852; Adams (Cambr.) B2232. IU, MH-L, NN-RB, PPL; Cambridge: UL, Munich: StB.
594/15

Botero, Giovanni. La prima[-seconda] parte delle Relationi universali . . . nella qual si contiene la descrittione di tutta la terra. *Bergamo: C.Ventura* 1594-95. 2v.;8vo. 1st publ., Rome, 1591-92. Sabin 6800; Streit I:199 & 202; Ind.aur.122.707; JCB (3) I:332. RPJCB.
594/16

Bozio, Tommaso. De signis ecclesiae Dei. *Lyons: P.Landry*, 1594. 3v.;8vo. 1st publ., Rome, 1590. Ind.aur.123.296; Baudrier (Lyons) V:340. RPJCB; BN, Berlin: StB.
594/17

Casas, Bartolomé de las, Bp of Chiapa. Histoire admirable des horribles insolences, cruautez, et tyrannies exercees par les Espagnols és Indes Occidentalles . . . Et nouvellement traduite & mise en langue françoise [par Jacques de Miggrode], pour l'utilité des bons François & l'instruction des mauvais. *Lyons:* 1594. 222p.;8vo. 1st publ. in this translation, Antwerp, 1579, under title *Tyrannies et cruautes des Espagnols*; here a reissue, with cancel t.p., of the [Paris?] 1582 edn. Hanke/Giménez 483. NN-RB.
594/18

Chytraeus, Nathan. Variorum in Europa itinerum deliciae. *Herborn:* [*C.Corvinus*] 1594. 864p.;8vo. On p.773-795 are reprinted the Latin legends of Sebastian Cabot's map, 1st publ., [Antwerp? ca. 1544?], as *Declaratio chartae novae*. Sabin 3037; Winship (Cabot) 75; Church 248; JCB (3) I:332. CSmH, CtY, IU, MH, MnU-B, NN-RB, RPJCB; BL, BN.
594/19

Clavius, Christoph. In Sphaeram Joannis de Sacro Bosco commentarius. Nunc quarto ab ipso auctore recognitus. *Lyons: G.Julliéron,for Gabiano Bros*, 1594. 551p.;illus.;4to. 1st publ., Rome, 1570; here a reissue of Lyons, 1593, edn with altered imprint date. Backer II:1213; Baudrier (Lyons) VII:230. DLC, NN-RB, BL, Paris: Ste Geneviève.
594/20

Davys, John. [The seaman's secrets. *London: T.Dawson*, 1594?]. Entered in the Stationer's Register, 3 Sept. 1594; no copy today is known. Subsequent editions contain refs to English explorers of the New World. Cf.Sabin 18842; cf.STC 6369.
594/21

Du Bartas, Guillaume de Salluste, seigneur.

L'Eden, ou Paradis terrestre de la Seconde semaine . . . Avec commentaires & annotations contenants plusieurs descriptions & deductions d'arbres, arbustes, plantes & herbes . . . Par Claude Duret. *Lyons: B.Riguard*, 1594. 114 numb.lvs;4to. 1st publ. with Duret's commentary, Nevers, 1591, under title *La seconde semaine;* Du Bartas's text 1st publ., Paris, 1584. Baudrier (Lyons) III:433. MH-A; BL, Paris: Ste Geneviève.
594/22

Estienne, Charles. De veltbouw ofte lantwinninghe. *Amsterdam: E.Muller,for C.Claeszoon*, 1594, 259p.;illus.;fol. 1st publ. in Dutch, Antwerp, 1566. Bibl.belg.,1st ser., X,E41. Amsterdam: UB.
594/23

Gabelkover, Oswald. Artzneybuch. *Tübingen: G.Gruppenbach*, 1594. 2 pts;4to. 1st publ., Tübingen, 1589, under title *Nützlich Artzneybuch*. DNLM, MBCo.
594/24

Hues, Robert. Tractatus de globis et eorum usu. *London: T.Dawson*, 1594. 28 lvs;8vo. Included are numerous refs to the New World. STC 13906. BL.
594/25

Hurault, Michel, sieur de Bélesbat et du Fay. Quatre excellent discours sur l'estat present de la France. [*Paris?*] 1594. 214 numb.lvs;12mo. 1st publ., [Paris?], 1593. ICN; BN.
594/26

Jesuits. Letters from missions. Annuae litterae (1590-91) 1594. Litterae . . . duorum annorum MDXC et MDXCI. *Rome: Jesuit College*, 1594. 919p.;8vo. Included are letters from the Mexican, Peruvian & Brazilian provinces. Streit I:202; Backer I:1288. NNH; Fulda:Sem.
594/27

——. Recueil de quelques missions des Indes Orientales, & Occidentales: extraict d'aucuns avertissemens, escrits és annees 1590. & 1591 . . . Traduict . . . d'italien [par Michel Coyssard?]. *Lyons: J.Pillehotte*, 1594. 172p.; 8vo. Transl. from Rome, 1592, *Ragguaglio d'alcune missioni*. Sabin 44965; Baudrier (Lyons) II:338-339; Cioranescu (XVI) 7083; Palau 154578. BL.
594/28

Laszcz, Martin. Judicium albo rossadek: ksiedza Milolaia Issjory [pseud.]. *Vilna: D.Leczycki*, 1594. 105p.;4to. Includes, p.37, a defense of Jesuits in the New World. Tazbir p.13; Backer IV:1548; Wierzbowski 1781.
594/29

LeRoy, Louis. Of the interchangeable course, or variety of things in the whole world. *London: C.Yetsweirt*, 1594. 130 numb.lvs;4to.

Transl. by Robert Ashley from LeRoy's *De la vicissitude ou varieté des choses*, 1st publ., Paris, 1575. STC 15488. CSmH, CtY, DLC, ICN, InU-L, MH, MiU. RPJCB; BL. 594/30

Léry, Jean de. Histoire d'un voyage fait en la terre du Bresil, autrement dite Amerique. [*Geneva:*] *Heirs of E.Vignon*, 1594. 382p.; 8vo. 1st publ., La Rochelle, 1578. Sabin 40151; Borba de Moraes I:405-406; Atkinson (Fr.Ren.) 368; JCB (3) I:333. DLC, MH, MnU-B, NN-RB, RPJCB; BL, BN. 594/31

——. Historia navigationis in Brasiliam quae et America dicitur. *Geneva: Heirs of E.Vignon*, 1594. 340p.; illus.; 8vo. 1st publ. in Latin, Geneva, 1586. Sabin 40154 (& 32041); Borba de Moraes I:405-406; JCB (3) I:333. DLC, InU-L, MB, MnU-B, NN-RB, PPL, RPJCB; Strasbourg: BN. 594/32

Lobo Lasso de la Vega, Gabriel. Mexicana . . . emendada y añadida por su mismo autor. *Madrid: L.Sánchez,for M. Martínez*, 1594. 304 numb.lvs; port.; 8vo. Contains 13 additional cantos not found in Madrid, 1588, edn. In verse. Sabin 39140; Medina (BHA) 354; Pérez Pastor (Madrid) 438; Palau 132559. NNH, RPJCB; Madrid: BN. 594/33

Lumnius, Joannes Fredericus. De vicinitate extremi judicii Dei libri duo. *Antwerp: J.van Keerberghen*, 1594. 270p.; 8vo. 1st publ., Antwerp, 1567. Cf.Sabin 42675; cf.Streit I:206; Adams (Cambr.) L1715. NNUT; Cambridge: UL, BN. 594/34

Mariz, Pedro de. Dialogos de varia historia em que sumariamente se referem muytas cousas antiguas de Hespanha. *Coimbra: A.de Mariz*, 1594. 244 numb.lvs; ports; 4to. In Dialogue iv, chapt.viii contains an account of the discovery of Brazil. Sabin 44608; Borba de Moraes II:21; Anselmo 905; Palau 152278. ICN, RPJCB; BL. 594/35

Molina, Luis de. De justitia tomus primus. *Venice: Society of Minims*, 1594. 1174 cols; fol. 1st publ., Cuenca (Spain), 1593. Adams (Cambr.) M1570; Palau 174616:I. Cambridge: Emmanuel, BN. 594/36

Morigia, Paolo. Historia de' personaggi illustri religiosi. *Bergamo: C.Ventura*, 1594. 344p.; port.; 4to. 1st publ., Bergamo, 1593; here a reissue with altered imprint date? IU; BL. 594/37

Neander, Michael. Orbis terrae divisio compendiaria et plana in partes et regiones suas praecipuas . . . Accessit etiam Chronicorum omnium aetatum, gentium & temporum compendium. *Wittenberg: [S.Gronenberg? for] J.Apel,at Leipzig*, 1594. 2 pts; 8vo. 1st publ., Leipzig, 1586. Sabin 52174n. MiU-C. 594/38

Paris. Lycée Louis-le-Grand. Defenses. de ceux du College de Clermont contre les requeste & plaidoyée contre eux. [*Paris?*] 1594. 2 pts; 8vo. A reply to Antoine Arnauld's *Plaidoyé* of this year, including refs to Spanish West Indies. MH. 594/39

Quad, Matthias. Europae universalis et particularis descriptio. *Cologne: L.Andreae,for J.Bussemacher*, 1594. 73 maps; fol. Of the maps the 1st depicts the world, incl. America. Sabin 66892. BL. 594/40

Rectorius, Livonius. Dissertatio apologetica de indole et qualitate guaiaci et sarsaparillae. *Bologna: G.Rossi* 1594. 107p.; 4to. A reply to L.Rectorius's 1593 *De indole . . . guaiaci*. BN. 594/41

Rivadeneira, Pedro de. Vida del .p. Ignacio de Loyola . . . y de los padres . . . Diego Laynez, y Francisco de Borja. *Madrid: P.Madrigal*, 1594. 3 pts; fol. Includes life of Loyola, 1st publ. in Spanish, Madrid, 1583, & that of Borgia, Madrid, 1592. Sabin 70781; Backer VI:1727; Pérez Pastor (Madrid) 457; Palau 266226; Adams (Cambr.) R467. NN-RB; BL. 594/42

——. Vita Ignatii Loiolae. *Lyons: J.Roussin*, 1594. 676p.; 8vo. 1st publ., Naples, 1572. NNUT. 594/43

Rosaccio, Giuseppe. Inestimabile et maravigliosa virtu del tabaco. *Florence: G.A.Caneo*, 1594. 4 lvs; 8vo. The earliest extant edn, an earlier Vicenza edn cited in imprint being unknown. Arents 45. NN-A. 594/44

——. Le sei eta del mondo. *Bologna: G.Rossi*, 1594. 63p.; map; 8vo. 1st publ., Brescia, 1593. Cf.Sabin 73197. NN-RB, RPJCB. 594/45

——. Teatro del cielo e della terra. *Florence: [F. Tosi]* 1594. 56p.; illus.,maps; 8vo. 1st publ., Brescia, 1592. Cf.Sabin 73198. DLC, InU-L, NN-RB, PPFr; BL. 594/46

——[Anr edn]. *Ferrara: V.Baldini*, 1594. 56p.; illus.,maps; 8vo. Sabin 73198. NN-RB. 594/47

Sánchez de Acre, Pero. Libro del reino de Dios, y del camino por donde se alcança. *Madrid: Widow of P.Madrigal*, 1594. 965p.; 4to. Written in Mexico, where Sánchez was the first Provincial of the Jesuit province, & licensed for printing, 13 May 1592, at Mexico City. Medina (BHA) 356; Backer VII:529;

Pérez Pastor (Madrid) 757. BL, Oviedo: BU.
594/48

Satyre Ménippée. Satyre, Menippee de la vertu du catholicon d'Espagne . . . A laquelle est adjousté un discours sur l'interpretation du mot de Higuiero d'infierno. [*Paris?*] 1593 [i.e.,1594]. 414 (394)p.;12mo. The 'Discours', not present in the earlier Tours edn of this year, identifies a Spanish drug 'appelée Higuiero d'infierno', referred to in the *Satyre*, as in fact the 'figuier des Indes' (prickly-pear cactus; Opuntia) found in the West Indies, & compares supporters of the League of French Catholics to the plant. Derived from the *Observations sur le titre . . . de la Satyre Menippee* of 1593. Cioranescu (XVI) 20347. MH.
594/49

—[Anr edn]. [*Paris?*] 1594. 274p.;8vo. CSt, MiU, WaU.
594/50

—[Anr edn]. [*Paris?*] 1594. 275p.;illus.;8vo. DFo.
594/51

—[Anr edn]. [*Paris?*] 1594. 325p.;illus.;12mo. Adams (Cambr.) S447. NjP; Cambridge: Emmanuel.
594/52

Schotus, Fridericus. Ander theil D. Joh. Fausti Historien darin beschrieben ist, Christophori Wageners, Fausti gewesenen Discipels auffgerichter Pact mit dem Teuffel . . . Neben einer feinen beschreibung der Newen Inseln . . . P[*rague?*]., 1594. 72 lvs;illus.;4to. 1st publ., P[rague?], 1593. Henning (Wagner) 2; Wolfenbüttel 115. Wolfenbüttel: HB.
594/53

—[Anr edn]. P[*rague?*]., 1594. 54 lvs;illus.;8vo. Henning (Wagner) 3. Zerbst: Oberschule.
594/54

—[Anr edn]. [*Frankfurt a.M.: N.Bassé*, 1594]. 56 lvs;illus.;8vo. Henning (Wagner) 4. CtY; Weimar: Zentralbibliothek der deutschen Klassik.
594/55

Soto, Domingo de. De justitia & jure libri decem. *Venice:* [*F.Prato,for?*] *Society of Minims,* 1594. 1006p.;4to. 1st publ., Salamanca, 1553. Possibly a reissue of Prato's 1584 edn. Palau 320163; Shaaber S499. PU. 594/56

Tabourot, Etienne. Les bigarrures . . . *Lyons: B.Riguad,* 1594. 167 numb.lvs;12mo. 1st publ., Paris, 1585. In verse & prose. Baudrier (Lyons) III:434. BN. 594/57

Tasso, Torquato. Il Goffredo, overo Gierusalemme liberata, poema heroico. *Venice: G.B.Ciotti,* 1594. 576p.;12mo. 1st publ.. with

American refs, Parma, 1581. Adams (Cambr.) T244. Cambridge: Jesus. 594/58

Verdugo y Sarria, Pedro. Libro de los mysterios de la missa. *Madrid: L.Sánchez,* 1594. 128 numb.lvs;4to. The author is described in the title as Prior of the Convent of Our Lady of the Rosary at Santa Fé in New Granada (i.e., Colombia). Medina (BHA) 357; Pérez Pastor (Madrid) 459; Palau 359983. Madrid: BU. 594/59

1595

Agrippa, Camillo. Nuove inventioni . . . sopra il modo di navigare. *Rome: D.Gigliotti,* 1595. 52p.;illus.,port.;4to. Included are refs to New World navigation. Ind.aur.101.828. NN-RB, NcU, RPJCB; BL, BN. 595/1

Anchieta, José de. Arte de grammatica da lingoa mais usada na costa do Brasil . . . Com licença . . . da Companhia de Jesu. *Coimbra: A.de Mariz,* 1595. 58 numb.lvs;8vo. Sabin 1371; Borba de Moraes I:28; Ind. aur.105.130; Anselmo 908; Palau 11834. BL. Madrid: BN. 595/2

Arnauld, Antoine. Oratio . . . pro Universitate Parisiensi actrice, contra Jesuitas reos. *Leyden: L.Elzevir,* 1595. 2 pts;4to. 1st publ. in Latin, Leyden, 1594. Ind.aur.108.870; Adams (Cambr.) A1989. CtY; Cambridge: UL, Munich: StB. 595/3

—[Anr edn]. Actio . . . pro Academia Parisiense actrice. *Paris:* [*M.Patisson?*] 1595. 85p.;8vo. Ind.aur.108.872; Adams (Cambr.) A1986. Oxford: Bodl., Munich: StB. 595/4

——. Plaidoyé . . . pour l'Université de Paris, demanderesse, contre les Jesuites defendeurs. *Paris:* [*M.Patisson?*] 1595. 88p.;8vo. 1st publ., Paris, 1594. Ind.aur.108.873. BN, Nuremberg: StB. 595/5

Bellinato, Francesco, supposed author. Discorso di cosmographia in dialogo. *Venice: A.Manuzio,* 1595. 48p.;8vo. 1st publ., Venice, 1573. Renouard (Aldus) 252,2; Ind.aur. 116.210; Adams (Cambr.) B527; JCB (STL) 17. MH, RPJCB; BL, BN. 595/6

Benzoni, Girolamo. Americae, das fünffte Buch, vol schöner unerhörter Historien auss dem andern Theil . . . gezogen: von der Spanier Wüten beyd wider ihrer Knecht die Nigriten, unnd auch die arme Indianer . . .

Sampt kurtzer and nützlicher Erklärung der Historien bey jedem Capitel. [*Frankfurt a.M.: T.de Bry*, 1595]. 113p.;illus.,map;fol (Theodor de Bry's *America.* Pt 5. German). 1st publ. in this translation by Nicolaus Höniger as bk 2 of the Basel, 1579, *Der Newen Weldt . . . History* but here supplemented by annotations supplied by Urbain Chauveton in the Basel, 1578, Latin *Novae Novi Mundi historiae,* here 1st translated; cf.earlier pt (bk 1) of 1594. Cf.Sabin 8784; cf.Church 186; JCB (3) I:395-396. CSmH, DLC, MH, MiU-C, NN-RB, PPL, RPJCB; BL, BN.   595/7

_____. Americae pars quinta . . . secunda sectionis Hispanorum, tùm in nigrittas servos suos, tum in Indios crudelitatem . . . Addita ad singula fere capita scholia, in quibus res Indiae luculenter exponuntur. [*Frankfurt a.M.: T.de Bry*] 1595. 92p.;illus.,map;fol. (Theodor de Bry's *America.* Pt 5. Latin). 1st publ., Geneva, 1578, as bk 2 (of 3) of Urbain Chauveton's translation, with annotations, of Benzoni's *Historia del Mondo Nuovo;* cf.earlier pt (bk 1) of 1594. Cf.Sabin 4799 & 8784; Church 156; JCB (3) I:395. CSmH, DLC, ICN, MH, MiU-C, NN-RB, RPJCB; BL, BN.   595/8

Boaistuau, Pierre. Histoires prodigeuses. *Antwerp: G.Janssens,* 1595. 720p.;12mo. 1st publ. with American ref. in section by François de Belleforest, Paris, 1571. Ind. aur.120.105. MH; BN.   595/9

Bock, Hieronymus. Kreütterbuch. *Strassburg: J.Rihel,* 1595. 470 lvs;illus.;fol. 1st publ. with illus., Strassburg, 1546; here ed. by Melchior Sebizius. Pritzel 866n; Nissen (Bot.) 182n; Ind.aur.120.601; Ritter (Strasbourg) 220. CSdS, NN-RB; BL, Strasbourg: BN.   595/10

Bodin, Jean. Methodus ad facilem historiarum cognitio . . . denuo recusa. [*Geneva:*] *J. Stoer,* 1595. 8vo. 1st publ., Paris, 1566. Ind. aur.120.853. ICN, NNC; Munich: StB.   595/11

Botero, Giovanni. Delle relationi universali . . . terza parte. *Rome: G.Faciotto,for G.Ferrari,* 1595. 328p.;4to. Section 'Dell'isole dell'Oceano Atlantico' mentions Brazil. Continues pts 1-2, 1st publ., Rome, 1591-1592. Cf.Sabin 6801; Streit I:203n; Ind.aur. 122.710; Adams (Cambr.) B2555. RPJCB; Cambridge: Trinity.   595/12

_____. Relatione universale de' continenti del Mondo nuovo. *Rome: [G.Faciotto?] for G.Ferrari,* 1595. 98p.;4to. Issued with the 3d pt of Botero's *Delle relationi universali* of this year. Sabin 6801-6802; cf.Streit I:203n; Ind.aur. 122.711. MBAt, MnU-B, NN-RB, RPJCB.   595/13

_____. Relatione universale dell'isole sino al presente scoverte. *Rome: B.Bonfadino,for G. Ferrari,* 1595. 161p.;4to. Amongst the islands are those of the New World. Issued with the 3d & 4th pts of Botero's *Delle relationi universali* of this year. Cf.Sabin 6801; cf.Streit I:203n; Ind.aur.122.709. MBAt, NN-RB, RPJCB.   595/14

_____. Le relationi universali. *Vicenza: G.Greco* (v.1) *& P.Dusinelli,at Venice* (v.2-3), 1595. 3v.;maps;4to. 1st publ., Rome, 1591-95. ICN.   595/15

Bozio, Tommasso. De signis ecclesiae Dei. *Lyons: P.Landry,* 1595. 3v.;8vo. 1st publ., Rome, 1591; here a reissue of Landry's 1594 edn. Streit I:205; Baudrier (Lyons) V:344; Ind.aur.123.299; Adams (Cambr.) B2642. Cambridge: UL, LeMans: BM.   595/16

Capelloni, Lorenzo. Les divers discours. *Troyes: J.LeNoble & M.Sonnius,at Paris,* 1595. 276 numb.lvs;12mo. Transl. by Pierre de Larivey from Genoa, 1576, Italian text. Ind.aur.131.535. CSmH, MH, MnU; BL, BN.   595/17

Carion, Johann. Chronique et histoire universelle . . . Dressee premierement par Jean Carion, puis augmentee . . . & enrichie . . . par Ph. Melanchton & Gaspar Peucer . . . Plus deux livres adjoustez de nouveau aux cinq autres. [*Geneva:*] *J.Stoer,for P.de Saint André,* 1595. 2v.;8vo. 1st publ. as here transl. & supplemented by Simon Goulart, Geneva, 1579. Jones (Goulart) 15(b); Ind.aur.132.380. BL, Berlin: StB.   595/18

Chute, Anthony. Tabaco. The distinct and severall opinions of the late and best phisitions . . . of the divers natures and qualities thereof. *London: A.Islip,for W.Barlow,* 1595. 54p.;illus.;8vo. Sabin 94165; Arents 46. CSmH, MWA, NN-A.   595/19

Davys, John. The worldes hydrographical discription . . . whereby appeares that from England there is a short and speedie passage into the South Seas . . . by northerly navigation. *London: T.Dawson,* 1595. 48 lvs;8vo.

Sabin 18843; STC 6372; Church 249. CSmH, DFo, ICN, NN-RB; BL.   595/20

Dodoens, Robert. A new herball; or, Historie of plants . . . Corrected and amended. *London: E.Bollifant,* 1595. 916p.;fol. 1st publ. in English, London, 1578. Pritzel 2345n; Nissen (Bot.) 516n; STC 6986; Henrey (Brit.bot.) 112; Arents (Add.) 19. CSmH, DFo, ICJ, MH, MiU, NN-A; BL.   595/21

Du Bartas, Guillaume de Salluste, seigneur. La divina settimana: cioè I sette giorni della creatione del mondo . . . Tradotta . . . dal signor Ferrante Guisone. Aggiuntovi di nuovo le figure intagliate in raine da Cristoforo Paulin. *Venice: G.B.Ciotti,* 1595. 12mo. 1st publ. in Italian, Tours, 1592. In verse. Holmes (Du Bartas) I:109 no.19n. BL, Paris: Mazarine.   595/22

En la causa que se trata entre el Arçobispo de Lima, y el Colegio de la Compañia de Jesus, de la dicha ciudad: . . . El licenciado Castro governador de aquellos reynos del Peru, aura veynte y dos años, que para que mejor se dotrinassen los Indios que bivian en aquella ciudad, de otros repartimientos escogio un sitio para fundar un lugar, que despues se llamo de Santiago. [*Madrid?* ca.1595?]. 3p.;fol. Medina (BHA) 8042; Streit II:1098. Lima: BN.   595/23

Estienne, Charles. L'agriculture et maison rustique, de mm. Charles Estienne et Jean Liebault. *Lyons: J.Roussin,* 1595. 4to. 1st publ., Paris, 1567. Thiébaud (La chasse) 349-350.   595/24

———. Dictionarium historicum, geographicum, poeticum. *Lyons: T.Soubron & M.Desprez,* 1595. 452 numb.lvs;4to. Includes entries for American areas not found in earlier edns. Baudrier (Lyons) IV:359. IU; BN.   595/25

Fioravanti, Leonardo. La cirurgia. *Venice: M.Bonibelli,* 1595. 182 numb.lvs;8vo. 1st publ., Venice, 1570. DNLM, ICU.   595/26

———. De capricci medicinali . . . Di nuovo, dall'istesso autore . . . ampliati . . . revisti, corretti, & ristampati. *Venice: M.Bonibelli,* 1595. 267 numb.lvs;illus.;8vo. 1st publ., Venice, 1561. Adams (Cambr.) F487; Moranti (Urbino) 1494. DNLM, RPB; Cambridge: UL, Urbino: BU.   595/27

Flurance, David Rivault, sieur de. Les estats, esquels il est discouru du prince du noble & du tiers estat. *Lyons: C.Morillon,for B.Rigaud,* 1595, 235p.;12mo. Includes identification of America as ancient kingdom of Tharsis, governed by kings. Sabin 24917; Baudrier (Lyons) III:440. BL.   595/28

Franck, Sebastian. Werelt-boeck, spieghel ende beeltnisse des gheheelen aerdtbodems . . . to weten Asia, Aphrica, Europa ende America. *Amsterdam: C.Claeszoon,* 1595. cxxxiiii lvs;fol. 1st publ. in Dutch, [Antwerp? 1550?]. Sabin 25470n; JCB (3) I:335-336. NN-RB, RPJCB.   595/29

Fuenmayor, Antonio de. Vida y hechos de Pio V. *Madrid: L.Sánchez,* 1595. 147 numb. lvs;4to. Included are minor refs to New World. Pérez Pastor (Madrid) 473; Palau 95240; Adams (Cambr.) F1130. NNH; BL, BN.   595/30

Gabelkover, Oswald. Artzneybuch. *Tübingen: G.Gruppenbach,* 1595. 2 pts;4to. 1st publ., Tübingen, 1589, under title *Nützlich Artzneybuch.* CLU-M, DNLM, NBC; London: Wellcome.   595/31

González de Mendoza, Juan, Bp. Historia de las cosas mas notables, ritos y costumbres del gran reyno de la China . . . Con un itinerario del Nuevo Mundo. *Medina del Campo: S.del Canto,for the Heirs of B.Boyer,* 1595. 348 numb.lvs;8vo. 1st publ., Rome, 1585. Sabin 47827 (& 27776); Medina (BHA) 361; Wagner (SW) 7aa; Streit IV:2031; Pérez Pastor (Medina del Campo) 230; JCB (3) I:336. CtY, MB, MnU-B, NN-RB, RPJCB; BL.   595/32

Goulart, Simon, comp. Le quatriesme recueil, contenant l'histoire des choses plus memorables avenue sous la Ligue. [*Geneva?*] 1595. 835p.;8vo. Includes the *Response à un avis,* 1st publ., [Paris?], 1589. Adams (Cambr.) F869. Cambridge: Clare.   595/33

——[Anr edn]. [*Geneva?*] 1595. 768p.;8vo. Jones (Goulart) 30(b); Adams (Cambr.) F873. MH; BL, BN.   595/34

Guarguante, Orazio. Tria opuscula. Hoc est: De theriacae virtutibus paraphrasis, De mechiocani radice opusculum, ac De ovo gallinarum. *Venice: G.B.Ciotti,* 1595. 61p.; 4to. DNLM; BL.   595/35

Heyns, Peeter. Epitome Theatri. *Antwerp:* 1595. See entry under Ortelius, Abraham, below.

Honter, Johannes. Rudimentorum cosmographicorum . . . libri iiii. *Prague: Schuman Press,* 1595. 48p.;illus.,maps;8vo. 1st publ. in this version, Kronstadt, 1542. In verse. DLC, MiU-C; BL. 595/36

Hurault, Michel, sieur de Bélesbat et du Fay. Quatre excellens discours sur l'estat present de la France. [*Paris?*] 1595. 214 numb.lvs;12mo. 1st publ., [Paris?], 1593. Cioranescu (XVI) 11797. BL, BN. 595/37

Klonowicz, Sebastian Fabian. Flies, to iest, Spuszczánie statków Wisla. [*Racow:*] *S.Sternácki* [1595]. 47p.;4to. In verse. Mentions recent discoveries of new worlds. Yarmolinsky (Polish Americana) 44 no.2; Graesse IV:29. 595/38

La Noue, François de. Discours politiques et militaires. *Lyons: D.Bellon*, 1595. 1019p.; 16mo. 1st publ., Basel, 1587. As with other edns of this work, the imprint is perhaps fictitious. Adams (Cambr.) L158; Baudrier (Lyons) I:29. ICU, MH; Cambridge: Clare. 595/39

La Popelinière, Lancelot Voisin, sieur de. The historie of France. *London: J.Windet*, 1595. 134 lvs;fol. Transl. from author's *Histoire de France . . . depuis lan 1550*, 1st publ., [La Rochelle], 1581. STC 11276. CSmH, DFo, ICN; BL. 595/40

Lavanha, João Baptista. Regimento nautico. *Lisbon: S.Lopez*, 1595. 37 numb.lvs;4to. Sabin 39232; Anselmo 813; King Manuel 243. NNH; BL, Lisbon: BN. 595/41

Linschoten, Jan Huygen. Reys-gheschritt. *Amsterdam:* 1595. See the year 1596.

Lucidarius. M.Elucidarius. Von allerhandt Geschöpffen Gottes . . . unnd wie alle Creaturen geschaffen seind auff Erden. *Frankfurt a.M.: Heirs of C.Egenolff*, 1595. [87]p.;illus.;4to. 1st publ., Strassburg, [ca. 1535]. Schorbach (Lucidarius) 66. BL, Munich: StB. 595/42

Medina, Pedro de. The arte of navigation, translated out of Spanish . . . by John Frampton. *London: T.Dawson*, 1595. 93p.;illus.; 4to. 1st publ. in English, London, 1581. Sabin 47347n; STC 17772; Palau 159681. CSmH, MBAt, NcU; London: Royal Institution of Naval Architects. 595/43

———. Primera, y segunda parte de Las grandezas y cosas notables de España . . . nuevamente, corregida y muy ampliada, por Diego Perez de Messa. *Alcalá de Henares: J.Gracián,for J.de Torres*, 1595. 334 numb.lvs; map;fol. 1st publ., Alcalá de Henares, 1548.

Medina (BHA) 362; García (Alcalá de Henares) 707; Palau 159686n. NNH; BL, Madrid: BN. 595/44

Mercator, Gerardus. Atlas, sive Cosmographicae meditationes. *Düsseldorf: A.Buys*, 1595. 3 pts;maps;fol. Included are a world map and one depicting America. In this edn the lvs for Gallia & Germania are signed. Sabin 47881; Koeman (Me) 13A; Phillips (Atlases) 3400. CSmH, DLC, MiU-C, NjP, RPJCB; BL, BN. 595/45

——[Anr edn]. *Düsseldorf: A.Buys*, 1595. Differs in reset text, etc. distinguishable by having lvs for Gallia & Germania unsigned. Koeman (Me) 13B. Cu-B; BL, Strasbourg: BN. 595/46

Montaigne, Michel Eyquem de. Les essais . . . edition nouvelle trouvee apres le deceds de l'autheur, reveüe et augmentee par luy d'un tiers plus qu'aux precedentes impressions. *Paris: A.L'Angelier*, 1595. 2 pts;fol. The earliest edn based on Montaigne's own annotated copy of Bordeaux, 1580, text. Tchémerzine VIII:408. CU, DLC, ICU, MH, NN-RB; BL, BN. 595/47

——[Anr issue]. *Paris: M.Sonnius*, 1595. Tchémerzine VIII:408. MWiW-C; BN. 595/48

——[Anr edn]. *Lyons: F.LeFèvre*, 1595. 1002p.; 12mo. Baudrier (Lyons) V:355. MH; BN. 595/49

Nash, Thomas. Pierce Pennilesse his supplication to the divell. *London: T.C[reede].,for N.Ling*, 1595. [72]p.;4to. 1st publ., London, 1592. STC 18375. CSmH, CtY, DFo; BL. 595/50

Ortelius, Abraham. Epitome Theatri . . . Praecipuarum regionum delineationes . . . continens. *Antwerp: A.Coninx,for P.Galle*, 1595. 109 numb.lvs;maps;obl.16mo. 1st publ. with Latin version of text by Peeter Heyns, Antwerp, 1585. Sabin 57690; Koeman (Ort.) 56; Adams (Cambr.) O345. DLC, ICN, MH, PPL, RPJCB; BL, Brussels: BR. 595/51

———. Theatrum orbis terrarum. *Antwerp: Plantin Office*, 1595. 337 lvs;illus.,port.,maps;fol. 1st publ., Antwerp, 1570. Koeman (Ort.) 29. CSmH, DLC, ICN, MiU-C, NN-RB, PPL; BL. 595/52

Pontaymeri, Alexandre de, sieur de Faucheron. Discours d'estat, ou la necessite & les moyens de faire la guerre en l'Espaigne sont exposez. *Paris: J.Mettayer & P.L'Huillier; The Hague: A.Henricszoon*, 1595. 15 lvs;8vo. In-

cludes ref. to 'le Pérou des Américains'.
Cioranescu (XVI) 17775. BL, BN.　595/53
___[Anr edn]. *Lyons*: 1595. 31p.;8vo. BN. 595/54

Quad, Matthias. Die Jahr Blum welch da
begreifft und in sich helt fast alle Jahren dieser
Welt. *Cologne: J.Bussemacher*, 1595. 39
numb.lvs;illus.;4to. In verse. On recto of lf 25
is a ref. to Vespucci. Baginsky (German Americana) 96. NN-RB.　　　　　　　　595/55

Ramírez, Juan, d. 1609. Advertencias . . . sobre el servicio personal al qual son forçados y
compelidos los Indios de la nueva España por
los Visorreyes. [*Madrid?* 1595?]. 4 numb.lvs;
fol. Dated at Madrid, 10 October 1595. Medina (BHA) 7743; Streit I:210.　　595/56
___. Paracer . . . sobre el servicio personal, y
repartimiento de los Indios . . . En Madrid, a.
20. de ottubre . . . 1595. [*Madrid?* 1595?]. 4
lvs;fol. Medina (BHA) 7744; Streit I:209.
　　　　　　　　　　　　　　　　595/57

Rivadeneira, Pedro de. Las obras . . . agora
de nuevo revistas y acrecentadas. *Madrid:
Widow of P.Madrigal,for J.de Montoya*, 1595.
943p.;8vo. Contains accounts of Francesco
Borgia (1st publ., Madrid, 1592) & Ignatius
Loyola (1st publ., Naples, 1572). Cf.Sabin
70779; Pérez Pastor (Madrid) 496; Palau
266195.　　　　　　　　　　　　595/58
___. Tratado de la religion y virtudes que deve
tener el prencipe christiano para governar y
conservar sus estados. Contra lo que Nicolas
Machiavelo y los politicos deste tiempo en-
señan. *Madrid: P.Madrigal,for J.de Mon-
toya*, 1595. 66p.;4to. In bk ii, chapts xi, xxxv
& xxxviii contain refs to the riches of the New
World, citing José de Acosta, mentioning
Cortés, etc. Pérez Pastor (Madrid) 497;
Backer VI:1735; Palau 266334. InU-L, MiU,
NcU; BL.　　　　　　　　　　　595/58a
___. Vita Ignatii Loiolae. *Lyons: J.Roussin*,
1595. 676p.;8vo. 1st publ., Naples, 1572. A
reissue with altered imprint date of printer's
1594 edn? Cf.Sabin 70782; Backer VI:1726;
Palau 266206n. BL.　　　　　　　595/59
___[Anr issue]. *Lyons: [J.Roussin,for] J.Gesselin,
at Paris*, 1595. Backer VI:1726; Palau
266206.　　　　　　　　　　　　595/60
___[Anr edn]. *Madrid: P.Madrigal*, 1595. 8vo.
Pérez Pastor (Madrid) 498; Palau 266207.
　　　　　　　　　　　　　　　　595/61

Roberts, Henry. Lancaster his allarums, honorable assaultes, and supprising of the block-

houses and store-houses belonging to Fernand
Bucke in Brasill. *London: A.J[effes].for
W.Barley*, [1595]. [24]p.;illus.;4to. Borba de
Moraes II:209-210; STC 21083; JCB (3) I:337.
CSmH, RPJCB.　　　　　　　　　595/62
___. The trumpet of fame: or Sir Fraunces
Drakes and Sir John Hawkins Farewell. *Lon-
don: T.Creede,& sold by W.Barley*, 1595.
12p.;4to. In verse. Sabin 71895; STC 21088.
CSmH.　　　　　　　　　　　　595/63

Román y Zamora, Jerónimo. Republicas del
mundo . . . Corregida y censurada por el Ex-
purgatorio del Santo Officio . . . Y tambien
van añadidas en esta segunda impression
diversas Republicas . . . y casi hechas otras de
nuevo por el mesmo author. *Salamanca:
J.Fernández,for J.de Terti*, 1595. 3v.;fol. Substantially enl. from edn 1st publ., Medina del
Campo. 1575. In v.3, bk 3 treats 'De la republica, de los Indios Occidentales'. The printing of this work was ostensibly shared by Fernández (responsible for v.1 & lvs 100 ff. in v.3)
with Diego Cosio (v.2) & with Sántiago del
Canto, at Medina del Campo (v.3, lvs 1-100).
Sabin 72895; Medina (BHA) 363; Streit I:211;
Pérez Pastor (Medina del Campo) 236. CtY,
ICN, InU-L, MH, NN-RB; BL. BN.　595/64

Romanus, Adrianus. Parvum theatrum ur-
bium, sive Urbium praecipuarum totius orbis
descriptio. *Frankfurt a.M.: N.Bassé*, 1595.
365p.;illus.;4to. 'De Novo Orbe, sive India
Occidentali': p.359-365. Sabin 73000; Adams
(Cambr.) R694; Shaaber R192. DLC, ICU,
MH, MnU-B, NN-RB, PU; BL, Strasbourg:
BN.　　　　　　　　　　　　　595/65

Rosaccio, Giuseppe. Il mondo e sue parti, cioe
Europa, Affrica, Asia, et America. *Florence:
F.Tosi*, 1595. 176p.;maps;8vo. Sabin 73195;
JCB (3)I:338. DLC, MnU-B, RPJCB; BL.
　　　　　　　　　　　　　　　　595/66
___. Le sei età del mondo, con brevita de-
scritte. *Florence: F.Tosi* [1595?]. 43p.;map;
8vo. 1st publ., Brescia, 1593. DFo, InU-L;
BL.　　　　　　　　　　　　　595/67
___[Anr edn]. *Venice*: 1595. 48p.;8vo. Sabin
73197. DFo; BN.　　　　　　　　595/68
___. Teatro del cielo e della terra. *Venice*:
1595. 56p.illus.,map;8vo. 1st publ., Brescia,
1592. Sabin 73198. DFo; BN.　　595/69

Salazar, Estéban de. Veynte discursos sobre el
Credo. *Alcalá de Henares: J.I.de Lequérica,for L.de La Puerta*, 1595. 248 numb.lvs;

4to. 1st publ., Granada, 1577-78. Medina (BHA) 365; Streit II:1128. Seville: BU. 595/70

Satyre Menippée. Satyre Menippée de la vertu de Catholicon d'Espagne. [*Paris?*] 1595. 2 pts;12mo. 1st publ., with American refs, [Paris? 1594]. Adams (Cambr.) S448. BL. 595/71

Satyre Menippée. English. A pleasant satyre or poesie . . . Newly turned out of French into English. *London: Widow Orwin, for T.Man,* 1595. 216p.;4to. Transl. by T.W[ilcox?]. from *Le satyre Menippée* as publ., [Paris? 1594], with 'Discours', in which French Leaguers are symbolized by the West Indian prickly-pear cactus (Opuntia). STC 15489. CSmH, CtY, DFo, MH; BL. 595/72

Spain. Sovereigns, etc., 1556-1598 (Philip II). El Rey. Lo que . . . se assienta y concierta . . . sobre la provision general que ha de hazer de esclavos negros, para todas las Indias Ocidentales. [*Madrid?* 1595?]. 11 numb.lvs;fol. Dated at Madrid, 30 Jan. 1595. Medina (BHA) 7745. Santiago, Chile: BN. 595/73

Staden, Hans. Waerichtige historie enn beschrijvinge eens landts, in America gheleghen, wiens inwoon ders wilt, naecht, seer godtloos, ende wreede menschen eeters zijn . . . Nu niews uut den hoochduytschen overgheset. *Amsterdam: C.Claeszoon,* 1595. 84 lvs;illus.; 8vo. 1st publ. in Dutch, Antwerp, 1558. Sabin 90042; Tiele-Muller 288. The Hague: KB. 595/74

Tasso, Torquato. La delivrance de Hierusalem, mise en vers françois . . . par Jean Du Vignau. *Paris: M.Guillemot,* 1595. 259 numb.lvs;port.;12mo. The earliest edn as here transl. from Tasso's *Gerusalemme liberata*, 1st publ. with ref. to Columbus, Parma, 1581. Racc. Tassiana 744; Cioranescu (XVI) 9430. CtY, DLC, ICU, MH, NIC; Bergamo: BC. 595/75

—[Anr issue]. *Paris: N.Gilles,* 1595. BN. 595/76

——. Il Goffredo, overo Gierusalemme liberata, poema heroico. *Venice: G.B.Ciotti,* 1595. 576p.;12mo. 1st publ. with American refs, Parma, 1581. Adams (Cambr.) T245. Cambridge: Emmanuel. 595/77

——. La Hierusalem . . . rendue françoise par B[laise]. d[e]. V[igenère]. b[ourbonnais]. *Paris: A.L'Angelier,* 1595. 326 numb.lvs; ports; 4to. Transl. from Tasso's *Gerusalemme liberata*, 1st publ. with ref. to Columbus, Parma,

1581. Racc.Tassiana 745; Cioranescu (XVI) 21749. BL, BN. 595/78

Tovar, Simón de. Examen i censura . . . del modo de averiguar las alturas de las tierras, por la altura de la estrella del norte, tomada con la ballestilla. *Seville: R.de Cabrera,* 1595. 91 numb.lvs;illus.;4to. Author's dedicatory letter refers to navigational errors in voyages to Indies. Medina (BHA) 366; Bibl.mar.esp. 222; Palau 338316. Madrid: BN. 595/79

1596

Acosta, José de. De natura Novi Orbis libri duo. Et de promulgatione evangelii apud barbaros. *Cologne: House of Birckmann, for A. Mylius,* 1596. 581p.;8vo. 1st publ., Salamanca, 1588. Sabin 120; Medina (BHA) 368; Streit I:212; Backer I:34; Ind.aur.100.460; Palau 1979; Shaaber A30; JCB (3) I:339. DLC, MH, PU, RPJCB; BL, BN. 596/1

——. Historia naturale, e morale delle Indie . . . Nuovamente tradotta della lingua spagnuola . . . da Gio. Paolo Galucci. *Venice: B.Basa,* 1596. 173 numb.lvs;8vo. Transl. from Spanish text, 1st publ., Salamanca, 1588. Sabin 124; Medina (BHA) 330n (I:501); Streit II:1138; Backer I:36; Pritzel 14n; Ind.aur. 100.461; Arents 48; JCB (3) I:339. CtY-M, DLC, MH, MiU-C, MnU-B, NN-RB, RPJCB; BL, Munich: StB. 596/2

Alberti, Leandro. Descrittione di tutta l'Italia. *Venice: P.Ugolino,* 1596. 495p.;4to. 1st publ., Bologna, 1550. Ind.aur.102.358; Adams (Cambr.) A479. CU, DCU, NN-RB, PPAN; Cambridge: St John's, BN. 596/3

Anania, Giovanni Lorenzo d'. L'universale fabrica del mondo, overo cosmografia. *Venice: A.Muschio,* 1596. 402p.;maps;4to. 1st publ., Naples, 1573. Sabin 1364n; Ind.aur. 105.090. CtY, DLC, NN-RB, RPJCB; BL, Göttingen: UB. 596/4

Bauhin, Kaspar. Φυτοπυναξ, seu Enumerato plantarum ab herbariis nostro seculo descriptarum. *Basel: S.Henricpetri* [1596]. 669p.; port.;4to. Includes discussion of numerous American plants, e.g. sarsaparilla, Guacatan (Guaiacum), Nicotiana (tobacco), the potato (Solanum tuberosum). Pritzel 505; Ind.aur. 114.861; Adams (Cambr.) B386. DNLM, ICJ, MH-A, MiU; BL, BN. 596/5

Beccari, Bernardino. Avviso del successo dell'armata inglese nel voler tentare l'impresa di Panama nel Perù. *Rome: N.Mutii,* 1596. [7]p.;8vo. Covers 2nd stage of Sir Frances Drake's final expedition to Caribbean. JCB AR25:32. RPJCB. 596/6

——. Avviso della morte di Francesco Drac [i.e., Drake], & del mal successo dell'armata inglese. *Rome: N.Mutii,* 1596. [8]p.;8vo. Covers last stage of Drake's final expedition to Caribbean. JCB AR25:32-33. RPJCB. 596/7

——. Relatione del successo dell'armata d'Inghilterra condotta da Fracesco Drac [i.e., Drake], & da Giovanni Achines [i.e.,Hawkins] generali, a S.Giovanni di Porto Ricco nella nuova Spagna, il di 23. di novembre 1595. *Rome: N.Mutii,* 1596. [8]p.;8vo. Covers 1st stage of Drake's final Caribbean expedition. Ind.aur.115.404; JCB AR25:31. RPJCB; Rome: BN. 596/8

Benzoni, Girolamo. Americae pars sexta. Sive Historiae . . . sectio tertia. *Frankfurt a.M.: T.de Bry,* 1596. 106p.;illus.;fol. (Theodor de Bry's *America.* Pt 6. Latin). 1st publ., Geneva, 1578, as bk 3 (of 3) of Urbain Chauveton's translation, with annotations, of Benzoni's *Historia del Mondo Nuovo;* cf.earlier pts 1-2, publ. in 1594 & 1595. Cf.Sabin 8784; Church 156; JCB (3) I:396-397. CSmH, DLC, ICN, MH, MiU-C, NN-RB, RPJCB; BL, BN. 596/9

Bigges, Walter. A summarie and true discourse of Sir Frances Drakes West Indian voyage. *London: W.Ponsonby,* 1596. 52p.;4to. 1st publ., London, 1589. Sabin 20842; cf.STC 3057; JCB AR58:13-14. MiU, NN-RB, RPJCB. 596/10

Boaistuau, Pierre. Het wonderlijcke schadtboeck der historien. *Amsterdam: C.Claeszoon,* 1596. 8vo. 1st publ. in Dutch, Dordrecht, 1592. Ind.aur.120.107. Amsterdam: UB. 596/11

Borough, William. A discourse of the variation of the cumpas. *London: E.Allde,for H.Astley,* 1562 [i.e.,1596]. 30 lvs;illus.;8vo. 1st publ., London, 1581. Ind. aur.122.492; STC 3391. NN-RB; BL. 596/12

Botero, Giovanni. Allgemeine Weltbeschreibung, das ist: Eigentliche und warhafftige Erzehlung aller der gantzen Welt vornembster Landschafften, Stätten unnd Völckern. *Cologne: J.Gymnich,the Younger,* 1596. 2v.;maps;fol. Transl. from pts 1-2 of author's *Relationi universali,* 1st publ., Rome,

1591-92. Borba de Moraes I:100; Streit I:216; Ind.aur.122.717; JCB (3) I:340. MnU-B, RPJCB; BN, Berlin: StB. 596/13

——. Della ragione di stato . . . quarta edizione. *Milan: P.da Ponte,for P.M.Locarno,* 1596. 2 pts;8vo. 1st publ., Venice, 1589. Ind.aur. 122.719. DFo, MB; Berlin: StB. 596/14

——.[Anr edn]. . . . Di nuovo in questa quarta editione dall'istesso autore in alcuni luoghi mutati & accresciuti. *Turin: G.D.Tarino,* 1596. 2 pts;8vo. Ind.aur.122.722. MoSW; BN. 596/15

——. Delle relationi universali . . . Parte quarta. *Rome: [G.Faciotto?] for G.Ferrari,* 1596. 153p.;4to. Deals principally with missionary activities in the New World. Streit I:213; Ind. aur.122.720. RPJCB. 596/16

——[Anr edn]. *Vicenza: Heirs of Perin,* 1596. NNH. 596/16a

——. Gründlicher Bericht, von Anordnung guter Policeyen und Regiments . . . auss Italianischer . . . Sprach gebracht. *Strassburg: L.Zetzner,* 1596. 440 numb.lvs;8vo. Transl. from Botero's *Della ragion di stato,* 1st publ., Venice, 1589. Ind. aur.122.721; Ritter (Strasbourg) 232. Berlin: StB. 596/17

——. Geographische Landtaffel dess Gebiets des grossen Türcken . . . mit . . . Beschreibung seines Einkommens Kräfften und . . . Regierung . . . und geographische Landtaffel darin das . . . Gebiet, des Königs zu Hispanien . . . Philippi von Oesterreich, für Augengestalt wirt. *Cologne: L.Andreae,* 1596. maps;fol. Transl. from pt 2, bk 4, of author's *Delle relationi universali,* 1st publ., Rome, 1591; cf. Botero's *Tabula geographica* from same printer of this year described below. Sabin 94185n; Ind.aur.122.716. BL. 596/18

——. Le relationi universali. *Venice: G.Angelieri,* 1596. 4v.;maps;4to. 1st publ., Rome, 1591-92. Ind.aur.122.726. CtY, DLC, ICN, NN-RB; Berlin: StB, Leyden: UB. 596/19

——[Anr edn]. *Bergamo: C.Ventura,* 1596. 4v.; 8vo. Streit I:214. Rome: B.Alessandrina. 596/20

——. Tabula geographica imperii Magni Turcae . . . Et tabula geographica . . . imperium Philippi Austriaci, Indiarum Hispaniarum &c. regis. *Cologne: L.Andreae,* 1596. [30]p.; maps;fol. Transl. from pt 2, bk 4, of author's *Delle relationi universali,* 1st publ., Rome, 1592. Sabin 94185. DLC, NN-RB. 596/21

____. Theatrum, oder Schawspiegel: darinn alle Fürsten der Welt, so Kräffte und Reichthumb halben namhafft seind, vorgestellt werden. *Cologne: L.Andreae,* 1596. fol. Transl. by Johann von Brüssel from pt 2 of author's *Delle relationi universali,* 1st publ., Rome, 1592. Ind.aur.122.715. DLC; Berlin: StB, Vienna: NB. 596/22

____. Theatrum principum orbis universi. *Cologne: L.Andreae,* 1596. [162]p.;maps;fol. Transl. from pt 2 of author's *Delle relationi universali,* 1st publ., Rome, 1592. Ind.aur. 122.714; Adams(Cambr.) B25. DLC, MnU-B, PBL; Cambridge: St John's, Copenhagen: KB. 596/23

Campana, Cesare. Delle historie del mondo . . . libri tredici, ne' quali si narrano le cose avvenute dall'anno 1580 fino al 1596. *Venice: G.Angelieri & Co.,* 1596. 2v.;4to. Included are accounts of Drake's expeditions of 1586 & 1595. Ind.aur.130.729 v.2; Adams (Cambr.) C465 v.2. DFo, ICU, NNC; BL, BN. 596/24

Casas, Bartolomé de las, Bp of Chiapa. Spieghel der spaenscher tyrannye in West Indien. *Amsterdam: N.Biestkens 'de jonge',for C.Claeszoon,* 1596. 43 lvs;map;4to. 1st publ. in Dutch, [Antwerp?], 1578. Cf.Sabin 11251; Knuttel 960. BL, The Hague: KB. 596/25

___[Anr edn]. *Amsterdam: N.Biestkens 'de Jonge',for C.Claeszoon,* 1596. 43 lvs;map;4to. Sabin 11251; Medina (BHA) 1085n (II:476); Streit I:219; Church 251; JCB (3) I:341. CSmH, ICN, NN-RB, RPJCB; BL. 596/26

Casmannus, Otho. Marinarum quaestionum tractatio philosophica. *Frankfurt a.M.: Z.Palthenius,* 1596. 444(ie., 244)p.;8vo. Sabin 11340; Adams (Cambr.) C827. BL. 596/27

Clavius, Christoph. In Sphaeram Joannis de Sacro Bosco commentarius. *Venice: B.Basa,* 1596. 483p.;illus.;4to. 1st publ., Rome, 1570. Backer II:1213; JCB AR20:1596. NN-RB, RPJCB, WU. 596/28

Clowes, William. A profitable and necessarie booke of observations . . . Last of all is adjoined a short treatise, for the cure of lues venerea. *London: E.Bollifant,for T.Dawson,* 1596. 229p.;ullus.;4to. The 'short treatise' was 1st publ. separately, London, 1579, as *A short and profitable treatise touching . . . the morbus gallicus.* Proksch I:19; STC 971. CSmH, CtY, DNLM; BL. 596/29

Conestaggio, Girolamo Franchi di. L'union du royaume de Portugal a la couronne de Castille. *Besançon: N.de Moingesse,* 1596. 478p.;8vo. Transl. by Thomas Nardin from author's *Dell'unione del regno di Portugallo,* 1st publ., Genoa, 1585. ICN, MH, NNH; BL, BN. 591/30

Cortés, Martín. The arte of navigation . . . Lastly corrected and augmented [by J.Tap]. *London: E.Allde,for H.Astley,* 1596. 90 numb.lvs;illus.,map;4to. 1st publ. in English, London, 1561. Sabin 16968n; STC 5803. CSmH, DLC, MBAt, NN-RB; BL. 596/31

Dávila Padilla, Agustín, Abp of Santo Domingo. Historia de la fundacion y discurso de la provincia de Santiago de Mexico, de la Orden de Predicadores, por las vidas de sus varones insignes, y casos notables de Nueva España. *Madrid: P.Madrigal,* 1596. 815p.; fol. Sabin 18780; Medina (BHA) 370; Streit II:1139; Pérez Pastor (Madrid) 509; JCB (3) I:341-342. DLC, MH, RPJCB; Madrid: BN. 596/32

Du Bartas, Guillaume de Salluste, seigneur. Hebdomas . . . a Gabriele Lermeo . . . latinitate donatum. Nova & repurgata editio. [*Geneva:*] *G.Cartier,* 1596. 261p.;12mo. 1st publ. in Latin, Paris, 1583. In verse. Holmes (DuBartas) I:107 no.4; Adams (Cambr.) D974. DFo; Cambridge: Emmanuel.596/33

____. La seconde sepmaine . . . reveue . . . et embellie en divers passages par l'autheur mesme. En ceste nouvelle est adjousté . . . explications . . . par S[imon]. G[oulart]. *Rouen: T.Mallard,* 1596. 3 pts;12mo. 1st publ., Paris, 1584. In verse. Holmes (DuBartas) I:85 no.8b; Jones (Goulart) 20(n). BN. 596/34

___[Anr issue]. *Rouen: [T.Mallard,for] R.Du Petit Val,* 1596. NIC. 596/35

Duchesne, Joseph. Opera omnia. *Lyons* [i.e., *Geneva*]: *J.Lertout,* 1596. 2v.;8vo. Included is Duchesne's *Sclopetarius,* 1st publ., Lyons [i.e.,Geneva], 1576. ICJ. 596/36

Durante, Castore. Il tesoro della sanita. *Venice: M.Bonibelli,* 1596. 326p.;8vo. 1st publ., Rome (?), 1586. MH; BN. 596/37

Du Verdier, Antoine. Les diverses leçons . . . suivans celles de Pierre Messie. *Tournon: C.Michel,* 1596. 611p.;port.;8vo. 1st publ., Lyons, 1577. Baudrier (Lyons) Suppl.(de la Perrière) I:178. BN. 596/38

Emili, Paolo. L'histoire des faicts, gestes et conquestes . . . de France . . . mise en françoise par Jean Regnart . . . avec la suite . . . tirée du latin de . . . Arnold Le Ferron.

Paris: F.Morel,for R.Fouet, 1596. 687p.;fol.
1st publ., Paris, 1581; here reissued with
cancel t.p. Ind.aur.100.842.   596/39

Ercilla y Zúñiga, Alonso de. Primera, segunda, y tercera parte de la Araucana. *Perpignan: S.Arbus,for J.Andres*, 1596. 323
numb.lvs;12mo. 1st publ. in all 3 pts, Madrid,
1590. Medina (BHA) 372; Medina (Arau.) 15.
BL, Madrid: BN.   596/40

Estienne, Charles. Dictionarium historicum,
geographicum, poeticum. [*Geneva:*] *J.Stoer*,
1596. 452 numb.lvs;4to. 1st publ. as here expanded, Lyons, 1595. ICU, MH, NNH, TxU.
                                          596/41

Fernel, Jean. Universa medicina. *Geneva: J.
de Laon*, 1596. 647p.;8vo. Includes both Fernel's *De abditis rerum causis*, 1st publ., Paris,
1548, and his *De luis venereae curatione*, 1st
publ., Antwerp, 1579. PBL.   596/42

Fioravanti, Leonardo. Del compendio de i
secreti rationali . . . libri cinque. *Venice:
A.Salicato*, 1596. 8 (i.e.,187) numb.lvs;8vo.
1st publ., Venice, 1564. DNLM.   596/43

Fitz-Geffrey, Charles. Sir Francis Drake, his
honorable lifes commendation, and his tragi-
call deathes lamentation. *Oxford: J.Barnes*,
1596. [106]p.;8vo. In verse. STC 10943;
Madan (Oxford) I:39-40. CSmH; BL. 596/44
—[Anr edn]. Newly printed with additions. *Oxford: J.Barnes*, 1596. [112]p.;8vo. STC 10944;
Madan (Oxford) I:40. Oxford: Bodl. 596/45

Flurance, David Rivault, sieur de. Les estats,
esquels il est discouru du prince, du noble &
du tiers estat. *Lyons: C.Morillon,for B.Ri-
gaud*, 1596. 392p.;12mo. 1st publ., Lyons,
1595; here a reissue with altered t.p. Cf.Sabin
24917; Baudrier (Lyons) III:442-443. NN-
RB; BN.   596/46

Franciscus Dracus redivivus. Das ist, Kurtze
Beschreibung aller vornehmbsten Reysen,
Schiffarten unnd Wasserschlachten, so der
weitberümbte Englische Admiral, Franciscus
Dracus . . . vollbracht . . . Erstlich getruckt
zu Amstertamb in Holland, durch Johann
Clausen. [*Cologne?* 1596]. [13]p.;ports,
maps;4to. The earlier Amsterdam edn is unknown. JCB AR58:8-13. RPJCB; BL. 596/47

Gabelkover, Oswald. Artzneybuch. *Tübingen: G.Gruppenbach*, 1596. 2 pts;4to. 1st
publ., Tübingen, 1589, under title *Nützlich
Artzneybuch*. DNLM, NNNAM; BL.   596/48

Gerard, John. Catalogus arborum, fruticum
ac plantarum tam indigenarum quam ex-

oticarum in horto Gerardi nascentium. *London: R.Robinson*, 1596. 18p.;4to. Includes
numerous American plants, identified as
such, amongst them the potato. Pritzel 3283;
STC 11748; Henrey (Brit.bot.) 152. RPB; BL.
                                          596/49

Giorgini, Giovanni. Il Mondo Nuovo . . .
Con gli argomenti in ottava rima del sig. Gio.
Pietro Coloni, & in prosa del sig. Girolamo
Ghisileri. *Jesi: P.Farri*, 1596. 153 numb.
lvs;4to. In verse. Sabin 27473; Adams (Cam-
br.) G625; Arents (Add.) 105; JCB (3) I:342.
CSmH, DLC, ICN, InU-L, MH, MnU-B,
NN-A, RPJCB; Cambridge: UL.   596/50

Giovio, Paolo, Bp of Nocera. Elogia virorum
bellica virtute illustrium . . . imaginibus exornata. *Basel: P.Perna*, 1596. 258p.;illus.,
ports;fol. 1st publ. as here illustrated, Basel,
1575. Sabin 36773n. CU, CtY, ICN, MH; BN.
                                          596/51

Gómara, Francisco López de. The pleasant
historie of the conquest of the West India, now
called new Spaine . . . Translated out of the
Spanish tongue, by T[homas]. N[icholas].
London: T.Creede, 1596. 405p.;4to. 1st publ.
as here translated, London, 1578. Sabin
27752; Wagner (SW) 2qq; Streit II:1140; STC
16808; JCB (3) I:346. CSmH, CtY, DLC,
ICN, InU-L, MH, MiU, NN-RB, RPJCB; BL.
                                          596/52

González de Mendoza, Juan, Bp. Historia de
las cosas mas notables . . . del gran reyno de la
China . . . Con un itinerario del nuevo Mun-
do. *Antwerp: P.Bellère*, 1596. 380p.;8vo. 1st
publ., Rome, 1585. Sabin 27777; Wagner
(SW) 7f; Streit IV:2039; Peeters-Fontainas
(Impr.esp.) 510; JCB (3) I:343. CU-B, DLC,
InU-L, MH, MnU-B, NN-RB, RPJCB; BL,
BN.   596/53

Grabowski, Piotr. Polska nizna. *Cracow*:
1596. 78 lvs;4to. Includes a ref. to the New
World. Wierzbowski 1822; Tazbir p.18. Poz-
nan: TPNB.   596/54

Grégoire, Pierre. De republica libri sex et
viginti. *Pont-à-Moussin: N.Claudet*, 1596.
1035p.;4to. Refers to Spanish in Hispaniola.
Rép.bibl.IV:43; Adams (Cambr.) G1092;
Moranti (Urbino) 1710. ICN; Cambridge:
UL, Nancy: BM.   596/55

Harangue d'un cacique indien, envoyee aux
François, pour se garder de la tyrannie de
l'Espaignol. Traduite par P.A. [*Paris?*] 1596.
8 lvs;8vo. The use of phrase 'cacique indien'

was solely a literary device, the text being without American substance. NN-RB. 596/56

Herburt, Jan. Zdanie o narodzie ruskim. *Cracow:* 1596. Refs to Spanish conquests in West Indies, p.1094-1095. Tazbir p.11-12. 596/57

Illescas, Gonzalo de. Historia pontifical y catholica, en la qual se contienen las vidas y hechos de todos los summos pontifices romanos . . . por el mismo author en muchas lugares añnadida en la quinta impression. *Barcelona: J.Cendrat, for R.Nogues & J.Genoves,* 1596. 2v.;fol. The earliest edn to contain refs to America, its discovery, Indians & missions, found in the lives of Clement V through Pius V. Streit I:218. MH, NNH; Granada: BU. 596/58

In memoriam celeberrimi viri domini Francisci Drake militis, qui . . . obiit. viz. 18. die Januarii . . . 1595 [i.e.,1596]. [*London: J. Windet,* 1596]. bds.;fol. In verse. London: Soc. of Antiquaries. 596/59

Kemys, Lawrence. A relation of the second voyage [of Sir Walter Raleigh] to Guiana. *London: T.Dawson,* 1596. 32 lvs;4to. Sabin 37686; STC 14947; Church 250; JCB (3) I:343. CSmH, DLC, MH, MiU-C, MnU-B, NN-RB, PBL, RPJCB; BL. 596/60

La Noue, François de. Discours politiques et militaires. [*Lyons?*] *F.LeFèvre,* 1596. 1090p.; 8vo. 1st publ., Basel, 1587. Adams (Cambr.) L159. Cambridge: Emmanuel. 596/61

___ [Anr edn]. [*Geneva:*] *J.Stoer,* 1596. 1020p.; 12mo. BN. 596/62

Linschoten, Jan Huygen van. Reys-gheschrift vande navigatien der Portugaloysers in Orienten . . . Item van China nae Spaenschs Indien, ende wederom van daer nae China; als oock van de custen van Brasilien . . . Item van't vaste landt, ende die voor eylanden (Las Antillas ghenaent) van Spaenschs Indien. *Amsterdam: C.Claeszoon,* 1595[-96]. 147p.; fol. Includes also with special t.p. dated 1596 'Een seker extract ende sommier van alle de renten . . . des Coninghs van Spangien'. Normally bound with, as issued, Linschoten's *Itinerario, voyage, ofte schipvaert* of 1596. Sabin 41356; Borba de Moraes I:416-417; Tiele-Muller 84-85; Church 252; JCB (3) I:344-345. CSmH, ICN, RPJCB; BL, BN. 596/63

___ . Beschryvinghe van de gantsche custe van Guinea . . . ende tegen over de Cabo de S.Augustijn in Brasilien . . . Volcht noch de beschryvinge van West Indien. *Amsterdam: C.Claeszoon,* 1596. 82p.;maps;fol. Normally bound with, as issued, Linschoten's *Itinerario, voyage, ofte schipvaert* of this year. Sabin 41356; Borba de Moraes I:416; Tiele-Muller 86-87; Church 252; JCB (3) I:344. CSmH, DLC, RPJCB; BL, BN. 596/64

Lodge, Thomas. A margarite of America. [*London:*] *J.Busbie,* 1596. 139p.;4to. A romance purportedly written during residence in the Straits of Magellan; otherwise without American relevance. Sabin 41765; STC 16660. BL, Oxford: Bodl. 596/65

___ . Wits miserie, and the worlds madnesse. *London: A.Islip; sold by C.Burby,* 1596. 59 lvs;4to. Included are 3 refs to tobacco. STC 16677; Pforzheimer 623; Arents (Add.) 102. CSmH, DFo, MH, NN-A; BL. 596/66

Lopes, Duarte. De beschryvinghe vant groot ende vermaert coninckrijck van Congo . . . beschreven door Philips Pigafetta in Italiaens ende overgheset in ons Nederlantsche spraecke, deur Martijn Everart B. *Middelburg: J.Willeboortsen, for C.Claeszoon, at Amsterdam,* 1596. [98]p.;illus.,map;4to. Transl. from *Relatione del reame di Congo,* 1st publ., Rome, 1591. Tiele-Muller 298. RPJCB; BL. 596/67

Lowe, Peter. An easie, certaine, and perfect method to cure and prevent the Spanish sickness. *London: J.Roberts,* 1596. 4to. Proksch I:20; STC 16872. BL. 596/67a

Marieta, Juan de. Historia ecclesiastica de todos los santos de España. *Cuenca: J.Masselin & P.del Valle, for C.Bernabe,* 1596,'94. 4 pts in 3 v.;fol. Includes accounts of missionaries active in America, e.g., Bartolomé de las Casas. Medina (BHA) 375; Streit I:221. BL. 596/68

Mattioli, Pietro Andrea. Herbárž. *Prague: D.Adam,* 1596. 476 numb.lvs;illus.;fol. 1st publ. in Czech, Prague, 1562. Pritzel 5993; Nissen (Bot.) 1315n. CtY-M, NNC; London: Wellcome. 596/69

Meteren, Emanuel van. Historia oder eigentliche und warhaffte Beschreibung aller Kriegshändel und gedenckwürdigen Geschichten, so sich in Niderteutschland . . . zugetragen haben. *Hamburg: F.Van Dortt,* 1596. 674p.; fol. Transl. from Dutch manuscript, itself 1st publ., Delft, 1599. Includes minor American refs, expanded in subsequent edns. Palau 166943; Graesse IV:506. NNH; BL. 596/70

Minadoi, Aurelio. Tractatus de virulentia venerea. *Venice: R.Meietti,* 1596. 284p.;4to. Proksch I:20; Adams (Cambr.) M1452. DNLM; BL, BN. 596/71

Monardes, Nicolás. Joyfull newes out of the new-found worlde. Wherein are declared, the rare and singular vertues of divers herbs, trees, plantes, oyles & stones . . . Englished by John Frampton. *London: E.Allde,assigns of B.Norton,* 1596. 187 numb.lvs;illus.;4to. 1st publ. as here translated, London, 1577. Sabin 49946; Medina (BHA) 237n (I:393); Guerra (Monardes) 32; STC 18007; Nissen (Bot.) 1397nc; Church 253; JCB (3) I:346. CSmH, CtY, DLC, ICJ, InU-L, MH, MiU-C, MnU-B, NN-RB, PPL, RPJCB; BL. 596/72

Nash, Thomas. Have with you to Saffron-Walden. *London: J.Danter,* 1596. 83 lvs;4to. Includes refs to tobacco. STC 18369; Pforzheimer 763; Arents (Add.) 103. CSmH, DFo, MH, NN-A; BL. 596/73

Norman, Robert. The newe attractive, containing a short discourse of the magnes or lodestone. *London: E.Allde,for H.Astley,* 1596. 2 pts;illus.;4to. 1st publ., London, 1581. Cf.Sabin 55496; STC 18650. Horblit; BL. 596/74

Nova novorum. Newe zeitungen aus östen, westen, von newen gefundenen Landen, newen Völkeren, newen handtierungen, ungehorten sprachen und schriften: von Francisci Draci, Indische expedition. Mit deren Landen eigentliche und wahre beschreibung. *Neuhofen:* 1596. [14]p.;illus.;4to. Palmer 314; Palau 76145; JCB AR39:16-18. RPJCB (illus. wanting); Berlin: StB. 596/75

Ortelius, Abraham. Thesaurus geographicus. *Antwerp: Widow of C.Plantin & J.Mourentorf,* 1596. 364 lvs;fol. 1st publ., Antwerp, 1578, under title *Synonymia geographica.* Sabin 57709; Adams (Cambr.) 0348; Moranti (Urbino) 2367; JCB (3) I:348. CU, DLC, IU, MnU-B, RPJCB; BL, BN. 596/76

Partitio magnitudinis universi orbis in jugera terrae, et significatio, quanta eorum pars colatur habiteturque . . . quo fine recensentur omnes Europae, Asiae, Africae et Americae provinciae, indicaturque. *Cologne: L.Andreae,* 1596. [7]p.;map;fol. Sabin 94185n. ICN, MiU-C, NN-RB. 596/77

Plat, Sir Hugh. Sundrie new and artificiall remedies against famine. *London: P.S[hort].,* 1596. 18 lvs;4to. Cites use by East [*sic*] Indian natives of tobacco for food; drawn from Monardes. STC 19996; Arents (Add.) 104; Hunt (Bot.) 174. CSmH, DFo, MH, NN-A; BL. 596/78

Ptolemaeus, Claudius. Geographiae universae tum veteris, tum novae, absolutissimum opus. *Venice: Heirs of S.Galignani,* 1596. 2v.; maps;4to. Edited with new maps by Giovanni Antonio Magini. Included are maps & text relating to America. Sabin 66492; Stevens (Ptolemy) 53; Phillips (Atlases) 403; JCB (3) I:348. CSmH, CtY, DLC, InU-L, MH, MiU-C, MnU-B, NN-RB, PPRF, RPJCB; BL, Strasbourg: BN. 596/79

Quad, Matthias. Europae, totius terrarum orbi parti praestantissime . . . descriptio, tabulis novem et sexaginta expressa. *Cologne: L.Andreae,for J.Bussemacher,* 1596. 66 (i.e., 69) maps;fol. 1st publ., Cologne, 1594. Cf.Sabin 66892. NjP, PPL. 596/80

Rabelais, François, Les oeuvres. *Lyons: J.Martin,* 1596. 12mo. Includes 'Le quart livre', 1st publ., Paris, 1552. Plan (Rabelais) 114; Adams (Cambr.) R9A. IU, OCl; BL. 596/81

—[Anr edn]. *Lyons: P.Estiard,* 1596. 2 pts;16mo. Plan (Rabelais) 115; Rothschild 1516; Adams (Cambr.) R9. IU, MH, MiU, RPB; Cambridge: Trinity Hall, BN. 596/82

Raleigh, Sir Walter. The discoverie of the large, rich, and bewtiful empyre of Guiana. *London: R.Robinson,* 1596. 112p.;4to. On p.&, line 12 begins 'upon it, there'. Sabin 67551; STC 20634. CSmH, DFo, NN-RB, PP; Manchester: Rylands. 596/83

—[Anr edn]. *London: R.Robinson,* 1596. 112p.;4to. On p.60, line 12 begins 'on it, there'. For variant states, see the STC. Sabin 67552-53; STC 20635. CSmH, DFo, MH, MiU-C, NN-RB; BL. 596/84

—[Anr edn]. *London: R.Robinson,* 1596. 112p.;4to. On p.60, line 12 begins 'it, there'. For variant states see the STC. Sabin 67554; STC 20636; Arents 49; Church 254; JCB (3) I:349. CSmH, CtY, DFo, ICN, NN-RB, RPJCB; BL. 596/85

Relacion del viage que hizieron las cinco fragatas de armada de su Magestad, yendo por cabo dellas Don Pedro Tello de Guzman, este presente año de novente y cinco. *Seville: R.de Cabrere* [1596]. 4 lvs;4to. On capture of ship from Drake's squadron off Guadeloupe. Kraus (Drake) 29 (p.202-203); Escudero

(Seville) 802; Palau 257253. H.P.Kraus.
596/86

Resende, García de. Choronica que tracta da vida e grandissimas virtudes . . . do . . . Dom João ho Segundo. *Lisbon: S.Lopez,* 1596. cxxxiiii lvs;fol. 1st publ., Lisbon, 1545. Sabin 70062n; Borba de Moraes II:200; Anselmo 816; King Manuel 247; Shaaber R79. MH, PU; BL, BN. 596/87

Reszka, Stanislaw. De atheismus et phalarismus evangelicorum. *Naples: G.G.Carlino & A.Pace,* 1596. 609p.;4to. Pages 502-503 refer to New World. ICN; BL, BN. 596/88

A rich store-house or treasury for the diseased . . . By A.T. *London: T.Purfoot,* 1596. 66 numb.lvs;4to. Section on French pox cites Guaiacum & sarsaparilla. STC 23606. CSmH, DFo, NNNAM; London: Wellcome. 596/89

Rivadeneira, Pedro de. De vita Francisci Borgiae Societatis Jesu . . . libri quattuor. *Rome: A.Zanetti,* 1596. 191p.;illus.;4to. Transl. by Andreas Schott from 1592, Madrid, Spanish text. Backer VI:1735; Palau 266310; Adams (Cambr.) R468. MH, NjP, RPJCB; Cambridge: UL. 596/90

——. La vie du pere François de Borgia . . . nouvellement tourné d'espagnol en françois. *Verdun: J.Wapy,* 1596. 311 numb.lvs;8vo. Transl. from Spanish text, 1st publ., Madrid, 1592; perhaps transl. by François Solier. Backer VI:1734; Cioranescu (XVII) 63230; Palau 266314. 596/91

—[Anr edn]. *Douai: B.Bellère,* 1596. 467p.;8vo. Here transl. by Michel d'Esne de Béthencourt. Backer VI:1734; Cioranescu (XVI) 9435. MoSU-D. 596/92

Rosaccio, Giuseppe. Il mondo e sue parti, cioe Europa, Affrica, Asia, et America. *Verona: F.dalle Donne & S.Vargnano,* 1596. 238p.; maps;8vo. 1st publ., Florence, 1595. Cf.Sabin 73195n. RPJCB. 596/93

—[Anr issue?]. *Verona: G.Discepolo,* 1596. Cf.Sabin 73195n. BL. 596/94

——. Le sei eta del mondo. *Milan: G.Ferioli,* 1596. 46p.;8vo. 1st publ., Brescia, 1593. ICN, MiU. 596/95

——. Teatro del cielo e della terra. *Brescia: V.Sabbio,* 1596. 56p.;illus.,maps;8vo. 1st publ., Brescia, 1592. Cf.Sabin 73198. MiU. 596/96

Roscius, Julius. Elogia militaria. *Rome: B.Bonfadini,for A.Ruffinelli,* 1596. 211p.; 4to. In verse. Included are poems on Ferdinand Cortés, &c. Sabin 73225 (& 33068); Adams (Cambr.) R779. DFo, ICN, NN-RB; BL. 596/97

Savile, Capt. Henry. A libell of Spanish lies: found at the sacke of Cales, discoursing the fight in the West Indies, twixt the English navie . . . and . . . the king of Spaines, and of the death of Sir Francis Drake. *London: J.Windet,* 1596. 47p.;illus.;4to. Included is Spanish text of letter of Bernardino Delgadillo de Avellanbeda, dated, Havana, 30 March 1596, followed by English translation, & in turn by Savile's answer. Sabin 77289; STC 6551; Palau 70045; Church 255; JCB (3) I:342. CSmH, CtY, DFo, ICN, MiU-C, NN-RB, RPJCB; BL. 596/98

Schylander, Cornelis. Cornelis Shilander his Chirurgerie . . . With an easie maner of drawing oyle out of wound-hearbes, turpentine, guaiacum and waxe. Translated out of Latin . . . by S[tephen]. Hobbes. *London: R. Jones,for C.Burby,* 1596. [56]p.;4to. Transl. from the author's *Practica chirurgiae;* 1st publ., Antwerp, 1577 as pt 2 of his *Medicina astrologica.* STC 21817. DNLM, MH, PPC; BL. 596/99

Spain. Laws, statues, etc. Provisiones, cedulas, capitulos de ordenanças, instrucciones, y cartas, libradas y despachadas . . . por sus Magestades . . . con acuerdo de los señores presidentes, y de su Consejo Real de las Indias . . . tocantes al buen govierno de las Indias. *Madrid: Imprenta Real,* 1596. 4v.;fol. Compiled by Diego de Encinas. Sabin 22550; Medina (BHA) 371; Streit I:222; Pérez Pastor (Madrid) 521; JCB (3) I:253. MH, RPJCB; BL(v.1), Madrid: BN. 596/100

Spain. Sovereigns, etc., 1556-1598 (Philip II). Instrucion para el virrey de la Nueva España. *Aranjuez:* 1596. [32]p.;fol. MiU-C. 596/101

Tagault, Jean. Institutione di cirurgia. *Venice: N.Moretti,* 1596. 421 numb.lvs;illus.;8vo. 1st publ. in Italian, Venice, 1550. DNLM, IaU. 596/102

Torquemada, Antonio de. Giardino di fiori curiosi . . . tradotto di spagnuolo . . . per Celio Malespina. *Venice: A.Salicato,* 1596. 262p.;4to. 1st publ., in Italian, Venice, 1590; here a reissue? Palau 334922n. 596/103

Zárate, Agustín de. Conqueste van Indien. De wonderlijcke ende warachtighe historie vant coninckrijck van Peru. *Amsterdam:*

C.Claeszoon, 1596. 154 numb.lvs;map;4to. 1st publ. in this translation by R.de Bacquère, Antwerp, 1563. Sabin 106257; Palau 379635; JCB (3) I:350. RPJCB.   596/104

1597

Augenio, Orazio. Epistolarum & consultationum medicinalium libri xxiiii. *Frankfurt a.M.: Heirs of A.Wechel, C.de Marne & J.Aubry*, 1597-1600. 3v.;port.;fol. 1st publ. with American refs, Venice, 1592. Ind. aur.109.850-851; Adams (Cambr.) A2127. CtY-M, DNLM; BL, Munich: StB.   597/1

Benzoni, Girolamo. Das sechste Theil der neuwen Welt. oder der Historien . . . das dritte Buch. *Frankfurt a.M.: J.Feyerabend, for T.de Bry*, 1597. 62p.;illus.,map;fol. (Theodor de Bry's *America*. Pt 6. German). 1st publ. in this translation by Nicolaus Höniger as bk 3 of the Basel, 1579, *Der Newen Weldt . . . History* but here supplemented by annotations supplied by Urbain Chauveton in the Basel, 1578, Latin *Novae Novi Mundi historiae*, here 1st translated; cf.earlier pts 1-2, publ. in 1594 & 1595. Cf.Sabin 8784; Church 188; JCB (3) I:397-398. CSmH, DLC, ICN, MH, MiU-C, NN-RB, RPJCB; BL, BN.   597/2

Blundeville, Thomas. M.Blundeville his exercises . . . The second edition. *London: J.Windet*, 1597. 392 numb.lvs;4to. 1st publ., London, 1594. Cf.Sabin 6024; STC 3147; Ind.aur.120.026; JCB (3) I:351. CSmH, CtY, ICN, MH, NIC, RPJCB; BL.   597/3

Boaistuau, Pierre. Histoires prodigeuses. *Antwerp: G.Janssens*, 1597. 720p.;8vo. 1st publ. with American ref. in section by François de Belleforest, Paris, 1571. Ind.aur.120.109. Vienna: UB.   597/4

Boissard, Jean Jacques. Icones quinquaginta virorum illustrium . . . cum eorum vitis descriptis. *Frankfurt a.M.; T.de Bry*, 1597-99. 4v.;ports;4to. In v.1 is a portrait of Columbus, with biography. Sabin 34160 (& 6161); Ind.aur.121.342; Adams (Cambr.) B2326-2329; JCB (3) I:353. DLC, MH, MdBJ-G, MiU, NN-RB, RPJCB; BL, BN.   597/5

Botero, Giovanni. Amphitheatridion, hoc est, Parvum amphitheatrum. *Cologne: L.Andreae*, 1597. 147p.;4to. 1st publ. in this Latin version, Cologne, 1596. under title *Mundus imperiorum*. Ind.aur.122.727. Vienna: NB.   597/6

———. Commentariolus parallelos . . . libellus . . . nunc primum . . . versus in latinum ex italo. *Cologne: L.Andreae*, 1597. [48]p.;4to. Extracted & transl. by C.Utenhove from Botero's *Delle relatione universali*, including description of New Spain. Sabin 6799 (& 98222); Ind.aur.122.728; Adams (Cambr.) B2546. BL, Munich: StB.   597/7

———. Delle relationi universali . . . Parte seconda. Revista et arrichita di molte cose memorabili dall' auttore. *Rome: G.Ferrari*, 1597. 289p.;4to. 1st publ., Rome, 1592. Cf.Sabin 6801; Streit I:223; Ind.aur.122.730. Rome: B.Alessandrina.   597/8

———. Discorsi sopra la ragione di stato. *Milan: P.Ponti, for P.M.Locarno*, 1597. 216p.;8vo. 1st publ., Venice, 1589, under title *Della ragion di stato*. Ind.aur.122.729. DLC, KU; Milan: BT.   597/9

———. Le relationi universali . . . Et si trata del continente del Mondo Nuovo . . . Nuovamente ristampate & corrette. *Venice: N.Polo* (pt 1); *G.Vincenti* (pts 2-3); *& Vicenza: G.Greco* (pt 4), 1597. 4 pts; maps;4to. 1st publ., Rome, 1591-95. Sabin 6804; Streit I:223; Ind.aur.122.731 (&,pt 4,122.732); Adams (Cambr.) B2556. CtY, DFo, MH, NN-RB; Cambridge: St John's.   597/10

Campana, Cesare. Delle historie del mondo . . . Volume secondo . . . dall'anno 1580, fino al 1596 . . . Seconda impressione diligentemente corrette. *Venice: G.Angelieri*, 1597. 774p.;4to. 1st publ., Venice, 1596; here designated as a 2nd vol. in anticipation of a 1st vol., covering years 1570-1580, not publ. till 1599. The latter is without American refs. Ind.aur.130.730 v.2; Adams (Cambr.) C466 v.2. DFo, InMunS, RPJCB; BL, BN.   597/11

Candidus, Pantaleon, pseud.? Tabulae chronologicae. *Strassburg: J.Rihel*, 1597. 172p.;4to. Adams (Cambr.) C505 &, P180; Moranti (Urbino) 776. CU, MB; Cambridge: Jesus, Urbino: BU.   597/12

Caro, Annibale. De le lettere familiari . . . volume primo. *Venice: G.Alberti*, 1597. 116(i.e., 176)p.;4to. 1st publ., Venice, 1572. Ind.aur.132.485; Adams (Cambr.) C745. DFo, NjP; Cambridge: UL, Venice: BN.   597/13

Casas, Bartolomé de las, Bp of Chiapa. Newe Welt. Warhafftige Anzeigung der Hispanier grewlichen, abschewlichen Tyranney, von ihnen inn den Indianischen Ländern . . . und die Newe Welt genennet wird, begangen . . . Hernacher in die frantzösische Sprach, durch Jacoben von Miggrode . . . gebracht: jetzt aber ins Hochteutsch, durch einen Liebhaber dess Vatterlands . . . ubergesetzt. [*Frankfurt a.M.:*] 1597. 158p.;4to. Transl. from Antwerp, 1579, French edn. Sabin 11277; Medina (BHA) 1085n (II:478); Streit I:225; Baginsky (German Americana) 99; JCB (3) I:354. DLC, NN-RB, RPJCB; BL.   597/14

Ciekliński, Piotr. Potrójny z plauta. *Zamosc: M.Leski,* 1597. 91p.;4to. Comedy, mentioning America. Tazbir p.8; cf.Wierzbowski 3030.   597/15

Crespin, Jean. Histoire des martyrs persecutez et mis à mort pour la verité de l'Evangile. [*Geneva? E.Vignon?*] 1597. 758 numb.lvs; fol. 1st publ. with American material, [Geneva], 1564; here enlarged by Simon Goulart. Borba de Moraes I:199n; Jones (Goulart) 23(b). ICN, NNH, NcD; BN.   597/16

Dresser, Matthaeus, comp. Historien und Bericht, von dem newlicher Zeit erfundenen Königreich China . . . Item, Von dem auch new erfundenen Lande Virginia. *Leipzig: Heirs of J.Beyer,for F.Schnellboltz,* 1597. 297p.;4to. Compiled & transl. from J.González de Mendoza's *Historia . . . de la China,* 1st publ., Rome, 1585, suppl. by Thomas Hariot's account of Virginia, 1st publ., London, 1588. Cf.Sabin 20926; Medina (BHA) 373n (I:548); Wagner (SW) 7v; Baginsky (German Americana) 100; cf.Streit IV:2044; Arents (Add.) 97; JCB (3) I:354-355. NN-RB, RPJCB; BL.   597/17

Du Bartas, Guillaume de Salluste, seigneur. Commentaires sur la Sepmaine . . . le tout diligement reveu et corrigé [par Simon Goulart]. *Rouen: T.Mallard,* 1597. 228 (i.e.,328) numb.lvs;12mo. 1st publ. in this form, including text of *La sepmaine* itself, Geneva, 1581. In verse. Holmes (DuBartas) I:74 no.24; Jones (Goulart) 20(n). BN.   597/18

_[Anr issue]. *Rouen:* [*T.Mallard,for*] *R.Du Petit Val,* 1597. Holmes (DuBartas) I:74 no.24(n); Adams (Cambr.) D971. Cambridge: Trinity.   597/19

Du Fail, Noël, seigneur da La Hérissaye. Les contes et discours d'Eutrapel. *Rennes: N.Glamet,* 1597. 223 numb.lvs;8vo. 1st publ.,

Rennes, 1585. Rép.bibl.,XIX:73-74. ICN, MH, NNPM; BN.   597/20

Durante, Castore. Il tesoro della sanita. *Venice: D.Farri,* 1597. 324p.;8vo. 1st publ., Rome (?), 1586. DNLM.   597/21

Ercilla y Zúñiga, Alonso de. Primera, segunda, y tercera partes de la Araucana. *Antwerp: A.Bacx,for P.Bellère,* 1597. 329 numb.lvs;12mo. 1st publ. in all 3 pts, Madrid, 1590. In verse. Sabin 22722; Medina (BHA) 379; Medina (Arau.) 17; Peeters-Fontainas (Impr.esp.) 391; JCB (3) I:355. DLC, MB, MoU, NNH, RPJCB; BL, Brussels: BR.
597/22

_[Anr edn]. *Madrid: P.V.de Castro,for M.Martínez,* 1597. 445 numb.lvs;8vo. Medina (BHA) 378; Medina (Arau.) 16; cf.Pérez Pastor (Madrid) 536. NN-RB, NNH. 597/23

_[Anr issue]. *Madrid: P.V.de Castro,for J.de Montoya,* 1597. Pérez Pastor (Madrid) 536; Shaaber E351. MiU-C, NN-RB, PU; Madrid: BN.   597/24

Estienne, Charles. L'agriculture et maison rustique, de mm. Charles Estienne et Jean Liebault. [*Geneva?*] *G.Cartier,* 1597. 842p.; illus.;8vo. 1st publ., Paris, 1567. Thiébaud (La chasse) 350. MH-A.   597/25

Falloppius, Gabriel. Kunstbuch. *Augsburg: M.Manger,* 1597. 466p.;8vo. 1st publ. in German, Augsburg, 1571. Shaaber F366. DNLM, NNC, PU.   597/26

Fernel, Jean. Universa medicina. *Lyons: T.Soubron & M.Desprez,* 1597. 2v.;8vo. Includes both Fernel's *De abditis rerum causis,* 1st publ., Paris, 1548, and his *De luis venereae curatione,* 1st publ., Antwerp, 1579. Sherrington (Fernel) 72.J16; Baudrier (Lyons) IV:361-362. CtY, DLC, MiU, MnU; London: Wellcome.   597/27

Fioravanti, Leonardo. Del compendio de i secreti rationali . . . libri cinque. *Venice: M.A.Bonibelli,* 1597. 8vo. 1st publ., Venice, 1564. IaU, MiU; BL.   597/28

Foglietta, Uberto. Dell'istorie di Genova . . . libri xii. Tradotte per m. Francesco Serdonati. *Genoa: Heirs of G.Bartoli,* 1597. 664p.;fol. Transl. from author's *Historiae Genuensium libri xii,* 1st publ., Genoa, 1585, the ref. to Columbus here appearing on p.562. DLC, InU-L, MH, MiU-C, NN-RB; BL.   597/29

Gerard, John. The herball or General historie of plantes. *London: E.Bollifant,for B.& J.Norton,* 1597. 1392p.;illus.;fol. Virtually a

translation by Robert Priest of Rembert Dodoens's *Stirpium historiae pemptades sex*, 1st
publ., Antwerp, 1583. Included are numerous
descriptions & illus. of American plants, with
refs to their origins. Amongst these is the
earliest illus. of the potato. Pritzel 3282;
Nissen (Bot.) 698; STC 11750; Henrey
(Brit.bot.) 154; Arents 50. CSmH, CtY, DLC,
ICN, MH, MiU-C, MnU-B, NN-A, RPJCB;
BL.   597/30

Grégoire, Pierre. De republica libri sex et
viginti. *[Frankfurt a.M.:] Z.Palthenius,for
Heirs of P.Fischer*, 1597. 1536p.;8vo. 1st
publ., Pont-à-Moussin, 1596. Adams (Cambr.) G1093. Cambridge: Jesus.   597/31

Hall, Joseph, Bp of Norwich. Virgidem-
iarum, six bookes. *London: T.Creede,for R.
Dexter*, 1597. 2 pts;4to. Included are refs to
tobacco in pt 2. STC 12716; Pforzheimer 444;
Arents (Add.) 106. CSmH, DFo, IU, MH,
NN-A; BL.   597/32

Honter, Johannes. Enchiridion cosmographiae, continens praecipuarum orbis regionum delineationes. *Zurich: J.Wolf*, 1597. 32
lvs;illus.;8vo. 1st publ. in this version, Kronstadt, 1542, under title *Rudimenta cosmographica*. In verse. BN.   597/33

Houtman, Cornelis de. Verhael vande reyse
by de Hollandtsche schepen gedaen naer Oost
Indien. *Middelburg: B.Langenes*, 1597.
62p.;illus.,maps;obl.4to. An account of a
voyage commanded by Houtman, supplemented by earlier reports; compilation attributed to the publisher. Includes mention of
Brazil & Strait of Magellan. Tiele 503; Tiele-
Muller 105. Amsterdam: NHSM.   597/34

Hues, Robert. Tractaet ofte Handelinge van
het gebruijck der hemelscher ende aertscher
globe. *Amsterdam: C.Claeszoon*, 1597.
67p.;illus.;4to. Transl. by Jodocus Hondius
from Hues's London, 1594, *Tractatus de
globis*. Sabin 33562. NN-RB; BL.   597/35

Jessenius, Johannes. De morbi gallici in-
vestigationes dissertationes septem. *Wittenberg*: 1597. 8vo. Proksch I:83   597/36

Jodelle, Etienne. Oeuvres et meslanges poetiques . . . Reveuës & augmentees en ceste
derniere edition. *Lyons: B.Rigaud*, 1597. 298
numb.lvs;12mo. 1st publ., Paris, 1574. Baudrier (Lyons) III:447. BL, BN.   597/37

Langham, William. The garden of health.
London: [Deputies of C.Barker] 1579 [i.e.,
1597]. 702p.;4to. Included are chapts on

Guaiacum & sarsaparilla. STC 15195. CSmH,
CtY, DNLM, MH, MiU; BL.   597/38

La Noue, François de. Discours politiques et
militaires. *Basel: F.Forest*, 1597. 710p.;16mo.
1st publ. Basel, 1587. MB.   597/39

Léry, Jean de. Historie van een reyse ghedaen
in den lande van Bresillien. *Amsterdam: C.
Claeszoon*, 1597 [colophon: 1596]. [222]p.;
illus.,map;4to. Transl. from Léry's French
text, 1st publ., La Rochelle, 1578. Sabin
40155 (& 32098); Borba de Moraes I:404-405.
DLC.   597/40

Lopes, Duarte. Regnum Congo, hoc est,
Warhaffte und eigentliche Beschreibung des
Konigreichs Congo . . . in . . . teutsche
Spraach transferieret . . . durch Augustinum
Cassiodorum. *Frankfurt a.M.: J.Sauer,for
J.T.& J.I.de Bry,Bros*, 1597. 74p.;illus.,
maps;fol. (J.T. de Bry's *India Orientalis*. Pt 1.
German). Transl. from Pigafetta's edn of
Lopes's *Relatione del reame di Congo*, 1st
publ., Rome, 1591. Church 226; JCB (3)
I:421. CSmH, IU, NN-RB, RPJCB; BL, BN.
    597/41

———. A report of the kingdome of Congo . . .
translated out of Italian by Abraham Hart-
well. *London: [J.Windet,fot] J.Wolfe*, 1597.
217p.;illus.,maps;4to. Transl. from author's
Relatione del reame di Congo, 1st publ.,
Rome, 1591. STC 16805. CSmH, CtY, DFo,
IU, MnU-B, NN-RB; BL.   597/42

López Madera, Gregorio. Excelencias de la
monarchia y reyno de España. *Valladolid:
D.Fernández de Córdova,for M.de Córdova*,
1597. 84 numb.lvs;fol. In ch.9 are accounts of
Spanish discoveries in New World. Alcocer
(Valladolid) 369; Palau 141348; Shaaber
L345. CU, MH, NN-RB, PU, RPJCB; BL,
Salamanca: BU.   597/43

Maiolo, Simeone, Bp of Volturara. Dies
caniculares seu Colloquia . . . quibus plera-
que naturae admiranda, quae aut in aethere
fiunt, aut in Europa, Asia atque Africa, quin
etiam in ipso Orbe Novo, & apud omnes Antipodas sunt, recensentur. *Rome: A.Zanet-
ti,for G.A.Ruffinelli*, 1597. 1177p.;4to. Contains numerous refs to natural history of New
World, drawn from P.M.d'Anghiera &
Oviedo. Sabin 44056; JCB (3) I:355. DLC,
ICN, MiU, NNE, RPJCB; BL.   597/44

Mariz, Pedro de. Dialogos. *Coimbra*: 1597.
See the year 1599.

Marlowe, Christopher. Tamburlaine the

Great. *London: R.Jones,* 1597. 2 pts;8vo. 1st publ., London, 1590. STC 17427. CSmH.

597/45

Matienzo, Juan de. Commentaria in librum quintum recollectionis legum Hispaniae. *Madrid: P.Madrigal,for J.de Sarría,* 1597. 485 numb.lvs;fol. 1st publ., Madrid, 1580. Medina (BHA) 380; Pérez Pastor (Madrid) 540; Palau 158226n. DLC, MH-L, NNH.

597/46

Mexía, Pedro. Vite di tutti gl'imperadori romani tratte per Lodovico Dolce dal libro spagnuolo. *Venice: O.Alberti,* 1597. 547 numb.lvs;4to. 1st publ. in enlarged form, Venice, 1561. Palau 167354n. BN. 597/47

Molina, Luis de. De justitia, tomus secundus de contractibus. *Cuenca: M.Serrano de Vargas,* 1597. 2143 cols;fol. In disp.398, 406 & 408, on monetary exchanges, refs occur to the New World, citing Brazil and Peru. Palau 174615:II. DCU; BL. 597/48

Neander, Michael. Orbis terrae partium succincta explicatio. *Leipzig: A.Lamberg,for J.Apel,* 1597. 583p.;8vo. 1st publ., Eisleben, 1583. Cf.Sabin 52175n; Adams (Cambr.) N115. Cambridge: Emmanuel, Strasbourg: BN. 597/49

Orta, Garcia da. Dell'historia de i semplici aromati, et altre cose, che vengono portate dall'Indie Orientali pertinenti all'uso della medicina, di Don Garcia dal'Horto . . . con alcune brevi annotationi di Carlo Clusio . . . Et due altri libri parimente di quelle cose che si portano dall'Indie Occidentali . . . di Nicolò Monardes . . . Hora . . . tutti tradotti . . . da m.Annibale Briganti. *Venice: Heirs of G.Scoto,* 1597. 525p.;illus.;8vo. 1st publ. in Italian, Venice, 1576. Sabin 57669; Guerra (Monardes) 33; Arents (Add.) 66; Palau 99521. DNLM, ICN, MH-A, NN-RB. 597/50

Osorio, Jerónimo, Bp of Silves. De rebus Emmanuelis Lusitaniae Regis . . . gestis, libri duodecim . . . Item Jo. Matalii Metelli . . . praefatio et emendata. *Cologne: House of Birckmann,for A.Mylius,* 1597. 368 numb. lvs;8vo. 1st publ. with Matal's preface, Cologne, 1574. Sabin 57804n; Adams (Cambr.) O383. DLC, InU-L, NN-RB; BL, Strasbourg: BN. 597/51

Pantaleon, Heinrich, pseud.? Tabulae chronologicae. *Strassburg: J.Rihel,* 1597. 4to. See Candidus, Pantaleon, above. 597/52

Pasquier, Etienne. Les lettres. *Lyons: [P. Roussin,for] J.Veyrat,* 1597. 438 numb. lvs; 8vo. 1st publ., Paris, 1586. Thickett (Pasquier) 21; Baudrier (Lyons) IV:402. CU, CtY, ICN, MiU, NNU; Oxford: Bodl., BN. 597/53

Plaintes des Eglises Reformees de France: sur les violences et injustices qui leur sont faites. *[Geneva?]* 1597. 172p.;12mo. Includes passage on cannibalism of Topinambas & Margajas, Indians of Brazil. Adams (Cambr.) F842. ICN, WU; Cambridge: Clare. 597/54

Plinius, Basilius. Carmen de venenis et venenatis in universum, et de morbi gallici investigatione. *Wittenberg:* 1597. 8vo. Proksch I:82. 597/55

Possevino, Antonio. Apparatus ad omnium gentium historiam. *Venice: G.B.Ciotti,* 1597. 260 numb.lvs;8vo. Extracted & enl. from author's *Bibliotheca selecta,* 1st publ., Rome, 1593. In section 6, ch.26, 'Indorum, sive de rebus Indicis', are listed those authors who have written on both Indies. Cf.Sabin 64450; Backer VI:1079; Adams (Cambr.) P1995. CtY, ICN, NN-RB, RPJCB; BL, BN. 597/56

Ptolemaeus, Claudius. Geographiae universae tum veteris, tum novae absolutissimum opus . . . commentariis uberrimis illustratus est à Jo. Antonio Magino patavino. *Cologne: P.Keschedt,* 1597. 2 pts;maps;4to. 1st publ. as ed. & suppl by Magini, Venice, 1596. Sabin 66493n (& 43822 & 59033); Stevens (Ptolemy) 54. DLC, ICN, InU-L, MH, NN-RB, RPJCB; Strasbourg: BN. 597/57

—[Anr issue]. [Colophon, pt 2:] *Arnhem: J.Janszoon,* 1597. Sabin 66493; Stevens (Ptolemy) 54; Phillips (Atlases) 404; Adams (Cambr.) M117; JCB (3) I:356. DLC, RPJCB; BL.

597/58

Rauw, Johann. Cosmographia, das ist: Eine schöne, richtige und volkomliche Beschreibung dess göttlichen Geschöpfs, Himmels und der Erden. *Frankfurt a.M.: N.Bassé,* 1597. 1031p.;illus.,port.,maps;fol. Sabin 67977. CtY, DLC, MiU-C, NN-RB; Strasbourg: BN.

597/59

Richeome, Louis. Trois discours pour la religion catholique, des miracles, des saincts & des images. *Bordeaux: S.Millanges,* 1597. 587p.;8vo. In bk 1, ch.23 discusses Brazil, Peru, etc. Backer VI:1817; Rép.bibl.I:57; Cioranescu (XVI) 59455. RPJCB; BN. 597/60

Rivadeneira, Pedro de. Tratado de la religion y virtudes que deve tener el principe christiano. *Antwerp: Plantin Office,* 1597. 437p.;8vo. 1st publ., Madrid, 1595. Backer VI:1735; Peeters-Fontainas (Impr.esp.) 1123; Adams (Cambr.) R462; Palau 266334. ICN, InU-L, MH; BL, BN. 597/60a

Ronsard, Pierre de. Oeuvres. *Paris: [L.Delas, for] Widow of G.Buon,* 1597. 10v.;ports; 12mo. 1st publ. as here collected, Paris, 1578. MH, MiU, NjP; BL, BN. 597/61

Rosaccio, Giuseppe. Le sei eta del mondo. *Venice:* 1597. 47p.;8vo. 1st publ., Brescia, 1593. Cf.Sabin 73197. BN. 597/62

____. Teatro del cielo e della terra. *Venice:* 1597. 64p.;maps;16mo. 1st publ., Brescia, 1592. Cf.Sabin 73198; JCB (3) I:356. NNH, RPJCB. 597/63

Santisteban Osório, Diego de. Quarta y quinta parte de la Araucana. *Salamanca: J. & A. Renaut,* 1597. 151, 252-400 numb.lvs;12mo. Continues A.de Ercilla y Zúñiga's *Araucana,* 1st publ. in all 3 pts, Madrid, 1590. Sabin 57801; Medina (Chile) 24; Palau 300190. MH, NN-RB. 597/64

Sassonia, Ercole. Luis venereae perfectissimus tractatus. *Padua: L.Pasquato,* 1597. 48 numb.lvs;4to. Proksch I:20-21; Adams (Cambr.) S535. CtY-M, DNLM, MnU-B, NNNAM, PPC; BL, BN. 597/65

Schmidel, Ulrich. Warhafftige unnd liebliche Beschreibung etlicher fürnemmen Indianischen Landschafften und Insulen . . . an Tag gebracht durch Dieterich von Bry. *[Frankfurt a.M.:] T.de Bry,* 1597. 31 numb.lvs;fol. (Theodor de Bry's *America.* Pt 7. German). 1st publ., Frankfurt a.M., 1567, as pt 2 of Sebastian Franck's *Warhafftige Beschreibunge aller theil der Welt.* At head of title: Das vii. Theil America. Cf.Sabin 8784; Church 191; JCB (3) I:399-400. CSmH, DLC, ICN, MH, MiU-C, NN-RB, RPJCB; BL, BN. 597/66

Talavera, Gabriel de. Historia de Nuestra señora de Guadalupe . . . milagrosa patrona de este sanctuario. *Toledo: T.de Guzmán,* 1597. 475 numb.lvs;illus.;4to. For the use of the Mexican shrine at Guadalupe. Sabin 94224; Pérex Pastor (Toledo) 426; Palau 326748; JCB (3) I:357. NN-RB, RPJCB; BL, BN. 597/67

Tasso, Torquato. Il Goffredo, overo Gierusalemme liberata, poema heroico. *Venice: G.B. Ciotti,* 1597. 570p.;12mo. 1st publ. with American refs, Parma, 1581. Racc. Tassiana 177. Bergamo: BC. 597/67a

Teixeira, José, supposed author. Traicte paraenetique. C'est à dire exhortatoire. Auquel se montre . . . le droit chemin & vrais moyens de resister à l'effort du Castellan [Philippe II] . . . Par un Pelerin espagnol . . . Traduict de langue castillane [et augmenté] . . . par J.D.Dralymont [i.e., Jean de Montlyard]. *Auch* [i.e.,*Paris?*]: 1597. 120 numb.lvs;12mo. Long & generally attributed to Teixeira, or to Antonio Pérez, the ascription is now believed erroneous. Described by Montlyard as transl. from a Castillian *Trattado paranaetico,* the latter is unknown in printed form. Included are numerous refs to New World. Cf.Sabin 96752; Cioranescu (XVI) 16061; cf.STC 19837.5; Palau 328874. MH; BN. 597/68

Torquemada, Antonio de. Giardino di fiori curiosi . . . tradotto di spagnuolo . . . per Celio Malespina. *Venice: G.B.Ciotti,* 1597. 208 numb.lvs;8vo. 1st publ. in Italian, Venice, 1590. Palau 334923. DLC, ICN. 597/69

Wytfliet, Corneille. Descriptionis Ptolemaicae augmentum, sive Occidentis notitia. *Louvain: J.Bogaert,* 1597. 104(i.e., 95)p.; maps;fol. Sabin 105696n; Koeman (Wyt) 1. CSmH, NN-RB. 597/70

__[2nd edn]. *Louvain: J.Bogaert,* 1597. 191p.;maps;fol. With errata note on p.[192]. Sabin 105696; Koeman (Wyt) 1B; Fairfax Murray (Germany) 446; JCB (3) I:357. DLC, RPJCB. 597/71

__[Anr issue of 2nd edn]. *Louvain: J.Bogaert,* 1597. Without errata note on p.[192]. Phillips (Atlases) 1140; JCB (3) I:357. DLC, MH, MiU-C, RPJCB. 597/72

1598

Acosta, José de. Geographische und historische Beschreibung der überauss grossen Landschafft America. *Cologne: J.Christoffel,* 1598. 51p.;maps;fol. Transl. from 1st two bks of the Cologne, 1596, edn of Acosta's *De natura Novi Orbis,* 1st publ. Salamanca, 1588. Sabin 26981 (&128); Streit II:1150; Backer I:34; Ind.aur.100.465; Baginsky (German Americana) 102; JCB (3) I:358. InU-L, NN-RB, RPJCB, TxU; BL. 598/1

____. Histoire naturelle et morale des Indes, tant Orientalles qu'Occidentalles . . . traduite par Robert Regnault, 1598. *Paris: M.Orry,* 1598.

375p.;8vo. Transl. from Acosta's *Historia natural y moral de las Indias,* 1st publ., Seville, 1590. Sabin 125; Medina (BHA) 330n (I:501); Streit II:1148; Backer I:36; Ind. aur.100.466; Arents 51; JCB (3) I:358. DLC, MH, NN-RB, OCl, RPJCB; BL, BN.   598/2

___. Historie naturael ende morael van de Westersche Indien . . . overgheset: door Jan Huyghen van Linschoten. *Haarlem: G.Rooman,for J.L.Meyn,at Enkhuizen,* 1598. 389 numb.lvs;8vo. Transl. from Acosta's *Historia natural y moral de las Indias,* 1st publ., Seville, 1590. Sabin 126; Medina (BHA) 330n (I:502); Streit II:1149; Backer I:35; Ind. aur.100.464; JCB (3) I:357. DLC, MnU-B, RPJCB; BL.   598/3

Apianus, Petrus. Cosmographie, oft Beschrijvinge der gheheelder werelt. *Amsterdam: C. Claeszoon,* 1598. 121 numb.lvs.;illus.,map; 4to. 1st publ. in this enlarged version, Antwerp, 1592. Ortroy (Apian) 64; Bibl.belg., 1st ser.,I:A44; Ind.aur.106.471; JCB (3) I:359. RPJCB; The Hague: KB.   598/4

Arfe y Villafañe, Juan de. Quilatador, de la plata, oro, y piedras, conforme a las leyes reales, y para declaracion de ellas. *Madrid: G.Drouy,* 1598. 144 (i.e.,244) numb.lvs; port.;8vo. 1st publ., Valladolid, 1572. Pérez Pastor (Madrid) 561; Ind.aur.107.218; Palau 16054. RPJCB; BL, BN.   598/5

Banchieri, Adriano. La nobilità dell'asino di Attabalippa dal Perù [pseud.]. *Venice: B.Barezzi,* 1598. 44 numb.lvs;4to. 1st (?) publ., [Bologna?], 1588; cf.1592 edn. Brunet I:540; Ind.aur.112.138. Warsaw: BU. 598/5a

Boaistuau, Pierre. Histoires prodigeuses. *Paris: Widow of G.Cavellat,* 1598,'97. 6v.; illus.;16mo. 1st publ. with American ref. in section by François de Belleforest, Paris, 1571. Ind.aur.120.116. DFo; BL, Vienna: NB.   598/6

___[Anr edn]. *Paris: Widow of G.Buon,* 1598. 1282p.;illus.;16mo. DNLM, PPC.   598/7

Bodin, Jean. Methodus ad facilem historiarum cognitionem, accurate denuo recusa. *Strassburg: L.Zetzner,* 1598. 550p.;8vo. 1st publ., Paris, 1566. Ind. aur.120.863. MH; Berlin: StB.   598/8

___. Les six livres de la Republique . . . ensemble une Apologie de René Herpin. *Lyons: Giunta Press,* 1598. 8vo. 1st publ., Paris, 1576. Ind.aur.120.858; Baudrier (Lyons) VI:423. Toulouse: BM.   598/9

Botero, Giovanni. Aggiunte fatte di Giovanni Botero alla sua Ragion di stato . . . Con una relatione del mare. *Rome: G.Ferrari,* 1598. 8vo. Contains in the 'Relatione del mare' numerous refs to the New World, e.g., to Mexico, the River Plate, etc. Ind. aur.122.737. Berlin: StB, Copenhagen: KB.   598/10

___[Anr edn]. *Pavia: A.Viani,* 1598. 95 numb.lvs;8vo. Ind.aur.122.736; Adams (Cambr.) B2549. ICU, InU-L, MiDW, NNC, RPB; Cambridge: UL, BN.   598/11

___[Anr edn]. *Venice: G.B.Ciotti,* 1598. 8vo. Ind.aur.122.738. Copenhagen: KB, Warsaw: BU.   598/12

___. Commentariolus parallelos. *Cologne: L. Andreae,* 1598. 27 lvs;maps;4to. 1st publ., Cologne, 1597, as here extracted & transl. from Botero's *Delle relatione universali,* 1st publ., Rome, 1591-95. Cf.Sabin 98222; Ind. aur.122.733. NIC, NN-RB; BN, Vienna: NB.   598/13

___. Della ragione di stato . . . Di nuovo in questa quinta editione dall'isteso autore in alcuni luoghi mutati & accresciuti. *Milan: P.Ponti,* 1598. 402p.;8vo. 1st publ., Venice, 1589. Ind.aur.122.735. MB, MiDW, MnU-B; Copenhagen: KB, Vienna: NB.   598/14

___[Anr edn]. *Venice: The Gioliti,* 1598. 376p.; 8vo. Ind.aur.122.739. ICU, InU-L, NcD; Berlin: StB.   598/15

___. Discorsi sopra la ragione di stato. *Venice: The Gioliti,* 1598. 8vo. 1st publ., Venice, 1589, under title *Della ragion di stato.* InU-L.   598/16

___. Mundus imperiorum, sive De mundis imperiis libri quatuor . . . a Guidone de Bruecqs, ex . . . italicis relationibus latine factum. *Cologne: B.Buchholtz,* 1598. 148p.;4to. Transl. from Botero's *Delle relationi universali,* 1st publ., Rome, 1591-95, Ind.aur. 122.734. BL, BN.   598/17

Capivaccio, Girolamo. Acroaseis de virulentia gallica, sive lue venerea. *Frankfurt a.M.: Heirs of C.Egenolff,* 1598. 119p.;8vo. 1st publ., Spira, 1590. Proksch I:20; Ind. aur.131.675. DNLM; BL, Berlin: StB. 598/18

Cartier, Jacques. Discours du voyage fait . . . aux Terres neufves de Canadas, Norembergue, Hochelague, Labrador, et pays adjacents, dite Nouvelle France. *Rouen: R.Du Petit Val,* 1598. 64p.;8vo. Probably transl. from Ramusio's *Navigationi et viaggi,* 1st publ., Venice, 1556; cf.Paris, 1545, *Brief recit.* Sabin 11140 (coliated, in error?, 72p.); Harrisse (NF) 7; JCB AR46:4-10. ICN, NHi, RPJCB; BN. 598/19

Casas, Bartolomé de las, Bp of Chiapa. Narratio regionum Indicarum per Hispanos quosdam devastarum verissima . . . hispanice conscripta . . . anno vero hac 1598 latine conexcuse [et iconibus illustrata a J.T. et J.I.de Bry]. *Frankfurt a.M.: T.de Bry & J.Sauer,* 1598. 141p.;illus.;4to. Transl. from the Paris, 1579, *Tyrannies et cruautez des Espagnols,* itself transl. from the *Brevissima relación,* 1st publ., Seville, 1552. Sabin 11283; Medina (BHA) 383; Streit I:228; Church 320; JCB (3) I:360. CSmH, DLC, MH, NN-RB, PPL, RPJCB; BL, BN. 598/20

Castillejo, Cristóbal de. Obras. *Antwerp: M.Nuyts,* 1598. 372 numb.lvs;12mo. 1st publ., Madrid, 1573. Peeters-Fontainas (Impr.esp.) 203; Palau 48017n. DFo, NNH; BL, BN. 598/21

—[Anr issue]. *Antwerp: [M.Nuyts,for] P.Bellère,* 1598. Peeters-Fontainas (Impr. esp.) 204; Palau 48017n; Adams (Cambr.) C953; Shaaber C248. MB, NNH, PU; Cambridge: UL, BN. 598/21a

Dresser, Matthaeus, comp. Historien und Bericht, von dem newlicher Zeit erfundenen Königreich China . . . Item, Von dem auch erfundenen Lande Virginia. *Leipzig: Heirs of J.Beyer,for F.Schnellboltz,* 1598 [colophon:1597]. 297p.;4to. 1st publ., Leipzig, 1597; here a reissue with altered imprint date. Sabin 20926; Baginsky (German Americana) 103. CtY, DLC, MiU-C, MnU-B, NN-RB; Wolfenbüttel: HB. 598/22

Du Bartas, Guillaume de Salluste, seigneur. The colonies of Bartas. With the commentarie of S[imon]. G[oulart]., enlarged by the translatour [William Lisle]. *London: R.F[ield].for T.Man,* 1598. 4to. In verse. Transl. from 4th pt of 2nd day of *La seconde sepmaine,* 1st publ., Paris, 1584. STC 21670. CSmH. 598/23

——. The second weeke, or Childhood of the world. *London: P.S[hort].,* 1598. [94]p.;8vo. Transl. from author's *La seconde sepmaine,* 1st publ., Paris, 1584. STC 21661. CSmH. 598/24

—[Anr enlarged edn]. *London: P.Short,for W. Wood,* 1598. STC 21661.5. DFo. 598/25

——. Suite des oeuvres . . . ascavoir, Les deux Sepmaines. [*Geneva:*] *G.Cartier,* 1598. In

verse. Holmes (DuBartas) I:74 no.25. ICU; BL. 598/26

Du Fail, Noël, seigneur de La Hérissaye. Les contes et discours d'Eutrapel. *Rennes: N.Glamet,* 1598. 452p.;12mo. 1st publ., Rennes, 1585. Rép.bibl.,XIX:74. BN. 598/27

—[Anr edn]. *Rennes: N.Glamet,* 1598. 549p.; 12mo. Rép.bibl.,XIX:74. DFo, MH; BL. 598/28

Emili, Paolo. L'histoire des faicts, gestes et conquestes . . . de France . . . mise en françois par Jean Regnart . . . avec la suite . . . tirée du latin de . . . Arnold Le Ferron. *Paris: F.Morel,* 1598. 687p.;fol. 1st publ., Paris. 1581; here a reissue with cancel t.p. Ind.aur.100.843. ICN, InU-L; BL. 598/29

Estienne, Charles. L'agriculture et maison rustique, de mm. Charles Estienne et Jean Liebault. *Paris: P.Bertault,* 1598. 394 numb.lvs;illus.;4to. 1st publ. as enl. by Liébault, Paris, 1567; here reprinted as expanded in 1583. Arents (Add.) 34. NN-A. 598/30

—[Anr issue]. *Paris: P.Chevalier,* 1598. Thiébaud (La chasse) 350. 598/31

—[Anr issue]. *Paris. J.DuPuis,* 1598. Thiébaud (La chasse) 350. 598/32

—[Anr issue]. *Paris: J.LeBouc,* 1598. Thiébaud (La chasse) 350. 598/33

—[Anr issue]. *Paris: M.Orry,* 1598. Thiébaud (La chasse) 350. 598/34

—[Anr edn]. *Rouen: J.Crevel,* 1598. 394 numb. lvs; illus.;4to. Thiébaud (La chasse) 350. 598/35

—[Anr issue]. *Rouen: T.Daré,* 1598. Thiébaud (La chasse) 350. 598/36

—[Anr issue]. *Rouen: J.Osmont,* 1598. Thiébaud (La chasse) 350. 598/37

——. XV. Bücher von dem Feldbau . . . von Carolo Stephano und Johanne Libalto . . . vom . . . Melchiore . . . Sebizio inn Teutsch gebracht. *Strassburg: Heirs of B.Jobin,* 1598. 763p.;illus.;fol. 1st publ. in German, Strassburg, 1579. Ritter (Strasbourg) 1358. MH, NjP; BL, Strasbourg: BN. 598/38

Florio, John. A worlde of wordes, or Most copious, and exact dictionarie in Italian and English. *London: A.Hatfield,for E.Blount,* 1598. 462p.;fol. Included are entries for tobacco. STC 11098; Arents (Add.) 108. CSmH, CtY, DLC, ICN, MH, MiU, NN-A, PU-F, RPB; BL. 598/39

France. Sovereigns, etc., 1589-1610 (Henry IV). Edict contenant le pouvoir donné au marquis de Cottenmael et de la Roche pour la conqueste des terres Canada, Labrador, isle de Sable, Noremberg et pays adjacens. *Rouen: R.Du Petit Val,* 1598. 24p.;8vo. Harrisse (NF) 8; Wroth & Annan 2.   598/40

Gabelkover, Oswald. Medecyn-boeck. *Dordrecht: A.Canin,* 1598. 456 (i.e.,556) p.;4to. Transl. by Carel Baten from German text, 1st publ., Tübingen, 1589, under title *Nützlich Artzneybuch.* DNLM, NNNAM.   598/41

Goulart, Simon, comp. Le cinquiesme recueil, contenant les choses plus memorables avenues sous la Ligue. *[Geneva?]* 1598. 835p.;8vo. Includes (p.635-640) the *Observations notables sur le titre . . . de la Satyre Menippee,* 1st publ., [Paris?], 1593. Jones (Goulart) 30(b). DLC, MH, MiU-C; BL, BN.   598/41a

Hakluyt, Richard. The principal navigations, voiages, traffiques and discoveries of the English nation . . . This first volume. *London: G.Bishop,R.Newbery& R.Barker,* 1598. 619p.;fol. Enl. from London, 1589, edn. Sabin 29595; Borba de Moraes I:328; Streit I:227; STC 12626; JCB (3) I:360-361. CSmH, CtY, DLC, ICN, InU-L, MH, MiU-C, MnU-B, NN-RB, PBL, RPJCB; BL, BN.   598/42

Hall, Joseph, Bp of Norwich. Virgidemiarum. The three last bookes of byting satyres. *London: R.Bradock,for R.Dexter,* 1598. 105p.;8vo. In verse. In bk 4, satire 3 has ref. to Guiana's gold & Orinoco; in bk 5, satire 2 refers to tobacco. STC 12716 pt 2; Arents (Add.) 106; Pforzheimer 444. CSmH, DFo, IU, MH, NN-A; BL.   598/43

Heurne, Johan van. De febribus liber. *Leyden: Plantin Press (C. Raphelengius),* 1598. 167p.;4to. Adams (Cambr.) H514; Proksch I:83. DNLM, ICJ, MnU-B; Cambridge: St John's, BN,   598/44

Heyns, Peeter. Epitome du Theatre. *Antwerp:* See entry under Ortelius, Abraham, below.

——. Le miroir du monde . . . Aggrandi & enrichi . . . de plusieurs belles cartes du Paisbas. *Amsterdam: Z.Heyns,* 1598. 97 numb. lvs;maps,port.;obl.4to. 1st publ., Antwerp, 1579. Atkinson (Fr.Ren.) 390; Koeman (Z.Hey) 1; Bibl.belg.,1st ser.,XII:H57. BL, BN.   598/45

——. Il theatro del mondo. *Brescia:* 1598. See entry under Ortelius, Abraham, below.

Houtman, Cornelis de. Diarium nauticum itineris Batavorum in Indiam Orientalem. *Middelburg: B.Langenes,* 1598. 40 lvs;illus., maps;obl. 4to. Transl. from the *Journael vande reyse der Hollandtsche schepen,* of this year; 1st publ., Middelburg, 1597, under title *Verhael vande reyse by de Hollandtsche schepen.* Tiele 505; Tiele-Muller 107. Amsterdam; NHSM.   598/46

——[Anr issue]. *[Middelburg: B.Langenes,for] J. Janszoon,at Arnhem,* 1598. Tiele 505n; Tiele-Muller 108n. OCl.   598/47

——[Anr issue]. *[Middelburg: B.Langenes,for] A.Périer,at Paris,* 1598. Tiele 505n; Tiele-Muller 108. DLC, ICN, NN; BL, Amsterdam: NHSM.   598/48

——. The description of a voyage made by certaine ships of Holland into the East Indies . . . translated out of Dutch . . . by W[illiam]. P[hillip]. *London: [J.Windet? for] J.Wolfe,* 1598. 116p.;maps;4to. Transl. from the *Journael vande reyse der Hollandtsche schepen* of this year; 1st publ., Middelburg, 1597, under title *Verhael vande reyse by de Hollandtsche schepen.* Tiele 506n; Tiele-Muller 122; STC 15193. CSmH, ICU, NN-RB; BL, Amsterdam: NHSM.   598/49

——. Journael van de reyse der Hollandtsche schepen ghedaen in Oost Indien. *Middelburg: B.Langenes,* 1598. 34 lvs;illus.,maps;obl.4to. 1st publ., Middelburg, 1597, under title *Verhael vande reyse by de Hollandtsche schepen;* here ed. by C.Gerritszoon. Tiele 504; Tiele-Muller 106. NN-RB; BL, Amsterdam: NHSM   598/50

——[Anr issue]. *[Middelburg: B.Langenes,for] J.van Waesberghe,at Rotterdam,* 1598. BL.   598/51

——. Journal du voyage de l'Inde Orientale, faict per les navires hollandoises. *Middelburg: B.Langenes,* 1598. 40 lvs;illus.,maps;obl.4to. Transl. from the *Journael vande reyse der Hollandtsche schepen,* Middelburg, 1598; 1st publ., Middelburg, 1597, under title *Verhael vande reyse by de Hollandtsche schepen.* Tiele 506; Tiele-Muller 109; Atkinson (Fr.Ren.) 387. BL.   598/52

——[Anr issue]. *[Middelburg: B.Langenes,for] A.Périer,at Paris,* 1598. CtY, NN-RB. 598/53

——. Kurtze warhafftige Beschreibung der newen Reyse oder Schiffahrt . . . Aus der niderlendischen . . . Sprach . . . verdolmetschet. *Nuremberg: C.Lochner,for L.Hulsius,* 1598. 71p.;illus.,maps;4to. (Levinus Hulsius's *Sammlung von Schiffahrten.* Pt 1). Transl. from the *Verhael vande reyse by de Hollandtsche schepen,* Middelburg, 1597. For what is described as a 2nd issue, see the Church catalogue. Sabin 33653; Tiele-Muller 122; Church 256; JCB (3) I:450. CSmH, NN-RB, RPJCB; BL. 598/54

Hurault, Michel, sieur de Bélesbat et du Fay. Le recueil des excellens et libres discours sur l'estat présent de la France. [*Paris?*] 1598. 2 pts;12mo. 1st publ., [Paris?], 1593, under title *Quatre excellens discours.* Adams (Cambr.) H1196. CU; Cambridge: UL. 598/55

Langenes, Barent. Caert-thresoor, inhoudende de tafelen des gantsche Werelts Landen. *Middelburg: B.Langenes;for sale by C.Claeszoon,Amsterdam* [1598]. 2v.;maps; obl.8vo. Included are 12 maps relating to America. Sabin 38880 (&9839); Koeman (Lan) 1. MiU-C; BL, Strasbourg: BN. 598/56

Linschoten, Jan Huygen van. Discours of voyages into ye Easte & West Indies. *London: J.Wolfe,* 1598. 462p.;illus.,maps;fol. Transl. by William Philip; 1st publ. in Dutch, Amsterdam, 1596. Sabin 41374; Borba de Moraes I:417; STC 15691; Arents (Add.) 110; Church 221; JCB (3) I:362. CSmH, CtY, DLC, ICN, InU-L, MH, MiU-C, MnU-B, NN-RB, RPJCB; BL. 598/57

Lodewijcksz, Willem. D'eerste boeck; Historie van Indien, waer inne verhaelt is de avontueren die de Hollandtsche schepen bejeghent zijn . . . Door G.M.A.W.L. *Amsterdam: C.Claeszoon,* 1598. 70 lvs;illus.,maps; obl.4to. Includes mention of Brazil. Tiele 507; Tiele-Muller 111. CtY, NN-RB; BL. 598/58

_____. Premier livre de l'Histoire de la navigation aux Indes Orientales, par les Hollandois . . . Par G.M.A.W.L. *Amsterdam: C.Claeszoon,* 1598. 53 numb.lvs;illus,maps;fol. Transl. from *D'eerste boeck; Historie van Indien* above. Tiele 511; Tiele-Muller 113; Atkinson (Fr.Ren.) 388; JCB (3) I:364. CSmH, DFo, MB, NN-RB, RPJCB; BL, BN. 598/59

_____. Prima pars descriptionis itineris navalis in Indiam Orientalem . . . Authore G.M.A.W.L. *Amsterdam: C.Claeszoon,* 1598. 51 numb. lvs;illus.,maps;fol. Transl. from *D'eerste boeck; Historie van Indien,* of this year above.

Tiele 510; Tiele-Muller 112; JCB (3) I:364. DLC, IEN, NjP, MnU-B, RPJCB; BL, Amsterdam: NHSM. 598/60

Loew, Conrad. Meer oder Seehanen Buch, darinn verzeichnet seind, die wunderbare . . . Reise und Schiffarhten . . . Auff und durch welche Schiffarten, ein Newe Welt gegen Nidergang . . . erfunden und entdeckt seind . . . auss andern Spraachen . . . gebracht, durch Conrad Löw. *Cologne: B.Buchholtz,* 1598. 110p.;maps;fol. Extracted & transl. from earlier accounts of European explorers of varied nationality. Sabin 42392; Baginsky (German Americana) 106; JCB (3) I:364-365. MnU-B, NN-RB, RPJCB; BL. 598/61

Lonitzer, Adam. Kreuterbuch . . . zum letzenmal von neuwem ersehen, und . . . gebessert . . . durch Adamum Lonicerum. *Frankfurt a.M.: J.Sauer,for Heirs of C.Egenolff,* 1598. ccclxxxii lvs;illus.,port.;fol. 1st publ. in German, Frankfurt a.M., 1557. Pritzel 5599n; Nissen (Bot.) 1228n. ICN, NN-RB. 598/62

Lopes, Duarte. Regnum Congo, hoc est Vera descriptio regni Africani . . . Latio sermone donata ab August. Cassiod. Reinio. *Frankfurt a.M.: W.Richter,for J.T. & J.I. de Bry,Bros,* 1598. 60p.;illus.,map;fol. (J.T.de Bry's *India Orientalis.* Pt 1. Latin). Transl. from author's *Relatione del reame di Congo,* 1st publ., Rome 1591; cf.de Bry's German version of 1597. Church 205; JCB (3) I:419. CSmH, CtY, ICN, NN-RB, RPJCB; BL, BN 598/63

Lucidarius. M.Elucidarius. Von allerhandt Geschöpffen Gottes . . . und wie alle Creaturen geschaffen seynd auff Erden. *Frankfurt a.M.: M.Becker,for Heirs of C.Egenolff,* 1598. [87]p.;illus.,map;4to. 1st publ., Strassburg, [ca.1535]. Schorbach (Lucidarius) 67. Munich: StB. 598/64

Marcos da Lisboa, o.f.m., Bp. Delle croniche de' Frati Minori del . . . p.S.Francisco. Parte terza . . . tradotta di lingua spagnuola . . . dal sig. Horatio Diola . . . Et in questa seconda impressione corrichita, & megliorata molto. *Venice: E.Viotti,* 1598. 342 numb.lvs; 4to. 1st publ. in Italian; Venice, 1591; transl. from Salamanca, 1570, Spanish text. Streit I:188. Rome: B.Alessandrina. 598/65

Marguérite d'Angoulême, Queen of Navarre. L'heptameron ou Histoires des amans fortunez. *Rouen: R.de Beauvais,* 1598. 589p.;12mo. 1st publ. in this version, Paris, 1559. Adams

(Cambr.) M568; Tchémerzine VII:395. BL.
598/66

___[Anr edn]. *Rouen: J. Osmont,* 1598. 578p.;
12mo. Tchémerzine VII:395. 598/67

Mariz, Pedro de. Dialogos. *Coimbra:* 1598.
See the year 1599.

Mattioli, Pietro Andrea. Opera quae extant
omnia. *Frankfurt a.M.: N.Bassé,* 1598. 2
pts;illus.;fol. Includes Mattioli's *Commentarii,* 1st publ., Venice, 1554, & his *Morbi
gallici . . . opusculum,* Bologna, 1533. Pritzel
5984; Nissen (Bot.) 1309; Arents (Add.) 27-A;
Shaaber M198a. CtY, DNLM, ICJ, MH-A,
MiU, NN-A, PU, RPB; BL, BN. 598/68

Mayr, Johann. Compendium cronologicum
seculi à Christo nato decimi sexti. *Munich:
N.Heinrich,* 1598. 159 lvs;4to. Included are
numerous refs to America. Sabin 47109;
Palmer 357. ICN, MnU-B, NSyU. 598/69

Meteren, Emanuel van. Historia belgica
nostri potissimum temporis . . . ad annum usque 1598. *[Antwerp?* 1598]. 623 [i.e.,643]p.;
ports,map;fol. Transl. from Dutch manuscript, itself 1st publ., Delft, 1599; cf.German
edn of 1596. Palau 166944; Adams (Cambr.)
M1366; Shaaber M321. CLU, DLC, ICN,
MH, MiU, MnU, NNH, PU, WU; BL(as
[1600?]), BN. 598/70

Montaigne, Michel Eyquem de. Essais . . .
édition nouvelle prise sur l'exemplaire
trouvé après le deceds de l'autheur. *Paris:A.
L'Angelier,* 1598. 1166p.;8vo. 1st publ., Bordeaux, 1580; 1st publ. with author's annotations, Paris, 1595. Tchémerzine VIII:409;
Adams M1623 (describing copy misdated 'cIc.
Ic. xcxviii'). IU, MH; Cambridge: Emmanuel,
BN. 598/71

Montemayor, Jorge de. Diana of George of
Montemayor . . . translated out of Spanish
. . . by Bartholomew Yong. *London:
E.Bollifant,for G.B[ishop].,* 1598. 496p.;fol.
Includes also Gaspar Gil Polo's *Enamored
Diana,* transl. from his *Diana enamorada,* 1,
1st publ., Valencia, 1564. STC 18044;
Shaaber M398. CSmH, CtY, DLC, ICN, MH,
MiU, MnU, NN-RB, PU-F, WU; BL. 598/72

Münster, Sebastian. Cosmographey: das ist
Beschreibung aller Länder. *Basel: S.Hen-
ricpetri,* 1598. 1461p.;maps;fol. 1st publ., Basel, 1544. Sabin 51395; Burmeister (Münster)
83. CU, DLC, MH, MiU, PPL, RPB, BL,
BN. 598/73

Ortelius, Abraham. Epitome du Theatre du

monde . . . Reveu, corrigé, & augmenté de
plusieurs cartes, pour la derniere fois. *Antwerp: Plantin Press,for P.Galle,* 1598. 118
numb.lvs;maps;obl.8vo. 1st publ. with French
text, by Peeter Heyns, under title *Le miroir du
monde,* Antwerp, 1579. Atkinson (Fr.Ren.)
389; Koeman (Ort.) 57. DLC, ICN, RPJCB;
BL, Antwerp: Plantin Mus. 598/74

____. Theatre de l'univers, contenant les cartes
de tout le monde . . . Le tout reveu, amendé.
Antwerp: Plantin Press, 1598. 119 maps;
illus.,port.;fol. 1st publ. in French, Antwerp,
1572. Atkinson (Fr.Ren.) 391; Koeman (Ort.)
32; Phillips (Atlases) 406; JCB (3) I:365. DLC,
MH, MiU-C, NN-RB, RPJCB; BL, BN.
598/75

____. Il theatro del mondo . . . ridotto dalla
forma grande . . . in questa piccola [da Pietro
Maria Marchetti]. *Brescia: Comp.Bresciana,*
1598. 213p.;maps;8vo. 1st publ. in Latin,
Antwerp, 1572. Sabin 57702 (misdated 1589);
Koeman (Ort.) 69; Phillips (Atlases) 408.
DLC, ICN, InU-L, MiU-C, NN-RB, RPJCB;
BL, BN. 598/76

____. Theatrum orbis terrarum. Opus nunc
denuo ab ipso auctore . . . commentariis auctum. *[Antwerp: Plantin Press,for] A.Ortelius,*
1598. 184 lvs;maps;fol. 1st publ., Antwerp,
1570. Koeman (Ort.) 31. MnHi; BL, The
Hague: KB. 598/77

Pasquier, Etienne. Les Lettres. *Arras: G.de La
Rivière,for G.Bauduin,* 1598. 812p.;12mo. 1st
publ., Paris, 1586. Thickett (Pasquier) 22.
DFo; Paris: Arsenal. 598/78

Passe, Crispijn van de. Effigies regum ac prin-
cipium, eorum scilicet quorum vic ac potentia
in re nautica . . . spectabilis est. *Cologne:*
1598. [19]p.;illus.,ports;fol. Included are
ports & notices of Columbus, Vespucci & Sir
Francis Drake. Sabin 58995. CSmH, InU-L,
NjP, PBL; BL. 598/79

Possevino, Antonio. Apparato all'historia di
tutte le nationi. *Venice: G.B.Ciotti,* 1598. 270
numb.lvs;8vo. Transl. by author from his *Apparatus ad omnium gentium historiam,*
Venice, 1597. Cf.Sabin 64450; Backer
VI:1079-80. CtY, DFo, ICN, RPJCB; BL.
598/80

Pretty, Francis. Beschryvinghe vande over-
treffelijcke ende wijdtvermaerde zeevaerdt
vanden . . . meester Thomas Candish . . .
Hier noch by ghevoecht de voyagie van . . .
Sire Françoys Draeck, en Sir Jan Haukens

. . . naer West-Indien. *Amsterdam: C.Claes-zoon*, 1598. 42 numb.lvs;map;obl.4to. Transl. by Emanuel van Meteren from English mss supplied him by Hakluyt. A reissue of the following item, supplemented by coast pilots, a letter of Cavendish, etc. Sabin 11605; Borba de Moraes I:148-149; Tiele-Muller 296 (c); JCB (3) I:366. DLC, MnU-B, NN-RB, RP-JCB; BL.   598/81

____. Descriptio vande heerlicke Voyagie ghed-aen door den Edelman m. Thomas Candish . . . Hier noch by ghevoecht de voyaghie van Sire Françoys Draeck, en Sire Jan Haukens . . . naer West Indien. *Amsterdam: C.Claes-zoon*, 1598. 26 numb.lvs;map;obl.4to. Transl. by Emanuel van Meteren from English mss sent him by Hakluyt. Cf.preceding item. NN-RB.   598/82

Ptolemaeus, Claudius. Geografia, cioè Descri-tione universale della terra . . . in due volumi . . . nuovamente . . . rincontrati, & corretti . . . [da] Gio. Atn. Magini . . . Opera . . . tradotta dal r.d. Leonardo Cernoti. *Venice: G.B. & G.Galignani*, 1598, '97. 2 pts;maps;fol. Transl. from Latin text as ed. by Magini, 1st publ., Venice, 1596. Sabin 66506; Stevens (Ptolemy) 55; Phillips (Atlases) 405; Adams (Cambr.) M118; JCB (3) I:366. CSmH, CtY, DLC, ICU, InU-L, MiU-C, MnU-B, NN-RB PPL, RPJCB; BL, BN.   598/83

____. Geografia . . . tradotta di greco . . . da Girolamo Ruscelli . . . et hora ampliata da Gioseffo Rosaccio. *Venice: Heirs of M.Sessa*, 1598. 3 pts;maps;4to. 1st publ. as ed. & transl. by Ruscelli, Venice, 1561. The 2nd pt, with special t.p., comprises Ruscelli's *Esposi-tioni . . . sopra la Geografia di . . . Tolomeo.* Sabin 66507n; Armstrong (Ptolemy) 41. CtY, DLC, ICN, MB, MiU-C, NN-RB; BL. 598/84

Raleigh, Sir Walter. Waerachtighe ende grondighe beschryvinge van . . . Guiana . . . ende den vermaerden zeevaerder Capiteyn Laurens Keymis. *Amsterdam: C.Claeszoon*, 1598. 47 numb.lvs;obl.4to. Transl. from Raleigh's *Discoverie of Guiana*, 1st publ., London, 1596. Lvs [31]-47, with special t.p., comprise Lawrence Kemys's *Waerachtighe ende grondighe beschryvinghe van . . . Guiana*, 1st publ. in English, London, 1596. Sabin 67595 (& 37687-88); Tiele-Muller 302-305; JCB (3) I:361-362. NN-RB, NcU, RPJCB; BL.   598/85

Rebello, Amador. Compendio de algunas car-tas que este anno de 97. vierão dos padres da

Companhia de Jesu, que residem na India . . . & nos reinos de China, & Japão, & no Brasil. *Lisbon: A.de Siqueira*, 1598. 240p.;8vo. Sabin 68329 (& 72499); Borba de Moraes II:174; Streit II:1322; Backer VI:1559; Anselmo 1071. RPJCB; Lisbon: BN.   598/86

Richeome, Louis. Trois discours pour la religion catholique . . . Reveus et augmentez en ceste seconde edition par l'autheur. *Bordeaux: S.Millanges*, 1598. 838p.;12mo. 1st publ., Bordeaux, 1597. Backer VI:1817; Rép.bibl.I:60. BN.   598/87

Rivadeneira, Pedro de. Trattato della religione, e virtute, che tener deve il principe christiano, per governare e conservare i sui stati. Contro quel, che Nicolo Macchiavelli, dannato autore, e i politici . . . empiamente insegnano . . . dall lingua spagnuola . . . tradotto per Scipione Metelli. *Genoa: G.Pa-voni*, 1598. 535p.;4to. Transl. from author's *Tratado de la religion*, 1st publ., Madrid, 1595. Backer VI:1735; Palau 266339. CtY, NNUT.   598/88

____. Vita Francisci Borgiae. *Antwerp: J.Trognesius*, 1598. 462p.;4to. 1st publ. as here transl. by A.Schott, Rome, 1596. Palau 266311; Adams (Cambr.) R469. NNUT; Cambridge: Sidney Sussex.   598/88a

____. Vita Ignatii Loiolae . . . brevissimis et utilissimis scholiis illustrata a Christiano Simone Litho. [*Paris?*] 1598. 193p.;8vo. 1st publ., Naples, 1572. Cf.Sabin 70782; Palau 266208; Adams (Cambr.) R466. BL.   598/89

Rosaccio, Giuseppe. Le sei eta del mondo. *Venice:* 1598. 47p.;8vo. 1st publ., Brescia, 1593. Cf.Sabin 73197. MB;BL.   598/90

____. Teatro del cielo e della terra. *Venice:* 1598. 64p.;illus.,maps;8vo. 1st publ., Brescia, 1592. Cf.Sabin 73198. MB, NN-RB; BL.

598/91

Ruscelli, Girolamo. Espositioni, et introdut-tioni universali . . . sopra la Geografia di Claudio Tolomeo. *Venice: Heirs of M.Sessa*, 1598. [53]p.;maps;4to. In C.Ptolemaeus, *La geografia*, Venice, 1598, q.v.; see also redated 1599 issue.   598/92

Ryff, Peter. Elementa sphaerae mundi, sive Cosmographiae: in usum scholae math-ematicae Basilensis. *Basel: J.Schroeter*, 1598. 2 pts;8vo. On p.46 is a ref. to America. MH, MiU; BL.   598/93

Santisteban Osório, Diego de. Quarta y quin-ta parte de la Araucana. *Barcelona: J.Amello, for M.Menescal*, 1598. 146 numb.lvs;12mo.

1st publ., Salamanca, 1597; continues A.de Ercilla y Zúñiga's *Araucana*. Sabin 57802; Medina (BHA) 387; Medina (Chile) 26; JCB (3) I:368. NN-RB, RPJCB; BL. 598/94

Scaliger, Julius Caesar. In libros duos, qui inscribuntur de plantis, Aristotele authore. *Marburg: P.Egenolff,* 1598. 498p.;8vo. 1st publ., Paris, 1556. Pritzel 8088n; Adams (Cambr.) S588. ICU, MB, NN-RB; BL. 598/95

Scholtz, Lorenz, comp. Consiliorum medicinalium. *Frankfurt a.M.: Heirs of A.Wechel & C.de Marne & J.Aubry,* 1598. 1164 cols;fol. Includes Johann Crato von Krafftheim's 'Commentarii de vera praecavendi et curandi febrem pestilentem contagiosam', 1st publ., Frankfurt, 1594, in his *Consiliorum & epistolarium medicinalium liber,* v.4. CtY-M, DNLM, MiU; BL. 598/96

Severt, Jacques. De orbis catoptrici, seu Mapparum mundi principis, descriptione ac usu, libri tres. Editio secunda. *Paris: A.Drouart,* 1598. 332(i.e., 232)p.;illus.;fol. 1st publ., Paris, 1590. JCB AR20:1598. CtY, MH, RP-JCB; BN. 598/97

—[Anr issue]. *Paris: L.Sonnius,* 1598. DLC, MdBJ; BL, BN. 598/98

Skarga, Piotr. Zywoty swiętych starego y nowego. 1598. 1148p.;fol. 1st publ., Vilna, 1579. Backer VII:1267. 598/99

Soto, Domingo de. Commentariorum . . . in quartum Sententiarum. Tomus primus[-secundus]. *Venice: G.Zenari,* 1598. 2v.;4to. 1st publ., Salamanca, 1557-60. Palau 320178; Adams (Cambr.) S1481; Moranti (Urbino) 3154; Shaaber S498. PU; Cambridge: Gonville & Caius, BN. 598/100

Spain. Sovereigns, etc., 1556-1598 (Philip II). Instruccion y forma que se ha de tener y guardar en la publicacion, predicacion, administracion, y cobrança de la bula de la Santa Cruzada, en los obispados de Guatemala, Onduras, Chiapa, Nicaragua, y Verapaz. *Madrid:* 1598. 16p.;fol. Cf.1588 edn. Palau 120127. 598/101

Surius, Laurentius. Commentarius brevis rerum in orbe gestarum, ab anno salutis 1500 usque in annum 1574. *Cologne: A.Quentel,* 1598. 837p.;8vo. 1st publ., Cologne, 1564, as supplement to Nauclerus's *Cronicon;* cf.Cologne, 1566, separate edn. MH. 598/102

Tarcagnota, Giovanni. Delle historie del mondo. *Venice: The Giuntas,* 1598. 3 pts in 5v.;4to. 1st publ. in this expanded version,

Venice, 1583. DFo, MH, NNH; BL, BN. 598/103

Tasso, Torquato. Il Goffredo, overo Gierusalemme liberata, poema heroico. *Venice: G.B.Ciotti,* 1598. 770p.;illus.;12mo. 1st publ. with American refs, Parma, 1581. Racc.Tassiana 178. Bergamo: BC. 598/104

Teixeira, José, supposed author. Tractaet paraeneticq. dat is te segghen: Onderwysinghe ofte vermaninghe . . . Door een Spaensch Pelgrim . . . Ghetranslateert uut de castiliaensche sprake in françoysche tale, door J.d.Dralymont [i.e., Jean de Montlyard] . . . ende nu in Nederduytsch overgeset, door C.P.Boeyt. Nu nieulijcks ghedruckt. [*Amsterdam?*] 1598. 42 numb.lvs;4to. Transl. from French version 1st publ., Agen (i.e., Paris?), 1597. On disputed authorship, see 1597 edn. Cf.Sabin 96752; Knuttel 1021. The Hague: KB. 598/105

—[Anr edn]. Tractaet paraeneticq . . . Nu nieuwelijcx ghedruckt. [*Amsterdam?*] 1598. 42 numb.lvs;4to. Knuttel 1023. The Hague: KB. 598/106

—[Anr edn]. Tractaet paranetiq . . . Nieuwelijcx ghedruckt. [*Amsterdam?*] 1598. 42 numb.lvs;4to. Knuttel 1022. MH; The Hague: KB. 598/107

—[And edn]. Tractaet paraeneticq . . . Nu nieuwelick ghedruckt. [*Antwerp?*] 1598. Belg.typ. (1541-1600) I:4553. Brussels: BR. 598/108

———. Traicté paranaetique, c'est à dire exhortatoire . . . auquel se montre . . . le droit chemin et vrais moyens de resister à l'effort du Castellan [Philippe II] . . . Par un Pelerin espagnol . . . Traduict de langue castellane . . . par J.d.Dralymont . . . Seconde edition augmentee. *Agen* [i.e.,*Paris?*]: 1598. 180 numb.lvs;12mo. 1st publ., Auch (i.e., Paris), 1597; here containing added material on Brazil. On disputed authorship, see 1597 edn. Palau 328876. MH; BN. 598/109

—[Anr edn]. [*London? Eliot's Court Press?*] 1598. 71 numb.lvs;8vo. STC 19837.5; Palau 328875. BL, BN. 598/110

———. A treatise paraenetical . . . wherein is shewed . . . the right way . . . to resist the violence of the Castilian king . . . by a Pilgrim Spaniard . . . Translated out of the Castilian tongue into the French by J.d.Dralymont [i.e., Jean de Montlyard] . . . and now Englished. *London:* [*R.Field,for*] *W.Ponsonby,* 1598. 160p.;4to. Transl. from French version with

title *Traicte paraenetique*, 1st publ., Paris, 1597. Sabin 96752; STC 19838; Palau 328878. CSmH, CtY, DFo, InU-L, MH, RPJCB; BL.
598/111

Vecellio, Cesare. Habiti antichi, et moderni di tutto il mondo . . . Di nuovo accresciuti di molte figure. *Venice: The Sessas*, 1598. 507 numb.lvs;illus.;8vo. 'Degli habiti dell'America': lvs 488-507. 1st publ., Venice, 1590, without American material. Sabin 98732; Shaaber V66; JCB (3) I:368-369. DFo, ICN, MH, MiU, PU, RPJCB; BL, BN.   598/112

Veer, Gerrit de. Diarium nauticum, seu Vera descriptio trium navigationum admirandarum. *Amsterdam: C.Claeszoon*, 1598. 43 numb.lvs.;illus.,maps;fol. Transl. by Charles de L'Ecluse from the author's *Waerachtige beschryvinghe van drie seylagien* below. Tiele-Muller 95; Tiele 1130; Adams (Cambr.) V316; JCB (3) I:369. DLC. MnU-B, NN-RB, RPJCB; BL, BN.   598/113

——. Vraye description de trois voyages de mer tres admirables.. *Amsterdam: C.Claeszoon*, 1598. 44 numb.lvs.;illus.,maps;fol. Transl. from the author's *Waerachtighe beschryvinghe* below. Tiele-Muller 96; Tiele 1131; JCB (3) I:369. MiU-C, NN-RB, RPJCB(imp.); BL, BN.   598/114

——. Waerachtighe beschryvinghe van drie seylagien. *Amsterdam: C.Claeszoon*, 1598. 61 lvs;illus.,maps;obl.4to. Includes mention of Columbus, Cortés, Brazil, West Indies, etc. Tiele-Muller 93; Tiele 1129. NN-RB; BL, Amsterdam: NHSM.   598/115

——. Warhafftige relation der dreyen newen unerhörten, seltzamen Schiffart, so die holländischen und seeländischen Schiff gegen Mitternacht . . . verricht . . . erstlich in niderländischer Sprach beschrieben . . . jetzt aber ins Hochteutsch gebracht durch Levinum Hulsium. *Nuremberg:C. Lochner, for L.Hulsius*, 1598. 146p.;illus.,maps;4to. Transl. from the author's *Waerachtige beschryvinghe van drie seylagien . . . schepen*, of this year above. Hulsius's preface here includes as well refs to American exploration. Sabin 33655; Baginsky (German Americana) 107; Church 266; JCB (3) I:452-453. NN-RB, RPJCB; BL, BN.
598/116

Vega Carpio, Lope Félix de. La Dragontea. *Valencia: P.P.Mey*, 1598. 273p.;8vo. Poem on Sir Francis Drake's exploits in Spanish America. Sabin 98768; Medina (BHA) 388;

Palau 356313. BL, Madrid: BN.   598/117

Verheiden, Willem. In classem Xerxis Hispani oratio. Ad serenissimam Elisabetham Angliae Reginam. *The Hague: A.Henricszoon*, 1598. [70]p.;4to. Though the dedicatory epistle is dated 'Kal. Ianuar. M.D.LXXXIX.' this posthumous publication probably represents a pious act of the author's brother, whose life of Willem was reprinted by the same press in this year; cf. however an undated edn (or issue?) entered at Knuttel 859 under year 1589, for which a data of ca.1600 appears more probable. In praising the English for defeating the Spanish Armada, refs to Philip's American possessions and to Francis Drake occur. RPJCB; BL, BN.   598/118

Vigo, Giovanni. de. La prattica universale in cirurgia . . . Di nuovo ristampata, & ricorretta. *Venice: D.Imberti*, 1598. 558p.;illus.;4to. Includes in Italian translation the author's *Practica in arte practica copiosa*, 1st publ., Rome, 1514. DNLM; London: Wellcome.
598/119

Wateson, George. The cures of the diseased, in remote regions. *London: F.Kingston,for H.Lownes*, 1598. [28]p.;4to. From author's observations in Spain, describes disease designated 'tabardilla' (possibly yellow fever and/or typhus) as prevalent in both Indies; also mentioned are pineapples, manioc & tobacco. In this state the dedication is signed 'W.G.'. Sabin 103258; STC 25106. BL, Cambridge: UL.   598/120

—[Anr state]. *London: F.Kingston,for H. Lownes*, 1598. Dedication signed 'George Wateson'. Sabin 103258n; STC 25106a. BL.
598/121

Wytfliet, Corneille. Descriptionis Ptolemaicae augmentum, sive Occidentis notitia commentario illustrata, et hac secunda editio sui parte aucta. *Louvain: G.Rivius*, 1598. 191p.;maps;fol. 1st publ., Louvain, 1597. Sabin 105697; Borba de Moraes II:381; Koeman (Wyt) 2; Phillips (Atlases) 3645; JCB (3) I:370. DLC, MiU-C, NN-RB, RPJCB; BL, Brussels: BR.   598/122

Zamorano, Rodrigo. Cort onderwijs vande conste der seevaert . . . Overgeset uut den spaenschen . . . deur Martin Everart. *Amsterdam: C.Claeszoon*, 1598. 48 numb.lvs;illus.; 4to. Transl. from author's *Compendio del arte de navegar*, 1st publ., Seville, 1582. The 1598 edn recorded by Sabin (106246) and Medina (BHA 389) implying a Spanish text is in fact perhaps the present translation. Palau 379253. CtY; BL, Brussels: BR.   598/123

Zárate, Agustín de. Conqueste van Indien. De wonderlijcke ende warachtighe historie vant coninckrijck van Peru. *Amsterdam: C.Claeszoón,* 1598. 154 numb.lvs;map;4to. 1st publ. in this translation by R.de Bacquère, Antwerp,, 1563; here a paginary reprint of 1596 edn. Sabin 106257; JCB (3) I:370. RP-JCB.   598/124

1599

Abbot, George, Abp of Canterbury. A briefe description of the whole worlde. *London: T.Judson,for J.Brown,* 1599. 34 lvs;4to. Sabin 21n; STC 24; Ind.aur.100.079. CSmH, NN-RB; BL.   599/1

—[Anr edn]. *London: T.Judson,for J.Brown,* 1599. 32 lvs;4to. MiU-C.   599/2

Aguilar, Gaspar Honorato de. Fiestas nupciales que la cuidad y reyno de Valencia han hecho en el . . . casamiento del Rey don Phelipe . . . III . . . con doña Margarita de Austria. *Valencia: P.P.Mey,for A.Aguilar,* 1599. 335(ie., 135)p.;8vo. In verse. Included are numerous refs to persons & places in the New World. Ind.aur.101.933; Palau 3576. NNH.   599/3

Aldrovandi, Ulisse. Ornithologiae libri xii. *Bologna: G.B. Bellagamba,for F.dei Franceschi,* 1599-1603. 3v.;illus.,ports;fol. Included are American birds, e.g., Brazilian magpie (Pica brasilica). Ind.aur.103.119-120; Adams (Cambr.) A647. CtY, DLC, ICN, MB, MnU-B, NN-RB, PPAN; BL, BN.   599/4

Alemán, Mateo. Primera parte de Guzman de Alfarache. *Madrid: V.de Castro,* 1599. 256 numb.lvs;port.;4to. For the numerous scattered refs to America, see M.J.Gray, *An index to Guzmán de Alfarache* (New Brunswick, 1948). Medina (BHA) 392; Pérez Pastor (Madrid) 615; Ind.aur.103.141. MH, NNH; BL.   599/5

—[Anr edn]. *Barcelona: S.de Cormellas,for A.Tabano,* 1599. 207 numb.lvs;8 vo. Medina (BHA) 393; Ind.aur.103.142. CtY.   599/6

—[Anr issue of preceding]. *Barcelona: G.Graells & G.Dotil,* 1599. Ind.aur.103.142n; Palau 6670. NNH.   599/7

—[Anr edn]. *Saragossa: J.Pérez de Valdivielso, for J.Bonilla,* 1599. 206 numb.lvs;8vo. Sán-

chez (Aragon) 833; Ind.aur.103.143. Oxford: Bodl., Vienna: NB.   599/8

Alonso de la Veracruz. Speculum conjugiorum. Cum appendice. Nunc primum in Italia typis excusum. *Milan: Heirs of P.da Ponte,* 1599. 2 pts;4to. 1st publ., Mexico City, 1556, with here added the *Appendix,* 1st publ., Madrid, 1571. Medina (BHA) 403; Streit I:232; Shaaber A180. CU-L, PU; BL, Seville: BU.   599/9

Banchieri, Adriano. La nobiltà dell'asino, di Attabalippa dal Perù [pseud.]. *Venice: B. Barezzi,* 1599. 44 numb.lvs;illus.;4to. 1st (?) publ., [Bologna?], 1588; here a reissue of Barezzi's 1598 edn? Graesse I:247; Ind.aur. 112.139; Adams (Cambr.) B142. CU, CtY, ICN, NNC; BL, BN.   599/10

Bodin, Jean. Methodus ad facilem historiarum cognitionem, accurate denuo recusa. *Strassburg: L.Zetzner,* 1599. 550p.;8vo. 1st publ., Paris, 1566; here a reissue of Zetzner's 1598 edn? Ind. aur.120.865; Adams (Cambr.) B2246; Ritter (Strasbourg) 224. MH; BL. Strasbourg: BN.   599/11

——. Les six livres de la Republique . . . [*Geneva?*] *G.Cartier,* 1599. 8vo. 1st publ., Paris, 1576. Includes also Bodin's Paris, 1578, *Discours.* Ind.aur.120.864. CU, ICU, RPB; Munich: StB.   599/12

Bosso, Fabrizio, marchese. In funere Philippi . . . II. Hispaniarum regis, oratio. *Milan: P.da Ponte,* 1599. [32]p.;4to. Includes ref. to Spanish expansion in West Indies under Philip. Ind.aur.122.649; Adams (Cambr.) B2539. BL.   599/13

Botero, Giovanni. Diez libros de la Razon de estado . . . Traduzido de l'italiano . . . por Antonio de Herrera. *Barcelona: J.Cendrat,* 1599. 175 numb.lvs;8vo. 1st publ. in Spanish, Madrid, 1593. Ind.aur.122.740. CtY, DLC; BN.   599/14

——. Raison et gouvernement d'estat . . . traduicts sur la 4.e impression italienne . . . par Gabriel Chappuys. *Paris: G.Chaudière,* 1599. 347 numb.lvs;8vo. Includes both the Italian text, 1st publ., Venice, 1589, with title *Della ragion di stato,* and Chappuys's translation. Ind.aur.122.746; Adams (Cambr.) B2551; Shaaber B635. NN-RB, PU, RPB; Cambridge: UL, BN.   599/15

——. Relationi universali . . . novamente reviste . . . corrette, & ampliate dall'istesso auttore. *Brescia: Comp. Bresciana,* 1599. 4v.;fol. 1st publ., Rome, 1591-95. Cf.Sabin 6803n; Bor-

ba de Moraes I:100; Ind.aur.122.744; Adams
(Cambr.) B2559. MiU-C, ViU; BL, BN.

599/16

__[Anr edn]. *Venice: G.Angelieri,* 1599. 5v.;
maps; 4to. Ind.aur.122.748. DLC, ICN, NN-
RB, PPL; BN.　　　　　　　　　　599/17

Braun, Georg. Civitates orbis terrarum libri
sex. *Cologne: B.Buchholtz,* 1599[-1618]. 6v.;
illus.;maps;fol. 1st publ., Cologne, 1572. Ind.
aur.123.972; Moranti (Urbino) 681. ICN,
MH; Bonn: UB, Vienna: NB.　　　599/18

Bruneau, N., sieur de Rivedoux. Histoire
veritable de certains voiages perilleux et
hazardeux sur la mer. *Niort: T.Portau,* 1599.
212p.;12mo. Relates chiefly to voyages to Peru
& along its coast. Atkinson (Fr.Ren.) 397;
Ind.aur.125.560; Rép.bibl.IV:23. BL, BN.

599/19

Bry, Theodor de, comp. Americae achter
Theil. In welchem erstlich beschrieben wirt
das . . . Königreich Guiana . . . Alles mit
fleiss beschrieben durch . . . Walthern Ralegh
. . . und . . . Lorentz Keymis . . . Zum
andern die Reyse dess edlen . . . Thomas Can-
disch [i.e., Cavendish] . . . Durch Frantzen
Prettie . . . auffgezeichnet. Und zum dritten
die letzte Reyss der gestrengen Edlen . . .
Frantzen Draeck und Johan Hauckens . . .
Alles erstlich in engelländischer Sprach
aussgangen jetzt aber auss der holländischen
translation in die hochteutsche Sprache
gebracht durch Augustinum Cassiodorum.
*Frankfurt a.M.: M.Becker,for Widow & Heirs
of T.de Bry,* 1599. 160p.;illus.,map.;fol.
(Theodor de Bry's *America.* Pt 8. German).
Cf.Sabin 8784; Baginsky (German Amer-
icana)108; Church 194; JCB (3) I:405. CSmH,
DLC, ICN, MH, MiU-C, NN-RB, RPJCB;
BL, BN.　　　　　　　　　　　　599/20

____. Americae pars viii. Continens Primo,
Descriptionem trium itinerum . . . Francisci
Draken . . . Secundo, iter . . . Thomae Can-
disch [i.e., Cavendish] . . . Tertio, duo itinera
. . . Gualtheri Ralegh . . . redacta, & in
latinum sermonem conversa, auctore m.
Gotardo Artus. *Frankfurt a.M.: M.Becker,for
Widow & Heirs of T.de Bry,* 1599. 2
pts;illus.;fol. (Theodor de Bry's *America.* Pt
8. Latin). Transl. from a variety of English
sources. For variant issues see refs cited.
Cf.Sabin 8784; Church 163; JCB (3)
I:401-402. CSmH, DLC, ICN, MH, MiU-C,
NN-RB, RPJCB; BL, BN.　　　　599/21

Buttes, Henry. Dyets dry dinner. *London:*
T.Creed,for W.Wood, 1599. [242]p.;illus.;
8vo. Final section discusses tobacco, citing
American source. STC 4207; Ind.aur.128.
358; Arents 53. CSmH, CtY, MH, MiU,
NN-A; BL, Berlin: StB.　　　　　599/22

Capaccio, Giulio Cesare. Oratio in obitu
Philippi II. Hispaniarum regis. *Naples: G.G.
Carlino & A.Pace,* 1599. 40p.;4to. Included
are refs to Spanish America. Sabin 10721;
Ind.aur.131.445. BL, Rome: B.Casanatense.

599/23

Casas, Bartolomé de las, Bp of Chiapa. Newe
Welt. Warhafftige Anzeigung der Hispanier
grewlichen, abschewlichen und unmensch-
lichen Tyranny von ihnen in den Indianischen Ländern. [*Frankfurt a.M.:*] 1599.
158p.; illus.;4to. 1st publ. in German, 1597.
Sabin 11278 (erroneously dated, with title
from added engraved t.p.) & 11279 (plates);
cf.Medina 1085n (II:478-479); Baginsky (German Americana) 109; Streit I:237; Shaaber
C202; JCB (3) I:371-372. NN-RB, PU, RP-
JCB; BL.　　　　　　　　　　　599/24

Chapman, George. A pleasant comedy entituled: An humerous dayes myrth. *London:
V.Simmes,* 1599. [59]p.;4to. Includes ref. to
tobacco. STC 4987; Greg 159; Arents 54.
CSmH, CtY, DFo, ICN, MH, NN-RB; BL.

599/25

Cheyne, James. Cosmographia sive Geographia . . . Accessit gemmae Phrysii . . . de orbis
divisione, & insulis recenter inventis. *Douai:
B.Bellère,* 1599. 2 pts;illus.;8vo. 1st publ.,
Douai, 1576, under title *De geographia libri
duo.* RPJCB.　　　　　　　　　　599/26

Chiabrera, Gabriello. Rime, *Genoa: G.Pa-
voni,* 1599. 12mo. Included is a poem on Columbus, 1st publ. in the author's *Canzonette,*
Genoa, 1591. Cf.Sabin 12614n. BL.　599/27

Chytraeus, Nathan. Variorum in Europa
itinerum . . . Editio secunda. [*Herborn:*] *C.
Corvinus,* 1599. 654p.;8vo. 1st publ., Her-
born, 1594. Winship (Cabot) 75n; Adams
(Cambr.) C1623. DFo, ICU, MH, MiU-C,
NN-RB: BL.　　　　　　　　　　599/28

Davys, John. The seaman's secrets. *London:
T.Dawson,* 1599. 2 pts;illus.;4to. 1st publ.,
London, [1594?]. Sabin 18842; cf.STC 6369.
CSmH, DLC.　　　　　　　　　　599/29

Diago, Francisco. Historia de la provincia de
Aragon de la Orden de Predicadores.
Barcelona: J.Cendrat,for S.de Cormellas,
1599. 294 numb.lvs;fol. Includes accounts of
Dominicans in New World. Streit I:236;

Adams (Cambr.) D384; Palau 71627. CtY, NNUT; BL, BN. 599/30

Dos informaciones hechas en Japon: una de la hazienda que Taycosama . . . mandò tomar de la nao S.Felipe . . . yendo de las Filipinas à Nueva España. [*Madrid?* 1599?]. 49 lvs;fol. Medina (BHA) 396: Streit IV:1910; Palau 75776. 599/31

Du Bartas, Guillaume de Salluste, seigneur. Commentaires et annotations sur la Sepmaine [par Simon Goulart]. *Rouen:* [*T.Mallard,for*] *T.Reinsart,* 1599. 228 (i.e.,328) numb.lvs; 12mo. 1st publ. in this form, including text of *La sepmaine* itself, Geneva, 1581; here a re-issue of Mallard's 1597 edn. In verse. Holmes (DuBartas) I:86-87 no.12; Adams (Cambr.) D972. CSt, MH, NjP; Cambridge: Magdalene. 599/32

____. La divina settimana, cioè I sette giorni della creatione del mondo . . . Tradotta . . . del signor Ferrante Guisone . . . Quarta impressione ricoretta. *Venice: G.B.Ciotti,* 1599. 1st publ. in Italian, Tours, 1592. In verse. Holmes (DuBartas) I:109 no.19n. Paris: Sorbonne. 599/33

____. La seconde sepmaine. *Rouen:* [*T.Mallard,for*] *T.Reinsart,* 1599. 3pts;12mo. 1st publ., Paris, 1584; here a reissue of Mallard's 1596 edn. In verse. Jones (Goulart) 20(o); MH; Zurich: StB. 599/34

Gabelkover, Oswald. Artzneybuch. *Tübingen: G.Gruppenbach,* 1599. 2 pts;4to. 1st publ., Tübingen, 1589, under title *Nützlich Artzneybuch.* DNLM, NNBG. 599/35

____. The boock of physicke . . . translated out of High-duche by . . . Charles Battus [i.e., Carel Baten] . . . and now nuelye translated out of Low-duche . . . by A.M. *Dordrecht: I.Canin,* 1599. 393p.;fol. Transl. from author's *Medecyn-boeck,* 1st publ., Dordrecht, 1598, itself transl. from his *Artzneybuch,* 1st publ., Tübingen, 1589, under title *Nützlich Artzneybuch.* STC 11513; Arents (Add.) 111. CLU-M, CtY, DFo, MBCo, NN-A, PPC, WU; BL. 599/36

Garzoni, Tommaso. La piazza universale di tutte le professioni del mondo. *Venice: R.Meietti,&G.A.Bertano,* 1599. 958p.;4to. 1st publ., Venice, 1587. ICN, MiU, NNC; BL. 599/37

Gerard, John. Catalogus arborum, fruticum ac plantarum tam indiginarum quam exoticarum in horto Gerardi nascentium. *London: R.Robinson,* 1599. 22p.;fol. 1st publ.,

1596. Pritzel 3283n; STC 11749; Henrey (Brit.bot.) 153; Arents 56. DFo, MH-A, MiU, NN-A; BM(Nat.Hist.). 599/38

Gesner, Konrad. The practise of the new and old phisicke . . . Newly corrected and published in English, by George Baker. *London: P.Short,* 1599. 255 numb.lvs;illus.;4to. 1st publ. in English, London, 1576, under title *The newe jewell of health.* STC 11798. CSmH, CtY-M, DLC, MH, MnU; BL. 599/39

Gómara, Francisco López de. Historia dell'Indie Occidentali, overo Conquista della provincia di Ucatan . . . Tradotta . . . da Lucio Mauro. *Venice: B.Barezzi,* 1599. 402 numb.lvs;8vo. 1st publ. in Italian, Venice, 1566, as here translated. Sabin 27745; Wagner (SW) 2cc; Streit II:1153; JCB (3) I:376. CtY, DLC, MB, NN-RB, RPJCB; BL. 599/40

Goulart, Simon, comp. Le sixiesme et dernier recueil, contenant les chose plus memorables avenues sous la Ligue. [*Geneva?*] 1599. 723p.;8vo. Includes Antoine Arnauld's *Plaidoyé . . . pour l'Université de Paris,* 1st publ., Paris, 1594, and Alexandre de Pontaymeri's *Discours d'estat,* 1st publ., Paris & The Hague, 1595. Jones (Goulart) 30(b); Adams (Cambr.) F869. DLC, MH, MiU-C; BL, BN. 599/40a

Guevara, Diego. Exercitatio academia de aetate et qualitate ordinandorum. *Madrid: L.Sánchez,* 1599. 4to. Guevara was Mexican-born. Medina (BHA) 395. 599/41

Guicciardini, Francesco. La historia d'Italia. *Venice: G.Polo,* 1599. 2v.;4to. 1st publ., Florence, 1561. Adams (Cambr.) G1517. DFo, ICN, ViU; BL. 599/42

____. The historie of Guicciardin: containing the warres of Italie and other partes . . . Reduced into English by Geffray Fenton. *London: R.Field,* 1599. 943p.;fol. 1st publ. in English, London, 1579. STC 12459. CSmH, CtY, DLC, InU-L, MH, MiU, PPL, RPJCB; BL. 599/43

____. De oorlogen van Italien. *Dordrecht: I.Canin,* 1599. 588 numb.lvs;4to. Transl. from the author's *L'historia d'Italia,* 1st publ., Florence, 1561. BN. 599/44

Hakluyt, Richard. The principal navigations, voyages, traffiques and discoveries of the English nation. *London: G.Bishop, R.Newbery & R.Barker,* 1599. 2v.;fol. 1st publ., London, 1589. For the contents, sources, and detailed bibliographical analysis, etc., see *The*

Hakluyt Handbook, ed. by D.B. Quinn (London, 1974). Vol.1 is here a reissue, with cancel t.p., of 1598 edn. Sabin 29596-97; STC 12626; Church 322; Shaaber H10; JCB (3) I:372-374. CSmH, ICN, MB, MiU-C, MnU-B, NNC, PU, RPJCB; BL.   599/45

Hall, Joseph, Bp of Norwich. Virgidemiarum. The three last bookes of byting satyres. Corrected and amended with some additions. *London*: [*R.Bradock*] *for R.Dexter,* 1599. 55 lvs;8vo. 1st publ., London, 1598. STC 12719; Arents (Add.) 107. CSmH, CtY, DFo, IU, MH, NN-A; BL.   599/46

Heurne, Johan van. Praxis medicinae nova ratio . . . Recognita & emendata ab auctore. *Leyden: Plantin Press (C.Raphelengius),* 1599. 643p.;illus.;8vo. 1st publ., Leyden, 1587. Arents (Add.) 86. DNLM, NN-A; BL.
599/47

Houtman, Cornelis de. Kurtze warhafftige Beschreibung der newen Reyse oder Schiffart . . . Secunda editio. *Nuremberg: L.Hulsius,* 1599. 76p.;illus.,maps;4to. (Levinus Hulsius's *Sammlung von . . . Schiffahrten.* Pt 1). 1st publ. in this version, Nuremberg, 1598. Sabin 33653n; Church 257; JCB (3) I:450. CSmH, RPJCB.   599/48

Iñíguez de Lequérica, Juan, comp. Sermones funerales, en las honras del Rey . . . Felipe II. *Madrid: V.de Castro,* 1599. 332 numb.lvs;4to. Among the 15 sermons here publ. is that of Mexican-born Agustín Dávila Padilla. Medina (BHA) 370n; Pérez Pastor (Madrid) 650.   599/49

Langenes, Barent. Caert-thresoor, inhoudende de tafelen des gantsche werelts landen. *Amsterdam: C.Claeszoon,* 1599. 2v.;maps; obl.8vo. 1st publ., Middelburg, 1598. Sabin 9839n; Koeman (Lan) 2. DLC, MB, MiU-C.
599/50

La Noue, François de. Discourses politiques et militaires. *Basel: F.Forest,* 1599. 701p.; 16mo. 1st publ., Basel, 1587. MiU.   599/51

Léry, Jean de. Histoire d'un voyage fait en la terre du Bresil, dite Amerique . . . Quatrieme edition. [*Geneva:*] *Heirs of E.Vignon,* 1599. 478p.;illus.;8vo. 1st publ., [La Rochelle?], 1574. Sabin 40151; Borba de Moraes I:404; Atkinson (Fr.Ren.) 398; Arents (Add.) 112. NN-A; BL, BN.   599/52

Linschoten, Jan Huygen van. Dritter Theil Indiae Orientalis. *Frankfurt a.M.: M.Becker,for J.T.& J.I.de Bry,* 1599. 233p.;illus., maps;4to. (J.T.de Bry's *India Orientalis.* Pt 3.

German). Included also is Willem Lodewijcksz's *Der Holländer Schiffahrt in die Orientalische Insulen,* transl. from his *D'eerste boeck; Historie van Indien,* 1st publ., Amsterdam, 1598, with its refs to Brazil. Church 230; JCB (3) I:427. CSmH, MBAt, NN-RB, RPJCB; BL, BN.   599/53

____. Navigatio ac itinerarium . . . in Orientalem sive Lusitanorum Indiam. *The Hague: A.Henricszoon,for the author & C.Claeszoon at Amsterdam, & sold by G.Elzivir, The Hague,* 1599. 2pts;illus.,maps,port.;fol. Transl. from the *Itinerario, voyage ofte Schipvaert,* 1st publ. Amsterdam, 1596, with its accompanying *Reysgheschrift.* The 2nd pt, with speical t.p., *Descriptio totius Guineae tractus,* is a truncated translation of Linschoten's *Beschryvinghe van . . . Guinea* of that year. Sabin 43166 (& 19699); Borba de Moraes I:418; Tiele-Muller 92; Adams (Cambr.) L735; JCB (3) I:375. CtY, DLC, MH-A, MiU-C, NN-RB, PU, RPJCB; BL, BN.599/54

Luisini, Luigi. Aprodisiacus, sive De lue venerea. *Venice: B.Barezzi & Co.,* 1599. 756p.;fol. 1st publ. as here collected, Venice, 1566-67, under title *De morbo gallico,* including also Lorenz Fries's *Epitome* & U. von Hutten's *De Guaici medicina.* Benzing (Fries) 25; Benzing (Hutten) 110. BN.   599/55

Magnus, Olaus, Abp of Upsala. De gentibus septentrionalibus historia. *Amberg: M.Forster,* 1599. 592p.;12mo. 1st publ. as here condensed by C.Scribonio, Antwerp, 1558. Collijn (Sver.bibl.) III:309; Adams (Cambr.) M145. CtY, MH, MnU-B, NNC; BL.   599/56

____. De wonderlijcke historie vande noordersche landen. *Amsterdam: C.Claeszoon* [1599]. 302 numb.lvs;illus.,maps;8vo. Transl. from Magnus's *Historia de gentibus septentrionalibus,* 1st publ., Rome, 1555. Included also is an appendix in which Frobisher's search for a Northwest passage is described. Sabin 57106; Collijn (Sver.bibl.) III:291-294. NN-RB.   599/57

Mariz, Pedro de. Dialogos de varia historia em que sumariamente se referem muytas cousas antiguas de Hespanha. *Coimbra: A.de Mariz,* 1597 [i.e.,1599]. 388 numb.lvs;ports; 4to. 1st publ., Coimbra, 1584; here enlarged with added matter on Brazilian history. Colophon, verso of prel.lf 11: Acabouse de imprimir a segunda vez, esta primeyra parte dos Dialogos . . . a 8. dias de Abril de 1599. . . . Sabin 44608n; Borba de Moraes II:21; Anselmo 915; King Manuel 264. MH, MnU-B; Lisbon: BN. 599/58

—[Anr issue]. *Coimbra: A.de Mariz,* 1598 [i.e.,1599]. Sabin 44608n; Borba de Moraes II:21n; Anselmo 915n; Adams (Cambr.) M603; King Manuel 264n. MH; Cambridge: UL, BN. 599/59

Medina Rincón, Juan. Vida admirable de fr. Juan Bautista Moya, una de los primeros religiosos Augustinos de la Nueva España. *Salamanca:* 1599. 4to. Streit II:1154. 599/60

Meteren, Emanuel van. Belgische ofte Nederlantsche historie van onsen tijden. *Delft: J.C.Vennecool,* 1599. 433p.;ports;fol. 1st publ. in unauthorized German translation, Hamburg, 1596. Palau 166945; Adams (Cambr.) M1365. Cambridge: UL. 599/61

Nash, Thomas. Nashes lenten stuffe. *London:* [*T.Judson & V.Simmes*] *for N.L*[*ing*].*& C.B*[*urby*]., 1599. 75p.;4to. Includes refs to tobacco. STC 18370; Arents 57; Pforzheimer 764. CSmH, CtY, DFo, ICN, MH, NN-A; BL, BN. 599/62

Panciroli, Guido. Rerum memorabilium iam olim deperditarum: & contrà recens atque ingeniose inventarum: libri duo . . . italicè primùm conscripti, nec unquam hactenus editi: nunc . . . latinitate donati . . . per Henricum Salmuth. *Amberg: M.Forster,* 1599. 752p.;8vo. Transl. from ms. text of author's *Raccolta breve d'alcune cose più segnalate,* itself not publ. till 1612, at Venice. The 2nd vol. of the present edn appeared in 1602. Includes discussion of pearls, mentioning Columbus & tobacco. Cf.Sabin 58411; Adams (Cambr.) P139. CU, PPL, RPJCB; BL, BN. 599/63

Ptolemaeus, Claudius. Geografia . . . tradotta di greco . . . da Girolamo Ruscelli . . . et hora nuovamente ampliata da Gioseffo Rosaccio. *Venice: Heirs of M.Sessa,* 1599,'98. 3 pts;maps;4to. 1st publ. as ed. & transl. by Ruscelli, Venice, 1561; here a reissue, with altered imprint date, of 1598 edn. The 2nd pt, with special t.p. dated 1598, comprises Ruscelli's *Espositioni . . . sopra la Geografia di . . . Tolomeo.* Sabin 66507; Stevens (Ptolemy) 56; Phillips (Atlases) 409; Adams (Cambr.) P2237; JCB (3) I:376. CSmH, CtY, DLC, ICN, InU-L, MB, MiU-C, MnU-B, NN-RB, PPRF, RPJCB; BL, BN. 599/64

Quad, Matthias. Enchiridion cosmographicum: dass ist, Ein Handtbüchlin, der gantzen Welt gelegenheit. *Cologne: W.Lützenkirchen,* 1599. 266p.;illus.,maps;4to. Sabin 66890; Palmer 374. CtY, DLC, NN-RB; BL. 599/65

Rabelais, François. Les oeuvres. *Lyons: J. Martin,* 1599. 3pts;12mo. Plan (Rabelais) 116. CU-B, OCl; BL, BN. 599/66

—[Anr edn]. [*Paris?*]: *Heirs of Simon Jean,* 1599. Plan (Rabelais) 117. 599/67

Raleigh, Sir Walter. Brevis & admiranda descriptio regni Guianae, auri abundantissimi, in America, seu Novo Orbe. *Nuremberg: C. Lochner,for L.Hulsius,* 1599. 13p.;illus., map;4to. Transl. from publisher's German edn of this year. Sabin 67546 (& 33658); Church 281; JCB (3) I:457. CSmH, DLC, InU-L, MnU-B, NN-RB, RPJCB; BL. 599/68

——. Kurtze wunderbare Beschreibung. dess goldreichen Konigreichs Guianae in America, oder newen Welt. *Nuremberg: C.Lochner, for L.Hulsius,* 1599. 16p.;illus.,map;4to. (Levinus Hulsius's *Sammlung von . . . Schiffahrten.* Pt 5). Transl. from *The discoverie of . . . Guiana,* 1st publ., London, 1596. Sabin 67562 (&33658); Church 274; JCB (3) I:455. CSmH, MH, MnU-B, NN-RB, RPJCB; BL. 599/69

Reisch, Gregor. Margarita filosofica . . . Tradotta nuovamente dalla lingua latina . . . da Giovan Paolo Gallucci. *Venice: G.A.Somasco,* 1599. 1138p.;maps;4to. Transl. from author's *Margarita philosophica,* 1st publ., Strassburg, 1503. Sabin 69132. DLC, ICN, MH, NN-RB; BL. 599/70

—[Anr edn?]. *Venice: B.Barezzi,* 1599. 4to. Sabin 69132n; Brunet IV:1201. 599/71

Richeome, Louis. Trois discours pour la religion catholique . . . Reveus et augmentez en ceste troisiesme edition. *Bordeaux: S.Millanges,* 1599. 839p.;12mo. 1st publ., Bordeaux, 1597. Backer VI:1817; Rép.bibl.I:62. 599/72

Rivadeneira, Pedro de. Trattato della religione, e virtuti, che deve haver il principe christiano . . . tradotto per Scipioni Metelli. *Brescia: Comp. Bresciana,* 1599. 541p.;8vo. 1st publ. in Italian, Genoa, 1598. Backer VI:1735-1736; Palau 266340. ICN; BN. 599/73

——. La vie du r.p. Ignace de Loyola . . . nouvellement traduite du latin . . . et enrichie de plusieurs choses tirees du r.p. Pierre Maffée [par Pierre Guirand]. *Avignon: J.Bramereau,* 1599. 596p.;8vo. Edited & transl. from Latin text, 1st publ., Venice, 1586. Cf.Sabin 72499;

Rép.bibl.VI:55; Palau 266248; Shaaber R122. PU; BN. 599/73a

Rocamora, y Torrano, Ginés. Sphera del universo. *Madrid: J.de Herrera,* 1599. 271 numb.lvs;4to. Variant issues contain 8, 14 or 16 prelim. lvs. Sabin 72282; Medina (BHA) 398; Pérez Pastor (Madrid) 647; Adams (Cambr.) R626. CtY, DLC, InU-L, MnU-B, NN-RB, RPJCB; BL. 599/74

Rosaccio, Giuseppe. Le sei età del mondo. *Florence: F.Tosi,* 1599. 46p.;8vo. 1st publ., Brescia, 1593. ICN, NN-RB 599/75

____. Teatro del cielo e della terra. *Florence: F.Tosi,* 1599. 52p.;illus.;8vo. 1st publ., Brescia, 1592. Cf.Sabin 73198. DLC, RPJCB. 599/76

Saavedra Guzmán, Antonio. El peregrino indiano, poema de los hechos de Hernan Cortes. *Madrid: P.Madrigal,* 1599. 347 numb.lvs; port.;8vo. Sabin 29380; Medina (BHA) 399 (VI:517); Pérez Pastor (Madrid) 648; JCB AR28:20-21. MH, NNH, RPJCB; BL, BN. 599/77

Sánchez de Acre, Pero. Libro del reyno de Dios, y del camino por donde se alcança . . . aora nuevamente enriquezido con quatro libros. *Madrid: L.Sánchez,* 1599. 520 numb. lvs;4to. 1st publ., Madrid, 1594. Cf.Medina (BHA) 356; Backer VII:529; Pérez Pastor (Madrid) 654. BL, Madrid: BU(S.Isidro). 599/78

Satyre Ménippée. Satyre Menippee de la vertu du catholicon d'Espaigne . . . Derniere edition. Augmentée . . . de l'interpretation du mot de Higuiero d'infierno. [*Paris?*] 1599. 2v.;illus.;12mo. 1st publ., [Paris? 1594]. Adams (Cambr.) M449. CSt, DLC, NNC; Cambridge: UL. 599/78a

Schmidel, Ulrich. Vera historia, admirandae cuiusdam navigationis, quam Huldericus Schmidel . . . in Americam vel novum Mundum, juxta Brasiliam & Rio della Plata, confecit. *Nuremberg: [C.Lochner, for] L.Hulsius,* 1599. 101p.;illus.,map,port.;4to. Transl. from Schmidel's *Neuwe Welt,* 1st publ., Frankfurt a.M., 1567. Sabin 33659 (&77679); Church 274; JCB (3) I:455. CSmH, DLC, MH, MnU-B, NN-RB, RPJCB; BL, BN. 599/79

____. Verissima et jucundissima descriptio praecipuarum quarundam Indiae regionum & insularum . . . ex germanico . . . conversa autore m. Gotardo Artus. [*Frankfurt a.M.:*] *T.de Bry,* 1599. 60p.;illus.;fol. (Theodor de Bry's *America.* Pt 7. Latin). Transl. from Schmidel's *Neuwe Welt,* 1st publ., Frankfurt a.M., 1567. At head of title: Americae pars vii. Cf.Sabin 8784; Church 139; JCB (3) I:399. CSmH, DLC, ICN, MH, MiU-C, NN-RB, RPJCB; BL, BN. 599/80

____. Warhafftige Historien einer wunderbaren Schiffart . . . von Anno 1534, biss 1554 in Americam oder Newenwelt, bey Brasilia und Rio della Plata gethan. *Nuremberg: C.Lochner, for L.Hulsius,* 1599. 103p.;illus.,map, port.;4to. (Levinus Hulsius's *Sammlung von . . . Schiffahrten.* Pt 4). 1st publ., Frankfurt a.M., 1567. Sabin 33656; Borba de Moraes I:349; Church 271; JCB (3) I:454. CSmH, DLC, ICN, MH, NN-RB, RPJCB; BL. 599/81

____[Anr edn]. Warhafftige unnd liebliche Beschreibung etlicher fürnemmen Indianischen Landschafften und Insulen . . . an Tag gebracht durch Dieterich von Bry. [*Frankfurt a.M.:*] *T.de Bry,* 1599. 31 numb.lvs;fol. (Theodor de Bry's *America.* Pt 7. German). Cf.Sabin 8784 ; Church 191; JCB (3) I:399-400. CSmH, DLC, ICN, MH, MiU-C, NN-RB, RPJCB; BL, BN. 599/82

Het secreet des Conincx van Spaengnien, Philippus den tweeden, achterghelaten aen zijnen lieven sone Philips de derde . . . Int licht ghebrocht door . . . Rodrigo D.A., ende nu overgheset uyt den Spaenschen door P.A.P. [*Amsterdam?*] 1599. [7]p.;4to. Includes refs to Spanish control of West Indies. Authorship has been attributed to Willem Usselinx. Knuttel 1058. MiU-C (assigned to Felipe II, King of Spain); The Hague: KB. 599/83

Sermones predicados a las honras del Rey . . . Philipo Segundo este año de 1598. *Seville: F.Pérez,* 1599. 4 pts;4to. Comprises sermons by Aguilar de Terrones, A.Cabrera, Juan Bernal, & Mexican-born Agustín Dávila Padilla. Cf.Medina (BHA) 370n & 7746; Palau 309659 (misdated 1598). BL. 599/84

Serres, Jean de. Histoire des choses memorables avenues en France, depuis l'an M.D.XLVII. jusques au commencement de l'an M.D.XCII . . . Derniere edition. [*Geneva?*] 1599. 794p.;8vo. Under year 1566 is a brief ref. to Villegagnon. DeU, MH, NIC. 599/85

Tabourot, Estienne. Les bigarrures. *Lyons: J.Anard, for Heirs of B.Rigaud,* 1599. 89

lvs;8vo. In verse & prose. 1st publ., Paris, 1585. Baudrier (Lyons) III:453. CtY, DFo, ICN, MH; BL. 599/86

Tasso, Torquato. Il Goffredo, overo Gierusalemme liberata, poema heroico. *Venice: G.B.Ciotti,* 1599. 576p.;illus.;8vo. 1st publ. with American refs, Parma, 1581. Racc.Tassiana 179. CU, MH, NIC; BN, Bergamo: BC. 599/87

Torquemada, Antonio de. Jardin de flores curiosas. *Medina del Campo: C.Lasso Vaca, for J.Boyer,* 1599. 286 numb.lvs;8vo. 1st publ., Salamanca, 1570. In verse. Pérez Pastor (Medina del Campo) 244; Palau 334913. 599/88

Vargas Machuca, Bernardo de. Milicia y descripcion de las Indias. *Madrid: P. Madrigal,* 1599. 186 numb.lvs;illus.,port.; 4to. Sabin 98604; Medina (BHA) 402; Pérez Pastor (Madrid) 662; Adams (Cambr.) V271; JCB (3) I:377. DLC, MH, NN-RB, RPJCB; BL, BN. 599/89

Veer, Gerrit de. Tre navigationi fatte dagli Olandesi, e Zelandesi . . . Descritte in latino . . . e nuovamente da Giovan Giunio Parisio tradotte. *Venice: G.B.Ciotti,* 1599. 79 numb.lvs;illus.,maps;4to. Transl. from de Veer's *Diarium nauticum,* 1st publ., Amsterdam, 1598. Adams (Cambr.) V317; Mortimer (Italy) 521; JCB (3) I:377. DLC, MH, NN-RB, RPJCB; Cambridge: UL. 599/90

—[Anr issue]. *Venice:* [*G.B.Ciotti,for*] *G.Porro & Co.*. 1599. Mortimer (Italy) 521. DLC, MH, NN-RB; BL, BN. 599/91

____. Trois navigations admirables faictes par les Hollandois & Aelandois. *Paris: G.Chaudière,* 1599. 366p.;8vo. Prob. transl. from de Veer's *Waerachtighe beschrijvinghe van drie seylagien* below; a pirated edn. Cf.the author's Vray description of 1598. Cf.Tiele-Muller 96; Rothschild 1962; JCB (3) I:377. DLC, MnU-B, NN-RB, RPJCB; BL, BN. 599/92

____. Vraye description de trois voyages de mer. *Amsterdam: C.Claeszoon,* 1600. 44 numb. lvs.;illus.,maps;fol. 1st publ. in this version, Amsterdam, 1598. Tiele-Muller 97; Adams (Cambr.) V318. Cambridge: UL, BN. 599/93

____. Waerachtighe beschrijvinghe van drie seylagien. *Amsterdam: C.Claeszoon,* 1599. 61 numb.lvs.;illus.,maps;obl.4to. 1st publ., Amsterdam, 1598. Tiele-Muller 94; Tiele 1129n; JCB (3) I:378. MnU-B, RPJCB; Amsterdam: NHSM. 599/94

Vega Carpio, Lope Félix de. Fiestas de Denia, al Rey catholico Felippo III. *Valencia: D.de La Torre,for J.Mora,* 1599. 71p.;8vo. 'La rica Persia, Arabia, Tracia, Armenia/La India en tierra firme . . . /Quisieran ofrecer a su grandeça'—p.70. Palau 356315. BL, Valencia: BM. 599/95

Wright, Edward. Certaine errors in navigation. *London: V.Sims* [*& W.White*], 1599. 2 pts;illus.;4to. Included are numerous refs to the Americas. Sabin 105572; STC 26019. CtY, NN-RB, RPJCB; BL. 599/96

—[Anr issue]. *London:* [*V.Sims & W.White*] *for E.Aggas,* 1599. A reissue with cancel t.p. of the preceding. Sabin 105572n; STC 26019a. CSmH; Oxford: Magdalen. 599/97

1600

Abbot, George, Abp of Canterbury. A briefe description of the whole worlde. *London: R.B*[*arker?*].*, for J.Brown,* 1600. 32 lvs;4to. 1st publ., London, 1599. Sabin 21n; STC 25; Ind.aur.100.080. DFo, ICN, MH, NN-RB; BL. 600/1

Acosta, José de. Histoire naturelle et moralle des Indes . . . traduite en françois par Robert Regnault. Derniere edition, reveue & corrigee de nouveau. *Paris: M.Orry,* 1600. 375 numb.lvs;8vo. 1st publ. in French, Paris, 1598. Sabin 125n; Medina (BHA) 330n (I:501); Atkinson (Fr.Ren.) 403; Streit II: 1325; Adams (Cambr.) A127; Ind.aur.100. 469; Arents 51-a; JCB (3) II:3. DLC, MH-A, MiU-C, NN-A, RPJCB; BL, BN. 600/2

____. New Welt, das ist: Vollkommen Beschreibung von Natur, Art und gelegenheit der Newen Welt, die man sonst America oder West-Indien nennet. *Cologne: J.Christoffel,* 1600. 51p.;maps;fol. 1st publ. in German, Cologne, 1598, under title *Geographische . . . Beschreibung der . . . Landschafft America.* Sabin 129; Ind.aur.100.468; Palau 1995. Munich: StB, Vienna: NB. 600/3

Alemán, Mateo. Guzman d'Alfarache. Divisé en trois livres . . . Faict françois, par Gabriel Chappuys. *Paris: N.& P.Bonfons,* 1600. 2

pts;12mo. Transl. from Spanish text, 1st publ., Madrid, 1599. Ind.aur.103.152; Cioranescu (XVI) 6367; Palau 6737. Paris: Arsenal.   600/4

___[Anr issue]. *Paris: R.Ruelle,* 1600. Shaaber A161. PU.   600/5

___. Primera parte de la vida del picaro Guzman de Alfarache. *Barcelona: S.de Cormellas,* 1600. 207 numb.lvs;8vo. 1st publ., Madrid, 1599. Medina (BHA) 409; Palau 6680. NNH; BN.   600/6

___[Anr edn]. *Barcelona: G.Graells & G.Dotil,for J.Genoves,* 1600. 207 numb.lvs;8vo. Cf.printers' 1599 edn. Palau 6670n.   600/7

___[Anr edn]. *Brussels: J.Mommaert,* 1600. 207 numb.lvs;8vo. Peeters-Fontainas (Impr.esp.) 32; Palau 6676. MB; Cambridge: Emmanuel, Paris: Mazarine.   600/8

___[Anr issue of preceding]. *Brussels: J. Mommaert & R. Velpius,* 1600. Medina (BHA) 407; Peeters-Fontainas (Impr.esp.) 31; Palau 6679. NNH; BL, BN.   600/9

___[Anr edn]. *Coimbra: D.G.Loureiro,* 1600. 207 numb.lvs;8vo. Medina (BHA) 410; Anselmo 822; Palau 6673. NNH; BL, BN.   600/10

___[Anr edn]. *Lisbon: J.Rodrigues,for S.Carvalho,* 1600. 120 numb.lvs;4to. Cf.Medina (BHA) 411; Palau 6672.   600/11

___[Anr issue of preceding]. *Lisbon: J.Rodrigues,for L.Peres,* 1600. Cf.Medina (BHA) 411; Anselmo 1003; Palau 6674.   600/12

___[Anr edn]. *Madrid: V.de Castro,* 1600. 276 numb.lvs;12mo. Adams (Cambr.) A655; Palau 6675. MH, NNH; BL, BN.   600/13

___[Anr edn]. *Madrid: V.de Castro,* 1600. 207 numb.lvs;4to. A reissue of printer's 1599 edn, with altered imprint date? Adams (Cambr.) A652. BL.   600/14

___[Anr edn]. *Madrid: Heirs of J.Iñiguez de Lequérica,* 1600. 255 numb.lvs;port.;4to. Medina (BHA) 406; Palau 6677. NNH.
                                               600/15

___[Anr edn]. *Paris: N.Bonfons,* 1600. 288 numb.lvs;12mo. Medina (BHA) 408; Palau 6678.   600/16

Alvarado, Alfonso de. Artium differendi ac dicendi indissolubili vinculo junctarum, libri duo. *Basel: S.König,* 1600. 2 pts;4to. The author is said to have been born in Peru. Medina (BHA) 412; Ind.aur.104.021; Palau 9089. Berlin: StB.   600/17

Bejarano, Pedro. Resolucion breve cerca de las monedas que corren en la Isla Margarita.

Lisbon: P.Craesbeeck, 1600. 16 numb.lvs;4to. Medina (BHA) 413; Ind.aur.115.826; Palau 26468. MH, NNH.   600/18

Benzoni, Girolamo. Novae Novi Orbis historiae, id est, Rerum ab Hispanis in India Occidentali hactenus gestarum . . . libri tres, Urbani Calvetonis opera . . . ex italicis . . . latini facti. [*Geneva:*] *Heirs of E. Vignon,* 1600. 480p.;8vo. 1st publ. in Latin, [Geneva], 1586. Sabin 4794; Medina (BHA) 414; Streit II:1326; Ind.aur.117.001; Adams (Cambr.) B687; JCB (3) II:5. DLC, NN-RB, RPJCB, WU; BL, Geneva: BP.   600/19

Bertius, Petrus. Tabularum geographicorum contractum libri quatuor, cum luculentis singularum tabularum explicationibus. *Amsterdam: C.Claeszoon;for sale by J.Janszoon at Arnhem,* 1600. 646p.;maps;obl.4to. Incorporates maps 1st publ. in Barent Langenes's *Caert-thresoor,* 1st publ., Middelburg, [1598]. Sabin 5014n; Koeman (Lan) 4; Ind.aur.118.053; Adams (Cambr.) B821. CtY, MiU-C; BL, BN.   600/20

Bonardo, Giovanni Maria, conte. La grandezza, larghezza, e distanza. di tutte le sfere . . . Con alcune chiare annotationi . . . di Luigi Groto. [*Venice:*] *G.Zoppini & Bros,* 1600. 136 numb.lvs;port.;8vo. 1st publ. with Groto's annotations mentioning New World, Venice, 1584. Ind.aur.121.674; Adams (Cambr.) B2380. DLC, NjP, RPJCB; BL, BN.
                                               600/21

___. La minera del mondo . . . Mandata in luce . . . da Luigi Grotto. *Venice: G.Zoppini & Bros,* 1600. 112 numb.lvs;8vo. 1st publ., Venice, 1585. Ind.aur.121.675. BL, BN.
                                               600/22

Botero, Giovanni. Amphitheatridion. Hoc est, Parvum amphitheatrum. *Lübeck: L.Albrecht,* 1600. 106 lvs;4to. 1st publ., Cologne, 1596, under title *Mundus imperiorum.* Ind. aur.122.749; Streit I:242; Adams (Cambr.) B2545. MdBJ, RPJCB; BL, Copenhagen: KB.
                                               600/23

___. Le relationi universali. *Venice: G. Angelieri,* 1600. 5 pts;maps;8vo. 1st publ., Rome, 1591-95. Sabin 6803n; Ind.aur. 122.751; Streit I:241; JCB (3) II:5. CtY, RPJCB; Copenhagen: KB.   600/24

Bruneau, N., sieur de Rivedoux. Histoire veritable de plusieurs voyages adventureux, & perilleux, faits sur la mer. *Rouen: J.Osmont,* 1600. 101 lvs;12mo. 1st publ., Niort, 1599;

here enl. with refs to West Indies, Florida & Brazil. Sabin 94153; Atkinson (Fr.Ren.) 411. NN-RB; Paris: Arsenal. 600/25

—[Anr issue]. *Rouen: P.Calles,* 1600. Atkinson (Fr.Ren.) 411n. BN. 600/26

Canini, Angelo. De locis S.Scripturae hebraicis . . . commentarius . . . Accessit Gaspari Varrerii . . . de Ophira regione in sacris litteris disputatio. *Antwerp: Widow & Heirs of J. Bellère,* 1600. 250p.;8vo. Barreiros's work, discussing America as Ophir, 1st publ., Coimbra, 1561, in his *Chorographia.* Sabin 3596n; Ind.aur.131.042; Adams (Cambr.) C507. BL, BN. 600/27

—[Anr edn]. *Louvain: G.Rivius,* 1600. 8vo. Ind.aur.131.043. Brussels: BR. 600/28

Castillejo, Cristóbal de. Obras. *Madrid: A.Sánchez,for P.de LaTorre,* 1600. 438 numb.lvs;8vo. 1st publ., Madrid, 1573. Pérez Pastor (Madrid) 679; Palau 48018. NNH; BN, Madrid: BN. 600/29

Clavius, Christoph. In Sphaeram Joannis de Sacro Bosco commentarius. *Lyons:* 1600. 4to. 1st publ., Rome, 1570. Backer II:1213.

600/30

Conestaggio, Girolamo Franchi di. The historie of the uniting of the kingdom of Portugall to the crowne of Castill. *London: A.Hatfield,for E.Blount,* 1600. 374p.;fol. Transl. by Edward Blount from author's *Dell'unione del regno di Portogallo,* 1st publ., Genoa, 1585. STC 5624. CSmH, CtY, DLC, ICN, InU-L, MH, MiU, MnU-B, NN-RB, RPCJB; BL. 600/31

——. L'union du royaume de Portugal à la couronne de Castille . . . prise de l'italien . . . par m. Th. Nardin. *Arras: G.Bauduin,* 1600. 591p.;8vo. 1st publ. in French, Besançon, 1596. BL, BN. 600/32

Dekker, Thomas. The pleasant comedie of Old Fortunatus. *London: S.S[tafford]. for W. Aspley,* 1600. 4to. Includes refs to tobacco. STC 6517; Pforzheimer 277; Greg 162; Arents (Add.) 113. CSmH, DFo, MH, NN-A; BL. 600/33

Du Bartas, Guillaume de Salluste, seigneur. Hadriani Dammanis a Bysterveldt . . . Bartasias; qui de mundi creatione libri septem; liberius tralati et acuti [!]. *Edinburgh: R.Waldegrave,* 1600. 112 (i.e., 312) p.;8vo. Transl. from author's *La sepmaine,* 1st publ., Paris, 1578. In verse. Holmes (DuBartas) I:107 no.6; STC 21657. CSmH, DFo, IU; BL, BN. 600/34

Duchesne, Joseph. Sclopetarius, sive De curandis vulneribus. *Lyons* [i.e.,*Geneva*]:*J. Lertout,* 1600. 209p.;8vo. (His *Opera medica,* v.2). 1st publ., Lyons [i.e., Geneva], 1576. DNLM. 600/35

Durante, Castore. Il tesoro della sanita. *Venice: Heirs of G.M.Leni,* 1600. 302p.;8vo. 1st publ., Rome (?), 1586. DNLM, MH-A; BL. 600/36

Estienne, Charles. L'agriculture et maison rustique, de mm. Charles Estienne et Jean Liebault. *Rouen: R.de Beauvais,* 1600. 394 numb.lvs;illus.;4to. 1st publ., Paris, 1567. Thiébaud (La chasse) 350-351. 600/37

—[Anr issue]. *Rouen: J.Osmont,* 1600. Thiébaud (La chasse) 350-351. 600/38

——. Maison rustique, or The countrie farme. Compiled in the French tongue by Charles Stevens and John Liebault . . . And translated . . . by Richard Surflet. *London: E.Bollifant,for B.Norton,* 1600. 901p.;illus.;4to. Transl. from *La maison rustique,* 1st publ., Paris, 1567. Thiébaud (La chasse) 357; STC 10547; Arents 58. CSmH, CtY, DFo, IU, MH, MnU-B, NN-RB, PPAN; BL. 600/39

Falloppius, Gabriel. Opera omnia. *Frankfurt a.M.: Heirs of A.Wechel, C.de Marne,& J. Aubry,* 1600. 2v.;fol. 1st publ. as here collected, Venice, 1584. DNLM; London: Wellcome, BN. 600/40

Fragoso, Juan. Aromatum, fructuum, et simplicium aliquot medicamentorum ex India utraque, et Orientali et Occidentali, in Europam delatorum . . . historia brevis . . . Nunc latine edita opera . . . Israelis Spachii. *Strassburg: J.Martin,* 1600. 115 numb.lvs;8vo. Transl. from Fragoso's *Discursos de las cosas aromaticas,* 1st publ., Madrid, 1572. Sabin 25418 (& 26005); Medina (BHA) 415; Pritzel 3000n. BL. 600/41

Freigius, Johann Thomas. Historiae synopsis, seu Praelectionum historicarum in Altofiano Noribergensium gymnasio delineatio. *Basel: S.Henricpetri,* 1600. 102p.;8vo. 1st publ., Basel, 1580. BN. 600/42

Genebrard, Gilbert, Abp of Aix. Chronographiae libri quatuor . . . Posteriores, e d. Arnaldi Pontaci Chronographia aucti . . . Emendatum, adauctum etiam cum appendice per Petrum Victorem Palmam Cajetanum. *Paris: G.Chaudière,* 1600. 3 pts in 1 v.;fol. 1st publ., Paris, 1567; Palma Cayet's Appendix contains ref. to Sir Francis Drake's seizure of

Cartagena. Adams (Cambr.) G400. MH; Cambridge: UL. 600/43

Gesner, Konrad. Quatre livres des secrets de medecine. *Rouen: P.Calles,* M.VI.C. [i.e., 1600?]. 352p.;illus.;4to. 1st publ. in French, Paris, 1573. IaAS. 600/44

———. Vogelbuch . . . Nachmals aber durch Rudolff Heusslein in hoch teutsch versetzt. *Frankfurt a.M.: J.Sauer, for Heirs of R.Cambier,* 1600. 556p.;illus.;fol. 1st publ., Zurich, 1557. Nissen (Birds) 351. CtY, ICJ, NIC; BL. 600/45

Giglio, Girolamo. Nuova seconda selva di varia lettione, che segue Pietro Messia. *Venice: The Guerras,* 1600. 198 numb.lvs;8vo. 1st publ., Venice, 1565. Adams (Cambr.) G608. Cambridge: UL. 600/46

Gilbert, William. De magnete, magneticisque corporibus. *London: P.Short,* 1600. 240p.;illus.;fol. The preface, by Edward Wright, contains refs to Sir Francis Drake, Thomas Cavendish, etc. Sabin 27356; STC 11883; JCB AR46:27-31. CSmH, CtY, DLC, IU, InU-L, MH, MiU, MnU-B, NN-RB, PPAN, RPJCB; BL. 600/47

González de Mendoza, Juan, Bp. Histoire du grand royaume de la Chine . . . ensemble un itineraire du nouveau monde, & le descouvrement du nouveau Mexique en l'an 1583 . . . mise en françois avec des additions . . . par Luc de la Porte. *Paris: Widow of G.Buon,* 1600. 308 numb.lvs;8vo. 1st publ in French, Paris, 1588. Sabin 27780n (&32009); Atkinson (Fr.Ren.) 409n. BN. 600/48

—[Anr issue]. *Paris: A.L'Angelier,* 1600. Sabin 32009; Wagner (SW) 7ee; Atkinson (Fr.Ren.) 409; Adams (Cambr.) G867. Cambridge: UL, Paris: Mazarine. 600/49

—[Anr issue]. *Paris: A.Périer,* 1600. Wagner (SW) 7ff. DLC, InU-L, MiU, NN-RB. 600/50

Goulart, Simon. Histoires admirables et memorables de nostre temps. Recueillies de plusieurs autheurs, memoires & avis de divers endroits . . . Premier livre. *Paris: J.Houzé,* 1600. 155 numb.lvs;12mo. Includes scattered refs to New World, derived from a variety of sources. For subsequent 2nd & 3rd pts, see the year 1601. Jones (Goulart) 54a. BN. 600/50a

Hakluyt, Richard. The third and last volume of the voyages, navigations, traffiques, and discoveries of the English nation . . . to all parts of the newfound world of America, or the West Indies. *London: G.Bishop, R.New-*bery & R.Barker, 1600. 868p.;map;fol. For the prior 2 vols, see the years 1598 & 1599. Sabin 29598; STC 12626; Arents (Add.) 94; Church 322; Shaaber H10; JCB (3) I:374; JCB AR29:23-25. CSmH, DLC, ICN, MH, MiU-C, NN-RB, PU, RPJCB; BL, BN. 600/51

Honter, Johannes. Rudimentorum cosmographicorum . . . libri iii . . . Quibus nunc primum accesère Instructiones de sphaera mundi . . . Universalis item chronici compendium novum: ab initio scilicet mundi, in praesentum usque annum . . . Opera Matthiae Quadi. *Cologne: W.Lützenkirchen,* 1600. 220p.; 8vo. 1st publ. in this version, Kronstadt, 1542. In verse. Borsa 98; Szabo 945. DLC. 600/52

Jonson, Ben. The comicall satyre of Every man out of his humor. *London: [A.Islip] for W.Holme,* 1600. 68 lvs;4to. Contains mentions of tobacco & its Cuban source & of French pox. STC 14767; Greg 163 (a). CSmH, MB; BL. 600/53

—[Anr edn]. *London: [P.Short] for W.Holme,* 1600. 64 lvs;4to. STC 14768; Greg 163(b). London: V.& A., Oxford: Bodl. 600/54

—[Anr edn]. *London: N.Linge,* 1600. [128]p.; 4to. Prob. printed later than 1600. STC 14769; Greg 163(c); Arents 59. CSmH, CtY, DFo, MH, NN-A; BL. 600/55

La Boétie, Etienne de. La mesnagerie de Xenophon . . . mise en lumiere avec quelques vers françois et latins. *Paris: C.Morel,* 1600. 131 numb.lvs;8vo. 1st publ., Paris, 1571; here a reissue of that edn with cancel t.p. BN. 600/56

Langenes, Barent. Thresor de chartes, contenant les tableaux de tous les pays du monde. *The Hague: A.Henricszoon, for C.Claeszoon at Amsterdam* [1600?]. 2 pts;illus.,maps;obl. 8vo. Transl. by Jean de La Haye from Langenes's *Caert-thresoor,* 1st publ., Middelburg, [1598]. Sabin 95757; Atkinson (Fr.Ren.) 408; cf.Tiele 225; Koeman (Lan) 6; Phillips (Atlases) 415. DLC, MH, NNH; Amsterdam: UB. 600/57

Leo Africanus, Joannes. A geographical historie of Africa, written in Arabicke and Italian . . . Translated and collected by John Pory. *London: [Eliot's Court Press, for] G.Bishop,* 1600. 420p.;map;fol. Supplementary text, derived from Ramusio, includes ref. to Portuguese slave trading with West Indies. Sabin 40047; STC 15481; JCB (3) II:6. CSmH,

CtY, DLC, ICN, MH, MnU, NN-RB, PBL. RPJCB; BL.   600/58

Léry, Jean de. Histoire d'un voyage fait en la terre de Bresil, dite Amerique. [*Geneva:*] *Heirs of E.Vignon,* 1600. 478p.;illus.;8vo. 1st publ., La Rochelle, 1578; here a reissue of 1599 edn with altered imprint date. Sabin 40152n; Borba de Moraes I:404; Atkinson (Fr.Ren.) 398; JCB (3) II:7. DLC, MH, NN-RB, RPJCB; BL, Paris: Mazarine.   600/59

Liscovinus, Vincentius. De lue venerea. *Basel:* 1600. Proksch I:83.   600/60

Maiolo, Simeone, Bp of Volturara. Dies caniculares; hoc est Colloquia tria et viginti. *Oberursel: C.Sutor,for J.T.Schönwetter,* 1600. 824p.;4to. 1st publ., Rome, 1597. Cf.Sabin 44056; Brunet III:1323. BL.600/60a

Matal, Jean. America, sive Novus Orbis, tabulis aeneis secundum rationes geographicas delineatus. *Cologne: S.Hemmerden,* 1600. 52 lvs;maps;fol. Sabin 48170. MH, NN-RB.
600/61

Mattioli, Pietro Andrea. Kreutterbuch . . . zum dritten mal . . . gemehret . . . durch J.Camerarium. *Frankfurt a.M.: Z.Palthenius,for J.Rosa,* 1600. 460 numb.lvs;illus.;fol. 1st publ., Frankfurt, 1586. Pritzel 5990n; Nissen (Bot.) 1311n; Shaaber M199. DNAL, MH-A, PU-D.   600/62

Memorial del hecho, cerca de la hoia de la minuta del testamento de don Christoval Colon. [*Madrid?* ca.1600?]. 25 lvs;fol. Sabin 14659; Palau 161695. BL.   600/63

Montaigne, Michel Eyquem de. Essais . . . édition nouvelle prise sur l'exemplaire trouvé après le deceds de l'autheur. *Paris: A.L'Angelier,* 1600. 1166p.;8vo. 1st publ., Bordeaux, 1580; 1st publ. with author's annotations, Paris, 1595. A reissue or perhaps paginary reprint of 1598 edn. Tchémerzine VIII:410. CU-A, ICN, MH, MiU; BL, BN.   600/64

Neck, Jacob Corneliszoon van. Journael ofte Dagh-register, inhoudende een waerachtigh verhael ende historische vertellinghe vande reyse, ghedaen door de acht schepen van Amsterdamme. *Amsterdam: C.Claeszoon* [1600]. 42 numb.lvs;illus.;obl.4to. Includes refs to Brazil, Lima, and tobacco from the West Indies. Tiele-Muller 123; Tiele 781; Muller (1872) 2210. NN-RB.   600/64a

Nuova raccolta di tutte le piu illustri et famose citta di tutto il mondo. *Venice: D.Rasicoti* [ca.1600?]. 160 pls;fol. Copper-plate views,

signed in part by Francesco Valesio. Included are views of Cuzco & Mexico City. Cf. Phillips (Atlases) 5390. RPJCB.   600/65

Oñate, Alonso de. Paracer de un hombre docto . . . de muchos años de experiencia en las cosas de las Indias, cerca del servicio personal de los Indios del Piru y Nueva España. [*Madrid?* 1600]. 11 numb.lvs;fol. Sabin 57305; Medina (BHA) 6691; Palau 201630; JCB (3) II:7. RPJCB.   600/66

Outgherszoon, Jan. Niewe, volmaeckte beschryvinghe der vervaerlijcker Strate Magellani. *Amsterdam: H.de Buck,for Z.Heyns* [1600]. [23]p.;illus.,maps;obl.4to. Issued with B.J. Potgieter's *Wijdtloopigh verhael* of this year. Sabin 57952 (& 22584); Tiele-Muller 11b; JCB (3) II:8. CSmH, NN-RB; RPJCB.   600/67

Pasini, Antonio. Annotationi, & emendationi nella tradottione dell'ecc. P. Andrea Matthioli de' cinque libri Della materia medicinale di Dioscoride Anazerbeo . . . Seconda edizione. *Bergamo: C.Ventura,for Heirs of T.Bozzola,* 1600. 252p.;4to. 1st publ., Bergamo, 1591. Cf.Pritzel 6964. CtY-M, DNLM.   600/68

Pons, Jacques. In Historiam generalem plantarum Rouillii . . . breves annotationes & animadversiones compendiosae. *Lyons: J.Pillehotte,* 1600. 59p.;8vo. The work here annotated is that of Jacques Dalechamps, 1st publ., Lyons, 1586. Pages 41-51 mention American plants. Pritzel 7263; Baudrier (Lyons) II:361; DNLM, MH-A, PPL, RPJCB; BL.   600/69

Potgieter, Barent Janszoon. Wijdtloopigh verhael van tgene de vijf schepen (die int jaer 1598. tot Roſterdam toegherust werden, om door de Straet Magellana haren handel te dryven) wedervaren is, tot den 7. September 1599. *Amsterdam: H.de Buck,for Z.Heyns* [1600]. [68]p.;illus.,maps;obl.4to. With this was issued J.Outgherszoon's *Nieuwe, volmaeckte beschryvinghe der vercaerlijcker Strate Magellani* of this year. Sabin 64581; Tiele-Muller 11a. MH, NN-RB, RPJCB.
600/70

Quad, Matthias. Compendium universi complectens geographicarum enarrationum libros sex. *Cologne: W.Lützenkirchen,* 1600. 714p.; 8vo. Cf.Quad's *Enchiridion cosmographicum,* Cologne, 1599. Section on America occupies p.590-665. Sabin 66889; Adams (Cambr.) Q4. DLC, IU, RPJCB; Cambridge: UL, BN.
600/71

_____. Geographisch Handtbuch, in welchem die Gelegenheit der vornembsten Lantschafften des gantzen Erdtbodems in . . . Taffeln furgebildt, mit beygefügter notwendiger Beschreibung und Auslegung derselben. *Cologne: J.Bussemacher*, 1600. [328]p.;maps; fol. Sabin 66894; Phillips (Atlases) 411; Baginsky (German Americana) 113. DLC, ICN, MnHi, NN-RB; BL, BN.   600/72

Rabelais, François. Les oeuvres. *Lyons: J. Martin*, 1558 [i.e.,ca.1600?]. 3 pts;12mo. Includes 'Le quart livre', 1st publ., Paris, 1552. Plan (Rabelais) 95. DFo; BN.   600/73

_____[Anr edn]. *Lyons: J.Martin*, 1558 [i.e., ca.1600?]. 3 pts;8vo. Plan (Rabelais) 96; Adams (Cambr.) R6. CtY, DNLM, MH; Cambridge: Christ's, Paris: Ste Geneviève.   600/74

_____[Anr issue?]. *Lyons: J.Martin*, 1600. 3 pts; 12mo. Plan (Rabelais) 118. DFo, DNLM, OCl.   600/75

Richeome, Louis. Trois discours pour la religion catholique. *Paris: P.Bertault*, 1600. 626p.;8vo. 1st publ., Bordeaux, 1597. Backer VI:1817. BN.   600/76

_____[Anr issue]. *Rouen: T.Reinsart*, 1600. RP-JCB; BN.   600/77

Rivadeneira, Pedro de. Vita del p. Francesco Borgia . . . Tradotta dalla lingua spagnuola dal commendatore F.Giulio Zanchini. *Florence: M.Sermatelli*, 1600. 294p.;fol. Transl. from author's *Vida del padre Francisco de Borja*, 1st publ., Madrid, 1592. Backer VI: 1734; Palau 266317. CtY, RPJCB.   600/78

_____. Zywot Bl. Oyca Ignacego Lojoli. [*Cracow?*] 1600. 'Par le p. Sim. Wysocki'—Backer. Backer VI:1731; Palau 266247.   600/79

Romancero general. Romancero general, en que se contienen todos los romances . . . en las nueve partes de romanceros. *Madrid: L.Sánchez,for M.Martínez*, 1600. 368 numb.lvs;4to. In verse. Based upon the *Flor de romances*, 1st publ., Lisbon, 1593. Included are scattered refs to the Indies, esp. Chile. Pérez Pastor (Madrid) 715; Palau 276978. CaBVaU, NNH.   600/80

Rowlands, Samuel. The letting of humors blood in the head-vaine. *London: W.White for W.F[erbrand].*, 1600. 4to. In verse. Includes adverse comments on tobacco. Post-1600 edns have title *Humors ordinarie*, etc. STC 21392.7. Oxford: Bodl.   600/81

_____[Anr edn]. *London: W.White for W.F[er-brand].*, 1600. 8vo. STC 21393 ('In title: "humours"; B2ʳ line 4: "feeelde" [sic].'). Oxford-Bodl.   600/82

_____[Anr edn]. *London: W. White for W. F[erbrand].*, 1600. 8vo. STC 21393.5 ('In title: "humours"; B2ʳ line 4: "fielde" '). BL.   600/83

Sassonia, Ercole. Tractatus triplex . . . Accessit ejusdem doctrina . . . De lue venerea, seu morbo gallico. *Frankfurt a.M.: S.Latomus,for J.T.Schonwetter*, 1600. 344p.;8vo. The 'De lue venerea' 1st publ., Padua, 1597. Cf.Proksch I:20; Adams (Cambr.) S536. BL, BN.   600/84

Satyre Ménippée. Satyre Menippee de la vertu de catholicon d'Espaigne . . . Derniere edition. Augmentée . . . de l'interpretation du mot de Higuiero d'infierno. [*Paris?*] 1600. [288]p.;illus.;12mo. 1st publ., [Paris? 1594]. Adams (Cambr.) M450. MH; Cambridge: Clare.   600/85

Serres, Jean de. Historia, oder Eigentliche warhaffte Beschreibung aller gedenckwirdigen Sachen die sich . . . von dem Jahr an 1547. biss zu Anfang des 1597. Jahrs . . . zugetragen. Newlich . . . in die teutsche Sprach . . . gebracht durch J.R.V.S. *Mümpelgart: J.Foillet*, 1600. 1056p.;8vo. Transl. from author's *Histoire des choses memorables avenues en France*, 1st publ., [Geneva?], 1599, with brief ref. to Villegagnon's attempted Brazil colony. BN.   600/86

_____. Inventaire general de l'histoire de France . . . jusques à present [13 septembre 1598]. *Paris: A.Saugrain & G.de Rues*, 1600. 8v.;8vo. An earlier, 1597, edn reached only the year 1422. Said here to have been continued by Jean de Montlyard. Under year 1555 is a brief ref. to Villegagnon's attempted Brazil colony. DFo, IU, NNC; BL, BN.   600/87

Spain. Sovereigns, etc., 1504-1516 (Ferdinand V). Carta del Rey Catholico a Pedra [sic] Arias Davila governador de Castilla del Oro, par la qual se conocera si pudo cortar la cabeça a su yerno el Adelantado Basco Nuñez de Balboa. [*Madrid? ca.1600?*]. 3p.; fol. Sabin 56338; Medina (BHA) 6327. 600/88

Tabourot, Estienne. Les bigarrures. *Lyons: J.Anard,for B.Rigaud*, 1600. In prose & verse. 1st publ., Paris, 1585. Baudrier (Lyons) III:454.   600/89

Tasso, Torquato. Godfrey of Bulloigne, or The recoverie of Jerusalem. Done into English heroicall verse, by Edward Fairefax. *London: A.Hatfield,for J.Jaggard & M. Lownes*, 1600. 392p.;fol. Transl. from Tasso's *Gerusalemme liberata*, 1st publ., with refs to Columbus, Parma, 1581. Racc.Tassiana 856; STC 23698; Shaaber T92. CSmH, CtY, DFo, ICN, MH, NN-RB, PU; BL, BN. 600/90

____. Goffredo, overo Gierusalemme liberata, poema heroico. *Venice: Heirs of F.dei Franceschi*, 1600. 2 pts;4to. 1st publ. with American refs, Parma, 1581. Racc.Tassiana 180; Shaaber T91. PU; Bergamo: BC. 600/91

—[Anr edn]. *Venice: G.B.Ciotti*, 1600. 2 pts; 4to. Racc.Tassiana 181. Bergamo: BC.600/92

Torquemada, Antonio de. Giardino di fiori curiosi, in forma di dialogo . . . tradotto di spagnuolo . . . per Celio Malespina. *Venice: G.B.Ciotti*, 1600. 208 numb.lvs;8vo. 1st publ. in Italian, Venice, 1590; cf.Ciotti's 1597 edn, of which this is perhaps a reissue. Cf.Palau 334923. RPJCB. 600/93

____. The Spanish Mandevile of miracles. Or the garden of curious flowers. *London: J. R[oberts].for E.Matts*, 1600. 158 numb.lvs; 4to. Transl. by Lewis Lewkenor, as ed. by Ferdinand Walker, from author's *Jardin de flores curiosas*, 1st publ., Salamanca, 1579. Palau 334927; STC 24135. CSmH, DLC, MH, NN-RB; BL. 600/94

Torres, Pedro de. Libro que trata de la enfermedad de las bubas. *Madrid: L.Sánchez*, 1600. 114p.;4to. Proksch I:21; Medina (BHA) 416; Pérez Pastor (Madrid) 720. DNLM; BL, BN. 600/95

Vargas Machuca, Bernardo de. Libro de exercicios de la gineta. *Madrid: P.Madrigal*, 1600. 121p.;8vo. On use of lance as developed in New World. Medina (BHA) 418; Pérez Pastor (Madrid) 722; Palau 352447. RPJCB; BL, BN. 600/96

Vaughan, William. Naturall and artificial directions for health. *London: R.Bradocke*, 1600. 46 lvs;8vo. Includes section on medicinal use of tobacco. STC 24612; Arents 60. NN-A; BL. 600/97

Velasco, Luis de. Las capitulaciones que el Virrey Don Luys de Velasco hizo con Don Juan de Oñate, Governador y Capitangeneral de las provincias de la Nueva Mexico en conformidad de las ordenanças reales para semejantes descubrimientos. [*Madrid?* 1600?]. [10]p.;fol. Sabin 98794; Wagner (SW) 11. Seville: Archivo de Indias. 600/98

Verheiden, Willem. In classem Xerxis Hispani oratio. *The Hague: A.Henricszoon* [ca.1600?]. [70]p.;4to. 1st (?) publ., The Hague, 1598. Though entered by Knuttel as a 1589 work on the basis of the dedication date, the printer is not found at The Hague prior to 1591; that this is a subsequent edn or impression with imprint date deleted seems probable. Knuttel 859. The Hague: KB. 600/99

Addenda

John, Prester. Botschafft des grossmechtig- sten konigs David, auss dem grossen und ho- hen Morenland. [*Bonn?* 1533?]. [38]p.;4to. Transl. from the *Legatio David Aethiopiae regis* (Bologna, 1533), itself lacking American refs but here supplemented by letter written from Mexico by Juan de Zumárraga, publ., Toulouse, 1532, in Antonio de Olave's *Passio gloriosi. . . Andree de Spoleto.* Sabin 106399; Harrisse (BAV) 177; Medina (BHA) 87n (I:135); Streit II:311; JCB (3) I:107. NN-RB, RPJCB; BL.   A533/1

__[Anr edn]. Bottschaft des grossmechtigsten konig David. *Dresden: W.Stoeckel*, 1533. [26]p.;4to. DLC, MnU-B, NN-RB.   A533/2

Bonsi, Lelio. Cinque lezioni . . . lette . . . publicamente nella Accademia fiorentina. *Florence: The Giuntas*, 1560. 112 numb.lvs; 8vo. On lvs 56, 57 & 66 refs to Columbus, Vespucci & Verrazzano appear. Ind.aur.122. 172. CtY, DFo, ICN, NN-RB, PU, RPJCB; BL, BN.   A560/1

Heresbach, Conrad. Rei rusticae libri qua- tuor. *Cologne: J.Birckmann*, 1570. 391 numb. lvs;8vo. In bk 4, on poultry, section 'De In- dicis avibus' describes turkey, said to have been unknown prior to 1530. DFo, MH, NN- RB, PPAmP; BL.   A570/1

Heresbach, Conrad. Rei rusticae libri qua- tuor. *Cologne: J. Birckmann*, 1571. 391 numb. lvs;illus.;4to. 1st publ., Cologne, 1570; here a reissue with altered imprint date? MB; BN   A571/1

Camões, Luiz de. Os Lusiadas. *Lisbon: A. Gonzalvez*, 1572. 186 numb.lvs;4to. In verse. In Canto X, the 1st stanza mentions 'Temisti- tao', i.e., Mexico; on lf 171r, in the 2nd stanza Brazil is cited. In this edn, generally consid- ered the 1st, the head of the pelican in border on t.p. is turned to the left. Anselmo 697; Ind. aur.130.693; King Manuel 136. MH, NNH; BL, BN.   A572/1

__[Anr edn]. *Lisbon: A. Gonzalvez*, 1572. 186 numb.lvs. In this edn the pelican in the t.p.

border faces the right. Presumably a forged piracy, perhaps publ. between 1580 & 1584. Anselmo 698; King Manuel 136. MH, RPJCB; BL.   A572/2

Heresbach, Conrad. Rei rusticae libri qua- tuor. *Cologne: Widow of J. Birckmann*, 1573. 713p.;illus.;8vo. 1st publ., Cologne, 1570. CU, CtY, DNAL, NNC; BN.   A573/1

Bourne, William. A regiment for the sea: conteyning most profitable rules, mathemati- cal experiences, and perfect knowledge of navigation. *London: T.Hacket* [1574]. 63 numb.lvs;4to. The imprint reads 'by Thomas Hacket'. America is mentioned only as a place on which Bourne has been unable to secure in- formation on magnetic response of compass. Taylor (Regiment) 442-443; STC 3422; Ind. aur.123.197. CSmH, DLC; Cambridge:Pepys.   A574/1

__[Anr issue]. *London: T.Hacket* [1574]. The imprint reads 'for Thomas Hacket'. Taylor (Regiment) 442. BN.   A574/2

Bourne, William. A regiment for the sea. *London: T.Dawson & T. Gardiner, for J. Wight* [1576]. 63 lvs;4to. 1st publ., London [1574]. STC 3423; Ind.aur. 123.198. BL.   A576/1

Bourne, William. A regiment for the sea. *London: T.Dawson & T.Gardiner, for J.Wight*, 1577. 76 lvs;4to. 1st publ., London [1574]. Taylor (Regiment) 443-444; STC 3424; Ind.aur.123.199. MB, PU; Oxford: Bodl.   A577/1

Heresbach, Conrad. Foure bookes of hus- bandry . . . Newely Englished, and increased, by Barnabe Googe. *London: R.Watkins*, 1577. 193 numb.lvs;illus.;4to. Transl. from Heresbach's *Rei rusticae libri quatuor*, 1st publ., Cologne, 1570, with discussion of tur- keys in bk 4. STC 13196. CSmH, CtY, DFo, IU, MH, NNC, WU; BL.   A577/2

The strange and marveilous newes lately come from . . . Chyna . . . Translated out of the Castlyn tongue, by T.N[icholas?]. *London: T.Gardiner, & T.Dawson* [1577]. [12]p.;8vo.

Said to have been originally written by a merchant in Mexico describing Pacific voyage of Spanish fleet, the Spanish text has not been traced. STC 5141. DFo.　　　　　　A577/3

Heresbach, Conrad. Foure bookes of husbandry . . . Newely Englished, and increased, by Barnabe Googe. *London: [H.Denham?], for J.Wight,* 1578. 193 numb.lvs;illus.;4to. Transl. from author's *Rei rusticae,* 1st publ., Cologne, 1570; 1st publ. in English, London, 1577. STC 13197. CSmH, CtY, DFo, MH-A, WU; BL.　　　　　　　　　　　A578/1

Escalante, Bernardino de. A discourse of the navigation which the Portugales doe make . . . Translated out of Spanish . . . by John Frampton. *London: T.Dawson,* 1579. 46 numb.lvs;4to. Transl. from Escalante's *Discurso de la navegacion,* 1st publ., Seville, 1577; refs to Spanish New World exploration appear solely in Frampton's dedicatory epistle. Sabin 22913; Streit IV:982; STC 10529; JCB (3) I:275. CSmH, DFo, MnU-B, NN-RB, PPRF, RPJCB; BL.　　　　　　　A579/1

Bourne, William. A regiment for the sea . . . Newly corrected and amended by the author. *London: T.East,for J.Wight,* 1580. 80 numb. lvs;4to. 1st publ., London, [1574], but with here added text containing numerous scattered refs to navigational matters relating to the Americas. Taylor (Regiment) 445-446; STC 3425; Ind.aur. 123.202. MH, NjP; Oxford:Bodl.　　　　　　　　　　A580/1

Camões, Luiz de. La Lusiada . . . Traducida en verso castellano de portugués, por . . . Luys Gomez de Tapia. *Salamanca: J.Périer,* 1580. 307 numb.lvs;8vo. Transl. from Camoes's *Os Lusiadas,* 1st publ., Lisbon, 1572. Silva (Camoes) 155; Ind.aur.130.695; Palau 41050. CtY, DLC, InU-L, MH, NNH; BL.

　　　　　　　　　　　　　　　A580/2

———. Los Lusiadas . . . Traduzidos . . . por Benito Caldera. *Alcalá de Henares: J.Gracián,* 1580. 198 lvs;4to. Transl. from Camões's *Os Lusiados,* 1st publ., Lisbon, 1572. In verse. Silva (Camões) 154; García (Alcalá de Henares) 552; Ind.aur.130.694. DLC, IU, MH, NNH, RPJCB; BL, Madrid: BN.　　　　　　　　　　　　A580/3

Guichard, Claude. Funerailles & diverses maniéres d'ensevelir des Rommains, Grecs, & autres nations. *Lyons: J.de Tournes,* 1581. 546p.;illus.;4to. Includes (p.437-466) chapt. on New World practices. Cartier (de Tournes)

616; Adams (Cambr.) G1545. CSt, DLC, MH, MnU-B, NNUT; BL, BN.　　　　A581/1

Bourne, William. A regiment for the sea . . . Newly corrected and amended y [sic] the author. *London: T.East,for J.Wight,* 1584. 76 numb.lvs;4to. 1st publ., London, [1574], but here reprinted from enl. 1580 edn. Taylor (Regiment) 447; cf.STC 3425. CtY, MH (imp.);Edinburgh:PL.　　　　　A584/1

Camões, Luiz de. Os Lusiadas . . . Agora de novo impresso. *Lisbon: M.de Lyra,* 1584. 280 numb.lvs;8vo. In verse. 1st publ., Lisbon, 1572. Anselmo 738; Ind.aur.130.696; King Manuel 178. DCU, MH, NNH; BL, Lisbon:BN.　　　　　　　　　　　A584/2

Garzoni, Tommaso. La piazza universale di tutte le professioni del mondo. *Venice: G.B.Somasco,* 1585. 4to. Includes brief chapter on America. BL.　　　　　　　　A585/1

Nicolay, Nicolas de. The navigations, peregrinations and voyages, made into Turkie . . . Translated out of French by T.Washington. *London: T.Dawson,* 1585. 161 numb.lvs; illus.;4to. The dedicatory epistle, by John Stell, mentions Columbus, Anghiera & Oviedo. STC 18574. CSmH, DLC, ICU, MH, NN-RB; BL.　　　　　　　　　　　　A585/2

Wecker, Johann Jacob. A compendious chyrurgerie: gathered, & translated (especially) out of Wecker . . . Published . . . by Jhon Banester. *London: J.Windet,for J.Harrison, the Elder,* 1585. 530 p.;12mo. Among the prescriptions offered, some employ Guaiacum. STC 25185. DNLM, WU; London:Wellcome.

　　　　　　　　　　　　　　　A585/3

———[Anr issue]. *London: J.Windet,for T.Man & W.Brome,* 1585. STC 25185a. DNLM, MBCo; BL.　　　　　　　　　　A585/4

Heresbach, Conrad. Foure bookes of husbandrie . . . Newly Englished, and increased by Barnabe Googe. *London: [H.Denham] for J.Wight,* 1586. 193 numb.lvs;illus.;4to. Transl. from author's *Rei rusticae,* 1st publ., Cologne, 1570; 1st publ. in English, London, 1577. STC 13198. CSmH, CtY, DFo, InU-L, MH-A; BL.　　　　　　　　　　A586/1

Bailey, Walter. A briefe discours of certain bathes in the countie of Warwicke. *[London: J.Charlewood?]* 1587. 36p.;8vo. Dedication signed by author. In preface, ref. is made to 'abuse of Mechoacan and divers other Indian and foreign medicines'. STC 1191; Ind. aur.111.663. DFo;BL.　　　　　　　A587/1

__[Anr state]. [*London: J.Charlewood?*] 1587. 8vo. The dedication is unsigned. STC 1192; Ind.aur.111.663. BL.   A587/2

Bourne, William. A regiment for the sea . . . Newly corrected and amended by the author. *London: T.East,for J.Wight,* 1587. 63 numb.lvs;4to. 1st publ., London, [1574], but here with enl. text of 1580. Taylor (Regiment) 449; STC 3426; Ind.aur.123.205. BL. A587/3

Dawson, Thomas. The good huswifes jewell. *London: J.Wolfe,for E.White,* 1587. 52 numb.lvs;8vo. Includes mention of potato. STC 6391. MH, MiU, NN-RB.   A587/4

Garzoni, Tommaso. La piazza universale di tutte le professioni del mondo . . . Nuovamente formata. *Venice: G.B.Somasco,* 1587. 957p.;4to. 1st publ., Venice, 1585. CtY, ICU, MH, NcD; BL.   A587/5

Botero, Giovanni. Delle cause della grandezza delle città, libri iii. *Rome: G.Martinelli,* 1588. 79p.;8vo. Contains numerous refs to cities, rivers & wealth of New World, incl. Canada, Brazil & Peru. Ind.aur.122.696; Adams (Cambr.) B2553. Cambridge:UL, Berlin: StB.
A588/1

The good huswives handmaid for cookerie. [*London: R.Jones,* 1588?]. 8vo. Mentions potato. STC 13853. BL.   A588/2

An answer to the untruthes, published and printed in Spaine . . . First written and published in Spanish . . . Faithfully translated by J[ames]. L[ea]. *London: J.Jackson,for T.Cadman,* 1589. 53p.;4to. Transl. from the anon. *Respuesta y desengano contra la falsedades* of this year described below. In addition to the ref. to Francis Drake in text he is mentioned in translator's preface & in poem on p.33. STC 17132 (M.,D.F.R.de). CSmH, DFo, MH, NN-RB; BL.   A589/1

Respuesta y desengano contra las falsedades publicadas e impresas en España enbituperio de la Armada Inglesa. *London: A.Hatfield, for T.Cadman,* 1589. 49p.;4to. On p.19 is a passage describing Drake's exploits in the West Indies. For an English translation of this year see the *Answer to the untruthes* above. STC 17131(M.,D.F.R.de). MH; BL. A589/2

The restorer of the French estate discovering the true causes of these warres in France . . . Translated out of French. *London: R.Field,* 1589. 172p.;4to. 'The Spaniard dayly bargaineth with infidels as well in Affrik, as, in India and in the New found world'—p.15.

Though the translator suggests that the unknown author was that of the *Discourse upon the present state of France*, of 1588, i.e., Michel Hurault, evidence for this has not been found, nor has the French original been identified. STC 11289. CSmH, CtY, DFo, ICN, MH; BL.   A589/3

Stow, John. A summarie of the Chronicles of England. *London: R.Newbery,* 1590. 760p.; 8vo. Under years 1576, 1577 & 1578 Frobisher's voyages are mentioned, under 1580, that of Francis Drake. STC 23325.2 (formerly 23327). CtY, DFo(imp.), MH, WU; BL.
A590/1

Camerarius, Philipp. Operae horarum succisivarum, sive Meditationes historicae . . . [Centuria prima]. *Altdorf: C.Lochner & J.Hofmann,* 1591. 509p.;4to. Includes ref. to new islands in west, & to the swiftness of Indians in chasing down stags. Note is also made of Peter Martyr d'Anghiera's mention of a place called 'Zauana', in 'Guaccaiarima'. For pts 2 & 3 see the years 1601 & 1609. Ind. aur.130.588; Adams (Cambr.) C450; cf. Jantz (German Baroque) 45. Cambridge: Trinity, Munich:StB.   A591/1

___[Anr issue?] *Nuremberg: C.Lochner & J.Hofmann,* 1591. 509p.;4to. Ind.aur.130. 589. Munich: StB, Warsaw:BJ.   A591/2

Camões, Luiz de. Os Lusiadas . . . Agora de novo impresso. *Lisbon: M.de Lyra,* 1591. 186 numb.lvs;8vo. In verse. 1st publ., Lisbon, 1572. Anselmo 757; Ind.aur.130.697; King Manuel 219. NNH; Lisbon: BN.   A591/3

Perceval, Richard. Bibliotheca hispanica. Containing a grammar, with a dictionarie in Spanish, English, and Latine. *London: J.Jackson,for R.Watkins,* 1591. [228]p.;4to. In the dictionary the word 'hamaca' (hammock), of Carib origin, appears. STC 19619. CSmH, DLC, ICN, MH, MiU, NN-RB; BL. A591/4

Bourne, William. A regiment for the sea . . . Newlie corrected and amended by Thomas Hood. *London: T.East,for J.Wight* [1592]. 79 numb.lvs;4to. 1st publ., London, [1574], but here based on enl. text of 1580. Taylor (Regiment) 450; STC 3427; Ind.aur.123.205. DFo, MWiW-C, NN-RB; BL.   A592/1

Ercilla y Zúñiga, Alonso de. Primera, segunda, y tercera partes de La Araucana. *Barcelona: Widow of H.Gotart,for S.de Cormellas, & G.Lloberas,* 1592. 3 pts;18mo. 1st publ. with all 3 pts, Madrid, 1590. Cf.Sabin 22722;

cf.Medina (BHA) 342; Medina (Arau.) 14; JCB (3) I:327. MB, NN-RB, RPJCB, ViU.

A592/2

Eytzinger, Michael von. Historica rerum intra septem menses in Europa gestarum relatio: Das ist, Ein historische Beschreibung. *Cologne: G.von Kempen,* 1592. 86p.;4to. Includes report of safe return of Spanish silver fleet from America. Jantz (German Baroque) 73. NcD(imp.);Göttingen:StUB. A592/2a

Greene, Robert. A disputation betweene a hee conny-catcher, and a shee conny-catcher. *London: A.J[effers]., for T.G[ubbin].,* 1592. 4to. Mentions the potato. STC 12234. CSmH; Oxford:Bodl. A592/3

_____. Philomela, the Lady Fitzwaters nightingale. *London: R.B[radock].& E.A[llde]., for E.White,* 1592. 4to. One 'most false Lutesio' is compared to 'the Hysop [i.e.,tobacco?], growing in America, that is liked of strangers for the smell'. STC 12296. CSmH, MH. A592/4

Stow, John. The annales of England, faithfully collected out of the most autenticall authors. *London: R.Newbery [& Eliot's Court Press,* 1592]. 1305p.;4to. Included are accounts of the exploits of Frobisher, Drake, Cavendish, &c. STC 23334. CSmH, CtY, DLC, ICN, MH, NN-RB, RPB; BL. A592/5

Antist, Vicente Justiniano. Adiciones a la historia del s.p.fr. Luis Beltran. *Valencia: P.P.Mey,* 1593. 175 numb.lvs;8vo. Cf. the author's *Verdadera relacion de la vida . . . del padre fray Luys Bertran,* 1st publ., Valencia, 1582. Cf.Medina (BHA) 347; Palau 13084.

A593/1

A book of cookerie: otherwise called The good huswifes handmaide for the kitchin. *London: R.Jones,* 1594. 8vo. On verso of lf 20 are directions 'To bake a Turkie'. STC 3298; Ind. aur.122.213. Oxford: Bodl. A594/1

Bourne, William. De const der zee-vaerdt. *Amsterdam: C.Claeszoon,* 1594. 55 numb.lvs; 4to. Freely transl. from London, 1592, edn of author's *A regiment for the sea.* Taylor (Regiment) 450-451. Amsterdam: NHSM. A594/2

Heresbach, Conrad. Rei rusticae libri quatuor. *Speyer: A.Smesmann,* 1594. 889p.;8vo. 1st publ., Cologne, 1570. DNLM, MH; BL.

A594/3

Flor de romances. Flor de romances nuevos recopilados de muchos autores por Pedro Flores. *Alcalá de Henares: J.Gracián,for*

M.Thomas, 1595. 1st publ., Lisbon, 1593, but here lacking Ercilla y Zúñiga's *Araucana,* pt 3. NNH. A595/1

Heresbach, Conrad. Rei rusticae libri quatuor. *Speyer: A.Smesmann,* 1595. 889p.;8vo. 1st publ., Cologne, 1570; here a reissue with altered imprint date of printer's 1594 edn? NcD; BL, BN. A595/2

Mexía, Pedro. De verscheyden lessen . . . Hier zijn noch by ghevoecht seven verscheyden tsamensprekinghen, van nieus overgheset wt den Fransoysche . . . tale. *Leyden: J.C.van Dorp,for J.Paedts Jacobszoon,* 1595. 2 pts;8vo. 1st publ. in Dutch, Antwerp, 1588; transl. from the author's *Les diverses leçons,* Lyons, 1577. Here included, with special t.p. & separate paging is Mexía's *De seven verscheyden tsamen sprekingen,* 1st publ. in Spanish, [Seville? 1547?], under title *Colóquios.* Cf.Palau 167339. TxU. A595/3

Spenser, Edmund. Amoretti and epithalamion. *London: P.S[hort]., for W.Ponsonby,* 1595. [134]p.;8vo. In the Amoretti, sonnet xv refers to search for treasure in both Indies. STC 23076; Church (Engl.lit.) 660; Pforzheimer 965. CSmH, DFo, TxU; BL. A595/4

Botero, Giovanni. Delle cause della grandezza delle cittá, libri iii. *Milan: Heirs of P.da Ponte,* 1596. 78p.;8vo. 1st publ., Rome, 1588. Ind.aur.122.718. DFo; BL. A596/1

Bourne, William. A regiment for the sea . . . Newly corrected and amended by Thomas Hood. *London: T.East,for J.Wight,* 1596. 79 numb.lvs;4to. 1st publ., London, [1574], but cf. 1592 edn. Taylor (Regiment) 452; STC 3428; Ind.aur.123.206. DFo, MnU-B, NN-RB, PHC; BL. A596/2

Dawson, Thomas. The good huswifes jewell . . . Newly set forth. *London: E.White,* 1596. 8vo. 1st publ., London, 1587. STC 6392. CSmH; BL, Oxford: Bodl. A596/3

Flor de romances. Varios romances nuevos por Pedro Flores. *Saragossa: L.de Robles,for A.Tabano,* 1596. 1st publ., Lisbon, 1593, but here lacking Ercilla y Zúñiga's *Araucana,* pt 3. NNH. A596/4

Harington, Sir John. A new discourse of a stale subject, called The metamorphosis of Ajax. *London: R.Field,* 1596. 120p.;illus.; 8vo. The 'Second section' includes refs to the 'river of Orenoque' & to the potato; in the 'Third section' is a passage on Guiana. These prob. derive from Sir Walter Raleigh's *Discoverie . . . of Guiana* of this year. STC 12779. CSmH, DFo, MH; BL.   A596/5

Heresbach, Conrad. Foure bookes of husbandrie . . . Newly Englished, and increased by Barnabe Googe. *London: T.East,for T.Wight,* 1596. 193 numb.lvs;illus.;4to. Transl. from author's *Rei rusticae,* 1st publ., Cologne, 1570; 1st publ. in English, London, 1577. STC 13199; Shaaber H80. DFo, MH-A, PU(imp.); Oxford: Bodl.   A596/6

Barlow, William. The navigators supply. *London: G. Bishop,R.Newberry & R.Barker,* 1597. [100]p.;4to. In the dedicatory epistle Francis Drake's West Indian exploits are mentioned. STC 1445; Ind.aur.113.176. CSmH; BL.   A597/1

A book of cookerie: otherwise called The good huswifes handmaide to the kitchin. *London: E.Allde,* 1597. 16mo. 1st publ., London, 1594. STC 3299. BL.   A597/2

Camões, Luis de. Os Lusiadas . . . Polo original antigo agora novamente impressos. *Lisbon: M.de Lyra,for E.Lopes,* 1597. 186 numb.lvs;8vo. In verse. 1st publ., Lisbon, 1572. Anselmo 770; Ind.aur.130.700; King Manuel 251. CSt, CtY, DCU, ICN, InU-L, MH, NN-RB; BL, BN.   A597/3

Dietterlin, Wendel. Architectura de constitutione symmetria ac proportione quinque columnarum. *Nuremberg: H.&B.Caymox,* 1598. 209 numb.lvs;illus.;fol. Perhaps transl. from Dietterlin's German edn of this year below. Brunet II:706. MH.   A598/1

———. Architectura von Ausstheilung, Symmetria und Proportion der fünff Seulen. *Nuremberg: B.Caymox,* 1598. 209 numb.lvs;illus.; fol. Fountain portrayed on 1f 200 includes Indian figures & inscriptions 'Presilia', Andes, Peru & Hispaniola. Cf.Latin edn above. Brunet II:706; Jantz (German Baroque) 56; Fairfax Murray (Germany) 134. DLC, NcD; BL, BN.   A598/2

———.[Anr issue]. *Nuremberg: H.& B.Caymox,* 1598. Brunet II:706. CU, DLC, ICN, NN-RB, PP.   A598/3

Shakespeare, William. The hystorie of Henrie the fourth [Pt 1]. [*London: P.Short,for A.Wise,* 1598]. 4to. In Act 2, Scene 1, turkeys are mentioned. STC 22279a; Greg 145(a). DFo(imp.).   A598/4

—[Anr edn]. The history of Henrie the fourth.

London: P.S[hort]. for A.Wise, 1598. 4to. STC 22280. CSmH; BL(imp.).   A598/5

Vega Carpio, Lope Félix de. Arcadia, prosas y versos. *Madrid: L.Sánchez,for J.de Montoya,* 1598. 312 numb.lvs;8vo. In bk 3 a statue, with its inscription, of Hernando Cortés is described. Pérez Pastor (Madrid) 613; Palau 356290. MB; Madrid: BN.   598/6

Aray, Martin. The discoverie and confutation of a tragical fiction devysed . . . by Edward Squyer . . . by M.A. preest. [*London?*] 1599. 14 numb.lvs;8vo. On verso of lf 5 is a ref. to Hawkins and Drake's West Indian voyage of 1595. STC 9; Allison & Rogers 35; Ind.aur.100.033. DFo.   A599/1

Bourne, William. De const der zee-vaerdt. *Amsterdam: C.Claeszoon,* 1599. 55 numb. lvs;4to. 1st publ. in Dutch, Amsterdam, 1594, as transl. from London, 1592, *A regiment for the sea.* Taylor (Regiment) 453; Ind. aur.123.207. BL.   A599/2

Camerarius, Philipp. Operae horarum succisivarum . . . [Centuria prima]. *Nuremberg: C.Lochner,* 1599. 524p.;4to. 1st publ., Altdorf, 1591. Ind.aur.130.590. DLC, NN-RB; Paris: Mazarin, Munich:StB.   A599/2a

Daniel, Samuel. The poeticall essayes . . . Newly corrected and augmented. *London: P.Short,for S.Waterson,* 1599. 108 numb.lvs; 4to. Includes, with special t.p., poem 'Musophilis' containing verses undoubtedly reflecting the New World: 'What worlds in th'yet unformed Occident May come refin'd with th'accents that our ours?'. STC 6261; Grolier Club (Langland to Wither) 59; Pforzheimer 245. CSmH, DLC, MH, NN-RB; BL.   A599/3

Perceval, Richard. A dictionarie in Spanish and English . . . Now enlarged and amplified . . . by John Minsheu. *London: E.Bollifant,* 1599. 391p.; fol. Greatly expanded version of that included in Perceval's 1591 *Bibliotheca hispanica,* including additional vocabulary relating to American terms. STC 19620. CSmH, CtY, DLC, ICN, MH, NN-RB, PPL; BL.

A599/4

Ribadeneira, Marcelo de. Historia de las islas del archipiélago, y reynos de la gran China . . . y de lo sucedido en ellos a los religiosos descalços, de la orden del . . . padre San Francisco, de la provincia de San Gregorio de las Philipinas. *Rome: N.Muschio,* 1599. 725p.;4to. Included in bk 6 is an account of a

Mexican-born friar, Felipe de Jesús. Cf.Sabin 76787n; cf.Medina (BHA) 593; Palau 266191.
A599/5

Shakespeare, William. The history of Henrie the fourth [Pt 1] . . . Newly corrected. *London: S.S[tafford]. for A.Wise*, 1599. 40 lvs; 4to. 1st publ., London, 1598. STC 22281. CSmH, DFo, MH(imp.); BL. A599/6

Stevin, Simon. Λιμενευρετικη, sive, Portuum investigandorum ratio. *Leyden: Plantin Press (C.Raphelengius)*, 1599. 21p.;illus.;4to. Transl. by Hugo Grotius from Stevin's *De haven-vinding* of this year below. Bibl. belg.,ser.1:XXIII:S139. BL, BN. A599/7

____. The haven-finding art, or The way to find any haven or place at sea. *London: G.B[ishop]., R.N[ewberry]., & R.B[arker].*, 1599. 27p.;illus.;4to. Transl. by E.Wright from Stevin's *De haven-vinding* of this year below. In addition to mention of America in author's text, Wright's preface includes further refs to it. STC 23265. CSmH, DLC, NNE(imp.); BL. A599/8

____. De haven-vinding. *Leyden: Plantin Press (C.Raphelengius)*, 1599. 28p.;illus.;4to. In 1st paragraph America is mentioned as a navigational goal. Bibl.belg.,ser.1:XXIII:S138. The Hague:KB. A599/9

____. Le trouve-port, traduit d'alleman en fran-çois. *Leyden: Plantin Press (C.Raphelengius)*, 1599. 30p.;illus.;4to. Transl. from Stevin's *De haven-finding* of this year above. BN.
A599/10

A true report of the gainefull, prosperous and speedy voiage to Java. *London: P.S[hort].for W.Aspley* [1599?]. 23p.;4to. On voyage of Jacob van Neck; cf. Neck's *Journael*, Amsterdam, [1600]. Included are mentions of Brazil & Peru. STC 14478; Tiele-Muller p.144. DFo, DLC, NN-RB; BL. A599/11

Vega Carpio, Lope Félix de. Arcadia, prosas y versos. *Madrid: L.Sánchez,for J.de Montoya*, 1599. 301(i.e.,312) numb.lvs;8vo. 1st publ., Madrid, 1598. Pérez Pastor (Madrid) 663; Palau 356291. NNH. A599/12

Stow, John. The annales of England . . . until 1600. *London: [Eliot's Court Press & F.Kingston,for] R.Newbery* [1600]. 4to. 1st publ. with refs to Frobisher & Drake, London, 1592. STC 23335. CU, ICU, PU-F: BL. A600/1

Vaughan, William. The golden-grove . . . a worke very necessary for all such, as would know how to governe themselves, their houses, or their countrey. *London: S.Stafford*, 1600. 8vo. In bk 3, chapt.26, the Council of the Indies is mentioned; in chapt.61, the cruelty of the Spanish to Indians. STC 24610. CSmH, DFo, NjP; Oxford: Bodl. A600/2

Appendix I

A Geographical Index of Printers and Booksellers & Their Publications

FICTITIOUS LOCATIONS————

Auch. *See* France—Paris—
Printer unidentified
Augusta: J.Faber. *See* Great
Britain—London—Smith
Basilisco, ausserhalb Madrill. *See*
Switzerland—Basel—Apiarius
Hierapoli. *See* Geneva: Printer
unidentified
India Pastinaca
   1545? Albergati, V. La
   pazzia
Rhuwart. *See* Germany—
Strassburg—Jobin, Bernhard
Timaripa. *See* Germany—
Cologne—Cervicornus,
Eucharius
Utopia: R.Arabalida
   1541 Ribaldus, P. Satyrarum
   liber prior

AUSTRIA————

VIENNA
Alantse, Leonhart
1518 Mela, P. De situ orbis
1520 Solinus, C.J. Joannis Camertis . . . in . . . enarrationes
Alantse, Leonhart & Lucas
1514 Albertus Magnus. De
   natura locorum
1515 Albertus Magnus. De
   natura locorum
1516 Orationes Viennae . . . ad
   divum Maximilianum
Singriener, Johann
1514 Albertus Magnus. De
   natura locorum
1514 Stiborius, A. Super requisitione . . . de romani calendarii
1515 Agricola, R. Ad Joachimum
   Vadianum epistola
1518 Mela, P. De situ orbis

1520 Solinus, C.J. Joannis Camertis . . . enarrationes
Vietor, Hieronymus
1514 Albertus Magnus. De
   natura locorum
1516 Orationes Viennae . . . ad
   divum Maximilianum
Winterburg, Johannes
1498? Steber, B. A mala franczos
   . . . praeservatio
1508 Dionysius, Periegetes. Situs
   orbis
1508? Fur die platern Malafrantsosa
1509 Catholic Church. Liturgy
   and ritual. Missal. Missale
   Pataviense
1512 Catholic Church. Liturgy
   and ritual. Missal. Missale
   Pataviensis

BELGIUM————

ANTWERP
Printer unidentified
1528 Mura, P.de. Catecismo . . .
   en lengua mexicana
1533? Gasser, A.P. Historiarum
   . . . epitome
1544? Cabot, S. Declaratio chartae
1550? Franck, S. Wereltboeck
1569 Gonsalvius, R. Historie van
   de Spaensche Inquisitie
1572 Arias Montanus, B. In
   Benedicti . . . adnotationes
1578 Casas, B.de las. Seer cort
   verhael
1579 Casas, B.de las. Spieghel
   der spaenscher tiranije
1585 Marnix, P.de. Pithie . . .
   exhortation. *See* Great
   Britain—London—
   Waldegrave, Robert

1587 Durante, C. Tractatus de
   usu radicis . . . Mechoacan
1598 Teixeira, J. Tractaet
   paraneticq (2)
**Ancxt, Marie, widow of J.van
Liesvelt**
1548 Brant, S. Sottenschip
Bacx, Andreas
1586 Ercilla y Zúñiga, A.de.
   Araucana
1597 Ercilla y Zúñiga, A.de.
   Araucana
Bellère, Jean
1554 Cieza de León, P.de.
   Chronica del Peru
1554 Gómara, F.L.de. Historia
   general de las Indias
1558 Alvares, F. Historiale
   description de l'Ethiopie
1562 Magnus, O. Historia de
   gentibus septentrionalibus
1565 Fregoso, B. Factorum, dictorumque memorabilium
1566 Apollonius, L. De Peruviae
   regionis
1567 Apollonius, L. De Peruviae
   regionis
1570 Magnus, O. Historiae de
   gentibus septentrionalibus
1572 Recueil, de la diversite des
   habits
1573 Sacro Bosco, J.de. Sphaera
   . . . emendata
1574 Apianus, P. Cosmographia
1575 Apianus, P. Cosmographia
   . . . corregida
1576 Baptista Mantuanus. Opera
1581 Apianus, P. Cosmographie
   ou description
1582 Sacro Bosco, J.de. Sphaera
   . . . emendata
1584 Apianus, P. Cosmographia
1587 Everard, G. De herba
   panacea (2)

1589? Ortelius, A. Theatrum oder Schawbuch

1598 Ortelius, A. Theatrum orbis terrarum

Parijs, Guillaem van

1570 Alderhande habijt

Plantin, Christophe

1555 Belon, P. Observations (2)

1555 Duval, P. De la grandeur de Dieu

1558 Alvares, F. Historiale . . . de l'Ethiopie (2)

1558 Magnus, O. Historia de gentibus septentrionalibus

1558 Staden, H. Warachtige historie . . . eens lants in America

1558 Thevet, A. Singularitez de la France Antarctique

1561 Magnus, O. Histoire des pays septentrionaux (2)

1562 Ayalá, G. Carmen pro vera medicina

1562 Magnus, O. Historia de gentibus septentrionalibus

1565 Du Bois, J. De morbi articularii curatione

1565 Estienne, C. Agriculture

1566 Dodoens, R. Frumentorum . . . historia

1566 Estienne, C. Landtwininge

1567 Orta, G.da. Aromatum

1568 Dodoens, R. Florum, . . . historia

1569 Arias Montanus, B. Rhetoricorum libri iiii

1569 Dodoens, R. Florum, . . . historia

1569 Dodoens, R. Historia frumentorum

1570 Magnus, O. Historiae de gentibus septentrionalibus

1571 Garibay y Zamalloa, E.de. Compendio historial

1572 Meerman, A. Theatrum conversionum gentium

1573 Meerman, A. Theatrum conversionum gentium

1574 Apianus, P. Cosmographia

1574 Capilupi, I. Carmina

1574 Dodoens, R. Purgantium . . . historiae

1574 Monardes, N. De simplicibus medicamentis

1574 Orta, G.da. Aromatum

1576 L'Ecluse, C.de. Rariorum aliquot stirpium

1576 L'Obel, M.de. Plantarum . . . historia

1576 Peña, P. Nova stirpium adversaria

1577 Heyns, P. Spieghel der werelt

1578 Ortelius, A. Synonomia geographica

1579 Bizzarri, P. Senatus populique Genuensis . . . historiae (2)

1579 Fernel, J. De luis venereae curatione

1579 Heyns, P. Miroir du monde

1579 Monardes, N. Simplicium medicamentorum ex Novo Orbe delatorum

1579 Orta, G.da. Aromatum.

1579 Ortelius, A. Additamentum Theatri orbis terrarum

1579 Ortelius, A. Theatrum orbis terrarum

1580 Ortelius, A. Additamentum Theatri orbis terrarum

1580 Ortelius, A. Theatrum oder Schawbuech

1581 L'Obel, M.de. Kruydtboeck

1581 L'Obel, M.de. Plantarum . . . icones

1581 Ortelius, A. Theatre de l'univers

1582 Costa, C.da. Aromatum et medicamentorum . . . liber

1582 Estienne, C. Landtwinnighe

1582 L'Ecluse, C.de. Aliquot notae

1582 Monardes, N. Simplicium medicamentorum ex Novo Orbe

1583 Dodoens, R. Stirpium historiae

1583 Heyns, P. Miroir du monde

1583 Heyns, P. Spieghel der werelt

1584 Dodoens, R. De sphaera

1584 Ortelius, A.Additamentum III. Theatri orbis terrarum

1584 Ortelius, A. Dritte Zusatz desz Theatri oder Schawbuchs

1584 Ortelius, A. Theatrum orbis terrarum

1585 Favolius, H. Theatri orbis terrarum enchiridion

1585 Pirckheimer, W. Descriptio Germaniae

1587 Ortelius, A. Theatre de l'univers

1587 Ortelius, A. Thesaurus geographicus

1587 Rivadeneira, P.de. Vita Ig-

natii Loiolae

1588 Ortelius, A. Epitome du Theatre du monde

1588 Ortelius, A. Theatro de la tierra universal

1589 Ortelius, A. Epitome Theatri

1589? Ortelius, A. Theatrum oder Schawbuch

1590 Ortelius, A. Epitome du Theatre du monde

Plantin, Christophe, Widow of

1591 L'Obel, M.de. Icones stirpium

1593 Orta, G.da. Aromatum

1596 Ortelius, A. Thesaurus geographicus

Plantin Office

1590 Ortelius, A. Additamentum IV Theatri orbis terrarum

1591 Ortelius, A. Vierde zusatzs desz Theatri oder Schawspiegels

1592 Ortelius, A. Theatrum orbis terrarum

1593 Ortelius, A. Theatro . . . ridotta in forma piccola

1595 Ortelius, A. Theatrum orbis terrarum

1597 Rivadeneira, P.de. Tratado de la religion

1598 Ortelius, A. Epitome du Theatre du monde

1598 Ortelius, A. Theatrum orbis terrarum

Rade, Gillis van den

1572 Recueil, de la diversite des habits

1573 Sacro Bosco, J.de. Sphaera . . . emendata

1574 Polo, G.G. Diana enamorada

1575 Braun, G. Civitates orbis terrarum

1575 Ortelius, A. Theatrum orbis terrarum

1587 Everard, G. De herba panacea (2)

Raphelengius, Franciscus

1579 Casas, B.de las. Tyrannies et cruautez

Richard, Jean

1544 Gemma, R. De principiis astronomiae

1552 Honter, J. Rudimentorum cosmographicorum . . . libri iii

1554 Honter, J. Rudimentorum

cosmographicorum . . . libri
iii (2)
1555 Boileau de Bouillon, G.
Sphere
1555 Honter, J. Rudimentorum
cosmographicorum . . . libri iii
1560 Honter, J. Rudimentorum
cosmographicorum . . . libri
iii (2)
1566 Sacro Bosco, J.de. Sphaera
. . . emendata
Roelants, Jan
1557 Paracelsus. Excellent tracktaet
1563 Staden, H. Warachtighe
historie . . . eens lants in
America
Ruault, Thomas
1591 Du Bartas, G.de S., seigneur. Commentaires. *See*
France — La Rochelle — Haultin, Jérome
Silvius, Willem
1562 Ayalá, G. Carmen pro vera
medicina
1562 Magnus, O. Wonderlijcke
historie van de noordersche
landen
1563 Zárate, A.de. Wonderlijcke
ende warachtighe historie . . .
van Peru
1564 Zárate, A.de. Wonderlijcke
ende warachtighe historie . . .
van Peru
1573 Zárate, A.de. Wonderlijcke
ende warachtige historie . . .
van Peru
Smits, Gérard
1575 Torquemada, A.de. Jardin
de flores curiosas
1578 Jode, G.de. Speculum orbis
terrarum
Steels, Gillis
1574 Polo, G.G. Diana enamorada
Steels, Jan
1533 Gasser, A.P. Historiarum
. . . mundi epitome
1536 Burchardus, de Monte Sion.
Descriptio terrae
1536 Gasser, A.P. Historiarum
. . . mundi epitome
1537 Carion, J. Chronica
1540 Carion, J. Chronica
1542 Boemus, J. Omnium gentium mores
1548 Gemma, R. De principiis
astronomiae

1553 Beausard, P. Annuli astronomici instrumenti
1553 Gemma, R. De principiis
astronomiae
1553 Tarafa, F. De origine . . .
regum Hispaniae
1554 Cieza de León, P.de.
Chronica del Peru
1554 Gómara, F.L.de. Historia
general de las Indias
1554 Lopes de Castanheda, F.
Histoire des Indes de Portugal
1555 Belon, P. Observations
1557 Alvares, F. Historia de . . .
Etiopia
Steels, Jan, Widow and Heirs of
1567 Polo, Gaspar Gil. Diana
enamorada
1570 Ulloa, A.de. Historie . . .
vanden . . . keyser Kaerle
1576 Lopes de Castanheda, F.
Histoire des Indes de Portugal
Strout, Pierre, pseud.
1568 Ronsard, P. de. Discours.
See France — Lyons — Rigaud,
Benoît
Tavernier, Ameet
1566 Apollonius, L. De Peruviae
regionis
1567 Apollonius, L. De Peruviae
regionis
Thielens, Antheunis
1567 Lumnius, J. De extremo Dei
judicio
1577 Schylander, C. Medicina astrologica
Trognaesius, Joachim
1592 Verstegen, R. Declaration
of the true causes
1598 Rivadeneira, P.de. Vita
Francisci Borgiae
Verwithagen, Jan, the Elder
1561 Apianus, P. Cosmographie
oft Beschrijvinghe
1563 Zárate, A.de. Wonderlijcke
. . . historie . . . van Peru
1564 Apianus, P. Cosmographia
1565 Hese, J.de. Peregrinatio
1571 Garibay y Zamalloa, E.de.
Compendio historial
1573 Apianus, P. Cosmographie
oft Beschrijvinghe
1573 Zárate, A.de. Wonderlijcke
. . . historie . . . van Peru
1574 Apianus, P. Cosmographia (3)
1575 Apianus, P. Cosmographia
. . . corregida (2)

1577 Schylander, C. Medicina astrologica
1581 Apianus, P. Cosmographie
ou description
1584 Apianus, P. Cosmographia (3)
Verwithagen, Jan, Widow of
1592 Apianus, P. Cosmographie,
oft Beschrijvinge
Vorsterman, Willem
1505? Vespucci, A. Mundus
novus
1540 Sylvius, P. Fundament der
medicinen

BRUSSELS

Mommaert, Jan
1600 Alemán, M. Guzman
d'Alfarache, pte la (2)
Velpius, Rutgerus
1600 Alemán, M. Guzman
d'Alfarache, pte la

GHENT

Keyser, Pieter de
1520 Baptista Mantuanus. Selectiora . . . opuscula

LIÈGE

Morberius, Gualterus
1585 Catholic Church. Pope,
1572-1585. Actes exhibez publiquement

LOUVAIN

Bogardus, Joannes
1565 More, Sir T. Opera
1566 More, Sir T. Opera
1567 Surius, L. Commentarius
brevis
1573 Soto, D.de. Commentariorum . . . in quartum
Sententiarum
1597 Wytfliet, C.van. Descriptionis Ptolemaicae augmentum (3)
Fowler, John
1570 Genebrard, G.
Chronographia
1572 Genebrard, G. Chronographia
Maes, Jean, the Elder
1573 Soto, D.de. Commentariorum . . . in quartum Sententiarum (2)
Martens, Thierry
1516 More, Sir T. Utopia

Rescius, Rutgerus
1539 Goes, D.de. Commentarii
1540 Goes, D.de. Fides, religio, moresque Aethiopum
1542 Goes, D.de. Hispania
1544 Goes, D.de. Aliquot opuscula
Rivius, Gerardus
1598 Wytfliet, C. Descriptionis Ptolemaicae augmentum
1600 Canini, A. De locis S. Scripturae
Velpius, Reinerus
1554 Haschaert, P. Morbi gallici . . . curatio
1569 Jesuits. Letters from missions (The East). Epistolae Japonicae
1570 Jesuits. Letters from missions (The East). Epistolae Japonicae
Waen, Jan
1554 Haschaert, P. Morbi gallici . . . curatio
Welle, Hieronymus
1573 Soto, D.de. Commentariorum
Zangrius, Petrus
1565 More, Sir T. Opera
1566 More, Sir T. Opera
Zassenus, Servatius
1530 Gemma, R. De principiis astronomiae
1548 More, Sir T. Utopia

CZECHOSLOVAKIA————

PILSEN
Bakalar, Mikulus
1505 Vespucci, A. Spis o nowych zemiech

PRAGUE
Printer unidentified
1593 Schotus, F. Ander theil D. Johann Fausti Historien
1594 Schotus, F. Ander theil D. Joh. Fausti Historien (2)
Adam, Daniel
1596 Mattioli, P.A. Herbar
Kosorsky, Jan, ze skosore.
1554 Münster, S. Kozmograffia czeska
Melantrich, Georg
1563 Mattioli, P.A. New Kräuterbuch
Melantrich, Jiri
1562 Mattioli, P.A. Herbárž

Schuman Press
1595 Honter, J. Rudimentorum cosmographicorum . . . libri iiii

FRANCE ————

Printer or place unidentified
1565 La Place, P.de. Commentaires de l'estat de la religion (3)
1590 Arnauld, A. Coppie de l'Anti-Espagnol
Jean, Simon, Heirs of, pseud.
1599 Rabelais, F. Oeuvres

AGEN. *See* Paris

ARRAS
Bauduin, Gilles
1598 Pasquier, E. Lettres
1600 Conestaggio, G.F.di. Union du royaume de Portugal
La Rivière, Guillaume de
1598 Pasquier, E. Lettres

AUCH. *See* Paris

AVIGNON
Bramereau, Jacques
1590 Pasquier, E. Lettres
1599 Rivadeneira, P.de. Vie du r.p. Ignace de Loyola
LaGrange, Gabriel de
1593 Montaigne, M.E.de. Essais
Vincent, Matthieu
1558 Cardano, G. De rerum varietate

BESANÇON
Moingesse, Nicolas de
1596 Conestaggio, G.F.di. Union du royaume de Portugal

BLOIS
Gomet, Barthélemy
1579 Du Bartas, G.de S., seigneur. Sepmaine

BORDEAUX
Printer unidentified
1586 Girard, B. Discours sur l'extreme cherté
1587 Girard, B. Discours sur l'extreme cherte
Chouin, Jean, pseud.
1579 Hoyarsabal, M.de. Voyages avantureux
Millanges, Simon
1576 Rondelet, G. Traité de

verole
1580 Montaigne, M.E.de. Essais
1582 Montaigne, M.E.de. Essais
1597 Richeome, L. Trois discours pour la religion catholique
1598 Richeome, L. Trois discours pour la religion catholique
1599 Richeome, L. Trois discours pour la religion catholique

CAEN
Le Chandelier, Pierre
1585 Du Bartas, G.de S., Seigneur. Oeuvres

CHARTRES
Cottereau, Claude
1591 Hurault, M. Discours sur l'estat de France

DIEPPE
Le Sellier, Jessé
1566 Le Challeux, N. Discours de l'histoire de la Floride

DOUAI
Bellère, Balthasar
1596 Rivadeneira, P.de. Vie du père Francois de Borgia
1599 Cheyne, J. Cosmographia sive Geographia
Bogard, Jean
1584 Du Bartas, G.de S., seigneur. Seconde sepmaine
Boscard, Jean, Widow of
1593 Jesuits. Letters from missions. Bref discours d'aucunes missions
Winde, Louis de
1576 Cheyne, J. De geographia

LANGRES
Des Preyz, Jean
1592 Girault, S. Globe du monde

LA ROCHELLE
Chuppin, Antoine
1578 Léry, J.de. Histoire d'un voyage . . . en . . . Bresil (2)
1585? Alfonce, J., i.e., J.Fonteneau. Voyages avantureux
Davantes, Pierre
1573 La Popelinière, L.V.de. Vraye . . . histoire. *See* Switzerland—Geneva—Stoer, Jakob
Haultin, Jérôme
1588 Du Bartas, G.de S.,

seigneur. Seconde semaine
1588 La Noue, F.de. Discours
politiques
1590 La Noue, F.de. Discours
politiques
1591 Du Bartas, G.de S.,
seigneur. Seconde sepmaine (5)
1591 Du Bartas, G.de S.,
seigneur. Commentaires sur la
Sepmaine (3)

Haultin, Pierre
1581 La Popelinière, L.V.de.
Histoire de France

Portau, Jean
1580? Alfonce, J., i.e.,
J.Fonteneau, known as. Voyages avantureux (2)
1583 Copie d'une lettre missive
1585? Alfonce, J., i.e.,
J.Fonteneau, known as. Voyages avantureux (2)

Villepoux, Martin
1580? Alfonce, J., i.e.,
J.Fonteneau, known as.
Voyages avantureux

LUNEVILLE

La Fontaine, Charles de.
1579 Estienne, C. Agriculture.
See Switzerland—Geneva—La
Fontaine, Charles de

LYONS

Printer unidentified
1501 Regimen sanitatis salernitanum
1552 Rabelais, F. Quart livres
1553 Rabelais, F. Quart livre
1556 Rabelais, F. Oeuvres
1559 Rabelais, F. Oeuvres
1564 Rabelais, F. Oeuvres
1564 Ronsard, P.de. Continuation du Discours
1565 Rabelais, F. Oeuvres
1585 Stella, G.C. Columbeidos.
See Great Britain—London—
Wolfe, John
1593 Duchesne, J. Grand miroir
du monde
1593 Montaigne, M.E.de. Essais
1594 Casas, B.de las. Histoire
. . . des horribles insolences
1595 Pontaymeri, A.de. Discours
d'estat
1600 Clavius, C. In sphaeram
Joannis de Sacro Bosco

Aleman, Balthazar
1552 Rabelais, F. Quart livre

Anard, Jean
1599 Tabourot, E. Bigarrures
1600 Tabourot, E. Bigarrures

Ancelin, Thibaud
1594 Arnauld, A. Fleur de lys
1594 Arnauld, A. Plaidoye . . .
pour l'Universite de Paris

Arnoullet, Balthazar
1546 Fuchs, L. De historia stirpium
1547 Fuchs, L. De historia stirpium (3)
1549 Fuchs, L. Plantarum effigies
1549 Fuchs, L. Stirpium imagines
1550 Fuchs, L. Histoire des
plantes
1551 Fuchs, L. Histoire des
plantes
1551 Fuchs, L. De historia stirpium
1551 Fuchs, L. Plantarum
eefigies [sic]
1552 Fuchs, L. Plantarum effigies
1554 Dioscorides, Pedanius. De
materia medica (4)
1554 Gesner, K. Thesaurus
Euonymi
1555 Gesner, K. Thesaurus
Euonymi (2)

Arnoullet, Balthazar, Widow of
1557 Gesner, K. Tresor des remedes secretz (2)
1558 Amatus Lusitanus. In Dioscoridis . . . De medica materia (4)
1558 Fuchs, L. Histoire des
plantes
1558 Gesner, K. Thesaurus
Euonymi
1559 Gesner, K. Thesauri
Euonymi
1559 Gesner, K. Tresor des remedes secretz

Ausoult, Jean
1547 Tagault, J. De chirurgica
institutione

Bacquenois, Nicolas
1550 Fracastoro, G. De sympathia . . . rerum

Balsarin, Guillaume
1498 Brant, S. Nef des folz
1499 Brant, S. Grant nef des folz

Barbier, Symphorien
1556 Fuchs, L. De componendorum . . . medicamento-
rum (2)

1560 Fontanon, D. De morborum
internorum curatione (2)
1561 Fuchs, L. De componendorum . . . medicamento-
rum (2)
1564 Sacro Bosco, J.de. Sphaera

Barbou, Jean
1537 Brasavola, A. M. Examen
omnium simplicium

Basignana, Etienne de
1516 Baptista Mantuanus. Fastorum libri

Bellon, Daniel
1595 La Noue, F.de. Discours
politiques

Béraud, Jean
1579 Torquemada, A.de. Hexameron

Béraud, Symphorien
1582 Soto, D.de. De justitia
1582 Vigo, G.de. Opera . . . in
chirurgia

**Béringen, Godefroy &
Marcellin**
1549 Manardo, G. Epistolarum
medicinalium libri

Bevilacqua, Simon
1516 Gatinaria, M. De curis egritudinum

Blanchard, Antoine
1528 Almenar, J. Libelli . . . di
morbo gallico
1529 Almenar, J. Libelli . . . di
morbo gallico (2)
1529 Hock von Brackenau, W.
Mentagra
1530 Vigo, G.de. Opera . . . in
chirurgia

Bonhomme, Macé
1554 Rondelet, G. De piscibus
marinis
1556 Merula, G. Memorabilium
1558 Amatus Lusitanus. In
Dioscoridis . . . De medica
materia
1558 Rondelet, G. Histoire entiere des poissons

Bonyn, Benoît
1525 Vigo, G. de. Practique et
cirurgie (2)
1532 Gatinaria, M. De curis egritudinum . . . practica

Boyer, Jacques
1557 Francisco de Vitoria. Relectiones theologicae

Cartier, Gabriel. For works purported to have been published
at Lyons by Cartier, *see*

Switzerland — Geneva — Cartier,
Gabriel

Cloquemin, Louis, the Elder
1571 Chaumette, F. Enchiridion
1572 Chaumette, F. Enchiridion
1572 Marguérite d'Angoulême.
   Heptameron
1572 Sarrasin, J.A. De peste
1578 Chaumette, F. Enchiridion
1578 Marguérite d'Angoulême.
   Heptameron
1579 Du Bartas, G.de S.,
   seigneur. Sepmaine
1580 Daneau, L. Geographiae
   poeticae
1581 Marguérite d'Angoulême.
   Heptameron

Constantin, Antoine
1545? Gasser, A.P. Epitome historiarum

Cotier, Gabriel
1561 Du Pinet, A. Historia plantarum
1561 Mattioli, P.A. Commentaires
1562 Mattioli, P.A. Commentarii
1563 Mattioli, P.A. Commentarii
1563 Mexîa, P. Diverses leçons

Cotier, Gabriel, Widow of
1566 Mattioli, P.A. Commentaires
1567 Du Pinet, A. Historia plantarum
1570 Mexîa, P. Diverses leçons
1572 Mattioli, P.A. Commentaires
1573 Mattioli, P.A. Commentaires

Crespin, Jean
1530 Vigo, G.de. Opera . . . in
   chirurgia

Desprez, Moyse
1595 Estienne, C. Dictionarium
   historicum
1597 Fernel, J. Universa medicina

Didier, Jean
1592 Parsons, R. Elizabethae . . .
   edictum
1593 Parsons, R. Elizabethae . . .
   edictum

Dubois, Michel
1554 Carion, J. Chronicorum
   libri (2)
1556 Brasavola, A. M. Examen
   omnium simplicium (2)

Duport, Ambroise
1586 Francisco de Vitoria. Relectiones theologicae

Du Ry, Antoine
1525 Vigo, G. de. Opera . . . in
   chirurgia

Edoard, Nicolas
1559 Soto, D. de. De justitia (2)

Estiard, Pierre
1571 Rabelais, F. Oeuvres
1573 Rabelais, F. Oeuvres (2)
1574 Rabelais, F. Oeuvres
1580 Rabelais, F. Oeuvres
1596 Rabelais, F. Oeuvres

Faure, Jacques
1554 Brasavola, A.M. Examen
   omnium loch
1555 Brasavola, A.M. Examen
   omnium loch

Ferdelat, Pierre
1594 Arnauld, A. Coppie de
   l'Anti-Espagnol

Flajollet, Jean
1539 Gatinaria, M. De curis
   egritudinum

Forest, François
1587 Duchesne, J. Grand miroir
   du monde

Fradin, François
1498 Baptista Mantuanus. De patientia

Fradin, Pierre
1556 Amatus Lusitanus. Curationum . . . centuriae . . . tertia & quarta

Frellon, Jean
1547 Ferri, A. De ligni sancti
1549 Fontanon, D. De morborum
   internorum curatione
1550 Fontanon, D. De morborum
   internorum curatione
1553 Fontanon, D. De morborum
   internorum curatione (2)
1554 Carion, J. Chronicorum
   libri
1554 Dioscorides, Pedanius. De
   materia medica
1556 Brasavola, A.M. Examen
   omnium simplicium
1556 Fuchs, L. De componendorum . . . medicamentorum
   ratione
1560 Fontanon, D. De morborum
   internorum curatione
1561 Fuchs, L. De componendorum . . . medicamentorum
   ratione

Frellon, Jean & François
1537 Brasavola, A.M. Examen
   omnium simplicium

1546 Brasavola, A.M. Examen
   omnium simplicium

Gabiano, David & Jean de, Bros
1593 Clavius, C. In Sphaeram
   Joannis de Sacro Bosco
1594 Clavius, C. In Sphaeram
   Joannis de Sacro Bosco

Gabiano, Jean François de
1556 Amatus Lusitanus. Curationum medicinalium centuriae
   . . . tertia et quarta

Gabiano, Scipion de & Bros
1536 Morbi gallici curandi ratio

Gazeau, Guillaume
1547 Fuchs, L. De historia stirpium
1550 Fracastoro, G. De sympathia . . . rerum
1550 Paradin, G. Histoire de
   nostre temps
1552 Paradin, G. Histoire de
   nostre temps
1554 Fracastoro, G. De sympathia . . . rerum
1554 Paradin, G. Histoire de
   nostre temps
1555 Fuchs, L. De historia stirpium
1558 Monteux, J.de. Halosis
   febrium
1558 Paradin, G. Histoire de
   notre tems

Giunta, Jacques
1521 Vigo, G.de. Opera . . . in
   chyrurgia
1525 Vigo, G.de. Opera . . . in
   chirurgia
1530 Vigo, G.de. Opera . . . in
   chirurgia, v.1
1530 Vigo, G.de. Opera . . . in
   chirurgia, v.2
1534 Vigo, G.de. Opera . . . in
   chyrurgia
1535 Sabellico, M.A.Coccio,
   called. Rapsodiae historiarum
   Enneadum
1538 Vigo, G.de. Opera . . . in
   chirurgia
1539 Gatinaria, M. De curis egritudinum . . . practica

Giunta, Jacques, Heirs of
1559 Soto, D.de. De justitia
1564 Sacro Bosco, J. de. Sphaera
1567 Sacro Bosco, J. de. Sphaera
1569 Soto, D.de. De justitia

Giunta, Jeanne
1582 Soto, D.de. De justitia et
   jure

Giunta Press
1586 Fernel, J. Universa medicina
1589 Maffei, G.P. Historiarum Indicarum libri
1598 Bodin, J. Republique
Gryphius, Antoine
1573 Valleriola, F. Observationum medicinalium libri
1581 Sánchez, F. Quod nihil scitur
Gryphius, Sébastien
1532 Manardo, G. Epistolarum medicinalium tomus secundus
1548 Cardano, G. Contradicentium medicorum
1552 Maffei, R. Commentariorum . . . libri
1554 Valleriola, F. Enarrationum medicinalium libri
1565 Botallo, L. Commentarii duo
Gryphius, Sébastien, Heirs of
1561 Giovio, P. Historiarum temporis sui
1562 Valleriola, F. Loci medicinae communes
Gueynard, Etienne
1520 Hutten, U.von. Guaiacum. L'experience . . . touchant la medicine
Guichard, Jacques
1591 Estienne, C. Agriculture
Guissio, Paul
1586 Fernel, J. Universa medicina
Harsy, Antoine de
1573 Fontanon, D. De morborum internorum curatione
1574 Fontanon, D. De morborum internorum curatione
1574 Saint-Gelais, M. de. Oeuvres poetiques
1578 Du Bartas, G. de S., seigneur. Sepmaine
1582 Soto, D.de. De justitia
1582 Torquemada, A.de. Hexameron
Honorat, Barthélemy
1577 Du Verdier, A. Diverses leçons
1577 Mexía, P. Diverses leçons
1580 Cardano, G. De rerum varietate
1580 Cardano, G. De subtilitate
1580 Du Verdier, A. Diverses leçons
1580 Mexía, P. Diverses leçons
1580 Tagault, J. Chirurgie
1582 Soto, D.de. De justitia

1584 Du Verdier, A. Diverses leçons
1584 Mexía, P. Diverses leçons
1584 Peucer, K. Devins
1585 Du Verdier, A. Bibliotheque
1587 Duchesne, J. Grand miroir du monde
Honorat, Sébastien
1554 Brasavola, A.M. Examen omnium loch
1555 Brasavola, A.M. Examen omnium loch
1561 Brasavola, A.M. Examen omnium loch
Huguetan, Gilles & Jacques
1542 Gatinaria, M. De curis egritudinum
Jouve, Michel
1572 Donati, M. Traite de . . . de Mechiaacan
Julliéron, Gaspard
1593 Clavius, C. In Sphaeram Joannis de Sacro Bosco
1594 Arnauld, A. Fleur de lys
1594 Arnauld, A. Plaidoye . . . pour l'Universite de Paris
1594 Clavius, C. In Sphaeram Joannis de Sacro Bosco
Juste, François
1529 Brant, S. Grand nef des folz
1534 Nouvelles . . . des isles du Peru
1539 Triumphe de . . . dame Verolle
Landry, Pierre
1586 Francisco de Vitoria. Relectiones theologica
1587 Francisco de Vitoria. Relectiones theologicae
1594 Bozio, T. De signis ecclesiae Dei
1595 Bozio, T. De signis ecclesiae Dei
La Place, Jean de
1517 Waldseemüller, M. Cosmographie introductio
La Porte, Hugues de
1541 Ptolemaeus, C. Geographicae enarrationis
Le Fèvre, François
1589 Valleriola, F. Enarrationum medicinalium libri
1591 Fracastoro, G. Operum pars prior-posterior
1595 Montaigne, M.E.de. Essais
1596 La Noue, F.de. Discours politiques

Lertout, Jean. For works purported to have been published by Lertout at Lyons, *see* Switzerland — Geneva
Lescuyer, Bernard
1516 Baptista Mantuanus. Fastorum libri
Marcorelle, Jean
1570 Mexía, P. Diverses leçons
1572 Gesner, K. Euonymus sive De remediis secretis
Mareschal, Jean
1583 Bodin, J. Methodus ad . . . historiarum cognitionem
Mareschal, Jean, Heirs of
1591 Bodin, J. Methodus ad . . . historiarum cognitionem
1592 Bodin, J. Methodus ad . . . historiarum cognitionem
Marion, Jean
1520 Albertini, F. Mirabilia Romae
Marsilius, Alexandre
1578 Fernel, J. Universa medicina
1581 Fernel, J. Universa medicina
1581 Tasso, T. Gerusalemme liberata
1582 Soto, D.de. De justitia
Martin, Jean
1565 Estienne, C. Agriculture
1567 Rabelais, F. Oeuvres
1569 Rabelais, F. Oeuvres
1584 Rabelais, F. Oeuvres (2)
1586 Rabelais, F. Oeuvres
1588 Rabelais, F. Oeuvres
1593 Rabelais, F. Oeuvres
1596 Rabelais, F. Oeuvres
1599 Rabelais, F. Oeuvres
1600 Rabelais, F. Oeuvres (3)
Michel, Etienne
1580 Cardano, G. De rerum varietate
1580 Cardano, G. De subtilitate
1580 Mexía, P. Diverses Leçons (2)
1582 Soto, D.de. De justitia
Michel, Pierre
1558 Paradin, G. Histoire de notre tems
1561 Brasavola, A. M. Examen omnium loch
Morillon, Claude
1594 Arnauld, A. Premiere Philippique
1595 Flurance, D.R., sieur de. Estats
1596 Flurance, D.R., sieur de. Estats

1558 Gesner, K. Tresor des remedes secretz
1559 Gesner, K. Thesauri Euonymi
1559 Gesner, K. Tresor des remedes secretz
1560 Fontanon, D. De morborum internorum curatione
1561 Fuchs, L. De componendorum . . . medicamentorum ratione

Vincent, Barthélemy
1572 Gesner, K. Euonymus sive De remediis secretis
1593 Bodin, J. Apologie de Rene Herpin
1593 Bodin, J. Republique

METZ
Faber, Abraham
1591 Boissard, J.J. Poemata

MONBÉLIARD
Foillet, Jean
1592 Bodin, J. Respublica . . . in Teutsch

MONTLUEL
Pesnot, Charles
1573 Rabelais, F. Oeuvres
1579 Rabelais, F. Oeuvres

NEVERS
Roussin, Pierre
1591 Du Bartas, G.de S., seigneur. Seconde semaine

NIORT
Porteau, Thomas
1599 Bruneau, N. Histoire . . . de certains voyages

ORLEANS
Printer unidentified
1565 Bref recueil de l'affliction
Gibier, Eloi
1559 Marguérite d'Angoulême. Heptameron

PARIS
Printer unidentified
1527 Dialogo aquae argenti
1531 Parmentier, J. Description nouvelle
1553 Postel, G. Des merveilles du monde
1553 Rabelais, F. Oeuvres
1559? Marguérite d'Angoulême. Heptameron

1560 Marguérite d'Angoulême. Heptameron
1566 Le Challeux, N. Discours . . . de la Floride (2)
1566 Requeste au Roy
1568 Histoire memorable . . . de la Floride
1584 Bruno, G. Spaccio. *See* Great Britain—London—Charlewood, J.
1584 Discours au Roi Henri III
1588 Advertissement certain
1588 Hurault, M. Discours sur l'estat de France (5)
1588 Hurault, M. Excellent et libre discours
1588 La Noue, F. de. Discours politiques (3)
1589 Hurault, M. Excellent . . . discours
1589 Pasquier, E. Remonstrance aux François
1589 Response a un avis
1590 Arnauld, A. Anti-Espagnol
1591 Hurault, M. Discours
1591 Hurault, M. Premier discours
1592 Arnauld, A. Antiespagnol
1593 Arnauld, A. Fleur de lys
1593 Hurault, M. Quatre excellent discours
1593 Observations notables
1594 Hurault, M. Quatre excellent discours
1594 Paris. Lycée Louis-le-Grand. Defenses de ceux du College de Clermont
1594 Satyre Menippee (4)
1595 Hurault, M. Quatre excellent discours
1595 Satyre Menippee
1596 Harangue d'un cacique indien
1597 Teixeira, J. Traicte paraenetique
1598 Hurault, M. Recueil des . . . discours
1598 Rivadeneira, P. de. Vita Ignatii Loiolae
1598 Teixeira, J. Traicte paraenetique (3)
1599 Satyre Menippee
1600 Satyre Menippee
Augereau, Antoine
1532 Novus Orbis regionum (2)
Auvray, Guillaume
1586 Laudonnière, R.G.de. Histoire notable de la Floride

1586 Maisonfleur, E.de. Cantiques spirituels
1587 Anghiera, P.M.d'. De orbe novo
Badius, Josse, Ascensius
1505 Baptista Mantuanus. De patientia
1509 Baptista Mantuanus. Opera nova
1509 Sabellico, M.A.Coccio, called. Rapsodie historiarum Enneadum
1511 Maffei, R. Commentariorum Urbanorum
1512 Eusebius Pamphili. Chronicon
1513 Baptista Mantuanus. De patientia
1513 Baptista Mantuanus. Opera
1513 Sabellico, M.A.Coccio, called. Rapsodie historiarum Enneadum
1515 Macrobius, A.A.T. Macrobius intiger
1515 Maffei, R. Comentarium Urbanorum
1516 Sabellico, M.A.Coccio, called. Rapsodie historiarum Enneadum
1519 Macrobius, A.A.T. Macrobius intiger
1526 Maffei, R. Commentarii Urbanorum (2)
1527 Sabellico, M.A.Coccio, called. Rapsodiae historiarum Enneadum
Baligault, Félix
1497 Brant, S. Nef des folz
1503 Vespucci, A. Petri Francisci de Medicis Salutem
Barbé, Jean
1545 Histoire de la terre neuve du Peru
Bertault, Pierre
1598 Estienne, C. Agriculture
1600 Richeome, L. Trois discours
Beys, Gilles
1578 Cardano, G. De la subtilité
Birckmann, Arnold, Widow of
1549 Fuchs, L. Histoire des plantes
Bogard, Jacques
1543 Fuchs, L. De historia stirpium
1546 Fuchs, L. De historia stirpium
1548 Carion, J. Chronicorum libri tres

1598 Montaigne, M.E.de. Essais
1599 Tasso, T. Hierusalem . . . rendue francoise
1600 González de Mendoza, J. Histoire . . . de la Chine
1600 Montaigne, M. E. de. Essais

L'Angelier, Arnoul
1552 Héry, T. de. Methode curatoire

L'Angelier, Charles
1550 More, Sir T. Utopie
1556 Cardano, G. De la subtilité

L'Angelier, Pierre
1583 Du Bartas, G. de S., seigneur. Commentaires . . . sur la Sepmaine
1590? Montaigne, M. E. de. Essais

Langres, Pierre de
1565 Pysière, G. de. Discours de . . . Floride

La Noüe, Guillaume de
1578 Cardano, G. De la subtilité
1581 Osório, J. Histoire de Portugal
1587 Osório, J. Histoire de Portugal

La Porte, Jean
1508 Baptista Mantuanus. Ad potentas christianos

La Porte, Maurice de
1530? Hutten, U. von. Experience . . . touchant . . . Guaiacum
1542 Vigo, G. de. Practique et cirurgie

La Porte, Maurice de, Heirs of
1557 Thevet, A. Les singularitez de la France Antarctique
1558 Thevet, A. Les singularitez de la France Antarctique

Laurens, Jean Le Petit. See Petit, Jean

Le Bouc, Hilaire
1579 Du Bartas, G. de S., seigneur. Beresithias

Le Bouc, Jean
1598 Estienne, C. Agriculture

Le Clerc, Antoine
1545 Cartier, J. Brief recit
1557 Couillard, A. Antiquitez . . . du monde

Le Fizelier, Robert
1583 Jodelle, E. Oeuvres
1584 Cardano, G. De la subtilité

Le Jeune, Martin
1557 Barré, N. Copie de quelques letres

1558 Barré, N. Copie de quelques letres
1561 Magnus, O. Histoire des pays septentrionaux
1563 Postel, G. De universitate
1566 Bodin, J. Methodus ad facilem historiarum cognitionem
1567 Genebrard, G. Chronographia
1568 Malestroict, J.C.de. Paradoxes
1572 Bodin, J. Methodus ad facilem historiarum cognitionem
1578 Malestroict, J.C. Paradoxes
1580 Genebrard, G. Chronographiae libri quatuor (3)
1580 Palissy, B. Discours . . . des eaux et fonteines

Le Mangnier, Félix
1587 Osório, J. Histoire de Portugal

Le Mangnier, Robert
1561 Osório, J. Histoire de Portugal

Le Noir, Guillaume
1554 Fontaine, C. Nouvelles et antiques merveilles
1556 Cardano, G. De la subtilité (3)

Le Noir, Michel
1516 Gaguin, R. Croniques de France

Le Noir, Philippe
1521 Fracanzano da Montalboddo. Nouveau monde
1530 Brant, S. Grand nef des folz
1530? Hutten, U. von. L'experience . . . touchant . . . Guaiacum
1530 Vigo, G. de. Practique et cirurgie

Le Petit. See Petit

Le Preux, Poncet
1514 Gaguin, R. Grandes chroniques
1515 Gaguin, R. Croniques de France

L'Huillier, Pierre
1574 Girard, B. de. Discours sur l'extrême cherté
1575 LeRoy, L. De la vicissitude . . . des choses
1575 Thevet, A. Cosmographie universelle
1576 LeRoy, L. De la vicissitude . . . des choses
1577 LeRoy, L. De la vicissitude

. . . des choses
1579 LeRoy, L. De la vicissitude . . . des choses
1582 La Popelinière, L.V., sieur de. Trois mondes (3)
1583 LeRoy, L. De la vicissitude . . . des choses
1584 Du Bartas, G.de S., seigneur. Seconde sepmaine (2)
1584 De Bartas, G.de S., seigneur. Sepmaine
1584 LeRoy, L. De la vicissitude . . . des choses
1595 Pontaymeri, A.de. Discours d'estat

Longis, Jean
1561 Paradin, G. Histoire de nostre temps

Loys, Jean
1542 Glareanus, H. De geographia (2)
1546 Sacro Bosco, J. de. Sphere . . . traduicte

Macé, Charles
1573 Rondelet, G. Methodus curandorum . . . morborum
1574 Rondelet, G. Methodus curandorum . . . morborum (2)
1575 Boaistuau, P. Histoires prodigeuses
1575 Rondelet, G. Methodus curandorum . . . morborum
1576 Boaistuau, P. Histoires prodigeuses
1584 Du Pinet, A. Histoire des plantes

Macé, Jean
1563? Rondelet, G. Methodus curandorum . . . morborum
1564 Cardano G. Contradicentium medicorum
1567? Rondelet, G. Methodus curandorum . . . morborum

Mallard, Olivier
1542 Bolognini, A. De la curation des ulceres

Mallot, Gervais
1570 Belleforest, F. de. Histoire universelle
1572 Belleforest, F. de. Histoire universelle

Marchant, Guy
1493 Colombo, C. Epistola (3)
1498 Sacro Bosco, J. de. Uberrimum sphere mundi
1500 Brant, S. Narren scip

Marnef, Geoffroy de
1497 Brant, S. Nef des folz

1498 Brant, S. Stultifera navis
Marnef, Jérôme de
1569 Sacro Bosco, J.de. Sphaera
1572 Sacro Bosco, J.de. Sphaera
1577 Sacro Bosco, J.de. Sphaera
1580 Boaistuau, P. Histoires
prodigeuses
1584 Sacro Bosco, J.de. Sphaera
. . . emendata
1585 Du Bartas, G.de S., seigneur. Sepmaine
1588 Belon, P. Observations
Marnef, Frères de
1509 Baptista Mantuanus. Opera
1513 Baptista Mantuanus. Opera
Mettayer, Jean
1595 Pontaymeri, A. de. Discours
d'estat
Micard, Claude
1566 Cardano, G. De la subtilité
1567 Mexía, P. Diverses leçons
1569 Mexía, P. Diverses leçons
1572 Mexía, P. Diverses leçons
1580 Mexía, P. Diverses leçons
1583 Du Verdier, A. Diverses
leçons
1584 Du Verdier, A. Diverses
leçons
Moreau, Baltasar
1590 Severt, J. De orbis catoptrici
Morel, Claude
1600 La Boétie, E.de. Mesnagerie
de Xenophon
Morel, Fédéric
1557 Duval, P. De la grandeur
de Dieu
1559 Terraube, G.de. Brief discours . . . en la cosmographie
1566 Discours . . . en la cosmographie
1566 Mexía, P. Trois dialogues
1566 Mizauld, A. Cosmographie
1566 Terraube, G.de. Discours
. . . en la cosmographie
1567 LeRoy, L. Consideration
sur l'histoire francoise
1567 Mexía, P. Trois dialogues
1567 Mizauld, A. Cosmographie
1568 LeRoy, L. Consideration
sur l'histoire francoise
1569 Terraube, G.de. Brief discours . . . en la cosmographie
1570 LeRoy, L. Consideration
sur l'histoire francoise
1570 Mexía, P. Trois dialogues
1571 La Boétie, E.de. Mesnagerie
de Xenophon
1571 LeRoy, L. Consideration

sur l'histoire francoise
1575 Terraube, G.de. Bref discours . . . en la cosmographie
1578 Mexía, P. Trois dialogues
1578 Toscana, G.M. Peplus
Italiae
1579 LeRoy, L. Consideration
sur l'histoire francoise
1579 Mexía, P. Trois dialogues
1581 Emili, P. Histoire des faicts
. . . de France
1582 La Boétie, E.de. Mesnagerie
de Xenophon
1588 LeRoy, L. Consideration
sur l'histoire francoise
1596 Emili, P. Histoire des faicts
. . . de France
1598 Emili, P. Histoire des faicts
. . . de France
Nivelle, Sébastien
1554 Amatus Lusitanus. Curationum medicinalium centuriae
. . . prima et secunda
1556 Jesuits. Letters from missions. Institution de loix
Normant, Vincent
1565 Coppie d'une lettre . . . de
la Floride
1567 Marguérite d'Angoulême.
Heptameron
Nyverd, Jacques
1530 Gaguin, R. Mer des cronicques
Ongois, Jean d'
1578 Centellas, J.de. Voyages
Orry, Marc
1598 Acosta, J.de. Histoire . . .
des Indes
1598 Estienne, C. Agriculture
1600 Acosta, J.de. Histoire . . .
des Indes
Parant, Jean
1576 Lopes de Castanheda, F.
Histoire des Indes de Portugal
1579 Du Bartas, G.de S., seigneur. Beresithias
1580 Gohory, J. Instruction . . .
de lherbe Petum
Patisson, Mamert
1574 Jodelle, E. Oeuvres
1579 Le Pois, A. Discours sur les
medalles
1583 Jodelle, E. Oeuvres
1594 Arnauld, A. Plaidoye . . .
pour l'Universite de Paris
1595 Arnauld, A. Actio . . . pro
Academia Parisiense
1595 Arnauld, A. Plaidoye . . .

pour l'Universite de Paris
Périer, Adrian
1598 Houtman, C.de. Diarium
nauticum
1598 Houtman, C.de. Journal du
voyage
1600 González de Mendoza, J.
Histoire . . . de la Chine
Périer, Jérémie
1588 González de Mendoza, J.
Histoire . . . de la Chine
1589 González de Mendoza, J.
Histoire . . . de la Chine
Périer, Thomas
1584 La Popelinière, L.V.de.
Amiral de France
1585 Botero, G. Epistolarum . . .
libri ii
1585 La Popelinière, I.V.de.
Amiral de France
1586 Botero, G. Epistolarum . . .
libri ii
Petit, Jean, the Elder
1498 Sacro Bosco, J.de. Uberrimum sphere
1505 Baptista Mantuanus. De patientia
1508 Sacro Bosco, J.de. Uberrimum sphaera
1509 Sabellico, M.A.Coccio,
called. Rapsodie historiarum
Enneadum
1509? Wollich, N. Enchiridion
musices
1511 Maffei, R. Commenta-
riorum Urbanorum
1513 Sabellico, M.A.Coccio,
called. Rapsodie historiarum
Enneadum
1515 Macrobius, A. Macrobius
intiger
1515 Maffei, R. Comentarium
Urbanorum
1515 Sacro Bosco, J.de. Sphere
textum
1516 Baptista Mantuanus. Opera .
1516 Sabellico, M.A.Coccio,
called. Rapsodie historiarum
Enneadum
1526 Maffei, R. Commentarii Urbanorum
1527 Gaguin, R. Mer des croniques
1527 Sabellico, M.A.Coccio,
called. Rapsodiae historiarum
Enneadum
Petit, Jean, the Younger
1532 Novus Orbis regionum

Le Prest, Jean
1551 Rouen. Deduction du somptueux ordre
Loyselet, Georges
1580 Mexia, P. Diverses leçons
Mallard, Martin & Honoré
1588 Macer Floridus. Fleurs . . . des vertus des herbes
1588 Monardes, N. Brief traite de la racine Mechoacan
Mallard, Robert
1573 Medina, P.de. Art de naviguer
1593 Fuchs, L. Histoire . . . des plantes
Mallard, Thomas
1578 Alfonce, J., i.e., J.Fonteneau, known as. Voyages avantureux
1589 Du Bartas, G.de S., seigneur. Commentaires sur la Sepmaine
1593 Du Bartas, G.de S., seigneur.Commentaires sur la Sepmaine
1596 Du Bartas, G.de S., seigneur. Seconde sepmaine (2)
1597 Du Bartas, G.de S., seigneur. Commentaires sur la Sepmaine (2)
1599 Du Bartas, G.de S., seigneur. Commentaires . . . sur la Sepmaine
Osmont, Jean
1598 Estienne, C. Agriculture
1598 Marguérite d'Angoulême. Heptameron
1600 Bruneau, N. Histoire . . . de plusieurs voyages
1600 Estienne, C. Agriculture
Pavie, Guillaume
1573 Medina, P.de. Art de naviguer
Petit, Jean
1545 Ferri, A. Methode curative
Reinsart, Théodore
1590 Gesner, K. Secrets de medecine
1599 Du Bartas, G.de S., seigneur. Seconde sepmaine
1599 Du Bartas, G.de S., seigneur. Commentaires . . . sur la Sepmaine
1600 Richeome, L. Trois discours pour la religion catholique
Retif, Pierre
1592 Du Bartas, G.de S., seigneur. Oeuvres

Valentin, Robert
1552 Rabelais, F. Le quart livre

ST. DIÉ
Lud, Gautier
1507 Waldseemüller, M. Cosmographiae introductio (5)

STRASBOURG. *See* GERMANY—STRASSBURG

TOULOUSE
Barril, Jean
1532 Antonio de Olave. Histoire et lettres
1532 Antonio de Olave. Passio gloriosi . . . Andree de Spoleto
1532 Díaz de Lugo, J.B. Lettres envoyees au chapitre general
Boudeville, Guy de
1553 Barot, J.de. Devis poictevin
Colomiès, Jacques
1532 Antonio de Olave. Histoire et lettres
1533 Antonio de Olave. Passio gloriosi . . . Andree de Spoleto
1553 Ferrier, A. De pudendagra
1562 Ronsard, P.de. Continuation du Discours

TOURNON
Michel, Claude
1596 Du Verdier, A. Diverses leçons
Mettayer, Jean
1592 Du Bartas, G.de S., seigneur. Divina settimana
1593 La Charlonye, G.de. De sphaera mundi

TROYES
Le Noble, Jean
1595 Capelloni, L. Divers discours
Vivant, Louis
1556 Rabelais, F. Oeuvres

VERDUN
Wapy, Jean
1596 Rivadeneira, P.de. Vie du père François de Borgia

VIENNE
Trechsel, Gaspar
1541 Ptolemaeus, S. Geographicae enarrationis libri octo

VILLEFRANCHE, PSEUD.
Du Mont, Claude, pseud.
1579 Du Bartas, G.de S., seigneur. Sepmaine. *See* France—Blois—Gomet, Barthélemy

GERMANY————

Place & Printer unidentified
1529 Karl V, Emperor of Germany, Ain Ernstliche red

ALTDORF
Lochner, Christoph & Johann Hofmann
1591 Camerarius, P. Operae horarum

AMBERG
Forster, Michael
1599 Magnus, O. De gentibus septentrionalibus
1599 Panciroli, G. Rerum memorabilium . . . libri duo

AUGSBURG
Printer unidentified
1520 Karl V, Emperor of Germany. Caroli . . . recessuri adlocutio
1522? Newe zeitung. von dem lande. das die Sponier funden haben (2)
1524 Recept von ainem holtz
1535 Copey etlicher brieff, so auss Hispania kummen seindt
1565 Lopes de Castanheda, F. Warhafftige und volkomene Historia
1577? Newe Zeytung auss den new erfundenen Inseln
Erfurt, Hans von
1519 Recept von ainem holtz
Franck, Matthäus
1565 Newe Zeytung von einem seltzamen Meerwunder
1566? Warhafftige Contrafey einer wilden Frawen
Froschauer, Hans
1505 Vespucci, A. Dise figur anzaight uns das volck (2)
Grimm, Sigmund
1518 Recept von ainem holtz
1518 Schmaus, L. Lucubratiuncula de morbo gallico
Manger, Michael
1571 Falloppius, G. Kunstbüch
1573 Falloppius, G. Kunstbüch
1588 Falloppius, G. Kunstbüch

Birckmann, Johann, Widow of
1573A Heresbach, C. Rei rusticae libri quatuor
Braun, Georg
1575 Braun, G. Civitates orbis terrarum
Buchholtz, Bertram
1598 Botero, G. Mundus imperiorum
1598 Loew, C. Meer oder Seehanen Buch
1599 Braun, G. Civitates orbis terrarum
Bussemacher, Johann
1594 Quad, M. Europae . . . descriptio
1595 Quad, M. Jahr Blum
1596 Quad, M. Europae totius terrarum . . . descriptio
1600 Quad, M. Geographisch Handtbuch
Calenius, Gerwin
1564 Nauclerus, J. Chronicon
1566 Surius, L. Commentarius brevis
1567 Surius, L. Commentarius brevis
1568 Surius, L. Commentarius brevis (2)
1568 Surius, L. Kurtze Chronick oder Beschreibung der vornembsten haendeln
1574 Anghiera, P.M.d'. De rebus oceanicis
1574 Jesuits. Letters from missions (The East). Rerum . . . in Oriente gestarum volumen
1574 Surius, L. Commentarius brevis (2)
1586 Surius, L. Commentarius brevis
Cervicornus, Eucharius
1523 Maximilianus, Transylvanus. De Moluccis insulis
1523 Schöner, J. De nuper . . . repertis insulis
1537 Vochs, J. Opusculum praeclara de omni pestilentia
Cholinus, Maternus
1566 Sacro Bosco, J.de. Sphaera
Cholinus, Peter
1590 Sacro Bosco, J.de. Sphaera
Christoffel, Johann
1589 Acosta, J.de. Geographische . . . Beschreibung der . . . Landschafft America
1600 Acosta, J.de. New Welt

Ciotti, Johann Baptist
1588 Mercado, L. De communi . . . praesidiorum artis medicae
1592 Mercado, L. De communi . . . praesidiorum artis medicae
Gottfried von Kempen. See Kempen, Gottfried von
Graminäus, Theodor
1572 Braun, G. Civitates orbis terrarum
Gymnich, Johann, the Elder
1532 Vives, J.L. De disciplinis
1536 Vives, J.L. De disciplinis
Gymnich, Johann, the Younger
1581 Genebrard, G. Chronographiae libri quatuor
1587 Thurneisser, L. Historia . . . plantarum omnium
1592 Bozio, T. De signis ecclesiae Dei
1596 Botero, G. Allgemeine Weltbeschreibung
Hemmerden, Stephan
1600 Matal, J. America . . . delineatus
Kempen, Gottfried von
1577 Braun, G. Civitates orbis terrarum
1578 Ptolemaeus, C. Tabulae geographicae
1579 Braun, G. Theatre des cites
1581 Peurbach, G.von. Theoricae novae planetarum
1582 Bazán, A.de. Historia successus
1582 Braun, G. Beschreibung . . . der vornembster Staet
1582 Braun, G. Civitates orbis terrarum
1588 Braun, G. Civitates orbis terrarum
1591A Eytzinger, M.von. Nova nova mensium
1592A Eytzinger, M.von. Historia rerum
1591 Peurbach, G.von. Theoricae novae planetarum
1593 Braun, G. Civitates orbis terrarum
Keschedt, Peter
1597 Ptolemaeus, C. Geographiae universae . . . opus
Landen, Johannes
1505 Vespucci, A. Mundus novus
Lützenkirchen, Wilhelm
1599 Quad, M. Enchiridion cos-

mographicum: das ist, Ein Handtbüchlin
1600 Quad, M. Compendium universi
Melchior von Neuss. See Neuss, Melchior von
Mylius, Arnold
1586 Osorio, J. De rebus Emmanuelis . . . gestis
1589 Maffei, G.P. Historiarum Indicarum libri xvi
1590 Maffei, G.P. Historiarum Indicarum libri xvi
1591 Peurbach, G.von. Theoricae novae planetarum
1593 Maffei, G.P. Historiarum Indicarum libri xvi
1596 Acosta, J.de. De natura Novi Orbis
1597 Osorio, J. De rebus Emmanuelis . . . gestis
Neuss, Melchior von
1532 Cortés, H. De insulis nuper inventis
1534 Trithemius, J. Liber octo quaestionum
Quentel, Arnold
1598 Surius, L. Commentarius brevis
Quentel, Heinrich, Sons of
1505 Sacro Bosco, J.de. Opus sphaericum
1508 Sacro Bosco, J.de. Opus sphericum
Quentel, Johann, Heirs of
1564 Nauclerus, J. Chronicon
1566 Surius, L. Commentarius brevis
1567 Surius, L. Commentarius brevis
1568 Surius, L. Commentarius brevis (2)
1568 Surius, L. Kurtze Chronick
1574 Anghiera, P.M.d'. De rebus oceanicis
1574 Jesuits. Letters from missions (The East). Rerum . . . in oriente gestarum volumen
1574 Surius, L. Commentarius brevis (2)
1586 Surius, L. Commentarius brevis
Schreiber, Nikolaus
1566 Alberti, L. Descriptio totius Italiae
Zierickzee, Cornelius von
1500 Grünpeck, J. Tractatus de pestilentiali scorra

JENA
Printer unidentified
1588 Hiel, L. Dissertatio . . . de
  morbo gallico

LANDSHUT
Apianus, Peter
1524 Apianus, P. Cosmo-
  graphicus liber
Weissenburger, Johann
1521? Apianus, P. Isagoge
1524 Apianus, P. Cosmo-
  graphicus liber
1524 Apianus, P. Kunstlich Instrument

LAUINGEN
Reinmichel, Leonhard
1582 Rauwolf, L. Aigentliche Beschreibung der Raiss
1583 Rauwolf, L. Aigentliche Beschreibung der Raiss

LEIPZIG
Printer unidentified
1500 Manardo, G. De erroribus
  . . . Pistoris
1500 Pollich, M. Castigationes in
  alabandicas declarationes
1501 Pistoris, S. Confutatio
  conflatorum
1501 Pollich, M. Responsio
Apel, Jakob
1594 Neander, M. Orbis terrae
  divisio compendiaris
1597 Neander, M. Orbis terrae
  partium succincta explicatio
Beyer, Johann, Heirs of
1597 Dresser, M. Historien . . .
  von dem . . . Königreich China
1598 Dresser, M. Historien . . .
  von dem . . . Königreich China
Blum, Michael
1532 Tollat von Vochenberg, J.
  Artzney Buchlein
Böttiger, Gregorius
1493? Maino, G.del. Oratio . . .
  apud . . . Alexandrinum
1496 Grünpeck, J. Tractatus de
  pestilentiali scorra
Brandis, Moritz
1498 Pistoris, S. Positio de malo
  franco
Deffner, Georg
1586 Neander, M. Chronicon
1586 Neander, M. Orbis terrae
  divisio compendiaria
1586 Neander, M. Orbis terrae
  partium succincta explicatio

1590 Neander, M. Chronicon
Kachelofen, Conrad
1500 Pistoris, S. Declaratio defensiva . . . de malo franco
1502? Sacro Bosco, J.de. Sphaera
Lamberg, Abraham
1589 Neander, M. Orbis terrae
  partium succincta explicatio
1597 Neander, M. Orbis terrae
  partium succincta explicatio
Landsberg, Martin
1502? Sacro Bosco, J.de. Sphaera
1506 Vespucci, A. Von den
  newen Insulen (2)
Lantzenberger, Michael
1592 Wittich, J. Bericht von den
  . . . bezoardischen Steinen
Schnellboltz, Franz
1597 Dresser, M. Historien . . .
  von dem . . . Königreich China
1598 Dresser, M. Historien . . .
  von dem . . . Königreich China
Steinmann, Hans, Heirs of
1589 Wittich, J. Bericht von den
  . . . Bezoardischen Steinen
Stöckel, Wolfgang
1499 Leoniceno, N. De epidemia
1505 Vespucci, A. Von den
  nuwen Insulen
1507 Wellendarfer, V. Decalogium . . . de metheorologicis
  impressionibus

LÜBECK
Albrecht, Lorenz
1600 Botero, G. Amphitheatridion
The Poppy printer
1497 Brant, S. Narren schyp

MAGDEBURG
Brandis, Moritz
1498 Grünpeck, J. Tractatus de
  pestilentiali scorra
Winter, Jakob
1506 Vespucci, A. Van den
  nygen Insulen
1507 Vochs, J. De pestilentia

MAINZ
Schöffer, Ivo
1533 Haselberg, J. Von den welschen Purppeln
Schöffer, Johann
1519 Hutten, U.von. De Guaiaci
  medicina
1524 Hutten, U.von. De Guaiaci
  medicina

1531 Hutten, U.von. De Guaiaci
  medicina

MARBURG
Egenolff, Christian
1543 Dioscorides, Pedanius. De
  medicinali materia
Egenolff, Paul
1598 Scaliger, J.C. In libros duos,
  qui inscribuntur de plantis
Kolbe, Andreas
1557 Staden, H. Varhaftige beschreibung eyner Landschafft
1557 Staden, H. Warhaftige Historia und beschreibung

MÜMPELGART
Foillet, Jakob
1600 Serres, J.de. Historia, oder
  Eigentliche . . . Beschreibung
  aller gedenckwirdigen Sachen

MUNICH
Printer unidentified
1586 Newe Zeitung auss Venedig
Berg, Adam
1571 Jesuits. Letters from missions. Sendtschreiben und warhaffte zeytungen
1582 Bazán, A.de. Warhaftige
  und gründliche Beschreibung
1583 Bazán, A.de. Gründlicher
  Bericht
1589 Conestaggio, G.F.di. Historien der Königreich, Hispanien, Portugal
Heinrich, Nikolaus
1598 Mayr, J. Compendium cronologicum
Schobser, Johann
1505 Vespucci, A. Von der neuwen gefunden Region

NEUHOFEN
Printer unidentified
1596 Nova novorum. Newe zeitungen aus oesten westen

NUREMBERG
Printer unidentified
1496 Ulsenius, T. Vaticinium in
  epidemicam scabiem
1505 Vespucci, A. Mundus novus
1534 Newe Zeytung aus Hispanien
1583? Bazán, A.de. Narratio
Andreae, Hieronymus
1552 Paracelsus. Von der Frant-

zösischen kranckheit

Berg, Johann vom

1551 Schöner, J. Opera mathematica

1561 Schöner, J. Opera mathematica

Berg, Johann vom, Heirs of

1580 Settle, D. Beschreibung der
Schiffart des . . . Martini

1580 Settle, D. De Martini
Forbisseri . . . navigatione

Caymox, H. & B.

1598A Dietterlin, W. Architectura de constitutione

1598A——Architectura von
Ausstheilung

Gerlach, Katharina

1580 Settle, D. Beschreibung der
Schiffart des . . . Martini Forbissher

1580 Settle, D. De Martini Forbisseri . . . navigatione

Glaser, Hans Wolf

1566? Warhafftige Contrafey
einer wilden Frawen

Gutknecht, Jobst

1514 Catholic Church, Liturgy
and ritual. Missal. Missale Pataviense

1518? Bewert Recept wie man
. . . Gnagacam . . . brauchen sol

Hain, Gabriel

1554 Renner, F. Köstlich und bewärtes Artzney Buechlein

1557 Renner, F. New wolgegründet nützlichs . . . Handtbüchlein

Heller, Jakob

1514 Catholic Church, Liturgy
and ritual. Missal. Missale Pataviense

Heussler, Christoph

1565 Paracelsus. Drey nützlicher
Bücher

1571 Renner, F. Sehr nützlichs
. . . Handtbüchlein

1572 Renner, F. Sehr nützlichs
. . . Handtbüchlein

Heussler, Leonhard

1582? Bazán, A.de. Königliche
Spanische Meerschlacht

Heyn, Gabriel

1559 Renner, F. New wol-
gegründet . . . Handtbüchlein

Hochfeder, Caspar

1496 Grünpeck, J. Von dem ursprung des Bösen Franzos

1496 Grünpeck, J. Tractatus de

pestilentiali scorra

Höltzel, Hieronymus

1514 Copia der Newen Zeytung
auss Presillg Landt

Hofmann, Johann

1590 Bigges, W. Narrationes . . .
expeditionis Francisci Draki

1591A Camerarius, P. Operae
horarum

Huber, Wolfgang

1506 Vespucci, A. Von der neu
gefunden Region

1506 Vespucci, A. Von der neu
gefunnden Region

Hulsius, Levinus

1598 Houtman, C.de. Kurtze . . .
Beschreibung der newen Reyse

1598 Veer, G.de. Warhafftige relation der dreyen newen . . .
Schiffart

1599 Houtman, C.de. Kurtze . . .
Beschreibung der newen Reyse

1599 Raleigh, Sir W. Brevis . . .
descriptio regni Guianae

1599 Raleigh, Sir W. Kurtze . . .
Beschreibung dess . . . Konigreichs Guianae

1599 Schmidel, U. Vera historia,
admirandae cuiusdam navigationis

1599 Schmidel, U. Warhafftige
Historien einer wunderbaren
Schiffart

Koberger, Anton

1493 Schedel, H. Liber chronicarum

Koberger, Johann

1525 Ptolemaeus, C. Geo-
graphicae enarrationis

Lochner, Christoph

1590 Bigges, W. Narrationes . . .
expeditionis Francisci Draki

1591A Camerarius, P. Operae
horarum

1598 Houtman, C.de. Kurtze . . .
Beschreibung der newen Reyse

1598 Veer, G.de. Warhafftige relation der dreyen newen . . .
Schiffart

1599A Camerarius, P. Operae
horarum

1599 Raleigh, Sir W. Brevis . . .
descriptio regni Guianae

1599 Raleigh, Sir W. Kurtze . . .
Beschreibung, dess . . . Konigreichs Guianae

1599 Schmidel, U. Vera historia,
admirandae cuiusdam navigationis

Neuber, Ulrich

1551 Schöner, J. Opera mathematica

1561 Schöner, J. Opera mathematica

Petrejus, Johann

1530 Pirckheimer, W. Germaniae
. . . explicatio

1532 Pirckheimer, W. Germaniae
. . . explicatio

1533 Schöner, J. Opusculum geographicum

1538 Rithaymer, G. De orbis terrarum situ

1543 Copernicus, N. De revolutionibus orbium

1550 Cardano, G. De subtilitate

Peypus, Friedrich

1512 Aristoteles. Meteorologia

1520 Auszug ettlicher sendbrieff

1524 Anghiera, P.M.d'. De
rebus, et insulis noviter repertis

1524 Cortés, H. Praeclara . . .
narratio

1524 Cortés, H. Tertia . . . preclara narratio

1529 Paracelsus. Vom Holtz
Guaiaco

1530 Paracelsus. Von der Frantzösischen kranckheit

Stuchs, Georg

1497 Brant, S. Stultifera navis

1505 Vespucci, A. Das sind die
new gefunden menschen

1508 Fracanzano da Montalboddo. Newe unbekanthe landte

1508 Fracanzano da Montalboddo. Nye unbekande Lande

Stuchs, Hans

1514 Ptolemaeus, C. Opere

1515 Schöner, J. Luculentissima
quaedam terrae . . . descriptio

1518 Schöner, J. Appendices . . .
in opusculum Globi astriferi

Wagner, Peter

1494 Brant, S. Narren Schyff

Weigel, Hans

1577 Weigel, H. Habitus praecipuorum populorum

PFORZHEIM
Anshelm, Thomas
1509 Seitz, A. Nutzlich regiment

REGENSBURG
Kohl, Peter
1522 Apianus, P. Declaratio (2)

REICHENAU
Haselberg, Hans
1515 Trithemius, J. Liber octo
　　questionum

REUTLINGEN
Greyff, Michael
1494 Brant, S. Narren Schyff (2)
1503? Grünpeck, J. Libellus . . .
　　de mentulagra

ROSTOCK
Barkhusen, Hermann
1505 Vespucci, A. Epistola . . .
　　De novo mundo
Dietz, Ludwig
1519 Brant, S. Nye schip van
　　narragonien
Gutterwitz, Andreas
1572 Honter, J. Rudimentorum
　　cosmographicorum . . . libri iii
Lucius, Jakob
1569 Baten, C. Propositiones
Moellemann, Stephan
1589 Beccadelli, A. De dictis . . .
　　Alphonsi regis
1591 Beccadelli, A. De dictis . . .
　　Alphonsi regis
Stöckelmann, Johann
1572 Honter, J. Rudimentorum
　　cosmographicorum . . . libri iii

SPEYER
Albinus, Bernardus
1587 Chassanion, J. De gigan-
　　tibus
1589 Marquardus, J. Practica
　　. . . morborum
1590 Capivaccio, G. De lue ven-
　　erea acroaseis
1592 Marquardus, J. Practica
　　theorica empirica morborum
Hist, Conrad
1502 Schellig, C. Kurtz Regiment
　　. . . wie man sich vor der Pes-
　　tilenz enthalten . . . sol
Schmidt, Jakob
1529 Grimaldi, G.B. Copey eynes
　　brieffes
Smesmann, Abraham
1594A Heresbach, C. Rei rusticae

libri quatuor
1595A Heresbach, C. Rei rusticae
　　libri quatuor

STRASSBURG
Printer unidentified
1534 Vives, J.L. Wannenher Ord-
　　nungen menschlicher Beywon-
　　ing
1573 Paracelsus. Chirurgia
　　magna. *See* Switzerland
　　—Basel—Perna, Peter
1589 Beuther, M. Warhafftiger
　　. . . Bericht
1592 Hurault, M. Exactissimi dis-
　　cursus de rebus gallicis
Beck, Balthasar
1541 Ferri, A. New erfundene
　　heylsame . . . Artzney
Cammerlander, Jakob
1534 Oppianus. Alieuticon
1535 Lucidarius
1539 Lucidarius
1545 Brant, S. Narren Spiegel
Emmel, Samuel
1559 Ferri, A. New erfundene
　　heylsame . . . Artzney
Fries, Augustin
1556 Giovio, P. Historiarum sui
　　temporis
Gran, Heinrich
1518 Sacro Bosco, J.de. Introduc-
　　torium . . . in tractatum
　　sphere
Grüninger, Johann
1494 Brant, S. Nuv schiff
1496? Brant, S. Nuw schiff
1497 Brant, S. Nuw schiff
1497 Brant, S. Stultifera navis
1497 Widman, J. Tractatus . . .
　　de pustulis
1498 Brant, S. Varia . . . car-
　　mina
1504 Reisch, G. Aepitomia omnis
　　phylosophiae
1507 Lud, G. Erclarnis und uss-
　　legung der . . . Welt
1507 Lud, G. Speculi orbis . . .
　　declaratio
1508 Reisch, G. Margarita phi-
　　losophica
1509 Vespucci, A. Diss buechlin
　　saget wie die zwen durch
　　luechtigsten herren (2)
1509 Waldseemüller, M. Cosmo-
　　graphie introductio
1509 Waldseemüller, M. Welt
　　kugel
1509 Waldseemüller, M. Globus

mundi
1511 Waldseemüller, M. Instruc-
　　tio manuductionem (2)
1512 Reisch, G. Margarita phil-
　　osophica
1515 Reisch, G. Margarita phil-
　　osophica
1519 Hutten, U.von. Von der
　　. . . Artzney des Holtz
　　Guaiacum
1520 Geiler, J. Narrenschiff
1522 Ptolemaeus, C. Opus Geo-
　　graphiae
1525 Fries, L. Ein clarer bericht
　　wie man alte scheden . . .
　　heylen soll
1525 Fries, L. Uslegung der Mer
　　carthen
1525 Ptolemaeus, C. Geo-
　　graphicae enarrationis
1527 Fries, L. Uslegung der Mer-
　　carthen
1529 Fries, L. Clarer bericht . . .
　　von dem holtz Guaiaco (2)
1530 Fries, L. Hydrographiae
1530 Fries, L. Underweisung. . .
　　der Cartha marina
Hupfuff, Matthias
1505 Vespucci, A. Be (i.e., De)
　　ora antarctica
1505 Vespucci, A. Von den
　　nuewen Insulen
1506 Vespucci, A. Von den
　　nüwen Insulen
1512 Brant, S. Narrenschiff
1520 Baptista Mantuanus. Fas-
　　torum libri
Jobin, Bernhard
1577 Fischart, J. Glückhafft
　　Schiff von Zürich
1578 Merckliche Beschreibung
　　. . . eynes frembden unbe-
　　kanten Volcks
1579 Estienne, C. Siben Bücher
　　von dem Feldbau
1580 Estienne, C. Siben Bücher
　　von dem Feldbaw
1587 Estienne, C. XV.Bücher von
　　dem Feldbau
1588 Estienne, C. XV.Bücher von
　　dem Feldbaw
1589 Hurault, M. Discours, ein
　　fürtreffliches frey . . . Be-
　　denken
1590 Arnauld, A. L'antiespagnol,
　　oder Ausfurliche Erklerunge
1590 Arnauld, A. Antihispanus
1592 Estienne, C. XV.Bücher von
　　dem Feldbauw

1598 Teixeira, J. Treatise
paraenetical
1599 Guicciardini, F. Historie
Gardener, Thomas
1576A Bourne, W. Regiment for
the sea
1577A Bourne, W. Regiment for
the sea
1577A Strange and marveilous
newes
Gubbin, Thomas
1592A Greene, R. Disputation
Hacket, Thomas
1563 Ribaut, J. Whole and true
discoverye
1566 Le Challeux, N. True and
perfect description
1568 Thevet, A. New found
worlde
1574A Bourne, W. Regiment for
the sea (2)
1587 Greepe, T. True and
perfecte newes
1590 Mela, P. Rare and singuler
worke
Hall, Rowland
1563 Ribaut, J. Whole and true
discoverye
Harrison, John, Sr.
1585A Wecker, J.J. Chyrurgerie
Harrison, Luke
1569 Hawkins, Sir J. True
declaration
Haslop, Henry
1587 Haslop, H. Newes out of
. . . Spaine
Hatfield, Arnold
1589A Respuesta y desengano
1598 Florio, J. Worlde of wordes
1600 Conestaggio, G.F.di. Historie
1600 Tasso, T. Godfrey of Bulloigne
Hester, John
1582 Fioravanti, L. Compendium
of . . . secretes
Hinde, John
1583 Peckham, Sir G. True reporte
Holme, William
1600 Jonson, B. Every man out of
his humor (2)
Howe, William
1581 Zárate, A.de. Strange and
delectable history
1587 Haslop, H. Newes out of
. . . Spaine
Islip, Adam
1595 Chute, A. Tabaco

1596 Lodge, T. Wits miserie
1600 Jonson, B. Every man out of
his humor
Jackson, John
1589A Answer to the untruthes
1591A Perceval, R. Bibliotheca
hispanica
Jaggard, John
1600 Tasso, T. Godfrey of Bulloigne
Jeffes, Abel
1592A Greene, R. Disputation
1592 Nash, T. Pierce Penilesse (2)
1592 Roberts, H. Our Ladys retorne
1593 Nash, T. Pierce Pennilesse
1595 Roberts, H. Lancaster his
allarums
Jones, Richard
1576 Gilbert, Sir H. Discourse of
a discoverie (2)
1581 Zárate, A.de. Strange and
delectable history (2)
1588A Good huswives handmaid
1590 Marlowe, C. Tamburlaine
1592 Nash, T. Pierce Penilesse
1593 Marlowe, C. Tamburlaine
1594A Book of cookerie
1596 Schylander, C. Chirurgerie
1597 Marlowe, C. Tamburlaine
Judson, Thomas
1599 Abbot, G. Briefe description (2)
1599 Nash, T. Nashes lenten
stuffe (2)
Jugge, Richard
1555 Eden, R. Decades of the
new world
1561 Cortés, M. Arte of navigation
1572 Cortés, M. Arte of navigation
1577 Anghiera, P.d'. History of
travayle
1579 Taisnier, J. Very necessarie
. . . book
1589 Cortés, M. Arte of navigation
Jugge, Richard, Widow of
1579 Cortés, M. Arte of navigation
1584 Cortés, M. Arte of navigation
Kingston, Felix
1598 Wateson, G. Cures of the
diseased (2)
1600A Stow, J. Annales of England

Kingston, John
1581 Borough, W. Discours . . .
of the cumpas
1581 Norman, R. New attractive
1581 Zárate, A.de. Strange and
delectable history
1582 Fioravanti, L. Compendium
of the rationall secretes
Lawe, Thomas
1585 Roberts, H. Most friendly
farewell
Ling, Nicholas
1595 Nash, T. Pierce Pennilesse
1599 Nash, T. Nashes lenten
stuffe
1600 Jonson, B. Every man out of
his humor
Lownes, Humphrey
1598 Wateson, G. Cures of the
diseased (2)
Lownes, Matthew
1600 Tasso, T. Godfrey of Bulloigne
Man, Thomas, Sr.
1585A Wecker, J.J. Compendious
chyrurgerie
1589 Banister, J. Antidotarie chyrurgicall
1595 Satyre Menippee. English.
1598 Du Bartas, G.de S., seigneur. Colonies
Mantell, Walter
1585 Roberts, H. Most friendly
farewell
Marsh, Thomas
1572 Münster, S. Briefe collection . . . of straunge and memorable thinges
1574 Münster, S. Briefe collection . . . of straunge and memorable thinges
1575 Banister, J. Needefull . . .
treatise of chyrurgerie
1576 Münster, S. Briefe collection . . . of straunge and memorable thinges
1581 Compendious . . . examination of . . . complaints (4)
Mattes, Edmund
1600 Torquemada, A.de. Spanish
Mandevile of miracles
Maunsell, Andrew
1578 Churchyard, T. Prayse and
reporte
1589 Martin, A. Second sound
Middleton, Henry
1571 Vigo, G.de. Most excellent
workes
1574 Serres, J.de. Commentar-

Ghirlandi, Andrea
1505? Vespucci, A. Lettera . . .
delle isole nuovamente trovate
Giunta, House of
1560A Bonsi, L. Cinque lizioni
1572 Sacro Bosco, J.de. Sfera
. . . tradotta . . . da Piervincenzio Dante
1579 Sacro Bosco, J.de. Sfera
. . . tradotta . . . da Piervincenzio Dante
Giunta, Bernardo, the Elder
1539 Giambullari, P.F. Apparato
et feste nelle noze dello . . .
Duca di Firenze (2)
1548 Opere burlesche
1549 Firenzuola, A. Rime
**Giunta, Bernardo, the Elder,
Heirs of**
1552 Opere burlesche
1566 Mellini, D. Descrizione
dell'entrata della . . . Reina
Giovanna (3)
Giunta, Filippo, the Elder
1507 Benivieni, A. De abditis
. . . morborum . . . causis
**Giunta, Filippo, the Elder,
Heirs of**
1519 Lucianus Samosatensis.
Opuscula
Giunta, Filippo, the Younger
1588 Maffei, G.P. Historiarum
Indicarum libri xvi
1589 Maffei, G.P. Istorie delle
Indie Orientali
1589 Poccianti, M. Catalogus
scriptorum florentinorum
**Giunta, Filippo, the Younger,
Heirs of**
1591 Lorenzini, N. Peccator contrito
Manzani, Domenico
1583 Cecchi, G.M. Lezione
Marescotti, Giorgio
1583 Cesalpino, A. De plantis
Mazochius, Antonius de
1533? González de Mercado, L.
Copia di una lettera . . . sopra
la presa . . . del Peru
Morgiani, Lorenzo de'
1493 Dati, G. Lettera dell isole
. . . trovate nuovamente
1495 Dati, G. Lettera dellisole
che ha trovato . . . el Re di
Spagna
Ortega de Carrion, Juan
1537 Sacro Bosco, J.de. Sphera
volgare

Pacini, Piero
1496 Lilio, Z. De origine et laudibus scientiarium
Petri, Johannes
1493 Dati, G. Lettera dell isole
. . . trovate nuovamente
1495 Dati, G. Lettera dellisole
che ha trovato nuovamente el
Re di Spagna
Sermatelli, Michelangelo
1600 Rivadeneira, P.de. Vita del
p.Francesco Borgia
Torrentino, Lorenzo
1549 Fornari, S. Spositione sopra
. . . l'Orlando furioso
1550 Giovio, P. Historiarum sui
temporis
1551 Amatus Lusitanus. Curationum medicinalium centuria
prima
1551 Giovio, P. Elogia virorum
bellica (2)
1551 Vittori, B. De morbo
gallico
1554 Giovio, P. Elogi vite . . .
d'huomini illustri di guerra (2)
1561 Guicciardini, F. Historia di
Italia
1561 Guicciardini, F.
Dell'historia d'Italia
Tosi, Francesco
1594 Rosaccio, G. Teatro del
cielo
1595 Rosaccio, G. Mondo e sue
parti
1599 Rosaccio, G. Sei eta del
mondo
1599 Rosaccio, G. Teatro del
cielo
Tubini, Antonio
1505? Vespucci, A. Lettera . . .
delle isole nuovamente trovate

Petruccio, Ottaviano
1513 Paulus Middelburgensis. De
recta Paschae celebratione

Bartoli, Girolamo
1585 Conestaggio, G.F.di. Dell'u-
nione del regno di Portogallo
1585 Foglietta, U. Historiae Genuensium
1586 González de Mendoza, J.
Dell'historia della China
1588 Bodin, J. Republica

1588 Foglietta, U. Clarorum
Ligurum elogia
1589 Conestaggio, G.F.di. Dell'u-
nione del regno di Portogallo
1590 Tasso, T. Gierusalemme
1591 Chiabrera, G. Canzonette
Bartoli, Girolamo, Heirs of
1597 Foglietta, U. Dell'istorie di
Genova
Bellone, Antonio
1537 Giustiniani, A. Castigatissimi annali
Bellone, Cristoforo
1579 Foglietta, U. Elogi . . .
degli huomini chiari della
Liguria
Bellone, Marc' Antonio
1576 Capelloni, L. Ragionamenti
varii
1578 Monardes, N. Herba tabaco
Paulus, Nicolaus Justinianus
1516 Bible. O.T. Psalms. Psalterium hebreum
Pavoni, Giuseppe
1598 Rivadeneira, P.de. Trattato
della religione
1599 Chiabrera, G. Rime.
Poggio, Giacomo del
1583 Antist, V. Vera relatione de
la vita . . . del p.f. Luigi Bertrando
Porrus, Petrus Paulus
1516 Bible, O.T. Psalms. Psalterium hebreum
Roccatagliata, Antonio
1583 Antist, V. Vera relatione de
la vita . . . del p.f. Luigi Bertrando

Farri, Pietro
1596 Giorgini, G. Mondo Nuovo (2)

Busdrago, Vincenzo
1551 Interiano, P. Inventione del
corso della longitudine
1551 Interiano, P. Ristretto delle
historie genovese
1558 Interiano, P. Ristretto delle
historie genovesi

Printer unidentified
1515 Vella, G. Consilium medicum . . . qui morbo gallico
laborant

Griffio, Cristoforo
1564 Fallopius, G. De morbo gallico
1564 Fracanzano, A. De morbo gallico
Meietti, Paolo
1580 Fernel, J. De luis venereae
1589 Nores, G.de. Discorso . . . intorno alla geographia
1582 Nores, G.de. Tavole . . . del mondo
Pasquato, Lorenzo
1570 Ambasciata del gran re de Chicorani
1597 Sassonia, E. Luis venereae . . . tractatus

PARMA
Viotti, Erasmo
1581 Tasso, T. Gerusalemme liberata (2)

PAVIA
Bartoli, Girolamo
1568 Dordoni, G. De morbi gallici curatione
Boscho, Joannes Andreas de
1496 Scillacio, N. De foelici philosophorum paupertate appentenda
Burgofranco, Jacobus de
1509 Gatinaria, M. De curis egritudinum . . . practica
Carcano, Antonius de
1493 Maino, G.del. Oratio habita apud . . . Alexandrinum
Garaldis, Bernardinus de
1516 Aureum opus
1521 Baviera, B. Consilia
Girardengus, Franciscus
1494? Scillacio, N. De insulis . . . nuper inventis
Moscheni, Francesco
1553 Natta, Marco Antonio. De pulchro
Viani, Andrea
1598 Botero, G. Aggiunte . . . alla sua Ragion di stato

PERUGIA
Petrucci, Pietro Giacopo
1579 Valadés, D. Rhetorica christiana
Rastelli, Giovanni Bernardino
1574 Sacro Bosco, J.de. Sfera tradotta da Pier-Vincentio Dante

PESCIA
Torrentino, Lorenzo
1555 Pico della Mirandola, G.F. Strega

PIACENZA
Bazzachi, Giovanni
1587 Anguisola, A. Compendium simplicium

ROME
Printer unidentified
1500? Maino, G.del. Oratio
1508 Téllez, F. Razonamiento delos embaradores de Espana
1516 Catholic Church. Pope, 1513-1521. Breve . . . Leonis . . . Pape
1520? Díaz, J. Provinciae . . . in India Occidentali noviter repertae
1533? Zumárraga, J.de. Universis et singulis R.P. ac fratribus . . . Salute
1537 Catholic Church. Pope, 1534-1549. De baptizandis incolis . . . Indiae
1537 Garcés, J. De habilitate et capacitate gentium
1593 Parsons, R. Elizabethae . . . edictum
Accolti, Vincente
1574 Foglietta, U. Clarorum Ligurum elogia
1581 Pamphilus, J. Chronica ordinis Fratrum Eremitarum S. Augustini
1585 Gonzalez de Mendoza, J. Historia . . . dela China
1588 Piccha, G. Oratio ad Sixtum V
Angeli, Giuseppe degli
1577 Foglietta, U. Clarorum Ligurum elogia
Basa, Domenico
1581 Clavius, C. In Sphaeram Joannis de Sacro Bosco commentarius
1585 Clacius, C. In Sphaeram Joannis de Sacro Bosco commentarius
1587 Gonzaga, F. De origine seraphicae religionis
Bericchia, Jacomo
1585 Durante, C. Herbario nuovo
1586 Durante, C. Tesoro della sanita

Besicken, Johann
1493? Almeida, F. Ad Alexandrinum . . . Oratio
1494 Dati, G. Secondo cantare dell India
1500 Torrella, G. Dialogus de dolore
1501 Alpharabius, J. Panaegyricus
1505 Manuel I, King of Portugal. Copia di una lettera del Re
1505? Pacheco, D. Obedientia potentissimi Emanuelis Lusitaniae Regis
1505 Torrella, G. Consilium de egritudine pestifera
1506 Maffei, R. Commentariorum urbanorum liber i-xxxviii
1506? Torrella, G. De morbo gallico
Blado, Antonio
1524 Ponti, A. Rhomitypion
1530 Beroaldo, F., the Younger. Carminum . . . libri iii
1531 Fracastoro, G. Syphilis
1534? Rio, B.del. Copia de una lettera . . . delle rechezze . . . ritrovato in India
1535? Letera de la nobil cipta . . . ritrovata alle Indie
1536 Brasavola, A.M. Examen omnium simplicium
1537 Ferri, A. De ligni sancti
1553 Jesuits. Letters from missions. Novi avisi di piu lochi de l'India
Blado, Antonio, Heirs of
1567 Catholic Church. Pope, 1566-1572. Bulla . . . extensionis
1567 Catholic Church. Pope, 1566-1572. Bulla confirmationis
1568 Catholic Church. Pope, 1566-1572. Bulla . . . extensionis
1570 Jesuits. Letters from missions (The East). Nuovi avisi
1572 Foglietta, U. Clarorum Ligurum elogia
1573 Foglietta, U. Clarorum Ligurum elogia
Bonfadini, Bartholomeo
1583 Gambara, L. De navigatione Christophori Columbi
1585 Durante, C. Herbario nuovo (2)

1585 Gambara, L. De navigatione Christophori Columbi
1595 Botero, G. Relatione universale de' continenti
1595 Botero, G. Relatione universale dell'isole
1596 Roscius, J. Elogia militaria

Calentano, Andrea
1586 González de Mendoza, J. Dell'historia della China

Calvo, Francesco Minizio
1523 Maximilianus, Transylvanus. Epistola
1524 Giovio, P. De romanis piscibus (2)
1524 Maximilianus, Transylvanus. Epistola
1525? Poliziano, A.A. Oratio pro oratoribus Senensium
1527 Giovio, P. De piscibus marinis (2)

Coattino, Francesco
1586 Esteve, J. Ad Sixtum Quint. . . . Oratio habita

Diani, Tito
1583 Gambara, L. De navigatione Christophori Columbi
1585 Durante, C. Herbario nuovo (2)
1585 Gambara, L. De navigatione Christophori Columbi

Donangeli, Ascanius & Hieronymus
1591 Bozio, T. De signis ecclesiae Dei, t.2

Dorici, Valerio & Luigi
1550 Sepulveda, J.G.de. Apologia . . . pro libro de justis belli causis
1552 Gambara, L. Chorineus
1552 Jesuits. Letters from missions (The East) Avisi particolari
1555 Cieza de León, P.de. Cronica del . . . Peru
1556 Gómara, F.L.de. Historia generale delle Indie Occidentali

Eliano, Vittorio
1570 Clavius, C. In Sphaeram Joannis de Sacro Bosco commentarius
1575 Clavius, C. In Sphaeram Joannis de Sacro Bosco commentarius

Faciotto, Guglielmo
1591 Botero, G. Delle relazioni universale
1595 Botero, G. Delle relazioni universali . . . terza pte
1596 Botero, G. Delle relazioni universali . . . Pte quarta

Ferrari, Giorgio
1581 Pamphilus, J. Chronica ordinis Fratrum Eremitarum S. Augustini
1591 Botero, G. Delle relazioni universale
1595 Botero, G. Delle relazioni universali . . . terza pte
1595 Botero, G. Relatione universale de' continenti
1595 Botero, G. Relatione universale dell'isole
1596 Botero, G. Delle relazioni universali . . . Pte 4ta
1597 Botero, G. Delle relazione universali . . . Pte 2da
1598 Botero, G. Aggiunte fatte . . . alla sua Ragion di stato

Freitag, Andreas
1493 Maino, G.del. Oratio habita apud . . . Alexandrinum

Gardano, Alessandro
1586 Esteve, J. Ad Sixtum Quint. . . . Oratio

Gigliotti, Domenico
1595 Agrippa, C. Nuove inventioni

Gigliotti, Giovanni, Heirs of
1587 Vera relazione di tutto quello che la flotta . . . ha portato
1590 Capilupi, I. Capiluporum carmina

Grassi, Bartolomeo
1585 González de Mendoza, J. Historia . . . dela China
1586 González de Mendoza, J. Dell'historia della China
1591 Lopes, D. Relatione del . . . Congo

Guileretus, Stephanus
1514 Vigo, G.de. Practica in chirurgia (2)

Jesuit College. See also **Society of Jesus**
1580 Jesuits. Compendium privilegiorum. Compendium Indicum
1583 Jesuits. Letters from missions. Annuae litterae (1582) 1584. Annuae litterae . . . MDLXXXI
1584 Jesuits. Letters from missions. Annuae litterae (1582) 1584. Annuae litterae . . . .M.D.LXXXII
1586 Jesuits. Compendium privilegiorum. Compendium facultatem et indulgentiarum
1586 Jesuits. Letters from missions. Annuae litterae (1584) 1586. Annuae litterae . . . .M.D.LXXXIV
1587 Jesuits. Letters from missions. Annuae litterae (1585) 1587. Annuae litterae . . . .M.D.LXXXV
1589 Jesuits. Letters from missions. Annuae litterae (1586-7) 1589. Litterae . . . M.D.LXXXVI et M.D.LXXXVII
1590 Jesuits. Letters from missions. Annuae litterae (1588) 1590. Annuae litterae . . . .M.D.LXXXVIII
1591 Jesuits. Letters from missions. Annuae litterae (1589) 1591. Annuae litterae . . . .M.D.LXXXIX
1594 Jesuits. Letters from missions. Annuae litterae (1590-91) 1594. Litterae . . . MDXC et MDXCI

Marsioni, Giovanni
1586 González de Mendoza, J. Dell'historia della China

Martin, of Amsterdam
1500 Torrella, G. Dialogus de dolore

Martinelli, Giovanni
1586 González de Mendoza, J. Dell'historia della China
1588A Botero, G. Delle cause della grandezza delle citta

Mayr, Sigismundo.
1493 Almeida, F. Ad Alexandrinum . . . Oratio
1494 Dati, G. Secondo cantare dell India

Mazochius, Jacobus
1510 Albertini, F. Opusculum de mirabilibus . . . Romae
1510 Albertini, F. Septem mirabilia . . . Romae
1514 Cataneo, G.M. Genua
1515 Albertini, F. Opusculum de mirabilibus . . . Romae
1520 Karl V. Emperor of Germany. Caroli. . . . recessuri adlocutio
1523 De Roma prisca et nova

Muschio, Nicolò
1599A Ribadeneira, M.de. Historia de las islas . . . de la gran China (2)

Mutii, Nicolò
1596 Beccari, B. Avviso del successo
1596 Beccari, B. Avviso della morte
1596 Beccari, B. Relatione del successo

Nani, Ercole
1514 Vigo, G.de. Practica in chirurgia (2)

Panizza, Valente
1574 Foglietta, U. Clarorum Ligurum elogia

Pelagallo, Vincenzo
1586 González de Mendoza, J. Dell'historia della China
1590 Botero, G. Della ragion di stato

Plannck, Stephan
1493? Carvajal, B.L. de. Oratio super praestanda
1493 Colombo, C. Epistola . . . de insulis Indie (2)
1493 Dati, G. Questa e la hystoria della inventione
1493? Maino, G.del. Oratio habita apud . . . Alexandrinum
1497 Widman, J. Tractatus . . . de pustulis

Rasimo, Cesaro
1586 González de Mendoza, J. Dell'historia della China

Rossi, Battista di
1552 Jesuits. Letters from missions (The East). Avisi particolari
1553 Jesuits. Letters from missions. Novi avisi . . . de l'India

Ruffinelli, Giovanni Antonio
1586 González de Mendoza, J. Dell'historia della China
1596 Roscius, J. Elogia militaria
1597 Maiolo, S. Dies caniculares

Santi, & Co.
1589 Stella, G.C. Columbeidos
1590 Stella, G.C. Columbeidos

Silber, Eucharius
1493 Colombo, C. Epistola . . . de insulis Indie
1493 Dati, G. Storia della inventione delle nuove insule
1498 Inghirami, T.F. De obitu illustrissimi Joannis Hispaniae

1500 Pintor, P. De morbo foedo
1504 Vespucci, A. Mundus novus
1505? Pacheco, D. Obedientia potentissimi Emanuelis Lusitaniae Regis
1516? Ferdinand V, King of Spain. Epistola

Society of Jesus. *See also* **Jesuit College**
1557 Jesuits. Letters from missions. Avisi particulari dell'Indie di Portugallo

Tornieri, Giacomo
1586 Durante, C. Tesoro della sanita
1591 Bozio, T. De signis ecclesiae Dei, t.1

Turre, Petrus de
1497 Torrella, G. Tractatus cum consilius contra pudendagram

Vatican Press
1593 Possevino, A. Bibliotheca selecta de ratione studiorum

Viottis, Giovanni Maria de
1555 Magnus, O. Historia de gentibus septentrionalibus

Vitali, Bernardino dei
1508 Ptolemaeus, C. Geographiae

Zanetti, Aloyse
1592 Jesuits. Letters from missions. Ragguaglio d'alcune missioni dell'Indie Orientali
1593 Parsons, R. Elizabethae . . . edictum
1596 Rivadeneira, P.de. De vita Francisci Borgiae
1597 Maiolo, S. Dies caniculares

Zanetti, Francesco
1579 Foglietta, U. Opera subsiciva
1581 Clavius, C. In Sphaeram Joannis de Sacro Bosco commentarius
1581 Gambara, L. De navigatione Christophori Columbi
1585 Clavius, C. In Sphaeram Joannis de Sacro Bosco commentarius
1586 Durante, C. Tesoro della sanita

SIENA
Printer unidentified
1515 Campani, N., Lo Strascino. Lamento . . . sopra il mal francioso

Bonetti, Luca
1593 Minetti, G. Quaestio . . . de sarzaparillae et ligni sancti viribus

TURIN
Printer unidentified
1590 Estienne, C. Agricoltura
1593 Jesuits. Letters from missions. Ragguaglio d'alcune missioni

Bevilacqua, Nicolò, Heirs of
1578 Costeo, G. De universali stirpium
1582 Estienne, C. Agricoltura
1583 Estienne, C. Agricoltura
1590 Bodin, J. Republica

Farine, Jérôme, pseud.
1578 Du Bartas, G.de S., seigneur. Sepmaine. *See* France—Lyons—Harsy, Antoine de

Morello, Matteo
1580 Falloppius, G. Secreti diversi

Ratteri, Giovanni Battista
1583 Estienne, C. Agricoltura

Tarino, Giovanni Domenico
1592 Fioravanti, L. Del compendio de i secreti rationali
1596 Botero, G. Della ragione di stato

Varonne, Giovanni
1580 Falloppius, G. Secreti diversi

VENICE
Printer unidentified
1520? Díaz, J. Littera mandata della . . . Cuba
1523? Maynardus, P. De preservatione . . . a pestiphero morbo
1526 Varthema, L.di. Itinerario
1527 Maynardus, P. De quiditate morbi gallici causis
1528? Delicado, F. Retrato de la Locana
1532 Bartolomeo da li Sonetti. Isolario
1532 Massa, N. Liber de morbo gallico
1534? Copia della lettere del prefetto della . . . nuova Spagna (2)
1539 Goes, D.de. Avisi de le case fatte da Portugesi

1540 Berni, F. Tutte le opere
1545? Albergati, V. Pazzia
1545? Albergati, V. India Pastinaca
1545 Berni, F. Tutte le opere
1546 Albergati, V. Pazzia
1565 Nel Bresil di san Vicenzo
1575 Foresti, J.F. Sopplimento delle croniche
1582 Tasso, T. Gierusalemme liberata
1590 Banchieri, A. Nobiltá dell'asino
1595 Rosaccio, G. Teatro del cielo
1597 Rosaccio, G. Sei etá del mondo
1597 Rosaccio, G. Teatro del cielo
1598 Rosaccio, G. Sei etá del mondo
1598 Rosaccio, G. Teatro del cielo e della terra
Alberti, Giovanni
1597 Caro, A. De le lettere familiari
1597 Mexía, P. Vite di tutti gl'imperadori
Aldine Press, *See also* The Manuzio family.
1575 Ulloa, A.de. Vita dell' . . . Imperator Carlo
1585 LeRoy, L. Vicissitudine o mutabile varietá delle cose
1589 Vairo, L. De fascino
1592 LeRoy, L. Della vicissitudine o mutabile varieta delle cose
Angelieri, Giorgio
1570 Tagault, J. Institutione di cirurgia
1573 Danti, A. Osservationi di diverse historie
1574 Guicciardini, F. Historia d'Italia
1575 Porcacchi, T. Isole piú famose
1576 Porcacchi, T. Isole piú famose
1583 Guicciardini, F. Historia d'Italia
1590 Porcacchi, T. Isole piú famose
1596 Botero, G. Relationi universali
1596 Campana, C. Delle historie del mondo

1597 Campana, C. Delle historie del mondo
1599 Botero, G. Relationi universali (2)
1600 Botero, G. Relationi universali
Arrivabene, Andrea
1539 Brasavola, A.M. Examen omnium simplicium
1550 Fernel, J. De abditis rerum causis
1555 Macchelli, N. Tractatus de morbo gallico
1556 Cieza de León, P.de. Istorie del Peru
1556 Macchelli, N. Tractatus de morbo gallico
1557 Gómara, F.L.de. Historie dell'India, pte 2da
Arrivabene, Giorgio
1496 Leonardi, C. Expositio canonum
Avanzi, Lodovico degli
1556 Rostinio, P. Trattato di mal francese
1559 Rostinio, P. Trattato del mal francese
1561 Alberti, L. Descrittione di tutta l'Italia
1561 Fioravanti, L. Capricci medicinali
1564 Fioravanti, L. De' capricci medicinali
1565 Fioravanti, L. De capricci medicinali
1568 Alberti, L. Descrittione di tutta Italia
1568 Fioravanti, L. De capricci medicinali
1573 Fioravanti, L. De capricci medicinali
Barezzi, Barezzo
1592 Banchieri, A. Nobiltá dell'asino
1598 Banchieri, A. Nobiltá dell'asino
1599 Banchieri, A. Nobiltá dell'asino
1599 Gómara, F.L.de. Historia dell'Indie Occidentali
1599 Reisch, G. Margarita filosofica
Barezzi, Barezzo, & Co.
1599 Luisini, L. Aprodisiacus, sive De lue venerea
Basa, Bernardo
1596 Acosta, J. de. Historia . . .

delle Indie
1596 Clavius, C. In Sphaeram Joannis de Sacro Bosco
Bascarini, Nicolò de
1544 Dioscorides, Pedanius. Historia, et materia medicinale
1548 Ptolemaeus, C. Geografia
Bayuera, Constantio
1505 Colombo, C. Copia de la lettera . . . mandata ali . . . Re
Benzoni, Gabriel
1565 Benzoni, G. Historia del Mondo Nuovo
Bertano, Giovanni Antonio
1580 Guicciardini, F. Della historia d'Italia
Bevilacqua, Nicolò
1563 Guicciardini, F. Historia d'Italia
1565 Guicciardini, F. Historia d'Italia
1568 Guicciardini, F. Historia d'Italia
Bindoni, Alessandro
1520? Angliara, J.de. Viaggio: col paese de lisola del oro trovato
1520 Capitulo over Recetta delo arbore
1528 Coppo, P. Portolano
Bindoni, Alessandro & Benedetto
1521 Gatinaria, M. De curis egritudinum . . . practica
Bindoni, Bernardino
1535 Foresti, J.F. Supplementum supplementi delle chroniche
1538 Ruel, J. De natura stirpium
1540 Foresti, J.F. Supplemento delle chroniche (2)
Bindoni, Francesco, the Elder
1534 Petrarca, F. Chronica delle vite de pontefici
1535 Varthema, L.di. Itinerario
1536 Massa, N. Liber de morbo neapolitano
1537 Apianus, P. Cosmographiae introductio
1537 Campani, N., Lo Strascino. Lamento . . . sopra il male incognito
1553 Guazzo, M. Cronica
Bindoni, Francesco, the Younger
1554 Apianus, P. Cosmographiae introductio

THE NETHERLANDS ──────

AMSTERDAM

Printer unidentified
1562 Franck, S. Wereltboeck
1587 Verheiden, W. Nootelijcke consideratien (3)
1588 Verheiden, W. Nootelijcke consideratien
1598 Teixeira, J. Tractaet paraeneticq (2)
1598 Teixeira, J. Tractaet paranetiq
1599 Secreet des Conincx van Spaengnien

Biestkens, Nikolaus, the Younger
1596 Casas, B.de las. Spieghel der spaenscher tyrannye (2)

Buck, Herman de
1600? Outgherszoon, J. Nieuwe . . . beschryvinghe der . . . strate Magellani
1600 Potgieter, B.J. Wijdtloopigh verhael van tgene de vijf schepen

Claeszoon, Cornelis
1576 Lopes, D. Beschryvinghe vant . . . coninckrijck van Congo
1588? Cavendish, T. Copye, overgeset
1588 Estienne, C. Veltbouw
1592 Apianus, P. Cosmographie, oft Beschrijvinge
1594A Bourne, W. Const der zeevaerdt
1594 Estienne, C. Veltbouw
1595 Staden, H. Waerichtige historie . . . eens landts, in America gheleghen
1596 Casas, B.de las. Spieghel der spaenscher tyrannye (2)
1596 Linschoten, J.H.van. Beschryvinghe van . . . Guinea
1596 Linschoten, J.H.van. Reysgheschrift vande navigatien der Portugaloysers in Orienten
1596 Zárate, A.de. Conqueste van Indien
1597 Hues, R. Tractaet . . . van het gebruijck der . . . globe
1597 Léry, J.de. Historie van een reyse . . . inden lande van Bresillien
1598 Apianus, P. Cosmographie, ofte Beschrijvinge
1598 Langenes, B. Caert-thresoor

1598 Pretty, F. Beschryvinghe vande . . . zeevaerdt vanden . . . Thomas Candish
1598 Pretty, F. Descriptio vande heerlicke voyagie ghedaen door . . . Thomas Candish
1598 Raleigh, Sir W. Waerachtighe . . . beschryvinge van . . . Guiana
1598 Veer, G.de. Diarium nauticum
1598 Veer, G.de. Vraye description de trois voyages de mer
1598 Veer, G.de. Waerachtighe beschryvinghe van drie seylagien
1598 Zamorano, R. Cort onderwijs vande conste der seevaert
1598 Zárate, A.de. Conqueste van Indien
1599A Bourne, W. Const der zeevaerdt
1599 Langenes, B. Caert-thresoor
1599 Linschoten, J.H.van. Navigatio . . . in Orientalim . . . Indiam
1599 Magnus, O. Wonderlijcke historie van de noordersche landen
1599 Veer, G.de. Waerachtighe beschrijvinghe van drie seylagien
1600 Bertius, P. Tabularum geographicorum contractum libri quatuor
1600 Langenes, B. Thresor de chartes
1600 Neck, J.C.van. Journael
1600 Veer, G.de. Vraye description de trois voyages de mer

Heyns, Zacharias
1598 Heyns, P. Miroir du monde
1600? Outgherszoon, J. Nieuwe . . . beschryvinghe der vervaerlijker strate Magellani
1600 Potgieter, B.J. Wijdtloopigh verhael van tgene de vijf schepen

Muller, Ewout
1594 Estienne, C. Veltbouw

Nicolai, C. See **Claeszoon, Cornelis**

ARNHEM

Janszoon, Jan
1598 Houtman, C.de. Diarium nauticum . . . in Indiam Orientalem

1600 Bertius, P. Tabularum geographicorum contractum libri quatuor

DELFT

Henricszoon, Albert
1583 Franck, S. Chronica, tytboeck en gheschiet bibel

Pafraet, Albert
1515 Baptista Mantuanus. De patientia

Pafraet, Richard
1498 Baptista Mantuanus. De patientia
1501 Baptista Mantuanus. De patientia
1503 Baptista Mantuanus. De patientia

DORDRECHT

Canin, Abraham
1598 Gabelkover, O. Medecynboeck

Canin, Isaack
1599 Gabelkover, O. Boock of physicke
1599 Guicciardini, F. Oorlogen van Italien

Verhaghen, Pieter
1585 Justificatie van den doorluchtigen Don Antonio

ENKHUIZEN

Meyn, Jacob Lenaertszoon
1598 Acosta, J.de. Historie naturael . . . van . . . Westersche Indien

HAARLEM

Rooman, Gilles
1598 Acosta, J.de. Historie naturael

THE HAGUE

Elzevir, Gillis
1599 Linschoten, J.H.van. Navigatio . . . in Orientalim . . . Indiam

Henricszoon, Albert
1594 Arnauld, A. Plaidoye . . . pour l'Universite de Paris
1595 Pontaymeri, A.de. Discours d'estat
1598 Verheiden, W. In classem Xerxis Hispani oratio
1599 Linschoten, J.H.van. Navigatio . . . in Orientalim . . . Indiam

SPAIN ——————————

Printer and place unidentified
1582 Bazán, A.de. Copia de una
carta
1582 Bazán, A.de. Relacion:
Copia de una carta
1585 Rio Riano, A.del. Tratado
de hidrografia

ALCALÁ DE HENARES
Angulo, Andrés de
1569 Catholic Church. Pope,
1566-1572. Bullas
1569 Gómez de Castro, A. De
rebus gestis
1572 Román y Zamora, J. Historia, 1a pte
Brocar, Arnão Guillén de
1516 Anghiera, P.M.d'. De orbe
novo
Brocar, Juan de
1539 Marineo, L. De las cosas
memorables
1543 Spain. Laws, statutes, etc.,
1516-1556. Leyes y ordenanças
1546 Cervantes de Salazar, F.
Obras
1553 García Matamoros, A. De
asserenda
Eguía, Miguel de
1526 Sacro Bosco, J.de. De
sphera mundi
1528 Spain. Laws, statutes, etc.
Pramaticas
1530 Anghiera, P.M.d'. De orbe
novo
1530 Anghiera, P.M.d'. Opus
epistolarum
1530 Marineo, L. De las cosas
memorables de España
1530 Marineo, L. De rebus Hispaniae
1533 Marineo, L. De las cosas
memorables
1533 Marineo, L. De rebus Hispaniae memorabilibus
Gracián, Juan
1573 Pérez de Moya, J. Tratado
. . . de astronomia
1574 Meneses, F.de. Luz de alma
christiana
1580A Camões, L.de. Lusiadas
1585 Cervantes Saavedra, M.de.
Galatea
1591 Salazar, E.de. Veynte discursos
1595 Flor de romances
1595 Medina, P.de. Grandezas

. . . de España
Gutiérrez, Luis
1566 Medina, P.de. Grandezas
. . . de España
1567 Meneses, F.de. Luz de alma
christiana
Iñiguez de Lequerica, Juan
1578 Alfonso X, el Sabio. Coronica general
1595 Salazar, E.de. Veynte discursos
Martínez, Diego
1578 Alfonso X, el Sabio. Coronica general
Martínez, Sebastián
1583 Bazán, A.de. Relación
Nebrija, Antonio de
1516 Anghiera, P.M.d'. De orbe
novo
Polono, Lanzalao
1503 Spain, Laws, statutes, etc.,
1479-1504. Algunas bullas
Puerta, Luis de la
1595 Salazar, E.de. Veynte discursos
Ramírez, Juan
1503 Spain. Laws, statutes, etc.,
1479-1504. Algunas bullas
Robles, Blas de
1585 Cervantes Saavedra, M.de.
Galatea
Robles, Pedro de
1566 Medina, P.de. Grandezas
. . . de España
Thomas, Mari
1595A Flor de romances
Torres, Juan de
1595 Medina, P.de. Grandezas
. . . de España
Villanueva, Juan de
1566 Medina, P.de. Grandezas
. . . de España
1567 Meneses, F.de. Luz de alma
christiana

ARANJUEZ
Printer unidentified
1596 Spain. Sovereigns, etc.,
1556-1598. Instrucion para el
virrey

BAEZA
Montoya, Juan Bautista de
1581 Guicciardini, F. Historia

BARCELONA
Printer unidentified
1493? Colombo, C. Letra enviada

al escrivano de Racio
Amello, Joan
1598 Santisteban Osoria, Diego
de. Araucana, ptes 4ta y 5ta
Amorós, Carles
1515 Téllez, F. Razonamiento de
las embaxadores de Espana
1534 Tomic, P. Historias . . .
dels . . . reys de Arago
1545 Ferrer, J. Sentencias catholicas
Bornat, Claud
1556 Jesuits. Letters from missions. Copia de diversas cartas
Cantarello, Ferdinando
1567 Catholic Church. Pope,
1566-1572. Bulla confirmationis
Cendrat, Jaime
1586 González de Mendoza, J.
Historia de la China (2)
1591 Acosta, J.de. Historia . . .
de las Indias (3)
1591 Salazar, E.de. Veynte discursos
1592 Calvo, J. Libro de medicina
1596 Illescas, G.de. Historia pontifical
1599 Botero, G. Razón de estado
1599 Diago, F. Historia de la
provincia de Aragon de la
Orden de Predicadores
Cormellas, Sebastián de
1592A Ercilla y Zúñiga, A.de.
Araucana, ptes 1a-3a
1599 Alemán, M. Guzman de Alfarache, pte 1a
1599 Diago, F. Historia de la
provincia de Aragon de la Orden de Predicadores
1600 Alemán, M. Guzman d'Alfarache, pte 1a
Cortey, Pablo
1566 Copia de una carta venida
de Sevilla
Dotil, Giraldo
1599 Alemán, M. Guzman de Alfarache, pte 1a
1600 Alemán, M. Guzman d'Alfarache, pte 1a
Genovés, Jerónimo
1596 Illescas, G.de. Historia pontifical
1600 Alemán, M. Guzman d'Alfarache, pte 1a
Gotart, Huberto, Widow of
1592A Ercilla y Zúñiga, A.de.
Araucana, ptes 1a-3a

1584 Spain. Sovereigns, etc., 1556-1598. Instrucion para la observacion de los eclipses de la luna

1585 Spain. Sovereigns, etc., 1556-1598. Instruction . . . para la descripcion de las Indias

1588 Spain. Sovereigns, etc., 1556-1598. Instruccion y forma . . . de la Bula de Santa Cruzada

1590 Vique Manrique, P. Vista que V[uestra]. S[eñoria]. vio en revista

1595? En la causa entre el Arcobispo de Lima, y el Colegio de la Compania de Jesus

1595? Ramírez, J. Advertencias . . . sobre el servicio personal al qual son forçados . . . los Indios

1595? Spain. Sovereigns, etc., 1556-1598. El Rey. Lo que . . . se assienta y concierta . . . sobre la provision . . . de esclavos negros

1598 Spain. Sovereigns, etc., 1556-1598. Instruccion . . . de la bula de la Santa Cruzada

1599? Dos informaciones hechas en Japon

1600? Memorial del hecho, cerca . . . del testamento de don Christoval Colon

1600 Oñate, A. de. Paracer de un hombre docto cerca del servicio personal de los Indios

1600? Spain. Sovereigns, etc., 1504-1516. Carta . . . a Pedra Arias Davila

1600? Velasco, L. de. Capitulaciones que el Virrey . . . hizo con Don Juan de Onate

Bogia, Esteban & Francisco

1587 Tasso, T. Jerusalem libertada

Castro, Pedro Várez de

1597 Ercilla y Zúñiga, A.de. Araucana, ptes 1a-3a (2)

1599 Alemán, M. Guzman de Alfarache, pte 1

1599 Iñíguez de Lequerica, J. Sermones funerales

1600 Alemán, M. Guzman d'Alfarache, pte 1 (2)

Cosín, Pierres

1569 Ercilla y Zúñiga, A.de.

Araucana, pte 1a

1571 Alonso de la Veracruz. Appendix ad Speculum conjugorum

1573 Castillejo, C.de. Obras

1578 Ercilla y Zúñiga, A. Araucana, ptes 1a-2a (2)

Drouy, Guillermo

1578 Informacion de derecho . . . de la Nueva Espana

1578 Velázquez de Salazar, J. Peticion

1591 Camões, L.de. Lusiadas

1591 Petrarca, F. Sonetos

1598 Arfe y Villafañe, J.de. Quilatador de la plata

Gerardo, Querino

1586 González de Mendoza, J. Historia de la China

1586 Zurita, F. Theologicarum de Indis quaestionum, enchiridion

Gómez, Alonso

1569 Venegas de Busto, A. Differencias de libros, 1a pte

1583 Rivadeneira, P.de. Vida del .p. Ignacio de Loyola

Gómez, Alonso, Widow of

1584 Rivadeneira, P.de. Vida del padre Ignacio de Loyola

1585 Ercilla y Zúñiga, A.de. Araucana, pte 1a

1586 Rivadeneira, P.de. Vida del padre Ignacio de Loyola

1586 Rivadeneira, P.de. Vita Ignatii Loiolae

1589 Castellanos, J.de. Elegias, pte 1a

1591 Suárez de Escobar, P. Espejo de vida christiana, pte 1a

Herrera, Juan de

1599 Rocamora y Torrano, G. Sphera

Ibáñez, Sebastián

1572 Fragoso, J. Discursos de la cosas aromaticas

Imprenta Real

1596 Spain. Laws, statutes, etc. Provisiones, cedulas

Iñíguez de Lequérica, Juan, Heirs of

1600 Alemán, M. Guzman d'Alfarache, pte 1a

Madrigal, Pedro, the Elder

1587 González de Mendoza, J. Historia . . . dela China

1587 Tasso, T. Jerusalem libertada

1588 Lobo Lasso de la Vega, G. Cortes valeroso

1589 Ercilla y Zúñiga, A.de. Araucana, pte 3a

1590 Ercilla y Zúñiga, A.de. Araucana, ptes 1a-3a

1590 Leo Hebraeus. Traduzion del Indio

1590 Lima (Ecclesiastical province). Council, 1583. Concilium

1591 Herrera y Tordesillas, A.de. Historia de Portugal

1591 Lima (Ecclesiastical province). Council, 1583. Concilium

1591 Spain. Laws, statutes, etc., 1556-1598. Ordenanças para remedio de los danos . . . de los navios

1592 Moles, J.B. Memorial de . . . San Gabriel

1592 Rivadeneira, P.de. Vida del .p. Francisco de Borja

1592 Rivadeneira, P.de. Vida del padre Francisco de Borja

1593 Rivadeneira, P.de. Vida del .p. Ignacio de Loyola

1594 Rivadeneira, P.de. Vida del .p. Ignacio de Loyola

Madrigal, Pedro, the Elder, Widow of

1594 Sánchez de Acre, P. Libro del reino de Dios

1595 Rivadeneira, P.de. Obras

Madrigal, Pedro, the Younger

1595 Rivadeneira, P.de. Tratado de la religion

1595 Rivadeneira, P.de. Vita Ignatii Loiolae

1596 Davila Padilla, A. Historia de la fundacion . . . de Santiago de Mexico

1597 Matienzo, J.de. Commentaria

1599 Saavedra Guzmán, A. Peregrino indiano

1599 Vargas Machuca, B.de. Milicia . . . de las Indias

1600 Vargas Machuca, B.de. Exercicios de la gineta

Martínez, Miguel

1597 Ercilla y Zúñiga, A.de. Araucana, ptes 1a-3a

1600 Romancero general

Montoya, Juan de

1591 Espinel, V. Diversas rimas

1591 Herrera y Tordesillas, A.de.

tentiarum
1570 Soto, D.de.
Commentariorum . . . in quartum Sententiarum
Terranova y Neyla, Alonso de
1577 Torquemada, A.de. Jardin de flores curiosas
1582 Soto, D.de. De justitia
1583 San Román, A.de. Consuelo de penitentes
Terti, Joan de
1595 Román y Zamora, J. Republicas del mundo

SARAGOSSA
Alterach, Juan de
1583 Antist, V.J. Verdadera relacion de la vida . . . del padre fray Luys Bertran
Bernúz, Pedro
1554 Gómara, F.L.de. Historia general delas Indias
1555 Gómara, F.L.de. Historia general de las Indias
Bonilla, Juan de
1599 Alemán, M. Guzman de Alfarache, pte 1a
Capila, Miguel
1553 Gómara, F.L.de. Historia general de las Indias
Coci, Jorge
1511 Sobrarius, J. Panegyricum carmen
1523 Cortés, H. Carta de relacion
Escarilla, Juan, Widow of
1590 Ercilla y Zúñiga, A.de. Araucana, pte 3a
Fuentes, Domingo de
1583 Bazán, A.de. Relacion de la jornada
Hernández, Diego
1548 Venero, A.de. Enchiridion de los tiempos
Hurus, Pablo
1499 Vagad, Gauberte Fabricio de. Coronica de Aragon
Millán, Agustín
1552 Gómara, F.L.de. Istoria de las Indias
1553 Gómara, F.L.de. Historia general de las Indias
1554 Gómara, F.L.de. Historia general delas Indias
1554 Gómara, F.L.de. Historia general delas Indias, pte 2da
1555 Gómara, F.L.de. Historia general de las Indias
1561 Alvares, F. Historia de las cosas de Etiopia

Millán, Juan
1567 Pulgar, H.del. Chronica de . . . Don Hernando y Doña Ysabel
1577 Polo, G.G. Diana enamorada, pte 1a
Millán, Juana, Widow of Diego Fernández
1549 Venero, A.de. Enchiridion
Nájera, Bartolomé de
1547 Mexía, P. Coloquios o dialogos
Nájera, Bartolomé de, Widow of
1562 Mexía, P. Coloquios
1571 Torquemada, A.de. Jardin de flores curiosas
Pérez de Valdivielso, Juan
1599 Alemán, M. Guzman de Alfarache, pte 1
Robles, Lorenzo de
1596A Flor de romances. Varias romances nuevos
Robles, Lorenzo & Domingo de, Bros
1582 Bazán, A.de. Succedido a la armada
1587 Gonzalez de Mendoza, J. Historia . . . dela China
1588 González de Mendoza, J. Historia . . . de la China
Soler, Juan
1577 Ercilla y Zúñiga, A.de. Araucana, pte 1a
1578 Ercilla y Zúñiga, A.de. Araucana, pte 1a
1578 Ercilla y Zúñiga, A.de. Araucana, pte 2a
1581 Vigo, G.de. Pratica en cirurgia
1583 Bazán, A.de. Relacion de la jornada
Suelves, Miguel de
1567 Pulgar, H.del. Chronica de . . . Don Hernando y Dona Ysabel
Tabano, Angelo
1596A Flor de romances. Varias romances nuevos
Zapila, Miguel de
1554 Gómara, F.L.de. Historia general delas Indias
1555 Gómara, F.L.de. Historia general de las Indias
1561 Alvares, F. Historia de las cosas de Etiopia

SEVILLE
Printer unidentified
1542 Rodríguez, J. Relacion cier-

ta . . . de una carta
1548 Gasca, P.de la. Traslado de una carta . . . embiada . . . del Cuzco
1553? Treslado de una carta embiado de . . . los Reyes
1556? Spain. Laws, statutes, etc., 1556-1598. Ultima nueva orden
1580 Calvo, J. Cirugia
1584? San José, G.de. Razones informativas
Alvárez, Antón
1551 Cortés, M. Breve compendio de la sphera
1556 Cortés, M. Breve compendio de la sphera
Alvárez, Cristóbal
1550 Chaves, J.de. Chronographia
1551 Mexía, P. Dialogos
Barrera, Alonso de la
1574 Riguel, H. Nuevas yslas del poniente
1582 Zamorano, R. Arte de navegar
Burgos, Andrés de
1542 Díaz de Isla, R. Tractado . . . contra el mal serpentino
1546 Enciso, M.F.de. Suma de geographia
Cabrera, Rodrigo de
1595 Tovar, S.de. Examen . . . del modo de averiguar
1596 Relacion del viage que hizieron las . . . fragatas de armada
Canalla, Juan
1552 Medina, P.de. Regimiento de navegacion
Carpintero, Simon
1563 Medina, P.de. Regimiento de navegacion
Carvajal, Andrés de
1553 Spain. Casa de Contratacion de las Indias. Ordenanzas reales
Cisneros, Juan Francisco de
1580 Cháves, J.de. Chronographia
Coca, Alonso de
1559? Martínez, A. Relacion . . . de los trabajos . . . del Rio de La Plata
1562? Díez, D. Relacion
Cromberger, Jacobo
1503 Polo, M. Cosmographia
1511 Anghiera, P.M.d'. Opera (2)
1519 Enciso, M.F.de. Suma de geographia

1532 Fries, L. Epitome opusculi de curandi pusculi

1532 Gasser, A.P. Historiarum . . . epitome

1533 Bellum Christianorum principum

1534 Dionysius, Periegetes. De totius orbis situ

1535 Gasser, A.P. Historiarum . . . epitome

1535 Reisch, G. Margarita philosophica

1537 Gatinaria, M. Summi medici omnes

1540 Ptolemaeus, C. Geographia universalis

1542 Ptolemaeus, C. Geographia universalis

1544 Münster, S. Cosmographia. Beschreibung aller Lender

1545 Münster, S. Cosmographia. Beschreibung aller Lender

1545 Ptolemaeus, C. Geographia universalis

1546 Münster, S. Cosmographia: Beschreibung aller Lender

1548 Münster, S. Cosmographia: Beschreibung aller Lender

1550 Münster, S. Cosmographei, oder beschreibung aller lander

1550 Münster, S. Cosmographiae universalis lib. vi

1552 Münster, S. Cosmographiae universalis lib. vi

1552 Münster, S. Cosmographie universelle

1552 Ptolemaeus, C. Geographiae . . . libri viii

1553 Cardano, G. De subtilitate

1553 Münster, S. Cosmographei, oder Beschreibung aller lander

1554 Münster, S. Cosmographiae universalis lib. vi

1555 Münster, S. Cosmographie universelle

1556 Münster, S. Cosmographei, oder beschreibung aller lander

1556 Münster, S. Cosmographie universelle

1557 Cardano, G. De rerum varietate (2)

1558 Münster, S. Cosmografia universale

1558 Münster, S. Cosmographei, oder beschreibung aller lander

1559 Cardano, G. Offenbarung der Natur

1559 Münster, S. Cosmographiae

universalis lib. vi

1560 Cardano, G. De subtilitate (2)

1560 Giovio, P. Historiarum sui temporis

1560 Münster, S. Cosmographie universelle

1561 Giovio, P. Descriptiones . . . regionum atque locorum (2)

1561 Münster, S. Cosmographei oder beschreibung aller lander

1561 Proclus, D. De sphaera

1564 Cardano, G. Ars curandi parva

1564 Mexía, P. Vilvaltige Beschreibung christenlicher . . . Keyseren

1564 Münster, S. Cosmographey oder beschreibung aller lander

1565 Münster, S. Cosmographie universelle

1566 Cardano, G. Ars curandi parva

1566 Copernicus, N. De revolutionibus orbium

1566 Guicciardini, F. Historiarum sui temporis

1567 Fregoso, G. Exemplorum, hoc est, Dictorum . . . memorabilium

1567 Giovio, P. Historiarum sui temporis

1567 Guicciardini, F. Historiarum sui temporis

1567 Magnus, O. Historia . . . de gentium septentrionalium

1567 Magnus, O. Historien der mittnaechtigen Laender

1567 Münster, S. Cosmographey oder beschreibung aller Lander

1569 Münster, S. Cosmographey, oder Beschreibung aller Lander

1571 Giovio, P. Descriptiones . . . regionum atque locorum (2)

1572 Brant, S. Stultifera navis

1572 Münster, S. Cosmographey, oder Beschreibung aller Lander

1572 Münster, S. Cosmographiae universalis lib. vi

1572 Pantaleon, H. Diarium historicum

1574 Guicciardini, F. Gründtliche . . . beschreibung

1574 Münster, S. Cosmographey,

oder beschreibung aller Lander

1575 Giovio, P. Elogia virorum bellica (2)

1577 Giovio, P. Musaei Joviani imagines

1578 Giovio, P. Opera . . . . omnia

1578 Münster, S. Cosmographey, oder beschreibung aller Lander

1580 Giovio, P. Icones . . . virorum bellica

Resch, Conrad

1535 Reisch, G. Margarita philosophica

Schott, Johann

1508 Reisch, G. Margarita philosophica

Schroeter, Johann

1598 Ryff, P. Elementa sphaerae

Waldkirch, Konrad von

1585 Paracelsus. Cheirugia

1586 Paracelsus. Cheirugia

1587 Beuther, M. Warhafftiger kurtzer Bericht

1588 Beuther, M. Warhafftiger kurtzer Bericht

1589 Thilo, V. Icones heroum bellica

Westheimer, Bartholomäus

1541 Fregoso, B. De dictis . . . memorabilibus

Wolff, Jakob

1493 Colombo, C. De insulis

Wolff, Thomas

1519 Albertini, F. Opusculum de mirabilibus . . . Romae

BERNE

Apiarius, Matthias

1540 Ryd, V.A. Catalogus annorum

1550 Ryd, V.A. Catalogus annorum

1574 Guicciardini, F. Gründtliche . . . beschreibung

GENEVA

Printer unidentified

1561? Response aux lettres de Nicolas Durant

1561 Histoire des choses memorables advenues en . . . Bresil

1561 Richer, P. Refutation des folles resveries . . . de Nicolas Durand

1561 Richer, P. Libri duo . . . ad refutandas naenias

1565 La Place, P.de. Commentaires de l'estat de la religion (3)

1568 Gonsalvius, R. Histoire de l'Inquisition d'Espagne

1574 Léry, J.de. Histoire . . . de Sancerre

1582 La Popelinière, L.V.de. Histoire de France

1590 Goulart, S. Premier recueil (2)

1590 Goulart, S. Second recueil (2)

1595 Goulart, S. Quatriesme recueil (2)

1597 Plaintes des Eglises Reformees de France

1598 Goulart, S. Cinquiesme recueil

1599 Goulart, S. Sixiesme . . . recueil

1599 Serres, J.de. Histoire des choses memorables avenues en France

Aubert, Pierre

1570 Crespin, J. Histoire des vrays temoins

Bérion, Jean

1579 Carion, J. Chronique

1580 Carion, J. Chronique

Bianchi, Antonio de'

1588 Valleriola, F. Observationum medicinalium lib.vi

Cartier, Gabriel

1582 Casas, B.de las. Histoire admirable des horribles insolences

1588 Bodin, J. Republique

1593 Bodin, J. Republique

1596 Du Bartas, G.de S., seigneur. Hebdomas

1597 Estienne, C. Agriculture

1599 Bodin, J. Republique

Chouët, Jacques

1581 Du Bartas, G.de S., seigneur. Sepmaine

1582 Du Bartas, G.de S., seigneur. Sepmaine

1588 Du Bartas, G.de S., seigneur. Sepmaine

1589 Du Bartas, G.de S., seigneur. Seconde sepmaine

1593 Du Bartas, G.de S., seigneur. Seconde sepmaine

1593 Du Bartas, G.de S., seigneur. Sepmaine

Chuppin, Antoine

1578 Settle, D. Navigation du

Capitaine . . . Forbisher

1580 Léry, J.de. Histoire d'un voyage . . . en . . . Bresil (2)

1581 Osório, J. Histoire de Portugal

1585 Léry, J. de. Histoire d'un voyage . . . en . . . Bresil

Crespin, Jean

1564 Crespin, J. Actes des martyrs

1565 Crespin, J. Actes des martyrs

1566 Scaliger, J.C. In libros de plantis Aristoteli inscriptos (3)

1570 Crespin, J. Histoire des martyrs

1582 Crespin, J. Histoire des martyrs

Durant, Jean

1581 Du Bartas, G.de S., seigneur. Sepmaine

1582 Du Bartas, G.de S., seigneur. Sepmaine

Durant, Jean, Widow of

1588 Du Bartas, G.de S., seigneur. Sepmaine

Estienne, François

1570 Estienne, C. Agriculture

1581 Osório, J. Histoire de Portugal

Forest, François

1587 La Noüe, F.de. Discours politiques

Grégoire, Jean

1571 Sarrasin, J.A. De peste commentarius

1572 Sarrasin, J.A. De peste commentarius (2)

Juge, Claude de

1577 Bodin, J. Republique

Köln, Wygand

1519 Sensuyent lordonnance des royaumes

La Fontaine, Charles de

1579 Estienne, C. Agriculture

Laon, Jean de

1596 Fernel, J. Universa medicina

Lertout, Jean

1576 Duchesne, J. Sclopetarius

1576 Duchesne, J. Traitte de la cure . . . des arcbusades

1588 Chaumette, J. Enchiridion chirurgicum

1591 Duchesne, J. Opera medica

1591 Duchesne, J. Sclopetarius

1596 Duchesne, J. Opera omnia

1596 Duchesne, J. Sclopetarius

1600 Duchesne, J. Opera medica

1600 Duchesne, J. Sclopetarius

Saint André, Pierre de

1595 Carion, J. Chronique

Stoer, Jacob

1573 La Popelinière, L.V.de. Vraye . . . histoire des troubles

1577 Fernel, J. Universa medicina

1578 Fernel, J. Universa medicina (2)

1579 Daneau, L. Geographiae poeticae

1580 Daneau, L. Geographiae poeticae

1580 Fernel, J. Universa medicina

1588 Airebaudouze, P.de. Orbis terrarum . . . epitome

1589 Airebaudouze, P.de. Orbis terrarum . . . epitome

1591 Bodin, J. De republica

1592 Airebaudouze, P.de. Orbis terrarum . . . epitome

1593 Grand dictionaire françois-latin

1595 Bodin, J. Methodus ad facilem historiarum cognitio

1595 Carion, J. Chronique

1596 Estienne, C. Dictionarium historicum

1596 La Noue, F.de. Discours politiques

Tournes, Jean de

1587 Maycrnc, L.T.dc. Histoire generale d'Espagne

1589 Sarrasin, J.A. De peste

1591 Boemus, J. Mores . . . omnium gentium

Vignon, Eustache

1570 Serres, J.de. Commentariorum de statu religionis

1570 Serres, J.de. Rerum in Gallia

1571 Serres, J.de. Commentariorum de statu religionis

1572 Serres, J.de. Commentariorum de statu religionis

1575 Serres, J.de. Commentariorum de statu religionis

1577 Serres, J.de. Commentariorum de statu religionis

1578 Benzoni, G. Novae Novi Orbis

1579 Benzoni, G. Histoire nouvelle du Nouveau Monde

1580 Serres, J.de. Commentariorum de statu religionis

1581 Benzoni, G. Novae Novi Orbis

1586 Benzoni, G. Historia Indiae
Occidentalis
1586 Léry, J.de. Historia navigationis in Brasiliam
Vignon, Eustache, Heirs of
1593 Duchesne, J. Grand miroir
du monde
1593 Guicciardini, F. Histoire des
guerres d'Italie
1594 Léry, J.de. Histoire d'un
voyage fait en . . . Bresil
1594 Léry, J.de. Historia navigationis in Brasiliam
1597 Crespin, J. Histoire des
martyrs
1599 Léry, J.de. Histoire d'un
voyage fait en . . . Bresil
1600 Benzoni, G. Novae Novi
Orbis
1600 Léry, J.de. Histoire d'un
voyage fait en . . . Bresil

LAUSANNE
Le Preux, François
1576 Guilandini, M. In C.Plinii
majoris capita aliquot . . .
commentarius

SAINT GALL
Straub, Leonhard
1583 Gesner, K. Köstlichen . . .
Schatzes Euonymi

ZURICH
**Froschauer, Christoph, the
Elder**
1534 Vadianus, J.von Watt,
called. Epitome trium terrae
partium (2)
1545 Gesner, K. Bibliotheca
universalis

1546 Honter, J. Rudimenta
cosmographica
1548 Gesner, K. Pandectarum
. . . libri xxi
1548 Honter, J. Rudimenta
cosmographica
1548 Honter, J. Rudimentorum
cosmographicorum . . . libri iii
1548 Vadianus, J.von Watt,
called. Epitome trium terrae
partium
1549 Honter, J. Rudimentorum
cosmographicorum . . . libri iii
1550? Vadianus, J.von Watt,
called. Epitome trium terrae
partium
1552 Honter, J. Rudimentorum
cosmographicorum . . . libri iii
1555 Gesner, K. Appendix
Bibliothecae
1555 Gesner, K. Historiae
animalium liber iii
1555 Gesner, K. Icones avium
1557 Gesner, K. Vogelbüch
1558 Honter, J. Rudimentorum
cosmographicorum . . . libri iii
1560 Gesner, K. Icones avium
1560 Gesner, K. Nomenclator
aquatilium animantian
1564 Honter, J. Rudimentorum
cosmographicorum . . . libri iii
**Froschauer, Christoph, the
Younger**
1565 Gesner, K. Euonymus de
remediis secretis
1565 Honter, J. Rudimentorum
cosmographicorum . . . libri iii
1569 Gesner, K. Euonymus sive
de Remediis secretis, pars
secunda
1570? Gesner, K. Euonymus sive
de Remediis secretis, pars

secunda
1570 Honter, J. Rudimentorum
cosmographicorum . . . libri iii
1572 Paracelsus. De medicamentorum simplicium
1573 Honter, J. Rudimentorum
cosmographicorum . . . libri iii
1574 Gesner, K. Bibliotheca . . .
in epitomen redacta
1575 Honter, J. Rudimentorum
cosmographicorum . . . libri iii
1577 Gesner, K. Epistolarum
medicinalium . . . libri iii
1578 Honter, J. Rudimentorum
cosmographicorum . . . libri iii
1581 Gesner, K. Vogelbuch
1581 Honter, J. Rudimentorum
cosmographicorum . . . libri iii
1583 Gesner, K. Bibliotheca . . .
in epitomen redacta
1583 Honter, J. Rudimentorum
cosmographicorum . . . libri iii
Froschauer, House of
1590? Honter, J. Rudimentorum
cosmographicorum . . . libri iii
Gessner, Andreas
1552 Gesner, K. Thesaurus
Euonymi
1554 Gesner, K. Thesaurus
Euonymi
Gessner, Andreas & Jakob
1555 Gesner, K. Schatz
1555 Gesner, K. Chirurgia
Gessner, Jakob
1583 Gesner, K. Köstlichen . . .
Schatzes Euonymi
Wolf, Johannes
1597 Honter, J. Enchiridion cosmographiae
Wyssenbach, Rudolph
1552 Gesner, K. Thesaurus
Euonymi

An Alphabetical Index of Printers and Booksellers
& Their Geographic Location

Accolti, Vincente (1574-1588): Rome

Ach, Heinrich von (1574-1576): Cologne

Adam, Daniel (1596): Prague

Aggas, Edward (1587-1599): London

Aguilar, Agustín (1599): Valencia

Alantse, Leonhart (1518-1520): Vienna

Alantse, Leonhart & Lucas (1514-1516): Vienna

Alberti, Giovanni (1597): Venice

Albinus, Bernardus (1597-1592): Speyer

Albrecht, Lorenz (1600): Lübeck

Aldine Press (1575-1592): Venice

Aleman, Balthazar (1552): Lyons

Allde, Elizabeth (1592-1597): London

Allde, John (1563?): London

Alterach, Juan de (1583): Saragossa

Alvares, António (1593): Lisbon

Alvares, Joào (1550-1561): Coimbra

Alvarez, Antón (1551-1556): Seville

Alvarez, Cristóbal (1550-1551): Seville

Amello, Joan (1598): Barcelona

Amorós, Carlos (1515-1545): Barcelona

Anard, Jean (1599-1600): Lyons

Ancelin, Thibaud (1594): Lyons

Ancxt, Marie (1548): Antwerp

Andreae, Hieronymus (1552): Nuremberg

Andreae, Lamberg (1594-1597): Cologne

Andres, Jean (1596): Perpignan

Andrysowicz, Lazarus (1581): Cracow

Angeli, Giuseppe degli (1577): Rome

Angelieri, Giorgio (1570-1600): Venice

Angulo, Andrés de (1569-1572): Alcalá de Henares

Anoke, John, pseud. (1589): London

Anshelm, Thomas (1509): Pforzheim; (1512-1513): Tübingen; (1519): Hagenau

Apel, Jakob (1594-1597): Leipzig

Apianus, Peter (1524): Landshut

Apianus, Peter & Georg (1532-1533): Ingolstadt

Apiarius, Matthias (1540-1574): Berne

Apiarius, Samuel (1590): Basel

Arbús, Sanson (1596): Perpignan

Arnoullet, Balthazar (1546-1555): Lyons

Arnoullet, Balthazar, Widow of (1557-1559): Lyons

Arrivabene, Andrea (1539-1557): Venice

Arrivabene, Giorgio (1496): Venice

Aspley, William (1599A-1600A): London

Astile, John, pseud. (1589): London

Astley, Hugh (1592-1596): Strassburg

Aubert, Pierre (1570): Geneva

Aubry, Jean (1592-1600): Frankfurt am Main

Augereau, Antoine (1532): Paris

Ausoult, Jean (1547): Lyons

Auvray, Guillaume (1586-1587): Paris

Avanzi, Lodovico degli (1556-1573): Venice

Avila, Gaspar de (1525-1540): Toledo

Ayala Cano, Juan de (1570): Toledo

B., R. (1600): London

Bacquenois, Nicolas (1550): Lyons

Bacx, Andreas (1586-1597): Antwerp

Badian Steps, At the (1582?): Florence

Badius, Josse, Ascensius (1505-1527): Paris

Bakalar, Mikulus (1505): Pilsen, Czechoslovakia

Baldini, Vittorio (1581-1594): Ferrara

Baligault, Félix (1497-1503): Paris

Ballard, Richard (1581-1585): London

Ballou, Daniel (1595): Lyons

Balsarin, Guillaume (1498-1499): Lyons

Barbé, Jean (1545): Paris

Barbier. Symphorien (1556-1564): Lyons

Barbou, Jean (1537): Lyons

Barezzi, Barezzo (1592-1599): Venice

Barezzi, Barezzo, & Co. (1599): Venice

Barker, Christopher, Deputies of (1597): London

Barker, Robert (1597A-1600): London

Barkhusen, Herman (1505): Rostock

Barley, William (1592-1595): London

Barlow, William (1595): London

Barnes, John (1596): Oxford

Barreda, Antonio de (1498): Salamanca

Barreira, António de (1593): Coimbra

Barreira, Joao de (1550-1554): Coimbra;
  (1563-1574): Lisbon

Barrera, Alonso de la (1574-1582): Sevi̇lle

Barril, Jean (1532): Toulouse

Bartoli, Girolamo (1568): Pavia; (1585-1591):
  Genoa

Bartoli, Girolamo, Heirs of (1597): Genoa

Basa, Bernardo (1596): Venice

Basa, Domenico (1581-1587): Rome

Bascarini, Nicolò de (1544-1548): Venice

Basignana, Etienne de (1516): Lyons

Basilea, Fadrique de. *See* Biel, Friedrich

Basse, Nikolaus (1588-1598): Frankfurt am Main

Bauchu, Jean (1591): Rouen

Bauduin, Gilles (1598-1600): Arras

Baum, Theodor (1567): Cologne

Bayuera, Constantio (1505): Venice

Bazzachi, Giovanni (1587): Piacenza

Beauvais, Romain de (1598-1600): Rouen

Bebel, Johann (1524-1538): Basel

Beck, Balthasar (1541): Strassburg

Beckler, Matthaeus (1598-1599): Frankfurt am
  Main

Belis, Bonaventure (1573): Rouen

Bellagamba, Giovanni Battista (1599): Bologna

Bellère, Balthasar (1596-1599): Douai

Bellère, Jean (1554-1587): Antwerp

Bellère, Jean, Widow & Heirs of (1600): Antwerp

Bellère, Pierre (1575-1598): Antwerp

Bellone, Antonio (1537): Genoa

Bellone, Cristoforo (1579): Genoa

Bellone, Marc' Antonio (1576-1578): Genoa

Benacci, Alessandro (1559-1593): Bologna

Benedictis, Hieronymus de (1520-1524): Bologna

Benedictis, Hieronymus de, Heirs of (1533):
  Bologna

Benzoni, Gabriel (1565): Venice

Béraud, Jean (1579): Lyons

Béraud, Symphorien (1582): Lyons

Berg, Adam (1571-1589): Munich

Berg, Johann vom (1551-1580): Nuremberg

Bergen, Gimel (1584-1591): Dresden

Berghen, Adriaen van (1533-1534): Antwerp

Bergmann, Johann (1494-1499): Basel

Bericchia, Jacomo (1585-1586): Rome

Béringen, Godefroy & Marcellin (1549): Lyons

Bérion, Jean (1579-1580): Geneva

Bernabé, Cristiano (1596): Cuenca, Spain

Bernuz, Pedro (1554-1555): Saragossa

Bertano, Giovanni Antonio (1580): Venice

Bertault, Pierre (1598-1600): Paris

Bertellio, Lucas (1566): Padua

Bertellio, Lucas, & Co. (1564): Padua

Berthelet, Thomas (1533-1540): London

Besicken, Johann (1493?-1506?): Rome

Bevilacqua, Nicolò (1563-1568): Venice

Bevilacqua, Nicolò, Heirs of (1578-1590): Turin

Bevilacqua, Simon (1516): Lyons

Beyer, Johann, Heirs of (1597-1598): Leipzig

Beys, Gilles (1578): Paris

Bianchi, Antonio de' (1588): Geneva

Biel, Friedrich (1500): Burgos

Biestkens, Nikolaus, the Younger (1596): Amsterdam

Bindoni, Alessandro (1520?-1528): Venice

Bindoni, Alessandro & Benedetto (1521): Venice

Bindoni, Bernardino (1535-1540): Venice

Bindoni, Francesco, the Elder (1534-1553): Venice

Bindoni, Francesco, the Younger (1554-1561):
  Venice

Bindoni, Gasparo (1562-1564): Venice

Birckmann, Arnold (1532): Cologne; (1533-1540):
  Antwerp

Birckmann, Arnold, Heirs of (1557-1566): Antwerp;
  (1567-1581): Cologne

Birckmann, Arnold, Widow of (1548): Antwerp;
  (1549): Paris

Birckmann, Johann (1570-1571): Cologne

Birckmann, Johann, Widow of (1573): Cologne

Birckmann, House of (1586-1597): Cologne

Bishop, George (1589-1600): London

Blado, Antonio (1524-1553): Rome

Blado, Antonio, Heirs of (1567-1573): Rome

Blanchard, Antoine (1528-1530): Lyons

Blount, Edward (1598-1600): London

Blum, Michael (1532): Leipzig

Böttiger, Gregorius (1493?-1496): Leipzig

Bogard, Jacques (1543-1548): Paris

Bogard, Jean (1584): Douai

Bogardus, Joannes (1565-1597): Louvain

Bogia, Esteban & Francisco (1587): Madrid

Bollaert, Roelant (1527-1529?): Antwerp

Bollifant, Edmund (1595-1600): London

Bonaccorsi, Francesco (1496)ː Florence

Bonardo, Cornelio (1586): Salamanca

Bonardo, Pellegrino (1564-1573): Bologna

Bonardo, Vincenzo (1536): Bologna

Bonelli, Giovanni Maria (1553-1576): Venice

Bonelli, Giovanni Maria, Heirs of (1572): Venice

Bonetti, Luca (1593): Rome

Bonfadini, Bartholomeo (1583-1596): Rome

Bonfadino, Giovanni Battista (1588): Venice

Bonfons, Nicolas (1575-1600): Paris

Bonfons, Nicolas & Pierre (1600): Paris

Bonhomme, Macé (1554-1558): Lyons

Bonibelli, Marc' Antonio (1597): Venice

Bonibelli, Michele (1595-1596): Venice

Bonilla, Juan de (1599): Saragossa

Bonte, Grégoire de (1530-1553): Antwerp

Bonyn, Benoît (1525-1532): Lyons

Bordeaux, Jean de (1571-1578): Paris

Borgominieri, Rutilio (1565): Venice

Bornat, Claud (1556): Barcelona

Borsano, Jo. Ambrosio da (1535): Milan

Boscard, Jean, Widow of (1593): Douai

Boscho, Joannes Andreas de (1496): Pavia

Bosello, Matteo (1573): Venice

Bosello, Pietro (1552-1560): Venice

Bottis, Christophorus de (1496): Venice

Bouchet, Jacques (1526): Poitiers

Bouchet, Jacques & Guillaume, Bros (1559): Poitiers

Boudeville, Guy de (1553): Toulouse

Boyer, Benito (1566-1573): Salamanca; (1579-1599): Medina del Campo

Boyer, Benito, Heirs of (1595): Medina del Campo

Boyer, Jacques (1557): Lyons

Boyer, Juan (1583): Valladolid

Bozzola, Giovanni Battista (1571): Bologna

Bozzola, Thomas, Heirs of (1600): Bergamo

Brachonier, Philippe (1583): Paris

Bradock, Richard (1592-1600): London

Bramereau, Jacques (1590-1599): Avignon

Brandes, Lüdeke (1590): Helmstadt

Brandis, Moritz (1498): Leipzig & Magdeburg

Braubach, Peter (1536): Hagenau

Braun, Georg (1572-1593): Antwerp; (1575): Cologne

Breton, Richard (1502-1567): Paris

Breyer, Lucas, the Elder (1561): Paris

Briganci, The (1579): Venice

Brocar, Arnão Guillén de (1511-1512): Logroño; (1516): Alcalá de Henares

Brocar, Juan de (1539-1553): Alcalá de Henares

Broome, Joan (1591): London

Broome, William (1583-1585): London

Browne, John, Sr. (1599): London

Brubach, Peter (1537-1539): Hall (Swabia)

Brucioli, Francesco & Bros. (1543): Venice

Brumen, Thomas (1578): Paris

Bruneau, Jean (1565-1567): Paris

Bruyn, Abraham (1586?-1589): Antwerp

Bry, Johann Theodor & Johann Israel de (1597-1599): Frankfurt am Main

Bry, Theodor de (1590-1599): Frankfurt am Main

Bry, Theodor de, Widow & Heirs of (1599): Frankfurt am Main

Brylinger, Nikolaus (1550-1561): Basel

Brylinger, Nikolaus, Heirs of (1568-1582): Basel

Buchholtz, Bertram (1598-1599): Cologne

Buck, Herman de (1600): Amsterdam

Bund, Sigmund (1557): Hagenau

Buon, Gabriel (1562-1587): Paris

Buon, Gabriel, Widow of (1597-1600): Paris

Burby, Cuthbert (1596-1599): London

Burges, Nicolas de. *See* Le Bourgeois, Nicolas

Burgofranco, Jacobus de (1509): Pavia

Burgos, Andrés de (1542-1546): Seville; (1554-1557): Evora

Busby, John, Sr. (1592-1596): London

Busdrago, Vincenzo (1551-1558): Lucca

Bussemacher, Johann (1594-1600): Cologne

Buys, Albert (1595): Düsseldorf

Bynneman, Henry (1568-1584): London

Cabrera, Rodrigo de (1595-1596): Seville

Cacchi, Giuseppe (1572-1573): Naples

Cadman, Thomas (1585-1589A): London

Cagnacini, Giulio Cesare (1582): Ferrara

Cagnacini, Giulio Cesare & Bros (1585): Ferrara

Calenius, Gerwin (1564-1586): Cologne

Calentano, Andrea (1586): Rome

Calles, Pierre (1600): Rouen

Calvarin, Simon (1566-1578): Paris

Calvo, Andrea (1522): Milan

Calvo, Francesco Minizio (1523-1527): Rome; (1540): Milan

Cambier, Robert (1585): Frankfurt am Main

Cambier, Robert, Heirs of (1600): Frankfurt am Main

Cammerlander, Jakob (1534-1545): Strassburg

Camocio, Giovanni Francesco (1557-1572): Venice

Campos, Hermão de (1516): Lisbon

Canacci, Antonio (1581): Casalmaggiore

Canalla, Juan (1552): Seville

Cancer, Mathias (1567): Naples

Caneo, Gian' Antonio (1594): Florence

Caneto, Joannes Arlonius de (1534): Naples

Canin, Abraham (1598): Dordrecht

Canin, Isaack (1599): Dordrecht

Canova, Alejandro de (1570): Salamanca

Canova, Juan de (1557-1565): Salamanca

Cantarello, Ferdinando (1567): Barcelona

Canto, Francisco del (1567-1589): Medina del
  Campo

Canto, Santiago del (1595): Medina del Campo

Capello, Giovanni Battista (1582): Naples

Capila, Miguel (1553): Saragossa

Carcano, Antonius de (1493): Pavia

Carlino, Giovanni Giacomo (1596-1599): Naples

Carlo, Giovanni Stefano di (1516): Florence

Carnaccioli, Andrea de (1556): Venice

Caron, Christoval (1556): Milan

Carpintero, Simón (1563): Seville

Carpo, Marco Antonio da (1536): Bologna

Cartier, Gabriel (1582-1599): Geneva

Carvajal, Andrés de (1553): Seville

Carvalho, Sebastiào (1600): Lisbon

Castiglione, Giovanni Antonio da (1556): Milan

Castro, Pedro de (1542?-1549): Medina del Campo

Castro, Pedro Várez de (1597-1600): Madrid

Cavalli, Giorgio de' (1564-1565): Venice

Caveiller, Jean (1558-1560): Paris

Cavellat, Gabriel, Widow of (1577-1588): Paris

Cavellat, Guillaume (1550-1572): Paris

Cavellat, Léon (1588): Paris

Cavellat, Pierre (1578-1584): Paris

Cawood, John (1570): London

Caymox, H. & B. (1598): Nuremberg

Cendrat, Jaime (1586-1599): Barcelona

Cervicornus, Eucharius (1523-1537): Cologne

Cesano, Bartolomeo (1551): Venice

Cesare, Cesare, & Bros (1582): Naples

Cesneros, Juan Francisco de (1580): Seville

Charlewood, John (1573-1592): London

Chaudière, Guillaume, the Elder (1571-1600): Paris

Chaudière, Regnault (1520): Paris

Chesneau, Nicolas (1574-1583): Paris

Chevalier, Pierre (1598): Paris

Chevallon, Claude (1526-1534): Paris

Chevillot, Pierre (1581-1583): Paris

Cholinus, Maternus (1566): Cologne

Cholinus, Peter (1590): Cologne

Chouët, Jacques (1581-1593): Geneva

Chouin, Jean, pseud. (1579): Bordeaux

Christoffel, Johann (1589-1600): Cologne

Chuppin, Antoine (1578-1585): Geneva;
  (1578-1585?): La Rochelle

Ciotti, Giovanni Battista (1591-1600): Venice. Cf.
  following item

Ciotti, Johann Baptist (1588-1592): Cologne. Cf.
  preceding item

Claeszoon, Cornelis (1576-1600): Amsterdam

Claudet, Nicolas (1596): Pont-à-Moussin, France

Clémence, Abel (1565): Rouen

Cloquemin, Louis, the Elder (1571-1581): Lyons

Cnipius, Joannes (1578-1584): Frankfurt am Main

Coattino, Francesco (1586): Rome

Coca, Alonso de (1559?-1562?): Seville

Coci, Jorge (1511-1523): Saragossa

Cock, Symon (1525?-1534): Antwerp

Coldock, Francis (1573-1574): London

Colines, Simon de (1525-1540): Paris

Colomiès, Jacques (1532-1562): Toulouse

Comin da Trino (1532-1572): Venice

Compagnia Bresciana (1598-1599): Brescia

Coninx, Arnout (1584-1595): Antwerp

Constantin, Antoine (1545?): Lyons

Coppens van Diest, Gillis, the Elder (1539-1572):
  Antwerp

Coppens van Diest, Gillis, the Younger (1573-1574):
  Antwerp

Corcuera, Pedro de (1567): Valladolid

Cordier, Jean (1575): Antwerp

Córdova, Martín de (1597): Valladolid

Cormellas, Sebastián de (1592-1600): Barcelona

Cornetti, Giacomo (1585-1587): Venice

Correa, Francisco (1566-1581): Lisbon

Correzet, Gilles (1553-1555): Paris

Cortey, Pablo (1566): Barcelona

Corvinus, Christoph (1582). See Rab, Christoph

Corvinus, Christoph (1594-1599): Herborn

Corvinus, Georg (1561-1574). See Rab, Georg

Cosín, Pierres (1569-1578): Madrid

Cosío, Diego (1595): Salamanca

Costantini, Balthazar (1553-1558): Venice

Costilla, Jorge (1510-1526): Valencia

Cotier, Gabriel (1561-1563): Lyons

Cotier, Gabriel, Widow of (1566-1573): Lyons

Cotinet, Denys (1584): Paris

Cottereau, Claude (1591): Chartres

Cousteau, Antoine (1525): Paris
Craesbeeck, Pedro (1600): Lisbon
Cratander, Andreas (1522-1532): Basel
Crato, Johann. *See* Krafft, Johann, Wittenberg
Creede, Thomas (1595-1600): London
Crespin, Jean, the Elder (1530): Lyons
Crespin, Jean, the Younger (1564-1582): Geneva
Crevel, Jean, the Elder (1573): Rouen
Crevel, Jean, the Younger (1598): Rouen
Cromberger, Jacobo (1503-1523): Seville
Cromberger, Jácome (1552): Seville
Cromberger, Juan (1530-1536): Seville
Cyaneus, Louis (1531): Paris

Dallier, Jean (1557): Paris
Danter, John (1596): London
Danza, Paolo (1534): Venice
Daré, Thomas (1598): Rouen
Davantes, Pierre (1572): Basel
David, Mathieu (1552-1558): Paris
Dawson, Thomas, Sr. (1576A-1599): London
Day, John (1559-1579): London
Deffner, Georg (1586-1590): Leipzig
Delas, Léger (1597): Paris
Delicado, Francisco (1529): Venice
Denham, Henry (1566-1586A): London
Denise, Estienne (1556): Paris
Des Preyz, Jean (1592): Langres, France
Des Prez, François (1567): Paris
Desprez, Mayse (1595-1597): Lyons
Des Rues, Guillaume (1600): Paris
Dewes, Garrat (1578): London
Dexter, Robert (1591-1599): London
Diani, Tito (1583-1585): Rome
Díaz, Fernando (1569-1588): Seville
Díaz, Juan (1582): Granada
Didier, Jean (1592-1593): Lyons
Dietz, Ludwig (1519): Rostock
Discepolo, Girolamo (1593-1596): Verona
Doesborch, Jan van (1506-1522?): Antwerp
Donangeli, Ascanius & Hieronymus (1591): Rome
Dongois, Jean. *See* Ongois, Jean d'
Doni, Anton Francesco (1548): Venice
Dorici, Valerio & Luigi (1550-1556): Rome
Dorp, Jan Claeszoon van (1598): Leyden
Dortelata, Neri (1544): Florence
Dotil, Giraldo (1599-1600): Barcelona
Drouart, Ambroise (1598): Paris
Drouy, Guillermo (1578-1598): Madrid

Dubois, Michael (1554-1556): Lyons
Du Bois, Simon (1528): Paris
Du Fossé, Nicolas (1589): Paris
Du Gort, Jean (1557): Rouen
Du Gort, Robert & Jean (1551): Rouen
Du Mont, Claude, pseud. *See* Gomet, Barthélemy
Du Petit Val, Raphael (1593-1598): Rouen
Duport, Ambroise (1586): Lyons
Du Pré, Galliot, the Elder (1514-1534): Paris
Du Pré, Galliot, the Younger (1572): Paris
Du Puys, Jacques, the Elder (1551-1589): Paris
Du Puys, Jacques, the Younger (1598): Paris
Du Puys, Mathurin (1546): Paris
Durant, Jean (1581-1582): Geneva
Durant, Jean, Widow of (1588): Geneva
Du Ry, Antoine (1525): Lyons
Dusinelli, Pietro (1595): Venice
Duval, Denys (1578): Paris

East, Thomas (1571-1596): London
Eder, Wolfgang (1580-1590): Ingolstadt
Edoard, Nicolas (1559): Lyons
Egenolff, Christian (1532-1564): Frankfurt am Main; (1543): Marburg
Egenolff, Christian, Heirs of (1566-1598): Frankfurt am Main
Egenolff, Paul (1598): Marburg
Eguía, Miguel de (1526-1533): Alcalá de Henares; (1527): Toledo; (1529): Logroño
Eliano, Vittorio (1570-1575): Rome
Eliot's Court Press (1592-1600): London
Elzevir, Gillis (1599): The Hague
Elzevir, Louis (1594-1595): Leyden
Emmel, Samuel (1559): Strassburg
Episcopius, Eusebius (1574): Basel
Episcopius, Nikolaus, the Elder (1531-1544): Basel
Episcopius, Nikolaus, the Younger (1561-1574): Basel
Episcopius, Nikolaus, the Younger & Eusebius (1563): Basel
Erfurt, Hans von (1519): Augsburg
Erlinger, Georg (1524): Bamberg
Escarilla, Juan, Widow of (1590): Saragossa
Escrivano, Alonso (1571-1577): Seville
Esparza, Martin de (1584): Valencia
Espinosa, Juan de (1541-1551): Medina del Campo; (1548): Toledo
Esquivivas, Alonso de (1520): Toledo
Estiard, Pierre (1571-1596): Lyons

Estienne, François (1538): Paris; (1570-1581): Geneva

Estienne, Henri, the Elder (1512-1518?): Paris

Estienne, Robert, the Younger (1579): Paris

Faber, Abraham (1591): Metz

Faber, Johann (1527-1528): Basel; (1530-1536): Freiburg

Facciotto, Guglielmo (1591-1596): Rome

Farine, Jérôme, pseud. *See* Harsy, Antoine de

Farri, Domenico (1555-1597): Venice

Farri, Pietro (1596): Jesi, Italy

Faure, Jacques (1554-1555): Lyons

Ferbrand, William (1600): London

Ferdelat, Pierre (1594): Lyons

Ferioli, Gratiadeo (1596): Milan

Fernández, Juan (1595): Salamanca

Fernández de Córdova, Alonso & Diego (1572): Valladolid

Fernández de Córdova, Diego (1574-1597): Valladolid

Fernández de Córdova, Francisco (1545-1567): Valladolid

Ferrari, Giorgio (1581-1598): Rome

Ferrariis, Johannes Jacobus (1509): Milan

Ferrer, Juan (1550-1557): Toledo

Février, Jean (1578-1583): Paris

Feyerabend, Hieronymus (1571-1591): Frankfurt am Main

Feyerabend, Johann (1590-1597): Frankfurt am Main

Feyerabend, Sigmund (1567-1591): Frankfurt am Main

Feyerabend, Sigmund, Heirs of (1592): Frankfurt am Main

Fezandat, Michel (1550-1552): Paris

Field, Richard (1589-1599): London

Fischer, Peter (1586-1594): Frankfurt am Main

Fischer, Peter, Heirs of (1597): Frankfurt am Main

Flores, Pedro (1593): Lisbon

Flajollet, Jean (1539): Lyons

Foillet, Jakob (1600): Mümpelgart

Foillet, Jean (1592): Monbéliard

Foquel, Guillermo (1588-1589): Salamanca

Forest, François (1587): Geneva; (1587): Lyons; (1587-1599): Basel

Forster, Michael (1599): Amberg, Germany

Foucher, Jean (1539-1563): Paris

Fouet, Robert (1596): Paris

Fowler, John (1570-1572): Louvain

Fradin, François. (1498): Lyons

Fradin, Pierre (1556): Lyons

Franceschi, Francesco dei (1571-1592): Venice; (1599): Bologna

Franceschi, Francesco, Heirs of (1600): Venice

Franceschi, Pietro dei (1575): Venice

Franceschini, Camillo (1576-1582): Venice

Franceschini, Camillo & Francesco (1565): Venice

Franck, Matthäus (1565-1566): Augsburg

Freitag, Andreas (1493): Rome

Frellon, Jean (1547-1561): Lyons

Frellon, Jean & François (1536-1546): Lyons

Fries, Augustin (1556): Strassburg

Friess, Wolfgang (1537): Basel

Frisius, Gemma (1544): Antwerp

Froben, Hieronymus, the Elder (1531-1544): Basel

Froben, Hieronymus, the Younger (1585): Basel

Froben, Johann (1518): Basel

Froben, Johann Erasmus (1538): Basel

Froben Office (1530-1556): Basel

Froschauer, Christoph, the Elder (1534-1564): Zurich

Froschauer, Christoph, the Younger (1565-1583): Zurich

Froschauer, Hans (1505): Augsburg

Froschauer, House of (1590?): Zurich

Fuentes, Domingo de (1583): Saragossa

Furter, Michael (1505-1517): Basel

Gabiano, David & Jean de, Bros (1593-1594): Lyons

Gabiano, Jean François de (1556): Lyons

Gabiano, Scipion de & Bros (1536): Lyons

Gadoulleau, Michel (1578): Paris

Galharde, Germão (1537-1553): Lisbon

Galignani, Giovanni Battista & Giorgio (1598): Venice

Galignani, Simone (1572-1576): Venice

Galignani, Simone, Heirs of (1590-1596): Venice

Galle, Philippe (1572-1598): Antwerp

Gara, Giovanni di (1586): Venice

Garaldis, Bernardinus de (1516-1521): Pavia

Garanta, Nicolò (1526): Venice

Gardano, Alessandro (1586): Rome

Gardano, Angelo (1578): Venice

Gardener, Thomas (1576-1577): London

Garrich, House of (1591): Gerona

Gast, Matías (1563-1570): Salamanca

Gast, Matías, Heirs of (1585): Salamanca

Gaudoul, Pierre (1525): Paris

Gaultherot, Vivant (1542-1553): Paris

Gaulthier, Pierre (1545-1552): Paris

Gazeau, Guillaume (1547-1558): Lyons

Gazeau, Jacques (1543-1549): Paris

Gemperlin, Abraham (1586-1592): Freiburg

Gengenbach, Pamphilus (1522?): Basel

Genovés, Jerónimo (1596-1600): Barcelona

Gerardo, Querino (1586): Madrid

Gering, Ulrich (1506): Paris

Gerlach, Katharine (1580): Nuremberg

Germain, Barthélemy (1579): Basel

Gesselin, Jean (1595): Paris

Gessner, Andreas (1552-1554): Zurich

Gessner, Andreas & Jakob (1555): Zurich

Gessner, Jakob (1583): Zurich

Ghelen, Jan van (III) (1584): Antwerp

Ghemart, Adrián (1567-1568): Valladolid

Ghirlandi, Andrea (1505?): Florence

Giaccarelli, Anselmo (1550-1553): Bologna

Gibier, Eloi (1559): Orléans

Giglio, Domenico (1564-1565): Venice

Giglio, Domenico & Alvise (1566): Venice

Giglio, Girolamo & Co. (1558): Venice

Gigliotti, Domenico (1595): Rome

Gigliotti, Giovanni, Heirs of (1587-1590): Rome

Gilles, Gilles (1558-1567): Paris

Gilles, Nicolas, the Younger (1595): Paris

Giolito de' Ferrari, Gabriel (1546-1571): Venice

Giolito de' Ferrari, Gabriel & Bros. (1552-1556): Venice

Giolito de' Ferrari, House of (1586-1598): Venice

Giraldo, Pedro (1497): Valladolid

Girardengus, Franciscus (1494?): Pavia

Girault, Ambroise (1525-1536): Paris

Giunta, Bernardo, the Elder (1539-1549): Florence

Giunta, Bernardo, the Elder, Heirs of (1552-1566): Florence

Giunta, Bernardo, the Younger (1587): Venice

Giunta, Bernardo & Bros (1581-1592): Venice

Giunta, Filippo (1591): Venice

Giunta, Filippo, the Elder (1507-1519): Florence

Giunta, Filippo, the Younger (1588-1589): Florence

Giunta, Filippo, the Younger, Heirs of (1591): Florence

Giunta, Jacques (1521-1539): Lyons

Giunta, Jacques, Heirs of (1559-1569): Lyons

Giunta, Jeanne (1582): Lyons

Giunta, Lucantonio (1520-1536): Venice

Giunta, Lucantonio, Heirs of (1543-1584): Venice

Giunta, Philippe de (1582): Burgos

Giunta, House of (1553-1598): Venice; (1560-1579): Florence

Giunta Press (1586-1598): Lyons

Glamet, Noël (1585-1598): Rennes

Glaser, Hans Wolf (1566?): Nuremberg

Glockner, Tomás (1493): Seville

Gomet, Barthélemy (1579): Blois

Gómez, Alonso (1569-1583): Madrid

Gómez, Alonso, Widow of (1584-1591): Madrid

Gonçalves, António (1571-1576): Lisbon

Gotart, Huberto, Widow of (1592): Barcelona

Gottfried von Kempen. *See* Kempen, Gottfried von, Cologne

Gourbin, Gilles (1554-1585): Paris

Gourmont, Gilles de (1506-1517): Paris

Gourmont, Robert de (1508): Paris

Gracián, Juan (1573-1595): Alcalá de Henares

Graells, Gabriel (1599-1600): Barcelona

Graf, Stephen Melchior (1543-1551): Freiburg

Graminäus, Theodor (1572): Cologne

Gran, Heinrich (1518): Strassburg

Granjon, Robert (1550-1551): Paris

Grapheus, Joannes (1528-1553): Antwerp

Grassi, Bartolomeo (1585-1591): Rome

Grave, Claes de (1533): Antwerp

Greco, Giorgio (1595-1597): Vicenza

Grégoire, Jean (1571-1572): Geneva

Gregoriis, Gregorius de (1526): Venice

Greyff, Michael (1494-1503?): Reutlingen, Germany

Griffio, Alessandro (1578): Venice

Griffio, Cristoforo (1564): Padua

Griffio, Giovanni (1552-1576): Venice

Grimm, Sigmund (1518): Augsburg

Gromors, Pierre (1543?): Paris

Gronenberg, Simon (1584-1594): Wittenberg

Grüninger, Johann (1494-1530): Strassburg

Gruppenbach, Georg (1594-1599): Tübingen

Gryphius, Antoine (1573-1581): Lyons

Gryphius, Sébastien (1532-1565): Lyons

Gryphius, Sébastien, Heirs of (1561-1562): Lyons

Gualteruzzi, Carlo (1551): Venice

Gualtieri, House of (1560): Venice

Guarin, Thomas (1567-1574): Basel

Gubbin, Thomas (1592): London

Gubisius, Urban (1582-1583): Eisleben, Germany

Gülfferich, Heinrich (1549-1555): Frankfurt am Main

Guerra, House of (1560): Venice

Guerra, Domenico & Giovanni Battista (1566-1571): Venice

Gueullart, Jean (1552): Paris

Gueynard, Etienne (1520): Lyons

Guichard, Jacques (1591): Lyons

Guileretus, Stephanus (1514): Rome

Guillard, Charlotte (1547): Paris

Guillard, Guillaume (1555): Paris

Guillemot, Mathieu (1595): Paris

Guissio, Paul (1586): Lyons

Gutiérrez, Juan (1566-1568): Seville

Gutiérrez, Luis (1566-1567): Alcalá de Henares

Gutknecht, Jobat (1514-1518?): Nuremberg

Gutterwitz, Andreas (1572): Rostock

Guzmán, Francisco de (1569): Toledo

Guzmán, Tomás de (1597): Toledo

Gymnich, Johann, the Elder (1532-1536): Cologne

Gymnich, Johann, the Younger (1581-1596): Cologne

Gysser, Hans (1507): Salamanca

Hacket, Thomas (1563-1590): London

Hagembach, Pedro, Successor of (1508): Toledo

Hain, Gabriel (1554-1557): Nuremberg

Hall, Rowland (1563): London

Haller, Jan (1506-1522): Cracow

Han, Weigand (1557-1562?): Frankfurt am Main

Han, Wiegand, Heirs of (1563-1566): Frankfurt am Main

Harrison, John, Sr. (1585): London

Harrison, Luke (1569): London

Harsy, Antoine de (1573-1582): Lyons

Harsy, Olivier de (1556-1580): Paris

Haselberg, Hans (1515): Richenau

Haslop, Henry (1587): London

Hatfield, Arnold (1589-1600): London

Haultin, Jérôme (1588-1591): La Rochelle

Haultin, Pierre (1581): La Rochelle

Hectoris, Benedictus (1498-1523): Bologna

Hectoris, Benedictus, Heirs of (1525): Bologna

Heinrich, Nikolaus (1598): Munich

Heller, Jakob (1514): Nuremberg

Hemmerden, Stephan (1600): Cologne

Henric, Jacques, pseud. See Haultin, Pierre, La Rochelle

Henricksen, Henrick (1580-1581): Antwerp

Henricpetri, Sixtus (1569-1600): Basel

Henricszoon, Albert (1583): Delft; (1595-1600?): The Hague

Hentzke, Michael (1578): Berlin

Herbst, Magnus (1493): Seville

Hernández, Diego (1548): Saragossa

Herrera, Juan de (1599): Madrid

Herwagen, Johann, the Elder (1532-1555): Basel

Herwagen, Johann, the Younger (1560): Basel

Hespanha, João de (1576): Lisbon

Hester, John (1582): London

Heussler, Christoph (1565-1572): Nuremberg; (1578): Frankfurt am Main

Heussler, Leonhard (1582?): Nuremberg

Heyn, Gabriel (1559): Nuremberg

Heyns, Zacharias (1598-1600): Amsterdam

Hillen, Michael (1522?-1533): Antwerp

Hinde, John (1583): London

Hispanus, Johannes. See Hespanha, João de

Hist, Conrad (1502): Speyer

Hochfeder, Caspar (1496): Nuremberg

Höltzel, Hieronymus (1514): Nuremberg

Hofmann, Johann (1590-1591): Nuremberg; (1591): Altdorf

Holme, William (1600): London

Honorat, Barthélemy (1577-1587): Lyons

Honorat, Sébastien (1554-1561): Lyons

Honter, Johannes (1541-1542): Kronstadt

Houzé, Jean (1584-1600): Paris

Howe, William (1581-1587): London

Huber, Wolfgang (1506): Nuremberg

Hubert, Adrian (1587-1592): Antwerp

Huet, Pierre (1583): Paris

Huete, Pedro de (1578): Valencia

Huete, Pedro de, Widow of (1582-1585): Valencia

Hüter, Simon (1567): Frankfurt am Main

Huguetan, Gilles & Jacques (1542): Lyons

Hulpeau, Jean (1572): Paris

Hulsius, Levinus (1598-1599): Nuremberg

Hupfuff, Matthias (1505-1520): Strassburg

Hurus, Pablo (1499): Saragossa

Hygman, Nicolas (1517): Paris

Ibáñez, Sebastián (1572): Madrid

Imberti, Domenico (1598): Venice

Imperadore, Bartolomeo & Francesco (1543-1553): Venice

Imprenta Real (1596): Madrid

Iñiguez de Lequerica, Juan (1578-1595): Alcalá de Henares

Iñiguez de Lequerica, Juan, Heirs of (1600): Madrid

Isengrin, Michael (1540-1556): Basel

Islip, Adam (1595-1600): London

Jackson, John (1589-1591): London

Jaggard, John (1600): London

Janot, Denis (1530-1536?): Paris

Janot, Jean (1515?): Paris

Janssens, Guislain (1594-1597): Antwerp

Janszoon, Jan (1598-1600): Arnhem, The Netherlands

Jean, Simon, Heirs of, pseud. (1599): France, n.p.

Jeffes, Abel (1592-1595): London

Jesuit College (1580-1594): Rome

João, Manuel (1567): Lisbon

Jobin, Bernhard (1577-1592): Strassburg

Jobin, Bernhard, Heirs of (1598): Strassburg

Jode, Gérard de (1578): Antwerp

Jode, Gérard de, Widow & Heirs of (1593): Antwerp

Jones, Richard (1576-1597): London

Jouan, Timothée (1582-1583): Paris

Jouve, Michel (1572): Lyons

Jucundus, Johannes, pseud. See Vignon, Eustache, Geneva

Judson, Thomas (1599): London

Juge, Claude de (1577): Geneva

Jugge, Richard (1555-1589): London

Jugge, Richard, Widow of (1579-1584): London

Julien, Guillaume (1578-1582): Paris

Julliéron, Gaspard (1593-1594): Lyons

Junta, Juan de (1529-1571): Burgos; (1542-1551): Salamanca

Junta, Philippe de (Burgos). See Giunta, Philippe de

Juste, François (1529-1539): Lyons

Kachelofen, Conrad (1500-1502?): Leipzig

Keerberghen, Jan van (1594): Antwerp

Kempen, Gottfried van (1577-1593): Cologne

Kerver, Jacques (1536-1577): Paris

Kerver, Jacques, Widow of (1584): Paris

Keschedt, Peter (1597): Cologne

Kessler, Nikolaus (1496-1509): Basel

Keyser, Martin de (1527-1536): Antwerp

Keyser, Pieter de (1520): Ghent

Kingston, Felix (1598-1600A): London

Kingston, John (1581-1582): London

Kistler, Bartholomäus (1497): Strassburg

Knoblauch, Johann, the Elder (1506-1519): Strassburg

Koberger, Anton (1493): Nuremberg

Koberger, Johann (1525): Nuremberg

Köbel, Jakob (1515): Oppenheim

Köln, Wygand (1519): Geneva

König, Samuel (1600): Basel

Kohl, Peter (1522): Regensberg

Kolbe, Andreas (1557): Marburg

Kosorsky, Jan, ze skosore (1554): Prague

Krafft, Johann (1554-1560): Wittenberg

Krafft, Johann, Heirs of (1585): Wittenberg

La Barre, Nicolas de (1518-1527): Paris

Laet, Hans de (1553-1566): Antwerp

La Fontaine, Charles de (1579): 'Luneville' (i.e., Geneva)

La Grange, Gabriel de (1593): Avignon

Lamberg, Abraham (1589-1597): Leipzig

Lambert, Jean (1503): Paris

La Motte, Pierre, pseud. See Cloquemin, Louis, Lyons

Lamparter, Nikolaus (1509): Basel

Landen, Johannes (1505): Cologne

Landry, Pedro (1582): Medina del Campo; cf. following entry

Landry, Pierre (1586-1595): Lyons; cf. preceding entry

Landsberg, Martin (1502?-1506): Leipzig

Langenes, Baernaerdt (1597-1598): Middelburg

L'Angelier, Abel (1581-1600): Paris

L'Angelier, Arnoul (1552): Paris

L'Angelier, Charles (1550-1556): Paris

L'Angelier, Pierre (1583-1590?): Paris

Langres, Pierre de (1565): Paris

La Nouë, Guillaume de (1578-1587): Paris

Lantzenberger, Michael (1592): Leipzig

Laon, Jean de (1596): Geneva

La Place, Jean de (1517): Lyons

La Porte, Hugues de (1541): Lyons

La Porte, Jean (1508): Paris

La Porte, Maurice de (1530?-1542): Paris

La Porte, Maurice de, Heirs of (1557-1558): Paris

La Rivière, Guillaume de (1598): Arras, France

Laso, Pedro (1578): Salamanca

Laso Vaca, Cristóbal (1599): Medina del Campo

Latomus, Sigmund (1600): Frankfurt am Main

Laurens, Jean Le Petit. See Petit, Jean, Paris

Lawe, Thomas (1585): London

Le Bouc, Hilaire (1579): Paris

Le Bouc, Jean (1598): Paris

Le Bourgeois, Nicolas (1545): Rouen

Le Chandelier, Pierre (1585): Caen

Lechler, Martin (1567-1577): Frankfurt am Main

Le Clerc, Antoine (1545-1557): Paris

Le Fèvre, François (1589-1596): Lyons; (1591): Basel

Le Fizelier, Robert (1583-1584): Paris

Legnano, Johannes Jacobus & Bros (1505-1519): Milan

Le Hoy, Robert (1551): Rouen

Le Jeune, Martin (1557-1580): Paris

Le Mangnier, Félix (1587): Paris

Le Mangnier, Robert (1561): Paris

Le Megissier, Martin, the Younger (1574): Rouen

Leni, Giovanni Maria (1575-1577): Venice

Leni, Giovanni Maria, Heirs of (1600): Venice

Leno, Francesco de (1540?): Venice

Le Noble, Jean (1595): Troyes

Le Noir, Guillaume (1554-1556): Paris

Le Noir, Michel (1516): Paris

Le Noir, Philippe (1521-1530): Paris

León, Juan de, the Elder (1545-1549): Seville

León, Juan de, the Younger (1585-1591): Seville

Le Petit. *See* Petit, Jean, Paris

Le Prest, Jean (1551): Rouen

Le Preux, François (1576): Lausanne

Le Preux, Poncet (1514-1515): Paris

Lertout, Jean (1576-1600): Geneva

Lescuyer, Bernard (1516): Lyons

Le Sellier, Jessé (1566): Dieppe

Le Signerre, Guillermus (1497): Milan

Leski, Martin (1597): Zamosc, Poland

L'Huillier, Pierre (1574-1595): Paris

Liechenstein, Petrus (1515): Venice

Lin, Wouter van (1533-1534): Antwerp

Ling, Nicholas (1595-1600): London

Lloberas, Gabriel (1592): Barcelona

Lobato, André (1586): Lisbon

Locarno, Pietro Martire (1596-1597): Milan

Locatellis, Bonetus (1516): Venice

Lochner, Christoph (1590-1599): Nuremberg; (1591): Altdorf

Loe, Hendrick van der (1578): Antwerp

Loe, Jan van der (1548-1563): Antwerp

Longis, Jean (1561): Paris

Lonicer, Adam (1578-1584): Frankfurt am Main

Lopes, Estevão (1597): Lisbon

Lopes, João (1576): Lisbon

Lopes, Simão (1590-1596): Lisbon

Lorenzini, Francesco (1559-1565): Venice

Loureiro, Diogo Gomes (1600): Coimbra

Lownes, Humphrey (1598): London

Lownes, Matthew (1600): London

Loys, Jean (1542-1546): Paris

Loyselet, Georges (1580): Rouen

Lucienberg, ____ (1573): Frankfurt am Main

Lucius, Jakob (1569): Rostock

Lucius, Ludwig (1554): Basel; (1573): Frankfurt am Main

Lud, Gautier (1507): St. Dié

Luere, Simon de (1505): Venice

Lützenkirchen, Wilhelm (1599-1600): Cologne

Lufft, Hans (1572-1580): Wittenberg

Lydanus, Theodorus (1571-1575): Antwerp

Lyra, Manuel de (1584-1597): Lisbon

Macé, Charles (1573-1584): Paris

Macé, Jean (1563?-1567?): Paris

Madrigal, Pedro, the Elder (1587-1594): Madrid

Madrigal, Pedro, the Elder, Widow of (1594-1595): Madrid

Madrigal, Pedro, the Younger (1595-1600): Madrid

Maes, Jean, the Elder (1573): Louvain

Magarino, Faustino de (1584): Seville

Maldonado, Fernando (1584): Seville

Mallard, Martin & Honoré (1588): Rouen

Mallard, Olivier (1542): Paris

Mallard, Robert (1573-1593): Rouen

Mallard, Thomas (1578-1599): Rouen

Mallot, Gervais (1570-1572): Paris

Mammarello, Benedetto (1590-1592): Ferrara

Mammarello, Domenico (1582): Ferrara

Man, Thomas, Sr. (1585-1598): London

Manger, Michael (1571-1597): Augsburg

Mangoni, Domenico (1583): Florence

Mantegatiis, Petrus Martyr de (1507): Milan

Mantegatiis, Petrus Martyr & Bros (1505): Milan

Mantell, Walter (1585): London

Manuzio, Aldo, the Elder (1497): Venice

Manuzio, Aldo, the Elder, Sons of (1551): Venice

Manuzio, Aldo, the Younger (1572-1595): Venice

Manuzio, Paolo (1547-1557): Venice

Marchant, Guy (1493-1500): Paris

Marchetti, Pier Maria (1591): Brescia

Marcolini, Francesco (1558): Venice

Marcorelle, Jean (1570-1572): Lyons

Marés, Matías (1585): Bilbao; (1588): Logroño

Mareschal, Jean (1583): Lyons

Mareschal, Jean, Heirs of (1591-1592): Lyons

Marescotti, Giorgio (1583): Florence

Maria, Marco di (1563-1565): Venice

Marini, Luis (1591): Barcelona

Marion, Jean (1520): Lyons

Mariz, António de (1594-1599): Coimbra

Marne, Claude (1592-1600): Frankfurt am Main

Marnef, Frères de (1509-1513): Paris

Marnef, Geoffroy de (1497-1498): Paris

Marnef, Jean de, the Second (1558?-1559): Poitiers

Marnef, Jean de, the Second & Enguilbert, Bros (1540-1546): Poitiers

Marnef, Jérôme de (1569-1588): Paris

Marsh, Thomas (1572-1581): London

Marsilius, Alexandre (1578-1582): Lyons

Marsioni, Giovanni (1586): Rome

Martens, Thierry (1493): Antwerp; (1516): Louvain

Martin, of Amsterdam (1500): Rome

Martin, Jean (1565-1600): Lyons

Martin, Jost (1600): Strasbourg

Martinelli, Giovanni (1586-1588): Rome

Martínez, Diego (1578): Alcalá de Henares

Martínez, Miguel (1597-1600): Madrid

Martínez, Sebastián (1583): Alcalá de Henares

Masselin, Juan (1593-1596): Cuenca

Mattes, Edmund (1600): London

Maunsell, Andrew (1578-1589): London

Mayer, Johann (1569): Heidelberg

Mayer, Sebald (1558): Dillingen

Mayr, Sigismundo (1493-1494): Rome; (1516): Naples

Mazochius, Antonius de (1533?): Florence

Mazochius, Jacobus (1510-1523): Rome; (1520): Mirandola

Meietti, Paolo (1580-1589): Padua

Meietti, Roberto (1596): Venice

Melantrich, Georg (1563): Prague

Melantrich, Jiri (1562): Prague

Melchior von Neuss. See Neuss, Melchior von

Melgar, Alonso de (1523-1526): Burgos

Mena, Hugo de (1568-1582): Granada

Menescal, Juan Pablo (1586): Barcelona

Menescal, Miguel (1598): Barcelona

Mersman, Herman, pseud. See Haultin, Jérôme, La Rochelle

Mettayer, Jean (1592-1593): Tournon; (1595): Paris

Mey, Juan (1546-1567): Valencia

Mey, Pedro Patricio (1593-1599): Valencia

Meyn, Jacob Lenaertszoon (1598): Enkhuizen, The Netherlands

Micard, Claude (1566-1584): Paris; (1596): Tournon

Michel, Etienne (1580-1582): Lyons

Michel, Pierre (1558-1561): Lyons

Middleton, Henry (1571-1577): London

Mierdman, Stephen (1551-1553): London

Millán, Agustín (1552-1561): Saragossa

Millán, Juan (1567-1577): Saragossa; (1577): Lérida

Millán, Juana, Widow of Diego Hernández (1549): Saragossa

Millanges, Simon (1576-1599): Bordeaux

Millis, Guillermo de (1544-1555): Medina del Campo

Minutianus, Alexander (1507): Milan

Miravet, Vicente de (1584): Valencia

Misch, Friedrich (1495): Heidelberg

Misintis, Bernardinus de (1497): Brescia

Moellemann, Stephan (1589-1591): Rostock, Germany

Moingesse, Nicolas de (1596): Besançon

Mollijns, Jan (1562?): Antwerp

Mommaert, Jan (1600): Brussels

Montesdoca, Martín de (1553-1570): Seville

Montoya, Juan de (1591-1599): Madrid

Montoya, Juan Bautista de (1581): Baeza, Spain

Mora, Juan (1599): Valencia

Morberius, Gualterus (1585): Liège

Moreau, Baltasar (1590): Paris

Morel, Claude (1600): Paris

Morel, Fédéric (1557-1598): Paris

Morello, Matteo (1580): Turin

Moreno, Juan (1559-1562): Salamanca

Moretti, Nicolò (1596): Venice

Morgiani, Lorenzo de' (1493-1495): Florence

Morhart, Ulrich, the Elder (1534-1542): Tübingen

Morhart, Ulrich, Widow of (1562): Tübingen

Morillon, Claude (1594-1596): Lyons

Morin, Romain (1520): Lyons

Moscheni, Francesco (1553): Pavia

Mourentorf, Jan (1591-1596): Antwerp

Moylin de Cambray, Jean (1519-1534): Lyons

Müller, Christian (1564-1578): Strasbourg

Müller, Kraft (1538): Strasbourg

Muller, Eiwout (1594): Amsterdam

Muschio, Andrea (1571-1596): Venice

Muschio, Nicolò (1599): Rome

Mussetti, Juan Pedro (1542-1543): Medina del Campo

Mutii, Nicolò (1596): Rome

Mylius, Arnold (1586-1597): Cologne

Myt, Jacques (1516-1521): Lyons

Nadler, Jörg (1508-1520): Augsburg

Nájera, Bartolomé de (1547): Saragossa

Nájera, Bartolomé de, Widow of (1562-1571): Saragossa

Nani, Ercole (1514): Rome

Navarro, Juan, Heirs of (1584): Valencia

Navò, Curtio & Bros (1538): Venice

Nebrija, Antonio de (1516): Alcalá de Henares

Neuber, Ulrich (1551-1561): Nuremberg

Neuss, Melchior von (1532-1534): Cologne

Newbery, Ralph (1584-1600): London

Newton, Ninian (1586): London

Nicolai, C. *See* Claeszoon, Cornelis, Amsterdam

Nicolini, Domenico (1563-1570): Venice

Nicolini, Domenico & Cornelio dei (1560): Venice

Nicolini da Sabbio, Giovanni Antonio dei
(1524-1540): Venice

Nicolini da Sabbio, Giovanni Antonio & Pietro dei
(1542): Venice

Nicolini da Sabbio, Giovanni Antonio dei & Bros
(1533): Venice

Nicolini da Sabbio, Giovanni Maria dei (1550):
Venice

Nicolini da Sabbio, Pietro & Giovanni Maria dei
(1550-1561): Venice

Nicolini da Sabbio, Pietro, Giovanni Maria & Cornelio dei (1547): Venice

Nicolini da Sabbio, Stefano dei (1535-1537): Venice

Nicolini da Sabbio, Stefano dei & Bros (1530):
Verona

Niergue, François, pseud. *See* Pesnot, Charles,
Montluel & Lyons

Nivelle, Sébastien (1554-1556): Paris

Nogués, Raphael (1596): Barcelona

Normant, Vincent (1565-1567): Paris

Norton, Bonham (1596-1600): London

Norton, Bonham & John (1597): London

Norton, William (1577-1580): London

Nourry, Claude (1520): Lyons

Núñez, Diego (1587): Seville

Nuyts, Martin (1547-1556): Antwerp

Nuyts, Martin, Widow of (1561-1564): Antwerp

Nuyts, Martin,. the Younger (1593-1598): Antwerp

Nyverd, Jacques (1530): Paris

Oeglin, Erhard (1508-1514): Augsburg

Ogerolles, Jean d' (1556-1585): Lyons

Olmo, Marcantonio (1572): Venice

Ongois, Jean d' (1578): Paris

Oporinus, Johann (1544-1570): Basel

Oporinus, Johann, Heirs of (1588): Basel

Orry, Marc (1598-1600): Paris

Ortega de Carrion, Juan (1537): Florence

Ortelius, Abraham (1580-1598): Antwerp

Orwin, Thomas (1587-1591): London

Orwin, Thomas, Widow of (1595): London

Osanna, Francesco (1584-1590): Mantua

Osmont, Jean (1598-1600): Rouen

Otmar, Johann (1504): Augsburg

Otmar, Silvan (1516?): Augsburg

Otmar, Valentin (1548): Augsburg

Pace, Antonio (1596-1599): Naples

Pacini, Piero (1496): Florence

Padovano, Giovanni (1535-1545): Venice

Padovano, Giovanni, Heirs of (1560): Venice

Paets, Jan Jacobszoon (1594-1595): Leyden

Pafraet, Albert (1515): Delft

Pafraet, Richard (1498-1503): Delft

Pagan, Mattio (1545-1562): Venice

Palthinius, Zacharias (1597-1600): Frankfurt am
Main

Panizza, Valente (1574): Rome

Parant, Jean (1576-1580): Paris

Parijs, Guillaem van (1570): Antwerp

Pasini, Maffeo (1534-1537): Venice

Pasquato, Lorenzo (1570-1597): Padua

Patisson, Mamert (1574-1595): Paris

Paulus, Nicolaus Justinianus (1540): Genoa

Pavie, Guillaume (1573): Rouen

Pavoni, Guiseppe (1598-1599): Genoa

Payan, Thibaud (1558-1568): Lyons

Paz, Agustín de (1541-1542): Zamora

Pederzano, Giovanni Battista (1524-1555): Venice

Pegnitzer, Juan (1493-1503): Seville

Pelagallo, Vincenzo (1586-1590): Rome

Pen, George (1582): London

Pencio, Jacopo (1499-1511): Venice

Penet, Hector (1535): Lyons

Perchacino, Gratioso (1568-1582): Venice

Peres, Luis (1600): Lisbon

Pérez, Bartolomé (1534): Seville

Pérez, Blas (1588): Toledo

Pérez, Francisco (1599): Seville

Pérez de Valdivielso, Juan (1599): Saragossa

Périer, Adrian (1598-1600): Paris

Périer, Jérémie (1588-1589): Paris

Périer, Juan (1580): Salamanca

Périer, Thomas (1584-1586): Paris

Perin, Heirs of (1596): Vicenza

Perna, Peter (1560-1596): Basel

Pescioni, Andrea (1582-1586): Seville

Pesnot, Charles (1573-1579): Montluel; (1575-1582): Lyons

Petit, Jean (1545): Rouen

Petit, Jean, the Elder (1498-1527): Paris

Petit, Jean, the Younger (1532): Paris

Petit, Nicolas (1535): Lyons

Petit, Oudin, the Elder (1542-1544): Paris

Petras, Ramón de (1526): Toledo

Petrejus, Johann (1530-1550): Nuremberg

Petri, Adam (1521): Basel

Petri, Andreas (1569): Eisleben, Germany

Petri, Heinrich (1529-1580): Basel

Petri, Johannes (1493-1495): Florence

Petrucci, Pietro Giacopo (1579): Perugia

Petruccio, Ottaviano (1513): Fossambrone

Peypus, Friedrich (1512-1530): Nuremberg

Philippe, Jean (1497): Paris

Philoponi, Philoterpsis & Clidanus (1569): Mantua

Picardo, Juan (1541-1543): Zamora

Pietrasanta, Plinio (1555-1581): Venice

Pillehotte, Jean (1593-1600): Lyons

Pincio, Aurelio (1534-1555): Venice

Piotrkowczyk, Andreas (1585-1590): Cracow

Pivard, Jean (1498): Lyons

Planes, Miguel de (1497): Valladolid

Planfoys, Jean (1525): Lyons

Plannck, Stephan (1493?-1499): Rome

Plantin, Christophe (1555-1590): Antwerp; (1585): Leyden

Plantin, Christophe, Widow of (1591-1596): Antwerp

Plantin Office (1590-1598): Antwerp

Poggio, Giacomo del (1583): Genoa

Polo, Girolamo (1599): Venice

Polo, Nicolò (1507): Venice

Polono, Lanzalao (1503): Alcalá de Henares; (1503): Seville

Ponsonby, William (1590-1598): London

Ponte, Gotardus da (1516-1535): Milan

Ponte, Pacifico da (1596-1599): Milan

Ponte, Pacifico da, Heirs of (1596-1599): Milan

The Poppy Printer (1497): Lübeck

Porràlis, Tomás (1578-1585): Pamplona

Porras, Juan de (1503?-1520): Salamanca

Porro, Girolamo (1572-1591): Venice

Porro, Girolamo & Co. (1599): Venice

Porrus, Petrus Paulus (1516): Genoa

Porta. *See* La Porte

Porta, Giovanni Battista (1581): Venice

Portau, Jean (1580?-1585?): La Rochelle

Porteau, Thomas (1599): Niort

Portonari, Francesco (1555-1566): Venice

Portonariis, Andreas de (1553-1565): Salamanca

Portonariis, Domingo de (1569-1576): Salamanca

Portonariis, Simón de (1569): Salamanca

Portonariis, Vincent de (1516-1535): Lyons

Portonariis, Vincente & Simón (1573-1574): Salamanca

Posa, Pedro (1493): Barcelona

Powell, William (1555): London

Prato, Fioravante (1584-1594): Venice

Prévost, Benoît (1553-1560): Paris

Prévost, Mathurin (1556): Paris

Printer of Lebrija's Gramática (1498): Salamanca

Prodocino, The (1569): Venice

Prüss, Johann, the Younger (1511-1539): Strassburg

Puerta, Luis de la (1595): Alcalá de Henares

Pullon, Jean (1544-1559): Lyons

Purfoot, Thomas (1569-1596): London

Pynson, Richard (1509): London

Quentel, Arnold (1598): Cologne

Quentel, Heinrich, Sons of (1505-1508): Cologne

Quentel, Johann, Heirs of (1564-1586): Cologne

Rab, Christoph (1582): Frankfurt am Main

Rab, Georg (1561-1574): Frankfurt am Main

Rabut, René (1581): Granada

Rade, Gillis van den (1572-1587): Antwerp

Ramírez, Juan (1503): Alcalá de Henares

Ramminger, Melchior (1522): Augsburg

Rampazetto, Francesco (1565-1570): Venice

Rampazetto, Francesco, Heirs of (1581): Venice

Rampazetto, Giovanni Antonio (1583): Venice

Raphelengius, Christoph (1598-1599): Leyden

Raphelengius, Franciscus (1579): Antwerp; (1586-1590): Leyden

Rasicoti, Donato (1600?): Venice

Rasimo, Cesaro (1586): Rome

Rastell, John (1520?): London

Rastelli, Giovanni Bernardino (1574): Perugia

Ratdolt, Erhard (1505): Augsburg

Ratteri, Giovanni Battista (1583): Turin

Ravenoldo, Andrea (1565-1566): Venice

Reffeler, Paul (1576): Frankfurt am Main

Regazzola, Egedio (1574): Venice

Regnault, François (1512?-1522): Paris

Reinmichel, Leonhard (1582-1583): Lauingen, Germany

Reinsart, Théodore (1590-1600): Rouen

Rembolt, Berthold (1506): Paris

Renaut, Juan & Andrés (1582-1597): Salamanca

Resch, Conrad (1519-1526): Paris; (1535): Basel

Rescius, Rutgerus (1539-1544): Louvain

Retif, Pierre (1592): Rouen

Ribeiro, António (1576-1588): Lisbon

Richard, Guillaume (1542): Paris

Richard, Jean (1544-1566): Antwerp

Richard, Thomas (1548): Paris

Richer, Jean, the Elder (1585-1588): Paris

Richter, Wolfgang (1598): Frankfurt am Main

Rigaud, Benoît (1559-1600): Lyons

Rigaud, Benoît, Heirs of (1599): Lyons

Rihel, Josias (1556-1597): Strassburg

Rihel, Theodosius (1567): Strassburg

Rihel, Wendelin (1536-1554): Strassburg

Rivius, Gerardus (1598-1600): Louvain

Robertis, Dominico de (1537-1549): Seville

Roberts, James (1596-1600): London

Robinot, Gilles, the Elder (1558-1560): Paris

Robinson, Robert (1588-1599): London

Robles, Blas de (1585): Alcalá de Henares; (1586-1587): Madrid

Robles, Lorenzo de (1596): Saragossa

Robles, Lorenzo & Domingo de, Bros (1582-1588): Saragossa

Robles, Pedro de (1566): Alcalá de Henares; (1574): Lérida

Roccatagliata, Antonio (1583): Genoa

Roce, Denys (1506-1513): Paris

Rodrigues, Jorge (1600): Lisbon

Rodrigues, Luis (1545): Lisbon

Rodríguez, Juan (1587): Toledo

Rodríguez, Miguel (1550-1569): Toledo

Rodríguez, Pedro (1588-1592): Toledo

Roelants, Jan (1557-1563): Antwerp

Roffet, Nicolas, Widow of (1586): Paris

Roffet, Ponce (1545): Paris

Roigny, Jean de (1540): Paris

Roigny, Michel de (1571-1574): Paris

Rollet, Pierre (1548-1551): Lyons

Rooman, Gilles (1598): Haarlem

Rosa, Jonas (1600): Frankfurt am Main

Rossi, Battista di (1552-1553): Rome

Rossi, Francesco, Heirs of (1581): Ferrara

Rossi, Giovanni (1594): Bologna

Rouillé, Guillaume (1547-1587): Lyons

Roussin, Jacques (1593-1595): Lyons

Roussin, Pierre (1572-1597): Lyons; (1591): Nevers

Roussin, Pierre, Heirs of (1593): Lyons

Ruault, Thomas (1591): Antwerp

Rubeis, Laurentius de (1497?): Ferrara

Ruberia, Giustiniano da (1497-1532): Bologna

Rubini, Bartolomeo (1573): Venice

Ruelle, Jean, the Younger (1572-1574): Paris

Ruelle, Réné (1600): Paris

Ruffinelli, Giacomo (1549): Mantua

Ruffinelli, Giovanni Antonio (1586-1591): Rome

Ruffinelli, Venturino (1535): Venice

Rufin, Etienne (1547): Lyons

Rusconi, Giorgio dei (1506-1521): Venice

Rusconi, Giorgio dei, Heirs of (1522): Venice

Rusconi, Giovanni Francesco & Giovanni Antonio dei (1524): Venice

Sabbio, Vincenzo di (1592-1596): Brescia

Sabon, Sulpice (1545?): Lyons

Sacon, Jacques (1498): Lyons

Sagete, Antonio (1585): Seville

Saint-André, Pierre de (1577): Lyons; (1595): Geneva

Saint Denis, Jean (1527): Paris

Salicato, Altobello (1583-1596): Venice

Salvador, Ventura de (1585): Venice

Salviani, Horatio (1573-1589): Naples

Sánchez, Andrés (1600): Madrid

Sánchez, Francisco (1572-1587): Madrid

Sánchez, Luis (1591-1600): Madrid

Sancto Ursio, Henrico de & I. Maria (1507): Vicenza

Sansovino, Francesco & Co. (1559-1560): Venice

Sansovino, Giacomo (1569): Venice

Santa Catalina, Fernando de (1548): Toledo

Santi & Co. (1589-1590): Rome

Santillana, Pedro de (1582): Burgos

San Vito, Anello (1576-1582): Naples

Sarria, Juan de (1597): Madrid

Sartorius, David (1586-1593): Ingolstadt

Sauer, Johann (1596-1600): Frankfurt am Main

Saugrain, Abraham (1600): Paris

Saugrain, Jean (1559-1566): Lyons

Saur, Johann. *See* Sauer, Johann

Savetier, Nicolas (1527): Paris

Scharffenberg, Crispin (1561): Breslau

Scharffenberg, Hieronymus (1554): Cracow

Scharffenberg, Marcus (1530-1534): Cracow

Schaur, Johann (1496): Augsburg

Schilders, Richard (1583-1584): Middelburg

Schirat, Michael (1567): Heidelberg

Schmidt, Bonaventura (1591): Zerbst, Germany

Schmidt, Jakob (1529): Speyer

Schmidt, Johann (1576): Frankfurt am Main

Schmidt, Peter (1583): Frankfurt am Main

Schnellboltz, Franz (1597-1598): Leipzig

Schobser, Johann (1505): Munich

Schöffer, Ivo (1533): Mainz

Schöffer, Johann (1519-1531): Mainz

Schöffer, Peter, the Younger (1532): Strassburg; (1542): Venice

Schönsperger, Johann (1494-1505): Augsburg

Schonwetter, Johann Theobald (1600): Frankfurt am Main

Schott, Johann (1503-1504): Freiburg; (1508): Basel; (1513-1539): Strassburg

Schreiber, Nikolaus (1566): Cologne

Schroeter, Johann (1598): Basel

Schürer, Matthias (1510-1515): Strassburg

Schuman Press (1595): Prague

Schwertel, Johann (1576): Wittenberg

Scinzenzeler, Joannes Angeles (1508-1519): Milan

Scoto, Girolamo (1569): Venice

Scoto, Girolamo, Heirs of (1574): Venice

Scoto, Gualtiero (1552-1557): Venice

Scoto, Gualtiero, Heirs of (1597): Venice

Scoto, Ottaviano, Heirs of (1516-1520): Venice

Secerius, Johannes (Johann Setzer) (1530): Hagenau

Seitz, Peter, Heirs of (1550): Wittenberg

Sergent, Pierre (1536): Paris

Sermatelli, Michelangelo (1600): Florence

Serrano de Vargas, Miguel (1597): Cuenca

Serres, William (1555): London

Sertenas, Vincent (1545-1560): Paris

Servain, Etienne (1592): Lyons

Sessa, Giovanni Battista, the Elder (1504): Venice

Sessa, Giovanni Battista & Melchiorre (1556-1560): Venice

Sessa, Melchiorre (1533-1551): Venice

Sessa, Melchiorre, Heirs of (1570-1599): Venice

Sessa, House of (1598): Venice

Severszoon, Jan (1534?): Leyden

Sevestre, Jean (1573-1582): Paris

Sheldrake, John (1590): London

Short, Peter (1592-1600): London

Siebeneycher, Jan (1593): Cracow

Siebeneycher, Matthias (1564): Cracow

Siebeneycher Press (1584): Cracow

Silber, Eucharius (1493-1516?): Rome

Silvius, Willem (1562-1573): Antwerp

Simmes, Valentin (1592): London

Singrenier, Johann (1514-1520): Vienna

Siqueira, Alexandre (1598): Lisbon

Smesmann, Abraham (1594A-1595A): Speyer

Smith, John (1592): London

Smits, Gérard (1575-1578): Antwerp

Society of Jesus (1557): Rome. *See also* Jesuit College

Society of Minims (1594): Venice

Solempne, A. (1569): Norwich

Soler, Juan (1577-1583): Saragossa

Somasco, Giacomo Antonio (1599): Venice

Somasco, Giovanni Battista (1585-1589): Venice

Sonnius, Laurens (1598): Paris

Sonnius, Michel, the Elder (1568-1587): Paris

Sonnius, Michel, the Younger (1588-1595): Paris

Soubron, Thomas (1592-1597): Lyons

Speranza, Sign of (1556): Venice

Spiess, Johann (1593-1594): Frankfurt am Main

Spinosa, Juan de. *See* Espinosa, Juan de

Stadelberger, Jakob (1501): Heidelberg

Stafford, Simon (1599A-1600): London

Stationers, Company of (1618): London

Steels, Gillis (1574): Antwerp

Steels, Jan (1533-1557): Antwerp

Steels, Jan, Widow & Heirs of (1567-1576): Antwerp

Steiner, Heinrich (1530-1544): Augsburg

Steinmann, Hans, Heirs of (1589): Leipzig

Steinmayer, Paul (1578-1584): Frankfurt am Main

Sternácki, Sebastian (1595): Racow, Poland

Stöckel, Wolfgang (1499-1507): Leipzig; (1533): Dresden

Stöckelmann, Johann (1572): Rostock, Germany

Stoer, Jacob (1573-1596): Geneva

Straub, Leonhard (1583): Saint Gall

Strout, Pierre, pseud. *See* Rigaud, Benoît, Lyons

Stuchs, Hans (1514-1518): Nuremberg

Suelves, Miguel de (1567): Saragossa

Sutton, Edward (1553-1555): London

Sybold, Heinrich (1530): Strassburg

Tabano, Angelo (1596): Saragossa; (1599): Barcelona

Tack, Heinrich (1586): Frankfurt am Main

Tacuinus, Joannes (1506): Venice

Tarino, Giovanni Domenico (1592-1596): Turin

Tavernier, Ameet (1566-1567): Antwerp

Temporal, Jean (1555-1556): Lyons

Terranova, Juan Bautista de (1569-1577): Salamanca

Terranova, Juan Maria de (1559-1570): Salamanca

Terranova y Neyla, Alonso de (1577-1583): Salamanca

Terti, Joan de (1595): Salamanca

Thielens, Antheunis (1567-1577): Antwerp

Thomás, Mari (1595): Alcalá de Henares

Thomasini, Giovanni Francesco (1575): Venice

Timoneda, Juan (1567): Valencia

Tinghi, Philippe (1578-1582): Lyons

Tini, Michele (1586): Milan

Tini, Pietro & Francesco (1572): Venice

Toldi, Francesco (1573-1574): Venice

Tornieri, Giacomo (1586-1591): Rome

Torre, Diego de la (1599): Valencia

Torre, Pedro de la (1600): Madrid

Torrentino, Lorenzo (1549-1561): Florence; (1555): Pescia

Torres, Juan de (1595): Alcalá de Henares

Torresano, Federico (1547-1556): Venice

Tosi, Francesco (1594-1599): Florence

Tottell, Richard (1556): London

Tournes, Jean de (1546-1582): Lyons; (1587-1591): Geneva

Toye, Robert (1555): London

Trammezzino, Francesco & Michele, Heirs of (1580): Venice

Tramezzino, Michele (1548-1573): Venice

Trechsel, Gaspar (1541): Vienne, France

Trepperel, Jean, the Elder, Widow of (1515?): Paris

Trepperel, Jean, the Younger (1530?): Paris

Treschel, Gaspard & Melchior (1532-1535): Lyons

Trincher, Francisco (1586): Barcelona

Trognaesius, Joachim (1592-1598): Antwerp

Trot, Barthélemy (1528-1534): Lyons

Trugillo, Sebastián (1552-1565): Seville

Tubini, Antonio (1505?): Florence

Turre, Petrus de (1497): Rome

Turrison, Bernard (1568): Paris

Ugolino, Paolo (1589-1596): Venice

Ulhart, Philipp (1548-1550): Augsburg

Ulricher, Georg (1534): Strassburg

Ulzina, Honorat (1562): Valencia

Unglerius, Florianus (1512-1514): Cracow

Valentin, Robert (1552): Rouen

Valgrisi, Felice (1584-1585): Venice

Valgrisi, Vincenzo (1544-1570): Venice

Valgrisi, Vincenzo, Heirs of (1573-1583): Venice

Valle, Pedro del (1596): Cuenca

Valvassori, Giovanni Andrea (1547): Venice

Valvassori, Giovanni, Antonio & Florio (1541-1543): Venice

Varela, Juan (1518-1529): Seville

Várez de Castro, Pedro. *See* Castro, Pedro Várez de

Vargnano, Stefano (1596): Verona

Varonne, Giovanni (1580): Turin

Vascovan, Michel de (1549-1577): Paris

Vatican Press (1593): Rome

Vautrollier, Thomas (1579): London

Veale, Abraham (1551-1556): London

Velpius, Reinerus (1554-1570): Louvain

Velpius, Rutgerus (1600): Brussels

Venge, Walter (1585): London

Ventura, Comino (1588-1600): Bergamo

Vercellensis, Albertinus (1503-1504): Venice

Vercellensis, Bernardinus (1504-1524): Venice

Verhaghen, Pieter (1585): Dordrecht

Verwithagen, Jan, the Elder (1561-1584): Antwerp

Verwithagen, Jan, Widow of (1592): Antwerp

Veyrat, Jean (1597): Lyons

Viani, Andrea (1598): Pavia

Viart, Pierre (1523): Paris

Victoria, Martín de (1578): Burgos

Vidali, Giacomo (1576): Venice

Vidoué, Pierre (1518-1519): Paris

Vietor, Hieronymus (1514-1516): Vienna; (1519): Cracow

Vignon, Eustache (1570-1586): Geneva

Vignon, Eustache, Heirs of (1593-1600): Geneva

Villaneuva, Juan de (1566-1567): Alcalá de Henares; (1574): Lérida

Villaquirán, Juan de (1520): Toledo; (1540-1542): Valladolid

Villepoux, Martin (1580?): La Rochelle

Villiers, Gilbert de (1525): Lyons

Viñao, Juan (1519): Valencia

Vincent, Antoine (1546-1561): Lyons

Vincent, Barthélemy (1572-1593): Lyons

Vincent, Matthieu (1558): Avignon

Vincenti, Giacomo (1597): Venice

Viotti, Erasmo (1581): Casalmaggiore; (1581): Parma; (1591-1598): Venice

Viottis, Giovanni Maria de (1555): Rome

Vitali, Bernardino dei (1501-1535): Venice; (1508): Rome

Vivant, Louis (1556): Troyes

Vorsterman, Willem (1505?-1540): Antwerp

Waen, Jan (1554): Louvain

Waesberghe, Jan van (1598): Rotterdam

Wagner, Peter (1494): Nuremberg

Waldegrave, Robert (1583): London; (1600): Edinburgh

Waldkirch, Konrad von (1585-1589): Basel

Walley, Robert (1587): London

Wapy, Jean (1596): Verdun

Ward, Roger (1589-1590): London

Warnerus, Petrus (1560?): Kampen, The Netherlands

Waterson, Simon (1599): London

Watkins, Richard (1577-1591): London

Wechel, André (1560-1567): Paris; (1574-1581): Frankfurt am Main

Wechel, Andreas, Heirs of (1584-1600): Frankfurt am Main

Wechel, Chrestien (1528-1551): Paris

Wechel, Johann (1585-1592): Frankfurt am Main

Wechel, Johann, Widow of (1594): Frankfurt am Main

Weigel, Hans (1577): Nuremberg

Weissenburger, Johann (1521?-1524): Landshut, Germany

Weissenhorn, Alexander & Samuel (1555): Ingolstadt

Welle, Hieronymus (1573): Louvain

Westheimer, Bartholomaus (1541): Basel

Whitchurch, Edward (1543-1550): London

White, Edward, Sr. (1587-1596): London

White, William (1599-1600): London

Wight, John (1576-1596): London

Wight, Thomas (1596-1600): London

Willeboortsen, Jeronimus (1576): Middelburg

Willer, Georg (1571-1583): Augsburg

Winde, Louis de (1576): Douai

Windet, John (1585-1598): London

Winter, Jakob (1506-1507): Magdeburg

Winterburg, Johannes (1498?-1512): Vienna

Wirsung, Marx (1518): Augsburg

Wise, Andrew (1598-1599): London

Wolf, Johannes (1597): Zurich

Wolfe, John (1585-1598): London

Wolff, Georges (1498): Paris

Wolff, Jakob (1493): Basel

Wolff, Thomas (1519): Basel

Wood, William (1598-1599): London

Woodcock, Thomas (1582): London

Worde, Wynkyn de (1509): London

Wright, William, Sr. (1581): London

Wykes, Henry (1565): London

Wyssenbach, Rudolph (1552): Zurich

Yetsweirt, Charles (1594): London

Yvañez, S. See Ibáñez, Sebastián. Madrid

Zaltieri, Marc' Antonio (1588): Venice

Zanetti, Aloyse (1592-1597): Rome

Zanetti, Bartholomeo (1537-1542): Venice

Zanetti, Cristoforo (1573-1575): Venice

Zanetti, Francesco (1579-1586): Rome

Zangrius, Petrus (1565-1566): Louvain

Zapila, Miguel de (1554-1561): Saragrossa

Zassenus, Servatius (1530-1548): Louvain

Zenaro, Damiano (1566-1592): Venice

Zenaro, Giovanni (1598): Venice

Zenaro, Giovanni & Andrea (1576-1589): Venice

Zenaro, Giovanni & Bros (1584): Venice

Zetzner, Lazarus (1596-1599): Strassburg

Zierickzee, Cornelius von (1500): Cologne

Ziletti, Francesco (1569-1585): Venice

Ziletti, Francesco, Heirs of (1589): Venice

Ziletti, Giordano (1557-1582): Venice

Zoppini, Fabio & Agostino (1581-1589): Venice

Zoppini, Giacomo & Bros (1600): Venice

Zoppino, Nicolò (1528-1540): Venice

Zoppino, Nicolò & Vincenzo di Paolo (1521-1523): Venice

Author, Title and Subject Index

In the preparation of this index it was believed that the user would be better served, not by references to entry numbers in the text, but by the fuller forms adopted, incorporating the year where a work is described and by which it can be located. This should facilitate a visual grasp in quantitative terms of the dissemination of a given work. We trust that our practices in such matters will be self-evident, but when publication dates span more than a single year, the entry will be found under the first given. Where a date appearing on a title page has proven in some way erroneous, the correct year and actual location is indicated by bracketed information. Those items with the letter A appended to the date will be found in the Addenda, while multiple editions or issues of a given item are indicated by a figure within parentheses following the year.

As we have had occasion to emphasize in our preface, the high proportion of works which appeared in multiple editions has led us to adopt the expedient of simply providing references from titles to the main entry. And under the subject entries (represented by use of full capitals) we have included only the earliest edition of a work and of its translations.

In many respects the provision of subject entries has been as vexing a problem as we have encountered. The diversity of the topics in question, the frequent vagueness of an author's intent, the use of terminology no longer meaningful, and the very obscurity of the reference involved have frequently conspired to impede the limited aim of providing a specific guide to an individual topic in some way American. That Dr Landis, chiefly responsible for this index, has succeeded in meeting this challenge as fully as he has merits acclaim.

A.,M.,Preest. *See* Aray, Martin

A mala franczos . . . praeservatio ac cura. *See* Steber, Bartholomaeus

Abbot, George, Abp of Canterbury. A briefe description of the whole worlde. London: T.Judson,for J.Brown, 1599 (2)

— —London: R.B.,for J.Brown, 1600

Abraham ben Mordecai Farissol. *See* Farissol, Abraham ben Mordecai

Abravanel, Judah. *See* Leo Hebraeus

The abridgment of the English chronicle. *See* Stow, John

Academiae veteris et novae . . . legatio. *See* Voerthusius, Joannes

Acerca de la materia medicinal. *See* Dioscorides, Pedanius

Acosta, Christovam d'. *See* Costa, Christovam da

Acosta, Emanuel. *See* Costa, Manuel da

Acosta, José de. Concilium provinciale Limense. *See* Lima (Ecclesiastical province). Council, 1583

—De natura Novi Orbis. Salamanca: G.Foquel, 1588

— —Salamanca: G.Foquel, 1589

— —Cologne: Birckmann Office, for A.Mylius, 1596

—Geographische und historische Beschreibung der . . . Landschafft America. Cologne: J.Christoffel, 1589

—Histoire naturelle et moralle des Indes. Paris: M.Orry, 1598·

— —Paris: M.Orry, 1600

—Historia natural y moral de las Indias. Seville: J.de León, 1590

— —Barcelona: J.Cendrat, 1591

— —Barcelona: J.Cendrat,for House of Garriach,at Gerona, 1591

— —Barcelona: J.Cendrat,for L.Marini, 1591

—Historia naturale, e morale delle Indie. Venice: B.Basa, 1596

—Historie naturael ende morael van . . . Westersche Indien. Haarlem: G.Rooman,for J.L. Meyn,at Enkhuizen, 1598

—New Welt. Cologne: J.Christoffel, 1600

ACOSTA, JOSÉ DE

—Rivadeneira, Pedro de. Tratado de la religion . . . que deve tener el prencipe christiano. Madrid: 1595

Acoubar, ou la Loyauté trahie. *See* Du Hamel, Jacques

—Curationum medicinalium centuria secunda. Venice: G.Griffio,for V.Valgrisi, 1552

—Curationum medicinalium centuriae duae: prima et secunda. Paris: B.Prévost,for G.Gourbin, 1554

— —Paris: B.Prévost,for S.Nivelle, 1554

— —Lyons: G.Rouillé, 1559

— —Lyons: G.Rouillé, 1560

— —Venice: V.Valgrisi, 1566

— —Lyons: G.Rouillé, 1567

— —Lyons: G.Rouillé, 1580

—Curationum medicinalium centuriae duae: tertia & quarta. Lyons: P.Fradin,for J.F.de Gabiano, 1556

— —Lyons: G.Rouillé, 1565

— —Lyons: G.Rouillé, 1580

—Curationum medicinalium centuriae quatuor. Basel: Froben Office, 1556

— —Venice: B. Costantini, 1557

—Curationum medicinalium . . . centuriae duae: quinta videlicet et sexta. Venice: V.Valgrisi, 1560

— —Lyons: G.Rouillé, 1564

— —Lyons: G.Rouillé, 1580

—De morbo gallico. *In* Luisini, Luigi. De morbo gallico omnia quae extant. Venice: 1566

—In Dioscoridis . . . De medica materia. Venice: G.Scoto,1553

— —Strassburg: W.Rihel, 1554

— —Venice: G.Scoto,for I.Zilleti, 1557

— —Lyons: Widow of B.Arnoullet, 1558

— —Lyons: Widow of B.Arnoullet,for M.Bonhomme, 1558

— —Lyons: Widow of B.Arnoullet,for T. Payen, 1558

— —Lyons: Widow of B.Arnoullet,for G.Rouillé, 1558

Ambasciata del gran re de Chicorani. Padua: L.Pasquato, 1570

Ambrogini, Angelo. *See* Poliziano, Angelo Ambrogini, known as

Amerbach, Georg. Threnodia de morte Caroli .v.. Dillingen: S.Mayer, 1558

America, sive Novus Orbis, tabulis aeneis . . . delineatus

See Matal, Jean

America, tertia pars: memorabilem provinciae Brasiliae historiam. *See* Staden, Hans.

AMERICA IN DRAMA. *See also* subheading 'Drama' under specific names & topics

—Cieklinski, P. Potrojny z plauta. Zamosc: 1597

AMERICA IN FICTION

—Alemán, M. Guzman d'Alfarache. Madrid: 1599

— —Guzman d'Alfarache (French). Paris: 1600

—Fischart, J. Das glückhafft Schiff von Zurich. Strassburg: 1577

—Letera de la nobil cipta nuovamente ritrovata. [Rome: 1535?]

—Rabelais, F. Le quart livre . . . du bon Pantagruel. Paris: 1552

AMERICA IN POETRY. *See also* subheading 'Poetry' under specific names & topics

—Boissard, J.J. Poemata. Basel: 1574

—Brant, S. Le grand nauffrage des folz. Paris [ca.1536?]

— — Das Narren Schyff. Basel: 1494

— —Dat Narren Schyp. Lübeck, 1497

— —Der Narren scip. Paris: 1500

— —La nef des folz du monde. Paris: 1497

— —The shyp of folys. London: 1509

— —Der sottenschip. Antwerp: 1548

— —Stultifera navis. Basel: 1497

—Du Bartas, G.de S., seigneur. Bartasias. Edinburgh: 1600

— —Beresithias. Paris: 1579

— —The colonies. London: 1598

— —Commentaires . . . sur La sepmaine. Paris: 1582

— —La divina settimana. Tours: 1592

— —L'Eden. Lyons: 1594

— —Hebdomas. Paris: 1583

— —The second weeke. London: 1598

— —La seconde sepmaine. Paris: 1584

— —La sepmaine. Paris: 1578

—Montesino, A. Cancionero.

Toledo: 1508

—Nature of the four elements. A new iuterlude. [London: 1520?]

—Teluccini, M. Artemidoro. Venice: 1566

Americae, das fünffte Buch. *See* Benzoni, Girolamo

Americae achter Theil. *See* Bry, Theodor de

Americae pars quinta. *See* Benzoni, Girolamo

Americae pars sexta. *See* Benzoni, Girolamo

Americae pars viii. *See* Bry, Theodor de

Amintae gaudia. *See* Watson, Thomas

L'amiral de France. *See* La Popelinière, Lancelot Voisin, sieur de

Amman, Jost, *illus. See* Weigel, Hans. Habitus praecipuorum populorum

Amoretti and epithalamion. *See* Spenser, Edmund

Amphitheatridion. *See* Botero, Giovanni

Anania, Giovanni Lorenzo d'. L'universale fabbrica del mondo. Naples: G.Cacchi, 1573

— —Venice: G.Vidali,for A.San Vito,at Naples, 1576

— —Venice: A.Muschio,for A.San Vito,at Naples, 1582

— —Venice: A.Muschio, 1596

—comp. & tr. Lo scoprimento dello stretto artico. Naples: G.B.Capello, 1582

Anastro Ysunza, Gaspar de, *tr. See* Bodin, Jean. La republica. Turin: 1590

Anatomia. *See* Berengario, Jacopo

Anchieta, José de. Arte de grammatica. Coimbra: A.de Mariz, 1595

Ander theil D. Joh. Fausti Historien. *See* Schotus, Fridericus

Andrés de Aguirre. *See* Aguirre, Andrés de

Anghiera, Pietro Martire d'. Opera: Legatio babylonica. Seville: J.Cromberger, 1511 (2)

—De nuper . . . repertis insulis . . . enchiridion. Basel: A.Petri, 1521

— —*In* Burchardus, de Mont

BERTRÁN, LUIS. *See* LUIS
BERTRÁN, SAINT
BERTRANDO, LUIGI. *See*
LUIS BERTRÁN, SAINT
Beschreibüng allerley
Gelegenheyte. *See* Magnus,
Olaus, Abp of Upsala
Beschreibung . . . der vornemb-
ster Staet. *See* Braun, Georg
Beschreibung der Reyss . . . in
die Morgenlaender. *See*
Rauwolf, Leonhard
Beschreibung der Schiffart des
Haubtmans Martini Forbissher.
See Settle, Dionyse
Beschreibuug [sic] . . . der
vornembster Statt. *See* Braun,
Georg
Beschryvinghe van de gantsche
custe van Guinea. *See*
Linschoten, Jan Huygen van
Beschryvinghe vande . . .
zeevaerdt vanden . . . Thomas
Candish. *See* Pretty, Francis
De beschryvinghe vant . . . co-
ninckrijck van Congo. *See*
Lopes, Duarte
Bessard, Toussainct de. Dialogue
de la longitude est-ouest.
Rouen: M.LeMégissier,the
Younger, 1574
Best, George. A true discourse.
London: H.Bynneman, 1578
Béthencourt, Jacques de. Nova
penitentialis quadragesima . . .
in morbum gallicum. Paris:
N.Savetier, 1527
Beuter, Pedro Antonio. Co-
ronica general, primera parte.
Valencia: J.Mey, 1546
—Cronica generale. Venice:
G.Giolito de' Ferrari & Bros,
1556
Beuther, Michael. Bildnisse.
Basel: P.Perna, 1582
—Warhafftiger kurtzer Bericht.
Basel: C.Waldkirch, 1587
— —Basel: C.Waldkirch, 1588
— —Strassburg: 1589
Eyn bewert Recept wie man das
holtz Gnagacam . . . brauchen
sol. [Nuremberg? J.Gutknecht?
1518?]
—[Bamberg: G.Erlinger] 1524
Bialobrzeski, Marcín. Postilla
orthodoxa. Cracow: L.An-
drysowicz, 1581
Bible. O.T. Psalms. Polyglot.
Psalterium hebreum. Genoa:

P.P.Porrus,for N.J. Paulus,
1516
BIBLIOGRAPHY. *See also* BIO-
BIBLIOGRAPHY
—Basse, N. Collectio in unum
corpus. Frankfurt a.M.: 1592
—Du Verdier, A. La biblio-
thèque. Lyons: 1585
—Gesner, K. Appendix
Bibliothecae. Zurich: 1555
— —Bibliotheca universalis.
Zurich: 1545
— —Elenchus scriptorum. Basel:
1551
— —Pandectarum . . . libri xxi.
Zurich: 1548
—La Croix du Maine, F.G., sieur
de. Premier volume de la
Bibliothèque. Paris: 1584
Bibliotheca . . . in epitome
redacta. *See* Gesner, Konrad
Bibliotheca hispanica. *See*
Perceval, Richard
Bibliotheca selecta de ratione
studiorum. *See* Possevino, An-
tonio
Bibliotheca universalis. *See*
Gesner, Konrad
La bibliothèque. *See* Du Verdier,
Antoine
Bielski, Marcín. Kronika. Cra-
cow: 1551
— —Cracow: H.Scharffenberg,
1554
— —Cracow: M.Siebeneychera,
1564
Les bigarrures. *See* Tabourot, Es-
tienne
Bigges, Walter. Expeditio Fran-
cisci Draki. Leyden: Plantin
Press (F.Raphelengius), 1588
—Narrationes . . . quam prima
continet diarium expeditionis
Francisci Draki. Nuremberg:
C.Lochner & J.Hofmann, 1590
—Relation oder Beschreibung
der Rheiss . . . durch . . .
Franciscum Drack. [Cologne]
1589
—A summarie and true discourse
of Sir Frances Drakes West In-
dian voyage. London: R.Field,
1589
— —London: R.Ward, 1589
— —London: W.Ponsonby, 1596
—Le voyage de messire François
Drake. Leyden: Plantin Press
(F.Raphelengius), 1588
— —*In* Goulart, Simon. Le

premier recueil, contenant les
choses plus memorables
advenues sous la Ligue.
[Geneva?] 1590
Bini, Giovanni Francesco.
Capitolo del mal francese.
1538. *In* Casa, Giovanni dalla,
Abp. Le terze rime. Venice:
1538
— —*In the same.* Tutte le opere.
Venice: 1540
— —*In the same.* Tutte le opere.
Venice: 1542
— —*In the same.* Tutte le opere.
Venice: 1545
— —*In* Opere burlesche. Flor-
ence: 1548
— —*In the same.* Florence: 1552
— —*In the same.* Venice: 1564
— —*In the same.* Venice: 1565
BIO-BIBLIOGRAPHY
—Possevino, A. Apparato
all'historia di tutte le nationi.
Venice: 1598
— —Apparatus ad omnium gen-
tium historiam. Venice: 1597
— —Bibliotheca selecta de ra-
tione studiorum. Rome: 1593
BIOGRAPHY—COLLECTIONS
—Castellanos, J.de. Elegias, pte
1a. Madrid: 1589
—Thevet, A. Les vrais pourtraits.
Paris: 1584
Biondo, Michelangelo. De
origine morbi gallici. *In*
Gesner, Konrad, comp.
Chirurgia. Zurich: 1555
—De partibus ictu sectis citissime
sanandis. Venice: G.A.& P.dei
Nicolini da Sabbio, 1542
—De ventis et navigatione.
Venice: Comin da Trino, 1546
BIRDS. *See also* PARROTS &
TURKEYS
—Aldrovandi, U. Ornithologiae
. . . libri xii. Bologna: 1599
—Gesner, K. Historiae
animalium liber iii. Zurich:
1555
— —Vogelbüch. Zurich: 1557
Bizzarri, Pietro. Historia . . .
della guerra fatta in Ungheria.
Lyons: G.Rouillé, 1568
— —Lyons: G.Rouillé, 1569
—Pannonicum belli. Basel: 1573
— —*In* Geuffroy, Antoine. Aulae
Turcicae . . . descriptio. Basel:
1573
—Senatus populique Genuensis

furt a.M.: 1588

—Thurneisser, L. Historia unnd Beschreibung . . . aller . . . Erdgewechssen. Berlin: 1578

——Historia, sive Descriptio plantarum omnium. Berlin: 1578

BOTANY, MEDICAL. *See also* GUAIACUM, SARSAPARIL-LA, TOBACCO, etc.

—Bonardo, G.M. La Minera del mondo. Venice: 1585

—Dioscorides, Pedanius. Acerca de la materia medicinal. Antwerp: 1555

——De materia medica. Lyons: 1554

——De medicinali materia. Marburg: 1543

——Historia, et materia medicinale. Venice: 1544

——Il Dioscoride. Venice: 1548

—Dodoens, R. Stirpium historiae. Antwerp: 1583

—Durante, C. Herbario nuovo. Rome: 1585

—Fioravanti, L. Della fisica. Venice: 1582

—Fragoso, J. Aromatum, fructuum, et simplicium aliquot medicamentorum . . . historia brevis. Strasbourg: 1600

——Discursos de la cosa aromáticas. Madrid: 1572

—Mattioli, P.A. Les commentaires sur les six livres des simples de Pedacius Dioscoride. Lyons: 1561

——Commentarii in libros sex Pedacii Dioscoridis. Venice: 1554

——De i discorsi . . . nelli sei libri di Pedacio Dioscoride. Venice: 1585

——De plantis epitome utilissima. Frankfurt a.M.: 1586

——I discorsi . . . ne i sei libri della materia medicinale. Venice: 1555

——Herbář. Prague: 1562

——Kreuterbuch. Frankfurt a.M.: 1586

——New Kräuterbuch. Prague: 1563

—Monardes, N. Brief traité de la racine Mechoacan. Rouen: 1588

——De simplicibus medicamentis. Antwerp: 1574

——Delle cose che vengono portate dall'Indie Occidentali. Venice: 1575

——Dialogo llamado Pharmacodilosis. Seville: 1536

——Dos libros. El uno trata de todos las cosas que traen de nostras Indias Occidentales. Seville: 1565

——Historia medicinal, ptes 1a-3a. Seville: 1574

——Joyfull newes out of the new-found world. London: 1580

——Libro de las cosas, pte 2a. Seville: 1571

——Modo et ordine come si ha de usare la radice Mechoacane. Milan: 1570

——Simplicium medicamentorum ex Novo Orbe delatorum. Antwerp: 1579

——The three bookes. London: 1577

—Orta, G.da. Aromatum. Antwerp: 1567

——Dell'historia de i semplici. Venice: 1576

—Pasini, A. Annotationi et emendationi nella tradottione dell'eccell. P.Andrea Matthioli. Bergamo: 1591

Botero, Giovanni. Aggiunte fatte di Giovanni Botero alla sua Ragion di stato. Pavia: A.Viani, 1598

——Rome: G.Ferrari, 1598

——Venice: G.B.Ciotti, 1598

—Allgemeine Weltbeschreibung. Cologne: J.Gymnich,the Younger, 1596

—Amphitheatridion. Cologne: L.Andreae, 1597

——Lübeck: L.Albrecht, 1600

—Commentariolus parallelos. Cologne: L.Andreae, 1597

——Cologne: L.Andreae, 1598

—Della ragion di stato. Venice: The Gioliti, 1589

——Ferrara: V.Baldini, 1590 (2)

——Rome: V. Pelagallo, 1590

——Milan: P.da Ponte,for P.M.Locarno, 1596

——Turin: G.D.Tarino, 1596

——Milan: P.da Ponte, 1598

——Venice: The Gioliti, 1598

—Delle cause della grandezza delle cittá. Rome: G.Martinelli, 1588A

——Milan: Heirs of P.da Ponte,

1596A

—Delle relatione universali . . . Parte seconda. Rome: G. Ferrari, 1597

—Delle relationi universale. Rome: G.Facciotto,for G.Ferrari, 1591

——Ferrara: B. Mammarelli, 1592

—Delle relationi universali . . . terza parte. Rome: G.Faciotto,for G.Ferrari, 1595

—Delle relationi universali . . . parte quarta. Rome: [G.Faciotto?] for G.Ferrari, 1596

——Vicenza: Heirs of Perin, 1596

—Discorsi sopra la ragione di stato. Milan: P.da Ponte,for P.M.Locarno, 1597

——Venice: The Gioliti, 1598

—Epistolarum . . . libri ii. Paris: T.Périer, 1585

——Paris: T.Périer, 1586

—Geographische Landtaffel. Cologne: L.Andreae, 1596

—Gründlicher Bericht. Strassburg: L.Zetzner, 1596

—Mundus imperiorum. Cologne: B.Buchholtz, 1598

—Raison et gouvernement d'estat. Paris: G.Chaudière, 1599 (2)

—Razon de estado. Madrid: L.Sánchez, 1593

——Barcelona: J.Cendrat, 1599

—Relatione universale de' continenti. Rome: B.Bonfadino, for G.Ferrari, 1595

—Relatione universale dell'isole. Rome: B.Bonfadino,for G.Ferrari, 1595

—Relatìoni universali. Bergamo: C.Ventura, 1594

——Bergamo: C.Ventura, 1596

——Venice: G.Angelieri, 1596

——Brescia: Comp.Bresciana, 1599

——Venice: G.Angelieri, 1599 (2)

——Venice: G.Angelieri, 1600

—Le relationi universali, pt 1. Vicenza: G.Greco, 1595

——Venice: N.Polo, 1597

—Le relationi universali, pts 2-3. Venice: P.Dusinelli, 1595

——Venice: G.Vicenti, 1597

—Le relationi universali, pt 4. Vicenza: G.Greco, 1597

—Tabula geographica. Cologne: L.Andreae, 1596
—Theatrum, oder Schawspiegel. Cologne: L.Andreae, 1596
—Theatrum principum. Cologne: L.Andreae, 1596
Botschafft des groszmechtigsten Konigs David. *See* John, Prester
Bourne, William. De const der zee-vaerdt. Amsterdam: C.Claeszoon, 1594A
——Amsterdam: C.Claeszoon, 1599A
—A regiment for the sea. London: T. Hacket, 1574A (2)
——London: T.Dawson & T.Gardiner,for J.Wight, 1576A
——London: T.Dawson & T.Gardiner, for J.Wight, 1577A
——London: T.East, for J.Wight, 1580A
——London: T.East,for J. Wight, 1584A
——London: T.East,for J. Wight, 1587A
——London: T.East,for J. Wight, 1592A
——London: T.East,for J. Wight, 1596A
Bozio, Tommaso. De signis ecclesiae Dei. Cologne: J. Gymnich,the Younger, 1592-93
——Lyons: P.Landry, 1594
——Lyons: P.Landry, 1595
—De signis ecclesiae Dei, v.1. Rome: G.Tornieri, 1591
——, v.2. Rome: A.& H.Donangeli, 1591
Brant, Sebastian. Eulogium de scorra pestilentiali. Basel: J.Bergmann, 1496
——1496. *In* Grünpeck, Joseph. Tractatus de pestilentiali scorra. Augsburg: 1496
—Le grand nauffrage des folz. Paris: D.Janot [ca.1536?]
—La grand nef des folz. Lyons: J.d'Ogerolles, 1579
—La grand nef des folz. Lyons: F.Juste, 1529
——Paris: D.Janot,for [P.LeNoir], 1530
—La grant nef des folz. Lyons: G.Balsarin, 1499
—Das gross Narren Schiff. Strassburg: J.Rihel, 1564

—Das Narren Schyff. Augsburg: J.Schoensperger, 1494
——Basel: [J.Bergmann], 1494
——Nuremberg: P.Wagner, 1494
——Reutlingen: M.Greyff, 1494 (2)
—Dat Narren schyp. Lübeck: [The Poppy printer], 1497
—Der Narren scip. Paris: G.Marchant, 1500
—Der Narren Spiegel. Strassburg: J. Cammerlander, 1545
——Strassburg: W.Rihel, 1549
—Das Narrenschiff. Basel: J.Bergmann, 1495
——Basel: J.Bergmann, 1499
——Basel: N.Lamparter, 1509
——Strassburg: M.Hupfuff, 1512
——Frankfurt a.M.: H.Gülfferich, 1553
——Frankfurt a.M.: H.Gülfferich, 1555
——Frankfurt a.M.: W.Han, 1560
——Frankfurt a.M.: G.Rab & Heirs of W.Han, 1566
—Navis stultorum oft, Der sotten schip. Antwerp: J.van Ghelen, 1584
——La nef des folz du monde. Paris: [F.Baligault? for] G.de Marnef & J.Philippe, 1497
——Lyons: G.Balsarin, 1498
—Das neu narren schiff. Augsburg: J.Schönsperger, 1498
—Das neu narrenschiff. Augsburg: J.Schönsperger, 1495
—Das nüu schiff. Strassburg: J.Grüninger, 1494
——Strassburg: [J.Grüninger] 1494 [i.e.,ca.1496?]
—Das nuw schiff. Strassburg: J.Grüninger, 1497
—Dat nye schip van narragonien. Rostock: L.Dietz, 1519
—Salutifera [sic] navis. Lyons: J.Sacon, 1498
—The shyp of folys. London: R.Pynson, 1509
—The shyppe of fooles. London: W.de Worde, 1509
—Der sottenschip. [Antwerp: M.Ancxt, 1548]
—Stultifera navis. Augsburg: J.Grüninger, 1497
——Augsburg: J.Schönsperger, 1497

——Basel: J.Bergmann, 1497 (2)
——[Nuremberg: G.Stuchs?] 1497
——Basel: J.Bergmann, 1498
——Paris: G.Wolff,for G.de Marnef, 1498
—Stultifera navis . . . The ship of fooles. London: J.Cawood, 1570
—Stultifera navis mortalium. Basel: H.Petri, 1572
—Varia . . . carmina. Basel: J.Bergmann, 1498
——Strassburg: J.Grüninger, 1498
—Welt Spiegel oder Narren Schiff. Basel: S.Henricpetri, 1574
Brasavola, Antonio Musa. De medicamentis Venice: Heirs of L.Giunta, 1552
—Examen omnium decoctionum. *See* Rostinio, Pietro. Trattato di mal francese. Venice: 1556
—Examen omnium loch. Venice: The Giuntas, 1553
——Lyons: J.Faure,for S.B.Honorat, 1554
——Lyons: J.Faure,for S.Honorat, 1555
——Lyons: J.Faure,for J.Temporal, 1555
——Lyons: P.Michel,for S.Honorat, 1561
—Examen omnium simplicium. Rome: A.Blado, 1536
——Lyons: J.Barbeu,for J.& F.Frellon, 1537
——Venice: Comin da Trino,for A.Arrivabene, 1539
——Lyons: J.Pullon, 1544
——Lyons: J.Pullon,for G.de Millis,at Medina del Campo, 1544
——Lyons: J.& F.Frellon, 1546
——Lyons: A.Vincent, 1546
——Lyons: M.Dubois,for J.Frellon, 1556
——Lyons: M.Dubois,for A.Vincent, 1556
—Examen simpl[icium]. Venice: V.Valgrisi, 1545
Brassicanus, Johannes Alexander. Pan [Greek.] Omnis. Hagenau: T.Anshelm,for J.Knobloch,at Strassburg, 1519
Braun, Abraham. *See* Bruyn, Abraham de

Calmetus, Antonius. *See*
Chaumette, Antoine
Calvo, Juan. Libro de medicina.
Barcelona: J.Cendrat, 1592
—Primera y segunda parte de la
cirugia. Seville: 1580
**Camerarius, Joachim, 1534-
1598.** Hortus medicus. Frank-
furt a.M.: J.Feyerabend,for
S.Feyerabend,H.Tack &
P.Fischer, 1588
Camerarius, Philipp. Operae
horarum succisivarum. Altdorf:
C.Lochner & J.Hofmann,
1591A
— —Nuremberg: C.Lochner &
J.Hofmann, 1591A
— —Nuremberg: C.Lochner,
1599A
Camilla, Giovanni. Enthosiasmo
. . . de' misterii, Venice:
G.Giolito de' Ferrari, 1564
Camões, Luiz de. La Lusiada.
Salamanca: J.Périer, 1580A
—Os Lusiadas. Lisbon: A.Gon-
zalvez, 1572A (2)
— —Lisbon: M.de Lyra, 1584A
— —Lisbon: M.de Lyra, 1591A
— —Lisbon: M.de Lyra,for E.
Lopez, 1597A
—Los Lusiadas. Alcalá de
Henares: J.Gracián, 1580
— —Madrid: G.Drouy, 1591
Campana, Cesare. Delle historie
del mondo. Venice:
G.Angelieri & Co., 1596
— —, v.2. Venice: G.Angelieri,
1597
**Campani, Niccolò, called Lo
Strascino.** Lamento . . . sopra
il mal francioso. [Siena?
ca.1515]
— —Venice: N.& V.di P.Zop-
pino, 1521
— —Venice: N.& V.di P.Zop-
pino, 1523
— —Venice: N.Zoppino, 1529
— —Venice: F.Bindoni &
M.Pasini, 1537
CANADA. *See also* FRENCH IN
CANADA *and* NEW FRANCE
—Cartier, J. Brief recit. Paris:
1545
— —Discours du voyage fait . . .
aux Terres-neufves. Rouen:
1598
— —A shorte and briefe narra-
tion. London: 1580
—Du Fail, N., seigneur de La

Hérissaye. Les contes . . .
d'Eutrapel. Rennes: 1585
—France. Sovereigns, etc.,
1589-1610 (Henry IV). Edict
contenant le pouvoir donné au
marquis de Cottenmael . . .
pour la conqueste des terres
Canada. Rouen: 1598
ÇANADA—DRAMA
—Du Hamel, J. Acoubar, ou la
Loyaute trahie. [Rouen? 1586]
CANADA—POETRY
—Ronsard, P.de. Continuation
du Discours des miseres de ce
temps. Paris: 1562
— —Discours des misères de ce
temps. Lyons: 1568
— —Oeuvres. Paris: 1567
Cancionero de diversas obras. *See*
Montesino, Ambrosio, Bp
Candidus, Pantaleon. Tabulae
chronologicae. Strassburg:
J.Rihel, 1597
Canini, Angelo. De locis S.
Scripturae hebraicis . . . com-
mentarius. Antwerp: Widow &
Heirs of J.Bellère, 1600
— —Louvain: G.Rivius, 1600
CANNIBALISM
—Ronsard, P.de. Continuation
du Discours des miseres de ce
temps. Paris: 1562
— —Discours des misères de ce
temps. Lyons: 1568
— —Oeuvres. Paris: 1567
CANNIBALISM—BRAZIL
—Lopes, D. De beschryvinghe
vant . . . coninckrijck van Con-
go. Middelburg: 1576
— —Regnum Congo, hoc est,
Vera descriptio regni Africani.
Frankfurt a.M.: 1598
— —Regnum Congo, hoc est,
Warhaffte . . . Beschreibung
des Konigreichs Con-
go.Frankfurt a.M.: 1597
— —Relatione del reame di Con-
go. Rome: 1591
— —A report of the kingdome of
Congo. London: 1597
—Montaigne, M.E.de. Les essais.
Bordeaux: 1580
—Plaintes des Eglises Reformees
de France. [Geneva?] 1597
Cantiques spirituels. *See*
Maisonfleur, Etienne de
Canzonette. *See* Chiabrera,
Gabriello
Capaccio, Giulio Cesare. Oratio

in obitu Philippi II. Naples:
G.G. Carlino & A.Pace, 1599
Capelloni, Lorenzo. Les divers
discours. Troyes: J.Le Noble &
M.Sonnius,at Paris: 1595
—Ragionamenti varii. Genoa:
M.A. Bellone, 1576
Capilupi, Ippolito, Bp of Fano.
Capiluporum carmina. Rome:
Heirs of G.O.Gigliotto, 1590
—Carmina. Antwerp: C. Plantin,
1574
Capiluporum carmina. *See*
Capilupi, Ippolito, Bp of Fano
Las capitulaciones que el Virrey
. . . hizo con Don Juan de
Oñate, Governador . . . de la
Nueva Mexico. *See* Velasco,
Luis de
Capitulo over Recetta delo ar-
bore. [Venice] A. Bindoni,
1520
Capivaccio, Girolamo. Acroaseis
de virulentia gallica. Frankfurt
a.M.: Heirs of C.Egenolff,
1598
—De lue venerea acroaseis.
Speyer: B.Albini, 1590
— —*In* Marquardus, Joannes.
Practica theorica empirica
morborum. Speyer: 1592
Capodivacca, Girolamo. *See*
Capivaccio, Girolamo
Capricci medicinali. *See*
Fioravanti, Leonardo
Caracciolo, Virgilio. Compendio
della descrittione. Naples:
M.Cancer, 1567
Caradog, of Llancarvan. The
historie of Cambria. London:
R.Newbery & H.Denham, 1584
Cardano, Girolamo. Ars curandi
parva. Basel: S.Henricpetri,
1564
— —Basel: S.Henricpetri, 1566
—Contradicentium medicorum.
Lyons: S.Gryphius, 1548
— —Paris: J.Macé, 1564-65
—De la subtilité. Paris:
G.LeNoir, 1556
— —Paris: [G.LeNoir,for]
J.Foucher, 1556
— —Paris: [G.LeNoir,for]
C.L'Angelier, 1556
— —Paris: S.Calvarin, 1566
— —Paris: C.Micard, 1566
— —Paris: G.Beys, 1578
— —Paris: S.Calvarin, 1578
— —Paris: G.Chaudière, 1578

—The Spanish colonie. London:
T.Dawson,for W.Brome, 1583

—Spieghel der spaenscher
tiranije. [Antwerp?] 1579

——Amsterdam: N.Biestkens 'de
jonghe' for C.Claeszoon, 1596

——Amsterdam: N.Biestkens 'de
Jonge' for C.Claeszoon, 1596

—Tratado comprobatorio.
Seville: S.Trugillo, 1553

—Tyrannies et cruautez. Antwerp: F.Raphelengius, 1579

——Paris: G.Julien, 1582

Casas, Gonzalo de las. Libro intitulado Arte para criar seda.
Granada: R.Rabat, 1581

Cassanionus, Joannes. *See* Chassanion, Jean

Castaldi, Giacomo di. *See*
Gastaldo, Jacopo

Castanheda, Fernão Lopes de.
See Lopes de Castanheda, Fernão

Castel-Branco, Juan Rodrigo de.
See Amatus Lusitanus

Castellanos, Juan de. Elegias, pte
1. Madrid: Widow of
A.Gómez, 1589

Castello Branco, João Rodrigues.
See Amatus Lusitanus

Castigationes in alabandicas
declarationes. *See* Pollich,
Martin

Castigatissimi annali. *See* Giustiniani, Agostino, Bp of Nebbio

**Castile. Laws, statutes, etc.,
1252–1284 (Alfonso X).** Las
siete partidas. Salamanca:
A.de Portonariis, 1555

——Salamanca: A.de Por-
tonariis, 1565

——Salamanca: D.de Por-
tonariis, 1576

——Valladolid: D.Fernández de
Córdova, 1587

Castillejo, Cristóbal de. Obras.
Madrid: P.Cosin, 1573

——Madrid: F.Sánchez, 1577

——Antwerp: M.Nuyts, 1598

——Antwerp: [M.Nuyts,for] P.
Bellère, 1598

——Madrid: A.Sánchez,for P.de
La Torre, 1600

Catalogus annorum et principum. *See* Ryd, Valerius
Anselmus

Catalogus arborum. *See* Gerard,
John

Catalogus scriptorum floren-

tinorum. *See* Poccianti,
Michele

Cataneo, Giovanni Maria.
Genua. Rome: J.Mazochius,
1514

Catecismo de la doctrina cristiana en lengua mexicana. *See*
Mura, Petrus de

Catholic Church. Commisarius
Generalis Cruciatae. *See* Spain.
Sovereigns, etc., 1556-1598
(Philip II).

**Catholic Church. Liturgy and
ritual. Missal.** Missale pro
Pataviensis eccl. ritu. Augsburg: E.Ratdolt, 1505

——Vienna: J.Winterburg, 1509

——Vienna: J. Winterburg, 1512

——Nuremberg: J.Heller,for
J.Gutknecht, 1514

—Missale Romanum. Venice:
L.Giunta, 1520

——Venice: Heirs of L.Giunta,
1546

—Missale Saltzeburgensis.
Venice: P.Liechenstein, 1515

**Catholic Church. Pope,
1492–1503 (Alexander VI).**
Alfonsus de Fonseca. [Madrid:
1530?]

——Bula de la concession.
[Madrid: 158-?]

—Copia de la bula de la concession. [Madrid: 158-?]

—Copia de la bula del decreto y
concession. [Logroño: A.G.de
Brocar?, 1511?]

—Copia dela bula dela concession. Logroño: A.G.de Brocar,
1511

**Catholic Church. Pope,
1513–1521 (Leo X).** Breve . . .
Leonis . . . Pape. Rome: 1516

**Catholic Church. Pope,
1534–1549 (Paul III).** De baptizandis incolis . . . Indiae.
Rome: 1537

**Catholic Church. Pope,
1566–1572 (Pius V).** Bulla . . .
extensionis. Rome: Heirs of
A.Blado, 1567

—Rome: Heirs of A.Blado,
1568

—Bulla confirmationis.
Barcelona: F.Cantarelli, 1567

——Rome: Heirs of A.Blado,
1567

—Bullas . . . confirmationis.
Alcalá de Henares: A.de

Angulo, 1569

—Confirmatio et nova concessio.
Seville: J.Gutiérrez, 1568

**Catholic Church. Pope,
1572–1585 (Gregorius XIII).**
Actes exhibez publiquement.
Liège: G.Morberius. 1585

CATHOLIC CHURCH— MIS-
SIONS. *See also* MISSIONS

—Holy Roman Empire.
Sovereigns, etc., 1519–1556
(Charles V). Carolus Quintus
divina favente clementia
Romanorum imperator.
Bologna: 1530

Causa aestus maris. *See* Sfondrati, Pandolfo

Cavendish, Thomas. Copye,
overgeset. Amsterdam:
C.Claeszoon, [1588?]

CAVENDISH, THOMAS

—Advertissement certain contenant les portes advenues en
l'armée d'Espagne. Paris: 1588

—Bry, T. de. Americae achter
Theil. Frankfurt a.M.: 1599

——Americae pars viii. Frankfurt
a.M.: 1599

—Gilbert, W. De magnete
magneticisque corporibus.
London: 1600 (2)

—Lopes, D. De beschryvinghe
vant . . . coninckrijck van Congo. Middelburg: 1576

——Regnum Congo, hoc est,
Vera descriptio regni Africani.
Frankfurt a.M.: 1598

——Regnum Congo, hoc est,
Warhaffte . . . Beschreibung
des Konigreichs Congo. Frankfurt a.M.: 1597

——Relatione del reame di Congo. Rome: 1591

——A report of the kingdome of
Congo. London: 1597

—Pretty, F. Beschryvinghe vande
. . . zeevaerdt vanden . . .
Thomas Candish. Amsterdam:
1598

——Descriptio vande heerlicke
Voyagie ghedaen door . . .
Thomas Candish. Amsterdam:
1598

—Stow, J. The annales of England. London: 1592A

Cayet, Pierre Victor Palma. *See*
Genebrard, Gilbert, Abp of
Aix. Chronographiae libri
quatuor. Paris: 1600

The complaint of England. *See* Lightfoot, William

Conciliorum omnium orthodoxorum. *See* Padilla, Francisco de

Concilium provinciale Limense. *See* Lima (Ecclesiastical province). Council, 1583

Conestaggio, Girolamo Franchi di. Dell'unione del regno di Portogallo. Genoa: G.Bartoli, 1585

— —Genoa: G.Bartoli, 1589

— —Venice: P.Ugolino, 1592

—Historie of the uniting . . . of Portugall. London: A.Hatfield,for E.Blount, 1600

—Historien der Königreich Hispanien, Portugal. Munich: A.Berg, 1589

—L'union du royaume de Portugal. Besançon: N.de Moingesse, 1596

— —Arras: G.Bauduin, 1600

Confutatio conflatorum. *See* Pistoris, Simon

Conqueste van Indien. De wonderlijcke ende warachtige historie. *See* Zárate, Agustín de

La conquista del Peru. Seville: B.Pérez, 1534

Conquista del Peru. Verdadera relacion. *See* Xérez, Francisco de

Consideration sur l'histoire françoise. *See* Le Roy, Louis

Consilia. *See* Baviera, Baverio

Consiliorum medicinalium. *See* Scholtz, Lorenz

Consilium de egritudine pestifera. *See* Torella, Gaspar

Consilium medicum pro egregio . . . Aloysio Mantuano. *See* Vella, Giorgio

De const der zee-vaerdt. *See* Bourne, William

Consuelo de penitentes. *See* San Román, Antonio de

Les contes . . . d'Eutrapel. *See* Du Fail, Noël, seigneur de La Hérissaye

Conti, Natale. Universae historiae sui temporis. Venice: D.Zenaro, 1581

Continuation du Discours des misères de ce temps. *See* Ronsard, Pierre de

Contradicentium medicorum. *See* Cardano, Girolamo

Contrafayt Kreuterbuch. *See* Brunfels, Otto

De contreyen vanden eylanden. *See* Cortés, Hernando

Cooper, Thomas, Bp of Winchester. Thesaurus linguae romanae et britannicae. London: H.Wykes, 1565

— —London: [J.Charlewood?] 1573

— —London: 1578

— —London: H.Bynneman, 1584

— —[London?] 1587

Copernicus, Nicolaus. De revolutionibus orbium. Nuremberg: J.Petrejus, 1543

— —Basel: H.Petri, 1566

COPERNICUS, NICOLAUS

—Bruno, G. La cena de la Ceneri. London: 1584

Copey etlicher brieff, so auss Hispania kummen seindt. [Augsburg? 1535]

Copey eynes brieffes . . . Ansoldo de Grimaldo. *See* Grimaldi, Giovanni Battista

Copia de diversas cartas de algunos padres. *See* Jesuits. Letters from missions

Copia de la lettera . . . mandata ali . . . Re. *See* Colombo, Cristoforo

Copia de una carta que Don Antonio escrivio. *See* Bazán, Alvaro de, marqués de Santa Cruz

Copia de una carta venida de Sevilla. Barcelona: P.Cortey, 1566

Copia de una lettera . . . delle richezze . . . ritrovato in India. *See* Río, Baldassare del, Bp

Copia de unas cartas de algunos padres. *See* Jesuits. Letters from missions

Copia de unas cartas embiadas del Brazil. *See* Jesuits. Letters from missions (Brazil)

Copia dela bula dela concession. *See* Catholic Church. Pope, 1492-1503 (Alexander VI)

Copia delle lettere del prefetto della India la nuova Spagna. [Venice?] 1534 (2)

—*In* Bordone, Benedetto. Isolario. Venice: 1547

Copia der Newen Zeytung auss Presillig Landt. Augsburg:

E.Oeglin [1514] (2)

—Nuremberg: H.Höltzel, 1514

Copia di una lettera . . . sopra la presa . . . del Peru. *See* González de Mercado, Luis

Copia di una lettera del Re di Portugallo. *See* Manuel I, King of Portugal

Copia di una lettera di Sybilia. [Florence? 1538]

Copie d'une lettre missive. La Rochelle: J.Portau, 1583

Copie de quelques letres. *See* Barré, Nicolas

Coppie d'une lettre venant de la Floride. Paris: V.Normant & J.Bruneau, 1565

Coppie de l'Anti-Espagnol. *See* Arnauld, Antoine

The coppie of the Anti-Spaniard. *See* Arnauld, Antoine

Coppo, Pietro. Portolano. Venice: A.Bindoni, 1528

Copye, overgeset. *See* Cavendish, Thomas

Córdoba, Antonio de. Opera. Venice: G.Ziletti (Toledo: J.de Ayala Cano) 1569 [i.e.,1570]

Córdoba, Francisco Hernández de. *See* Fernández de Córdoba, Francisco

CORN. *See* MAIZE

Corónica de Aragon. *See* Vagad, Gauberte Fabricio de

Corónica de la Orden de Predicadores. *See* Cruz, Juan de la, fray

Corónica de las Indias. *See* Oviedo y Valdés, Gonzalo Fernandez de

Corónica general, 1a pte. *See* Beuter, Pedro Antonio

Corónica general de España. *See* Alfonso X, el Sabio, King of Castile and León

Corónica geral. *See* Sabellico, Marco Antonio Coccio, called

Corrunnus, Joannes. Enarrationes. 1516. *See* Baptista Mantuanus. Exhortatio. Paris [1512?]

Corsali, Andrea. Lettera . . . allo illustrissimo signore Duca Juliano de Medici. Florence: G.S.di Carlo, 1516

— —*In* Alvares, Francisco. Historiale description de l'Ethiopie. Antwerp: 1558

——Madrid: P.V.de Castro,for
M.Martínez, 1597

——Madrid: P.V.de Castro,for
J.de Montoya, 1597

——*See also* Santisteban Osorio,
Diego de. Araucana, ptes 4ta y
5ta

Erclarnis und usslegung der . . .
Welt. *See* Lud, Gualtherus

Ernstighe vermaninghe vanden
standt ende gheleghentheyt.
See Marnix, Philippe de,
seigneur de Sainte-Aldegonde

Ain ernstliche red Keyserlicher
Maiestet. *See* Karl V, Emperor
of Germany

Errata recentiorum medicorum.
See Fuchs, Leonhart.

Erudita et elegans explicatio. *See*
Casas, Bartolomé de las, Bp of
Chiapa

Escalante, Bernardino de. A
discourse of the navigation
which the Portugales doe
make. London: T.Dawson,
1579A

ESKIMOS—NEWFOUNDLAND
—Warhafftige Contrafey einer
wilden Frawen. Nuremberg
[1566?]

Espejo, Antonio de. Histoire des
terres nouvellement
descouvertes . . . nommées le
nouveau Mexico. Paris: Widow
of N.Roffet, 1586

——*In* González de Mendoza, J.
Histoire . . . de la Chine.
Paris: 1588

——*In the same.* Paris: 1589 (2)

——*In the same.* Paris: 1600 (2)

—New Mexico. London: T.Cad-
man [1587]

——*In* González de Mendoza.
The historie . . . of China.
London: 1588

—El viaje que hizo Antonio de
Espejo. Paris: R.Hakluyt, 1586

——*In* González de Mendoza, J.
Historia . . . dela China.
Madrid: 1586

——*In the same.* Madrid: 1587

——*In the same.* Medina del
Campo: 1595

Espejo de vida christiana, pte 1a.
See Suárez de Escobar, Pedro

Espinel, Vicente. Diversas rimas.
Madrid: L.Sánchez, 1591

——Madrid: L.Sánchez,for J.de

Montoya, 1591

Espositioni et introduttioni
universali. *See* Ruscelli,
Girolamo

Les estats. *See* Flurance, David
Rivault, sieur de

Este es traslado . . . de una carta
de privilegio. *See* Spain.
Sovereigns, etc., 1479-1504
(Ferdinand V and Isabella I)

Este es un traslado de una carta
. . . embiada . . . del Cuzco.
See Gasca, Pedro de la

Esta es un tratado. *See* Casas,
Bartolomé de las, Bp of
Chiapa

Estete, Miguel de. La relacion
del viaje. *In* Oviedo y Valdés,
Gonzalo Fernández de. Co-
rónica de las Indias. Salamanca: 1547

**Estève, José, Bp of Orihuela &
of Vesti.** Ad S.D.N. Sixtum
Quintum . . . oratio habita.
Milan: M.Tini, 1586

——Rome: A.Gardano & F.Coat-
tino, 1586

Estienne, Charles. L'agricoltura.
Venice: A.Manuzio, the
Younger, 1581

——Turin: Heirs of N.Bevilac-
qua, 1582

——Turin: Heirs of N.Bevilac-
qua,for G.B.Ratteri, 1583

——Turin: 1590

——Venice: A.Manuzio, the
Younger, 1591

—L'agriculture. Paris: J.DuPuys,
1564

——Antwerp: C.Plantin, 1565

——Lyons: J.Martin, 1565

——Paris: J.DuPuys, 1565

——Paris: J.DuPuys, 1567

——Paris: J.DuPuys, 1570

——Paris: J.DuPuys [i.e.,Geneva:
F.Estienne] 1570

——Paris: J.DuPuys, 1572

——Paris: J.DuPuys, 1573

——Paris: J.DuPuys, 1574

——[Lyons: Printed for]
J.DuPuys,at Paris, 1576

——[Lyons: Printed for]
J.DuPuys,at Paris, 1578

——Luneville [i.e.,Geneva?]:
C.de La Fontaine, 1579

——Lyons: [Printed for]
J.DuPuys,at Paris, 1583

——Paris: J.DuPuys, 1583

——Lyons: [Printed for]
J.DuPuys,at Paris, 1586

——[Lyons: Printed for]
J.DuPuys,at Paris, 1589

——Lyons: J.Guichard, 1591

——Lyons: J.Roussin, 1595

——[Geneva?] G.Cartier, 1597

——Paris: P.Bertault, 1598

——Paris: P.Chevalier, 1598

——Paris: J.DuPuys, 1598

——Paris: J.LeBouc, 1598

——Paris: M.Orry, 1598

——Rouen: J.Crevel, 1598

——Rouen: T.Daré, 1598

——Rouen: J.Osmont, 1598

——Rouen: R.de Beauvais, 1600

——Rouen: J.Osmont, 1600

—Dictionarium historicum.
Lyons: T.Soubron & M.DuPré,
1595

——[Geneva:] J.Stoer, 1596

—XV Bücher von dem Feldbau.
Strassburg: B.Jobin, 1587

——Strassburg: B.Jobin, 1588

——Strassburg: B.Jobin, 1592

——Strassburg: Heirs of B.Jobin,
1598

—De landtwininge. Antwerp:
C.Plantin, 1566

——Antwerp: C.Plantin, 1582

—Maison rustique, or The countrie farme. London: E.Bolli-
fant, for B.Norton, 1600

—— *See also* Monardes, Nicolás.
Three bookes. London: 1577

—Siben Bücher von dem Feldbau. Strassburg: B.Jobin, 1579

——Strassburg: B.Jobin, 1580

——*In* Crescenzi, Pietro de. New
Feldt und Ackerbaw. Frankfurt
a.M.: 1583

—Sylva, frutetum, collis. Paris:
F.Estienne, 1538

—De veltbouw. Amsterdam:
C.Claeszoon, 1588

——Amsterdam: E.Muller,for
C.Claeszoon, 1594

Eulogium de scorra pestilentiali.
See Brant, Sebastian

Euonymus de remediis secretis.
See Gesner, Konrad

Europae totius terrarum orbi parti praestantissime . . . descriptio. *See* Quad, Matthias

Europae universalis et particularis
descriptio. *See* Quad, Matthias

**Eusebius Pamphili, Bp of
Caesarea.** Chronicon. Paris:

H.Estienne,for J.Badius, 1512
— —[Paris?] H.Estienne [1518?]
Everaert, Martin, tr. *See* Medina,
Pedro de. De zeevaert oft
Conste van ter zee te varen.
Antwerp: 1580
Everard, Giles. De herba
panacea. Antwerp: G.van den
Rade,for J.Bellère, 1587 (2)
Every man out of his humor. *See*
Jonson, Ben
Exactissimi discursus de rebus
gallicis. *See* Hurault, Michel,
sieur de Belesbat et du Fay
Examen i censura . . . del modo
de averiguar. *See* Továr,
Simon de
Examen omnium loch. *See*
Brasavola, Antonio Musa
Examen omnium simplicium. *See*
Brasavola, Antonio Musa
Examen simplicium. *See*
Brasavola, Antonio Musa
Examen vanitatis doctrinae gen-
tium. *See* Pico della Miran-
dola, Giovanni Francesco
Excelencias de la monarchia y
reyno de Espana. *See* Lopéz
Madera, Gregorio
Excellent . . . discours sur l'estat
present de la France. *See*
Hurault, Michel, sieur de
Belesbat et du Fay
An excellent discourse upon the
. . . present estate of France.
See Hurault, Michel, sieur de
Belesbat et du Fay
Een excellent tracktaet. *See*
Paracelsus
An excellent treatise touching
howe to cure the French-
pockes. *See* Paracelsus
Exemplorum, hoc est, Dictorum
factorumque memorabilium.
See Fregoso, Battista
Exercitatio academia. *See*
Guevara, Diego
Exhortatio. *See* Baptista Man-
tuanus
Expeditio Francisci Draki. *See*
Bigges, Walter
L'experience et approbation . . .
touchant la medicine du boys
dict Guaiacum. *See* Hutten,
Ulrich von
Explanatio veri ac legitimi juris.
Leyden: C.Plantin, 1585
Explanation of the true and law-

full right. Leyden: C.Plantin,
1585 (2)
EXPLORERS. *See also the
names of individual explorers*
—Freigius, J.T. Historiae synop-
sis. Basel: 1580
—Thevet, A. Les vrais pourtraits
vies des hommes illustres.
Paris: 1584
EXPLORERS, ENGLISH
—Verstegen, R. A declaration of
the true causes of the great
troubles. Antwerp: 1592
EXPLORERS, ENGLISH—
POETRY
—Watson, T. Amintae gaudia.
London: 1592
Expositio canonum. *See*
Leonardi, Camillus
Extraict ou recueil des isles. *See*
Anghiera, Pietro Martire d'
**Eytzinger, Michael, Freiherr
von.** Historia rerum . . .
relatio. Cologne: G.von
Kempen, 1592A
—Nova . . . relatio. Das ist, Ein
newe Beschreibung. Cologne:
G.von Kempen, 1591A
Factor, Nicolas. Testimonios de
la santidad . . . del Padre Fr.
Luis Bertran. Valencia: Heirs
of J.Navarro, 1584
Factorum, dictorumque memora-
bilium. *See* Fregoso, Battista
The faerie queene. *See* Spenser,
Edmund
Fallopius, Gabriel. Opera.
Frankfurt a.M.: Heirs of
A.Wechel, 1584
— —Venice: F.Valgrisi, 1584
— —Frankfurt a.M.: Heirs of
A.Wechel,C.de Marne &
J.Aubry, 1600
—De morbo gallico. Padua:
L.Bertello & Co.,& C.Griffio,
1564
— —Venice: F.Lorenzini, 1565
— —*In his* Opuscula. Padua:
1566
— —Venice: E.Regazzola, 1574
— —*In his* Opera. Venice: 1584
— —*In his* Opera. Venice: 1600
—Künstbuch. Augsburg: M.Man-
ger,for G.Willers, 1571
— —Augsburg: M.Manger,for
G.Willers, 1573
— —Augsburg: M.Manger, 1588
— —Augsburg: M.Manger, 1597

—Opuscula. Padua: L.Bertellio,
1566
—Secreti diversi. Venice: M.di
Maria, 1563
— —Venice: M.di Maria, 1565
— —Venice: G.F.Camozio, 1572
— —Venice: A.Gardano, 1578
— —Turin [G.Varrone &
M.Morello?] 1580
— —Venice: C.Franceschini, 1582
— —Venice: V.de Salvador, 1585
— —Venice: M.A.Zaltieri, 1588
The famous West Indian
voyadge. *See* Boazio, Baptista
A farewell. Entituled to the . . .
generalls of our English forces.
See Peele, George
**Farissol, Abraham ben
Mordecai.** [Iggereth orhoth
'olam. Venice: G.di Gara,
1586]
Fastorum libri. *See* Baptista
Mantuanus
Favolius, Hugo. Theatri orbis
terrarum enchiridion.
Antwerp: C.Plantin,for
P.Galle, 1585
Federmann, Nicholas. In-
dianische historia. Hagenau:
S.Bund, 1557
FELIPE DE JESUS
—Ribadeneira, M.de. Historia de
las islas . . . de la gran China.
Rome: 1599A (2)
Ferdinand V, King of Spain.
Epistola . . . ad Carolum
Regem Castilie. [Augsburg:
S.Otmar, 1516?]
— —[Rome? E.Silber?, 1516?]
Fernández, Diego. Historia del
Peru. Seville: F.Díaz, 1571
Fernández de Córdova, Alonso.
Por don Alonso Fernandez de
Cordova. [Madrid? 158-?]
FERNÁNDEZ DE CÓRDOBA,
FRANCISCO
—Ein auszug ettlicher sendbrieff.
Nuremberg: 1520
Fernández de Enciso, Martín. *See*
Enciso, Martín Fernández de
Fernández de la Gama, Juan, ed.
See Orden de Santiago. Com-
pilacion de los establecimientos
de la Orden de la Caballeria.
Seville: 1503
Fernández de Oviedo y Valdés,
Gonzalo. *See* Oviedo y Valdés,
Gonzalo Fernández de

Fernández de Santaella, Rodrigo, tr. *See* Polo, Marco. Cosmographia

—*See also* Polo, Marco. Libro . . . delas cosas maravillosas que vido. Logroño: 1529

Fernel, Jean. Cosmotheorica. Paris: S.de Colines, 1527 [i.e.,1528]

— —Paris: S.de Colines, 1528

—De abditis rerum causis. Paris: C.Wechel, 1548

— —Venice: P.& G.M.Nicolini da Sabbio,for A.Arrivabene, 1550

— —Paris: C.Wechel, 1551

— —Paris: C.Wechel,for J.DuPuys, 1551

— —Paris: A.Wechel, 1560

— —*In his* Opera medicinalia. Venice: 1566

— —*In the same.* Paris: 1567

— —Frankfurt a.M.: A.Wechel, 1574

— —*In his* Universa medicina. Frankfurt a.M.: 1574

— —Frankfurt a.M.: A.Wechel, 1575

— —*In his* Universa medicina. Frankfurt a.M.: 1575

— —Frankfurt a.M.: A.Wechel, 1577

— —*In the same.* Frankfurt a.M.: 1577

— —*In the same.* Geneva: 1577

— —*In the same.* Geneva: 1580

— —Frankfurt a.M.: A.Wechel, 1581

— —*In his* Universa medicina. Frankfurt a.M.: 1581

— —*In the same.* Lyons: 1586

— —Frankfurt a.M.: Heirs of A.Wechel,C.de Marne, & J.Aubry, 1592

— —*In his* Universa medicina. Frankfurt a.M.: 1592

— —Frankfurt a.M.: Heirs of A.Wechel,C.de Marne,& J.Aubry, 1593

— —*In his* Universa medicina. Frankfurt a.M.: 1593

— —*In his* Universa medicina. Geneva: 1596

— —Lyons: ˙T.Soubron & M.Desprez, 1597

—De luis venereae curatione. Antwerp: C.Plantin, 1579

— —Padua: P.Meietti, 1580

— —*In his* Universa medicina. Geneva: 1580

— —*In the same.* Frankfurt a.M.: 1581

— —*In the same.* Lyons: 1586

— —*In the same.* Frankfurt a.M.: 1592

— —*In the same.* Frankfurt a.M.: 1593

— —*In the same.* Geneva: 1596

— —*In the same.* Lyons: 1597

—Monalosphaerium. Paris: S.de Colines, 1526

—Opera medicinalia. Venice: R.Borgominieri, 1565

— —Venice: F.Portonariis, 1566

—Universa medicina. Paris: A.Wechel, 1567

— —Frankfurt a.M.: A.Wechel, 1574

— —Frankfurt a.M.: A.Wechel, 1575

— —Frankfurt a.M.: A.Wechel, 1577

— —[Geneva:] J.Stoer, 1577

— —Frankfurt a.M.: A.Wechel, 1578

— —Geneva: J.Stoer, 1578

— —[Geneva: J.Stoer,for] A.Marsilius,at Lyons, 1578

— —Geneva: J.Stoer, 1580

— —Frankfurt a.M.: A.Wechel, 1581

— —[Frankfurt a.M.: A.Wechel,for] A.Marsilius,at Lyons, 1581

— —Lyons: Heirs of J.Giunta & P.Guissio, 1586

— —Frankfurt a.M.: Heirs of A.Wechel,C.Marne & J.Aubry, 1592

— —Frankfurt a.M.: Heirs of A.Wechel,C.Marne & J.Aubry, 1593

— —Geneva: J.de Laon, 1596

— —Lyons: T.Soubron & M.Desprez, 1597

Ferrer, Jaume, de Blanes. Sentencias catholicas. Barcelona: C.Amorós, 1545

Ferrerius, Augerius.*See* Ferrier, Auger

Ferri, Alfonso. De l'administration du sainct-boys. Poitiers: J.& E.de Marnef, 1540

— —Poitiers: J.& E.de Marnef, 1546

—De ligni sancti . . . medicina.

Rome: A.Blado, 1537

— —Basel: J.Bebel, 1538

— —Paris: J.Foucher, 1539

— —Paris: J.Foucher, 1542

— —Paris: V.Gaultherot, 1542

— —Paris: J.Foucher, 1543

— —Paris: V.Gaultherot, 1543

— —Lyons: J.Frellon, 1547

—Methode curative. Rouen: J.Petit,for N.LeBourgeois [ca.1545]

—Ein new Artzeneybuch. Dresden: [G.Bergen] 1584

—New erfundene heylsame . . . Artzney. [Strassburg: B.Beck] 1541

— —Strassburg: S.Emmel, 1559

Ferrier, Auger. De lue hispanica. Paris: G.Gilles, 1564

—De morbo gallico. *In* Liébault, Jean. Thesaurus sanitatis. Paris: 1577

—De pudendagra. Toulouse: J.Colomiès,the Elder, 1553

— —Antwerp: Widow of M.Nuyts, 1564

Ferron, Arnoul. *See* Le Ferron, Arnoul

Fidalgo d'Elvas. *See* Relaçam, verdadeira dos trabalhos . . . Fernando de Souto

Fides, religio, moresque Aethiopum. *See* Goes, Damião de

Fiestas de Denia. *See* Vega Carpio, Lope Félix de

Fiestas nupciales que la ciudad y reyno de Valencia han hecho. *See* Aguilar, Gaspar Honorato de

Fioravanti, Leonardo. Capricci medicinali. Venice: L.degli Avanzi, 1561

—La cirurgia. Venice: Heirs of M.Sessa, 1570

— —Venice: Heirs of M.Sessa, 1582

— —Venice: M.Bonibelli, 1595

—A compendium of the rationall secretes. London: J.Kingston, for G.Pen & J.H[ester]., 1582

—De' capricci medicinali. Venice: L.degli Avanzi, 1564

— —Venice: L.degli Avanzi, 1565

— —Venice: L.degli Avanzi, 1568

— —Venice: L.degli Avanzi, 1573

— —Venice: Heirs of M.Sessa, 1582

——Rome: G.degli Angeli, 1577
——*In his* Opera subsiciva.
Rome: 1579
——Genoa: G.Bartoli, 1588
—Dell'istorie di Genova. Genoa:
Heirs of G.Bartoli, 1597
—Gli elogi . . . degli huomini
chiari della Liguria. Genoa:
C.Bellone, 1579
—Historiae Genuensium. Genoa:
G.Bartoli, 1585
—Opera subsiciva. Rome:
F.Zanetti, 1579
Fontaine, Charles. La descrip-
tion des terres trovées de nostre
temps. Lyons: J.Pullon,for
B.Rigaud, 1559
—Les nouvelles & antiques mer-
veilles. Paris: G.Le Noir, 1554
Fontanon, Denys. De morborum
internorum curatione. Lyons:
J.Frellon, 1549
——Lyons: J.Frellon, 1550
——Lyons: J.Frellon, 1553
——Lyons: J.Frellon,for A.Vin-
cent, 1553
——Venice: G.Griffio,for
B.Costantino, 1553
——Lyons: S.Barbier,for
J.Frellon, 1560
——Lyons: S.Barbier,for A.Vin-
cent, 1560
——Lyons: A.de Harsy, 1573
——Lyons: A.de Harsy, 1574
FOREIGN EXCHANGE
—Molina, L.de. De justitia,
tomus secundus de contrac-
tibus. Cuenca: 1597
**Foresti, Jacopo Filippo, da
Bergamo.** Novissime hystori-
arum omnium repercussiones.
Venice: A Vercellensis, 1503
—Noviter historiarum omnium
repercussiones. Venice: G.dei
Rusconi, 1506
—Sopplimento delle croniche.
Venice: 1575
—Suma de todas las cronicas.
Valencia: G.Costilla, 1510
—Supplemento delle chroniche.
Venice: B.Bindoni [for
M.Sessa] 1540 (2)
—Supplemento supplementi de le
Chroniche. Venice: G.dei
Rusconi, 1508
—Supplementum supplementi
chronicarum. Venice: G.dei
Rusconi, 1513

—Supplementum supplementi de
le Chroniche. Venice: G.dei
Rusconi, 1520
——Venice: G.F.& G.A.dei Rus-
coni, 1524 (2)
——Venice: B.Bindoni, 1535
——Venice: B.& F.Imperadore,
1553
Fornari, Simone. La spositione
sopra . . . l'Orlando furioso.
Florence: L.Torrentino,
1549[-50]
Fortsetzung der Zeytungen und
historischen Berichts. *See*
Jesuits. Letters from missions
Fossetier, Julien. De la glorieuse
victoire. [Antwerp? S.Cock?,
1525?]
Foucher, Jean, o.f.m.
Itinerarium catholicum.
Seville: A.Escrivano, 1574
Foure bookes of husbandrie. *See*
Heresbach, Conrad
Fracan, M. *See* Fracanzano da
Montalboddo
Fracanzano da Montalboddo.
Itinerarium Portugallensium e
Lusitania. [Milan:
J.A.Scinzenzeler, 1508?]
—Newe unbekanthe landte.
Nuremberg: G.Stuchs, 1508
—Le nouveau monde et naviga-
cions. Paris: G.Du Prê [1516]
—Nye unbekande Lande.
Nuremberg: G.Stuchs, 1508
—Paesi novamente retrovati,
Vicenza: H.& I.M.Sancto Ur-
sio, 1507
——Milan: J.A.Scinzenzeler,for
J.J.Legnano & Bros, 1512
——Venice: G.dei Rusconi, 1521
—Paesi nuovamente retrovati.
Milan: J.A.Scinzenzeler,for
J.J.Legnano & Bros, 1508
——Venice: G.di Rusconi, 1517
——Milan: J.A.Scinzenzeler,for
J.J.Legnano & Bros, 1519
—Sensuyt le Nouveau monde.
Paris: J.Janot [1515?]
——Paris: [Widow of J.Trep-
perel, 1515?] (3)
——Paris: P.Le Noir [1521]
——Paris: D.Janot [ca. 1535]
Fracanzano, Antonio. De morbo
gallico. Bologna: P.Bonardo,
1564
——Padua: C.Griffio, 1563 [i.e.,
1564]

——Venice: F.Lorenzini, 1565
—De morbo gallico tractatus. *In*
Fallopius, Gabriel. De morbo
gallico. Padua: 1564
——*In* Fallopius, Gabriel. De
morbo gallico. Venice: 1565
——*In* Fallopius, Gabriel. De
morbo gallico. Venice: 1574
Fracastoro, Girolamo. Opera
omnia. Venice: Heirs of
L.Giunta, 1555
——Venice: Heirs of L.Giunta,
1574
——Venice: Heirs of L.Giunta,
1584
—Operum pars prior-posterior.
Lyons: F.LeFèvre, 1591
—De sympathia et antipathia
rerum. Venice: Heirs of
L.Giunta, 1546
——Lyons: N.Bacquenois,for
G.Gazeau, 1550
——Lyons: J.de Tournes &
J.Gazeau, 1554
—Syphilis, sive Morbus gallicus.
Verona: [S.dei Nicolini da Sab-
bio & Bros] 1530
——Paris: L.Cynaeus, 1531
——Rome: A.Blado, 1531
——Basel: J.Bebel, 1536
——*In* Ferri, Alfonso. De ligni
sancti. Paris: 1542
——*In the same.* Paris: 1543
——*In the same.* Lyons: 1547
Fragoso, Juan. Aromatum, fruc-
tuum, et simplicium aliquot
medicamentorum . . . historia
brevis. Strassburg: J.Martin,
1600
—Discursos de la cosas aromat-
icas. Madrid: F.Sanchez,for
S.Ibáñez, 1572
**France. Sovereigns, etc.,
1589-1610 (Henry IV).** Edict
contenant le pouvoir donné au
marquis de Cottenmael . . .
pour la conqueste des terres
Canada. Rouen: R.Du Petit
Val, 1598
Francesco da Bologna, o.f.m.
La letera mandata dal rev.
padre frate Francesco da
Bologna. Venice: P.Danza
[1534]
FRANCISCANS—MISSIONS
—Fricius, V. Indianischer
Religionstandt der gantzen
newen Welt. Ingolstadt: 1588

Fuchs, Leonhart. Commentaires tres excellens de l'hystoire des plantes. Paris: J.Gazeau, 1549

— De componendorum miscendorumque medicamentorum ratione. Lyons: [S.Barbier, for ?] J.Frellon, 1556

— — Lyons: [S.Barbier,for ?] A. Vincent, 1556

— — Lyons: S.Barbier,for J.Frellon, 1561

— — Lyons: S.Barbier,for A.Vincent, 1561

— De historia stirpium commentarii insignes. Basel: M.Isengrin, 1542

— — Paris: J.Bogard, 1543

— — Paris: J.Gazeau, 1543

— — [Lyons:] B.Arnoullet,for M.DuPuys,at Paris, 1546

— — Paris: J.Bogard, 1546

— — Paris: O.Petit, 1546

— — Lyons: B.Arnoullet, 1547

— — Lyons: B.Arnoullet,for G.Gazeau, 1547

— — Paris: J.Foucher, 1547

— — Paris: V.Gaultherot, 1547

— — Paris: C.Guillard, 1547

— — Lyons: B.Arnoullet, 1549

— — Lyons: B.Arnoullet, 1551

— — Lyons: J.de Tournes & G.Gazeau, 1555

— De usitata huius temporis componendorum . . . ratione. Basel: J.Oporinus [1555]

— Errata recentiorum medicorum. Hagenau: J.Secerius, 1530

— Histoire des plantes. Paris: Widow of A.Birckmann, 1549

— — Lyons: B.Arnoullet, 1550

— — Lyons: B.Arnoullet, 1551

— — Lyons: Widow of B.Arnoullet,for G.Rouillé, 1558

— — Lyons: C.Pesnot, 1575

— Histoire générale des plantes. Rouen: R.Mallard, 1593

— Historia de las yervas, y plantas. Antwerp: H.de Laet,for Heirs of A.Birckmann, 1557 (2)

— Läbliche abbildung und contrafaytung aller kreüter. Basel: M.Isengrin, 1545

— New kreuterbuch. Basel: M.Isengrin, 1543

— Den nieuwen Herbarius. Basel: M.Isengrin [ca. 1545]

— Plantarum effigies. Lyons: B.Arnoullet, 1549

— — ('eefigies'). Lyons: B.Arnoullet, 1551

— — Lyons: B.Arnoullet, 1552

— Primi de stirpium historia. Basel: M.Isengrin, 1545

— — Basel: M.Isengrin, 1549

— Stirpium imagines. Lyons: B.Arnoullet, 1549

Fuenmayor, Antonio de. Vida y hechos de Pio V. Madrid: L.Sánchez, 1595

Fuentes, Alonso de. Summa de philosophia natura. Seville: J.de León, 1547

Fulgosus, Baptista. *See* Fregoso, Battista

Tfundament der medicinen. *See* Sylvius, Petrus

Funerailles & diverses manieres d'ensevelir. *See* Guichard, Claude

FUNERAL RITES AND CEREMONIES

— Guichard, C. Funerailles. Lyons: 1581A

Fur die platern Malafrantsosa. [Vienna: J.Winterburg, ca.1508?]

Fusch, Remaclus. Morbi hispanici . . . curandi. Paris: C.Wechel, 1541

Gabelkover, Oswald. Artzneybuch. Tübingen: G.Gruppenbach, 1594

— — Tübingen: G.Gruppenbach, 1595

— — Tübingen: G.Gruppenbach, 1596

— — Tübingen: G.Gruppenbach, 1599

— The boock of physicke. Dordrecht: I.Canin, 1599

— Medecyn-boeck. Dordrecht: A.Canin, 1598

— Nützlich Artzneybuch. Tübingen: 1589

Gabriel de San José. *See* San José, Gabriel de

Gabrielli, Giulio, of Gubbio. Orationum et epistolarum . . . libri duo. Venice: F.Ziletti, 1569

Gaebelkover, Oswald. *See* Gabelkover, Oswald

Gaguin, Robert. Les croniques de France. Paris: G.Du Pré, 1515

— — Paris: P.LePreux, 1515

— — Paris: Michel LeNoir, 1516

— Les grandes chroniques. Paris: P.LePreux,& G.Du Pré, 1514

— La mer des croniques. Paris: N.de La Barre, 1518

— — Paris: R.Chaudière [1520]

— — Paris: P.Gaudoul [1525]

— — Paris: [A.Girault, 1525]

— — Paris: N.de La Barre,for J.de Saint Denis, 1527

— — Paris: N.de La Barre,for J.Petit, 1527

— — Paris: J.Nyverd [1530]

— — Paris: [A.Girault] 1536

— — Paris [J.Kerver?] 1536

— — Paris [P.Servent?] 1536

Galard-Terraube, Gallard de. *See* Tarraube, Galard de

Galatea. *See* Cervantes Saavedra, Miguel de

Gallo, Antonio. De ligno sancto. Paris: S.de Colines, 1540

Gallucci, Giovanni Paolo. Theatrum mundi. Venice: G.B.Somasco, 1588

— — Venice: G.B.Somasco, 1589

Galvão, António. Tratado . . . dos diversos e desvayrados caminos. [Lisbon:] J.de Barreira, 1563

Gambara, Lorenzo. Chorineus. Rome: V.&L.Dorici, 1552

— De navigatione Christophori Columbi. Rome: F.Zanetti, 1581

— — Rome: B.Bonfadini & T.Diani, 1583

— — Rome: B.Bonfadini & T.Diani, 1585

Gante, Pedro de. *See* Mura, Petrus de

Ein gar schon . . . Büchlin. *See* Vives, Juan Luis

Garcés, Julien, Bp of Tlaxcala. De habilitate et capacitate gentium. Rome: 1537

Garcéz, Henrique, tr. Camoes, Luis de. Lusiadas. Madrid: 1591

—, **tr.** Patrizi, Francesco, Bp of Gaeta. De reyno, y de la institucion del que ha de reynar. Madrid: 1591

—, **tr.** Petrarca, Francesco. Los sonetos y canciones. Madrid: 1591

--Lyons: G.Rouillé, 1561

--Paris: O.de Harsy, 1570

--Paris: [O.de Harsy,for] J.DuPuys, 1570

--Paris: [O.de Harsy,for] J.DuPuys, 1580

-Historia . . . de nuestro tiempo. Salamanca: A.de Portonariis, 1562-63

-Historiarum sui temporis. Florence: L.Torrentino, 1550-52

--, t.1. Venice: G.Griffio,for P.Bosello, 1552

--, t.2. Venice: Comin da Trino, 1552

--Paris: M.de Vascovan, 1553-54

--[n.p.] 1555

--Strassburg: A.Fries, 1556

--Paris: M.de Vascovan, 1558-60

--Basel: H.Petri & P.Perna, 1560

--Lyons: Heirs of S.Gryphius, 1561

--Basel: [H.Petri & P.Perna] 1567

-Historie del suo tempo. Venice: D. Farri [for P.Pietrasanta] 1555

--, pte 1a. Venice: Comin da Trino, 1558

--, pte 2nda. Venice: Comin da Trino, 1557

-Icones sive Imagines virorum bellica. [Basel: P.Perna & H.Petri? ca.1580]

-Istorie del suo tempo, t.1. Venice: B.& F.Imperadore, 1551

--t.2. Venice: B.Cesano, 1553

-Libro de las historias y cosas acontescidas en Alemana. Valencia: J.Mey,for H.Ulzina, 1562

-Libro de pesci romani. Venice: The Gualtieri, 1560

-Musaei Joviani imagines. Basel: P.Perna & H.Petri, 1577

-Regionum et insularum . . . descriptiones. Basel: P.Perna, 1578

-Ein warhafftige beschrybung aller nammhafftigen geschichten. Basel: 1560

-Warhafftige Beschreibunge aller Chronickwirdiger Historien. Frankfurt a.M.:

G.Rab,for P.Perna,at Basel, 1570

Girard, Bernard de, sieur du Haillan. Discours sur l'extreme cherté. Paris: P.L'Huillier, 1574

--Bordeaux: 1586

--Bordeaux: 1587

Girault, Simon. Globe du monde. Langres: J.Des Preyz, 1592

Girava, Gerónimo. La cosmographia y geographia. Venice: G.Ziletti, 1570

-Dos libros de cosmographia. Milan: G.A.da Castiglione & C.Caron, 1556

Giustiniani, Agostino, Bp of Nebbio. Castigatissimi annali. Genoa: A.Bellone, 1537

-,ed. See Bible. O.T. Psalms. Polyglot. Psalterium hebreum. Genoa: 1516

Glareanus, Henricus. Brevissima totius habitabilis terrae descriptio. Paris: C.Wechel, 1542

-Compendiara Asiae . . . descriptio. In Pius II, Pope. Asiae . . . descriptio. Paris: 1534 (2)

-De geographia. Basel: J.Faber, 1527

--Basel: J.Faber, 1528

--Freiburg i.Br.: J.Faber, 1530

--Freiburg i.Br.: J.Faber, 1533

--Venice: G.A.dei Nicolini da Sabbio,for M.Sessa, 1534

--Freiburg i.Br.: J.Faber, 1536

--Venice: G.A.dei Nicolini da Sabbio,for M.Sessa, 1538

--Freiburg i.Br.: J.Faber, 1539

--Venice: G.A.dei Nicolini da Sabbio, 1539

--Paris: J.Loys, 1542

--Paris: J.Loys,for G.Richard, 1542

--Freiburg i.Br.: S.M.Graf, 1543

--Venice: P.,G.M.,& C.dei Nicolini da Sabbio,for M.Sessa, 1549

--Paris: G.Cavelat, 1550

--Freiburg i.Br.: S.M.Graf, 1551

--In Peurbach, Georg von. Theoricae novae planetarum. Cologne: 1581

--In the same. Cologne: 1591

Globe du monde. See Girault, Simon

Globus mundi. See Waldseemüller, Martin

Das glückhafft Schiff von Zürich. See Fischart, Johann

Godfrey of Bulloigne. See Tasso, Torquato

Godoy, Diego de. See Cortés, Hernando. La quarta relacion

Goes, Damião de. Aliquot opuscula. Louvain: R.Rescius, 1584

--In Anghiera, Pietro Martire d'. De rebus oceanicis et novo orbe. Cologne: 1574

-Avisi de le case fatte da Portugesi. Venice: 1539

-Chronica do . . . rei Dom Manuel. Lisbon: F.Correa, 1566

-Commentarii rerum gestarum . . . a Lusitanis. Louvain: R.Rescius, 1539

-Fides, religio, moresque Aethiopum. Louvain: R.Rescius, 1540

--Paris: C.Wechel, 1541

--In Boemus, Johann. Mores, leges, et ritus omnium gentium. Lyons: 1582

--In the same. Geneva: 1591

-Hispania. Louvain: R.Rescius, 1542

--In Beale, Robert. Rerum Hispanicarum scriptores. Frankfurt a.M.: 1579

Il Goffredo. See Tasso, Torquato

Gohory, Jacques. Instruction de la congnoisce . . . de lherbe Petum. Paris: J.Parant, 1580

-Instruction sur l'herbe Petum. Paris: G.Du Pré, 1572

GOLD

-Karl V, Emperor of Germany. Caroli. Ro. regis, recessuri adlocutio. Rome: 1520

-Marlowe, C. Tamburlaine the Great. London: 1590

The golden-grove. See Vaughan, William

Gómara, Francisco López de. Hispania victrix. Medina del Campo: G.de Millis, 1553

-Histoire generalle des Indes Occidentales. Paris: M.Sonnius, 1568

--Paris: M.Sonnius, 1569

--Paris: B.Turrisan, 1569

— —Paris: M.Sonnius, 1577

— —Paris: M.Sonnius, 1578

— —Paris: M.Sonnius, 1580

— —Paris: M.Sonnius, 1584

— —Paris: M.Sonnius, 1587

—Historia dell'India, pte 2da. Venice: G.Ziletti, 1565

—Historia dell'Indie Occidentali. Venice: B.Barezzi, 1599

—Historia delle nuove Indie Occidentali. Venice: G.Bonadio, 1564

—Historia delle nuove Indie Occidentali . . . Parte seconda. Venice: P.Bosello, 1560

— —Venice: F.Lorenzini, 1560

— —Venice: C.Franceschini, 1576

—Historia di Don Ferdinando Cortés. Venice: F.Lorenzini, 1560

— —Venice: G.Bonadio, 1564

— —Venice: C.Franceschini, 1576

—Historia di Messico. Venice [G.Ziletti?] 1573

—Historia general de las Indias. Saragossa: A.Millán,for M.Capila, 1553

— —Antwerp: H.de Laet,for J.Bellère, 1554

— —Antwerp: H.de Laet,for J.Steels, 1554

— —Antwerp: M.Nuyts, 1554

— —Saragossa: P.Bernuz & A. Millán,for M.de Zapila, 1554

— —Saragossa: P.Bernuz & A.Millán,for M.de Zapila, 1555

—La historia generale delle Indie Occidentali. Rome: V.&L. Dorici, 1556

—Historie dell'India, pte 2da. Venice: D.Farri,for A.Arrivabene, 1557

— —Venice: D.Farri,for G.Ziletti, 1557

—Historie dell'Indie, pte 3a. Venice: G.Ziletti, 1566

—La istoria de las Indias. Saragossa: A.Millán, 1552

—The pleasant historie of the conquest of the Weast India. London: H.Bynneman, 1578

— —London: T.Creede, 1596

—La segunda parte dela historia general delas Indias. Saragossa: A.Milán, 1554

—Voyages et conquestes du Capitaine Ferdinand Courtois.

Paris: A.L'Angelier, 1588

Gómez de Castro, Alvár. De rebus gestis a Francisco Ximeno Cisnerio. Alcalá de Henares: A.de Angulo, 1569

— —Frankfurt a.M.: A.Wechel, 1581

Gómez de Ciudad Real, Alvár. El vellocino dorado. Toledo: J.de Ayalá, 1546

Gonsalvius, Reginaldus, Montanus. A discovery and playne declaration. London: J.Day, 1568

— —London: J.Day, 1569

—Der heiligen hispanischen Inquisition. Heidelberg: J.Mayer, 1569

—Der heyliger Hispanischer Inquisitie. [Norwich, Eng.? A.Solempne?] 1569

—De heylighe Spaensche inquisitie. London: J.Day, 1569

—Histoire de l'Inquisition d'Espagne. [Geneva?] 1568

—Historie van de Spaensche Inquisitie. [Antwerp?] 1569

—Inquisitio hispanica. Eisleben: A.Petri, 1569

—Sanctae Inquisitionis Hispanicae. Heidelberg: M.Schirat, 1567

Gonzaga, Francisco, Bp. De origine seraphicae religionis. Rome: D.Basa, 1587

— —*In* Fricius, Valentinus. Indianischer Religionstandt der gantzen newen Welt. Ingolstadt: 1588

Gonzales de Merchado, Luigi. *See* González de Mercado, Luis

González de Mendoza, Juan, Bp. Dell'historia della China. Genoa: G.Bartoli, 1586

— —Rome: A.Calentano & C.Rasimo, 1586

— —Rome: B.Grassi, 1586

— —Rome: G.Marsioni, 1586

— —Rome: G.Martinelli, 1586

— —Rome: V.Pelagallo, 1586

— —Rome: G.A.Ruffinelli, 1586

— —Venice: A.Muschio, 1586

— —Venice: A.Muschio, 1588

— —Venice: A.Muschio, 1590

—Histoire . . . de la Chine. Paris: J.Périer, 1588

— —Paris: N.du Fosse, 1589

— —Paris: J.Périer, 1589

— —Paris: Widow of G.Buon, 1600

— —Paris: A.L'Angelier, 1600

— —Paris: A.Périer, 1600

—Historia . . . dela China. Rome: V.Accolto,for B.Grassi, 1585

— —Valencia: Widow of P.de Huete, 1585

— —Barcelona: J.Cendrat,for P.Menescal, 1586

— —Barcelona: J.Cendrat,for F.Trincher, 1586

— —Madrid: Q.Gerardo,for B.de Robles, 1586

— —Madrid: P.Madrigal,for B.de Robles, 1586 [i.e.,1587]

— —Saragossa: L.& D.de Robles, 1587

— —Venice: A.Muschio [i.e.,London: J.Wolfe] 1587

— —Saragossa: L.& D.de Robles, 1588

— —Medina del Campo: S.del Canto,for the Heirs of B.Boyer, 1595

— —Antwerp: P.Bellère, 1596

—The historie . . . of China. London: J.Wolfe,for E.White, 1588

—Historien. *See* Dresser, Matthias

—Itinerario . . . de la China. Lisbon [A.Lobato?] 1586

—Ein neuwe . . . Beschreibung dess . . . Konigreichs China. Frankfurt a.M.: S.Feyerabend, 1589

—Nova . . . historia de . . . regno China. Frankfurt a.M.: [S.Feyerabend?] 1589

González de Mercado, Luis. Copia di una lettera . . . sopra la presa del'India del Peru. Florence: A.de Mazochius [1533?]

González de Montes, Raimundo. *See* Gonsalvius, Reginaldus, Montanus

The good huswives handmaid for cookerie. [London: R.Jones, 1588A]

The good huswifes jewell. *See* Dawson, Thomas

Goulart, Simon. Le cinquiesme recueil contenant les choses plus memorables avenues sous la Ligue. [Geneva?] 1598

—Histoires admirables et memo-
rables de nostre temps. Paris:
J.Houzé, 1600
—Le premier recueil, contenant
les choses plus memorables
advenues sous la Ligue.
[Geneva?] 1590 (2)
—Le quatriesme recueil, conte-
nant l'histoire des choses plus
memorables avenue sous la
Ligue. [Geneva?] 1595 (2)
—Le second recueil, contenant
l'histoire des choses plus
memorables advenues sous la
Ligue. [Geneva?] 1590 (2)
—Le sixiesme et dernier recueil,
contenant les choses plus
memorables avenues sous la
Ligue. [Geneva?] 1599
—*See also* Carion, Johann.
Chronique et histoire univer-
selle
—*See also* Crespin, Jean. Histoire
des martyrs
—*See also the numerous edns of*
Guillaume de Salluste, seigneur
Du Bartas's La sepmaine *as ed.*
& annotated by Goulart, 1st
publ., Geneva, 1581, & subse-
quently reprinted under title
Commentaires . . . sur La sep-
maine
Gourgues, Dominique de. His-
toire memorable de la reprinse
. . . de la Floride. Paris: 1568
Grabowski, Piotr. Polska nizna.
Cracow: 1596
Gracián, Jerónimo. Stimulo dela
propagacion dela fee. Lisbon:
A.Lobato, 1586
Grammatica, o Arte de la lengua
general de los Indios. *See*
Domingo de Santo Tomás
Le grand dictionaire françois-
latin. Geneva: J.Stoer, 1593
Le grand miroir du monde. *See*
Duchesne, Joseph
Le grand nauffrage des folz. *See*
Brant, Sebastian
La grand nef des fols. *See* Brant,
Sebastian
Les grandes chroniques. *See*
Gaguin, Robert
Las grandezas y cosas notables de
España. *See* Medina, Pedro de
La grandezza, larghezza, e dis-
tanza di tutte le sfere. *See*
Bonardo, Giovanni Maria,

conte
La grant nef des folz. *See* Brant,
Sebastian.
Le grant voyage. *See* Breyden-
bach, Bernhard von
GREAT BRITAIN—COLONIES
—Dee, J. General and rare
memorials. London: 1577
Greene, Robert. A disputation
betweene a hee conny-catcher,
and a shee conny-catcher. Lon-
don: A.Jeffes,for T.Gubbin,
1592A
—Philomela. London: R.Bradock
& E.Allde,for E.White, 1592A
GREENLAND
—Magnus, O., Abp of Upsala.
Beschreibueng allerley
Gelegenheyte. Strassburg: 1567
——De gentibus septentrionali-
bus. Amberg: 1599
——Histoire des pays septen-
trionaux. Antwerp: 1561
——Historia de gentibus septen-
trionalibus. Rome: 1555
——Historia de gentibus septen-
trionalibus . . . a C.Scribonio
. . . redacta. Antwerp: 1558
——Historien der mittnaechtigen
Laender. Basel: 1567
——Storia . . . de' costumi de
popoli settentrionali. Venice:
1561
——De wonderlijcke historie van
de noordersche landen. Ant-
werp: 1562
—Ziegler, J. Quae intus continen-
tur. Syria . . . Schondia.
Strassburg: 1532
——Terrae sanctae . . . Syriae.
Strassburg: 1536
Greepe, Thomas. The true and
perfecte newes of the . . . ex-
ploytes performed . . . by . . .
Syr Frauncis Drake. London:
J.Charlewood,for T.Hackett,
1587
Grégoire, Pierre. De republica.
Pont-à-Moussin: N.Claudet,
1596
——[Frankfurt a.M.:]
Z.Palthenius,for Heirs of
P.Fischer, 1597
Gregorius XIII, Pope. *See*
Catholic Church. Pope,
1572-1585 (Gregorius XIII)
GRENVILLE, SIR RICHARD
—Parsons, R. Elisabethen, der

Koenigin . . . Edict. In-
golstadt: 1593
——Elizabethae, Angliae reginae
. . . edictum. Lyons: 1592
——Responce a l'injuste . . .
edict d'Elizabeth reyne
d'Angleterre. Lyons: 1593
GRIJALVA, JUAN DE
—Ein Auszug ettlicher sendbrieff.
Nuremberg: 1520
—Díaz, J. Littera mandata della
insula de Cuba. [Venice?
1520?]
——Provinciae sive regione in In-
dia Occidentali noviter reper-
tae. [Rome? 1520?]
—Varthema, L.di. Itinerario . . .
ne lo Egypto ne la Suria.
Venice: 1520
——Itinerario . . . Buelto de
latin en romance. Seville: 1520
Grimaldi, Giovanni Battista.
Copey eynes brieffes . . .
Ansaldo de Grimaldo. [Speyer:
J.Schmidt, 15]29
Das gross Narren Schiff. *See*
Brant, Sebastian
Den groten herbarius. *See* Hortus
Sanitatis, Minor
Groto, Luigi. *See* Bonardo,
Giovanni Maria, conte. La
grandezza, larghezza, e
distanza di tutte le sfere; *and*
the latter's La minera del
mondo
Grotto, Luigi. *See* Groto, Luigi
Grünbeck, Joseph. *See* Grünpeck,
Joseph
Gründlicher Bericht, von
Anordnung guter Policeyen.
See Botero, Giovanni
Gründlicher Bericht, wellicher
gestallt . . . *See* Bazán, Alvaro
de, marqués de Santa Cruz
Gründtliche und rechte Under-
weisung der Chirurgie. *See*
Tagault, Jean
Gründtliche unnd warhafftige
beschreibung. *See* Guicciar-
dini, Francesco
Grünpeck, Joseph. Ein hübscher
Tractat von dem ursprung des
Bösen Franzos. Augsburg:
J.Schaur, 1496
——Nuremberg: C.Hochfeder,
1496
—Libellus . . . de mentulagra.
[Reutlingen? M.Greyff? 1503?]

Schuman Press, 1595

Horto, Garcia del. *See* Orta, Garcia da

L'horto dei semplici. *See* Cortusi, Giacomo Antonio

Hortop, Job. The rare travailes. London: [T.Scarlet] for W.Wright, 1591

Hortorum libri triginta. *See* LeCourt, Benoît.

Hortus medicus. *See* Camerarius, Joachim, 1534–1598

Hortus Sanitatis, Minor. Den groten herbarius. Antwerp: C.de Grave, 1533

Houtman, Cornelis de. The description of a voyage made by certaine ships of Holland. London: [J.Windet?] for J.Wolfe, 1598

—Diarium nauticum itineris Batavorum in Indiam Orientalem. Middelburg: B.Langenes, 1598

— —[Middelburg: B.Langenes,for] J.Janszoon at Arnhem, 1598

— —[Middelburg: B.Langenes,for] A.Périer,at Paris, 1598

—Journael van de reyse der Hollandtsche schepen. Middelburg: B.Langenes, 1598

— —[Middelburg: B.Langenes,for] J.van Waesberghe, at Rotterdam, 1598

—Journal du voyage de l'Inde Orientale. Middelburg: B.Langenes, 1598

— —[Middelburg: B.Langenes,for] A.Périer,at Paris, 1598

—Kurtze warhafftige Beschreibung der newen Reyse. Nuremberg: C.Lochner,for L.Hulsius, 1598

— —Nuremberg: L.Hulsius, 1599

—Verhael vande reyse by de Hollandtsche schepen. Middelburg: B.Langenes, 1597

Hoyarsabal, Martin de. Les voyages avantureux. Bordeaux: J.Chouin, 1579

Ein hübscher Tractat von dem ursprung des Boesen Franzos. *See* Gruenpeck, Joseph

Huerto, Garcia del. *See* Orta,

Garcia da

Hues, Robert. Tractaet . . . van het gebruijck der . . . globe. Amsterdam: C.Claeszoon, 1597

—Tractatus de globis. London: T.Dawson, 1594

Hulsius, Levinus. Sammlung von . . . Schiffahrten, pt 1. Houtman, Cornelis de. Kurtze warhafftige Beschreibung der newen Reyse. Nuremberg: 1598

— — — —Nuremberg: 1599

— —, pt 4. Schmidel, Ulrich. Warhafftige Historien einer wunderbaren Schiffart. Nuremberg: 1599

— —, pt 5. Raleigh, Sir Walter. Kurtze wunderbäre Beschreibung dess . . . Konigreichs Guianae. Nuremberg: 1599

An humerous dayes myrth. *See* Chapman, George. A pleasant comedy

HUNTING

—Argote de Molina, G. Libro de la monteria. Seville: 1582

Hurault, Michel, sieur de Belesbat et du Fay. Discours sur l'estat de France. [Paris?] 1588 (5)

— —Chartres: 1591

— —[Paris?] 1591

—Discours, ein fürtreffliches frey . . . Bedencken. Kleine Rhuwart: H.Windstill [i.e.,Strassburg? B.Jobin?] 1589

—A discourse upon the present state of France. [London: J.Wolfe] 1588 (2)

—Exactissimi discursus de rebus gallicis. [Strassburg] 1592

—An excellent discourse upon the . . . present estate of France. London: [J.Wolfe] 1592

—Excellent et libre discours sur l'estat present de la France. [Paris?] 1588 (5)

— —[Paris?] 1589

—Premier discours sur l'estat de la France. [Paris?] 1591

—Quatre excellent discours sur l'estat present de la France. [Paris?] 1593

— —[Paris?] 1594

— —[Paris?] 1595

—Le recueil des . . . discours sur l'estat present de la France. [Paris?] 1598

Hurtado de Toledo, Luis, joint author. *See* Carvajal, Miguel de. Cortes d' casto amor. Toledo: 1557

Hutten, Philipp von. *See* Cortés, Hernando. Von dem Newen Hispanien. Augsburg: 1555

Hutten, Ulrich von. De admiranda guaiaci medicina. *In* Liber de morbo gallico. Venice: 1535

—De Guaiaci medicina. Mainz: J.Schöffer, 1519

— —[Paris:] P.Vidoué,for C.Resch, 1519

— —Bologna: H.de Benedictis, 1521

— —Mainz: J.Schöffer, 1524

— —Mainz: J.Schöffer, 1531

— —*In* Luisini, Luigi. De morbo gallico. Venice: 1566

— —*In* Luisini, Luigi. Aprodisiacus, sive De lue venerea. Venice: 1599

—De morbo gallico. London: T.Berthelet, 1533

—L'experience et approbation . . . touchant la medicine du boys dict Guaiacum. Paris: M.de LaPorte [ca.1530?]

— —Paris: P.LeNoir [ca.1530?]

— —Paris: J.Trepperel [ca.1530?]

—Guaiacum. L'experience . . . touchant la medicine du . . . Guaiacum. Lyons: E.Gueynard,for C.Nourry [ca.1520]

—Of the wood called Guaiacum. London: T.Berthelet, 1536

— —London: T.Berthelet, 1539

— —London: T.Berthelet, 1540

—Von der wunderbarlichen Artzney des Holtz Guaiacum. Strassburg: J.Grüninger, 1519

HUTTEN, ULRICH VON

—Brunfels, O. Herbarum. Strassburg: 1530

Huttich, Johann, comp. *See* Novus Orbis regionum. Die new welt. Strassburg: 1534

Hydrographia la mas curiosa. *See* Poza, Andrés de

Hydrographiae; hoc est, Charta marinae. *See* Fries, Lorenz

Leo Africanus, Joannes. A geographical historie of Africa. London: [Eliot's Court Press, for] G.Bishop, 1600
—Historiale description de l'Afrique. Lyons: J.Temporal, 1556
Leo Hebraeus. La traduzion del Indio. Madrid: P.Madrigal, 1590
Léon, Jean. See Leo Africanus, Joannes
León, Juan de. Relacion de lo que se truxo del Peru. Medina del Campo: 1534
LEÓN, JUAN DE
—Gonsalvius, R. Der heiligen hispanischen Inquisition, etliche . . . ränck. Heidelberg: 1569
——A discovery and playne declaration. London: 1568
——De heylighe Spaensche inquisitie. London: 1569
——Histoire de l'Inquisition d'Espagne. [Geneva?] 1568
——Historie van de Spaensche Inquisitie. [Antwerp?] 1569
——Inquisitio hispanica. Eisleben: 1569
——Sanctae Inquisitionis Hispanicae. Heidelberg: 1567
Leonardi, Camillus. Expositio canonum. Venice: G.Arrivebene, 1496
Leone, Giovanni. See Leo Africanus, Joannes
Leoniceni, Niccolò. De curatione morbi. In Almenar, Juan. Libelli duo di morbo gallico. Lyons: 1528
—De curation morbi. In the same. Lyons: 1529
—De epidemia. See Liber de morbo gallico. Venice: 1535
—De morbo gallico. Milan: G.Le Signerre,for J. Legnano, 1497
——In Gatinaria, Marco. Contenta in hoc volumine. Venice: 1516
—Libellus de epidemia. Venice: A.Manuzio, 1497
——[Leipzig: W.Stöckel, ca.1499]
——In Aureum opus. Pavia: 1516
——In Massa, Niccoló. Liber de morbo gallico. [Venice?] 1532

—Opuscula. Basel: A. Cratander & J.Bebel, 1532
Le Paulmier de Grentemesnil, Julien. De morbis contagiosis. Paris: D.Duval, 1578
Le Pois, Antoine. Discours sur les medalles. Paris: M.Patisson,for R.Estienne, 1579
LeRoy, Louis. Consideration sur l'histoire françoise. Paris: F.Morel, 1567
——Lyons: B.Rigaud, 1568
——Paris: F.Morel, 1568
——Paris: F.Morel, 1570
——Paris: F.Morel, 1571
——Paris: F.Morel, 1579
——Paris: F.Morel, 1588
—De la vicissitude ou varieté des choses. Paris: P.L'Huillier, 1575
——Paris: P.L'Huillier, 1576
——Paris: P.L'Huillier, 1577
——Paris: P.L'Huillier, 1579
——Paris: P.L'Huillier, 1583
——Paris: P.L'Huillier, 1584
—Della vicissitudine o mutabile varietá delle cose. Venice: Aldine Press, 1592
—Of the interchangeable course, or variety of things. London: C.Yetsweirt, 1594
—La vicissitudine of mutabile varietá delle cose. Venice: Aldine Press, 1585
Léry, Jean de. Histoire d'un voyage fait en la terre du Bresil. La Rochelle: A.Chuppin, 1578 (2)
——Geneva: A.Chuppin, 1580 (2)
——[Geneva:] A. Chuppin, 1585
——[Geneva:] Heirs of E.Vignon, 1594
——[Geneva:] Heirs of E.Vignon, 1599
——[Geneva:] Heirs of E.Vignon, 1600
—Histoire memorable de la ville de Sancerre. [Geneva:] 1574
—Historia de Schiffart. In Staden, Hans. Dritte Buch Americae, darinn Brasilia . . . auss eigener erfahrung in Teutsch beschrieben. Frankfurt a.M.: 1593
—Historia navigationis in Brasiliam. [Geneva:] E.Vignon, 1586

——Geneva: Heirs of E.Vignon, 1594
—Historie van een reyse ghedaen inden lande van Bresillien. Amsterdam: C.Claeszoon, 1597
—Narratio. In Staden, Hans. America tertia pars memorabilem provinciae Brasiliae historiam. Frankfurt a.M.: 1592
Letera de la nobil cipta nuovamente ritrovata alle Indie. [Rome: A.Blado, 1535?]
La letera mandata dal rev. padre frate Francesco da Bologna. See Francesco da Bologna, o.f.m.
Letra enviada al escrivano de Racio. See Colombo, Cristoforo
Lettera de la nobil città nuovamente ritrovata alle Indie. [Florence? 1536?]
—[Florence? 1539?]
Lettera . . . allo illustrissimo signore Duca Juliano de Medici. See Corsali, Andrea
Lettera . . . delle isole nuovamente trovate. See Vespucci, Amerigo
Lettere . . . della conquista del paese. See Avilá, Pedro Arias d'.
Lettere di principi. See Ruscelli, Girolamo
The letting of humors blood. See Rowlands, Samuel
Lettres du Japon. See Jesuits. Letters from missions
Lettres envoyées au chapitre general. See Dîaz de Lugo, Juan Bernardo, Bp
Lexicon, o Vocabulario de la lengua general de Peru. See Domingo de Santo Tomás
Ley de como ham de hir armados os navios. See Portugal. Laws, statutes, etc.
Leyes y ordenanças nuevamente hechas . . . por la governacion de las Indias. See Spain. Laws, statutes, etc., 1516-1556 (Charles I)
Leyes y ordenanzas . . . para la governacion de las Indias. See Spain. Laws, statutes, etc., 1516-1556 (Charles I)
Leys, e provisões. See Portugal. Laws, statutes, etc.

Las leys y prematicas hechas en las Cortes de Toledo. *See* Spain. Laws, statutes, etc., 1516-1556 (Charles I)

Lhoyd, Humphrey. *See* Llwyd, Humphrey, tr.

A libell of Spanish lies. *See* Savile, Capt. Henry

Libelli duo di morbo gallico. *See* Almenar, Juan

Libellus . . . de mentulagra. *See* Grünpeck, Joseph

Libellus ad evitandum . . . morbum gallicum. *See* Almenar, Juan

Libellus de cura ulcerum. *See* Bolognini, Angelo

Libellus de epidemia. *See* Leoniceno, Niccolo

Libellus geographicus. *See* Eisenmenger, Samuel, called Siderocrates

Liber chronicarum. *See* Schedel, Hartmann

Liber de morbo composito, vulgo gallico appelato. *See* Paschalis, Joannes

Liber de morbo gallico. Venice: G.Padovano & V.Ruffinello, 1535

— *See also* Massa, Niccolò

Liber de morbo neapolitano. *See* Massa, Niccolò

Liber geographiae. *See* Ptolemaeus, Claudius

Liber octo questionum. *See* Trithemius, Johannes

Libretto de tutta la navigatione. *See* Anghiera, Pietro Martire d'

Libri de piscibus marinis. See Rondelet, Guillaume

Libri de situ orbis. *See* Mela, Pomponius

Libri duo apologetici ad refutandas naenias. *See* Richer, Pierre

Libro, o Practica en cirurgia. *See* Vigo, Giovanni de

Libro . . . delas cosas maravillosas que vido. *See* Polo, Marco

Libro . . . nel qual si ragiona de tutte l'isole. *See* Bordone, Benedetto

Libro de exercicios de la gineta. *See* Vargas Machuca, Bernardo de

Libro de grandezas y cosas memorables de España. *See* Medina, Pedro de

Libro de la cosmographia. *See*

Apianus, Petrus

Libro de la monteria. *See* Argote de Molina, Gonzalo

Libro de las cosas. *See* Monardes, Nicolás

El libro de las costumbras de todas las gentes del mundo, y de las Indias. *See* Tamara, Francisco

Libro de las historias y cosas acontescidas en Alemana. *See* Giovio, Paolo, Bp of Nocera

Libro de los mysterios de la missa. *See* Verdugo y Sarría, Pedro

Libro de medicina. *See* Calvo, Juan

Libro de pesci romani. *See* Giovio, Paolo, Bp of Nocera

Libro de reyno de Dios. *See* Sánchez de Acre, Pero

Il libro del mal francese. *See* Massa, Niccolò

Libro del muy esforçado . . . cavallero don Claribalte. *See* Oviedo y Valdés, Gonzalo Fernández de

Libro del reino de Dios. *See* Sánchez de Acre, Pero

Libro delas quatro enfermedades cortesanos. *See* Lobera de Avilá, Luis

Libro detto Strega. *See* Pico della Mirandola, Giovanni Francesco

Libro en que esta copiladas algunas bullas. *See* Spain. Laws, statutes, etc., 1479-1504 (Ferdinand V and Isabella I)

Libro intitulado Arte para criar seda. *See* Casas, Gonzalo de las

Libro llamado Thesoro de virtú. *See* Isla, Alonso de la

Libro que trata de la enfermedad de las bubas. *See* Torres, Pedro de

Liébault, Jean. Thesaurus sanitatis. Paris: J.DuPuys, 1577

— *See also* Estienne, Charles. L'agriculture *& its translations.*

Lightfoot, William. The complaint of England. London: J.Wolfe, 1587

Lilio, Zaccaria, Bp. De origine et laudibus scientiarius. Florence: F.Bonaccorsi,for P.Pacini, 1496

Lima (Ecclesiastical province). Council, 1583. Concilium provinciale Limense. Madrid:

P.Madrigal, 1590

— —Madrid: P.Madrigal, 1591

LIMA—CHURCH HISTORY. *See also* PERU—CHURCH HISTORY

—En la causa que se trata entre el Arçobispo de Lima, y el Colegio de la Compania de Jesus. [Madrid? 1595?]

Linschoten, Jan Huygen van. Beschryvinghe van de gantsche custe van Guinea. Amsterdam: C.Claeszoon, 1596

—Discours of voyages into ye Easte and West Indies. London: J.Wolfe, 1598

—Dritter Theil Indiae Orientalis. Frankfurt a.M.: M.Becker,for J.T. & J.I.de Bry, 1599

—Navigatio ac itinerarium . . . in Orientalem . . . Indiam. The Hague: J.H.van Linschoten, 1599

— —The Hague: A.Henricszoon,for C.Claeszoon & G.Elzevir, 1599

—Reys-gheschrift vande navigatien der Portugaloysers in Orienten. Amsterdam: C.Claeszoon, 1595 [i.e., 1596]

Lisboa, Marcos da. *See* Marcos de Lisboa, Bp, o.f.m.

Liscovinus, Vincentius. De lue venerea. Basel: 1600

Littera mandata della insula de Cuba. *See* Díaz, Juan

Livre . . . de la curation des ulceres. *See* Bolognini, Angelo

Livro . . . que tracta da vida . . . do . . . Rey don Joam ho segundo. *See* Resende, Garcia de.

Llwyd, Humphrey, tr. *See* Caradog, of Llancarvan. The historie of Cambria. London: 1584

L'Obel, Matthias de. Icones stirpium. Antwerp: Widow of C.Plantin & J.Mourentorf, 1591

—Kruydtboeck. Antwerp: C.Plantin, 1581

—Plantarum . . . historia. Antwerp: C.Plantin, 1576

—Plantarum . . . icones. Antwerp: C.Plantin, 1581

Lobera de Avila, Luís. Libro delas quatro enfermedades cortesanos. Toledo: J.de Ayala,

——Frankfurt a.M.: M.Becker, for Heirs of C.Egenolff, 1598
—Eyn newer M.Lucidarius. Strassburg: J.Cammerlander [ca.1535]
——Strassburg: J.Cammerlander [ca.1539]
Lucubrationes. *See* More, Sir Thomas
Lucubratiuncula de morbo gallico. *See* Schmaus, Leonardus
Luculentissima quaedam terrae totius descriptio. *See* Schöner, Johann
Lud, Gualtherus. Erclarnis und usslegung der . . . Welt. Strassburg: J. Grüninger, 1507
—Speculi orbis . . . declaratio. Strassburg: J.Grüninger, 1507
Lugo, Juan Bernardo Díaz de. *See* Díaz de Lugo, Juan Bernardo, Bp
Luis venereae curandae ratio. *See* Botallo, Leonardo
Luis venereae perfectissimus tractatus. *See* Sassonia, Ercole
LUIS BERTRAN, SAINT
—Antist, V.J. Vera relatione de la vita . . . del p.f. Luigi Bertrando. Genoa: 1583
——Verdadera relacion de la vida . . . del padre fray Luis Bertran. Valencia: 1582
—Factor, N. Testimonios de la santidad . . . del padre fr. Luis Bertran. Valencia: 1584
—Martí L. Historia del bienaventurado padre Luys Bertran. Valencia: 1584
Luisini, Luigi. Aprodisiacus, sive De lue venerea. Venice: B.Barezzi & Co., 1599
—De morbo gallico. Venice: G.Ziletti, 1566
Lumnius, Joannes Fredericus. De extremo Dei judicio. Antwerp: A. Thielens, 1567
——Venice: D.Farri, 1569
—De vicinitate extremi judicii Dei. Antwerp: J.van Keerberghen, 1594
La Lusiada. *See* Camões, Luiz de
Lusiadas. *See* Camões, Luis de
Luz de alma christiana. *See* Meneses, Felipe de
Lyly, John. Pappe with an hatchet. London: J.Anoke &

J.Astile,for [T.Orwin] 1589 (3)
Lysandro y Rosellia. *See* Muñon, Sancho de. Tragicomedia de Lysandro y Rosellia. Salamanca: 1542
Lyvro . . . que trata da vida . . . don Joào o segundo. *See* Resende, Garcia de
M.,D.F.R.de. *See* An answer to the untruthes, published and printed in Spaine & *the* Respuesta y desengano contra las falsedades publicadas . . . en España, London: 1589A
M.Blundeville his exercises. *See* Blundeville, Thomas
M.Elucidarius. *See* Lucidarius
Macchelli, Niccolò. Tractatus de morbo gallico. Venice: A.Arrivabene, 1555
——Venice: A.Arrivabene, 1556
Macer Floridus. Les fleurs du livre des vertus des herbes. Rouen: M.& H.Mallard, 1588
Macer, Joannes. Indicarum historiarum . . . libri tres. Paris: G.Guillard, 1555
—Les trois livres de l'Histoire des Indes. Paris: G.Guillard, 1555
Macrobius, Ambrosius Aurelius Theodosius. Macrobius intiger. Paris: J.Badius,for J.Petit, 1515
——Paris: J.Badius, 1519
MADOG AB OWAIN GWYNEDD
—Caradog, of Llancarvan. The historie of Cambria. London: 1584
Maffei, Giovanni Pietro. Historiarum Indicarum libri xvi. Florence: F. Giunta, 1588
——Cologne: House of Birckmann,for A.Mylius, 1589
——Lyons: The Giuntas, 1589
——Venice: D.Zenaro, 1589
——Bergamo: C.Ventura, 1590
——Cologne: House of Birckmann,for A.Mylius, 1590
——Cologne: House of Birckmann,for A.Mylius, 1593
—Le historie delle Indie Orientali. Venice: D.Zenaro, 1589
——Le istorie delle Indie Orientali. Florence: F.Giunta, 1589
—Selectarum epistolarum ex India quatuor. Venice: D.Zenaro, 1588
Maffei, Raffaele. Commen-

tariorum urbanorum liber i-xxxviii. Rome: J.Besicken, 1506
——Paris: J.Badius,for himself & J.Petit, 1511
——Paris: J.Badius,for himself & J.Petit, 1515
——Paris: J.Badius,for himself, J.Petit,C.Chevallon & C.Resch, 1526
——Basel: Froben Office, 1530
——Basel: H.Froben & N.Episcopius, 1544
——Lyons: S.Gryphius, 1552
MAGALHAES, FERNAO DE
—Barros, J.de. Terceira decada da Asia. Lisbon: 1563
—Beccadelli, A. De dictis . . . Alphonsi regis. Wittenberg: 1585
—Bessard, T.de. Dialogue de la longitude est-ouest. Rouen: 1574
—Lopes de Castanheda, F. Historia . . . da India, t.6. Coimbra: 1554
——Historia dell'Indie Orientali. Venice: 1577
—Lumnius, J.F. De extremo Dei judicio. Antwerp: 1567
——De vicinitate extremi judicii Dei. Antwerp: 1594
—Maximilianus, Transylvanus. De Moluccis insulis. Cologne: 1523
——Epistola de admirabili et novissima Hispanorum . . . navigatione. Rome: 1524
——Il viaggio fatto da gli Spagniuoli atorno del mondo. Venice: 1536
—Medina, P.de. Las grandezas y cosas notables de España. Alcalá de henares: 1595
——Libro de grandezas y cosas memorables de España. Alcalá de Henares: 1548
—Mexîa, Pedro. Colóquios o dialogos. Seville: 1547
——Dialoghi. Venice: 1557
——Los dialogos o colóquios. Seville: 1548
——Les diverses leçons. Paris: 1556
——A pleasaunt dialogue concerning phisicke. London: 1580
——Trois dialogues. Paris: 1566
——De verscheyden lessen.

—Medicinales epistolae. Strassburg: J.Schott, 1529

MANATEES
—Rondelet, G. L'histoire entière des poissons. Lyons: 1558
— —Libri de piscibus marinis. Lyons: 1554

MANIOC
—Wateson, G. The cures of the diseased. London: 1598

MANNERS & CUSTOMS. *See also* INDIANS—SOCIAL LIFE & CUSTOMS
—Boemus, J. Gli costumi, le leggi, et l'usanze di tutti le genti. Venice: 1558
— —Mores, leges, et ritus. Lyons: 1582
— —Omnium gentium mores. Antwerp: 1542
—Tamara, F. El libro de las costumbras. Antwerp: 1556

Mantuanus Baptista. *See* Baptista Mantuanus

Manuel I, King of Portugal. Copia di una lettera del Re di Portugallo. Milan: P.M. de Mantegatiis & Bros,for J.J. Legnano & Bros, 1505
— —Rome: J.Besicken, 1505

Manuzio, Paolo. De elementis. Paris: M.David, 1558
—De gli elementi. Venice: P.Manuzio, 1557

Marcos da Lisboa, o.f.m., Bp. Delle chroniche de Frati Minori. Venice: E. Viotti, 1591
— —Venice: E.Viotti, 1598
—Tercera parte de las Chronicas. Salamanca: A.de Canova, 1570

Margallo, Pedro. Phisices compendium. Salamanca: [J.de Porras?], 1520

Margaret, of Angouleme, Queen of Navarre. *See* Marguérite d'Angoulême, Queen of Navarre

Margarita filosofica. *See* Reisch, Gregor

Margarita philosophica. *See* Reisch, Gregor

MARGARITA ISLAND
—Bejarano, P. Resolucion breve cerca de las monedas. Lisbon: 1600

A margarite of America. *See* Lodge, Thomas

Marguérite d'Angoulême, Queen of Navarre. L'Heptameron. [Paris: 1559?]

— —Paris: B.Prévost,for J.Caveiller, 1559
— —Paris: B.Prévost,& E.Gibier, at Orléans, 1559
— —Paris: B.Prévost,for V.Sertenas, 1559
— —Paris: B.Prévost, 1560
— —Paris: B.Prévost,for J.Caveiller, 1560
— —Paris: B.Prévost,for G.Robinot, 1560
— —Paris: B.Prévost,for V.Sertenas, 1560
— —[Paris?] 1560
— —Lyons: G.Rouillé, 1561
— —Paris: G.Gilles, 1561
— —Paris: G.Gilles, 1567
— —Paris: V.Normant & J.Bruneau, 1567
— —Paris: M.de Roigny, 1571
— —Lyons: L.Cloquemin, 1572
— —Paris: M.de Roigny, 1574
— —Lyons: L.Cloquemin, 1578
— —Lyons: L.Cloquemin, 1581
— —Paris: G.Buon, 1581
— —Paris: A.L'Angelier, 1581
— —Rouen: R.Beauvais, 1598
— —Rouen: J.Osmont, 1598
—Histoires des amans fortunez. Paris: J.Caveiller, 1558
— —Paris: G.Gilles, 1558
— —Paris: G.Robinot, 1558
— —Paris: V.Sertenas, 1558

Mariana, Juan de. Historiae de rebus Hispaniae. Toledo: P.Rodríguez, 1592 (2)

Marieta, Juan de. Historia ecclesiastica de todos los santos de España. Cuenca: J.Masselin & P.del Valle,for C.Bernabé, 1596

MARIGOLDS. *See also* BOTANY
—Guilandini, M. Papyrus. Venice: 1579

Marineo, Lucio, Siculo. De Hispaniae laudibus. Burgos: F.Biel, 1500
—De las cosas memorables de España. Alcalá de Henares: M.de Eguía, 1530
— —Alcalá de Henares: M.de Eguía, 1533
— —Alcalá de Henares: J.de Brocar, 1539
— —*See also* Gómez de Ciudad Real, Alvár. El vellocino dorado. Toledo: 1546
—De rebus Hispaniae mem-

orabilibus. Alcalá de Henares: M.de Eguía, 1530
— —Alcalá de Henares: M.de Eguía, 1533
— —*In* Beale, Robert. Rerum Hispanicarum scriptores. Frankfurt a.M.: 1579
—Sumario dela serenissima vida . . . de . . . don Fernando y doña Ysabel. Seville: D.de Robertis, 1545

MARITIME LAW
—Spain. Laws, statutes, etc., 1556-1598 (Philip II). Ordenanças . . . sobre el despacho de las flotas de Nueva España. Madrid: 1585

Mariz, Pedro de. Dialogos de varia historia. Coimbra: A.de Mariz, 1594
— —Coimbra: A.de Mariz, 1599 (2)

Marlowe, Christopher. Tamburlaine the Great. London: R.Jones, 1590
— —London: R.Robinson,for R.Jones, 1593
— —London: R.Jones, 1597

Marniz, Philippe de, seigneur de Sainte-Aldegonde. Ad potentissimos ac serenissimos reges. [Middelburg R. Schilders] 1583
— —[Middelburg? R.Schilders?] 1584
— —Ernstighe vermaninghe vanden standt ende gheleghentheyt. [Middelburg? R.Schilders?] 1583
—A pithie and most earnest exhortation. Antwerp [i.e.,London: R.Waldegrave] 1583
—Remonstrance serieuse sur l'etat de la chrestienté. [Middelburg? R.Schilders?] 1583

Marquardus, Joannes. Practica theorica empirica morborum. Speyer: B.Albinus, 1589
— —Speyer: B.Albinus, 1592

Marten, Anthony. *See* Martin, Anthony

Martí, Luis. Historia del bienaventurado padre Luys Bertran, pte la. Valencia: V.de Miravet & Heirs of J.Navarro, for M.de Esparza, 1584

Martín de Valencia. *See* Antonio de Olave,o.f.m. Histoire et lettres. Toulouse: 1532; *and also*

—Durante, C. Tractatus de usu radicis et foliorum Mechoacan. Antwerp: 1587

—Gohory, J. Instruction sur l'herbe Petum. Paris: 1572

—Guarguante, O. Tria opuscula . . . De Mechioacani radice opusculum. Venice: 1595

—Wecker, J.J. Practica medicinae generalis. Basel: 1585

MECHOACAN — POETRY

—Tabourot, E. Les bigarrures. Paris: 1585

Medecyn-boeck. *See* Gabelkover, Oswald

Medici libelli. *See* Paracelsus

Medicina astrologica. *See* Schylander, Cornelis

Medicinales epistolae. *See* Manardo, Giovanni

Medina, Pedro de. L'art de naviguer. Lyons: G.Rouillé, 1553

— —Lyons: G.Rouillé, 1554

— —Lyons: G.Rouillé, 1561

— —Lyons: G.Rouillé, 1569

— —Rouen: J.Crevel,B.Belis, G.Pavie & R.Mallard, 1573

— —Lyons: G.Rouillé, 1576

—Arte de navegar. Valladolid: F.Fernández de Córdova, 1545

—Arte del navegar. Venice: A.Pincio,for G.B.Pederzano, 1554

— —Venice: A.Pincio,for G.B. Pederzano, 1555

—The arte of navigation. London: T.Dawson, 1581

— —London: T.Dawson, 1595

—Las grandezas y cosas notables de España. Alcalá de Henares: J.Gracián,for J.de Torres, 1595

—Libro de grandezas y cosas memorables de España. Alcalá de Henares: D.de Robertis, 1548

— —Seville: D.de Robertis, 1549

— —Alcalá de Henares: P.de Robles & J.de Villanueva,for L.Gutiérrez, 1566

—Regimiento de navegacion. Seville: J.Carnalla, 1552

— —Seville: S.Carpintero, 1563

—De zeevaert oft Conste van ter zee te varen. Antwerp: H.Hendricksen, 1580

Medina Rincón, Juan. Vida admirable de fr. Juan Bautista Moya. Salamanca: 1599

Meditatiunculae. *See* Cabrera, Cristobal

Meer oder Seehanen Buch. *See* Loew, Conrad

Meerman, Arnould. Theatrum conversionum gentium. Antwerp: C.Plantin, 1572

— —Antwerp: C.Plantin, 1573

Megiser, Hieronymus. Specimen quadraginta diversarum linguarum. Frankfurt a.M.: J.Spiess, 1593

Meinardus, Johannes. *See* Manardo, Giovanni

Mela, Pomponius. Cosmographia. Salamanca: [Printer of Lebrija's Gramatica] 1498

—De orbis situ. Basel: A.Cratander, 1522

— —Paris: [C.Wechel] 1530

— —Paris: J.Roigny, 1540

— —Paris: C.Wechel, 1540

—Libri de situ orbis. Vienna: J.Singriener,for L.Alantse, 1518

—The rare and singuler worke. London: T.Hacket, 1590

Mellerstadt, Martin. *See* Pollich, Martin

Mellini, Domenico. Descrizione dell'entrata della . . . Reina Giovanna. Florence: Heirs of B.Giunta, 1566 (3)

Memorabilium. *See* Merula, Gaudenzio

Memoriae nostrae libri quatuor. *See* Paradin, Guillaume

Memorial de la provincia de San Gabriel. *See* Moles, Juan Bautista

Memorial del hecho, cerca . . . del testamento de don Christoval Colon. [Madrid? 1600?]

Meneses, Felipe de. Luz de alma christiana. Seville: M.de Montesdoca, 1555

— —Medina del Campo: G.de Millis, 1555 [i.e.,1556]

— —Seville: S.Trugillo, 1564

— —Alcalá de Henares: J.de Villanueva,for L.Gutiérrez, 1567

— —Medina del Campo: F.del Canto, 1567

— —Medina del Campo: F.del Canto, 1570

— —Seville: M.Montesdoca, 1570

— —Alcalá de Henares: J.Gracián, 1574

— —Salamanca: P.Lasso, 1578

— —Medina del Campo: F.del Canto,for B.Boyer, 1582

— —Medina del Campo: F.del Canto,for P.Landry, 1582

Menezes, Philippe de. *See* Meneses, Felipe de

Mentagra. *See* Hock von Brackenau, Wendelin

La mer des cronicques. *See* Gaguin, Robert

Mercado, Luis. De communi . . . praesidiorum artis medicae. Valladolid: D.Fernández de Córdova, 1574

— —Cologne: J.B.Ciotti, 1588

— —Cologne: J.B.Ciotti, 1592

Mercado, Thomás de. De' negotii, et contratti de mercati. Brescia: P.M.Marchetti, 1591

—Summa de tratos, y contratos. Seville: F.Díaz, 1571

— —Seville: F.Díaz,for D.Núñez, 1587

—Tratos y contratos de mercaderes. Salamanca: M.Gast, 1569

Mercator, Gerardus. Atlas, sive Cosmographicae meditationes. Düsseldorf: A.Buys, 1595 (2)

— —Düsseldorf: A.Buys, 1595

—, **ed.** Ptolemaeus, Claudius. Tabulae geographicae . . . emendatae per Gerardum Mercatorem. Cologne: 1578

Merckliche Beschreibung . . . eynes frembden unbekanten Volcks. Strassburg: B.Jobin, 1578

Mermannius, Arnoldus. *See* Meerman, Arnould

Merula, Gaudenzio. Memorabilium. Lyons: M.Bonhomme, 1556

Merveilleux et estrange rapport . . . des commoditez qui se trouvent en Virginia. *See* Hariot, Thomas

La mesnagerie de Xenophon. *See* La Boëtie, Estienne de

The metamorphosis of Ajax. *See* Harington, Sir John. A new discourse

Metellus, Joannes Matalius. *See* Matal, Jean

Meteorologia. *See* Aristoteles

Methode curative. *See* Ferri, Alfonso

La methode curatoire de la mala-

Opera mathematica. *See*
Schöner, Johann

Opera medica. *See* Duchesne,
Joseph

Opera medicinalia. *See* Fernel,
Jean

Opera subsiciva. *See* Foglietta,
Uberto

Opera Rapsodiae historicae
Enneadum. *See* Sabellico,
Marco Antonio Coccio, called

Opera: Legatio babylonica. *See*
Anghiera, Pietro Martire d'

Operae horarum succisivarum.
See Camerarius, Philipp

Opere burlesche. Florence:
B.Giunta, 1548

—Florence: Heirs of B.Giunta,
1552-55

—Venice: D.Giglio, 1564-66

—Venice: D.Giglio, 1565

OPHIR

—Barreiros, G. Chorographia.
Coimbra: 1561

—Du Bartas, G.de S., seigneur.
La seconde semaine. Nevers:
1591

Oppianus. Alieuticon, sive De
piscibus. Strassburg:
J.Cammerlander, 1534

OPUNTIA (CACTUS). *See*
PRICKLY PEAR

Opus chirigicum. *See* Paracelsus

Opus epistolarum. *See* Anghiera,
Pietro Martire d'

Opus sphaericum. *See* Sacro
Bosco, Joannes de

Opus sphericum. *See* Sacro
Bosco, Joannes de

Opusculum de mirabilibus . . .
Romae. *See* Albertini,
Francesco

Opusculum de sphera mundi. *See*
Sacro Bosco, Joannes de

Opusculum geographicum. *See*
Schöner, Johann

Opusculum geographicum
rarum. *See* Myritius, Johannes

Opusculum praeclara de omni
pestilentia. *See* Vochs, Joannes

Oratio . . . pro Universitate Parisiensi. *See* Arnauld, Antoine

Oratio ad Sixtum V. *See* Piccha,
Gregorio

Oratio habita apud . . . Alexandrinum. *See* Maino, Giasone
del

Oratio in funere . . . Caroli V.

Augusti. *See* Robortello,
Francesco

Oratio in funere Regis Catholici.
See Magno, Marco Antonio

Oratio in obitu Philippi II. *See*
Capaccio, Giulio Cesare

Oratio pro oratoribus Senensium.
See Poliziano, Angelo Ambrogini, known as

Oratio super praestanda. *See*
Carvajal, Bernardino Lopez
de, Cardinal

Orationes Viennae Austriae ad
divum Maximilianum. Vienna:
H.Vietor,for L.& L.Alantse,
1516

Orationum et epistolarum . . .
libri duo. *See* Gabrielli, Giulio,
of Gubbio

Orbis terrae divisio compendiaria. *See* Neander, Michael

Orbis terrae partium succincta
explicatio. *See* Neander,
Michael

Orbis terrarum synoptica epitome. *See* Airebaudouze,
Pierre de, seigneur du Cest

Orden de Santiago. Compilación
de los establecimientos de la
Orden de la Caballeria. Seville:
J.Pegnitzer, 1503

Ordenanças . . . sobre el despacho de las flotas de Nueva
Espana. *See* Spain. Laws,
statutes, etc., 1556-1598
(Philip II)

Ordenanças para remedio de los
danos . . . de los navios, que
navegan a las Indias Ocidentales. *See* Spain. Laws, statutes, etc., 1556-1598 (Philip II)

Ordenanças reales del Consejo de
las Indias. *See* Spain. Consejo
de las Indias.

Ordenanças reales, para la Casa
de la contractacion. *See* Spain.
Casa de Contratación de las
Indias

Ordenanças reales para los
juezes. *See* Spain. Casa de
Contratación de las Indias

Ordenanzas para el Prior. *See*
Seville. Universidad de los mercaderes tratantes en las Indias

Ordenanzas reales del Consejo de
las Indias. *See* Spain. Consejo
de las Indias

Ordenanzas reales para la Casa

de contractacion. *See* Spain.
Casa de Contratación de las
Indias

Ordinancie inhoudende die oude
en nieuwe poincten. *See* Antwerp

Ordonantie inhoudende de niew
poincten. *See* Antwerp

L'ordonnance des royaumes . . .
appertenans à . . . Charles. *See*
Sensuyt lordonnance des
royaumes

Ornithologiae . . . libri xii. *See*
Aldrovandi, Ulisse

ORNITHOLOGY. *See* BIRDS

Orta, Garcia da. Aromatum.
Antwerp: C.Plantin, 1567

— —Antwerp: C.Plantin, 1574

— —Antwerp: C.Plantin, 1579

— —Antwerp: Widow of C.Plan-
tin,& J.Mourentorff, 1593

—Coloquios dos simples. Goa:
J.de Endem, 1563

—Dell'historia de i semplici.
Venice [G.& A.Zenari?] 1576

— —Venice: F.Ziletti, 1582 (2)

— —Venice: G.& A.Zenari, 1589

— —Venice: Heirs of F.Ziletti,
1589

— —Venice: Heirs of G.Scoto,
1597

—*See also* Wittich, Johann.
Bericht von den wunderbaren
bezoardischen Steinen. Leipzig:
1589

Ortelius, Abraham. Additamentum Theatri orbis terrarum.
Antwerp: [C.Plantin] 1579

— —Antwerp: [C.Plantin] 1580

—Additamentum III. Theatri
orbis terrarum. Antwerp:
[C.Plantin?] 1584

—Additamentum IV Theatri
orbis terrarum. Antwerp: Plantin Office, 1590

—Cosmographia; das ist, Warhaffte . . . beschreibung dess
gantzen erdbodens. Frankfurt
a.M.: P.Reffeler,for S.Feyera-
bend, 1576

—Der dritte Zusatz dess Theatri
oder Schawbuchs desz Erdbodems. Antwerp: [C.Plantin?]
1584

—Epitome du Theatre du
monde. Antwerp: C.Plantin,for
P.Galle, 1588

— —Antwerp: C.Plantin,for

Nicolay, Nicolas de. The navigations . . . made into Turkie. London: 1585A

Ruscelli, Girolamo. Delle lettere di principi. Venice: 1581

—Epistres des princes. Paris: 1572

——Paris: 1574

—Lettere di principi. Venice: 1564

——Venice: 1570

——Venice: 1572

——Venice: 1573

——Venice: 1574

Pacecchus, Dieghus. See Pacheco, Diogo

Pacheco, Diogo. Obedientia potentissimi Emanuelis Lusitaniae Regis. [Rome: J.Besicken, 1505?]

——[Rome: E.Silber, 1505?]

Padilla, Francisco de. Conciliorum omnium orthodoxorum. Madrid: F.Sánchez, 1587

Padilla, Juan de. Los doce triumfos. Seville: J.Varela, 1521

——Seville: J.Varela, 1529

Padilla, Thomas de, tr. Alvares, Francisco. Historia de las cosas de Etiopia. Antwerp: 1557

———Saragossa: 1561

PADUA. UNIVERSITÁ. ORTO BOTANICO

—Cortusi, G.A. L'horto dei semplici. Venice: 1591

Paesi novamente retrovati. See Francanzano da Montalboddo

Palissy, Bernard. Discours admirables de la nature des eaux et fonteines. Paris: M.LeJeune, 1580

Pamphilus, Josephus, Bp of Segni. Chronica ordinis Fratrum Eremitarum S. Augustini. Rome: G.Ferrario,for V.Accolti, 1581

Pan [Greek]. Omnis. See Brassicanus, Johannes Alexander

Panaegyricus. See Alpharabius, Jacobus

Panciroli, Guido. Rerum memorabilium . . . libri duo. Amberg: M.Forster, 1599

Pandectarum . . . libri xxi. See Gesner, Konrad

Panegyricum carmen. See Sobrarius, Joannes

Panormita, Antonius. See Beccadelli, Antonio

Pantaleon, Heinrich, pseud.? Chronographia christianae ecclesiae. Basel: N.Brylinger, 1550

——Basel: N.Brylinger, 1551

——Basel: N.Brylinger, 1561

———Basel: Heirs of N.Brylinger, 1568

—Diarium historicum. Basel: H.P[etri]., 1572

—Tabulae chronologicae. See Candidus, Pantaleon

Papel del pleyto. See Silva, Joanna de Saavedra de

Pappe with an hatchet. See Lyly, John

Papyrus. See Guilandini, Melchior

Paracelsus. Cheirugia. Warhafftige Beschreibunge der Wundartzney . . . Der ander Theil. Basel: C.Waldkirch, 1585

——Basel: C.Waldkirch, 1586

—Chirurgia magna. Strassburg [i.e.,Basel: P.Perna] 1573

—De medicamentorum simplicium. Zurich: C.Froschauer, 1572

—De morbe gallico. Warhaffte Cur der Frantzosen. Strassburg: C.Müller, 1578

—Drey Bücher. Strassburg: C.Müller, 1565

—Drey nützlicher Bücher. Nuremberg: C.Heussler, 1565

—Der dritte Theil der . . . Wundtartzney. Frankfurt: W.Han & G.Rab [1562?]

—Een excellent tracktaet. Antwerp: J.Roelants, 1557

—An excellent treatise touching howe to cure the Frenchpockes. London: J.Charlewood, 1590

—Holtzbüchlein. Strassburg: C.Müller, 1564

—Kleine Wundartzney. Basel: P.Perna, 1579

—Medici libelli. Cologne: A.Birckmann, 1567

—Opus chirigicum. Basel: P.Perna, 1581

—Schreiben von der Frantzosen. Basel: P.Perna, 1577

—Vom Holtz Guaiaco. Nuremberg: F.Peypus, 1529

—Von der Frantzösischen kranckheit. Nuremberg: F.Peypus, 1530

——Nuremberg: H.Andreae, 1552

——Frankfurt a.M.: H.Gülfferich, 1553

Paracer . . . sobre el servicio personal . . . de los Indios. See Ramírez, Juan

Paracer de un hombre docto cerca del servicio personal de los Indios. See Oñate, Alonso de

Paradin, Guillaume. Histoire de nostre temps. Lyons: J.de Tournes & G.Gazeau, 1550

——Lyons: J.de Tournes & G.Gazeau, 1552

——Lyons: J.de Tournes & G.Gazeau, 1554

——Lyons: P.Michel, 1558

——Lyons: J.de Tournes & G.Gazeau, 1558

——Paris: L.Breyer, 1561

——Paris: J.Longis & R.Le Mangnier, 1561

—Memoriae nostrae libri quatuor. Lyons: J.de Tournes, 1548

Les paradoxes. See Malestroict, Jehan Cherruyt de

Paraphrase de l'astrolabe. See Focard, Jacques

Paris. Lycée Louis-le-Grand. Defenses. de ceux du College de Clermont. [Paris?] 1594

Parmenius, Stephanus, Budeus. De navigatione . . . Humfredi Gilberto. London: T.Purfoot, 1582

Parmentier, Jean. Description nouvelle des merveilles de ce monde. Paris: 1531

PARROTS

—Muñón, S.de. Tragicomedia de Lysandro y Rosellia. Salamanca: 1542

Parsons, Robert. A declaration. See Verstegen, Richard. A declaration of the true causes of the great troubles. Antwerp: 1592

—Elisabethen, der Königin . . . Edict. Ingolstadt: D.Sartorius, 1593

—Elizabethae, Angliae reginae

La relacion que dio Alvar Nuñez, Cabeça de Vaca. *See* Núñez Cabeza de Vaca, Alvaro

Relacion verdadera de los trabajos . . . del Rio de La Plata. *See* Martínez, Andrés

Relacion verdadera del felice sucesso . . . contra la armada. *See* Bazán, Alvaro, marqués de Santa Cruz

La relacion y comentarios del governador Alvar Nuñez Cabeça de Vaca. *See* Núñez Cabeza de Vaca, Alvaro

Relation oder Beschreibung der Rheiss . . . durch . . . Franciscum Drack. *See* Bigges, Walter

A relation of the second voyage to Guiana. *See* Kemys, Lawrence

Relatione del reame di Congo. *See* Lopes, Duarte

Relatione del successo. *See* Beccari, Bernardino

Relatione universale de' continenti. *See* Botero, Giovanni

Relatione universale dell'isole. *See* Botero, Giovanni

Le relationi universali. *See* Botero, Giovanni

Relectiones theologicae xii. *See* Francisco de Vitoria

Relectiones theologicae tredecim. *See* Francisco de Vitoria

Relectiones tredecim. *See* Francisco de Vitoria

Relectiones undecim. *See* Francisco de Vitoria

Remonstrance aux François sur leur sedition. *See* Pasquier, Etienne

Remonstrance serieuse sur l'état de la chrestienté. *See* Marnix, Philippe de, seigneur de Sainte-Aldegonde

Renner, Franz. Ein köstlich und bewärtes Artzney Büchlein. Nuremberg: G.Hain, 1554

—Ein new wolgegruendet nützlichs . . . Handtbüchlein. Nuremberg: G.Hain, 1557

— —Nuremberg: G.Heyn, 1559

—Ein sehr nützlichs und heilsams . . . Handtbüchlein. Nuremberg: C.Heussler, 1571

— —Nuremberg: C.Heussler, 1572

—Wundartzneybuch. Frankfurt

a.M.: C.Heussler, 1578

A report of the kingdome of Congo. *See* Lopes, Duarte

A report of the truth of the fight about the iles of Açores. *See* Raleigh, Sir Walter

Reportorio dos tempos. *See* Avelar, André do

La republica. *See* Bodin, Jean

La republica . . . dell'isola Eutopia. *See* More, Sir Thomas

Republicas del mundo. *See* Román y Zamora, Jeronimo

La republique. *See* Bodin, Jean

La republique d'Utopie. *See* More, Sir Thomas

Requeste au Roy, faite en forme de complainctes par les femmes vefves. [Paris?] 1566

Rerum a Societate Jesu in oriente gestarum volumen. Jesuits. *See* Letters from missions(The East)

Rerum Hispanicarum scriptores. *See* Beale, Robert

Rerum in Gallia. *See* Serres, Jean de

Rerum memorabilium . . . libri duo. *See* Panciroli, Guido

Rescius, Stanislaus. *See* Reszka, Stanislaw

Resende, García de. Chronica que tracta da vida . . . do . . . Dom Joao ho Segundo. Lisbon: S.Lopez, 1596

—Lyvro . . . que trata da vida . . . don João o segundo. Lisbon: L.Rodriguez, 1545

— —Evora: A.de Burgos, 1554

Reski, Stanislav. *See* Reszka, Stanislaw

Resolucion breve cerca de las monedas. *See* Bejarano, Pedro

Resolutio dialectica. *See* Aristoteles. Organum. Latin

Responce . . . aux remonstrances faictes a la Royne mère. *See* Villegagnon, Nicolas Durand de

Responce a l'injuste . . . edict d'Elizabeth reyne d'Angleterre. *See* Parsons, Robert

Response a un avis qui conseille aux François de se rendre sous la protection du Roi d'Espagne. [Paris?] 1589

—*In* Goulart, Simon. Le quartriesme recueil. [Geneva?] 1595

La response aux lettres de Nicolas Durant, dict le chevalier de Villegaignon. [Geneva? 1561?]

—Paris: A.Wechel, 1561

Response aux libelles d'injures. *See* Villegagnon, Nicolas Durand de

Responsio . . . in superadditos errores Simoni Pistoris. *See* Pollich, Martin

Respublica in . . . Teutsch . . . gebracht. *See* Bodin, Jean

Respuesta y desengano contra las falsedades publicadas . . . en España. London: A.Hatfield, for T.Cadman, 1589A

The restorer of the French estate. London: R.Field, 1589A

Reszka, Stanislaw. De atheismus. Naples: G.G.Carlino & A. Pace, 1596

Retrato de la Loçana. *See* Delicado, Francisco

Rettung der Jesuiter Unschuld. *See* Scherer, Georg

Reusner, Jeremias. Decisiones. Basel: Heirs of N.Brylinger, 1582

Reys-gheschrift vande navigatien der Portugaloysers in Orienten. *See* Linschoten, Jan Huygen van

Die Reyse van Lissebone. *See* Springer, Balthasar

Rhetorica christiana. *See* Valadés, Diego

Rhetoricorum libri iiii. *See* Arias Montanus, Benedictus

Rhomitypion. *See* Ponti, Antonino

Ribadeneira, Marcelo de. Historia de las islas . . . de la gran China. Rome: N.Muschio, 1599A

Ribadeneira, Petrus. *See* Rivadeneira, Pedro de

Ribaldus, Petrus, Peruanus, pseud. Satyrarum liber prior. Utopia: R.Arabalida, 1541

Ribaut, Jean. The whole and true discoverye of Terra Florida. London: R.Hall, for T.Hacket, 1563

RIBAUT, JEAN

—Flores, B.de. Obra nuevamente compuesta. Seville: 1571

—La Popelinière, L.V., sieur de.

Santo Tomás, Domingo de. *See* Domingo de Santo Tomás

SANTO DOMINGO. *See also* HISPANIOLA

—Greepe, T. The true and perfecte newes of the . . . exploytes performed . . . by . . . Syr Frauncis Drake. London: 1587

SANTO DOMINGO—CHURCH HISTORY. *See* DOMINICANS IN SANTO DOMINGO

Sanuto, Livio. Geografia . . . distinta in xii libri. Venice: D.Zenaro, 1588

Sarrasin, Jean Antoine. De peste commentarius. Geneva: J.Grégoire, 1571

——[Geneva:] G.Grégoire, 1572

——[Geneva: G.Grégoire,for] L.Cloquemin,at Lyons, 1572

——Geneva: J.de Tournes, 1589

SARSAPARILLA

——Anguisola, A. Compendium simplicium. Piacenza: 1587

—Bauhin, K. Phytopinax. Basel [1596]

—Cardano, G. Contradicentium medicorum. Lyons: 1548

—Cesalpino, A. De plantis. Florence: 1583

—Dodoens, R. Purgantium . . . historiae. Antwerp: 1574

—Ferrier, A. De pudendagra. Antwerp: 1564

—Fioravanti, L. Capricci medicinali. Venice: 1561

——A compendium of the rationall secretes. London: 1582

——De' capricci medicinali. Venice: 1564

——Del compendio de i secreti rationali. Venice: 1564

—Fracanzano, A. De morbo gallico. Padua: 1564

—Langham, W. The garden of health. London: 1597

—Luisini, L., comp. De morbo gallico. Venice: 1566

—Minetti, G. Quaestio non minus pulchra . . . de sarzaeparillae et ligni sancti viribus. Şienna: 1593

—Porta, G.B.della. Phytognomonica. Naples: 1588

—Rectorius, L. Dissertatio apologetica de indole . . . guaiaci et sarsaparillae. Bologna: 1594

—A rich store-house or treasury for the diseased. London: 1596

—Turner, W. Herbal. Cologne: 1568

—Wittich, J. Bericht von den wunderbaren bezoardischen Steinen. Leipzig: 1589

Sassonia, Ercole. Luis venereae perfectissimus tractatus. Padua: L.Pasquato, 1597

—Tractatus triplex. Frankfurt a.M.: S.Latomus,for J.T. Schonwetter, 1600

Satyrarum liber prior. *See* Ribaldus, Petrus, Peruanus, pseud.

Satyre Menippée. Satyre, Menippee. [Paris?] 1594 (4)

——[Paris?] 1595

——[Paris?] 1599

——[Paris?] 1600

—**English.** A pleasant satyre or poesie. London: Widow Orwin,for T.Man, 1595

Savile, Capt. Henry. A libell of Spanish lies. London: J.Windet, 1596

Saxonia, Hercules. *See* Sassonia, Ercole

Scaliger, Julius Caesar. In libros de plantis Aristoteli inscriptos, commentarii. [Geneva:] J.Crespin, 1566 (2)

——[Geneva: J.Crespin,for] G.Rouillé,at Lyons, 1566

—In libros duos, qui inscribuntur De plantis, Aristotele autore. Paris: M.de Vascovan, 1556

——Marburg: P.Egenolff, 1598

Scanaroli, Antonio. Disputatio utilis de morbo gallico. Bologna: [B.Hectoris] 1498

Scandianese, Tito Giovanni. I quattro libri della caccia. Venice: G.Giolito de' Ferrari, 1556

Schaller, Georg. Thierbuch. Frankfurt a.M.: J.Feyerabend,for Heirs of S.Feyerabend, 1592

Schatz. *See* Gesner, Konrad

Schedel, Hartmann. Liber chronicarum. Nuremberg: A.Koberger, 1493

——Augsburg: J.Schönsperger, 1497

Schellig, Conrad. In pustulas

malas. [Heidelberg: F.Misch, 1495/96?]

—Ein kurtz Regiment wie man sich vor der Pestilenz enthalten sol. Heidelberg: [J.Stadelberger] 1501

——[Speyer: C.Hist, 1502]

Scherer, Georg. Rettung der Jesuiter Unschuld. Ingolstadt: D. Sartorius, 1586

Die Schiffung. *See* Angliara, Juan de

Schitler, Joannes. Tractatus methodicus de morbo gallico. Breslau: C.Scharffenberg, 1561

Schmaus, Leonardus. Lucubratiuncula de morbo gallico. Augsburg: S.Grimm & M.Wirsung, 1518

Schmidel, Ulrich. Neuwe Welt. Frankfurt a.M.: M.Lechler,for S. Feyerabend & S.Hüter, 1567

—Vera historia, admirandae cuiusdam navigationis. Nuremberg: [C.Lochner,for] L.Hulsius, 1599

—Verissima et jucundissima descriptio . . . Indiae. [Frankfurt a.M.:] T.de Bry, 1599

—Warhafftige unnd liebliche Beschreibung etlicher . . . Indianischen Landschafften. [Frankfurt a.M.:] T.de Bry, 1597

——[Frankfurt a.M.:] T.de Bry, 1599 (2)

—Warhafftige Historien einer wunderbaren Schiffart. Nuremberg: L.Hulsius, 1599

Schmidt, Ulrich. *See* Schmidel, Ulrich

Eyn schön hübsch lesen von etlichen insslen. *See* Colombo, Cristoforo

Ein schöne newe zeytung so Kayserlich Mayestet auss Indiat yetz newlich zükommen seind. [Augsburg: M.Ramminger, 1522]

Schöner, Johann. Appendices . . . in opusculum Globi astriferi. Nuremberg: H.Stuchs, 1518

——Antwerp: M.de Keyser,for R.Bollaert, 1527

—De nuper sub Castiliae ac Portugalliae regibus . . . reper-

—Ordenanças reales para los juezes. Madrid: F.Sánchez, 1585

Spain. Consejo de las Indias. Ordenanças reales. [Madrid: 1571?]

—Ordenanzas reales. Madrid: F.Sánchez, 1585

SPAIN. CONSEJO DE LAS INDIAS

—Spain. Laws, statutes, etc. Provisiones, cedulas, capitulos de ordenanças. Madrid: 1596

Spain. Cortes. Quaderno de las cortes. Burgos: A.de Melgar, 1523

— —Burgos: J.de Junta, 1529

— —Burgos: J.de Junta, 1535

— —Salamanca: J.de Junta, 1551

— —Salamanca: J.à Cánova, 1561

Spain. Laws, statutes, etc. Las pragmaticas del reyno. Seville: J.Varela, 1520

— —Alcalá de Henares: M.de Eguía, 1528

— —Valladolid: J.de Villaquirán, 1540

—Pragmaticas y leyes. Medina del Campo: P.de Castro, 1549

—Provisiones, cedulas, capitulos de ordenanças. Madrid: Imprenta Real, 1596

—Recopolación de algunas bullas. Toledo: J.Ferrer, for M.Rodríguez, 1550

SPAIN. LAWS, STATUTES, ETC.

—Matienzo, J.de. Commentaira [i.e.,Commentaria] in librum recollectionis. Madrid: 1580

Spain. Laws, statutes, etc., 1479-1504 (Ferdinand V & Isabella I). Libro en que esta copiladas algunas bullas. Alcalá de Henares: L.Polono, for J.Ramírez, 1503

— —[Salamanca? J.de Porras? 1503?]

Spain. Laws, statutes, etc., 1504-1516 (Ferdinand V). [Declaracion y moderacion de las ordenanzas hechas para el buen gobierno de las Indias. Valladolid? 1513?]

Spain. Laws, statutes, etc., 1516-1556 (Charles I). Las cortes de Toledo. Burgos: A.de Melgar, 1525

—Leyes y ordenanças nuevamente hechas . . . por la governacion de las Indias. Alcalá de Henares: J.de Brocar, 1543

— —Madrid: F.Sánchez, 1585

—Las leys y prematicas hechas en las Cortes de Toledo. Burgos: A.de Melgar, 1526 (2)

— —Burgos: J.de Junta, 1531

— —Salamanca: J.de Junta, 1550

—Las pregmaticas y capitulos . . . en las Cortes . . . en Valladolid. Valladolid: F.Fernández de Córdova, 1549 (2)

Spain. Laws, statutes, etc., 1556-1598 (Philip II). Ordenanças . . . sobre el despacho de las flotas de Nueva Espana. Madrid: F.Sánchez, 1585

—Ordenanças para remedio de los daños . . . de los navios, que navegan a las Indias Ocidentales. Madrid: P.Madrigal, 1591

—La ultima nueva orden y ordenanças. [Seville? 1556?]

Spain. Sovereigns, etc., 1479-1504 (Ferdinand V & Isabella I). Este es treslado . . . de una carta de privilegio. [Burgos: 1497?]

Spain. Sovereigns, etc., 1504-1516 (Ferdinand V). Carta del Rey Catholico a Pedra Arias Davila. [Madrid? ca.1600?]

Spain. Sovereigns, etc., 1556-1598 (Philip II). El Rey. Lo que . . . se assienta y concierta . . . sobre la provision . . . de esclavos negros. [Madrid? 1595?]

—Instruccion para la observacion del eclypse de luna. [Madrid? 1577]

— —[Madrid? 1582?]

—Instruccion y forma . . . en la publicacion . . . de la Bula de Santa Cruzada. Madrid: 1588

— —Madrid: 1598

—Instruccion y orden para la publicacion . . . de la Bula de la Santa Cruzada. [Madrid? 1573]

—Instrucion para el virrey de la Nueva España. Aranjuez: 1596

—Instrucion para la observacion

de los eclipses de la luna. [Madrid? 1584]

—Instruction, y memoria de las relaciones . . . para la descripcion de las Indias. [Madrid: 1577]

— —[Madrid? ca.1585]

SPANISH AMERICA. *See also* LATIN AMERICA

—Bosso, F. In funere Philippi . . . oratio. Milan: 1599

—Capaccio, G.C. Oratio in obitu Philippi II. Naples: 1599

—Francisco de Vitoria. Relectiones theologicae. Lyons: 1557

—Verheiden, W. In classem Xerxis Hispani oratio. The Hague: 1598

SPANISH AMERICA— BIOGRAPHY

—Cervantes Saavedra, M.de. Galatea. Alcalá de Henares: 1585

SPANISH AMERICA— COMMERCE

—The restorer of the French estate. London: 1589A

SPANISH AMERICA— DESCRIPTION & TRAVEL

—González de Mendoza, J.; Bp. Dell'historia della China. Rome: 1586

— —Histoire . . . de la Chine. Paris: 1588

— —Historia . . . dela China. Rome: 1585

— —The historie . . . of China. London: 1588

— —Itinerario . . . de la China. Lisbon: 1586

—Sensuyent lordonnance des royaumes. Geneva: 1519

SPANISH AMERICA— DISCOVERY & EXPLORATION. *See also* COLOMBO, CRISTOFORO; VESPUCCI, AMERIGO; DISCOVERIES— SPANISH; *etc.*

—Bordone, B. Libro . . . nel qual si ragiona di tutte l'isole. Venice: 1528

SPANISH AMERICA— HISTORY

—Mayerne, L.T.de. Histoire generale d'Espagne. Geneva: 1587

—Oviedo y Valdés, G.F.de. Coronica de las Indias. Salamanca: 1547

Szyszkowski, Matthias. Pro religiossimis Societatis Jesu patribus. Cracow: A.Piotrkowczck, 1590

Tabaco. *See* Chute, Anthony

Tabernaemontanus, Jacobus Theodorus, called. *See* Theodorus, Jacobus, called Tabernaemontanus

Tabourot, Estienne. Les bigarrures. Paris: J.Richer, 1585

— —Paris: J.Richer, 1586

— —Paris: J.Richer, 1588

— —Rouen: J.Bauchu, 1591

— —Lyons: B.Rigaud, 1594

— —Lyons: J.Anard,for Heirs of B.Rigaud, 1599

— —Lyons: J.Anard,for B.Rigaud, 1600

Tabula geographica. *See* Botero, Giovanni

Tabulae chronologicae. *See* Candidus, Pantaleon

Tabulae geographicae . . . emendatae per Gerardum Mercatorem. *See* Ptolemaeus, Claudius

Tabularum geographicorum contractum libri quatuor. *See* Bertius, Petrus

Tagault, Jean. La chirurgia. Venice: M.Tramezzino, 1550

—La chirurgie. Lyons: B.Honorat, 1580

—Der chirurgijen instructie. Antwerp: [Heirs of A.Birckmann, ca. 1560?]

—De chirurgica institutione. Paris: C.Wechel, 1543

— —Venice: V.Valgrisi, 1544

— —Lyons: E.Rufin & J.Ausoult, for G.Rouillé, 1547

— —Lyons: G.Rouillé, 1549

— —Venice: V.Valgrisi, 1549

— —*In* Gesner, Konrad. Chirurgia. Zurich: 1555

— —Lyons: G.Rouillé, 1560

— —Lyons: G.Rouillé, 1567

—Gründtliche und rechte Underweisung der Chirurgie. Frankfurt: G.Rab & S.Feyerabend, 1574

—Institutione di cirurgia. Venice: G.Angelieri, 1570

— —Venice: N.Moretti, 1596

—Les institutions chirurgiques. Lyons: [P.Rollet,for] G.Rouillé, 1549

—*See also* Banister, John. A needefull . . . treatise of chyrurgerie. London: 1575

Taisnier, Joannes. A very necessarie and profitable book concerning navigation. London: R.Jugge [1579]

Talavera, Gabriel de. Historia de Nuestra Señora de Guadalupe. Toledo: T.de Guzmán, 1597

Tallat von Vochenberg, Johann. *See* Tollat von Vochenberg, Johann

Tamara, Francisco. El libro de las costumbras de todas las gentes del mundo, y de las Indias. Antwerp: M.Nuyts, 1556

Tamburlaine the Great. *See* Marlowe, Christopher

Tannstetter von Thannau, Georg. Super requisitione Leonis Papae X. *See* Stiborius, Andreas. Super requisitione Leonis Papae X . . . de romani calendarii correctione consilium. Vienna: 1514

—*See* Albertus Magnus, Saint, Bp of Ratisbon. De natura locorum

Tarafa, Francisco. De origine, ac rebus gestis regum Hispaniae liber. Antwerp: H.de Laet,for J.Steels, 1553

Tarcagnota, Giovanni. Delle historie del mondo. Venice: M.Tramezzino, 1562

— —Venice: M.Tramezzino, 1573

— —Venice: The Giuntas, 1585

— —Venice: F.dei Franceschi, 1592

— —Venice: The Giuntas, 1598

—Delle historie del mondo . . . Supplemento. Venice: Heirs of F.& M.Tramezzino, 1580

Tasso, Torquato. La délivrance de Hierusalem. Paris: N.Gilles, 1595

— —Paris: M.Guillemot, 1595

—Gerusalemme liberata. Casalmaggiore: A.Canacci & E.Viotti, 1581

— —Ferrara: V.Baldini, 1581

— —Ferrara: Heirs of F.Rossi, 1581

— —Lyons: P.Roussin, for A.Marsilius, 1581

— —Parma: E.Viotti, 1581 (2)

— —[Venice?] 1582

— —Mantua: F.Osanna, 1584

— —Venice: A.Salicato, 1584

— —Ferrara: G.C.Cagnacini & Bros, 1585 (2)

— —Genoa: G.Bartoli, 1590

—Gierusalemme liberata. *See* Gerusalemme liberata *above*

—Godfrey of Bulloigne. London: A.Hatfield,for J.Jaggard & M.Lownes, 1600

—Il Goffredo. Venice: G.Perchacino, 1581

— —Ferrara: D.Mammarelli & G.C.Cagnacini, 1582

— —Naples: G.B.Cappelli, 1582 (2)

— —Naples: H.Salviani & C.Cesare & Bros, 1582 (2)

— —Venice: G.Perchacino, 1582

— —Venice: F.dei Franceschi, 1583

— —Ferrara: G.C.Cagnacini & Bros, 1585

— —Venice: A.Salicato, 1585

— —Venice: A.Salicato, 1588

— —Venice: A.Salicato, 1589

— —Venice: A.Salicato, 1590

— —Venice: A.Salicato, 1592

— —Venice: A.Salicato, 1593

— —Venice: G.B.Ciotti, 1594

— —Venice: G.B.Ciotti, 1595

— —Venice: G.B.Ciotti, 1597

— —Venice: G.B.Ciotti, 1598

— —Venice: G.B.Ciotti, 1599

— —Venice: G.B.Ciotti, 1600

— —Venice: Heirs of F.dei Franceschi, 1600

—La Hierusalem . . . rendue françoise. Paris: A.L'Angelier, 1595

— —Paris: A.L'Angelier, 1599

—Jerusalem libertada. Madrid: P.Madrigal,for E.& F.Bogia, 1587

Tavole . . . del mondo. *See* Nores, Giasone de

Taye Peilhot, baron de. *See* Barot, Jean de, baron de Taye Peilhot

Teatro del cielo e della terra. *See* Rosaccio, Giuseppe

Teixeira José, supposed author, Tractaet paraeneticq. [Amsterdam?] 1598 (4)

— —[Antwerp?] 1598

—Traicté paraenetique. Auch [i.e.,Paris?]: 1597